Children Today

Second Canadian Edition

Grace J. Craig
University of Massachusetts

Marguerite D. Kermis
Canisius College

Nancy L. Digdon
Grant MacEwan College

Prentice
Hall

Toronto

Canadian Cataloguing in Publication Data

Craig, Grace J.
  Children today

2nd Canadian ed.
Includes bibliographical references and index.
ISBN 0-13-099085-X

1. Child development. I. Kermis, Marguerite D., 1948– .
II. Digdon, Nancy Linda, 1958– . III. Title.

HG767.9.C73 2001   305.231   C00-930426-6

ISBN 0-13-099085-X

Vice President, Editorial Director: Michael Young
Acquisitions Editor: Jessica Mosher
Marketing Manager: Judith Allen
Developmental Editor: Lise Dupont
Production Editor: Avivah Wargon
Copy Editor: Marcia Miron
Production Coordinator: Wendy Moran
Page Layout: Susan Thomas/Digital Zone
Photo Research: Lisa Brant
Art Director: Mary Opper
Interior Design: Lisa LaPointe
Cover Design: Lisa LaPointe
Cover Image: PhotoDisc
Cover Photographs: Lisa LaPointe, Yolanda de Rooy, Phyllis Seto, Wendy Moran, Tammie Hui, Candace Hill, Sarah Battersby

4 5   06 05 04

Printed and bound in the United States of America

Brief Contents

Contents

Part Two   The Beginnings of Human Life   62

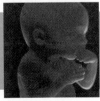

CHAPTER 3
Heredity and Environment
62

CHAPTER 4
The Prenatal Period
94

CHAPTER 5

Childbirth and the Neonate
124

Part Three   Infancy: The First Two Years of Life 154

CHAPTER 6

Infancy: Physical, Motor, and Cognitive Development
154

CHAPTER 7

Infancy: Developing Relationships 194

CHAPTER

14

Middle Childhood: Personality and Social Development 430

Part Six   Adolescence   464

CHAPTER

15

Adolescence: A Time of Transition 464

CHAPTER

16

Adolescence: Social and Personality Development 494

Preface

Like its predecessor, the Second Canadian edition of *Children Today* is aimed at a cross-section of students varying in academic background, career interests, and past experiences with the social sciences. Many will seek a future in child-related fields, such as social work, education, counselling, nursing, speech therapy, school psychology, program administration, and many others. Some students are already coaches, counsellors, tutors, or parents. Many will be parents at some time. Most have a strong curiosity about their own childhood and adolescence. This text aims to provide a sound, thought-provoking introduction to contemporary child development research and theory, as well as its application. The text draws on many fields—anthropology, sociology, history, nursing, public health, and of course, psychology—to portray the current key issues, topics, and controversies in child development.

Goals of the Second Canadian Edition

In the Second Canadian Edition of *Children Today*, we had three primary goals: to solidify the research base throughout the text, to extend the Canadian content, and to strengthen the applied focus of the text. We attempted to accomplish these goals without making the book longer and unwieldy for use in a typical course.

Research

More than 220 recent references have been added to this edition. The interdisciplinary nature of child development is apparent in that new references have been chosen from a number of disciplines, including psychology, nursing, medicine, social work, sociology, neurosciences, anthropology, early childhood, child and youth care, and education.

Canadian Content

We have expanded the Canadian content of the first edition by adding an additional 115 Canadian references. Like its predecessor, the Second Canadian Edition of *Children Today* has been specially created for Canadian students, with a number of characteristics that give the book a Canadian perspective:

1. We have included appropriate Canadian demographics and statistics throughout, and when available, have updated those presented in the first edition. Findings from the ongoing Canadian project, National Longitudinal Survey of Children in Youth, have been incorporated throughout the book.

2. Many of the examples and discussions reflect the multicultural nature of Canada. For example, the language chapter mentions Cree, Inuktitut, and Chinese, and includes a discussion of French immersion programs that have been pioneered in Canada.

3. Canadian government policies that affect development have been mentioned throughout the book. See, for example, the discussions of birthing practices, educational practices, day-care standards, health and physical development, tobacco advertising, and young offenders. We have tried to make students aware of aspects of development that are unique to the Canadian context.

4. We wanted students to gain an appreciation of the breadth and quality of developmental research taking place in Canada. To that end, we added more discussions of the work of Canadian researchers. Discussions of Canadian research appear in every chapter.

Applied Focus

The second Canadian edition has a strong focus on application, both in the main body of the text, and in the 21 Applications boxes found throughout the book. Although these Applications boxes should be of interest to a broad range of students, some of the boxes are especially relevant to particular programs. Application boxes and other boxes particularly relevant to **early childhood educators** include the following:

*   Observing Children in Child-Care Centres (Chapter 1)
*   Health Inspections of Child-Care Centres in Toronto (Chapter 7)
*   Setting Standards for Quality Day Care in Canada (Chapter 7)
*   Why Do Children Talk to Themselves? (Chapter 8)
*   Measuring Bacteria Levels in Ball Pit Play Areas (Chapter 9)
*   Setting Up Play Centres to Foster Dramatic Play (Chapter 10)

Boxes of particular interest to **nurses** and other health care professionals include the following:

*   Reproductive Technology: What Are the Options? (Chapter 4)
*   Smoking and Alcohol: The Effects on the Fetus (Chapter 4)
*   The "Kilogram Kids" (Chapter 5)
*   Sudden Infant Death Syndrome (SIDS) (Chapter 6)
*   Trends in Breast-Feeding and Bottle-Feeding Around the World (Chapter 6)
*   Helping Children Manage Pain (Chapter 9)
*   A Young Child's Conception of Death (Chapter 10)
*   Children's Concepts of Their Bodies (Chapter 12)
*   Chronic Illness and Children's Peer Relationships (Chapter 12)
*   Anorexia and Bulimia (Chapter 15)

Boxes that will be of special interest to **teachers** and **teacher assistants** include the following:

- Keeping the Fun in Sport (Chapter 12)
- Math Achievement Test Scores in Canadian Elementary Schools (Chapter 13)
- Canadian Research on Playground Aggression and Bullying (Chapter 14)
- After-School Care Programs and Children's Social Development (Chapter 14)
- Changing Sleep Habits in Adolescence (Chapter 15)
- What Do Parents in Southern Ontario Think About Sex Education in School? (Chapter 15)
- Why Do Adolescents Drop Out of School? (Chapter 15)

Boxes that are especially relevant for students in **social work, child and youth care,** and other community service programs include the following:

- Adolescent Depression Considered from Different Theoretical Perspectives (Chapter 2)
- Attachment in Infants Afraid of Their Mothers (Chapter 7)
- Romanian Orphanage Children Adopted by Families in British Columbia (Chapter 7)
- Children's Eyewitness Testimony (Chapter 10)
- Stress Reactions in Children (Chapter 12)
- Stepfamilies and Blended Families (Chapter 14)
- Are Adolescents the Victims of Raging Hormones? (Chapter 15)
- Youth Gambling in Quebec (Chapter 16)
- Adolescent Suicide (Chapter 16)
- Prevention of Youth Violence (Chapter 16)

Boxes that would be particularly helpful for **parents** (and prospective parents) include the following:

- Recognizing Operant Conditioning in Everday Life (Chapter 2)
- The Nurture Assumption: Why Children Turn Out the Way They Do (Chapter 2)
- Emerging Fatherhood: Changing Roles (Chapter 5)
- Infant Waking, Fussing, Crying, Feeding, and Sleeping: What Is the Range of "Normal"? (Chapter 5)
- Right from Birth: Building Your Child's Foundation for Life (Chapter 5)
- "Hothouse" Babies (Chapter 6)
- Mothers Who Work Outside the Home in Atlantic Canada (Chapter 7)
- Looking for Causes of Difficult Temperament in Canadian Infants and Toddlers (Chapter 7)
- Successful Toilet Training (Chapter 7)
- Children's Food Preferences (Chapter 9)
- To Spank or Not to Spank? (Chapter 11)
- Could a Child Who Has Wandered Off Find the Way Home? (Chapter 13)
- Out-of-School Care of Young Adolescents (Chapter 16)

New Pedagogical Features

We kept a number of pedagogical features from the first edition: chapter outlines, definitions of key terms in the margins, chapter summaries, and questions for review. Other pedagogical features of the first edition have been improved. For instance, Questions to Ponder are now in the margins next to the relevant sections to encourage students to consider them while they are reading. All of the Web sites have been updated, and we have included links to major Canadian sites. Other pedagogical features are new to this edition. We've added "Summing Up" development summaries at the end of Parts 3, 4, 5, and 6. These part-ending spreads will be valuable study aids as students progress through the text. The suggested readings sections that have been included in the first edition have been updated and moved from the textbook to the Instructor's Manual and the Companion Website.

Here's a more detailed look at the changes to specific chapters:

Chapter 1 This chapter has been reorganized, consistent with comments from reviewers, to emphasize *application* of research. Discussions of developmental processes and research designs have been condensed, clarified, and updated. The historical, socioeconomic, and cultural perspectives have been expanded. There is a new Focus on an Issue box, "Canadian History and the Experiences of Children"; a new Applications box, "Observing Children in Child-Care Centres"; more examples of Canadian applications; and increased coverage of longitudinal designs.

Chapter 2 The ecological model has been moved here from Chapter 1; the Vygotsky section has been totally rewritten; and learning and cognitive sections have been condensed. Details about specific stages are now summed up in tables; there is a new Focus on an Issue box on the Nurture Assumption and a new section on humanistic psychology. The section on neuroscience has been expanded; the discussion of controversial issues has been clarified; and the section on the "Limitations of Developmental Theories" has been moved from the beginning to the end of the chapter, as it will be more meaningful to students after they had read about the theories. The language used in the concept summary tables has been simplified, and a new concept summary table (Table 2-7) highlights the key features of each of the theories.

Chapter 3 The genetics section has been almost completely rewritten; there is a new Applications box, "The Human Genome Project"; the genetic disorders section has been reorganized for ease of study, and the coverage of the disorders has been increased. There are new figures of Punnett Squares; the section on prenatal screening has been moved to Chapter 4; and the section on culture and family has been condensed, with more Canadian references added to it.

Chapter 4 The section on teratogens has been expanded to include more on the father's occupation and participation in the Gulf War, as well as Canadian studies about exposure to mercury and PCBs. The section on prenatal screening has been moved from Chapter 3 to this chapter. The box on reproductive technology has been updated and there is a new discussion of the development of children conceived with the assistance of reproductive technology. The section on developmental trends has been condensed.

Chapter 5 In response to reviewer requests, the cross-cultural discussion has been expanded, and there is a new section on brain development. More Canadian examples have been added in addition to a new Focus on Diversity box on infant behaviours across cultures and a new Focus on Application box, "Right from Birth: Building Your Child's Foundation for Life."

Chapter 6 There is more in-depth discussion of a few studies, particularly in the sections on perceptual and cognitive development. More subheadings have been introduced throughout to make the material more digestible, especially in the section on vision. The section on brain development has been rewritten, and there are updates and more Canadian references throughout.

Chapter 7 More Canadian research on attachment has been added (including the works of Pederson, Moran, Symons, Moss, Tarabulsky, and colleagues). New additions include a Focus on Diversity box, "Attachment in Infants Afraid of Their Mothers"; a new Focus on Diversity box, "Mothers Who Work Outside the Home in Atlantic Canada"; a new Focus on Application box, "Health Inspections of Child-Care Centres in Toronto; and a new Focus on Diversity box, "Looking for Causes of Difficult Temperament in Canadian Infants and Toddlers." There are also new discussions of aggression and shyness in toddlers, a revised section on toilet training, and a new discussion of Greenspan's research on self-concept.

Chapter 8 A new Focus on an Issue box, "The Study of Speech Perception in Infants Too Young to Speak," highlights the research of Janet Werker at UBC. The section on multilingualism has been updated, and there is a new detailed discussion of the preservation of Aboriginal languages.

Chapter 9 The section on development of neurons has been moved to Chapter 6; the section on environmental hazards and accidents has been updated, and new Canadian references have been added. Table 9-2, "Environmental Hazards and the Well-being of Children," is new and the section on lead poisoning has been rewritten and includes Canadian references. There is a new section on unintentional poisonings, a new Focus on Application box, "Measuring Bacteria Levels in Ball Pit Play Areas"; updated Canadian references on poverty; an updated discussion of asthma; and an updated discussion of the psychological effects of chronic health problems.

Chapter 10 The section on the theory of mind has been expanded so that key studies are presented in more detail. The box on children's eyewitness testimony has been largely rewritten and focuses on critical research issues. The section on play has been condensed, and there is a new section on the Reggio Emilia approach to early childhood education.

Chapter 11 The section on three theories revisited has been updated to include current theories, and the descriptions of older theories have been condensed; the section on defence mechanisms has also been condensed, and defence mechanisms that are not used by preschoolers have been deleted; the discussion of emotional regulation has been updated; the section on autonomy, mastery, and competence has been condensed and updated; the section on aggression and prosocial behaviour has been condensed, and new references added; new Canadian references have also been added to the sections on peers and social skills and on the family context; and the Focus on Diversity box, "To Spank or Not to Spank? Cultural Differences in Attitudes toward Spanking" has been revised and moved to this chapter from Chapter One.

Chapter 12 The section on rough-and-tumble play has been updated; and the section on obesity has been expanded to incorporate Mendelson's studies relating obesity to self-esteem. New additions include a Focus on Application box, "Chronic Illness and Children's Peer Relationships"; a discussion of Morrongiello's research on the influence of friends on accident risk; and a discussion of the cognitive benefits of physical education.

Chapter 13 A new Focus on Application box, "Math Achievement Test Scores in Canadian Elementary Schools," has been included; the section on information processing has been condensed and a new Canadian study added; the section on new demands and expectations has been condensed and new Canadian references have been added; the research on phonics has been updated; multicultural Canadian research has been added to the section on parental influences on school success; and the section on learning disabilities has been updated and includes new Canadian references.

Chapter 14 The section on theoretical overview has been deleted, and the section on continuing family influences has been updated and contains new Canadian references (especially in the subsections on divorce, child abuse, and poverty). There are two new boxes, Focus on Diversity, "Stepfamilies and Blended Families," and Focus on an Issue, "Canadian Research on Playground Aggression and Bullying."

Chapter 15 The section on development in a cultural and historical context has more Canadian content. There is a new section on work and school in the new millennium; a new Focus on an Issue Box, "Changing Sleep Habits During Adolescence"; new Canadian research on sexual behaviour and attitudes; a new Focus on an Issue Box, "What Do Parents in Southern Ontario Think About Sex Education in Schools?"; and new references, including a Canadian one, in the section on teen parents. The Focus on an Issue box "Why Do Adolescents Drop Out of School?" has been expanded and new sections on Aboriginal concerns and preventing school drop-out have been added, as well as many new Canadian references throughout.

Chapter 16 This chapter contains new Canadian references on parent–adolescent relationships; a new Focus on Application box on youth gambling (which includes Canadian data); a new Focus on Application box, "Preventing Youth Violence" (which includes Canadian studies); new Canadian references on risk-taking and drug usage; and new Canadian references on sexual behaviour.

Pedagogical Features

Part-ending Development Summaries (new to this edition) visually summarize chronological development for that development stage.

Questions to Ponder (now in the margins) for each major section of the text encourage students to stop, think about, and evaluate the section they have just read.

Chapter Opening Quotations spark student interest in the chapter topic.

Chapter Outline acts as a road map for the chapter.

Running Glossary in the margins makes studying key terms easier.

Concept Summary Tables summarize key concepts and theories presented in the chapters.

Focus on Applications boxes feature interesting topics for educators, caregivers, or both.

Focus on an Issue boxes highlight interesting, cutting-edge topics in the discipline.

Focus on Diversity boxes feature many of the contemporary diversity issues relevant to child development.

Summary and Conclusions sections at the end of the chapter provide a concise summation of the chapter's main points.

Questions to Review for self-study help students know they've absorbed the chapter content.

Weblinks lead students to major Canadian sources of information about child development.

Chronological Organization

In the field of child development, there is always the question of whether to organize developmental research and theory by topics, such as cognition, genetics, and moral development, or to present child development as it happens chronologically, emphasizing the holistic, interrelated nature of these topics. We have chosen to present child development as primarily organized into the classic chronological periods of infancy, early childhood, middle childhood, and adolescence. In each age-defined section, there is a balanced presentation of physical, motor, cognitive, and social-emotional development. Yet some topics are singled out for special emphasis. In the infancy section, there is a full chapter on childbirth and the competence of the newborn. Similarly, in the early childhood section, there is a full chapter on language development, showing the continuity of this crucial area of development from infancy to middle childhood. One central theme in the study of child development is the complex interplay of biological and environmental factors that produce development. Consequently, near the beginning of the text there is another full chapter on heredity and environment. Here we define the contemporary issues around the processes of development in today's multiple cultural contexts. Up-to-date research helps define the current topics.

Instructor Supplements

Instructor's Manual The Instructor's Manual accompanying *Children Today* assembles the relevant teaching material for each chapter and provides teaching tips, chapter outlines, activities, additional discussion questions, lecture suggestions, transparency masters to enhance your classroom experience, and more.

Test Item File A comprehensive Test Item File has been prepared for this edition. Available in both printed and computerized form, the file contains more than 2500 questions. A variety of questions are provided, including multiple-choice, true-false, and essay. Questions cover a balance of conceptual, applied, and factual material from the text. Pearson Test Manager is a test generator designed to allow the creation of personalized exams. Test questions can be added to the Test Item File and existing questions can be edited using a personal computer. The Test Manager also offers an Online Testing System, which is the most efficient, time-saving examination aid on the market, allowing the instructor to administer, correct, grade, record, and return computerized exams over a variety of networks.

Student Supplement

Companion Website A comprehensive online Study Guide for the Second Canadian Edition of *Children Today* features a three-part review and self-test format that effectively reinforces learning. Exercises for each chapter progress from basic factual recall, through conceptual understanding, to application of concepts.

Acknowledgments

Children Today incorporates the contributions of many individuals: people of all ages who have participated in classrooms, clinical encounters, and interviews; students and research assistants; colleagues, teachers, and mentors; family members and friends. Their experiences, ideas, and insights are reflected in this text. Thanks also to all the reviewers who reviewed the Second Canadian Edition: Gordon Beckett, Sheridan College of Applied Arts; Wanda Boyer, University of Victoria; Deborah Collins, St. Lawrence College; Patricia Corson, Ryerson Polytechnic University; Lanalee Hardacre, Conestoga College; Mary Knight, Durham College; Sue Martin, Centennial College and YMCA of Greater Toronto; Rosemary Mills, University of Manitoba; Renée Ouelette, St. Clair College; David R. Pederson, University of Western Ontario; and Ann Robson, University of Western Ontario.

I am especially grateful to people who responded to my devnet posting for Canadian references. Your willingness to alert me to your work and to send me reprints certainly made my job easier. It has been a privilege to cite the quality research being conducted across this country. At times, though, the breadth of quality Canadian research presented me with a dilemma. It was not possible to include it all without exceeding the length restrictions of the book.

At Pearson Education Canada, there are a number of people who have contributed enormously to this project: Nicole Lukach, aquisitions editor; Dawn du Quesnay, senior developmental editor; Lise Dupont, developmental editor; Avivah Wargon, production editor; and Marcia Miron, copy editor. It has been a pleasure collaborating with all of you.

Last, but not least, I want to acknowledge the inspiration and love of my husband, Michael Dawson, and my children, Michele and Christopher.

N.L.D

Your Internet companion to the most exciting, state-of-the-art educational tools on the Web!

The Pearson Education Canada Companion Website is easy to navigate and is organized to correspond to the chapters in this textbook. The Companion Website comprises seven distinct, functional features:

1) **Customized Online Resources**

2) **Student Centre**

3) **Faculty Centre**

4) **Communication**

5) **Contents**

6) **About the Authors**

7) **Ordering Info**

Explore the seven areas in this Companion Website. Students and distance learners will discover resources for indepth study, research, and communication, empowering them in their quest for greater knowledge and maximizing their potential for success in the course.

A NEW WAY TO DELIVER EDUCATIONAL CONTENT

1) Customized Online Resources

Our Companion Websites provide instructors and students with a range of options to access, view, and exchange content.

- **Syllabus Manager** provides *instructors* with the options of creating online classes and constructing an online syllabus linked to specific modules in the Companion Website.

- **Mailing lists** enable *instructors* and *students* to receive customized promotional literature.

- **Preferences** enable *students* to customize the sending of results to various recipients, and also to customize how the material is sent, e.g., as HTML, text, or as an attachment.

- **Help** includes an evaluation of the user's system and a tune-up area that makes updating browsers and plug-ins easier. This new feature will enhance the user's experience with Companion Websites.

www.pearsoned.ca/craig

2) Student Centre

Online Interactive Study Guide modules form the core of the student learning experience in the Companion Website. These modules are categorized according to their functionality:

- Objectives
- Multiple-Choice
- Fill-in-the-Blanks
- Matching
- Essay
- Glossary

The Multiple-Choice, Fill-in-the-Blanks, and Matching modules provide students with the ability to send answers to our grader and receive instant feedback on their progress through our Results Reporter. Coaching comments and references back to the textbook ensure that students take advantage of all resources available to enhance their learning experience.

3) Faculty Centre

This Companion Website provides a password-protected centre featuring the Instructor's Manual that accompanies this book.

4) Contents

Click here to view the detailed Table of Contents.

5) Communication

Companion Websites contain the communication tools necessary to deliver courses in a **Distance Learning** environment. **Message Board** allows users to post messages and check back periodically for responses. **Live Chat** allows users to discuss course topics in real time, and enables professors to host online classes.

Communication facilities of Companion Websites provide a key element for distributed learning environments. There are two types of communication facilities currently in use in Companion Websites:

- **Message Board** – this module takes advantage of browser technology providing the users of each Companion Website with a national newsgroup to post and reply to relevant course topics.

- **i-Chat** – enables instructor-led group activities in real time. Using our chat client, instructors can display Website content while students participate in the discussion.

6) About the Authors

Click here to find out more about the backgrounds of the authors.

7) Ordering Info

Click here to be linked to the catalogue description and the necessary ordering information for this title.

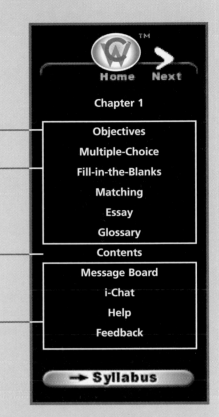

Note: Companion Website content will vary slightly from site to site depending on discipline requirements.

The Companion Website can be found at:

www.pearsoned.ca/craig

PEARSON EDUCATION CANADA

26 Prince Andrew Place
Don Mills, Ontario M3C 2T8

To order:
Call: 1-800-567-3800
Fax: 1-800-263-7733

For samples:
Call: 1-800-850-5813
Fax: (416) 447-2819
E-mail: phcinfo.pubcanada@pearsoned.com

Child Development: Perspectives, Processes, and Research Methods

Science is built up with facts,
as a house is built with stones.

HENRI POINCARÉ

Outline

CHAPTER 1

Objectives

By the time you have finished this chapter, you should be able to do the following:

✔ Discuss the goals of those who study child development.

✔ Identify developmental domains.

✔ Define biological and environmental processes of development, and explain how these two types of developmental processes interact.

✔ Explain how historical, socioeconomic, and cultural factors influence our understanding of human development.

✔ Describe the research methodology used in the study of human development.

✔ Describe the major categories of developmental research and explain their similarities and differences and their impact on cause-and-effect conclusions.

✔ Discuss the ethical principles that researchers should follow when conducting research with children.

In our house, we savour many memories as we go up and down the stairs. You see, along the walls we have photographs of our children taken over the years, from the time they were newborns. From time to time, my children will stop to inspect the pictures: "Will I always be shorter than my friends?" "Why didn't I have any hair when I was a baby?" "Is that me or Michele in your stomach, Mom?"

Sometimes their questions get me thinking about the study of development. Like most parents who have more than one child, I am struck by how similar my two children are. Whenever the younger one enters a new phase, he often reminds me of the older one when she was that age. Yet, at the same time, I am impressed by their individuality—even from their baby pictures it is readily apparent "who is who." And, as I noticed the other day, their individuality can be detected in the nature of the photographs themselves. The ones of Michele, my quieter, more serious child, often catch her reading, admiring animals, or engaging in other solitary pursuits. Those of her younger brother, Chris, a more outgoing child, often show him clowning around and surrounded by a horde of friends (Digdon).

The photographs of my children bring to mind three simple questions that motivate much of the study of development: What are the qualities of people the same age that set them apart from others who are older or younger? In what ways do individuals the same age differ from one another? What processes are responsible for the way people develop?

The Goals of Developmental Science

Complex and rich, full of quest and challenge, the process of human development is the product of many strands—the blending of the biological and the cultural, the intertwining of thought and feeling, the synthesis of inner motivations and external

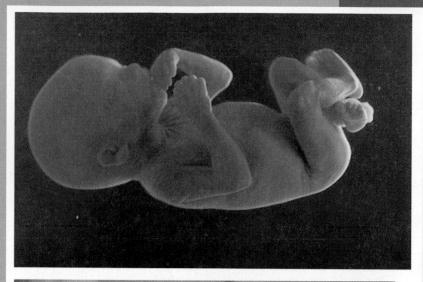

The life span stages depicted in this text are prenatal development, infancy, early childhood, middle childhood, and adolescence.

pressures. The process begins with conception and continues throughout the life of the individual.

In this book, our aim will be to examine developmental trends, principles, and processes across several disciplines as they affect children's development. We shall investigate the growing child at all ages and stages, from conception to adolescence, with attention to biology, anthropology, sociology, and psychology.

Understanding, Explanation, and Application

The goal of studying child development is to discover, amid all the complexities, some consistent common processes and major influences that affect behaviour. We begin with careful observations and descriptions of children's growth and behaviour. Then we generate hypotheses, test these hypotheses, and, we hope, progress to clear explanations and greater understanding. This understanding can often lead to applications aimed at improving the lives of children. "The test of true understanding of a phenomenon is the ability to change it" (Hetherington, 1998, p. 94).

In this country alone, there are many examples of people applying developmental research to help change children's lives for the better. Dr. Fraser Mustard, a founder of the Canadian Institute for Advanced Research, for example, is using research on preschool development to help design interventions for children at risk for school failure. Research has shown that children who are behind in kindergarten tend to lag behind their classmates in later years as well. In order to prevent this outcome, Dr. Mustard and the Toronto District School Board established an early intervention program aimed at providing at-risk preschool children with enrichment and parents with education about child development. Other communities across the country have also established early intervention programs, such as the Aboriginal Headstart program in northern Canada, a school-readiness program that was created to meet the cultural needs of Aboriginal children. Some early intervention programs start as early as the prenatal stage because this is a period of rapid growth (infants born small are at risk for a number of health problems), including the growth of the brain. Examples of prenatal programs are the Healthiest Babies Possible program in Vancouver, the Babies Best Start program in Toronto, and the Montreal Diet Dispensary program for pregnant women. The Good Food Box program in Kingston, Ontario, benefits pregnant women by providing nutritious foods to low-income families. These programs, like several others in the country, demonstrate the ways that developmental research is being applied in Canadian communities.

Key Terms and Concepts Related to the Study of Development

Before we go any further, there are some important terms and concepts used in the psychology of child development that you will need to understand.

Developmental Domains

development The changes over time in structure, thought, or behaviour of a person as a result of both biological and environmental influences.

Development refers to the changes over time in the structure, thought, or behaviour of a person owing to both biological and environmental influences. Usually these changes are progressive and cumulative, and they result in increasing organization and function.

Development occurs in three areas, or domains: the physical, the cognitive, and the psychosocial. The *physical domain* refers to physical characteristics such as size and shape, as well as to sensory capacities and motor skills. The *cognitive domain* (from the Latin word for "to know") involves all mental abilities and activities and even the organization of thought. This domain includes such activities as perception, reasoning, memory, problem solving, and language. The *psychosocial domain* refers to personality characteristics and social skills. This area of development includes the child's unique style of behaving, feeling, and reacting to social circumstances. For each child, development in these three domains occurs concurrently and interdependently.

The various domains of the child's existence interact in complex and unique ways. Development, therefore, is not piecemeal or haphazard; rather, it is holistic. Each aspect of development in normal, healthy children involves mutual and interactive changes in all three domains. Concept Summary Table 1-1 summarizes the three domains.

The study of children who are blind underscores the holistic nature of development. Research is showing that the effects of blindness are not limited to physical development; blindness also affects psychosocial and cognitive development. Ann Bigelow, a psychologist at St. Francis Xavier University, in Nova Scotia, has done a number of studies on babies and children born blind (see, for example, Bigelow, 1995, 1996). She has found that babies who are blind have difficulty with social interaction because they cannot see the reactions of people around them—they cannot return a smile they do not see. They are delayed in reaching for objects (because they cannot see them), and so are slow to learn about them. They are also delayed in crawling and walking, though not in sitting or standing. The features of their language—and the way they learn it—are quite different from those of other babies. For example, compared with sighted babies, babies who are blind are more limited in what they talk about. They refer almost exclusively to their own needs and actions and do not talk about things in their environment. They require their parents (or other people) to play a more directive role in pointing out new vocabulary.

Developmental Processes

Central to the concerns of developmental psychologists are the processes by which change takes place. There is no clear agreement on precisely how development happens, for example, on how children acquire a nearly complete grammar of their language by age 5 or on how they learn to read, to assume a sex role, or to express love, grief, and hostility. Developmental researchers investigate biological, environmental, distal, and proximal processes, as well as interactions among processes, the timing of development, and socialization. Let us look briefly at each of these aspects of development.

Biological Influences on Development All living organisms develop according to a genetic code or plan. In some organisms, such as moths and butterflies, the plan is precise and allows for little physical or behavioural alteration. When psychologists refer to the process of growing according to a genetic plan, they use the term **maturation.** The maturation process consists of a series of preprogrammed changes not only in the organism's form, but also in its complexity, integration, organization, and function. Faulty

> **maturation** The physical development of an organism as it fulfills its genetic potential.

Concept Summary

Table 1-1 An Overview of the Developmental Domains Organizing Growth and Behavioural Change	
The physical domain	Involves the basic growth and changes that occur in the individual's body. Changes can be external, such as in height and weight, as well as internal, such as in muscles, glands, the brain, and sense organs. Physical health and motor skills (for example, walking, crawling, and learning to write) are included in this domain.
The cognitive domain	Involves the mental processes related to thinking and problem solving. Changes include those in perception, memory, reasoning, creativity, and language.
The psychosocial domain	Involves the development of personality and interpersonal skills. These two areas are interrelated and include self-concept and emotions, as well as social skills and behaviours.

nutrition or illness may delay maturation, but proper nutrition, good health, and even encouragement and teaching will not necessarily speed it dramatically. This principle seems to be true for the human life span and for such processes as an infant's motor development and an adolescent's development of secondary sex characteristics.

Environmental Influences on Development   Our environment influences us every minute of the day. Light, sound, heat, food, drugs, anger, gentleness, severity—these and millions of other influences may fulfill basic biological and psychological needs, cause severe harm, attract our attention, or provide the components for learning. Some environmental influences are temporary and limited to just one situation, for example, a case of chicken pox at age 4. Others may be permanent, such as the sustained interaction with parents, or recurrent, as in the case of a grandparent who periodically enters the child's life.

Interaction of Biological and Environmental Influences   Some psychologists continue to debate how much of our behaviour is due to maturation and how much to learning. An infant first sits up, then stands, and finally walks primarily because of maturational processes. But even this behaviour can be obstructed by drugs, poor diet, fatigue, disease, restriction, or emotional stress. Certain behavioural limitations or characteristics are inherited in the genetic code; however, all behaviour develops within a specific environment. Robert Plomin (1990) points out, for example, that environmental factors can trigger an inherited susceptibility to a disease, such as asthma or diabetes. The disease may also affect socialization and intellectual development if it prevents participation in social or athletic events and interferes with school attendance. The same type of interaction can be seen in the relationship between inherited physical characteristics (such as body type, skin colour, and height) and a person's self-concept and social acceptance. Behaviour may be based on stereotypical expectancies (for example, fat people are jolly, adolescents are awkward) that the individual, as well as others, holds.

critical period The only point in time when a particular environmental factor can have an effect.

Timing   The interaction of biological and environmental processes may depend on exactly when an environmental effect occurs. There are various **critical periods** in human development—time spans when, and only when, a particular environmental factor can have an effect. Several critical periods occur during prenatal development, when certain chemicals, drugs, and diseases can adversely affect the development of specific body organs (see Chapter 4). For example, if a pregnant woman who lacks im-

Through the process of socialization, children everywhere learn the attitudes, beliefs, customs, values, and expectations of their society.

Before a child can learn to read, he must be ready to read.

munity to the rubella (or German measles) virus is exposed to the virus two months after conceiving, severe birth defects, such as deafness, or even spontaneous abortion (miscarriage) may result. If, however, that same woman were to be exposed to the virus six months after conceiving, no effects would occur.

Other periods exist during which the individual is more or less sensitive to environmental influences. An **optimal period** is similar to a critical period. It is the particular time span when a specific behaviour develops most successfully as a result of the interaction of maturation and learning. But an optimal period does not have the all-or-nothing quality of a critical period. Although there is an optimal time for a behaviour to develop, the behaviour can be learned at an earlier or later date. **Readiness** refers to the point at which individuals have matured sufficiently to learn a specific behaviour. They may be unable to learn the behaviour fully and efficiently before this maturational point, but it is not crucial that they learn it at the moment of readiness. For example, some children may be ready to learn subtraction at about 7 years of age. If, for some reason, they are not taught to subtract until age 8 or 10, however, the opportunity will not have been lost forever, as would be true of a process for which a critical period exists. The precise nature of timing in human development is still unknown. Are there critical periods for learning certain behaviours? Are there optimal periods for learning to read, to be a gymnast, or to speak a foreign language?

Socialization: A Reciprocal Process **Socialization** is the general process by which the individual becomes a member of a social group—a family, a community, a tribe, or the like. This process includes learning the attitudes, beliefs, customs, values, roles, and expectations of the social group. It is a lifelong process that helps individuals live comfortably and participate fully in their culture or in their cultural group within the larger society (Goslin, 1969).

Socialization is generally recognized as a two-way process. In the past, researchers saw children's behaviour as almost entirely the result of how parents and teachers treated the children. For example, researchers believed that children passively identified with and then imitated adults who were influential in their lives. More recently, many studies have focused on how parents and children mutually influence one another's behaviour (Hetherington & Baltes, 1988). Infants are socialized by their experience within the family, but their very presence, in turn, forces family members to learn new roles. Perhaps the following example will help to illustrate this point.

optimal period The time during which a behaviour is most easily developed. However, an optimal period does not have the all-or-nothing quality of a critical period.

readiness A point in time when an individual has matured enough to benefit from a particular learning experience.

socialization The general process by which the individual becomes a member of a social group.

Question to Ponder

Can you think of instances of reciprocal socialization that apply to your life? How have your parents socialized you? How have you socialized your parents?

The birth of a baby socializes every other family member into new roles.

proximal processes Factors that affect an individual's development through his direct interactions with others, such as critical interactions with family or peers. The focus of study zooms in on the details of the interactions.

distal processes The broader context of development, including outside factors that can influence how individuals interact with others. The focus of study is like a wide-angle lens.

norms Average development for children of certain ages.

Paul and June were a professional couple in their forties who had been married for 16 years before the birth of their first child. They were happy about the arrival of their daughter but found that having a baby led to many changes in their lifestyle. For example, they could no longer spontaneously decide to go out to dinner and a movie after work. They had to first find a babysitter, and then pick her up. They had to be home by a set time, and then return to the sitter's house before stumbling into bed. To make matters worse, they could no longer sleep in! The days of a carefree "dinc" (double-income-no-children) lifestyle were over. Nevertheless, after several months of adjustment, they could no longer imagine life without their daughter.

The arrival of a child helped change Paul and June into "parents" with new roles and behaviours that reflect their new responsibility and with some ability to defer their wants. In this way, current views of socialization stress the two-directional or shared experience of socialization.

Proximal and Distal Processes   Psychologists use the terms **proximal** and **distal processes** to explain behaviour. Proximal processes are factors that are present at the time the behaviour occurs and that have a direct effect upon it. Distal processes are factors that are not present at the time of the behaviour and that affect the behaviour indirectly. For example, when trying to understand why bullies target some children and not others, researchers look at both proximal and distal processes. To study proximal processes, researchers focus on how the bullied child interacts with peers, as if using a zoom lens to look at the interactions in detail. In this type of study, researchers in Montreal found that some bullied children are overly submissive and come across as easy targets who are unlikely to defend themselves (Hodges, Boivin, Vitaro, & Bukowski, 1999). To study distal processes, researchers look beyond the immediate context of the bullying to other factors that might explain why children are overly submissive. It is like using a wide-angle lens to view the "bigger picture." For example, a distal factor related to bullying might be the bullied child's relationship with his parents. One study found that bullied boys were overly dependent on parents and were socialized to be nonassertive (Ladd & Ladd, 1998). The boys' relationships with their parents affected how they interacted with peers. Developmental psychologists focus on both proximal and distal processes in order to gain a more complete understanding of behaviour.

Developmental Norms and Pathways

The study of development sometimes focuses on an individual child, often a special case, such as Helen Keller or the Dionne quintuplets. Without necessarily generalizing the conclusions to other children, researchers have studied these cases in detail to see how the children developed in their unusual circumstances. Most of the time, though, researchers do not focus on an individual child, but instead try to reach conclusions that will apply to many children. To draw conclusions, researchers study a group of children and report the average performance of the group. These averages are called **norms.** Most textbooks on development, including this one, report developmental norms or averages. For example, the norm for babies learning to walk is 12 months. We must also realize, though, that not all babies learn to walk at exactly 12 months; there is normal variation around the average. Learning to walk at 9 months or at 15 months is well within the normal range. It is important to be aware of this normal variation in the timing of development—not all children develop at the same rate. The establishment of norms, though, can help us identify children who are outside the range of normal variation. Establishing norms can be useful, for example, in designing programs to help children who are developmentally delayed or gifted.

In addition to identifying norms, the study of development describes how children change from one age to the next, outlining the typical *pathway*, or course of development. We must be cautious, though, in assuming that all children follow the same path of development. More and more, developmental psychologists are recognizing that there are many different pathways, rather than a single one. Thus, not only are there variations in the rate at which children develop, but there are also differences in how they develop, making the study of development more complex.

The study of development is also complicated by the diverse range of environmental factors that influence how children develop. Children live in families, which are part of communities, which are part of societies at particular times in history, all of which can affect development.

Historical, Socioeconomic, and Cultural Perspectives

The study of child development views both the individual and society as entities that change with the passage of time. Societies change over time in response to historical events, such as industrialization, and also in response to variations in the population structure, such as the baby boom. Individuals change biologically, personally, and socially over time. In addition to these patterns of change, there are differences in how societies and individuals interact. For example, children born in different cultures have different experiences. Developmental psychologists have, therefore, developed a number of ways of taking historical, socioeconomic, and cultural influences into account.

Historical Perspectives

Looking at child development from a historical perspective gives us a richer understanding of development by identifying developmental trends that are consistent over time, as well as aspects of development that are unique to a historical period. It is important to identify common historical trends so that we appreciate how the present is affected by the past. For instance, we may wonder why Canada does not have a nationally funded child-care system today. Part of the reason lies in our history. A deeply rooted belief in our society is that families, not governments, are most responsible for the care of children. This belief is not deeply rooted in some other countries, such as Sweden, which has developed a national child-care system.

A historical perspective is valuable, as well, because it shows us whether aspects of development that seem "normal" today are persistent through history or whether they are unique to our time. A good example is the recommended age for toilet training. In the 1950s, it was common for people to toilet train infants who were less than a year old, and most infants would be trained by 18 months. Today, the Canadian Paediatric Association recommends that toilet training be initiated between 2 and 2½ years, and some children are not toilet trained until they are 3 or 4 years old. This circumstance is so common that makers of disposable diapers and "pull ups" have added new larger sizes. A historical perspective toward toilet training helps us to appreciate that today's advice might be as changeable as the advice that came before it. What will people a hundred years from now think of our current attitudes toward children and child rearing?

A number of events in Canadian history have had a profound impact on Canadian society and on the care of its children. These events are summarized in greater detail in the box "Canadian History and the Experiences of Children."

Socioeconomic Perspectives

The socioeconomic perspective looks at the social effects of varying degrees of prosperity in society. This analysis includes global factors that affect most of the society, as well as factors that affect only a subgroup within the society. In hard economic times, governments cut back spending on education, health, and social assistance. More parents

Question to Ponder

Can you think of examples of current changes in Canadian society that might affect child development?

In the late 1800s, it was common for Canadian children to work to help support the family.

FOCUS ON AN ISSUE

Canadian History and the Experiences of Children

THE TIME OF CONFEDERATION

In 1867, when Canada became a country, most citizens assumed that the care of children was private—they believed that it was more the responsibility of families and communities than of governments. Canadians of European heritage were pioneers who valued the self-sufficiency of the family. Most lived in rural areas and provided for their own needs; when they could not meet their needs, they turned to extended family, friends, and the church. There was no official government support for families in need. Similarly, the care of children in Aboriginal communities emphasized the self-sufficiency of local communities. Because families and communities were seen as self-sufficient, the government did not have a need to develop social programs. The need for social programming changed, though, as Canada became more industrialized and urban.

INDUSTRIALIZATION

Between 1880 and 1900, the urban population of Canada more than doubled, going from 14 percent to 37 percent of the total populace (Wallace, 1995). Urban families found it difficult to be self-sufficient because most jobs were low-paying factory positions. Poor families required their children to do manual labour in the factories to supplement the family income, and children as young as 6 years routinely worked 9- to 10-hour days. In Montreal, children too young to work often were placed temporarily in church-run or-

phanages until the family could afford to take them back. In small communities in Nova Scotia, work was scarce, and older children had to leave the community to find work, often in western Canada or in the United States.

Gradually, public outcry erupted over the harsh treatment of children and the lack of government intervention. In 1888, Ontario passed An Act for the Protection and Reformation of Neglected Children, which overrode the rights and privileges of parents by allowing children to be removed from

---

Over one million Canadian children live in poverty today.

---

abusive or neglectful homes (Howe, 1995). Other provinces soon followed Ontario's lead, and by the early 1900s all provinces had similar child welfare and child protection laws.

Around this time, schools became more available. There was a move from private schools that served children from privileged families to public schools that provided free education for all children. Interestingly, there was public backlash against the schools because they conflicted with the value that child rearing is a private, family responsibility. "It (public school) kills the sense of duty in the parent, who is naturally bound to educate, as well as to feed and clothe the children whom he brings into the world" (Heaton, 1886, as quoted in Wallace, 1995).

THE WAR YEARS AND THE DEPRESSION

Deaths on the battlefields of World War I led to a decline in the population and to a significant increase in the number of fatherless families. Provincial governments responded by introducing mother's allowances (government cheques given to mothers to help them support their children); the first province to do so was Manitoba, in 1916. Mother's allowances were thought to serve numerous purposes: to reduce infant mortality (and thus increase the population), to help families afford to let their children stay in school rather than work, and to reduce juvenile delinquency. In offering mother's allowances, governments showed commitment to the family, rather than to institutions such as orphanages and industrial schools, as the place for raising children.

Foster homes were established to care for children whose biological families were unable to do so. The government no longer left the raising of children entirely to the discretion of families. The Canada Council on Child Welfare published a number of pamphlets on child-rearing issues and sent them to mothers so that they would know how to parent "properly." For example, mothers were advised, "Remember that a child is born without habits. Teach him only good ones.... If you pick him up each time he stirs, you will teach him to cry whenever he is lying down" (Strong-Boag, 1983, pp. 164–165).

However, the government adopted a different attitude toward the up-

---

are unemployed, and more families live in poverty (we will discuss the effects of poverty in Chapter 9).

A number of economic factors affect Canadian children. For instance, in 1997 the Canadian Labour Congress reported that of industrialized countries, Canada has one of the highest rates of low-paid employment for women (as cited in Freiler & Cerny, 1998). The minimum wage is below the poverty line in every province and territory. Furthermore, the rate of poverty among single-parent families headed by women has been 56 to 57 percent since 1980, one of the highest rates in the industrialized world. In addition to low minimum wages, the rules associated with social assistance contribute to the poverty of women and their children. Single mothers on social assistance are

bringing of Aboriginal children. Instead of focusing on strengthening Aboriginal families, the government removed children from their homes and sent them to residential schools, often far away from their parents and communities. Children at the schools were forbidden to speak their Aboriginal languages and lost most of their culture and traditional ways, and consequently their pride in their heritage. (Residential schools remained in operation until the 1970s.)

After World War I, the Great Depression led to an increase in the number of children growing up in poverty. Poverty was so widespread that it challenged people's beliefs about its causes. Prior to the Depression, many assumed that laziness or weakness caused poverty. The Depression forced people to reconsider and to entertain the idea that poverty was caused by economic and societal conditions, not by deficiencies in people. This change in perception was important because different interpretations of the cause of poverty led to a move toward more humane treatment of the poor.

WORLD WAR II AND THE POSTWAR YEARS

World War II, in 1939, led to an increase in mothers working outside the home, often employed in the war industry and in positions vacated by men enlisted in the military. The federal government offered support for mothers by providing day nurseries for children under age 5 and day cares for older children. Child-care centres were established in Ontario and Quebec but not in the other, less-industrialized provinces. During the war, child-care centres were viewed as a legitimate government expenditure because the mothers were helping the war effort. Child-care centres were also seen as a way to prevent poor health and juvenile delinquency (the goal of preventing juvenile delinquency is a recurring theme in Canadian history).

After the war attitudes changed, and there was strong resistance to the use of nonparental care. Society assumed that only desperate families deserved help with child care and that mothers who were not in financial straits but desired child care were neglectful. Interestingly, there was a political side to government-funded child care. Many of the most outspoken advocates for child care were members of the Canadian Communist Party; thus, government-funded child care began to be seen as a communist threat (Finkel, 1995). On April 1, 1946, the federal government stopped funding child care and passed the responsibility on to provincial governments, who, in turn, passed it on to municipalities. At the same time, governments developed more stringent standards of care, forcing many centres to close because they could not afford to meet these standards. By 1962, the network of wartime child-care centres had almost entirely disappeared.

During the late 1940s, government support shifted from child-care centres (for children of working mothers) to nursery schools (for children of full-time homemakers). The purpose of nursery school was education, not the prevention of juvenile delinquency or the preservation of families, as was the case with wartime child-care centres. Trustees of boards of education often were opposed to social programs in the schools, as they believed that the sole mandate of schools was to educate. For instance, in 1947 a Toronto trustee spoke against providing free milk in schools because it would result in "the loss of initiative and entrepreneurship on the part of the children.... Free milk was going to do far more harm than good because we want to teach our children to get what they want by themselves" (quoted in Finkel, 1995, p. 266). Given this intolerance of dependency in children, imagine what was thought of parents who were not self-sufficient!

Recently, there has been more support for the idea that Canadian society has a responsibility to protect the rights and well-being of children. For example, in 1991 Canada approved the charter from the United Nations Convention on the Rights of the Child. The charter focused on children's rights in the areas of identity, learning and self-expression, family and community, mental and physical well-being, and protection. By approving the charter, Canada agreed to submit progress reports to the United Nations and submitted the first in 1994, which resulted in the publication of *The Progress of Canada's Children, 1996* (CCSD, 1996). We will be referring to some of the findings of this report in later chapters. Compared with earlier times, the lot of many Canadian children has improved dramatically. However, there is room for improvement because not all Canadian children have experienced better living conditions—over one million Canadian children live in poverty today.

expected to work once their youngest child reaches a certain age, which varies from province to province (ranging from 6 months in Alberta to 7 years in British Columbia).

One of the most recent socioeconomic concerns of Canadian families is the need to balance work and family life (Canadian Council on Social Development [CCSD], 1996). Workplace initiatives, such as on-site child care, job sharing, and flex-time, can make it easier for parents to juggle the demands of work with the responsibilities of parenting. Initiatives such as these, currently being implemented in many workplaces across the country, are in part a result of looking at child development from a socioeconomic perspective.

Cultural Perspectives

In order to understand how children develop, we must be knowledgeable about their cultures. The same behaviour can have very different meanings in different cultures. For instance, children from European backgrounds are socialized to show respect by making eye contact when an adult is speaking to them. When children look away, they are reprimanded: "Look at me when I am talking to you." However, maintaining eye contact with adults is not a universal sign of respect. Aboriginal children in Canada, as well as children in Japan and in Lebanon, among other countries, are expected to show respect by averting their gaze. Too much eye contact is disrespectful. One of my students who grew up in Lebanon recalls her mother scolding her, "Don't you dare look at me when I am talking to you" (Digdon).

It is important that we be aware of the ways that culture affects development so that we do not misinterpret a child's behaviour.

We also must be informed about differences in physical development related to a child's heritage. Hispanic or Asian babies often develop a bluish birthmark across their buttocks at birth or a few weeks after birth. It would be easy for people who are unaware of what the birthmark is to mistake it for a bruise. The birthmark usually fades with time.

Parental decisions about how to raise children can be affected by cultural values. For instance, many Canadian parents expect their infants to learn to sleep alone through the night. The parents encourage the infants to develop comfort habits, such as sucking on a pacifier or thumb, to help them soothe themselves if they awaken during the night. But in many other cultures around the world, it is unusual for babies to sleep alone. Instead, babies sleep with their mothers and breast-feed on demand throughout the night (Morelli, Rogoff, Oppenheim, & Goldsmith, 1992). It is important that in studying human development we take into account cultural variations such as these, which can have an impact on the course of development.

Children in some cultures, such as this Japanese girl, are expected to show respect by not maintaining eye contact with adults.

The Systematic Study of Human Development

The search for reliable, verifiable facts about human development is a complicated one. What are the differences between the evidence of our personal experience and the researcher's data? At what point does the researcher stop looking for more evidence? Both the casual observer and the researcher must decide what constitutes reliable evidence and when enough has been gathered to support a theory. Personal experience can be useful and important, but it must be tested in a more systematic way before others are likely to believe it. We rarely prove anything with absolute certainty. Nevertheless, if we can gather enough convincing evidence, it is possible that other people will come to similar conclusions.

Asking Good Questions

Thoughtful questions and astute observation have stimulated most breakthroughs in the natural and social sciences. Someone noticed something intriguing and different, asked probing questions, continued to observe it, and then systematically tested the phenomenon before arriving at some basis for generalization and prediction. Suppose, for example, that we look at the pictures of a house and some human beings as drawn by a 5½-year-old (see Figure 1-1). On closer observation, we notice that the house sits directly on the ground but the chimney leans at a strange angle. Looking at the small figures at the bottom, we notice that the bodies and the heads are combined and that their limbs are out of proportion. (These kinds of human figures are often called "tadpole people.") Are these just common "errors" caused by a child's poor motor coordination? Are they the idiosyncrasies of a particular child?

Jean Piaget, who developed a comprehensive theory of cognitive development through his astute observations of children, suggested that children's drawings are not just awkward reproductions of what they see; instead, they are representations of the way children think and construct "reality." After collecting drawings from many children, he proposed that pictures reveal the unique quality of children's understanding, as well as their lack of understanding about relationships between objects and the world. When compared with adults, young children appear to have cognitive limitations. In fact, these are not deficiencies but rather differences in the cognitive structures adults and children use. Unlike adults, children may see things from only their own point of view (egocentrism), or they may focus on only one relationship at a time (centration). In the child's experience, things "on" something else are usually related in a particular way. Therefore, their houses sit flat on the ground, and their chimneys rise perpendicular to the angles of the roofs.

What about the "tadpole people"? Do children really think that people's faces are on their abdomens? No, say Piaget and some others. The child's drawing is a representation of what the child considers important things about people (Freeman, 1980). Rather than being like a photograph, the drawing is the child's symbolic representation of her thinking and understanding of the world. Not all researchers agree with Piaget's interpretation of children's drawings. But Piaget was able to demonstrate certain common features often found in the drawings of children at different age levels, and he was able to stimulate others to do systematic research on children's thinking as expressed in their art (Winner, 1986).

Using the Scientific Method

Conducting research serves diverse and important purposes in our daily lives, but it principally serves to help us assess the truth of our beliefs regarding others, the nature of the world, and ourselves. Developmental research, in particular, is a means of amassing a body of knowledge regarding child growth and development to help us determine

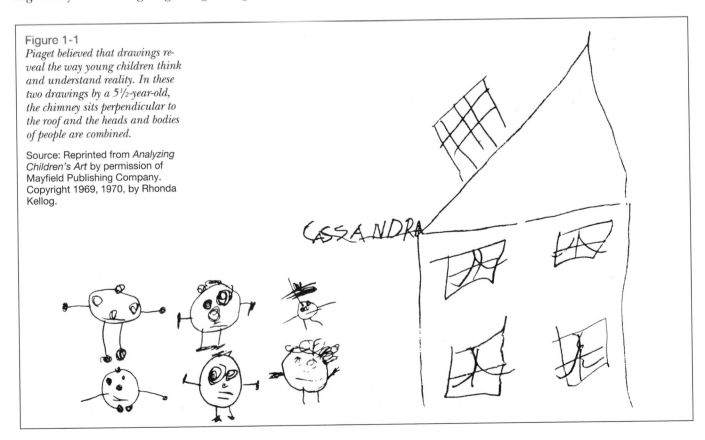

Figure 1-1
Piaget believed that drawings reveal the way young children think and understand reality. In these two drawings by a 5½-year-old, the chimney sits perpendicular to the roof and the heads and bodies of people are combined.

Source: Reprinted from *Analyzing Children's Art* by permission of Mayfield Publishing Company. Copyright 1969, 1970, by Rhonda Kellog.

whether social and educational interventions really work. In short, research and its appropriate methodologies are the sole source of an efficient, verifiable, and accurate study of human development (Kermis, 1984).

Research in child development follows the same scientific method used in any other branch of the social and behavioural sciences. Researchers may have different ideas about what to observe and how best to measure it, but most research essentially consists of four steps:

1. *Define the problem.* Determine specifically what you, the researcher, are interested in studying.
2. *Formulate hypotheses about the suspected causes of the problem.* Predict what is producing the behaviour you are interested in.
3. *Investigate the hypothesis.* First, collect the data, and second, analyze the data, using appropriate statistical measures.
4. *Draw conclusions.* Demonstrate the causal relationships suggested in your initial hypotheses.

A brief discussion of these steps may help us to understand the way research is designed.

Define the Research Problem The study of child development is full of interesting questions. What does the newborn infant see? How soon does the infant see the garden in the way we see it? Is adolescence necessarily a period of storm and stress, or can it be a smooth transition to adulthood? What are the differences in moral development demonstrated by adolescent boys and girls? How do these differences manifest themselves in adolescent social behaviour? Interesting as they may be, such broad questions are not effective research questions. Before we can conduct a study, we need to narrow the problem to something testable. "How do children learn language?" is too broad. "How does the child begin to understand metaphor, sarcasm, or other forms of nonliteral language?" is a narrower question, but it is not yet testable.

In a recent series of studies, the researchers were interested in how children learn to understand sarcasm. Sarcasm is, after all, a complicated language form. When the airline loses your luggage and your best friend says, "Well, this must be your lucky day!" he is being sarcastic. The speaker does not literally intend what he says. There is subtlety, irony, and nuance to the meaning of the literal words. There may be humour or cruelty in sarcasm. Adults detect sarcasm using two cues: (1) the context contradicts what the speaker has said, and (2) the speaker often uses tone of voice to signal the meaning. But young children tend to miss these cues; they understand things literally. Researchers can ask, "Which of these cues does the child first understand, and at what age, and in what context?" The researchers have now formulated a testable question (Capelli, Nakagawa, & Madden, 1990).

Develop a Hypothesis In most studies, researchers specify their expectations in the form of a hypothesis. They make a prediction about what will happen in the study. In the study on children's understanding of sarcasm, the researchers predicted that children would be able to use intonation or tone of voice much sooner than they would understand the contextual cues. Even very young children listen to vocal expressions as a clue to emotions. But for them to understand the contrast between the context and the literal meaning of the speaker is a much more difficult task.

Test the Hypothesis To test whether the hypothesis is correct, researchers choose a specific procedure, decide on a setting, determine a measurement, and select certain aspects of the situation to be controlled. Researchers must be careful to design the observations so that they are measuring the behaviour systematically and without bias. In the study on understanding sarcasm, the researchers invented several stories. Each story had two versions: a sarcastic one and a serious one. They tape-recorded these stories in two ways: sometimes the punch line was said in a mocking, sarcastic way, and sometimes it was delivered in a neutral tone of voice. Then they played these stories, some serious and some sarcastic, to third graders, sixth graders, and adults, and compared their reactions on a systematic questionnaire (Capelli, Nakagawa, & Madden, 1990).

Draw Conclusions Based on the evidence collected, researchers must draw conclusions that neither overstate nor understate what they have found. In the study of sarcasm, the adults clearly identified all sarcastic responses whenever there were context cues (lost luggage), intonation cues (a mocking tone of voice), or both types of cues available. Sixth graders had considerable difficulty when there was no change in intonation, and third graders almost never understood the sarcasm unless there was a sarcastic tone of voice. The authors concluded that children initially depend much more heavily on intonation than on context to recognize sarcasm (Capelli, Nakagawa, & Madden, 1990).

> **Question to Ponder**
>
> What do you think are the advantages and disadvantages of using the scientific method to study child development?

Collecting Data in Developmental Psychology

Research studies produce widely varying findings, depending on the measurements used and the individuals selected for study. Subjects may be observed in real-life situations, or they may be tested in controlled, contrived situations. They may take written tests to determine their level of achievement, their ability to solve problems, or their creativity. The researchers may observe their behaviour directly or ask the participants to report on it. It may be helpful if we examine some of the specific types of research designs.

The three most commonly used research methods are naturalistic observations, correlations, and experiments.

Naturalistic Observations
Studies that use **naturalistic observations** involve observing children in their natural environments, such as at home, in school, or on the playground. The researcher simply records the ongoing behaviour, without in any way attempting to control or change it. For example, Pepler and Craig (1995) recorded the aggressive behaviours of children on a school playground in Toronto. They used video cameras with zoom lenses so that they could record the behaviour from a distance to prevent children from reacting to their presence. As well, they attached wireless microphones to the children's clothing to pick up conversations. Using this method, Pepler and Craig were able to observe more subtle forms of aggression, such as verbal aggression in girls. The method worked well with younger children (6- to 10-

> **naturalistic observations**
> Recording the ongoing behaviour of children in their natural environments without attempting in any way to change or control the environments.

Naturalistic observation is one of the most commonly used research methods in child psychology.

FOCUS ON APPLICATION

Observing Children in Child-Care Centres

Child-care workers are experts at observing children and use a number of special observational methods, such as anecdotal records, running records, and time sampling.

Anecdotal records are descriptions of a key event or behaviour. Descriptive, objective language is used so that people reading the anecdotal record get a sense of "being there." The focus is on what the child-care worker saw and heard the child do, rather than on inferences of what the child was thinking or feeling. Here is an example of an anecdotal record that describes the interaction between two 3-year-olds and their teacher while the children were getting dressed to go outside:

> Recorded by Mary Shaw on May 18, 1999, 10:30 a.m.: Sherri, Dana, and Teacher. In cubbies dressing for outdoor play. Sherri bends over with eyes close to Dana's coat zipper. She puts the two parts together, but when she tried to pull it up, it slips out. She grits her teeth, stomps her foot, looks up at teacher. "I tan't dit it." Teacher bends down and says to Dana, "Dana, you put this part in and hold it so Sherri can put this little part in the slot." She does. Dana says, "Thanks Sherri. You're my buddy, right?" Sherri says, "Right Dana." (Nilsen, 1997, p. 38)

Child-care workers are experts at observing children.

Notice that the anecdotal record includes who made the recording, the date and time, and a play-by-play description of what took place and what was said (word for word, attempting to capture the child's pronunciation). Anecdotal records enable the child-care worker to document the behaviour of individual children. These records can be kept in the child's file so that workers can monitor the children's development. They also can be considered when child-care workers plan curricula. In this example, the teacher could plan to bring in dress-up clothing with zippers for the dramatic play area to follow up on the children's interest in mastering zippers.

Running records are similar to anecdotal records but are not limited to one event or behaviour. Running records cover a longer period of time, from half an hour to several months. Sometimes recordings are made every day; other times they are made a day here and there. Keeping a running record is like creating a movie of the child's behaviour. Running records are useful for placing a problem behaviour in the context of what came immediately before it (the antecedents) and immediately after it (the consequences). They can reveal possible causes for children's behaviour. The disadvantage of running records is the extra effort and time they take to create, but the advantage is their completeness.

---

year-olds) but not older children (11- and 12-year-olds). The older children were more aware of the microphones and were more self-conscious about being observed.

Studies that use naturalistic observations often go to great lengths to ensure that the observer does not affect the behaviour of the observed. Therefore, the main advantage of naturalistic observations is that they allow us to learn about the everyday behaviours of children. This quality of reflecting real life is called **ecological validity.** These studies provide rich descriptions of behaviour but do not allow us to uncover its causes. Hypotheses about the causes of behaviour can be tested in experiments.

Sometimes observers form relationships with the people they wish to observe. For example, in *ethnography,* a research method commonly used in anthropology, anthropologists live among other cultural groups, becoming participant observers of the way of life within the group. The main advantage of ethnography is that it attempts to get an insider's view. For example, Sibylle Artz, through the Youth Violence Project in Victoria, used ethnography to study violent girls. Over the course of a year, she spent hundreds of hours with six of the girls and with their parents, teachers, counsellors, and law enforcement officers. One of the interesting findings from the study was that the girls saw themselves more as victims of violence (and they were—both at home and with peers). They downplayed the negative effects of their own violent behaviour and justified it by saying that the victim deserved it. In the words of one girl, "It just kinda happened after she mouthed me off, I was just totally freaked with her. I wouldn't necessarily kill her, but I'd get her good. I just want to teach her a lesson. I'd beat the crap out of her. She's pissed me off so badly, I just want to give her two black eyes. Then I'd be fine. I'd have gotten the last word in" (Artz, 1998, p. 89).

ecological validity The results of a study give an accurate portrayal of the behaviour in the "real world."

Time sampling provides a record of how often a behaviour occurs, rather than a description of the behaviour. The following is an example of a grid that could be used to do time sampling of how often children go to different play areas during free play sessions.

During each five minute interval, the child-care worker scans the room to see where each child is playing. Time samples provide information about all of the children. Where does a particular child spend most of her time? Does she play with one child more than others? Is any child consistently left out? In addition to providing information about the children, time samples tell us about the popularity of different play areas.

Time (in five-minute intervals)

Play areas	10:05	10:10	10:15	10:20	10:25	10:30
Artwork	Geoff Paul Sarah	Geoff Karl	Susan Brittany	–	–	–
Dress-up clothes	Susan Brittany	Susan Brittany Tina	Tina Sarah	Susan Brittany Tina Sarah	Susan Brittany Tina Sarah Maggie	Geoff Karl Paul Maggie
Puzzles	Karl	Paul Sarah	Geoff Karl Paul	–	–	Susan Brittany Colin Kevin
Water table	Todd Amin	Todd Amin	Maggie Beth	Maggie Beth Geoff Karl	Beth Geoff Karl Todd	Beth Todd Amin
Blocks	Colin Tina Beth	Maggie Beth	Todd Amin	Paul Todd	Paul Amin	–
Reading centre	Maggie	Ana Chen	–	Amin	–	Ana
Indoor slide	Kevin Ana	Colin Kevin	Ana Chen Colin	Ana Colin Kevin	Ana Colin Kevin	–
Watching	Chen	–	Kevin	Chen	Chen	Chen

Correlations These studies look for relationships between variables. A *variable* is any measure that can take on different values. An example is the amount of violent television children watch—some children watch more than others. In a study of **correlations,** the researcher simply measures how much violent television children watch to determine whether this amount is related to other variables, such as the number of times children behave aggressively. Do children who watch more violent television also act more aggressively? If so, there is a *direct relationship* between the variables, or a *positive correlation*. However, if children who watch more violent television behave less aggressively than other children, there is a *negative correlation*. And if there is no association between television viewing and aggression, there is a *zero correlation*.

It is important to note that the researcher does not control the variables in correlational studies (for example, the researcher does not regulate children's television viewing habits). This lack of control makes it difficult to determine whether one variable caused the other. Correlational studies simply prove whether variables are related (or unrelated). Suppose there is a positive correlation between viewing violent television and behaving aggressively. There are three equally plausible explanations: (1) television caused the aggression, (2) children who were more aggressive preferred violent television, and their aggression caused them to watch more of it, or (3) watching violent television and aggression were not causally related at all but were correlated because of a third variable. For example, perhaps children who did not spend much time interacting with parents watched more television and behaved more aggressively because of the lack of parent monitoring. Correlational studies do not allow us to distinguish which interpretation is correct. To determine causes, researchers have to conduct an experiment.

correlations Relationships between variables. Correlations do not prove cause and effect.

independent variable The variable that experimenters manipulate in order to observe its effects on the dependent variable.

dependent variable The variable in an experiment that changes as a result of manipulating the independent variable.

designing experiments An experiment requires the manipulation of an independent variable in a controlled setting to see whether the independent variable causes changes in a dependent variable. Greatest control is achieved by conducting the experiment in a tightly controlled environment, such as a laboratory. When experiments are properly controlled, they allow researchers to determine the causes of behaviour.

Experiments In an experiment, the researchers systematically change some of the conditions, or **independent variables,** and observe the resultant behaviour, or **dependent variables.** For example, an experiment could be conducted to see whether violent television makes children aggressive. To do this experiment, the researchers could control the children's exposure to violent television, the independent variable. The children might be randomly assigned to one of two conditions. In one condition, the children could be shown violent television; in the other, children could be shown nonviolent television. As well, the researchers would have to ensure that the children's experiences in the two conditions were identical except for the presence or absence of violence. That way, any differences in the children's aggression could not be explained by other factors.

Designing experiments, however, can be challenging and not without problems. Consider the following example: a first-year student arrives at university never having had an alcoholic drink. The student feels pressured by peers to try some alcohol, so he decides to do an experiment. The first night he drinks wine mixed with soda, and the next morning he has a headache. The second night he tries rum mixed with soda, and the following morning he has a headache and an upset stomach. The third night he drinks Scotch mixed with soda, and the next morning he is so ill that he cannot get out of bed. "Great," he says with relief, "I have learned my lesson. No more soda for me!"

Experiments can be tricky because sometimes there is an uncontrolled variable that is causing the results, rather than the independent variable. Uncontrolled variables are called *confounds.* Sometimes, in order to control all the confounds, the experiment becomes so artificial that it does not resemble behaviour in the real world.

In 1979, Urie Bronfenbrenner described developmental psychology as "the science of the strange behavior of the child in a strange situation with a strange adult for the shortest period of time" (p. 19). He said this because at the time there was a strong preference for studying children through experiments in laboratories, rather than through other types of studies. Since that time, developmental psychology has come to recognize the importance of the context in which development occurs (Elder, Modell, & Parke, 1994; Kagitcibasi, 1996; Magnusson, 1996; Moen, Elder, & Luscher, 1995). Researchers are increasingly attempting to combine the precision of laboratory experiments with the ecological validity of naturalistic settings.

Research conducted in natural settings enables researchers to study the everyday lives of children, but it often lacks the appropriate controls to allow conclusions about cause and effect.

Some topics in developmental psychology cannot be studied through experiments. To do an experiment, the researcher must manipulate the variable of interest, and some variables cannot be manipulated. For example, researchers wanting to understand the effects of parent death on child development obviously could not control this variable. The researcher could, however, use naturalistic observations or correlational studies. Therefore, developmental psychology needs both experiments and other designs to adequately study the range of topics addressed in the field.

Longitudinal, Cross-Sectional, and Sequential Designs As we mentioned earlier, development is a continual, dynamic, and lifelong process, and so developmental studies, in contrast to other types of research, focus on change over time. Any field of study concerned with time-associated or age-associated change is considered a developmental discipline. Developmental psychology, therefore, focuses on the description, explanation, prediction, and modification of age-associated behaviour change.

Let us now look at three types of research designs that are used in developmental psychology. The differences among these designs are summarized in Concept Summary Table 1-2.

LONGITUDINAL DESIGNS

In a **longitudinal design,** scientists study the same individuals at different points in their lives. The time period during which people are studied varies from a few months to several years. Longitudinal studies of infants tend to involve a shorter time frame because development happens so rapidly in infancy. For example, Daphne Maurer and Terri Lewis, at McMaster University, have conducted longitudinal studies of blind babies who have had surgery to restore their sight (1993). Each baby's vision is tested shortly after surgery and again on later occasions, up to several months after surgery. Other longitudinal studies, however, can last for decades. Lewis Terman and collaborators conducted a longitudinal study of high-IQ children that lasted for over 60 years. The children were first tested in 1922, again in 1928, and then approximately every five years until the mid-1980s (Elder, Modell, & Parke, 1994).

Longitudinal designs are especially appealing to the developmental psychologist. Because individuals are compared with themselves at different points in time, test subjects do not have to be sorted and carefully matched. Some developmental processes can be looked at closely by studying these individuals every week, or even every day. In the study of language development in the second or third year of life, for example, a small

> **longitudinal design** A study in which the same people are observed continually over a period of time.

Concept Summary

Table 1-2   Common Developmental Research Designs

Longitudinal designs	Groups of participants are studied repeatedly over time; multiple times of testing occur at different ages. *Asset:* Shows relationships between early and late behaviours. *Liability:* Possibility of age changes being misinterpreted because of selective dropout, familiarity with testing materials, and cohort effects.
Cross-sectional designs	Groups of participants of different ages are tested at the same time. *Asset:* Conducted more quickly and more efficiently than the longitudinal design. *Liabilities:* Age differences are studied rather than age changes because of the single test time; does not permit the study of growth trends; cohort effects may influence age differences.
Sequential designs	Two or more groups of children born at different times are tested repeatedly over time. *Assets:* Permits both longitudinal and cross-sectional comparisons of children's performance; allows researchers to measure the existence of cohort effects. *Liabilities:* May have some of the problems of both cross-sectional and longitudinal studies, but the design helps to identify these difficulties; more expensive and longer time frame is necessary to collect data.

FOCUS ON APPLICATION

Quiz on Being a Critical Consumer of Information

Try to answer each of the following questions before you read the answer key.

1. A newspaper headline reads, "Heavy Drinkers Get Lower College Grades." What would you conclude from this headline? Did the drinking cause the lower grades?

2. A private school advertises that its students score 10 points higher in math than do children in public school. What can you conclude from this advertisement?

3. Your psychology text states that people who were abused as children are more likely than others to become child abusers. Did their history of abuse cause them to become abusive?

4. A television documentary claims that some hyperactive children perform better in school if they take medication such as Ritalin. How can this conclusion be proved?

5. According to a magazine article, children who attend day care are more aggressive than children raised at home. Does day care make children aggressive?

We cannot draw cause-and effect conclusions from quasi-experiments

ANSWER KEY

1. We cannot automatically conclude that the drinking caused the lower grades, as the study reported in the headline was most likely based on correlation rather than on experiment. An experiment would not be ethical because the researcher would have to control the students' drinking, forcing some students to drink heavily and then observing the effects of the drinking on their grades. All we can conclude from the headline is that heavy drinking is associated with lower grades. We cannot conclude that drinking caused the lower grades because other plausible interpretations have not been ruled out. Perhaps students drink more because they get lower grades. Or perhaps drinking and grades appear related only because they are both related to the degree of student commitment to being in school.

2. This study does not prove that the private schooling per se causes the higher math scores. To prove this hypothesis, researchers would have to do an experiment and control who goes to private school and who

group of children can be studied every week for a detailed picture of their emerging language, enabling the researchers to witness development as it unfolds. This kind of longitudinal study is called a *microgenetic study* because it uncovers the steps involved in the genesis of the behaviour. Recently, this type of study was used to explore how children learn to crawl and walk (Adolph, Vereijken, & Denny, 1998).

One type of longitudinal design, called a *prospective design*, monitors children before and after environmental changes to see the effects on development. This is a powerful method for studying the effects of environmental changes that researchers cannot manipulate. For example, researchers in Sweden did a prospective longitudinal study to examine the effects of day care on children's cognitive development (Broberg, Wessels, Lamb, & Hwang, 1997). The study began before any of the children were in day care and was continued after some were enrolled in day care and others remained at home. In this way, the researchers could see whether any differences between the children in day care and those reared at home originated early (before the children were even in day care) or later (only after exposure to day care). In this particular study, the researchers were especially interested in cognitive development. Interestingly, the groups of children had similar cognitive development before and during day care. But by the time the children were 8 years old, those who had been in day care had more advanced cognitive development than did the other children. The researchers called the positive effect of day care a "sleeper effect" because it did not become evident until the children were older.

Another use of longitudinal designs is to monitor development of family members from one generation to the next (Serbin & Stack, 1998). In 1976, Jane Ledingham and Alex Schwartzman started the Concordia Longitudinal Project, which studied children from low-income, inner-city neighbourhoods in Montreal. The children, who are now in their 20s and early 30s, are still being studied today. Furthermore, a number of them have become parents, and their children are also being studied. For instance, re-goes to public school (this is the independent variable) to ensure that the two groups of children were equivalent at the outset. Parents would never agree to this type of study, so the researcher would have to study pre-existing groups of children. This is called a *quasi-experiment* —on the one hand, it resembles an experiment because it compares groups, but on the other hand, the researcher does not control group membership. We cannot draw cause-and-effect conclusions from quasi-experiments because they do not rule out other plausible conclusions. Perhaps the students from private school are more likely to practise math on the computer at home. It may be this home activity, rather than experiences at school, that leads to the higher math scores.

3. We cannot prove that history of abuse makes people abusive because it would be unethical to do the appro-

priate experiment. The researcher would have to control who was abused, perhaps by randomly assigning children to abusive and nonabusive groups. Abuse can be studied only by correlation. Therefore, we must be cautious in assuming any causal association between experiencing abuse as a child and perpetrating it as an adult.

4. The effectiveness of a drug can be proved by an experiment that uses a double-blind design. In this type of design, the researcher would choose at random some hyperactive children to be given the drug, and others to be given a placebo that looks like the drug but has no active ingredient. The placebo would be needed as a control to ensure that any behavioural changes from the drug were due to its active ingredients and not simply to the children's belief that a pill would work. Therefore, children would not be

told whether they had received the drug or the placebo. Similarly, it would be important that the researchers who evaluated the children's behaviour not be aware whether each child had received the drug or the placebo in order to prevent researcher bias.

5. We cannot conclude that day care makes children aggressive because it would be impossible to conduct the required experiment. To do the experiment, the researcher would have to control whether children went to day care or were raised at home. Instead, the researcher is able to compare only pre-existing groups of day-care and home-reared children. This is an example of a quasi-experiment that does not allow unequivocal cause-and-effect conclusions. Perhaps the children were more aggressive before they started day care.

searchers examined children born to teen mothers (Serbin, Cooperman, Peters, Lehoux, Stack, & Schwartzman, 1998). Characteristics of the mother—her level of education and her history of childhood withdrawal or aggression—predicted whether her children were referred to clinics for aggressive or withdrawn behaviour. Of children whose mothers dropped out of school, 82 percent required a clinic referral, compared with 25 percent of those whose mothers completed high school. Furthermore, children were more likely to be perceived as withdrawn or aggressive if their mothers had a history of these problems.

Longitudinal studies also have several drawbacks. They require a great deal of time from both researchers and subjects. Subjects may become ill, go on vacation, move away, or simply stop participating in the research project. Some subjects become used to taking the tests and tend to do better than those being examined for the first time. As well, longitudinal studies, such as Terman's long-term study of high-IQ children, provide a detailed account of the development of one generation of people, but it is often unclear whether other generations would show a similar pattern of development.

CROSS-SECTIONAL DESIGNS

Cross-sectional designs have the advantage of being more quick, inexpensive, and manageable than longitudinal studies. In a cross-sectional design, researchers study children of different ages at one point in time. For example, a researcher might be interested in how well children of different ages understand "knock, knock" jokes ("Knock, knock. Who's there? Jamaica. Jamaica who? Jamaica this bad knock, knock?"). The researcher might conduct her entire study in the year 2000 by testing 5-year-olds, 7-year-olds, and 9-year-olds, and then comparing the different age groups. Cross-sectional studies provide conclusions about age differences, but they do not allow us to make strong conclusions about age changes because we are comparing different children.

cross-sectional design A method of studying development in which a sample of individuals of one age are observed and compared with one or more samples of individuals of other ages.

SEQUENTIAL DESIGNS

sequential design A combination of cross-sectional and longitudinal research designs in which individuals of several different ages are observed repeatedly over an extended period of time.

Some researchers combine both approaches in a **sequential design.** They start with a cross-section of ages (as in a cross-sectional study) and then study each of the age groups over time (as in a longitudinal design). An example of a sequential design is the National Longitudinal Survey of Canadian Children and Youth (NLSCY)/(Human Resources Development Canada & Statistics Canada [HRDC & Stats Can], 1996). The study began in 1994, when the researchers collected information about a number of age groups (newborns to 11 years). Since 1994, the same children have been studied every two years. This study is particularly ambitious because it is following approximately 23 700 children, documenting aspects of the children's development, as well as aspects of the environments in which they are being raised. We will examine results from this study in later chapters.

The sequential design is able to solve problems associated with interpreting the results of cross-sectional and longitudinal designs. The difficulty in cross-sectional designs is that the subjects in the different age groups are different children. It is unclear whether the younger children will be similar to the older ones when they get to be that age. The sequential design makes this factor clear because the same children are studied at different ages. As well, the difficulty with longitudinal studies is that only one group of children is followed over time, so it is uncertain whether the findings associated with each age apply to other generations. The sequential design, however, can distinguish whether results are general to an age group or peculiar to one group of children. For example, from the NLSCY study we can distinguish the characteristics of 5-year-olds that are common to all the 5-year-olds studied (including those who were 5 in 1994, 1996, 1998, and so on) from those that are unique to one group of 5-year-olds (such as those who were 5 during 1996). This is a powerful method because it enables researchers to study the effects of environmental changes. For example, did children who were 5 at the time of government cutbacks to kindergartens develop differently from children who were 5 when there was a more extensive kindergarten program? The sequential design can be used to answer this question.

Interpreting the Evidence

Three witnesses to a robbery, or to the same research study, may submit three different reports. We do not all interpret evidence in the same way. In the scientific study of child development, it is necessary to establish dependable, repeatable, and consistent procedures that lead to similar conclusions. Otherwise, it becomes impossible for the field to progress and knowledge to expand.

Blocks to Good Observation

OBSERVER BIAS

Many of us see what we expect or want to see; this bias is called *subjectivity.* We either do not notice or refuse to believe whatever conflicts with our preconceptions. Whether it results from cultural assumptions, prejudice, stereotyping, or inexperience, a bias will invalidate the conclusions of an observation. Observing without a bias is called *objectivity.* An observer of female athletic skills, for instance, may not be completely objective if convinced that girls either cannot or should not be skilled in this area.

INSENSITIVITY

When we observe the same thing every day, we often become so accustomed to it that we fail to recognize its significance. For example, the seats that students choose in a classroom may tell us something about their popularity, leadership, feelings of isolation, and social groups to which they belong. But if we see these students in the classroom several times a week, we may overlook this readily available information. Another example may be our inability to recognize signs of distress in those to whom we are closest, or most intimate.

LIMITED HYPOTHESIS

Another obstacle to good observation is the tendency to look at too large, too small, or too arbitrary a piece of behaviour. If, for example, we wanted to know something about memory in children or adolescents, we might choose a number of approaches. We might observe some individuals in this group following the routine of a typical day and note how many times they forget things. But this method is too arbitrary to measure memory functions precisely. Such observations would not reveal, for example, how well the subjects had learned the things they had forgotten or what they did know. A laboratory setting might provide more accurate results.

Limiting Conclusions

It is easy to go beyond the data and to conclude more than was actually found in a study. Overrating conclusions can happen in a number of ways, but we might be particularly on the alert for three of them.

Problems of Definition In research, we normally have two kinds of definitions: a theoretical definition and an operational definition. A *theoretical definition* of a particular variable is based on the theorist's hypothetical construction. For example, a theoretical definition of intelligence might be "the ability to adapt to one's environment." In contrast, an *operational definition* specifies the particular variable in terms of how it is measured. In this case, an operational definition of intelligence might be "those behaviours that the Stanford-Binet intelligence test measures." Researchers with different ideas of what intelligence means get different results when interpreting the same material. If the researchers want to be sure they are talking about the same thing, they need to agree on a definition that describes the techniques of observation and measurement to be employed in their study. That is an operational definition. But their work is more meaningful if they also provide a theoretical definition.

To illustrate, let us consider the problem of studying aggression. We might be able to agree on a theoretical definition of aggression as "behaviour that is intended to injure or destroy." But how do we measure intent? What do we observe? To answer these questions, we need an operational definition of our research topic. One researcher might measure hitting, kicking, punching, and other physical acts against another person. A second researcher might measure verbal insults. A third might measure a teacher's rating of the child's aggressiveness on a five-point scale from high to low. A fourth might measure the aggressive content in a child's storytelling. But the child who scores high in fantasy aggression may be quite low in actual physical aggression as measured by the first researcher. These researchers are measuring different things.

Generalization beyond the Sample Research is conducted in a particular setting and under specific conditions, with particular individuals from a certain sociocultural context. The results of any study, therefore, must be limited to similar individuals in similar situations. For example, children who experience a great deal of sarcasm in their daily lives may learn the cues for this behaviour much more quickly than those who grow up in families where sarcasm is a rare event.

Correlation or Causality Strong conclusions about **causality** can be made only from well-controlled experiments that rule out other explanations. It is tempting, though, to draw causal conclusions from correlational studies. Even researchers sometimes do this. For example, in studying poor readers, researchers found that reading difficulties were positively correlated with abnormal eye movements when the children scanned a line of print. Children with more reading difficulties had more of the abnormal eye movements. Some researchers, then, wrongly assumed that the abnormal eye movements were causing the reading problems, and so the researchers designed remedial programs to train readers in proper eye movements (Stanovich, 1986). But, as it turned out, the abnormal eye move-

causality A relationship between two variables in which change in one brings about an effect or result in the other.

Abnormal eye movements are correlated with reading problems, but that does not mean they cause them. In fact, the reading problems cause the abnormal eye movements, rather than the other way round.

ments were not the cause of the reading problems—the reading problems were the cause of the abnormal eye movements. No wonder the treatments were ineffective.

Research Ethics

It hardly needs to be said that researchers should follow ethical principles when conducting research with human beings. They should never knowingly harm anyone or violate basic human rights. Following ethical practice is especially important when conducting research on dependent groups, such as children. Nevertheless, issues of individual rights and what may be harmful to research participants are more complex than they may appear—as the following hypothetical research situation illustrates.

> Three-year-old Emma, who is newly separated from her mother in her first preschool class, sits in a room with an unfamiliar adult who is wearing a white lab coat. The researcher asks her to sit on a high chair and place her head into a helmet-like device, through which she will look at some pictures. In order to hold her head still, Emma must place her mouth over a hard rubber bite bar. Emma balks, frowns, and begins to tremble. Despite the urging of her teacher's aide to do what the "doctor" says, she seems unable to follow the instructions. Soon, tears appear on her cheeks.

This scenario could be an example of a research study comparing eye movements and visual processing in preschool boys and girls. The anxiety created by any test situation is familiar to all of us, but it may be more problematic for a child who is relatively unfamiliar with evaluative situations. Such a study raises broad ethical questions. Are the results of this kind of experiment important enough to justify putting vulnerable people under stress? Is it ethical to test people without giving them information that they can understand about the purposes of the experimentation?

Guidelines for Ethical Research Practice

Most of us agree that some experiments using human beings as research subjects are necessary if we are to understand and control the impact of potentially harmful environmental events. However, these potential benefits must be balanced with the rights of individual research participants. According to the 1991 revision of the Canadian Code of Ethics, the most important principle guiding research should be respect for the dignity of the participants.

Do you think that the case about Emma, the little girl crying in the research lab, follows this principle? What else could the researchers have done to ensure that Emma's dignity was respected? Not only do researchers need to protect the dignity of participants, but they also must adhere to other ethical principles. For example, the basic principles espoused by the Society for Research in Child Development (1990) are fundamental rules that would guide any reputable and honest researcher. They include the following principles:

- *Protection from harm.* No treatment or experimental condition given to the child as part of the study should be mentally or physically harmful.
- *Informed consent.* Informed consent of the child, if old enough, or from the parents or others who act on the child's behalf (such as school officials) should be obtained for any research involving children. Adults and children should be free to discontinue their participation in the research at any time.
- *Privacy.* Confidentiality of the information obtained in the study must be preserved. No agencies or individuals outside of the researchers will have access to the participants' records.
- *Knowledge of results.* Children and their parents have the right to be informed of the results of research in terms understandable to them.

- *Beneficial treatments.* Each child who participates in the study has the right to profit from beneficial treatments provided to other participants in the study. For example, if a child is in a control group of a study to develop a new vaccine, he is entitled to that vaccine at a later time.

A close look at several of these guidelines will help in understanding the ethical principles involved in research with children.

The Right to Informed Consent All major professional organizations hold that people should participate voluntarily, should be fully informed of the nature and possible consequences of the experiment, and should not be offered excessive inducements such as large amounts of money. Infants and young children do not offer their consent—their parents do. It is hoped that parents have the best interests of their children in mind. Children over the age of 8 and adults should give their own consent. Researchers should be sensitive to other forms of inducement. How easily, for example, can a 9-year-old in school say no to someone who looks like a teacher or another authority figure (Thompson, 1990)?

The Right to Privacy or Confidentiality We all have a right to privacy; therefore, researchers must keep confidential information about our private lives, thoughts, and fantasies. Also, test scores must be protected from inappropriate use by those outside the research project. Test scores may be categorized using phrases such as "dull-normal intelligence," "pre-delinquent," "weak ego control," or "impulsive." When such labels are shared with parents or teachers, they can be easily misinterpreted. Labels also can become self-fulfilling—if teachers are told that a child has limited intelligence, they may treat the child in a way that makes that description come true.

The Right to Protection from Psychological Harm Everyone agrees that researchers should never knowingly harm their subjects. While physical injury is easily avoided, it is often difficult to determine what is psychologically harmful. For example, in studies of obedience, is it reasonable to give children orders just to see if they will follow them? In the numerous studies of infants' responses to novelty, is it reasonable to expose children for long periods to increasingly novel items?

Another example concerns test failure. Sometimes a researcher wants to demonstrate that a 7-year-old can understand a particular concept but a 5-year-old cannot. All the 5-year-old children, knowingly or unknowingly, experience repeated failure. Should children have to go through the needless confusion of trying to solve what, for them, are unsolvable problems? How does the researcher debrief such children or make them feel that they did well no matter what the outcome?

Most research organizations currently have screening committees to make sure that their studies are not harmful to the participants. Guidelines for social and psychological research with children usually specify that the study should have only minimal risk: that is, the risk of harm should be no greater than that experienced in daily life or in the performance of routine psychological tests. These screening committees are becoming more stringent in their protection of the participants. Many committees, for example, feel that they have a responsibility to protect people's rights to self-esteem and to expose them only to test situations that will enhance their self-concept (Thompson, 1990).

Benefits to the Participant It may not be enough for researchers to seek the voluntary, informed consent of their participants, respect their confidentiality, and protect them from physical and psychological harm. Perhaps researchers need to supply some positive benefits to individuals in return for their participation. At the very least, researchers should try to make participation fun, interesting, or informative or try to create a positive situation in which the person can be heard, supported, understood, and respected. The rights of participants in research are still being explored and defined. Indeed, many studies considered permissible even two decades ago are no longer viewed as ethical.

Question to Ponder

If you had to rank the ethical principles, which one would you consider most important? Do you think this list includes all the important ethical principles related to research? What is missing?

Summary and Conclusions

The goal of studying child development is to discover and understand common processes and major influences from conception through adolescence. Those of us who study child development consider the impact of historical change, socioeconomic factors, and cultural factors on children. But the process is complementary. Not only do cultural and social factors affect the children who are exposed to them, but they also help to shape attitudes toward the children. Attitudes toward children, and toward the child-rearing practices associated with them, not only have changed historically, but vary across cultural and socioeconomic groups.

Both biology and environment influence development to produce change in the structure, thought, or behaviour of a person. Development occurs in three domains of a child's existence: the physical, cognitive, and psychological domains. Some of the changes are primarily biological, while others are more strongly environmentally determined. In practice, however, much of development involves an interaction between heredity and environment. Development also involves both proximal and distal processes. As well, socialization is reciprocal—parents socialize children, and children socialize parents.

To be able to fully understand development, we must systematically study it using the scientific method. Research designs that allow precise measurement of behaviour have evolved in the laboratory and naturalistic settings. Various sorts of designs have evolved to study development: cross-sectional designs, which test people of different ages at one time; longitudinal designs, which test the same people repeatedly at different ages; and sequential studies, which combine these two approaches.

Despite the greater control possible through experimental design, certain barriers still exist to interpreting the data correctly. Factors serving as barriers to good research include the researcher's objectivity, sensitivity to detail, and selection of an appropriate level of analysis. Furthermore, unless the variables have been operationally defined, conclusions may not be replicable. We also must be careful to avoid confusing correlation (the relationship between two variables) and causation. Sometimes two variables may be closely related, yet neither causes the other.

Finally, in testing vulnerable individuals such as children, it is essential to keep in mind generally accepted ethical principles. Such principles include voluntary consent, the right to privacy or confidentiality, the right to freedom from psychological harm, and the right to receive any beneficial results from the experiment. We need to always safeguard the cognitive, emotional, and physical health of the children we study.

Key Terms and Concepts

causality (p. 25)
correlations (p. 19)
critical period (p. 8)
cross-sectional design
   (p. 23)
dependent variable (p. 20)

designing experiments
   (p. 20)
development (p. 6)
distal processes (p. 10)
ecological validity (p. 18)
independent variable
   (p. 20)

longitudinal design (p. 21)
maturation (p. 7)
naturalistic observations
   (p. 17)
norms (p. 10)
optimal period (p. 9)

proximal processes (p. 10)
readiness (p. 9)
sequential design (p. 24)
socialization (p. 9)

Questions to Review

1. What are the goals of developmental science?
2. What is meant by the term *development,* and what roles do biological processes and environmental influences play in bringing about development?
3. What is the difference between proximal and distal processes?
4. What are developmental norms?
5. How would you explain the relationship between biological and environmental development processes?

What roles do timing and readiness play in this relationship?

6. Compare the contributions of historical, socioeconomic, and cultural perspectives to the understanding of human development.

7. List four basic steps involved in the scientific method.

8. Describe the major categories of developmental research and list their strengths and limitations.

9. List and describe the factors that must be considered in order to interpret evidence.

10. Describe the ethical factors that researchers must consider when conducting research with children.

Weblinks

www.ccsd.ca/
Canadian Council on Social Development
"One of Canada's most authoriative voices promoting better social and economic security for all Canadians." This site has statistics, reports, and news releases related to social issues such as child poverty.

www.cfc-efc.ca/
Child & Family Canada
This extensive site is the result of the collaboration of 52 Canadian nonprofit organizations. It has a plethora of information on a wide range of topics related to child development, special programs, and social policy.

www.ciar.ca/
The Canadian Institute for Advanced Research
This site has links to a number of papers related to human development and social policy.

Theories of Child Development: An Introduction

Putting on the spectacles of science in expectation of finding the answer to everything looked at signifies inner blindness.

J. FRANK DOBIE
THE VOICE OF THE COYOTE, 1949

Outline

CHAPTER 2

Objectives

By the time you have finished this chapter, you should be able to do the following:

✔ Describe and compare the major theories of child development.

✔ Be familiar with major terms and concepts employed by each theory of child development.

What makes every child a unique person? How do parents, teachers, television characters, and even imaginary friends contribute to the process of development? How do the social, physical, and cognitive realities of children interact to move them toward more advanced skills? These questions and their answers form the basis for theories of development.

What then is the essence of human nature? Are we primarily rational and goal oriented? Or are we driven by passions? How do we learn—by discovery, by insight, or by small, sequential steps of increasing complexity? How do reward, pain, curiosity, or inner drives motivate us? What is a "conscience," and how does it develop? Do we have control over it? Or do external and internal forces that we cannot control shape it? Sometimes we study developmental psychology to seek answers to these basic questions. Any answer that we find will be based on a particular theory of human development—on a set of assumptions or principles about human behaviour that provides a framework for a particular mass of data.

If you think about the questions raised above, you will probably realize that you have your own "theories" about the answers to them. Your answers probably have a lot to do with your thoughts about other people. For example, you may view young offenders either as being responsible for their actions or as victims of their environment or early training. You may believe that 6-year-olds are able to decide for themselves what they should study in school, or you may think that at this age they cannot be expected to know what they want. You probably have assumptions about the degree to which each person is responsible for his behaviour and the degree to which we can rely on human rationality to direct our actions wisely.

Why Study Theories of Development?

Why is it important to understand the theories of human behaviour? A broad understanding of various theories creates the detachment that lets us evaluate our own views, actions, and reactions. It is important for us to re-examine the assumptions behind our beliefs to see whether they make sense, whether they fit with the evidence, and what follows from them. A familiarity with the major theories, then, allows us to examine, evaluate, and discipline our intuition and our own theories about human behaviour.

Theories give shape to otherwise large and unmanageable collections of data. Social scientists use theories to help formulate significant questions, to select and organize their data, and to understand the data within a larger framework. The resulting body of information, together with the broader theory, allows social scientists to make new predictions about future human behaviour.

As with any scientific endeavour, those who build theories do not always agree with one another. Nor do they all choose the same area of development to explore. Some theorists, such as Freud and Erikson, focus on personality development, while others, such as Piaget, study the development of thinking in children. Each theorist brings a unique background of training and interests to the study of child development, which is then incorporated into the premises of the theories they are constructing. Each theory, therefore, becomes a reflection of the personality, thought, and values of the individual who designed it.

Our personal theories also affect the kinds of questions we ask about development. Sometimes in class I ask students if they have a theory about why newborn babies smile (a delightful sight if you are fortunate enough to see it). Some students think that newborns smile because they have gas. These students then are likely to pay attention to the newborn's feeding and bowel movements. Other students think that smiling is insignificant—nothing more than random muscle movements. These students are likely to ignore infants' smiling. Still other students think that smiling is a social gesture. They focus on what the newborn was experiencing or looking at, such as the smiling faces of mom and dad (Digdon). As you can see, theories are critical because they influence how (and if) we choose to study particular topics in development.

Three Controversial Issues

There are three controversial issues that theories of child development address: nature versus nurture, continuities versus discontinuities, and the organismic versus mechanistic nature of human beings (i.e., the extent to which people have control over the course of their development). When theories differ, it is often because of the way they deal with these issues.

nature Stresses the role of heredity and maturation in development.

nurture Stresses the role of upbringing and environment in development.

Nature versus Nurture   Nature versus nurture refers to the question of which factors are most significant in determining development—those related to heredity or those related to environment. Theorists who focus on **nature** view heredity as the major influence on development. Theorists who emphasize **nurture,** on the other hand, view environmental factors, such as maternal behaviour, crowding, temperature, and cultural factors, as the major determinants of children's development of behaviours. A nature theorist and a nurture theorist would look at the same behaviour and describe very different processes by which it developed. For example, a theorist who emphasizes heredity and biology as the determinants of behaviour might say that the level of cognitive maturity of the child causes a preschooler to invent imaginary friends. A theorist who emphasizes nurture might look to environmental factors such as isolation, lack of responsive caretakers, or the absence of siblings as the cause of the behaviour.

Continuity versus Discontinuity The question of continuities versus discontinuities is also crucial for developmental researchers. **Continuities** of development emphasize quantitative change, with behaviours building continually on each other. The change can be either an increase (e.g., developing a larger vocabulary) or a decrease (e.g., becoming less physically aggressive). Some theories, such as learning theories, view all development as involving quantitative changes. Development is seen as gradual, with small changes in amount, rather than changes that transform the person into a qualitatively different one. Qualitative changes are complete—for example, a caterpillar that changes into a butterfly undergoes a qualitative change. Do qualitative transformations occur in human development? If so, development is described as **discontinuous.** Theories that view development as discontinuous usually have clearly defined stages (like those in the theories of Piaget, Freud, and Erikson). When children pass from one stage to the next, it is assumed that they have changed qualitatively.

Organismic versus Mechanistic Factors The final question—whether human nature is basically organismic or mechanistic—is derived from philosophy. **Organismic** theorists believe that humans are active organisms who fully participate in the process of development. Individuals interact with other individuals and events and are changed by these interactions. In turn, they act on the objects and events and change them. Organismic theorists, like Piaget, who study cognition, believe that as we take in information, we are transformed by it, enabling us to act more competently in subsequent interchanges. In this theoretical framework, humans are seen as acting on their world. The **mechanistic** viewpoint, on the other hand, describes humans as passive reactors to environmental events, internal drives, or motivation. This viewpoint is most clearly expressed by the behaviourists, who see humans as being controlled by rewards or punishment.

Learning Theories

Learning theories find the key to a person's nature in the way that she is shaped by the environment. According to these theories most behaviour is acquired, and it is acquired by learning. Learning is a pervasive process. It is not confined simply to formal schooling or instruction; it also includes the acquisition of morality, biases, and mannerisms, such as gestures. Learning, therefore, covers a broad spectrum of behaviour. The learning theorist sees child development as a gradual, step-by-step accumulation of knowledge, skills, memories, and competencies. The child becomes an adolescent and then an adult primarily by the gradual, continuous addition of experiences and learning, which lead, in turn, to more skills and knowledge. As noted in our earlier discussion of controversial issues in child development, learning theories emphasize nurture, continuity, and the mechanistic nature of development.

Behaviourism

Learning theories have roots in an approach to psychology called *behaviourism* (researchers who adopt behaviourism are called *behaviourists*). Behaviourism is based on the philosophical notion of tabula rasa (clean slate), suggested by the English philosopher John Locke. This notion proposed that all human beings are born without any innate ideas. Therefore, people learn appropriate behaviours, thoughts, and feelings through the influence of their environments.

Question to Ponder

What is your opinion of the nature versus nurture debate?

continuity Development is ongoing, occurring in small steps and not in distinct stages, as a tree grows wider and develops more branches.

discontinuity Development progresses through distinct stages, as a caterpillar transforms into a butterfly.

organismic A person plays an active role in her development.

mechanistic A person's development is shaped by factors beyond his control.

mechanistic model In learning theory, the view of human beings as machines that are set in motion by input (stimuli) and that produce output (responses).

deterministic model The view that a person's values, attitudes, behaviours, and emotional responses are determined by past or present environmental factors.

classical conditioning A type of learning in which a neutral stimulus comes to elicit a response by repeated pairings with an unconditioned stimulus.

The infant becomes conditioned to suck at the sight of the nipple because it is associated with milk in the mouth.

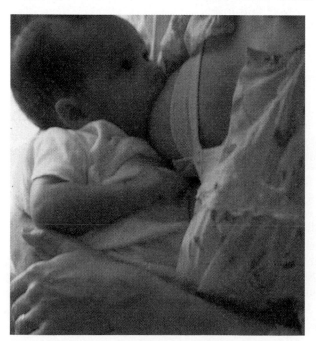

The Notion of Reactive Beings Behaviourists assume that human nature is neither bad nor good; people are reactive—they simply respond to their environment. Every individual is shaped by the process of associating stimuli and their responses or associating behaviours and their consequences. Therefore, the learning process occurs automatically. Some people consider that this **mechanistic model** views people as machines that are set in motion by input (a stimulus) and that then produce output (a response). Behaviourists are not concerned with analyzing what happens between the stimulus and the response. The mind itself cannot be easily observed and described from the outside. Behaviourists do not trust people to give accurate reports of their subjective thoughts and feelings. Consequently, they do not give much attention to the mind and do not subscribe to unconscious or genetic determinants of behaviour.

Behaviourism has also been described as a **deterministic model.** According to the behaviourist, everything in the individual's behaviour, including values, attitudes, and emotional responses, is determined by either the past or present environment. Therefore, such concepts as blame, respect, and dignity are considered irrelevant. According to behaviourism, because people are products of their past learning history, they deserve neither credit nor blame for their actions. This principle was eloquently stated by John Watson, one of the early behaviourists:

> Give me a dozen healthy infants, well-formed, and my own specified world to bring them up in and I'll guarantee to take any one at random and train him to become any type of specialist I might select—doctor, lawyer, merchant-chief, and yes, even beggar-man or thief, regardless of his talents, penchants, tendencies, vocations, and race of his ancestors. (1930, p. 104)

(In case you are curious, Watson never did carry out the experiment.)

Behaviourists are interested in how people and animals form associations. One type of association is learned through **classical conditioning.** Ivan Pavlov developed classical conditioning in 1928, while he was studying how dogs salivate when presented with food and new stimuli that they come to associate with food, such as the sound of a bell. Classical conditioning applies to reflexes and automatic reactions. An example of a reflex is the knee-jerk reflex, which doctors test by gently tapping the edge of the seated patient's kneecap with a small hammer. The patient responds by kicking his leg out. This reflex happens automatically and is not under the patient's conscious control. Because it is automatic and innate, it is called an *unconditioned response* (*conditioned* means "learned," so *unconditioned* means "not learned"). If the doctor keeps testing the knee-jerk reflex over and over, eventually the patient will kick his knee out at the sight of the hammer, before it even touches his knee. In this case, the patient has learned to anticipate the tap on the kneecap at the sight of the hammer. This response is called *conditioned* because it is learned.

Emotional reactions can be acquired through classical conditioning. In a classic example in 1920, the well-known behaviourists John B. Watson and Rosalie Rayner conditioned an 11-month-old infant named Albert to fear rats. Albert was confronted with a white rat. At first, he showed no fear of the animal, but then Watson made a loud clanging noise every time he showed the rat to Albert, causing the baby to cry and crawl away. It did not take many pairings of the previously neutral stimulus of the rat with the unpleasant loud noise for Albert to respond with anxiety and fear to the rat alone. Reportedly, other white or furry objects, even a Santa Claus beard, soon frightened Albert. This spread of a response to other similar stimuli is called *stimulus generalization.*

Albert's case was a dramatic example of conditioning with stimulus generalization, although the experiment was cruel, unethical, and imprecise (Harris, 1979). We can see clear parallels in children's everyday lives. Doctors' white uniforms or medicinal smells may arouse fear in children because they associate these things with unpleasant experiences, such as painful injections. This association of the pain of injections with white coats is so well recognized that many pediatricians have their nurses give immunizations to small children rather than themselves giving them. In this way, the painful procedures are not associated with the pediatrician. Positive emotional reactions can be conditioned in the same way as negative ones. Reactions of relaxation or pleasure are easily associated with previously neutral stimuli, such as an old song that brings back all the memories of a sunny day at the beach or the excitement of a high school dance.

Classical conditioning, therefore, helps us to understand the occurrence of emotional responses, such as fear, in young children. Other learned emotional responses undoubtedly also develop in this manner.

Operant Conditioning The foregoing examples have illustrated classical conditioning. But these procedures do not apply so well to more complex behaviour, such as learning to drive a car, play baseball, or recite poetry. These are all examples of predominantly voluntary, or *operant,* behaviour. The key difference between operant and classical conditioning is that in **operant conditioning,** behaviour cannot be elicited automatically. The behaviour must occur on its own. After the behaviour occurs, operant conditioning influences whether it will occur again. In operant conditioning, behaviours that are rewarded or reinforced are likely to reoccur, and behaviours that are not reinforced are less likely to reoccur. (See the box "Recognizing Operant Conditioning in Everyday Life.") The key theorist associated with operant conditioning is B.F. Skinner.

Many of the principles of operant conditioning have been applied to child rearing.

How can operant conditioning be used to teach a complex act? Most often, the final behaviour must be built bit by bit, or shaped. In **shaping,** successive approximations of the final task are rewarded. Suppose a child is learning to put on socks. At first, the parent puts on one sock nearly all the way, lets the child pull it up, and then praises the child. The next day, the parent may put the sock on halfway and let the child finish a bit more of the task. It is not long before the child is putting on socks with no help. Similar principles may be used to toilet train infants, to teach children to swim, or to mould a shy adolescent into an accomplished public speaker.

> **operant conditioning** A type of conditioning that occurs when an organism is reinforced for voluntarily emitting a response. What is reinforced is then learned.
>
> **shaping** Systematically reinforcing successive approximations to a desired act.

Operant conditioning has been used as a tool to study infants' perceptions and understandings. For example, Schneider, Trehub, and Bull (1979) studied sound perception and preference in 6-, 12-, and 18-month-old infants. They first rewarded the infants for turning their heads in the direction of a tone. When the infants had learned to do this, the experimenters varied the intensity of the tones and their frequency. Using this methodology, the researchers were able to determine that infants can detect sounds higher than those typical of speech, and in the high frequencies, their perception approaches that of adults. Perception is poorer at the lower frequencies. The researchers, therefore, determined that most auditory development after infancy takes place in the lower-frequency sounds.

Contemporary Behavioural Analysis Today, the systematic study and application of classical and operant conditioning principles is called *behavioural analysis.* Numerous educational and therapeutic programs have been established to train or retrain individuals to behave in a more appropriate or desirable way. Shaping human behaviour for therapeutic goals is called *behaviour modification.* One effective way to modify behaviour is through the use of a token economy. Imagine a residential facility for delinquent adolescents. The adolescents can buy with tokens the rewards in this controlled

To avoid the unpleasant stimulus of being scolded, this child may behave differently from now on.

world, such as tasty food, time in the gym, a semiprivate or private bedroom, current magazines to read, and, eventually, a weekend pass. However, they must earn these tokens for very precise, carefully defined behaviours in the classroom and in the work setting. The tokens now become effective reinforcement for paying attention and making progress in school, following the rules, and being productive in the workplace. But they are effective only when the trainer remembers operant conditioning principles, such as rewarding small incremental steps toward the achievement of the final goal.

Extensive research has shown that token economies can be used successfully with retarded and autistic people, children in classrooms and at home, and delinquents and psychiatric inpatients (Baker & Brightman, 1989). The aim of training with tokens is to improve a trainee's skills to the point at which these skills are so useful to the trainee in the real world that tokens are no longer required. To this end, any token economy must have a plan for weaning trainees off the tokens as early as possible. Otherwise, they may become so dependent on the token economy that the effectiveness of the behaviour modification program is lost.

Social-Learning Theory   Social-learning theorists have tried to enlarge the scope of learning theory to explain complex social patterns. To do so, they have gone well beyond

---

FOCUS ON APPLICATION

Recognizing Operant Conditioning in Everyday Life

Read each of the following scenarios and see if you can use operant conditioning to help you interpret them.

1. A father is watching the Stanley Cup final on television while his children play noisily in the same room. The father gives each child a loonie to go to the store so that he can watch the game in peace. What will the children do the next time their father wants to watch television?

2. A child who has been playing quietly on her own goes over and starts fiddling with the CD player. Her mother says, "Oh, I guess you are bored. Let's go to the park." What will the child do in the future when she wants to go to the park?

3. Two families have trouble with children throwing temper tantrums for candy at the grocery store checkouts. The first family has a history of giving in and buying the candy every time the child has a tantrum. The second family has a history of sometimes ignoring the tantrum but other times giving in, perhaps because the parents have headaches or are embarrassed. Which child's tantrums will be easier to eliminate?

4. A child seems to deliberately do things that will lead people to yell at him. Why might this child be acting this way?

5. A mother asks a child to pick up her toys. The child does not comply. The mother asks seven more times, her voice becoming a little louder each time. The child still does not comply. The mother is becoming angry and threatens to put all the toys in the garbage. Still the child refuses to comply. Now the mother does one of two things—she explodes in anger or she picks up the toys herself. What has the child learned?

Children need attention.

ANSWERS

1. The father has reinforced the children for playing noisily. They will likely be noisy the next time the father wants to watch television.

2. The mother has reinforced the child for fiddling with the CD player but did not reinforce her for playing quietly on her own. Parents often forget to reinforce children for desirable behaviours. Parents are advised to catch children being good. Reinforcing the good behaviour will cause it to occur more often, will leave less time for misbehaviour, and will create a more positive tone

in the parent–child interactions.

3. It will be easier to eliminate the tantrums of the child who received the candy every time she threw a tantrum. Behaviours that are reinforced every time they occur are easier to eliminate than behaviours that are reinforced intermittently.

4. Children need attention. Perhaps this child was not receiving any attention for positive behaviour and has learned that the only way to get attention is to misbehave. Being yelled at is better than being ignored. Children, like adults, show individual differences in reinforcers; thus, for some children, being yelled at can become a reinforcer.

5. The child has learned to gamble. If she perseveres, her mother might pick up her toys for her. To change this situation, the mother should break this long activity cycle of repeated requests and threats. Instead, the mother should make one request, and if the child does not comply, give one warning of the consequences. If the child does not comply, the consequences should be delivered. Perhaps the child should be sent to time-out or lose a privilege.

a seemingly "automatic" conditioning process. Albert Bandura (1977), a leading social-learning theorist, points out that in daily life people notice the consequences of their own actions—that is, they notice which actions succeed and which fail or produce no result—and adjust their behaviour accordingly. Through such observed response consequences they gain information, incentive, and conscious reinforcement. They are able to hypothesize about what is appropriate in which circumstances and to anticipate what may happen as a result of certain actions. Unlike the more mechanistic learning theorists, social-learning theorists give conscious thought a larger role in guiding behaviour.

IMITATION AND MODELLING

Just as people learn directly from experiencing the consequences of their own behaviour, they also learn by watching another person's behaviour and its consequences (Bandura, 1977; Bandura & Walters, 1963). People derive basic principles from their observations and formulate rules of action and behaviour. All of us, not just children, learn a wide variety of behaviours from observing and imitating (or avoiding) the actions of others around us. In their early years, children learn the many aspects of sex-appropriate roles and the moral expectations of their community. They also learn how to express aggression and dependency, along with prosocial behaviours like sharing. As they grow to adulthood, they will learn career-appropriate attitudes and values, social-class and ethnic attitudes, and moral values.

In a well-known example of modelling, Bandura (1977) conducted a series of experiments in which children watched various levels of aggressive behaviour in short films. One group of children saw the aggressive behaviour rewarded, a second group saw it punished, a third group saw a film of nonaggressive play, and a fourth group saw no film at all. The children who saw aggression rewarded were significantly more aggressive in their own play, whereas those who saw the behaviour punished were less aggressive. There is no question that children may learn to express aggression in a particular way from the behaviour they see on television programs. (Imitation and modelling are discussed at length in Chapter 6.) A recent study showed that 9- to 12-year-old children learned some fears, such as the fear of animals or of criticism, by modelling the fear responses of their mothers (Muris, Steerneman, Merckelbach, & Meesters, 1996).

SOCIAL LEARNING AND COGNITION

Bandura (1986) has compiled an updated summary of social-learning theories, which he now calls **social cognitive theory.** *Cognition* means "thinking," and this name change reflects a new emphasis on thinking as part of learning. Social-learning theorists still talk about rewards and punishments, but they recognize that children observe their own behaviour, the behaviour of others, and the consequences of these behaviours. Children also can anticipate consequences based on past events. They form opinions about themselves and others and then behave in a fashion that is consistent with these opinions (Miller, 1989). This shift in emphasis by social-learning theorists has moved them away from their study of only observable behaviour, making them more similar to the cognitive theorists, whom we will also discuss.

> **social cognitive theory** The belief that people are not passive recipients of reinforcement. From observing the consequences of their own behaviour and that of others, people can anticipate the consequences of future behaviour. Thinking is a part of learning.

An Evaluation of Learning Theories

Learning theories, including behaviourism, contemporary behavioural analysis, and social-learning theory, have made major contributions to our understanding of human development. These theories focus on the situational factors that affect behaviour. They specify the situation carefully and make predictions based on past research. In fact, their principles are probably more easily tested than those of any other theory. Some of their predictions have been demonstrated repeatedly. For instance, Skinner and his followers have shown that many types of behaviour are indeed affected by reinforcement. Several techniques, such as modelling and various types of behaviour modification, have been quite effective in changing behaviour when skillfully applied in schools, weight-control programs, and homes for disturbed children.

Despite this precision, learning theorists may be attempting to explain too large an area of human development. For the most part, they have neglected to pay enough attention to thought, emotions, personality, and the understanding of the self. They tend to seek universal processes and to ignore individual differences.

Finally, learning theorists have been baffled by one major human learning achievement. The laws of learning do not adequately account for the complex way in which young children learn a language. Rather than simply involving imitation and reward, the development of language depends on a complex interaction of the individual child's language-learning abilities and his language environment. In explaining language development and the learning of other aspects of culture, learning theorists seem unable to describe and account for the complexity of the naturalistic setting. Their behavioural predictions work best in the laboratory, where it is possible to control the stimulus environment closely (Miller, 1989). Concept Summary Table 2-1 presents the key aspects of the behavioural theories.

Cognitive Theories

Unlike early learning theorists, who saw human beings as passive machines acted upon by the environment, cognitive theorists see human beings as rational, active, alert, and competent. For them, human beings do not merely receive information—they also process it. Therefore, each person is a thinker and a creator of her reality. People do not simply respond to stimuli—they also give such stimuli structure and meaning. Cognitive theorists emphasize the organismic nature of human development. In addition, they focus on the influences of both nature and nurture. They are split, though, on the issue of continuity and discontinuity of development. Some cognitive theories, such as Piaget's theory, emphasize discontinuity; others, such as information processing, focus more on continuity.

Piaget

Jean Piaget was a theorist interested in cognitive development. Piaget's interests in the mind were both biological and philosophical. To Piaget, the mind, like any other

---

Question to Ponder

Should developmental researchers strive to develop grand theories that attempt to explain all aspects of development or more modest theories that focus on only one aspect of development? What would be the strengths or weaknesses of either approach?

Concept Summary

Table 2-1   Key Aspects of the Behavioural Theories

- Behavioural theories stress that development follows the laws of learning and is determined largely by environmental events.

- Classical conditioning refers to involuntary responses elicited by some naturally occurring stimulus, which is then paired with another unrelated stimulus. Over the course of several pairings, the unconditioned response becomes conditioned to occur in the presence of the second, or conditioned, stimulus.

- It is likely that classical conditioning is involved in the learning of fears, emotional responses, and other similar behaviours. Classical conditioning has also been used to condition involuntary, or autonomic, nervous system responses, such as changes in blood pressure and skin temperature.

- The main proponent of modern behaviourism, B.F. Skinner, developed the notion of operant conditioning.

- Skinner's theory states that behaviour is a function of its consequences. Operant behaviours are controlled by what follows them.

- Behaviours that are reinforced are more likely to occur again; behaviours that are not reinforced are less likely to occur again.

- Operant conditioning procedures have been very useful in child-raising, education, and clinical practice settings.

living structure, does not simply respond to stimuli, but rather grows, changes, and adapts to the world. Piaget and other cognitive psychologists have been called **structuralists** because they are concerned with the structure of thought (Gardner, 1973b). Three major cognitive theorists are Jean Piaget, Jerome Bruner, and Heinz Werner; here, we shall focus on Piaget.

structuralism A branch of psychology concerned with the structure of thought and the ways in which the mind processes information.

Piaget's investigations grew out of his work with Theodore Simon and Alfred Binet at their lab in Paris, where he worked on creating standardized versions of the IQ test that they had developed. The French government had commissioned these two psychologists to create a standardized test to determine the intelligence of school children. While testing children, Piaget became more interested in the patterns he found in the children's wrong answers than in their right answers. These patterns seemed to provide a clue to the way thought processes develop in children. He theorized that the differences between children and adults are not confined to *how much* they know, but rather occur in the *way* they know. According to Piaget, qualitative as well as quantitative differences separate the thinking of children from that of adults. At this point, Piaget began to diverge from the quantitative, or psychometric, approach to intelligence.

Piaget's approach to intelligence is quite different from the IQ-testing approach with which we are all familiar. Piaget and his colleagues felt that standardized questions frequently led to stereotyped and uninteresting answers. Therefore, he proposed using clinical or probing interview techniques. Such an interview approach reveals the child's or adolescent's thought processes in answering a question, rather than the specific knowledge the child has accumulated. The interview reveals these thought processes by requiring the child to either answer questions or manipulate materials. From interviews, Piaget concluded that logic models can be used to describe the development of integrated thought processes in children.

To illustrate his theory, Piaget devised one of his most famous problems to test conservation. **Conservation** was Piaget's term for the awareness that physical quantities remain constant despite changes in their shape or appearance. In this test, he showed a child two identical glasses, each containing the same amount of liquid. After the child agreed that the amount of liquid in each glass was the same, Piaget poured the liquid from one of the glasses into a tall, narrow glass. He then asked the child how much liquid was in the tall glass: Was it more or less than in the original glass, or was it the same amount? Most children aged 6, 7, or older answered that the amount was the same. But children under 6 said that the tall glass held more, even when they watched the same liquid being poured back and forth between the original glass and the tall glass. This experiment has been conducted with children of many cultures and nationalities, and the results are nearly always the same.

conservation A cognitive ability described by Piaget, in which the child is able to judge changes in amounts based on logical thought instead of mere appearances; thus, she judges that an amount of water will remain the same even when it is poured into a glass of a different shape and size.

Piaget reasoned that until they reach a certain stage, children form judgments based more on perceptual than on logical processes. In other words, they believe what their eyes tell them. To the younger children, the liquid rose higher in the tall glass, so there was more of it. Children 6 years or older, on the other hand, barely glanced at the glasses. They knew that the amount of liquid remained the same, regardless of the size or shape of the glass it was in. When children demonstrated this ability, they were said to be able to conserve. They did not base their judgments solely on perception; they also used logic. Their knowledge came from within themselves, as much as from outside sources.

The Active Mind According to Piaget, the mind is neither a blank slate on which knowledge can be written nor a mirror that reflects what it perceives. If the information, perception, or experience presented to a person fits with a structure in his mind, then that person understands, or assimilates, that information, perception, or experience. If the information, perception, or experience does not fit, the mind rejects it (or if the structure is ready to change, it changes itself to accommodate the information or experience). According to Piaget, **assimilation** is interpreting new experiences in terms of existing mental structures, without changing them. **Accommodation,**

assimilation In Piaget's theory, the process of making new information part of one's existing mental structures.

accommodation Piaget's term for the act of changing our thought processes when a new object or idea does not fit our concepts.

In Piaget's conservation experiment, a child is shown liquid from two identical glasses poured into a short, wide glass and a tall, narrow glass. When asked which has more or less liquid, children under 6 say that the tall glass holds more.

equilibration Piaget's term for the basic process in human adaptation, in which individuals seek a balance, or fit, between the environment and their own structures of thought.

on the other hand, is changing existing mental structures to integrate new experiences. Let us consider an example of how a toddler might use assimilation and accommodation to extend and modify his concept of "dog." Initially, the toddler might think that all four-legged, furry animals are dogs. Gradually, he will refine this concept. Suppose he lives in a neighbourhood where large dogs are common. There might be a German shepherd, a dalmation, a golden retriever, and a black lab. There are also a number of cats in the neighbourhood. From this experience, the toddler might develop a concept of dog that requires a dog to be a minimum size (bigger than a cat). When the toddler meets other, larger dogs, such as Rottweilers, he will call them "dogs," readily assimilating them into his existing concept of dog. But when he meets small dogs, such as Pekingese, he is faced with a contradiction. He must accommodate his concept of dog to encompass a wider range of sizes; some dogs are as small as cats. Life experiences change mental structures. And, equally important, mental structures influence how we interpret life experiences. Therefore, we could say that there is a two-way interaction between mental structures and life experiences—they both affect each other.

The mind always tries to find a balance between assimilation and accommodation, to eliminate inconsistencies or gaps between reality and its picture of reality. This process, called **equilibration,** is basic to human adaptation and, indeed, to all biological adaptation. But, for Piaget, the growth of intelligence is merely an important example of biological adaptation. Piaget believed that these invariant functions of adaptation, assimilation, and accommodation form the basis of the human intellectual adaptation to the environment that allows our species to survive.

Piaget's Stages of Cognitive Development The process of intellectual development, according to Piaget, proceeds through four stages, which are outlined in Concept Summary Table 2-2. (We will study these stages in detail in later chapters.)

Piaget's stages reflect his emphasis on the discontinuous nature of development. According to Piaget, children in one stage think and interpret the world differently than do children in other stages because each stage has a unique set of cognitive structures. It is like the different ways that a pre-reader and a reader respond to a page of

Concept Summary

Table 2-2   Piaget's Stages of Mental Development

STAGE	AGE	ILLUSTRATIVE BEHAVIOUR
Sensorimotor	birth to 18 months or 2 years	Infants know the world only by looking, grasping, mouthing, and other actions.
Preoperational	2 to 7 years	Young children form concepts and have symbols such as language to help them communicate. These images are limited to their personal (egocentric), immediate experience. Preoperational children have very limited, sometimes "magical" notions of cause and effect and have difficulty classifying objects or events.
Concrete operational	7 to 11 years	Children begin to think logically, classify on several dimensions, and understand mathematical concepts, provided they can apply these operations to concrete objects or events. Concrete operational children achieve conservation.
Formal operational	12 years and beyond	Individuals can explore logical solutions to both concrete and abstract concepts. They can think systematically about all possibilities, project into the future or recall the past, and reason by analogy and metaphor.

print. To the pre-reader, it is a jumble of shapes. To the reader, it is the gateway to words and ideas. Children in different stages interpret the same environmental input differently. Another important feature of the stages is that they are arranged in a fixed order—children do not skip stages or go through them in different orders because later stages are built out of early ones. Concept Summary Table 2-3 summarizes the key points of Piaget's cognitive development theory.

Neo-Piagetian Theories   Juan Pascual-Leone, now at York University in Toronto, first established neo-Piagetian theories in 1963 (see Pascual-Leone, 1987). There have since been a number of other theories, such as that of Robbie Case. These theories, like Piaget's, posit that cognitive development proceeds through a number of general stages; however, unlike Piaget's, the stages are not based on logical structures. Pascual-

Concept Summary

Table 2-3   Key Aspects of Piaget's Theory of Development

- Piaget's theory is based on the belief that the child is active, rather than merely reactive, in the process of development.

- Development is a biologically based process that causes changes to the child's mental structures.

- Intelligence is an example of biological adaptation.

- Adaptation includes two complementary processes; assimilation, by which the individual takes information into already existing structures, and accommodation, by which the individual modifies existing structures to meet the demands of the changing environment.

- Piaget's theory has four stages. There are qualitative differences between stages and later stages build on earlier ones. For that reason, the stages occur in a fixed order.

Leone's stages are based on age-related changes in attention (Pascual-Leone, 1996). Robbie Case's stages are based on age-related changes in concepts and understanding, which are influenced by what the child is thinking about (Case, 1992). According to Case's theory, children can reason differently in various contexts. According to Piaget, however, children's cognitive structures would cause them to reason the same across contexts. Case's theory, unlike Piaget's, can explain inconsistencies in children's reasoning (see Brainerd, 1978, for a review). As well, neo-Piagetians emphasize the role of social factors, such as tutoring, in facilitating cognitive development.

Information-Processing Theory

Piaget has many critics, among them, the *information-processing theorists.* Like Piaget, they are cognitive psychologists because they study thought and the mind. Unlike Piaget, they are skeptical of a theory based on qualitatively different stages. They believe human development, including human cognitive development, is a continuous, incremental progression, not a discontinuous one. These theorists resemble learning theorists because they, too, are trying to develop a science of human behaviour. Information-processing theorists want to identify basic processes, such as perception, attention, or memory, and to describe precisely how these processes function.

Humans constantly process information. We selectively attend to something—perhaps the letters on this page. We translate the letters into words and the words into ideas. We then store these ideas for later reference. Many information-processing theorists, therefore, have used the computer as a model of the human brain. The computer has hardware—the machine itself—and software—the programs that instruct its operation. The mind also has hardware—the cells and organs of the brain—and software—the learned strategies for processing information. The computer must process input, perform certain operations on the information, store it, and generate output. The mind, too, must selectively attend and perceive, then associate, compute, or oth-

FOCUS ON AN ISSUE

Piaget in the Preschool

George Forman and Fleet Hill (1980) have used Piaget's theories to design toys for use in the preschool. The Silhouette Sorter is one of these toys. It is a sorting box designed to improve on commercially made sorting boxes. A commercially made sorting box consists of a box with holes of various shapes cut in it and blocks of various shapes to be put through the appropriate holes. These sorting boxes do not encourage children to think about how shapes can change.

The Silhouette Sorter is a box with three holes and one block. Each hole shows a different perspective of the block. For example, the child may place an animal-shaped block through a hole on the side of the box which is the shape of the side silhouette of the

block. The top of the box shows a top silhouette of the same animal-shaped block; the rear of the box has a rear silhouette of the same block. While playing with the Silhouette Sorter, the child

The Silhouette Sorter is a box with three holes and one block. Each hole shows a different perspective of the block.

learns that the identity of the animal-shaped block stays the same, whereas the shape or perspective of that block can change.

Some of the points that educators stress when applying the theories of

Piaget include the following:

1. Children need to learn through experience.

2. Children need cognitive conflict as part of the process of equilibration.

3. Children need an open environment in which they can pose and test their questions.

4. Children should be helped to construct relationships between objects and the forms the objects can take (Forman & Fosnot, 1982).

The Silhouette Sorter and similar toys address these points by providing children with the learning experiences they need to think about objects and their environment.

erwise "operate" on the information. Routinely, the mind must store in the memory and later retrieve information. Finally, it must generate output in the form of responses—words and actions.

Some information-processing theorists have turned their attention to children as a way of studying how these processes develop. Some have been particularly interested in a cognitive activity that they call *encoding*—the process of identifying key aspects of an object or event in order to form an internal representation of it (Siegler, 1986). This internal representation is something like Piaget's "mental image." Some developmental questions might be: Do children of different ages select different aspects or fewer aspects of an event or object to store in a mental image? Do they select different strategies for encoding or retrieving information? *Retrieval* is the process of receiving information from memory stores.

Information-processing thoerists ask whether children of different ages encode events or objects differently.

There are numerous studies on the information-processing capabilities of infants, children, and adolescents. We will be looking at several of these studies throughout the book. Only in recent years have information theorists designed these studies to examine the question of how information processing develops or, in the words of some, how the "computer" reprograms itself to work with new material (Klahr, Langley, & Necher, 1987).

Cognitive Development in Social Context

For Piaget, the image of the child is one of an "active scientist" who interacts with her physical environment and forms increasingly complex thought strategies. This active, constructing child seems to be working alone at problem solving. Increasingly, however, psychologists are recognizing that the child is a social being who plays and talks with others and learns from this interaction (Bruner & Haste, 1987). In the psychologist's lab, children may work alone at solving the problem that the researcher gives them. Yet, outside of the lab, children will experience real events in the company of adults and older, more experienced peers, who will translate or make sense of these events for them. Hence, children's cognitive development is an apprenticeship in which they are guided in their understanding and skill by more knowledgeable companions (Rogoff, 1990). In fact, these more advanced companions, parents, teachers, and others produce disequilibrium in the child's thinking, which challenges the child to adopt more complex thought patterns.

Vygotsky   The Russian psychologist Lev Vygotsky (1896–1934) developed his theory of development during the late 1920s and early 1930s. It was not widely available, though, until several years later because the Soviet government banned Vygotsky's writings from 1936 until 1956 for political reasons. After the ban was lifted, his writings were translated into English and made available outside the Soviet Union. Researchers in Canada started reading translations of Vygotsky's work in about 1970.

A key feature of Vygotsky's theory is his recognition of the important roles that cultures and societies play in cognitive development. He acknowledged the importance of maturation, but he stressed that maturation was an insufficient explanation of cognitive development. According to Vygotsky, development cannot be explained without taking into consideration the culture and society in which the person lives. Vygotsky's theory fits well with studies that have found differences in thinking styles within Canada's multicultural society. For example, Tharp (1994) found that Inuit elders in the Yukon had a different thinking style than did teachers from European backgrounds. The elders used holistic thinking, which means putting learning into a

Question to Ponder

Do you use more holistic thinking or analytic thinking? Does your style of thinking change depending on what you are thinking about?

Vygotsky believed that adults and older, more experienced peers act as guides by helping children develop their understanding and skills.

signs The symbols, such as speech and written language, that are used in a culture to influence the behaviour of other people and one's own behaviour. According to Vygotsky, different cultures may use different signs.

broad context (i.e., looking at the big picture). For example, when asked to prepare a 16-week unit plan for teaching children how to make moccasins of caribou skin, the elders spent 14 weeks focusing on background related to the caribou, including its relation to the land and the hunting of caribou. The elders did not emphasize moccasins until the 15th week of the program. Teachers of European heritage, on the other hand, started with the moccasin, laying out the separate steps required to make it. They used analytic thinking—breaking a larger problem up into small parts. Clearly, cultural background influenced the thinking styles of teachers and elders.

One of the reasons that people from diverse backgrounds think differently is their societies have developed different tools to assist thinking. For example, Polynesian sailors use star patterns as a tool to help navigate ships to distant islands. They do not have compasses or high-tech navigational tools. Their thinking about navigation is not the same as the thinking of Canadian sailors, who use maps, compasses, and modern technology. Children's thinking will develop in distinct ways in societies that use different tools.

Another reason that people think differently is societies have developed different signs to help them think. **Signs** are symbolic systems such as spoken languages, written languages, numbering systems, and drawings. For example, children in societies that have both spoken and written language learn to think more abstractly than do people in illiterate societies. Children learn signs through interactions with other people in their society. For example, they learn spoken language from listening to other speakers. The way language is spoken in the community influences how children learn to communicate with others, as well as with themselves. Children talk to themselves aloud, and they gradually learn to talk to themselves covertly through the "voice" inside their heads.

The development of self-talk is important because it can be used for self-control. A good example can be found by listening to children talk about their drawings. Preschool children talk while they draw, but their speech does not seem to control what they draw. It is common for preschoolers not to name what they have drawn until after they have finished the drawing. I remember when my daughter was 2 and created a long, oval shape attached to a line. Several minutes later, she excitedly told me that she had drawn me an owl (Digdon). Older children, however, use speech to plan and control what they draw. They say things like, "I am going to draw an owl. I think I'll make its head first so I can do the big eyes...." According to Vygotsky, the most important cognitive development occurs when problem solving, tool usage, and speech become interconnected. He called this occurrence *mediation*, as speech and tools mediate problem solving.

Vygotsky was interested in the development of signs among children of different ages within the same society. Younger children rely on external signs (i.e., signs that are in the world outside their minds), whereas older children can use internal signs (i.e., signs that operate inside their heads). Young children can use symbols, but the symbols must be external. Child-care workers sometimes reinforce this ability by making each child his own symbol. When my son was in a child-care program, all his belongings were labelled with a drawing of a sun. He could readily use this external sign to distinguish his things from those of other children (Digdon).

Vygotsky's theory has implications for education. Vygotsky stressed that learning should be matched with the child's developmental level. He distinguished two separate developmental levels. One was the level that the child reached when working independently, and the other was the level the child was able to master when given guidance—such as hints, demonstrations, or leading questions—from adults or more experienced peers. He called the range between the two developmental levels the **zone of proximal development.** Vygotsky thought that teachers should aim their lessons at the level the child is able to master with guidance, rather than at the level he has attained working independently. Vygotsky used an analogy of fruit and blossoms (1978). The level the child can reach in independent work is like the fruit—it is already developed. The level the child can reach with guidance is like the blossom. The teacher can help the child turn the blossom into a fruit. "What a child can do with assistance today, she will be able to do herself tomorrow" (Vygotsky, 1978, p. 86). My son's piano teacher provides an excellent example of the use of the zone of proximal development. She guides children to higher levels of playing by demonstrating ("Here, let me play this for you"), by giving hints ("Maybe if you say the words 'bumbleberry pie, bumbleberry pie,' it will help you get the timing of this section"), and by asking leading questions ("What are you going to remind yourself to do when you get to this bar?"). Through her instruction, children learn to play better. They also start to imitate her teaching strategies so that they learn ways to "teach" themselves how to play better (Digdon). Researchers are currently exploring how taught skills can become internalized and act as mediators in the child's regulation of her own behaviour (Karpov & Haywood, 1998).

> **zone of proximal development**
> The difference between children's actual performance when they work alone and their potential performance when more knowledgeable adults or peers assist them.

An Evaluation of Cognitive Theories

Cognitive theorists criticize learning theory because they find that the emphasis on repeated practice and positive reinforcement is too simplistic to explain much of human thought and understanding. According to cognitive theorists, when people solve problems, they are motivated by their own basic competence, not by a mere stimulus–response reinforcement (Bruner & Haste, 1987).

Cognitive theorists respect human rationality and project an optimism that is absent in learning theories. They consider the human being of any age to be an integrated person who can plan and think through a problem. In addition, they account for the roles that understanding, beliefs, attitudes, and values seem to play in so much behaviour. Many psychologists feel that cognitive theories, in dealing with language and thought, begin where learning theories end.

Cognitive theories have been widely applied to education. They have been especially useful in helping educators plan instruction to fit children's stages of development (see the box "Piaget in the Preschool"). The theories suggest ways to determine when a child is ready for a certain subject and which approaches to it are most appropriate for a specific age. Donaldson (1979), however, suggests that Piaget may have been too distinct in his stages of development, which may make educators too rigid in their ideas of what children can understand.

Cognitive theories are concerned mainly with intellectual development, and thus far they have been unable to explain all of human behaviour. Some key areas still to be investigated include social, emotional, and personality development. Although cognitive theorists look chiefly at the development of perceptual abilities, language, and complex thought, they have not yet explored the individual's potential for dependence, nurturance, aggression, and sexuality. Psychoanalytic theory, which studies emotions and their relation to personality development, traditionally has been concerned with these areas.

The Psychoanalytic Tradition

psychoanalytic tradition Based on the theories of Freud, whose view of human nature was deterministic. He believed that personality is motivated by innate biological drives.

The theories of Sigmund Freud, the neo-Freudians, and the ego psychologists form what we call the **psychoanalytic tradition.** The driving force behind this tradition was the work of Sigmund Freud, who provided the primary source of data for these theories through his clinical case studies. Freud's notion of human nature is a deterministic one, resembling the view of the learning theorists, but it emphasizes the determinism of innate drives instead of the determinism of the environment. According to psychoanalytic theory, human beings are driven creatures who constantly try to redirect or channel potent inner forces. These forces, evident from childhood, are transformed as individuals develop various forms of behaviour. The psychoanalytic theories, therefore, propose that personality development has strong ties to the physical maturation of the body. Modern psychologists of the psychoanalytic tradition, such as Erik Erikson, no longer see animal drives (for example, sex and aggression) as the sole basis for human behaviour, but they still draw heavily from the traditions of Freud and the neo-Freudians.

Freud

Sigmund Freud (1856–1939), the founder of modern psychoanalysis, was born in Vienna and conducted most of his work in Europe. Freud's concern was human emotional life, as this part of the self was kept well hidden in the society in which he lived. Freud emphasized the unconscious as a determinant of behaviour. He believed that the biological, or animal, drives are the primary forces behind human behaviour. Freud's assertion that humans are biologically directed, along with his systematic study of the animal components of human nature, was significant historically in opening the way for a scientific study of human behaviour. Much of Freud's theory looked to childhood for clues about the underlying nature of the personality.

Freud's theory is divided into three components: the dynamic, which focuses on the action of psychic energy; the structural, which focuses on the elements of personality; and the sequential, which focuses on the manner in which instincts are gratified across the life cycle. Regarding the dynamic component, Freud believed that psychic energy—the energy that operates the different components of development—powers the instincts that drive the whole psychic system (Salkind, 1981). These instincts consist of *thanatos,* the death instinct, and *eros,* the life instinct.

Freud believed that death is unpredictable but that it is also the only absolute thing in existence. From his medical and biological training, he concluded that there is constant conflict between the individual's basic tendency or push toward death and the erotic forces promoting life, reproduction, and growth.

The instinctual needs of organisms, according to Freud, are essentially asocial. Society, therefore, attempts to control them. Since needs and goals are found mostly in the external, social world, a person must adapt to society. But that adaptation frequently has costs, including anxiety and neurosis. Hence, the drives become subconscious and are transformed into slips of the tongue, humour, or dreams. Psychoanalytic theory posits that the early failures of adaptation have long-lasting results. This approach, therefore, concentrates on the early developmental history of individuals—the period between birth and 5 years of age—for clues to the underlying nature of the personality.

According to Freud's theory, much of the development of the personality occurs in the period between birth and entering school. A child is born pure *id,* the primitive, hedonistic component of personality structure. The id is based on the *pleasure principle*— that is, the id forces individuals to seek constant, immediate gratification of their impulses. As the child matures biologically, the *ego* develops. The ego is based on rational contact with the external world, or the *reality principle.* The ego encourages the individual to conform to society's directives and to learn to defer gratification in order to achieve broader social goals. Finally, between the years of 3 and 6, the *superego* emerges. The superego is the "policeman," or conscience, that thereafter is constantly in conflict with the id, while the ego attempts to achieve a sense of balance for the personality.

Freud's Psychosexual Stages According to Freud, the personality develops in several **psychosexual stages.** The first three stages occur well before puberty: in them, children focus their pleasure in different erogenous zones of their bodies. The *oral stage* is the first, and it occurs in early infancy. Here, the child's mouth becomes the centre of sensual stimulation and pleasure; infants love to suck things and to mouth toys. Later, during the *anal stage* (ages 1½ to 3) and the *phallic stage* (ages 3 to 5), the focus of pleasure moves from the mouth to the genital area.

psychosexual stages Freud's stages of personality development.

If children experience too much frustration or too much gratification at any psychosexual stage, they may become fixated on the needs of that stage. Furthermore, the parents' reactions to any of these stages may profoundly affect the child's personality development. For example, if parents are too harsh in treating mistakes in toilet training during the anal stage, the child may become a compulsively neat and overcontrolled adult.

The oral, anal, and phallic stages are part of the *pregenital period,* in which the child's sexual or sensual instincts are not yet directed toward reproduction. The *latency period,* lasting from about ages 6 to 12, is a time of relative calm. Girls play primarily with girls, boys play primarily with boys, and the focus is on acquiring knowledge and skills. Freud believed that latency was a period during which drives are directed toward the development of social skills and so sexual urges are unexpressed or nonexistent.

Freud's final stage of personality development is the *genital stage,* which begins during adolescence. Owing to biological maturation, the old submerged sexual feelings, together with stronger physical drives, emerge. The goal of this stage is the establishment of a mature adult sexuality that will eventually be accompanied by biological reproduction. If things go well, the individual becomes capable of creating a mature balance between love and work. But the resolution or lack of resolution of earlier stages profoundly shapes this stage, like the others. Unresolved earlier conflicts may re-emerge periodically as adult neurotic behaviour.

Freud's theory is far more complex than this short summary suggests. But instead of considering it in any more detail, we shall move on to the neo-Freudians,

Figure 2-1
The Unconscious
Freud believed that potent inner forces determine human behaviour.

Concept Summary

Table 2-4   Summary of Key Aspects of Freud's Psychoanalytic Theory

- Freud focused on personality development.

- Freud thought that most psychic energy came from the instincts, which are based on the organism's biological needs.

- The structure of personality has three parts: the id, which is the most primitive and motivates the person to seek immediate pleasures; the ego, which is the person's sense of "me"; and the superego, which represents the internalized standards and rules of society.

- Freud's theory has five psychosexual stages: the oral stage (birth to 1½ years), the anal stage (1½ to 3), the phallic stage (3 to 5), the latency stage (6 to 12), and the genital stage (puberty to death).

who have also had a great influence on modern psychology. One of the most interesting and important of the neo-Freudians was Erik Erikson.

Erikson

Erik Erikson (1904–1994) was a third-generation Freudian. He was introduced into the Vienna Circle, the hand-picked training group for psychoanalysis, by Freud's daughter, Anna. He became a practitioner and originally treated children. Like many others, he left Vienna in the 1930s because of the negative political climate and immigrated to the United States.

The theory of personality development Erikson developed has much in common with Freud's, but it is marked by some important differences. Erikson became disenchanted with psychoanalytic theory because he believed it dealt with extremes of behaviour. He saw the development of the individual as occurring in several stages, many of which corresponded to those of Freud. His model, however, was **psychosocial,** not psychosexual. In other words, Erikson believed that personality arises from the manner in which social conflict is resolved during key interaction points in development, for example, feeding during infancy and toilet training. This viewpoint differs from Freud's emphasis on psychosexual maturation as the determinant of personality.

> **psychosocial model** Erikson's theory that personality arises from the manner in which social conflict is resolved.

Although Erikson agreed with Freud that early experiences are extremely significant, he saw personality development as a dynamic and continuing process from birth to death, as can be seen in Concept Summary Table 2-5.

Erikson extended Freud's theory of psychosexual development to include what he referred to as *psychosocial development.* Erikson emphasized the cultural or social influences on development, rather than the influence of pleasure derived from stimulation of erogenous zones. The core concept of Erikson's theory is the acquisition of *ego identity,* which loosely means self-knowledge. He believed ego identity was accomplished differently from culture to culture. Erikson believed that for today's youth, development of their ego identity, self-image, and self-concept is more important and has largely superseded Freud's theme of sexuality. Sexuality was important to Erikson, but as only one of a series of developmental issues to be resolved.

According to Erikson, autonomy needs are especially important to toddlers.

Erikson's stages expand on the drives within the individual and the way in which parents and others in society treat these forces. In addition, under Erikson's theory, the stages are seen as periods of life during which the individual's capacities for experience dictate that he must make a major adjustment to the social environment and the self. Although parental attitudes do affect the way the individual handles these conflicts, the social milieu is extremely important, too. For instance, within the context of our multicultural society, many Aboriginal people today experience identity crises and are confused about the society to which they belong. Erikson's model expands on Freud's in another key way: Erikson's eight stages of development encompass all ages of human life.

Erikson's book *Childhood and Society* (1963) presents his model of the eight stages of human development. In Erikson's view, everyone experiences eight crises or conflicts in development; the adjustments a person makes at each stage can be altered or reversed later. For example, children who are denied affection in infancy can grow to normal adulthood if they are given extra attention at later stages of development. But adjustments to conflicts do play an important part in the development of personality. The resolution of these conflicts is cumulative—that is, a person's manner of adjustment at each stage of development affects the way he handles the next conflict.

According to Erikson, specific developmental conflicts become

Concept Summary

Table 2-5   Erikson's Psychosocial Stages

PSYCHOSOCIAL STAGE	TASK OR CRISIS	SOCIAL CONDITIONS
Stage 1 (birth to 1 year)	Trust versus mistrust	From early caregiving, infants learn about the basic trustworthiness of the environment. If their needs are met—if they receive attention and affection and are handled in a reasonably consistent manner—they form a global impression of a trustworthy and secure world. If, on the other hand, their world is inconsistent, painful, stressful, and threatening, they learn to expect more of the same and believe that life is unpredictable and untrustworthy.
Stage 2 (2 to 3 years)	Autonomy versus shame and doubt	Toddlers discover their own bodies and how to control them. They explore feeding and dressing, toileting, and many new ways of moving about. When they succeed in doing things for themselves, they gain a sense of self-confidence and self-control. But if they fail continually and are punished or labelled messy, sloppy, inadequate, or bad, they learn to feel shame and self-doubt.
Stage 3 (4 to 5 years)	Initiative versus guilt	Children begin to explore beyond themselves. They discover how the world works and how they can affect it. For them, the world consists of both real and imaginary people and things. If their explorations, projects, and activities are generally effective, they learn to deal with things and people in a constructive way and gain a strong sense of initiative. Again, if they are criticized severely or punished, they learn to feel guilty for many of their own actions.
Stage 4 (6 to 11 years)	Industry versus inferiority	Children begin to develop numerous skills and competencies in school, at home, and in the outside world of their peers. According to Erikson, children's sense of self is enriched by the realistic development of such competencies. Comparison with peers is increasingly important. A negative self-evaluation compared with others is especially damaging at this time.
Stage 5 (12 to 18 years)	Ego identity versus ego diffusion	Before adolescence, children learn a number of different roles, such as the role of student or friend, older brother, Christian, Italian, athlete, or the like. During adolescence, it is important to sort out and integrate these various roles into one consistent identity. Adolescents seek basic values and attitudes that cut across these various roles. If they fail to integrate a central identity or cannot resolve a major conflict between two major roles with opposing value systems, the result is what Erikson calls ego diffusion.
Stage 6 (young adulthood)	Intimacy versus isolation	In late adolescence and young adulthood, the central developmental conflict is that of intimacy versus isolation. The intimacy that Erikson describes concerns more than sexual intimacy. It is an ability to share one's self with another person of either sex without fear of losing one's own identity. Success in establishing this intimacy will be affected by the resolution of the five earlier conflicts.
Stage 7 (adulthood)	Generativity versus self-absorption	In adulthood, after the earlier conflicts have, in part, been resolved, men and women are free to direct their attention more fully to assisting others. Parents sometimes find themselves by helping their children. Individuals can direct their energies without conflict to the solution of social issues. But failure to resolve earlier conflicts often leads people to be preoccupied with themselves—with their own health, psychological needs, comfort, and the like.
Stage 8 (maturity)	Integrity versus despair	In the last stages of life, it is normal for adults to look back over their lives and judge them. If people look back over their lives and are satisfied that they have had meaning and involvement, then they have a sense of integrity. But if their lives seem to have been a series of misdirected energies and lost chances, they have a sense of despair. Clearly, this final resolution is a cumulative product of all the previous conflict resolutions.

critical at certain points in the life cycle. During each of the eight stages of personality development, a specific developmental task or conflict will be more significant than any other (see Concept Summary Table 2-5). Yet, although each conflict is critical at only one stage, it is present throughout life. For instance, autonomy needs are especially important to toddlers, but throughout life people must continually test the degree of autonomy they can express in each new relationship. As presented, these stages are extremes. No one will actually become entirely trusting or mistrustful; rather, people will develop varying degrees of trust or mistrust throughout life. The key aspects of Erikson's psychosocial theory are presented in Concept Summary Table 2-6. We will examine some of the stages in more detail in later chapters.

An Evaluation of the Psychoanalytic Tradition

Although the psychoanalytic tradition is often thought of in historical terms, it continues to make significant contributions to the study of human behaviour. Its strength lies in the richness of its holistic approach: its willingness to look at the whole individual, including both conscious and unconscious mental activities, and to deal specifically with emotions. Its emphasis on unconscious processes allows it to explore important areas of human behaviour that many other traditions barely touch. It is also a rich theory for dealing with interpersonal relationships, particularly the relationships of childhood and those in the primary family unit.

The basic weakness of psychoanalytic theory is inseparable from its strength. Although the theory explores the depths of personality, it is precisely this area that is almost impossible to define or to validate by experiment. The theory draws much of its data from case studies of adults, who must subjectively reconstruct their childhoods. Psychoanalytic theory, therefore, is often described as unscientific, vague, and difficult to test.

Humanistic Psychology

Humanistic psychology developed in the 1950s as a reaction against the way that Freud's theory and learning theories approached the development of personality. Many perceived these approaches as too deterministic and one-sided. Humanists, such as Abraham Maslow and Carl Rogers, claimed that there is more to personality than learned responses and instincts. Humanistic psychology advocates a holistic approach to the study of personality that considers the person's inner thoughts, feelings, goals, and dreams. The goal is to study the person "from the inside out" to get a sense of how that person experiences the world.

Question to Ponder

Do Erikson's stages seem to apply to your life? Do you think they are universal?

---

humanistic psychology A holistic approach to the study of personality that considers the person's inner thoughts, feelings, goals, and dreams. According to this approach, humans are spontaneous, self-determining, and creative.

Concept Summary

Table 2-6 Key Aspects of Erikson's Psychosocial Theory of Development

- Erikson's theory has eight psychosocial stages. The stages cover the whole lifespan.

- Each stage is marked by a psychosocial crisis that must be resolved.

- Psychological development results from an interaction between the individual's biological needs and societal demands.

- Erikson extended the scope of his theory beyond the early years to include young adulthood, middle age, and late life.

- While both Freud and Erikson present theories derived from the psychoanalytic tradition, Freud's theory may be called psychosexual, while Erikson's is primarily psychosocial.

An important humanistic psychologist is Abraham Maslow. His theory, proposed in 1954, stresses each person's innate need for *self-actualization*, which means "becoming the best you can be." According to Maslow, a person does not have the luxury of becoming self-actualized if other needs, such as safety, love, food, and shelter, have not been met. For example, a hungry child's preoccupation with food detracts from higher needs, such as learning and self-actualization.

Humanistic psychology has had an impact in several ways. It acts as a spur to other developmental approaches, for it stresses the significance of keeping in touch with real life in all its richness. It has helped promote child-rearing approaches that respect the child's uniqueness and educational approaches that "humanize" the interpersonal relationships within schools. It has broadened the scope of curricula. In the words of a modern humanistic psychologist, "Children do not simply learn through their minds, but through their feelings and concerns, their imaginations and their bodies" (Miller, 1990, p. 153). Educational approaches that share the holistic view of humanistic psychology include Montessori, Waldorf, Reggio Emilia, progressive, and open education. We will look at these approaches in Chapter 10.

> **Question to Ponder**
>
> Do you think that humanistic psychology has had an influence on schools that you attended?

Ethology

Ethology is a branch of biology that studies patterns of animal behaviour. Among psychologists, it has stimulated a renewed interest in the biological characteristics that humans have in common with animals. Ethologists stress the importance of studying both people and animals in their natural settings. Just as ethologists choose to study the social relationships of baboons in the wild, instead of in wire cages, they also insist on observing children at play during school recess, rather than in contrived laboratory settings.

> **ethology** The study of animal behaviour, often observed in natural settings and interpreted in an evolutionary framework.

Ethologists use the same theoretical principles in studying the behaviour of humans and animals. They see many similarities between animal and human behaviour, and they believe that a similar evolutionary experience has preserved certain behavioural traits in humans that are common to animals, too. Ethologists also propose that, like other animals, all human beings demonstrate species-specific patterns of behaviour that are similar despite cultural differences. Even blind, deaf children smile and babble at the appropriate age, and they demonstrate pouting and laughing throughout their lifetime, despite being unable to imitate models (Eibl-Eibesfeldt, 1989).

The idea that social behaviour is largely determined by an organism's biological inheritance is the major feature of *sociobiology*, a branch of ethology. Like ethologists, sociobiologists see similarities between animal and human behaviour, but they go further and claim that complex patterns of social behaviour are genetically determined in both animals and humans (Wilson, 1975). To support this claim, sociobiologists cite examples of birds' nest building—a complex pattern of behaviour that birds exhibit at the right time without the benefit of learning. Sociobiologists generalize from this and other complex unlearned social patterns of insects, birds, and lower mammals to suggest a similar basis for human behaviour patterns. They believe that many human behaviour patterns that are used to express dominance, territoriality, nurturance, mating, and aggression show a thin veneer of learned culture on top of a genetically inherited biological pattern of behaviour. This theory has caused vigorous debate among psychologists, most of whom say that human social behaviour is learned.

The ethologist's interest in inherited behaviour patterns resembles that of the psychoanalyst in drive theory, but there is a major difference. The psychoanalyst sees human drives as remnants of archaic, biological drives that threaten to destroy civilization. Ethologists and sociobiologists, on the other hand, view the drives (and the behaviour that results from the drives) as an integral part of civilization itself. Perhaps the successful civilization is the one that does not attempt to restrict human biological heritage (Hess, 1970).

Ethology adds another important dimension of analysis. Most developmental psychologists look at the situational and historical causes of behaviour. The ethologist sees these aspects but considers an adaptive function as well—the function the behaviour serves in preserving the individual or the species. For example, a baby cries. The situational cause may be that the baby is in pain. The historical cause may be that the baby has been rewarded by care after crying in the past. The immediate function is to alert the mother and to trigger her nurturance. Therefore, crying is an innate behaviour pattern directed toward the specific target of nurturance. Finally, the evolutionary function of crying is survival of the infant. The infant cries because he does not have other available responses, such as talking or walking, that would elicit adult attention. His survival depends on adult nurturance. Ethologists emphasize the evolutionary function of many behaviour patterns, such as adult responsiveness to creatures that look babyish, flirting behaviour as part of a courtship pattern, or aggressive posturing as part of territorial defence (Bowlby, 1982; Eibl-Eibesfeldt, 1989). Ethologists analyze the seemingly universal as well as the culture-specific aspects of this behaviour.

Ethology's way of looking at human nature is making its mark on psychology. The process of infant–caretaker attachment has been extensively examined through this perspective (see the further discussion in Chapter 7). Mary Ainsworth and John Bowlby are key attachment researchers who have an ethological perspective. They have conducted numerous studies on peer interaction, with a focus on dominance patterns in human groups. Ethologists suggest that a dominance hierarchy among children may decrease aggressive conflicts in the playground, as has been found in other primate groups (Eibl-Eibesfeldt, 1989).

Ethologists also examine cognitive development, but here they pay considerable attention to the biological, species-specific component of learning and thinking. Ethologists suggest that the human brain is prepared for certain kinds of learning, but not for others. Complex learning, like that of language, may be done more easily in certain sensitive periods of development than in others (Bornstein, 1987). Even problem solving is influenced by the human brain's innate sensitivity to only certain aspects of a problem. Studies suggest that 4-year-olds solve problems in a trial-and-error fashion

Question to Ponder

Do you believe in the nurture assumption?

FOCUS ON AN ISSUE

The Nurture Assumption: Why Children Turn Out the Way They Do

Have you ever wondered why children turn out the way they do? According to the *nurture assumption,* the way parents raise children has an enormous impact on how children develop. Does this assumption sound reasonable to you? If it does, you are not alone; most people in our society share this assumption. However, Judith Rich Harris, author of *The Nurture Assumption,* suggests that parents have less of an impact on children than we assume. In her book, she presents evidence that seems to suggest that peers, not parents, are the main socializing agents. She refers to the following examples:

1. Immigrant children, whose parents have the culture and language of the "old country," grow up with the culture and language of the "new country." They speak with the accent of their peers, not that of their parents. How is this possible if the nurture assumption is true?

Will the nurture assumption ... stand the test of time?

2. In Britain, it is customary for upper-class boys to be cared for primarily by a nanny or governess until age 6, when they are shipped off to boarding school. By the time the boys are men, they bear an uncanny resemblance to their fathers—they have the same upper-class accent and demeanour. At first glance, this evidence may seem to be in favour of the nurture assumption, which would predict that children resemble their parents; however, the fathers provided virtually none of the nurture. The boys do not resemble those who provided most of the nurture—the nanny or governess and the teachers. Why do the boys resemble their fathers? According to Harris, it is because their fathers attended the same boarding schools, where norms of behaviour are consistent between generations, and the boys at the schools socialize one another.

3. According to the nurture assumption, girls learn to be women by imitating their mothers, just as boys learn to be men by imitating their fathers. Does this actually happen? Are children rewarded for imitating parents?

similar to the method chimpanzees use. Yet, 8-year-old children in all cultures have distinctly human strategies for problem solving (Charlesworth, 1988).

Neuroscience

Neuroscience first emerged over the last century to "understand how the brain produces the remarkable individuality of human action" (Kandel, Schwartz, & Jessell, 1995, p. xv). Researchers have invented a number of methods that allow them to study the brain more easily and less invasively. Specialized scans, such as CT, MRI, and PET, provide pictures of the brains of living people. They show the size and structure of the brain, and some even show which parts of the brain are most active. Brain scans are used to compare children with developmental disorders, such as autism or attention deficit hyperactivity, with children who do not have the disorders (Filipek, 1999). This is an exciting new area of research that might lead to advances in diagnosis and treatment.

Research in neuroscience is having a major impact on the study of development. Researchers can study the brains of developing children and see how environmental stimulation affects brain development. If children are deprived of stimulation, adequate nutrition, or nurture during the first five years, their brains develop differently than do those of other children. These differences can affect the child for life (Guy, 1997). Ironically, the more we learn about the brain's biology, the more we realize the importance of the environment. We cannot understand brain development without considering environmental influences.

Through methods discovered in the neurosciences, researchers are now better able to study the behaviour of fetuses. They can watch them on ultrasound or listen to their movements and heart rate by using special Doppler stethoscopes (Smotherman &

neuroscience The interdisciplinary study of the brain and behaviour.

According to Harris, many of the things children see parents doing—making messes, bossing people around, lighting matches, coming and going as they please—are inappropriate behaviours for children. Children are often discouraged, rather than encouraged, from behaving like their parents. In most societies, children who behave like adults are considered poorly behaved. According to Harris, children do not learn rules of social behaviour from watching their parents; they learn them from watching other children.

If you believe in the nurture assumption, you might be saying to yourself, "These are just three examples. Perhaps they are the exceptions." We also need to examine evidence that seems to support the nurture assumption. This evidence comes mainly from studies looking at whether the way parents treat children is related to how the children behave (we will describe these studies in more detail in Chapter 13). Essentially, parents who are warm and affectionate with their children and who set limits for their children's behaviour have children who are judged to be better adjusted than other children in our society. From this evidence, it would seem that parents' nurturing makes a difference. Can we conclude that it causes the children to be better adjusted? No, because the studies are correlational, rather than controlled experiments. The studies are *consistent* with the nurture assumption, but they do not *prove* it. There could be other explanations, not the least of which is the shared genetic makeup passed from parent to child—socially competent parents produce socially competent children.

Harris states that the nurture assumption is fairly recent and is not universal to cultures around the world. She traces its origin to Freud's theory—the notion that nurturing during the first 5 or 6 years sets the foundation for personality and can cause effects that last a lifetime—and to behaviourism—the idea that parents mould children by doling out reinforcement and punishment. Before these two theories were put forth, most people did not believe in the nurture assumption. Perhaps the nurture assumption, then, is no more than a cultural myth. The fact that most people believe it does not necessarily mean that it is true; it may be like other assumptions that people used to hold but that we know today are false.

It will be interesting to see the fate of the nurture assumption. Will it ultimately be replaced by a new assumption, perhaps Harris's assumption that peers are a critical influence on development? Or will the nurture assumption ultimately be proved and stand the test of time?

Robinson, 1996). They are exploring links between prenatal behaviour and behaviour after birth. This is an important new direction because many experiences in the womb, such as exposure to toxins, can have a profound impact on later development (Jacobson & Jacobson, 1996). We will explore prenatal development in more detail in Chapter 4.

In addition to creating new research frontiers, neuroscience methods have allowed researchers to study the biological underpinnings of topics that were traditionally studied from other theoretical perspectives. For example, memory in infants, traditionally studied from a cognitive perspective, now can be examined from a biological perspective to see what is happening in the brain (Nelson, Henschel, & Collins, 1993). Similarly, individual differences in temperament, an aspect of personality, are now being related, in part, to inherited differences in brain chemicals and the reactivity of the nervous system (Kagan, 1994). Very shy children have different brain chemistries than do more outgoing children.

Perry (1995) describes how abuse and neglect in early childhood can change the child's biological reaction to stressful events. The changed biological reaction can be long lasting. "The seeds of adult aggression and lack of emotional control may be sown in the brain wiring of some children who receive very little care and nurturing in their early years" (Guy, 1997, p. 5). Other neuroscience research has monitored the presence of stress hormones in children who are enrolled in child care (see Tout, deHaan, Campbell, & Gunnar, 1998). The researchers collected samples of children's saliva and assessed them for the presence of stress hormones (cortisol). Interestingly, hormone levels were higher in the morning than in the afternoon. As well, changes in hormone levels predicted aggressive or anxious behaviour in boys, but they did not predict behaviour in girls.

Neuroscience has also affected the study of development by fostering collaboration between psychologists working with experts in other fields, such as genetics, pharmacology, biology, medicine, and computer science, thereby broadening the thinking about development. This interdisciplinary collaboration is important because "no single discipline has the expertise to comprehensively address the complex questions with which the scientific community is now confronted" (Leavitt & Goldson, 1996, p. 389). For example, Thomas Shultz and his colleagues at McGill University have combined Piaget's theory of cognitive development with ideas from computer science to better explain how children develop from one stage to the next (Shultz, Mareschal, & Schmidt, 1994; Shultz, Schmidt, Buckingham, & Mareschal, 1995).

Question to Ponder

Are there any topics in development that cannot be studied from a neuroscience perspective?

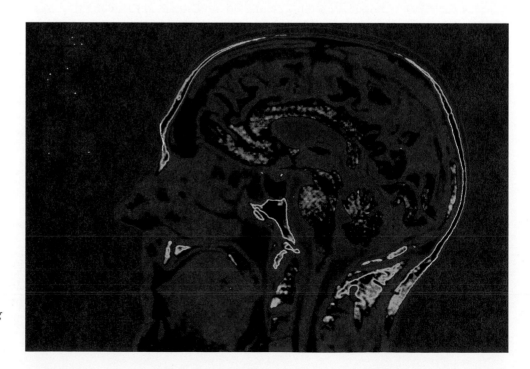

Research in neuroscience is having a major impact on the study of development.

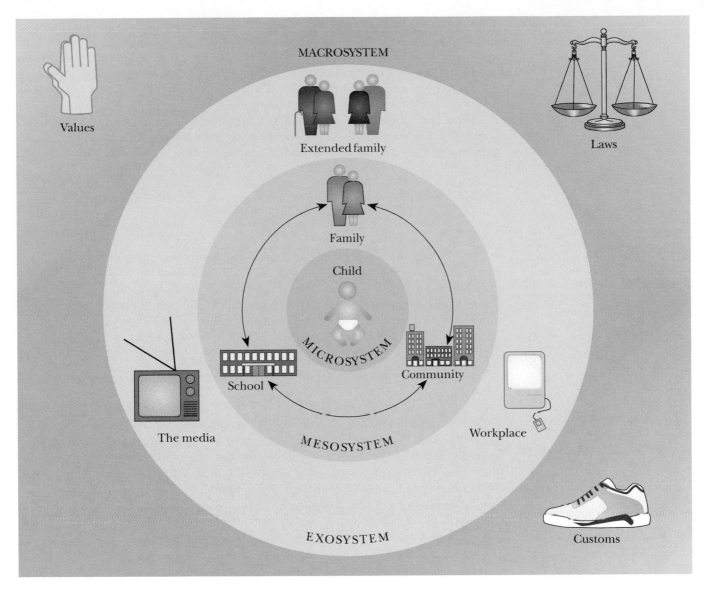

Figure 2-2
Bronfenbrenner's
Ecological Model.

Ecological Systems Theory

Today, perhaps the most influential theory of human development is that of the American psychologist Urie Bronfenbrenner. When he first articulated his theory, in the 1970s, he called it the **ecological systems theory** (Bronfenbrenner, 1979, 1989). He emphasized understanding how the environment influences a child's development and determining how the developing child affects her environment. Therefore, he described development as a dynamic, two-directional, reciprocal process. In addition, Bronfenbrenner expanded the concept of environment to include four distinct levels of analysis, as pictured in Figure 2-2. Let us now look at each of the levels.

> **ecological systems theory** A theory that focuses on how different levels of the environment affect child development and on how the child alters his environment. Development is viewed as a dynamic, two-directional process.

The Microsystem

The first level, or **microsystem,** refers to the activities, roles, and interactions of the child and his immediate single setting, such as the home, day-care centre, or school. For example, in the home, the child's development may be encouraged by the mother's sensitivity to his moves toward independence. In turn, his moves toward independence may encourage the mother to think of new ways to promote this kind of behaviour. The microsystem is the environmental level most frequently studied by psychologists.

> **microsystem** The immediate environments, such as home and school, in which the child spends the most time.

The Mesosystem

mesosystem The interactions among different microsystems.

A key feature of the model is that the various microsystems are not isolated from each other. The **mesosystem,** or second level, comprises the interrelations among two or more microsystems. In this level, the child's development is affected by the formal and informal connections between home and school, or among home, school, and her neighbourhood peer group. For example, a child's progress at day care may be affected positively by her parents' close communication with the teachers there. Similarly, the attentiveness of her day-care teachers is likely to benefit the child's interactions at home.

The Exosystem

exosystem The indirect environmental influences on a child, such as policies in the parent's workplace.

The **exosystem,** or third level, refers to the social settings or organizations beyond the child's immediate experience that nevertheless affect him. Examples range from formal settings, such as his parents' workplaces and the community health and welfare system, to less formal organizations, like the child's extended family or his parents' social network of friends. For example, his mother may work for a company that allows her to work at home several days a week. Such flexibility may enable her to spend more time with her child, and so the company indirectly promotes his development. At the same time, her being able to be with him more may make her less tense and, therefore, more productive on the job.

The Macrosystem

macrosystem The environmental influences at the level of the society. They include values, laws, and customs.

Unlike the other levels, the **macrosystem,** or outermost level, does not refer to a specific setting, but rather comprises the values, laws, and customs of the culture or society the child lives in. For example, laws providing for the inclusion of children with disabilities in mainstream classes are likely to profoundly affect the educational and social development of all children in such classes. The success or failure of mainstreaming, in turn, may encourage or discourage other governmental efforts to integrate the two groups.

Although interventions to encourage development can occur at all levels, Bronfenbrenner (1989) suggests that interventions at the macrosystem are especially critical because the macrosystem has the power to affect every other level. For example, China has a policy to restrict families to one child. This policy has caused parents to change some of their child-rearing values and has made them more likely to overprotect or overindulge their child (Jing, 1996). Therefore, state policy changes can affect the folkways of people.

In Canada, many provinces are struggling to maintain funding for adequate education. Some provinces might respond by eliminating programs such as kindergarten or physical education. These changes could have a profound impact on the development of individual children. On a more positive note, the Northwest Territories recently extended high schools into smaller communities so that students do not have to leave home to finish their schooling. This change has caused an enormous increase in enrolment in senior high school, an increase of 128 percent from the 1983–1984 to 1993–1994 school years (Jewison, 1995).

The Bioecological Model

In recent years, Bronfenbrenner has expanded his original theory. He now calls it a *bioecological system* (Bronfenbrenner, 1995) to emphasize the development of individual children in particular environments. He recognized that children differ biologically and psychologically and that these differences affect how children respond to their environments. He was especially interested in how children interact with key people whom they see regularly in their immediate environments, such as parents or peers. Bronfenbrenner called these interactions *proximal processes* and hypothesized that understanding these interactions was the key to understanding development. Of course, he recognized that proximal processes do not occur in isolation, but rather are influenced by the changing natures of the people involved in the interactions and by all levels of the environment. They are also influenced by the historical time in which they occur.

The Limitations of Developmental Theories

Our current theories of development are incomplete. They do not tell us about age-related changes across the lifespan, nor do they tell us about how behaviours can be modified. Many theories define only one area of development, such as personality, rather than development in general. We do have many good theories that predict and explain limited aspects of behaviour or behaviour in specific stages of the lifespan. Nevertheless, most developmental psychologists agree that what is needed is a unifying theory of development that encompasses biological, behavioural, and social factors, as well as their interactions. The current theory that comes closest to this goal is the ecological model.

No one theory fully explains developmental processes and behaviours. That does not mean that these theories are irrelevant or inadequate. Theories, which usually follow a number of observations, generally play two major roles. First, they organize the observations into some kind of defined pattern. Second, they develop a rational explanation of how or why the observed phenomenon occurs. Because of the complexity of developmental processes, different theories address discrete aspects of the process. Each theory may be valid and worth studying in its own right, but it may fail to explain the cause of the developmental process. Each has its positive and negative aspects, but none is likely to be "the" theory of development. It still remains for some research to successfully integrate the disparate natures of these theories into a core explanation of child development.

As we have seen, the process of human development is complex and open to many interpretations. Theories of development have been remarkably diverse in their content and underlying beliefs. Why is it important to understand the theories of child behaviour? A broad understanding of various theories creates the detachment that lets us evaluate our own views, actions, and reactions. A familiarity with the major theories, then, allows us to examine, evaluate, and discipline our intuition and our own "theories" of children's behaviour.

Besides helping us understand our own ways of thinking, knowledge of the major theories makes us more eclectic. By acquainting ourselves with several theories, we can examine behaviour from more than one frame of reference and can see the value of other explanations. Many psychologists, too, are eclectic. They select from numerous theories those particular aspects that will help them in their work. Almost all psychologists have been influenced by others' theories. Therefore, in describing the various theories given in this chapter, we do not intend to label or pigeonhole psychologists; instead, we intend to simply present the basic outlines of some of the most popular beliefs. For review, the major theories of development are contrasted in Concept Summary Table 2-7.

Which theories match your basic assumptions about development? Are your assumptions consistent with just one theory, or are you eclectic, sharing assumptions with more than one theory? Is there any theory that you do not match with at all? It is important to consider your personal assumptions, you will likely find that theories you share the most assumptions with seem to make the most sense to you, but theories that have different assumptions will seem foreign.

Question to Ponder

How are developmental theories influenced by the historical time and the society in which they evolve?

Question to Ponder

Which developmental theories are most compatible with your intuition about development?

Concept Summary

Table 2-7 An Overview of the Theories

THEORY	KEY CONCEPTS AND IDEAS
Learning Theories	
Conditioning (Pavlov, Watson, Skinner)	Development is deterministic and mechanistic (shaped by the environment). Development occurs continuously.
Social cognitive (Bandura)	Children learn through imitation and modelling. Children's thinking and interpretations of situations affect learning.
Cognitive Theories	
Piaget and Neo-Piagetian (Piaget, Case, Pascual-Leone)	Both nature and nurture affect development. Children play an active role in their own development (organismic). They progress through cognitive stages (discontinuous). The main processes of development are assimilation and accommodation.
Information processing	Uses a computer metaphor. Cognitive development is seen as continuous. As children develop, they improve in how they encode, store, process, and retrieve information.
Social context (Vygotzsky)	Cognitive development is affected by the society in which children live. Children learn to use the signs and tools that are available in their society. The zone of proximal development has implications for education.
Psychoanalytic Theories (Freud)	Development is strongly influenced by biological drives beyond the person's control (determinism). Development is discontinuous. Children progress through psychosexual stages.
(Erikson)	Development is discontinous and lifelong. People progress through psychosocial stages.
Humanistic Theories (Maslow)	Focuses on the intrinsic aspects of development (a person's dreams, goals, motives, and imagination). In order to become self-actualized, people must first satisfy "lower needs."
Ethology	Emphasizes the evolutionary significance of behaviours. Behaviours evolve because they improve the chances of survival.
Neuroscience	The interdisciplinary study of the brain and behaviour. Neuroscience recognizes that the environment can affect how the brain develops.
Ecological Model (Bronfenbrenner)	In order to understand development, we must consider characteristics of the child and how they interact with different aspects of the environment (the microsystem, mesosystem, exosystem, and macrosystem).

FOCUS ON DIVERSITY

Adolescent Depression Considered from Different Theoretical Perspectives

One of the best ways to understand the role of theories is to consider a concrete example of a topic that has been studied from different theoretical perspectives. One such topic is adolescent depression. Depression is much more than simply the sad mood that most adolescents experience from time to time. Adolescent depression, like depression in adults, is a syndrome that has a variety of symptoms affecting the person's mood, behaviour, and physical well-being. Symptoms most common in depressed adolescents are hypersomnia (sleeping much more than normal), hopelessness, helplessness, self-criticism, and low self-esteem (Kutcher, Marton, & Boulos, 1993). Approximately 4 to 8 percent of adolescents are depressed, and they are twice as likely to be female than male (Kutcher, Marton, & Boulos, 1993). It is important to understand the causes of adolescent depression because depressed adolescents have a high risk of suicide, and if they survive, are at risk for depression in adulthood. Each of the major theories in psychology provides different insights into the causes of depression. Let us look at five of the theories: the psychoanalytic, behavioural, cognitive, neuroscience, and ecological models.

The psychoanalytic theories, as first described by Freud in 1917, conceptualize depression in terms of the inner conflict caused by a major loss. The depressed person is angry about the loss but turns the anger inward. His self-esteem depends more on the opinions and approval of others than on his own judgment. Rado, as cited in Mendelson (1990), describes depression as a "great despairing cry for love" (p. 25). According to the psychoanalytic tradition, resolving inner conflicts treats depression.

Behavioural theories relate depression to lack of reinforcement (Lewinsohn, 1974). The availability of reinforcement can be altered by a number of situations, such as changes in the environment (e.g., adolescents may lose a relationship that used to be reinforcing), lack of social skills (e.g., adolescents who are overly withdrawn or aggressive may not receive much reinforcement from peers), or changes in the perceived relationship between the person's behaviour and reinforcement (e.g., adolescents who perceive that there is no relationship between effort and grades often become helpless and give up). According to behavioural theories, depression is treated by making reinforcement more available.

Depressed adolescents have a high risk of suicide.

Cognitive theories focus on the maladaptive thinking of depressed people. For example, Beck (1972) summarized the essential elements of the thinking of a depressed person as a cognitive triad: (1) a negative view of self, (2) a negative view of the world, and (3) a negative view of the future. The negative thinking affects the depressed person's reactions to everyday events. For instance, many teenagers occasionally experience peer rejection (e.g., they ask a classmate out and are turned down). Depressed teenagers would overreact and start thinking that they are unlovable and ugly (and a host of other negative attributes), that the world is unfair, and that they will never get a date in the future. To treat the depression, then, according to cognitive theories, requires altering the negative thinking.

The neurosciences examine the biological bases of depression. In particular, they focus on chemical imbalances in the brain, most often caused by abnormal levels of neurotransmitters. Neurotransmitters allow cells in the brain, called neurons, to communicate with each other. Drugs such as Prozac or Zoloft, which alter neurotransmitters, especially one called serotonin, could be used to treat depression.

Bronfenbrenner's ecological model considers interactions among biological, psychological, and social factors that operate within the microsystem, mesosystem, exosystem, or macrosystem. Factors within the macrosystem (i.e., at the level of the culture) may be especially relevant to understanding why some subgroups of adolescents are more at risk for depression than others are. The rate of depression among Aboriginal adolescents is high, and they have a higher rate of suicides than do other adolescents (Canadian Institute of Child Health [CICH], 1994). Why? Perhaps we need to look beyond the individual to the larger social context, especially since many suicides among Aboriginal youth form a cluster, in which several young people in the same community attempt suicide around the same time (Armstrong, 1993).

Having different theoretical perspectives is a mixed blessing. On the one hand, it encourages specialization so that researchers can examine a few aspects of depression in detail. But, on the other hand, it is as though each theory looks at depression from a different vantage point, much like the six blind men who encountered the elephant. One grabbed the trunk and judged the elephant to be a snake; another grabbed a leg and thought it was a tree; and so on. We need to integrate the theories so we can glimpse the whole elephant.

Summary and Conclusions

Everyone has a theory about human nature, but not everyone has considered the way in which human nature develops in all its complexity across a variety of domains. For this reason, we study many different theories to enlarge our perspective and to look for ways of integrating their diversity.

Behaviourism is a philosophy that underlies the learning theories, which are based on the belief that the environment is the most significant factor in human development. In classical conditioning, for example, new stimuli become conditioned so that they elicit established responses. It is believed that many of our emotional responses are learned in this manner. In operant conditioning, the behaviour must occur before it can be strengthened by reinforcement; operant conditioning has been applied to education and to behaviour management programs. Social-learning theory applies learning principles to social behaviour. Much of this learning occurs through the processes of modelling and observation. In this way, children learn sex roles, social attitudes, and moral judgments, according to the learning theorists. Overall, although learning theory has much practical utility, it fails to explain many complex behaviours, such as language.

The cognitive theories see the mind as active, alert, and possessing innate structures that process and organize information. Piaget's theory of cognitive development is essentially an interactional model that sees intelligence as an example of adaptation to environmental demands. This adaptation occurs through the complementary processes of assimilation (bringing in information with existing structures) and accommodation (changing structures to meet environmental demands). For Piaget, mental structures, called schemes, form the basis for this incorporation of new knowledge. Piaget proposed that cognitive development occurs in four stages. In each of these, children use qualitatively different structures to solve problems.

Information-processing theorists tend to be critical of Piaget's theory. They use computer models to study lifelong mental processes, such as attention, perception, and memory. Unlike Piaget, these theorists are not looking for qualitative differences in cognition based on maturity. Vygotsky and his followers also have disagreements with Piaget's theory. According to Vygotsky, cognitive development is greatly influenced by the culture and society in which the child lives. Children learn the signs and tools of their culture through social interaction. Speech is an example of a sign. Children's social speech forms the basis for how children will later learn to talk to themselves. Children use self-talk to regulate their own behaviour. Vygotsky's concept of the zone of proximal development has implications for education.

Freud's psychoanalytic theory is based on principles of determinism. In this theory, behaviour and personality are controlled by innate sexual and aggressive drives. Personality develops in several psychosexual stages. During each stage, children must solve certain conflicts and reach a balance between frustration and gratification of their needs. The success or failure to resolve each stage will determine a child's future personality.

Erik Erikson disagreed with Freud about the importance of sexuality in determining personality. Erikson believed that the main motivation for personality development is the acquisition of an ego identity. He proposed that this identity seeking is a process that lasts from birth to death and occurs in eight psychosocial stages. The needs of each period are critical at different ages, but the needs are present throughout life.

Humanistic psychology was a reaction against the determinism of learning and psychoanalytic theories. Humanists focused on people's roles in their own development—on their motives, goals, dreams, and imagination. Maslow emphasized the concept of self-actualization.

Ethology, the branch of biology that studies animal behaviour, has contributed to developmental psychology. Ethologists study social behaviour in natural settings and consider its adaptive function for individuals and groups. Sociobiologists have been criticized for assuming that complex human behaviour is as genetically determined as some animal behaviour.

Neuroscience has broadened the study of development through the discovery of new methods and extensive interdisciplinary collaboration.

The ecological model, developed by Bronfenbrenner, expanded the concept of the environment to include four levels: the microsystem (the immediate environment, such as the home), the mesosystem (interactions among microsystems), the exosystem (broader environmental influences, such as the media), and the macrosystem (environmental influences that relate to the whole society). He viewed development as being affected by interactions between characteristics of the child and different levels of the environment.

The breadth and scope of those theories that address developmental questions is impressive. Although none presents a comprehensive look at development in general, together, they contribute to our understanding of individual aspects of development, such as cognition or personality. In the future, we will undoubtedly see more attempts to integrate theories and to combine the biological and environmental components of behavioural determinism. In our discussion of the effects of heredity and environment on development, in Chapter 3, we will begin to look at the ways in which this integration might occur.

Key Terms and Concepts

accommodation (p. 39)
assimilation (p. 39)
classical conditioning (p. 34)
conservation (p. 39)
continuity (p. 33)
deterministic model (p. 34)
discontinuity (p. 33)
ecological systems theory (p. 55)

equilibration (p. 40)
ethology (p. 51)
exosystem (p. 56)
humanistic psychology (p. 50)
macrosystem (p. 56)
mechanistic (p. 33)
mechanistic model (p. 34)
mesosystem (p. 56)
microsystem (p. 55)

nature (p. 32)
neuroscience (p. 53)
nuture (p. 32)
operant conditioning (p. 35)
organismic (p. 33)
psychoanalytic tradition (p. 46)
psychosexual stages (p. 47)

psychosocial stages (p. 48)
shaping (p. 35)
signs (p. 44)
social cognitive theory (p. 37)
structuralism (p. 39)
zone of proximal development (p. 45)

Questions to Review

1. When studying human development, why is it important to have a broad understanding of the various theories on the subject?
2. What are some of the basic assumptions about human behaviour made by learning theorists?
3. How would you compare classical and operant conditioning?
4. Explain how social-learning theorists have expanded the scope of learning theory.
5. How are the concepts of imitation and modelling employed in social-learning theory?
6. Explain information-processing theory. How is it similar to learning theories?
7. What are some criticisms of learning theories?
8. How do cognitive theories differ from learning theories?
9. Describe Piaget's conservation experiment. What is the significance of its results?
10. What does Piaget mean by the "active mind"?
11. Describe Piaget's concepts of assimilation, accommodation, and equilibration.

12. According to Vygotsky, how do children learn to control their own behaviour?
13. Describe the zone of proximal development and how it relates to education.
14. What are some limitations of cognitive theories?
15. List some of Freud's assumptions about personality development.
16. How is Erikson's theory of personality development different from Freud's?
17. What are the strengths and weaknesses of the psychoanalytic tradition?
18. How has humanistic psychology affected the study of development?
19. What contributions has the field of ethology made to the study of human development?
20. How has neuroscience broadened the study of development?
21. Describe Bronfenbrenner's concepts of the microsystem, mesosytem, exosystem, and macrosystem.

Weblinks

www.ldb.org/setting.htm
A Comment on Settings in Health Promotion
This online paper was published in the Internet Journal of Health Promotion. It shows how Bronfenbrenner's theory of development has led to changes in thinking about health care.

www.neurosciencefoundation.ca/about.php3
NeuroScience Canada Foundation
Where is neuroscience research being undertaken in Canada? This Web site has information on programs,
universities, and affilitated institutes, as well as media releases related to neuroscience.

fcis.oise.utoronto.ca/~rcase/mathfunctions.html
Applying Neo-Piagetian Theory to the Teaching of Math
Robbie Case and Mindy Kalchan, at OISE in Toronto, have posted a copy of their paper "Teaching Mathematical Functions in Primary and Middle School: An Approach Based on Neo-Piagetian Theory."

Heredity and Environment

It's breeding and training and something much more that drives you and carries you home.

DAN FOGELBERG
RUN FOR THE ROSES

Outline

CHAPTER 3

Objectives

By the time you have finished this chapter, you should be able to do the following:

✔ Explain the principles and processes of molecular genetics.

✔ Describe the causes and characteristics of genetic abnormalities, and discuss the application of genetic research and counselling.

✔ Describe methods used in the field of behavioural genetics.

✔ Explain different types of gene–environment interactions.

✔ Describe the influence of cultures and families on development.

Shortly after Leonardo da Vinci died in 1519 at the age of 67, his younger half-brother Bartolommeo set out to reproduce a living duplicate of the great painter, sculptor, engineer, and author. Since he and Leonardo were related, the father that Bartolommeo chose was himself. He chose as his wife a woman whose background was similar to that of Leonardo's mother: She was young and came of peasant stock, and had also grown up in the village of Vinci. The couple produced a son Piero, who was then carefully reared in the same region of the Tuscan countryside, between Florence and Pisa, that had nurtured Leonardo. Little Piero soon displayed an artistic talent, and at the age of 12 he was taken to Florence, where he served as an apprentice to several leading artists, at least one of whom had worked with Leonardo. According to Giorgio Vasari, the leading art historian of the period, the young Piero "made everyone marvel ... and had made in five years of study that proficiency in art which others do not achieve save after length of life and great experience of many things." In fact Piero was often referred to as the second Leonardo.

At the age of 23, however, Piero died of a fever and so it is impossible to predict with certainty what he might have gone on to achieve—though there is some indication in that Piero's works have often been attributed to the great Michelangelo. Nor is it possible to say positively how much of Piero's genius was due to heredity and how much to environment. Full brothers share, on the average, 50 percent of their genes, but Bartolommeo and Leonardo were half-brothers and so would have had only about a quarter of their genes in common. Piero's mother and Leonardo's mother do not appear to have been related, but in the closely knit peasant village of Vinci it is quite possible that they had ancestors in common and thus shared

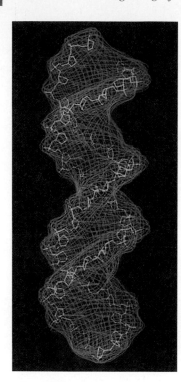

DNA contains the genetic code that regulates the functioning and development of the organism. The code is contained in a sequence of base pairs.

genes. On the other hand, a strong environmental influence cannot be ruled out. The young Piero was undoubtedly aware of his acclaimed uncle; and certainly his father, Bartolommeo, provided every opportunity that money could buy for the boy to emulate him. But Bartolommeo's efforts to give the world a second Leonardo by providing a particular heredity and environment might, after all, have had little influence. Piero possibly was just another of the numerous talented Florentines of his time. (From Peter Farb, *Humankind* [Boston: Houghton Mifflin, 1978], pp. 251–252. Reprinted by permission of Houghton Mifflin Co. and Jonathan Cape, Ltd.)

Any parent has inevitably been greeted at some time or other with the statement, "She looks just like her father!" or "You can certainly tell that they are brothers— they look alike, walk alike, and even sound alike!" The typical response is generally one of pride: "Yes, there is a certain similarity—she even has some of my movements and mannerisms." The statement invariably leads to some ruminations on the wonders of genetics.

This example illustrates the age-old question of heredity versus environment, which has long fascinated historians and novelists—not to mention developmental psychologists. At one time, people focused most on distinguishing how much of a trait came from heredity and how much came from environment. They tried to quantify the separate effects of the two contributors (for example, concluding that IQ scores are 50 percent genetics and 50 percent environment). Today, however, the focus is not so much on separating the effects as it is on understanding how genetics and environment work together to produce a trait or behaviour (Plomin & Rutter, 1998). Almost any behaviour requires both inherited capacity and environmental circumstances. The key issue is not whether nature or nurture has the greater impact on human development, but rather how genetics and environment interact in the shaping of an individual.

The genetic code, or genetic plan, present at birth is one starting point. Through this plan we inherit certain physical and behavioural traits from our parents and ancestors. The unfolding, or maturation, of the genetic plan requires a supportive (or at least not harmful) environment, as we will see in the discussion of the prenatal period in Chapter 4. The environment, or the culture, is the other starting point. Our socialization, or what we learn from our culture and how this learning affects us and every other individual, depends on many cultural factors and on how, when, and by whom we are exposed to these factors.

It is possible, moreover, for the environment to produce devastating effects on the developing fetus that rival those produced by genetic effects. A child, for example, may be born with a cleft lip and palate because of some unknown genetic error or because of steroids the mother took during a crucial period of prenatal development. Although one cause is based on heredity and the other on environment, they both produce the same severe malformation.

Principles and Processes of Molecular Genetics

Cells, chromosomes, genes, DNA, RNA, base pairs, and *codons* are all terms that are used when we discuss heredity. Therefore, a brief review of their definition and significance should be helpful before we discuss the processes of inheritance.

Location of the Genetic Material

chromosome   A DNA molecule; human cells have 23 pairs of chromosomes, making a total of 46.

DNA (deoxyribonucleic acid) The material that contains the genetic code that regulates the functioning and development of the person.

The entire genetic code is contained within the nucleus of each cell. The terms *DNA, chromosomes,* and *genes* all describe the code, but they are referring to different levels of detail. At the most general level are the **chromosomes,** which are depicted in Figure 3-1. Each chromosome is made from a **DNA** molecule. Furthermore, along each chromosome, strands of the DNA can be divided into separate genes.

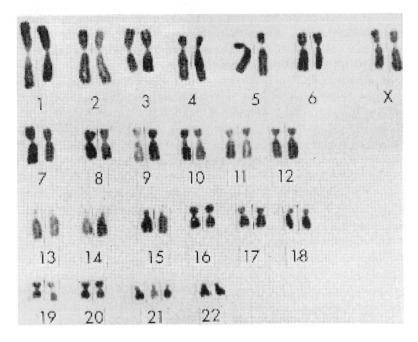

Figure 3-1
A karyotype showing the chromosomes arranged according to type. Note that there are three number 21 chromosomes, which indicates an individual with Down syndrome.

Chromosomes There are four key points to remember about chromosomes:

1. The number of chromosomes in each cell is important. All human cells with a nucleus have 46 chromosomes, except for ova and sperm, which have 23. Different species have different numbers of chromosomes. Changes to the number of chromosomes result in genetic disorders or in miscarriages.

2. Chromosomes are arranged in pairs. The 46 chromosomes in human cells make 23 pairs, which are referred to by their number. Figure 3-1 shows the pairs of chromosomes. One member of each chromosome pair was inherited from the mother and the other from the father.

3. Chromosome pairs 1 to 22 are called **autosomes.** They do not distinguish between males and females. The 23rd chromosome pair has the sex chromosomes. These chromosomes are named X and Y (they look like the letters). Females have two X chromosomes; males have one X and one Y chromosome. Sex chromosomes contain genes that control the development of the primary and secondary sex characteristics and various other sex-linked traits.

4. The ova and sperm have only half the genetic material of the parent cell. Each time ova and sperm are produced, the chromosomes are rearranged, as cards are shuffled and dealt. Ova and sperm are created through a type of cell division called **meiosis.** The chance that any two siblings may receive the same assortment of chromosomes is about one in 281 trillion. This figure does not even allow for the fact that the individual genes on a chromosome often make a **crossover** to the opposite chromosome during cell division. It is, therefore, virtually impossible for the same combination of genes to occur twice, except in identical twins, who develop from the same ova and sperm.

Genes and the Production of Protein

Each chromosome contains tens of thousands of **genes.** The total number of genes on all the chromosomes combined is close to a million (Kelly, 1986). Genes are important because they contain the directions for making proteins. Proteins are essential for life. Body cells are largely made up of proteins, as are a number of chemicals used throughout the body, such as hormones, enzymes, and brain neurotransmitters. Genes ensure that cells produce the "proper" proteins. Errors in the genes can cause genetic disorders, not so much because of the presence of a "faulty" gene but because the error leads to abnormal protein production (Hawley & Mori, 1999).

autosomes The chromosomes of a cell, excluding those that determine sex. It includes the first 22 pairs.

meiosis The process of cell division in reproductive cells that results in an infinite number of different chromosomal arrangements.

crossover The process during meiosis in which individual genes on a chromosome cross over to the opposite chromosome. This process increases the random assortment of genes in offspring.

genes Strands of DNA that code for a particular trait, such as eye colour.

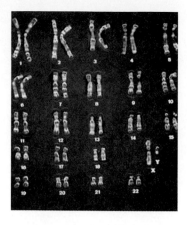

To develop a normal human baby, the zygote must have 23 pairs of chromosomes, or 46 chromosomes.

base pairs The "rungs" of the DNA molecule. All DNA has the same four types of bases, and this is enough to provide the codes for all life forms.

codons A group of three consecutive base pairs. The sequence of codons controls protein synthesis.

It is interesting that all of a person's cells contain the same genes. For instance, genes for brain neurotransmitters are found not just in brain cells, but also in liver cells, hair cells, and so on. One of the fascinating features of genetics is that there are regulator genes within each cell that control the other genes, telling some to produce their proteins and others to be inactive. Furthermore, there are regulators that tell genes to produce their proteins at one stage of development and not at other stages. For instance, during puberty, genes in the glands get "turned on" so that more protein can be produced to make hormones. It is important to note that the presence of a gene is not enough to ensure that the "right" proteins are synthesized. Genes must be turned on or off at the appropriate time in development. Development, then, may be described as a "complex program of expressing genes in some cell types and not in others at specific times during development" (Hawley & Mori, 1999, p. 3).

The expression of genes results in the synthesis of proteins. As we mentioned earlier, genes are made up of strands of DNA. Let us take a strand of DNA and look at it under great magnification so that we can examine its structure (see Figure 3-2). DNA has a double helix shape—it looks like two spirals woven together. Inside the spirals, we can distinguish rungs that connect one spiral to the other. The rungs contain the directions for protein synthesis. Each rung is made up of two bases—one attached to the spiral on the right, the other attached to the spiral on the left. The two bases are attracted to each other, forming a bond, which connects the two spirals. Two bases bonded together are called a **base pair.** There are only two types of base pairs found in DNA: (1) cytosine and guanine and (2) thymine and adenine. Because of their chemistry, cytosine always bonds with guanine (C and G), and thymine always bonds with adenine (T and A).

Let's now look at the base pairs that run along the inner edge of one of the spirals. One molecule of DNA (a chromosome) has about 65 million base pairs, which can be divided up into individual genes. Each gene has several hundred or thousand bases. Furthermore, the base pairs within a gene are organized into groups of three, called **codons.** Each codon codes for an amino acid (amino acids are used to make proteins) or for signals indicating where one protein code stops and the next one begins. The sequence of codons provides the blueprint for all possible proteins in the same way that combinations of letters of the alphabet can be used to express all the words in a language. If you change the sequence of codons, you change the protein

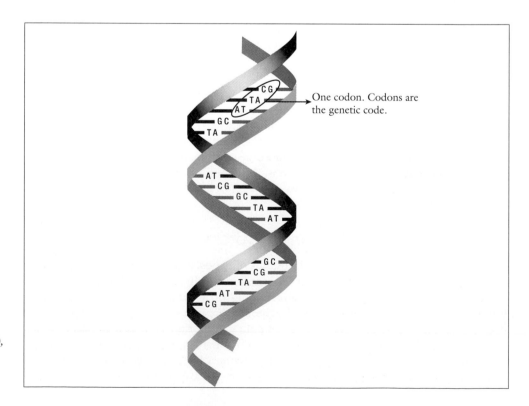

One codon. Codons are the genetic code.

Figure 3-2
DNA Molecule
The strands of the molecule are bonded together by base pairs: cytosine (C) joined to guanine (G), and thymine (T) joined to adenine (A).

Concept Summary

Table 3-1 Review of Genetics

- The human genetic code is located on the 46 chromosomes, which are in the cell nucleus.

- The 46 chromosomes are organized into 23 pairs (one member of the pair came from the mother, and the other came from the father).

- Each chromosome is made from one molecule of DNA.

- Strands of DNA can be divided into genes.

- Genes consist of a sequence of base pairs that form codons, which are the blueprint for proteins.

- The synthesis of the "proper" proteins is required for normal development.

- Mutations are changes in the genetic code.

(in the same way that changing the order of letters changes the word). Sometimes changes do occur. They are called **mutations.** Mutations can result in changes that are beneficial, harmful, or inconsequential. We will look at some mutations when we look at genetic disorders. It is important to keep in mind, though, that not all mutations are harmful.

Cells go to great lengths to protect the genetic code. Chromosomes, DNA, and genes—the keepers of the code—are unable to leave the nucleus of the cell. Therefore, RNA makes a copy of the code and takes it out of the nucleus to the part of the cell where proteins are made. Other types of RNA are responsible for bringing the appropriate amino acids to the site of protein production.

The box "The Human Gene Project" has information on how scientists around the world are identifying human genes.

mutations Changes in the sequence of codons within the gene. Mutations may be harmful, beneficial, or inconsequential.

RNA (ribonucleic acid) A substance formed from and similar to DNA. It acts as a messenger in a cell, bringing the genetic code to the site of protein production. It also brings the appropriate amino acids.

Genes: Dominant and Recessive Alleles

Chromosomes are organized into pairs. The first 22 pairs are called the *autosomes.* All of the genes on one chromosome have a corresponding gene on the other chromosome in the pair. The pair of genes code for the same thing, such as eye colour. The genes may be identical (e.g., both code for blue eyes) or they may be different (e.g., one codes for blue eyes and the other codes for brown eyes). Alternate forms of the same gene are called **alleles.** Examples of alleles for eye colour are blue, brown, black, green, or hazel. A single gene pair carries some hereditary traits, such as eye colour. Other traits are carried by a pattern of several interacting gene pairs. For eye colour, a child might inherit an allele for brown eyes (B) from the father and an allele for blue eyes (b) from the mother. The child's **genotype,** or gene pattern, for eye colour would therefore be Bb. But how do these genes combine? What colour will the child's eyes be? Gregor Mendel, an Austrian monk who founded the field of genetics, discovered that when two competing traits are inherited, one will be expressed. It is called the **dominant** trait. The other trait will not be revealed. It is called the **recessive** trait. In eye colour, the allele for brown eyes (B) is dominant and that for blue eyes (b) is recessive. When a gene is dominant, its presence in a gene pair will cause that specific trait to be expressed. Therefore, an individual with either the genotype Bb or BB has brown eyes. The expressed trait, brown eyes, is called the **phenotype.** People with blue eyes have the genotype bb.

In another example, let us assume that the father's genotype is Bb (brown eyes) and the mother had blue eyes (which must be the genotype bb). All the children of

alleles A pair of genes, found on corresponding chromosomes, that affect the same trait.

genotype The genetic makeup of a given individual.

dominant In genetics, one gene of a gene pair that will cause a particular trait to be expressed.

recessive In genetics, one gene of a gene pair that determines a trait in an individual only if the other member of that pair is also recessive.

phenotype In genetics, those traits that are expressed in the individual.

FOCUS ON APPLICATION

The Human Genome Project

Scientists around the world have been working on the Human Genome Project since 1990. Their goal is to map all the human genes (i.e., the genome) and to eventually identify those genes and combinations of genes that cause particular disorders. This $3 billion (US) research effort was expected to take 15 years, but according to Francis S. Collins, director of the (US) National Center for Human Genome Research, the project will be completed in the year 2003, a full two years ahead of schedule (Beardsley, 1996). By 1998, there were more than 16 354 genes on the map—more than triple the number there were in 1994. Researchers at Canadian universities and hospitals have contributed to the project. Ronald Worton, at Ottawa General Hospital, mapped the gene for Duchenne muscular dystrophy. Diane Cox, at the University of Alberta's Department of Medical Genetics, cloned the gene for a liver disease called Wilson disease. Michael Hayden, at the University of British Columbia, developed a diagnostic test for Huntington's disease. Lap Chee Tsui, at Toronto's Hospital for Sick Children, cloned the gene for cystic fibrosis. And Leigh Field, at the University of Calgary, was instrumental in the discovery of a gene related to dyslexia. Researchers have developed and refined a number of methods for studying the human genome.

OBTAINING SAMPLES OF GENES

In order to study genes, researchers must obtain samples of body cells, from which they extract the DNA. Blood samples—either fresh or frozen—are commonly used. DNA extracted from human blood can be kept safely in the freezer and used years later. Genetic researchers who study children sometimes obtain cells by rubbing the inside of the cheek with cotton because this procedure is less invasive than using a needle (Plomin & Rutter, 1998). Other samples are taken from clippings of finger- and toenails. Samples are durable enough to be shipped by mail to research labs. For instance, Dr. Gulliver

---

Researchers have developed and refined a number of methods for studying the human genome.

---

in St. John's is collecting samples from psoriasis patients in Newfoundland so that they may be shipped to California for genetic analysis (Abraham, 1998). Psoriasis is a skin disorder that causes red, flaky patches. Its severity ranges from mild to life-threatening. Newfoundland's psoriasis rate is five to ten times the national average. Many have an inherited form of the disorder that can be traced back two hundred years to their English and Irish ancestors.

SEARCHING SAMPLES FOR SPECIFIC GENES

After researchers have the sample, they search for specific genes within the sample. *Linkage* is one method used to search for genes among family members, including some who have the disorder or trait and others who do not have it. Researchers look for sequences of base pairs in the DNA (called *markers*) that distinguish those who have the disorder from those who do not. This method can be used to scan the entire genome, and it is especially advantageous when researchers are not sure where the gene is located. Researchers used linkage to find the genes for Huntington's disease and for PKU (phenylketonuria). Scanning the whole genome is an enormous feat, as you will recall that there are 65 million bases to scan on one chromosome alone. Fortunately, most of the scanning has been automated through technological advances. Linkage identifies the general area on the chromosome where the gene is located, rather than zooming in precisely on the gene.

Another method that is used to search for genes is *association*, which compares genes. This method is better at looking at a portion of the genome in finer detail than at scanning the entire genome. Researchers use association when they want to compare a group of people who have a disorder with a control group of people from the general population. For example, the method was used to compare children with attention deficit hyperactivity disorder (ADHD) with children who do not have the disorder (as described in Rutter, Silberg, O'Connor, & Simonoff, 1999a).

Question to Ponder

What ethical issues will need to be resolved as the Human Genome Project maps out our genetic code?

these parents will inherit a recessive gene for blue eyes from the mother. From the father, however, they may inherit either the dominant gene for brown eyes (B) or the recessive gene for blue eyes (b). Therefore, the children will be either blue-eyed (bb) or brown-eyed (Bb). If we know the genotypes of the parents, we can determine all the possibilities of genotypes and phenotypes—and the probabilities of each—for their children. See the example of a Punnett square in Figure 3-3. These squares readily reveal the probabilities of different phenotypes, given the genotypes of the parents. The columns are labelled with the alleles in the mom's genotype. (Uppercase letters are used to signify a dominant allele. Lowercase letters stand for recessive alleles.) The rows are labelled with the alleles in the dad's genotype. Each of the boxes within the square is filled in with the alleles of its row and column coordinates. See if you can

Using association, researchers were able to discover a gene, called DRD4, which may play a role in the disorder. The gene has a sequence of 48 base pairs that repeat, either a few times (five or less) or many times (six or more). If it repeats more than five times, there is a strong likelihood that the person is described as someone who seeks novelty or who is constantly attracted to new stimulation. Novelty seeking and the presence of the DRD4 gene was more common in the children who had ADHD than in other children. This does not mean, however, that researchers found the sole cause of ADHD. The DRD4 gene did not discriminate perfectly between children with and without the disorder. Some children in the control group had the gene; as well, some children with ADHD did not have the gene. Studying the possible genetics of ADHD is complex because the disorder is likely not caused by a single gene, but rather by a combination of genes and environmental influences. "Genes interact with their environment at all levels, including the molecular; there is virtually no interesting aspect of development that is strictly 'genetic,' at least in the sense that it is exclusively a product of information contained in the genes" (Elman, Bates, Johnson, Karmiloff-Smith, Parisi, & Plunkett, 1996).

DISCOVERING THE EFFECTS OF THE GENES

Once researchers isolate a gene, they clone it and use sophisticated methods to determine the role of the gene in protein synthesis. The DRD4 gene has been linked to a protein that is used in a type of brain receptor called a *dopamine receptor.* The significance of this finding is not yet clear. One hypothesis is that the protein causes the receptor to be less sensitive, which leads the person to seek novelty as a way to increase dopamine (Rutter et al., 1999a).

GENE THERAPIES

Corrective **gene therapy**—the repair or substitution of individual genes to correct certain defects—is proceeding at a careful pace. Geneticists have made amazing advances in genetic engineering experiments on plants, bacteria, and even other animals. Scientists can transplant genetic materials from one species into the cell of another species. The result is a hybrid with characteristics of both donors. This gene-splicing technique has been used to create new plants. It is also possible to create a strain of bacteria that will produce a human growth hormone (Garber & Marchese, 1986). Through a process called *cloning,* scientists have been able to duplicate some laboratory animals from just one of the somatic, or body, cells. But the use of such genetic engineering techniques on humans would involve a number of risks and challenges—physical, psychological, social, and ethical. It is appropriate that most professionals are advancing with extreme caution.

In at least a few cases, however, gene therapy is progressing well and with little public outcry. In the 1970s, a boy named David became famous because he lived in a sterile bubble. He had a severe inherited disorder in his immune system that meant he was liable to die from the slightest infection. This rare condition, called severe combined immunodeficiency (SCID), has now become the target of the first government-approved clinical trials in the United States for human gene therapy. In September 1990, a 4-year-old girl with SCID began receiving a billion or so gene-altered immune system cells intravenously in a saline solution. The results have been good so far. By 1993, the young girl's body was producing its own immunities and she was healthy. A couple of years later, she was featured in a *Scientific American* article as a healthy, active 9-year-old (Beardsley, 1996).

Many other diseases are under study for effective techniques in gene therapy. The most promising candidates are those diseases caused by a single gene that can be isolated, cloned, and transplanted. For cystic fibrosis, the gene treatment may be by an aerosol spray applied directly to the lungs. For sickle-cell anemia, the cure would be a little more complicated. There must be delivery of the healthy gene to the blood cells, along with another gene capable of deactivating the damaged version. Ideally, scientists aim to remove the patient's damaged cells and then alter and return them to the patient. In each case, the genes must reach the right target, for example, the bone marrow, the liver, or cells in the skin. The process is extremely complex (Verma, 1990). Attempts to treat cystic fibrosis and Duchenne muscular dystrophy with gene therapy have largely failed because patients' cells did not take up enough of the transplanted genes (Beardsley, 1996).

complete the boxes in the Punnett square shown in Figure 3-4. What are the probabilities of each of the phenotypes?

Genetics would be straightforward if all alleles followed a dominant/recessive pattern. This is not the case, though. Some alleles have a co-dominance relationship. For example, the combination of straight and curly hair results in wavy hair. As well, there are other factors that make genetics more complicated. For example, some genes, referred to as *jumping genes,* move around, recombine with other genes at different points in development, and give rise to proteins that regulate the expression of other genes (Elman et al., 1996). Hence, the genetic code is not static, but can change over the course of development.

gene therapy The manipulation of individual genes to correct certain defects.

Figure 3-3
Punnett squares are used to predict the genetic makeup of the children of parents with particular genotype combinations.

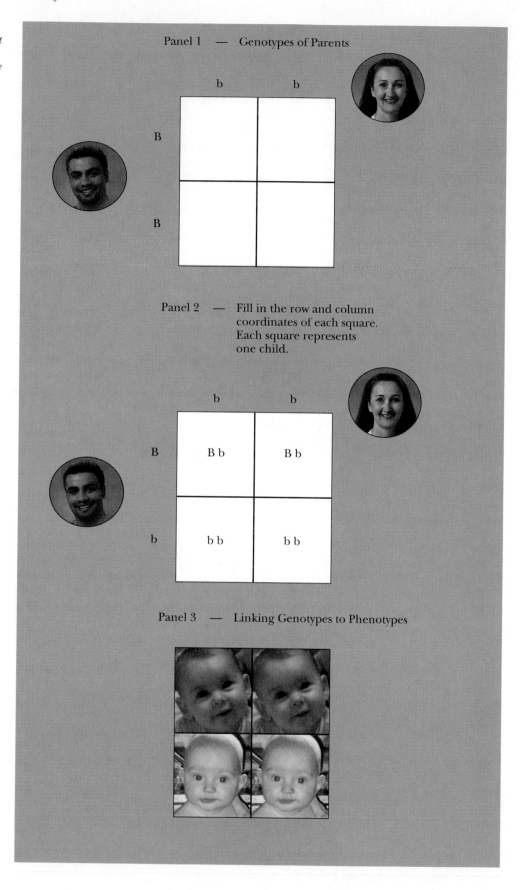

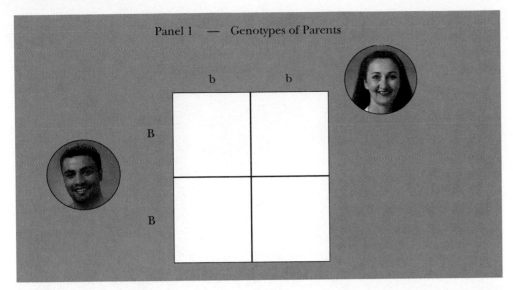

Panel 1 — Genotypes of Parents

Figure 3-4
Fill in the genotype and phenotype for each child. What is the probability that the child will have brown eyes? What is the probability that she will have blue eyes?

(Answer: All of their children will have brown eyes.)

Polygenetic System of Inheritance

Most traits, including eye colour, do not usually result from a single gene pair, but from a combination of many gene pairs—with and without dominance—that interact in a number of ways. For the characteristic of height, for instance, several genes or gene pairs seem to combine with others to create larger or smaller people, with larger or smaller limbs and other parts. Gene pairs may also interact in such a way that one gene pair either allows or inhibits the expression of another gene pair. A system of various types of interaction among genes and gene pairs is called a **polygenic inheritance** system. Such systems frequently give rise to phenotypes that differ markedly from those of either parent.

> **polygenic inheritance** A trait caused by an interaction of several genes or gene pairs and interactions between genes and environmental influences.

Genetic Abnormalities

Genetic abnormalities originate in the ova or the sperm. There are different types of genetic abnormalities. Some are caused by an abnormal number of chromosomes. In other cases, the number of chromosomes is normal, but there are one or more abnormal genes on the chromosomes. And in some cases, the abnormality is restricted to just a portion of a gene—i.e., part of the sequence of base pairs is abnormal. Abnormal numbers of chromosomes are more common in ova, whereas mutations of the genes are more common in sperm (Hawley & Mori, 1999). Genetic abnormalities often can be traced to problems with cell division, either meiosis or mitosis. In meiosis, cells with 46 chromosomes divide to produce ova and sperm that have 23 chromosomes. Problems with meiosis can affect the number of chromosomes. In mitosis, cells divide to produce cells that have the same number of chromosomes as the original cell. Problems with mitosis are associated with mutations to genes.

The effects of genetic abnormalities vary in severity. Some are so severe that the fetus cannot sustain life and is miscarried early in the pregnancy. Others are "silent," not producing any detectable effects in the person's phenotype—the person develops "normally." And others result in genetic disorders. We will now look at some of the different types of disorders.

Chromosomal Defects

Down Syndrome This is the most common chromosomal defect and occurs once for every 800 births. It usually, but not always, is inherited from the mother and becomes

Some children with chromosomal abnormalities may have nearly normal intelligence.

progressively more common the older the mother. For example, in women 45 and older, the occurrence is once for every 25 births. People who have Down syndrome have an extra chromosome 21, which either floats freely in the cell nucleus or is situated on top of another chromosome in piggy-back fashion. It causes improper physical and mental development.

Children with Down syndrome often are severely developmentally delayed and may have serious cardiac and respiratory system problems. Nevertheless, they are often happy children who enjoy music and group play. Recently, there has been a discouraging finding concerning these individuals, however. It appears that many individuals with Down syndrome develop Alzheimer's disease in adulthood (Kermis, 1986). While this is certainly not good news, it has helped to narrow the search for the genetic origins of Alzheimer's disease to chromosome 21, since this is the locus for Down syndrome.

A variation of Down syndrome is known as "mosaic" Down syndrome because the person has a mosaic, or pattern, of normal and abnormal cells. The normal cells have 46 chromosomes and the abnormal ones have 47 (including the extra 21st chromosome). The abnormal cells occur because of problems when cells are dividing. A cell divides improperly, allocating 47 chromosomes to one new cell and only 45 to the other. Cells with only 45 chromosomes cannot survive, but those with 47 develop alongside normal cells with 46 chromosomes (Koch & Koch, 1974). Children with this genotype have both normal cells and cells with a Down syndrome pattern. Their impaired learning ability and the extent of their other Down syndrome traits depend on the number of abnormal cells that are produced; these, in turn, depend on how early the developmental error occurred. Some of these people may have nearly normal intelligence. Even those children with more classic Down syndrome vary in the amount of mental retardation or the number of physical symptoms that they display (Turkington, 1987).

Abnormalities of the Sex Chromosomes Several abnormalities may occur in the arrangement of the sex chromosomes.

KLINEFELTER'S SYNDROME

This abnormality occurs when males have at least one, and possibly more, extra X chromosomes, yielding an XXY arrangement. This disorder occurs once in every 1000 live born males. This phenotype usually includes sterility, small external male sex organs, undescended testicles, and breast enlargement. Approximately 25 percent of men with Klinefelter's syndrome have mental retardation. These defects generally worsen as more Xs are added to the genotype. This disorder is eased in its physical manifestations by hormonal replacement therapy after the usual age of puberty. This therapy, which involves testosterone (male sex hormone) injections, must be continued for the remainder of the individual's life to maintain the secondary sex characteristics.

TURNER'S SYNDROME

This disorder affects females and occurs once in every 10 000 female births. In this condition, one X chromosome is either absent or inactive, making an XO arrangement. Individuals with Turner's syndrome usually have an immature female appearance (because they do not develop secondary sex characteristics), and they lack internal reproductive organs. They may be abnormally short and are sometimes mentally retarded. Once the disorder is discovered, usually at puberty, when the girl fails to develop normal secondary sex characteristics, hormone replacement therapy may be initiated to help her appear more normal. However, she will remain sterile.

SUPERMALE SYNDROME

This abnormality results when males have one or more extra Y chromosomes, producing the XYY pattern. This pattern appears about once in every 1000 men in the general population, but four times in every 1000 men in prison populations. Physically, men with this pattern tend to be taller than average, and they have a greater incidence of acne and minor skeletal abnormalities. In most studies, the average XYY subject has slightly lower intelligence than the XY control group does. It was hypothesized that men in this genotype have a more aggressive personality and develop differently from males with the normal genotype. More extensive examination has indicated that this hypothesis was exaggerated. Although on average these men have a little less impulse control and some are more aggressive with their wives or sexual partners, there is little or no difference between XYY males and XY males in a broad range of aggression measurements (Theilgaard, 1983).

FRAGILE X SYNDROME

This disorder results when one of the X chromosomes has a piece broken off its tip. That X chromosome is susceptible to breakage because of a defect in a portion of one gene, the FMR1 gene (Hawley & Mori, 1999). Within the gene, a sequence of three base pairs (cytosine, guanine, guanine) is repeated more times than is normal. Thus, fragile X, although grouped as a chromosomal disorder, could also be classed as a disorder that is caused by a portion of a gene. It occurs once in every 1200 live born males and once in every 2000 live born females. Individuals with this syndrome may have growth abnormalities. Babies may have large heads, higher-than-normal birth weights, large, protruding ears, and long faces. Some have unusual behavioural patterns that may include hand clapping, hand biting, hyperactivity, or poor eye contact. This syndrome is associated with mental retardation and various forms of learning disorders, but also with some cognitive strengths in vocabulary and some types of memory (Hagerman, 1996). It is estimated that fragile X is second only to Down syndrome as the most common chromosomal defect associated with mental retardation.

Because the fragile X disorder is on the X chromosome, it affects males and females differently. As males have only one X chromosome, many more of them are affected. They also suffer much more seriously than do females, who have a second X chromosome that is normal and may counter the negative impact of the abnormal X. This particular disability is very curious and is under considerable study by geneticists.

It is interesting to note that almost 20 percent of the males who carry the fragile X chromosome do not experience the syndrome. This outcome is very unusual for an X-linked defect (Barnes, 1989).

Sex-Linked Inheritance The combining of the X and Y chromosomes provides opportunities for some unusual genetic events to occur. Most of the genes on the X chromosome are unable to pair with a corresponding gene on the much shorter Y chromosome. Males, therefore, express all traits, dominant and recessive alike, that appear on the X chromosome for which there are no mates, or alleles, on the Y chromosome. These single genes are known as *sex-linked genes*, and the traits that are related to them are called **sex-linked traits.**

> **sex-linked traits** Traits carried by genes on either of the sex-determining chromosomes.

HEMOPHILIA

Also called bleeder's disease, hemophilia is probably the most dramatic example of a sex-linked genetic abnormality. Although it is quite rare, occurring once in every 4000 to 7000 male births, it has assumed considerable media prominence because of its association with AIDS. Since hemophiliacs have episodes of bleeding that require transfusions, many hemophiliacs who received transfusions before procedures were developed to safeguard the blood supply developed AIDS. Hemophilia is carried as a recessive gene on the X chromosome. Hemophiliacs are deficient in an element of the blood plasma called Factor VIII, which is needed for normal blood clotting. They may bleed for hours from a small wound that would normally clot within five minutes; internal bleeding is especially dangerous, as it may go unnoticed and cause death. Because hemophilia is a disorder that is recessive on the X chromosome, females usually are not affected, but all of their daughters will be carriers, and 50 percent of their sons will be afflicted.

Hemophilia was common among the royal families of Europe, and it has been traced to the mother of Queen Victoria (1819–1901) of England. Victoria, herself, was not hemophilic, but she transmitted the defect. (Women suffer from the disease in the very rare instance when they inherit the recessive trait from both parents; otherwise, the gene for normal clotting is dominant.) Victoria had four sons and five daughters; the recessive gene was passed to her youngest son, who had mild hemophilia, and to three of her daughters. As transmitters, the daughters spread the disease throughout the royal families of Europe.

RED-GREEN COLOUR BLINDNESS

A girl will be colour blind only if she receives the same gene from both parents. This means that her father must be colour blind and her mother must carry the gene for the defect. A boy will be colour blind if he inherits the recessive gene on the X chromosome from his mother. He cannot inherit the trait from his father because he inherits only the Y chromosome from his father, and none of the traits of colour blindness are expressed on it. There are three or four types of colour blindness, some with different patterns of inheritance.

SEX-LINKED TRAITS ON THE AUTOSOMES

Other kinds of sex-related traits occur as a result of genes on other chromosomes. A beard is an example of a sex-related trait. Women normally do not have beards, but they carry the genes necessary to produce them. Therefore, a son inherits traits that determine the type of beard he will grow from both his mother and his father. The dominant traits may actually be inherited through the mother, so that the beards of father and son may be completely different.

Nonsex-Linked Traits The vast majority of inherited traits are carried not on the sex chromosomes, but on the other 22 pairs, the autosomes. Either recessive or dominant genes may carry disorders. (Examples of these disorders are presented in Table 3-1.)

Many disorders are carried as single recessive genes. In order for such disorders to be expressed, a child must inherit the recessive gene from both parents—that is, both parents must be carriers of the **nonsex-linked autosomal trait.** When both parents are carriers of such a disease, approximately 25 percent of the children will inherit the disorder, 50 percent will be carriers, and another 25 percent will not inherit the recessive genes at all.

An interesting characteristic of these disorders is that they occur almost solely within a specific nationality, race, or ethnic group. This limitation usually results because the gene pool has become small enough through intermarriage that the risk of carriers marrying increases significantly.

> **nonsex-linked autosomal trait**
> Trait caused by genes on the non-sex-determining chromosomes (autosomes).

TAY-SACHS DISEASE

This severe genetic disorder results in early death for those children afflicted with it. The child, who appears normal at birth, begins to show a slight but noticeable physical weakness by 6 months. By 10 months the disorder is readily obvious. Children who had been happy, who recognized their parents, and who ate and slept well regress. They become too weak to move their head, are irritated by sound, and are unable to control their eye movements. After age 1, there is a steady physical decline. Convulsive seizures usually begin at 14 months, and by 18 months such children are being tube fed. Their tiny bodies lie limp and frog-legged. Their head starts to enlarge. They usually die of pneumonia somewhere between the ages of 2 and 4. It is a heartbreaking disorder for parents and other loved ones to observe.

In the case of Tay-Sachs disease, there is believed to be one gene that controls the production of one enzyme. This gene is faulty, and the enzyme, *hex a enzyme*, does not break down the fatty substances in brain cells (called *sphingolipids*) as it is supposed to. These substances build up in the cells to lethal concentrations, resulting in subsequent cell death. This disorder is uncommon in the general population, occurring once in every 200 000 to 500 000 births. However, in the Ashkenazi Jews, it occurs once in every 5000 births because one in 30 Ashkenazi Jews are carriers of the disorder, and they are more likely to marry someone from the same heritage.

SICKLE-CELL ANEMIA

This disorder predominantly affects African-Americans in the United States. Because 10 percent of African-Americans are heterozygous (carry only one gene for the trait), they have the sickle-cell trait but it goes undetected unless there is severe oxygen deprivation. Only 0.2 percent of the African-American population actually has sickle-cell anemia. These people show all the symptoms of the disorder—pain in the joints, blood clots, infections—and may not survive to age 20. Since 10 percent of African-Americans are carriers, one out of every 100 pregnancies involves two partners who are carriers. This couple has a 25 percent risk of having an afflicted child. A blood test is currently available that determines if an individual is a carrier of the sickle-cell trait.

CYSTIC FIBROSIS

This is another severe genetic disease of childhood. The symptoms of the disease focus on the function of the exocrine glands, which produce mucus throughout the body, such as in the lungs and digestive tract, and which are also responsible for sweat production to aid in cooling the body. Cystic fibrosis often results in death by the time of young adulthood. To survive, children with the disease require extensive physical therapy to loosen mucus several times a day, which is a very fatiguing and time-consuming procedure. Having a cystic child may make it difficult for parents to readily allocate time to other children in the family, as well as to each other. Such a child, therefore, requires an incredible family commitment. If the individual survives, fertility is often compromised. For example, most males are sterile, and the women, while fertile, have continuing respiratory problems throughout pregnancy that affect fetal health.

PHENYLKETONURIA (PKU)

This is an example of the effects of environmental manipulation on the phenotype of a disorder. PKU is a defect in amino acid metabolism caused by the inability of the body to remove phenylalanine from the body—this amino acid has recently received considerable "product recognition" as it is a component of artificial sweeteners, such as Nutrasweet. You will notice that diet soft drinks and other such products often have warning labels informing phenylketonurics of the risks associated with consumption. PKU is manifested by the build-up of phenylalanine in the brain, which causes cells to become damaged and die. This cell destruction results in a variety of severe neurological symptoms, including irritability, athetoid motion (uncontrollable muscle twitches and movements), hyperactivity, and convulsive seizures. Afflicted children often have an odd, reddish-blond colouring in their skin and hair because of the excess of phenylalanine.

This disorder is detectable by a blood test given to the baby at birth. If the test is positive, the child is immediately started on a diet to rigidly control phenylalanine. This diet controls the manifestation of the worst symptoms of the disorder, such as the profound retardation that was its usual end result. Phenylketonurics may have normal life expectancies and the ability to reproduce. However, fertile females with PKU are considered to have very high risk of miscarriage or birth defects because the fetus grows in an abnormal uterine environment.

Some abnormalities are carried by dominant genes instead of by the pairing of recessives. In other words, some abnormalities may be caused by only one gene inherited from one parent.

HUNTINGTON'S CHOREA

This disease is characterized by progressive dementia, random, jerking movements, and a lopsided, staggering walk. This disorder does not appear until the victims reach middle age or later (for women, after the childbearing years). Those who eventually develop this disease may have been unaware that they were carrying the defective gene and have had children who also inherited the dominant gene.

The discovery that one is carrying a defective gene is a distressing experience. However, a carrier should acknowledge the possibility of transmitting the disease to future generations when considering marriage or deciding whether to have children. Most people never know what kind of defective genes they carry, although everyone probably harbours from five to eight potentially lethal ones at the very least. Most recessive and nonsex-linked genes will probably never be expressed. Still, people can obtain a great deal of information about their genetic inheritance, and about that of a potential partner, to make intelligent and responsible decisions.

INHERITED FORM OF RETINOBLASTOMA

This disorder is a type of cancer in which tumours form on the back of the eye, causing blindness. A single dominant gene causes about 40 percent of the cases of retinoblastoma. The gene causes cells to divide, resulting in the growth of tumours. For a short time, the growth of tumours is prevented by other genes in the cells, called *tumour suppressing genes* (Hawley & Mori, 1999). Over time though, these tumour suppressing genes become inactive (because they mutate), and the dominant gene for retinoblastoma is expressed. Eventually, everyone who has the retinoblastoma gene will develop the cancer.

Multifactoral Genetic Disorders

Causes of these disorders are complex—they include several genes, environmental factors, and the interplay between genes and the environment. Asthma and ADHD are examples of multifactoral genetic disorder (see the box "The Human Genome Project," on page 68, for a discussion of ADHD).

Question to Ponder

The example of PKU shows that the environment can modify the expression of a genetic disorder. Is it possible that the environment might also cause some genetic disorders by increasing the number of genetic mutations? What is happening in communities such as Chernobyl, Russia, which has experienced nuclear contamination?

Table 3-1 Brief Descriptions of Genetic Diseases and Conditions

Cystic fibrosis	Lack of enzyme produces abnormally thick mucus that obstructs lungs and digestive tract; recessive inheritance; 1:2100 Caucasian births; more common in individuals of northern European descent; extensive therapy and immediate treatment of infections allows many to survive into adulthood and reproduce.
Diabetes mellitus	Deficient metabolism of fats and sugar owing to body's failure to produce insulin; controllable by insulin, exercise, and restricted diet; two of the main forms of this disease are sex linked; 1.1 per 1000 Canadian children under the age of 14 are diabetic; polygenic inheritance.
Phenylketonuria	Inability to neutralize a harmful amino acid, phenylalanine, which is contained in many food proteins; causes hyperactivity and severe retardation; treatable by placement on a restrictive diet immediately; 1:8000 to 12 000 births.
Sickle-cell anemia	Abnormal sickling of red blood cells, causing oxygen deprivation, pain, swelling, and tissue damage; 50 percent of children die by age 20; recessive inheritance; more common in African-Americans.
Marfan syndrome	Tall, slender build with thin, long arms and legs; heart defects and eye abnormalities; excessive lengthening of the body leads to skeletal malformations; death from heart failure common in young adulthood; dominant inheritance; 1:20 000 births.
Muscular dystrophy	Degenerative muscle disease, causing abnormal gait, loss of ability to walk and eventually of most motor abilities; occasionally causes death; one type, Duchenne muscular dystrophy, is sex linked; other types are recessive; 1:4000 males has Duchenne muscular dystrophy.
Thalassemia (also called Cooley's anemia)	Abnormal red blood cells, leading to listlessness, enlarged liver and spleen, and retarded physical growth; occasionally death occurs; treatable by blood transfusions; recessive inheritance; 1:500 births to parents of either Mediterranean or subtropical and tropical Asian descent.

Sources: Adapted from McKusick, 1988; CICH, 1994.

Inherited deafness is a type of multifactoral genetic disorder that is caused by two gene pairs described as loss of function genes. A person will be deaf if they inherit two loss of function genes in either or both pairs. Suppose two people with inherited deafness have children. If the mother and father have the same affected gene pair, then all of their children will be deaf. But, it is possible that the mother has one defective gene pair and the father has the other one. In this case, all of their children will have hearing.

Genetic Counselling

genetic counselling Counselling that helps potential parents evaluate their risk factors for having a baby with genetic disorders.

Once we know the dangers inherent in certain types of gene pairings and the tragic consequences of various chromosomal abnormalities, what can we do to avoid them? **Genetic counselling** is now a widely available resource that can help potential parents evaluate such risk factors in childbearing and thus enable them to make intelligent decisions (Garber & Marchese, 1986). When the knowledge of genetics was in its infancy, prospective parents with a family history of inherited disease were faced with a serious dilemma: Should they try to have children and risk passing on the disease, or should they decide against having children at all? This situation occurred because doctors and researchers had little understanding of how genetic diseases were transmitted. Today, a potential parent asking the question, "Will my child have a genetic defect?" has many more answers.

Predicting a baby's vulnerability to any of the nearly 5000 genetic disorders that have been identified so far is frequently a complicated process. The potential parents' complete medical records are examined to uncover diseases that can be traced to a genetic abnormality. Each parent is given a complete physical examination, including biochemical and blood tests. A family pedigree is prepared to show which members of the family have been afflicted by any disorder and whether the inheritance pattern is dominant, recessive, or X-linked. If an inheritable genetic abnormality is found, a genetic counsellor evaluates a couple's risk of having a baby with the genetic disorder, puts the risk in perspective, and suggests reproductive alternatives (such as adoption or artificial insemination of a donor egg) if the couple decides the risk is too great. Fortunately for many parents, the risk of bearing a child with a disease that makes living a normal life difficult has been considerably reduced by new prenatal-testing methods. Table 3-2 shows the characteristics of persons who are candidates for genetic counselling.

Ethical Issues in the New Reproductive Genetics

While tremendous strides are being made in genetic research, many ethical issues remain to be solved as they relate to this new research in human genetic engineering. The Human Genome Project (see the box on page 68) is designed to map all the human genes and identify those genes and combinations that cause particular disorders. When we gain this knowledge, what shall we, as a society, do with it? We shall certainly try to prevent such severe disorders, but how? Who will decide whether a high-risk couple may carry a child with a severe disability to full term? And shall we value such a child less than other children or blame the parents for failing to prevent the birth? What about the use of procedures such as amniocentesis and abortion for reasons of personal preference

---

Table 3–2 Characteristics of Candidates for Genetic Counselling

- Anyone who is aware of a family history of inherited genetic disorders or who actually has a genetic disorder or defect.

- The parents of a child who either has a serious congenital abnormality or genetic defect.

- A couple who has experienced more than three miscarriages or a miscarriage in which the fetal tissue analysis indicated chromosomal abnormality.

- A pregnant woman over age 35 or a father over age 44, who because of age has an increased risk of chromosomal damage.

- Prospective parents belonging to certain ethnic groups that are at high risk for certain disorders, such as Tay-Sachs, sickle-cell anemia, or thalassemia.

- A couple who is aware of parental exposure to an excessive dose of radiation, drugs, or other environmental agents that can result in birth defects

---

Source: Adapted from Lauersen, 1983.

rather than health—for example, selectively aborting female babies, a procedure that has been documented as occurring in India, China, and other Asian countries? Is such use of this technology justifiable and ethical? Although we can do nothing about the policies or practices in other countries, the World Health Organization (WHO) and other similar bodies have issued statements that using prenatal diagnosis for sex selection is an improper use of the technology.

Other advances in medical technology are affecting sex selection. Procedures such as the sperm separation methods originally developed by Ronald Erikksen for use with cattle breeding are becoming more reliable with humans. Depending on the father's sperm count, these costly procedures claim an 80 to 90 percent success rate in producing sons or daughters for families willing to undergo the rigorous medical protocols necessary to conceive a child of either sex. The procedure is based on the fact that the Y-chromosome-bearing sperm are smaller and faster swimmers than the larger, X-chromosome-bearing sperm. In this methodology, the sperm are first washed and centrifuged to remove faulty sperm and impurities and next allowed to "swim" through a series of solutions. The woman is then artificially inseminated with the man's sperm during ovulation.

Genetic counselling is now a widely available resource to help potential parents evaluate risk factors.

Technology now allows us to distinguish "healthy" from "unhealthy" sperm, but some people are concerned that it may be extended to distinguishing "optimal" sperm (or ova) from "nonoptimal" sperm. Will people try to select for other traits, such as height, physical attractiveness, intelligence, and personality? Will people be tempted to engineer a better human race? This goal can be dangerous, as demonstrated by the history of World War II and the Holocaust. Around the time of World War II, the eugenics movement became popular in Canada. *Eugenics* is selective breeding to ensure that the fittest in the society have children and the "unfit" do not. This movement led to Canadian laws that allowed the government to sterilize people judged to be mentally defective, without their consent. In Alberta, these laws were still in effect until the early 1970s. Is it right for the government to decide who may have children and who may not?

Another ethical issue involves the use of nondirective versus directive counselling by genetic counsellors. Although the majority of counsellors believe in nondirective approaches, for example, "not making decisions for patients, but supporting any decision they make" or "telling patients that reproductive decisions that they make are theirs alone," a majority find these principles difficult to apply. Many tell patients what others have done in their situation or what the counsellor would do. Truly nondirective counselling may even violate the goals of public health programs, as the following remarks indicate:

> Ordinarily, public health targets an at-risk population, for example, heavy smokers, and tries to change their behavior. There is no question of nondirectiveness. The health educator does not say, "I will support whatever decision you make about smoking," but instead says, "Don't smoke." If public health programs in genetics are aimed at prevention, as many appear to be, they come into direct conflict with nondirectiveness. To say to parents at high risk, "Don't have children" could be regarded as a limitation of basic freedom and an insult to human dignity in many societies, but to say, "We support your decision to have children even if there is a high risk for serious disorders" may be going too far in the opposite direction. (Wertz, 1992, p. 502)

Genetic counselling for disorders such as Huntington's disease, a severe, degenerative disorder that results in death, involves other ethical issues. The gene for

Huntington's has been discovered, and doctors can screen people to see whether they carry the defective gene. Because a dominant gene causes it, anyone who carries the gene will develop the disorder, usually in middle age. Should healthy people be told that they carry this gene? The situation is even more complicated when family members from different generations are tested. Consider three generations—grandmother, mother, and daughter. Suppose the grandmother died of Huntington's. The mother does not want to be tested to see if she carries the gene. The granddaughter is tested for the gene and has it. Therefore, the mother must have it too, unless Huntington's runs on both sides of the family. Should the granddaughter be told that she carries the gene? Telling her will result in her knowing that both she and her mother will develop Huntington's. Does giving her this knowledge violate her mother's right to privacy?

Other ethical issues arise because some genetic disorders are more common among people from certain heritages. Robert Hegele, a professor of medicine and biochemistry at the University of Western Ontario, discovered a mutated gene in people of the Oji-Cree First Nation of Sandy Lake, in Northern Ontario. The mutated gene makes them prone to Type 2 diabetes (Unland, 1999). This information can have positive effects on the community, as members can be educated about diet and lifestyle factors that contribute to Type 2 diabetes, with the goal of preventing it. Interestingly, these people have carried the gene for generations, but only in recent generations has the gene led to diabetes. Their ancestors' healthy diet and high levels of exercise prevented the onset of diabetes. Could this genetic information ever be used to discriminate against people from Aboriginal backgrounds? For example, could insurance companies charge them more because of possible health risks? As we learn more and more about genetics, we must consider ways in which that information can be used and misused.

Behavioural Genetics

It is one thing to consider the impact of genetics on the shape of a person's nose or the colour of someone's eyes, but it is quite another to wonder if short-tempered aggressiveness is, in part, genetically determined. Human behaviour seems nowhere near as prescribed or preprogrammed as animal behaviour is, and what patterns do exist seem highly modifiable, depending on the culture and the circumstance. Nevertheless, the study of the genetic components of behaviour has been highly controversial for decades.

Researchers first look at genetic influences on the development of behaviour for the whole human species. These influences include the typical patterns of growth, along with perceptual and motor skill patterns. The genetic influence is evident beyond the prenatal period. In fact, genetic programming is involved throughout development. Pubescence, for example, occurs in adolescence as the person becomes capable of sexual reproduction. There are physical aspects of this change that are genetically programmed, as well as some behavioural tendencies that are part of this sequence. Although certain tendencies can be altered slightly with health care and nutrition, the underlying pattern remains (Scarr & Kidd, 1983).

A second approach to the study of behavioural genetics concentrates on individual differences. Over the years, for instance, researchers have examined individual differences in intelligence. It is clear that intelligence is a measure of both heredity and environment—people exercise their inherited capacities within an environmental context. But the study of intelligence has generated heated debate. Consequently, researchers have shifted recently to the study of personality, where having more of a trait, such as sensitivity or impulsivity, is not necessarily better, but simply makes a person different. Researchers hope to be able to analyze inherited differences in personality, interests, or even learning style more objectively (Plomin, 1983; Scarr & Kidd, 1983).

Inherited differences in behaviour are assumed to follow a polygenic system of inheritance. The behaviour results from the effects of several genes, environmental factors, and interactions among genes and environment. Behavioural geneticists use special methods to study genetic and environmental influences on behaviour. Two of these

---

Question to Ponder

Who is ultimately responsible for making decisions about ethical issues related to genetics: the society or the individuals involved in the particular decision?

One research strand behavioural geneticists have focused on is the impact of heredity on individual differences such as intelligence. However, because the study of intelligence provoked controversy, researchers are now concentrating on analyzing inherited differences in personality traits.

methods—adoption studies and twin comparisons—have been used for many years. Mavis Hetherington developed the third method—blended family studies—during the 1990s. All three methods are designed to separate genetic from environmental effects.

Adoption Studies

In these studies, adopted children are compared with members of their adopted families (shared environments but genetically unrelated) and with members of their biological families (genetically related but different environments). In the Minnesota Adoption Studies, for instance, adopted children were compared on a number of dimensions with their biological parents, their adoptive parents, and the biological children of their adoptive parents (Scarr & Weinberg, 1983). In addition, the adoptive parents were compared with their biological children. When the researchers compared test scores of adopted children with the scores of nonadopted peers, findings showed that adoptive families were influential; as a group, the adopted children had higher IQs and achieved more in school. But when they analyzed individual differences within the group, the researchers found that test scores were more closely related to the intellectual abilities of biological parents than to the abilities of adoptive parents.

Adoption studies have begun to focus on differences in attitudes, interests, personality, and behaviour patterns, such as alcoholism (Fuller & Simmel, 1986). It might be assumed that such characteristics would be predominantly generated and nurtured within the child-rearing environment—that is, in the adoptive home. Nevertheless, according to several studies, some attitudes, vocational interests, and personality traits seem resistant to the adoptive family environment (Scarr & Weinberg, 1983). In a recent series of studies, Cadoret and his colleagues followed the children of biological parents who had antisocial personalities, substance abuse problems, or both (Cadoret, Yates, Troughton, Woodworth, & Stewart, 1995a, 1995b). Even though these children were adopted at birth, they had higher rates of behavioural problems than average, including antisocial personality disorder and substance abuse problems related to their biological backgrounds.

We must be aware of possible shortcomings in adoption studies. Researchers are studying adopted children in order to make conclusions about genetics and environment that apply to the general population. However, adopted children may not

Question to Ponder

Which method—adoption studies, twin comparisons, or blended family designs—would you use if you were a researcher?

twin comparisons Comparing the degree of similarity between identical twins with that between fraternal, same-sex twins.

Some studies suggest that identical twins are more similar than fraternal twins are in personality traits like sociability, emotionality, and activity level. But how much of this similarity can be attributed to genetic influence and how much to the environment?

be representative of the general population (Rutter, Silberg, O'Connor, & Simonoff, 1999b). Adopted children are more likely to be born to younger mothers who received less obstetric care. Adoptive parents are better educated and more socially advantaged than parents in general. Adoption studies are becoming more difficult to conduct because most adoptions involve older children or special needs children. The logic of adoption studies requires the children to be adopted shortly after birth.

Twin Comparisons

Identical twins, called *monozygotic* or *MZ twins,* result from a single fertilized egg that separates to form two people and, thus, have identical genetic makeup. Fraternal twins, called *dizygotic* or *DZ twins,* result from two eggs being fertilized by different sperm during the same month. Therefore, fraternal twins are like siblings and share only about 50 percent of their genetic makeup. But unlike other siblings, fraternal twins share more similar environments because they are born into the family at the same time. Both fraternal twins and identical twins have similar environments, so if identical twins are more similar to each other than are fraternal twins, one could argue it is because of their genetic relatedness.

Repeatedly, **twin comparisons** find that a wide range of personality traits are at least partly inherited. Three frequently inherited characteristics are emotionality, sociability, and activity level, sometimes called the *EAS traits* (Goldsmith, 1983; Plomin, 1990). Emotionality is the tendency to become aroused easily to fear or anger. Sociability is the extent to which individuals prefer to do things with others rather than on their own. More recent studies of twins have revealed that child and adolescent psychiatric disorders have genetic components (Edelbrock, Rende, Plomin, & Thompson, 1995; Gottesman & Goldsmith, 1994; Rutter et al., 1999b). As well, self-reported delinquency seems to have genetic causes (Rowe & Rogers, 1995).

Can you think of potential problems with twin comparisons? One problem is whether the method controls for environmental similarity. Twin comparisons are based on the assumption that fraternal twins share the same degree of environmental similarity as do identical twins because both types of twins are born into a family at the same time. Is this assumption valid? Perhaps identical twins, who look more similar, are treated more similarly than are fraternal twins, who do not bear as close a resemblance to each other. Therefore, identical twins may have more similar environments, as well as more genetic similarity. Another problem with twin comparisons relates to acquiring the sample of twins. About 30 percent of twins contacted to participate in the studies decline to do so (Rutter et al., 1999b). Moreover, twin samples underrepresent children from ethnic minority backgrounds and from socially disadvantaged backgrounds. Will the findings from twin studies be applicable to twins from other backgrounds who were not studied?

Blended Family Design

Hetherington, Reiss, and Plomin (1994) initiated the use of blended families in behavioural genetics. Blended families, or stepfamilies, are useful because children in the same family differ in biological relatedness. There are full siblings (born to the same parents), half-siblings (having one parent in common), and genetically unrelated siblings (having no parent in common). Are siblings who are more genetically related more similar?

An advantage of this method is that blended families are more common than adopted families or families with twins. Of Canadian families, 4 percent are blended families (HRDC & Stats Can, 1996). A disadvantage of this method is that some of the preliminary results are difficult to interpret (Rutter et al., 1999b).

FOCUS ON AN ISSUE

Identical Twins Reared Apart

Oskar Stöhr was raised as a Catholic in Hitler's Germany and became a Nazi youth. Jack Yufe grew up in the Caribbean as a Jew and spent many years on an Israeli kibbutz. Identical twins who were separated at birth, Stöhr and Yufe did not meet until they became adults. Their lives, although markedly different in some superficial ways, show some startling similarities. Both men doze off while watching television; love spicy foods, liqueurs, and buttered toast dipped in coffee; have overbearing, domineering relationships with women, whom they yell at when they are angry; and think it is funny to sneeze in a crowd of strangers. They also have amazingly similar mannerisms, temperaments, and tempos, and, when tested, showed very similar personality profiles (Holden, 1980).

Striking similarities have shown up in other pairs of identical twins separated at birth. Kathleen and Jenny sat in the same positions and laughed and wept over the same things. Both Olga and Ingrid stopped menstruating at the age of 18, when each assumed she was pregnant, arranged to marry the man responsible, found out she wasn't pregnant, and started menstruating again around the time of the wedding (Farber, 1981). When Bridget and Dorothy, both housewives, met for the first time at age 38, each wore seven rings on carefully manicured hands, two bracelets on one wrist, and a watch and bracelet on the other wrist (Holden, 1980).

How many of these similarities are pure coincidence? How many are the product of similar backgrounds? And how many are linked in some unknown way to the hereditary code locked in the genes?

To discover where the truth lies, Thomas Bouchard and his colleagues at the University of Minnesota have been conducting a study of 48 pairs of identical twins who were separated at birth. The researchers have compared the sets of identical twins reared apart with a small group of fraternal twins reared apart and with a large sample of identical and fraternal twins reared

---

When Bridget and Dorothy, both housewives, met for the first time at age 38, each wore seven rings on carefully manicured hands, two bracelets on one wrist, and a watch and bracelet on the other wrist.

---

together (Tellegen, Lykken, Bouchard, Wilcox, Segal, & Rich, 1988). In most cases, the IQ scores of the identical twins were remarkably similar, and even their brainwave tracings were almost the same (Bouchard, 1987). By comparing these twins with fraternal twins, researchers have concluded that perhaps 50 percent of measured intelligence in adulthood is due to heredity (Plomin, 1990).

Several personality traits were also quite similar in the identical twins who were reared apart. All of the twins in the study answered extensive self-report personality questionnaires. The correlation of traits for the identical twins

reared apart was surprisingly high. Traits that were quite similar included sense of well-being, social potency, reactions to stress, feelings of alienation, aggressiveness, self-control/cautiousness, harm avoidance, and absorption/imagination. Some traits had lower correlations, including achievement (working hard) and social closeness (intimacy). Whether they had been reared together or apart, the fraternal twins showed far less similarity in all of these traits.

Many of the identical twins also had similar neuroses. Even when they were brought up in totally different emotional environments, they shared mild depressions, phobias, and hypochondriacal traits. These similarities sparked the researchers into thinking about the role that heredity plays in common neurotic illnesses—a role that has already been established for psychoses.

The researchers themselves are the first to warn against drawing too many conclusions from these findings. They point to the problems—the size of their sample and the fact that most of the identical twins grew up in similar environments, so their similarities may not be traceable to their genes alone. Moreover, they warn, there is a tendency among researchers and lay people alike to look for and find similarities in the twins' behaviour even when differences are more informative. Bouchard and his colleagues also say these differences show that there is no one answer and that human behaviour is a result of both our genetic inheritance and the environment that shapes us (Bouchard, 1987).

The Interaction of Genetics and Environment

Although studies in behavioural genetics offer considerable evidence for a genetic influence on temperaments, personality styles, and disorders, they are unable to tell us how the genetic components interact with the environment. A quiet, easygoing child experiences a different environment than an impulsive, angry, assertive child does.

The child helps shape or trigger the environment, which, in turn, limits and moulds how the child expresses her feelings. Examples of the way the environment responds to an easy and a difficult child might help us to conceptualize this interaction.

Abbie is an aggressive 4-year-old girl. When observed in her Montessori pre-school classroom, she is in constant motion—disrupting the work of other children, attempting to start fights with both boys and girls, staring opponents down when the fights are stopped. The two teachers in the room direct most of their attention at undoing the negative effects of Abbie's behaviour. Since it is attention she is seeking through her aggressiveness, the teachers' actions only fuel her disruptiveness. The consequences are that the other children are beginning to avoid her and the teachers are losing patience with her antics. Her parents have been asked to withdraw her from the program.

Christopher is a quiet, introspective 4-year-old boy. When observed in his preschool classroom, he is actively involved in working with a teacher on a project. His smiling face reveals his interest and enjoyment. The teacher's enthusiasm is enhanced by his receptiveness. He has made friends with all the children in the room, even the more aggressive ones, because of his interest in them and his willingness to listen to their stories. The consequence is that teachers and children who value his sense of outgoing enjoyment of his daily activities seek him out.

These examples indicate the tremendous impact that children's personalities can have on their environments. In Christopher's case, the psychosocial environment (the people with whom interaction occurs) facilitates his continued growth by positive stimulation. This positive feedback allows him to more fully engage in learning from more of the classroom environment. Abbie's negative behaviour, on the other hand, minimizes her positive learning experience in the classroom. Moreover, her behaviour is beginning to limit future opportunities for growth, as she is labelled difficult. It becomes clear that temperament and personality help to structure those aspects of the environment that the child experiences, while, in turn, the environment—in terms of the people and objects in it—shapes the future capabilities of the child.

Our physical appearance—whether we are tall or short, dark or light, plain or beautiful—is largely genetically determined, but the way in which our culture views these physical attributes can profoundly affect personality development. In Western culture, for example, people who are tall are frequently given more power and authority, not necessarily because they are worthy of it, but because they literally stand "head and shoulders" above the rest of us. For the same sort of cultural reasons, a beautiful, muscular child with learning disabilities who appears to have no disabling characteristics may be treated as if he has no handicap at all. In other words, inherited traits may be admired or not, depending on current cultural attitudes toward physical appearance, making it even more difficult to separate the effects of genetics and culture. For instance, the muscular, handsome boy who is not particularly intelligent may develop more self-confidence and become a more capable person because everyone around him believes that muscular, handsome males must be capable. On the other hand, the beautiful, intelligent blond girl may develop a confused self-concept because everyone around her thinks of her as beautiful but dumb.

The interaction of heredity and environment may begin immediately with the newborn infant. T. Berry Brazelton and his students have spent several years studying individual differences in newborn infants all over the world. They've studied African, Asian, Latin American, European, and American infants. In one study, Brazelton compared Zambian infants and white American infants (Lester & Brazelton, 1982). Many of the newborn Zambian infants were undernourished and dehydrated at birth. Their behaviour reflected this physical state. They exhibited poor visual following and less motor activity, and they had poor head control. But because the Zambian culture expects newborns to be vigorous, the parents ignored the limp behaviour of their infants and handled them as if they were more responsive than they actually were. The infants were breast-fed frequently and on demand and showed rapid weight gain. Within a couple of weeks, they had become highly responsive, sturdy infants. The American infants, on the other hand, were considerably stronger at birth. Most stayed in the hospital for three days (the Zambian infants went home the day after they were born) and were handled gently at home. The American babies were fed every three or four hours and were involved in little play activity. They changed very little in their general responsiveness or activity over the first two weeks.

It seems apparent, then, that genetic endowment by itself does not determine neonatal behaviour. The genetic endowment, the prenatal environment, the mother's reproductive and obstetric history, and the caregiving system all play a role in determining behaviour.

Types of Gene–Environment Interactions

Children interact with their environment in three ways, depending on their individual genetic predispositions. There are passive, evocative, and active interactions.

Passive Interactions In the passive interaction pattern, the parents give and the child accepts both the genes and the environment, either favourable or unfavourable, for the development of particular abilities. A musical child in a musical family, for instance, receives an enriched musical environment in which to develop his skills. There is a tendency for the parent's genetic makeup (e.g., musical aptitude) to be related to the environment she provides for her children (e.g., musical enrichment). Another example is hockey skills. Suppose Wayne Gretzky's son Ty grows up to be a gifted hockey player, like his father. Ty is a recipient of a passive interaction, acquiring athletic aptitude from his father, as well as an environment rich in hockey experience.

Evocative Interactions In an evocative interaction pattern, the child evokes particular responses from his parents and others based on his genetically influenced behaviour. An active, sociable, extroverted child will demand responses from parents and teachers. A quiet, passive, shy child may be ignored. Ge, Cadoret, Conger, and Neiderhiser (1996) show that the simple evocative interaction pattern should be extended to a mutually evocative interaction pattern between the child and the parents. Genetic differences in the child and the parents influence the interaction between them. Evocative interactions support the idea that socialization is reciprocal—parents influence children's behaviour, and equally important, children influence parents' behaviour.

The study of evocative interactions has been extended to adoptive families, such as those in the Colorado Adoption Project (O'Connor, Deater-Deckard, Fulker, Rutter, & Plomin, 1998). The children in this study were adopted within days of birth. Some adopted children came from biological mothers who had a history of antisocial behaviour. These children were described as "at risk." They had more behavioural problems than did other adopted children, even though the types of homes they were adopted into were similar to those of other adopted children. Furthermore, the behaviour of the adoptive parents changed in reaction to their children's behavioural problems. The parents used more negative control (guilt induction, hostility, and withdrawal from the relationship with the child). They were also more inconsistent in disciplining the children. Therefore, the at-risk children had more behavioural problems, and these problems evoked more negative parenting in their adoptive parents, which, in turn, made the children's behavioural problems worse.

It is important to note that evocative interactions are not solely responsible for a person's behaviour. Environmental factors can have a strong impact on parent–child interaction. For instance, parents who respond negatively to a child may not necessarily be reacting to the child's behaviour, but rather may be influenced by other factors, such as marital distress (Conger, Patterson, & Ge, 1995).

Question to Ponder

Should adoptive parents be told that their children's biological parents have a history of antisocial behaviour? What would be the advantages and disadvantages of telling them?

Active Interactions An active relationship may exist between the child and his environment; that is, the child may actively seek specific environments (peers or opportunities) that are compatible with his temperament, talents, or predispositions. However, biological factors (e.g., chronic illness), environmental influences (e.g., parental pressure), cultural elements (e.g., racism), or individual characteristics (e.g., shyness) may limit potential niches for an individual (Wachs, 1996).

The Influence of Culture and Family on Development

Question to Ponder

Do you think there are any unique aspects of Canadian society that might affect the development of children in this country?

Two conclusions are strongly supported by recent studies in behavioural genetics: (1) genetic factors play a crucial role in development and (2) environmental influences are also critical. In order to understand development, we must appreciate the interplay between genes and the environment. (See the box "Male–Female Differences.") The environment includes physical factors (e.g., nutrition, presence of toxins) and social factors (e.g., relationships and upbringing). Two important social influences are the culture and the family.

Although we speak of a culture and a social environment, we must keep in mind that these are not single, fixed entities. An individual's social environment, already complex at the moment of birth, changes constantly. Infants are born into many social groups—a family, perhaps a tribe, a social class, a racial or ethnic unit, a religious group, and a community. Each of these social entities has some shared ideas, beliefs, assumptions, values, expectations, and appropriate patterns of behaviour. These shared expectations form the culture of the group.

Although some cultural characteristics are universal—food taboos and funeral rites, for example (Farb, 1978)—we shall focus here on cultural diversity and the rich variety of cultural patterns. In examining differences between cultures, however, many people find it difficult to avoid being ethnocentric. **Ethnocentrism** is the tendency to assume that one's own beliefs, perceptions, and values are true, correct, and factual and that other people's beliefs are false, unusual, or downright bizarre. For instance, some people may regard members of "primitive" tribes as simple, unintelligent, exotic, and uncivilized; others may see them as "noble savages," untainted by the evils of civilization and industrialized society. These oversimplifications miss both the complexity and the richness of unfamiliar cultures. But if it is difficult to be objective about distant cultures, it is even harder to suspend judgment on the cultural diversity close at hand. A visitor from abroad who speaks English with a pronounced accent may be accepted with fascination, but a neighbour who speaks with a regional or ethnic accent may be treated with indifference or even hostility.

ethnocentrism The tendency to assume that one's own beliefs, perceptions, customs, and values are correct or normal and that those of others are inferior or abnormal.

Alternative Family Styles

The type of family into which a child is born can dramatically affect the expectations, roles, beliefs, and interrelationships that she will experience throughout life (Hartup, 1989). Here, we shall examine three basic family styles and the cultural patterns that underlie them.

Extended Families In an extended family (one having many relatives and several generations close by), children may be cared for by a variety of people—uncles, aunts, cousins, grandparents, or older siblings, as well as parents. Extended family living is especially important in Aboriginal cultures. Many children have deep bonds with aunties and grandmothers who played a main role in their upbringing. Recent immigrants from Asia, southern Europe, Africa, and the Caribbean also are likely to value extended family relationships (Baker, 1996). Qureshi and Qureshi (1983) describe the experiences of Islamic Pakistani Canadians who started immigrating to Canada in the 1950s. Many of the families, accustomed to a rich social network involving extended family, found

Children who are part of an extended family have many more people to interact with and learn from.

themselves isolated in Canada and had to create new social ties. Adapting to life in Canada was especially difficult for women, who had a more traditional role in the home. In Canada, the women did not have the benefit of sisters, aunts, cousins, and so on, for daily support. The family was incomplete without extended family.

Communal Families Communal social systems are found in various forms in Israel, the former Soviet Union, China, and some parts of Europe and North America. In this type of system, the social relationships take a different form from those of the extended family. The peer group is usually an intensely powerful force in the socialization of young children. Communal societies reinforce conformity and cooperation, while discouraging individualism and significant deviance from group standards.

The Israeli kibbutz represents one of the most sustained and studied efforts to institutionalize communal child care in any modern progressive society. The kibbutzim were founded by self-declared idealists in open rebellion against their own families. They sought, among other things, to dismantle traditional family structures, to liberate women from sex-stereotyped roles, and to raise children in a collective, unpossessive way. The early kibbutzim were designed to prevent children from identifying strongly with their individual family units. To foster this collective spirit, the kibbutzim relied on a system in which many adults supervised all of the children's activities. In each house, four to eight children of the same age were cared for according to group-approved child-rearing methods. Boys and girls were treated alike. The children were taught to share, to consider group interests before individual desires, and to value their roles in the kibbutz society. Children benefited from the attention of the child-care specialists and from their relationships with their own parents, whom they saw daily during extended visiting periods.

Communes exist in Canada, but they are not part of mainstream society. Examples are Hutterite colonies in southern central Alberta and Mennonite communities in the Kitchener-Waterloo region of Ontario. Hutterite children are taught at a young age to respect the needs of the colony and to accept that individuals have little control over their lives (Bonta, 1997). By the time children are 3 years old, they are expected to accept that the colony is more important than the individual and that older people are more important than younger ones. "Children 3 years old can no longer scream lustily; they must be quiet around adults and even have to cry quietly. They are readily dismissed from activities when adults or older children do not want them around" (Bonta, 1997, p. 302).

FOCUS ON *DIVERSITY*

Male–Female Differences

How do males and females differ? The first obvious difference occurs at conception—males have an XY for the 23rd chromosome pair, and females have an XX. The X chromosome is larger than the Y chromosome and has more genes. Therefore, some of the genes on the X chromosome do not have complements on the Y chromosome. This feature of the X chromosome is the reason that genetic disorders caused by recessive genes on the X chromosome are more common in males than in females. Colour blindness is an example of this type of disorder.

But having the XY pair does not guarantee that the baby will be born looking male. Surprisingly, both males and females are genetically programmed to develop female bodies; genetic males develop male bodies only because of the presence of chemicals at critical times in prenatal development. Six weeks after conception, the Y chromosome of the male triggers the release of a chemical (H-Y antigen) that causes testes to form (Haqq et al., 1994). Three months later, the testes secrete a hormone called *testosterone*, which causes the development of a penis and scrotum. The absence of testosterone results in the development of ovaries and a vagina. Most of the time, development proceeds normally, in that people with the XY pair look male and people with the XX pair look female. But there are some rare cases in which chemical imbalances have caused mismatches. Money and colleagues have studied some unusual cases in which people with the XY pair look female and people with the XX pair look masculine (Money & Ehrhardt, 1972). Genetic males will develop female genitals if they are insensitive to testosterone. This disorder is called *androgenic insensitivity syndrome* (testosterone is a type of androgen hormone). Testosterone affects not only the genitals, but also brain development (Gorski, 1985). Genetic males insensitive to testosterone will develop female brains, look female, and be treated as females. Therefore, it is not surprising that they often live normal lives as females, although they are sterile (Jones & Park, 1971). Similarly, genetic females exposed to testosterone will develop masculinized genitals. If detected at birth, this condition can be treated with surgery to feminize the genitals and with ongoing hormone therapy. Genetic females treated for exposure to testosterone can live normal lives as females, although they are often reported to be tomboyish (Ehrhardt, Epstein, & Money, 1968).

But what about the vast majority of children who develop normally? Are there differences between males and females? Studies have shown that male babies, on average, are born slightly longer and heavier than are female babies. Newborn girls have slightly more mature skeletons, and they seem to be a bit more responsive to touch. By age

---

By age 3 many children have learned some sex-specific behaviours.

12, the average girl is well into the adolescent growth spurt and maturation, while the average boy is still considered physically a preadolescent. By age 18, the average female has roughly 50 percent less muscular strength than the average male. In adulthood, the male body carries more muscle and bone, while the average female body carries more fat as insulation. There are built-in health advantages for women, including more pliable blood vessels and the ability to process fat more efficiently. By middle age, males are succumbing much more quickly to health hazards, such as emphysema, arteriosclerosis, heart attacks, liver disease, homicide, suicide, or drug addiction. By age 65, there are only 68 men alive for every 100 women; at age 85, women outnumber men almost two to one. At the age of 100, there are five times as many women as there are men (McLoughlin, Shryer, Goode,

& McAuliffe, 1988).

In addition to studying physical differences between males and females, researchers have also examined possible sex differences in mental abilities and behaviour. Research conducted before 1980 often found sex differences in cognitive abilities and social behaviours (see, for example, Maccoby and Jacklin, 1974, for a review). The studies consistently found that females had better verbal skills and that males had better mathematical and spatial skills. In addition, males were more aggressive. However, studies conducted in the last 15 years do not report consistent gender differences in cognitive abilities (see, for example, Linn & Hyde, 1991), and the extent and interpretation of gender differences in aggression are controversial (Knight, Fabes, & Higgins, 1996).

In figuring out whether there are gender differences, researchers compare the average (called the *mean*) for females to that of males. Therefore, findings of gender differences, when they exist, apply to averages, not necessarily to individuals. Even when gender differences are found, there may still be considerable overlap between males and females, as shown in Figure 3-5.

Other research has consistently found no differences between the average male and female in sociability, self-esteem, motivation to achieve, or even rote learning and certain types of analytical skills (Ruble, 1988).

Discussion of sex differences would not be complete without discussing possible differences in the socialization of girls and boys. In most cultures, children display clear sex-typed behaviour by 5 years of age. Indeed, by age 3 many children have learned some sex-specific behaviours (Weinraub, Clemens, Sockloff, Ethridge, Gracely, & Myers, 1984). In nursery schools, for example, girls are often observed playing with dolls, helping with snacks, and showing greater interest than boys in art and music. Boys in nursery schools can be found building bridges, roughhousing, and playing with cars and trucks. Pitcher and Schultz (1983) found this clear differentiation among 2- and 3-year-olds, noting that sex-specific behaviours became stronger by the time children reached age 4 or 5.

Sometimes, these sex-typed behaviours are exaggerated or stereotypical. Gender-role stereotypes are rigid, fixed ideas of what is appropriate masculine and feminine behaviour. They imply a belief that "masculine" and "feminine" are two distinct categories and that an individual's behaviour must reflect one or the other category. These ideas pervade nearly every culture. For instance, many parents expect their male children to be "real boys"—reserved, forceful, self-confident, tough, realistic, and assertive—and their female children to be "real girls"—gentle, dependent, high strung, talkative, frivolous, and impractical (Bem, 1975). Some children are put under strong social pressure to conform to these gender-role stereotypes, regardless of their natural dispositions.

The learning of gender roles begins in infancy. Kagan (1971) reports that mothers respond more physically to their boys but more verbally to their girls when their infants babble. These differences in how the two sexes are treated are obviously detectable by the time a child is 6 months old, at least in Kagan's Boston-area study. A similar study conducted 20 years later in Montreal finds that the rooms and toys provided for infants of each sex are stereotypical. Parents still expect active, vigorous play with objects from their boys and quieter play with dolls from their girls (Pomerleau, Bolduc, Malcuit, & Cossette, 1990). In many cases, however, studies are unnecessary. Many caregivers recognize that their responses toward a 1-year-old boy differ from those toward a 1-year-old girl. It is not simply a matter of pink and blue blankets; often, it is hundreds of little things every day—the way children are held, how often they are picked up, how they are talked to, the kinds of things that are said to them, the amount of help they are given, how caregivers respond to crying. All of these behaviours are frequently subtly influenced by the child's sex.

How are gender roles learned? The processes of reward and punishment and modelling for appropriate or inappropriate behaviour begin early in infancy. Society's baby boys are socialized toward a masculine stereotype of physical activity and prowess. Smith and Lloyd (1978) studied the behaviour of mothers with 6-month-old infants who were not their own. The babies were "actors": girls were sometimes presented as boys, and boys were sometimes presented as girls. Invariably, mothers encouraged the perceived boys more than the perceived girls in walking, crawling, and other physical play. Girls were handled more gently and encouraged to speak. As children get older, parents consistently react more favourably when their children engage in behaviour that is appropriate to their sex.

Fathers may be especially important in the development of the child's gender role (Honig, 1980; Parke, 1981). While fathers teach children of both sexes to become more independent and autonomous, they also, more than mothers, teach specific gender roles by reinforcing femininity in daughters and masculinity in sons. It was once thought that fathers were influential only in teaching their sons masculine behaviour, and this seems to be somewhat true in the preschool period. Boys whose fathers have left before they reach age 5 are often more dependent on their peers and are less assertive (Parke, 1981). For girls, the effect of a father's absence is more evident during adolescence. Effective fathers help their daughters learn to interact with men in appropriate ways (Lamb, 1979; Parke, 1981).

Peers also socialize children. Maccoby (1995) argues that the peer culture is a major factor in the development of sex-typed behaviour. Indeed, I remember asking my son, when he was 4 years old and attending day care several days a week, if he wanted to take a favourite doll for nap time. He looked at me with horror in his eyes, replying, "No, Mom. The kids would laugh at me" (Digdon).

Figure 3-5
Suppose the pink curve stands for girls' performances on a vocabulary test and the blue curve stands for boys' performances on the same test. Although the girls' average is significantly higher, notice the considerable overlap between the two curves. Many tests that indicate sex differences show similar patterns of overlapping curves.

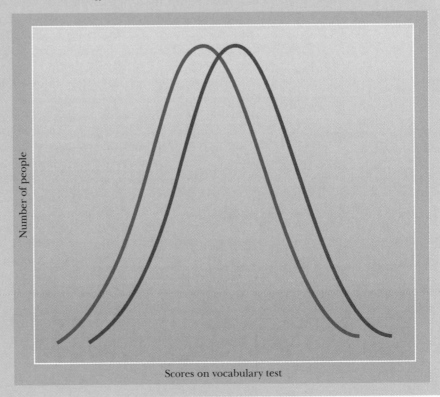

Nuclear Families Nuclear families are hard to define because they are diverse. In the past, *nuclear* referred to a biological family, consisting of a husband, a wife, and their unmarried children, all of whom live as a unit apart from relatives, neighbours, and friends. This definition, though, is too narrow. In Canada, 79 percent of nuclear families are composed of children living with both biological parents; 16 percent are lone-parent families; 4 percent are stepfamilies; and 1 percent are adoptive or foster parent families (HRDC & Stats Can, 1996). Family composition is less important than other factors, such as the family's financial well-being and the types of relationships that family members share with one another. Well-functioning families have enough income to meet their needs and have relationships that are supportive. Poverty, abuse, and neglect hinder the ability of families to function well (United Nations, 1996).

The Family as Transmitter of Culture

Besides integrating the individual child into the family unit, parents or caregivers in all of the family styles discussed above also interpret for the child the outside society and its culture. Religion, ethnic traditions, and moral values are conveyed to children at an early age. In a cohesive, homogeneous society, like the Israeli kibbutz, people outside the family reinforce and expand parental teachings. There is little contradiction between the family's way of doing things and the customs of the community at large. But in a more complex, multi-ethnic society, many cultural traditions are often opposed. Some parents struggle to instill their own values so that their children will not become assimilated into the culture of the majority. Parents express many cultural values to their children in their attitudes toward such daily choices as food, clothing, friends, education, and play.

Family Systems

Families are more than the sum of the individuals within them. They have structure and a hierarchy of authority and responsibility. They have rules for behaviour, both formal and informal. They have customs, rituals, and patterns of relationships that persist over time (Kreppner & Lerner, 1989). Each family member may have a specific role in interactions with other family members. An older sibling may be responsible for younger siblings. Each family member may have alliances with some family members, but not with others. Two sisters, for example, may frequently take the same side against their brother. The network of interrelationships and ongoing expectations is a major influence on the child's social, emotional, and cognitive development.

Patterns of mutual influence within the family are extremely complex. This is true even in small families. Siblings in the same family may share many experiences, such as having an overly strict mother or growing up with middle-class, suburban family values. Yet there is also a set of nonshared experiences and relationships. In one series of studies, the relationships between parents and their first-born and parents and their second-born were compared over a period of time (Dunn, 1986). As one might expect, the relationships between mother and first-born were often quite close and intense, at least until the birth of the second child. Things then became more complicated. If the first-born child had an affectionate relationship with the father, this affection tended to increase, as did the conflict and confrontation between the mother and this first-born. If the mother gave a good deal of attention to the second child, the conflict between the mother and the first child escalated. In fact, the more the mother played with the 1-year-old second baby, the more the siblings quarrelled with each other a year later (Dunn, 1986).

Clearly, members of the same family do not necessarily experience the same environment. When adolescents are asked to compare

Similarity of interests may cause more intimacy between certain family members.

their experiences with those of their siblings, they often note more differences than similarities. Although they may see some similarity in family rules and expectations, there are many differences concerning the timing and impact of the events—a divorce, for instance. Even larger differences occur in how each sibling is treated by the other siblings (Plomin, 1990). In a recent study, parents and adolescents were asked to rate their family environment. There was some agreement on whether or not the family was well organized, had a strong religious orientation, or was often in conflict. But considerable disagreement existed between parents and their adolescent children on how cohesive the family was, how much expressiveness or independence was allowed, and whether or not there was an "intellectual" family orientation (Carlson, Cooper, & Spradling, 1991). It becomes apparent that as each child enters a family, the nature of the family and consequent interactions within it change, as the following comments indicate:

> It became very clear to me that the family into which I was born as the first daughter was very different from that of my fourth sibling. He was 10 years younger and had been born when my parents were older. I was the experimental child—didn't have a bicycle until I was in high school, had curfews, and was very responsible for the other children in the family. I had the sense that I had to be the peacemaker and keep my parents happy. I guess today I would say that I always had a strong need for their approval.
>
> My brother, on the other hand, was different. I thought he got away with murder. He had no curfews, he had a car in high school, my parents were never harsh with him in terms of academic expectations. He is a very engaging guy, but there is something about him that is slow to grow up. He has sort of a Peter Pan quality. He married late, at age 34. He and his wife are definitely socially and materially oriented and are putting off the decision to have children. I was afraid that being the last one home he would have trouble moving off on his own. After my father died, I thought for a time that he would "inherit" Mom. He's just now beginning to come into his own and I'm very proud of him for it. He's finally growing up.

The family may be an important microcosm in which the child learns about the broader cultural community, but the transmission of its culture is not simple. This difficulty is due partly to the complex nature of the family system itself, and partly to the complexity of the society in which we live. The more diverse the social fabric, the more pressure on the family system. It also becomes more difficult to transmit values when values are unfocused and in transition. This is perhaps the main challenge that Canadian families face today.

As each child enters a family, the nature of the family and consequent interactions within it change.

Summary and Conclusions

In this chapter we have presented the key aspects of molecular genetics. Genetic material is contained on the 23 pairs of chromosomes. Chromosome pairs 1 to 22 are called the autosomes. The 23rd pair is the sex chromosomes—XX in females, and XY in males. Each chromosome is a DNA molecule. Strands of DNA form genes. Different variants of a gene are called alleles. Some alleles are dominant, whereas others are recessive. Dominant genes are always expressed in the phenotype. Recessive genes are expressed in the phenotype only if the person has two recessive genes at that gene location. Genes contain sequences of base pairs that may be grouped into codons. The sequence of codons gives the directions for protein synthesis. Proteins are essential for life. Normal development requires the production of the appropriate protein at the right stage of development.

Genetic abnormalities can occur because of abnormal numbers of chromosomes. Down syndrome, Klinefelter's syndrome, Turner's syndrome, supermale syndrome, and fragile X syndrome are examples. Other disorders are called sex-linked disorders because recessive genes on the X chromosomes cause them. Females are carriers, and males are more likely to have the disorder. Examples are hemophilia and red-green colour blindness. Recessive genes on the autosomes carry other disorders. Examples are Tay-Sachs disease, sickle-cell anemia, cystic fibrosis, and PKU.

Dominant genes may also carry disorders, such as Huntington's and retinoblastoma. Finally, disorders such as asthma follow a polygenic system of inheritance. Several genes, environmental factors, and the interplay between genes and environment cause them.

Genetic counselling is a new specialty in medicine that apprises potential parents of the risks associated with their planned pregnancy. Genetic counselling is especially suggested for older parents, parents with a recognized genetic defect in their family, or couples that have suffered three or more miscarriages. We should note that the rapid developments in reproductive genetics have led to concern over ethical dilemmas. Some researchers have suggested that these dilemmas will form a major research and theoretical focus for the first half of this century.

A child's behaviour is not determined solely by genetics, however. The effects of culture and socialization cannot be underestimated. Research with adopted children and twins, for example, has pointed out the strong contributions of both heredity and environment to behaviour. There are three types of gene–environment interactions: passive, evocative, and active.

The effects of genes need to be considered in the context of the person's environment. The culture and the family are critical environmental influences.

Key Terms and Concepts

alleles (p. 67)

autosomes (p. 65)

base pairs (p. 66)

chromosome (p. 64)

codons (p. 66)

crossover (p. 65)

DNA (deoxyribonucleic acid) (p. 64)

dominant (p. 67)

ethnocentrism (p. 86)

genes (p. 65)

gene therapy (p. 69)

genetic counselling (p. 78)

genotype (p. 67)

meiosis (p. 65)

mutations (p. 67)

nonsex-linked autosomal trait (p. 75)

phenotype (p. 67)

polygenic inheritance (p. 71)

recessive (p. 67)

RNA (ribonucleic acid) (p. 67)

sex-linked traits (p. 74)

twin comparisons (p. 82)

Questions to Review

1. Describe the genetic code in terms of chromosomes, DNA, genes, base pairs, and codons. How are these terms interrelated?

2. What is the difference between genotype and phenotype?

3. Why is protein synthesis important?

4. What are some abnormalities caused by chromosomal defects? What is known about the causes and symptoms of these defects?

5. How are sex-linked disorders transmitted? What are some examples of sex-linked disorders, and who is most likely to manifest these disorders?

6. What are some diseases caused by nonsex-linked autosomal traits? Describe the characteristics of these disorders.

7. Explain genetic counselling.

8. Describe ethical issues associated with advances in genetics.

9. What twin comparisons are used in behavioural genetics?

10. How are adoption studies used to study genetic influences on behaviour?

11. What is an advantage of the blended family design, as compared with adoption or twin studies?

12. How do passive gene–environment interactions differ from evocative or active ones?

13. Give examples of ways that the family is a transmitter of culture.

14. Define *unshared environment* within a family.

Weblinks

www.cprn.ca/

Canadian Policy Research Networks, Inc.

This site has information on Canadian policies related to family, health, and work. It includes links to free online publications.

www.ornl.gov/hgmis/

Human Genome Project

This is the official site for the international Human Genome Project. It has extensive information on the project, genetics, and genetic disorders and on ethical, legal, and social issues.

www.statcan.ca/start.html

Statistics Canada

This site provides information on social trends, culture, and family.

The Prenatal Period

The history of man for the nine months preceding his birth would, probably, be far more interesting and contain events of greater moment than for all the three score and ten years that follow it.

SAMUEL TAYLOR COLERIDGE

Outline CHAPTER 4

Objectives

By the time you have finished this chapter, you should be able to do the following:

✔ **Understand factors that affect the likelihood of conception.**

✔ **Describe three prenatal developmental periods.**

✔ **Describe the reproductive alternatives provided by modern technology, including the emotional, legal, and moral issues they raise.**

✔ **Describe the general trends that occur in prenatal growth and development.**

✔ **Explain the importance of critical periods in prenatal development.**

✔ **List the factors that influence prenatal development.**

✔ **Understand why it is difficult to isolate the effects of specific teratogens.**

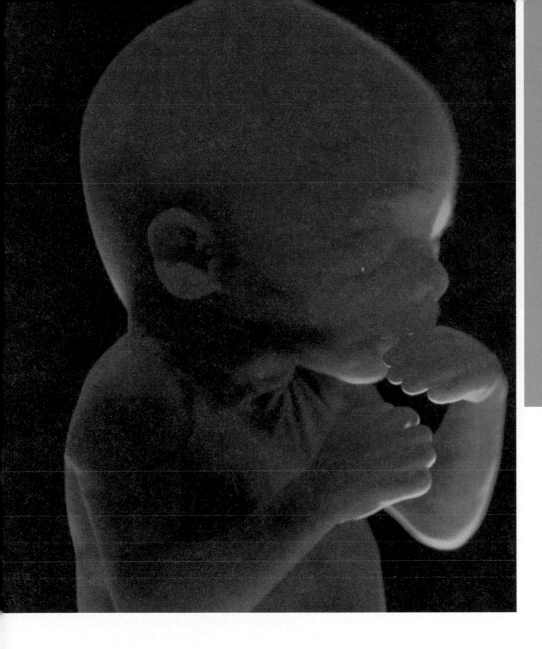

Conception and Infertility

How old are you? Chances are you will tell me your age since your date of birth. But in ancient China, people used to judge their ages from the presumed dates of conception. Sometimes we forget about the extensive development that has already taken place before we first breathe air in the world outside our mothers. The prenatal period, lasting about 38 weeks, is the time of the most rapid growth and development in a person's life. In fact, a single fertilized egg increases its original weight by more than a billion times from conception to birth.

As in our chapter on genetics, we shall study here the interaction of heredity and environment, this time in connection with the prenatal period. The fetus inside the womb of the mother is very much affected by the physical environment in which its parents live—the amount and quality of food they consume, the immediate safety of their home and community, the work its mother does, perhaps even the music the parents listen to, and other factors. Prolonged stress that the mother experiences has an effect on the developing fetus, as do viruses, radiation, temperature, and other factors. This interaction of heredity and environment is so intimate during the prenatal period that an embryo that is perfect genetically can be terribly damaged by a virus the pregnant woman is exposed to—an environmental factor.

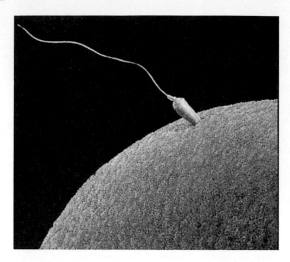

A living human ovum at the moment of conception. Although some sperm cells have begun to penetrate the outer covering of the ovum, only one will actually fertilize it.

Prenatal development—the unfolding of inherited potential—is one of the most dramatic examples of maturation. The prenatal maturation of human infants occurs within a highly controlled environment—the uterus—and it follows an orderly, predictable sequence. But even in the uterus there are environmental influences that affect development. Almost from the moment of conception, children are part of an environmental context. They do not begin life with a "clean slate." The expectations and anxieties, riches and deprivations, stability and disruptions, health and illnesses of the families into which they are born affect not only their life after birth, but also their prenatal development. These factors may even affect the chances that this baby would be conceived at all. In this chapter, we will explore a couple's decision to have children and what may happen if they are unable to conceive. We will then examine the biological and maturational processes during the prenatal period, as well as the environmental influences on these processes.

Prenatal Development

The development of each unique human being begins at the moment of conception. A one-celled, fertilized egg that can hardly be seen carries all of the genetic information needed to create a new organism. But the journey of the next nine months is complex and, at times, perilous. It is estimated that over 50 percent of all fertilized eggs are lost within the first two weeks (Grobestein et al., 1983). We will now look at the process of fertilization and at the intricate sequence of development over the next nine months.

Conception and Fertilization

ovum The female reproductive cell (the egg or gamete).

Fallopian tubes Two passages that open out of the upper part of the uterus and carry the ova from the ovary to the uterus.

ovulation The release of the ovum into one of the two Fallopian tubes; occurs approximately 14 days after menstruation.

sperm The male reproductive cell (or gamete).

fertilization The union of an ovum and a sperm.

About the tenth day after the beginning of the average woman's regular menstrual period, an **ovum,** or egg cell, that has developed in one of her two ovaries is stimulated by hormones and enters a sudden period of growth that continues for three or four days. By the end of the thirteenth or fourteenth day of growth, the follicle surrounding the ovum breaks, and the ovum is released to begin its journey down one of two **Fallopian tubes.** This release of the ovum from the ovary is called **ovulation.**

In most women, then, ovulation occurs about the fourteenth day after the onset of menstruation. The mature ovum survives for only two or three days. A man's **sperm,** deposited in a woman's vagina during sexual intercourse, also survives for as long as three days. A viable sperm, moving from the vagina through the uterus and up the Fallopian tube and reaching the ovum during the critical 48- to 72-hour period, can fertilize the ovum. Otherwise, the ovum continues down the Fallopian tube to the uterus, where it disintegrates.

The sperm and ovum are single cells, each containing half of the hereditary potential of the individual. The union of the two cells to produce a human being is quite a remarkable achievement. Some 300 million sperm are deposited in the vagina during intercourse, yet only one of these may fertilize an ovum. The sex and inherited traits of the child depend on which of these millions of sperm cells survives to penetrate the ovum. For the sperm cells, the trip to the ovum is long and difficult. The microscopic sperm cells must work their way upward through a foot-long passage, through acidic fluids that can be lethal to them, through mucus and other obstacles—and finally one arrives at the proper place at the proper time. It is at that moment of **fertilization** "when, out of a billion possibilities, the DNA of one individual, specific person is created" (Silber, 1991, p. 73).

Infertility

A variety of factors can cause infertility, including infections in the woman, ranging from common yeast infections to venereal diseases, which lead to scarring in her reproductive system; a medical condition in the mother called *endometriosis,* which causes menstrual flow to back up the Fallopian tubes, blocking them and causing tumour-like growths in the abdomen; and the mother's age, as fertility starts declining after age 30, and by age 40 the woman is appreciably less fertile. All of a woman's eggs are present at birth. By the time she is 40, a woman has older eggs that are often damaged, preventing conception or, if they are fertilized, they can produce abnormalities that result in miscarriage. Although it is possible for men to fertilize an egg at any age, it becomes more difficult with increasing age. Older sperm are less mobile, slower swimmers, and more likely to have abnormalities that either prevent conception or lead to early miscarriage. Lowered sperm counts (sperm counts are lower in fathers-to-be who wear unusually tight pants) or sperm damage caused by environmental factors, including high temperatures or chemicals such as alcohol, also contribute to infertility.

Because of problems with infertility, approximately 1 in 12 couples will be able to conceive only with special medical intervention (Mosher & Pratt, 1990). Fertilization that occurs outside of the womb is called *in vitro* **fertilization (IVF).** Ovum and sperm are united in a petri dish (not in a test tube, as implied by the now common phrase *test-tube babies*). This new ovum, which has been fertilized in solution, grows for the first few days with rapid cell division and then must be promptly implanted in a human uterus to survive.

> *in vitro* **fertilization (IVF)** Fertilization of a woman's egg outside the womb.

We may see a fuller discussion of this new reproductive technology in the box "Reproductive Technology: What Are the Options?" These procedures are no longer experimental, but are clinically approved, with established guidelines ("In-vitro," 1984). The guidelines ensure the safety of the procedure and aid in the selection of couples who can be helped to achieve fertilization using this technology. There are now dozens of fertility clinics in the United States and a number in Canada—at least ten in the Toronto area, one in Nova Scotia, one in Alberta, and two in British Columbia (Fine, 1999).

We can describe much of what happens in fertilization and in the following development of the fetus, but there are still many things we do not fully understand about the outcome of fertilization. Researchers are working on some interesting questions. For instance, for every 100 girls conceived, approximately 160 boys are conceived. Why are more male sperm successful in penetrating the ovum than female sperm? We know, for example, that compared with the female, the male sperm has a smaller, rounder head and a longer tail, it swims faster, it is more affected by an acid environment, and it tends to live for a shorter period of time (Rosenfeld, 1974a; Silber, 1991). Although many more boys are conceived, however, only 105 boys are born for every 100 girls. Why do more boys than girls die during the prenatal period? And why do ovulation induction procedures seem to produce an increase in girls, unless the sperm is introduced directly into the uterus by an insemination procedure? These are just some of the many challenging questions that are being investigated.

> **germinal period** Includes conception, the period of very rapid cell division, and initial cell differentiation. This period lasts approximately two weeks.
>
> **embryonic period** The second prenatal period, which lasts from the end of the second week to the end of the second month after conception. Most of the major structures and organs of the individual are formed during this time.
>
> **fetal period** The final period of prenatal development, lasting from the beginning of the third month after conception until birth. During this period, all organs, limbs, muscles, and systems become functional.

Periods of Prenatal Development

The nine months of prenatal development are divided into three periods based on the extent of development. The first period, called the **germinal period,** starts at conception and ends about two weeks later, when the fertilized egg is securely attached to the wall of the uterus. The second period, called the **embryonic period,** extends from the end of the second week to the end of the second month. It is the time when most body parts are starting to form. The third period, called the **fetal period,** extends from the start of the third month until birth. It is a time of rapid growth and the elaboration of body parts laid down during the embryonic period.

Let us now look at each of the periods in a bit more detail.

FOCUS ON AN ISSUE

Reproductive Technology: What Are the Options?

Modern advances in reproductive technology have given infertile couples several new alternatives. The oldest and still widely used technique is artificial insemination. Simply stated, artificial insemination is the impregnation of a woman by the artificial introduction of semen. This process can take several forms.

A woman can be artificially injected with the sperm of her husband, or if the sperm is diseased or weak, with sperm donated by a stranger and kept frozen until used. Another technique that infertile couples can try is *in vitro* fertilization (IVF), which involves fertilizing a woman's egg with a man's sperm in a laboratory dish, then placing the fertilized egg in the woman's uterus (Wallis, 1984). The first "test-tube baby" was Louise Brown, who was born in 1978 in the United Kingdom.

IVF has become an increasingly popular method of dealing with infertility—about 1 percent of first-born children in Western societies are conceived through the use of IVF (van Balen, 1998). IVF children seem to develop similarly to children who were conceived "naturally"; they do not dif-

fer in the rate of congenital problems (van Balen, 1998). However, preterm births, lower birth weight, and multiple births are more common in IVF pregnancies. The causes of these effects are unclear because there are several potential causes, including the age of the mother (IVF mothers tend to be older), the mother's medical history

---

IVF children do not seem to be affected psychologically by their method of conception.

---

related to her infertility, or the IVF treatment (van Balen, 1998).

IVF children do not seem to be affected psychologically by their method of conception (Chan, Raboy, & Patterson, 1998; Golombok, Cook, Bish, & Murray, 1995). For instance, parents and teachers assessed 7-year-old IVF children and found that they were similar in psychosocial adjustment to other children (Chan et al., 1998). A problem with IVF, however, is that the method often fails; it has a 26.2 percent chance

of success in American clinics, reported to be one of the best in the world (Fine, 1999). The odds are less clear in Canada because the government does not require clinics to publicize success rates (McIlroy, 1999). As well, clinics may vary in the populations that they treat. Some may have lower success rates because they treat people who have more severe fertility problems.

A newer method of IVF referred to as the GIFT Protocol has been found to have a 46 percent chance of success. In this procedure, too, the egg is fertilized by the sperm in a petri dish, the cells are allowed to grow somewhat, and then the embryo is placed in the Fallopian tube in the site where fertilization normally occurs. This procedure has a success rate approximately two times greater than that of the technique of implanting embryos in the uterus.

A recent development of *in vitro* fertilization, known as *donated eggs*, involves fertilizing an egg donated by a stranger with the sperm of the father-to-be's, then implanting the egg in the prospective mother's uterus. The technique of donated eggs makes it possible for an otherwise infertile woman to

Germinal Period

zygote A fertilized ovum.

blastula The hollow, fluid-filled sphere of cells that forms several days after conception.

implantation The embedding of the prenatal organism in the uterine wall after its descent through the Fallopian tube.

Question to Ponder

What are advantages and disadvantages of the use of reproductive technology?

The fertilized egg, called a **zygote,** begins to divide just hours after conception, producing two cells. About two days later, these cells divide, producing four cells. Then they divide so that there are eight cells. The cell divisions continue, so that by the end of the fourth day, there are sixty or seventy cells. The cells become organized into a ball that has a fluid-filled centre surrounded by two layers of cells. This ball is called a **blastula.** (You will notice that the name of the baby-to-be keeps changing as it progresses through the prenatal periods.)

The blastula is associated with two important aspects of prenatal development: (1) the blastula migrates from the site of conception in the Fallopian tube to the uterus (see Figure 4-1) and (2) the dividing cells start to differentiate so that daughter cells are not identical to mother cells. Cell differentiation begins about four or five days after conception. Interestingly, both the baby's body parts and the support system required to sustain the baby (that is, the placenta, umbilical cord, and fluid-filled amniotic sac) all eventually develop from the blastula. The outer layer of cells of the blastula develops into the support system, the inner layer of cells into the baby.

Once in the uterus, the blastula must attach itself to the wall. This process is called **implantation.** If implantation does not occur, the blastula will be flushed from the mother's body during her next menstrual period. This expulsion is called a **miscarriage,** or

have the experience of bearing a child, regardless of her age. With better understanding of the hormonal control of ovulation, it is now possible for postmenopausal women to carry and deliver babies, and it is an alternative for couples who cannot conceive but can carry children. Another option available to couples who might be able to conceive but cannot carry children is to enter into a contract with a surrogate mother who will carry a child to term for them. This was the alternative chosen by the Sterns when they signed a contract with Mary Beth Whitehead to have her bear a child for them.

The unravelling of the arrangements between Whitehead and the Sterns, known as the Baby M case, brought to prominence the emotional, ethical, and legal issues raised by solutions to the infertility problem. These issues have by no means been resolved. In 1989, the federal government created the Royal Commission on New Reproductive Technologies to study the legal, ethical, social, and health issues. In the years since 1989, the commission has published reports and has made recommendations. In 1996, the federal government introduced legislation to prohibit practices such as

using technologies for selecting the sex of the baby or using donor eggs and sperm from cadavers. According to the legislation, licences would be required for the storage and handling of human eggs, sperm, and embryos; for *in vitro* fertilization; and for donor insemination (McIlroy, 1999). This legislation was not passed, however, because of the election call in 1997. Similar legislation is expected to come before the government in the fall of 1999. Canada lags behind other countries, such as the United States and the United Kingdom, which already have legislation in place (McIlroy, 1999).

Because the technology involved is so new, there is little hard data on the psychological after-effects of carrying someone else's child or of rearing a child that someone else bore at the legal parents' request. Nor does anyone yet know the eventual effects on the child. Most difficult of all are the moral questions raised by reproductive technology and its relation to traditional values. Is it right to hire a woman's uterus or a man's sperm so that some other couple can have a chance to raise a child? What are the implications of raising children for whom only one of the parents is a bio-

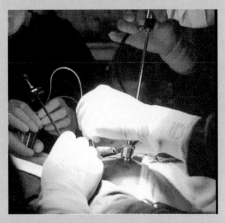

In vitro *fertilization.*

logical parent? On the other hand, is it right to deny a childless couple the opportunity that modern technology makes possible to raise children and to have a full family life? Is adoption an alternative that could reduce the need for reproductive technology? Finally, we cannot ignore the trauma that infertile couples experience as they deal with miscarriage and innumerable visits to infertility specialists to achieve their goal of having a healthy baby (Beck, 1988). As a society, we have not yet resolved these issues, just as we have not yet resolved other issues connected with reproductive rights.

spontaneous abortion, and resembles a heavy period with cramping. Miscarriages are more common in blastulas that have abnormalities, and it is estimated that about 50 percent of blastulas are miscarried, often without the woman being aware that she was ever pregnant.

At the end of the germinal period, the blastula is implanted in the wall of the uterus. Although it has over one hundred separate cells, it is no bigger than a period on a typed page (about .015 of a centimetre long). Implantation marks the transition from the germinal period to the embryonic period.

> **miscarriage (spontaneous abortion)** Expulsion of the prenatal organism before it is viable.

Embryonic Period

Generally, the embryonic period is considered to extend from near the end of the second week to the end of the second month after conception. It is a crucial time, when much that is essential to the baby's further prenatal development and future lifetime development occurs. During the embryonic period, all the tissues and structures that will house, nurture, and protect the embryo (and later the fetus) for the remainder of the nine months are formed. In addition, the development begins, in form at least, of all organs and most features of the embryo itself. During the embryonic period, this very tiny being develops arms, legs, fingers, toes, a face, a heart that

Figure 4-1
The journey of the fertilized egg is shown as it moves from ovary to uterus. Fetal development begins with the union of sperm and egg high in the Fallopian tube. During the next few days, the fertilized egg, or zygote, travels down the Fallopian tube and begins to divide. Cell divisions continue for a week until a blastula is formed. By this time, the blastula has arrived in the uterus and, within the next few days, will implant itself in the uterine wall.

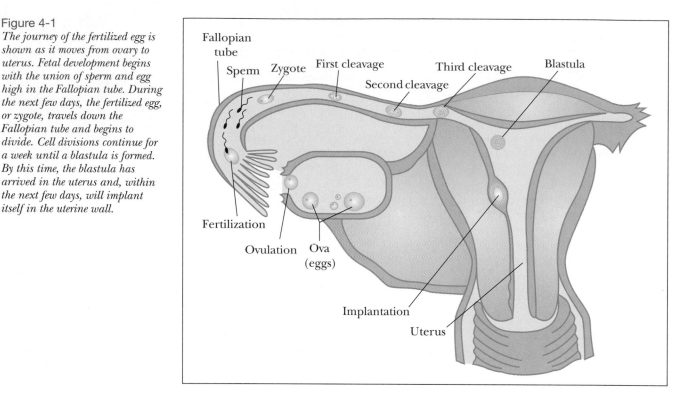

amniotic sac A fluid-filled membrane that encloses the developing embryo or fetus.

placenta A disk-shaped mass of tissue that forms along the wall of the uterus, through which the embryo receives nutrients and discharges wastes.

chorion The protective outer sac that develops from tissue surrounding the embryo.

umbilical cord The rope of tissue connecting the placenta to the embryo; this rope contains two fetal arteries and one fetal vein.

ectoderm In embryonic development, the outer layer of cells that becomes the skin, sense organs, and nervous system.

mesoderm In embryonic development, the middle layer of cells that becomes the muscles, blood, and excretory system.

endoderm In embryonic development, the inner layer of cells that becomes the digestive system, lungs, thyroid, thymus, and other organs.

beats, a brain, lungs, and all the other major organs. By the end of the embryonic period, the embryo is a recognizable human being.

The embryo develops within an **amniotic sac** filled with amniotic fluid; it is then nourished by means of an organ called the **placenta,** which develops specifically to assist the growth of the new organism. The placenta is a disk-shaped mass of tissue growing from the wall of the uterus; it is formed partly from the tissue of the uterine wall and partly by the **chorion,** the outer layer of tissue that surrounds the embryo and the amniotic sac.

The placenta starts to develop at the moment of implantation and continues to grow until about the seventh month of pregnancy. It is connected to the embryo by the **umbilical cord,** a "rope" of tissue containing two fetal arteries and one fetal vein. The placenta allows the exchange of materials between mother and embryo, keeping out large particles of foreign matter but passing on nutrients. Enzymes, vitamins, and even immunities to disease pass from the mother to the embryo, while the resulting waste products in the embryo's blood are passed to the mother for final elimination. Sugars, fats, and proteins also pass through to the embryo, but some bacteria and some salts do not. It is important to note that the mother and child do not actually share the same blood system. The placenta allows the exchange of nutritive and waste materials across cell membranes without the exchange of blood cells.

During this period, the embryo itself grows rapidly and changes occur daily. Immediately after implantation, the embryo develops into three distinct layers: the **ectoderm,** or outer layer, which becomes skin and the nervous system; the **mesoderm,** or middle layer, which becomes muscles, blood, and the excretory system; and the **endoderm,** or inner layer, which becomes the digestive system, lungs, and glands. Simultaneously, the neural tube (the beginning of the nervous system and the brain) and the heart start to develop. At the end of the fourth week of pregnancy, and only two weeks into the embryonic period, the heart is beating; the nervous system, in its somewhat primitive form, is functioning; and both are contributing to the development of the entire embryo. Frequently, all of these developments occur before the mother is even aware that she is pregnant.

During the second month, all of the structures that we recognize as human develop rapidly. The arms and legs unfold from small buds on the sides of the trunk. The eyes become visible, seemingly on the sides of the head, at about a month, and the full face changes almost daily during the second month. The internal organs—the lungs, digestive system, and excretory system—are being formed, although they are not yet functional. We may see the growth of the embryo depicted in Figure 4-2.

Many miscarriages occur during the embryonic period. They are usually caused by inadequate development of the placenta, the umbilical cord, and/or the embryo (Beck, 1988). Because the embryo receives its nutrients from the mother through the placenta, an inadequate diet or the poor health of the mother may adversely affect the developing child. It is important for us to keep these phases of prenatal development in mind when we discuss later in this chapter environmental factors that can affect the embryo and fetus. It becomes obvious that, depending on the timing of exposure, damage will occur to broadly different aspects of fetal development.

In some cases the first division of the zygote produces two identical cells, which then separate and develop into two individuals (monozygotic or identical twins). In other cases, two ova are fertilized by different sperm and the result is fraternal or dizygotic twins.

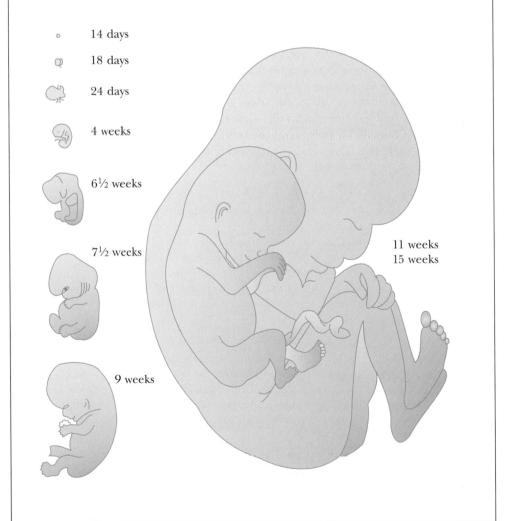

14 days

18 days

24 days

4 weeks

6½ weeks

7½ weeks

9 weeks

11 weeks
15 weeks

Figure 4-2
The embryonic period. This is a lifesize illustration of the growth of the human embryo and fetus from 14 days to 15 weeks.

Fetal Period

The fetal period lasts from the beginning of the third month until birth—or for about seven months—versus an average total **gestation period** of 266 days. It is during the fetal period that the organs, limbs, muscles, and systems become functional. The fetus begins to kick, squirm, and turn its head and, eventually, its body. Even with its eyes sealed shut, the fetus starts to squint, frown, move its lips, open its mouth, swallow a little amniotic fluid, suck its thumb, and make sucking motions.

During the third month, the first external signs of sex differentiation become apparent. The penis and scrotum in the male or the beginning of the labia in the female can be detected, although the male organs develop sooner than do those of the female. At the same time, the male fetus develops a prostate gland, vas deferens, and epididymis, while the female develops Fallopian tubes and ovaries with their full complement of approximately 400 000 eggs.

The eyes, still set toward the sides of the head, develop their irises, and all of the nerves needed to connect the eye to the brain are now in place. Teeth form under the gums; ears begin to appear on the sides of the head; fingernails and toenails form. The fetus develops a thyroid gland, a thymus gland, a pancreas, and kidneys. The liver begins to function, and the lungs and stomach begin to respond. By the twelfth week, the vocal cords have developed, the taste buds have formed, and ribs and vertebrae have begun to ossify (turn from cartilage to bone). The fetus, although unable to survive on its own, has acquired almost all of the systems and functions necessary for a human being. And at this point, it is only about 7.6 centimetres long and weighs around 114.2 grams.

During the fourth to sixth months (the second trimester), all of the processes begun in the first trimester continue. (The nine months before birth are divided into three equal segments of three months each, called **trimesters**.) The body becomes longer, so the head does not look as out of proportion as it did during the preceding month. The face develops lips, and the heart muscle strengthens, beating from 120 to 160 times a minute. In the fifth month, the fetus acquires a strong hand grip and increases the amount and force of its movements. The mother will be able to feel an elbow, a knee, or the head, as the fetus moves around during its waking periods. This feeling of movement is a very important experience for many pregnant women, as the following comments indicate:

> I remember the day I first felt my daughter move inside of me. It was initially a soft, tickling sensation—much like I would imagine a butterfly's wing to feel. It was such a wonderful feeling. As time went by, the movements became more intense ... it seemed as though whenever I finally sat down to rest in the evening, she would wake up and want attention. Sometimes I would play with her; I would push in one spot and then she would push back. One time when I was eight months pregnant and giving a lecture she decided to flip right over. Luckily, I had a podium in front of me or the flip would have been visible.

> I remember my sister telling me to watch the movements my daughter made after she was born. I would see her making the movements she had been making inside of me for all those months. Sure enough, I saw her pushing those arms and legs out and squirming around. I'm sure she was glad to finally be out in the open, away from the tight confines of the sac and uterus.

During the fifth month, the fetus is also undergoing a process of skin-cell replacement. Oil glands form and secrete a cheesy coating, called the *vernix caseosa*, which protects the skin from the amniotic fluid. The fetus also develops a hairy covering on its body, referred to as *lanugo hair*, and begins to grow eyebrows and eyelashes.

In the sixth month, the fetus grows to about 30 centimetres in length and weighs approximately .7 kilograms. The eyes are completely formed, and the eyelids can open.

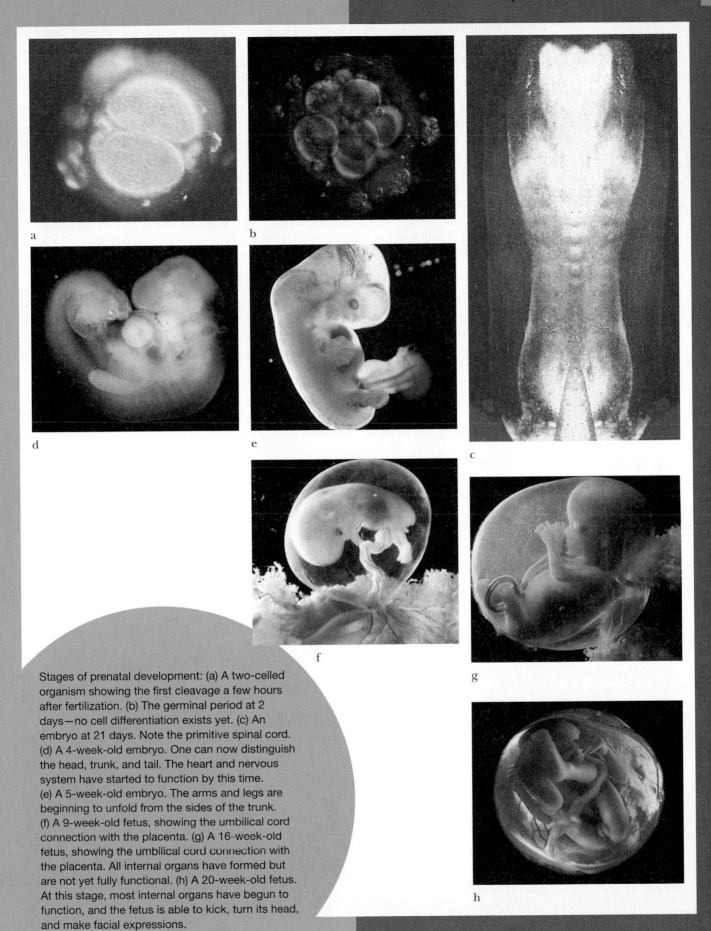

Stages of prenatal development: (a) A two-celled organism showing the first cleavage a few hours after fertilization. (b) The germinal period at 2 days—no cell differentiation exists yet. (c) An embryo at 21 days. Note the primitive spinal cord. (d) A 4-week-old embryo. One can now distinguish the head, trunk, and tail. The heart and nervous system have started to function by this time. (e) A 5-week-old embryo. The arms and legs are beginning to unfold from the sides of the trunk. (f) A 9-week-old fetus, showing the umbilical cord connection with the placenta. (g) A 16-week-old fetus, showing the umbilical cord connection with the placenta. All internal organs have formed but are not yet fully functional. (h) A 20-week-old fetus. At this stage, most internal organs have begun to function, and the fetus is able to kick, turn its head, and make facial expressions.

Bone formation progresses, hair on the head continues to grow, and the fetus begins to straighten out its posture so that the internal organs can shift to their proper positions.

By the beginning of the third trimester (that is, after 24 weeks of development in the uterus), a healthy fetus is considered **viable**—it might survive outside the mother's body if it were placed in an incubator and given special, intensive care. With modern medical advances, however, some special care units for premature infants have been able to sustain babies who are born even earlier than this. Perhaps as many as 20 percent of fetuses born at 24 weeks survive, provided they are in the best-equipped neonatal intensive care units. At 29 weeks, fully 90 percent survive in such units (Kantrowitz, 1988). Such care is very expensive, however, especially for very premature infants with multiple problems who must be cared for in newborn intensive care units (NICUs).

By the seventh month, the fetus weighs about 1.4 kilograms, and its nervous system is mature enough to control breathing and swallowing. During this seventh month, the brain develops rapidly, forming the tissues that localize the centres for all of the senses and motor activities. The fetus is sensitive to touch and can feel pain; it may even have a sense of balance.

A frequently raised question is whether or not a fetus hears. It has long been known that a fetus is startled by very loud sounds occurring close to the mother but hardly at all by moderate sounds. The reason is that the fetus is surrounded by a variety of sounds. There are digestive sounds from the mother's drinking, eating, and swallowing. There are breathing sounds. Also, there are circulatory system sounds that correspond to the rhythm of the mother's heartbeat. The fetus can hear loud conversational speech from outside the body, but the sound is muffled. In fact, the internal noise level in the uterus is thought to be as loud as that of a small factory (Armitage, Baldwin, & Vince, 1980; Aslin, Pisoni, & Jusczyk, 1983). Noise does affect the fetus, however, as the following mother's comment indicates:

> I'll never forget the day we went to a modified sports car race at a local track. We were sitting on metal bleachers in the upper section just under a metal roof. I was seven months pregnant at the time. The noise was ab-

viable After twenty-four weeks of development, the ability of the fetus to live outside the mother's body, provided it receives special care.

FOCUS ON AN ISSUE

Does the Fetus Learn?

Is the fetus capable of learning? Can we train the unborn child, and can this training give the child a head start on its later learning? What has the fetus already learned about its mother? For centuries, people have wondered about how experiences in the womb may affect the unborn child. The Greek philosopher Aristotle thought the fetus could acquire sensation (Hepper, 1989). In medieval Europe, some even believed that the fetus might possess ideas. If Aristotle and these others are correct, how does the fetus acquire these sensations or ideas? Is there evidence that either supports or debunks these beliefs?

First, let us review what we already know about fetal capabilities. Researchers generally agree that the fetus is sensitive to touch and vibration and can hear in the final two months before birth (Hepper, 1989; Poole, 1987). It must be noted, however, that sounds coming from outside of the mother must compete with sounds inside the mother's body in order to be

Can we train the unborn child, and can this training give the child a head start on its later learning?

heard. Researchers who placed microphones in the wombs of sheep were shocked to discover the rather high volume of noise inside the sheep (Armitage, Baldwin, & Vince, 1980). With the rhythmic noises of the circulatory system, the steady beat of the mother's heart, and the various rumblings of the mother's digestive system, the fetal environment seems to be as loud as a small factory. Researchers speculate that sounds coming from outside the mother's body must be quite muffled.

The fetus adapts to its noisy environment through a simple form of learning called *habituation*. Quite simply, the fetus learns to respond to certain sounds. Repetitive sounds, such as a steady heartbeat, are soothing. The fetus is startled by sudden new sounds and vibrations but seems to calm down as the sounds continue. Researchers have discovered that after birth, the sound of a metronome set to the pace of the mother's heartbeat is soothing to the newborn.

What does the fetus learn from the outside world? Peter Hepper (1989)

solutely incredible. I finally put ear plugs on to muffle some of the noise. The amazing thing was that our poor baby had no ear plugs. He seemed to be upset by the noise because he was moving very strongly inside of me. I finally had to leave the race because my body hurt from the pummelling he was giving me.

Some researchers suggest that if mothers read to children rhythmically or play certain music before birth, the child prefers those experiences after birth. A study was conducted in which certain books, like Dr. Seuss's *The Cat in the Hat,* were read aloud by mothers to their unborn babies. Others played classical music, such as Vivaldi or Bach. In all cases, after birth the babies preferred these "familiar" patterns to unfamiliar patterns. They were more likely to be soothed by them and sucked a nipple or pacifier more upon hearing them. These studies demonstrated that prenatal auditory experiences influence postnatal auditory preferences (DeCasper & Spence, 1992). See the box "Does the Fetus Learn?" for a more complete discussion of this type of research.

Researchers have determined that the human organism does much more than just develop physically during the prenatal period. As early as 15 weeks, the fetus can grasp, frown, squint, and grimace. Reflex movements result from the touching of the soles of the feet or the eyelids. By 20 weeks, the senses of taste and smell are formed. By 24 weeks, the sense of touch is more fully developed, and there is response to sound. By 25 weeks, the response to sound grows more consistent. At 27 weeks, a light shone on the mother's abdomen sometimes causes the fetus to turn its head. In any case, a brain scan will show that the fetus has reacted to the light. All of these behaviours—facial expressions, turning, kicking, ducking actions—that occur late in the seventh month occur in the womb and may be purposeful movements that make the fetus more comfortable (Fedor-Freybergh & Vogel, 1988).

In the eighth month, the fetus may gain as much as .24 kilograms a week and begins to ready itself for the outside world. Fat layers now form under the skin in order to protect the fetus from the temperature changes that it will encounter at birth. Although the survival rate for infants born at eight months is better than 90 percent

Question to Ponder

What are the practical implications of fetuses learning in the womb?

---

created an interesting experiment with a group of expectant mothers in London. Hepper asked these mothers how often they watched Britain's most popular television soap opera, *Neighbours* (on BBC1). He selected one group who watched the program nearly every day and another group who virtually never watched it. Within hours of the babies' births, Hepper played the theme music from the show to the newborns while they were crying. As soon as they heard the music, the babies in the first group stopped crying and became alert. Newborn babies of the mothers who had not watched the program showed no reaction. There seemed to be little doubt that the newborns who had been habituated to the music of the television program had learned something.

But what exactly did the fetus learn? Some people, such as Rene Van de Carr, founder of a prenatal academic head-start program in California, claim that prenatal stimulation can make babies more alert and smarter (Poole, 1987). How could they prove these claims? Remember from Chapter 1 that researchers have to conduct experiments to prove cause and effect. Let me describe a study, and you guess whether it is an experiment: A researcher, convinced that fetuses learn in the womb, had a group of mothers play classical music loud enough so that the fetuses could hear it several hours a day for the last three months of the pregnancies. After birth, the researchers found that the fetuses recognized the music. Ten years later, they found that more of the fetuses exposed to classical music had grown up to become musical prodigies than had children who were not part of the special prenatal music program. Can we conclude that the prenatal music exposure caused the musical talent? No. Mothers who participated in

the prenatal music program might have had more musical talent and valued music more than did other mothers. Therefore, the experiences of the two groups of babies after birth might have been quite different. Babies from the prenatal music program might have been more likely to inherit greater musical aptitude and to be exposed to a rich musical environment. Either of these factors, rather than the prenatal music exposure, might have caused the babies from the prenatal music program to become musical prodigies. To rule out these other factors, the researcher would have had to include a control group of mothers who had similar aptitudes and interests in music to those of the mothers in the prenatal program. Babies from the prenatal music program would then be compared with babies from the control group who did not participate in a prenatal music program.

in well-equipped hospitals, these babies do face risks. Breathing may still be difficult; initial weight loss may be greater than for full-term babies; and, because their fat layers have not fully formed, temperature control could be a problem. For these reasons, babies born at this developmental stage are usually placed in incubators and are given the same type of care as babies born in the seventh month.

Fetal sensitivity and behaviour also develop rapidly in the eighth month. At the middle of the month, it is thought that the eyes open in the uterus, and the fetus may be able to see its hands and environment, although it is dark. Some doctors think that awareness starts at about 32 weeks, when many of the neural circuits are quite advanced. Brain scans show periods of dream sleep. As the fetus moves into the ninth month, it develops daily cycles of activity and sleep, and its hearing becomes quite mature (Shatz, 1992).

During the ninth month, the fetus continues to grow and begins to turn to a head-down position in preparation for the trip through the birth canal. The vernix cascosa starts to fall away, and the hairy coating dissolves. Immunities to disease pass from the mother to the fetus and supplement the fetus's own developing immune reactions. One to two weeks before birth, the baby "drops" as the uterus settles lower into the pelvic area. The weight gain of the fetus slows, the mother's muscles and uterus begin sporadic, painless contractions, and the cells of the placenta start to degenerate—all is ready for birth.

We may see the accomplishments of the various stages of prenatal development presented in Table 4-1.

Developmental Trends

The whole process of prenatal development that we just described seems orderly and predictable. Nevertheless, each fetus develops with its own differences in size and shape, in skin tone, in strength and proportions, in developmental pace, and so on. For example, the gestation period (the time for a full-term pregnancy as measured from the mother's last menstrual flow to the day of childbirth) is usually 40 weeks. But normal full-term infants are born as early as 37 weeks or as late as 43 weeks.

cephalocaudal developmental trend The sequence of growth in which development occurs first in the head and progresses toward the feet.

proximodistal developmental trend The directional sequence of development that occurs from the midline of the body outward.

differentiation In embryology, the process in which undifferentiated cells become increasingly specialized.

integration The organization of differentiated cells into organs or systems.

What general trends do we see in this process of prenatal development? Usually—although with some exceptions—development proceeds from the top of the body downward. This "head-to-tail" development is called the **cephalocaudal developmental trend.** (It is not a rule, a law, or even a principle, but just a trend.) The cephalocaudal trend explains the top-heavy appearance of embryos and fetuses. At nine weeks gestation, the head is about the same length as the rest of the body combined. Similarly, development usually proceeds from the middle of the body outward. This "near-to-far" development is the **proximodistal trend.** The embryo develops the trunk, and then buds for arms and legs begin to form. The buds for arms grow from the shoulder outward to the fingers. Similarly, legs grow outward from the hips to the toes.

Finally, there are the developmental processes of **differentiation** and **integration.** In the biology of prenatal development, cells become differentiated into distinct and specialized layers. The embryo has three layers—the ectoderm, mesoderm, and endoderm. Cells within the layers soon become integrated into organs or systems, such as the heart and circulatory system.

Prenatal Influences and Teratogens

So far in our study of prenatal development, we have described only normal developmental processes. The predictable and predetermined sequence outlined would presumably occur under ideal environmental conditions. These ideal conditions include a well-developed amniotic sac with a cushioning of amniotic fluid; a fully functional placenta and umbilical cord; an adequate supply of oxygen and nutrients; and freedom from disease organisms and toxic chemicals. What we have not considered is the effect on the fetus of any alteration in these conditions.

Table 4-1 Three Stages of Prenatal Development

	TIME	DEVELOPMENT
GERMINAL PERIOD	**0–2 WEEKS**	
Fertilization	0	Ovum impregnated by sperm
		Fertilized egg is called a zygote
Rapid cell division	2hrs–12th day	Ball of 70+ cells forms
Implantation	12th–14th days	Blastula embedded in wall of uterus
EMBRYONIC PERIOD	**2 WEEKS–2 MONTHS**	
Nourishing structures	1st–4th weeks	Amniotic sac, placenta, chorion, and umbilical cord form
Cellular structures	1st–4th weeks	Ectoderm, mesoderm, and endoderm evolve
Heart and nervous system	3rd–4th weeks	Start to form and function
Head	3rd–4th weeks	Forms and grows rapidly
Organs and limbs	4th–8th weeks	Arms, legs unfold; lungs and digestive, excretory systems form
Facial features	4th–8th weeks	Eyes move to side of head; mouth, ears form
FETAL PERIOD	**2 MONTHS–9 MONTHS**	
Eyes	8th–12th weeks	Irises and nerves are in place
Teeth	8th–12th weeks	Form under the gums
Ears	8th–12th weeks	Develop
Fingernails and toenails	8th–12th weeks	Appear on limbs
Sex organs	8th–12th weeks	Penis and scrotum in male, labia in female appear
Glands	8th–12th weeks	Thyroid and thymus form
Internal organs	8th–12th weeks	Pancreas, kidneys develop; liver, lungs, stomach start to work
Bone structure	12th week	Ribs and spine begin to change from cartilage
Vocal cords and taste buds	12th week	Are formed
Body	4th–6th months	Lengthens, is covered by hairy fuzz, replaces skin cells, starts moving so mother feels it
Face	4th–6th months	Grows lips, eyebrows, and eyelashes
Heart muscle	4th–6th months	Beats 120–160 times per minute
Hands	5th month	Acquire strong grip
Skin/oil glands	5th month	Secrete protective coating called vernix caseosa
Hair	5th month	Develops fine body hair (languo), eyebrows, eyelashes
Eyes	6th month	Completely formed, eyelids can open
Head	6th month	Hair grows
Fetus	24th–26th weeks	Viable, may survive outside mother's body if in incubator
Body	7th month	Weighs 1.4 kilograms, nervous system can control breathing and swallowing
Brain	7th month	Forms tissues for sensory, motor activities; can experience pain, touch, and sound
Body	8th month	Increases in length to 43 or 46 centimetres, weighs 1.8 to 2.7 kilograms, forms fatty layers under skin for use after birth
Baby	9th month	Continues to grow, turns in head-down position for birth, loses fuzzy body covering, weight gain slows, "drops"
Mother	Last week or two before birth	Uterus settles lower in pelvic area, muscles begin painless contractions, placenta starts to break down

Most pregnancies result in full-term, healthy, well-developed babies. In most cases, the protective system of shielding in the uterus and filtering through the placenta works efficiently. However, some babies (from 5 to 8 percent of live births) are born with birth defects. These defects range from gross anomalies that spell certain and almost immediate death for the newborn to minimal physical or mental defects that may have little impact on the child's future development. Although we might like to assume that birth defects happen only to other people's babies and are probably caused by some inherited traits, they can happen to anyone, and only a small proportion are the result of inherited factors. The majority of birth defects are caused by environmental influences during the prenatal period or childbirth or by the interaction of heredity and environmental influences (see Chapter 3).

The study of developmental abnormalities is called **teratology** (derived from the Greek word *tera*, which means "monster"). A teratogenic agent, or **teratogen,** is the specific agent that disturbs the development of the fetus—a virus or chemical, for example. In revealing the causes of abnormalities in infants, teratology also helps us to understand the normal process of development and to prevent defects and abnormalities whenever possible.

Early studies of teratogens tended to focus on physical birth defects, visible at birth and assumed to be caused by the mother's exposure to teratogens during the pregnancy. More recent studies, however, are much broader, examining the following kinds of teratogens:

1. Teratogens that affected the mother before she conceived the baby. For example, the drug Accutane, used to treat severe acne, remains in the body for several months after the last dose because it is stored in fat. Therefore, a fetus could be exposed to Accutane, even though the mother had stopped taking the drug months before conceiving. Women on Accutane are advised to wait at least six months to a year after their last doses before trying to get pregnant (Gravelle, 1990).

2. Teratogens that affect the baby through the father, either directly by altering his sperm or indirectly by transferring from the father to the pregnant mother. For example, dangerous chemicals on the father's clothes can be transferred to the pregnant woman if she handles his clothing. Men who smoke have a higher risk of fathering a child with kidney and urinary tract defects (Li et al., 1996). An ambitious study of 22 192 children born with birth defects in British Columbia showed that fathers who were firefighters had a higher rate of babies born with heart defects (Olshan, Teschke, & Baird, 1990). Firefighters are often exposed to carbon monoxide and other chemicals in smoke and soot, and these chemicals are suspected to be teratogens. Other teratogens associated with the father's workplace are lead, solvents in paint, and chemicals used in the petroleum industry (Kantor, Curnen, Meigs, & Flannery, 1979; Savitz & Chen, 1990; Taskinen et al., 1989). Many people believe that chemicals used in the Gulf War caused birth defects, but a recent study fails to confirm this conclusion (Cowan, DeFraites, Gray, Goldenbaum, & Wishik, 1997). The rate of birth defects among children fathered by Gulf War veterans did not differ from that among children fathered by military personnel who did not fight in the Gulf War.

3. Teratogens that produce behavioural, learning, and psychological problems, rather than physical birth defects. For example, babies exposed to heroin or methadone prenatally are born addicted and have to go through drug withdrawal. Withdrawal symptoms include irritability, sweating, jitteriness, diarrhea, and vomiting. In addition, these babies often have learning and behavioural problems by the time they reach school-age (Zuckerman & Brown, 1993).

4. Teratogens that produce effects that do not become apparent until the person is much older. For example, mothers who took the hormone diethylstilbestrol (DES) to help prevent miscarriage have daughters who have an increased risk of developing vaginal and cervical cancers in early adulthood. Sons of these mothers have an increased risk of developing testicular cancer in early adulthood (Briggs, Freeman, & Yaffe, 1986).

teratology The study of developmental abnormalities or birth defects.

teratogens The toxic agents that cause these disturbances.

Critical Periods

During prenatal development, the effects of many environmental conditions depend on the relative stage of development, that is, the point in the developmental sequence when the change in the prenatal environment occurs. Unfortunately, many environmental effects on prenatal development occur before a woman is even aware of her condition. She may not be particularly concerned about her nutritional needs, not especially worried about minor diseases like rubella (German measles) or influenza, not thinking about the potential harmful effects of any drugs that she may be taking. In short, the damage is often done before a woman knows that there is an unborn child to worry about.

A critical period is the time when an organ, a structure, or a system is most sensitive to a particular influence. Figure 4-3 illustrates the critical periods in prenatal development, highlighting when specific organs and systems can be most seriously harmed.

The timing and nature of critical periods can be seen in the range of effects of the drug thalidomide. Thalidomide was prescribed as a mild tranquilizer for pregnant women, mostly in Great Britain and Germany in 1959 and 1960. It relieved insomnia and nausea and other symptoms of morning sickness. Within the next two years, as many as 10 000 deformed babies were born, and the deformities were attributed to the mothers' intake of thalidomide. A careful study of the history of these pregnancies showed that the nature of the deformity was determined by the timing of the mother's use of the drug. If the mother took the drug between the 34th and 38th day after her last menstrual period, the child had no ears. If she took the drug between the 38th and 47th days, the child had missing or deformed arms. If she took the drug between the 40th and 45th days, the child had defects in the intestines or gall bladder. If she took the drug between the 42nd and 47th days, the child had missing or deformed legs (Schardein, 1976).

Figure 4-3

Critical periods in prenatal development. Green represents highly sensitive periods; blue represents less sensitive periods.

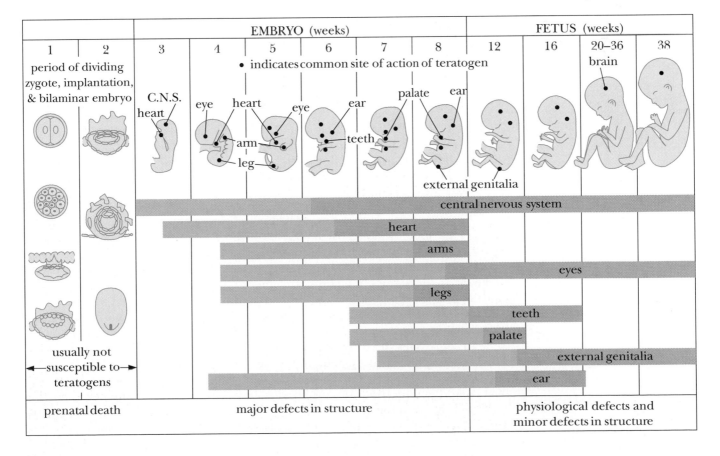

Exposure to the same teratogen, therefore, has different outcomes in the three periods of prenatal development. In the germinal period, the baby-to-be is either unaffected or affected so severely that it is miscarried. In the embryonic period, there is the greatest risk of physical birth defects. At this stage, the baby is most vulnerable to teratogens. And in the fetal period, functioning of organs (especially the brain) is most affected. Of course, as in most aspects of development, there are exceptions. For example, malnutrition has a greater effect in the last three months of the pregnancy than in the embryonic stage (Bauerfeld & Lachenmeyer, 1992).

Types of Prenatal Influences

What factors influence prenatal development? According to some common myths, the fetus is a perfect parasite, completely protected within the mother's uterus. But according to other common myths, practically everything the mother experiences affects the fetus—for instance, a child's bright red birthmark may be attributed to the strawberries the mother ate while pregnant. Current thinking about teratogens falls between the extremes of common myths. Some teratogens, like alcohol, affect the fetus directly by passing from the mother's blood into the placenta. Other teratogens influence the fetus indirectly by changing the uterine environment (that is, by changing the temperature or level of oxygen available from the mother's blood).

The variety of factors that have been found to influence prenatal development is impressive—even frightening. Nutrition, drugs, diseases, hormones, blood factors, radiation, maternal age at the time of conception, stress, and type of prenatal care all play a part in the development of the child. There is some concern that even though we know about the effects of many environmental factors, there are still drugs and other agents whose influences on the fetus have not yet been determined. It is relatively easy to study the direct effects of a drug like thalidomide on the infant's physical structure. However, it is much more difficult to discover the subtle neurological changes that lead to a learning disability at age 7 as a result of heavy air pollution (Needleman, Schell, Bellinger, Leviton, & Alfred, 1990). Table 4-2 summarizes the effects of different teratogens.

Nutrition   One of the most important elements of the prenatal environment is nutrition. As the following excerpt points out, the effects of a lack of proper prenatal nutrition can extend throughout an individual's life span:

> A fetus, malnourished in the womb, may never make up for the brain cells and structures that never came properly into being. Malnutrition both before and after birth virtually dooms a child to stunted brain development and therefore to considerably diminished mental capacity for the rest of his life. (Rosenfeld, 1974b, p. 59)

A mother's imbalanced diet, a vitamin deficiency, or deficiencies in the metabolism of the mother may cause fetal malnutrition. Folic acid is a type of B vitamin found in dark green vegetables, beans, peas, nuts, liver, and oranges. Deficiencies in folic acid increase the risk of spina bifida, a type of neural tube defect that can cause paralysis. In 1998, the Canadian government took steps to prevent folic acid deficiencies by passing regulations requiring that white flour be enriched with folic acid. The intent of the regulation is to reduce the number of children born with neural tube defects—currently about four hundred a year, according to Health Canada.

In some cases the fetus is unable to use the nutrients supplied by the mother. This complication may happen because of metabolic disorders, genetic abnormalities, or problems in the placenta. The most notable symptoms of fetal malnutrition are low birth weight, smaller head size, and smaller size overall, compared with newborns who have been in utero for the same amount of time (Metcoff et al., 1981; Simopoulos, 1983). Malnourished pregnant women also often have spontaneous abortions, give

Table 4-2 Summary of the Effects of Teratogens

TYPE OF TERATOGEN	INCREASED RISKS
Diseases and conditions of the mother	
Rubella	— Blindness, deafness, microcephaly (unusually small head and brain), mental retardation, cerebral palsy, heart defects
	— Risk is greatest in the first twelve weeks of the pregnancy (52 percent affected) and near zero risk in the last three months of the pregnancy
Chicken pox	— Facial or limb deformities
Lyme disease	— Heart defects, brain damage
Diabetes	— Delayed growth, spina bifida, cardiovascular abnormalities, malformed legs
Toxoplasmosis (a parasite found in cat feces and raw meat), herpes virus, syphilis, cytomegalovirus	— Blindness, deafness, brain damage, mental retardation, heart defects
Major life stresses (loss of job or spouse, victim of violence)	— Preterm labour and delivery
	— Low birth weight
Malnutrition	— Most risk in the last three months of the pregnancy; preterm labour and delivery
	— Low birth weight; newborn is apathetic, anxious, withdrawn, and irritable
Folic acid vitamin deficiency	— Spina bifida in people who are genetically vulnerable to this disorder
AIDS	— Some babies are born HIV positive
Mother's exposure to environmental toxins	
Radiation from atomic bombs	— Effects vary with distance from the explosion
	— Within .8 kilometres—miscarriage
	— Within 2 kilometres—microcephalic (unusually small head and brain)
	— Beyond 3.2 kilometres—born healthy, but risk of later developing leukemia
Radiation from cancer cobalt treatments	— Brain damage
Mercury-contaminated fish	— Malformations, mental retardation
Lead	— Mental retardation
PCBs (found in chemical transformers)	— Premature labour and delivery, low birth weight
	— Babies have weak reflexes, startle easily, and experience motor delays
Drugs taken by the mother during the pregnancy	
Tetracycline (type of antibiotic)	— Staining of the baby's teeth
Accutane (used to treat severe acne)	— Head and facial deformities
Dilantin (anticonvulsant used to treat epilepsy)	— Malformed arms and legs
	— Facial deformities
Methotrexate (type of chemotherapy used to treat cancer)	— Deformities of the eyes, ears, head, and skeleton
Thalidomide (antinausea drug prescribed in the late 1950s and early 1960s)	— Deformed or missing arms, missing ears, deformed or missing legs, defects in the intestines and gall bladder
Alcohol	— Fetal alcohol syndrome in heavy drinkers (see the box "Smoking and Alcohol: The Effects on the Fetus")
	— Exposure in the first twelve weeks is associated with physical malformations
	— Exposure later in the pregnancy is associated with small size, learning difficulties, lack of coordination, and behavioural problems
	—Breech birth
	— Problems persist into adulthood

Table 4-2 Summary of the Effects of Teratogens *(continued)*

TYPE OF TERATOGEN	INCREASED RISKS
Drugs taken by the mother during the pregnancy *(continued)*	
Marijuana	— Low birth weight
	— Babies have tremors, decreased responsiveness, and a high-pitched cry
	— At age 4 years score low on tests of memory and verbal abilities
Cocaine	— Low birth weight, brain damage, preterm labour and delivery, malformed limbs
	— Newborn is excessively sleepy, irritable, easily overstimulated, and responds poorly
	— At school-age, preliminary findings of learning disabilities and behavioural problems
Heroin (type of opiate)	— No known birth defects but baby is born addicted and must go through withdrawal (can cause death)
	— Withdrawal symptoms include irritability, sweating, jitteriness, diarrhea, vomiting
	— Growth retardation, brain abnormalities
Methadone (type of opiate)	— Baby is born addicted and goes through withdrawal similar to that of heroin
	— Baby may show signs of restlessness, agitation, tremors, and sleep disturbance for three to six months after withdrawal
	— Babies are difficult to console when crying
	— Poor motor coordination and seizures
	— Growth retardation (but less than for heroin), abnormal brain development
	— When school-aged, often require special education, repeat grades, have behavioural problems, are inattentive, and have poor self-discipline
Smoking tobacco	— Miscarriage, low birth weight, stillborn, sudden infant death syndrome, kidney problems, defects of the abdominal wall, brain damage
	— At school-age, learning difficulties
Barbiturates (type of tranquilizer)	— Learning disabilities
Aspirin in large doses	— Excessive bleeding
DES (hormone to prevent miscarriage)	— Abnormal genitals
	— Later risk of vaginal and cervical cancer in females and testicular cancer in males, sterility in males
Father's exposure to teratogens	
Smoking tobacco	— Damage to the kidneys and urinary tract
Drinking alcohol	— Abnormal sperm with damaged DNA
	— Behavioural problems
Exposure to lead, some anticancer drugs, nuclear radiation, toxic smoke, chemicals used in waste treatment plants, dioxin-containing herbicides	— Miscarriage
	— Variety of birth defects

Sources: Abel, 1990, 1992, 1995; Bauerfeld & Lachenmeyer, 1992; Briggs, Freeman, & Yaffe, 1986; Gravelle, 1990; Gray & Yaffe, 1986; Li et al., 1996; Morse, Lessner, Medvesky, Glebatis, & Novick, 1991; Nordentoft et al., 1996; Purvis, 1990; Zuckerman & Brown, 1993.

birth prematurely, or lose their babies shortly after birth; even less-severe nutritional deficiencies can cause problems that last a lifetime (Bauerfeld & Lachenmeyer, 1992).

In countries ravaged by famine or war, the effects of malnutrition on child development are clear. There are high rates of miscarriages and stillbirths, and children born to malnourished mothers quickly develop diseases and fail to thrive unless immediate dietary adjustments are made. Even in developed societies, it is estimated that from 3 to 10 percent of all live births show indications of fetal malnutrition (Simopoulos, 1983). According to Zeskind and Ramey (1978), most cases of fetal malnutrition occur in low-income families. The truly unfortunate outcome is that reduced brain development in the late fetal period and early infancy probably is never overcome. However, if previously well-nourished mothers go through a temporary

The effects of malnutrition on child development are painfully apparent in countries ravaged by famine or war.

period of malnutrition during pregnancy, but the baby has a good diet and responsive caregivers after birth, there may be no long-lasting deficits (Stein & Susser, 1976).

Therefore, if the period of malnourishment has been relatively short, it can sometimes be compensated for with infant nutrition programs or with combined health, nutrition, and child-care programs. H.G. Birch and J.D. Gussow (1970) have cited a range of studies in which carefully controlled nourishment programs for expectant mothers resulted in full-term, healthy babies. Research indicates that short-term malnutrition of the mother during pregnancy may have relatively minor effects on the fetus. Evidence is based on a study of pregnant women who, during the blockade in Holland in World War II, were on limited rations for as long as three months during their pregnancies. These women were not starving, but they were seriously undernourished. Although there was a slight rise in the rate of stillborn babies and spontaneous abortions, those infants who survived were remarkably healthy once food was readily available, and they made up their initial low weight. Follow-up tests of these individuals at age 19 indicated no apparent reduction in intelligence and no marked behavioural abnormalities (Stechler & Shelton, 1982).

Research with animals demonstrates that the mother can buffer the fetus from the effects of malnutrition by drawing on her own stored resources, and she can also protect her own tissues from serious long-term drain. Both mother and fetus, therefore, appear capable of recovery from limited malnutrition (Jones & Crnic, 1986). But if the mother becomes pregnant shortly after the birth of the first child, the second pregnancy may further deplete her body's reserves and compromise the health of the second child.

The importance of nutrition during pregnancy is widely known and has fuelled the creation of a number of programs for pregnant women and infants in several Canadian communities. The Montreal Diet Dispensary provides nutritional counselling and food supplements to low-income pregnant women. In Toronto and Vancouver, the Healthiest Babies Possible program provides milk supplements and nutritional counselling to pregnant women who are at risk for malnutrition (Guy, 1997).

Drugs and Chemical Agents Drugs administered during pregnancy may adversely affect the developing fetus and neonate. Harmful drugs include not just illicit ones, but also prescription drugs and nonprescription over-the-counter medications. Before taking any drugs, pregnant women should consult their physicians. The majority of Canadian women report taking no prescription or over-the-counter drugs during

FOCUS ON AN ISSUE

Smoking and Alcohol: The Effects on the Fetus

Few people these days encourage pregnant women to smoke or drink. Since 1957, when the first reports appeared on the effects of cigarette smoking on fetal development, the link between smoking and fetal abnormalities has become increasingly clear. But as recently as the mid-1970s, many doctors advised their patients that moderate drinking was harmless or even good for their mental health. We are now learning that this is not so.

SMOKING

Each time the mother smokes a cigarette, the heart of the fetus beats more quickly. Among heavy smokers, a rate much higher than the norm is found for spontaneous abortions, stillbirths, and prematurity. Babies born to heavy smokers tend to weigh less at birth than those born to nonsmokers (Nordentoft et al., 1996; Streissguth, Sampson, Barr, Darby, & Martin, 1989; Vorhees & Mollnow, 1987). Richard Naeye (1979, 1980, 1981) has examined the extensive research studies on smoking conducted over the past 25 years, and makes the following points:

1. Newborns whose mothers smoke during pregnancy weigh approximately 200 grams less than newborns whose mothers do not smoke.

2. The more cigarettes a mother smokes per day, the smaller the newborn.

3. This growth disadvantage may continue for several years after birth.

4. Mothers who stop smoking during pregnancy often have normal-sized babies.

5. Smoking during pregnancy can also

lead to congenital malformations, neonatal pneumonia, and a higher rate of newborn mortality. Li et al. (1996) recently found a higher rate of kidney and urinary tract problems in babies born to smokers.

Richard Naeye continues to examine the effects of maternal smoking during pregnancy. In a large follow-up study conducted on thousands of children, he has found that 7-year-olds whose mothers smoked 20 or more cigarettes per day scored lower on tests of spelling and reading and had a shorter attention span than did chil-

Each time the mother smokes a cigarette, the heart of the fetus beats more quickly.

dren of light smokers or nonsmokers (Vorhees & Mollnow, 1987).

How does smoking damage fetuses? Research points to the placenta. The placenta is the site of an exchange between the blood of the mother and of the fetus. The mother's blood provides nutrients and oxygen to the fetus, along with many other substances. The fetus, in turn, passes waste materials out of its system to the mother's, where they can be dissipated. Some forms of damage to the placenta occur only among women who smoke, and other forms of damage occur often among women who smoke (Naeye, 1981). Researchers also suggest that smoking can constrict blood vessels in the uterus, reducing the flow of nutrients

to the placenta (Fried & Oxorn, 1980). Both effects can reduce the amount of oxygen and nutrients supplied to the fetus, leading to reduced birth weight and possible fetal damage.

In light of the potential for harm, many doctors urge women who are trying to become pregnant not to smoke and those who are already pregnant to stop for the duration of the pregnancy. But nicotine dependence can be powerful. Only 25 percent of pregnant women who attempt to quit smoking are successful (Oncker, 1996). Moreover, the use of nicotine gum or the patch is not recommended because

pregnancy (HRDC & Stats Can, 1996). From mothers' reports, it seems that about one in four Canadian children are exposed to over-the-counter or prescription drugs in utero. Another concern for pregnant women is exposure to chemicals, such as pesticides and paints, in the environment.

Developing structures are usually more vulnerable to drugs and chemicals than are structures that have already developed. Furthermore, some drugs may cross the placental barrier only to be trapped in the primitive system of the embryo or fetus. For example, fetal systems may be unable to handle a drug as efficiently as the maternal system can. Instead of being passed as a waste, the drug may accumulate in an organ

their effects on the fetus are unclear (Oncker, 1996).

According to the National Longitudinal Survey of Children and Youth, 23.6 percent of Canadian women smoked during their pregnancy, and 84.1 percent of this group did so throughout the entire pregnancy (McIntyre, 1996).

In addition to being affected by maternal smoking, the fetus may be affected by the mother's exposure to second-hand smoke. Nonsmoking mothers' exposure to second-hand smoke was measured by assessing nicotine levels in their hair. Those with higher levels were more likely to give birth to babies who were small for their gestational age (Nofstad, Fugelseth, Qvigstad, Zahlsen, Magnus, & Lindemann, 1998).

ALCOHOL CONSUMPTION

The consumption of alcoholic beverages by pregnant women is also being examined more closely. Since 1968, a growing body of research has indicated a relationship between drinking during pregnancy and problems with spontaneous abortion, birth defects, and learning disabilities. By the mid 1970s, it was obvious that as many as a third of the infants born to heavy drinkers (alcoholics) showed marked congenital abnormalities (Ouellette, Rosett, & Rosman, 1977). These abnormalities have been identified as part of the **fetal alcohol syndrome (FAS)** and include small size and low birth weight, mental retardation, and neurological abnormalities. Certain distinct facial characteristics also are common, such as a small head, a thin upper lip, a poorly developed indentation above the upper lip, a wide space between the margins of the eyelids, and flat cheek-

bones (Rosett, Weiner, & Edelin, 1981).

Canadian studies of FAS have been conducted in British Columbia, the Yukon, and recently Saskatchewan (Habbick, Nanson, Snyder, Casey, & Schulman, 1996). In Saskatchewan, the rate of FAS has been fairly steady since 1973, with an average of 0.585 per 1000 births. Overall, in Canada there is a higher rate of FAS in Aboriginal babies than in other babies. For instance, between 1992 and 1994, 86 percent of babies born with FAS were Aboriginal (Habbick et al., 1996). Habbick and colleagues discuss several cultural factors that might explain the high rate of FAS in Aboriginal babies, including differences in "patterns of alcohol consumption and abuse, child bearing at a later maternal age when alcohol abuse is likely to be greater, and perhaps dietary and metabolic influences" (1996, p. 206).

FAS almost always occurs among mothers who drink heavily, defined as consuming 118 or more millilitres of alcohol daily. What, then, is the effect of light to moderate drinking on the developing embryo or fetus? (Moderate drinking may be defined as consuming from 29.5 to 118 millilitres per day.) Many researchers believe that FAS is simply the worst of many abnormalities that can result from drinking during pregnancy. Similar, yet milder, abnormalities are usually called *fetal alcohol effects (FAE)* (Vorhees & Mollnow, 1987). In 1996, a new term—*alcohol-related neurodevelopmental disorder (ARND)*—was coined for FAE and subtle abnormalities associated with prenatal exposure to alcohol (Streissguth & Kanter, 1997).

Since the mid-1970s, Dr. A.P. Streissguth and her colleagues have followed a group of over 1500 children who were born in the Seattle area. They have conducted a longitudinal study to de-

termine the effects of the pregnant mother's drinking and smoking on the child's later behaviour. Even in moderate amounts, alcohol seems to be related to the increased occurrence of heart rate and respiratory abnormalities in the newborn, to the newborn's difficulty in adapting to normal sounds and lights, and to lower mental development scores at 8 months. These findings cannot be attributed to nicotine or caffeine because both were carefully controlled for in this project. At 4 years of age, the children of moderate alcohol users were less attentive and less compliant with their parents and performed less well on a laboratory test of visual attention than did children of nondrinking mothers (Streissguth, Barr, & MacDonald, 1983). While the subjects were in elementary school, Streissguth and others found evidence suggesting that learning disabilities, attention problems, and hyperactivity may be more common among children born to mothers who were defined as moderate drinkers than those born to nondrinking mothers (Briggs, Freeman, & Yaffe, 1986; Streissguth et al., 1989; Streissguth & Kanter, 1997).

Reviewing all of this evidence, many experts now advise that pregnant women abstain from alcohol. According to the National Longitudinal Survey of Children and Youth, 82.6 percent of Canadian women reported that they abstained from alcohol while pregnant; 7.1 percent reported drinking alcohol throughout the pregnancy; and 2.8 percent said that they drank alcohol only during the first three months of the pregnancy (McIntyre, 1996). The validity of these self-reports has not been confirmed. They may be accurate, or the women may be reporting one thing and doing another. This is a problem with self-report data in general.

or a system of the fetus. Although a drug has been found "safe" for use by adults, it does not necessarily follow that it will not harm the fetus.

Many chemical substances in the mother's environment may be harmful to the fetus, yet pregnant women have little or no control over some of them. For example, in the late 1950s, an industrial plant in Japan discharged waste containing mercury into the ocean. People living in the surrounding community had children born with profound retardation and neurological impairment. It was found that the mercury had worked its way up the food chain in the ocean's system and had become deposited in the larger fish. Fish was the principal food source for many of these people (Reuhl &

fetal alcohol syndrome (FAS)
Congenital abnormalities, including small size, low birth weight, certain facial characteristics, and possible mental retardation, resulting from maternal alcohol consumption during pregnancy.

Chang, 1979). Mercury is also present in birds and marine mammals, such as seals and beluga whales. Marine mammals are staples in the diets of Aboriginal peoples in Canada's north. Recently, researchers found high levels of mercury in blood samples taken from the umbilical cords of Canadian infants born to mothers who eat the fat of marine mammals or the eggs of mercury-infected birds (Muckle, Dewailly, & Ayotte, 1998). The researchers also found high levels of another teratogen, polychlorinated biphenyls (PCBs). The main approach to preventing human exposure to these teratogens has been an attempt to reduce their presence in the environment. The production of PCBs is no longer permitted in Canada. Another approach would be to change the diet of people who eat mercury- and PCB-contaminated food. However, changing people's diets would open up a whole new set of problems because marine mammals provide essential vitamins, proteins, minerals, and other nutrients. If they are no longer part of the diet, "communities could see a higher incidence of premature births, dental decay, anemia in children and adults, diabetes, and problems associated with obesity and heart illness" (Muckle et al., 1998, p. 24).

Another environmental concern is lead poisoning of mothers and infants. The exposure to moderate levels of lead, either prenatally or after birth, impairs infants' cognitive development. Affected children have slower reaction time, have difficulty maintaining attention, and are more distractible, disorganized, and restless. Even in the 1980s, when we had reduced the levels of lead in car emissions, infants born in our cities had high enough levels of lead in their blood to produce lifelong behavioural deficits (Vorhees & Mollnow, 1987).

The damaging effects of mercury and lead are well established. Several other chemicals found in the environment are suspected to have negative effects. One study compared newborns whose mothers consumed fish contaminated with PCBs (a common set of compounds found in electrical transformers and paint) during pregnancy with a control group of normal infants (Jacobson, Jacobson, Schwartz, Fein, & Dowler, 1984). The infants exposed to this toxic substance showed weak reflexes and motor immaturity, and they startled more. Also, more babies than normal were born prematurely or were small for their gestational ages. Research continues into a wide range of other potential environmental toxins, including food preservatives, insecticides, and even some cosmetics and hair dyes.

In summary, then, the effects of drugs are difficult to predict. What may have no effect on animals or on women who are not pregnant may be very harmful to a rapidly developing fetus. In addition, there are wide individual differences in infants and mothers in their vulnerability to drugs. It is generally advised that women be extremely cautious in ingesting drugs during pregnancy—and even while breast-feeding.

Diseases Many diseases do not appear to affect the embryo or fetus at all. For example, most kinds of bacteria do not cross the placental barrier, so even a severe bacterial infection in the mother may have little or no effect on the fetus. On the other hand, many viruses—particularly rubella, syphilis, herpes, poliomyelitis, and many varieties of viral colds—do cross the placental barrier. The example of rubella (or German measles) has been carefully studied. This disease may cause blindness, heart defects, deafness, brain damage, or limb deformity, depending on the specific time in the developmental sequence that the mother contracts it.

In general, disease may produce infections that gain entry to the fetus by one of two routes: the transplacental route—taken by infections such as AIDS and rubella—and the ascending cervical-amniotic route—taken by venereal diseases, such as syphilis and gonorrhea. The cervical-amniotic route essentially infects the amniotic fluid first, and then the fetus. Maternal infections may affect the fetus in a variety of ways. They may infect the fetus and produce miscarriage, stillbirth, or severe deformity. They may produce death in infancy or defective or malformed tissues and organs. Or, they may produce no effect at all—especially in women who have immunities for the diseases to which they are exposed. It is important to remember that once an infection reaches the fetus it may produce extremely severe effects, since the fetus lacks an immune system to battle it.

Question to Ponder

Newspapers across the country carried the story of a judge in Winnipeg who ordered a pregnant woman into treatment for sniffing glue. Is this order ethical? Is society more responsible for protecting the rights of the unborn child or for respecting the freedom of the woman to regulate her own behaviour?

FOCUS ON AN ISSUE

Critical Thinking about Teratogens and Birth Defects

It is difficult to study the effects of teratogens because it is unethical to manipulate them in experiments on humans. Some animal experiments have been done (see Bauerfeld & Lachenmeyer, 1992, for a review), but it is often unclear whether the results would generalize to humans. All of the studies on humans are correlational; thus, it is more difficult to determine cause and effect. Interpreting the effects of teratogens is complicated for the following reasons:

1. Exposure to the same teratogens at the same points in development can exert different effects on different fetuses. Individual differences in vulnerability are, in part, genetically determined, as are differences in vulnerability after birth, such as the tendency to sunburn (children who inherit darker skin can stay in the sun longer without burning). Abel (1995) recently found individual differences in the effects of alcohol on fetuses, perhaps mediated by differences in how alcohol affected the mothers.

2. It is difficult to study the effects of illicit drugs, such as cocaine or marijuana, because mothers may be reluctant to report using them. It is particularly difficult to accurately measure alcohol consumption during pregnancy. Alcohol passes through the mother's body relatively

---

It is difficult to link teratogens to later problems.

---

quickly, so after only a short time it can no longer be detected in her blood or breath. Most studies on alcohol have to rely on the mother's own reports of her drinking habits (Russell, Martier, Sokol, Mudar, Jacobson, & Jacobson, 1996). Russell et al. found that asking indirect questions, such as "How many drinks does it take to make you feel high?" or "How many drinks can you hold?" provided more reliable responses than direct questions, such as "How much do you drink?"

3. It is difficult to isolate the effects of a particular illicit drug because many drug users are multiple drug users. For example, people who smoke marijuana may also smoke tobacco and drink alcohol. As well, parents who use illicit drugs are more likely to be under emotional disturbance and psychological stress (Jacobson & Jacobson, 1996). They also may be malnourished. Thus, these factors associated with drug use, or a combination of several factors, may in reality cause perceived drug effects. A recent study on the effects of cocaine described them as "cocaine-polydrug effects" because of the difficulty in isolating the use of one drug in human studies (Brown, Bakeman, Coles, Sexson, & Demi, 1998).

4. It is difficult to link teratogens to later problems, such as learning and behavioural difficulties in school, because babies exposed to particular teratogens may also have different experiences after birth that contribute to the problems.

Stress Regardless of what folklore may say, a mother's momentary thoughts will not affect the fetus. If a woman "thinks bad thoughts," her baby will not be born with some sort of psychic burden; if she is frightened by a snake, a spider, a bat, or some other creature, the child will not begin life with a personality defect or a birthmark. In other words, a mother's grief, worry, surprise, or other short-term emotional problems will not have an effect on her unborn child.

Prolonged and intense emotional stress during pregnancy, however, can affect the developing child. During the prenatal period, the family makes adjustments for the impending birth. Sometimes this stress and change influence the emotional or nutritional state of the mother. Indeed, a family struggling with unemployment, illness, marital discord, or difficult relationships with in-laws may find a new child—especially an unplanned or unwanted one—too much of a burden. Similarly, newly married prospective parents who are still adjusting to each other's needs may not be ready to take on the additional responsibilities of parenthood. Single mothers face particularly difficult problems concerning financial and living arrangements; social support is important at this time, when they feel most alone. Teenage mothers may also face these problems, as well as the equally difficult ones involving interrupted school and social lives, parental disapproval, and the assuming of responsibilities for which they are not ready.

Prolonged stress during pregnancy may cause an expectant mother to neglect her diet, become frail or physically ill, ignore medical advice, or take harmful drugs. Furthermore, prolonged and intense emotional stress during pregnancy may cause either

The hormonal balance and tissue development in older first-time mothers may be a factor in the higher incidence of prenatal defects or abnormalities reported for this population.

chemical changes—secretions of hormones from the endocrine system—or muscular tensions that can affect the environment of the developing child (Montagu, 1950).

Rh Factor Sometimes there is incompatibility between the mother's blood and that of the developing fetus. The most well known and well studied component of blood is the Rh factor. The Rh factor is a component of the blood found in almost 85 percent of whites and nearly 100 percent of blacks; its presence makes a person's blood Rh positive, its absence, Rh negative. The two Rh types are genetically inherited and are incompatible under certain conditions. If a mother's blood is Rh negative and her baby's is Rh positive, the trouble begins.

Some of the baby's blood "leaks" into the mother's system, and the mother's body builds up antibodies that then leak back into the baby's system and attack its blood cells. No danger exists for the mother, only for the unborn child. Furthermore, the antibody build-up does not usually happen quickly enough to affect a first child, only those born later. Today, with modern obstetrical care, an Rh-negative mother can be treated after her first Rh-positive pregnancy to prevent future incompatibility problems (Freda, Gorman, & Pollack, 1966; Kiester, 1977; Queenan, 1975).

Radiation Excessive doses of radiation in early pregnancy, through the use of repeated X-rays, radium treatment administered to cancer patients, or high levels of radiation in the atmosphere (resulting from nuclear explosions, for example), have produced marked effects on prenatal development (Sternglass, 1963). Careful review of the evidence in animals, as well as in humans, indicates that moderate levels of radiation cause structural damage during the embryonic period (from two to eight weeks), and tend to cause mental retardation or mild central-nervous system damage in the period from eight to fifteen weeks of pregnancy. The effects of lower levels of radiation are not well established (Jensh, 1986).

Maternal and Paternal Age The age of the mother can have an effect on the prenatal development of the child. Over 80 percent of Canadian babies are born to mothers who

Table 4-3 Risk of Conceiving an Infant with Down Syndrome by Maternal Age

MATERNAL AGE	FREQUENCY OF DOWN SYNDROME INFANTS AMONG BIRTHS
30	1/885
31	1/826
32	1/725
33	1/592
34	1/465
35	1/365
36	1/287
37	1/225
38	1/176
39	1/139
40	1/109
41	1/85
42	1/67
43	1/53
44	1/41
45	1/32
46	1/25
47	1/20
48	1/16
49	1/12

Source: Baird & Sadovnick, 1987.

are 20 to 34 years old, about 5 percent are born to teen mothers, and about 15 percent are born to mothers over 34 (HRDC & Stats Can, 1996). The incidence of prenatal defects or abnormalities is higher for first-time mothers over 35 years of age and teenage mothers than for mothers between these ages. Although the precise reason for this difference is unclear, it is suspected that the hormonal balance and tissue development in the mother may play a role. For instance, Down syndrome occurs most often in children of mothers over age 35. As we can see in Table 4-3, the risk of Down syndrome is almost 10 times greater at age 40 than at 30. Although we understand the cause of the abnormality (an incorrect number and pairing of chromosomes), we do not yet know why it occurs more frequently to mothers in this age group. It may have to do with increasing damage to the eggs because of time for greater exposure to mutating agents, problems with meiosis in older eggs, or other unknown factors (Baird & Sadorvick, 1987).

Male factors also underlie failure to conceive or to bear a healthy child. Older men, like older women, have an increased risk of spontaneous mutations or gene replication errors during meiosis. The risk may be even greater for older men than for older women, since divisions in the male germ cell line occur with greater frequency than in females. For example, the cells lining the testicles divide throughout a man's life to provide the cells necessary for spermatogenesis (sperm production). There are relationships between paternal age and the increased incidence of cleft lip and palate, aneuploidy (abnormal chromosome numbers), and missing X chromosomes. It has also been documented that cytomegalovirus, a virus capable of producing significant birth defects, shows viral transmission through semen (Gunderson & Sackett, 1982). In addition, it has been shown that the sperm carries the extra chromosome in about 25 percent of Down syndrome conceptions (Magenis, Overton, Chamberlin, Brady, & Lorrien, 1977).

Perinatology

A new branch of medicine, **perinatology,** considers childbirth not as a single point in time but as a span of time that begins with conception and goes on through the prenatal period, delivery, and the first few months of life. In order to deal with the multifaceted health problems of this period, many specialists—including obstetricians, pediatricians, geneticists, endocrinologists, biochemists, surgeons, social workers, and psychiatrists—work in teams. Perinatologists are specialists in the management of high-risk pregnancies and deliveries. In addition to their regular medical training, these physicians must have an additional two years of training that focuses on the latest research and management of high-risk pregnancies.

The perinatologist and perinatal team work intensively with women who have high-risk pregnancies. A pregnancy may be defined as high risk if the mother has a chronic medical condition (such as diabetes, high blood pressure, or kidney disease); if the mother develops a pregnancy-induced medical condition (such as toxemia or gestational diabetes); if the mother is on medications (such as those for epilepsy or schizophrenia); if the placenta is inadequate; if there is a threatened miscarriage; if the mother is a teenager or over 40; or if the fetus is not developing normally. The majority of pregnancies are not high risk. For instance, according to the National Longitudinal Survey of Children and Youth, 6.5 percent of Canadian mothers had diabetes, 10 percent had high blood pressure, and 18.3 percent reported some other physical health problem (McIntyre, 1996). Because of the need to closely monitor high-risk mothers and fetuses, perinatal teams are usually associated with major hospitals, which have the resources necessary to support such pregnancies. Perinatal teams often are consulted prior to the pregnancy and then help the expectant mother and her baby throughout the pregnancy and delivery. They use high-tech prenatal-screening procedures, which allow for the early diagnosis

perinatology A branch of medicine that deals with the period from conception through the first few months of life.

The safety and reliability of ultrasound imagery used to inspect the fetus makes this technique popular among the medical profession.

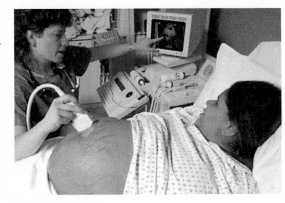

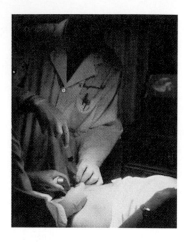

In amniocentesis, a needle is inserted into the mother's abdominal wall to obtain a sample of amniotic fluid. The cells in the fluid are then examined for genetic abnormalities.

amniocentesis A test for chromosomal abnormalities that is performed during the second trimester of pregnancy; it involves the withdrawal and analysis of amniotic fluid.

ultrasound A technique that uses sound waves to produce a picture of the fetus while it is still in the mother's uterus.

chorionic villi sampling (CVS) A prenatal screening test that involves the analysis of fetal cells for genetic disorders. It provides earlier results than amniocentesis but has a greater risk of miscarriage.

fetoscope A long, hollow needle with a small lens and light source at its end that is inserted into the amniotic sac for observation of the fetus.

alphafetoprotein A protein that when found in elevated levels in mother's blood sample may indicate abnormalities in the fetus.

and prompt medical treatment of potential problems. These techniques include amniocentesis, ultrasound, the use of fetoscopes, and maternal blood analysis.

Amniocentesis involves the withdrawal of a small amount of amniotic fluid by means of a long, thin needle with a syringe attachment. This is a relatively painless procedure in which the needle is inserted through the mother's abdominal wall into the amniotic sac. Doctors can then examine fetal cells in the fluid for various genetic defects. This procedure is usually not done until the fifteenth week of pregnancy, and it takes one to two weeks for all of the tests to be completed. An increased risk of miscarriage is associated with amniocentesis, but the risk of fetal loss is less than the risk of miscarriage by natural causes at age 35. Obstetricians routinely recommend amniocentesis for women older than 35 because of the increased incidence of birth defects found in babies born to women over this age.

The use of **ultrasound** in prenatal screening provides further information about the growth and health of the fetus. Pictures produced by ultrasound mapping show the location, position, size, and movement of the fetus. Ultrasound pictures can assist in amniocentesis by revealing a safe place to insert the needle. As early as seven weeks after conception, ultrasound pictures can diagnose pregnancy, and they can monitor the fetus's heartbeat, breathing, and movements throughout the rest of the pregnancy. Ultrasound images are used to judge the maturity of the fetus by helping to determine whether its size is proper for the number of weeks into the gestation period. They can also be used to identify a number of prenatal conditions, including defects of the fetus's neural tube, abnormal growth or development, and multiple pregnancies (Knox, 1980). As ultrasound pictures are a reliable and safe way to inspect fetuses, physicians and hospitals are using them with increasing frequency.

A newer procedure called **chorionic villi sampling (CVS)** can be conducted much earlier than amniocentesis, at around eight to twelve weeks. In this procedure, cells are drawn from the membranes surrounding the fetal tissue and are analyzed in a fashion similar to that in amniocentesis. Because more cells are collected in this procedure, the tests can be completed within a few days. This procedure involves more risk than either of the other procedures, however. A small proportion of fetuses abort spontaneously after CVS (Wyatt, 1985). When this information is given to mothers who are at high risk for a genetic defect, about half choose to wait and use amniocentesis together with ultrasound as a screening technique (Reid, 1990). When CVS is done within the first ten weeks of the pregnancy, the risk of the procedure causing limb abnormalities and fetal death increases. However, there is greater success in avoiding fetal damage in hospitals that frequently perform the procedure (Kuliev, Modell, & Jackson, 1992). If there is a serious likelihood of a genetic defect, it is clearly an advantage to have test results ten weeks into a pregnancy instead of eighteen weeks. Early abortions (before twelve weeks) are much safer and are psychologically easier for the woman.

Fetoscopy is a procedure used to inspect the fetus for limb and facial defects. In this procedure, a needle larger than that employed in amniocentesis and containing a light source is inserted into the uterus to directly view the fetus. This procedure may allow a sample of the fetal blood or tissue to be withdrawn, allowing for the prenatal diagnosis of disorders such as sickle-cell anemia, thalassemia, and hemophilia. Fetoscopy is usually not done before fifteen to eighteen weeks after conception and involves a greater risk of miscarriage and infection than does amniocentesis.

Since some of the fetus's cells enter the maternal blood stream early in pregnancy, maternal blood analysis is often a helpful diagnostic tool eight weeks after conception. The substance looked for in this test is **alphafetoprotein,** which is elevated in the presence of kidney disease, abnormal esophagus closure, or severe central-nervous system defects.

A new and exciting method of prenatal diagnosis has now been developed, called *preimplantation genetic diagnosis*. This procedure is associated with *in vitro* fertilization, in which sperm and ova are mixed together outside of the mother's body and then reimplanted in either the uterus or the Fallopian tubes. In preimplantation diagnosis, cells are removed from the embryo and analyzed for defects before the embryo is implanted inside the mother's body. In 1992, a baby girl was born to parents who were carrying the cystic fibrosis gene, detected through this procedure (Handyside, Lesko, Tarin, Winston, & Hughes, 1992). The British researchers responsible for her healthy birth suggest that this costly procedure may be helpful in prenatal diagnosis of such disorders as Duchenne muscular dystrophy, sickle-cell disease, and Tay-Sachs.

Summary and Conclusions

The prenatal period is a time of rapid growth and development that begins when the ovum and sperm unite in the Fallopian tubes. Such a union is not possible for couples who have fertility problems. Fortunately, advances in medical technology have created alternatives, so that fertilization can occur outside the Fallopian tubes. Fertilization outside the woman's body is called *in vitro* fertilization.

Once fertilization occurs, the new life starts its journey toward birth. During the germinal period, the fertilized egg continues to divide and moves slowly down the Fallopian tubes and into the uterus. Once implantation occurs, the embryonic period has begun. This period lasts until the third month. During the embryonic period, 95 percent of the body parts become differentiated and begin to function. The embryo becomes recognizably human, although very small. Development follows cephalocaudal (head downward) and proximodistal (centre outward) trends. Once the fetal bones start to ossify, the fetal stage begins. During this stage, the body of the fetus continues to develop, body parts begin to function, sensation occurs, and the fetus becomes heavier and larger. By 24 weeks after conception, the fetus is able to exist—with tremendous medical support—outside the body of its mother. During the last three months, the fetus gains new skills, grows, and starts to process information from its environment, which facilitates the maturation of its nervous system. Usually between 37 to 40 weeks after the mother's last menstrual period, the baby is born. Some obstetricians allow pregnant women to go to 43 weeks if all is well with the baby.

This maturational process is far from automatic. A number of things can go wrong. Environmental factors can work alone or combine to produce malformed or malfunctioning organs. Drugs, radiation, age, disease, and various internal factors can affect the fetus. Any factor that can affect the fetus is called a teratogen. Teratogens can exert their influence through the mother or by altering the father's sperm. Teratogens can cause physical and behavioural changes apparent at birth or later in development. It is difficult to isolate the effects of particular teratogens because studies of them are correlational. Perinatology is a new branch of medicine that focuses on high-risk pregnancies. It sometimes involves the use of prenatal screening procedures, such as amniocentesis, ultrasound, CVS, fetoscopy, and analysis of the mother's blood for alphafetoprotein.

Key Terms and Concepts

alphafetoprotein (p. 120)

amniocentesis (p. 120)

amniotic sac (p. 100)

blastula (p. 98)

cephalocaudal developmental trend (p. 106)

chorion (p. 100)

chorionic villi sampling (CVS) (p. 120)

differentiation (p. 106)

ectoderm (p. 100)

embryonic period (p. 97)

endoderm (p. 100)

Fallopian tubes (p. 96)

fertilization (p. 96)

fetal alcohol syndrome (FAS) (p. 115)

fetal period (p. 97)

fetoscope (p. 120)

germinal period (p. 97)

gestation period (p. 102)

implantation (p. 98)

integration (p. 106)

in vitro fertilization (IVF) (p. 97)

mesoderm (p. 100)

miscarriage (spontaneous abortion) (p. 99)

ovulation (p. 96)

ovum (p. 96)

perinatology (p. 119)

placenta (p. 100)

proximodistal developmental trend (p. 106)

sperm (p. 96)

teratogens (p. 108)

teratology (p. 108)

trimesters (p. 102)

ultrasound (p. 120)

umbilical cord (p. 100)

viable (p. 104)

zygote (p. 98)

Questions to Review

1. After a woman ovulates, what is the period of time during which she can become pregnant? Describe the process that occurs if the ovum is fertilized, and contrast it with the fate of an unfertilized ovum.

2. What is *in vitro* fertilization?

3. What is the germinal period, and what important processes do cells begin at this time?

4. What is the embryonic period? What important developments take place during this period?

5. What is the fetal period? List and describe the developmental processes of this period.

6. What are some of the advances in reproductive technology? What are the dilemmas they raise?

7. What is the purpose of the vernix caseosa?

8. Describe the cephalocaudal and proximodistal prenatal developmental trends.

9. What is a teratogen or a teratogenic agent?

10. How do environmental factors affect fetal development?

11. What is the relationship between thalidomide and the timing and nature of critical periods?

12. List the factors that have been found to influence prenatal development.

13. What is fetal alcohol syndrome?

14. What is the effect of cigarette smoking on a fetus?

15. How does prolonged and intense stress affect the environment of a fetus?

16. Why is it difficult to prove the effects of specific teratogens?

17. What methods of prenatal screening are used in perinatology?

Weblinks

www.poetsrx.com/art/ivf.html
Assisted Reproductive Technology
This site, intended for a general audience, gives more detail about the procedures involved in assisted reproductive technologies. It also has links to general information on infertility and its diagnosis and treatment.

www.pregnancycalendar.com/
Pregnancy Calendar
This informative site has articles on a wide range of topics related to pregnancy, prenatal development, birth, and infant care. As well, there is an interactive component: pregnant women may get a free, personalized pregnancy calendar.

www.acbr.com/fas/
Fetal Alcohol Syndrome
This extensive Canadian site, sponsored by the Triumf Project and the Fetal Alcohol Support Network of Toronto and Peel, has links to numerous articles and organizations related to fetal alcohol syndrome.

Childbirth and the Neonate

Hold a baby to your ear
As you would a shell:
Sounds of centuries you hear
New centuries foretell
Who can break a baby's code?
And which is the older—
The listener or his small load?
The held or the holder?

E.B. WHITE
"CONCH"

Outline CHAPTER 5

Objectives

By the time you have finished this chapter, you should be able to do the following:

✔ List and describe the three stages of childbirth.

✔ Describe the benefits and liabilities of medical advances in childbirth.

✔ Describe the neonate, including the following: neonatal adjustment, neonatal assessment, infant states, infant capacities, and temperamental differences.

✔ List the special needs of premature infants.

The Sequence of Childbirth

Childbirth is not an isolated event. It is part of a process initiated when the woman first discovers she is pregnant—or even before, as in the case of couples who plan pregnancies. Successful labour and delivery begin months before she enters the labour room. In fact, successful childbirth depends on the care the mother takes of herself and on the quality of medical attention she receives.

Labour and delivery often involve the teamwork of the father, the mother, the midwife (if she is part of the birthing process), the obstetrician, and the obstetric nurse. Labour and delivery that are most successful from a developmental viewpoint occur naturally, smoothly, and gently, with time to bond closely after the birth. However, since every pregnancy involves individuals, there is room for considerable variation, as the following comment indicates:

> Few pregnancies seem as though they could have been lifted right from the pages of an obstetrical manual—with morning sickness that vanishes at the end of the first trimester, first fetal movements felt at precisely 20 weeks, and lightening that occurs exactly two weeks before the onset of labor. Likewise, few childbirth experiences mirror the textbook—commencing with mild regular contractions, widely spaced, and progressing at a predictable pace to delivery. (Eisenberg, Murkoff, & Hathaway, 1984)

There are certain events in the last few weeks that lead up to the onset of labour. One of the first signs of impending labour is the descent of the baby's head into the birth canal, an event called *lightening*. This term refers to the sensation that the pregnant woman experiences of feeling less burdened. But with this downward movement by the baby comes the increased need for urination, since pressure is now placed on the bladder. One or two days prior to delivery the pregnant woman may experience intermittent contractions. Meanwhile, the baby's movement typically declines significantly. Once its head is engaged in the pelvis, the baby is more constricted. Finally, in response to changes in hormonal secretions, the process of childbirth begins.

We usually describe the process of childbirth as occurring in three stages: labour, the birth itself, and the delivery of the afterbirth.

Labour

labour The first stage of childbirth, typically lasting 12 to 18 hours and characterized by uterine contractions during which the cervix dilates to allow for passage of the baby.

Labour, the first stage, is the period during which the cervix of the uterus dilates to allow for the passage of the baby. Although labour can last from a few minutes to over 30 hours, it typically takes 12 to 18 hours for the first child and somewhat less for later children. It begins with mild uterine contractions, generally spaced 15 to 20 minutes apart. As labour progresses, the contractions increase in frequency and in intensity until they occur only 3 to 5 minutes apart. The muscular contractions of labour are involuntary, and the mother can best help herself by trying to relax during this period.

Labour is typically divided into three sections also. The first phase, called *latent labour,* is the longest and least intense phase of labour. Gradually, the cervix stretches and becomes dilated, creating an opening to allow for passage of the baby through the birth canal. The second phase, *active labour,* is usually shorter than the first, lasting an average of 2 to 3½ hours for first babies and often less time for later-born children. During this phase, the contractions become stronger and more frequent, usually occurring 3 to 4 minutes apart and lasting 40 to 60 seconds. The final stage, referred to as *advanced active* or *transitional labour,* is the most demanding and exhausting phase. This stage may last only 5 to 10 minutes, but the intensity of contractions picks up dramatically. They become very strong, occurring 2 to 3 minutes apart and lasting 60 to 90 seconds, with intense peaks that continue for most of the contraction. By the end of this phase, the cervix is fully dilated and the final pushing is ready to begin.

false labour Painful contractions of the uterus without dilation of the cervix.

birth The second stage of childbirth, which is the time between full cervix dilation and the time when the baby is free of the mother's body.

Some mothers experience **false labour,** especially with the first child. It is often difficult to distinguish false labour from real labour, but one test that often works is to have the expectant mother walk about. Real labour usually becomes more uncomfortable with simple exercise, but the pains of false labour tend to diminish. In addition to the false labour around the due date, during the last four to six weeks many women have increasing numbers of usually painless contractions, which are caused by the pressure of the heavier baby on the abdominal muscles and its increasing pressure on the pelvis.

During labour, two other events must occur. First, a mucous plug that covers the cervix is released. This process is called *showing* and may cause some bleeding. Second, the amniotic sac, or "bag of waters," which has enclosed the fetus, may break and some amniotic fluid may rush forth. Generally, the rush of water stops when the woman stands up because the baby's head blocks the flow. The rupture of membranes before labour begins is uncommon and occurs in less than 15 percent of pregnancies.

Two types of breech presentation. Delivery in this position is difficult for both mother and baby.

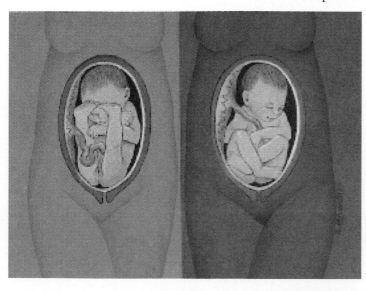

Birth

The second stage of childbirth is the actual birth of the baby. **Birth** is usually distinguished as the period between the time that the cervix is fully dilated and the time when the baby is free of the mother's body. This stage usually lasts from 10 to 40 minutes, and, like labour, it tends to last longest for a first birth. Contractions are regular, with one every two to three minutes, and they are of greater intensity and longer duration than those occurring during labour. Each birth contraction lasts about one minute, and the mother can actively assist in the birth by bearing down with her abdominal muscles during each contraction.

Normally, the first part of the baby to emerge from the birth canal is the head. It *crowns*, or becomes visible, and emerges more and more with each contraction until it can be grasped. The tissue of the mother's **perineum** (the region between the vagina and the rectum) must stretch considerably to allow the baby's head to emerge. In Western cultures, and especially in hospitals in the United States, the attending doctor often makes an incision, called an **episiotomy**, to enlarge the vaginal opening. It is believed that this incision can heal more neatly than the jagged tear that might occur if the incision were not made. Episiotomies are much less common in western Europe. Obstetricians occasionally use a steel or plastic tool, called *forceps*, or a *vacuum extractor* (a cup placed on the baby's head and connected to a suction device) to grasp the head and hasten the birth, should complications arise. Like episiotomies, forceps and vacuum extractor deliveries are more common in the United States than Europe. Recent statistics suggest that 20 to 30 percent of American births use either of these instruments, whereas only 5 percent of European births do so (Korte & Scaer, 1990).

In most normal births, the baby is born head first in a face-down position. After the head is clear, the baby's face turns to one side so that its body emerges with the least resistance. More difficult births occur when the baby is positioned in a **breech presentation** (buttocks first) or a **posterior presentation** (facing toward the mother's abdomen instead of toward her back). In each of these cases, the baby is usually assisted to prevent unnecessary injury to the mother or the infant.

Afterbirth

The expulsion of the placenta, the organ developed especially to nourish the fetus, and related tissues marks the third stage of childbirth, the delivery of the **afterbirth.** This stage is virtually painless and generally occurs within 20 minutes after the delivery. Again, the mother can help the process by bearing down. The placenta and umbilical cord (together known as the afterbirth, once they have been expelled from the uterus) are then checked for imperfections that might signal damage to the newborn.

Childbirth in Different Settings

The birth of a child follows the same biological timetable in every society, but attitudes toward childbirth differ widely from one culture or historical period to another. Among the Navaho Indians of the southwest United States, for example, women typically give birth in public, with everyone in attendance (Raphael-Leff, 1991). In traditional Laotian culture, relatives and friends visited the woman in labour. They played musical instruments, told jokes, and even made licentious comments to divert her attention (Reinach, 1901). In contrast, some cultures keep childbirth hidden. The Cuna of Panama tell their children that babies are found in the forest between deer horns; children never witness even the preparations for childbirth (Jelliffe, Jelliffe, Garcia, & DeBarrios, 1961). The cultural ideal among the !Kung-San, a tribal society in northwest Botswana, is that women tell no one about their initial labour pains and go into the bush alone to give birth. They deliver the baby, cut the cord, and stabilize the newborn—all without assistance (Komner & Shostak, 1987). The Arapesh of New Guinea focus on the "dirtiness" of birth. Labouring women are sent to the edge of the village to give birth in a place reserved for birth, menstruating women, excretion, and foraging pigs. Women need to be cleansed and purified after giving birth. Postpartum purification ceremonies are common in other societies, such as among the Hottentots in South Africa, in villages in Jordan, in the Caucasia region of Russia, in India, and in Vietnam (Raphael-Leff, 1991).

Question to Ponder
Why do you think babies are born head first?

perineum The region between the vagina and the rectum.

episiotomy An incision made to enlarge the vaginal opening during childbirth.

breech presentation The baby's position in the uterus, such that the buttocks will emerge first; assistance is usually needed in such cases to prevent injury to the mother or the infant.

posterior presentation A baby is positioned in the uterus facing the mother's abdomen rather than her back.

afterbirth The placenta and related tissues, following their expulsion from the uterus during the third stage of childbirth.

Giving Birth in Canadian Hospitals

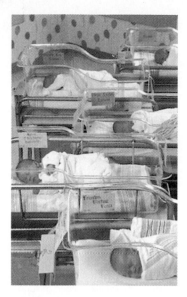

Although the technological sophistication of hospital maternity care has saved many high-risk and premature babies, it has also tended to isolate the mother and newborn from their traditional support system.

cesarean section A surgical procedure used to remove the baby and the placenta from the uterus by cutting through the abdominal wall.

Most babies in Canada are born in hospitals, out of view of society. The reason is not that our society dictates extreme modesty, such as we see among the Cuna, but rather, that hospital conditions have greatly reduced the hazards of childbirth for both infant and mother. Some deliveries require major medical intervention in the case of problems such as improper fetal position and prematurity. About 1.1 percent of all births in Canada and the United States are babies weighing less than 1500 grams, or about three pounds (Pharoah & Alberman, 1990). These babies are at least eight weeks premature and normally remain in hospital until they have reached their original due dates (Minde, 1993). In the past 40 years, obstetrical medicine has made dramatic progress in dealing with difficult deliveries. Infants who would not have survived in 1960 are now thriving in record numbers.

The new medical advances include drugs, microsurgery, diagnostic tools, and preventive measures. For instance, a vaccine given to an Rh-negative woman immediately after her first delivery can completely prevent blood incompatibility problems in future pregnancies. As we have seen in Chapter 4, procedures like amniocentesis, ultrasound, and fetoscopy can help diagnose conditions prenatally, and steps can then be taken to treat the fetus or the newborn. During high-risk labours, many hospitals routinely measure fetal heart rate using a device called a *fetal monitor*. The heart rate can alert the obstetrician to problems such as pressure on the umbilical cord, lack of oxygen, or fetal distress ("Fetal Monitoring," 1979). A fetus in distress can be delivered surgically through an incision in the mother's abdomen. This process is called a **cesarean section**, or C-section. According to the National Longitudinal Survey of Children and Youth, 18 percent of Canadian births in 1994 were by cesarean section, and 12.4 percent of vaginal births required interventions such as the use of forceps (6.9 percent) or suction (5.5 percent).

Often a hospital birth involves the mother's lying flat on her back, with her feet in stirrups. This position is useful if the mother is heavily sedated or if frequent pelvic exams are required. However, this is not the most common birthing posture around the world. In most societies women sit, stand, or walk while in labour and squat or kneel while giving birth. When women are in these postures, gravity pulls the baby downward, assisting in delivery. Women who give birth in hospitals are often encouraged not to eat while in active labour, in case they require surgery for the delivery or for complications. Instead of eating, women typically suck on ice or lollipops, and they may have intravenous (IV) if the labour is prolonged or complicated. In other, more traditional societies, labouring women are given special foods or drinks thought to open the body for childbirth, including honey, soups, herbal tea, and foods rich in vitamin B1 (Raphael-Leff, 1991). As you can see, the labour and birth experience can be quite different depending on where the woman gives birth.

Making the Hospital Experience More Natural Giving birth in hospital has had some important social side effects. Among these consequences is the removal of childbirth from the family and the community, which has resulted in the loss of rich social support. The new mother, in many cases separated even from her husband and family except during hospital visiting hours (which are typically extended for fathers), is apt to feel alone, exposed, and unsupported in one of life's major events. Segregating the mother also means that children grow up knowing little about the birth process, except what they learn from second-hand reports. Consequently, new parents are sometimes surprised at the appearance of their newborn infants—small, often wrinkled creatures, whose soft-boned heads may be misshapen after the passage through the birth canal.

In the past two decades, there has been much negative talk and writing about childbirth as a medical and surgical event, rather than as a natural and family-centred event. As a result, customs are changing.

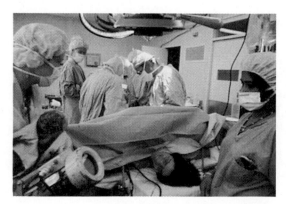

Although most births occur through the birth canal, in cases where this is either difficult or dangerous a cesarean section is advised.

In "natural" childbirth classes, parents learn to prepare as much as possible for the actual course of birth.

For example, most Canadian hospitals now have special birthing rooms that are designed to create a more relaxed, homelike setting. As well, mothers have more choices in managing the pain associated with labour and delivery. Choices range from drugs to relaxation, distraction, and breathing exercises. Concern over the effect of drugs given during pregnancy and childbirth is one of the reasons that doctors such as Grantly Dick-Read (1953) and Fernand Lamaze (1970) first suggested **"natural" childbirth.** Essentially, "natural" childbirth (we put the word in quotation marks because here it means a good deal more than having babies naturally) involves three things: (1) teaching the mother and father about labour and delivery and about exercises that can help manage the pain of labour, (2) limiting the use of medication during labour and delivery, and (3) encouraging the active participation of the mother in the birth. For instance, the monitoring of contractions better allows a woman to control and coordinate the timing of breathing and pushing with her expulsive labour contractions (Leventhal, Shacham, & Easterling, 1989). "Natural" childbirth often encourages the father to play a more active role in helping the mother through the labour and delivery and in caring for the newborn. Many hospitals permit the newborn to "room-in" with the mother, so that the family has more privacy in caring for the baby. As well, several Canadian hospitals have implemented a "short-stay" program, in which a mother and a baby without complications are sent home early, sometimes a mere 12 hours after the birth, often with follow-up nursing support in the home.

"natural" childbirth A childbirth method that involves the mother's preparation (including education and exercises), limited medication during pregnancy and birth, and the mother's (and perhaps father's) participation during the birth.

Using Midwives

Midwives, childbirth assistants who remain with a mother throughout her labour, are increasingly relieving obstetricians in supervising births with no expected complications. Midwives treat labour and delivery as natural, healthy events, and they use massage, exercises, and other nondrug techniques to help the woman cope. Midwives deliver 80 percent of the world's babies and are especially common in Sweden, Denmark, Finland, Holland, and Japan (Smith, 1987). Although midwives practise in Canada, there are some legal ambiguities about their roles and credentials (Hatem-Asmar, Blais, Lambert, & Maheux, 1996). Different types of midwives exist, the three most common being the nurse-midwife, the professional-midwife (someone who has formal training in midwifery but is not a nurse), and the lay-midwife (someone who has unregulated training and experience). Many provinces, including Alberta, New Brunswick, the Northwest Territories, and Quebec, recently initiated task forces to define the common knowledge base and skills of midwives. Two provinces, Ontario and British Columbia, passed legislation for the licensing and funding of midwifery (Clelland, 1999). As of April 1,

midwife A childbirth assistant who remains with a mother throughout labour and who can supervise births where no complications are expected; nurse-midwives have had training in hospital programs, where they have studied obstetrics.

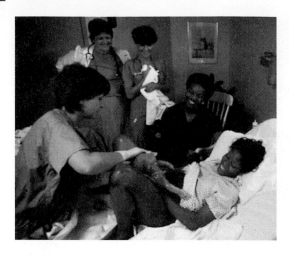

When delivery takes place at home, the mother is usually attended by a midwife.

Question to Ponder

Do you think the use of midwives in Canada will increase or decrease in the next 10 years? Which factors do you think will influence the rate at which midwives are used?

1999, midwives in British Columbia need a bachelor's degree or the equivalent. The only midwifery education programs in Canada are in Ontario (Clelland, 1999). Canada is one of only eight countries in the WHO that has not officially recognized midwifery as a legitimate medical practice (*Canada Year Book,* 1997).

Midwife-Attended Home Birth Home birth is controversial among health professionals, government, and the Canadian public. Those against it argue that it puts the mother and baby at risk. For instance, the Canadian Medical Association, as reported in Tyson (1991), described home birth as "an irresponsible act" (p. 14). Those for it argue that low-risk deliveries are better managed in comfortable surroundings that put the mother at ease and involve other family members in the birth process. Despite the controversy, the number of home births has increased in recent years. Tyson (1991) studied 1001 couples in Toronto who planned home births between 1983 and 1988. The vast majority (83.5 percent) delivered the babies at home without complication. The others (16.5 percent) required the mother, baby, or both to be transferred to hospital during the labour or shortly after the birth. Two of the infants transferred to hospital died of complications.

It is difficult for researchers to determine the relative merits of hospital and home births. In order to do so, they would have to do an experiment in which the researchers controlled which women gave birth in hospital and which at home. It is unlikely that women would agree to participate in this type of study or that the study would get ethical approval. As it stands, most studies are quasi-experiments, in that they compare women who give birth in hospital with those who do so at home. But the groups are self-selected and may have other differences that could explain differences in birth outcomes. Therefore, when researchers cite findings from these studies, they do so cautiously. The studies are not well enough controlled to enable the researchers to make strong conclusions about the merits of one type of birth practice over another.

The Infant's Experience

In this discussion of the experience of childbirth, we have almost ignored the infant's experience. If the mother has been heavily anesthetized, the infant, too, will be groggy and may need to be revived. Often, mucus is removed from the nose and mouth with a syringe. Also, it is common for the infant to cry at birth, indicating its vigorous responsiveness. Sometimes, however, the birth process is calmer than this.

Frederick Leboyer (1976), a French obstetrician, has developed a method of childbirth intended to make the birth process less stressful for the infant. He strongly objects to the bright lights, the noise, and the practice of holding the infant upside down and slapping it. He recommends that childbirth take place in a quiet, dimly lit room, that the cord remain connected for several minutes so that the infant's breathing will not be rushed, and that the baby be placed on the mother's abdomen, where the mother can gently fondle and caress her child. After a short time, the baby should be given a warm bath to relax.

Most hospitals still use bright lights and do not use the warm bath. However, most place the newborn on the mother's abdomen or chest. The cutting of the cord is more leisurely than in the past, and many infants nurse at the breast within minutes of birth (Nilsson, 1990; Young, 1982).

Even with new hospital procedures, childbirth is a remarkably stressful event for the newborn. But despite this stress, the full-term baby is well equipped to handle the event (Gunnar, 1989). In the last few moments of birth, the infant produces a major surge of adrenalin and noradrenalin, the stress hormones. The adrenalin shock counteracts any oxygen deficiency and prepares the baby for breathing through the lungs. Almost immediately, as the infant experiences the bright, noisy delivery room and the cold air, there is a first cry. The first breaths may be difficult because the fluid that was in the lungs must be expelled, and millions of little air sacs in the lungs must be filled. Yet, within minutes, most infants have established fairly regular breathing, typically with a lusty cry.

What about pain? The newborn has relatively high levels of a natural painkiller called beta-endorphins circulating in its blood system. Perhaps as a result of this substance, most infants experience a period of unusual alertness and receptivity shortly after birth. Many experts have suggested that this period of extended alertness, which may last an hour or more, is an ideal time for parents and infant to get acquainted (Nilsson, 1990).

Parent–Infant Bonding

Within minutes after birth, infant, mother, and father—if he is present—begin the process of **bonding,** or of forming an attachment. After the initial birth cry and filling of the lungs, a newborn calms down with time to relax on the mother's chest. After a little rest, she may struggle to focus her eyes on a face. She seemingly pauses to listen. The parents watch in fascination and begin talking to this new creature. They examine all of the parts—the fingers and the toes, the funny little ears. There is close physical contact, cradling, stroking. Many infants find the breast and almost immediately start to nurse, with pauses to look about. An infant who has had little or no anesthetic may enjoy a half-hour or more of heightened alertness and exploration, as his mother or father holds him close, establishes eye contact, and talks to him. The infant seemingly wants to respond. It has now been clearly established in at least eight independent laboratories and in five countries that babies are capable of doing some limited imitation of a parent. They move their heads, open and close their mouths, and even stick out their tongues in response to the facial gestures of their parents (Meltzoff & Moore, 1989).

It is now known that the baby's physical responses trigger significant physical processes within the mother's body. When the baby licks or sucks on a breast nipple, it causes increased secretion of prolactin, a hormone important in nursing, and oxytocin, another hormone that contracts the uterus and decreases bleeding. The infant also benefits from early breast-feeding. Although milk is not yet available, the mother produces a substance called *colostrum*. This substance appears to help clear the infant's digestive system.

Some psychologists believe that these early parent–infant interactions are psychologically significant in helping to establish a strong bond (see the box "Emerging Fatherhood: Changing Roles"). In one study (Klaus & Kennell, 1976) of 28 first-time, low-income, high-risk mothers, the hospital staff provided half of the mothers with 16 extra hours of infant contact in the first three days after birth. The two groups of mothers and infants were later examined at one month, one year, and two years. Over the two-year period, the extra-contact mothers consistently showed significantly greater attachments to their babies. They were more affectionate and attentive. Early extra contact may be particularly useful for teenage mothers or those who have had little or no experience with newborns, and for mothers of premature and high-risk infants, as these mothers are more likely to experience slow bonding patterns at birth owing to the difficulties of accepting their babies' shortcomings. But some researchers feel that early bonding is not quite so essential. They have found that, except for high-risk mothers and infants, the increased contact following birth made little or no difference (Field, 1979).

In general, the initial excitement and bonding is merely a foreshadowing of the depth of emotion that is to come—at least with emotionally sound parents. As one mother comments:

> I am a career woman who has always valued my logical and rational abilities. I was absolutely unprepared for the feeling I felt when I first held my

bonding Forming an attachment; refers particularly to the developing relationship between parents and infant that begins immediately after birth.

daughter. It was an overwhelming sense of wonder and thankfulness that she was alive and healthy. By the end of the first year, however, the feeling had grown to be all-encompassing. I could not imagine what life had been like before she arrived. I am aware of her every moment during my day—whether at work or with her. My husband has similar feelings. This is truly bonding ... what we felt initially was only a tiny portion of our current feelings today.

In any case, mothers and fathers who spend the early period with their babies report more self-confidence in their ability as parents and greater self-esteem. Goldberg (1983) notes the value of these feelings. She points out that because parenthood is a major transition, it is particularly important for parents to be encouraged in their new roles. She also suggests that as parents typically have an idealized image of what their baby will be like, parent–infant contact during the first few hours and days following birth may help them to adjust their expectations concerning the appearance and behaviour of their infant. Furthermore, if parents are to become attached to their baby, they need to become acquainted. Why should they delay in getting to know each other? Goldberg concludes, however, that if things do not go well in those first few days, or if the infant is premature or handicapped or the mother is ill or sedated, the relationship is not doomed—attachments can form later.

The Neonate

neonate A baby in the first month of life.

During the first month of life, a baby is known as a **neonate.** The first month is a very special period in a baby's life. It is distinguished from the rest of infancy because during this time, the baby must adjust to leaving the closed, protected environment of the mother's womb to live in the outside world. The first month is a period of both recovery from the birth process and adjustment of vital functions, such as respiration, circulation, digestion, and body-heat temperature regulation.

At birth, the average full-term baby weighs between 2.5 and 4.3 kilograms and is between 48 and 56 centimetres long. The baby's skin may be covered with the vernix caseosa, a smooth and cheeselike coating that developed during the fetal period. This coating is present especially in a cesarean delivery because it has not been wiped off during the tight passage through the birth canal. The baby's skin also may be covered with fine facial and body hairs that drop off during the first month. Temporarily, the newborn's head may look misshapen and elongated as a result of the process called *moulding*. In moulding, the soft, bony plates of the skull, connected only by cartilage, are squeezed together in the birth canal. Also, the external breasts and the genitals of both boys and girls may look enlarged. This enlargement is temporary, too. It is caused by the mother's female hormones, which passed to the baby before birth. The general appearance of the newborn, then, may be a bit of a shock to new parents, who expect to see the plump, smooth, 3- to 4-month-old infant shown in advertisements.

The Period of Adjustment

Despite their appearance, full-term neonates are sturdy little beings who are already making the profound adjustment to their new lives—from having their mothers do everything for them to functioning on their own as separate individuals. Four critical areas of adjustment are respiration, circulation of blood, digestion, and temperature regulation.

The birth cry traditionally symbolizes the beginning of the neonate's life. It also signals a major step in the child's development, for with the first breaths of air, the lungs are inflated for the first time, and they begin to work as the basic organ of the child's own respiratory system. During the first few days after birth, the neonate experiences periods of coughing and sneezing that often alarm the new mother, but they serve the important function of clearing mucus and amniotic fluid from the infant's air passages.

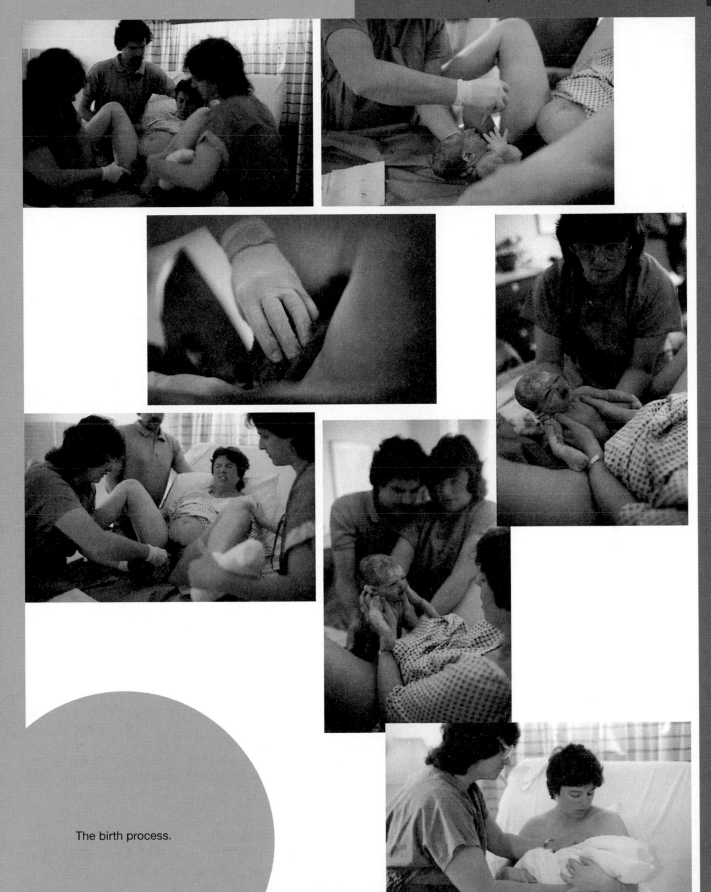

The birth process.

FOCUS ON AN ISSUE

Emerging Fatherhood: Changing Roles

George Russell awoke again feeling queasy. Ever since his wife, Kate, became pregnant and has had morning sickness, he too has felt ill in the morning. This morning was no different. George is going through what many other men with pregnant wives have experienced. Studies have indicated that between 10 and 15 percent of first-time fathers-to-be mimic some of the symptoms of their pregnant wives. They too occasionally experience nausea, abdominal discomfort, and strange cravings (Parke, 1981).

Some first-time fathers-to-be undergo a fair amount of stress as their wives go through pregnancy. It seems that mild depression, anxiety, and feelings of inadequacy are common. Among the natives of the Yucatan in Mexico, for example, pregnancy is confirmed when the woman's mate has nausea, diarrhea, vomiting, or cramps (Pruett, 1987). Not only do expectant fathers crave dill pickles with ice cream, they also have deeply troubling dreams and disturbing changes in sexual activity. It is obvious that these husbands have identified with their wives (Pruett, 1987).

Certainly, not all fathers experience such symptoms. Yet many fathers find the period of their wife's first pregnancy a time of anticipation, uncer-

---

Fathers who develop a strong bond with their infants are usually more sensitive to the child's changing needs and interests in later years.

---

tainty, changing attitudes, and changing roles. The definition of an appropriate role for fatherhood in our society has expanded in recent years.

Many fathers are now urged and encouraged by their wives and even their friends to participate directly in their child's birth. In childbirth classes, they have learned techniques of physical and emotional support for their wives. They can coach the mother through childbirth and then immediately start getting to know the newborn infant. As one mother who had had a cesarean section commented, "It was amazing. While they were stitching me up, they were taking the baby to the nursery to be bathed, weighed, and so forth. My husband disappeared with her. When he came back two hours later, he had given the baby her first bath, diapered her, and was all set to show me how to take care of babies!"

Fathers who have participated in their child's birth report an almost immediate attraction to the infant, with feelings of elation, pride, and increased self-esteem (Greenberg & Morris, 1974). Some studies report that these fathers are more deeply involved with and attached to their infants than are those who do not participate in birth and early care (Pruett, 1987). They also feel a closer relationship to their wives

---

The onset of breathing marks a significant change in the neonate's circulatory system, too. The baby's heart no longer needs to pump blood to the placenta for aeration. Instead, a valve in the baby's heart closes to redirect the flow of blood to the lungs to receive oxygen and to eliminate carbon dioxide (Pratt, 1954; Vulliamy, 1973). The circulatory system is no longer fetal; rather, it becomes entirely self-contained. The shift from fetal to independent circulatory and respiratory systems begins immediately after birth but is not completed for several days. Lack of oxygen for more than a few minutes at birth or during the first few days of adjustment may cause permanent brain damage.

Before birth, the placenta provided nourishment, as well as oxygen, for the infant. Once free of the womb, the infant must activate his own digestive system. This change is a longer, more adaptive process than are the immediate and dramatic changes in respiration and circulation.

Another gradual adjustment involves the neonate's temperature regulation system. Within the uterus, the baby's skin was maintained at a constant temperature. After birth, however, the baby's skin must constantly work to provide insulation from even minor changes in external temperature. During the first few days of life, babies must be carefully covered. Soon, they become better able to maintain their own body-heat temperatures, aided by a healthy layer of fat that accumulates during the first weeks of life.

Neonates are not all equally equipped to adjust to the abrupt changes brought about by birth, and it is essential to detect any problems at the earliest possible moment. Great advances have been made in this area in recent years. At one time, babies were considered healthy if they merely "looked" healthy. Then, in 1953, Virginia Apgar

because of this shared experience. New fathers who do not participate in childbirth and early infant play frequently feel more distant from their wives and feel somewhat ignored when the baby arrives. Often, the companionship between husband and wife is sharply reduced while the mother's focus is on the infant (Galinsky, 1980).

Many studies report that fathers who have begun a relationship with their newborns continue to provide more direct care and more play to their developing infants. This somewhat newer role of the nurturing father has many benefits for family development. In one study, infants whose fathers were actively involved in caregiving scored higher on motor and mental development tests (Pederson et al., 1979). In another, such infants were found to be more socially responsive than average (Parke, 1979). Couples report less tension, more joint goals, and shared decision making when both of them actively parent the infant. But, in evaluating these studies, we must remember that fathers who choose to have early contact with their infants may differ in many other ways from those who do not choose such contact (Palkovitz, 1985).

Actively involved fathers generally relate to their infants differently from the way mothers do. More often than not, these fathers play with their babies, while mothers wash, diaper, and feed them. Even when these fathers are involved in caretaking activities, they generally play while tending to their infants. Furthermore, the father's style of play is much different from the mother's. Fathers tend to play vigorously—tossing their babies in the air, moving their arms and legs to-and-fro, and bouncing them on papa's knee. Mothers, on the other hand, tend to coo at their babies, babble baby talk, and usually play more gently. At a very early age, infants look to their fathers with great expectations. "At only six weeks of age, babies will hunch their shoulders and lift their eyebrows, as though in anticipation that 'playtime has arrived' when their fathers appear" (Brazelton & Yogman, 1984).

Fathers who develop a strong bond with their infants are usually more sen-

sitive to the child's changing needs and interests in later years. These fathers also tend to have more influence over the child. Children are more likely to look up to and listen to these fathers because of the close, complex relationship established. It becomes clear from the research on fathers and their children in middle childhood and adolescence that fathers are instrumental in the gender identity of both their sons and daughters, and also in the achievement motivation and drive of both. The new research on fathers certainly contradicts Margaret Mead's statement, "Fathers are a biological necessity but a social accident."

devised a standard scoring system, and hospitals were able to evaluate an infant's condition quickly. We may see this scoring system, the **Apgar score,** presented in Table 5-1. The Apgar score is taken at one minute and again at five minutes after the baby's birth. The attendant observes the pulse, breathing, muscle tone, general reflex response, and colour of the skin (or the mucous membranes, palms, and soles for non-white babies). A perfect Apgar score is 10 points, with a score of 7 or more considered normal. Scores below 7 generally show that some bodily processes are not functioning fully and require at least watching and perhaps special attention. A score of 4 or less requires immediate emergency measures.

Apgar score An assessment scale of the newborn's physical condition.

Competencies of the Newborn

What can newborns do? What can they hear? How much do they see? What can they learn? We are still discovering some of the fascinating capabilities and skills that newborns possess. With the new emphasis on family interaction, parenting, and bonding, it is helpful to understand these competencies in order to see the infant as a fully participating partner in the family's social interactions.

Until the 1960s, psychologists thought that neonates were incapable of organized, self-directed behaviour. In fact, it was not uncommon to find the infant's world being described as a "booming, buzzing confusion." It was common to read in psychological literature that infants did not use the higher centres of the brain until they were almost a year old, or that newborns saw light and shadow but not objects or patterns. Behaviour in the first weeks of life was considered almost entirely reflexive. Later

Table 5-1 Apgar Scoring System for Infants

| | SCORES | | |
	0	1	2
Pulse	Absent	Less than 100	More than 100
Breathing	Absent	Slow, irregular	Strong cry
Muscle tone	Limp	Some flexion of extremities	Active motion
Reflex response	No response	Grimace	Vigorous cry
Colour*	Blue, pale	Body pink, extremities blue	Completely pink

*For nonwhites, alternative tests of mucous membranes, palms, and soles are used.

Source: From "Proposal for a New Method of Evaluating the Newborn Infant" by V. Apgar, Anesthesia and Analgesia. 1953, 32, 260. Used by permission of the International Anesthesia Research Society.

experiments have shown that we had significantly underestimated newborns. We now know that neonates are capable of organized, predictable responses and mental activity that is more complex than was expected of them. They have definite preferences and show a striking ability to learn. Moreover, they are able to attract attention to their needs. We introduce some of these concepts in this chapter, but we will more fully explore them in Chapter 6.

The key to this new understanding of infants lies in the development of more precise and creative ways of observing them. Early studies were poorly designed. They employed inadequate measurements and frequently put the infant at a disadvantage. Even adults who are placed flat on their backs to stare at a white ceiling while being covered up to their necks with blankets are not their most perceptive or responsive selves. When infants are placed tummy down on the mother's skin in a warm room, however, they will display an engaging repertoire of behaviours (Prechtl & Beintema, 1965). This and other new study techniques allow infants to respond fully to testing.

Child development researchers now know that infants are capable of more complex responses and mental activities than was previously believed.

Infant States When we watch sleeping newborns, we notice that at certain times they lie calmly and quietly, and at other times they twitch and grimace, although their eyes remain closed. Similarly, when awake, babies may be calm but are still capable of thrashing about wildly and crying.

By observing infants' activity over a considerable time, P.H. Wolff (1966) was able to separate and identify six newborn behavioural states: regular sleep, irregular sleep, drowsiness, alert inactivity, waking activity, and crying. The infant spends most of the day in either regular or irregular sleep. As the infant matures and the cortex of the brain "wakes up," these percentages shift. For example, by 4 weeks to 8 weeks of age, the typical baby is sleeping more during the night and less during the day. By the end of the first year, the typical baby is sleeping through the night. Once this occurs, parents begin to relax more and find the experience of parenting far more workable. As one working mother reported, "I no longer feel like a zombie." We can see the behaviours typical of these states presented in Concept Summary Table 5-1.

These states have a regular duration and seem to follow predictable daily cycles of waking and sleeping. The level of responsiveness in newborns depends largely on their particular behavioural state. For example, Wolff found that babies in a state of alert inactivity reacted to stimulation by becoming more active. Babies who were already in an active state had a different response: they seemed to calm down when stimulated. It is very important, therefore, to consider the state of newborns when trying to assess their reactions to outside events. In addition, since newborns spend approximately 70 percent of their time sleeping, research should be timed to their awake and alert phases. As we can see, timing of research may be difficult.

Ability to Be Soothed Crying is the infant state that causes parents and caregivers the most worry; it challenges them to discover the cause and then invent ways to stop it. Of the many techniques used to soothe babies, three stand out in their effectiveness: picking them up, providing constant rhythmic movement, and, for some, reducing the amount of stimulation that they receive from their own bodies by swaddling them in blankets. (The reason some infants sleep so well when wrapped up and taken for a ride in a car is likely that they are getting a combination of physical security and rhythmic movement.)

Newborns differ greatly in how easily they can be soothed and by which methods. Many infants quiet easily, either with their own self-comforting methods or to the sounds of an adult voice; other infants require more active soothing (Brazelton, Nugent, & Lester, 1987). Most important, some match must exist between the parents' technique

Concept Summary

Table 5-1	The Classification of Infant States
Regular sleep	The infant's eyes are closed, and he is completely relaxed. Breathing is slow and regular. The face looks relaxed, and the eyelids are still.
Irregular sleep	The infant's eyes are closed, but she engages in gentle limb movements of various sorts—writhing, stirring, stretching, and so forth. Grimaces and other facial changes occur. Breathing is irregular and faster than in regular sleep. Rapid eye movements occasionally occur.
Drowsiness	The baby is fairly inactive. The eyes are open but often close. Breathing is regular but faster than regular sleep. When the eyes are open they may have a dull, glazed quality.
Alert inactivity	The eyes are open, bright, and shining. They follow moving objects and can make good quality movements together (conjugate movement). The baby is fairly inactive, with a face quiet and not grimacing.
Waking activity	The baby frequently engages in motor activity involving the whole body. The eyes are open, and the breathing is highly irregular.
Crying	The baby has crying vocalizations combined with vigorous, disorganized motor activity.

for soothing the baby and the baby's ability to be soothed. When the match is wrong, awkward, or nonexistent, both mother and child may get themselves into behavioural patterns that later are hard to change (Brazelton, Nugent, & Lester, 1987).

Reflexes   Full-term infants confront the world with a number of complex **reflexes** and combinations of reflexes, as described in Table 5-2. It is believed that these reflexes have evolutionary survival value and reflect behaviours that have been in the past—and may still be in some ways today—necessary for the infant's ability to survive. Most of these reflexes disappear after three or four months because of increased brain development. Reflexes are regulated by primitive parts of the brain in the brain stem and are performed involuntarily. But as other parts of the brain mature, the baby gains conscious control over behaviours, and many of the reflexes drop off. Thus, an older baby who still has all of the newborn reflexes would need a neurological examination to ensure that the brain is developing properly.

The *Moro reflex* is the newborn's reaction to being startled. When newborns are startled, as by a loud sound, they react first by extending both arms to the side, with fingers outstretched as if to catch onto someone or something. They then gradually bring their arms back to the midline. Some have thought the Moro reflex to be a remnant of our ape ancestry—in the event of a fall, infant apes who grasped their mothers' hair were the most likely to survive. Another body reflex is the *tonic neck reflex*. It occurs when babies' heads are turned sharply to one side. They react by extending the arm and leg on the same side while flexing the arm and leg on the other side, in a kind of fencing position. The *stepping reflex* occurs when newborn babies are held vertically with their feet against a hard surface. They lift one leg away from the surface, and, if tilted slightly from one side to the other, they appear to be walking. The *grasping reflex* applies to newborns' toes, as well as to their fingers. Babies will close their fingers over any object, such as a pencil or finger, when it is placed on their palm. Some neonates can grasp with such strength that they support their full weight for up to a minute (Taft & Cohen, 1967).

reflex An unlearned, automatic response to a stimulus. Many reflexes disappear after three or four months.

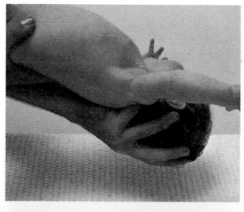
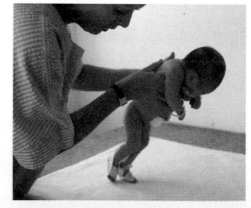

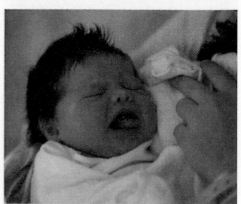

Some reflexes of the newborn: top left, Moro reflex; top right, stepping reflex; bottom left, sucking reflex; and bottom right, rooting reflex.

Table 5-2 Reflexes of the Newborn

REFLEX	DESCRIPTION
Moro (startle)	When infants are startled by loud sounds or by being suddenly dropped a few inches, they will first spread their arms and stretch out their fingers, then bring their arms back to their body and clench their fingers. Disappears after about 4 months.
Tonic neck	When infants' heads are turned to one side, they will extend the arm and leg on that side and flex their arm and leg on the opposite side, as in a fencing position. Disappears after 4 months.
Stepping (walking)	When infants are held upright with their feet against a flat surface and are moved forward, they will appear to walk in a coordinated way. Disappears after 2 or 3 months.
Placing	Similar to the stepping reflex. When infants' feet are put against a table edge, they will attempt to step up onto it. Disappears after 2 months.
Grasping (palmar)	When a pencil or a finger is placed in infants' palms, they will grasp it tightly and increase the strength of the grasp if the object is pulled away. Disappears after about 5 months.
Babkin	If objects are placed against both palms, infants will react by opening their mouths, closing their eyes, and turning their heads to one side. Disappears after 4 months.
Plantar	Similar to the grasping reflex. When an object or a finger is placed on the soles of infants' feet near the toes, they will respond by trying to flex their feet. Disappears sometime after 9 months.
Babinski	If the soles of infants' feet are stroked from heel to toes, infants will spread their small toes and raise the large one. Disappears after 6 months.
Rooting	If infants' cheeks are touched, they will turn their heads toward the stimulus and open their mouths, as if to find a nipple. Disappears after 3 or 4 months.
Sucking	If a finger is put in infants' mouths, they will respond by sucking and making rhythmic movements with the mouth and tongue. This reflex is permanent.
Swimming	Infants will attempt to swim in a coordinated way if placed in water in a prone position. Disappears after 6 months.
Ocular neck	Infants will tilt their heads back and away from a light shining directly into their eyes. This reflex is permanent.
Pupillary	The pupils of infants' eyes will narrow in bright light and when infants go to sleep, and will widen in dim light and when infants wake up. This reflex is permanent.

A useful reflex of the mouth is the rooting reflex. When one cheek is touched, babies "root," or move the mouth toward the stimulus. This movement aids them in finding the nipple. A mother who is unfamiliar with this response may try to push the infant's head toward the nipple. Because the reflex is toward, not away from, the stimulation, the baby will move toward the hand that pushes, thus seeming to reject the breast. The better maternal response to rooting is to hold the nipple and touch the baby's cheek with it. In this way, the baby turns and finds the nipple. The rooting reflex disappears by the third or fourth month (Taft & Cohen, 1967). The sucking reflex, like the rooting reflex, is clearly necessary for infant survival. Like some other reflexes, sucking begins in the uterus. Cases have been reported of babies born with thumbs already swollen from sucking.

Newborns' eyes are also capable of several reflex movements and motor patterns. The lids open and close in response to stimuli. The pupils widen in dim light and narrow in bright light; they also narrow when infants are going to sleep and widen when they wake up. Even an infant who is only a few hours old is capable of following a slow-moving object, such as a bright red ball, with its eyes (Brazelton, 1969).

Many other reflexes govern the behaviour of the newborn. Some, like sneezing or coughing, are necessary for survival. Others seem to be related to the behaviour patterns of our primate ancestors. Still others are not yet understood.

Brain Development and Experience   Recent studies in neuroscience have proved the critical role of early experiences in brain development (Shore, 1997). The brain does not develop automatically, but is dependent on environmental inputs such as proper nutrition and adequate sensory stimulation. Thus, early life experiences may have lasting effects because they change how the brain develops.

The brain normally follows a predictable sequence of development. During prenatal development, all the brain cells—called *neurons*—are produced in the centre of the brain (next to the fluid-filled ventricles), but they then must migrate to the appropriate spot in the brain. Neurons must be in the right spot so that they can form appropriate connections with other neurons. After migration, the neurons grow and differentiate (specialize). Prenatal experiences, depending on what they are and when they occur, can interfere selectively with the production, migration, or differentiation of neurons. For example, early exposure to alcohol slows the production of neurons, so that the brain is considerably smaller than normal, and causes neurons to migrate to the wrong spot (Nowakowski, 1993). Some of the intellectual impairment found in children with FAS can be attributed to abnormal brain development.

At birth, the brain is about 25 percent of the size and weight of an adult brain. It has virtually all of its neurons, which have already migrated to various places in the brain. After birth, the neurons must grow, differentiate, and form connections with other neurons; brain growth occurs both as the neurons themselves grow in size and as the number of connections between them increases (Shatz, 1992). Connections among neurons, sometimes referred to as the "wiring" of the brain, are essential because they determine how the brain will function. Many theorists believe that the brain is "prewired" for certain basic sensory and motor functions. However, this prewiring must be used in order to be fine-tuned and even, in some cases, to continue to exist. Many connections are lost through disuse, and others are strengthened by use (Bertenthal & Campos, 1987; Greenough, Black, & Wallace, 1987; Shatz, 1992). Sometimes students are surprised that normal brain development is not just the creation of new connections, but is also the elimination, or pruning, of faulty connections.

From numerous animal studies, we know that there are links between sensory and motor experience and actual brain growth. For instance, kittens who are raised in an environment where there are vertical lines but no horizontal lines actually lose the ability to make accurate perceptual judgments about horizontal lines. The kitten that lives in a deprived visual environment has fewer brain cells that respond to that kind of visual input after the period of deprivation. The environment, therefore, plays a significant role in early perceptual development. Although the visual system is functional at birth, without light, the neural connections between the eye and the brain, which are present at birth, will not be maintained. Moreover, the early learning of skills contributes to further learning and development. Early experiences—in the last two prenatal months and the first three years after birth—have a dramatic effect on brain development, influencing both the size of the brain and its organization.

The environment also plays a role in the development of normal human vision. Early visual experiences are crucial. Studies of babies blinded from birth because of cataracts show that there are multiple sensitive periods during which visual deprivation can disrupt human visual abilities (Maurer & Lewis, 1993). If stimulation is absent during the sensitive period, the brain will not develop normally. Surprisingly, after surgery to remove the cataracts, babies who had had cataracts in only one eye showed more visual abnormalities than did babies who had had cataracts in both eyes. Apparently, some of the abnormalities were due to competition between the eyes, and patching the normal eye for extensive periods can reduce these abnormalities.

Recent research has looked at the impact on brain development of experiences other than visual stimulation (Shore, 1997). Sensitive caregiving (i.e., responding to the infant's physical and social needs) facilitates brain development, but neglect and abuse

Question to Ponder

How could the findings on neonates help new parents adjust to their babies?

hinder it (Perry, 1995). Emotional experiences, such as developing trust in a caregiver, have a lasting impact on brain development (Ramey & Ramey, 1999). It is important to note that *sensitive caregiving* is a general term that refers to a collection of individual caregiving styles; there is no one "right" way to care for a baby. Ramey and Ramey (1999) developed a list of seven essential principles to guide caregivers of infants. These principles are described in the box "Right from Birth: Building Your Child's Foundation for Life."

Sensory and Perceptual Capacities Can newborn babies see the details of an object directly in front of them? Can they see patterns? Can they see colour and depth? Can they hear a low whisper? Are they sensitive to touch, or are they rather numb? Research indicates that all of the senses are operating at birth, but perception is limited and selective. **Perception** is the active process of interpreting sensory information. Visual perception is not just seeing; for example, it involves giving meaning to what we see. When infants turn their heads to selectively look at one thing and not another, or when they position themselves to get a better view of something in particular, they are exhibiting some perceptual competence. In Chapter 6, we will discuss the perceptual competencies of infants in greater detail. At this point, let us look briefly at the sensory and perceptual capacities of the newborn.

> **perception** The complex process by which the mind interprets and gives meaning to sensory information.

FOCUS ON APPLICATION

Right from Birth: Building Your Child's Foundation for Life

In their book *Right from Birth: Building Your Child's Foundation for Life,* Ramey and Ramey (1999) articulate seven essential principles for caregivers of infants which foster healthy development.

1. *Encourage exploration.* Infants learn by exploring their world. Provide them with sights and sounds and, as they get older, with objects to manipulate. Sensitive caregivers respond to the infant's cues for stimulation, providing stimulation when the infant is alert, but withdrawing it when the infant is uninterested or overstimulated.

2. *Mentor through actions.* Infants learn the ins and outs of life by observing the behaviour of trusted caregivers. "They learn from what they see and hear their parents *do*—how parents make things work, how they solve problems, what behaviour is acceptable or not, what types of cues and words win positive responses" (p. 149). There is also an emotional side of mentoring, which can lead to a love of learning.

3. *Celebrate developmental progress.* Express pleasure when infants accomplish a developmental task, however small. This response teaches infants that they are noticed and that what they do matters; it also makes it more likely that infants will react to their own learning with pleasure. The experience of pleas-

---

Infants learn by exploring their world.

---

ure with learning alters brain chemistry in a way that facilitates learning.

4. *Rehearse.* Provide opportunities for infants to practise skills over and over, in the same and different ways. Allow infants to learn through trial and error. "Build on your infant's interests and accomplishments, rather than push a predetermined list of skills to be learned at some set age or stage" (p. 156).

5. *Protect.* Infants need positive interactions with people. They should never be treated harshly, teased, or cared for in an insensitive way. "Punishment absolutely cannot be effective for babies of this age (birth to 18 months). Worse, it can bring out negative emotions or cause withdrawal and disengagement, and the wrong lessons are learned" (p. 159).

6. *Communicate with infants.* Talk to them, sing to them, gesture to them, smile at them, read to them. "Bring your baby into the wonderful world of language and its many uses" (p. 161).

7. *Guide infant behaviour.* Formal discipline is not appropriate at this age, but early practices can lay the foundation for later behaviour. Establish consistent routines. Model appropriate behaviours. "Punishments, timeouts, and withholding positive things aren't appropriate in the first year of life, other than minor withholding of signs of pleasure. Techniques that can be effective with a three-year-old will be confusing and seem random to a twelve-month-old" (p. 166).

VISION

The visual system consists of the eyes, the optic nerve linking the eyes to the brain, and numerous interconnected parts of the brain that make sense of the visual input. Most parts of the eye are fairly well developed at birth, so that even newborns are sensitive to light and darkness. Their pupils already contract in bright light and dilate in darkness. But some of the visual parts of the brain are still primitive. For example, Johnson (1993) describes how information from the eye connects to four distinct pathways in the brain, each responsible for a different aspect of vision. One of the pathways regulates reflexive eye movements, so that people can visually track a moving object. This pathway, regulated by lower parts of the brain, is mature at birth. Therefore, newborns are able to track slowly moving stimuli, such as a face or a doctor's penlight. The eye movements are initially short and jerky and are limited to a short distance. The location of the moving target affects how well the newborn can track it. The visual field is divided in half—the half moving toward the nose is called the *nasal visual field,* whereas the side toward the temples is called the *temporal visual field.* Newborns are better at orienting toward targets in the temporal field than in the nasal field (Goldberg, Mauer, & Lewis, 1996). Newborns have difficulty changing focus from one object to another. This difficulty is described as "sticky fixation" (Goldberg et al., p. 3). As well, the newborn's eye follows slightly behind the moving target (called *pursuit movement*), unlike the eye of an older baby, which sometimes looks slightly ahead of the moving target, anticipating its location. Anticipating the location of an object requires other visual pathways. These other pathways, involving higher parts of the brain, are very immature at birth and affect the newborn's ability to see the shapes, colours, and details of objects.

The lens of the newborn's eye does not function as well as it will a few months later. The newborn's ability to focus on objects, therefore, varies with the distance of the objects from the eye. The newborn can focus optimally within a narrow range of 17.8 to 25.4 centimetres, with objects beyond this distance appearing blurred. Interestingly, many close objects are socially significant. For instance, a feeding baby held in a parent's arms would have a clear view of the parent's face. As well, the newborn enjoys looking at mobiles dangling over the crib because they are close enough to see. Exquisite pictures hanging on the wall across the room from the crib are too far away for the baby to see clearly. The visual acuity for distance is estimated to be about 20/600, as compared to the normal 20/20 vision of an adult. Consequently, newborns are nearly blind to details across the room (Banks & Salapatek, 1983), since 20/600 vision translates into seeing an object 20 feet away as though it were 600 feet away. Furthermore, newborns sometimes lack **convergence** of the eyes—they are unable to focus both eyes on the same point. They will not be able to do so consistently until the end of the second month (Fantz, 1961). Lack of convergence probably limits depth perception.

convergence The ability to focus both eyes on one point.

We know that newborns are able to perceive their environment by the fact that they are selective about what they watch. Newborns clearly prefer to look at complex patterns. They look particularly at the edges and contours of objects, especially curves (Roskinski, 1977). Newborn babies are also exceptionally responsive to the human face (Fantz, 1958) and can recognize a face even after a delay (Pascalis & de Schonen, 1994). It is not surprising, then, that they develop an early recognition of their mothers' faces. An experiment by Carpenter (1974) showed a newborn's preference for her mother's face at 2 weeks. Carpenter presented each infant with pictures of her mother and another woman. At 2 weeks, the infants preferred to look at the familiar face. In some cases, they turned their heads completely away from the strange pictures, perhaps because the stimulus was too strong or too unfamiliar (MacFarlane, 1978).

One of the more startling examples of visual perception in neonates is their seeming ability to imitate facial expressions. A team of psychologists has run a series of experiments with infants, who are sometimes no more than 2 or 3 days old, to demonstrate imitation. First, the researchers find a time when the neonate is in a calm, alert state (a condition that is not always easy to find). The infant and adult look at each other, and the adult goes through a series of expressions in random order. He purses his lips, sticks out his tongue, opens his mouth wide, opens and closes his hand. In between, the adult pauses and wears a neutral expression. Both infant and adult are videotaped. Later, observers view the videotape of both the adult and the baby, and they try to match what the baby was imitating. Meltzoff and Moore (1989) find remarkable consistency. It appears that many of these babies match their expressions and hand movements to those of the adults. However, some researchers find slightly different results or argue that infants open their mouths wide to a variety of stimuli. Anisfeld (1996) recently reviewed the literature on neonatal imitation and concluded that there was strong evidence that neonates imitate tongue protrusion but that there is no convincing evidence that they imitate other expressions.

The visual sensitivity and preferences of newborns depend not only on the objects they are shown but also on their own state of arousal. Most visual preference studies must be done when the infant is awake, alert, and not too hungry. Newborns who have been fed will watch stimulating displays, such as rapidly flashing lights, nearly twice as long as awake, alert newborns who are being tested before their feeding (Gardner & Karmel, 1984).

It is important for us to keep in mind in our later discussion of infant social development that behavioural competencies, such as gazing at familiar objects (like the mother's or father's face) and imitating—or seeming to imitate—facial expressions, are important factors in developing and sustaining attachment between the infant and parents. The baby who alertly explores her mother's face, or who soothes when held by a familiar father, is the baby with whom the parents will find it easier to sustain attachment.

HEARING

We are certain that newborns can hear. They are startled by loud sounds, and they often turn toward a voice. Newborns are soothed by low-pitched sounds, such as lullabies, and they fuss after hearing high-pitched squeaks and whistles. Clearly, therefore, babies are responsive to the sounds in their environment. But how well developed is this hearing?

The anatomical structures for hearing are rather well developed in the newborn (Morse & Cowan, 1982). For the first few weeks, however, there is still excess fluid and tissue in the middle ear, and until it is reabsorbed, hearing is believed to be somewhat muffled—much the way you may hear if you have a bad cold. Moreover, the brain structures for transmitting and interpreting hearing are not fully developed. In fact, brain structures will continue to develop until the child is about 2 years old (Aslin, 1987; Morse & Cowan, 1982; Shatz, 1992). Despite these limitations, newborns are capable of responding to a wide range of sounds. Even in the first month of life, they are especially sensitive to speech sounds (Eimas, 1975; Werker, 1995). They also seem to show preference for the human voice. For instance, they will listen to a song sung by a woman rather than the same song performed on a musical instrument (Glen, Cunningham, & Joyce, 1981). Infants also seem to be able to localize sound. Even in their first few days, they will turn their heads toward a sound or a voice. One researcher has found that babies who turn toward a sound in the first few weeks of life seem to lose this ability during the second month and then pick it up again in the third month (Muir & Field, 1979).

OTHER SENSES

We know less about newborns' senses of taste, smell, and touch than we do about seeing and hearing. Some studies suggest that these three senses are finely tuned. Although evidence indicates that newborns may have reduced sensitivity to pain for the first few days, the senses of taste and smell are operating fully. Newborns discriminate between sweet, salty, sour, and bitter tastes through clearly differentiated facial responses to the four taste groups (Rosenstein & Oster, 1988). Also, newborns react negatively to strong odours, whereas they are selectively attracted to positive odours, such as a lactating female (Makin & Porter, 1989). As early as 6 days, the infant can distinguish the smell of its mother from the odour of another woman. This reaction is based on body odour, not just milk or breast odour, and naturally the infant shows a preference for the familiar scent (MacFarlane, 1978; Makin & Porter, 1989).

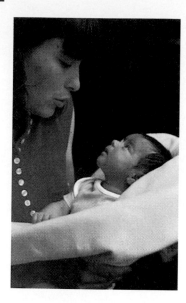

The newborn's senses are finely tuned. For example, an infant can recognize his mother by her smell.

The sense of touch is especially important to the comfort of newborns. The simple act of holding the arms or legs or pressing the abdomen often will be enough to quiet infants. Swaddling, as already mentioned, has a similar effect (Brazelton, 1969).

Maurer and Mondloch (1996) recently developed an interesting hypothesis about the integration of sensory information in the newborn. They suggested that in very young infants, stimulation in one sense modality triggers both perception in that modality and a specific perception in another modality. For example, coloured lights might lead to both visual and auditory perceptions, to "hearing colours." This unusual ability, found in some adults, is called *synesthesia*. Neuroscience studies of adults with synesthesia have revealed two unusual patterns of brain activity: (1) reduced activity in many higher parts of the brain that are normally more active in other adults and (2) increased activity in parts of the brain that deal with other sense modalities (Paulesu et al., 1995). For example, the person who reports hearing sounds when looking at coloured lights would show high activity in both visual and auditory parts of the brain. Interestingly, this pattern of brain activity observed in adults with synesthesia resembles the pattern of normal activity in the neonate's brain (Chugani, 1994; Neville, 1995). However, researchers cannot ask neonates if they "hear colours" or "see sounds." Instead, researchers must develop ingenious methods to figure out what the newborn perceives. Maurer and Mondloch are currently tackling that challenge.

Learning and Habituation We have already seen considerable evidence of infant learning. The neonate quiets to a familiar sound, song, or lullaby, or even to a familiar soap opera theme song (see the box "Does the Fetus Learn?" in Chapter 4). The neonate's ability to imitate facial expressions demonstrates some learning. Improved methods of observation have yielded useful information about the capacities of infants to learn some fairly complex responses. The newborns' ability to turn their heads has been used in many learning experiments. Some pioneering conditioning studies were conducted by Papousëk (1961). In these experiments, newborns were taught to turn their heads to the left to obtain milk whenever they heard a bell. For the same reward, they also learned to turn their heads to the right at the sound of a buzzer. Then, to complicate the situation, the bell and the buzzer were reversed. The infants quickly learned to turn their heads according to the rules of the new game.

Because sucking is well developed in the neonate, this ability has also been used in studies of neonatal learning and visual preferences. Kalnins and Bruner (1973), in an expansion of an earlier study by Siqueland and DeLucia (1969), wanted to determine whether infants could control sucking when it was linked to rewards other than feeding. Pacifiers were wired to a laboratory slide projector. If the infants sucked, the slide came into focus; if they did not suck, the picture blurred. Bruner noted that the infants learned quickly to focus the picture and also adapted quickly if conditions were reversed—that is, they learned to stop sucking to get the picture into focus. In other words, the infants—some as young as 3 weeks old—not only coordinated sucking and looking but also effectively controlled the focus of the slide show. Their reward was clear, rather than blurred, visual stimulation. Bruner concluded that infants had been greatly underestimated in terms of both their perceptual capabilities and their ability to solve problems voluntarily.

Papousëk's (1961) experiments involved more than the buzzers and bells discussed earlier. He also used light to reveal a key facet of newborn behaviour. Infants were taught to turn on a light by turning their heads to the left. Infants would turn their heads several times during a short period in order to turn on the light. But then an interesting thing happened—the infants seemed to lose interest in the game. Papousëk found that he could revive their interest by reversing the problem, but they soon became bored again. Papousëk's findings were important for two reasons: they supported Bruner's (1971) belief that competence, instead of immediate reward, motivates much of human learning, and they demonstrated a second learning phenomenon: **habituation.**

habituation The process of becoming accustomed to certain kinds of stimuli and no longer responding to them.

Infants habituate—they become accustomed to certain kinds of stimuli and then no longer respond to them. The process of habituation serves an important adaptive function. Infants need to be able to adapt to or ignore nonmeaningful stimuli, like the hissing of a radiator or the light touch of their clothing. Researchers use this process of habituation to find out a number of things about the perceptual capacities of infants. For example, a newborn's response at the onset of a moderately loud sound is a faster heartbeat, a change in breathing, and sometimes crying or general increased activity. As the sound continues, however, the infant soon habituates, or stops responding. When we change the sound stimulus, by even a small degree, and the response begins anew, it is clear that the infant perceives the change and reacts to the small difference. This habituating ability has been the basis of many experiments that have provided information about the sensory capacities and perceptual skills of newborns.

Assessment During the first few days of a baby's life, most hospitals provide an extensive evaluation of the newborn, possibly including a neurological examination and a behavioural assessment. Brazelton's neonatal behavioural assessment scale (1973) has been used increasingly by many hospitals. The 44 separate measures on this test can be grouped into seven behavioural clusters similar to the competencies discussed in this chapter. The seven clusters are habituation, orientation, motor tone and activity, range of state, regulation of state (that is, self-soothing ability), autonomic stability (that is, noting whether the infant reacts to stimulation with unusual tremors or startles), and reflexes. The scale includes the usual neurological tests, but it is designed primarily to assess the newborn's behavioural capabilities.

Newborns differ in their responses to new, prolonged, or slightly annoying stimuli. Some can easily detect, attend to, and habituate (grow accustomed) to changes in their environment. Others may be less responsive, or they may be overly responsive and too easily irritated—behaviours that decrease their attention spans and adaptability to changes. By assessing the newborn's competencies and ways of responding, the Brazelton scale may supply early information about a child's future personality and social development. Parents who observe a physician administer the Brazelton scale become much more sensitive to the capabilities and individuality of their own neonates (Parke & Tinsley, 1987).

Individuality of the Newborn

From the moment of birth, infants demonstrate their uniqueness and their variability. Parents with more than one child are usually quite aware of differences in their children's personalities, although all of the children were seemingly brought up more or less the same way. Many times these differences can be noted even before a child is born. One fetus may kick actively, whereas another will shift position gently or cautiously. The following infant profiles demonstrate the great differences that may occur.

Patrick was a happy and placid baby. He slept in a regular pattern, was good about feeding, and was easily soothed. He had accepted a pacifier and usually relaxed immediately once he started sucking on it. When awoken he would often lie in the infant carrier and quietly look around the room. If anyone approached him he would quietly turn to them and appear to be studying them. When picked up, even by new adults, he would mould against them and relax. At bedtime, his mother turned on the music box and turned down the lights, and he promptly fell asleep.

Megan was temperamentally very different from her twin brother, Patrick. She fussed frequently and had trouble with feeding. She would not stay sucking very long at the breast, so her mother switched her at 6 weeks to a bottle. Even after this change, she took extended periods of time to finish her feeding. She refused to accept a pacifier and was difficult to soothe. She did not sleep in any regular pattern and tended to be up several times a night. In fact, she had trouble going to sleep in the evening. Her pediatrician had suggested to her parents that they let her cry for 15 to 20 minutes at night before picking her up. She sometimes fell asleep before then but often persisted in her crying for extended periods of time.

How profound are these differences in the temperament styles of neonates? What does the newborn's behaviour tell us about his future personality? What are the dynamics between the baby's personality and the parents', and what are their effects? The individuality of the newborn has been the subject of many studies.

Temperament Most researchers agree that there are strong constitutional differences in temperament that appear early, that are probably inherited, and that are stable throughout much of the life span. But there is little agreement on which of these aspects of temperament can be reliably identified in the neonate (Bates, 1987). One of the simpler models of individuality lists just three characteristics that are present at birth—emotionality, activity level, and sociability (Buss & Plomin, 1984; Plomin, 1990). *Emotionality* refers to the ease and strength with which an infant is aroused by a stimulus to a behaviour and to emotional expression. *Activity level* is the amount of energy that the infant expends as a normal part of his waking day and the speed at which he expends this energy. *Sociability* refers to the infant's preference for being with others and to his ability to be rewarded by this interaction. Extremely high or low levels of any of these temperamental characteristics are not necessarily advantageous or disadvantageous, but are merely ways in which infants differ.

In contrast, Chess (1967) identified nine criteria to differentiate neonatal behaviour: activity level, biological regularity, positive–negative responses to new stimuli, adaptability, intensity of reaction, threshold of responsiveness, quality of mood (overall amount of pleasure versus displeasure displayed), attention span and persistence, and distractibility.

Chess used these criteria to study 136 children. She found that children could be divided into three basic types. She also determined that qualities seen as early as 2 or 3 months of age could be traced throughout childhood. The largest of Chess's three groups consisted of the "easy children"—babies (and later, children) who were biologically regular and rhythmical. The easy child has regular sleeping and eating schedules, accepts new food and new people, and is not easily frustrated. "Difficult children" form a smaller group. They withdraw from new stimuli and adapt slowly to change; their mood is often negative. A third type is the "slow-to-warm-up child." Children in this group withdraw from activities quietly, whereas the difficult child does so actively and noisily. Slow-to-warm-up children will show interest in new situations only if they are allowed to do so gradually, without pressure. Chess found no evidence that these temperamental types were influenced by parental behaviour.

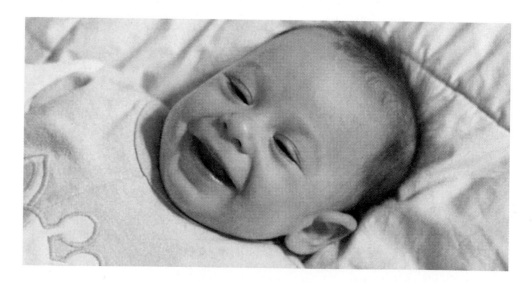

According to Chess, one of the characteristics of "easy children" is their ability to easily adapt to new situations.

FOCUS ON DIVERSITY

Infant Waking, Fussing, Crying, Feeding, and Sleeping: What Is the Range of "Normal"?

Some parents are concerned that their baby fusses too much, does not eat enough, or sleeps far too little. They wonder whether their baby's behaviour falls within the normal range and whether the baby will simply outgrow the problems.

In order to address parent concerns, we must look at longitudinal studies that monitor the behaviour of several infants over time. One study in the United Kingdom had two hundred mothers keep 24-hour diaries of how much time their babies spent fussing, crying, sleeping, and feeding (St James-Roberts & Plewis, 1996). Recordings were made when infants were 2, 6, 12, and 40 weeks old.

As well, at each of the ages, some of the mothers did recordings for three consecutive days. The table below shows the average amount of time infants spent in each activity. In addition, the table gives the standard deviations (SD). Standard deviations measure individual differences—the larger the standard deviation, the greater the individual differences.

The table depicts how the average amount of time spent on each behaviour changes from 2 weeks to 40 weeks. Averages, though, do not tell us about individual infants or about subgroups of infants. After doing more detailed analyses, St James-Roberts and Plewis

---

First-born infants fussed more and slept less than later-borns.

---

reached the following conclusions:

- There is considerable day-to-day variability in infants' sleeping, waking, fussing, and crying. "Infancy is predominately a period of adaptation, so that an infant's behaviour on successive days will resemble that in other infants more than it resembles the infant's own behaviour on the first day" (St James-Roberts & Plewis, 1996, pp. 2536–2537).
- Despite the day-to-day variability, there was a developmental trend in which infants gradually spent less

time sleeping, fussing, crying, and feeding from the time they were 2 weeks until they were 40 weeks old.

- Stable individual differences were apparent for crying, fussing, and sleeping. Birth order accounted for some of the individual differences in fussing and sleeping.
- First-born infants fussed more and slept less than later-borns. Sex differences accounted for some of the individual differences in crying—on average, boys cried about 5 minutes more a day than girls. In general, fussing and sleeping were the most stable infant behaviours. Infants who fussed more than average at 2 weeks continued to do so at 40 weeks. Similarly, infants who slept less than average at 2 weeks continued to do so at 40 weeks. The stability of fussing and sleeping suggests that these two behaviours may be related to temperament.

Amount of Time Spent in Behaviours per 24-Hour Day

	Age 2 weeks		Age 6 weeks		Age 12 weeks		Age 40 weeks	
	Average	SD	Average	SD	Average	SD	Average	SD
Sleeping	14 hrs. 16 min.	2 hrs. 20 min.	13 hrs. 28 min.	1 hr. 50 min.	13 hrs. 37 min.	1 hr. 28 min.	13 hrs. 9 min.	1 hr. 29 min.
Waking	3 hrs. 44 min.	1 hr. 36 min.	3 hr. 30 min.	1 hr. 55 min.	5 hrs. 6 min.	1 hr. 36 min.	8 hrs. 14 min.	1 hr. 23 min.
Feeding	4 hrs. 8 min.	1 hr. 14 min.	2 hrs. 29 min.	1 hr. 18 min.	2 hrs. 36 min.	50 min.	1 hr. 48 min.	39 min.
Fussing	1 hr. 17 min.	53 min.	1 hr. 28 min.	56 min.	1 hr. 7 min.	38 min.	39 min.	27 min.
Crying	1 hr. 1 min.	52 min.	40 min.	40 min.	29 min.	21 min.	11 min.	11 min.
Crying and fussing	2 hrs. 18 min.	1 hr. 17 min.	2 hrs. 8 min.	1 hr. 10 min.	1 hr. 37 min.	44 min.	50 min.	32 min.

Self-Regulation One of the major developmental tasks for the newborn infant is self-regulation. As we have seen, the full-term neonate is well equipped with a variety of ways to respond and adjust to outside stimulation. For instance, infants are capable of habituating to repeated stimuli and of comforting themselves in response to stress. But these self-regulating mechanisms vary with individual temperaments. Some infants are easily overstimulated; others are more difficult to arouse. Some respond best to auditory stimulation, others to touch. Some are hypersensitive to particular types of stimulation.

Sensitive caretakers help the babies focus their reactions to sensory experiences and moderate overexcitement or underarousal (Greenspan & Greenspan, 1985).

Although the basis of newborn individuality is not entirely understood, researchers agree generally that widely different personality styles are apparent at birth and that these differences increase over the first few months of life. During this same early period, infants and parents will establish a relationship based on their own distinct personalities (Lewis & Rosenblum, 1974). Many studies suggest that infants' temperaments and behavioural styles influence parental behaviour and partially determine the quality of early interactions (Bates, 1987).

Researchers regularly find that babies differ greatly in the amount of attention they evoke from their parents, with irritable infants receiving more parental stimulation than overly placid ones. Such attentiveness, however, may be accompanied by feelings of anger, bewilderment, or self-pity in the caregiver when numerous efforts to soothe or amuse the baby have failed. Babies who are easily quieted and amused may cause their parents to feel competent and satisfied in their caregiving (Segal & Yahraes, 1978). Therefore, the predictability of an infant's behaviour also affects the caregiver. Mild personality differences between parent and infant are fairly common, and even the most willing and enthusiastic parent needs time and patience to become acquainted with the infant's unique personality. The development of mutuality, reciprocity, and a symbiotic relationship between parent and infant is certainly not automatic or instinctive, as we shall see in Chapter 7.

The Premature Infant

premature Having a short gestation period (less than 37 weeks) and/or low birth weight (less than 2.5 kilograms).

So far, we have discussed only the development of healthy, full-term babies. A substantial number of newborns, however, are considered to be **premature**—a condition that can pose serious problems for infants and caregivers alike. About 1.1 percent of babies born in the United States and Canada weigh less than 1500 grams (about 3 pounds) (Pharoah & Alberman, 1990).

Two indicators of prematurity are frequently confused. The first is gestational time. The infant born before a gestation period of 37 weeks is considered premature. The second indicator is low birth weight. Because the average birth weight is 3.4 kilograms, an infant who weighs less than 2.5 kilograms is usually classified as premature, or in need of special attention, although only half of such infants have a gestation period of less than 37 weeks. Low-birth-weight babies, even when full term, often have problems resulting from fetal malnutrition, for example. Therefore, both cutoff points—2.5 kilograms and 37 weeks—are used in classifying babies as premature (Babson & Benson, 1966). The WHO defines a premature infant as one weighing less than 2.5 kilograms at birth. But it is obvious that there are significant differences between, for example, a 28-week fetus weighing 1.6 kilograms and a low-birth-weight, full-term infant. The 28-week fetus may require intensive care to sustain it. It may have immature lungs and still need considerable development. The low-birth-weight, full-term infant may have neurological damage but overall should be as mature as other full-term infants. Prematurity can occur for a number of reasons. The most common reason is multiple birth, when two or more infants are born at the same time. Other causes include diseases or disabilities of the fetus, the mother's smoking and/or drug taking, and malnutrition. In addition, diseases of the mother, such as diabetes or polio, may lead a doctor to deliver a baby before full term.

Immediately after birth, premature infants usually have greater difficulty making adjustments than do full-term babies. Their adaptation to the basic processes of circulation, respiration, and temperature control is more complicated. Temperature control, in particular, is a common problem. Premature infants have few fat cells and thus poorly maintain body heat. Therefore, in industrialized nations, newborns weighing less than 2.5 kilograms are usually placed in incubators immediately after birth. Another common problem is the feeding of premature infants. In their first few months, they seem unable to catch up in weight and height with full-term infants.

FOCUS ON AN ISSUE

The "Kilogram Kids"

There is an "elite club" of perhaps 10 000 infants born each year who spend their first few months following birth fighting for their lives. These infants are born 2½ and to 3 months ahead of schedule, and they weigh less than 1000 grams.

Three decades ago, virtually all of these infants would have died. In the past 30 years, though, obstetrical medicine has made dramatic progress in dealing with difficult deliveries. Infants who would not have survived in 1960 are now thriving in record numbers. For example, in well-equipped hospitals with intensive care units for newborns, the survival rate is generally more than 25 percent for infants weighing between 500 and 750 grams, more than 50 percent for those weighing between 751 and 1000 grams, and 90 percent for infants weighing between 1001 and 1500 grams (Minde, 1993).

But what is the experience of these tiny creatures and their families over the first several months of life? The infants may lie in a waterbed in an incubator, connected by wires and tubes to banks of blinking lights and digital displays. The several electronic and computerized devices monitor or adjust temperature, respiration and heart rates, blood gases, and brain waves. Parents are encouraged to visit their infants often, and they are usually al-

lowed to stroke and caress their children through the gloved portholes in the incubator. In many of these intensive care units, an effort is made to provide a homelike, personal atmosphere (Fincher, 1982).

Daily life-threatening crises are not unusual—these tiny beings need nutrients and struggle to function in their alien environment. Excess fluid strains the heart and lungs, yet too little may lead to dehydration and disruption of the sodium and potassium balance.

For parents, the premature birth of a child is traumatic.

The tiny bones need calcium for bone development, but too much calcium clogs tubes and tiny blood vessels.

For parents, the premature birth of a child is traumatic. According to neonatologist Ron Cohen, the parents are "in shock, mourning, grieving, going through denial, anger" (Fincher, 1982, p. 72). They are forced to deal with one crisis after another and hope that relatively little permanent damage will occur during this period. The staff in the special care units are very much aware of the parents' state and try to help them cope.

Is there any way to avoid the struggle of premature birth and the enormous emotional and financial costs of saving the lives of these tiny newborns? Several studies have demonstrated that over 50 percent of very early births could have been prevented with regular prenatal medical care, beginning at 12 weeks (Knobloch, Malone, Ellison, Stevens, & Zdeb, 1982; Monmaney, 1988). Even in those cases where very early birth cannot be prevented, the chances of survival are dramatically higher if the mother has had regular medical care.

In one study, 72.7 percent of the mothers of premature survivors had regular medical care, compared with only 25.2 percent of the mothers of nonsurvivors. It is much easier to treat a mother's ill health or poor nutrition early in pregnancy and thus reduce the risk of complex medical problems encountered by the neonate (Rahbar, Momeni, Fumufod, & Westney, 1985).

It seems almost impossible to match the nutritional conditions of the late fetal period to produce a growth rate outside the uterus comparable to that inside.

It is often believed that the effects of prematurity may last long after infancy. Several studies have indicated that premature infants suffer more illnesses in their first 3 years of life, score lower on IQ tests, and are slightly more prone to behavioural problems than are full-term babies (Knobloch, Pasamanick, Harper, & Rider, 1959). More recent research seems to indicate that this finding is true for only a small proportion—less than one-quarter—of premature infants (Bennett, Robinson, & Sells, 1983; Klein, Hack, Gallagher, & Fanaroff, 1985). Researchers have found a high rate of prematurity among children later diagnosed as being learning disabled, having reading problems, or being distractible or hyperactive (Minde, 1993).

All such reports, however, must be very carefully interpreted. It cannot be concluded, for example, that prematurity causes any of these defects. Although the immature birth condition of babies may make them less able to adjust to the shock of birth, prematurity has a more complex association with problems in later life. For instance, conditions like malnutrition, faulty development of the placenta, or crowding

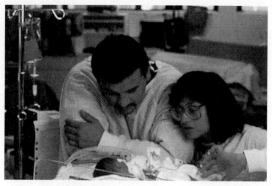

Even though there are obstacles to bonding with the premature infant in the first weeks after birth, many parents try to interact with their newborns as much as possible.

Question to Ponder

What can hospital staff do to facilitate parent–infant bonding with premature infants?

in the uterus may result in a number of symptoms—only one of which is premature birth. In such cases, the prematuring is merely a symptom of a disability or malfunction; it is not a cause.

Bonding with a Premature Infant

Some of the later problems of premature infants also may arise from the way that they are treated during the first few weeks of life (see the box "The 'Kilogram Kids'"). Because they are kept in incubators under conditions that are free of harmful micro-organisms, they receive less of the normal physical contact experienced by most newborns. There is little opportunity to enjoy the early contact after delivery that Klaus and Kennell found to be so important in promoting bonding. Few premature infants are breast-fed, few are held even while being bottle-fed, and some are unable to suck at all for the first few weeks. These infants miss the social experiences of normal feeding, which establish an early mutuality between the caregiver and the full-term infant. The caregiver may become less responsive because the infant appears unattractive or sickly or has a high-pitched, grating cry. These are great obstacles to effective parent–infant bonding in the early weeks of life.

The consequences of faulty bonding owing to prematurity are apparent throughout infancy (Goldberg, 1979). Preterm infants are held farther from the parent's body, touched less, and cooed at less. Later, these infants tend to play less actively than babies born full term and have difficulty absorbing as much external stimuli.

Studies conducted in the 1970s typically found that many of the differences between premature and full-term infants had disappeared by the end of the first year (see, for example, Goldberg, 1979). This catch-up was attributed to the efforts of parents who compensated for the premature infant's lack of responsiveness with more active parenting and intervention. But in the last 20 years, smaller and smaller premature babies have survived (Minde, 1993). Recent studies of premature infants include babies that are significantly smaller, younger, and at higher risk than babies in earlier studies. Studies of infants with very low birth weights (under 1000 grams) find that their problems are more pronounced over time (Mangelsdorf et al., 1996). Mangelsdorf and colleagues examined the relationship between infants with very low birth weights and their mothers when the infants were 14 months and 19 months old. The researchers rated relationships as secure or insecure. There were more insecure relationships at 19 months than at 14 months. The researchers speculated that parents compare their baby's progress with that of other babies, but that the comparison group changes. In the first year, they compare their baby with other premature babies in hospital. But by the second year, they compare their baby's progress with that of full-term age mates who are considerably advanced in walking, talking, and other developmental milestones. Comparing the premature infant with more advanced full-term age mates may adversely affect the parent–infant relationship.

In many hospitals, parents are encouraged to become more involved with the care of premature infants. They can put on masks and gowns and enter the intensive care unit to help with feeding, diaper changes, and other care. They can stimulate the baby by gently stroking and talking to it. Parents' taking part in the care of their infants in hospital promotes better bonding and caretaking when the baby is sent home.

There have been several follow-up studies of premature infants whose parents became actively involved in their care while these infants were in hospital. The parents learned early on to be responsive to the subtle behaviour of their premature infants. As these children grew up, they improved at each stage. Even as infants, they showed more progress in social and intellectual development compared with premature infants who did not have as extensive parental involvement in their care. They continued to be more advanced socially and intellectually, and they were still ahead at age 12 (Beckwith & Cohen, 1989; Goldberg, Lojkasek, Gartner, & Corter, 1988).

Some of the potentially detrimental effects of prematurity may be offset by an enriched environment during the first year of life. Zeskind and Ramey (1978) ran a pilot program for infants born premature because of fetal malnourishment. These infants were provided with full-service day care in addition to the necessary medical and nutritional services. Most of them reached normal performance levels by 18 months. Another matched group of fetally malnourished infants received the same medical and nutritional services but were cared for at home, not in the day-care program. These infants were slower to reach normal levels, and deficits in their performance were still apparent at 2 years. Zeskind and Ramey's study shows that with proper medical care, nutrition, and caregiving during their early development, premature infants need not be seriously disadvantaged by the conditions of their birth.

High-risk infants present similar problems in early bonding. They are likely to be segregated from their mothers' room for medical reasons and often have developmental problems that interfere with their ability to signal and reward parents for successful caregiving. The result is often a fussy, unresponsive baby and an overattentive mother. Sometimes, bonding patterns and mutual responses improve if the mother imitates her baby's behaviour instead of providing completely new stimuli that overwhelm and confuse the infant (Field, 1979).

Bonding between parents and an infant with disabilities is extremely difficult. While facing problems similar to those encountered with premature infants, such as early separation of infant and parents, there are other obstacles that must be overcome. The nature of the handicap may severely impair the baby's ability to respond. Moreover, parents frequently need to go through a period of mourning for the perfect child that did not arrive before they can accept, nurture, and become emotionally attached to the one that did. This is a case in which support groups made up of other parents with handicapped infants can be very helpful. Taking part in these groups helps the parents realize that they are not alone in their situation. In addition, others going through similar experiences often have techniques they can suggest that prove helpful.

Let us remember that almost 90 percent of all births go smoothly, without complications in either pregnancy or delivery. Many women consider giving birth one of the most important and psychologically significant experiences in their lives. They are more likely to have this sense of deep satisfaction if they are involved in choosing various birthing procedures and can be surrounded by loved ones. They appreciate prepared childbirth for the opportunity it offers to be alert and actively engaged with the infant in the first few hours of life. Parents who share the childbirth experience frequently report a deepening of their marriage and a strong sense of elation. Childbirth is indeed a peak experience for many, a time for reaffirming ideals and values.

Summary and Conclusions

Childbirth occurs in three stages: labour, which prepares the mother's body for the passage of the baby; the actual birth, which is usually completed in less than two hours; and delivery of the afterbirth, in which the placenta and related tissues are expelled from the uterus. The stages of childbirth have been handled differently at various times in history and in different cultures. Currently, most Canadian babies are born in hospitals that are equipped to deal with complications involving the mothers or the babies. However, many hospitals are trying to balance these safety concerns with the social needs of mothers and families. Many provinces are exploring the use of midwife-attended births, but only Ontario has fully legalized midwifery.

Once the baby is born, he is called a neonate for the first month. Neonates spend part of this time adjusting to the new world and to the new functions their bodies will be responsible for without their mothers' assistance—breathing, temperature regulation, digestion, and others. Newborns have behavioural states that regulate their interactions with this new world. Initially, they spend most of the time in sleep. Then gradually they spend more and more time in quiet alertness.

Newborns have well-established sensory capabilities. They see, although not sharply; they hear, although in a somewhat muffled fashion; and they have well-developed senses of taste and smell. The newborn's brain is developing rapidly, forming connections among neurons and pruning faulty connections. This development is affected by environmental experiences. Various assessment instruments have been developed, including Brazelton's neonatal behavioural assessment, to examine the individual infant's responsiveness and receptivity to stimuli from the environment.

Newborns, like the rest of us, are all individuals, with unique approaches to the world. Temperamental qualities also vary. Some newborns are easy, others difficult, and still others are slow to warm. Researchers have recently begun to study the effects of such temperamental qualities on parental interaction and attachment.

Finally, not all infants are healthy at birth, although the majority are. Some are either born preterm or have low birth weight for term—both classifications of the WHO category of prematurity. Premature infants often pose a challenge for parents. They do not look like the "perfect baby" the parents hoped for, they require extensive care that allows little interaction, and once home they frequently require continued special care and attention.

Key Terms and Concepts

afterbirth (p. 127)

Apgar score (p. 135)

birth (p. 126)

bonding (p. 131)

breech presentation
   (p. 127)

cesarean section (p. 128)

convergence (p. 142)

episiotomy (p. 127)

false labour (p. 126)

habituation (p. 144)

labour (p. 126)

midwife (p. 129)

"natural" childbirth
   (p. 129)

neonate (p. 132)

perception (p. 141)

perineum (p. 127)

posterior presentation
   (p. 127)

premature (p. 148)

reflex (p. 138)

Questions to Review

1. Compare and contrast the attitudes toward childbirth among different cultures.

2. Describe the three stages of childbirth.

3. List the three fundamental keys to "natural" childbirth.

4. List and describe the available options that a pregnant woman has when delivering her baby.

5. Describe Leboyer's method of childbirth.

6. What is bonding, and what do studies find significant concerning this interaction between parent and child?

7. What are the major physical developments that occur in the neonate immediately following birth?

8. Describe the Apgar score and explain what it measures.

9. List the six newborn behavioural states that were identified by Wolff in 1966.

10. What is the Moro reflex? List and describe other infant reflexes.

11. What is infant habituation? How does this ability provide information about the sensory capacities of the newborn?

12. What are two indicators of premature birth? What are the effects of prematurity on the development of the child?

Weblinks

www.birthpartners.com/CANADA.HTM

Birth Partners

This Canadian site has links to information on midwives, doulas, and lactation. It includes a directory of professionals in each province, as well as the names and addresses of related associations.

www.babycenter.com/refcap/174.html

Natural Childbirth

This site, sponsored by the Baby Centre, has information on methods of natural childbirth, such as Lamaze and the Bradley method. It also provides personal accounts of birthing experiences. What was it like to experience natural childbirth?

matweb.hcuge.ch/matweb/endo/cours_4e_MREG/Neonatology_guidelines.htm

Neonatology

This site supplies links to medical articles on gynecology, obstetrics, neonates, and preterm infants.

Infancy: Physical, Motor, and Cognitive Development

The child is a little
    inspector when it
    crawls
It touches and tastes
    the earth
Rolls and stumbles
    toward the object
Zigzags like a sail
And outmaneuvers the
    room.
I am learning the child's
    way
I pick up wood pieces
    from the ground
And see shapes into
    them

I notice a purple velvet
    bee resting on a
    flower
And stop to listen to its
    buzz
They have included me
And though I will not be
    put away to rock
    alone
And don't roll down the
    plush hills
Nor spit for lunch
I am learning their way
They have given me
    back the bliss of my
    senses.

HY SOBILOFF
"THE CHILD'S SIGHT"

Outline CHAPTER 6

Objectives

By the time you have finished this chapter, you should be able to do the following:

✔ Describe the developing competencies of the infant during the first 2 years.

✔ Contrast breast-feeding and bottle-feeding.

✔ Describe the nutritional needs of the infant.

✔ Describe the infant's perceptual development during the first year.

✔ Explain and critique Piaget's theory of cognitive development in the infant.

✔ Describe the infant's understanding of the properties of objects.

✔ Describe the effect of environmental stimulation on infant competency.

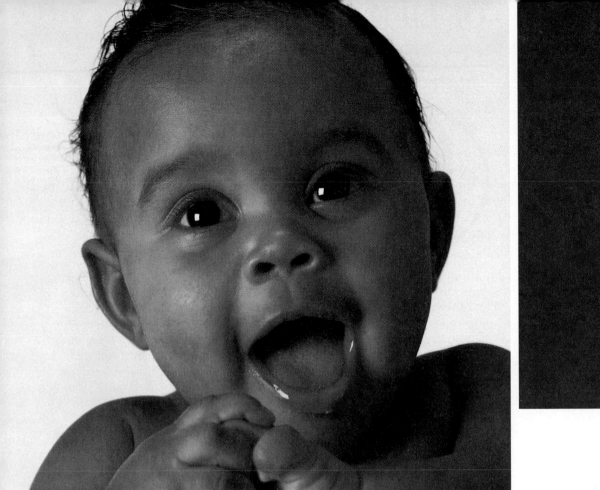

Within a day or two of birth the infant can lift his head in a gentle, bumbling motion and squint at objects close to him. He snuggles against his mother's breast, tasting the warm milk, and smelling the familiar good scents he associates with her. As he sucks, he often seems to softly stroke her breast in the tight-fisted way infants have. As we saw in Chapter 5, neonates come into the world able to sense and respond to their environment. They can see and hear, taste and smell, feel pressure and pain. They are selective in what they like to look at, and they are able to learn. They are still physically immature and dependent, however, and have limited cognitive ability. In the next 2 years, infants change more rapidly and more dramatically than during any other 2-year period. Some of these changes are obvious: infants crawl, sit, walk, and talk. Other changes are more difficult to detect: it is difficult to see the brain grow and become more specialized, and it is difficult to tell just what the infant sees, hears, and thinks.

In this chapter, we will highlight what we know about physical, motor, perceptual, and cognitive development in infants and toddlers. Although norms and averages of growth and behaviour have been established for children at various stages of development, children essentially develop in their own style, at their own pace, and in response to the tasks of their specific social context, as the following cases illustrate:

At 12 months of age, Tina was very active and independent. She had been walking for a month, but she often crawled when she wanted to get somewhere in a hurry. She cried whenever her mother tried to restrain her. From birth on, she was fussy. She slept irregularly and was given to long crying spells. At 8 months, Tina frequently howled when things did not go as she expected. She knew at an early age which toys, food, and people she preferred, and she did not like changes in her environment.

Her sister, Lana, born a year later, had developed in a different way. By the end of 12 months, she was quiet and placid, and she was content to sit in her playpen or crib for long periods of time. She had been able to pull herself upright at 7 months. She showed no signs of temper, frustration, or anxiety other than crying when someone unknown to her came near.

From the outset, these sisters differed on the three basic dimensions of temperament that we described in Chapter 5. Tina is more emotional and intense than is Lana, and she has a higher activity level than her sister does. However, Tina is also less sociable than Lana is. These individual differences become clearer as the children grow older.

At 18 months, Tina's active, sensitive, and intense nature became even more distinct. She usually played alone. She enjoyed lining up small sticks, stones, and toys and endlessly rearranging them. She continued to disturb her mother's sleep occasionally with her sudden waking and howling. Her fussiness and unpredictability began to show in her eating habits; she sometimes refused to eat food that she had always enjoyed. She was often upset when she was taken out of her home, sometimes crying uncontrollably when her mother took her for a visit to friends. Her expressions of surprise, joy, and anger were always intense, which puzzled her mother, who was a quiet, calm person herself. Tina firmly resisted all attempts at toilet training.

Lana, at 18 months, continued to be an easygoing, gentle child, but she had become more outgoing and friendly. She laughed and smiled whenever she was picked up and played with, especially by those who came to visit. She knew the names of some objects in the room and the parts of the body. She got hungry at regular intervals and would sleep peacefully most nights. She kept her even temper, but she was afraid of loud music or sudden noises. She was easily distracted from whatever she was doing. At 24 months, she had almost toilet trained herself by imitating her older sister.

This brief description of Tina and Lana at 12 and 18 months indicates that although common developmental changes occur during the first 2 years of life, great variations exist in temperament, interests, personality, and even the social context that infants experience. Parent–child relationships will differ based on reactions to numerous events and on each infant's birth order and temperament. The older sister must take the lead in learning new skills. The younger sister has both the advantage of following a more competent model and the disadvantage of losing in competition with her more competent sister.

Even in the same family, the social context of development is not identical. Parents will often wonder, "How did it happen that our children have two such different personalities, when we raised them the same … or, when they were raised in the same family?" The reality is that as more children are added to the same family, the family itself changes.

Infant and Toddler Competencies: An Overview

Infancy is a time of perceptual and motor discovery. Infants learn to recognize faces, food, and familiar routines. They explore flowers, insects, toys, and their own bodies. Every day is a discovery of the people, objects, and events that make up their environment. Such discovery is not only exciting, but it is also helpful in learning how to adapt to one's environment.

For decades, developmental psychologists have carefully studied the characteristics of infants and children. Arnold Gesell, a pioneer in the field, observed hundreds of infants and children. He recorded the details of when and how certain behaviours emerged, such as crawling, walking, running, picking up a small pellet, cutting with

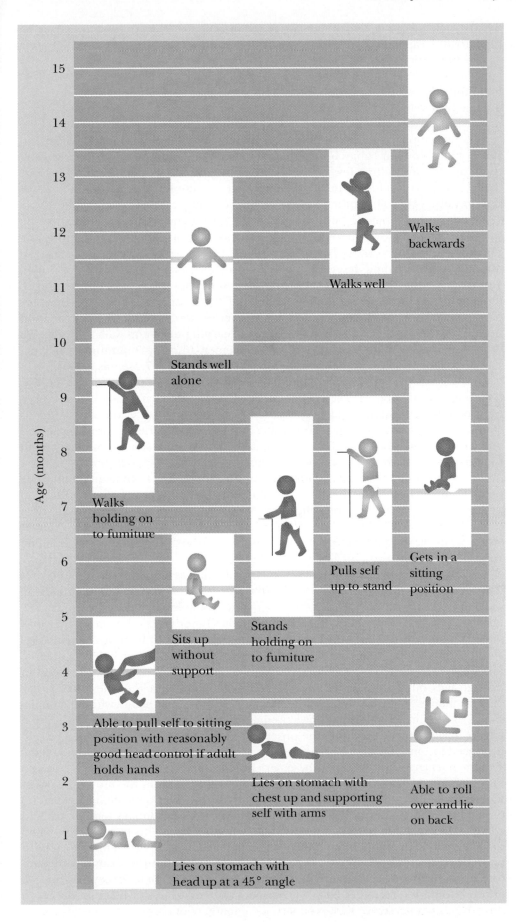

Figure 6-1
Examples of developmental tasks in infancy. The lower edge of each box represents the age at which 25 percent of all children perform each task; the line across the box, 50 percent; the upper edge of the box, 75 percent.

scissors, managing a pencil, or drawing the human figure. From the resulting data, he reported the capabilities of "average" children at varying ages. By 15 months, for example, his "average" children were able to walk; by 18 months, they could walk fast and run stiffly; at 21 months, they were able to kick a large ball (Gesell, 1940). Gesell, like others in the 1940s, believed that biological maturation mostly caused this sequence of development; thus, he largely ignored environmental effects. But today's researchers have shown that the infant's environment also affects development.

Stimulation enhances motor development. For example, Kipsigi parents in Kenya stimulate their babies by propping them up into a sitting position and holding them upright in the first few months after birth (Bul & Sabatier, 1986). It appears that this stimulation fosters motor development because Kipsigi infants, on average, sit and walk earlier than other babies. Infants' clothing or living arrangements can affect motor development. For example, at the turn of the 20th century infants typically wore long dresses. It would be difficult to crawl in a long dress without getting tangled. Interestingly, most of the infants dressed this way never crawled, but instead moved by sitting up and dragging their bottoms (Burnside, 1927, as cited in Adolph, Vereijken, & Denny, 1998). A lack of adequate stimulation can have devastating effects on motor development (and on virtually all other aspects of development). For example, infants raised in poor-quality orphanages—where they get minimal attention beyond feeding and cleaning—are delayed in learning to sit and walk (as well as in other milestones) and engage in unusual movements, such as continuous rocking, that appear to be self-stimulatory or self-soothing (Ames, 1997; Dennis, 1960).

It is clear that environmental experiences affect development. However, this does not mean that environmental effects are unrestricted—that infants can be taught to reach milestones earlier and earlier. Certainly, there are physical constraints. Infants cannot be taught to sit without support at 2 months because their spines are soft and bend, causing them to droop forward. Similarly, 2-month-old babies cannot be taught to walk because their heads are too heavy relative to the rest of their bodies, making it impossible for them to balance upright. As well, attempting to train an infant to be precocious can be stressful for the infant (see the box "Hothouse Babies" at the end of this chapter). Sensitive caregiving of infants does not involve a race to teach them the skills of older children. Ramey and Ramey (1999) developed a list of seven essential principles to guide caregivers of infants (see the box "Right from Birth: Building Your Child's Foundation for Life" in Chapter 5).

Gesell's sequence of milestones is still useful today, as long as we do not interpret it too rigidly. We must remember that there is a normal range of developmental pathways, rather than one path. For example, sequences of milestones typically describe infants as crawling before they walk. But some babies never do crawl. Instead, they may scurry about on their bottoms like crabs, using their arms to help push themselves along (Adolph et al., 1998). As well, it is noteworthy that babies reach developmental milestones at different rates, as shown in Figure 6-1. The milestones usually focus on average ages, but many babies developing normally will achieve the milestones earlier or later than average. It is important, though, to be aware of babies who reach milestones exceptionally quickly or slowly, as development in one sphere can have ripple effects in others. For example, the onset of crawling, or of other variations of self-produced locomotion, changes emotional and cognitive development. Emotional development changes because the baby experiences independence, but the baby may also experience anger and frustration owing to limit-setting from the mother, who attempts to ensure the baby's safety (Futterweit & Ruff, 1993). Despite its physical independence, the infant remains close to the mother by continually looking back to monitor her reaction before approaching something new. This behaviour is called *social referencing*. Cognitive development changes because the crawling infant begins to pay more attention to the spatial features of the environment (for example, the bottom stair is considerably lower than the top one), as this becomes necessary to move around safely. Interestingly, babies do not develop a wariness of heights and drops until they have experienced self-produced locomotion of one sort or another (Campos,

Question to Ponder

How do you think an infant's level of physical and cognitive development affects how adults respond to the infant?

Berenthal, & Kermoian, 1997). As well, the crawling infant can move to explore objects and places out of reach. There are fewer restrictions on his exploration.

The effects of motor development on emotional and cognitive development remind us of the holistic nature of development, as was discussed in Chapter 1. Developments in one domain interact with those in other domains. In order to get a sense of the "whole" child, we will now give a brief overview of competencies found in babies and toddlers of different ages. Keep in mind, though, that we are describing what is typical—individual differences are normal at all ages.

The First 4 Months

At the end of 4 months, most infants resemble the chubby, appealing babies seen in magazine advertisements. Since birth, they have nearly doubled in weight, from 2.7 to 3.6 kilograms to somewhere between 5.4 and 6.8 kilograms, and they have probably grown 10 centimetres or more in length. Their skin has lost the newborn look, and their fine birth hair is being replaced by new hair. Their eyes have begun to focus; when awake, they babble contentedly and smile in response to pleasant stimulation.

At birth, the size of an infant's head represents about one-quarter of the total body length. Around the age of 4 months, however, the body starts to grow and lengthen much more rapidly than the head, and these proportions change markedly (see Figure 6-2). By 12 years, a child's head is only one-eighth the length of the body, and by 25 years, only one-tenth of the total body length.

The infant's teeth and bones are also beginning to change. In some children, the first tooth erupts at 4 or 5 months, although the average age for this event is closer to 6 or 7 months. Many bones are not yet hard and heavily calcified but are still soft cartilage. They tend to be pliable under stress and rarely break. Muscles, however, may pull easily and be injured, as well-meaning adults occasionally discover when hoisting infants up by the arms and swinging them in play (Stone, Smith, & Murphy, 1973).

Much to the delight of parents and caregivers, by 4 months the average baby is usually sleeping through the night. This sleep pattern sometimes begins as early as 2 months. Gradually, the baby settles down into the family routine, daytime as well as nighttime. This is not to say that all babies sleep through the night that early. Many continue to awaken during the night until they are a year old or more. Each infant has her own rhythm and pattern of sleep and wake periods, as the following comments indicate:

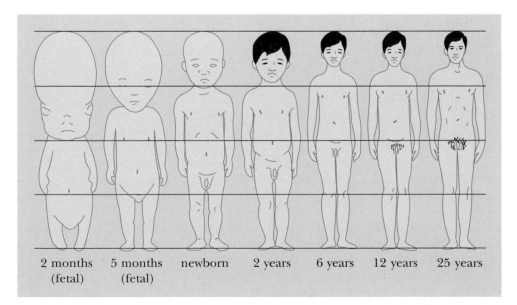

2 months (fetal)   5 months (fetal)   newborn   2 years   6 years   12 years   25 years

Figure 6-2
The cephalocaudal (head-downward) and proximodistal (centre-outward) development that we saw in prenatal growth continues after birth, and the proportions of the baby's body change dramatically during infancy.

Our first child slept through the night when she was 1 month old, and today at 4 she still is a very sound sleeper. Our second child arrived 11 months later, and she never slept through the night until she was 14 months old. My friends and pediatrician made many suggestions of ways to get her to sleep—none worked. I was becoming frustrated—and a real zombie at work—since she was up every three hours all night. Finally, I decided to consider the time she was up and taking a bottle to be "our" special time, when our other child was not needing attention at the same time. I really came to enjoy those late evening hours we spent together—and became much more human when I started adjusting my own sleep cycle to fit hers.

When 4-month-olds are placed in a stomach-down position, they can generally hold up their chests, as well as their heads. In a sitting position, they hold the head steady and observe very carefully everything that is going on.

Average infants of this age can roll over from stomach to back and from back to stomach (Dargassies, 1986; Stone, Smith, & Murphy, 1973). Most of the reflexes that are found in the newborn seem to dissolve by the time they are 2 or 3 months old and are gradually replaced by voluntary actions. The well-coordinated stepping reflex, for example, is replaced by seemingly more random, less-coordinated kicking (Thelen, 1989). This is also the time when **sudden infant death syndrome (SIDS)** is most common (see the box "Sudden Infant Death Syndrome").

Self-discovery usually begins about this time. Infants discover their own hands and fingers and spend several minutes at a time watching them, studying their movements, bringing them together, grasping one hand with the other. Some 4-month-olds also discover their feet and manipulate them in much the same way. It is quite normal, however, for some infants to be 5 or 6 months old before becoming aware of their feet, especially if they reach this age during the winter, when they are heavily bundled.

> **sudden infant death syndrome (SIDS)** The sudden death of an apparently healthy infant or child in whom no medical cause can be found in a postmortem examination.

From 5 to 8 Months

By 8 months, babies have gained another 1.8 to 2.3 kilograms and have grown about 7.6 centimetres, but their general appearance does not differ dramatically from that of 4-month-olds. They probably have at least two teeth, and perhaps a few more. The first teeth are usually the four front ones on the bottom, followed later by front ones on the top. Their hair is thicker and longer. By this time, too, their legs are oriented so that the soles of their feet no longer face each other.

At about 5 months, most infants achieve something called a *visually guided reach.* Before this age, they have possessed many of the component skills, such as a reflex grasp and then a more voluntary grasp, that are needed to perform this visually guided reach. They have been able to reach out toward an attractive object and have visually examined a variety of objects. It is a difficult task, however, to put all of these components together—to look, reach out, and successfully grasp an attractive object. Yet, in some ways, this one achievement transforms the world of the infant. Now begins a period of more systematic exploration of objects—with the hands, the eyes, and the mouth used individually or in combination (Rochat, 1989).

Most 8-month-old babies are able to pass objects from hand to hand, and some are able to use the thumb and finger to grasp. They may delight in filling both hands, and they are usually able to bang two objects together—a feat often demonstrated joyfully and endlessly. Most 8-month-olds can get themselves into a sitting position, and nearly all babies of this age can sit without support once they are placed in position. If they are put on their feet, well over half of the 8-month-olds can stand while holding on to some support, and about half can pull themselves into a standing position. A few may even begin to sidestep around the crib or playpen while holding on, and some babies may be walking, using furniture for support. This is a phenomenon referred to as *cruising.*

During the period from 5 to 8 months, most babies develop some form of locomotion. This is the time when the family dog is no longer safe, and all valuables

a

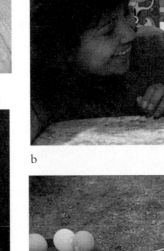

b

c

d

e

(a) At 4 months, infants can lift their chests as well as their heads and can carefully observe what is happening around them.

(b) Many 8-month-olds start to play social games like peek-a-boo.

(c) By 12 months, many infants are actively exploring their environment.

(d) At 18 months, most toddlers are able to walk alone, and they like to carry or pull toys with them.

(e) Two-year-olds walk, run, and can usually pedal a tricycle.

FOCUS ON AN ISSUE

Sudden Infant Death Syndrome (SIDS)

One of the most shattering events parents may experience is the sudden and unexplained death of their baby. Yet this is the most common cause of death among infants between 1 month and 1 year of age (CCSD, 1996). For example, in Canada there are approximately four hundred deaths annually from what is known as the sudden infant death syndrome, or SIDS (CICH, 1994). SIDS is defined as the sudden death of an apparently healthy infant or child in whom no medical cause can be found in a postmortem examination. SIDS has been called a diagnosis of exclusion because its victims can be identified only through an autopsy that rules out all other explainable causes of death. SIDS, sometimes called *crib death*, tends to happen without warning, while the child is asleep. The high incidence of SIDS has produced a great deal of concern within the medical profession.

Researchers have been unsuccessful in finding the precise cause but have found circumstances in which SIDS is common. Mothers under 20 years of age who have delayed or neglected to seek prenatal care run a higher than normal risk of having a child with SIDS. This risk is also increased if the mother had been ill during her pregnancy, had

a short interval between pregnancies, or had earlier experienced the loss of her fetus. In addition, smoking and the abuse of narcotics by the mother are often connected with SIDS. Smoking mothers who are also anemic run a particularly high risk of having a child with SIDS (Bulterys, Greenland, &

Because of this and other research linking sleeping position and SIDS, the American Academy of Pediatrics now recommends putting babies at risk to sleep on their backs or propped on their sides against pillows.

Kraus, 1990). In a Swedish study of all Swedes born between 1983 and 1985, it was found that smoking doubled the risk of SIDS and that the more the mother smoked, the greater her infant's risk of SIDS. In addition, maternal smoking was found to influence the time of death, as infants of smokers died at an earlier age. The researchers concluded that in countries such as

Sweden, smoking may be the single most important preventable risk for SIDS (Haglund & Cnattingius, 1990).

Recent research by Buck and her team from the University at Buffalo Medical School found that there was a sevenfold increased risk for SIDS associated with vaginal breech delivery and more than twice the risk for SIDS when mothers were in labour 16 hours or longer (Buck et al., 1989). Their research was conducted on 132 948 mothers from upstate New York who gave birth in 1974. It appears that the majority of breech SIDS infants were single footling deliveries (a rare type of breech presentation, with the baby emerging one foot first). The more common form of breech birth was not associated with an increased risk of SIDS. The researchers suggest that an earlier problem in the infant's development, not the breech birth itself, may be the primary causal factor. Buck (1991) observes that SIDS babies may have experienced a previous central nervous system insult in utero since they often show signs of subtle growth retardation, including reduced birth weight and length.

Babies who have been born prematurely or who were underweight at

---

should be placed above the infant's reach. They may learn to crawl (with body on the ground) or creep (on hands and knees). Other infants develop a method called "bear walking," which employs both hands and feet; still others scoot in a sitting position. The components of crawling are developing for several months beforehand. The infant is looking at more distant attractive objects and is reaching for them. There is a change in the pattern and flexibility of kicking and in other types of leg activity. Also, just before crawling, many infants have periods during which they rhythmically rock forward and backward. All these pieces of behaviour need to be integrated into the task of crawling across the floor toward an attractive, distant object (Goldfield, 1989).

Many babies of 8 months begin to play social games, such as peek-a-boo, bye-bye, and patty-cake, and most enjoy handing an item back and forth to an adult. Another quickly learned routine is that of dropping an object and watching someone pick it up and hand it back. This game is usually learned accidentally by both baby and adult, but the baby is often the first to catch on to the possibilities for fun.

birth run a higher than average risk of SIDS. They generally have greater than average difficulty breathing and often need support from respiratory devices.

There are significant provincial differences in the rate of SIDS. The rates in Alberta, British Columbia, Saskatchewan, Nova Scotia, Newfoundland, the Northwest Territories, and the Yukon are higher than those in other provinces (CICH, 1994). As well, the rate of SIDS is three times higher in First Nations babies and four times higher in Inuit infants than in other Canadian babies (*Canada Year Book*, 1997).

Frequently, in the week prior to the occurrence of SIDS, infants have severe breathing and digestive problems. Second and third children also run more risks of SIDS than does the average first-born. Babies who are part of multiple births also run above average risks, particularly triplets and the second child in twin births. "Several twin pairs, both [fraternal and identical], have died on the same day. Among 32 twin pairs recorded, 3 were found dead together" (Shannon, Kelly, Akselrod, & Kilborn, 1987).

Infants who later died of SIDS have been observed to be less active and less responsive than their siblings. Some have also been described as having had a strange cry. Deaths frequently occur at night when the infant is asleep and lying in any position (Shannon, Kelly, Akselrod, & Kilborn, 1987). Recent research from Tasmania has indicated, however, that babies put to sleep in a prone position (on their stomachs) may be at greater risk for SIDS (Dwyer, Ponsonby, Newman, & Gibbons, 1991). Because of this and other research linking sleeping position and SIDS, the American Academy of Pediatrics now recommends putting babies at risk to sleep on their backs or propped on their sides against pillows (AAP Task Force, 1992). We should note, however, that the American Academy of Pediatrics believes that the risk is very low for healthy babies who sleep in prone positions.

SIDS seems to occur most often in winter. Although medical researchers have not yet found a physiological cause, they suspect irregularities in the autonomic nervous system, especially as it relates to breathing and heart functions (Shannon, Kelly, Akselrod, & Kilborn, 1987). Recent research has found that some infants apparently are born with a degree of respiratory centre immaturity that, in combination with other problems, such as illness, head colds, and exposure to cold air or smoke, may result in cessation of breathing. Vestibular stimulation by rocking has been shown to be beneficial for premature babies in reducing apnea (halting of breathing). There appear to be additional benefits of rocking for premature infants, including more rapid maturation of the nerve cells of the cerebellum, which is still developing during the first 6 months of life. Shannon and his colleagues suggest that SIDS may be reduced by the use of automatically rocking cribs, especially during the night, when most deaths occur.

The occurrence of an infant's seemingly unexplained death has a devastating effect on the family and on everyone else connected with the child. All those associated with keeping the infant alive experience guilt, loss, and a sense of powerlessness (Mandell, McClain, & Reece, 1987). The family grief and loss are often mixed with anger and frustration: "Who is to blame?" "Why did this happen?" The family needs as much information as possible, as well as support in their sorrow and reassurance that there is a 98 percent certainty that later infants will not have SIDS (Chan, 1987). Until we understand the causes of SIDS, we shall still fail to identify many infants at risk and fail to monitor them effectively.

From 9 to 12 Months

At 12 months, most infants are about three times heavier than they were at birth, and they have grown about 22.9 to 25.4 centimetres in length. Throughout this first year, girls tend to weigh slightly less than boys do.

By 9 months, most infants have some form of locomotion; most have pulled themselves to a stand, and half of them are beginning to take steps while holding on to furniture. By 12 months, about half are standing alone and are starting to take their first few steps. The age at which free-walking begins varies widely, depending on both individual development and cultural factors. Over 50 years ago, Shirley (1931) and Gesell (1940) found that 15 months was the average age for free-walking to begin. Since 1967, however, researchers have observed that the period between 11 and 13 months is the average time for this behaviour to begin in healthy, well-fed infants who are given the opportunity and the encouragement to exercise (Frankenburg & Dodds, 1967).

The ability to stand and walk gives the infant a new visual perspective. Locomotion allows for more active exploration. Infants can get into, over, and under things. They can clean out a bureau drawer (in 10 seconds or less) and can follow their mother into the

About half of all 8-month-olds can pull themselves into a standing position.

pincer grasp The method of holding objects, developed around the age of 12 months, in which the thumb opposes the forefinger.

toddler The infant in the second year of life who has begun to walk—the child has a somewhat top-heavy, wide stance and walks with a gait that is not solidly balanced or smoothly coordinated.

kitchen. Infants of this age who are placed in "jolly jumpers" or "johnny jump-ups,"—spring-supported seats that hang from doorways—will turn to follow their mother as she moves from room to room and will even bounce to whatever music happens to be playing. Their world is broadened once again. The infant's motor development is spurred on by the new and exciting things that he can see and hear. His ability to explore at new levels and with new abilities spurs on his cognitive and perceptual development (Thelen, 1989).

Twelve-month-olds actively manipulate the environment. They are able to undo latches, open cabinets, pull toys, and twist lamp cords. Their newly developed **pincer grasp**—where the thumb opposes the forefinger—allows them to pick up grass, hairs, matches, and dead insects. They can turn on the television set and the stove, and they can explore kitchen cupboards, open windows, and poke things into electrical outlets. Because children are so busy exploring the environment, caregivers must set limits on their explorations. They have to strike a balance between too much restriction and sufficient control in order to keep the baby safe. "No" becomes a key word in the vocabulary of both the child and caregivers—although most pediatricians suggest concentrating on the "major no's" and baby-proofing the house to assist in maintaining the baby's safety. As one parent comments:

When our son was born, friends gave us a basket of various devices to help make our home safer for him as he grew. There were plugs to block electric outlets, seals for the refrigerator and toilet to prevent prying hands from opening them, locks for the cupboards, a gate for the stairway ... and a sign that read "This too shall pass!" We used all of them during his first 18 months!

At 12 months, babies are frequently able to play games and can "hide" by covering their eyes. They can roll a ball back and forth with an adult and can throw small objects, making up in persistence what they lack in skill. Many children of this age begin to feed themselves, using a spoon and holding their own cup for drinking. While this is not the neatest process, it contributes to the child's development toward autonomy.

The 12-month-old is on the verge of language. Infants of this age are usually struggling either to walk or to utter their first words—but generally not both. Most infants achieve control of walking first, then they start talking. Some 12-month-old children, however, can manage "mama," "dada," and two to eight other words, such as "no," "baby," "bye-bye," "hi," and "bow-wow." In Chapter 8, we will discuss in detail the infant's acquisition of language.

As they enter the second year, children become aware of themselves as individuals separate from their mothers (or caregivers); they increasingly exercise choice and preference. They may suddenly and vehemently refuse a food that they have always liked. They may protest loudly at bedtime, or they may engage in a battle of the wills with someone over a formerly trouble-free event, such as getting into a snowsuit or being placed in a high chair. Infants in their second year of life, once they have begun to walk, are usually referred to as **toddlers.**

Age 18 Months

The 18-month-old usually weighs between 9.9 and 12.2 kilograms, an indication that the rate of weight increase has slowed. The average height at this age is 78 to 83 centimetres. Almost all children at this age are walking alone. When walking, they generally like to push or pull something with them or carry something in their hands. They seldom drop down on all fours now, although walking may actually take more of their time and effort. Some are not yet able to climb stairs, and most have considerable difficulty kicking a ball, because their unsteadiness does not permit them to free one foot for kicking. Children of this age also find pedalling tricycles or jumping nearly impossible.

At 18 months, children may be stacking from two to four cubes or blocks to build a tower, and they can often manage to scribble with crayon or pencil. They have improved their ability to feed themselves and may be able to undress themselves partly. (The ability to put clothes on generally comes later.) Many of their actions are imitative of those around them—"reading" a magazine, sweeping the floor, or chatting on a toy telephone.

Most 18-month-olds have made strides in language and may have a vocabulary of several words and phrases. They usually combine two words to make a single sentence, and they can point to and name body parts and a few very familiar pictures. They may now begin to use words effectively. (For more on language development, see Chapter 8.)

Age 24 Months

By their second birthdays, toddlers have added approximately another 5 centimetres and .9 kilograms. Again, the rate of gain is tapering (see Figure 6-3).

Because, until recently, 2-year-olds were usually considered too young for most nursery schools and yet too old for regular monthly visits to a doctor, relatively few studies had been made on this age group. Toddlers stayed with their families and their caregivers and were seen around the neighbourhood, but they were generally out of the range of most research psychologists. Several studies show the 2-year-old as a fascinating active learner, just beginning to break through into new areas of skill, social understanding, and accomplishment (Bronson, 1981).

Children at 2 years not only walk and run, but they can usually pedal a tricycle, jump in place on both feet, balance briefly on one foot, and accomplish a fairly good overhand throw. They climb up steps and, sometimes, come down again with assistance. They crawl into, under, around, and over objects and furniture; they manipulate, carry, handle, push, or pull anything they see. They put things into and take things out of large containers. They pour water, mould clay, stretch the stretchable, and bend the bendable. They transport items in carts, wagons, carriages, or trucks. They explore, test, and probe. All of this exploration provides a vital learning experience about the nature and possibilities of their physical world, as the following comments suggest.

My husband and I were making the final preparations for our sabbatical housing and needed to make a lengthy long-distance telephone call. Our two

Figure 6-3
The weight and height of about 50 percent of the infants at a given age will fall in the blue regions; about 15 percent will fall in each of the white regions. Thus, on average, 80 percent of all infants will have weights and heights somewhere in the blue and white regions of the graphs. Note that as the infants age, greater differences occur in weight and height within the normal range of growth.

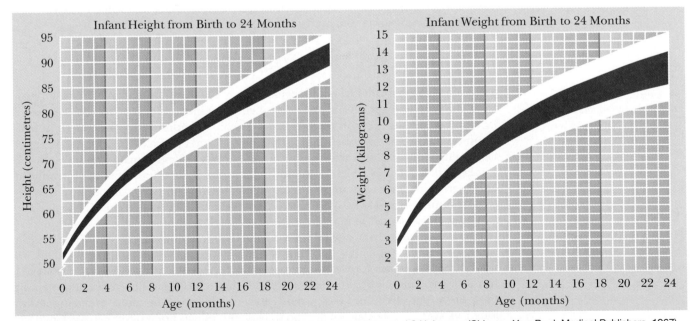

Source: Adapted from *Growth and Development of Children*, 5th ed., by E.H. Watson and G.H. Lowrey (Chicago: Year Book Medical Publishers, 1967).

daughters, aged 2 and 3, needed to be kept busy, so I innocently suggested that they take their bean bag chair up to their bedroom and pretend that their beds were boats and the bean bag was an island. They happily set off up-stairs to play.

Forty-five minutes later, we finished our call and noticed that it was sur-prisingly quiet in the house. My husband went upstairs to check on the kids. He called down, "Sherry, you've got to come up here and see this!" When I opened the kids' door, the entire room looked like it was filled with fog. Their brown carpet was white, the air was white, and our little 2-year-old looked like a ghost—her hair, clothes, eyelashes, everything was white.

When piecing together what happened, we were told by our 3-year-old that they had been pretending that the bean bag was a water tube and since it was going so fast, they had to put powder (a brand new large bottle of it) on their hands to make their grip better. Once they squeezed the bottle, the powder shot out about four feet. They varied how hard they squeezed and it went farther and shorter. In no time, the whole room—and their bod-ies—were coated with baby powder! (An unanticipated benefit? The room smelled baby powder fresh for weeks afterward!)

The language development of most 2-year-olds shows some marked gains. They are able to follow simple directions, name more pictures, and use three or more words in combination; some even use plurals. Given a crayon or pencil, 2-year-olds may create scrib-bles and be fascinated briefly with the magical marks. They may stack from six to eight blocks or cubes to build towers, and they can construct a three-block "bridge." Their spontaneous block play shows matching of shapes and symmetry. If they are willing, 2-year-olds can take off most of their own clothing, and they can put on some items.

Physical, motor, and cognitive development during the first 2 years is a com-plex, dynamic process. For infants to thrive, they must have their basic needs met by their environment. They must get enough sleep, feel safe, receive consistent care, and have appropriate stimulating experiences. Each developing system—perceptual or motor skills, for example—supports the others. A blind child does not crawl or walk as soon as the seeing child does. There is no lure of a distant toy or of a parent's face. There is no visual feedback to guide this child's motor action. Cognitive devel-opment, too, depends on the information that the child receives from her actions and sensory explorations. What is more, these interacting systems are helped or hin-dered by the social context in which the infant develops (Hazen & Lockman, 1989; Thelen & Fogel, 1989). In the next few sections, we will look at some of these com-ponents of infant development.

Nutrition and Malnutrition

malnutrition An insufficiency of total quantity of food or of certain kinds of food.

Two kinds of **malnutrition** generally occur. One is due to an insufficient total quantity of food, and the other to an insufficiency of certain kinds of food. Starvation or severe lack of food results in a condition called *marasmus*. Children with this pattern of mal-nutrition have a diet that is deficient in both protein and total calories. Considerable mus-cle wasting and loss of subcutaneous fat accompanies this type of malnutrition. However, if it lasts for a relatively short period of time, supplemental foods may be introduced and there is no long-term negative impact of the poor nutrition. Another type of se-vere malnutrition, called *kwashiorkor* (from the Swahili for "deposed child"), is caused by an insufficiency of protein in relation to total calories. Kwashiorkor more typically occurs in children 18 months of age or older who are no longer breast-feeding. The Swahili word for this type of malnutrition comes from the African tradition of placing a child in the home of relatives for weaning if the mother becomes pregnant. Once removed from the protein-rich breast milk, such children often suffer a deficiency of protein in their diets. The effects of kwashiorkor have been found to be more damaging in the long run, since the shortage of protein significantly affects brain development. Children with kwashiorkor, from such areas as Somalia, Ethiopia, or the African Sahel, are often presented in media accounts of starvation. They have large, protruding stomachs, and their arms and legs are often extremely thin.

Although more common in Third World nations, severe malnutrition can occur in Canadian children living in poverty or in severely neglectful circumstances. Over one million Canadian children live in poverty (CCSD, 1996). In addition, even if children receive adequate calories and protein, they can still be malnourished if they lack vitamins and minerals (Brown & Pollit, 1996). For instance, vitamin D deficiency results in rickets, the most pronounced symptoms being bowed legs that interfere with walking, swollen wrists, and enlarged heads (Binet & Kooh, 1996). Binet and Kooh recently documented the persistence of rickets in babies of recent African and Asian immigrants living in Toronto and attributed the vitamin D deficiency to feeding and child-rearing practices. All of the babies were exclusively breast-fed without vitamin supplements for 6 to 18 months. Breast milk does not contain adequate vitamin D, so breast-fed babies normally get the required amount through supplements or through daily skin exposure to sunlight. But babies born to African and Asian immigrants in Toronto during the winter rarely went outside because the parents were not accustomed to the cold and feared for their babies' safety. Also, darker-skinned babies require more exposure to sunlight in order to produce adequate vitamin D because the increased melanin (pigment) in their skin interferes with the synthesis of vitamin D. Thus, these babies were especially vulnerable to vitamin D deficiency.

Another type of malnutrition is iron-deficiency anemia, caused by a diet that is deficient in iron-rich foods, including leafy green vegetables, cereals, eggs, and red meat. It can occur at any age, but it is most common in 6- to 24-month-old infants and is estimated to affect 20 to 25 percent of the world's babies (Lozoff, Klein, Nelson, McClish, Manuel, & Chacon, 1998). This type of malnutrition is common among Canadian infants living in poverty. Canada has the second-highest rate of child and infant poverty among industrialized nations—second only to the United States (CCSD, 1996). Iron-deficiency anemia can cause the infant to appear pale and lethargic. It also affects cognitive and motor development; anemic infants score below average on tests of mental abilities and motor skills (Lozoff et al., 1998). In addition, the infant's lethargy elicits different adult reactions. During motor tests, examiners made fewer attempts to get the infants to perform tasks than they did with nonanemic infants (Lozoff et al., 1998). In play, caregivers of anemic infants show less obvious pleasure in the infant and less affection (Lozoff et al., 1998). Lozoff and colleagues (1998) did home observations of anemic and nonanemic infants. Compared with nonanemic infants, anemic infants were more likely to be asleep, irritable, doing nothing, being carried, or in bed and less likely to be walking or playing. If anemic infants were playing, it was most likely solitary play, at a distance from their mothers, whereas nonanemic infants were more likely to play with their mothers. Thus, anemic infants appear somewhat isolated and receive less stimulation than other infants.

Anemic infants can be treated with iron supplements. However, even after successful treatment, their motor and cognitive deficits persist. It is unclear why the negative effects of iron-deficiency anemia are so long lasting. One possibility is that the malnutrition causes long-lasting effects on early brain development that are not reversed by treatment. For example, decreased levels of iron in the brain impair the production of some neurotransmitters (especially dopamine) and the myelination of neurons (Felt & Lozoff, 1996). Another possibility is that despite being treated for anemia, the infants continue to live in poverty, and other factors associated with social disadvantage perpetuate the cognitive and motor deficits. More research is needed to clarify the reason for long-term effects of iron-deficiency anemia.

Breast-Feeding versus Bottle-Feeding

Milk is the major source of nutrients for infants. It is used almost exclusively in the diet for the first 6 months and together with solid foods for the next 6 to 12 months. Many women throughout the world choose to breast-feed their infants. The breast milk of

FOCUS ON DIVERSITY

Trends in Breast-Feeding and Bottle-Feeding around the World

Studies have shown that mid-20th-century mothers, both in the developed and less-developed countries of the world, have shifted from breast-feeding to bottle-feeding in record numbers. Mothers in the United States led this decline in breast-feeding as infant formulas became more available in the 1940s, 1950s, and 1960s. By 1971, less than 10 percent of babies born in the United States were breast-fed after the first 3 months of life. Although it has generally caused no hardship or nutritional problems for the great majority of infants in developed countries, the shift to commercial infant formula has resulted in widespread malnutrition and high infant mortality in poorer countries. Some recent statistics illustrate this shift: over 90 percent of the infants in Chile were breast-fed in 1960, and in 1968, less than 10 percent were breast-fed. In Mexico, 95 percent of 6-month-old infants were breast-fed in 1960; in 1966, only 40 percent were breast-fed. In Singapore, 80 percent of 3-month-old infants were breast-fed in 1951; in 1971, only 5 percent were breast-fed. In the poorer countries of the world, bottle-fed babies had a much higher mortality rate than did those who were breast-fed (Latham, 1977). Malnutrition occurs when people lack the money to buy expensive milk substitutes; in addition, many babies die when the commercial formula is diluted with contaminated

---

Recently, in response to the efforts of major national and world health organizations, many women have returned to breast-feeding their infants.

---

water, thereby transmitting intestinal disease to the infants.

Recently, in response to the efforts of major national and world health organizations, many women have returned to breast-feeding their infants. The rate of breast-feeding in Canada rose from 25 percent in 1970–1972, to 75 percent in 1982 and 87 percent in 1990 (Health and Welfare Canada, 1993). A recent study of Vancouver mothers found that 82.9 percent breast-fed their babies, but over half had stopped by the end of the first month, and only 18.2 percent had breast-fed for nine months or more, as recommended by the WHO (Williams, Innis, & Vogel, 1996). In fact, the WHO recommends that breast-feeding be continued for two years or more to improve the baby's immune system (Newman, 1995), although most Canadian women do not breast-feed for this length of time. In the Williams et al. study, mothers who breast-fed longest were most likely to be married or living common law, to have more education, and to have higher family incomes. The levels and trends of breast-feeding vary widely across socioeconomic, cultural, and religious groups. It is more popular in the western United States and is less popular in the southeastern states. Breast-feeding practices are also influenced by family and cultural ideas about how mothers should care for their children, by the amounts of time and money that are available, and by the advice mothers receive from health-care professionals.

Curiously, the increase in the number of working mothers was not a major cause in the decrease, and then

---

a reasonably well fed mother contains a remarkably balanced combination of nutrients, as well as antibodies that protect the infant from some diseases (Newman, 1995). Even a malnourished mother's milk provides nearly adequate nutrients, often at cost to her own health. If breast-feeding goes on for extended periods of time during severe malnutrition, the mother is no longer able to produce milk. In addition, if pregnancies occur in close sequence, with each subsequent child, both mother and child have more nutritional risk. This is why the WHO proposes family planning with a two- to three-year break between pregnancies as the ideal situation.

The content of breast milk suits most babies, and breast-fed babies tend to have fewer digestive disturbances. Additionally, breast milk is always fresh and ready at the right temperature, does not need refrigeration, and is absolutely sterile. Unless the mother is very ill, has an inadequate diet, or uses a lot of drugs or alcohol, breast milk is better for a baby's health. A recent study has raised concerns about smoking and breast-feeding (Mascola, Van Vunakis, Tager, Speizer, & Hanrahan, 1998). A number of chemicals in tobacco (such as nicotine and cotinine) pass into the breast milk.

For further discussion of breast-feeding, see the box "Trends in Breast-Feeding and Bottle-Feeding around the World."

increase, in the trend toward breast-feeding. Breast-feeding declined among women who did not work between births, as well as among those who did. In developing countries, where there are high infant mortality rates, the large percentage of bottle-fed babies is still a major public health concern. Here, too, despite extensive educational campaigns by the WHO and other groups, the decision of whether to breast-feed and, if so, for how long, is personal and is embedded in the sociocultural context. In Korea, boys are much more likely to be breast-fed than girls are (Nemeth & Bowling, 1985). In Nigeria, mothers with more education breast-feed less often, and Christian mothers breast-feed for a much shorter period of time than do Moslem mothers (Oni, 1987). In the Democratic Republic of the Congo (formerly Zaire) and many other countries, rural women use breast-feeding as a form of birth control, and, hence, they may continue it for several years (Mock, Bertrand, & Mangani, 1986). (It is important to note that this method of birth control is not 100 percent effective.) In a Canadian study conducted in Vancouver, the decision to breast-feed was made early in or even before the pregnancy and was largely based on personal choice (Williams, Innis, Vogel, & Stephen,

1999). Mothers who breast-fed their infants for less than three months often cited being concerned for the baby's nutrition or uncomfortable with breast-feeding as the reasons for weaning to formula.

Another Canadian study—part of the Better Beginnings, Better Futures Project—examined factors related to breast-feeding among low-income women living in disadvantaged communities in Ontario (Evers, Doran, & Schellenberg, 1998). At birth, 77 percent of the mothers reported breast-feeding. Mothers were more likely to breast-feed if they had attended prenatal classes, had higher levels of education, were married, and were not experiencing financial stress (defined as having enough money to live on). By the time their infants were 3 months, though, a third of the mothers had already weaned their babies to formula, citing "not enough milk," "baby rejected it," and "baby seemed hungry" as the main reasons for weaning. Those who breast-fed longer were more likely to be older nonsmokers with more education and to have participated in a home visitor program. It is interesting that the home visitor program, which is part of the Better Beginnings, Better Futures Project, enhanced breast-feeding because it was not designed to help with breast-feeding per se. Rather, the

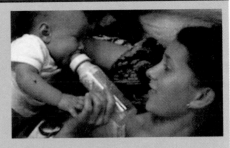

The shift from breast- to bottle-feeding occurred in less-developed countries, as well as in Canada and the United States.

home visitors offered to assist the parents with the problems that low-income parents often confronted. Problems were related to housing, child care, health care, transportation, and parenting. Providing general support may enable new mothers to concentrate on breast-feeding by reducing other demands on her time.

Why do some mothers choose to breast-feed, whereas others prefer to bottle-feed? It appears that good nutrition is only one of the many factors that influence this choice. Obviously, cultural factors, personal factors (such as the allocation of time to work and child care, the social schedule the mother keeps, and the availability of a peer group that is accepting of breast-feeding), and even national policies may have an effect, such as the length of paid maternity leave.

Weaning and the Introduction of Solid Foods

Some mothers in developed countries begin weaning babies from the breast at 3 or 4 months, or even earlier; others continue breast-feeding for as long as 2 or 3 years. Although such extended breast-feeding is rare among middle- to upper-class mothers in Canada, 2 or 3 years is not rare for certain Canadian subcultures or, as previously indicated, for some other cultures.

Normally, at about 3 to 6 months of age, infants gradually start to accept some strained foods. Usually, they begin with the simple cereals, such as rice, and expand to a variety of cereals and puréed fruits, followed somewhat later by strained vegetables and meats. It is possible that some infants may be allergic to one or a variety of foods, and it is therefore advised that caregivers introduce foods slowly. Other infants seem to take to almost everything that is offered. By 8 months, most infants are eating a broad range of specially prepared foods, and their milk consumption is usually reduced. As they acquire teeth, infants start on finger foods, sometimes beginning even earlier if manual dexterity is sufficient. Foods such as cheese strips, for example, readily dissolve in the mouth even without teeth, and infants seem to enjoy

Many babies today are not given solid food until around 6 months, unlike babies a generation ago, who were offered solid food much earlier. Doctors today often advise delaying the introduction of solid food to prevent food allergies and to ensure that the babies drink sufficient milk.

Question to Ponder

How might early feeding experiences have lasting effects on development? What types of effects would you look for?

novelty paradigm A research plan that uses infants' preferences for new stimuli over familiar ones in order to investigate their ability to detect small differences in sounds, patterns, or colours.

the experience of picking up and placing cheese strips in the mouth.

Weaning is a crucial time for the onset of malnutrition, as we saw earlier in this chapter. Particularly vulnerable are 1-year-olds who have already been weaned from the breast and whose families have insufficient money for milk or other nutritious foods. These children may survive on diets composed of potato chips, dry cereals, and cookies—foods that typically provide calories for energy but few nutrients. Even with enough milk or a variety of nutritious foods available, 1-year-olds may be unwilling to drink a sufficient amount of milk from a cup; they also may prefer crackers to the more wholesome snacks of cheese and meat. It is important to note that contrary to advertising slogans, children do not require sugared cereals. Children tend to like the crunchiness and taste of whole grain cereals without sugar and prefer sugared cereals only once they are introduced to them.

In cases of severe malnutrition during infancy, serious remedial programs of food supplementation, combined with education, can produce dramatic results. In a study done in Bogotá, Colombia, children were provided with food supplements for their first 3 years. The food supplements were accompanied by periodic home visits. These children showed much less growth retardation and revealed all-around better functioning than the control groups—even three years after the supplements were discontinued (Super, Herrera, & Mora, 1990). A recent study found that malnourished children in Guatemala had delayed intellectual development, but nutritional supplements alone were insufficient to reverse the delays because the children also lacked educational and medical resources (Brown & Pollit, 1996). A more comprehensive intervention that included nutrition, education, and medical resources was required to overcome the intellectual delays.

We have examined the typical development patterns and nutritional needs of infants during their first 2 years. We will now analyze the process of perceptual and cognitive development.

Perceptual Competence

As explained in Chapter 5, perception is a complex process of interpreting our sensory environment. This process takes time to develop (Gibson & Spelke, 1983). The whole notion of talking about infant competence reflects a significant change in our view of the infant. Through hard work and the use of imaginative research techniques, psychologists have discovered that human infants are far more complex and have many more competencies than had once been supposed.

New technology has helped researchers in their studies. Today, it is possible to measure certain basic physiological reactions of a baby to the environment and to specific stimulation. Heart activity, brain wave activity, and the electrical response of the skin can provide useful information about what infants perceive and about how much they understand. Researchers can also gather information from highly refined pictures of an infant's movements—for example, eye movement or hand manipulation. But new technology is only part of the answer. A good research plan, or paradigm, is more important. As we saw in Chapter 2, the classical and instrumental conditioning paradigms have been used to assess infant sensory and memory capabilities. The basic premise is that an infant cannot be conditioned to respond to stimuli that he cannot perceive.

Another useful strategy to measure infant competence is the **novelty paradigm.** It is well known that babies quickly tire of looking at the same image or playing with the same toy. Infants habituate (adapt to) repeated sights or sounds (see Chapter 5).

Also, very young infants often show their lack of interest by looking away. If given a choice between a familiar toy and a new one, most infants will choose the new one. Even if there is only a small difference in the new toy, the infant will choose it. Researchers have been able to use this information in setting up experiments to determine how small a difference in sound, pattern, or colour the infant is capable of detecting. It is important that researchers use strict procedural controls when studying infant perception because subtle differences can influence infant performance. For example, Nnubia, Maurer, and Lewis (1992) found that 1- and 2-month-old infants responded differently depending on whether or not they were sucking on pacifiers.

The **surprise paradigm** is another useful way to study the infant's understanding of the world. Human beings tend to register surprise—through facial expression, physical reaction, or vocal response—when something happens that they did not expect or, conversely, when something does not happen that they did expect. Researchers are able to determine infants' surprise reactions by measuring changes in their breathing, heartbeat, or galvanic skin response or by simply observing their expressions or bodily movements. Researchers can design experiments to test precisely what infants expect and what events violate their expectations (Bower, 1974). Because of such research techniques, we know that even though newborns have limited sensory and perceptual competence, these abilities improve dramatically during the first 6 months. All of these paradigms allow us to determine infant competencies, even though infants do not use language.

> **surprise paradigm** A research technique used to test infants' memory and expectations. Infants cannot report what they remember or expect, but if their expectations are violated, they respond with surprise. For example, if the doll is not under the cloth where the infants saw it hidden, they are surprised.

Vision

Humans are visually oriented organisms. In adults, vision is the most highly developed sense and tends to dominate human environmental interactions. During the first 4 to 6 months, infants' visual abilities develop rapidly. Even before grasping or crawling is possible, they explore the world visually. As we saw in Chapter 5, newborns can visually track a moving penlight and can discriminate between different shapes; however, they prefer to focus on complex patterns and human faces (Fantz, Ordy, & Udelf, 1962).

Visual Acuity Visual acuity is the ability to see a focused, clear image at various viewing distances. People who cannot see clearly up close are far-sighted; those who cannot see clearly at a distance are near-sighted. Newborns are extremely near-sighted. Targets that are more than 25.4 centimetres away appear blurry to them. Interestingly, the face of a person cradling the infant in a feeding position is within the range of the infant's best visual acuity, as is a mobile dangling over the side of his crib. Visual acuity improves rapidly and is nearly adult-like by 6 months. You might be curious about how researchers measure visual acuity in infants. Obviously, infants cannot read out the letters on a Snellen chart (a chart that has a big *E* on top, followed by rows of letters in increasingly smaller type). Infants are tested with a novelty paradigm in which they are first shown a picture of a single vertical stripe. They are shown it repeatedly until they habituate to it. Now they are given a test. They are shown a picture that has two vertical stripes. If they can detect both stripes, this picture will be novel, and the infant will attend to it. If the infant's acuity is poor, the two stripes will be so blurry that they appear joined. It will be like another trial of a picture with one stripe. In this case, the infant will not attend to it because he is habituated to pictures with one stripe. In the picture that has two stripes, researchers vary the distance between the stripes, bringing them closer and closer together, until the infant treats them as though they were one. Whereas newborns discriminate stripes 3.2 millimetres apart and 25.4 centimetres away, 6-month-olds discriminate stripes .8 millimetres apart from that same distance (Banks & Dannemiller, 1987; Fantz, Ordy, & Udelf, 1962).

Seeing in Colour Colour discrimination improves steadily over the first year. Even newborns can see bright colours, such as yellow, orange, red, green, and turquoise.

For the first 1 to 2 months, they actually prefer black-and-white patterns over coloured ones, probably owing to the greater contrast. The colour images may appear a bit blurry or washed out to the infant because of the lack of contrast. By 2 months, the infant picks up more subtle colours, such as blue, purple, or chartreuse, when compared with grey. Infants' colour vision and preference for colour improve rapidly. By 4 months, they discriminate between most colours, and, by 6 months, their colour perception nearly equals that of adults (Bornstein, 1978; Maurer & Maurer, 1988; Teller & Bornstein, 1987).

Selective Attention Infants are selective in what they look at from the beginning. They look at novel and moderately complex patterns and at human faces. Some changes take place during the first year, however, in exactly what attracts their attention. Newborns look predominantly at the edges of a face. By 2 to 3 months, there is a transition in what infants look at. Now, they scan the features inside the face. They are especially attracted to eyes and are attentive for longer periods of time. Making eye contact is important socially, as the infant develops relationships with caregivers. By 4 months, infants prefer a regularly arranged face over a distorted face. By 5 months, infants look at the mouth of a person who is talking, and by 7 months, they respond to the whole face and facial expressions. They prefer happy facial expressions over sad or angry ones. Also, as infants mature, they show increasing preference for greater complexity or contour over simpler designs. As well, between 9 and 12 months, infants gradually develop more control over what they look at and for how long (Ruff & Rothbart, 1996). The toddler is able to sustain attention for a longer period of time, and she has more control over shifting her attention from one object to another. While playing with an adult, she can shift attention back and forth between the adult and a toy. Toddlers are especially interested in what others are looking at and will look in the same direction. Toddlers' attention is less impulsive. It is more planned and self-regulated. Between 18 and 24 months, there is another major transition in attention (Ruff & Rothbart, 1996). Now, the toddler can use language to regulate and plan his attention.

Researchers wonder what causes these changes in selective attention. They seem to be due partly to the ways in which the neural system matures. Bornstein (1978), for example, discovered that 4-month-old infants prefer "pure" colours to other shades and look for a longer time at perpendicular lines than at slanted lines. He suggests that infants select these colours and lines because they trigger more "neural firing" in the brain. In other words, infants look at the things available that excite the most neural activity. Johnson (1993) has made a connection between the infants' visual preferences and abilities and the extent of maturation in four separate visual pathways in the brain. Ruff and Rothbart (1996) suggest that the increasing control over attention is possible because of the maturation of the cortex, especially the frontal lobe (see the section in this chapter on brain development and experience).

Eye Movements and Scanning A number of other improvements in vision occur during the first 6 months. Compared with newborns, older infants are better able to control their eye movements; they can track moving objects more consistently and for longer periods of time (Aslin, 1987). They also spend more time scanning the environment. During the first month of life, infants spend only 5 to 10 percent of their time in scanning, whereas they spend nearly 35 percent in scanning at 2½ months (White, 1971). Although newborns are attracted to bright lights and objects, provided the objects are not too bright, 4-month-olds are able to see and respond to dimmer objects.

There are individual differences in scanning efficiency. As early as 4 months, some infants are able to recognize objects after scanning them quickly, but other infants require considerably more time (Frick & Colombo, 1996). These early differences may prove significant, as some researchers are trying to relate them to differences in intellectual functioning once the children are school-aged (see, for example, Rose, Feldman, & Wallace, 1992).

Seeing Objects Do infants see objects the way adults see objects? It was once thought that infants had difficulty separating the object from the background. But, in reality, this problem is rare. Infants may not "see" that a cup is separate from a saucer without picking up the cup, but they can "see" that the cup and saucer are separate from the background. By 3 or 4 months, infants have had many visual experiences in which their head moves or the object moves. They will notice, for example, that a milk bottle, from another angle, is still a milk bottle. Infants can use motion, as well as space, to help define the objects in their world (Mandler, 1990; Spelke, 1988).

Depth Perception Humans see things in three dimensions. We see that some things are closer and that others are farther away. Even with one eye closed, we can tell the approximate distance of objects. The objects that are close to us appear larger, and they block our view of more distant objects. If we close one eye and hold our heads still, the view resembles a two-dimensional photograph. But, if we move our head, the world comes to life with its three-dimensional aspect. If we use both eyes (binocular vision), we really don't have to move our heads. The left-eye view and the right-eye view differ slightly. The brain integrates these two images, giving us information on distance and relative size.

Do infants have **depth perception**? Are their brains preprogrammed to integrate the images from two eyes in order to gain information about distance or relative size? Can they use the information that they gather by moving their heads to see the world in three dimensions?

It appears that the infant's brain can integrate two images in rudimentary form. Because the newborn's eyes are not well coordinated and because the infant has not learned how to interpret the information transmitted by the eyes, depth perception is probably not very sophisticated. It seems to take about 4 months for binocular vision to emerge (Aslin & Smith, 1988).

What is the evidence of developing depth perception? Even infants as young as 6 weeks use spatial cues to react defensively to potentially dangerous situations. Infants seem to dodge, blink, or show some form of avoidance reaction when an object appears to be coming directly at them (Dodwell, Humphrey, & Muir, 1987). By 2 months, infants react defensively to an object on a collision, but not near-miss, course. In addition, they prefer three-dimensional to two-dimensional figures. At 4 months, infants are able to swipe with reasonable accuracy at a toy that is dangled in front of them. By 5 months, they have a well-controlled, visually guided reach for objects that are close to them. However, infants at 5 months who are wearing a patch over one eye are slightly less accurate at reaching for objects. Similarly, when given the choice of two objects, one slightly closer than the other, they don't always pick the closer object (Granrud, Yonas, & Petterson, 1984).

One of the best-known experiments to test infants' depth perception is the **visual cliff.** Gibson and Walk (1960) created a special box to simulate depth. On one side, a heavy piece of glass covered a solid surface. On the other side, the heavy glass was 60 to 90 centimetres above a floor, simulating a cliff effect. Infants 6 months or older refused to crawl across the surface that appeared to be a cliff. Younger infants who were not yet able to crawl showed interest but not distress, as indicated by heart rate changes, when they were placed on the cliff side of the box (Campos, Langer, & Krowitz, 1970). This heart rate change indicated that younger infants are able to discriminate the spatial cues but do not show a marked fear response to the greater depth.

Further studies by Joseph Campos and his colleagues have focused on how children learn not to cross the cliff side. A baby who has barely learned how to crawl can sometimes be coaxed across the cliff, provided it is not too deep. The same baby will later refuse to cross if her mother has signalled to her that it is dangerous. She may tell her in an anxious voice not to cross, or she may simply express a look of fear, anxiety, or even horror. If these mothers do not show such a fear response themselves, but are rather encouraging, the babies can be coaxed to cross the deep side to reach their parent (Kermoian & Campos, 1988). It appears that the visual cues for depth perception are

depth perception The integration of images from the two eyes to gain information about distance or relative size, and the movement of the head to see the world in three dimensions.

visual cliff An experimental apparatus that tests depth perception of infants by simulating an abrupt drop-off.

Even when coaxed by their mothers, infants will not crawl over the edge of the visual cliff.

developed within the first 4 to 6 months (Yonas & Owsley, 1987). Infants learn the particular meaning of the information about distance or depth more gradually, especially as the child begins to move about his environment (Campos, Berenthal, & Kermoian, 1997). This is an excellent example of the way in which maturation and the psychosocial environment combine to produce the behaviours we observe in infants and children.

Hearing

The anatomical development of the auditory system is virtually complete before the end of gestation. Within the first few months, infants' hearing acuity improves considerably. At birth, the middle ear is filled with fluid and tissue, most of which disappears after the first few weeks. Despite this blockage, newborns show changes in heart rate and respiration in response to moderate sounds (for example, 60 decibels—the noise level of a normal telephone conversation). At 3 months, they respond to much softer sounds (43 decibels), and at 8 months to even softer tones (34 decibels) (Hoversten & Moncur, 1969). We also know by changes in their heart rates that infants detect fairly large changes in loudness, pitch, and duration of sound. They may even detect much smaller changes or hear much softer tones, although it is difficult to measure this degree of hearing, except through hospital experimentation. This measurement is done by a study of the electrical activity of the brain using EEG (electroencephalogram) readings (Hecox, 1975).

Infants do respond in other ways to sounds. They can be soothed, alerted, or distressed by them. Low-frequency or rhythmic sounds generally soothe infants. Loud, sudden, and high-frequency tones cause them distress. Infants also show—by turning their heads—that they can locate the source of the sound. These and other behaviours indicate that infants have fairly well developed auditory perception within their first 6 months of life.

As with vision, babies show auditory preferences early in development. Infants are especially attentive to human voices. Remarkably, one study found that newborns (3 days old or younger) preferred their mother's voice to that of another woman (DeCasper & Fifer, 1980). You might wonder how the researchers discovered this preference. Their procedure was simple, yet elegant, and included a number of controls. Infants were set up to suck on a pacifier while wearing headphones that played a tape either of their mothers reading a Dr. Seuss story or of another woman reading the same story. Infants could control which tape was played by changing their sucking rates. When infants suck on a pacifier, they do so in bursts, sucking for a while, pausing, then sucking again. The researchers monitored the length of the pauses between sucking bursts. First, they measured the length of pauses when infants wore headphones that were turned off. This average, called a *baseline condition,* was measured to establish the median length of time that an infant normally paused between sucking bursts. After the baseline was measured, the headphones were turned on. Now, the infant's sucking caused the tape either of the mother or of the other woman to be turned on, depending on how long the infant paused between sucking bursts. If he had a long pause, the tape of his mother played; if he had a short pause, the tape of the other woman played. Infants had more long pauses than short ones, so they got to listen to their mothers' voices more than the other voice. Does this result prove that the infants preferred their mothers' voices? The answer is no. These results are ambiguous. Infants may be pausing longer to hear mom's voice, or they may be pausing because they are tiring. Can you think of a control that could be added to this experiment to rule out the second interpretation? As you might have guessed, the researchers included another group of infants as a control. These infants heard their mothers' voices after short pauses and the other voice after long pauses—the reverse of the first group of infants. Interestingly, infants in the second group took shorter, not longer pauses. Thus, infants varied the length of their pauses so that they could hear their mothers' voices more often than the other one—whether it meant taking longer or shorter pauses. Now, do these findings prove that the infants prefer their mothers' voices? You might be curious about the tape of the other woman's voice. Is it possible that infants were sucking to hear their mothers' voices more, not because they preferred them, but because they found the other woman's voice aversive and were trying to avoid it? The researchers controlled for this possibility by using the voice of one of the other mothers as the other voice. For instance, Baby A modified her sucking to hear her mother's voice more often than the voice of Baby B's mother. But Baby B did the opposite—he modified his sucking to hear his mother's voice more often than that of Baby A's mother.

By 4 months, infants' preference for their mothers' voices is more obvious. They will smile more in response to their mothers' voices than to another female voice. By 6 months, they show distress upon hearing their mothers' voices if they cannot see them. This is the age at which the mother's mere talking to her baby from another room—perhaps while preparing food or a bottle—no longer is an effective soother. The infant must both see and hear her to stop crying. By 10 months, if the infant hears the mother's voice on tape she will look at her; if she hears another female voice, she will look at the other female. Infants at this age also vocalize more after hearing their mothers' voices (Mandler, 1990).

An important aspect of infants' hearing during the first year is their seemingly inborn ability to differentiate between speech and nonspeech sounds. As early as 1 month, infants can detect subtle differences between speech sounds called *phonemes* (the shortest speech segment in which a change also produces a change in meaning, such as *lip* and *lap*) (Eimas, 1975; Werker, 1995). In fact, one researcher was amazed to find that infants in the first year could pick up differences in language that even she could not pick up. She had borrowed a tape containing sounds used in the Czech language. After listening to it repeatedly, she could detect no differences. When she called the language lab to complain, they told her that she was mistaken. She then played this tape to her Canadian babies, who detected the differences immediately (Maurer & Maurer, 1988). It is clear that infants' sensitivity to speech sounds helps them learn how to speak. This sensitivity and their ability to recognize familiar voices help strengthen infants' attachment bond to parents and caregivers.

Integration

Researchers have generally agreed that at birth an infant's vision, hearing, and senses of touch, taste, and smell are nearly complete and that they improve rapidly over the next 6 months. In contrast, there has been great disagreement about whether there is integration of these senses during early infancy. How do we ask infants if they know that a particular sound comes from a particular object? How do infants acknowledge that the bumpy thing they just felt is now the same thing they are looking at? It is difficult to design experiments for the first 6 months of life. Recent imaginative work, however, suggests that either the senses are interrelated at birth or the necessary learning is extremely rapid.

As you will recall from Chapter 5, newborns will turn their heads to look at the source of a sound. They do not necessarily know what they will see, but there is a mechanism in place that will help them learn this. Some creative experiments have been done on **sensory integration.** In one study, infants were allowed to suck on either of two different kinds of pacifiers: one was covered with bumps, and the other was smooth. When the pacifier was removed and the infants were shown both kinds of pacifiers, they looked longer at the nipple that they had just felt in their mouth (Meltzoff & Borton, 1979). In another experiment, infants at 4 months were shown two films of complex events that they had not seen before and that had only one soundtrack. The infants turned to look at the film that matched the sound. Next, the film was

sensory integration The linking of information across sense modalities, for example, the recognition that a mother's voice (auditory information) comes from her face (visual information).

simplified so that only two speakers' faces were shown, and it looked as if both speakers were talking at exactly the same time. The infants were still able to pick out the speaker's face that matched the soundtrack (Kuhl & Meltzoff, 1988). In a recent study conducted by researchers at the University of British Columbia, 4½-month-old infants looked more at the lip movements that matched the vowel sound they were listening to than at lip movements for a different vowel sound (Patterson & Werker, in press). It is remarkable that infants that young can associate lip movements with individual speech sounds.

Other experiments have shown that infants expect faces to be responsive. They react differently to faces that are expressive than to those that are expressionless (see, for example, Kisilevsky et al., 1998). These experiments use the still-face paradigm, which has three phases. In the first phase, the infant spends one to two minutes interacting face-to-face with a responsive adult who smiles, talks, and touches the infant. Infants usually smile, vocalize, and look at the adult. Then, in the second phase, the adult suddenly becomes unresponsive to the infant for a minute or two. This behaviour is called the *still-face effect* (the adult mimics a statue). Infants usually stop smiling and vocalizing, and they often become distressed. Gradually, they turn away from the unresponsive adult. Finally, in the third phase, the adult resumes responsive interactions with the infant. The infant follows the adult's lead and starts smiling, vocalizing, and looking at the adult more than during the still-face effect. The third phase is a necessary control because it shows that the reduction in the infant's responsiveness is a reaction to the still-face effect and not just a reaction to prolonged face-to-face interaction. By 3 months, infants show a still-face effect while interacting with mothers, fathers, or strangers. The still-face effect is of interest to researchers who study how infants form social relationships (see Braungart-Reiker, Garwood, Powers, & Notaro, 1998). Of concern are infants who are constantly exposed to non-responsive interactions, perhaps because their caregivers are depressed. What does the infant learn from these interactions (or lack of interactions)? We will look at infants' social relationships in Chapter 7.

Much sensory integration must, of course, be learned. Infants must learn which sounds go with which sights, what the soft fur feels and looks like, what the noisy puppy looks like, and so forth. Nevertheless, it appears that infants have a built-in tendency to seek these links. Integration advances rapidly over the first year. In another study, Rose, Gottfried, and Bridger (1981) found that even though 6-month-olds could sometimes visually identify an object that they had touched or were touching, their cross-modal transference (tactual–visual) was not as strong as older infants'. Some of the research on the visual cliff makes a similar point about the integration of emotion and perception. Although young infants did recognize the depth in the visual cliff, and they noticed that one side was different from the other, they did not necessarily recognize that it was something unsafe or something not to be crawled across. They were more interested than afraid. Older infants who had a higher level of integration were more wary of the visual cliff. This result does not indicate that higher levels of integration cause the older infants to be afraid, but it does demonstrate that behaviour and emotions become linked over time—perhaps because of experience, maturation, or some combination of both.

Integration, then, is a process that becomes increasingly efficient and effective over the first year of the infant's life. One of the milestones in this process is the coordination of vision with reaching, a seemingly simple accomplishment that takes several months.

The Visually Guided Reach

If 1-month-old infants are shown an attractive object, they will do a number of things. Often, they will open and close their hands and wave their arms in a seemingly random way. Sometimes, they will open their mouths as if they are about to suck. They may even look intently at the object. But they cannot coordinate any of these reflexes by reaching out, grasping the object, and bringing it to their mouths. It takes at least 5 months to develop this skill.

Successful reaching requires a number of abilities: accurate depth perception, voluntary control of grasping, voluntary control of arm movements, and the ability to organize these behaviours in a sequence (Bruner, 1973). Throughout the first 5 months, infants are learning about objects with their mouths and hands and then linking visual information to direct the exploration of the fingers (Rochat, 1989). Finally, in the **visually guided reach,** infants combine many bits and pieces of behaviour; they functionally integrate and subordinate them to the total pattern. When they are first learning the guided reach, children must attempt individually the acts of reaching, grasping, and mouthing. Later, the reach itself becomes a means to an end, and children can then turn to a larger task—like stacking blocks. Their reaching is then functionally integrated and subordinated to block building.

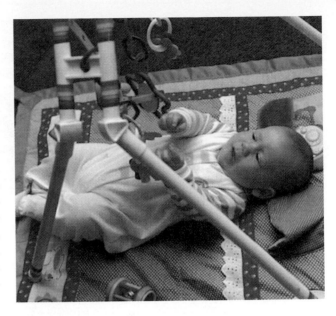

The coordination of vision with reaching—the visually guided reach—is one of the milestones in development.

Brain Development

Let us first look at brain development at the level of the cell. As we have seen in Chapter 4, as early as 2 weeks after conception, the specialized cells that will form the nervous system differentiate from those cells that will make up the skeleton, muscles, and other organs of the body. During the embryonic and early fetal period, there is rapid production of the basic nerve cells called **neurons.** The human brain has 100 to 200 billion neurons that store and transmit information.

Neurons are able to receive and transmit information because they have two types of branches off the main part of each cell: *dendrites* to receive information, and an *axon* to transmit messages to other neurons, as shown in Figure 6-4. All neurons form in a central part of the brain and then must migrate to where they belong, as was discussed in Chapter 5. Newly formed neurons do not start to grow dendrites and axons until after migration. A neuron's axon grows at the rate of about a millimetre per day, and its dendrites grow even more slowly (Kolb, 1995). Axons and dendrites grow to enable connections between neurons. These connections are called **synapses.** The pattern of synapses among neurons is sometimes referred to as the wiring of the brain. During the first year of life, new synapses develop rapidly. Curiously, the 1-year-old's brain has more synapses than the adult's brain. Many of the 1-year-old's synapses, though, are faulty or extra connections. A major part of brain development between the ages of 1 and 16 is the elimination of faulty or unused connections. Synapses that are used are kept; those that are not used are eliminated (Kolb, 1995). Environmental stimulation plays a critical role in brain development because it influences which neurons are used and preserved. Therefore, early experiences have lasting effects because they alter brain development.

Fewer than half of the cells in the brain are neurons; the others are *glial cells*. Glial cells provide a support system for the neurons, which are highly fragile. For example, the glial cells maintain favourable chemical environments for the neurons, clean up damaged areas of the brain, and insulate the neurons to improve communication. They provide insulation by forming a myelin sheath around the axons; this process is called **myelination.** Parts of the brain are myelinated at different rates. Myelination of pathways for motor reflexes and vision occurs in early infancy. More complex movement pathways follow, and, finally, the pathways and structures that control attention, self-control, memory, and learning are formed. Myelination continues into adolescence.

In summary, at a cellular level, two of the key brain developments during infancy are the refinement of synapses and myelination. Although these developments occur throughout the brain, their timing varies from one part of the brain to another.

visually guided reach Accurate reaching made possible by the functional integration of visual input.

neurons Cells in the nervous system that are responsible for communication. They form prenatally and continue to grow, branch, and make connections throughout life.

synapses Sites of communication between neurons.

myelination The formation of the myelin sheath covering the axons of neurons. This sheath increases the speed of transmission and the precision of the nervous system.

Figure 6-4
Neurons and Synapses
Neurons are specialized to receive and transmit messages. They receive signals through dendrites and transmit them down the axon. At the end of the axon, neurons form synapses with other neurons. The synapse is where information is conveyed from one neuron to the next.

Source: Adapted from Robert A. Baron (1998). *Psychology* (4th ed.). Needham Heights, MA: Allyn and Bacon, p. 45.

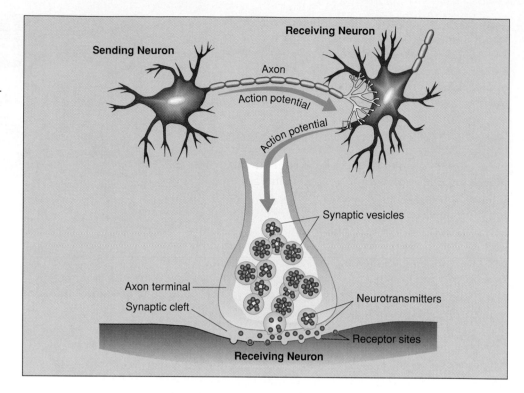

They occur very early—before birth—in parts of the brain that control vital functions, such as breathing and heart functioning, as well as basic reflexes. These functions are located in the brain stem (see Figure 6-5). However, even at birth the sensory areas of the brain are fairly mature, so that the infant is able to process sensory information immediately after birth.

During the first year, sensory areas mature first, followed by motor areas, and then by parts of the brain that link the two. At around 6 months, parts of the brain involved in reasoning, language, and memory become more active. A major transition occurs between 7 and 9 months, when the frontal lobe of the cerebral cortex (see

Figure 6-5
Parts of the Brain

Source: Adapted from Neil R. Carson, William Buskist, Michael E. Enzle and C. Donald Heth (2000), *Psychology: The Science of Behaviour*, Canadian Edition. Scarborough, Ont.: Allyn and Bacon Canada, p. 106.

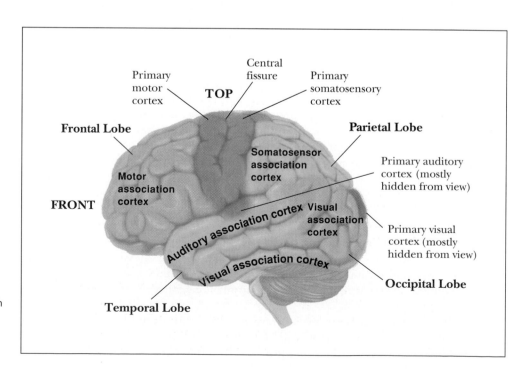

Figure 6-5) becomes considerably more active. Frontal lobe activity enables the infant to gain more control over her behaviour and to plan sequences of actions, which are critical steps toward goal-directed behaviour.

Cognitive Development

Cognition is the process by which we gain knowledge of our world. Cognition encompasses the processes of thinking, learning, perceiving, remembering, and understanding. Cognitive development refers to the growth and refinement of this intellectual capacity. Many theorists believe that infants take an active role in their own cognitive development. The problem is in finding out what infants do know and think about. When subjects cannot talk to you and tell you what they are thinking, how can you study their developing intellect?

The individual most influential in the study of emerging infant intelligence has probably been Jean Piaget. As was discussed in Chapter 2, Piaget was one of the few psychologists who had woven a design large enough to encompass all human intellectual development. Piaget was fascinated with the human mind, a passion that fuelled his natural talents as an observer of behaviour. Part of his work focused on the interaction between heredity and the environment, and part on the ways in which children manipulate the environment to exercise and develop their cognitive abilities.

As detailed in Chapter 2, Piaget saw humans as active, alert, and creative beings who possess mental structures, called schemes, that process and organize information. Over time, these schemes develop into more complex cognitive structures. Intellectual development occurs in four qualitatively different sequential periods that begin in early infancy and go on for the next 12 to 15 years into adolescence and beyond. His first period of intellectual development is called the **sensorimotor period.**

> **cognition** The process by which we know and understand our world.

> **sensorimotor period** Piaget's first stage of cognitive development.

The Sensorimotor Period

Infants come into the world prepared to respond to the environment with the perceptual capacities just discussed and with a few ready-made motor patterns—sucking, crying, kicking, and making a fist. For Piaget, these sensorimotor patterns form the infant's schemes—the infant's only way of processing information from the environment.

But what about thoughts and concepts? How do infants develop an understanding of objects, people, or relationships? How do they code and store things in their memory without any words? What, after all, is infant intelligence? According to Piaget, these ready-made schemes—looking, visually following, sucking, grasping, and crying—form the building blocks for cognitive development. They are transformed over the next 18 months into some early concepts of objects, people, and the self. Piaget considered sensorimotor behaviour to be the beginning of intelligence. From observing their actions, we can make inferences about infants' knowledge of the physical world.

> **adaptation** In Piaget's theory, the process by which infant schemes are elaborated, modified, and developed.

> *Infants have a limited number of behavioural schemes in their repertoire. Looking, mouthing, grasping, and banging are the ways they interact with their environment.*

Adaptation

Piaget viewed the sensorimotor period as comprising six fairly discrete stages. Because other researchers have found some variations in the course of events, we will not discuss this period by these discrete stages but rather by some of the processes of development that occur during it.

Infant schemes are elaborated, modified, and developed by a process that Piaget called **adaptation** (1962). He described how his 7 month-old daughter, Lucienne, played with a pack of cigarettes. Unlike a 2-year-old, who might take out a cigarette and pretend to smoke it, Lucienne had no such behaviours in her repertoire. She treated the pack of cigarettes as if it were any other toy or object that

she had been used to handling. Looking, mouthing, grasping, and banging were her only ways of interacting with the world: these were her toy-manipulating schemes. In other words, she assimilated the pack of cigarettes into her existing schemes. With each new object, children make minor changes in their action patterns, or schemes. The grasp and the mouth must accommodate the new object. Gradually, through assimilation and accommodation, these action patterns become modified, and the infant's basic sensorimotor schemes develop into more complex cognitive capacities.

Piaget noted a specific form of adaptation in infancy that he called a **circular response.** Much of what infants learn begins quite by accident. An action occurs, and then infants see, hear, or feel it. For example, some babies may notice their hands in front of their faces. By moving their hands, they discover that they can change what they see. They can prolong the event, repeat it, stop it, or start it again. Infants' early circular responses involve the discovery of their own bodies. Later circular responses concern how they use their bodies or themselves to change the environment, as in making a toy move.

According to Piaget, at the end of the sensorimotor period, most infants will have achieved a number of simple but fundamental intellectual abilities. These abilities include forming concepts about the uses of familiar objects, understanding object permanence, improving memory development, and learning some beginning ways to symbolically represent things, people, and events. Each of the following sections examines a part of this development.

Play with Objects

Although they are often unnoticed by parents or caregivers, accomplishments in object play are important to children's cognitive development. By 4 or 5 months, infants generally reach out, grasp, and hold objects. These seemingly simple skills—together with their advanced perceptual skills—equip them for more varied play with objects. In their play with objects, infants and young children demonstrate a memory for repeated events, match their actions appropriately with various objects, and develop their understanding of the social world through pretending and imitation. Play, in other words, lays the groundwork for further complex thinking and language.

Object play goes through definite stages, starting with simple explorations by about 5 months and moving to complex imitative and pretending behaviour by the end of 3 years (Garvey, 1977). By 9 months, most infants explore objects; they wave them around, turn them over, and test them by hitting them against something nearby. But they are unaware of the use or function of the things that they are handling. By 12 months, they stop first and examine objects closely before putting them in their mouths. By 15 to 18 months, they try to use objects as they were intended—for example, they might pretend to drink from a cup, brush their hair with a toy brush, or make a doll sit up. By 21 months, they generally use objects appropriately. They try to feed a doll with a spoon, put a doll in the driver's seat of a toy truck, or use keys to unlock an imaginary door. The play becomes still more realistic by 24 months. Toddlers take dolls out for walks and line up trucks and trailers in the right order. By 3 years, preschool children may make dolls into imaginary people with independent wills. They might have a doll go outdoors, chop wood, bring it back inside, and put it in an imaginary fireplace (Bornstein & O'Reilly, 1991; Fein, 1981).

Imitation

The object play of 2-year-olds is rich with imitations of their world. Infants' imitations—of actions, gestures, and words—are not as simple as they might appear to adults.

Within the first 3 months, infants do some sporadic imitation in the context of play with the caregiver. For example, an infant may imitate facial expressions, or she may stick out her tongue and match the sound or pitch of the mother's voice. Normally, mothers begin this game by imitating the infant. In fact, it is sometimes hard to tell who

circular response A particular form of adaptation in Piaget's theory, in which the infant accidentally performs some action, perceives it, then repeats the action.

is imitating—mother or child (Uzgiris, 1984). Interestingly, babies as young as 5 to 8 weeks are much more likely to imitate mouth movements of their mothers than similar movements produced by an object simulating mouth movements (Legerstee, 1991). For example, to stimulate opening and closing the mouth, Legerstee used a big blue box with a red interior. One side of the box was hinged, so that it could open and close, revealing the red interior. Babies who were shown the box opening and closing were far less likely to imitate the movement than were babies who were shown a human mouth opening and closing. Thus, even very young babies model familiar human targets more than inanimate ones. In addition, infants as young as 3 months are able to imitate the vowel sounds of speech and are already aware of the connection between mouth movements and sound (Legerstee, 1990). By 6 or 7 months, however, infants are much better at imitating gestures and actions. The first hand gestures to be imitated are those for which they already have action schemes: grasping, reaching, and so on. By 9 months, they can imitate novel gestures, such as banging two objects together. During the second year, infants begin to imitate a series of actions or gestures, even some that they have seen sometime previously. At first, children imitate only those actions they choose themselves. Later, they imitate those who show them how to brush their teeth or how to use a fork or spoon. Some toddlers even train themselves to use the toilet with relatively little struggle by imitating an older child.

Have you ever noticed that when adults see someone look off to the side, they often imitate, looking in the same direction? This action is called *gaze turning* and *joint visual attention*. Chris Moore and colleagues at Dalhousie University in Halifax have found that infants as young as 10 months also spontaneously engage in gaze turning and joint visual attention (Corkum & Moore, 1997). The infants can follow the mothers' lead, paying attention to the various things in the environment that the mothers are focusing on, thus facilitating communication before the use of language. Even infants as young as 6 months can turn their heads in the general direction that their mothers are looking, but the younger infants are not as adept at focusing on the specific target of the mothers' gaze and cannot be trained to do so until about 8 months (Corkum & Moore, 1997; Moore, Angelopoulos, & Bennett, 1997).

Does imitation require a mental representation of the action? Is it thinking? Piaget believed that even simple imitation was a complex match of action patterns. He predicted that infants would not imitate novel action until they were at least 9 months old. **Deferred imitation**—imitating something that happened hours or days before—requires memory of an image or some use of symbolic representation. Piaget predicted that this ability would not occur until the age of 18 months. But infants seem to be able to imitate novel action somewhat earlier than Piaget predicted. For instance, children of deaf parents begin to learn and use sign language as early as 6 or 7 months (Mandler, 1988). Imaginative researchers, using novel toys, have demonstrated deferred imitation well before 18 months. One such study used a box with a hidden button. If the infant found the button, a beep was heard. There was another box with an orange light panel on top. If the infant leaned forward and touched the light panel with her head, a light went on. There was also a bear that danced when jiggled with a string. Infants were shown these actions but were not given an opportunity to play with the toys immediately. Infants at 11 months could imitate these actions 24 hours later, and infants at 14 months could imitate them a week later. Infants who had not seen the demonstration did not spontaneously perform these actions (Meltzoff, 1988a, 1988b). It seems that infants have more ability to remember and imitate an action sequence than we had previously thought.

deferred imitation Imitation after a delay.

Object Permanence

According to Piaget, **object permanence** is the primary accomplishment of the sensorimotor period. This ability is an awareness that an object exists in time and space regardless of one's own perception of it. Infants do not fully develop object permanence

object permanence According to Piaget, the realization in infants at about 18 months that objects continue to exist when they are out of sight, touch, or some other perceptual context.

By 6 or 7 months, infants are greatly improved in their ability to imitate gestures and actions.

until they are about 18 months old. According to Piaget, during the first year, "out of sight, out of mind" seems literally true for them. If they do not see something, it does not exist. Therefore, a covered toy holds no interest, even if an infant continues to hold on to it under the cover.

To understand how infants develop the idea of object permanence, Piaget (1952) and other researchers investigated infant search behaviour. They found that most infants do not sustain a successful search for an object that they have just seen until 18 months of age. They do, however, form an idea of their mothers' (or caregivers') permanence somewhat before this, but they do not generalize this insight to all other external objects until later. At 6 and 8 months, more infants search for their mothers than for objects or for female strangers; by 10 months, infants are equally competent at searching for any of the stimuli (Legerstee, 1994).

Infants understand object permanence months before they are able to demonstrate it by searching for hidden objects. To search successfully, infants not only have to understand object permanence, but they also have to coordinate reaching movements and inhibit reflexes, such as the grasping reflex, that interfere with finding the object. This skill is not possible until the front part of the brain (frontal lobes) is sufficiently matured, usually at around 8 months (Diamond, 1993).

The development of object permanence, therefore, involves a series of accomplishments. First, infants must develop a recognition of familiar objects, which they do as early as 2 months; for example, they become excited at the sight of a bottle or their caregivers. Second, infants about 2 months old may watch a moving object disappear behind one edge of a screen and then shift their eyes to the other edge to see if it reappears. Their visual tracking is excellent and well timed, and they are surprised if something does not reappear. But they do not seem to mind when a completely different object appears from behind the screen. In fact, infants up to 5 months will accept a wide variety of objects with no distress (Bower, 1971).

Infants older than 5 months are more discriminating "trackers." They will be disturbed if a different object appears or if the same object reappears but moves faster or more slowly than before. Even these older infants, however, can be fooled in an experiment. Imagine two screens side by side with a gap in the middle. An object disappears behind one screen; it does not appear in the gap, but it does reappear from behind the outer edge of the second screen. It is not until infants are 9 months old that they will expect the object to appear in the intervening gap. In fact, they are then surprised if it does not (Moore, Borton, & Darby, 1978).

As stated earlier, infants do form the complete idea of person permanence somewhat before object permanence, but the first developmental stages remain almost the same as for objects. T.G.R. Bower (1971) arranged mirrors so that infants would see multiple images of their mothers. He found that most infants less than 5 months old were not disturbed at seeing more than one mother—in fact, they were delighted. Infants older than 5 months or so, however, had learned that they had only one mother, and they were very disturbed at seeing more than one.

Infants learn more about objects when they begin to search for hidden objects. Searching behaviour proceeds through a predictable sequence of development, and it begins at about 5 months. Infants younger than 5 months do not search or hunt; they seem to forget about an object once it is hidden. Hunting behaviour begins somewhere between 5 and 8 months. Infants of this age enjoy hiding and finding games; they like being hidden under a blanket or covering their eyes with their hands and having the world reappear when they take their hands away. As we have seen, they are surprised if one object vanishes behind a screen and another emerges on the other side. If a toy

In Bower's multiple mothers experiment, infants younger than 20 weeks are not disturbed by seeing more than one mother. But older infants become upset at the sight of such images.

disappears through a trap door and another reappears when the door is opened again, they are also surprised, but they accept the new toy. Older infants, between 12 and 18 months, are puzzled, and they search for the first toy.

Some irregularities occur in 1-year-olds' hunting behaviour, however. If a toy is hidden in place A and they are used to finding it there, 1-year-olds will continue looking for it in place A, even when they have seen it hidden in place B. Piaget (1952) suggests that infants of this age seem to have two memories—one of seeing the object hidden (the seeing memory) and another of finding it (the action memory). Not everyone agrees with Piaget's interpretation of this "hiding" experiment, however. Mandler (1990) has suggested that there are other explanations for the irregularities in 1-year-olds' hunting behaviour.

The final attainment of object permanence occurs at about 18 months and seems to depend on infants' locomotive ability. When infants crawl and walk, they can pursue their guesses and hypotheses more actively. If a ball rolls away, they may follow it and find it. If mother is out of sight, they may go and find her. In this way, they test the properties of the world around them through their own actions.

The Properties of Objects

Physical Properties There is more to understanding objects than object permanence. Do infants understand physical properties of objects? For instance, do they know what to expect when one object collides with another, such as a toy car bumping into another? Do they know how objects need to be positioned in order to be stacked on top of each other? Do they understand why some objects, but not others, fit in a container? Renee Baillargeon and colleagues have done a number of studies to address these questions (see Baillargeon, 1997, for a review). One set of studies focused on infants' understanding of stacking objects on top of each other. Infants at 3 months believe that an object will support another, as long as the objects touch. But the infants are not aware that the extent or position of contact is important. Therefore, they think that a block can rest precariously on the edge of another. By 6½ months, though, they will understand that the amount and type of contact will determine whether the object will balance on the other. The researchers found a similar pattern for other physical properties, such as collision: even 2-month-olds expect a little toy bug to move when a cylinder bumps it. But they do not appreciate that heavier cylinders will cause the bug to move farther. This more subtle awareness is acquired between 5½ and 6½ months. A recent study with slightly older infants (8½ months) found that the infants understood which objects would fit in a container (Aguiar & Baillargeon, 1998). Infants realized that wide objects could not be inserted into narrow containers unless the objects were compressible (like a sponge). Infants showed this understanding in two different situations: (1) when the object and container were visible simultaneously so that infants could compare their relative sizes and (2) when the object and container were shown separately so that the infant had to compare his memory of the size of the object to the size of the container.

Baillargeon related the infant's increasing knowledge about the physical properties of objects to changes in the infant's daily experiences. For example, 3-month-olds understand that objects that do not touch cannot support each other because infants of this age have observed countless examples of objects falling from midair (seeing soothers drop from their open mouths, or their mothers tossing toys into boxes or diapers into pails). But by 6½ months, they will also understand the extent of contact required for one object to support another. They reach this understanding because, by this age, they will have experienced manipulating objects (observing how much of their bottom must be on the chair before they tumble off, or observing how to position blocks to make a tower).

Social Properties Remarkably, infants as young as 2 months are already distinguishing between objects and people (Legerstee, Pomerleau, Malcuit, & Feider, 1987). Infants smile and vocalize more to people than to objects, even when the object is a doll (Legerstee, Corter, & Kienapple, 1990; Legerstee, Pomerleau, Malcuit, & Feider, 1987). Even at this young age, the infant seems to know that people are communication partners and that objects are not. We have already seen one example of this understanding in the still-face effect, described earlier in this chapter. Infants become distressed when people become unresponsive. Interestingly, though, they do not become as distressed when moving toys stop moving (Legerstee, 1997). There are also differences in infants' imitation of movements, depending on whether a person or an object makes the movement (Legerstee, 1991). Infants are more likely to imitate mouths opening and closing than they are boxes doing the same motion.

In a recent study at York University, Maria Legerstee and colleagues showed 5- and 8-month-old infants videos of themselves, another infant, and a doll (Legerstee, Anderson, & Schaffer, 1998). Infants clearly discriminated among the three. There was a novelty effect. They looked the most at the other infant (who was a stranger) and the least at themselves (all of the infants had regular experience looking in a mirror). By 5 months, infants showed early signs of distinguishing themselves from others. As well, infants reacted differently to the different faces. They smiled and vocalized more to the real faces (i.e., their own and the other infant's) than to the doll's face. In a follow-up study, infants also reacted differently to sounds from the different sources. When listening to tape recordings of their own voice, a peer's voice, or chiming bells and synthesizer music, they spent more time looking in the direction of voices than in the direction of the other sounds. They looked more in the direction of the novel voice (that of the other infant) than in the direction of their own. Even though they preferred to look at novel stimuli, they did not smile and vocalize more at them. It seems that smiling and vocalizing have social significance. Infants smiled more when hearing voices than the other sounds. As well, they vocalized more in response to voices, especially their own.

Forming Categories Mandler and colleagues used a variant of the novelty paradigm to assess infants' knowledge of categories (Mandler & McDonough, 1998). In this paradigm, researchers showed the infants a number of objects, one at a time, and then measured how long the infants spent examining each item. The first several objects belonged to the same category, such as the category "animals." For example, the researchers showed the infants a plastic horse, a plastic seated cat, a wooden bird with outstretched wings, and a plastic dog. The researchers showed them each of these objects three times, so that the infants tired of them and spent less time examining them (as in habituation, in the novelty paradigm). Then, the researchers showed the infants new items in two test trials. On the first trial, they showed the children a new instance of the same category (e.g., a plastic whale) and on the second, an instance from another category (e.g., an airplane). If the infants had formed a global category of animals, they should have spent less time examining the whale (because they had been habituated to animals) than the airplane. These categories required a conceptual understanding and were not based solely on perceptual features. For example, the airplane looked more like one of the original animals (the bird with outstretched wings) than the whale did. Infants who were 7 to 11 months old distinguished among the categories of animals, vehicles, and furniture. By 9 months, infants were able to distinguish between two categories of animals (e.g., dogs and birds). By 11 months, infants' categories were even more refined. They categorized plants as distinct from animals or vehicles, and furniture as distinct from kitchen utensils. They distinguished between types of mammals (e.g., cats and dogs). Interestingly, though, even at 11 months, infants did not distinguish between types of furniture (e.g., beds and chairs). From this research, it appears that infants first form global concepts (such as of animals and vehicles), and then later refine them by forming more specific concepts (distinguishing between cats and dogs, for example). Research is currently being done to determine why infants form some categories before others.

Memory

Most of the sensorimotor abilities discussed so far require some form of memory. We have seen how 4-month-old infants prefer to look at new objects, which shows that they have already established some memory for the familiar (Cohen & Gelber, 1975). An infant who imitates must be able to remember the sounds and actions of another person. Infants who search for a toy where they have seen it hidden are remembering the location of that toy. Although sensorimotor abilities have been studied thoroughly, the role that memory plays in them has not.

Very young infants seem to have powerful visual memories (Cohen & Gelber, 1975; McCall, Eichorn, & Hogarty, 1977). Habituation studies have shown that infants as young as 2 months store visual patterns (Cohen & Gelber, 1975). Fagan (1977) found that 5-month-olds recognize patterns 48 hours after the first presentation, and they can remember photographs of faces after two weeks. He discovered, too, that 5- to 6-month-olds who had previously recognized facial photographs after a delay of two weeks had trouble recognizing the photos if they had been shown similar photos in the meantime (Fagan, 1977). This effect could be reversed, however, by briefly presenting the original image.

A few studies have indicated that infants have some long-term memory, at least for dramatic events. For instance, children who participated in an unusual experiment at a very young age remembered the actions that took place when reintroduced to that setting several months later (Rovee-Collier, 1987). Indeed, in one study, children recalled aspects of their experiment two years later (Myers, Clifton, & Clarkson, 1987). These children were able to repeat their actions, although four out of five children could not verbally report them. These studies indicate that memory for sights, for actions, and even for events develops early and is relatively robust.

Symbolic Representation

During infancy, some of the earliest forms of representation are actions. Infants smack their lips before their food or bottle reaches their mouths. They may continue to make eating motions after feeding time is over. They may drop a rattle, yet continue to shake the hand that held it. They may wave bye-bye before they are able to say the words. These actions are the simplest forerunners of **symbolic representation**—the ability to represent something not physically present.

Question to Ponder

Do you think the types of memory that infants form are different than the types of memory that adults form? Do you think that adults can retrieve memories that were encoded during infancy?

symbolic representation The use of a word, picture, gesture, or other sign to represent past and present events, experiences, and concepts.

Imitating, finding hidden objects, and pretending all point to an underlying process of symbolic representation (Mandler, 1983). Between 6 and 12 months, children begin pretending, that is, using actions to represent objects, events, or ideas. They may represent the idea of sleeping by putting their heads down on their hands. As we have seen in object play, toward the end of the second year children use objects appropriately; they may, for example, have a doll drive a truck, which is represented by a shoe box. Such pretending behaviour shows that children of this age create symbols independent of their immediate surroundings—a forward step in cognitive growth.

Pretending behaviour, too, develops in a predictable sequence (Fein, 1981; Rubin, Fein, & Vandenberg, 1983). The first stage occurs by about 11 or 12 months; most children of this age pretend to eat, drink, or sleep—all familiar actions. In the next few months, there is a dramatic increase in the range and number of pretend activities. At first, infants do not need objects to pretend, as when a child pretends to sleep, curled up on a rug. But as they grow older, they use toys and other objects, too. By 15 to 18 months, they feed brothers and sisters, dolls, and adults with real cups and with toy cups, spoons, and forks. At this point, children need realistic objects to support their pretend games. By 20 to 26 months, they may pretend that an object is something other than what it is; a broom may become a horse, a paper sack a hat, a wood floor a pool of water. Such forms of pretending represent a further step in cognitive development. By noting the rough similarities between a horse and a broom, children combine a distant concept with a familiar one and thus establish a symbolic relationship between the two. (Language, of course, is the ultimate system of symbolic relationships, as we shall see in Chapter 8.)

Critique of Piaget's Theory

Piaget's theory of infant cognitive development has fuelled 40 years of research and debate. His careful, naturalistic observations of infants have challenged others to look more closely. His emphasis on the interaction of maturation and experience and on the infant's active, adaptive, constructive role in her own learning brought a new respect to infant research. For Piaget, the toddler is a "little scientist" who tests and discovers the nature of physical objects and of the social world. The younger infant wiggles and kicks and varies her motions to make interesting sights last. Or, she repeats and extends and varies her voice just to enjoy the sound of her own babbling. For some observers, Piaget made the infant more human—more like us—and definitely worthy of our study.

But Piaget was not correct in everything he found. Many critics feel he overemphasized motor development and ignored perceptual development. Some of his stages are probably wrong. It appears, for instance, that infants can imitate much earlier than Piaget would have imagined. Indeed, some newborns appear to imitate an adult sticking out his tongue. Even the development of object permanence may not occur precisely in the fashion that Piaget describes. In fact, some critics suggest that infants may have more sophisticated knowledge of objects based on their perceptual development but that their motor development may lag behind. Hence, young infants might be able to show evidence of object permanence if they are given tests that do not require coordinated actions (Baillargeon, 1987; Gratch & Schatz, 1987; Mandler, 1990).

Children generally start pretending between 6 and 12 months.

Environmental Stimulation and Infant Competencies

The environment exerts a powerful influence on the development of infant competencies. The presence or absence of stimulation can speed up or slow down the acquisition of certain behaviours. In addition, motivation, timing of stimulation, and the quality of caregiving also affect infant development. A number of questions can be raised about the effects of early experience on infant competencies. Do normal patterns of behaviour—motor, intellectual, and social—emerge in a predetermined fashion, regardless of the nature of the infant's early experiences? Or are there minimal experiential conditions that are necessary for proper development? What about the timing of experience; for example, are early experiences more crucial than later experiences? Can patterns established early be modified later?

Early experience can affect structural development, intersensory coordination, and behavioural maturation, as we have already seen. Even motor behaviours whose onset is maturational can be developmentally retarded in severely restricted institutionalized infants. Clearly, malnutrition affects cognitive development. However, most homes provide an adequate enough environment to allow cognitive competencies to grow. There is also a body of research indicating that when deprivation occurs, serious and often permanent damage may be done to the infant's intellectual abilities.

Deprivation

The home environment can have a significant impact upon the well-being and general development of children. There is essentially a continuum of environments that exist—ranging from optimal environments to seriously deprived environments, such as barren institutions. As would be expected, the more restricted and deprived the environment, the more profound the developmental delay of the child exposed to it. Being deprived of normal experiences can have a marked and sometimes prolonged effect on infant development. Wayne Dennis (1960, 1973; Dennis & Najarian, 1957) found that institutionalized children were severely retarded even in such basic competencies as sitting, standing, and walking when they had no opportunities to practise these skills. And because of the almost total lack of stimulation in their environment, these children were also delayed in language, social skills, and emotional expression:

> As babies they lay on their backs in their cribs throughout the first year and often for much of the second year.... Many objects available to most children did not exist.... There were no building blocks, no sandboxes, no scooters, no tricycles, no climbing apparatus, no wagons, no teeter-totters, no swings, no chutes. There were no pets or other animals of any sort.... They had no opportunities to learn what these objects were. They never saw persons who lived in the outside world, except for rather rare visitors. (Dennis, 1973, pp. 22–23)

In follow-up studies 15 and 20 years later, Dennis (1973) found that even those children who were adopted showed some developmental retardation in maturity. Those who remained in barren institutions showed marked retardation throughout life.

The Family Environment

The general effect of environment on the development of children has been demonstrated in several studies. A recent longitudinal study of children with sex-chromosome abnormalities contrasted the outcomes of children with such anomalies from competent, nondysfunctional families with those from dysfunctional families. In this study, the dysfunctional families had such characteristics as ineffective parenting and multiple stresses affecting the family, such as poverty, drug and alcohol abuse, or

FOCUS ON AN ISSUE

"Hothouse" Babies

We now know quite a bit about the infant's emerging competence. We know it is important to have a responsive environment and to match the environmental stimulation to the infant's current abilities. We know that infants are learning and making associations from the day they are born, and perhaps even before. Knowing these things, why not create the best possible environment, one that maximizes the opportunity for learning? Why not create a "hothouse" environment that provides early training in academics and other skills, with the aim of developing a "superbaby"? Several researchers, in fact, have tried. Perhaps the most well known is Glenn Doman, in his Better Baby Program (Moore, 1984). Doman has written several books, such as *How to Teach a Baby to Read* (1963), and he provides a weeklong course for parents on how to stimulate advanced mental development. He believes that regular and systematic

---

Just as tomatoes grown out of season taste flat, perhaps a hothouse child will be a flat, unexciting individual.

---

stimulation and early training accelerate brain growth. His program urges brief training sessions in reading and mathematics, beginning at 1 year. These training sessions, with flashcards, are to last five or ten minutes at first and then are to be extended as the child grows older. Later, toddlers and 2-year-olds study Japanese or modern art or learn to play the violin.

Other programs of infant stimulation are much less intense but instruct parents on how to maximize the learning opportunities in daily routines. You might be surprised, for example, to discover how much a toddler can learn from kicking, from banging toys, or from making a peanut butter sandwich (Lehane, 1976).

What are the results of these training programs? There have been some remarkable case studies. Many 3- or 4-year-old children have been taught to read at a second- or third-grade level. There are children who play the violin at 4 years. But the results are inconsis-

death of a family member. In general, both groups of children showed some motor and cognitive problems when compared with their normal siblings. However, the nature and extent of these problems were more pronounced if the child came from a multidysfunctional family. (Bender, Linden, & Robinson, 1987).

Another study followed the entire population of 670 children born on Kauai in the Hawaiian Islands in 1955 (Werner, 1989). At birth, 3 percent of the infants showed severe birth complications, 13 percent moderate complications, 31 percent mild complications, and 53 percent no complications. At the age of 2 years, a general assessment was done of their overall functioning. Of these 2-year-olds, 12 percent were rated as deficient in social development, 16 percent deficient in intellectual functioning, and 14 percent deficient in health. As is typical, the more severe the birth complications had been, the lower the developmental level of the children. Of special interest, however, was the relationship between birth complications and environmental factors. In general, the infants coming from dysfunctional families, especially those with low socioeconomic status, showed the greatest negative effect stemming from birth complications. For example, infants born with the most severe birth complications who were living in dysfunctional, poor families with mothers of low intelligence showed a difference of 19 to 37 points in their average IQ scores when compared with those infants with mild or moderate complications. On the other hand, infants with severe birth complications who were born into stable families with higher socioeconomic status showed only a 5- to 7-point difference when compared with their peers who had been born with mild or moderate deficiencies.

What specifically is there about these environments that produces such a negative effect? Part of the answer lies in the notion of family dysfunction—where there is great stress that tends to be persistent or insoluble in families, the members tend to focus on their personal needs rather than on the collective good of the family. If such a family is placed in poverty, essential factors such as access to health care, ability to gather information about dealing with problems, and often knowledge of what options might exist to improve the situation of their child with special needs are also removed.

tent, and there are some dangers. Sometimes an overeager parent teaches a child by the age of 2 to avoid anything that looks remotely like a flashcard. Children who spend a great deal of time in rote learning have less time to explore the world around them and to initiate activities with other children, as well as with adults. There are fewer opportunities for simply discovering. Finally, an overemphasis on cognitive development can have negative effects on social and personality development. Children can become insecure or overly dependent on their parents. Some children may become anxious because of the high expectations placed on them at an early age.

Several child development experts have gathered together in a symposium to discuss the challenges and problems of the trend toward "hot housing" infants and young children. One of them defines "hot housing" as "inducing infants to acquire knowledge that is typically acquired at a later developmental level" (Sigel, 1987, p. 212). David Elkind (1981) calls them hurried children. Most of these experts agree that structured training of infants and young children too early in academic tasks tends to have serious negative side effects on social and emotional development. These children not only lose play time, but they suffer from achievement anxiety and have limited informal social skills. Some have limited cognitive development, as well, with gaps in their understanding of the physical world, despite their rote memory for complex definitions or their advanced skills in reading. Professor Sigel suggests that hot housing is a wonderful metaphor, as it reminds one of the tomato plant in the greenhouse, in an artificial climate, protected and sterile, and with chemicals and alien forces that force growth "out of season." He asks, "Who really likes hothouse tomatoes?" (Sigel, 1987, p. 218). Professor Sigel suggests that, just as tomatoes grown out of season taste flat, perhaps a hothouse child will be a flat, unexciting individual. Similarly, early harvesting of hothouse children may stunt full development, depress their emotional range, and limit their ability to explore, create, and even problem solve in new environments. He suggests that parents provide a rich and varied growth environment for children, complete with social supports, and that they make ample room for the child to self-select and self-pace cognitive development, together with social awareness, a strong self-concept, and positive ways of socially interacting (Sigel, 1987).

Normal versus Optimal Environments

Studies such as those done with institutionalized infants may be criticized on methodological grounds, but the consensus is that deprived early experience has a devastating effect on the developing child. The questions then remain: What about the effects of normal environments? What is there in the normal or even enriched environment that may contribute to the social and intellectual growth of children?

A moderately enriched environment seems to promote optimum cognitive growth in infants.

Motivation

The vast majority of infants seem motivated to develop their skills with self-rewarding experiences. For example, children show considerable persistence in learning to walk for the sheer satisfaction of walking. Infants learn skills not only because they are intrinsically motivated, but also because the environment responds. They learn to push a toy simply to see it move. They practise motor skills to experience and master a task.

The responsiveness of the environment is crucial. In one study, three groups of infants were presented with three different types of crib decorations (Watson & Ramey, 1972). Infants in the first group were given a mobile that they could control. The second group was given a stabile, which did not move. The third group was given a mobile, but the wind, not the infants, made it move. Infants in the third group were then allowed to control the mobile; they performed poorly both immediately and six weeks later. They had already learned that their behaviour had no effect—the environment did not respond.

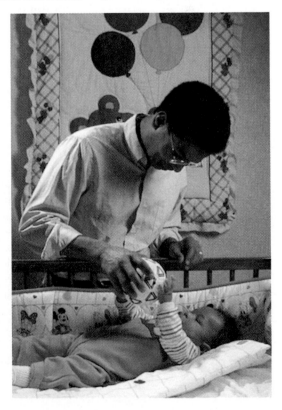

Variety and Timing of Stimulation

On the other hand, and contrary to the belief of some parents, grandparents, and other caregivers (and most toy manufacturers), infants do not require a vast assortment of toys or a massively enriched environment to develop cognitive skills (Yarrow, Rubenstein, Pedersen, & Jankowski, 1972). Instead, a moderately enriched environment, in which infants are given stimulating objects slightly ahead of the time that they would normally use them, seems to promote optimum growth (White & Held, 1966). The goal is to match the task with the child's development. Slightly accelerated stimulation, therefore, encourages growth and development; greatly accelerated stimulation confuses children. They will ignore or reject a task that is too difficult.

The Caregiver

A stimulating environment is created by a concerned adult caregiver. As we shall see in Chapter 7, the interpersonal relationship with the caregiver is a major influence on a child's mental development. In the course of feeding, diapering, bathing, and dressing their infants, parents and other caregivers provide a constant source of stimulation; by talking with infants and playing games, they demonstrate relationships between objects as well as between people. Even simple behaviours such as imitation occur most often in a rich dialogue of social play between adult caregiver and infant (Uzgiris, 1984). When development goes well, the infant competencies develop at the approximate ages described.

There is a great need for children to be raised in a responsive social environment if they are to show optimal developmental outcomes. When we contrast the children raised in institutions or dysfunctional families with those raised in optimal family environments, this relationship becomes especially clear. Children raised in institutions or in dysfunctional families grow up without a responsive caregiver who adjusts care-taking activities to the unique and special needs of individual children. In both cases, there is likely to be a lack of contingent feedback from caregivers; that is, the infant's behaviour is unlikely to produce immediate results, but interaction is more typically done on a schedule. Such infants, therefore, get little chance to shape and alter their environmental inputs. They receive little direct encouragement in the form of consistent and contingent feedback for emerging social skills and language skills such as smiling, crying, and vocalizing. Many of these infants appear to grow up to be children who have learned that they cannot control their environment—and they therefore cease trying. They often become passive or aggressive as the situation and their frustration demand.

Early Intervention

Some of the most hopeful and exciting applications of our knowledge of infant development have been the success stories from a number of early intervention programs. It is possible now to identify at birth (or even before) infants who fall into certain high-risk groups. Perhaps they are premature, malnourished, or developmentally delayed. Their mothers may be alcoholics or users of crack cocaine, or they may be emotionally disturbed. Also, poverty restricts the diets, the health care, and the quality of care some infants are likely to receive. Without help, many of these infants will have persistent learning disabilities or emotional scars. In addition, they may have health problems and are at greater risk for premature death.

Over the past two and a half decades, several programs have offered a variety of supportive services to parents and infants in these high-risk groups. Because adequate funding is limited, however, many of these programs service less than half of the children who need them. Thus, it is possible to compare the progress of infants and their families within the programs with others who are not enrolled. By and large, these

Question to Ponder

In optimal circumstances, caregivers affect infants by providing contingent feedback. Can you think of ways that infants affect their caregivers by providing contingent feedback?

programs have demonstrated a real difference. They show that an optimal environment is critical for the high-risk child to flourish and thrive (Horowitz, 1982; Korner, 1987).

Ira Gordon developed one of the first major home-based, parent-oriented intervention programs for infants in the late 1960s (Gordon, 1969). Working with poor families in rural Florida, Gordon set the goal of enhancing the intellectual and personality development of the infants and the self-esteem of the parents. He trained women from the community in child development, and they served as weekly home visitors. The women learned about the particular curriculum or activities to be offered at the appropriate developmental time for the infants they visited, and they learned interviewing skills. Intelligence tests showed that those infants who regularly participated in the weekly program for two or three years demonstrated significantly more advanced development over matched controls. Also, in follow-up measures, fewer children who had participated for at least two years were placed in special classes in public schools than were children from the control group.

Early intervention programs also have been established for children with more severe handicaps (Broussard, 1989; Sasserath, 1983). These programs offer a number of supports to both infant and family. Certainly, they help by demonstrating developmentally appropriate activities to capture the child's attention and to enhance learning. Also, they help parents to be aware of the milestones of development and sometimes the very small milestones of the severely delayed or retarded child. Beyond that, they help parents to be responsive to the child's needs and to the child's discoveries. But such programs also must meet the parents' needs. Parents should be supported in their adjustment to and parenting of a difficult or disabled child. Most experts on infant development would recommend a balanced program—even for the potentially gifted child. The National Association for the Education of Young Children (NAEYC) (1986) recommends to parents and infant day-care workers that infants need:

1. A secure, predictable environment so that they can learn to anticipate events and to make choices.

2. An intimate, stable relationship with a warm, responsive caregiver who is sensitive to the child's interests, needs, and rhythms.

3. Respect for the infant as an active participant in the dialogue of living rather than a passive recipient of training.

4. Ample space to explore, objects to handle, and other children to observe, to imitate, and to socialize with.

When all of these factors are in balance, the child has been provided with a nurturing environment. Such an environment encourages the development of skills and abilities, brings out the child's natural inquisitiveness, and provides a sense of active exploration with which to approach learning opportunities throughout life.

After reviewing the literature on early intervention, Ramey and Ramey (1998) identified six principles that influence the effectiveness of early intervention:

1. *Timing.* Interventions that start earlier and continue longer are optimal. Although this is true, there is no evidence for an absolute critical period such that interventions cannot be effective beyond a certain age.

2. *Intensity.* More intensive interventions are more effective than less intensive ones. One study found that children improved in cognitive skills when they had three intervention sessions a week, but not when they had fewer.

3. *Treating children directly.* Children who receive direct instruction from early intervention specialists show larger and more enduring gains than do children in programs that rely on training parents and other caregivers to do the intervention. Ramey and Ramey caution, though, that this does not mean parents are unimportant. "The recognition and celebration of parents and other family members as natural providers of young children's early learning experiences is profoundly important and should be encouraged. The practical question for the field of early intervention, however, is whether parent education and general family support programs can be justified if they do not produce child benefits" (Ramey & Ramey, 1998, p. 116).

Question to Ponder

Some children who require early intervention are enrolled in day care. Do you think early intervention should be integrated into the day care or offered to the children in independent programs outside of day care?

These fathers are attending a parent-training camp.

4. *Program breadth and flexibility.* Comprehensive programs produce more gains than do programs that are narrower in focus. An example of a comprehensive program is one that has a strong educational program for the child, as well as ongoing health and social services and practical supports (e.g., transportation, meeting family needs).

5. *Individual differences in program benefits.* Different programs may be needed to produce gains in children with different risk factors.

6. *Environmental supports to maintain gains.* Early intervention programs do not "cure" the at-risk child. The long-term effects of early intervention are brought about not just by the intervention program, but also by the child's environment during and after the intervention. Is there enough support to maintain the gains that were made during intervention? "Poor school environments, suboptimal health, a seriously dysfunctional home environment, economic depression, and many other contextual conditions are known to influence the behavior of children and, indeed, adults at all ages. Thus, longitudinal inquiry about the long-term effects of early intervention must take into consideration children's environments and experiences both during and after early intervention" (Ramey & Ramey, 1998, p. 118).

Summary and Conclusions

The notion of competencies developing during infancy is relatively new for those who study children. It is now recognized that predictable changes occur in the physical and cognitive development of infants and toddlers. However, there is also considerable variability in the timing of these behaviours—associated with varying levels of responsiveness and control of the environment, and caregivers to whom the child is exposed. There has been disagreement about the causes of such diversity. Arnold Gesell and his colleagues, for example, believed that maturation was the predominant cause, while Piaget saw it as a combination of maturity and experience.

Children grow in their abilities in all the behavioural domains as they grow toward adulthood. Each skill builds on previous actions and experiences, and, in turn, becomes the foundation on which future behaviours grow. Certain environmental factors influence this growth, such as malnutrition. It becomes clear that infants require a well-balanced diet during the first 2 years. This is essential since early malnutrition can permanently retard growth, particularly in the brain and central nervous system.

The development of sensory and perceptual competence also seems to consist of an interaction between maturation and experience. In general, infants are born with a sensory apparatus that is functional but in need of refinement. This refinement proceeds throughout the remainder of

life. It now appears as though the senses of infants are preprogrammed to work together. Immediately after birth, infants begin to link sights, sounds, and touch. Eye-hand integration accelerates after 5 months, once the visually guided reach is achieved.

Cognitive development, according to Piaget and others, begins with the elaboration of sensorimotor schemes. Infants build their own intelligence by elaborating and modifying these schemes in the process of adaptation. Of special interest is the type of adaptation called a circular response. This is the means by which infants discover their bodies and use them to intentionally change the environment. Using this model, infants acquire a number of fundamental intellectual abilities during the first 2 years. These include concepts about the use of familiar objects, imitation, the understanding of object permanence, memory, and symbolic representation.

It is important to realize that while maturation and brain development are vital factors in the acquisition of these competencies, so too is the environment. The environment has a powerful effect on the development of infant competencies. An environment that is responsive to the child's skills and stimulation—timed slightly ahead of the child's developmental level—will accelerate a child's normal progress. Lack of stimulation and an unresponsive environment retard the child's sensorimotor and cognitive development.

Key Terms and Concepts

adaptation (p. 179)

circular response (p. 180)

cognition (p. 179)

deferred imitation (p. 181)

depth perception (p. 173)

malnutrition (p. 166)

myelination (p. 177)

neurons (p. 177)

novelty paradigm (p. 170)

object permanence (p. 181)

pincer grasp (p. 164)

sensorimotor period
(p. 179)

sensory integration (p. 175)

sudden infant death
syndrome (SIDS)
(p. 160)

surprise paradigm (p. 171)

symbolic representation
(p. 185)

synapses (p. 177)

toddler (p. 164)

visual cliff (p. 173)

visually guided reach
(p. 177)

Questions to Review

1. Describe the developing competencies of the infant during the first 2 years.

2. Describe the effects of different types of malnutrition.

3. Why is breast-feeding recommended?

4. What are the nutritional needs of the infant during the first 2 years?

5. Discuss and compare the novelty paradigm and the surprise paradigm.

6. Describe brain development during the first 2 years.

7. Describe Piaget's theory of cognitive development. What have been some of the major criticisms of this theory?

8. What do infants understand about the physical properties of objects?

9. What is symbolic representation, and what is its significance for infant development?

10. Explain the effect of deprivation on infant development.

11. What factors influence the effectiveness of early intervention programs?

Weblinks

www.cps.ca/
Canadian Paediatric Society
This site has information on programs and issues related to children's health, including immunization, street smarts, healthy eating, childhood infections, choosing car seats for preterm infants, and injury prevention.

www.geocities.com/HotSprings/Falls/1136/
Breastfeeding Committee for Canada
Sponsored by Health Canada, this site has position papers, newsletters, and press releases related to breast-feeding and healthy infant development.

www.ciap.cpha.ca/
Canadian Immunization Awareness Program
This site has information on types of immunization, schedules, and Canadian statistics on rates of immunization, as well as discussions of facts and myths related to immunization.

Infancy: Developing Relationships

Where are you going, my little one, little one ...
Where are you going, my baby, my own?
Turn around, and you're two ...
Turn around, and you're four ...
Turn around and you're a young girl
Going out of the door.

Outline CHAPTER 7

Objectives

By the time you have finished this chapter, you should be able to do the following:

✔ Describe attachment and separation behaviours.

✔ Describe stranger anxiety and the theory that attempts to explain this behaviour.

✔ Describe the effect on emotional development when a child does not form an attachment relationship or when a child's progress toward attachment is interrupted.

✔ Describe the factors that affect the quality of the relationship between the infant and the caregiver.

✔ Describe adjustments that a family must make for a special needs infant.

✔ List different bonding disorders.

✔ Describe the differences and similarities between father–child interaction and mother–child interaction.

✔ Describe infants' emotional development in the context of a family system.

✔ Describe the effects of day care on development.

✔ Compare the effects of child-rearing patterns on infants' development.

Four-month-old Maria lay in her carrier on the sofa and observed the activities in the room. She was the focus of much attention. Her older sister would frequently come over and gently place her nose on her sister's and then give a big smile. The baby would broadly smile back—after an initial wide-eyed startle. Her mother was folding clothes but often would approach her to stroke her face or quietly say something to her. She too was greeted with a smile. Even the dog was part of the action—he would wander over to give her a friendly sniff. Finally, in walked Dad. The smile she gave to him lit up the room, as well as his face. After greeting the others, he quickly picked her up to cuddle her.

Human infants are born into an environment rich with expectations, norms, attitudes, beliefs, values, traditions, and ways of doing things. A cultural heritage, complete with value systems and standards for social behaviour, awaits them. Family members, of course, are already aware of their relationships to the infant, but newborns do not realize their relationships to those around them. At birth, Maria, described above, has no awareness of herself either as an individual or as an organism that can interact with the environment. She cannot recognize herself in a mirror. She does not know that her hands are part of her body or that she is actually the agent responsible for her own movement. She has not developed trust or mistrust and has no expectations concerning those who care for her. She is not conscious of being female. But she is beginning that process of mutual interaction that will lead to trust and to a particular understanding of herself and others.

A dramatic series of changes takes place during the first 2 years of human life, as was mentioned in Chapter 6. Within this period, the unaware newborns become toddlers. They become aware of their environment and of the ways in which they can act on it; aware of whether the world around them is responsive or unresponsive to their needs; aware that they can do some things for themselves or seek help when necessary. They become aware of various family relationships and of what is good and what is bad. They become conscious of being a girl or a boy and begin to learn how a sex designation imposes a certain style of behaviour.

Babies come into the world with certain response styles. Some are more sensitive to light or to sudden, loud sounds than are others. Some react more quickly to discomfort than do others. Some infants are fussy; some are placid; some are active, assertive, and vigorous. By age 2, the child has elaborated or restricted these basic response styles within a cultural context to produce what is called a *personality*.

In this chapter, we shall look at how the infant personality develops within relationships. We shall focus on primary, or first, relationships—those that establish patterns for the development of future relationships and for the acquisition of basic attitudes, expectations, and behaviour.

Attachment and Separation

attachment The bond that develops between a child and another individual as a result of a long-term relationship. The infant's first bond is usually characterized by strong interdependence, intense mutual feelings, and vital emotional ties.

In the course of a lifetime, most individuals are involved in a number of significant interpersonal relationships. The first and undoubtedly most influential bond is the one that immediately begins to grow between the infant and the mother or caregiver. The bond becomes firmly established by the time the child reaches 8 or 9 months of age. Since the mid-1960s, many psychologists have applied the term **attachment** to the process of development of this first relationship. Attachment is characterized by strong interdependence, intense mutual feelings, and vital emotional ties.

Attachments, as well as losses or separations, actually occur and affect us throughout life. The infant's first attachment, however, goes through several phases that lay the groundwork for future development. The process involves a characteristic series of events as the infant progresses from earliest awareness to the development of trust and confidence in the caregiver. Later, an equally characteristic sequence of events takes place in reaction to the loss of the relationship. These first responses to attachment and loss lay the foundation for later relationships, whether with peers, relatives, other adults, spouses, or lovers.

Question to Ponder

Why do you think infants do not develop attachments until around 7 months?

Imprinting and Attachment Behaviours

The psychologist Mary Ainsworth (1983) defines *attachment behaviours* as those that primarily promote nearness to a specific person to whom the infant is attached. Attachment behaviours include signalling (crying, smiling, vocalizing), orienting (looking), making movements related to another person (following, approaching), and engaging in active physical contact (clambering up, embracing, clinging). These behaviours indicate attachment only when they are specifically directed toward one or two caregivers, rather than toward people in general.

According to Ainsworth, attachment cannot develop without these particular behaviours. Consider, for example, how difficult it would be to develop the sense of emotional closeness to an infant who constantly stiff-armed the caregiver when she was picked up. Or what if an infant engaged in no smiling or vocalizing in response to the caregiver's appearance? Ainsworth and others (1979) have found that when a disability such as blindness occurs—or when the baby finds touch aversive—bonding between that infant and the caregiver is at risk. Such situations may require special intervention of pediatric psychologists or psychiatrists to suggest alternative ways of developing the first relationships. For example, psychiatrist Stanley Greenspan has written extensively on the high-risk caregiver/infant pairs he has assisted in developing these crucial first relationships (Greenspan & Greenspan, 1985).

The important point is that the infant must act in order for attachment to take place. The infant's initial behaviour seems to invite nurturing responses from the caregiver. She (or he) not only feeds, diapers, and generally cares for the infant's physical needs, but also communicates with the baby by talking, smiling, touching, and nuzzling. The attachment process, then, is mutual—the baby's behaviour prompts the caregiver to act in certain ways, and the caregiver's actions set off responses in the baby.

Why does attachment occur? Is it a conditioned response, or is there an innate need to establish a relationship? For a long while, developmental psychologists thought that babies formed attachments to their caregivers only because they fulfilled the babies' primary needs. It was thought that children learned to associate the caregiver's nearness with the reduction of primary drives, such as hunger (Sears, 1963). Much of this early stance derives from Freud's theory, which stated that there was nothing innate in a child's attachment drive. Attachment was determined merely by a caregiver's gratifying the child's needs. Through this process the infant formed a permanent, positive inner image of the mother, which he could rely on during short absences. In this process, the infant was a passive recipient of caregiver behaviours. Research—conducted primarily with animals—now indicates that the satisfaction of their primary needs is only a small part of infants' forming of attachments.

We can probably better understand infants' first relationships with their caregivers if we look at some of the relationships that other animals have with their mothers. This relationship has been studied most extensively in ducks and geese.

Orphaned goslings nurtured by Konrad Lorenz during the critical imprinting period follow him as if he were their real mother.

Imprinting Imprinting refers to the process by which newly hatched birds form a relatively permanent bond with the parent in the period immediately following birth. More than 40 years ago, Konrad Lorenz, an Austrian zoologist, observed that goslings began to follow their mother almost immediately after hatching. This bond between goslings and parent was important in helping the mother protect and train her offspring. Interestingly enough, Dr. Lorenz also found that orphaned greylag goslings that he nurtured during their first 24 hours after hatching—the critical period for imprinting—developed a pattern of following him, rather than another goose. This pattern was relatively permanent—and sometimes annoyingly persistent. Some of Lorenz's greylag geese much preferred to spend the night in his bedroom than on the banks of the Danube (Lorenz, 1952).

imprinting The instinctual learning process by which newly hatched birds form a relatively permanent bond with the parent in a few hours or days.

The critical period for imprinting occurs after hatching, when the gosling is strong enough to get up and move around, but before it has developed a strong fear of large, moving objects. If imprinting is delayed, the gosling will either fear the model parent or simply give up and grow limp, tired, and listless.

Researchers disagree about the similarities and differences between imprinting on birds and bonding behaviour in humans. There is no clear evidence that a critical period exists for human bonding. As we saw in Chapter 5, parents and infants may be particularly receptive to bonding in the first few days after birth, but this is hardly a critical period. On the other hand, it is clearly necessary for human infants to establish some kind of relationship with one or more major caregivers within the first 8 months or so in order for adequate personality development to occur. What we know about imprinting in birds provides promising parallels to human attachment, but the behaviours are not identical.

In Harlow's studies of attachment, young monkeys showed a distinct preference for the cloth-covered surrogate mother over the wire mother, regardless of which one supplied food.

Attachment in Monkeys Harry Harlow (1959) conducted an important series of studies on social deprivation in monkeys. Because monkeys have closer biological ties to humans than birds have, studies of their social development are more relevant to humans than are studies of goslings. An important series of observations began somewhat accidentally when Harlow was studying learning and conceptual development in monkeys. When he was setting up his laboratory conditions, he decided that it would be best to rear each young monkey without its mother in order to control the total learning environment. The mother was an uncontrolled variable. She taught the baby certain skills, and she rewarded and punished certain behaviours. She also served as a model for the baby to imitate. Harlow wanted to get at the basic process of learning, and to

do this, he felt it necessary to remove the mother from the cage. In doing so, however, he stumbled upon a new and more exciting area of study.

Separation from the mother had a disastrous effect on the young monkeys. Some died. Others were frightened, irritable, and reluctant to eat or play. Obviously, the monkeys required something more than regular feeding to thrive and develop. Harlow experimented with surrogate monkey mothers, wire forms designed to hold a bottle (Harlow & Harlow, 1962). Some of the surrogates were covered with soft cloth, while others were bare wire. Regardless of which surrogate supplied the food, all the young monkeys showed a distinct preference for the cloth form, clinging and vocalizing to it, especially when frightened. The infant monkeys developed bonds with their cloth surrogates and would not accept substitutes. The object they looked at and clung to was the focus of their psychological attachment, regardless of the food source.

Monkeys with cloth surrogates did not exhibit the extremely fearful, neurotic behaviour of the completely orphaned monkeys, but they failed to develop normally, nonetheless. As adults, they had difficulty establishing peer relationships and engaging in normal sexual activity. They were poor parents to their own offspring as well, despite Harlow's attempt at "psychotherapy"—he put them with "normal" monkeys. Subsequent research found that the improved social interactions of the surrogate-raised monkeys were enhanced by having a moving surrogate, for example, a cloth-covered bleach bottle that swung up and down and sideways. Such movement may foster the growth of the cerebellum, a portion of the brain that appears to be involved in emotional development.

Further studies in this series have indicated that peer contact among infant monkeys at least partially makes up for the deprivation of the infant–adult attachment bond (Coster, 1972). Infant monkeys who are raised with surrogate mothers and who have adequate opportunity to play with other infant monkeys develop reasonably normal social behaviour. Therefore, mutually responsive social interaction is crucial for normal development in monkeys; one would suspect that this is true for humans, too, because they are also a social species. In fact, research on twins and orphaned children seems to support this contention. These children often become attached to each other in a manner that may even preclude attachment to adults.

The Ethology of Human Attachment   Ethological theory, which looks at the similarity between behaviours across species, recognizes that babies actively contribute to the ties established with their parents. Ethologists assume that many of the behaviours that have evolved over time for various species have done so because they have survival value. John Bowlby (1973), who was originally trained as a psychoanalyst, was intrigued by Lorenz's research on imprinting. He believes that human babies are also born with preprogrammed behaviours that function to keep parents close in order to increase the probability of the infant's being protected from danger.

Bowlby proposes that attachment is based on built-in behaviours in both the infant and the caretaker. He believes that attachment is initiated by these preprogrammed behaviours but is maintained by pleasurable environmental events, such as physical closeness of the mother and child, the reduction of hunger, and comfort. In this way, his theory combines elements of both heredity and the environment in the development and maintenance of attachment.

Bowlby worked with Mary Ainsworth (Ainsworth, 1973; Ainsworth, Blehar, Wates, & Wall, 1978) to develop this theory. Ainsworth and Bowlby propose that the development of attachment goes through four phases or periods:

1. *The presocial or preattachment phase* (birth to 6 weeks). During this time, the infant engages in those attachment behaviours also described by Ainsworth—gazing, babbling, clinging, smiling, and grasping at the adult. Once the adult responds to these signals, the baby encourages the adult to remain close to her by continuing to emit those behaviours that serve to "rope the adult in." At this age, the infant directs such behaviours at all adults, even though she recognizes the mother's voice, smell, and manner. Although many parents believe the behaviours of their infants are

directed only at them, Bowlby believes that this phase is not true attachment, since infants at this age are indiscriminate.

2. *The social or attachment-in-the-making phase* (6 weeks to 6 to 8 months). During this phase, the infant begins to distinguish between particular people. The infant learns to trust in the environment and the people in it. Along with this trust comes the expectation that these people will respond to the infant's needs. Generally, even though infants can distinguish their mother and are beginning to respond differentially to her, they will not cry when separated from her during this phase.

3. *The clear-cut attachment phase* (6 to 8 months to 2 years). During this phase, the child will attempt to keep in proximity or closeness those people whom he has discriminated. True attachment to a caregiver is evident in the **stranger or separation anxiety** that many infants exhibit when the caregiver leaves. Separation anxiety appears to be a universal phenomenon, occurring at around 6 months of age and increasing until about 15 months. This time frame parallels that in cognitive development when object permanence develops. It appears that infants who have not yet achieved object permanence fail to show separation anxiety.

   In this phase, the older infant or toddler actively tries to keep his mother close. He will climb to follow her, turn in a jolly jumper as she moves from room to room, and cry when she leaves. Often, infants use their mothers as secure bases from which to launch their explorations. Mothers become the emotional support to which they return.

4. *The reciprocal relationship or goal-corrected system* (18 months to 2 years, and continuing from that time onward). Once the child's cognitive level allows her to understand why mother or father leaves, what factors influence the absence, and that they will certainly return, the final phase of attachment begins. In this phase, the caregiver and child mutually work out what is appropriate separation behaviour and what is not. The mother, for example, indicates that temper tantrums are inappropriate, but she works with her child to create a ritual that eases the separation. A mother might bathe her child and cuddle while reading a story prior to her leaving. A father may have a quiet talk or help the child to work a puzzle, and so forth.

Bowlby and Ainsworth believe that the nature of the parent–child interaction that emerges from the development of attachment in the first 2 years of life forms the basis for all future relationships. The new friendships in school, the teen peer structures, and the intimate bonding to a spouse all bear the marks of this first relationship between parent and child.

> **stranger or separation anxiety** An infant's fear of strangers or of being separated from the caregiver. Both occur in the second half of the first year and indicate, in part, a new cognitive ability to detect and respond to differences in the environment.

Stranger Anxiety

One of the developmental landmarks of the attachment relationship, as previously indicated, is the appearance of both stranger anxiety and separation anxiety. Pediatricians and psychologists often make no distinction between the two and refer to both as "7-months anxiety," because they often appear rather suddenly at about 7 months. Babies who have been smiling, welcoming, friendly, and accepting suddenly become more shy and fearful in the presence of strangers. They become extremely upset at the prospect of being left alone in a strange place, even for a minute. No traumatic event, sudden separation, or frightening encounter is necessary for this behaviour to emerge. Children at this stage of attachment cry and cling to their caregivers; they only cautiously turn around to explore a stranger. Stranger anxiety continues through the rest of the first year and much of the second year, with varying degrees of intensity.

The Discrepancy Hypothesis If no event is needed to bring on such anxiety, why does it first occur, almost without fail, in most children at about the same age? Most psychologists see stranger and separation

At about 7 months, infants become shy and fearful in the presence of strangers. Stranger anxiety is a landmark in the infant's social development.

discrepancy hypothesis A cognition theory according to which infants acquire, at around 7 months, schemes for familiar objects. When a new image or object is presented that differs from the old, the child experiences uncertainty and anxiety.

anxieties as a sign of intellectual development in infants. As infants' cognitive processes mature, they develop schemes for the familiar and notice anything that is new and strange. They can distinguish caregivers from strangers, and they become keenly aware of the absence of the primary caregiver. When they detect a departure from the known or the expected, they experience anxiety (Ainsworth, Blehar, Waters, & Wall, 1978); this theory is known as the **discrepancy hypothesis.**

The anxiety is based on the infant's new awareness that the caregiver's presence coincides with safety. Things seem secure when familiar caregivers are around, but uncertain when they are not. Hence, anxiety at 7 months can be viewed as a demonstration of the baby's more complex and sophisticated expectations. The infant's anxiety and distress vary a bit, based on a number of factors. Most infants are more distressed if the stranger is a male or if he towers over them. They are less distressed if the mother is close by or if the stranger is a child or a midget (Boccia & Campos, 1989).

Some psychologists believe that, at least by 9 months, the anxiety reaction is complicated by the learning that has already occurred. Bronson (1978) found that 9-month-old babies sometimes cry when they first notice a stranger, and even before the stranger has gotten close. This behaviour implies that children may have learned from negative experiences with strangers and may be anticipating another disturbing encounter. But the learning may be more subtle than that. Perhaps the mother signals to her baby by her facial expression or tone of voice. In one study, mothers of 8- to 9-month-old babies were carefully trained to knit their eyebrows, widen their eyes, pull down their lips, and demonstrate worry on their faces while greeting the stranger with a worried "hello." The control group was trained to demonstrate a pleased, smiling face and a cheery "hello" to the stranger. As predicted, these 8- to 9-month-old infants picked up their mothers' signals quite accurately. Infants whose mothers posed joy were more positive toward the stranger, smiled more, and cried less when they were picked up by the stranger than did those infants whose mothers displayed worry (Boccia & Campos, 1989). This kind of emotional signalling by the mother is called *social referencing.*

It is likely, then, that by the time infants are a year old, stranger and separation anxiety are influenced both by their ability to differentiate between the familiar and the strange and by their past experiences with strangers and with their mothers' reactions to strangers. Parents can assist their infants and toddlers in adjusting to strangers by modifying their own emotional reactions and by giving the children time to get to know the strangers (Feiring, Lewis, & Starr, 1984).

Stranger anxiety is a milestone in the attachment process and in social development (Bretherton & Waters, 1985). Once children learn to identify the caregiver as a source of comfort and security, they feel free to explore new objects in the caregiver's reassuring presence. Children who fail to explore, preferring to hover near their mothers, may not feel a secure attachment and thus miss out on new learning. On the other hand, some infants are too readily comforted by strangers or show wariness when returned to their mothers. This is a second kind of social maladjustment; it indicates uncertainty about the caregiver's ability to support the infant (Sroufe & Fleeson, 1986). These children are likely to suffer a more pervasive and unresolved anxiety that interferes with further development.

Separation and Loss

If, as was discussed, the attachment relationship is an essential part of normal development—and if that relationship progresses through a series of predictable, nearly universal stages—what happens to the child who does not have such a relationship or whose progress toward attachment is interrupted? What happens to the child who is brought up in an orphanage and is handled by numerous, changing caregivers during the first few years? What happens to the infant who must spend a prolonged period in hospital? And what about the child who has begun to establish a relationship and is suddenly separated from the caregiver?

In Chapter 6, we saw that prolonged institutionalization retards the development of cognitive and sensorimotor competencies in infants. Social deprivation has an even more devastating effect on the young child's emotional development. Infants who are cared for by continually changing caregivers who meet only their basic physical needs are unable to develop an attachment relationship. The mutual responses between child and primary caregiver do not occur consistently, and the social interaction that permits expression of emotion is missing (Bowlby, 1973, 1980, 1988). Profound apathy, withdrawal, and generally depressed functioning result and, in time, lead to inadequate personality development.

The child who has formed a full attachment relationship responds quite differently to separation from the primary caregiver than does the child who has never established such a relationship. The attached child goes through a series of dramatic reactions to both brief and prolonged separation.

John Bowlby (1973) divides the separation reaction of hospitalized, fully attached toddlers into three stages: protest, despair, and detachment. During the protest stage, children refuse to accept separation from the attachment figure. They may cry, scream, kick, bang their heads against their beds, and refuse to respond at all to anyone else who tries to care for them.

During the second stage, which may come a few hours or even several days after the initial reaction, the children appear to lose all hope. They withdraw and become very quiet. If they cry, they do so in a monotonous and despairing tone, rather than with the anger they exhibited earlier.

Eventually, separated children begin to accept attention from the people around them and appear recovered from their misery. If they are visited by the primary caregiver, they react with detachment or even lack of interest, as described by John Bowlby:

> A child living in an institution or hospital who has reached this state will no longer be upset when nurses change or leave. He will cease to show feelings when his parents come and go on visiting day; and it may cause them pain when they realize that, although he has an avid interest in the presents they bring, he has little interest in them as social people. He will appear cheerful and adapted to his unusual situation and apparently easy and unafraid of anyone. But this sociability is superficial: he appears no longer to care for anyone. (1960, p. 143)

When faced with the first two stages of a child's separation reaction, well-meaning adults often try to subdue what they see as inappropriate behaviour. But such adults underestimate the complexity of young children's reactions. These children need patient understanding and warm nurturance to help weather the stress. In fact, the child's response to separation is a prototype of behaviour later in life. It foreshadows the turmoil that adolescents go through over the loss of a first love and the grief that adults experience upon the death of a spouse or a child. Both young children and adults need to work through these emotional reactions in order to come to terms with the inevitable separations that occur throughout life. Only if they are allowed to express these feelings can children reach a level of detachment that will permit them to survive emotionally in their new situation and eventually form new attachments.

Patterns of Early Relationships

Most children, in most cultures, form a basic attachment within the first year of life. Infants all over the world show similar responses to their social environments; gradually, they establish an attachment relationship with their specific caregivers. Although the sequence of development of this first relationship occurs fairly consistently across cultures, the details of it vary dramatically depending on the personality of the parents, their child-rearing practices, the values of their culture, and the unique contribution of the child.

In most cultures, children form a basic attachment within the first year of life, but the intensity of bonding and anxiety varies according to specific child-rearing practices. Children reared in a kibbutz (below) are less attached to their caregivers than are children in other cultures who spend much of their infancy strapped to their mother's back.

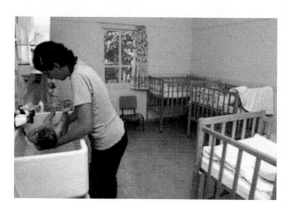

The Quality of the Relationship

strange situation test A laboratory test procedure used to measure attachment.

secure attachment The use of the attachment figure as a secure base for exploration.

insecure avoidant attachment A type of insecure attachment characterized by exceptional independence and indifference toward the attachment figure.

insecure ambivalent attachment A type of insecure attachment characterized by clingy, anxious behaviour and by a lack of exploration.

Measuring Attachment Differences Mary Ainsworth and colleagues developed the "strange situation" test to measure attachment differences in a controlled laboratory setting; the test takes about 20 minutes to complete (Ainsworth, Blehar, Waters, & Wall, 1978). During the test, as outlined in Table 7-1, the infant's behaviour is observed in a number of episodes that are designed to trigger exploratory or attachment-seeking behaviours. For instance, the baby is first observed alone in the room with the mother to see whether the baby explores the room and the extent to which the baby involves the mother in the exploration. Later, the baby is observed as a stranger enters the room and the mother departs to see whether attachment-seeking behaviours are triggered. From the infant's behaviour in the **strange situation test,** Ainsworth and colleagues distinguished three different types of attachment: **secure** (also called type B), **insecure avoidant** (type A), and **insecure ambivalent** (type C).

Infants with secure attachments show the following pattern of behaviour in the strange situation test: when alone in the rooms with their mothers, they explore, constantly looking back, vocalizing, or returning to their mothers and continually involving them in their play. The attachment literature describes this behaviour as using the mothers as secure bases for exploration. When the strangers enter the room, the infants show some wariness, but not distress. When the mothers leave the room, the infants become anxious; when the mothers return, the infants seek contact with them and appear happy at the reunion.

Infants with avoidant attachments are extraordinarily independent in the strange situation test and appear indifferent to their mothers' behaviour. For instance, when alone in the room with their mothers, they explore without involving their mothers. They are not wary of strangers and do not act upset when their mothers leave the room, nor do they seek contact with their mothers when they return.

Infants with ambivalent attachments cling extraordinarily to their mothers in the strange situation test. For instance, when they are alone in the rooms with their mothers, they stick close to them, often maintaining physical contact, and do not explore the rooms. When the strangers arrive, the infants show extreme wariness, and

Table 7-1 Ainsworth's Strange Situation Paradigm

EPISODE	EVENTS	VARIABLES OBSERVED
1	Experimenter introduces parents and baby to playroom and then leaves.	
2	Parent is seated while baby plays with toys.	Parents as a secure base.
3	Stranger enters, seats self, and talks to parent.	Reaction to unfamiliar adult.
4	Parent leaves. Stranger responds to baby and offers comfort if baby is upset.	Separation anxiety.
5	Parent returns, greets baby, and offers comfort if needed. Stranger leaves.	Reaction to reunion.
6	Parent leaves room; baby is alone.	Separation anxiety.
7	Stranger enters and offers comfort.	Ability to be soothed by stranger.
8	Parent returns, greets baby, offers comfort if needed. Tries to reinterest baby in toys.	Reaction to reunion.

Note: Each episode lasts about three minutes, but the separation episodes may be cut short if the baby becomes too distressed.

Source: Ainsworth et al., 1978.

when the mothers leave the room, the infants become so distressed that the episodes might be cut short for ethical reasons. Curiously, though, when the mothers return, the infants show ambivalence—approaching their mothers to be picked up, but once picked up, wanting down or behaving aggressively toward them. They do not seem comforted by their mothers' presence.

In most studies conducted in Canada and the United States, approximately two-thirds of infants are securely attached to their mothers, and the rest are either avoidant or ambivalent or do not fit one of the patterns. A new attachment category, **disorganized/disoriented** (type D), was created for those infants who do not fit any of the other patterns (Main & Solomon, 1990). Their behaviour in the strange situation test is contradictory. On the one hand, they seek to be close to their mothers, but on the other hand, they act afraid of them and show more stress reactions when their mothers are present (Carlson, 1998). They also show signs of freezing and other unusual behaviours. *Freezing* is defined as "the holding of movements, gestures, or positions in a posture that involves active resistance to gravity. For example, the infant sits or stands with arms held out waist high and to the sides" (Carlson, 1998, p. 1124). Freezing is like being in a trance. See the box "Attachment in Infants Afraid of Their Mothers" for a more detailed discussion.

Although the strange situation test is still widely used, it is no longer the only measure of infant attachment. The Q-sort measure was developed in 1985 (Waters & Deane, 1985). This measure consists of a stack of 90 cards. Each card describes an attachment behaviour that could be observed in the home, such as "cries when left alone." A parent (or another person familiar with the infant) reads the cards and sorts them into 9 10-card piles that range from most to least like the infant. To derive a measure of control, the sorting is compared with the typical sorting expected of securely attached infants. An advantage of the Q-sort measure over the strange situation test is that it can be used more easily with older children. The Q-sort is a stable measure of attachment from age 2 to 5 (Symons, 1998). This age range is important, because researchers are currently studying attachment beyond infancy. Indeed, they are even studying it in adults using another new measure—the adult attachment interview (George, Kaplan, & Main, 1985, as cited in Bakermans-Kranenburg & van Ijzendoorn, 1993).

David Pederson and Greg Moran at the University of Western Ontario developed another new measure of attachment in 1995. It measures attachment by observing

disorganized/disoriented attachment A new attachment category that is common in infants who have been abused. Infants act in a contradictory way: they seek closeness to their mothers, yet they fear them and are stressed in their presence.

FOCUS ON DIVERSITY

Attachment in Infants Afraid of Their Mothers

Some infants show a bizarre pattern of contradictory behaviour in the strange situation test. Although they seek closeness to their mothers, they also appear afraid of them. In addition, they show unusual behaviours such as freezing. This type of attachment is called disorganized/disoriented (type D).

Why do infants develop this type of attachment? Does it have long-term effects on development? To answer these questions, Carlson (1998) did a prospective longitudinal study that lasted for about 20 years and involved the collection of a wide range of data.

The study was started early, before the infants were born. Pregnant women were recruited to participate in the study. The researchers took a number of measures:

- They documented the woman's medical histories before and during pregnancy, the presence of

---

Children who had a disorganized/disoriented attachment had a higher rate of problems.

---

birth complications, and the woman's relationship or marital status at the time of the birth.

- They noted whether the woman had a history of abuse or psychological problems.

- They interviewed mothers to assess their risk for inadequate parenting. This measurement was based on "their knowledge of development, expectations and preparation for the baby, and motivation to care for the baby" (p. 1112).

- After birth, they assessed the infants for physical abnormalities and for behaviour and reflexes.

- When the infants were 3 months old, the researchers took two more measures: (1) a measure of infant temperament and (2) a home ob-

mothers and infants at home, where mother–infant interactions are more natural (Pederson & Moran, 1996). During the interaction, mothers are required to juggle attending to their infant with completing forms for the researcher. The mother's behaviour is not scripted, as it is in the strange situation test. A trained observer records interactions between the mother and infant and their relationship is classified as secure (B), avoidant (A), or ambivalent (C), as in the strange situation test. However, here is an additional, more detailed level of classification than in the strange situation test. Each category is subdivided: there are four subtypes of secure attachment (B1, B2, B3, B4), three of avoidant (A1-teaching, A1-ignoring, A2), and two of ambivalent (C1, C2). Pederson and Moran (1996) compared attachment at 12 months, as assessed with home observations, to attachment at 18 months, as assessed with the strange situation test. There was 84 percent consistency. However, secure and avoidant attachments were more consistent than were ambivalent ones. It is unclear whether the lack of consistency in ambivalent attachment is due to measurement error or to the instability of this relationship.

After distinguishing the different types of attachment, researchers then study the infants over time (that is, they use longitudinal studies, as described in Chapter 1) to see whether type of attachment is associated with differences in later behaviour. Many differences have emerged.

Using Type of Attachment to Predict Differences in Later Behaviour   Research conducted from the 1970s to the 1990s (see Belsky & Cassidy, 1994, for a review) suggests that, in general, securely attached infants show more positive development as preschoolers and school-aged children than do infants with any of the other types of attachment. For instance, as preschoolers, securely attached infants typically get along well with peers (for example, sharing, resolving conflicts without becoming aggressive, and playing harmoniously) and with adults (for example, complying more with parents and other adults), and they are unlikely to have behavioural problems (such as excessive tantrums, withdrawn behaviour, or aggression). In school, securely attached infants typically are better liked by peers, are less likely to be either bullies or victims, are less aggressive, and are rated by teachers as more socially competent. However, infants with the other types of attachment, often lumped together in a category la-

servation of mother–infant interactions during feeding.

- When the infants were 6 months old, the researchers observed them while the infants were played with and fed by their mothers to provide measures of the mothers' cooperation with and sensitivity toward their infants.

- The researchers assessed abuse and neglect through home observations and interviews with the mothers on numerous occasions from the time the infants were 3 days old until they were 1 year old.

Infant attachment to mother was measured at 12 and 18 months, using the strange situation test. Interestingly, of all the earlier measures, only those that related to the mother's interactions with her infant predicted the development of a disorganized/disoriented attachment. Disorganized/disoriented attachment was more common in infants born to mothers who lived alone with no support, who were judged to be at risk for inadequate parenting, who were observed to be insensitive during interactions with her infant, and who mistreated the infant through abuse or neglect.

It appears that infants learn to fear their mothers because of their early interactions with them. There is no indication that the infants are born with constitutional differences that develop into this type of attachment. A strength of this study is that it included a wide range of measures and was able to prove that only some were associated with disorganized/disoriented attachment.

How does disorganized/disoriented attachment affect the infant in the long term? Carlson continued to assess the infants for problems during the preschool, elementary school, and high school years. At every age, children who had a disorganized/disoriented attachment had a higher rate of problems. During the preschool years they had a poorer relationship with their mothers. During the school years, they had more behavioural problems. By adolescence, they had a higher rate of a type of mental disorder called dissociative disorder (related to multiple personality disorder).

belled *insecurely attached,* have higher risks of developing a variety of problems, including aggression, noncompliance, social withdrawal, excessive whining and temper tantrums, and difficulties interacting with peers. Some studies have found that avoidant infants, in particular, are more likely to have later problems with aggression (Londerville & Main, 1981; Troy & Stroufe, 1987). However, these studies were older and did not include the disorganized/disoriented category of insecure. More recent studies that have included this category do not find a relationship between avoidant attachment and aggression (Moss, Rousseau, Parent, St-Laurent, & Saintonge, 1998). Instead, these studies associated avoidant attachment with passive, withdrawn behaviour. Some studies have found that ambivalent infants are more likely to be socially withdrawn (Cassidy & Berlin, 1994). Others have found them to be more aggressive (Moss et al., 1998). Newer studies that have included a separate disorganized/disoriented category have found that these infants are especially prone to behavioural disorders (Lyons-Ruth, Repacholi, Alpern, & Connell, 1991).

Why is type of attachment associated with later development? It is difficult to answer this question because all of the research is correlational rather than experimental (as described in Chapter 1). Perhaps attachment differences cause the later differences in behaviour. Or perhaps attachment and later development appear related because some other factor, such as ongoing parenting style or infant temperament, influences both. For example, researchers in Montreal compared the level of parenting stress and depression in mothers whose school-aged children had different types of attachment (Moss et al., 1998). Mothers of ambivalent children reported the most stress and the highest levels of depression. It is difficult to isolate the effects of the attachment relationship from enduring differences in the mothers. Nevertheless, researchers are interested in understanding the kinds of factors associated with developing one type of attachment over others because, at the very least, type of attachment is a reasonably reliable indicator of infants at risk for later problems. One such factor is the responsiveness of mothers, as described in the next section.

Responsiveness In her studies of children in Uganda, Ainsworth (1967) found that children who showed the strongest attachment behaviour had a highly responsive relationship with their mothers. Back in the United States, she reported that securely attached 1-year-olds had mothers who were more responsive to their cries, more affectionate, more tender, less inept in close bodily contact, and more likely than mothers of insecure 1-year-olds to synchronize their rate of feeding and their play behaviour with the baby's own pace (Ainsworth et al., 1978). Since that time, researchers have consistently found that infants who were securely attached at age 1 had mothers who were more responsive to their physical needs, to their signals of distress, and to their attempts to communicate with facial expressions or vocalization (Bornstein, 1989).

But other researchers have found that maternal responsiveness is only weakly or not at all associated with security of attachment (Rosen & Rothbaum, 1993; Seifer, Schiller, Sameroff, Resnick, & Riordan, 1996). Interestingly, these discrepancies across studies might be due, in part, to a change in research strategy. For instance, early studies, such as those conducted by Ainsworth and colleagues, tried to isolate the effects of maternal responsiveness without considering how it might relate to other factors. But more recent studies typically examine the effects of maternal responsiveness while simultaneously considering the effects of other factors, such as infant temperament, that might interact, complicating the results (see, for example, Seifer et al., 1996).

Lack of maternal responsiveness can arise in different contexts and be influenced by other factors, often called *distal processes*. One example of a distal process is maternal depression. Mothers who are depressed are less responsive to their infants than are other mothers (Radke-Yarrow, Cummings, Kuczynski, & Chapman, 1997). Another example of a distal process is culture-related differences in child rearing. For example, Sagi, van Ijzendoorn, Aviezer, Donnell, and Mayseless (1994) studied the child-rearing practices of different Israeli kibbutzim. In some kibbutzim, infants spent nights in special infants' houses, cared for by rotating watchwomen. The mothers, although often responsive to the babies in the daytime, were unavailable at night, and when the babies awakened, the watchwomen responded to them less promptly and less consistently than did their mothers. More than half of the infants raised on this type of kibbutz developed insecure (especially ambivalent) attachment relationships to their mothers. In contrast, infants on other kibbutzim whose mothers cared for them at night often had much lower rates of insecure attachments to their mothers, despite having equivalent daytime care. Thus, differences in attachment were attributed to differences in the responsiveness of the nighttime care.

A Mutual Dialogue   In studying attachment, it is not enough to look at just the mother's behaviour. Infants, too, contribute to the interaction. The behaviours of both evolve gradually, one responding to the other. This emphasis on mutual influence between mother and infant represents a new conceptual approach. Yet, clearly, an infant who is sociable and who derives pleasure from close proximal contact can encourage even the most tentative new mother. In contrast, a fussy and irritable baby interrupts a caretaker's best efforts at soothing or verbal give-and-take (Belsky, Garduque, & Hrncir, 1984; Lewis & Feiring, 1989). According to Seifer et al., "Some combination of individual and contextual factors will be required to fully appreciate the development of attachment relationships" (1996, p. 23).

Schaffer (1977) has investigated the way in which **mutuality,** or interactive **synchrony,** between infant and caregiver is achieved. He observed that most infant behaviour followed an alternating on-off pattern—for instance, while visually exploring new objects, babies stared and then looked away. Some caregivers responded to these patterns with more skill than others did. Films of mothers face to face with their 3-month-old infants revealed a pattern of mutual approach and withdrawal; they took turns looking and turning, touching and responding, vocalizing and answering.

It is this rare kind of synchrony between infant and caregiver during the first few months that predicts a secure relationship at age 1 and also more sophisticated patterns of mutual communication at that time (Isabella, Belsky, & Von Eye, 1989).

Caregivers do not merely respond to the behavioural rhythms of the child. They also change the pace and nature of the dialogue with a variety of techniques: introducing a new object, imitating and elaborating on the infant's sounds or actions, or

mutuality (synchrony) The pattern of interchange between caregiver and infant in which each responds to and influences the other's movements and rhythms.

A warm, supportive relationship established in infancy between caregiver and child offers the child a firm base from which to learn competencies.

making it easier for the child to reach something of interest. By monitoring the baby's responses, caregivers gradually learn when the child is most receptive to new cues from them. No matter which technique is used, the mutual process takes many months to develop fully.

Some techniques seem to be especially effective in developing synchrony (Field, 1977; Paulby, 1977). Field compared infant reactions to three different maternal behaviours: the mother's spontaneous behaviour, her deliberate attempts to catch and hold the child's attention, and her imitation of the child. The infants responded most enthusiastically to the imitations, perhaps because of the slowed-down, exaggerated nature of imitative action. The closer the similarity between maternal and infant behaviour, the less discrepancy babies have to deal with, and the more attentive they will be. Furthermore, each mother carefully observed her infant's cutoff, or gaze-away, point. Field suggested that respecting the child's need for a pause is one of the earliest rules of "conversation" that a caregiver must learn.

Some parents frequently overstimulate their infant despite signals from the baby that should indicate this. Babies turn away, hide their heads, close their eyes, and in general try to get a few minutes of pause. Some parents fail to stop the overstimulation until the child actually cries. Other parents frequently understimulate their infant. They ignore their baby's smiles and babbling or other bids for attention. An infant whose cues for attention are ignored will soon give up trying unless he really needs it, and then the child is liable to cry. Often, parents have mixed patterns of sensitivity. Sometimes they overstimulate, sometimes they understimulate, and sometimes they misidentify the cues or signals from the infant. This mixed pattern tends to be particularly true of abusive mothers (Kropp & Haynes, 1987), of depressed mothers (Field, 1986), of some adolescent mothers (Lamb, 1987), and of mothers whose temperament is considerably different from that of the infant's (Weber, Levitt, & Clark, 1986).

The behaviour of a very sensitive and responsive mother changes as the infant grows older (Crockenberg & McCluskey, 1986). Indeed, some have used the word *scaffolding* to describe the mother's or father's role in progressively structuring the parent–child interaction (Ratner & Bruner, 1978; Vandel & Wilson, 1987). That is, the parents provide the framework around which they and their infant interact. They pick specific games, such as imitation or peek-a-boo. As the child becomes older, the game becomes more sophisticated. Therefore, early turn-taking, games, and free play gradually become structured by the parent. The child learns increasingly complex

Early mutuality and signalling lay the foundation for long-term patterns of interaction.

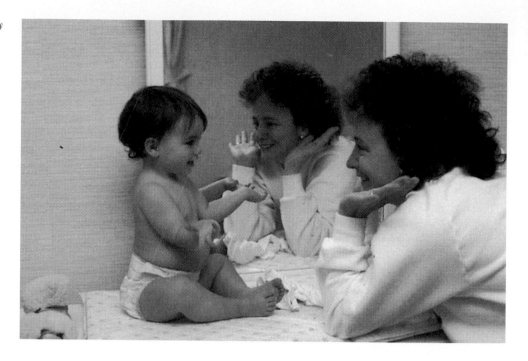

rules of social interaction—pacing and give-and-take, observing and imitating, maintaining the game, and so forth.

Researchers at Laval University in Quebec watched mothers teach their 12- to 16-month-old toddlers how to play with four new toys (Tarabulsy, Tessier, Gagnon, & Piche, 1996). The researchers monitored the mothers' behaviours to see which ones resulted in the toddlers' focusing on the mothers' instructions and complying with their commands. Interestingly, toddlers with different types of attachment responded differently to their mothers' behaviours. Securely attached toddlers responded positively when mothers were positive (showed encouragement or approval) or helpful (gave commands or structured the toys to facilitate toddlers' play). Avoidant toddlers responded positively when their mothers were positive but not when they tried to be helpful. Avoidant toddlers' focus on the toys was independent of their mothers' attempts to facilitate learning. Furthermore, mothers' smiles and laughs suppressed positive behaviour in avoidant infants. Avoidant toddlers may not respond positively to their mothers' smiles and laughs because they associate them with overstimulation or rejection, which are characteristic of how their mothers interact with them. Ambivalent toddlers reacted positively to their mothers' positive and helping behaviours, as well as to when their mothers interfered or disrupted their play or tried to coerce them to perform a behaviour. Ambivalent toddlers seemed "compliant at all costs," perhaps because they had a history of interacting with mothers who were minimally or inconsistently responsive.

Early mutuality and signalling lay the foundation for long-standing patterns of interaction, as has been illustrated in studies of maternal responses to crying. Mothers who respond promptly and consistently to their infants' crying in the first few months are most likely to have infants who cry less by the end of the first year. A quick response gives babies confidence in the effectiveness of their communications and encourages them to develop other ways of signalling to their mothers (Bell & Ainsworth, 1972). Infants who are exceptionally irritable are at risk for insecure attachment, in part because mothers tend to be less involved with them (Van den Boom, 1994). Van den Boom trained mothers to respond more sensitively to their irritable babies, and as a result of this intervention the infants became more sociable, better able to soothe themselves, and more likely to engage in cognitively advanced exploration.

When maternal care is inconsistent, infants fail to develop confidence and become either insistent or less responsive. Mutuality blossoms into a variety of behaviours in the second year of life. Some toddlers exhibit spontaneous sharing behaviour, both with parents and with other children—showing a new toy, placing it in someone's lap, or using it to invite another child to play. Such behaviour indicates toddlers' interests in the properties of toys, their delight in sharing, and their realization that others can see the same things that they see.

Children apply skills acquired in the mother–child dialogue to a wider social context. For instance, if they perceive their mothers as providing loving and sensitive care, they are more likely to perceive themselves as loveable. They may then expect more positive interactions from peers, perhaps producing a self-fulfilling prophecy (Cassidy, Kirsh, Scolton, & Parke, 1996). But children who perceive their parents as rejecting are more likely to expect peers to be hostile. These children are more likely to act defensively, perhaps contributing to problems in interacting with peers (Kerns, Kelpac, & Cole, 1996).

Multiple Attachments or Exclusivity Infants who have a relatively exclusive relationship with a parent or caregiver tend to exhibit intense stranger and separation anxieties. They also show these anxieties at an earlier age than do infants whose relationship with the caregiver has not been as exclusive (Ainsworth, 1967). A child who is constantly with the parent, sleeps in the same room at night, and is carried in a sling on the parent's back during the day experiences a dramatic and intense separation reaction. On the other hand, the child who has had a number of caregivers from birth tends to accept strangers or separation with far less anxiety (Maccoby & Feldman, 1972).

A question often asked is, If care is distributed among a number of caretakers, as well as parents, is the development of attachment impaired? This question is especially crucial when we consider that there are over 5.5 million children yearly being cared for in day-care centres. If the quantity of attachment is crucial, then children with less time with their parents will suffer—or so it would appear. Research, however, indicates that day care and multiple caregivers may have no adverse effects on attachment. Rather, these children often form multiple attachments (Clarke-Stewart & Fein, 1983; Welles-Nystrom, 1988). For example, infants attach not only to mothers, but also to fathers, siblings, and peers.

It would appear that the infant's social network is an amazingly complex and diverse one. The power of peers as attachment figures was revealed in a famous study by Anna Freud (Freud & Dann, 1951) of six German-Jewish orphans, who were separated from their parents at an early age during World War II. They were placed in a country home at Bulldog Banks, England, which had been transformed into a nursery for war children. This was their first experience in a small, intimate setting; previously they had been in larger institutions.

Because of their past experiences, the children were either hostile toward or ignored their adult caregivers, but they were solicitous and concerned in their behaviour toward each other. For example, a caregiver had accidentally knocked over one of the smaller children. Two of the other children threw bricks at the caregiver and called her names. Moreover, the children resisted being separated, even for special treats such as pony rides. The children were even able to overcome frightening situations to help one another: "On the beach in Brighton, Ruth throws pebbles into the water. Peter is afraid of waves and does not dare to approach them. In spite of his fear, he suddenly rushes to Ruth, calling out: 'Water coming, water coming,' and drags her back to safety" (Freud & Dann, 1951, pp. 150–168).

When toddlers first attend a day-care program, they often experience considerable separation distress. This seems to be particularly true when they are between 15 and 18 months old. But, even at this vulnerable age, some toddlers adjust more readily than others. Toddlers who have had an exclusive relationship with only one person have an especially difficult time. Conversely, those who have had too many separations and too many caregivers also experience a good deal of separation distress. Adjustment is easiest for toddlers who have had some experience with other caregivers and who have had a moderate degree of separation experience with several opportunities for reuniting (Jacobson & Wille, 1984).

The Infant with Special Needs

Severe stresses in mutuality often occur with infants with special needs and caregivers. Blind infants cannot search caregivers' faces or smile back. Deaf babies may appear to be disobedient. Infants with other severe handicaps cannot respond to signals as normal babies do. Obvious handicaps that are evident from birth, such as Down syndrome and cerebral palsy, are certain to create serious adjustment problems for all family members. Until recently, we too often ignored the way that an infant affects a caregiver and concentrated instead on the impact of the caregiver's behaviour on the child. In the past decade, researchers have begun to devote more attention to the former situation. When we study how infants' behaviours influence the adults around them, we begin to notice all the subtle means by which these small people help in maintaining the fundamental links that seem so essential to their later socialization.

Visually Impaired Infants Visual communication between caregiver and child is usually a prominent element in the establishment of attachment relationships. Caregivers depend heavily on subtle responses from their infants—looking back, smiling, and visually following—to maintain and support their own behaviour. Caregivers often feel, unconsciously, that a blind infant is unresponsive. It is essential for both that they establish a mutually intelligible communication system that overcomes this disability.

In early life, one of the normal infant's best developed resources for learning is the visual-perceptual system. Babies look at and visually follow everything new and have distinct preferences. They particularly like to look at human faces. Blind infants, however, cannot observe the subtle changes in their caregivers' facial expressions or follow their movements. Consequently, visually impaired infants fail to receive information that sighted babies use in formulating their own responses.

Caregivers of sighted infants rely on visual signals of discrimination, recognition, and preference. However, otherwise competent blind infants do not develop signals for "I want that" or "Pick me up" until near the end of the first year. The first few months of life are extremely difficult for both caregiver and infant. The child's seeming lack of responsiveness can be emotionally devastating for the caregivers unless they are wisely counselled by experienced people. The great danger is that communication and mutuality will break down and that the caregiver will start to avoid the child (Fraiberg, 1974).

Babies who are blind do not develop a selective, responsive smile language as early as sighted children; they do not smile as often or as ecstatically. They have very few facial expressions. Yet they rapidly develop a large, expressive vocabulary of hand signals for their caregivers. Eventually, they are able to direct and relate these signals to unseen people and objects. Training parents and caregivers of visually impaired infants to watch for and interpret hand signals greatly enhances the parent–child dialogue, attachment formation, and all subsequent socialization (Fraiberg, 1974).

Hearing-Impaired Infants The developmental difficulties of deaf infants follow a pattern that differs from those of blind infants. In the first few months of life, their well-developed visual sense generally makes up for the problems imposed by deafness. These children are visually responsive. After the first 6 months, however, communication between parents and infants sometimes begins to break down. The children's responses are not full enough to meet the parents' expectations. Often, the discovery of the child's deafness does not occur until the second year. By this time, the child has already missed a good deal of communication. One of the first indications of hearing impairment in a 1-year-old is apparent disobedience, as well as frequent startling when people approach. (The child does not hear them coming.) In 2-year-olds, there may be temper tantrums, frequent disobedience (or, conversely, severe withdrawal), together with widespread failure to develop normal expectations about the world around them. The diagnosis of deafness may come as a shock to parents who have been "talking to my child all along." Like parents of visually impaired children, they need special training

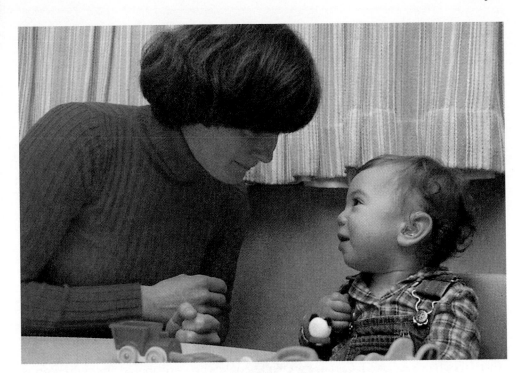

The diagnosis of deafness may come as a shock to parents who have been talking to their children all along. These parents need special training and counselling to help their children with disabilities develop fully.

and counselling to help the child develop fully. Without careful attention during infancy, deafness can result in poor communication during the preschool years and in severe social, intellectual, and psychological deficits later (Meadow, 1975).

Severe Handicaps When an infant is born with a severe handicap, such as cerebral palsy, there is a high risk of maternal rejection, withdrawal, and depression. A severely handicapped infant strains marital ties and may trigger a variety of disturbances in other children in the family. Child-care workers can help almost immediately with a family's early adjustment problems, and they should be consulted at once. Early success or failure in coping with initial traumas will greatly affect parents' abilities to make wise decisions about the care and education of this child (Turnbull & Turnbull, 1990).

Infants with Very Low Birth Weight More and more infants born up to 3 months prematurely and weighing under 1000 grams are surviving because of advances in medical technology, as discussed in Chapter 5. But these infants' early social experiences are much different from those of other infants. They often remain in hospital until several months after birth and are less socially responsive and more irritable than other infants (Mangelsdorf et al., 1996), so they are often more challenging for parents to nurture. Mangelsdorf et al. compared mother–infant attachments for very low birth weight infants to those of normal weight infants when the infants were 14 and 19 months old. At 14 months, there were no significant differences between the groups, but by 19 months, the very low birth weight infants had a higher rate of insecure attachments than did the normal weight infants.

Another study compared parent interactions with healthy preterm infants to that with full-term infants when the infants were 3 and 12 months old (Harrison & Magill-Evans, 1996). Parents interacted less with the preterm infants than with the full-term infants, even though the preterm infants in this study were healthy and as responsive as the full-term infants. Therefore, parents were not responding to differences in infant behaviour. Instead, the researchers suggest that the parents were influenced by their perception of preterm infants as more vulnerable and perhaps had lower expectations for interacting with them.

Bonding Disorders

Occasionally, caregivers and infants encounter serious problems when they try to establish their relationship. Such problems are known as *bonding disorders*. The failure-to-thrive infant and the abused or neglected infant are products of such relationships. Failure-to-thrive infants are usually small and emaciated. They appear to be quite ill and unable to digest food properly. Sometimes, they start eating very soon after arriving in hospital; at other times, they are listless and withdrawn, almost immobile. These infants often avoid eye contact by staring with a wide-eyed gaze, actively turning away, or covering their face or eyes. By definition, failure-to-thrive infants weigh in the lower 3 percent for their age group and show no evidence of any disease or abnormality that would explain their failure to grow. Often, disruption in the home and social environment of these infants is indicated. In addition, there is some evidence of developmental retardation among these infants, but it can generally be reversed with appropriate feeding (Barbero, 1983; Drotar, 1985).

In many cases, the mother of failure-to-thrive and abused or neglected infants is mentally or physically ill, depressed, alcoholic, or using drugs. She may have experienced some recent crisis that has had a prolonged emotional impact. An important finding is that the parents of these children have experienced similar deprivations when they were infants. Some studies show that as many as 85 percent of abusive or neglectful parents have had very negative early childhood experiences themselves; that is, they, too, were abused or neglected. Certainly, not all people who were abused as children grow up to abuse their children. But, too often, the cycle repeats itself (Helfer, 1982).

Based on their extensive clinical experience, Zeanah, Mammen, and Lieberman (1993) proposed five types of attachment disorder:

1. *Nonattached attachment disorder.* The child fails to develop a preferred attachment figure. This disorder is seen in extreme cases of neglect or in cases of multiple changes in caregivers.

2. *Indiscriminate attachment disorder.* The child shows indiscriminate superficial friendliness toward any adult, even a stranger, and does not use the mother or another attachment figure as a secure base for exploration. Some children engage in risky behaviours without checking back with their attachment figures, so they tend to be accident prone. This disorder is seen in children who have had multiple foster placements.

3. *Inhibited attachment disorder.* These children are unwilling to venture away from their attachment figures and show either excessive clinging and anxiety or compulsive compliance and fear of punishment. This disorder is seen in some children who have been abused by their attachment figures.

4. *Aggressive attachment disorder.* These children display high levels of aggression toward their attachment figures and sometimes toward themselves; aggression takes the form of head banging or scratching. This disorder is most common in children from homes with high levels of domestic violence.

5. *Role-reversed attachment disorder.* The child treats the attachment figure as though she were the child, being either overly nurturant or controlling and punitive. This role reversal often happens when the attachment figure is faced with high levels of stress but does not have adequate support, so she turns to the child for nurturance.

Zeanah and colleagues (1993) are studying possible links between attachment disorders and the development of other disorders, such as conduct problems or depression. Other researchers are relating quality of infant attachment to adult relationships and behaviour. For instance, West and Sheldon-Keller (1994) related quality of attachment to problems encountered by adults in intimate relationships. Mikulincer and Orbach (1995) related quality of attachment to the way that people deal with emotionally upsetting memories.

Question to Ponder

What type of interventions do you think would help children with bonding disorders?

Fathers, Siblings, and the Family System

Most research in child development has focused on the relationship between mother and child and has neglected the rest of the family. Evidence shows that infants form strong early attachments to fathers, as well, particularly when they have regular, close contact from birth. And infants securely attached to both parents are more socially competent at older ages than are infants securely attached to only one parent (Belsky, Garduque, & Hrncir, 1984). The stronger the early attachment, the more influence the father will have on later socialization. Belsky (1996) recently found that various factors that shape the quality of care provided by the father influence the development of a secure father–son attachment. These factors include the father's personality, coordination of work and home life, and marital satisfaction.

Siblings, too, form strong long-term bonds that often last a lifetime. The popular literature frequently highlights the competitive rivalry between siblings and downplays the positive, supportive, mutual-caring roles. But throughout life, siblings frequently protect and help one another. Many families also have a variety of other family members who play a strong role in the infant's development, including grandparents, aunts, uncles, and cousins. Indeed, most children develop in a social context that allows several early attachments. The strength of certain relationships can make up for some of the inadequacies of others. The infant has an opportunity to choose and discriminate between these relationships. His evolving emotional development is not attendant on the strengths and weaknesses of any one attachment bond.

Fathers and Fathering

During the 1980s, much was learned about fathers and fathering in the American family system. There is some evidence that fathers are spending more time with their infants than they did in the past (Pleck, 1985; Ricks, 1985). Fathers are quite capable of routine child care: they can bathe, diaper, feed, and rock, sometimes as skillfully as the mother performs these tasks. They can be as responsive to the infants' cues as mothers are (Parke, 1981), and infants can become as attached to them as they are to their mothers. Fathers who spend more time taking care of young children form strong attachments to them, and the children benefit from this extended time (Ricks, 1985). Despite these similarities, however, fathers are not, by and large, taking over the major responsibility for infant care, and the nature of the father's relationship with the infant is different from the mother's (Parke & Stearns, 1993).

Fathering The style of interaction between the father and infant differs from the interaction between the mother and infant. Whereas mothers are likely to hold infants for care-taking purposes, fathers are more likely to hold infants just to play with them (Parke, 1981). Fathers are also more often physical and spontaneous. Play between fathers and infants occurs in cycles that have peaks of high excitement and attention, followed by periods of minimal activity. Mothers engage their infants in subtle, shifting, gradual play, or they initiate such conventional games as pat-a-cake or peek-a-boo (Parke, 1996). Fathers, however, tend to initiate unusual, vigorous, and unpredictable games, which infants find most exciting (Lamb & Lamb, 1976). The exception to this pattern occurs when the father is the primary caregiver—he then tends to act more as mothers do (Field, 1978).

A recent Canadian study assessed how mothers and fathers interacted with their 2- to 12-month-old infants (Harrison, Magill-Evans, & Benzies, 1999). The researchers used the *nursing child assessment teaching scale* (Sumner & Spietz, 1994), which scores parents on sensitivity to infant cues, response to infant distress, behaviours to promote infant social-emotional growth, and behaviours to promote infant cognitive growth. Fathers and mothers were equally sensitive to infant cues, but fathers scored lower than mothers on the other scales. In addition, compared with mothers, fathers were less

FOCUS ON DIVERSITY

Romanian Orphanage Children Adopted by Families in British Columbia

In 1989 Romania had a revolution, and the world became aware of thousands of Romanian children living in poor-quality orphanages, as vividly described by Elinor Ames (1997). Imagine, if you can, a windowless room packed with rows of 15 white metal cribs. In each of the cribs, there is a baby, awake but rarely making a sound, simply lying there. From time to time, some of the older babies might get up on their hands and knees and rock repetitively back and forth. The babies do not interact with each other, nor do adults talk to or play with them. They spend 18 to 20 hours a day alone in their cribs. They are taken out only to be fed and cleaned. Feeding time is extraordinary. They are taken from their cribs and laid side by side in a large, communal playpen. An adult comes by and pops bottles into their mouths. All of their food is ground up so that it can be given through bottles with nipples that have extra-large holes. No one burps the babies, cuddles them, or encourages them to eat. They have to guzzle their food down quickly, because after about five minutes, the adult will take the bottles away.

When the children turn 3, toilet training begins. Imagine a room with 15 3-year-olds all being toilet trained at the same time. There is no allowance for individual differences. There is a row of 15 little potties, and four times a day, all of the children are set on the potties. They all sit there for 30 minutes, regardless of when they have completed their business. They are side by side, yet not interacting. They do not talk; they do not play; they do not venture off the potties. When they have play times, they simply sit and hold toys.

At the time of adoption, all of the children showed at least some developmental delays.

Many people around the world were touched by these children and set out to Romania to adopt them. Since 1990, Canadian families have adopted a number of the children. And since that time, Elinor Ames and numerous colleagues have been studying the development of children adopted by families in British Columbia (see Ames, 1997; Chisholm, 1998; Chisholm, Carter, Ames, & Morrison, 1995; Fisher, Ames, Chisholm, & Savoie, 1997; Morrison, Ames, & Chisholm, 1995). At the time

of adoption, all of the children showed at least some developmental delays and unusual behaviours. This was not surprising, given their extreme deprivation. But would these children be able to overcome their early experiences? To answer this question, Ames and colleagues have been studying the children longitudinally.

The time that the children spent in the orphanage was a critical factor. Those who were there for fewer than four months did much better than those who had been there longer. Those who had been in the orphanage for eight months or more had a number of problems to overcome. They had medical problems, including hepatitis B, intestinal parasites, anemia, and scabies. They had unusual behaviours, such as repetitive rocking. Interestingly, babies sometimes use repetitive rocking, but it is not normally seen in older children. The Romanian orphans retained that infant behaviour long past the time when other children have stopped it. They may have learned to use it in the orphanage to self-soothe or self-stimulate. Or their rocking on hands and knees may have started as a normal precursor to crawling, but persisted because the infant did not progress to normal crawling—there is not much

contingent in their interactions with their infants, meaning that the fathers did not react consistently to infant cues. Nonetheless, infants were more responsive when interacting with their fathers than with their mothers. According to the researchers, the infant might prefer dad because he is more novel (not the primary caregiver) and more of his interactions are playful, rather than caregiving. You might recall from Chapter 6 that infants have a preference for novel stimuli in general.

As infants get older and require less direct care, father–infant interaction is likely to increase. Fathers may engage in more rough-and-tumble play and interact more frequently with the young child in public places, such as zoos or parks (Lewis, 1987). Fathers' parenting interactions are related to their acceptance of their own childhood experiences and to their marital support (Onyskiw, Harrison, & Magill-Evans, 1997). Fathers who report having received more acceptance in childhood were more likely to be more responsive to their infants. Fathers who report less acceptance in childhood react differently toward their infants, depending on fathers' marital satisfaction. Those who have satisfying marriages are more responsive to their

opportunity to crawl when infants are confined to their cribs. They had difficulty eating because they refused solid food. This is not surprising, given that they had been exclusively bottle-fed in the orphanage. They had to be given puréed foods and gradually worked up to solids, just as people normally feed much younger babies. Once the children had started eating solids, they ate voraciously, not recognizing the internal cues for fullness. They were difficult to nurture because they did not seek adult attention. If they fell and bumped their heads, they would not come for comfort. If they awakened in the morning, they would not get up or call out for attention. They had learned this passivity in the orphanage. In addition, the amount of stimulation in their Canadian environments often overwhelmed them. They were frequently afraid of peers, siblings, flushing toilets, water draining out of bathtubs, and animals.

What were these children like after they had been with their Canadian families for a few years? Ames and colleagues did extensive observations and tests of the children when they were about 4½ years old. A year after adoption, children who had spent minimal time in the orphanage (i.e., less than four months) were doing so well that they were virtually indistinguishable from a comparison group of Canadian-born children. All of the children who had spent longer than four months in the orphanage were small for their ages, and 85 percent were below the tenth percentile for weight. They were screened for developmental delays in fine motor, gross motor, personal and social development, and language skills. All of the children had at least some delays, but they differed in the extent of their delays. Children with fewer delays were more likely to have spent less time in the orphanage, and they were more likely to have been in an orphanage that had better conditions, for example, one where the children were kept clean.

About a third of the children also had serious behavioural and emotional problems. They had changed from being withdrawn and anxious to acting out. They acted like they were in the terrible twos—they bit, hit, kicked, scratched, stole, and did not share, cooperate, or take turns. Not surprisingly, other children did not like to interact with them. As well, the adopted children had an unusual attachment relationship with their mothers, categorized as the disorganized/disoriented pattern (type D). They were extremely friendly to adults but did not discriminate between familiar people and strangers. This indiscriminate friendliness is often interpreted as a sign of attachment disorder (Zeanah, Mammen, & Lieberman, 1993). Its presence in children from the Romanian orphanage is difficult to interpret, though, because it was seen in orphanage children with insecure attachments, as well as in those with secure ones. Children with either type of attachment would approach and go off with strangers, showing no signs of concern or wariness. On occasion, they might even say to strangers, "I like you. Can I go and live with you and be your little girl now?" Imagine how this must have shocked and hurt their loving adoptive parents, about a third of whom became depressed and doubted their parenting competence.

Why did a third of the children have such severe problems when other adopted children were doing much better? Ames and colleagues found that the following factors increased the risk for serious problems: (1) spending more time in the orphanage (each month made a difference); (2) being adopted into a family that had two of the orphans rather than one; (3) being adopted into a family that had lower socioeconomic status and lower family income, and thus perhaps fewer financial resources to provide for the child's special needs or to afford parental relief; (4) being adopted into a family with a younger mother (the average age of the mothers of children with serious problems was 31, compared with an average age of 39 for the other adoptive mothers); and (5) being selected from the orphanage by the father alone, even though both parents would be raising the child.

infants than are those who are dissatisfied with their marriages. Therefore, marital satisfaction can counteract negative effects of the parent's less optimal childhood experiences on his parenting interactions.

Fathers who frequently interact with their infants, who are responsive to their signals, and who become significant individuals in their children's world are likely to develop into forceful agents of socialization later on. As the child grows older, the father becomes an important role model. He also may become an admirer and advocate of the child's achievements. There seems to be a link between paternal interaction in infancy and interaction in later childhood. Fathers who are inaccessible to their infants may have difficulty establishing strong emotional ties later on. It is even possible that they will have a negative influence as the child grows older (Ricks, 1985).

Fathers who are the most influential in their young children's lives not only spend time with them, but are also sensitive to their wants, cries, and developmental needs (Esterbrook & Goldberg, 1984; Parke, 1981). Indeed, fathers are increasingly taking the time to broaden their parenting role, even when their children are infants

(Lamb, Pleck, Charnov, & Levine, 1987; Parke, 1981). Because of this greater involvement, infants are more likely to use both their mothers and their fathers for *social referencing*. Social referencing denotes the process by which infants seek affective cues or signals from an adult figure to help them resolve their uncertainty, form an appraisal, and regulate their subsequent behaviour (Hirshberg & Svejda, 1990). The referencing process is an important avenue of parental influence in socioemotional development. It appears from the research that fathers play a big role in shaping their infants' responses when the children are uncertain about what the appropriate behaviour should be.

Fathers and the Family System There are social and psychological reasons why fathers are usually not equal partners in infant care. In one study, mothers and fathers were recruited from a childbirth class where, at least initially, the fathers were active participants and were expected to continue sharing infant care with their wives. But it did not work out that way (Grossman, Pollack, & Golding, 1988). Very soon after the birth of the child, both mothers and fathers rated the fathers as less competent in most infant-care skills. Fathers were then relegated to the role of "helping" the mother. No father in this study ever talked about the mother's "helping" the father take care of the infant. The more competent one—the mother—generally assumed the chief responsibility for the infant and, therefore, got more practice in performing infant care and interpreting the baby's signals. If someone feels incompetent, they do not enjoy doing a job (Entwisle & Doering, 1988). Most families deal with this inequality by selecting complementary roles for father and mother. Less successful couples tend to become impatient with each other. In these cases, it is common for the father to play with the infant but to serve as a reluctant and occasional helper. We should note here that sometimes the designated caregiver is the father because his nurturing skills are better than the mother's.

The father's indirect influence on the infant and, indeed, on the whole family is considerable. Numerous studies have indicated that a father's emotional support of the mother during pregnancy and during early infancy is important to the establishment of positive beginning relationships. The absence of a father during infancy creates considerable stress on the whole family system (Lewis, 1987).

Although in our culture the father is often a secondary caregiver, he plays an important part in a complex system of interactions. It is not enough just to study the ways in which a mother and baby or a father and baby interact. We must look at the way the three of them affect one another's behaviour. Clarke-Stewart (1978), in her study of the three-way pattern in many families, finds that the mother's influence on the child is usually direct, whereas the father's is often indirect, through the mother. The child usually influences both parents quite directly.

The addition of an infant, especially a first-born child, to a family affects the marriage itself. Studies have shown that the birth of the first child can create considerable stress on the marital relationship. A newborn makes heavy demands on the time and energy of both mother and father. Complementary roles need to be established. Decisions must be made about child-care arrangements, the mother's return to work, and so forth (Baruch & Barnett, 1986). The stress on the marriage may be greater if the infant is demanding, frequently sick, or handicapped. It is possible for stress to bring the couple closer together (Turnbull & Turnbull, 1990). Yet, if the marriage was vulnerable to begin with, the stress may cause increased dissatisfaction and turmoil.

Siblings

Siblings form significant and long-lasting attachments to one another beginning in infancy, although younger siblings are often more attached to the older siblings than the reverse (Lewis, 1987). Infants often form very strong attachments to a somewhat older sibling and are upset with the loss of that sibling, even when the separation is only overnight (Dunn & Kendrick, 1979). Older siblings become important social mod-

As more fathers become more involved parents, infants are increasingly likely to look to them for social referencing.

els. Children learn how to share, cooperate, help, and empathize by watching their older siblings. They learn appropriate sex roles and family customs and values. In some cultures, the older siblings perform a major caretaking role, sometimes being the principal caretaker of the younger child (Whiting & Whiting, 1975). In many families, the positive aspects of sibling roles—helping, protecting, and providing an ally—last a lifetime. It is somewhat surprising, therefore, that the negative aspects of sibling relationships have received more attention (Lewis, 1987).

Two negative aspects of sibling relationships are sibling rivalry and the dethroning of the older sibling with the birth of the new infant. It is clear that the birth of the second child makes a profound impact on the first or older sibling. Parents pay less attention, time, and energy to the first child. The role of the older child must shift. Parents' attitudes in handling this change influence the degree of sibling strife, competition, and rivalry (Dunn & Kendrick, 1979; Lewis, 1987; Lewis, Feiring, & Kotsonis, 1984). For example, if the parents attempt to enlist the older sibling in the care of the newborn from the onset, an alliance is often created both between the siblings and between the older sibling and the parents. The mother and father may refer to the newborn as "our baby." In addition, it is important that special time be created for the first child to have alone with the parents. This exclusive time makes the older child feel special rather than discarded. The following story illustrates this point:

> Our second daughter was born 11 months after our first. When the older one had her first birthday, there was already another child there. We made the decision that we would include her in everything we did for the new baby. She "helped" us change her, feed her, and cuddle her. We talked about "her" baby. Nearly 2 years later, she announced to the pediatrician on one visit, "My baby has a sore bottom. We need some medicine!" Now, at 3 and 4, they are still close. They share a room and play together constantly. When one is upset, the other comforts her.

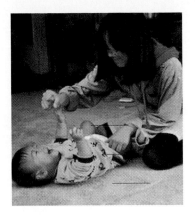

Siblings tend to form strong bonds and mutual caring roles that often last a lifetime.

Question to Ponder

How do you think relationships with siblings differ from those with peers?

Grandparents and Others

In many cultures, including our own, grandparents have considerable contact with their adult children and grandchildren—often on a weekly basis. In families where both

In families where both parents work, grandparents are frequently the primary caregivers for much of the time.

parents work, grandparents are frequently the primary caregivers for much of the time. The grandparent's role is usually somewhat different from that of the parent, and a different attachment relationship is formed. Grandparents frequently offer more approval and support, or empathy and sympathy, and less discipline. Sometimes, the relationship is more playful and relaxed (Lewis, 1987). Grandparents also have the time to tell the child the stories of when they—or their parents—were little. These stories help to create a sense of family identity and tradition.

Maternal Employment

The Social Ecology of Child Care

In modern societies, child care for young children is a complex issue. In 1993, 61.1 percent of Canadian mothers with children under age 3 worked outside of the home, compared with 44.4 percent in 1981 (Baker, 1996). A similar trend is found in other countries, such as Sweden and the United States, but the social context of working mothers is quite different in these countries. In Sweden, public child care is provided for every family that requests it. There are day-care centres, or day nurseries, and there are also family day-care providers (so-called day mothers). Both the day-care centres and the day mothers are hired and licensed by the municipalities. There is also a system of open preschools, where mothers or day mothers may take their children to meet and play with other children and receive advice and support in their caring roles. In other words, there is a publicly funded child-care system that provides support to families with infants and young children (Andersson, 1989; Hwang and Broberg, 1992).

In most communities in the United States, there is a quite different social ecology for the raising of infants and young children. Parents often are expected to make their own decisions about what type of child care they want and how much of it they will receive. They are financially responsible for providing supplemental child care and are assisted in this responsibility only if they have a low income. Many U.S. families face the difficult decision of finding suitable alternative child care at affordable prices.

Question to Ponder

Who is responsible for ensuring quality child care? Parents? Government? Child-care workers? Society at large?

FOCUS ON DIVERSITY

Mothers Who Work Outside the Home in Atlantic Canada

Women in the Maritimes, like women in other parts of the country, make a variety of family/employment arrangements after the birth of a baby. Doug Symons, at Acadia University, compared three groups of mothers from rural communities in Atlantic Canada: (1) those who returned to work before their baby was 6 months old, (2) those who returned to work after 6 months or longer at home, and (3) those who were full-time homemakers for the baby's first 2 years. His main research question was whether women with different patterns of postpartum employment would have different types of relationships with their 2-year-old

infants. How should he design his study? Should he start the study when the infants are 2, or should he start it when they are younger? Does it mat-

Mothers who returned to work after 6 months appeared to be doing exceptionally well.

ter? Symons's study is an excellent example of a prospective longitudinal design, as was discussed in Chapter 1. He started collecting data a few days after the baby's birth and continued

to follow the families for two years. Starting the study early was important because he was able to see whether there were pre-existing differences among the groups of mothers and could take these differences into account when he tried to isolate the effects of postpartum employment. If he had started the study when the infants were 2, he would have been unable to separate effects of postpartum employment from other differences among the women. In this case, the pre-existing differences could bias the results and would be confounds, as were discussed in Chapter 1.

What were the results of Symons's

Infant Day Care

In Canada, employers must provide 25 weeks of paid parental leave (Symons & Carr, 1995), compared with 9 months in Sweden (Welles-Nystrom, 1988) and 12 weeks in the United States. The 12 weeks' paid leave in the United States is allowed only to parents who have worked for at least 12 months, for at least 25 hours per week, and for employers of 50 employees or more (Symons & Carr, 1995); other women in the United States have no guaranteed leave. According to Volling and Belsky (1993), only 3 percent of U.S. mothers receive paid leave after the birth of a baby. Consequently, for financial reasons, more mothers in the United States are likely to return to work sooner than mothers in Canada. It is important to note this difference because most studies of infant day care have been conducted in the United States and may not apply to Canada or other countries. For instance, in 1986, Jay Belsky, a leading American researcher, caused a furor when he published a paper showing that infants in the United States who started day care before their first birthdays and attended for at least 20 hours per week were twice as likely to develop insecure attachments to their mothers than infants cared for at home. It is unclear whether these results would also be found in Canada, especially given that Canadian day cares are more regulated than those in the United States (Howe & Jacob, 1995). As well, fewer Canadian day cares are rated as providing inadequate care compared with U.S. day cares (Schliecker, White, & Jacobs, 1991) (see the box "Setting Standards for Quality Day Care in Canada").

It is difficult to draw strong conclusions about the effects of day care on development because the research is correlational, rather than experimental. Often, researchers are unable to separate the effects of day care from other differences, such as family experiences, attitudes, and income, which also influence development. Even if they could isolate these effects, there would still be different interpretations of why day care influences development.

Other recent research has found that such results are affected by children's gender, the family's economic status, and the kind of child care. Poor children seem to do better when cared for by their mothers or grandmothers, while, in more affluent families, girls do better with babysitters and boys do better with their mothers (Baydar &

study? First, he looked for preexisting differences between women who returned to work outside the home before their infants reached 6 months, who returned to work after 6 months, or who remained full-time homemakers. He collected this data before infants turned 6 months old. It is interesting to note that the groups *did not differ* on a number of measures, including age of mother, age of father, marital status of parents (married, not married), family socioeconomic status, infant's birth weight, difficulty of birth, type of birth (vaginal or C-section), gender of infant, and parity (no siblings, siblings). The groups did differ, however, on one measure: women who returned to work before 6 months were more likely to express fewer concerns about balancing work and family life

than were other women. Symons took this difference into account when he analyzed other results.

When infants were 2, Symons did a comprehensive assessment that included measures of the strength of attachment security of the mother–infant relationship, the mother's degree of sensitivity toward her infant, the mother's stress level, the mother's coping responses to stress, and the infant's behavioural problems. Interestingly, mothers who returned to work after 6 months appeared to be doing exceptionally well compared with other mothers—they showed more sensitivity toward their infants, were less stressed by their infants, and coped well with stress. Their infants had the most secure attachments and had fewer behavioural problems.

It is important to note that mothers and infants in other groups were not below average or found to be abnormal on these measures. They just were not doing as well as the group of mothers who returned to work after 6 months.

How far can we generalize from the results of this study? Would the findings apply to families in other communities? All of the families in this study relied on family-based child care (such as day homes) because their communities did not have child-care centres for children under 2 years. Would a similar study of infants in child-care centres get the same results?

FOCUS ON APPLICATION

Health Inspections of Child-Care Centres in Toronto

Children who attend child-care centres often experience more infectious illnesses, such as colds, flus, and gastrointestinal infections. It is crucial that child-care staff be aware of risky practices and of steps that they can take to lessen the risk of infection among the children in their care.

In 1992, the Canadian Paediatric Society published a manual called *Well Beings: A Guide to Promote the Physical Health, Safety and Emotional Well-Being of Children in Child Care Centres and Family Day Care Homes,* which outlined a strategy for infection control. Here is a summary of the main recommendations (as cited in Ying, Braithwaite, & Kogon, 1998):

- *Policies:* Child-care centres should have written health policies.

- *Daily health observation:* Child-care staff should observe children for symptoms of illness when they arrive and throughout the day.
- *Immunization:* Records should be up-to-date.

The recommendations alert child-care staff to possible areas for intervention.

- *Managing bodily substances:* Child-care staff should follow safe procedures when handling bodily substances.
- *Handwashing:* Children should be trained to wash their hands properly.

- *Diaper change:* Child-care staff should follow a set procedure for changing diapers and for cleaning the area afterwards. The diaper area should be next to a sink.
- *Toy cleaning:* All "mouthed" toys should be cleaned and sanitized before being used by another child. Other toys should be cleaned at least weekly.
- *Water-play table:* Water in the water-play table should be changed daily, and children and staff should wash their hands before and after water play. Disinfectants, such as bleach or vinegar, should not be added to the water in the water-play table.
- *Food quality:* Staff preparing food should not be doing diaper changes. While preparing food, staff should

Brooks-Gunn, 1991). Other studies suggest that the timing of a mother's return to work is crucial. Some babies whose mothers went back before they were 1 did less well on cognitive and behavioural measures than did infants whose mothers waited until they were 1. Other studies seem to indicate that when mothers returned to work earlier, their children were less affected than the children of mothers who waited until the second quarter of the first year (Baydar & Brooks-Gunn, 1991; Field, 1991). Additional research is needed to clarify these issues. Indeed, for many parents who must return to work quickly to support their families after the birth of a child, the results may be irrelevant, since they must use whatever care is available when they need it.

What is the process that leads to trouble for some infants who have nonparental care for more than 20 hours per week beginning at age 1? Jaeger and Weinraub (1990) suggest two models. One model is the maternal separation model. According to this model, the infant experiences daily, repeated separations from the mother as either maternal absence or maternal rejection. The infant comes to doubt the mother's availability or responsiveness. It is the absence of the mother that leads to insecurity.

The other model is called the quality of mothering model. In this perspective, it is not maternal employment or separation, per se, that determines the infant's outcome, but rather how maternal employment affects maternal behaviour. The employed mother is unable to be as sensitive and responsive a caregiver as she might be if she had more time and practice or if she had no regular interruptions. It is this change in the maternal behaviour that produces insecurity in the infant. Current research based on the quality of mothering model focuses on the competing demands of the mother's work and family; the quality of the child care, and whether she has to worry about it; the characteristics of the infant; and whether the mother thinks that her infant is sturdy, can adjust, and is capable of coping with the situation. What is the general quality of the mother's life? Does she find pleasure in her varying roles, in her employment status, and in being a mother? How much role conflict, marital strain, or fatigue is there? If the mother feels strong separation anxiety when she leaves her child each day, the child tends not to do well (McBride, 1990).

follow strict temperature and time control to prevent food poisoning.

- *Animal control:* Staff are advised to not keep pets in the child-care centre, and if they do, to never allow children to handle the animals without adult supervision.

- *Pest control:* Pests should be controlled by cleaning and regular maintenance. Pesticides should be used only when children are not present in the centre.

- *Sun safety:* The length of time children spend in the sun should be restricted, and shade should be provided. Staff should ensure that children use sun screen with SPF 15 or higher, wear hats or visors, and have drinks before and after time outdoors.

- *Injury prevention and security:* Child-care staff should follow a weekly,

monthly, and annual check of the physical environment to ensure that it is safe. Children should be supervised at all times. The hot water temperature should not be set hotter than 43 degrees to prevent scalding.

Using these recommendations as a guideline, health inspectors assessed 235 child-care centres in Toronto in 1994 (Ying et al., 1998). From their inspections, they identified the following priorities for public health interventions:

1. *Written health policies:* Although 91 percent of the centres had health policies, some of the policies needed refinement. For example, 24 percent of the policies did not require staff to record the health reason when children were too sick to attend. Therefore, their records would not assist in the early detection of the outbreak of contagious diseases.

2. *Handling bodily substances:* Only 62 percent of child-care supervisors had adequate understanding of procedures for handling bodily substances. This rate is alarming, given recent concern over HIV and hepatitis infections.

3. *Cleaning:* Many centres had inadequate cleaning practices related to diaper change, toys, and water-play tables.

4. *Injury prevention:* Safety checks, although present, often were not comprehensive. (See Ying et al.'s paper for a list of 20 safety items that should be included in a safety check.)

Although this study was restricted to child-care centres in Toronto, the authors suggest that the results would likely apply to centres in other Canadian communities. At the very least, the recommendations alert child-care staff to possible areas for intervention.

It is difficult to interpret studies on attachment differences between children in day cares and home-reared children. Attachment is usually measured with the strange situation test, as described earlier in this chapter. But this test may measure different things in day-care children, who are routinely separated from their mothers, than in home-reared children, who are separated from their mothers less often. Therefore, Waters and Deane (1985) developed the Q-sort (sometimes called Q-set) procedure, which uses a broad range of home observations of parent and infant interactions to assess attachment. Some researchers have found the same pattern of results using either the strange situation test or the Q-sort (for example, research conducted in Ontario by Pederson, Moran, Bento, & Buckland, 1992). But others have found a different pattern of results across the two methods (Mangelsdorf et al., 1996; Seifer et al., 1996). Current researchers face the challenge of untangling these discrepant results. Belsky, Campbell, Cohn, and Moore (1996), using the strange situation test, measured mother–infant attachments when the infants were 12 and 18 months old, as has been done in numerous studies in the 1970s and 1980s. In these earlier studies, type of attachment was stable from 12 to 18 months for 75 percent of the infants (see Thompson, 1996, for a review of these studies). But in the Belsky et al. study, conducted in the mid-1990s, when more mothers were employed, type of attachment was stable for only 50 percent of the infants. It would be interesting to see whether the same pattern of results would be found using the Q-sort method.

In summary, the potential effects of early day care likely involve many factors, including the quality of day care, family dynamics, the infant's temperament, and the broader social ecology of child rearing in a community.

Child Rearing and Personality Development

Commonly asked questions about child rearing by both parents and researchers include whether to breast-feed or bottle-feed, when or how to wean, whether to pick up babies immediately when they cry or to let them cry for a while, whether to allow thumb

FOCUS ON AN ISSUE

Setting Standards for Quality Day Care in Canada

In the 1970s, when researchers started to study the effects of day care on child development, they tended to make conclusions about day care in general. In fact, they often studied only high-quality, university-affiliated day cares. Researchers have since recognized that there are a range of day cares, some higher quality than others. What factors affect quality of day care? Nina Howe and Ellen Jacobs (1995), at Concordia University in Montreal, have outlined a model for Canadian standards for quality day care.

The model focuses on how the licensing and regulation of day cares and the standards of teacher education influence quality of child care and, ultimately, child development. In addition, the model recognizes that more global aspects of Canadian society influence licensing and regulation of day care and the standards of teacher education. We will now outline some of the particular aspects of quality that Howe and Jacobs included in their model.

DAY-CARE STANDARDS

Each province sets its standards, but standards tend to be similar from province to province. They typically include the following:

1. Maintaining minimum teacher–child ratios. The NAEYC recommends no more than 4 infants per teacher, 6 toddlers per teacher, or 10 preschoolers per teacher.

2. Maintaining smaller group sizes. Children in smaller groups interact more with peers and teachers, are more cooperative, and engage in more sophisticated play.

3. Maintaining adequate equipment and a clean, safe environment.

4. Requiring day-care teachers to have adequate training in child develop-

---

The NAEYC recommends no more than 4 infants per teacher, 6 toddlers per teacher, or 10 preschoolers per teacher.

---

ment, behaviour management, and first aid. Specialized training is a strong predictor of positive teacher–child interactions. Trained teachers are more sensitive to the needs of individual children, are more likely to design an age-appropriate program, and are more skilled at behaviour management and at encouraging children to become self-sufficient rather than overly dependent.

5. Creating positive work environments to facilitate job satisfaction among teachers and to prevent high rates of staff turnover. Better-paid teachers, often employed in nonprofit centres, report more job satisfaction and are less likely to quit. Children who attend centres with high staff turnover are less likely to develop secure attachments to teachers. They spend more time wandering aimlessly about the centre and less time interacting with peers.

6. Ensuring that Canadian day cares are sensitive to the multicultural and multilinguistic background of the children they serve.

7. Upholding provincial laws that require the licensing, monitoring, and inspection of day cares. Unannounced inspections tend to be more reliable than announced visits.

8. Maintaining some nonprofit day cares. In 9 of the 12 provinces and territories, there is a higher percentage of nonprofit than for-profit day-care spaces. The vast majority are nonprofit in Saskatchewan and Manitoba, but the majority are for-profit in Newfoundland and Alberta. On average, staff in nonprofit centres are better paid, report more job satisfaction, and are more likely to stay at their jobs and to provide stable, consistent, high-quality care.

9. Making day care more available in rural and northern communities and to seasonal or shift workers.

---

sucking or blanket carrying, what to do about temper tantrums, when to toilet train and how. If we look at these specific practices separately, we tend to get answers that are contradictory. It is hard to put them together to form a clear theory of good child rearing. We often conclude, for example, that it does not matter much whether children suck their thumbs or carry a blanket.

Yet such practices, when viewed in the context of the total pattern of child-rearing practices, clearly do matter. These patterns have a strong influence on later personality development. The way that we convey our culture to our children, beginning in infancy, is not at all subtle. We try to instill in our children from birth attitudes and values about the nature of their bodies—the acceptability of self-stimulation, the degree of physical closeness that is desirable, the amount of dependency allowed, and the goodness or badness of both their behaviour and their basic nature as human beings. These attitudes and values, communicated through many child-rearing practices, have a wide-ranging effect on personality development.

We shall examine specific child-rearing practices in the context of broad, cross-cultural child-rearing patterns. We shall concentrate on three particular aspects of child-rearing practices during the infancy period. First, we shall study the development of trust and nurturance in infants. As you will recall from Chapter 2, this aspect refers to the initial stage of Erikson's theory and to such questions as, What do infants learn about the basic trustworthiness of their social environment? Is the environment consistent and predictable? Is it responsive to the child's needs? Second, we shall examine how children's attempts at autonomy are met. When toddlers start to get up and move around, to do things for themselves, to control their bodies, and to try to control their environment, how are their needs satisfied? Third, we shall look at child-rearing practices during infancy in terms of their effect on growing self-awareness in childhood. Children who are heavily swaddled during the first year or who are bound to a cradleboard, for example, cannot explore their bodies as can children who are relatively free to move about. Children who have no access to a mirror do not discover their own images. But there are pervasive attitudes toward the body and the self that children learn each day.

Trust and Nurturance

If we look at infant care in other societies, we see dramatic differences both in approach and results. One study, for example, suggested a difference between the attitudes of American mothers and Japanese mothers toward their infants (Caudill & Weinstein, 1969). In general, the American mother viewed the infant as passive and dependent. Her goal was to make her child independent. The average Japanese mother held the opposite opinion of her infant. She saw her child as an independent organism who needed to learn about the dependent relationships within the family.

Such differences in attitude have resulted in two different child-rearing practices. American infants are ideally put in cribs in their own rooms, whereas Japanese infants traditionally share a bedroom with their parents. In the study, the Japanese mother tried to respond quickly when the baby cried, and she fed her child on demand. The American mother tended to let her child cry for a short while in the hope of establishing a regular, mature feeding schedule. The Japanese mother felt the need to soothe and quiet her baby often, whereas the American mother wanted to stimulate her baby to smile and vocalize. As a result of these different approaches, the Japanese baby quickly became less vocal and active than the American baby. But some of these differences may be due in part to the infant's initial temperament, as was mentioned in Chapter 5.

Feeding, Weaning, and Comfort Whether or not a mother breast-feeds or bottle-feeds her infant, the important question for psychological development is how the feeding method fits into the total pattern of nurturant care that the infant receives. Feeding time allows for the closeness between mother and child, and it expresses sensitivity and responsiveness between caregiver and child.

In some cultures, the transition period between the infant's birth and separation from the mother lasts for three years or more. Feeding is an integral part of this prolonged relationship (Mead & Newton, 1967). Children may sleep close to their mothers, be carried around in a sling during most of the first year, and be breast-fed until the age of 3 (Richman, LeVine, New, Howrigan, Welles-Nystrom, & LeVine, 1988). In other cultures, especially in North America, some infants may be separated from their mothers almost immediately by being given a separate bed and room and through early weaning. Somewhat in jest, Mead and Newton described the transition period for some North American babies as lasting less than a minute—until the umbilical cord is cut! In Sweden, maternal leave has been extended to nine months at 90 percent salary, with an additional nine months at reduced salary, mandated by laws discussed

One of the most popular comfort devices children use is a beloved blanket.

FOCUS ON DIVERSITY

Looking for Causes of Difficult Temperament in Canadian Infants and Toddlers

As part of the National Longitudinal Survey of Children and Youth (NLSCY), Canadian parents of 1- and 2-year-olds answered questions about their children that related to difficult temperament: "How easy or difficult is it for you to soothe your child when he or she is upset?"; "How many times per day, on average, does your child get fussy and irritable?"; "How often does your child smile and make happy sounds?"; and "How would you rate the overall degree of difficulty your child would present for the average parent?" This survey was conducted in 1994–1995. Since that time, two papers have published the survey's results related to difficult temperament (Normand et al., 1996; Ross, Scott, & Kelly, 1996). Here is a summary of the results.

There was some good news. The vast majority of parents rated their children as low in difficult temperament. Less than 10 percent of parents gave their children a high enough score to be considered difficult temperament. Parents' perceptions of children's behaviour are valuable because they may influence how parents interact with their children. It is important to keep in mind, though, that parents' ratings are subjective. Children rated difficult by parents may not necessarily be troublesome or unmanageable.

What factors might explain why some children are rated difficult and others are not? A number of physical factors related to the mother's pregnancy and delivery were considered: whether the mother had high blood pressure; whether she used tobacco and alcohol; whether she took medication; whether her baby was born by C-section; whether her baby required intensive care after birth; or whether she had postpartum complications, such as infection, excessive bleeding, or high blood pressure. None of these physical factors were associated with difficult temperament. Other physical factors, including low birth weight (2300 grams or less), preterm birth, and gestational diabetes, were associated with an increased chance of difficult temperament. On the other

---

Parent hostility was the strongest predictor of difficult temperament.

---

hand, forceps delivery reduced the risk of difficult temperament.

A number of psychosocial factors were considered and were found to have a greater influence on difficult temperament than did the physical factors. Factors associated with an increase in difficult temperament were lower family functioning, fewer positive parent–child interactions, the presence of siblings (especially a highly hyperactive sibling), postpartum depression in the mother, mothers who were much younger than average, and parents who were hostile. Of these factors, parent hostility was the strongest predictor of difficult temperament. "In the most hostile families, the odds [of difficult temperament] were 765 percent greater than in families with average hostility

scores" (Normand et al., 1996, p. 60). These results do not prove that hostility causes difficult temperament—they prove only that they are related (remember our discussion of correlations and causation in Chapter 1). It may be that the cause is bidirectional: hostile parenting causes the infant to be difficult, and cranky and difficult infants cause their parents to be hostile. In any case, the results indicate that psychosocial factors, rather than physical factors, are most associated with parental perceptions of difficult temperament. "The major clinical implication of these findings is that when a parent complains to a health or social service practitioner about having a difficult baby, the professional needs to assess parenting practices, family functioning and the mental health of the parent. It is not enough for physicians to look for potential medical causes or ascribe difficult temperament to teething, sleep deprivation or intolerance to certain foods" (Normand et al., 1996, p. 62).

From a developmental perspective, these findings have implications for the prevention of difficult temperament. Interventions aimed at improving family functioning can start even before the infant is born.

What are the long-term effects of difficult temperament? The NLSCY will be able to address this question in future studies because it will be assessing the same families every two years. Will children judged in 1994–1995 as having a difficult temperament be different from other children in later years?

---

earlier in this chapter. There is a public campaign that urges mothers to stay home with their children for at least nine months in order to provide continuity of care and nurturance. Despite the fact that Sweden has perhaps the lowest infant mortality rate in the world, mothers are concerned about the vulnerability of their infants, and both mothers and fathers pay close attention to the diet and health of the infant (Welles-Nystrom, 1988).

In Italy, the nurturance of the infant is a social affair. Mothers and infants are rarely alone. Mothers do most of the feeding, dressing, and cleaning of their infants in an indulgent and caring fashion. The family, friends, and neighbours all contribute to the social interaction with the infant. In one study, 70 percent of the time, although the mother was present, other people were also tending to the baby—hugging, talking, teaching, and even teasing the infant. The American observer was surprised at the amount of teasing that occurred, sometimes to the point of tears on the part of the infant. Infants were spanked; pacifiers were held just out of reach; candy was offered and then taken away. Adults said, "Here comes Daddy!" only to laugh and declare "He isn't here anymore!" and then swoop the tearful infant up to hug and kiss him amidst the laughter of onlookers. Even nap time was not sacred, as infants were jiggled and pinched to wake up when adults wanted to play with them. Despite this large amount of attention and stimulation, the infants seemed to learn to cope remarkably well (New, 1988).

Considerable research has been devoted to thumb sucking and other comfort devices, but remarkably few definitive conclusions have been reached about them. For the most part, sucking seems to be a natural need. Yet parents have responded to this need in a variety of ways (Goldberg, 1972; Richman et al., 1988). In much of early 20th-century Europe, thumb sucking was considered a dirty habit and harmful to a child's general personality development. Elaborate devices, vile-tasting applications, or simple sleeves were used to cover a child's hand to prevent thumb sucking. This era, with its strong fear of pleasure and of sense exploration, seems to be over. Today, some children are given a pacifier to suck, on the assumption that they can more easily give up the pacifier than they can give up the thumb. Most children who use either thumbs or pacifiers, however, give them up as regular comfort devices by the end of the preschool years; those who remain avid thumb suckers or avid comfort seekers generally have other needs that are not being met. Evidence that thumb sucking causes major damage to the dental arch is inconclusive. Most of this damage seems to occur in children who are still sucking at age 5, 6, or 7, when they are getting their second teeth.

Children use a wide variety of comfort devices and comfort-seeking behaviours. Cuddling favourite blankets, toys, and other objects and twisting and rubbing their hair or skin all provide familiar sensations. Through their reactions to comfort seeking, parents and caregivers convey their values and attitudes toward the child's body, toward self-stimulation, and toward what they feel is an acceptable level of closeness and dependency. From such reactions, children learn whether they are considered good or bad, whether they should feel anxious or guilty, and when they should feel comfortable and secure. They learn a great deal more than merely whether they should suck their thumbs or carry a blanket. Some bright children have learned the abstract words their parents use to give meaning to these behaviours, as the following comment indicates.

> A bright 3-year-old who had developed a fondness for her pacifier was asked by the pediatric dentist to stop using the "binky." Her comment to him was, "I can't stop, Doctor, it's a habit!"

Social Referencing and Cultural Meaning

One important avenue of parental influence on the infant is a process called **social referencing.** In situations of uncertainty, infants look to the parent's face to detect an emotional signal as to whether this situation is safe or unsafe, good or bad. We have seen the effectiveness of social referencing in encouraging an infant to cross a visual cliff or in deciding whether to become sociable with a stranger, for instance. But infants seem to look for an emotional signal under a wide range of circumstances, including how far to wander away from mother or whether or not to explore a strange toy. Infants look to fathers, as well as mothers, for emotional signals, and, although they look more to mothers than at fathers when both are present, the father's signals seem to be equally effective in regulating the infant's behaviour (Hirshberg & Svejda, 1990).

What happens if mother and father give conflicting emotional signals to their

Question to Ponder

The 1998 volume of the journal *Child Development* contains a Canadian study about infant social behaviour. All of the infants involved in the study were from Ontario, yet their backgrounds were described as "European American." Do you think this is an accurate label? Why or why not?

social referencing In ambiguous situations, infants look to their parents' emotional expressions to learn how to respond.

infant? What are the consequences of one parent encouraging the child to explore an unusual toy and the other frowning and displaying worry? In a study conducted with 1-year-olds, parents were coached to give consistent or conflicting emotional signals. The infants adapted much more easily to consistent signals, such as to both parents being happy or to both being fearful, than they did to conflicting emotional signals. In fact, when they were given conflicting facial responses—happy responses from mother and fearful responses from father, for example—the infants expressed their confusion in a wide range of anxious behaviours. Some did agitated sucking or rocking, and some avoided the situation altogether. Others wandered aimlessly or seemed disoriented. It seems that 1-year-olds are remarkably sensitive to the emotional signals from their parents. Some infants were more able to handle the conflict than were others (Hirshberg, 1990).

What are some of the messages that parents are already teaching their children at age 1? In a series of studies, anthropologists have intensely observed the !Kung San, a group of hunters and gatherers in Botswana. In this culture, the sharing of objects is an important value. When the anthropologists looked at mothers and their 10- to 12-month-old infants, they were surprised to find that, in contrast to many American parents, these parents seemed to pay no attention to the infant's exploration of objects. They did not talk about the objects and did not smile—but they neither punished nor frowned as children picked up twigs, grass, parts of food, nut shells, bones, and the like. They used an expression that meant "He's teaching himself." However, there was one activity with objects to which they did pay attention. The adults focused on the sharing and the giving and taking of objects. In fact, grandmothers began symbolic training by guiding the giving of special beads to relatives. When adults paid attention to objects at all, they encouraged sharing with expressions such as "Give it to me" or "Here, take this" (Bakeman & Adamson, 1990). It appears that, through social referencing, games, and selective attention, parents are already teaching their 1-year-olds the values of their culture.

Autonomy, Cooperation, and Discipline

By the time infants are 1 year old, their parents or caregivers have taught them some guidelines for acceptable behaviour, especially for their dependency needs and their needs for physical closeness. But, when the infants turn 2, caregivers cope with a whole new set of issues. Again, their personalities, as well as their cultural backgrounds, will affect their attitudes and methods of dealing with the toddler. To appreciate the diversity of problems facing those who care for toddlers, let us consider some typical 2-year-olds.

> He explores the qualities and possibilities of almost everything in his environment. She discovers the delights of pulling the toilet paper roll—endlessly. He uses pencil and crayon on walls, floors, and furniture. She enjoys picking up small things, from cigarette butts to crumbs to pebbles; many of these things will be given a taste test. He wedges his body into, under, or over any space that looks interesting. She picks up and carries around glass figurines, as well as toys. He alternates between clinging dependence and daring exploration, often within the space of a few minutes. She walks and runs and climbs for the sheer sensation of walking and running and climbing. He tries to cheer up another child by sharing his bottle, or he wilfully refuses to share. She is docile and eager to please one minute, and she challenges authority and routine the next. He wants to feed and dress himself on one occasion and wants everything done for him on the next. She may rebel at bedtime, protest at bath time, refuse to have her shoes or snowsuit put on, or reject a food that she has always enjoyed. He learns to say "No!"

Although the above examples are typical of toddlers, it is important to note that some toddlers are more socially competent than others. Researchers are especially concerned about toddlers who are exceptionally aggressive or antagonistic toward peers (Rubin, Hastings, Chen, Stewart, & McNichol, 1998). These toddlers may be rejected by peers and may be at risk for behavioural problems, school difficulties, and mental illness. (We shall discuss the long-term effects of peer rejection in Chapter 14.) A recent study, conducted in southwestern Ontario, observed pairs of 2-year-olds playing while their mothers were present (Rubin et al., 1998). The toddlers varied in how often they provoked aggressive conflicts with peers. Differences in aggressiveness were predicted by three factors: the toddler's gender (boys were more aggressive), the toddler's temperament, and the way that the mother interacted with her toddler. More aggressive toddlers had a dysregulated temperament, which means that they had poor self-control. They were easily frustrated and prone to anger. They also showed more social fearfulness. Their mothers were more likely to be domineering and negative while interacting with them. Toddlers most at risk for high aggression were boys who had poor self-control and who had mothers who were negative and domineering.

In addition to being concerned about overly aggressive toddlers, researchers have focused on toddlers who react to new situations with excessive shyness and fear (Rubin, Hastings, Stewart, Henderson, & Chen, 1997). Rubin and colleagues did a study on toddlers in southwestern Ontario. Each toddler was exposed to three new situations that might trigger shyness. In the first situation, the toddler and his mother were taken to an unfamiliar room with novel toys. A toddler was considered shy if he spent most of the time close to his mother and little time venturing away to explore the room. In the second situation, an adult stranger carrying an attractive toy entered the room. A toddler was considered shy if he was reluctant to approach the stranger or the toy. In the third situation, the toddler was observed playing with another toddler who was a stranger. A toddler was considered shy if he was wary of the other toddler. Interestingly, many toddlers appeared shy in one situation, but not in others; thus, it seemed that shyness in toddlers often depends on the context. However, 10 percent of the toddlers were consistently shy in all three situations. Consistent shyness was predicted by two factors: the toddler's temperament and the way the mother interacted with the toddler. Consistently shy toddlers had fearful temperaments and were highly distressed when separated from their mothers. Their mothers were described as overprotective. They tried to shield their toddlers from distress by becoming affectionate or controlling. Consistently shy toddlers may be at risk for social withdrawal. We will discuss the long-term effects of social withdrawal in Chapter 14.

In summary, research has consistently shown that the toddler's temperament and the caregiving she receives at home influence her development of socially competent behaviour. But what about toddlers who attend child-care centres? Which, if any, factors—such as type of care, quantity of care, quality of care, or stability of care—predict toddlers' social development? This question was addressed in a study that sampled over 1000 toddlers from 10 cities across the United States (National Institute of Child Health and Human Development [NICHD], 1998). Toddlers' self-control, cooperation, and management of aggressive and antisocial impulses were measured at age 2 and at age 3. Before evaluating the effects of child-care factors, the researchers controlled for background factors, such as the family's socioeconomic status and characteristics of the parents and the toddlers. Quality of care predicted toddlers' social development better than did the type or quantity of care. But even so, its effects were weak compared with the effects of the characteristics of the child and her experiences at home. All of the child-care factors combined explained less than 3 percent of the variation in children's social behaviour.

What transpires in the family appears to be more important in explaining children's early social and emotional development than whether children are cared for by someone other than their mothers on a routine basis or the quality, quantity, stability, and type of care or age of entry into such care. This is not to say, however, that these features of child care exerted no influence upon the children ... quality of care was the most consistent child-care predictor, with higher quality of care relating to greater social competence and cooperation and less problem behaviour at both 2 and 3 years of age. More time in care and more care arrangements (i.e., less stable care) were negative predictors of some outcomes at 2 years of age. And, finally, greater experience in groups with other children predicted more cooperation and fewer problems at both 2 and 3 years of age. (NICHD, 1998, p. 1168)

Another finding of interest in the study is that different results were apparent at age 2 than at age 3. For example, 2-year-olds who spent more time in child care were reported by their mothers to be less cooperative, and child-care staff reported that those 2-year-olds had more behavioural problems. However, by the time the children were 3, neither their mothers nor the child-care staff reported them as being different from other children. How should we interpret these results? One interpretation is that the effects were only short lived. Another interpretation is that the effects may be apparent at ages considered more stressful because they involve a transition. Age 2 is often considered a transitional age between infancy and preschool. The next transitional age is 5 or 6, when the child starts school. If the effects of child care at age 2 were due to it being a transitional age, will these effects resurface at age 5 or 6? It is important that researchers monitor the effects at different ages to determine whether effects are short term or whether they fluctuate. As well, it is possible for effects to be "sleeper effects," meaning that they are revealed for the first time only at an older age, as was discussed in the Broberg et al. (1997) study mentioned in Chapter 1. In that study, children who had attended child-care centres had better cognitive skills than did other children, but these differences did not become apparent until the children were 8 years old.

Toilet Training Toilet training is universal—children around the world learn to control the passing of wastes from their bodies. What is not universal, though, is the approach to toilet training. Different approaches are a reflection of many factors, including the personality of the adult doing the training, the temperament of the child, and the values and norms of the culture. Some adults start toilet training early, adopting an intensive training regime that can last for several months. Other adults adopt a laid-back approach, letting the child train himself. Still other adults strike a balance between the two

FOCUS ON APPLICATION

Successful Toilet Training

Current advice from the experts to parents about toilet training goes something like this: because newborns and young infants have no bladder control, they urinate reflexively in response to a full bladder. Young infants are unaware of urinating. Gradually, the nerves connecting the bladder and brain develop, and older infants begin to sense when their bladders are full. Now they can start to inhibit the release of urine. In general, toilet training should not be undertaken before children have adequate physical development, show interest in the process, have been dry at night, or show by gestures that they are aware that they are having a bowel movement or urinating (Langlois, 1998; Maizels, Rosenbaum, & Keating, 1999; Welford, 1998).

Once these behaviours have arrived indicating readiness, then it is time to begin the process. According to the

---

Mark, aged 2½, wanted to go to the preschool his older brother was attending. However, Mark had been resisting toilet training.

Canadian Paediatric Society and the College of Family Physicians of Canada, most children are ready for toilet training around age 2 or 2½. Interestingly, this age for toilet training is later than it was a generation ago. In the 1950s, it was common for toilet training to begin

before the infant was 1 year old. Perhaps earlier attempts were favoured because laundering diapers in the 1950s—using wringer washers and clotheslines—was arduous. In any case, infants who started training earlier did not achieve independent mastery until about the same age as those who started later. Young infants could be conditioned to perform on the potty if they were placed on it often and at key times, such as right after eating. However, they could not learn to control their bodily functions until they had matured.

There is no one right approach to toilet training, although more people now favour a low-key approach to a strict, disciplinarian one. Here are some practical suggestions recommended by today's experts:

approaches. Ultimately, most children will become toilet trained, regardless of the approach to training. Sometimes psychologists are interested in toilet training because it is related to other attitudes toward child rearing. Toilet training is just one aspect of behaviour affected by adult attitudes toward children's explorations and handling of their own bodies, as well as toward children's need for autonomy.

Those who are severe and harsh in toilet training are usually just as strict about other behaviours requiring self-mastery and independence, such as feeding, dressing, and general exploring. Some adults demand that a child have early and total control of bowel and bladder; they regard "accidents" as intolerable and dirty. Such people are likely to be severe when children break a plate, play in the dirt, explore new places and objects, and attempt to feed themselves (see the box "Successful Toilet Training").

Discipline How does a parent or caregiver set limits on a child's behaviour? Some, afraid that any kind of control over their children's behaviour will prevent creative exploration and independence, helplessly stand by while their 2-year-olds do whatever they please. Discipline, when it comes, is often harsh, reflecting the adults' own feelings of frustration. Others, determined not to "spoil" their children and convinced that 2-year-olds should act like responsible little citizens, set so many limits on behaviour that their children, literally, cannot do anything right. Although it is easy to see the errors in these extremes, it is not quite so simple to provide a set of guidelines that will be effective for every occasion. For example, adults who encourage exploration and manipulation may have to cope, sooner or later, with a child who wants to stick pins into electrical outlets. Obviously, adults must temper their guidelines with common sense and must consider children's needs for safety, as well as for independence and creative experience. Children permitted to run, jump, and climb can also be taught to walk quietly, to hold someone's hand, or to allow themselves to be carried in public places.

One important technique to help raise a child with a sense of self-discipline is to provide parental feedback. Parents need to show the children how they are coming across to others. Children need this feedback if they are to become sensitive to the

- Buy training pants or the disposable pull-ups.
- Place the child on the potty frequently, initially to help him make the association.
- Give rewards for success—stickers work well, as do pennies or hugs. Often, a reinforcer may be the attainment of something the child must be "big enough" to participate in, as the following examples suggest.

Mark, aged 2½, wanted to go to the preschool his older brother was attending. However, Mark had been resisting toilet training. His mother told him that he would go to school when he was potty trained. He learned within three days.

Mattie, who was 3, desperately wanted to wear "big girl" underpants, like her older sisters. She learned to use the toilet reliably within a day of wearing her first pair.

Ernestine, aged 3½, was still in a crib. She stopped wearing diapers and had no accidents when she was put into her own twin bed.

In each of these examples, the children were physiologically and psychologically ready for toilet training. They were also mature enough to remember to use the toilet when they felt the urge. However, for most children, accidents occasionally occur—especially when they are engaged in an activity they do not want to halt. Because occasional accidents are typical and because it is common for young children to have an urgent need to use the toilet ("I have to go right now!"), many Canadian parents choose to toilet train children during warmer months, when children are wearing less clothing. Accidents are best dealt with by quietly cleaning the child, setting her immediately on the potty, and then explaining that "we will work on it harder for the next time." Criticism accomplishes nothing except making the child self-conscious and overly stressed about the process. When accidents occur publicly in a child-care centre, staff need to handle them matter-of-factly so that the child is not embarrassed or teased. The opportunity to observe and imitate an older child often speeds the learning.

needs of others. Feedback might consist of praise for good behaviour, such as, "I like the way you help me set the table." Or it might be in terms of a mild scolding, such as, "I am upset that you opened my purse and took money without my permission." The key to feedback is that behaviour is criticized and guidance is given, but the child is never criticized.

Children who have developed a strong attachment relationship and whose needs are met through loving interaction with an adult are neither spoiled by lots of attention nor frightened or threatened by reasonable limits. They are stronger and more confident because they have a trustworthy relationship from which to venture forth into independence.

Development of the Self

At first, infants cannot differentiate between themselves and the world around them. Gradually, however, they begin to realize that they are separate and unique beings. Much of infancy is devoted to making this distinction. From 3 to 8 months, the infant actively learns about his body. First, the child discovers his hands, his feet, and some of the things he can do with them. Later, the child acts on the world and sees what happens. At 7 or 8 months, the infant makes a couple of significant advancements. He becomes particularly wary of strangers. That means he is discriminating of those he knows well and of those he doesn't. He also becomes able to delay his actions, even for a short time. This ability allows him the beginnings of self–other schemes. Infants now become more deliberate in their testing and exploring of their own responses and results. Also, by observing the behaviour of those around them, infants learn the beginnings of how they should behave. They can imitate. They begin to know what is expected. In the period from 12 to 18 months, the infant is hard at work learning these social expectations and learning what happens when he tests or explores the social world. By the end of this period, he clearly recognizes himself in pictures and in the mirror. One way that researchers test the infant's self-recognition is through the rouge test. A dot of red rouge is smeared on the infant's nose. Then, the infant is shown his reflection in the mirror. An infant who recognizes his own face will bring his hand to his nose to explore the mysterious red spot. However, younger infants, under a year, who have less self-awareness, will not touch their noses. They may do nothing, or they may touch their reflections in the mirror. Once the infant has self-awareness, he is capable of some of the social emotions, such as pride or embarrassment. He is ready for more detailed socialization (Lewis & Feinman, 1991). Finally, from 18 to 30 months, the child is developing considerable knowledge about himself with respect to the social world, about his gender, about his physical features and characteristics, about his goodness and badness, about what he can and cannot do. He recognizes that he has feelings, intentions, and thoughts and that these differ from those of other people (Shatz, 1994).

Possibly the sense of ownership that toddlers display is necessary to complete their sense of self.

By the end of the second year, the child's language has considerable self-reference. Children know their names and use them, often describing their needs and feelings in the third person: "Terri wants water." The words *me* and *mine* assume new importance in the vocabulary, and the concept of ownership is clearly and strongly acted out. Even in families in which sharing is emphasized and ownership is minimized, and despite many spontaneous demonstrations of sharing, toddlers show fairly extensive evidence of possessiveness. It may be that they need to establish a concept of ownership in order to round out their definition of self. Sharing and cooperation come more easily once toddlers are confident about what is theirs.

Self-awareness is a result of self-exploration, cognitive maturity, and reflections about self. Toddlers can frequently be heard talking to and admonishing themselves ("No, Lee, don't touch!") and rewarding themselves ("Me good girl!"). They incorporate cultural and social expectations into their reflections, as well as into their behaviour, and begin to judge themselves and others in light of these expectations. If they enjoy consistent, loving interaction with the caregiver in an environment that they are free to explore and can begin to control, they learn to make valid predictions about the world around them. According to Dr. Stanley Greenspan, a world-renowned expert in early childhood, the child's early emotional interactions with caregivers form the basis for self-development, as well as for intellectual and moral development (Greenspan, 1997). In the United States, the National Centre of Infants, Toddlers and Families published a report titled *Zero to Three,* in which they argue that "babies' emotional exchanges with caregivers, rather than their ability to fit pegs into holes or find beads under cups, should become the primary measuring rod of developmental and intellectual competence" (Greenspan, 1997, p. 9). Through sensitive caregiving, the infant or toddler learns initiative because her intentions and actions have a positive effect on others. For example, she learns that when she reaches out to her mother, her mother picks her up and comforts her. She feels secure when her mother gives her a hug. On the other hand, another child might experience rejection when he reaches out to his mother for comfort. His mother may withdraw or jerk away when he attempts physical closeness. He learns to fear closeness. According to Dr. Greenspan, these types of early interactions lay the foundations for later life experiences, as demonstrated in the following instance:

> Twelve-month-old Jason, for example, reaches repeatedly for closeness with his mother, but each time his demands make her feel tense and overwhelmed, and she withdraws from him. The active, energetic child soon learns to seek in stimulation the satisfaction he cannot find in intimacy. He becomes more aggressive, more and more impulsive. As he grows older he responds belligerently whenever he feels the loss, sadness, and vulnerability first experienced at his mother's rejection. When a friend moves away, a favourite teacher misses several days of school, or his parents ignore him, Jason gives no thought to his sadness or loneliness. Rather he applies the solution he learned as a baby: aggression, counter-rejection, and the attitude that is later expressed as "I don't need anyone." (Greenspan, 1997, p. 62)

From early interactions, children gradually establish a perception of themselves—perhaps as acceptable, competent individuals.

At 9 months, an infant greets the baby in the mirror. Between 16 and 18 months, infants make the amazing discovery of an independent self.

Summary and Conclusions

During infancy and toddlerhood, the first relationships between the infant and caregiver occur. This first relationship forms the basis for all later personality development. It is unclear to what extent the determinants of these first relations are genetic or environmental, but in general, an interaction is assumed. Ethologists who compare behaviour across species have studied imprinting in animals as a possible mechanism to explain attachment in humans. In animals, the timing of exposure to stimulation is crucial. Although in humans the development of a trust relationship during the first 6 months of life is important, there does not seem to be the same sort of critical period for its development.

Babies can develop different types of attachment: secure, avoidant, ambivalent, or disorganized/disoriented. There is a relationship between type of attachment and later development. Secure attachment is associated with more positive development, whereas the other types are associated with an increased risk for a variety of problems.

As attachment develops, stranger anxiety also arises. Somewhere between 6 to 8 months of age, the infant gains the cognitive ability to detect discrepancies between the familiar caregiver and all others. At similar ages, the infant may experience separation anxiety and the sense of loss when the caregiver is absent. The degree of separation and stranger anxiety in normal children varies according to the exclusivity and intimacy of the early relationships. When the attachment process has been interrupted or is dysfunctional, children may suffer from impaired personality development and from subsequent emotional difficulties.

The patterns of early relationships are affected by individual differences in the temperaments and environments in which they occur, by whether or not the child has a disability, and by any dysfunction existing in the bonding of the parent and child. When mutuality and interactive synchrony mark the communication between caregiver and infant, the attachment that develops is strong. When there is mutuality between the caregiver and child, the positive dialogue that develops is transferred to the larger social environment in which the child participates. Interactions with peers and with other adults show the same trust and prosocial behaviour. When something goes wrong in the communication dialogue because of physical or psychological abnormalities, the subsequent difficulties can produce devastating effects on the child's personality and mental health. Special counselling may be needed to compensate for and overcome such developmental problems.

Although much of the research on the development of attachment focuses on mother–child interactions, recent research has focused on the role of fathers. Infants can form strong attachments to a variety of people and objects in the environment. When fathers play a significant role in the lives of infants and toddlers, the attachment may be as strong as it is to the mother. The nature of the paternal role tends to be that of playmate, rather than caregiver and nurturer. However, when fathers assume the primary caregiver role, they more closely resemble mothers in terms of their smiling, imitating, and vocalizing with the infant.

The entire family changes when an infant is born. Patterns of communication, recreation, and responsibility shift. The way in which the couple handle these new demands either brings the couple closer or disturbs the marriage. If the marriage is strong and the couple negotiate the new demands with equanimity, humour, and mutual respect, then the relationships between the child and parents—and future children—will also be strong.

One difficult task that many families confront is how to provide infant and preschooler care if the mother works. Over 61 percent of Canadian mothers work, and their children are placed in a variety of day-care situations, including home care, care in the home of another, or formal day care. It is important to identify standards for quality care.

Child-rearing practices reflect cultural beliefs and, in turn, influence later personality development. The manner in which parents handle such early transitions as feeding, toilet training, discipline, and comfort devices conveys fundamental messages to their children. Children learn attitudes about their bodies, such as the acceptability of self-stimulation or of physical closeness. Family patterns in handling dependency and autonomy also have pervasive effects on the child's personality and self-concept. The social experiences—both within and outside the family—to which the child is exposed in the first two years essentially shape the growing understanding about the social world and the attitudes that children have about themselves.

Key Terms and Concepts

attachment (p. 196)

discrepancy hypothesis (p. 200)

disorganized/disoriented attachment (p. 203)

imprinting (p. 197)

insecure ambivalent attachment (p. 202)

insecure avoidant attachment (p. 202)

mutuality (synchrony) (p. 206)

secure attachment (p. 202)

social referencing (p. 225)

stranger or separation anxiety (p. 199)

strange situation test (p. 202)

Questions to Review

1. What are attachment behaviours, and what is the significance for the relationship between infant and caregiver?

2. What is imprinting, and when does it take place?

3. What is stranger anxiety? When and why does it occur?

4. Compare what happens to a child who does not form an attachment relationship or one whose progress toward attachment is interrupted with a child who has formed an attachment relationship.

5. How does an exclusive relationship affect the adjustment of the infant?

6. Describe how a responsive environment can affect the development of attachment behaviour and emotional development.

7. How did Schaffer define mutuality, or synchrony, and what effect does it have on infant development?

8. Compare and contrast the securely attached infant, the avoidant infant, and the ambivalent infant.

9. How does the special needs infant influence the attitude of the caregiver?

10. List several bonding disorders.

11. Describe the differences and similarities between father–child interaction and mother–child interaction.

12. What are the negative and positive effects of sibling relationships?

13. What is the grandparent's role in the development of the infant?

14. Why is it difficult to study the effects of day care on infant development?

15. List several factors to consider when evaluating a day-care centre.

16. Describe some of the child-rearing practices that vary from culture to culture, and explain how these different patterns influence later personality development.

Weblinks

www.dadscan.org/
Dads Can
This site, sponsored by Health Canada, promotes responsible and involved fathering by providing information on fathering tools, a chat room, and general information related to effective fathering.

home.istar.ca/~ccaac/closer.html
Child Care Advocacy Association of Canada
This organization promotes accessible, affordable, quality nonprofit child care.

members.tripod.com/~JudyArnall/
The Whole Family Attachment Parenting Association
This site, developed in Calgary, has information on parenting styles that focus on an infant's or a child's need for trust, empathy, and affection to create secure, peaceful, and enduring relationships. There are links to several parenting resources.

Summing Up...

Infancy

Physical

- Gains height and loses baby fat
- Nearly doubles in weight at 4 mos
- Changes in body proportions—less top heavy
- Gets first tooth (6 to 7 mos)
- Rolls from stomach to back and from back to stomach (4 mos)
- Uses voluntary actions instead of reflexes (4 mos)
- Discovers hands (4 mos) and feet (5 or 6 mos)
- Develops visually guided reach (5 to 8 mos)
- Can pass objects from hand to hand (5 to 8 mos)
- Starts cruising (5 to 8 mos)
- Develops locomotion (5 to 8 mos)
- Can pull to stand (9 mos)
- Walks independently (11 to 13 mos)
- Uses pincer grasp (9 to 12 mos)
- Can stack 2 to 4 cubes in a tower (18 mos)
- Brain develops—growth and pruning of synapses; myelination
- Frontal lobe develops (7 to 9 mos)
- Brain is 90% of adult size by age 8
- Corpus callosum matures
- Improves strength, speed, and coordination required for gross motor skills
- Develops fine motor skills

Psychosocial

- Improves self-feeding and dressing (18 mos)
- Goes through presocial or preattachment phase (birth to 6 wks)
- Goes through social or attachment-in-the-making phase (6 wks to 6 to 8 mos)
- Goes through clear-cut attachment phase (6 to 8 mos to 2 yrs)
- Forms reciprocal relationships (18 mos to 2 yrs)
- Develops stranger anxiety (7 mos)
- Forms trust
- Uses social referencing (1 yr)
- Becomes toilet trained (2 to 3 yrs)
- Develops self-awareness (3 to 8 mos)
- Learns social expectations (12 to 18 mos)

Cognitive

- Increases control over visual attention (9 to 12 mos)
- Increases control over eye movements (6 mos)
- Develops visual acuity—nearly adult-like by 6 mos
- Prefers to look at high-contrast patterns (1 to 2 mos)
- Prefers to look at faces (4 mos)
- Develops depth perception—reacts defensively to collisions (2 mos), swipes toys accurately (4 mos), uses visual cues (4 to 6 mos)
- Attends to human speech since birth
- Shows distress at still face effect (3 mos)
- Goes through sensorimotor stage—uses circular responses, imitation, symbolic representation
- Develops object permanence—recognizes familiar objects (2 mos), searches for hidden mother (6 to 8 mos), searches for a wide range of stimuli (10 mos)
- Distinguishes between self and others (5 mos)
- Learns concepts—distinguishes global concepts (7 mos)

Language: The Bridge from Infancy

And always behind my eyes
is the image of my daughter at age three asking
do butterflies have babies—
Or is it the other way round?

ELSIE MACLAY
"GREEN WINTER"

Outline

CHAPTER 8

Objectives

By the time you have finished this chapter, you should be able to do the following:

- ✔ List three major dimensions of language.

- ✔ Describe the role of early experience in language acquisition.

- ✔ Describe the sequence of language development in young children.

- ✔ Explain the influence of caregivers on their children's language development.

- ✔ Describe the multilingual nature of language learning in Canada.

Jason: *Maria broke the toy, didn't she?*

Mother: *Yes, dear. She did.*

Jason: *I don't break toys. I'm a good boy, ain't I?*

Mother: *I'm a good boy,* aren't *I?*

Jason: *Nah, you're a* girl!

The infant's first word is one of the highlights of infancy—indeed, parents rank it alongside the first time the baby sleeps through the night—especially if the first word is "dada" or "mama." Before that first word, however, even newborns communicate. It doesn't take long for them to discover how to let their parents know that they are hungry, wet, or bored. By about 1 year of age, most children begin to talk; by 4½, most have developed amazing verbal competence. Their vocabulary may be limited and their grammar far from perfect, but their implicit grasp of language structure is remarkable. They not only know the words with which to designate things and communicate thoughts, but they also exhibit a sophisticated understanding of the rules that govern the combinations and uses of these words. They speak in full sentences with phrases, clauses, and appropriate grammatical constructions, such as proper tenses and plural forms. This is a startling cognitive achievement when we think of the enormous complexity of the underlying rules of syntax and semantics. Language is an elaborate system of symbols. To manipulate the symbols properly, a child must first master basic cognitive concepts.

The complexity and originality of the 4½-year-old's speech are perhaps best illustrated by the *tag question,* which is a direct statement followed by a tag, or a request to confirm the statement: "Maria broke the toy, didn't she?" This apparently simple question actually involves a number of grammatical processes. In order to form the tag "didn't she," Jason had to understand several different rules. He had to know how to copy, or supply, the correct subject pronoun for "Maria," how to supply the auxiliary verb (the proper form of "do"), how to negate the auxiliary verb, and how to invert the word order of the auxiliary verb and pronoun. Somewhat younger children may have the general idea of the tag question but may not yet be able to master all of the grammatical processes. Therefore, they might say, "Maria broke the toy, unh?"

Language development is more than a purely cognitive achievement, however. It also involves social growth. Children must learn a specific language, with all of its cultural ramifications. While they learn syntax and vocabulary, children also absorb social values, such as politeness, obedience, and gender roles. Therefore, language acquisition involves both cognitive and social development; it is a bridge between infancy and childhood. When children can understand and communicate their wants, needs, and observations, the world deals with them in quite a different way.

Language Development

Language involves the use of symbols for communicating information. The acquisition of language is a complex yet natural process. Perhaps better than any other single accomplishment, it illustrates the range and potential of the human organism. For this reason, it is a particularly fascinating area of psychological development. To understand this phenomenon fully, we first should be aware of some of its most basic elements.

Aspects of Language

content The meaning of any written or spoken message.

form The particular symbol used to represent content.

use The way in which a speaker employs language to give it one meaning as opposed to another.

phonemes The smallest units of sound—vowels and consonants—that combine to form morphemes and words.

morphemes The minimal units of meaning in language that form basic words, prefixes, and suffixes.

grammar A complicated set of rules for building words, as well as the rules for combining words to form phrases and sentences.

morphology The set of rules for building words that is present in all languages.

syntax The rules for combining words to form phrases and sentences.

We often think of language as having three major dimensions: content, form, and use (Bloom & Lahey, 1978). **Content** refers to the meaning of any written or spoken message. **Form** is the particular symbol used to represent that content—the sounds, the words, the grammar. **Use** refers to the social interchange, or exchange, between two people: the speaker and the person spoken to. The details of that social exchange depend on the situation, on the relationship between the speaker and the listener, and on the intentions and attitudes of the two participants. In the example at the beginning of this chapter, Jason is talking about who broke the toy (content). He is using an especially sophisticated grammatical form—a tag question. Jason is concerned about receiving reassurance from his mother that he is a good boy, whereas his mother is interested in correcting his grammar. In this simple exchange, a great deal has been communicated. The information is conveyed in a particular form, in a fashion that reflects the relationship and intention of both participants. The form and the use, therefore, also contribute to the meaning of the message.

Form can be examined on three levels. **Phonemes** are the basic sounds—the vowels and the consonants—that combine to form words. English has 46 separate phonemes: vowels *(a, e, i, o,* and *u);* consonants such as *p, m, k,* and *d;* and blends of the two consonants like *th.* Other languages use different groups of phonemes. Sounds used in one language may even be absent in another. **Morphemes** are the meaning units—the basic words, prefixes, and suffixes. The sentence, "Mommy warmed the bottles" can be divided into six morphemes: *Mommy, warm, ed, the, bottle,* and *s.* Finally, every language has a **grammar**—a complicated set of rules for building words (**morphology**), as well as the rules for combining words to form phrases and sentences (**syntax**). In English, however, grammar is primarily concerned with syntax, and the two terms are often used interchangeably. The number of combinations of sounds or sentences in English is, for all practical purposes, infinite. It should be noted that aspects of form also convey meaning. "The dog bit the baby" is different from "The baby bit the dog" simply because of word order. Children learn such distinctions at an early age.

The social use of language is complex. Children learn to be polite and deferential

Expressing feelings and establishing and maintaining contact with others are some of the uses of speech.

to their elders, to simplify their language for babies, to take turns when they are involved in a conversation, and to understand indirect and direct speech. They learn to determine the speaker's intention, as well as to understand the actual words. For example, a sentence such as, "What is this?" can have different meanings, depending on the situation. It can serve as a simple request for information, but it also can be an expression of horror.

We use speech for a number of purposes. We use it to satisfy wants and needs; to control others; to maintain contact with other people; to express feelings; to imagine, pretend, or create; and to inquire and describe (Halliday, 1973). Young children are exposed to and implicitly learn these functions of language, as well as specific words and forms.

The Processes of Language Learning

Just how do humans progress from crying to babbling to speaking the infinite forms of adult language? Over the years this question has prompted considerable debate, especially between behaviourists and linguists. Behaviourists, most notably B.F. Skinner (mentioned in Chapter 2), emphasized that children learn language by being reinforced for imitating other speakers of the language. The child who says the word "cookie" and gets one is likely to use the word again. Behaviourists considered language learning no different from any other type of learning. In contrast, linguists such as Noam Chomsky studied the structures and meanings of different languages. They concluded that language learning cannot occur unless the child has an innate ability to look for grammar in the language. These linguists considered language learning different from any other type of learning. Today, it is recognized that language acquisition requires both experience with language, as suggested by the behaviourists, and innate abilities, as suggested by the linguists (Gleitman & Newport, 1995; Pinker, 1995).

Early Experience with a Language Environment Obviously, experience plays a role in language acquisition because children learn the languages they hear, not others among the 5000 or so human languages. Children in English communities learn English; children in Chinese communities learn Chinese. Children obviously learn first words—often simple labels—by hearing and imitating. In fact, they must learn most early vocabulary in this way; children cannot invent words and make themselves understood.

It is also clear that children who are not exposed to language do not learn it. Unfortunately, there are children who live in environments without language during their early years, such as described later in this chapter in the box "Is There a Critical Period for Learning Language?" These children tend to be mute. Interestingly, though, when they are later exposed to language, they are unable to learn it beyond the level of a typical 2-year-old. It seems that the timing of exposure to language is critical—it must happen within the first 6 years or so.

The importance of early experience with language also applies to deaf children's learning sign language. Deaf children born to deaf parents who sign and who are therefore exposed to sign language from birth learn to sign at the same rate that hearing children learn to speak. But other deaf children, those born to hearing parents, may not be exposed to sign language until much later and may be language delayed. Newport (1990) studied deaf adults who had been using sign language for at least 30 years and found that some were more fluent than others. Interestingly, the most fluent signers all had been exposed to sign language before age 6, and the less fluent signers after age 6.

The timing of language experience is also important in understanding the acquisition of second (and even third or fourth) languages. Johnson and Newport (1989) tested native Chinese and Korean speakers who had immigrated to the United States and started learning English 20 years ago. Some of the immigrants were children (the youngest was 3 years old) and others were adults (the oldest was 39 years old) when they first encountered English. Interestingly, more than 20 years later, differences were evident between those who were first exposed to English before the age of 7 and those who were first exposed when they were older; the people exposed before the age of 7 had a better grasp of English grammar and were able to speak the language without an accent.

Why do children who experience language early learn it better than adults? After all, this goes against the grain. In practically all other types of learning, adults learn better and faster than children. Why is language learning different? One explanation has to do with the development of the brain. According to Lenneberg (1967), the child's brain is flexible, so she can learn any language. But the mature brain has lost much of this flexibility. Differences in brain flexibility are apparent in the abilities of children and adults to recover from brain damage. When adults have damage to the

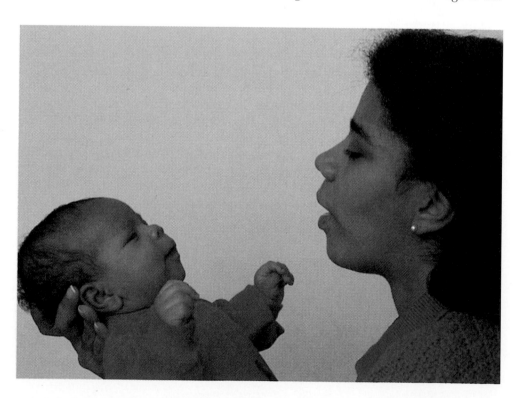

Obviously, experience is important because babies learn the languages of their parents.

left side of the brain (left hemisphere), they lose the ability to produce language or to understand it, or a combination of the two. Language deficits caused by brain damage are called **aphasia.** Sometimes aphasia is permanent in adults. But when young children have similar damage to the left hemisphere, they either experience temporary aphasia or none at all. Apparently, the child's brain is still flexible enough to process language in the remaining parts. This flexibility is described as *plasticity.*

aphasia Language impairment caused by brain damage.

According to Chomsky (1993), children come prepared to learn any language and to recognize language patterns. For example, in English we expect the subject of a sentence to come first, followed by the verb and the object ("The girl played Nintendo"). But in Japanese the object comes before the verb ("The girl Nintendo played"). English uses prepositions ("in the tickle trunk"); Japanese uses postpositions ("the tickle trunk in"). English puts question words at the beginning of the sentence ("What is the macarena?"); Japanese puts question words at the end ("Is the macarena what?"). Thus, English follows a different pattern from Japanese. Young children seem capable of learning any language pattern, but as their brains mature, they lose that flexibility. They expect new languages to conform to the language patterns that they already know. It is as though early experience with language "sets the switches" in the brain for particular language patterns.

How do children learn from early experience with language? The answer to this question is still a mystery. Imagine an adult telling a toddler, "See the glug," as the child watches a Christmas parade. How does the toddler know what the adult is referring to? Does "glug" mean Santa Claus, reindeer, sled, red suit, furry, man, snow? It is amazing that children are so good at picking out the intended referents.

Landau and Gleitman (1985) studied blind children who were learning language. Blind children face an interesting problem—they cannot see what words refer to, yet surprisingly, they learn language as well as sighted children do. The blind children, though, had unique meanings for words associated with vision, such as *see* or *look.* When asked to look up, they raised their hands rather than their eyes. When asked what they saw, they reported what their fingers were feeling.

Where Does Grammar Come From? How do children learn grammar? Or do they learn it? Skinner and other behaviourists assumed that children learned grammar by copying adults and by recognizing analogies. For example, the child might hear the sentence, "I coloured the watermelon green," interchangeably with, "I coloured the green watermelon." The child might then form the rule that "green" can occur before or after "watermelon" and later use this as an analogy for a similar sentence, "I tasted the green watermelon." He might assume that this sentence could also be expressed, "I tasted the watermelon green." Whoops. The analogy does not work. How does the child know when an analogy will work and when it will not?

Children's early language is charming because it contains examples of grammar that the child could not possibly be copying from adults. Consider the following examples of toddler talk: "I maked my bed, Mommy," "My want to go too," "Him hit me with the truck," or "The policeman will under arrested you." It seems that the child is attempting to construct a grammar, rather than merely parroting what she has heard. Even children at elementary school age invent their own grammar. I have heard them say "tooken" (meaning "took") and "usen" (meaning "used"), overapplying the English ending *en* found in words like *chosen.* I have heard them make up the word "discluded" (meaning "excluded") (Digdon).

Bickerton (1975) studied children raised in an unusual language environment, where the adult language had no grammar. In Suriname, South America, former slaves escaped from their masters' plantations to form their own communities. But the adults in these new communities had no common language. They made do with a pidgin language that borrowed vocabulary from various languages, and they used extensive nonverbal communication. This pidgin language lacked grammar. Interestingly, children growing up hearing pidgin did not learn to speak it. Instead, they automatically added grammar to the pidgin, creating a new language called **Creole.**

"What's the big surprise? All the latest theories of linguistics say we're born with the innate capacity for generating sentences."

It is important to note that humans learn grammar implicitly, without intention or awareness. Our speech follows rules of grammar, yet we often are unable to articulate these rules. It is like knowing that a pear tastes different from an apple, but being unable to explain how the two differ.

Language Beginnings

Language development involves learning to speak or produce oral or signed language, learning the meaning of words, and learning the rules of grammar—how words can be combined into sentences to communicate ideas. During the preschool years, there are two key processes involved in language development. **Receptive language** is a child's understanding of the spoken, signed, or written word. **Productive language** is what the child says, signs, or, later, writes. These interrelated processes evolve simultaneously. Often, receptive language, or language comprehension, develops a little bit ahead of language production. For example, a parent may ask her 14-month-old the following question, "Will you go into the kitchen and bring back the cookies?" The child may return with the cookies but be unable to produce such a sentence—or even the words "bring cookies"—himself.

Before the First Words

The production of language begins with an undifferentiated cry at the moment of birth. Soon after, infants develop a range of different cries and, by about 6 weeks, a variety of cooing sounds. At the time of birth, infants have developed a large area in the left hemisphere of the brain (the hemisphere that controls language) that allows them to listen to and respond to language from the very beginning (Brooks & Obrzut, 1981). By the second or third month, infants are sensitive to speech and can distinguish between such similar sounds as *b* and *p* or *d* and *t* (Eimas, 1974). Curiously, compared with adults, infants are able to hear differences among a wider range of speech sounds, including phonemes that are not part of their native languages (Werker, 1995). Infants, therefore, are language universalists who can distinguish all the sounds of human

---

Question to Ponder

How much language do you think babies understand before they are old enough to speak? How does their language understanding differ from that of animals such as dogs or apes?

Creole A new language created by children in communities where the adults do not have a common language. The adults communicate with pidgin, a form of speech that lacks grammar. Children automatically add grammar to pidgin, and a new language is born.

receptive language The repertoire of words and commands that a child understands, although she may be unable to say them.

productive language The spoken or written communication of children.

languages; adults are language specialists who can distinguish only sounds that are relevant to their languages, unless the sounds occur in a nonlanguage context.

One difficulty with speech perception is that slightly different sounds are sometimes treated as the same (we recognize the *t* sound, regardless of whether the speaker is male or female, even though the speakers say the sound differently). And other times, similar sounds are treated as distinct (we recognize *t* as different from *d,* even though they are similar). Interestingly, different languages recognize different sound distinctions. By the time we are 1 year old, we are better at hearing the sound distinctions of our languages, while we ignore other distinctions that might interfere with our native languages (Werker, 1995). For example, the Cree language does not have separate phonemes for *t* and *d,* so a speaker whose first language is Cree would hear the English words "tear" and "dare" as sounding the same. For more information on speech perception, see the box "The Study of Speech Perception in Infants Too Young to Speak."

Another challenge in speech perception is figuring out where one word stops and the next begins. "There are no completely reliable cues to the presence of word boundaries in fluent speech. The neat white spaces separating words on the page simply do not exist in spoken language" (Myers, Jusczyk, Kemler-Nelson, Charles-Luce, Woodward, & Hirsh-Pasek, 1996). Steven Pinker, in his 1994 book, *The Language Instinct,* gives excellent examples of sequences of sounds that can be organized into more than one set of words. For example, the sentences, "The good can decay in many ways" and "The good candy came anyways" are the same sounds. We will hear one sentence instead of the other, depending on the context. But no matter how fast people speak, we can perceive separate words, even without pauses between them. Infants are not able to do this until about 11 months (Myers et al., 1996).

Social Communication As we learned in Chapters 6 and 7, throughout the first year, infants have been learning nonverbal aspects of communication in the "mutual dialogue" between parent and infant. They have been learning to signal, to take turns, to

Babbling between caregiver and infant can be a pleasurable experience for both.

FOCUS ON AN ISSUE

The Study of Speech Perception in Infants Too Young to Speak

It may surprise you that researchers are able to study an infant's language perception months before she utters her first word. Janet Werker and colleagues at the University of British Columbia have done a number of studies to see whether preverbal infants perceive the different sounds and rhythms of languages (LaLonde & Werker, 1995; Pegg & Werker, 1997; Polka & Werker, 1994; Werker & Desjardins, 1995; Werker & Tees, 1999). These researchers also have studied how the infant's sensitivity to speech sounds changes as she starts to learn words or to coordinate hearing with lip reading and talking (Desjardins, Rogers, & Werker, 1997; Werker & Tees, 1999).

How do you think Werker and colleagues study speech perception in infants who are too young to speak and thus cannot tell them what they hear? Werker and colleagues get infants to *show* them by using two tasks: the conditioned head turn task and the habituation/dishabituation task. The conditioned head turn task is based on operant conditioning (discussed in Chapter 2). In the conditioned head turn task, the infant sits on her mother's lap, facing the researcher sitting across from them. The infant listens to a recording that is made up of a sequence of two sounds, such as "ba" and "da." For example, the infant might hear the sequence "ba ba ba da da da da ba ba da." The goal is to see

whether the infant can discriminate between the two sounds. Whenever the sound changes (from "da" to "ba" or from "ba" to "da"), an attractive toy to the side of the infant lights up, moves, and makes a noise. Naturally, infants will turn and look in the direction of this dazzling display. The key to this procedure is that the infant can learn to expect the toy to become activated whenever there is a change in the sound she is listening to. In anticipa-

---

Researchers are able to study an infant's language perception months before she utters her first word.

---

tion of the toy becoming activated, the infant will turn toward the toy, seconds *before* it begins its display. This is the behaviour that indicates to the researchers that the infant can distinguish between the two sounds. Infants who do not perceive the sound change will turn toward the toy display only after it has been activated.

To measure head turning at a sound change, the researcher must ensure that the infant is looking forward before the sound changes. The procedure will not work if the infant is constantly looking in the direction of the toy that becomes activated. The re-

searcher distracts the infant by holding other toys in front of her. The researcher also has to control for the infant's turning toward the dazzling toy display for reasons other than hearing a sound change. For example, the researcher or the mother may react in anticipation of the toy lighting up. The infant might be responding not to the sound change directly, but rather to the mother's or the researcher's reaction to the sound change. To control this factor, the researcher and the mother wear headphones that prevent them from hearing the sequence of sounds that the infant is listening to.

The other procedure uses the habituation/dishabituation task, discussed briefly in Chapter 5. In this procedure, the infant hears two sounds, such as "ba" and "da." The goal is to see whether the infant can distinguish between the sounds. One of the sounds is repeated (e.g., "ba ba ba ba ba …") until the infant habituates to it. Then the infant hears the other sound (e.g., "da"). If the infant can distinguish "da" from "ba," he will respond to "da" because it is a new sound. If the infant cannot perceive a difference between "ba" and "da," he will remain habituated to "da." Researchers are looking to see whether infants exposed repeatedly to the same sound (e.g., "ba") respond differently to a new sound (e.g., "da") than they do to another repetition of the initial sound (e.g., "ba").

---

use gestures, and to pay attention to facial expressions. Infants learn a lot about communication while playing simple games like peek-a-boo (Ross & Lollis, 1987). Indeed, some parents are very skillful at structuring social games with their infants that help them learn many aspects of the conversation in a most enjoyable fashion. Parents who do this well provide a structure for the game, or a scaffolding, that helps the child learn the rules of give and take and turn-taking (Bruner, 1983). But the social communication with the infant goes far beyond parents' games. Certainly, by 1 year of age, most healthy infants are alert to the people around them, including strangers, and they respond appropriately to the varied emotional expressions of adults (Klinnert, Emde, Butterfield, & Campos, 1986).

Babbling From the earliest moments, infants explore a variety of sounds. They gurgle, giggle, grunt, and sigh. They can communicate their hunger or discomfort by cry-

By using the conditioned head turn and habituation/dishabituation tasks, researchers have made counterintuitive and fascinating discoveries about infant speech perception. Infants are born with the ability to distinguish sounds used in their native language and, perhaps surprisingly, the sounds used in other languages but not in their native language. For example, the Aboriginal language Nthlakampx (a Salish language spoken in British Columbia) makes a distinction between two *k* sounds that is not made in English. Anglophone adults cannot distinguish these two *k* sounds; however, anglophone infants can at 6 to 8 months, but not at 10 to 12 months. Why does this change in speech perception occur? Werker and colleagues hypothesize that it is related to brain development. The areas of the brain that process language do not develop in isolation; rather, their development is influenced by the infant's exposure to language and by general cognitive development. The infant's exposure to his native language causes his brain to develop in a way that makes him especially tuned to the sound categories that are part of his language. Therefore, it is difficult for the older anglophone infant to distinguish the two Nthlakampx *k*s because English has only one *k* category and the infant's brain has become organized to fit *k*-like sounds into this one category. The 10-month-old infant hears the two Nthlakampx *k*s as "funny *k*s," but he does not hear them as distinct from

each other. It is not the case, though, that the older infant has lost the ability to discriminate non-native speech sounds in general. If the older anglophone infant hears language sounds that are totally unrelated to English sounds (such as "clicking" sounds from the African Zulu language), he can readily distinguish one type of click from another, as can anglophone adults.

The change in infant speech perception occurs around the same time as other cognitive changes, such as an improvement in the ability to form categories of objects and to search for hidden objects. Therefore, developmental changes in speech perception may reflect general cognitive changes that occur at around 10 months. As well, the influence of cognitive development may explain one difference between the speech perception of 10-month-olds and that of adults. Anglophone adults and infants were exposed to two English sounds: the *d* sound in the word "dash" and the *t* sound in the word "stash." Try saying the word "stash," omitting the first *s*. Can you distinguish the *t* sound in this word from the *d* in "dash"? Interestingly, 6- to 8-month-old infants can, but 10- to 12-month-old infants cannot. The distinction between this *t* and *d* is physically present but is never associated with a change of meaning in English words; thus, the 10- to 12-month-olds ignore it. Adults, on the other hand, can distinguish the sounds in some contexts but not in others. Adults have developed more flexibility

in their interpretation of sounds, perhaps reflecting their general cognitive maturity. However, 10-month-old infants appear not to have this flexibility.

Recently, Werker and colleagues have combined their studies of speech perception with studies of word learning. After all, learning to distinguish sounds is just one part of learning a language. Infants must learn to distinguish combinations of sounds (i.e., words) and to link the words to what they stand for. In one study, 14-month-old infants were shown two objects, one labelled with the nonsense word "lif," the other with the nonsense word "neem." Infants easily learned to associate the word "lif" with one object and the word "neem" with the other. These words were easy to distinguish because they sound so different. When the words sounded more similar, though, 14-month-olds had trouble distinguishing them. For example, infants shown objects labelled "bih" and "dih" were unable to make the distinction. When faced with the complex task of learning word–object associations, the infants did not attend to the fine distinction between *b* and *d*, even though they could easily distinguish these sounds in a standard speech perception task that did not involve word learning. When infants first start learning words, they do not attend to as much phonetic detail. According to Werker, as infants connect sounds to words and their meanings, their perception of speech sounds is reorganized.

ing. It is not until about 6 weeks that they start to produce speech sounds. They start with vowel sounds. This form of communication is called *cooing*, as it resembles the cooing of doves. By 4 or 5 months, the infant produces front-of-the-mouth consonants: "Ahh, bahh, bahh, bahh." This mixture of consonant and vowel sounds is called *babbling*. At first, the infant's babbling is the simple repetition of a couple of phonemes ("Bahh bahh bahh"). By 6 months, infants have a much more varied and complex repertoire. They can string together a wide range of sounds, draw them out, cut them off, and vary the pitch and rhythm. Increasingly, they seem to exert control over these vocalizations. They purposefully repeat sounds, elongate them, and pause in a kind of self-imitating pseudo talk, sometimes called **iteration.**

Sometime after 6 months, many parents hear something suspiciously like "Ma-ma" or "Da-da" and report this as their precocious infants' first words. Usually, however, these are chance repetitions of sounds that have no real meaning. Around this time, babbling

iteration Infants' purposeful repetition, elongation, and pause in sounds that imitate speech.

expressive jargon A term used to describe the babbling of an infant when the infant uses inflections and patterns that mimic adult speech.

Question to Ponder

Why do you think babies babble? Does babbling have a purpose?

takes on inflections and patterns much like those of the parents' language. In fact, the babbling begins to sound so much like adult speech that parents may strain to listen, thinking that perhaps it is coherent language. This highly developed babbling is what Arnold Gesell has termed **expressive jargon.** Such patterns of babbling appear to be the same for infants in all language groups (Roug, Landberg, & Lundberg, 1989).

Just how important is babbling? In what ways does babbling prepare a baby for speaking? A baby's babbling is an irresistible form of verbal communication, and caregivers throughout the world delight in imitating and encouraging these vocalizations. It appears that in the course of babbling, babies are learning how to produce the sounds they will later use in speaking. Thus, the sounds or phonemes that babies produce are influenced by what they hear before they use words. Although babbling is a means for babies to communicate and interact with other people, it is also a problem-solving activity. Babies babble as a way to figure out how to make the specific sounds needed to say words. This may be why babies do not stop babbling when they start producing words. In fact, new words seem to influence babbling, while babbling in turn affects the preferred sounds babies use in selecting new words (Elbers & Ton, 1985).

Comparisons of the babbling of hearing babies and deaf babies also indicate the importance of what the baby hears for the child's language development, even at the babbling stage. Although the babbling of groups of hearing babies and deaf babies is initially comparable, only the babbling of the hearing infants moves closer to the sounds of words used in their language (Oller & Eilers, 1988). Moreover, the babbling of deaf babies appears to lessen significantly after 6 months, when language production begins to be facilitated by reinforcement.

Babbling appears to play a key role in babies' learning to use the specific sounds needed to speak the language of their caregivers. For example, when the babbling of 10-month-old infants in Paris, London, Hong Kong, and Algiers was analyzed, researchers discovered that differences in how these infants pronounced vowel sounds paralleled the vowel sound pronunciations found in their native languages—French, English, Cantonese, and Arabic (de Boysson-Bardies, Halle, Sagart, & Durand, 1989).

What if a baby's babbling is atypical? In specific cases, atypical babbling has been associated with delays in beginning to speak (Stoel-Gammon, 1989). However, there is still much to be learned about the role of babbling in both normal and problematic speech development.

In all cultures, some children develop a fairly extensive vocabulary of pseudo-words. They use a particular range of specific vocalizations, usually paired with gestures, that have specific meanings (Reich, 1986).

Receptive Vocabulary Caregivers and researchers generally agree that very young children understand words before they can say them. Infants as young as 1 year are able to follow some directions from adults and to show by their behaviour that they know the meaning of words like "bye-bye." Infants' comprehension of speech, however, is a difficult area for psychologists and linguists to study. Although it is relatively easy to listen to children speak and to record them, it is much more difficult to identify and describe concepts that very young children associate with specific words. Even when the evidence seems clear—for example, when a 1-year-old follows the instruction "Put the spoon in the cup"—the child's understanding may be nowhere near as complete as we conclude. It is, after all, hard to put the cup in the spoon. Also, children may receive clues, such as gestures, that help them to perform tasks correctly. Parents of very young children often say that their children understand far more words at home, in familiar surroundings, than in unfamiliar testing rooms. Although this may be true, it is also true that parents use gestures and context clues to help convey their message. Parents also will frequently accept vague signals as evidence that their children understand instructions.

By the time children are 3 to 4 years old, they will readily begin to ask what the meaning of sentences, concepts, or phrases is—especially if they have been reinforced and encouraged to ask questions. The following exchange indicates the way in which this development proceeds:

Mother (singing): *Suzanne takes you down to a place by the water.... She gets you on her wavelength and lets the river answer....*

5-year-old girl: *Mommy, what does "wavelength" mean?*

Mother: *It means that you and another person have really understood each other ... that you've both felt the same way when you were talking to each other. Does that make sense, honey?*

5-year-old girl: *Sure, Mom. It's like when we were talking about how we couldn't wait for the snow to be gone and the flowers to come up. We both felt really happy.*

In this case, a verbal young child has fully engaged in discussion with her mother and has learned a new word in the process. Other times, vocabulary learning is not as straightforward. When my son, Chris, was in kindergarten, he learned about the different food groups in the Canada Food Guide. This class prompted a discussion between him and my husband about foods that could be classified in more than one group. My husband told Chris that cooks call tomatoes vegetables but biologists call them fruits. Later that day, Chris informed me of the discussion. I then asked Chris if he knew what a biologist was. He replied, "Of course I do, Mom. It is someone who doesn't know anything" (Digdon).

First Words

Most children utter their first words around the end of the first year. They then add single words, slowly at first, and much more rapidly by the middle of the second year. As children approach age 2, single words give way to two-word and then three-word sentences.

There is wide individual variation in the rate at which language learning progresses. Toddlers who seem to be progressing slowly in this area are not necessarily developmentally delayed; they may be busy with other tasks, as the following example indicates.

My second child, a boy, was really remarkable. He didn't walk until he was almost 18 months old. But could he talk! He would stand in his crib and yell, "Get me out of here," but he wouldn't try to get out. Our third child, Norma, was just the opposite. She was cruising around the living room at 7 months and walking at 9 months. She didn't talk until she was 14 months old.

Some children start late but catch up quickly; others seem stuck at particular stages for long periods of time. Regardless of the pace of language learning, the sequence of language development follows a regular and predictable pattern. This pattern appears not only in English, but in every language. Analysis of language acquisition in many countries has revealed remarkably consistent patterns (Slobin, 1972).

Early Words and Meanings Throughout the world, infants' first utterances are single words, most often nouns and usually names of the people, things, or animals in the immediate environment. But children learning Chinese first acquire more verbs than nouns (Tardif, 1996). In the beginning, children simply do not have the ability to use words in combination. Some psycholinguists feel that despite this restriction in language production, children can conceive full sentences, and their early utterances are actually **holophrastic speech**—single words meant to convey complex ideas. Therefore, in different contexts, with different intonations and gestures, "mama" may mean "I want my mother" or "Mama, tie my shoe," or "There she is, my mama." Other psycholinguists warn against overinterpreting brief utterances.

What words form an infant's early vocabulary? Because the caregivers of each infant use different words and the process of development is individual, the vocabularies that infants learn differ. But the types of words that infants first use fall into

holophrastic speech In the early stages of language acquisition, the young child's use of single words, perhaps to convey full sentences.

Among the first words infants use are nouns such as "car."

categories. Names—that is, nouns that refer to specific things, such as "dada," "bottie," and "car"—make up much of a child's early vocabulary (Nelson, 1974). However, children at the one-word stage also use words that indicate function or relationship, such as "there," "no," "gone," and "up," possibly even before they use nouns (Bloom, Lifter, & Broughton, 1985). The individual words and category of words a child uses most may depend on the child's personal speech style. Nelson (1981) identified children with a *referential style* as those who tended to use nouns, and children with an *expressive style* as those who learned more active verbs and pronouns.

Katherine Nelson was one of the first researchers to study differences in language-learning styles among children. By the age of 18 months, when children had vocabularies of approximately 50 words, the two distinct groups mentioned above had emerged. The referential children had vocabularies that were dominated by naming words—mostly nouns indicating persons or objects but few actions. The expressive children, on the other hand, had learned the naming words, but they also knew a higher percentage of words used in social interactions (for example, "Go away," "I want it," "Give me," and so forth). Thus Rachel, a referential child, had 41 name words in her 50-word vocabulary, but only 2 words in the social interaction or question-asking categories; Elizabeth, an expressive child, had a more balanced vocabulary, with 24 name words and 14 words in the social interaction and question-asking categories. The later language development of expressive and referential children also differs. Expressive children typically have smaller vocabularies and are more likely to use pronouns than nouns (Nelson, 1981). In addition, expressive children tend to create and use "dummy words"—words with no apparent meaning—to substitute for words they do not know.

Early speech grows out of the prelinguistic gestures that every baby uses to communicate (Gopnik, 1988). A child's first words appear to be social in nature. The child speaks in order to influence other people; he wants to get his mother's attention, to eat a cookie instead of an apple, or to indicate that he will not sit down in his bath. Later, in the one-word stage, when the child's abilities to think and to remember are more developed, the same types of words have been found to express intrapersonal thoughts and ideas (Gopnik & Meltzoff, 1987).

Overextensions and Underextensions When a child first uses a word, it usually refers to a specific person, object, or situation. The word "goggy" may apply to a child's own pet. The child may then use it when naming other dogs or other four-legged animals. But when this child learns new words, such as "horsie" or "kitty," she will redefine all of the animal categories she had previously learned (Schlesinger, 1982). This is an example of overextending a word. Children tend to overextend, underextend, or overlap the categories they use to determine what words refer to because they often do not share adults' knowledge of culturally appropriate functions and characteristics of objects. Instead, they may emphasize aspects of objects that adults have come to ignore when categorizing objects (Mervis, 1987). Some interesting examples of children's overextensions are given in Table 8-1.

Other times children use words as though they have more limited meanings than the conventional ones. For example, toddlers often think that the word "girl" means a female at least as old as they are. A baby cannot be a girl. This is an example of an underextension.

As children learn additional contrasting names for objects, such as kitty, cat, lion, and tiger, they reassign words to more specific and increasingly hierarchical categories (Clark, 1987). In other words, a lion and a tiger are different. They are both examples of the more general "cat" category. Over time, the child's linguistic categories take on the language use structure of the adults in that linguistic culture. The

Table 8-1 The Overextension of Words

CHILD'S WORD	FIRST REFERENT	EXTENSIONS	POSSIBLE COMMON PROPERTY
Bird	Sparrows	Cows, dogs, cats, any moving animal	Movement
Mooi	Moon	Cakes, round marks on window, round shapes in books, tooling on leather book covers, postmarks, letter O	Shape
Fly	Fly	Specks of dirt, dust, all small insects, his own toes, crumbs, small toad	Size
Koko	Cockerel crowing	Tunes played on a violin, piano, accordion, phonograph, all music, merry-go-round	Sound
Wau-wau	Dogs	All animals, toy, dog, soft slippers, picture of old man in furs	Texture

Source: de Villiers & de Villiers, 1979.

process of categorizing language appears to follow the same general pattern as that of intellectual or cognitive development (Chapman & Mervis, 1989).

Children's words and their meanings are closely linked to the concepts the children are developing. A child who applies the word "moon" to everything round has some concept of "round." But which comes first—the word and its meaning or the concept? Researchers differ in their interpretation of the evidence. Some, including Piaget, believe that most of the time the concept forms first. The child discovers a concept and then finds a name to attach to it, whether learned or of his own creation. Evidence for this theory includes the findings that twins have been known to create their own private language and that deaf children create signs or gestures even when they are not taught sign language. These findings would suggest that concepts come first and words afterward (Clark, 1983). Other researchers believe that words help shape our concepts. When a young child names the family pet "dog," he is simply naming that object. When he extends and refines his categories, he is learning the concept of "dog" (Schlesinger, 1982). In fact, both processes are probably true and serve to complement each other as the child learns language.

Two-Word Sentences

Toward the end of the second year, most children begin to put words together. Often, the first attempts are simply two words that represent two ideas: "Mommy see," "Sock off," or "More milk." This is a fascinating period in language development because implicit rules of syntax appear. In recent years, psycholinguists have studied the development of language production by recording and analyzing lengthy samples of children's speech, collected at daily or weekly intervals. Valuable insights have been gained about such features as sentence length, the kinds of grammatical rules children use, and the types of meanings children express at any given stage.

Telegraphic Speech When children start putting words together, their sentences seem to be sharply limited in length. At first, they seem restricted to two elements, then three, and so on. At each stage, the number of words or thoughts in a sentence is limited—children retain high information words and omit the less significant ones. The

telegraphic speech The utterances of 1- and 2-year-olds that omit the less significant words and include the words that carry the most meaning.

result is what Brown (1965) calls **telegraphic speech.** The informative words, which Brown terms *contentives*, are the nouns, verbs, and adjectives. The less important words are known as *functors* and are the inflections, auxiliary verbs, and prepositions.

When children first put two words together, they do it in a consistent way. They may say, "See dog" or "See truck" as they point at things. But they never say, "Truck, see." Even in the two-word sentence, we can find certain consistencies. What sort of grammar is being used? A number of models have been identified.

Pivot Grammar   Among the first significant grammatical analyses was the study by Braine (1963), which identified a **pivot grammar** at the two-word phase. *Pivot words* are usually action words ("go"), prepositions ("off"), or possessives ("my"). They are few in number and occur frequently in combination with *x-words,* or open words, which are usually nouns. "See," for example, is a pivot word that can combine with any number of open words to form two-word sentences: "See milk," "See Mommy," or "Mommy see." Pivot words almost never occur alone or with other pivots (McNeill, 1972). X-words may, however, be paired or used singly. These prohibitions and combinations are not random, but result from children's limited comprehension and production of language. The length restriction is apparently the main barrier to their expression of complex grammatical notions in more adult-sounding forms.

pivot grammar A two-word sentence-forming system used by 2-year-olds and involving action words, prepositions, or possessives (pivot words) in combination with x-words, which are usually nouns.

Case Grammar   Children seem able to express a number of relationships by word order: agent (who did it), patient (to whom), instrument (with what), location (where), and so forth (Fillmore, 1968). They are expressing a **case grammar.** Because of the variety of relationships that a two-word sentence can be used to express, the child's utterance must be interpreted in context. Lois Bloom (1970) noted that a child she was studying said, "Mommy sock" one time to indicate that her mother was putting on a sock and another time to communicate that she had found her mother's sock.

case grammar The use of word order to express different relationships.

With the help of gestures, tone, and context, children can communicate numerous meanings with a small vocabulary and limited syntax. Dan Slobin (1972) studied the variety of meanings conveyed by two-word sentences spoken by 2-year-olds. Although his young conversants were from different linguistic cultures, speaking English, German, Russian, Turkish, or Samoan, the children used speech in the same ways. Among the concepts that the 2-year-olds were able to communicate by two-word utterances were the following:

Identification: *See doggie.*

Location: *Book there.*

Nonexistence: *Allgone thing.*

Negation: *Not wolf.*

Possession: *My candy.*

Attribution: *Big car.*

Agent-action: *Mama walk.*

Action-location: *Sit chair.*

Action-direct object: *Hit you.*

Action-indirect object: *Give papa.*

Action-instrument: *Cut knife.*

Question: *Where ball?*

Language Complexities

Throughout the preschool years, children are rapidly expanding their vocabularies, their use of grammatical forms, and their understanding of language as a social act. Here, we look at a sampling of these many accomplishments.

Expanding Grammar

One of the more influential works in the study of language acquisition was written by Roger Brown (1973). Brown and his colleagues studied many children but recorded at length the speech patterns of three young children—Adam, Eve, and Sarah. Taking a developmental approach, Brown identifies five distinct, increasingly complex stages. He views development in terms of **mean length of utterance (MLU)**—the average length of the sentence that the child produces—instead of age, because children learn at very different rates. Eve, for example, progressed nearly twice as fast as Adam and Sarah. Yet the sequence is similar for most children. Certain skills and rules are apparently mastered before others, and certain errors are peculiar to specific stages.

mean length of utterance (MLU) The average length of the sentences that a child produces.

Stage 1 The first stage is characterized by two-word utterances, which we have discussed. This is the period in which telegraphic speech and pivot and open words emerge. Brown, however, goes beyond this structure to focus on the meaning that children are attempting to convey with word order and position—the concepts of existence, disappearance, and recurrence and of possession, agency, and attribution.

Stage 2 This stage of language acquisition is characterized by utterances slightly longer than two words. In addition to learning prepositions, articles, and case markers, children begin to generalize the rules of **inflections** to words they already know. Children at this stage are able to form the regular past tense of many verbs, such as "play/played," and the regular plurals of many nouns. To determine whether children have reached a more complex language stage and are not just relying on memory, Berko (1958) devised a test using nonsense words (see Figure 8-1). For instance, "This is a wug. Now there is another one. There are two of them. There are two_____." The subjects had to supply the correct inflection by generalizing what they knew about plurals. The tests, which have since been given to children even younger than Berko's preschool and first-grade subjects, reveal a surprising grasp of rules for conjugating verbs and forming plurals and possessives. In fact, children often overgeneralize. In spite of the fact that they may have already learned the forms of some irregular verbs, such as "go/went/gone," children produce words like "goed." They are applying the rule for forming the regular past tense to every verb. Although technically an error, such usages demonstrate children's extraordinary ability to generalize a complex language principle. This ability is called **overregularization.**

inflections Changes in form that words undergo to designate number, gender, tense, mood, and case.

overregularization The generalization of complex language principles, typically by preschool children rapidly expanding their vocabularies.

Stage 3 In the third stage, children learn to modify simple sentences. They create negative and imperative forms, ask yes-no questions, and depart in other ways from the simple statements of earlier stages. The negative form is an excellent example of how complex language learning can be. It also reveals children's ability to create original forms without depending on a model. The concepts for using negatives seem to exist quite early—long before the third stage. At first, children negate by putting the negative word at the beginning of an utterance; they express concepts such as nonexistence ("no pocket"), rejection ("no more"), and denial ("no dirty"), but they cannot use auxiliary verbs or embed a negative form within a sentence. By the third stage, however, children easily say such sentences as, "Paul didn't laugh" and "Jeannie won't let go" (Klima & Bellugi, 1966). In fact, they often use double and triple negatives, throwing them in wherever possible to emphasize a point.

Children also begin to learn to use active and passive voice during the third

Figure 8-1
One of Berko's Tests of
Children's Syntax
*Nonsense words are used to avoid
interference from memorization.*
Source: U. Bellugi and R. Brown
(1964), *The Acquisition of Language*,
Monographs of the Society for
Research in Child Development,
19(1), 43–79. Copyright © 1964 by
the Society for Research in Child
Development, Inc.

This is a wug.

Now there is another one.
There are two of them.
There are two _____ .

stage. Bellugi, Brown, and Fraser (1970) developed a test of children's understanding of these forms. They gave their subjects stuffed animals and asked them to act out "The cat chases the dog" and "The dog chases the cat." The 3-year-old subjects had no trouble demonstrating these simple declarative sentences. However, when shown two pictures illustrating "The boy is washed by the girl" and "The girl is washed by the boy," the children seldom identified the picture that corresponded to the sentence they heard. They had not yet mastered the passive concept. Their comprehension was limited to the more typical word order of agent-action-object.

Stages 4 and 5 In the fourth and fifth stages, children learn to deal with increasingly sophisticated structures. They begin to use subordinate clauses and fragments within compound and complex sentences. By the age of 4½, children have a good grasp of syntax, but they continue to learn for many years. Carol Chomsky (1969) tested subjects between the ages of 5 and 10 and found that children are actively acquiring syntax within those years. Such structures as, "John asked Bill what to do" are learned very late; some 10-year-olds did not clearly understand the subject of "do." And, of course, many adults have great difficulty with certain constructions.

More Words and Concepts

Throughout the preschool period, children are learning words rapidly—often at a rate of two or three a day. Some words have meaning only in context. For example, "this" and "that." Some words express relationships between objects: "softer," "lower," and "shorter." Frequently, children understand one concept, such as "more," much earlier than they know the word or the concept that contrasts directly with it—in this case, "less." A 3-year-old may easily be able to tell you which dish has more candy, but not which dish has less.

Often, children want to say things, but they do not know the right word, or they cannot recall it. At these times, children invent words. They use nouns in place of verbs, as in, "Mommy, needle it" ("Mommy, sew it"). Or a child trying to fold paper might ask, "How do you flat it?" Also, children invent complex words like "sweep-man" (someone who sweeps).

At least through age 3, children also have difficulty with pronouns and their use. By ages 4 to 5, most children have mastered them. For example, a child might say "my want to go out" or "us need to take a nap." Even when corrected, these errors persist for some time, as the following conversation between Rachael, age 3, and her mother indicates:

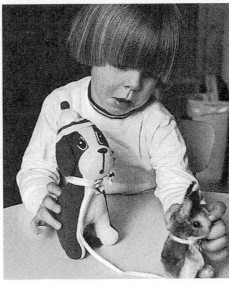

This 3-year-old is able to demonstrate the sentence, "The rabbit chases the dog" but not, "The dog is chased by the rabbit." Children of this age have not yet mastered the passive concept.

Rachael: *My need to use the potty, Mommy.*

Mother: *You mean, I need to use the potty.*

Rachael: *Mommy have to go too?*

Mother: *No, honey, but I'll go with you.*

Rachael: *Ya, Mommy! Us can go together.*

At times during this phase, many parents find themselves participating in a "who's on first" game that they have absolutely no chance of winning. The 3-year-old will invariably wear them down.

Some children also have difficulty pronouncing certain words, even though they can often recognize the correct pronunciation; for example, a child may understand that "I smell a skunk" is the correct form, but she may be able to say only, "I mell a kunk." Another difficult word for children is also one of their favourite foods: "pisghetti."

Influence of Parents' Speech

To gain and hold the attention of prelinguistic children, adults often use a particular mode of speaking that has been dubbed "motherese" (also called infant-directed speech or baby talk). When using motherese, adults (both men and women) exaggerate their vowels, speak in pitches higher than normal, and create words composed of repeated syllables, such as "bye-bye" and "nighty-night." They use short, simple sentences and talk about what is happening at the moment. While watching her infant try to stand, a mother might verbalize his progress: "Sabir falls down.... Bump.... Sabir sits up.... Can Sabir stand up?" The caregiver exaggerates intonation and stress, pauses between sentences, and often repeats earlier words and sentences (Ferguson & Snow, 1977). She also uses exaggerated facial expressions and movements. Infants prefer motherese to "regular" speech, even for languages other than their native one. For example, a study conducted in Vancouver found that infants of English-speaking parents preferred the Cantonese version of motherese to English motherese (Werker, Pegg, & McLeod, 1994).

The simple, exaggerated qualities of motherese probably make it easier for young children to understand and learn language. Short sentences are useful because young children have short memories. Simple sentences help children find the important words. Pauses help them separate words and sentences (Hirsh-Pasek, Nelson, Jusczyk, & Wright, 1986). Interestingly, deaf mothers signing to their deaf babies use a form of sign language that is similar to the motherese of spoken language (Masataka,

1996). When signing to infants, they go more slowly, use more repetition, and use more exaggerated movements than when they are signing to other adults.

It was once thought that the frequent use of motherese played a key part in the language development of the young child. But now researchers view motherese as only one of a variety of ways to interact verbally with the child. The simplified speech characteristic of motherese comes naturally to an adult speaking with anyone who does not yet speak fluently. In other words, motherese is not primarily a tool used to teach a baby language. Rather, the simplified way that caregivers speak to the child appears to be a reaction to the child's language abilities, not a strategy to improve them (Bohannon & Hirsh-Pasek, 1984). Looking at how young children learn to speak in other cultures confirms the idea that motherese is not critical to language development. In the Pacific Kaluli (Schieffelin & Ochs, 1983) and the Quicke Mayan cultures (Ratner & Pye, 1984), for instance, children learn to speak without extensive use of motherese.

Yet every culture successfully transmits language to its children. There appear to be many methods of talking and relating to infants that facilitate language development. Each culture has integrated some of these strategies into the patterns of social interaction with children (Snow, 1989). Although children do pick up specific words from their caregivers, the critical aspect of adults' speaking to children is that they provide children with information about language. Children generalize from what they hear, enabling them to understand words and syntax.

Researchers looking at children in the United States found that caregivers ask questions to check for children's understanding, expand children's utterances, and use ritualized play speech. Adults often speak for the children by expressing children's wants, wishes, and actions in syntactic English. The child's language develops most from everyday communication with adults who seek to communicate—that is, to understand and to be understood (Schacter & Strage, 1982).

It is unclear how the use of language by parents and the child's language development are related (Chesnick, Menyuk, Liebergott, Ferrier, & Strand, 1983). Of course, it is critical that parents both talk and listen to their children regularly. Differences between individuals in language development have been shown to be inherited to some extent. But they are also influenced by the environment. For example, twins typically have delayed language development. Studies have shown that these children receive significantly less verbal input from their mothers than do children who are not twins because the mothers of twins have to divide their attention between the two children (Tomasello, Mannle, & Kruger, 1986).

It is also interesting to make cross-language comparisons. For example, English-speaking parents rarely use the passive voice ("The candy was eaten by the children") when talking to toddlers. And so English-speaking children do not learn to use the passive until relatively late (Brown's Stage 3, discussed earlier in this chapter). But Inuit mothers speaking Inuktitut use the passive voice often when talking to their toddlers. Inuit children, therefore, learn the passive voice much earlier than do English-speaking children (Allen & Crago, 1996).

When parents speak with their children, however, they communicate far more than words, sentences, and syntax. They are demonstrating how thoughts are expressed and how ideas are exchanged. They are teaching the child about categories and symbols and about how to translate the complicated world into ideas and words. These conceptual tools provide a scaffold for the child to create her own form of expression (Bruner & Haste, 1987). Researchers at York University in Toronto, for example, related mothers' scaffolding to their toddlers' vocabulary at 15 months and found that more scaffolding was associated with a larger vocabulary (Stevens, Blake, Vitale, & MacDonald, 1998). Long before they can speak, children are initiated into their culture and language by the speech of their parents and caregiver. For a situation in which this interaction went awry, see the box "Is There a Critical Period for Learning Language?"

As we saw in earlier chapters, some research indicates that children are introduced to the language of their culture even before birth. DeCasper and Spence (1992), for example, reported that *prosody,* which is a combination of rhythm, intonation, and

Question to Ponder

Why do you think some cultures use motherese and others do not?

In all cultures parents, by speaking to infants, provide them with information about language.

inflection in speech, appears to be recognized and stored prenatally. Babies whose mothers had read *The Cat in the Hat* aloud while they were in the womb preferred that story to unfamiliar ones that they heard after birth. They sucked more in response to the familiar story than to unfamiliar readings. Whether or not further research supports this finding, it is more than likely that reading aloud aids children's introduction to their own languages by showing them the timing and inflections of more formal speech. Interestingly, looking at picture books can facilitate the production of language. Senechal, Cornell, and Broda (1995) found that 9-month-old infants vocalized more when their parents talked to them about picture books that had no words than when they read infants stories.

Children's Conversations

Children do more than say words or sentences. They have conversations—with adults, with other children, and even with themselves (see the box "Why Do Children Talk to Themselves?" later in this chapter). Conversations typically follow a certain pattern.

Monitoring the Message

First, it is necessary to gain the other person's attention. A child just learning the art of conversation may yank on somebody's clothing. As time passes, the same child may instead say something like, "Know what?" Children then learn that conversations often have a beginning, a middle, and an end. They discover, too, that in conversations people take turns; they talk on the same subject, they make sure the other person is listening or understanding, and they make sounds or nod to indicate that they understand what the other person is talking about (Garvey, 1984).

By casually listening to children's conversations, one notices that they do not run smoothly. Children often stop to see if the other person is listening and if they are understood. Children pause, repeat themselves, correct themselves. They ask questions. Indeed, this is a normal part of developing effective communication (Garvey, 1984; Reich, 1986). Even school-age children sometimes have considerable difficulty communicating all of the appropriate information to a listener. First- and second-grade children have difficulty comprehending one another fully, finding the part of the message

FOCUS ON AN ISSUE

Is There a Critical Period for Learning Language?

In 1970, a 13-year-old girl named Genie was discovered in Los Angeles. Her condition was startling. Since the age of 20 months, Genie had been a virtual prisoner in a small, curtained room in her house. For most of her days, she was strapped in a pottychair, where she was able to move only her hands and her feet. At night, she was laced into a kind of straitjacket and enclosed in a cagelike crib. Treated like an animal, Genie had no bowel or bladder control and could not stand erect. She was severely malnourished and was unable to chew solid food. She was also mute: she could neither speak nor understand language.

Since the first days of her imprisonment, Genie was never spoken to—a rule enforced by her father. She was fed by her brother, whom she saw for only a few minutes a day, but no words ever passed between them. The only sounds she heard were her father's doglike barks on some of the occasions when he beat her for crying or making noise.

Genie knew almost no language and had no understanding of grammar.

After she was removed from this situation, Genie was cared for by doctors at the Los Angeles Children's Hospital; the doctors took care of her immediate bodily needs, nursed her back to health, and calmed her fears. Psychologists were called in to try to evaluate her mental state and abilities, including how much she understood and how much language she had learned. They next had the task of teaching her language. Many psychologists feel that there is a critical period for learning language—a time during a child's early years when language learning must begin if it is to occur at all. Genie gave researchers a unique opportunity to study this critical period theory.

Genie knew almost no language and had no understanding of grammar. Researchers approached teaching her in much the same way they would approach teaching a younger child—through direct exposure to language during daily activities. She made only one- or two-word utterances at first, but she soon progressed. Within a year of her release, she began to string two and sometimes three words together to

---

they don't understand, and asking appropriate questions to help one another repair messages (Beal, 1987).

Finally, children must learn to adjust conversations to reduce friction, conflict, and embarrassment. This means using courtesy markers like "please" and "thank you," paying attention, and selecting the proper forms of address, appropriate phrasing, and suitable topics, which usually involves noting the status of the other person. Children spend a good deal of time learning these social refinements, and they are aided with reminders like, "Don't talk to your grandmother like that" (Garvey, 1984). It reminds me of the time I gave my friend's 2-year-old daughter, Sasha, juice and put only a little in the cup in case of spills. My friend prompted Sasha, "And what do you say to Nancy?" Sasha quickly blurted out, "More!" This was not exactly the answer her mother was looking for (Digdon). In the next section, we review other ways that children learn to be sensitive to social situations and to people with whom they are talking.

The Social Context of Language

The way that language is used depends on the situation and on the intentions of a speaker and a listener who have some kind of social relationship. Social relationships, in turn, involve mutual considerations of both role and status. We show our awareness of another person's status by our tone of voice, grammar, and mode of address, among other things. For example, an elderly neighbour may expect children to be quiet and calm and conveys these expectations in his speech. The neighbourhood children, in response, will show deference in their speech by modulating their voices and using polite forms of address. In general, children are quick to learn nuances of speech and to conform to social roles. They are also quick to perceive degrees of status and the attendant speech behaviour in a wide variety of social settings.

Therefore, children recognize early on that people are meant to be treated in different ways, based on their characteristics. Being able to interpret the social world ac-

make phrases like "clear white box." She soon began to use these phrases to form simple agent-action-object sentences, and she learned to add the word "no" to the beginning of the sentence to express a negative thought.

Despite this progress, it soon became apparent that Genie's language learning was severely limited. Even after four years of training, she had not learned many of the rudiments of grammar or articulation most children learn before the age of 4—rudiments that could transform her garbled messages into easily understood speech. She could use neither personal pronouns nor the demonstrative adjectives "this" and "that." In addition, despite her teachers' prodding, she never asked questions in the way a normal 3- or 4-year-old would. Unlike normal children, she never experienced the explosive spurt of language develop-

ment that quickly transforms a child's first words into full grammatical sentences. On the contrary, her progress was painfully slow. After four years, she could hardly be understood, and after seven years, she had learned as much language as a normal child learns in two or three years.

Nevertheless, the fact that any progress was made disproved the theory that language can be learned only during a critical developmental period between the age of 2 and puberty. Genie did learn a limited amount of language after this time. Because her language development has fallen far short of that of a normal child, however, it may still be true that optimum language development is tied to this critical period—but there is no way to know this for sure. Because Genie experienced severe physical and emotional deprivation in her childhood, it is impossible to determine whether her

language difficulties reflect her speech deprivation alone or whether the malnutrition, physical and emotional abuse, and social isolation she suffered also played a part.

By 24 years of age, Genie had received years of special education, rehabilitation, and foster care. She also had been closely observed and tested as psychologists attempted to find other clues to the mystery of language acquisition. Yet, despite this care and attention, her language still lacked many of the aspects of a 5-year-old's. Her case has provided many insights but no answers. Indeed, some believe that it has added even more fuel to the issue of whether a critical period in language development exists (de Villiers & de Villiers, 1979; Pines, 1981).

curately is a critical task for children. But in all cultures, commonly accepted social lessons are accompanied by unspoken attitudes that children also absorb. While the child expands her world by comprehending how she relates to others, she is acquiring the particular beliefs that compose the world view of her culture (Ochs, 1986).

One researcher examined how children between the ages of 4 and 7 modify their speech to correspond to different social situations and roles (Anderson, 1979). Twenty-four children were given an opportunity to act out several roles with the use of puppets. Three different situations were used: father-mother-child, physician-nurse-patient, and teacher-student-foreign student. In each setting, the children manipulated two puppets while the researchers worked the third. In improvising the various parts, the children spontaneously revealed how much they had already learned about social relationships and the social and cultural characteristics of speech.

Anderson found that although methods of portrayal varied with age, even the youngest children had a clear understanding of social context and power relationships, and they adjusted their vocabulary and speech accordingly to reflect these notions. Four-year-olds expressed their social understanding mostly by changing the pitch and volume of their speech. Those who role-played authority figures, such as fathers and physicians, stretched out their vowels and talked at a lower pitch than those who role-played lower-status figures. Children portraying low-status persons, on the other hand, used a higher and softer tone of voice, asked more questions, and deferred politely to the authority figure. "Mothers" spoke in higher, sometimes singsong voices. And every child, when speaking to a foreign student, spoke in a slow, flat monotone. Those who role-played young children simplified their speech, leaving out consonants and articles.

Slightly older children were able to modify appropriately the vocabulary and context of their speech. "Doctors" used medical terms like "hernia" and "temperature," often without knowing their meaning. A "patient" might say, "Doctor, do I have a hernia?" and the "doctor" might reply, "No, but I'll go out and get you one." Older children who played authority figures had learned techniques for maintaining control of a conversation.

Question to Ponder

In what ways does a child's language development affect his social development?

Through play, children can practise their conversational skills—for example, they learn to take turns speaking.

They would use floor holders, such as "Well...," "Now...," or "Then...," to prevent others with lower status from talking too much; they also made syntactic changes in their speech. "Fathers" would use imperatives, such as, "Have this done by tomorrow!" "Mothers," at least when played by girls, would use expressions of endearment and polite forms, such as, "Would you mind if I...?" As boys' ages increased, so did their reluctance to play dependent, less authoritative roles, such as those of young children.

Do children understand telephone communication? Do they know to adjust their speech when talking on the phone with people who cannot see them? I remember when my daughter was 2 and answered her grandmother's questions over the phone by nodding or shaking her head without saying a word (Digdon). At the University of New Brunswick in Fredericton, Cameron and Lee (1998) observed how children tried to teach adults to solve four-piece puzzles when the adults sat next to them or when the adults were not present but were talking with the children over the phone. Interestingly, 3-year-olds and 7-year-olds modified their instructions. They gave clearer instructions over the phone than in person. Over the phone, they were more likely to refer directly to unique features of the puzzle pieces (for example, "Move the red piece," when only one of the pieces was red) than to give directions that required nonverbal cues, such as pointing (for example, "Move this piece over there"). Although both 3-year-olds and 7-year-olds adjusted their instructions when using telephones, the 7-year-olds, in general, gave the clearer instructions. In another study, 4-, 6-, and 8-year-olds were shown the picture book *Frog, Where Are You?* illustrated by Mercer Mayer (Cameron & Wang, in press). The book has no text, so the children were asked to look at the pictures and to tell the story about finding the missing frog. Children told their stories to a listener face to face and to the same listener over the phone. Children created longer, more accurate stories over the phone than face to face. They also embellished their telephone stories with descriptions of the pictures. Their telephone stories were more goal directed. Goal-directed stories had three components: they mentioned events that caused the character to search for the frog (initiating events), events that were part of the search (unfolding events), and whether the frog was found (resolution). Clearly, children as young as 4 were able to adjust their message to the medium, telling different stories face to face than over the phone.

Bilingualism and Multilingualism

Canada is a land of many languages, including the two official ones, English and French. The other most common languages spoken by Canadians are Italian, Chinese languages, German, Portuguese, Ukrainian, Polish, Spanish, Punjabi, Dutch, and Greek. Many Canadians also speak one of over a hundred other languages. The fastest-growing languages in Canada are the Chinese ones (*Canada Year Book,* 1997). When we examine the language development of Canadian children, we must consider this multilingual feature of Canadian society. Multilingualism introduces a number of questions: How is language development affected when a child's family speaks a language different from the majority language of the community? Can children learning more than one language in the family do so without mixing up the languages? Can children living in English-speaking communities learn enough French in school to become bilingual? Can French children living in English-speaking communities retain their French language? Let's now look at research related to these questions.

Bilingual Toddlers

Fred Genesee and his colleagues at McGill University in Montreal have been studying children raised in a family where the mother is dominant in one language (English or French) and the father is dominant in the other. Often, the mother addresses the child in one language and the father in another. As former Canadian prime minister Louis St. Laurent remarked, "I didn't know at first that there were two languages in Canada. I just thought that there was one way to speak to my father and another way to speak to my mother" (*Canada Year Book,* 1997, p. 68).

Nicoladis and Genesee (1996) did a longitudinal study of four children raised in English/French bilingual homes that began when the children were about 1 year and 6 months and continued until they were 3. The researchers wanted to see when the children would start to differentiate the two languages, speaking one to their mothers and the other to their fathers. At the beginning of the study, none of the children were differentiating the languages, but all of them were by the end. Interestingly, the children learned to differentiate the languages at different rates, varying from 1 year and 9 months to 2 years and 4 months. Two of the children did so when they were still at the one-word stage. The toddlers were able to learn *translation equivalents,* synonyms for words in the other language. The French word "chien" is a translation equivalent for the English word "dog" because the words refer to the same concept. It is interesting that toddlers can learn translation equivalents because children learning a single language often resist using more than one word to refer to the same thing. For example, a child might argue that his budgie cannot be an animal because it is a bird. Somehow, a toddler learning two languages is able to accept that her budgie is a bird and "un oiseau."

As well, the toddlers were good at distinguishing between the languages and rarely mixed the two (2.05 percent of the time), such as in the example "doggy dodo" ("dodo" means "sleeping" in French). Genesee, Nicoladis, and Paradis (1995) found that children were more likely to mix the languages if they were speaking the language they knew less well. But when they spoke their dominant language, the other language intruded less.

Does learning two languages during the preschool years affect how children think? Ellen Bialystok at York University in Toronto found that bilingualism improved children's selective attention (Bialystok, 1999). Four and five-year-old children who spoke both Chinese and English were better at ignoring distractions than were children who spoke only English. Improved selective attention was demonstrated on a language task and on a nonlanguage card-sorting task. It seems that the benefits of bilingualism are not limited to language, but extend to more general aspects of thinking.

> ## Question to Ponder
>
> We know that toddlers can learn two languages at the same time. Is there a limit to the number of languages that children can learn simultaneously?

French Immersion Programs

French immersion programs began in Canada in St. Lambert, a suburb of Montreal, in 1965 (Lambert & Tucker, 1972). The St. Lambert project, as it was called, "quickly became a landmark in second-language teaching methodology not only in Canada but around the world" (Safty, 1995, p. 329). Immersion programs are now available in many communities across the country. In a typical immersion program, children take all subjects in French during the early years. English instruction is then gradually introduced between grades four and six until it accounts for 50 percent of the instruction time.

Numerous studies, conducted in different provinces, have found that the English skills of children in French immersion are at least as good, if not better, than those of English-speaking children in standard English programs. For instance, the French immersion students do as well in math and science (Swain, 1978), tests of English morphology for past tense and plurals (Gray & Cameron, 1980), writing (Laing, 1992), and tests of reading comprehension (Dank & McEachern, 1979). One interpretation of these results is that there is **cross-language transfer,** so that "a foreign language facilitates mastering the higher forms of the native language" (Vygotsky, 1966, p. 110). Another interpretation is that French immersion programs attract better students, and their high performance might therefore have nothing to do with the programs. Most of the studies attempt to rule out this second interpretation by collecting data on children's IQs and family backgrounds (see, for example, Gray & Cameron, 1980).

Earlier studies, such as the original St. Lambert project, were largely restricted to bright, middle-class children, so it was unclear whether the results would generalize

> **French immersion** School instruction that is mostly in French for English-speaking children.

> **cross-language transfer** The learning of a foreign language that improves mastery of the native language.

to other students. But other studies have looked at the experiences of a wider range of students in French immersion programs. For instance, Bruck (1978) found that children with learning difficulties performed the same in English whether they were in French immersion or in standard English programs. And the students in the immersion programs had the added advantage of greater mastery of French. Therefore, Bruck (1978) argued that children with learning problems should not automatically be excluded from immersion programs. As Genesee (1976) pointed out, it is not just academic aptitude that influences success in immersion programs. Children's motivations, personalities, and attitudes also influence their success in French immersion, as does their mastery of other languages. Interestingly, Swain and Lapkin (1992) found that children who read and wrote non-English heritage languages—such as Italian, Armenian, Croatian, Czech, Greek, Polish, or Ukrainian—learned more French than did unilingual English children or heritage language children who could speak but not read and write their native languages.

How much French do immersion children learn? By grade six, children in the original St. Lambert project could understand spoken and written French as well as native speakers (Lapkin, Swain, & Argue, 1983). But we need to keep in mind that these children lived outside Montreal and had the advantage of a vibrant French community and culture close by. Other studies have not been as promising. For example, Romney, Romney, and Menzies (1995) found that grade five immersion students in Calgary scored below average on tests of French reading achievement. As well, the children did not read in French for pleasure or watch French television. They attended school in French, but they conducted every other part of their lives in English. It is important to note that the effects of French immersion programs might vary, depending on the role of French in the family and the community. This factor highlights the importance of considering Bronfenbrenner's concept of the mesosystem, described in Chapter 2.

Should children enter French immersion programs in kindergarten or in a later grade? Is it too stressful for kindergarten children to be confronted by a teacher who speaks a different language? A recent study in Toronto found that kindergarten children in French immersion adjusted as well to school as did children in English kindergarten (Pelletier, 1998). Interviews with the children indicated that the immersion children, like the other children, had learned the school routines and what to expect in the classroom, even though the routines were in French. Classroom observations revealed that children in immersion classrooms engaged in similar types of play as children in English classrooms. Immersion children did not appear to be more stressed than children in English programs.

Some studies have compared children who started immersion in grade one (early immersion) with those who started it in grade seven (late immersion) (see Day

& Shapson, 1992, for a review). Studies in Montreal and New Brunswick find that children in the late immersion programs do as well in French as children in early immersion. But studies in Manitoba, Ottawa, and some districts in British Columbia find that children in early immersion do better in French than those in late immersion. French immersion programs in different school districts can be more or less effective because of subtle differences in programming or in the role of French in the larger community. More research is needed on the effectiveness of different immersion programs (see Safty, 1992).

In evaluating the amount of French learned by children in immersion, researchers are undecided about what the appropriate comparison group should be. On the one hand, when immersion children are compared with native French speakers, their French often appears inferior (Carey, 1984). Hector Hammerly, a researcher at Simon Fraser University, found that graduates of French immersion often speak a peculiar form of French; they use a combination of French vocabulary and English grammar dubbed "Frenlish" (Hammerly, 1989). He is concerned that French immersion programs are not true immersion, as children are not immersed in a community of native speakers. Rather, there is one native speaker (the teacher) and a number of fledgling speakers who do not use "proper" French. Children copy the mistakes of their peers. On the other hand, when they are compared with English-speaking children learning French in other programs, the French immersion children show greater mastery of French (Mackay, 1972). French immersion children are more likely to have acquired "functional bilingualism." They have enough knowledge of French to get by in daily interactions and in the workplace. According to Romney et al. (1995), French immersion children develop better oral than written French.

Preservation of Minority Languages

Parents whose native languages are different from those of the community face the challenge of teaching their children their native languages. Landry, Allard, and Theberge (1992) studied French families living in English communities in western Canada. They found that the use of French in the families and attendance in French schools that had a rich French atmosphere influenced the amount of French the children learned and their attitudes toward their native language. Some children learned English at the expense of their native French language. This result is called **subtractive bilingualism.** Such children often understand French better than they can speak or read and write it. As one 4-year-old Edmonton boy told me, "My ears know French, but my mouth doesn't," much to the disappointment of his French-speaking mother (Digdon). Parents who want to ensure their children learn their heritage languages need to make those languages dominant in the home. But 35 percent of French families living outside Quebec reported that they spoke English at home more often than they did French (*Canada Year Book,* 1997).

subtractive bilingualism The learning of a foreign language that interferes with the learning of a native language.

Loss of heritage language has become a major problem among Canadian Aboriginal peoples. At one time, more than 60 Aboriginal languages were spoken in Canada. Of these languages, 8 are already extinct, and 13 are close to extinction because they have fewer than 40 speakers. As well, 23 are seriously endangered because they have only a few hundred speakers (Kirkness, 1999). At the current rate of decline, Kirkness (1999) predicts that only 4 Aboriginal languages—Cree, Ojibwa, Inuktitut, and Dakota—have a reasonable chance of surviving through the next century. Loss of Aboriginal languages was accelerated when Aboriginal children were sent to residential schools that forbade them to speak their languages. In 1951, 87.4 percent of Aboriginal Canadians listed an Aboriginal language as their mother tongue. By 1986, the number had dropped to 29.3 percent (Kirkness, 1999). In 1991, most Aboriginal families were not speaking their heritage language—51 percent of adults and 71 percent of children reported never having learned it. What happens when people lose their heritage language? Do they lose their culture?

Most of culture is in the language and is expressed in the language. Language is best able to express most easily, most accurately and most richly, the values,

FOCUS ON AN ISSUE

Why Do Children Talk to Themselves?

Josh is alone in his room playing a game in which he tries to fit pieces into a puzzleboard. If we look in on him, we might overhear Josh say to himself, "This piece doesn't fit. Where's a round one? No, it doesn't. It's too big. This one is small...." Children between the ages of 4 and 8 have been observed directing their talk to themselves about 20 percent of the time in school environments that permit it (Berk, 1985). This is a high percentage. Why do they do so?

Psychologists call talking aloud to oneself *private speech*. All people, young and old, talk to themselves. But, unlike adults, young children do so in public situations, such as at school or in a playground. Young children often sing words to themselves about what they are doing ... songs they have generated spontaneously rather than the words to group songs. They also talk to themselves far more often than adults do. Some of the early observations of private speech among preschool children were made by Jean Piaget. He suggested that the private speech of young children indicated their immaturity. Social speech was more difficult because it re-

quired consideration of the listener's perspective. He called this talking to oneself *egocentric speech* (Piaget, 1926).

Piaget's observation stimulated other researchers to record the way children use social language and private speech. Early findings tended to

---

Numerous researchers have reported an apparent relationship between intelligence and the amount and quality of children's use of private speech.

---

raise questions about Piaget's explanation. Observers found that the amount of private speech varied a great deal depending on the situation, but even the youngest children used far more social speech to communicate and exchange ideas with others than they used private speech. Perhaps, private speech served a separate purpose.

Lev Vygotsky suggested that private

speech often mirrored adult social speech and helped to develop inner thought and self-direction (1966). When observing children engaged in private activity, researchers have found three stages in the development of the children's private speech. In its earliest stage, private speech occurs after an action—"I made a big one." At the second stage, talking to oneself accompanies an action—"It's getting darker and darker with lots of paint." Later, in the third stage, it precedes an action—"I want to make a scary picture with dark paint." Private speech in each of these stages seems to serve the purpose of controlling or guiding a child's behaviour in performing a task. The progression corresponds, researchers believe, to the developing thought process in a child's mind. At the final stage, when speech comes before behaviour, the child is planning a course of action. The changes in private speech from stage 1 to stage 3 illustrate the development of thought processes in guiding the child's behaviour and its accompanying linguistic development. The child's use of language progresses from simply

---

customs and overall interests of the culture. If you take language away from the culture, you take away its greetings, its curses, its praises, its laws, its literature, its songs, its riddles, its proverbs, its cures, its wisdom, its prayers. You are losing those things that essentially are the way of life, the way of thought, the way of valuing, and a particular human reality. (Fishman, as cited in Kirkness, 1999, pp. 1–2)

What can be done to preserve Aboriginal languages? The United States and New Zealand passed federal legislation to protect Aboriginal peoples' language rights. As of 1999, no such legislation has been passed in Canada. The Northwest Territories has passed legislation to protect the six languages spoken there (1990 Northwest Territories Official Languages Act). Similar legislation is needed in other Canadian jurisdictions to ensure that language preservation is funded and that policies and programs are developed. An example of a program developed in the Northwest Territories is the Dene Yati Project, initiated in 1993 in the small community of Lutsel'Ke (see CCSD, 1996). Because of concerns about young people not speaking the Dene language (part of the Chipewyan language family), the Dene Cultural Institute and members of the community invited families to participate in activities, such as hunting, fishing, camping, and picnics, that were conducive to Dene culture. They provided opportunities for children to speak Chipewyan, and children's use of the language improved. "Family members felt closer to one another and stronger in their culture. And the ability to make change happen made everyone feel empowered" (Joanne Barnaby,

mirroring adult speech in stage 1 to internally structuring the child's behaviour in stage 3.

Many studies have supported the idea that the function of private speech is to guide the child in performing a task (Duncan & Pratt, 1997). But some studies have failed to show a connection between private speech and the development of performance abilities. These studies were done in traditional school environments, where children were not encouraged to integrate private speech with their activities. Later research has shown that when children are given verbal tasks and encouraged to speak, they talk to themselves quite a bit (Frauenglass & Diaz, 1985). Other researchers have found that children in comfortable school environments tend to accompany academic tasks with private speech if adults are not present.

Numerous researchers have reported an apparent relationship between intelligence and the amount and quality of children's use of private speech. It seems that the brighter the child, the more private speech is used and the more mature is its content. Children's talking aloud to themselves seems to follow a curve. It increases at first as the child develops self-control, peaks at age 4 or 5,

and then diminishes drastically by age 8 (Diaz & Lowe, 1987). The private speech of bright children seems to peak at an earlier age than that of average children (Berk, 1985).

Further research has confirmed that there are connections between private speech, behaviour, and thought. As children grow older and internalize their speech, they become quieter and pay more attention to their tasks. This development suggests that, as they internalize private talk, children bring their behaviour under the control of thought. There is now evidence indicating that talking to oneself is related to the quality of performance, especially among brighter children. Impulsive primary school children who have difficulty with self-control and persistence can even be helped by training them to use self-directed verbal commands to regulate their own behaviour (Diaz & Lowe, 1987).

Learning to think and self-guidance are not the only functions of private speech. For example, children seem to talk to themselves as a means of playing and relaxing, expressing feelings, and absorbing emotions and ideas. Young children take great pleasure in word play, which is an important means

Often, young children talk out loud while they work or play. Sometimes the talk is pretend dialogue, but more often it fulfills other functions.

of learning language. Children tell themselves fantasies or speak to an imaginary playmate or talk to inanimate objects (Berk, 1985). Private speech is thus a way children have to express their feelings, to gain understanding of their environment, and to develop language, as well as to develop self-control and inner thought.

Executive Director of the Dene Cultural Institute, as cited in CCSD, 1996, p. 43).

Schools can play a role in preserving heritage languages. For instance, educators in the Northwest Territories are incorporating Inuktitut in the school curriculums (Maguire & McAlpine, 1996). In a similar vein, schools in many Aboriginal communities are adding Aboriginal language and culture courses to their curriculums. The Kativik School Board in Nunavik, northern Quebec, has two stated mandates: (1) to provide a curriculum rich in Inuit tradition, culture, and language and (2) to prepare students to participate in the modern world where the languages and cultures of southern Canada are dominant (Fuzessy, 1999). Bicultural and bilingual Inuit graduates from Nunavik adjusted well to postsecondary education in Montreal in English or French CEGEPs (first-year college) (Fuzessy, 1999). At the same time, they retained their Inuit language and culture. In order to preserve other heritage languages, many larger Canadian communities now have special school programs for languages such as the Chinese languages, German, Arabic, Ukrainian, and Hebrew.

English as a Second Language

There are a growing number of children who have recently arrived in Canada and cannot speak either English or French. Many of these children speak Chinese languages. It is therefore important to be aware of differences between Chinese languages and English so that English as a Second Language (ESL) programs can be most effective. To that end,

Ann Cameron and colleagues at the University of New Brunswick in Fredericton have studied children whose first language was Chinese (Mandarin) and who were first exposed to English when they were 5 or 6 years old (Cameron & Lee, 1999). The children were studied longitudinally to see when they acquired different English morphemes. The results were puzzling. Some English morphemes (such as the prepositions *in* and *on*) that have counterparts in Chinese were acquired early, perhaps facilitated by the child's understanding of the morphemes in Chinese. But other English morphemes with counterparts in Chinese (future and past tense of verbs) were acquired late. Other English morphemes, such as articles (*a, the*) and suffixes (*s, es*) to make nouns plural, have no equivalents in Chinese yet are acquired early, perhaps because of their novelty. It is interesting to compare the children's language acquisition to that of Chinese adults learning English. Adults typically find English morphemes, such as articles, hard to learn, yet 5- and 6-year-old children master them early. After a mere six months of exposure to English, the children had already acquired 10 of the major English morphemes. And after 18 months of exposure, they were using almost 24 morphemes in their speech. In other research, Tardif (1996) found that toddlers who are native speakers of Chinese learn more verbs than nouns, but those who are native speakers of English learn more nouns than verbs.

Summary and Conclusions

Human beings are highly verbal creatures. Once the human infant is able to actively engage in language, a whole new developmental phase emerges. Furthermore, once language begins, it often explodes into being—with the child's vocabulary by age 3 having several hundred words.

Language is a complex accomplishment. Psycholinguists study three basic elements of language: content, the meaning of written or spoken messages; form, the particular symbols used to represent the messages; and use, the way in which a speaker employs language to give it a particular meaning. Form itself consists of phonemes, the basic sounds; morphemes, the basic word forms; and syntax, the sentence structure.

Language acquisition requires early exposure to language and an innate sensitivity to grammar. Children deprived of language during their first 6 years are unable to learn it beyond the level of a toddler, even with extensive language training. Early exposure also facilitates second-language learning. Young children are better able than adults to learn the grammars of second languages and to speak them without accents. Children do not learn grammar by parroting adults. Instead, they are born prepared to look for a grammar when they encounter language. Children raised by adults who speak pidgin, a type of speech that lacks grammar, will automatically bring grammar to the speech and create a new language called Creole.

Children understand language before they can pro-duce it. Many aspects of interpersonal communication exist in infants before they speak. These include signalling, turn-taking, and gesturing. Language production begins with babbling and iteration. Early babbling produces a universal, wide variety of sounds, some of which are outside the parents' native language. After 6 months, infant babbling takes on the inflection phonemes and patterns of the parents' language. Also, deaf infants babble less than hearing children. At this age, infants' language development becomes more closely linked to the language around them.

Most children are producing some words by 1 year. All children—regardless of culture—utter single words, usually nouns, first. These words are believed to represent holophrastic speech, that is, they are meant to convey complex ideas. Children make common errors during language acquisition. Two such errors are overextension and underextension, which deal with the child's notions of concepts and the words to represent them. Following single-word utterances, all children begin to produce two-word sentences. The first use of case grammar, the expression of relationships by using word order, occurs here. During the second and third year, children rapidly begin to form longer sentences. These sentences often are examples of telegraphic speech, in which the child uses high-information words. Pivot words—such as action words and possessives—also are key aspects of language at this age.

Not all theorists emphasize age as the main determinant of language. Roger Brown proposes that language development should be measured by average sentence length. He states that language development occurs in five distinct, sequential stages: two-word utterances; longer phrases, marked by inflection; simple sentences that use negative and imperative forms; and two final stages that involve mastering complex, compound, and subordinate structures. Brown suggests that true mastery of syntax is not complete before age 10.

To understand the language development of Canadian children, we have to be aware of the multilingual features of Canadian society. Some Canadian toddlers learn English and French simultaneously because one parent speaks one language and the other parent speaks the other. Amazingly, these children are able to differentiate the languages. Some children learn second languages in school. Children in French immersion are able to learn French without jeopardizing their mastery of English. Other children's families speak languages different from the language of their community. Both the family and schools play a role in preserving heritage languages.

Often, young children talk out loud while they work or play. Sometimes the talk is pretend dialogue, but more often it fulfills other functions.

Key Terms and Concepts

aphasia (p. 241)

case grammar (p. 250)

content (p. 238)

Creole (p. 242)

cross-language transfer (p. 259)

expressive jargon (p. 246)

form (p. 238)

French immersion (p. 259)

grammar (p. 238)

holophrastic speech (p. 247)

inflections (p. 251)

iteration (p. 245)

mean length of utterance (MLU) (p. 251)

morphemes (p. 238)

morphology (p. 238)

overregularization (p. 251)

phonemes (p. 238)

pivot grammar (p. 250)

productive language (p. 242)

receptive language (p. 242)

subtractive bilingualism (p. 261)

syntax (p. 238)

telegraphic speech (p. 250)

use (p. 238)

Questions to Review

1. List three major dimensions of language.

2. Differentiate between phonemes and morphemes.

3. Describe four components of language development.

4. Describe the role of early experience in language acquisition. Where does grammar come from?

5. Discuss the sequence of language development in infancy.

6. Differentiate between receptive and productive language. How are these processes related, and when do they evolve?

7. What is babbling, and how important is it to the infant's language development?

8. Contrast the language development of twins versus singletons.

9. Describe holophrastic speech.

10. Differentiate between overextensions and underextensions. How are a child's words and meanings closely linked to the concept the child is learning?

11. What is telegraphic speech? What are its two major components? What types of grammar are used in telegraphic speech?

12. Describe the five stages of language acquisition as identified by Roger Brown.

13. Describe the influence of parents' speech on the infant.

14. Describe the process by which a child's language acquisition develops into conversational skills.

15. Describe the language learning of children in French immersion.

Weblinks

www.pch.gc.ca/offlangoff/english/index.html

Canadian Heritage: Official Languages

This site has information on language learning, linguistic policy, action plan 1999–2002, French immersion, and provincial language programs and issues, as well as a youth corner.

www.lang.uiuc.edu/r-li5/esl/

English as a Second Language

This is a resource site for teachers and students. It has lesson plans, descriptions of class activities, chats, dictionaries, quizzes, and discussions of issues.

www.umanitoba.ca/cm/cmarchive/vol19no1/frenchimmersion.html

French Immersion: Recommended Canadian Children's Books

This site has an extensive annotated bibliography of French books for children in French immersion programs. The list was compiled by Irene Aubrey, chief of the Children's Literature Service at the National Library of Canada.

Early Childhood: Physical Development

Child art is an art which only
the child can produce.
There is something that the child can also perform,
but it is not art.
It is imitation, it is artificial.

FRANZ CIZEK

Outline CHAPTER 9

Objectives

By the time you have finished this chapter, you should be able to do the following:

✔ Describe the physical development of the preschool child.

✔ Describe brain development during the preschool years and its impact on motor skills.

✔ Describe the changes in motor and fine motor skills during early childhood.

✔ Describe the role of art in children's development of fine motor skills.

✔ Discuss the variables influencing physical development, including nutrition and health.

✔ List the major types of illness and disabling conditions affecting young children and their impact on children and their families.

✔ Explain the relationship between poverty and health in early childhood.

✔ Describe the factors that encourage the development of resilient children.

"Mommy, watch me! Watch me!"

"Daddy, did you see me jump off that swing? Wasn't I brave?"

"Come on, Heather, let's slide down the stairs on our tummies—head first!"

For most adults, it is fascinating to watch young children at play or exploring their world. Their laughter and open smiles are contagious. Their activities may also be heart-stopping to watch at times. Children at this stage often are daredevils—after they overcome their initial fears. Active exploration, climbing, running, awkward skipping, and all the other motor activities young children perform form the basis for later physical development. Skills learned now are practised and refined in later periods of life. Future athletes, artists, and musicians arise from the physical explorations of early childhood.

In this chapter, we will concentrate on the dimension of physical development during early childhood. During this period, from 2 years through 5 years of age, the physical-motor skills of children rapidly develop. Children also make dramatic discoveries about the world around them by using their growing cognitive abilities.

As we look at each type of physical development, it is important to remember that the different aspects of the process do not really occur separately. For example, when a child begins to walk or skip, she is motivated to do so, she has the information needed, and she has the physical capacity to carry out her idea. Therefore, the ways in which a child behaves and thinks can be viewed as an integrated system (Thelen, 1989). Looking carefully at specific aspects of development offers many ways to understand the process by which children grow and change.

As we discussed earlier in Chapter 6, many researchers in physical development, including Esther Thelen (1992), believe that children's motor skills, such as walking

A motor skill like reaching is the culmination of a variety of component processes and structures assembled by the child to perform a specific task.

and reaching, emerge as the culmination of various component processes and structures that each child assembles to accomplish a particular task—for example, the child crosses the room to grab a desired toy. Some components are in place very early; others emerge more slowly. For the toddler to walk, for example, leg strength must be sufficient to allow him to shift balance and support to a single leg. Until he has attained that leg strength, the child will be incapable of independent walking.

The child must learn to adapt his stepping, lifting, or throwing patterns to his changing physical body and to the immediate environment (Thelen, 1992). When a child is motivated and ready to practise a specific skill, or to put some of the components together, the child may work at self-paced exploration with considerable persistence. The following example illustrates one child's skill development through play.

One spring afternoon, Tommy, aged 2 ½, visited the pond on his grandparents' farm. While grandpa repaired the boat, Tommy and his older brother ventured out onto a small dock a few steps away. His brother picked up a large stone and tossed it into the water. Tommy lingered, watching the circular patterns of widening waves while his brother left to play with a neighbour. Tommy started back toward his grandfather (who was watching him carefully) but then stopped to pick up a pebble, returned cautiously to the dock, and dropped it into the calm water. Surprise! He too had made the plop sound and that fascinating circle of widening waves. He smiled and watched transfixed until it disappeared. He turned to fetch another stone and then another and another. Most of the afternoon, despite the urging of his grandmother to come inside, he carried one stone after another to the pond. He lifted tiny pebbles and threw them as far as he could into the water. He lifted larger stones he could barely carry and struggled to simply drop them in. His grandfather marvelled at Tom's persistence and wondered about the common notion that 2-year-olds have short attention spans.

Thelen and others believe that the key process underlying motor development is *exploration*. Thelen (1992) defines this physical exploration as an active testing or problem solving by the child in order to choose which actions will best match the functional needs. Indeed, many researchers now believe that skill acquisition may involve the selection of appropriate and efficient actions from a larger pool of possible coordinated patterns (Thelen, 1989). We can see from this explanation of children's motor development that motivation and cognition are both involved in the development of motor abilities. It is, therefore, important for us to remember that while we will focus on physical-motor skills in this chapter, this is a somewhat artificial distinction.

Physical Growth and Change

Those who study the maturation of children have long been interested in variations in their physical size and proportions and shapes of their bodies—as well as variations in the timing of growth. In general, this study has followed one of two paths: first, and most frequently, it has focused on the measurement of body shape, stature, muscle, and fat tissue; second, it has focused on the psychological measurement of motor activities. Studies included in this second category have focused on children's feelings about their bodies—their perceptions of its shape, size, and capacities. But both paths often interact to study the efforts growing children make while engaging in physical activities and the satisfaction or dissatisfaction these efforts are likely to produce in terms of their self-concept (Cratty, 1986).

Even our own daily observations of growing children's play and peer interactions suggest the close interaction of mind and body. We have all seen thin, shy, withdrawn children, just as we have all seen the stereotypical muscular, confident bully. In general, research has found that children's satisfaction with their bodies and with themselves depends on how closely their bodies conform to societal ideals. Furthermore, the literature documents the relationship between athletic prowess and the achievement of social recognition in childhood and adolescence. Young children's changing bodies and their continual adjustments to how they feel about those bodies form an inseparable duo. Because of this, we shall present information in this chapter not only on the physical changes in young children's bodies, but also on the psychological adjustments associated with those changes.

Body Size and Proportion

Interest in the body size and proportion of children and youth has been stimulated by many factors. Extreme deviations in growth rates may be a cause for medical concern and may lead to interventions to accelerate or delay unusual rates of change. Physical educators and developmental psychologists have been interested in variations in the physique of young children because of the possible relationship with exercise tolerance, power, and strength, as well as with personality and the manner in which the child's body develops. Finally, coaches and scientists interested in high-level athletic performance, such as in the Olympic Games, often study the highly specialized body builds that seem most associated with success in particular events and their precursors in early childhood (Cratty, 1986).

Growth Changes The rate of growth in humans is not uniform. For most infants, the first year and a half of life is marked by extremely rapid growth. The growth rate levels off by the ages of 2 through 6 and remains fairly stable until the growth spurt associated with adolescence. Cratty (1986) and others have suggested that this stable pattern of growth is the reason that children in early and middle childhood are able to acquire so many new skills so rapidly. "Somehow such children do not have to worry about sudden changes in stature and can concentrate on using their relatively unchanging bodies to full advantage" (Cratty, 1986, p. 50).

We get a very different picture of growth, however, when we study individual children. Each child's growth is the result of the child's genes, nutrition, and opportunity to play and exercise. There are also gender differences in growth rates and patterns. These gender differences are small and insignificant in early childhood.

Body Proportions During the period of physical growth from birth to maturity, the proportions of body segments to total body size also change dramatically, as we may see in Figure 9-1. At birth, for example, the head makes up one-quarter of the body length. By maturity, despite the fact that the head has doubled in size, it makes up only one-eighth the body length. The legs increase fivefold to make up half the body length at maturity. The arms increase their length by four times at maturity, while the body's trunk shows a threefold increase.

Not all parts of the body grow at the same rate. Body segments have their own growth spurts at various stages during the growing years. For example, the 3- to 4-year-old's relatively short, stubby fingers begin to grow longer, which makes object handling much easier for the 6- to 7-year-old.

Changes in body proportions also affect the location of the body's centre of gravity, or weight centre. In children, the centre of gravity is higher than in adults, since children carry a higher proportion of their weight in their upper body. Boys have a slightly higher centre of gravity than do girls. During the school years, the centre of gravity descends to the pelvic area as changes in stature occur. Since young children tend to be more top heavy, controlling the body is more difficult. They will lose balance more quickly because of their higher centre of gravity; thus, coming to a quick stop without falling is quite difficult. Ball-handling, especially with larger balls, also may be negatively affected by this easy loss of balance. For example, when a young child catches a ball, the ball's weight shifts his centre of gravity forward and upward, depending on the level at which he receives the ball. This movement may result in a loss of balance in the direction of the ball's movement, which causes the child to either fall over backwards or to drop the ball after momentary possession (Nichols, 1990).

Figure 9-1
Changing Body Proportions in Girls and Boys from Birth to Maturity

Source: Nichols, B. (1990). *Moving and learning: The elementary school physical education experience.* St. Louis, MO: Times Mirror/Mosby College Publishing.

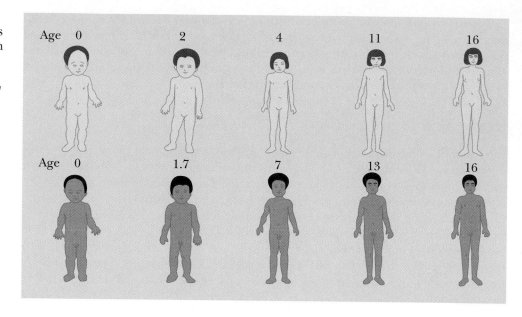

epiphysis The cartilaginous growth centre at the end of each bone.

Their higher centre of gravity often causes young children to lose their balance.

Skeletal Maturation Bones begin as soft tissue or cartilage and then harden, or *ossify*, as the body matures. Ossification begins before birth and continues until late adolescence. At birth, the ossification process has progressed to include the entire shaft of the long bones. At the end of each bone is a cartilaginous growth centre called the **epiphysis.** Between the epiphysis and the shaft of the bone lies the growth plate, where bone continually grows until maturation. The closure of the growth plate varies depending on the sex of the child. In general, girls mature sooner than boys. During these preschool years, therefore, girls are usually more advanced by a few months in bone maturation than are boys.

Skeletal age, which is determined by bone maturation, is typically measured by X-rays of the bones of the wrists. These X-rays show the degree of ossification, or progress of maturity, of the bones. Skeletal age may vary by as much as four years in children of the same chronological age. For example, the skeletal age of 6-year-olds may vary from four to eight years (Nichols, 1990).

While vigorous activity is essential to stimulate normal bone growth, there is growing concern today about potential injury to growing bones during the developing years, especially damage to the epiphysis. There is also increasing evidence that the stress of overtraining may have some lasting effect on bone growth. Injuries to mature children may produce little disturbance, but injury to young children may result in greater growth disturbance, since the younger child has many more years of growth before maturity (Nichols, 1990). We shall describe injuries in greater detail in Chapter 12 when we discuss organized sports in middle childhood.

Internal Bodily Changes Besides the obvious changes in height and weight that occur in early childhood, internal bodily changes also affect the child's physical development. These changes include differences in fat and muscle tissue and cardiovascular changes.

The rate at which fatty tissue is deposited in the body increases for a brief period from birth to 6 months and then decreases until 6 to 8 years of age. The decrease is more marked in boys. An increase in the rate of fat deposition for both sexes then occurs just before the adolescent growth spurt. There are also gender differences in the rate and placement of fatty tissues. These differences account for the variations in contours in boys and girls in middle childhood, which become more obvious at adolescence.

During early and middle childhood, muscle tissue increases in length, breadth, and width. The number of muscle fibres is largely determined by heredity and will not appreciably change during an individual's lifetime. Muscle weight increases about 40 times from birth to maturity. At birth, muscle weight makes up approximately one-fifth to one-fourth of the body's weight; by early adolescence, it accounts for one-third of the body's weight, and by maturity, it increases to two-fifths.

Since muscle growth lags behind increases in height in young children, it is not possible to judge their strength by their size. Children grow taller and heavier before they become stronger. There is little difference in the strength of boys and girls before puberty. The major differences in strength occur after the adolescent growth spurt. Since there are no major differences in strength during early and middle childhood between boys and girls, the two sexes are on a relatively equal footing in physical activity. Despite this equality, girls often perceive themselves as weaker than boys, while boys see themselves as stronger than girls. This myth may have an impact on participation in physical activities. Parents and preschool teachers may help children develop a realistic view of their own potential to allow them to develop to their fullest, whatever their gender.

There are also significant changes in cardiovascular function during early childhood. The heart rate, which is the number of heart beats per minute, undergoes considerable change during the life of an individual. At rest, children's heart rates are consistently higher than those of adults. For example, the heart rate of children under 6 years of age averages 100 beats per minute, while for the average adult it is about 70 for men and 80 for women. The higher heart rate of young children is probably due to their smaller stroke volume, the amount of blood each contraction of the heart ejects into circulation. Since younger children have smaller hearts and their hearts contract with less force, their stroke volume is less than that of adults. Because of these differences, cardiac output is also lower for children. Cardiac output is the amount of blood that can be pumped out of the heart each minute.

These changes significantly affect the amount of physical activity that young children can perform. Most children are highly motivated to engage in playing games, running, and other motor activities. They tend to work hard at these activities but also tire easily. Young children seem to handle physical activity well. They play hard, then rest or slow down before returning to full activity again. But they are also more susceptible to the negative effects of heat and cold, so adults need to be cautious when young children engage in vigorous physical activity where there are extremes of temperature (Nichols, 1990).

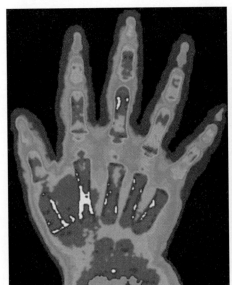 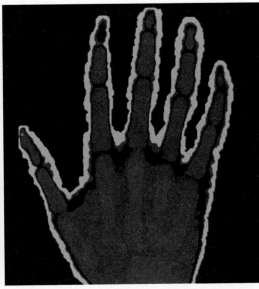

(Left) X-ray of 2-year-old's hand and wrist. (Right) X-ray of 6-year-old's hand and wrist. Note the greater degree of ossification in the older child's bones.

Brain Development

During early childhood, children develop a broad variety of skills, ranging from physical coordination and perception to memory and language. These complex capabilities are closely linked to corresponding aspects of brain development. Brain development supports increasingly complex learning; in turn, perceptual and motor activity, as well as problem solving and language learning, create and strengthen the child's network of neural connections.

Lateralization   The cortex, or surface, of the human brain is divided anatomically into two cerebral hemispheres—the left and the right. The hemispheres have different ways of processing information that may be very striking—a phenomenon referred to as **lateralization.** Roger Sperry (1970), among others, discovered many of these important properties of the cerebral cortex through surgery designed to reduce epileptic seizures. By cutting the connection between the two hemispheres, he reduced patients' seizures without noticeably impairing their ability to perform daily activities. Subsequent experiments indicated that each hemisphere of the brain was strong in some areas and weak in others. Sperry was awarded a Nobel Prize in medicine for his research revealing hemispheric specialization, and he also developed lifesaving techniques for brain surgery. We may see these areas illustrated in Figure 9-2.

As we can see, the left side of the brain controls the right side of the body, while the right side of the brain controls the left side. The left hemisphere is largely responsible for speech, language, writing, logic, math, and science. The right side is responsible for spatial construction, creative thinking, fantasy, art, and music appreciation (Cratty, 1986; Hellige, 1993). The hemispheres of the brain, therefore, may be thought of as two general information-processing subsystems with different biases and abilities (Hellige, 1993). But researchers are now beginning to emphasize the way in which the brain "puts itself back together" to allow these two differently organized subsystems to coordinate their activities. Therefore, while the brain's hemispheres have separate or complementary functions, the main point is that they almost always work together.

lateralization The process whereby specific skills and competencies become localized in particular hemispheres of the brain.

Figure 9-2
The Functions of the Right and Left Cerebral Hemispheres

Source: Shea, C.H., Shebilske, W.L., & Worchel, S. (1993). *Motor learning and control.* Englewood Cliffs, NJ: Prentice-Hall, p. 38.

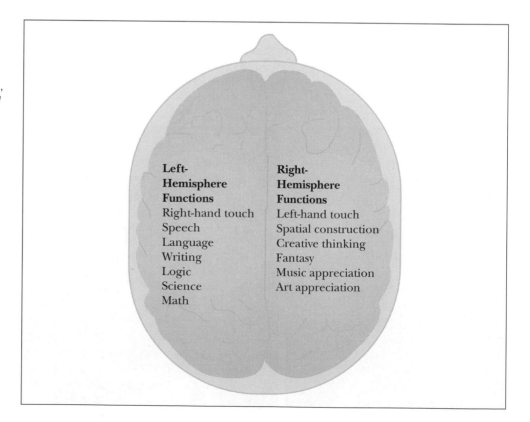

Left-Hemisphere Functions
Right-hand touch
Speech
Language
Writing
Logic
Science
Math

Right-Hemisphere Functions
Left-hand touch
Spatial construction
Creative thinking
Fantasy
Music appreciation
Art appreciation

When we observe the way in which children's skills develop, it is not surprising to learn that the different hemispheres of the brain develop at different times (Thatcher, Walker, & Guidice, 1987). For example, language develops very quickly during early childhood. Language skills are housed in the left hemisphere, which shows accelerated growth during the period from 3 to 6 years and then levels off. The right hemisphere, on the other hand, matures more slowly during early childhood and then accelerates slightly in growth between 8 and 10 years of age. This developmental difference is also reflected in the growth of children's skills in middle childhood. Spatial skills, such as drawing, finding directions, and recognizing geometric shapes, are slow to develop across childhood and adolescence. Research indicates that lateral specialization continues throughout childhood and into adolescence.

Handedness Researchers have long been intrigued by the fact that children tend to prefer to use one hand over another. Handedness is not the only asymmetry noted during development. Most children show head-turning responses and foot preferences—and even ear and eye preferences—that favour one side of the body over the other (Cratty, 1986). For the most part, children exhibit a preference for right-side head turns, handedness, and footedness. For most children, this right-side preference is associated with left-sided cerebral dominance. (Remember that the right side of the body is controlled by the left side of the brain, and vice versa.) However, of special concern over the years have been those children who prefer to use their left hand. The left hand has been associated in some cultures with deviancy or evil—hence, the word *sinister*, which is also the Latin word for "left." However, despite these preferences, there is only a weak relationship between preference in motor functions and the dominant cerebral hemisphere—the hemisphere that possesses greater capacity to carry out skilled motor action.

Research on cerebral dominance has found that for the majority of right-handed people, language is localized on the left side of the brain. However, for the remaining 10 percent of the population who are left-handed, language is often shared between the two sides of the brain, rather than being located predominantly on one side. This research indicates that the brains of left-handed people may be less strongly lateralized than those of right-handed persons (Hiscock & Kinsbourne, 1987). Furthermore, many left-handed people appear to be *ambidextrous*, or able to use both hands with fairly good dexterity.

For most children, there is a gradual acquisition of preferred hand usage that becomes fairly ingrained by early to middle childhood (Gesell & Ames, 1947). Coren and Porac (1980) documented the increased use of the right hand beginning from the nursery school years through adulthood. This finding may indicate increased pressure or training by parents and teachers to use the right hand, as well as increased brain specialization. A majority of 3- to 5-year-olds show a well-established foot preference. However, in one-third to one-fourth of the children, this growth continues beyond the age of 5. Some researchers have suggested recently that since "footedness" is less culturally influenced than handedness, foot preference may actually be a more sensitive indicator of developmental motor and cognitive delays (Bradshaw, 1989; Gabbard, Dean, & Haensly, 1991).

While many parents are concerned about what effect left-handedness will have on their children, it is important to note that research shows that few left-handed individuals have any developmental problems. They appear to be normal in all respects. In fact, some research suggests that children who have the ability to use both hands may best adapt to sports requiring mixed preferences. Examples may be the switch-hitting baseball player, the soccer player who uses both feet equally well, or the left-handed baseball pitcher. There is also a tendency for left-handed or mixed preference children to attain greater mathematical talents than their right-handed peers (Benbow, 1986). Some researchers contend that left-handed children are more creative than right-handers because of the more balanced involvement of both hemispheres in the completion of various tasks. Both Benjamin Franklin and Leonardo da Vinci were highly creative left-handed individuals.

Question to Ponder

Why do you think people develop a dominant hand? Why isn't everyone ambidextrous?

For most children there is a gradual acquisition of preferred hand usage that becomes fairly ingrained by early to middle childhood.

Physical-Motor Development

gross motor skills Capabilities involving large body movements.

fine motor skills Capabilities involving small body movements.

Because of changes in children's growing bodies and in their ability to concentrate and refine activities, children's **gross motor skills**—capabilities involving large body movements, such as running, hopping, and throwing—improve markedly (Clark & Phillips, 1985). **Fine motor skills**—capabilities involving small body movements—develop more slowly. Nonetheless, children eventually are able to put together a wooden puzzle, draw with a pencil, and use a spoon and fork.

Separating physical-motor and perceptual development from cognitive development in preschool children is difficult. Children's understanding of the world depends on the information they receive from their own bodies, perceptions, and motor activity and on the ways in which they experience themselves. Almost everything that a child does from birth through the first few years lays the foundations, in some way, not only for later physical-motor skills, but also for cognitive processes and social and emotional development. Looking, touching, exploring, babbling, bouncing, scribbling—all form the basis for the performance of more complex developmental tasks. Although much of what preschool children do—making mud pies, crawling, or hanging upside down—appears to be sheer sensory exploration, experts in development consider all of their actions to be purposeful, or directed toward some goal (von Hofsten, 1989). For example, children explore places and objects to find out what they feel like, to see them, and to hear them. Sensory exploration leads to concepts like "up," "down," "straight," and "tight." For instance, when a girl walks on a log at the beach, she learns not only how to balance, but also the cognitive concept "narrow" and the emotional concept "confidence."

Many aspects of development proceed from a physical-motor base. Some developmental sequences are continuous, as in the natural progression from scribbling to writing; others seem somewhat discontinuous. For example, children may explore different textures and weaves of material randomly with their fingers and eyes before they are ready to sort and classify or compare and contrast the materials. Similarly, they must sort and compare thoughts before they can deal with complex ideas. Another example is the relationship between early infant crawling experience and later motor skill development. Crawling triggers psychological development, especially the perception of spatial concepts, since the experiences associated with crawling provide a foundation for visual-spatial perception (McEwan, Dihoff, & Brosvic, 1991). The process of crawling provides "a state of eye-hand coordination, vestibular processing,

Although they take longer to develop than gross motor skills, fine motor skills such as those involved in putting together the pieces of a wooden puzzle now emerge.

improvement of balance and equilibrium, spatial awareness, tactile input, kinesthetic awareness, and social maturation" (McEwan, Dihoff, & Brosvic, 1991, p. 75).

Some developmental sequences involve **functional subordination.** Actions that at first are performed for their own sake later become part of a more complicated, purposeful skill. For example, a child's simple, fine motor explorations with crayon and paper have value in and of themselves, at first. Later, putting marks on paper becomes functionally subordinated to more complex skills, such as writing, drawing, creating designs, or even carpentry. The roots of complex thought are not always obvious; nevertheless, a look at physical-motor development is a good starting point from which to seek out these roots.

> **functional subordination** The integration of a number of separate simple actions or schemes into a more complex pattern of behaviour.

Ages 2 and 3

Compared with infants, 2-year-olds are amazingly competent creatures. They can walk, run, and manipulate objects. When we see one beside a 4- or 5-year-old, however, we recognize the younger child's limitations. At 2 years old—and even 3 years old—children are still rather short and a bit rounded. They walk with a wide stance and a body sway. Although they can climb, push, pull, and hang by their hands, they have little endurance. This is a fact recognized by parents who have spent 15 minutes dressing toddlers in every layer of warm clothing they own in preparation for the 10 minutes spent outside. Toddlers also are inclined to use both arms or both legs when only one is required (Woodcock, 1941). Thus, when a 2-year-old's mother offers him one cookie, he is likely to extend two hands.

By the age of 3, children's legs stay closer together during walking and running, and they no longer need to keep a constant check on what their feet are doing (Cratty, 1970). They run, turn, and stop more smoothly than they did as 2-year-olds, although their ankles and wrists are not as flexible as they will be at ages 4 and 5 (Woodcock, 1941). At 3 years, children are more likely to extend one hand to receive one item, and they begin to show a preference for using either the right or left hand.

Ages 4 and 5

At age 4, children are able to vary the rhythm of their running. Many 4-year-olds can also skip rather awkwardly and execute a running jump and a standing broad jump (Gesell, 1940). The average child of 4 is probably able to work a button through a

The gait of 2-year-olds is characterized by a wide stance and a body sway. They love to walk and run but have little endurance. In contrast, the legs of 3-year-olds stay closer together when they run.

buttonhole and can use a pencil or crayon to draw lines, circles, and simple faces.

By the time they are 5, children can skip smoothly, walk a balance beam confidently, stand on one foot for several seconds, and imitate dance steps (Gesell, 1940). They manage buttons and zippers and may be able to tie shoelaces. Many children can throw a ball overhand and catch a large ball thrown to them (Cratty, 1970). But accurate throwing and effective catching will show many changes over the next few years (Robertson, 1984).

Whereas 3-year-olds may push a doll carriage or a large truck for the fun of pushing it, 4-year-olds have functionally subordinated their pushing into a fantasy of doll play or a cars-and-trucks game. While 3-year-olds daub and smear paint with abandon and stack blocks one on top of another, 4-year-olds make a "painting" or use blocks to build houses, space stations, or farms. At age 4, children are still exploring some physical-motor activities for their own sake—for example, they may accurately pour liquid into tiny cups or operate a syringe and a funnel—but much of their play is embedded in the acting out of complex roles or in the purposeful construction of objects or games. We can see the motor development of preschool children presented in Concept Summary Table 9-1.

Fine Motor Skills

Fine motor skills involve the refined use of the hand, fingers, and thumb. The development of various abilities in which the hands are involved is part of a series of overlapping processes beginning before birth. At the sixth fetal month, a grasp response may be elicited. Near the end of the third year, a new manual ability emerges when the child begins to integrate and coordinate manual schemes with other motor, perceptual, or verbal behaviours. For example, 4-year-olds will be able to run, watch a ball, and simultaneously position the hands and fingers to catch the ball. Another example may be found in the preschool child's ability to carry on a dinner conversation while successfully manipulating a fork (Cratty, 1986). The development of self-care skills also falls under this set of skills.

The final period of manual activity, lasting from early to middle childhood, is marked by children's efforts to expand their artistic abilities. Young children play musical instruments, and they are able to represent their thoughts with increasing sophistication using artistic expression through sculpting, drawing, and clay modelling (Kellogg, 1969).

Concept Summary

Table 9-1	Motor Development of Preschool Children		
2-YEAR-OLDS	**3-YEAR-OLDS**	**4-YEAR-OLDS**	**5-YEAR-OLDS**
Walk with wide stance and body sway.	Keep legs closer together when walking and running.	Can vary rhythm of running.	Can walk a balance beam.
Can climb, push, pull, run, hang by both hands.	Can run and move more smoothly.	Skip awkwardly; jump.	Skip smoothly; stand on one foot.
Have little endurance.	Smear and daub paint; stack blocks.	Have greater strength, endurance, and coordination.	Can manage buttons and zippers; may tie shoelaces.
Reach for objects with two hands.		Draw shapes and simple figures; make paintings; use blocks for buildings.	Use utensils and tools correctly.

Preschoolers often practise tying shoelaces; by age 5, some children are able to complete this task.

Self-Care Skills As children gain fine motor skills, they become increasingly able to take care of themselves and complete their daily activities independently. From 2 to 3 years of age, for example, children are able to put on and remove simple items of clothing. They can also zip and unzip large zippers. The average child of this age is able to use a spoon effectively, may string large beads, and can open doors by turning the knob.

The 3- to 4-year-old child can fasten and unfasten large buttons and is able to independently serve food—although still with minor "messes" on occasion. He is also able to use scissors to cut paper and can copy simple shapes using pencil and paper. By the time children are 4 to 5 years of age, they are able to dress and undress themselves without assistance. They can use a fork very well and have sufficient manual dexterity to cut the lines of shapes with scissors. The 5- to 6-year-old can use a knife to cut soft food and can tie a simple knot. By age 6, children are able to tie their own shoelaces—although many of them consider this a very difficult task to learn.

From Scribbling to Writing Scribbling has been described as a type of "motor babbling" (Cratty, 1986). As the child matures, the forms that arise from scribbling gradually become transformed into printing and writing—in much the same way as the sounds produced by babbling eventually combine to form words. In Table 9-1, we may see the stages through which children pass between scribbling and learning to write and draw.

Children's Art Rhoda Kellogg has extensively studied the development of children's art. In the course of her work as an early childhood educator, she has amassed a collection of over half a million children's drawings from all over the world—tracing children's artistic development from age 2 to 8. She has shown that the expressive gestures of children, from the moment that they first record them with crayon or pencil, evolve in universal ways from basic scribbles to consistent symbols. Kellogg (1969) believes that every child, in her discovery of a model of symbolization, follows the same graphic evolution.

According to Kellogg, all children begin their artistic life producing a basic set of scribbles. Out of these shapeless scribblings eventually emerge first the circle, the upright cross, the diagonal cross, the rectangle, and other common forms. Then two or more of these basic forms are combined into that comprehensive symbol, the *mandala*, a circle divided into quarters by a cross. Over several years of development such basic patterns gradually become the child's conscious representation of familiar objects.

Question to Ponder

How much does practice influence the development of fine motor skills, such as learning to tie shoelaces? Should children who can't tie their shoelaces be provided with unlaced shoes until they are older and more ready to learn?

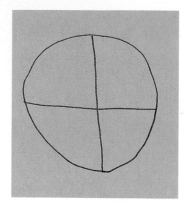

The mandala symbol is found in children's art around the world.

By age 3, the child begins to form face shapes, and by age 4, humans. By 4 to 5 years of age, the child achieves a human form with arms and legs, and, eventually, the suggestion of a trunk and clothes. By age 4 and 5, some children add other pictorials, such as houses, animals, boats, and other objects.

How Adults Affect Children's Art   Kellogg (1969) sees a crisis of sorts at age 5, with kindergarten training that begins to shape the child's art to the adult's cultural standards. The child begins to produce art that "sells," or elicits adult approval. This is also the point at which many children cease being creative, and only some children are seen as "artists." Kellogg feels that artistic endeavours should be free and spontaneous, unlike training in mathematical and word symbols, which must be less arbitrary.

Most art instruction conveys the message that it should be pictorial (or pure design) and functional in some way. Most adults do not consider children's drawing "art," and they attempt to shape it into what they consider art. In any event, by the age of 9 or 10, most children have lost the ability to simply produce what aesthetically pleases them. As Kellogg comments, "Adults do not scribble and most adults do not function at all in art. Therefore, the child has difficulty taking seriously his artistic self-education" (1969).

Motor Skills and Overall Development

Children's early motor experiences vary considerably. For some children, early childhood holds a wealth of motor experiences, including the opportunity to attempt to master diverse locomotor, climbing, and manipulative skills. Other children find their experiences limited during this important phase of development—because of either environmental or physical constraints. Opportunity for balanced and varied activity helps a child effectively and efficiently execute skills (Nichols, 1990).

Success at performing physical activities also has an impact on young children's self-concepts. Children's self-concepts include feelings about their bodies and their physical skills. Often, physically proficient young children are sought out by peers and become leaders at early ages. This valued skill level may give them the self-confidence and assurance to lead their classmates (Nichols, 1990).

Table 9-1 The Child's Progression from Scribbling to Writing and Drawing

1. A child may either hold a writing implement or use it to make marks on paper and on other surfaces.

2. The child creates crude scribbles—seemingly random marks without any coherent design.

3. The child reacts to what she draws; she may produce lines or squares or may balance a scribble on one side of a piece of paper with a figure drawn on the other.

4. The child draws simple geometric figures, beginning with crude crosses and simple spirals.

5. The child draws more exact geometrical figures, places two or more figures in combinations, and colours with increasing accuracy.

6. The child creates more complex designs, such as houses, people, and other familiar objects.

7. In school, the child learns block printing and cursive writing.

8. With proper training and/or interest, the child draws complex three-dimensional pictures and figures.

Learning Physical-Motor Skills

The physical-motor skills that preschool children learn are usually everyday actions, such as tying shoes, cutting with scissors, feeding themselves, buttoning and zipping up clothes, using a crayon or pencil, skipping, and jumping. These skills increase the young child's ability to move around, to take care of herself, and to express herself creatively. They expand the child's world and her ability to act upon it. Some young children also learn more highly skilled activities, such as gymnastics, how to play the piano or violin, and even how to ride a horse. Although there is debate over the value of early training, psychologists have identified the important conditions for physical-motor learning. These conditions are readiness, motivation, activity, attention, and some kind of feedback. It is helpful to look closely at these factors before deciding whether or not to train a young child.

For a young child to learn a highly skilled activity like playing the piano, certain conditions have to be in place, including readiness, motivation, and attention.

Readiness Any new skill or learning generally requires a state of readiness on the part of the child. A certain degree of maturation, some prior learning, and a number of preliminary skills must be present before the child can profit from training. The classic twin study of Myrtle McGraw (1935) demonstrated that although early training in the normal motor skills, such as cutting, buttoning, or climbing stairs, accelerated the acquisition of those skills, the gains were only temporary. The research method for these studies, called *co-twin control studies,* involved training only one twin in a particular skill. The training itself consisted of daily practice or drill three times a week, with the researcher praising and assisting the child, as well as demonstrating whenever necessary. It was assumed that such a concentrated and enriched training program would produce a permanent advantage in the skill being taught. But the researchers found that upon reaching the proper stage of maturation, or readiness, for the task involved, the untrained twin learned it very quickly and caught up with the trained twin within a few weeks.

The study revealed that early training—training given before the child has reached the appropriate maturation point—produces no lasting advantage, at least not for those skills that are phylogenetic in nature. *Phylogenetic skills* are behaviours that all normal members of a species possess, for example, crawling, sitting, walking, and so forth. *Ontogenetic skills,* which are individually learned behaviours, do appear to be affected by training. These behaviours include roller skating, skiing, bicycle riding, and other such activities. The twin who received the specialized training did engage in the ontogenetic activities at an earlier age and continued to outperform the untrained twin in these activities.

The difficulty for parents and teachers is knowing when children have reached the readiness point. American and Soviet studies have indicated that if children are introduced to new physical-motor learning at the optimal point of readiness, they learn quickly with little training or effort (Lisina & Neverovich, 1971). Children at the optimal readiness point want to learn, enjoy the practice, and get excited over their own performance. Children are frequently the best indicators of when they have reached the point of optimal readiness, as they begin to imitate particular skills on their own. Readiness also becomes a factor in the age at which children should start formal academic tasks such as writing.

Competence Motivation Another strong motive in motor-skill acquisition is **competence motivation** (White, 1959). Children try things out just to see if they can do them, to perfect their skills, to test their muscles and abilities, and to enjoy the way it feels. They run, jump, climb, and skip for the pleasure and challenge of these activities. This kind of motivation is *intrinsic;* it comes from within the child and is generated by the activity. *Extrinsic* motivation also can play a part in skill development. Parental encouragement, peer competition, and the need for identification can prompt a child to attempt, and then to perfect, a certain skill. Adults can boost the self-confidence of a child if they are encouraging and set goals that the child is able to accomplish.

But what if young children are pushed to develop skills through organized

competence motivation A need to achieve in order to feel effective as an individual.

physical activities? Team sports often emphasize competition and may communicate criticism and pressure. Experts in sports medicine recommend avoiding formal sports for young children. They encourage adults to help children to initiate their own active play. Such play experiences lead to a positive attitude toward developing skills. Physical activity becomes associated with well-being and with doing one's best (Rice, 1990).

The best motivation parents can provide may be doing physical activities year-round themselves. Research shows that the level of physical activity of preschool children is significantly related to the amount of time their parents spend in physical exercise (Poest, Williams, Witt, & Atwood, 1989).

Activity Activity is essential to motor development. Children cannot master stair climbing unless they climb stairs. They cannot learn to throw a ball unless they practise throwing. When children live in limited and restricted environments, the development of their physical-motor skills will lag. Children raised in crowded surroundings often show a delay in developing skills of the large muscles. They lack strength, coordination, and flexibility in running, jumping, climbing, balancing, and the like. Children who are hampered in their ability to use activity to learn—because they have few objects to play with, places to explore, or tools to use, as well as few people to imitate—may have trouble developing their motor skills. On the other hand, given a rich, meaningful environment full of objects to handle, open space to explore, and active people to imitate, children will generally have the necessary stimulation to pace their own learning. They will imitate a task, often repeating it endlessly. They will stack blocks and discover ways to make shapes. They will pour water repeatedly from one container to another to explore the concepts of "full" and "empty," "fast" and "slow," "spilling drops" and "making streams." Such self-designed and self-paced schedules of learning often are more efficient than adult-programmed lessons (Karlson, 1972).

Attention Physical-motor learning is also enhanced by attention. Paying attention requires an alert and engaged state of mind. But how can children's attention be increased? Young children cannot just be told what to do and how to do it. Rather, children at age 2 or 3 learn new physical skills most effectively by being led through the activity. In the former Soviet Union, exercises and games were used to teach children to move their arms and legs in a desired fashion. These techniques show that children

Activity is essential to motor development—for example, children cannot learn how to climb unless they practise that activity.

between the ages of 3 and 5 frequently can focus their attention most effectively by active imitation. Varying types of follow-the-leader games are fun and reasonably successful. Gradually, the teacher can add verbal reminders to help children focus on a particular aspect of the physical activity. Finally, when children are 6 or even 7, they can attend closely to verbal instructions and follow them reasonably well, at least when participating in familiar tasks and activities (Zaporozlets & Elkonin, 1971; Zelazo & Reznick, 1991).

Researchers have recently explored the relationship between children's ability to follow the rules of a game or activity and their developmental age. Previously, researchers had successfully determined the rules that governed children's behaviour, but they had largely ignored the notion of *execution*, which is the translation of knowledge into behaviour. Younger children's inability to execute rules may have multiple causes. They may lack the ability to control their attention, which therefore impedes their following of rules. And, even if they have the necessary attention, younger children may have difficulty following rules because they can't inhibit irrelevant responses (Zelazo & Reznick, 1991).

Feedback The course of learning motor skills is also motivated by feedback. **Extrinsic feedback** comes in the form of rewards, such as cookies, candy, or praise given for a task well done. Specific feedback, such as "Now you've got a strong grip on the bar," is more useful than general praise. The anticipation or promise of rewards is the extrinsic motivation previously discussed. **Intrinsic feedback** is a crucial monitor for skill development. Children discover that there are certain natural consequences to their actions and that these results may be more precise than arbitrary extrinsic feedback. For example, when climbing a jungle gym, they may derive pleasure from feeling tension in their muscles or from experiencing being up high and seeing things that they cannot see from the ground. If they feel a bit wobbly, they will try to stabilize themselves. The "wobble" is intrinsic to the task and is usually more effective in making children aware of their need for safety than being told by an adult to be careful (which is extrinsic). Parents and teachers can help to point out the natural consequences of an action, but the learning process is most effective when a child has the experience itself.

Early childhood education programs often provide opportunities for daily practice of gross motor and fine motor skills. By and large, this practice is usually individual and self-motivated, not teacher directed. Considerable research suggests that self-paced and active play results in higher levels of physical-motor development (Johnson, Christie, & Yawkey, 1987). Furthermore, there is evidence that certain kinds of playgrounds and indoor play environments designed according to these principles support higher levels of play and of motor development (Frost & Sunderline, 1985). Teachers ideally prepare an environment that allows for active exploration and interaction with other children and with materials. Children are encouraged to express themselves freely and loudly in outdoor environments and to develop small muscle skills and endurance with a wide variety of materials.

extrinsic feedback Rewards of praise given for performing a task well.

intrinsic feedback Feedback that comes from experiencing the natural consequences of performing a task.

Environmental Factors Influencing Physical Development

Many factors influence the development of physical abilities in infants and young children. These factors may be separated into two major groups: first, those influences that cause normal variations in physical development, such as inherited size and body conformation, and second, environmental influences that produce optimal or abnormal patterns of physical development. This second group includes such factors as nutrition, illness, accidents, or a combination of factors that might, for example, be present for a homeless family. We shall focus on this second set of variables in this section of the chapter.

Nutrition

Nutritional problems have significant effects on the physical development of children. Poor nutrition may limit the size of children's bodies and brains. As we have seen in earlier chapters, sustained periods of malnutrition during crucial phases of brain development may permanently reduce children's cognitive abilities. Similarly, prolonged deprivation of essential nutrients may have pronounced effects on children's movement capacities and physical development.

Since children often appear to eat very little, parents may worry that their children are not eating enough. Despite this concern, children's nutritional requirements are easily satisfied. The necessary protein may come from milk or meat (including fish, cheese, or eggs). Carrots, green vegetables, or egg yolks supply vitamin A. Vitamin C can come from citrus fruits, tomatoes, and leafy green vegetables. Calcium may come from

FOCUS ON APPLICATION

Children's Food Preferences

Eating or ingesting food, besides breathing and excretion, is one of the most frequent human activities. Eating is also a very personal activity. Food is one of the major sources of pleasure for human beings and has great emotion attached to it. We tend to remember tastes and smells with fondness—for example, the scent of warm chocolate chip cookies or cinnamon—or with distaste—for example, the odour of soured milk or sewage. Food selection is also an important human activity. Searching for, selecting, and preparing food invariably take more time than ingesting it. A good example is the time spent preparing a holiday dinner compared with the relatively short time spent in eating it.

There are developmental differences in food selection and in the individual's ability to make good food selections. For the fetus, for example, the main source of nutrition is placentally delivered blood. After birth—in a relatively abrupt manner—the main food is maternally delivered milk, from either the breast or the bottle. Finally, and more gradually, the wide range of food products available to adults are introduced. In fact, the weaning process is often considered one of life's major transitions. What is of interest to researchers is the manner in which the child, after weaning, selects foods to consume. In some cases, children are

influenced by parents' specific instruction into the nature of foods and their appropriateness, while in other cases children are influenced by parents' modelling, without specific instruction (Rozin, 1990).

Another aspect of development is learning which substances are edible and which are inedible. Toddlers younger than 2 years of age tend to place everything in the mouth. Researchers offered children ranging

---

Toddlers younger than 2 years of age tend to place everything in the mouth.

---

from 18 months to 5 years of age a variety of items in a "cafeteria" setting. These items included normal foods, inedible items (sponge and paper), items offensive to adults (a whole dried fish, human hair, imitation dog feces), and dangerous items (imitation soap). Children under 2 years of age placed all of the items, except for hair, in their mouths. By 3 years of age, children refused many of the items that adults also rejected (Rozin et al., 1986). Given the tendency of young children to mouth any object, we may sometimes wonder how they safely negotiate young childhood without ingesting toxins, sharp

objects, and other unsafe items.

There are also cultural differences in food preferences. For example, foods such as eggs and grains, which may be present at any meal in developing countries, are limited to breakfast in the United States. Preschool children are also likely to combine foods they like regardless of the appropriateness of the context. For example, many preschoolers believe that if they like two foods, such as beef and whipped cream, then they will like these foods when they are combined. Many parents have suffered through meals where their children put apple sauce on beef or gravy on ice cream.

In general, various ways have been suggested to encourage good nutrition in early childhood. Offering a well-balanced array of foods, attractively served, is helpful. Given the size of young children's stomachs, a combination of small portions at meals and snacks at various times of the day are more likely to provide good nutrition. A pleasant mealtime experience, with little discussion of disliked foods or table manners, is beneficial to children's eating patterns. Finally, sugary foods and desserts generally provide calories—with little or no nutritional benefit—at considerable cost. Fruit is a better alternative for snacks or meals (Kendrick, Kaufmann, & Messenger, 1991).

cheese, yogurt, milk, figs, or broccoli (Kendrick, Kaufmann, & Messenger, 1991). Providing an assortment of fresh fruits, vegetables, and grains, along with low amounts of meat, provides enough protein, vitamins, and minerals for young children's health. No one food is essential for a child's diet or health. The key lies in offering attractively presented foods throughout the day—combined with not forcing children to eat when they refuse. Despite the message of television commercials that foods high in sugar and fat are "good," these foods are low in nutrients and do not provide the most nutritious source for children's growth (see the box "Children's Food Preferences").

Environmental Hazards and Accidents

Information about the child's motor development can determine when certain problems may occur and the points at which interventions should be introduced for at-risk children, for example, providing children with car seats:

> The young child (0–3 years) lacks the motor control (e.g., balance, coordination, strength) necessary to ensure his or her safety when riding in an automobile. In addition, the physical development of the infant renders him or her more susceptible to brain injury because of softer brain consistency and skull construction and because a greater proportion of body weight centred in the head pulls the head forward in collisions. Because of these vulnerabilities, it becomes particularly critical that prevention measures be taken by adults for restraining infants and young children in car seats. (Maddux, Roberts, Sledden, & Wright, 1986, p. 27)

Because of an awareness of motor development, pediatricians often engage in anticipatory guidance with parents—pointing out what sorts of accidents and hazards must be avoided at which ages. In general, the three greatest environmental hazards for preschoolers are automobiles, their own homes, and swimming pools. Each year, many young children die because of motor vehicle accidents, because they ingested toxic or caustic substances found in their houses or garages, or because they fell into a swimming pool and were unable to swim. Some other common environmental hazards are summarized in Table 9-2.

These accidental deaths are easily prevented. Infant car seats, fences around pools, and placement of dangerous substances in locked or very high cabinets effectively protect small children from their own inquisitiveness or lack of physical abilities. In addition, young children require careful monitoring during their play—whether indoors or outside—since they lack the cognitive ability to follow safety rules and may let their natural curiosity and urge to explore drive their behaviour.

Canadians have recently become aware that children's clothing can present a hazard. Between 1982 and 1993, at least seven Canadian children have died from suffocation when their jacket drawstrings got caught on playground equipment or fences (Francescutti, as cited in Thomson, 1996). Dr. Francescutti and other physicians are lobbying governments to ban drawstrings on children's clothing. Often, Velcro can easily replace the drawstrings.

Another hazard has to do with putting children in shopping carts, unrestrained. Some children attempt to stand or climb out and can fall on their heads, causing brain damage or death. Children should never be left unrestrained and unattended in shopping carts.

Lead Poisoning One specific environmental hazard that has evoked considerable concern is *lead poisoning*—damage caused by too much lead in the body. Even small amounts of lead can interfere with

Although preschoolers are especially vulnerable to accidents in the car, in their own homes, and in swimming pools, these accidents often can be prevented.

Table 9-2   Environmental Hazards and the Well-Being of Children

- Falls are the leading cause of injury-related hospitalization among 1- to 4-year-olds. Over 80 percent of falls happen in the home while children are playing, walking, or running. The most common situation is falling down stairs. Another common situation is running and falling onto something sharp or hard, such as the corner of a coffee table, fireplace, or cement basement floor. Children also trip and hurt themselves on objects in their hands or mouths, such as lollipops.

- Between 1982 and 1995, at least six Canadian children age 2 to 9 died from inhaling a latex balloon. In attempting to blow up a balloon, some children inhale instead of exhale and suck the balloon into their throats, causing suffocation. Other instances of choking and near choking involve seeds, nuts, bones, fruits, vegetables, candy, coins, and toys (such as marbles and small figurines).

- On Canadian farms, 50 percent of fatal machinery-related accidents happen to preschool children. The supervision of children on farms can be difficult because farms are often large, including several buildings, fields, and animal enclosures. Children can quickly wander off to explore parts of the farm that are unsafe. The type of machinery most commonly involved in accidents is the tractor. Other machinery involved in accidents are hay wagons, conveyors and elevators, grain augers, combines and harvesters, balers, and manure spreaders.

- Aboriginal preschoolers have a high rate of injuries (perhaps as a result of poor living conditions and unsafe housing). Compared with other Canadian preschoolers, Aboriginal children are five times more likely to die from their injuries.

- About 40 percent of children under the age of 6 live in a home with a regular smoker. Smoking indoors significantly worsens air quality. Smoke aggravates respiratory problems, such as asthma.

- Between 1974 and 1992, Canada made important gains in improving the quality of outdoor air. There was a decline in sulphur dioxide (found in emissions from power plants), nitrogen dioxide (found in emissions from automobiles), lead, dust, and smoke. Other hazardous toxins, such as ozone, have not improved or have increased. Ground-level ozone creates fog and is the most serious air pollution problem in some parts of Canada, including Toronto, Vancouver, Saint John, the lower Fraser Valley in British Columbia, and the region that stretches from Windsor, Ontario, to Quebec City.

- Today's children have a 1 in 120 chance of developing malignant melanoma, the most deadly form of skin cancer. They have a 1 in 7 chance of developing another type of skin cancer.

Sources: CCSD, 1996; Raizenne, Dales, & Burnett, 1998; *For the Safety of Canadian Children and Youth,* 1997.

children's learning and behaviour. In larger amounts, lead causes serious damage to the brain, kidneys, nervous system, and red blood cells. Because of young children's natural curiosity and their tendency to engage in hand-to-mouth activity, they are at the greatest risk of lead poisoning.

The major source of contamination from lead is lead-based paint that becomes chips or dust for children to swallow. Since the mid-1970s, paints have not contained lead, but older homes and buildings may contain layers of lead-based paint. Children become poisoned from eating, chewing, or sucking on objects coated with lead dust or chips. Soil also may be contaminated from paint that has weathered or has been sanded or scraped off buildings. In addition, auto exhaust of leaded gasoline may cause lead to accumulate in the soil. When children get contaminated dirt on their hands and then put their hands in their mouth, they may become lead poisoned (Kendrick, Kaufmann, & Messenger, 1991). Sometimes, household objects contain lead. For example, in the fall of 1996, many Canadians removed mini-blinds from their homes after it was announced that they contained lead. In the fall of 1998, Health Canada issued warnings about the presence of lead in some plastics and vinyl used to make knapsacks, children's baseball gloves, infant toys, and cables (for information on specific products, contact Health Canada at 1-888-774-1111 or check their Web site at www.hc-sc.gc.ca/advisory). Compared with older children and adults, preschool children and infants are more at risk for lead poisoning for two reasons: they are more likely to put lead-containing substances in their mouths, and they absorb more of the lead. Suppose people of different ages swallowed the same amount of lead. Through digestion, infants would absorb about 42 to 53 percent of the lead into their bloodstreams; 2- to 6-year-olds would absorb 30 to 40 percent; 6- to 7-year-olds would absorb 18 to 24 percent; and adults would absorb only 7 to 15 percent (Chance & Harmsen, 1998).

A number of steps can be taken to prevent lead poisoning. In 1997, government representatives of G7 countries met in Miami, Florida, to write the 1997 Declaration of the Environment Leaders of the Eight on Children's Environmental Health (cited in *Canadian Journal of Public Health,* 1998). They recommended eliminating lead from products intended for use by children or from products that come into contact with food or drinking water. They also advocated regular blood testing to monitor lead levels in children at risk for lead poisoning. Some preventive steps have already been taken. For example, many countries, including Canada, have restricted the use of lead in gasoline and paint. Some Canadian communities, such as Riverdale in southeast Toronto, have done major clean-ups to remove lead contaminated soil from residential areas and have instituted public education programs about lead poisoning (Chaudham, 1998).

The major psychological and behavioural effects of lead poisoning are encountered only when high levels of lead are present. Since the major contamination from lead has been reduced, the usual effects are subtle behavioural ones detectable only in fairly large studies (Berney, 1993). These effects include lower intellectual achievement and less appropriate school behaviour than that shown by the general population.

Unintentional Poisonings Unintentional poisoning refers to the ingestion, skin absorption, or inhalation of toxic solids, liquids, or fumes. Children of the ages 1 to 4 have the highest reported rate of unintentional poisoning in Canada (*For the Safety,* 1997). More than 90 percent of these poisonings occurred during unsupervised play. According to the Canadian Hospitals Injury Reporting and Prevention Program (CHIRPP, 1994), over 97 percent of poisonings occurred in the home. Over 40 percent happened in the bedroom or living room, 16.7 percent in the kitchen, and 11.4 percent in the bathroom. Fifty-nine percent involved medications, 14.4 percent resulted from household products, and 13.2 percent involved berries and fungi. Examples of verbatim reports given to Canadian Poison Control Centres are "[the child] was playing with little brother, opened the medicine cabinet and swallowed some acetaminophen syrup" and "was playing in the livingroom and swallowed 12 cigarettes." Sometimes adults mistakenly assume that 3- and 4-year-olds know better than to eat or drink poisons because the children are articulate and bright. This is a misconception. Even 4-year-olds are tempted to ingest pills or liquids if they resemble candies and favourite drinks.

What steps can be taken to prevent accidental poisonings in preschool children? *For the Safety of Canadian Children and Youth* (1997) recommends three steps. First, better public education about the risks of poisoning is required. Education should target parents and other child-care providers, children, and health-care professionals. Organizations that may be involved in education are the Red Cross, Canada Safety Council, provincial poison control centres, health-care workers, pharmacists, prescribing physicians, and pharmaceutical and chemical companies. Second, more use of child-resistant packaging is necessary. The Canadian government should amend its legislation so that child-resistant packaging is required for all potentially hazardous products. They should also restrict the size of child-resistant containers. Third, early treatments need to be available for home use. In the case of a poisoning, it is important to act quickly to prevent absorption into the bloodstream. Until recently, the best-known method was to administer ipecac syrup, which is available for home use in Canada. There is now a better method—the use of activated charcoal, which is used in Canadian hospitals and needs to be more available for home use.

The Problems of Low Income and Homelessness

One effect of the economic crises of the 1980s and 1990s has been an increase in the number of children living in poverty. By 1991, over 1.2 million Canadian children

FOCUS ON APPLICATION

Measuring Bacteria Levels in Ball Pit Play Areas

Preschool children love to jump into ball pits and toss balls around them or burrow their bodies underneath a pile of balls. However, according to nursing researchers, these public play areas may be the perfect breeding grounds for illness-causing bacteria (Davis et al., 1999). "The high turnover of children who play in the ball pits, the close contact that children have with each other, and the difficulty of disinfecting every ball within the ball pits pose a potential public health risk within the pediatric population" (Davis et al., 1999, p. 151). Ball pits in restaurants are of concern because children may alternate between playing and eating without washing their hands between the two activities.

The nursing researchers assessed the levels of bacteria in three randomly

---

These public play areas may be the perfect breeding grounds for illness-causing bacteria.

---

selected ball pit play areas in a mid-Atlantic city in the United States. They found a number of types of bacteria that were in high enough concentrations to cause illnesses such as diarrhea or infections. Infected children show symptoms of illness 5 to 10 days after exposure.

The researchers recommended three preventive measures: (1) develop better cleaning practices for ball pits to ensure that all balls, as well as the bottom of the pit, are sanitized; (2) insist that children wash their hands before playing so they do not introduce more bacteria into the play area; and (3) require children to wash their hands after play to remove any acquired bacteria.

---

were living in poverty, compared with just over 760 000 in 1981, an increase of almost 500 000 (CICH, 1994). In 1991, the highest rate of child poverty was in Manitoba, where one in three children under the age of 7 lived in poverty. The next highest rates were in Newfoundland and Saskatchewan, where one in four children under the age of 7 lived in poverty (CICH, 1994). "Canada has the second highest rate of child poverty among industrialized countries, second only to the United States" (CCSD, 1996, p. 22). At this point, we need to note that low income by itself is not a health hazard. Certainly, many families confront the challenges of limited income and with the help of friends and the community provide adequate food, health care, supervision, and education for their children.

Yet for some families, the risks of prolonged low income are too high, and they experience the cycle of poverty depicted in Figure 9-3. Poverty often becomes a cycle in which health, poor or inadequate nutrition, and school failure are interrelated, leading in turn to unemployment, environmental inadequacy, and other debilitating conditions that can be passed on to the next generation. Researchers have begun to focus on the life-course dynamics of poverty (McLoyd, 1998). The timing and duration of poverty are critical. Poverty during the first 5 years is the most detrimental to a child's schooling. It increases the risks for school failure and dropping out, more so than does poverty in middle childhood or adolescence. As well, persistent poverty is more damaging than a single, short-lived bout of poverty.

The effects of poverty on children are mediated by a number of factors. For example, children of fathers who have lost their income are often irritable, negative, and moody (Elder, Nguyen, & Caspi, 1985). The effects on the children occur not because the father lost his income, but because the father's behaviour changed. He became moodier, more irritable, tense, and explosive. He became more punitive and inconsistent in disciplining his children. In this way, children feel the effects of their parents' loss of income through changes in parenting behaviour.

The effects of poverty vary, depending on the neighbourhood that children live in (McLoyd, 1998). Good neighbourhood resources, such as strong schools and recreational programs, can lessen the negative effects of poverty. But dangerous neighbourhoods that lack resources can magnify the negative effects of poverty.

Bronfenbrenner's ecological model, discussed in Chapter 2, provides a useful framework for understanding the effects of poverty. Effects of poverty can be examined at all levels of Bronfenbrenner's model—microsystem, mesosystem, exosystem, and macrosystem. At the level of the microsystem, we look at how the child's home life contributes to the negative effects of poverty. Poor children are at risk for inadequate or unsafe housing, parents stressed by financial worries, and a lack of educational resources, such as books and computers. At the mesosystem level, we look at interactions among microsystems. Coming from a poor home has an effect on school. Poor children who come to school poorly dressed and hungry are at risk for being teased by other children and for academic difficulties. At the exosystem level, we look at social settings beyond the child's immediate experience that nonetheless affect him. For example, poor children are at risk for living in neighbourhoods that have gangs and organized drug trading. At the macrosystem level, we look at laws, customs, and values. Zoning bylaws affect poor children if they allow industrial development or high traffic density next to low-income housing. Both factors can worsen air quality and pose safety risks. Cultural notions about the cause of poverty affect government policies that affect low-income families. Do governments provide social safety nets and supports for needy families? Do they set minimum wages that are livable?

Of particular concern today are the increasing numbers of children who are not only poor, but also homeless. Badly housed or homeless children are at risk for a variety of physical and psychological problems. Lead poisoning and exposure to structural, electrical, and sanitation hazards associated with substandard housing are an example of these risks. Homeless children also face educational disruption, as they may change schools or school districts often. Some homeless children are separated from family members in the family's efforts to find shelter. Finally, homeless children are exposed to considerable emotional stress. The results of this sustained emotional stress have been compared with post-traumatic stress disorder. Young homeless children may have short attention spans, weak impulse control, speech delays, or sleep disorders. They may be either withdrawn or aggressive. Many regress to earlier behaviours, such as unusual dependency on parents or siblings (Children's Defense Fund, 1992). Some studies have found serious psychosocial problems in preschool homeless children. Anxiety, depression, and learning difficulties have been reported (Bassuk & Rosenberg, 1990).

Homeless children also often have potentially serious health problems. Intestinal parasites causing severe diarrhea, unmet acute and chronic medical needs, hepatitis,

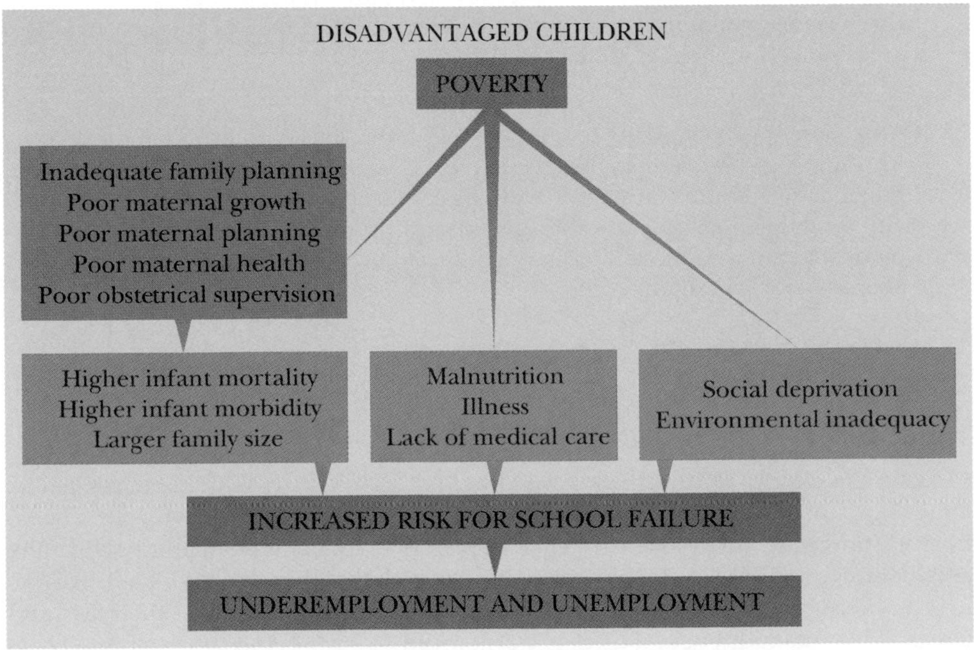

Question to Ponder

What causes poverty? How can we lessen its negative impact on children?

Figure 9-3
The Consequences of Poverty in Children

Source: Garmezy, N. (1991). Resiliency and vulnerability to adverse developmental outcomes associated with poverty. *American Behavioral Scientist, 34*(4), 419.

and AIDS have been found in homeless young children—who also exhibited developmental and school problems (Bass, Brennan, Mehta, & Kodzis, 1990). Homeless children are three times as likely as other children to have missed immunizations (Bassuk, 1991).

Resilient Children When discussing the effects of low income on children, there is often a tendency to overemphasize the negative impact on children. While poverty may challenge children, the majority will develop normally. In fact, considerable evidence suggests that despite the exposure to stressful and high-risk environments, many children do overcome life's difficulties. According to Werner, "Even in the most terrible homes, and beset with physical handicaps, some children appear to develop stable, healthy personalities and to display a remarkable degree of resilience, i.e., the ability to recover from or adjust easily to misfortune or sustained life stress" (1984, p. 87).

Most research, unfortunately, has focused on the negative outcomes associated with stresses, such as poverty and homelessness. But it is now clear that the protective factors that exist may modify these stresses. These protective factors include the following:

- Temperament.
- Reflectiveness in meeting new situations.
- Cognitive coping skills.
- Positive responsiveness to others.
- Warmth and cohesiveness of families.
- The presence of a caring adult.
- The presence of external support, such as a caring teacher or church that fosters ties to the larger community (Garmezy, 1991).

resilient children Children who develop normally despite exposure to persistent and/or prolonged stress.

Resilient children—children with these protective factors active in their lives—demonstrate unusual psychological strength, despite a history of severe or prolonged psychological stress. The following children are typical of these resilient individuals:

These were children like Michael for whom the odds, on paper, did not seem very promising. The son of teenage parents, Michael was born prematurely and spent his first three weeks of life in the hospital, separated from his mother. Immediately after Michael's birth, his father was sent with the Army to Southeast Asia for almost two years. By the time Michael was 8, he had three younger siblings and his parents were divorced. His mother left the area and had no further contact with the children.

And there was Mary, born to an overweight, nervous, and erratic mother who had experienced several miscarriages, and a father who was an unskilled farm labourer with only four years of education. Between Mary's fifth and tenth birthdays, her mother had several hospitalizations for repeated bouts with mental illness, after having inflicted both physical and emotional abuse on her daughter.

Yet both Michael and Mary, by age 18, were individuals with high self-esteem and sound values, caring for others and liked by their peers, successful in school and looking forward to their adult futures. (Werner, 1984, p. 87)

Of the positive attributes displayed by children in poverty, some are instilled by family or schools or other social institutions, such as churches. Others appear to be inherently present in children as a function of their temperament or cognitive skills. One persistent characteristic of resilient children is the faith that things will work out. This belief can be sustained if children encounter people who give meaning to their lives and a reason for commitment and caring (Werner, 1984). For instance, the Centre Locale

Service Communautaire (CLSC), Hochelaga Maisonneuve's mission in Montreal, aims to help families at the fringes of society, battling isolation, sexual abuse, family violence, illiteracy, addiction, delinquency, and crime (Vanier, 1996). In addition to providing services to the parents, the mission focuses on the children and on the families as a whole. The children are involved in social and academic programs, such as homework help, and early interventions for language and behavioural problems, as well as family-oriented social events.

The research on resilient children points out the need to avoid categorically labelling poor children as disadvantaged. Many of them, with the appropriate environmental and emotional supports, may well be resilient. Research on these children focuses on the "self-righting" tendencies that appear to move some children to normal development despite persistently adverse environmental conditions. "Children who do well have adults who care for them, brains that are developing normally, and, as they grow older, the ability to manage their own attention, emotions, and behaviour" (Masten & Coatsworth, 1998, p. 215). But, at the same time, it is important to note that poor children are more likely to become ill and have more serious illnesses, as shown in Table 9-3. This tendency results from increased environmental risk associated with poor housing, hazardous neighbourhoods, poor nutrition, and inadequate preventive care. The higher rates of serious illness and of death from diseases of childhood also reflect poor access to medical care.

The presence of at least one caring adult helps children to modify the negative effects of constant stress.

Health and Illness

Illness

Young children are healthy by adult standards because, on average, they have fewer chronic disabling or life-threatening disorders than adults. But children are also in a different developmental phase than adults. Ill health may be manifested by delays or reversals in development—by delays in the child's achieving developmental milestones. In addition, the implications of labelling are greater for children than for adults. For example, a health status measure that emphasizes handicaps may make children appear to be more disabled than they are. Children have inherently greater developmental potential and greater capacity to adapt or compensate for their infirmities than do adults (Starfield, 1992).

During early childhood, the most common acute conditions are upper respiratory problems. Asthma accounts for more hospital admissions of Canadian preschool-age children than any other illness (CICH, 1994). The second and third most common types of conditions are problems of the digestive system and injury. The frequencies for both illness and injury are greater for males than females during the preschool years. The most common problem, affecting 12 percent of children in a single year, is allergy. Ear infections and nonspecific symptoms, such as skin rashes, headache, or anemia, also occur quite frequently. Chronic medical conditions are present in about 7 percent of children. These conditions include asthma, heart conditions, arthritis, epilepsy, and diabetes.

In the past, the common view was that children with severe chronic illness die in childhood. However, current estimates of survival suggest that at least 90 percent of children—even with very severe long-term illnesses—survive to adulthood. This change is largely due to improved medical and surgical technologies, as well as to the availability of sophisticated medical care. The focus of health care for such children today is on improving the quality of their lives, rather than merely ensuring their survival. Many of them are unable to participate actively in most aspects of life.

Table 9-3 Relative Frequency of Health Problems in Low-Income Children Compared with Other Children

HEALTH PROBLEM	RELATIVE FREQUENCY IN LOW-INCOME CHILDREN
Low birth weight	double
Delayed immunization	triple
Asthma	higher
Bacterial meningitis	double
Rheumatic fever	double to triple
Lead poisoning	triple
Neonatal mortality	1.5 times
Postneonatal mortality	double to triple
Child deaths owing to accidents	double to triple
Child deaths owing to disease	triple to quadruple
Complications of appendicitis	double to triple
Diabetic ketoacidosis	double
Complications of bacterial meningitis	double to triple
Percent with conditions limiting school activity	double to triple
Lost school days	40 percent or more
Severely impaired vision	double to triple
Severe iron-deficiency anemia	double

Source: Starfield, 1992.

Chronic Illness

The total prevalence of chronically ill or disabled children in the population has been estimated at between 10 and 30 percent (Perrin, Guyer, & Lawrence, 1992). The majority of these conditions are mild and have little impact on children's daily activities or use of health services. About 10 percent of children with chronic illnesses, however, have their quality and quantity of life seriously affected by their illness or disabling condition. Among this group, only asthma and congenital heart disease occur with any great frequency. Other conditions—such as leukemia, epilepsy, kidney failure, or arthritis—are rare. For these children, the low numbers fail to accurately reflect the disproportionately greater strain on them and on their families imposed by their chronic illness or disability. Diseases such as leukemia (cancer of the white blood cells), muscular dystrophy (a progressive loss of motor functioning leading to death), or cerebral palsy (a disorder of muscles producing varying degrees of movement impairment) and disabilities such as blindness or deafness all occur in less than 1 percent of the population, but their effects may be devastating at worst and challenging at best for the child and family.

Two of the more common chronic illnesses children encounter are diabetes and asthma. In addition, AIDS has emerged as a concern in early childhood, although the number of affected children remains low. We shall briefly discuss some key aspects of these chronic illnesses and their impact on the children experiencing them.

Diabetes Diabetes is a disorder of metabolism caused by the failure of the pancreas, a gland located behind the stomach, to produce a chemical called *insulin*. Insulin helps the body store and use glucose (sugar) and metabolize fat. Without insulin, cells in the body cannot use the body's glucose and thus obtain insufficient nourishment.

When children have diabetes, they usually require adding insulin to their bodies every day through injections—typically one in the morning and one in the late afternoon. Diabetic children also need to follow a special low sugar, low fat diet, which

Although young children are healthier than adults, they still get sick. Chronic conditions affecting children include asthma and arthritis.

must be balanced with exercise. Food makes glucose rise in the blood, while insulin and exercise make it decrease. Children with diabetes often have difficulty balancing their blood sugar and may swing between hypoglycemia (low blood sugar) and hyperglycemia (blood sugar levels that are too high). Sugar levels that are too high may result in a diabetic coma; however, this outcome is rare in children who are being adequately monitored for their sugar levels. The more common hypoglycemic or insulin reaction may result in unconsciousness and convulsions if not treated promptly. The usual treatment is to provide sugar immediately in the form of orange juice or sugar tablets (Kendrick, Kaufmann, & Messenger, 1991). Parents of diabetic children report that most children as young as 5 years know when they are hypoglycemic and how to treat it (Faulkner, 1996).

One of the challenges of managing diabetes in children is ensuring that they comply with the dietary restrictions and that they eat at regular times. As well, the children have to put up with insulin injections and regular blood tests. Some preschoolers may find the frequent needles difficult. (See the box "Helping Children Manage Pain.") By the time they are 12 years old, many diabetic children have started to give their own injections and have assumed responsibility for other aspects of the diabetic routine (Faulkner, 1996).

Asthma Asthma is a chronic lung disease involving the restriction of air flow into the lungs. It can be mild or severe, and in rare cases it is life threatening. The symptoms of an asthma attack usually include wheezing, breathing difficulties, coughing, and a feeling of constriction in the chest. For most asthmatic children, antihistamines or bronchial dilators successfully control their symptoms most of the time.

It is important to consider asthma from a developmental perspective because having asthma can affect the child's development and the child's age can affect his reactions to asthma and its treatments (Ladebauche, 1997). Asthmatic infants often are more at risk for serious complications that require hospitalization during attacks. Hospitalization is especially stressful to 7- to 9-month-old infants if it involves separation from parents and being treated by hospital staff who are strangers. Wariness of strangers is normal at this age.

As infants develop into toddlers, the developmental issues associated with asthma change. The toddler's more advanced physical development is usually associated with wider airways and decreased risk of an asthmatic attack leading to respiratory distress. Toddlers experiencing asthma attacks may become frightened and may panic and cry. Emotional support for toddlers is critical. It is normal for toddlers to become assertive ("No!" is a favourite expression). They may resist treatments or insist, "I can do

For most asthmatic children, antihistamines or bronchial dilators successfully control their symptoms most of the time.

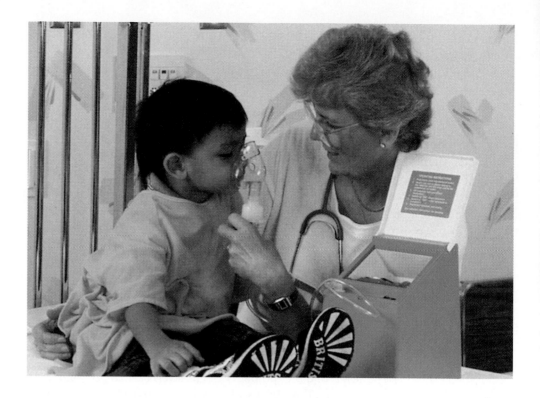

it myself." When possible, toddlers should be active in their treatment. Toddlers who have frequent or severe asthma attacks may start to act like infants. This stress reaction, called *regression,* is normal and transient. A toddler's sense of security can be increased by maintaining rituals (such as bedtime rituals) and routines so that the child has some predictability in his life.

Preschool children with asthma need to be given as many opportunities as possible to participate in "normal" activities and to interact with peers so that the children develop a healthy sense of initiative. Preschool children are able to understand more about asthma and treatment than toddlers, but they still have difficulty understanding the cause of their asthma. Preschool children sometimes see illness as punishment. They may feel they are to blame for their asthma attacks.

In the elementary school years, asthma can affect the child's body image and self-concept. The peer group's reaction to the asthma symptoms and treatment can have a major effect on the child's social development.

Many children outgrow asthma as they mature but may still show evidence of exercise-induced asthma as adults. Since physical activity often brings on asthma attacks, children with asthma have frequently been restricted in their physical activity by their parents and may have anxiety about participating in such activities (Nichols, 1990).

AIDS As of December 1995, there have been a total of 118 cases of acquired immune deficiency syndrome (AIDS) in children reported in Canada (*Canada Year Book,* 1997). It is important to note that not all children with AIDS are affected in the same way. Some children, infected prenatally by their mothers, develop severe symptoms before their first birthdays. The symptoms include severe failure to thrive, frequent infections, abnormal brain development, and a particular type of pneumonia called PCP (Riddel & Moon, 1996). These babies are critically ill and do not live long. But other children with AIDS develop their first symptoms after the age of 1 year. It is unclear how these children contracted AIDS—perhaps prenatally from their mothers or after birth from blood transfusions, breastfeeding, or sexual abuse. In any case, the disease progresses much more slowly in these children, and a study in Italy reports that 45.5 percent of them are still alive at age 9 (Riddel & Moon, 1996). In the United States, Riddel and Moon report that many children with AIDS now live to adolescence. Therefore, some children with AIDS will have chronic courses of illness and will have to cope with a variety of physical, psychological, and social problems.

The physical problems associated with AIDS are varied and somewhat unpredictable. Individual children show different patterns of problems. The most common effects include skin rashes; yeast infections (candida) of the esophagus, making it painful to swallow; digestive problems and recurrent diarrhea; anemia; pneumonia; infected sinuses that cause severe headaches; and chronic ear infections (Boland & Oleske, 1995). Many of these problems cause severe pain and discomfort. (See the box "Helping Children Manage Pain.")

The physical problems often are severe enough to cause frequent absences from school and hospitalization. Consequently, children may find it difficult to keep up with their school work and social lives. In addition, between 40 and 90 percent of AIDS-infected children have neurological impairment from AIDS (Henna & Mintz, 1995). Younger children with neurological impairment show extreme developmental delays. Older children lose the ability to pay attention and concentrate, become uncoordinated, and may develop some unusual behaviours.

Children with AIDS often have a number of psychological and social problems to deal with—more so than children with other types of chronic illness. For example, many AIDS-infected children also have to face the deaths of parents from AIDS. Boland and Oleske (1995) found that 76 percent of AIDS-infected children had lost a parent to AIDS by the time they were 9 years old. Children with AIDS also have more conflict over the disclosure of the diagnosis because of the stigma attached to AIDS (Pollock & Thompson, 1995). Children may encounter hostile reactions from other children and adults and may be excluded from their social settings. Some people, afraid of contracting the illness themselves, may avoid all contact with AIDS-infected children, even though no studies have shown that AIDS can be contracted through casual interactions. In fact, a study of 25 AIDS-infected preschool children and their 89 family members found that none of the family members became infected, even though they shared many items, hugged, kissed, slept in the same beds, and bathed with the infected children (Rogers et al., 1990).

Teachers need up-to-date information about AIDS, so that they are adequately informed about teaching children with the disease. A study of day-care workers in Quebec found that 56 percent of teachers felt ready to work with children infected with HIV (Renaud, Ryan, Cloutier, Urbanek, & Haley, 1997). However, after receiving educational sessions about HIV and AIDS, 86 percent of teachers felt ready to work with HIV-infected children. A slightly older study in Manitoba found that only 41 percent of public school teachers believed that they had sufficient resources for HIV-infected students, and only 34 percent of the teachers believed that teachers should accept HIV-infected students like any other students with special needs (Lebrun & Freeze, 1995).

Chronic Health Problems and the Family

Families provide the bulk of care for children with chronic and disabling conditions. Mothers of chronically impaired children are significantly less likely than the mothers of healthy children to be employed outside the home. In the past, children cared for at home were likely to be moderately impaired. With today's medical technology, severely impaired children requiring respirators or intravenous or tube feeding also are likely to receive care at home. Many of these children require extensive nursing care, monitoring, and the use of complex equipment on a 24-hour basis.

Serious illness or disability has a significant impact on the lives of affected children and their families. The following features have been found in families caring for seriously impaired children:

- Disruptions in school attendance and achievement for the child and siblings.
- Decreased peer contacts and friendships.
- Adjustment problems in both the child and siblings.

FOCUS ON AN ISSUE

Helping Children Manage Pain

Children with chronic illnesses often experience pain from the illnesses and from the medical procedures used to monitor and treat them. In the past, children were undertreated for pain because of the common misconception that children do not feel as much pain as adults and because of concerns about pain medications being too strong, and potentially dangerous, for children. Even as recently as 1998, a nursing study conducted in British Columbia found problems with pain control in children after surgery (Boughton et al., 1998). A quarter of the children received no pain relief, and another quarter received only partial relief with medication.

One way to improve pain control is to refine the use of medications. In addition, a number of psychological methods have been developed to treat pain in children:

1. *Distracting children.* This method involves directing the children's attention away from the pain and is particularly useful with preschool children who face painful or frightening medical procedures, such as blood tests (venipuncture). Blowing bubbles and singing are especially good distracters because they also help the children stay relaxed, and people experience less pain when relaxed than when tense or anxious. When children blow bubbles or sing, they must breathe slowly, and so they will not hyperventilate. Other ways to distract children include reading them stories (especially pop-up books), touching or massaging them on body parts other than where the pain is, rocking them, and playing them movies or music.

2. *Employing children's imaginations.* Older children can cope with pain by using their imaginations. For example, children can imagine that they put on magic gloves that have the power to lessen pain in whatever body parts they touch. Surprisingly, this technique works for some children (Torrance, Lewis, La Brie, & Czarniecki, 1995). Perhaps it works because pain is complicated—it is

Older children can cope with pain by using their imaginations.

more than just physical sensations, involving also fear and emotional suffering. Other techniques children can use include imagining that they are superheroes or superheroines who can conquer the pain; imagining that they can leave their bodies and go to places where there is less or no pain; imagining that they have switches they can use to turn down or off the pain; and imagining that they have magic wands that can make the pain disappear.

3. *Educating children about illnesses and treatments.* Children need clear and age-appropriate information about their illnesses and treatments. Otherwise, they may develop mistaken ideas about why they are sick

Children can be taught techniques to help them cope with pain.

and receiving treatment. For example, a child may assume that he developed asthma because he went outside with wet hair after swimming and was warned that if he did so, he would get sick. Or the child might think he is ill because he ate gum off the sidewalk or did not eat all his vegetables, or because he is being punished for some misbehaviour. Confused and frightened children will be more anxious and experience more pain. Children need information to prevent them from inventing their own explanations and to help make their illnesses and treatments more predictable, so that they can feel more in control. For instance, many pediatric cancer clinics have books for children that explain cancer and its treatment in language children can understand. Cancer clinics also have dolls, toy needles, and other medical apparatus that children can play with to help them deal with their illnesses and treatments.

Question to Ponder

How do you think children's physical development affects their psychological development?

- Depression and anxiety in the mother.
- Marital stress and disruption for the father and mother. (Varni & Babani, 1986)

In general, the successful mainstreaming of chronically ill and disabled children depends on their social competence skills and social acceptance. Controlling the level of stress within the family also assists in the child's overall adjustment—both within and outside of the family setting. Self-help or support groups often help families with ill or disabled children to reduce the stress and sense of isolation associated with caregiving.

Psychological Effects of Chronic Health Problems About 80 percent of children with chronic health problems are amazingly resilient and adapt well to the stresses of their health conditions (Vessey, 1999). The other 20 percent, however, experience behavioural, achievement, or psychiatric problems. Many studies have found that children with chronic health problems have twice the risk of having significant behavioural and psychiatric problems than healthy children. These studies have also found that the severity of the chronic disorder does not seem to raise or lower this risk—any chronic health problem carries the same relative risk (Perrin, Guyer, & Lawrence, 1992).

Children with chronic illnesses also have difficulty participating in preschool and school activities. In addition, many developmental disabilities require that special education services be provided to meet the child's special educational and physical needs. For the most part, however, chronic illnesses do not create a direct impact on the child's actual ability to learn. The effects are rather indirect and include excessive fatigue or the effect of medication on the child's abilities.

The most common problems chronically ill children face are absence from normal daily activities, such as school, preschool, or social groups. Children with recurring acute episodes such as those associated with asthma may often miss extended blocks of activities. As was stated recently,

> Many years ago, when the issue for these children was planning for premature death, schooling was considered unimportant; today, with most children surviving to adulthood, there is a great need to improve educational opportunities and to diminish the effects of illness or its treatment on the child's participation in school. (Perrin, Guyer, & Lawrence, 1992, p. 72)

Early Intervention As with many social or intellectual problems, prevention is the best way to deal with children's health problems. For example, preventing children's contracting AIDS is a better alternative than treating the child until death. However, since prevention is not always possible, early intervention is the next most desirable alternative.

When children with significant health problems and their families receive early diagnosis and treatment, the child's potential for optimal development is maximized, and she is less likely to suffer developmental delays. The family often becomes part of a support network of health-care providers, rehabilitation experts, and lay people that may help reduce the stress of family members, while enhancing their caregiving capabilities. If disabled children and toddlers receive early intervention, the educational costs to society are reduced by minimizing the need for special education and related

Early intervention helps this child develop the skills to participate fully with his peers.

services after they reach school age. Furthermore, early intervention minimizes the likelihood that disabled or seriously ill children will be institutionalized and increases the opportunities for more independent living in society after the child matures. Positive results have been achieved in child–adult interactions when parents have been trained to work with their children. The earlier this positive dialogue occurs, the better the developmental outcome (Gallagher, 1989).

The emphasis of intervention is generally on helping the parent or offering direct help to the child—based on the underlying belief that the child is a capable individual who, with effort, will succeed at a variety of tasks, ranging from the concrete to the abstract. The focus is often on proactive planning—planning ahead to prepare the child with basic skills that will allow him to successfully participate in various activities both within and outside of the family. Another focus is self-efficacy—preparing the child to do things alone, with assistance if need be, but with the child as the primary agent. The most effective programs appear to be those involving parent education, long duration of support and follow-up, and tasks that strongly encourage active hypothesis testing by the child so that he maintains high levels of motivation and effort (Cratty, 1986).

Summary and Conclusions

The period of early childhood is one of expanding skills. An example of this development may be found in comparing the relatively incompetent toddler at 2 years to the relatively mature child at 6 years. Although there is still a great deal to learn and a long way to go, the 6-year-old is well on her way. The average 2- to 3-year-old is embarking on a period of rapid learning and growth. Parents and students tend to expect more of children this age—particularly in terms of physical skills and in understanding the adult world—than they are capable of performing. The achievement of language has a tendency to make many adults view children as slightly smaller versions of themselves.

While this chapter has emphasized the physical development of early childhood, in fact, this is a somewhat arbitrary distinction, since children develop holistically. Physical, cognitive, and social aspects of child development are closely linked. The child grows and learns as one "dynamic system." The child's actions reflect her intentions and understandings of the world around her. Conversely, the child's physical size and physical activities, for example, affect her understanding of her world and her social behaviour, as well as the reactions of her parents and the social acceptance by her peers—which in turn affect her physical activities, and so it goes.

In terms of physical growth, early childhood presents the child's transition from a chubby, wide-stance toddler to the taller, more slender 6-year-old. On average, boys are slightly heavier and taller than girls, and girls naturally have a bit more fatty tissue. However, when size is controlled, boys and girls show equal strength and overall physical prowess. Although girls and boys tend to attribute greater strength to boys, it is in reality untrue.

Important internal changes also occur during early childhood. Cartilage hardens into bone in many growth areas of the body. New bones are formed in the wrist, hand, ankle, and foot. All this skeletal growth adds protection to the child's growing internal organs and gives the child a firmer shape. Internal organs, such as the lungs and circulatory system, increase in capacity and hence cause the child to have greater stamina and resistance to disease. Muscles and ligaments grow stronger gradually and pace the way for more advanced motor skills.

Considerable growth also occurs in the brain and central nervous system. The right and left hemispheres become specialized for different functions in a process called lateralization. As major areas of the brain develop, attention, balance, and the control of body movement also improve.

Growth has slowed for young children, so they usually have smaller appetites than before and often become picky eaters. Because calorie intake is small, the need for a high-quality diet for preschoolers is important. A balance of milk and milk products, meat or meat alternatives, vegetables, fruit, and bread and cereals is required.

Some children are at particular risk for problems in physical development, as well as cognitive and social development. These children include those from low-income families, especially the homeless, and children with chronic illness or disabling conditions. In general, the interventions suggested to enhance these children's overall health and physical functioning are broad based. They include parent education, remedial education for the child, and a network of appropriate agencies to help address the complex needs of the families of children with special needs.

Finally, it is important to note that not all children who are raised in environments of poverty, poor nutrition, or violence will be negatively affected. In many cases, resilient children arise in these settings, that is, children who develop normally despite the various negative conditions around them. These children have strong self-concepts, good coping skills, and warm temperaments. In addition, they have often benefited from an individual—whether teacher, parent, or other—who cared specially for them. Research on resilient children suggests new directions for future interventions with children at risk.

Key Terms and Concepts

competence motivation (p. 279)

epiphysis (p. 270)

extrinsic feedback (p. 281)

fine motor skills (p. 274)

functional subordination (p. 275)

gross motor skills (p. 274)

intrinsic feedback (p. 281)

lateralization (p. 272)

resilient children (p. 288)

Questions to Review

1. Describe the relationship between physical-motor development and cognitive development in preschool children. Distinguish between continuous, discontinuous, and functionally subordinate developmental sequences.

2. Compare and contrast the physical development of 2- and 3-year-olds and that of 4- and 5-year-olds.

3. What important conditions are required for physical-motor learning?

4. What environmental variables influence physical development in children?

5. Discuss environmental hazards that pose a risk for the safety and well-being of preschool children.

6. How does poverty affect health in early childhood? What sorts of illnesses occur disproportionately among poor children? What effect do they have on physical development?

7. How does serious chronic illness or a disabling condition affect young children? What special problems do their families face?

8. Describe the individual and environmental factors that are believed to produce resilient children. How could these factors be used to develop intervention programs for children who are at risk in early childhood?

Weblinks

www.vifamily.ca/
The Vanier Institute of the Family
This Canadian site examines issues and trends that are critical to the well-being and healthy functioning of Canadian families. It supplies information on poverty and families with special needs.

www.cpha.ca/clearinghouse_e.htm
The Canadian HIV/AIDS Clearinghouse
This is an up-to-date site on HIV/AIDS in Canada. Information is provided on prevention and on support for health-care workers and schools that deal with HIV infection. As well, the site has links to publications, policies, program descriptions, and news releases.

www.sass.ca/
Stay Alert … Stay Safe
This site provides resources for children and adults and includes information on Canada's leading street-proofing program for children ages 7 to 10.

Early Childhood: Developing Thought and Action

Thou straggler into loving arms,
Young climber up of knees,
When I forget thy thousand ways,
Then life and all shall cease.

MARY ANNE LAMB
"A CHILD"

Outline

CHAPTER 10

Objectives

By the time you have finished this chapter, you should be able to do the following:

✔ Describe the aspects and limitations of preoperational thought.

✔ Explain Piaget's view of preschool children and the strengths and weaknesses of his theory.

✔ Describe the memory capabilities of preschool children.

✔ Describe the development of children's theory of mind.

✔ Describe the major types of children's play and how they influence childhood development.

✔ Describe the role of art in childhood development.

✔ Understand the positive role of cognitive immaturity in children's cognitive development.

✔ Describe the different approaches to early childhood education.

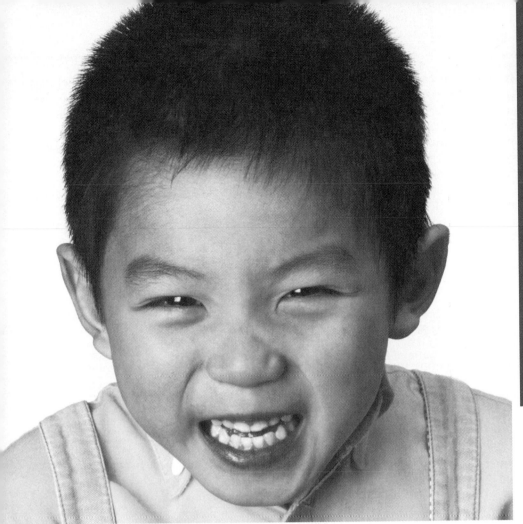

"Mother, who was born first, you or I?"

"Daddy, when you were little, were you a boy or a girl?"

"What is a knife—the fork's husband?"

The mother was breast-feeding her newborn daughter. Her 5-year-old son observed her closely and asked with utter seriousness, "Mommy, do you have coffee there sometimes, too?" (Chukovsky, 1963, pp. 21, 22, 24)

Preschool children, relative newcomers in this world, often demonstrate their thinking in ways that are both amusing and thought provoking. These comments, collected by Kornei Chukovsky, a Russian poet and observer of children's behaviour, reveal more about children than the fact that they make errors and have limited knowledge. They also show what an enormous distance preschool children must cover between the ages of 2 and 6 in order to develop the thought processes necessary for them to begin school. During this four-year period, young children change from "magicians," who can make things appear by turning their heads or disappear by closing their eyes, to concept-forming, linguistically competent realists (Fraiberg, 1959). They discover what they can and cannot control. They try to generalize from experience. Their reasoning changes from simple association to the beginnings of logic, and they acquire the language necessary to express their needs, thoughts, and feelings.

Conversations with preschoolers run the gamut from the hilarious to the frustrating—hilarious because of questions and word use, as in the examples above, and frustrating because of difficulties in deciphering what the child is saying. Sometimes parents may even have to ask their 4-year-old what their 3-year-old is saying. This questioning can lead to a knowing smile between the children, who are somewhat pleased with their alliance. A child may—in all seriousness—say, "Mom, I'm worried because my teacher says I have fossils!" The worried parent, who is looking for any evidence of ossified bony protuberances on her child, suddenly realizes that what he means is freckles! Communication can be challenging for the parents of young children.

In this chapter, we will concentrate on the different dimensions of developing cognitive competence during early childhood. As we saw in Chapter 9, this is the period during which the physical-motor skills of children rapidly develop. Children also make dramatic discoveries about the world around them by using their growing cognitive abilities. It is often difficult to disentangle the contributions of physical and cognitive development, but in this chapter we shall focus on the growth in cognition that occurs during early childhood.

Cognitive Development

In his pioneering investigation of how logical thinking develops in children, Jean Piaget described the course of development in terms of discrete periods that children pass through on the way to a logical understanding of the world (see Chapter 2). Piaget formulated a theory about how the process of thinking, or cognition, develops. Piaget's theory is based on the premise that human beings actively construct a personal understanding of the world. Children build their own reality based on their level of thinking. For instance, a child's understanding of a particular event, such as her mother's walking out the front door and waving good-bye, will vary depending on whether the child understands that her mother will continue to exist when the child doesn't see her.

Piaget viewed children as little scientists working diligently to figure out how the world works. According to this view, children do not merely absorb knowledge passively. Instead, they actively explore their surroundings, trying to comprehend new information based on their current patterns of understanding. Piaget studied the development of children's thinking by focusing on four stages, or periods, of intellectual development.

The first stage, the sensorimotor period of infancy, was discussed in depth in Chapter 6. The infant's intelligence is composed of sensory and action schemes used to explore the world. Toward the end of the sensorimotor period, children begin to show the capacity to understand the world through symbolization. The child's most dramatic use of symbols occurs during the beginning of language use.

Piaget called the second period, which generally spans ages 2 to 7, preoperational. The exact ages associated with the stage can vary from child to child, but the stage always occurs in the same order, that is, after the sensorimotor stage and before the concrete operational stage. During the preoperational period, children continue to expand their understanding of the world, using their increasing language and problem-solving skills. But Piaget theorized—based on his now-famous cognitive experiments—that during this age period children have not yet achieved the mental capacities necessary to understand many basic logical operations needed to correctly interpret reality. These operations include most concepts of number, cause and effect, time, and space. (According to Piaget's cognitive theory, these operations will be accomplished during the concrete operational stage, which comes after the preoperational period.)

We shall first discuss the dramatic cognitive advances made by preschool children in terms of Piaget's preoperational stage of development. Then we will present theories that challenge some of Piaget's conclusions about young children's cognitive abilities and how they develop. These theories also address aspects of cognitive development not covered by Piaget. We will look at children's memory and theory of mind. While not all researchers may agree on the exact nature of cognitive development, there is consensus on the tremendous increase in cognitive abilities during early childhood. Children, who enter this period with only rudimentary language and thought abilities, leave it asking questions such as, "Where did grandpa go when he died?" or "Do you see the butterfly lights on the houses at night?" The transition is both exciting and challenging.

Aspects of Preoperational Thought

The preoperational period lasts from about ages 2 to 7 and is divided into two parts—the *preconceptual stage* (from age 2 to about age 4) and the *intuitive*, or *transitional*, *stage* (from about ages 5 to 7).

The preconceptual stage is highlighted by the increasing use of symbols, symbolic play, and language. Previously, thought was limited to the infant's immediate environment. Now, the use of symbols and symbolic play marks the child's ability to think about something not immediately present. This ability gives the mind greater flexibility (Siegler, 1991). Similarly, words now have the power to communicate, even in the absence of the things they name. Children in the preconceptual stage still have difficulty with major categories, however. They cannot distinguish between mental, physical, and social reality. For instance, they think anything that moves is alive—even the moon and clouds—a cognitive pattern called *animism*. Children expect the inanimate world to obey their commands, and they do not realize that physical law is separate from human moral law. These traits stem partly from children's self-centred view of the world, or **egocentricity**; they are unable to separate clearly the realm of personal existence and power from everything else (Brown, 1965; Siegler, 1991).

The intuitive, or transitional, stage begins roughly at age 4. The transitional child begins to separate mental from physical reality and to understand mechanical causation apart from social norms. For example, before this stage of development, children may think that everything was created by their parents or some other adult. Now, they begin to grasp the significance of other forces. Intuitive children are beginning to understand multiple points of view and relational concepts, although in an inconsistent and incomplete way. Their comprehension of arrangements by size, numbers, and spatial classification is incomplete. Transitional children are unable to perform many basic mental operations.

One of the critical activities throughout the preoperational period is the development of symbolic representation. Without it, there could be no symbolic play, no language, not even a basic understanding of multiple points of view. Symbolic representation involves the child's taking an external object or event and creating an internal representation of it—in some cases, this may be a sort of "picture" of the person or event, while in others, it may be the creation of something that represents the person or event, such as a word.

egocentricity Having a self-centred view of the world—viewing everything in relation to oneself.

Representation

The most dramatic cognitive difference between infants and 2-year-olds is the ability to use symbols—that is, to use actions, images, or words to represent events or experiences. This ability is seen most clearly in the development of language (covered in Chapter 8) and in pretend, or symbolic, play (Flavell, Miller, & Miller, 1993). Two-year-olds are able to imitate past events, roles, and actions. By gestures in play, preschoolers may act out an extensive sequence that represents a car ride. Given other props, they may act out a family dinner or imitate a babysitter or a favourite book or television character.

The ability to use numbers to represent the quantity of objects in a particular array is another use of representation that we will discuss in more detail later in this chapter. The acquisition of skills in drawing and artistic representation also begins during this period.

Two-year-olds develop the ability to use symbols to represent actions, events, and objects—one of the milestones in cognitive development. This young businessperson is reading her newspaper during her commute to work.

sociocentric Emphasizing the shared or social interpretation of a situation, as opposed to an egocentric view, which ignores the reality of others.

sociodramatic play Pretend play in which children take on the personas, actions, and scripts of other persons or objects to play out a temporal drama.

Question to Ponder

Children often are asked to give eyewitness accounts of crimes they allegedly observed. How can you tell whether a child is giving an accurate or an inaccurate account?

Although symbolic representation starts at the end of the sensorimotor period, it is a continuing process; a child is much better at symbolization at age 4 than at age 2. In experiments with young children, Elder and Pederson (1978) found that the youngest children (2½ years old) needed props similar to the real object for their pretending games. But the 3½-year-olds were able to represent objects with quite different props or to act out a situation without props. For instance, they could pretend that a hairbrush was a pitcher and even pretend to use a pitcher with no props at all.

Once children begin to use symbols, their thought processes become more complex (Piaget, 1950, 1951). They show that they perceive the similarity between two objects or two events by giving them the same name; they become aware of the past and form expectations for the future; and they distinguish between themselves and the person they are addressing. Fein (1981) suggests that symbolic play may help children in two other ways:

1. It may help them become more sensitive to the feelings and points of view of others.
2. It may help them understand how an object can change in shape or form and still be the same object.

This increased sensitivity to others helps the child make the transition into more **sociocentric**, rather than egocentric, thinking, which involves understanding what others think or feel. While this kind of thinking requires many more years to mature, it begins in the new symbolic representational abilities of the preschooler.

Pretend and Real

When children are involved in pretend play, they usually participate in two levels of representation, or meaning—the level of the reality-based meaning of actions and objects, and the level of the pretend meaning of actions and objects. According to Bateson (1955), children must maintain two meaning frames: a real frame and a play frame. When in the real frame, children playing cops and robbers know that they are actually children and that they are riding broomsticks. But, simultaneously, they participate in the pretend frame of the cops and robbers story. When there are problems or disagreements, children often "break frame" to resolve their disputes before continuing with their make-believe.

Researchers now studying children's make-believe play find that preschool children in all cultures become increasingly sophisticated in making distinctions between what is pretend and what is real (Rubin et al., 1983). They are able to make greater and greater leaps from the real to the pretend meaning of a particular object or action, and they can extend the duration and complexity of their pretend roles and activities. This kind of representation seems to follow a predictable sequence.

The capacity for **sociodramatic play,** in which the child acts out a pretend interchange, increases dramatically beginning at about age 2 to 2½ years. By the age of 5, the simple gestures and imitations become part of intricate systems of reciprocal roles, improvisations of material, coherent plots, and interweaving of themes (Flavell et al., 1993). This play represents a complex and dynamic interplay of cognitive skills—often between two or more children. As Bretherton states, "Children must become co-playwrights, co-directors, and vicarious actors, without getting confused about which of their roles they or a playmate is momentarily adopting" (1989, p. 384).

The Appearance–Reality Distinction Another type of symbolic representation that contains dual meanings is known as the *appearance–reality distinction.* If, for example, a cat wears a dog mask, is he a cat or a dog? When Charlie Brown is dressed as a ghost for Halloween, is he really Charlie Brown or is he really a ghost? And what about a joke store sponge that looks like a solid piece of granite, or a red toy car covered with a green filter that makes it look black? Flavell, Green, and Flavell (1986) showed objects like these to children ages 3 to 7 and asked them, "What is this really and truly? Is it a

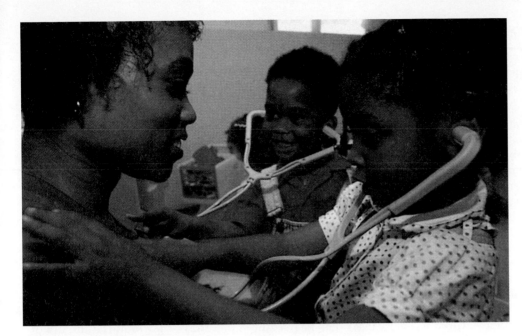

When in the real frame, these children playing doctor know that they are actually children, but at the same time they are participating in the pretend frame of doctor and patient.

rock or a sponge? Is it red or is it black?" They then asked the children, "What does this look like?" The 3-year-olds were quite confused by such questions. In some situations, the young children insisted that the car looks black and the car is black. In others, they reported that the sponge is a sponge and looks like a sponge. They clearly experienced difficulty with the two kinds of meanings. Most children of 5 or 6, however, are much better at these appearance–reality distinctions.

The appearance–reality distinction can help us understand how children decide what is safe to eat. Krause and Saarnio (1993) asked 3-, 4-, and 5-year-olds to choose things that were edible. The choices included obvious foods (a cookie, a Hershey's candy "kiss," a peanut, a carrot, a lollipop, and an apple), obvious non-foods (a key chain, a magnet, an eraser, a rock, a pen, and a candle), and other non-foods that were made to look like foods (a key chain that looked like a cookie, a magnet that looked like a piece of candy, an eraser that looked like a peanut, a pencil sharpener that looked like an ice cream cone, a pen that looked like a lollipop, and a candle that looked like an apple). The 3-year-olds made errors with the obvious foods, obvious nonfoods, and nonfoods that looked like foods. The 4- and 5-year-olds were good at distinguishing obvious foods from obvious nonfoods, but they still made mistakes with the nonfoods that looked like foods. They falsely assumed that these objects were edible. This finding has important implications for the prevention of accidental poisoning. Even 5-year-olds might be tempted to try nonfoods that bear strong resemblances to foods (for example, cleaning fluids that look like pop, or pills that look like little candies).

The appearance–reality distinction is complicated because children have to apply different rules to living things than to artefacts (nonliving things). Changing the appearance of an artefact can change its identity. A two-litre milk carton can become a bird feeder, for instance. But the identity of a living thing cannot be changed. A white horse painted with black stripes does not become a zebra, nor does a boy wearing a dress become a girl. Gelman (1990) found that kindergarten children falsely assume that the identity of a living thing can be changed by changing its appearance. But by grade two, most children understand that the identity of a living thing remains constant.

There seems to be a relationship between pretend play and appearance–reality distinctions. Children who have had a lot of practice with pretend play at 3 and 4 years are better able to understand that objects can look like something else (Flavell, Flavell, & Green, 1987; Flavell, Green, & Flavell, 1986). Some have found that children who have had a lot of experience with pretend play are also better at taking someone else's

FOCUS ON APPLICATION

Children's Eyewitness Testimony

In the early 1990s, children attending day care in a small Saskatchewan community made newspaper headlines across the country because they accused their day-care teachers of horrendous physical and sexual abuse. In these trials and similar ones across North America, children's testimonies were used as evidence to convict or acquit the accused parties. At times, psychologists were called to the courtrooms as expert witnesses to offer an opinion about whether the children's testimonies were likely to be valid. Evaluating children's testimony about abuse is contentious because the stakes are high. If people believe the child's testimony and it is untrue, this may cause an innocent person to be wrongly convicted. If people do not believe the child's true testimony, a child abuser may be acquitted and remain a danger to children. Some experts seem to speak as advocates for the wrongly convicted. These experts stress that children are unreliable witnesses because they have difficulty distinguishing fantasy from reality and are susceptible to coaching by authority figures (see Gardner, 1989). Other experts appear to be advocates for the children. They contend that children can be effective witnesses, that they strongly resist suggestion and are unlikely to lie (see Goodman & Bottoms, 1993). And yet others recognize that children's testimonies can be highly accurate or inaccurate, depending on whether the children are interviewed in a neutral manner or in a biased way (Bruck, Ceci, & Hembrooke, 1998; Ceci & Bruck, 1993). To arrive at an opinion, the experts study the research literature on children's memory.

The literature on children's memory is vast. Most of the studies published before the 1980s were about children's memory for words, stories, and events that were not emotionally charged. Many psychologists felt uncomfortable using the results from these studies as the basis for making inferences about the accuracy of children's memories of abuse. Perhaps memory for stories and other neutral materials is different from memory for traumatic experiences because emotional arousal affects memory. Researchers faced a challenge. They needed to design studies of children's memory that would be relevant to understanding children's memory

---

Evaluating children's testimony about abuse is contentious because the stakes are high.

---

for abuse. But how can researchers study memory for abuse? Obviously, they cannot expose children to abuse in a study. And if they study children who were allegedly abused, there is usually no corroborating evidence that confirms whether the children were indeed abused.

Researchers have developed some ingenious new designs. One approach was to study children who have experienced somewhat traumatic events that can be corroborated. One study involved interviewing 3- to 7-year-old children who had pediatric examinations that required them to take off their clothes or that involved their genitals (Baker-Ward, Gordon, Ornstein, Larus, & Clubb, 1993). The children were asked open-ended questions ("Tell me what the doctor did to you") and specific questions ("Did the doctor check your eyes?"), as well as misleading questions about something that never happened ("Did the doctor sit on top of you?"). They were interviewed immediately after the examination, then once more after a delay of either one, three, or six weeks.

In the initial interview, the 3-year-olds recalled less than 5-year-olds, who recalled less than 7-year-olds. In addition, the 3-year-olds provided little detail in response to general, open-ended questions—they required the use of specific probes. Although many details of the 3-year-olds' accounts were accurate, they also included details that were false. They were more often misled by leading questions than were the older children. Young children made two types of errors: errors of omission (i.e., did not include as much detail) and errors of commission (i.e., included false details). All age groups recalled more information in response to specific probes than to open-ended questions. But their responses to open-ended questions were more accurate than were those to specific probes.

In the second interview, children's accounts were mostly consistent with their initial accounts, although consistency was higher for 7-year-olds (94.2 percent consistent) than for 5-year-olds (85.4 percent consistent), who were more consistent than 3-year-olds (70 percent consistent). It is important to interview the children more than once because in court cases, children may be interviewed a dozen or more times. This study has shown that 3-year-olds, even those telling the truth, provide less consistent accounts than do older children. Young children do not have a good under

perspective or understanding someone else's feelings. Researchers suggest that seemingly innocent make-believe play provides important experiences for children's development of structured knowledge (Flavell, 1985; Garvey, 1977).

standing of time, so they may be inconsistent in their reports of when or how often events occurred. As well, if there are several months between accounts, the children may appear to alter their stories because they have developed more mature language to express them.

Another key finding in this study was that young children forgot details of the examination more quickly than did older children. The study showed that 3-year-olds showed significant forgetting by one week after the examination, and 5-year-olds by three weeks after it. The 7-year-olds did not show significant forgetting, even six weeks after the examination.

In another study of traumatic events, Carole Peterson and Michael Bell interviewed children who had been treated at St. Johns' Children's Hospital for stitches, fractures, second-degree burns, crushed fingers, or dog bites (Peterson & Bell, 1996). The children, who ranged in age from 2 to 13 years, and their parents were interviewed at home within a few days of their hospital visit, and then again six months later. The results of this study were similar to those of the study on pediatric examinations: older children remembered more than younger ones, and children's immediate memory was better than their memory after a delay.

This study also addressed issues that were not included in the study on pediatric examinations. The researchers checked whether children who were more stressed at the time of their injury had differences in memory than did other children. To the researchers' surprise, stress at time of injury was not a significant factor. But level of distress while being treated in hospital was significant—more distressed children remembered less than did other children. This finding must be interpreted cau-

tiously, though, because there was a confound. More distressed children tended to be younger, and younger children tend to remember less.

Another innovative aspect of this study is that the researchers categorized children's accounts to include central information (information directly related to the injury and its treatment) and peripheral information (the general context of the injury and treatment, such as time of day, location, and people present). Not surprisingly, children tended to recall more central than peripheral information. An interesting finding, however, was that categorizing information as central or peripheral seems to be different for children than for adults. Peterson and Bell cite an example of peripheral information—the colour of popsicle children were given after their treatment. This seemingly trivial detail was not trivial to the children; it was as well remembered as central information.

Another type of study involves staging events that have similar features to the kinds of situations that children typically give eyewitness accounts of in real life. It is important to keep in mind, though, that staged events are limited to those that are ethical. In one study, children were taken to a library and asked to put on and take off loose cotton shirts over their clothing (Oates & Shrimpton, 1991). In another study, two children were left in a trailer with an adult stranger. The adult dressed one of the children in a clown suit and photographed the child in front of the other child (Rudy & Goodman, 1991). In another study, day-care children between the ages of 3 and 6 briefly met a man named Sam Stone, who visited the day-care centre (Leichtman & Ceci, 1995). None of the children knew him (he was part of the experiment); he was simply introduced to the children

during story time. He did not interact with the children. The next day, their teacher showed them a soiled teddy bear and a ripped book and told them that Sam Stone did it. Every two weeks for the next three months, some of the children were told misinformation about Sam Stone and were asked misleading questions, such as "When Sam Stone tore the book, did he do it on purpose, or was he being silly?" Other children were not told the misinformation. After three months, all the children were questioned by a new interviewer about what actually happened during Sam Stone's visit. Children who had been repeatedly told misinformation about Sam Stone were more likely to wrongly say that they had seen him rip the book and soil the teddy bear during his visit to the day care. The children had formed a negative stereotype of Sam Stone and insisted that he was guilty and that he was bad. There were age differences in vulnerability to forming negative stereotypes. Compared with 5- and 6-year-olds, 3- and 4-year-olds were more likely to insist that they saw Sam Stone do the bad deeds and to persist in making this false claim, even when challenged by the interviewer. Such studies of staged events have revealed the critical influence of interviewing techniques on children's eyewitness accounts. Children are susceptible to outside influences, such as misleading questions, negative stereotyping, interviewer bias, and threats or inducements to give certain accounts (Bruck, Ceci, & Hembrooke, 1998). Therefore, in order to understand children's eyewitness accounts, it is not enough to just understand developmental factors that influence memory. We must also understand factors external to the child, such as the context in which children are interviewed.

Limitations of Preoperational Thought

Even with the development of symbolic representation, preoperational children still have a long way to go before they become logical thinkers. First, by adult standards, their thought processes are quite limited. Preoperational children cannot deal with abstractions.

irreversibility The belief that events and relationships can occur in only one direction, which is characteristic of preoperational thought.

They are concerned with the here and now, with physical things they can represent easily (see the box "A Young Child's Conception of Death").

Second, their thinking often is irreversible. For young children, events and relationships occur in only one direction. They cannot imagine how things would be if returned to their original state or how relationships can go in two directions. The following exchange provides an example of **irreversibility** in a preoperational child's thought:

A 3-year-old girl is asked, "Do you have a sister?" She says, "Yes."

"What's her name?" "Jessica."

"Does Jessica have a sister?" "No."

In this example, the relationship is one-way only; it is irreversible—the younger girl knows she has a sister, but she does not yet recognize that *she* is Jessica's sister. We will see more examples of irreversibility in Piaget's conservation experiment later in this chapter.

Third, preoperational children's thought is more egocentric, or centred on their own perspective so that they are less able to take into account another person's point of view. Preoperational children concentrate on their own perceptions and often assume that everyone else's outlook is the same as theirs. Piaget (1954) made an

FOCUS ON APPLICATION

A Young Child's Conception of Death

Imagine a 4-year-old who has just been told that a beloved and recently active, caring grandmother has died. Given what we know about young children's thinking, what reactions can we expect? What aspects of the situation are particularly difficult to understand? Are there specific fears and anxieties the child might experience? Finally, how should caregivers reassure the child?

A number of researchers have studied the differences between young children's understanding of death and how older children and adults view death (Speece & Brent, 1984). They have focused on three major aspects of the death concept:

1. Death is always irreversible, final, and permanent.
2. The absence of life functions is characteristic of death.
3. Death is universal—everyone must die.

The researchers found that children under the age of 5 lack all three of these components in their concept of death. They interviewed children of different ages and asked them a variety of questions. Sometimes, they asked

general questions, such as, "What is death?" But more often, they asked specific questions. Such questions might include, "Can a dead person come back to life?" "Can a dead person talk, feel, see, dream, or think?" "Does everyone die?" "Can you think of someone who might not die?"

Children who are told that death is like sleep may be afraid to close their eyes at night in fear that they, too, will die.

Young children frequently see death as a temporary state, like sleeping or "going away." They will sometimes suggest that dead people wake up or come back to life after a while. Is this a belief in reversibility? Some researchers suggest that it does not mean that children see death as reversible in all cases, but rather that they have not yet established distinct categories of "dead" and "alive." After all, when a person is asleep he is also alive, so why not when he is dead?

Young children also do not seem to understand that all functions cease when a person is dead. But they may think that there is reduced functioning. One child suggested that "you can't hear very well when you're dead." Often, children think that the deceased can't do visible things, such as eat and speak, but they can do less visible things, such as dream and know. Finally, young children do not yet realize that death is universal. They frequently believe that death can be avoided by being clever or lucky and that certain people are exempt from death, such as teachers, members of their immediate family, or themselves. Some children believe that people can do magical things to keep from dying—for example, a child may think that if she prays a lot she won't die. Is it any wonder that it is so difficult to explain the death of a friend or relative to a child who is under the age of 5?

Researchers generally agree that the concept of death develops between the ages of 5 and 7. Most 7-year-olds have at least a rudimentary knowledge of the three basic components of death. This development seems to parallel the transition in the child from Piaget's stage

interesting study that demonstrates this limitation of thought in his Three Mountain task. He seated children in front of a plaster model of a mountain range and showed them pictures of the mountain range, each taken from a different angle. He asked them to select the picture that represented their view of the mountains, then to select the picture that represented what a doll would see if seated facing the mountains from another angle. Most children had no trouble picking the picture matching their own viewpoint, but they could not put themselves in the doll's place and imagine the doll's view of the mountains. Based on children's responses in this experiment, Piaget concluded that preoperational children assume that their perspective is the only one.

But other researchers question whether children are as egocentric as they appeared to be in the Three Mountain task. Perhaps this task was especially difficult, not because it measured perspective taking, but because it required spatial skills. For example, the children had to distinguish whether a mountain was on the right or the left, but the average 3-year-old does not yet know right from left. Interestingly, Borke (1975) designed a perspective-taking task that demanded fewer spatial skills than the Three Mountain task. In Borke's task, the children were shown a farm scene, and Grover (from *Sesame Street*) drove around the farmyard, making various stops. At each stop, children were asked what Grover would see. Even the 3-year-olds answered correctly 80 percent of the time. Yet, when these same children tried the

of preoperational thought to concrete operational thinking (Speece & Brent, 1984).

Explaining the death of a grandmother to a young child does not just involve coping with the child's limited cognitive understanding. The reality of someone's death is difficult for adults, as well as children. Adults may intellectually understand the reality of death—its finality and permanence, its absence of life functions, and its universality. But, emotionally, they must struggle to cope with their loss. Young children, too, face emotional upheaval while trying to understand the realities of death. However, there are a number of factors that further complicate the adjustment for children. First, they are to some extent egocentric—they will be primarily concerned with how situations and events affect them. Second, they have trouble understanding cause and effect. Hence, when a young child asks, "Why did Grandma die?" she may not be asking what we think she is asking. She may not want to know about disease and old age; she may be wondering, instead, why her grandmother left her. Children wonder if they control such situations: "Did she leave because I was bad?" "If I'm good, will she come back?" "Will Mommy or Daddy die and leave me?" They may feel anger or guilt, or they

may wonder if their own angry thoughts caused the death. Children who are told that death is like sleep may be afraid to close their eyes at night in fear that they, too, will die. Children who are told that the angels took someone to heaven may develop other fears, as the following example suggests:

> Four-year-old Carlos was very attached to his grandfather, who had lived with him. His parents told Carlos that angels had come to take grandpa home. Later that week, Carlos became very upset when his parents tried to get him to play outside or go outside with them. He would cry, fall to the ground, and be visibly very frightened. Upon talking with a counsellor who worked extensively with children, it turned out that Carlos had become afraid that the angels would come to get him too if he went outside. He felt that he was safe as long as he had a roof over his head that prevented their entry. Within a short period of time with the counsellor, he came to accept his grandfather's death and to understand that he was safe outside.

Sometimes, young children will either try to get a deceased loved one to

return or attempt to protect themselves with a variety of magical strategies. They may make a bargain with God that if they are very good, the loved one will return. They may engage in rituals to protect themselves from dying also. These rituals may include positioning toys, stuffed animals, or furniture in special places in their rooms to create a place of safety for themselves.

It becomes clear that adults need to be sensitive in dealing with death when children are young. Mahler (1950) described grief reactions in children as differing from adult bereavement. Following the initial sorrow from the loss or separation, children may be angry at life or even at the deceased person, as the child may feel that it is unfair to be left behind.

All of these factors influence children's understanding of death. The preschool child needs simple, correct information combined with ample reassurance and emotional support to cope with the reality of death. Psychologists and pediatricians generally agree that adults must be honest. Children's anxiety is lessened if they know what is going on around them and if they perceive that people are being truthful.

Figure 10-1

Depending on how perspective taking is measured, preschool children may appear more or less competent. On this task, most 3-year-olds can interpret the farm scene from the doll's perspective, even when it is different than their own.

Figure 10-2

This is Piaget's classic Three Mountain task, which requires children to determine how the mountains would appear to the doll. Preschool children typically find this perspective-taking task more difficult than the one depicted in Figure 10-1.

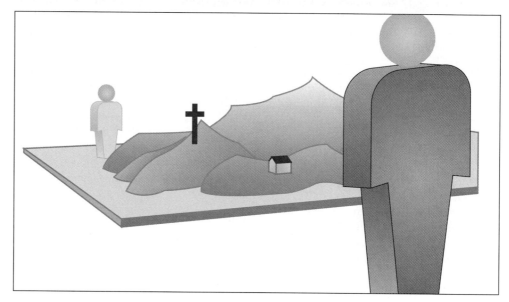

centration The focusing on only one aspect or dimension of an object or situation, which is characteristic of preoperational thought.

Three Mountain task, they answered correctly only 42 percent of the time. Therefore, children's perspective-taking skills vary, depending on the type of task they are given.

Fourth, preoperational children's thought tends to be centred on only one physical aspect or dimension of an object or a situation. They cannot hold several aspects or dimensions of a situation in mind at the same time. This limitation—called **centration**—is best seen in the class inclusion problem, a classic task used to study pre-operational thought. Young children have difficulty comparing a part with the whole. For example, if they are shown a collection of wooden beads, some red and some yellow, and are asked whether there are more red beads or more wooden beads, they will be unable to handle the problem. They cannot simultaneously consider colour and the broader category of wooden beads.

Fifth, preoperational children focus on present states, rather than on processes of change or transformation. They judge things according to their appearance in the present, not how they came to be that way.

Sixth, preoperational children assume that all events have single, direct causes. This limitation is called *finalism*. They do not understand that some events happen by chance. They will not understand why their friends' names, and not theirs, were picked in draws for prizes. Even adults sometimes have trouble understanding chance events (lotteries capitalize on this tendency). Preoperational children never understand chance events, and they search for single, direct causes for any events in their lives. The favourite question of preoperational children is "Why?" This characteristic has implications for the need to communicate with children about changes in their lives. Suppose children are faced with divorces of their parents, deaths of parents, or major illnesses. Children will search for causes, often ones that involve themselves as key players. For example, children might think that because they did not clean their rooms their parents are getting divorced.

Piaget's Conservation Experiments Several of these preoperational limitations can be seen in one of Piaget's classic experiments on the *conservation of matter*. In Chapter 2, one of these experiments was described. A child is shown two identical glasses holding the same amount of liquid. After the liquid from one of the glasses is poured into a taller glass, the child says the taller glass holds more water. In a second experiment, presented in Figure 10-3, a child is presented with two identical balls of clay. As the child watches, one ball of clay is transformed into various shapes while the other remains untouched. One ball might be rolled into a sausage, broken into five little balls, or flattened into a pancake. At each transformation, the child might be asked which has more clay, the untouched ball or the one that has become a sausage, five little balls, or a pancake. The child might say at one time that the untouched ball has more clay because it is fatter. But the child might also say that the sausage has more because it is longer, or the little balls because there are more of them, or the pancake because it is all spread out. At no time has a child said that the two are identical, although she has witnessed the whole transformation process. Clearly, preoperational children focus on the current state of the object, not on the process of transformation. They centre on one dimension at a time, such as either fatness or "spreadoutness." Their thinking is based on direct experience in the here and now. Their view of the process is irreversible. All of these cognitive limitations make preoperational children nonconservers.

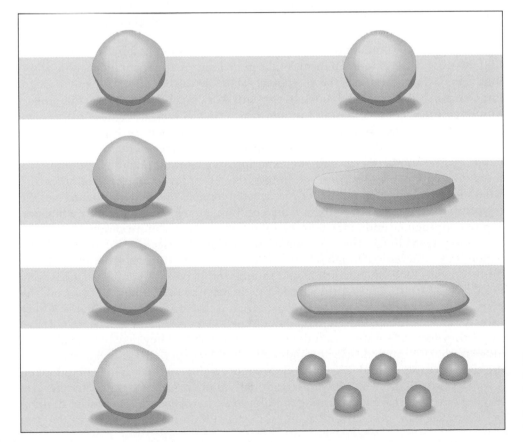

Figure 10-3
In this conservation experiment, a child is shown two identical balls of clay. One ball remains the same, while the other is transformed into various shapes.

classification The dividing of a large group into subgroups that have similar features.

Classification Preoperational children have a problem with **classification**—putting together those events or objects that go together. Young children have trouble with classification tasks because of their relatively short memories and attention spans. They may forget why they are putting things together before they finish a task. A preschooler may move a chair toward a table, then think about a friend to sit in the chair, then think of her hair, and run off to find a comb. Going into the bathroom for it, she sees a bar of soap—she thinks about playing in water, turns on the tap, and remembers that she is thirsty. So she goes to her mother, who wonders what happened to the table-and-chair project. Other problems in classification arise because of the confusing variety of reasons for which things, events, and people can be classified. Use, colour, texture, size, sound, and smell are criteria for classification that are readily apparent to an adult, but a child who has no trouble grouping plates, forks, and cups on the basis of use may not see the possibility of grouping plates according to size or cups according to colour. One basis, or reason, for classification may block another.

Seriation Sequences or series of any kind are difficult for young children to manage. For example, when presented with six sticks of graduated length, children can usually pick out the shortest or the longest. They may even be able to divide the sticks into piles, putting shorter sticks in one pile and longer sticks in the other. But young children have considerable difficulty lining the sticks up from shortest to longest because such a task requires a simultaneous judgment that each stick is longer than the next but at the same time is shorter than another (Flavell, 1963).

Early in the preoperational stage, between ages 2 and 4, children have difficulty correctly ordering the sticks. They might arrange two subsets, for example, long and short sticks, but have difficulty integrating the subsets. Later in the preoperational stage, between 4 and 7 years, children can correctly order the set of sticks, but they have difficulty inserting an additional stick of the same height into the sequence. Piaget proposed that the problem such children had was one of centring on a single dimension of an array. In order to correctly insert an additional stick, the child would have to perceive it as larger than the one just smaller than it, and smaller than the one just larger than it. The preoperational child finds this task very difficult (Flavell et al., 1993).

Number The development of numerical abilities in children is an intriguing area—both because of the amount of formal educational time that is spent in teaching about numbers, and also because of the great practical use to which numbers are put throughout a person's life. Piaget did much of the early work on children's understanding of numbers. In his conservation of number task, which is seen in Figure 10-4, the experimenter arranges two rows of six candies with a one-to-one correspondence, with one of the rows directly above the other. Once the child agrees that the two rows contain the same number of candies, the experimenter shortens one of the rows and removes one of the candies from the longer row. In order to conserve number, the child must recognize that the longer row actually contains one fewer candy, despite the row's appearance. Children younger than 5 or 6 are often fooled by the misleading perceptual appearance and judge that the longer row contains more candy.

Judging the longer row as having more may be influenced by children's cultural experiences. Interestingly, high school science students in Nunavut showed Inuit children two rows that contained the same number of marbles (Digdon, personal communication with students at the Canada Wide Science Fair, 1999). In one row, the marbles were bunched close together, whereas in the other row, the marbles were spread out. The Inuit children judged the bunched together row as having more because they focused on increased density, not on length. They may have learned to judge number through density through their everyday experiences, such as evaluating the size of a caribou herd. Bigger herds are more tightly packed, rather than longer.

Despite this problem with conservation of number, Rochel Gelman and her colleagues have determined that younger children do have more competencies in number than Piaget proposed. Gelman and Gallistel (1986), for example, identified two

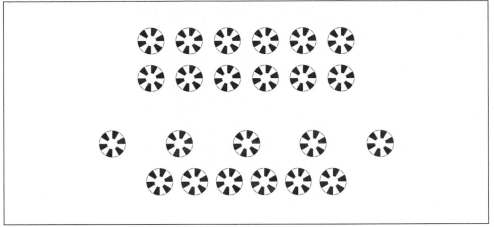

Figure 10-4
Piaget's Experiment on the Conservation of Numbers
When shown the arrangement of candies in the top two rows and asked whether one line has more or both lines are the same, the 4- or 5-year-old will generally answer that both lines contain the same number of candies. Using the same candies, an adult then removes a candy from the upper row and spreads out the remaining candies, so that the row looks longer. The adult does not change the number of candies in the lower row but simply pushes them closer together, so that the row looks shorter. The child has watched this operation and has been told that she may eat the candies in the line that contains more. Even preoperational children who can count will insist that the longer line has more, although they have gone through the exercise of counting off the candies in each line.

major types of numerical skills that young children possess: *number-abstraction abilities* and *numerical-reasoning principles*. Number-abstraction processes refer to cognitive processes by which the child arrives at the number of an array of objects. For example, a 3-year-old might count the number of cookies on a table and arrive at the number four. Numerical-reasoning principles allow the child to determine the correct way to operate on or transform an array (Flavell et al., 1993). For example, the child might come to realize that the only way that number can be increased in the conservation task presented earlier is to add an additional object. Simply spreading out the objects is an irrelevant transformation. These two types of numerical skills develop at different rates. Not until the child has gained some understanding of basic reasoning principles is he capable of adding, subtracting, multiplying, and dividing (Becker, 1993). As well, the child who knows that $2 + 3 = 5$ will not automatically understand that $3 + 2 = 5$ or that $5 - 3 = 2$.

Young children also have difficulty understanding money. They often assume that bigger coins are worth more, and older siblings can easily con them into trading a dime for a nickel. As well, they often assume that more coins means greater value. I remember when my 5-year-old son insisted on paying for a candy bar with his two-dollar coin (toonie) instead of his loonie, so that he would get more change back and have more money (Digdon).

Time, Space, and Sequence A 3-year-old may be able to say, "Grandma will come to visit next week." Even a 2-year-old may use words that seem to indicate a knowledge of time and space: *later, tomorrow, last night, far away, next time.* A child of 2 or 3, however, has very little appreciation of what these terms mean. And when questioned, might reply, "No, not that tomorrow, Mom. The other one." *Noon* may mean lunchtime, but if lunchtime is delayed an hour, it is still noon to the young child. Waking from a nap, a child may not even know whether it is the same day. The concepts of weeks and months, minutes and hours are difficult for children to grasp; a date such as Wednesday, April 14, is too abstract a concept for them.

Perhaps an example of children's understanding of daily activity sequences would be helpful. Recently, a series of experiments has been conducted to determine children's ability to time sequences related to their daily activities. Three kinds of tasks were used: placing elements in backward order, judging order from changing reference points (for example, if it is lunchtime, judging what the child has already completed and what activities are still left to do during the day), and estimating the lengths of intervals separating parts of activities.

When preschoolers were asked to perform these tasks, interesting differences emerged in their behaviour. By age 5, for example, children exceeded chance levels on the backward order test—they were able to indicate, beginning at the end of the day, what they had accomplished earlier, as well as order their day from multiple reference

Even though this preschooler is pointing to a number on the clock, the concept of minutes and hours is difficult for her to understand.

By crawling under the easel, this preschooler is learning the meaning of such words as far, near, over, under, to, far, inside, *and* outside.

points. Younger children were unable to do this. By age 4 to 5, children surpass chance levels on the judgment of time intervals (Friedman, 1990).

This study shows how difficult time concepts are for young children. At the age of 5, they have just mastered the ordering of their activities. To teach children to recite the days of the week or months in the year simply involves the rote memorizing of abstract material. Some contend that drilling children on such factors as order of days or months may actually get in the way of the time concept that underlies this knowledge.

When children are repeatedly drilled on a content, these drills may constitute the preponderance of operations that they perform. Thus, recitation of the days of the week and months during the school years probably encourages verbal-list representations of these contents. This might actually delay the development of the more flexible operations that imagery permits.... (Friedman, 1990, p. 1411)

With only a limited sense of time, young children have very little idea of cause-and-effect sequences. In fact, their early use of the words *'cause* and *because* may have nothing to do with the customary adult understanding of these terms. The same is true of the word *why*—the 4-year-old's favourite question. Children may repeat the question "Why?" endlessly, perhaps because they are trying to abstract words or communicate vague feelings. Their associations often are egocentric or unconnected. A child may ask her mother why Daddy isn't home. The mother may answer, "It isn't time" or "He's still working." These may not be the answers the child is looking for because of what she associates with her father's evening arrival—dinner, special games, or even punishment.

Spatial relations are another set of concepts that must be developed during the preschool period. The meanings of words such as *in, out, to, from, near, far, over, under, up, down, inside,* and *outside* are learned directly in the process of the child's experience of her own body (Weikart, Rogers, & Adcock, 1971). Weikart and associates suggest that the usual progression is for children to learn a concept first with their bodies (crawling under a table) and then with objects (pushing a toy truck under a table). Later, they learn to identify the concept in pictures ("See the boat go under the bridge!") and are able to verbalize it.

Beyond Piaget: Social Perspectives

In recent decades, some of Piaget's conclusions about the mental capabilities of young children have been challenged. His specific conclusions about the limitations of children's thoughts at different ages have been called into question. Critics have disputed his view of the child as a solitary explorer attempting to make sense of the world. Instead, these developmental psychologists argue, learning takes place within a framework of relationships with parents, caretakers, and peers. Furthermore, such interaction occurs within the context of the beliefs and rules in the child's specific culture. Piaget saw the developing child as an "active scientist" who learns as he goes along by experimenting with solutions to problems. Piagetian tasks were purposely devised to isolate ideas, such as conservation of number or quantity, to determine whether the child could use the concept in the experimental condition.

Since Piaget developed his theory about how children think, some developmental psychologists have looked at children from a very different perspective. Rather than the "active scientist" described by Piaget, these psychologists emphasize that a child is a social being. According to these psychologists, a child figures out how to interpret his experiences by interacting with more experienced people—parents, teachers, older children. In the course of daily interaction, the adults in the child's life pass on the rules and expectations of their particular culture (Bruner & Haste, 1987). Some theorists conclude that the process of growth is not strictly divisible into a series of specific stages (Bornstein & Bruner, 1986).

Piaget used complex materials and problems to determine a child's conceptual abilities. If the ability to solve a problem is linked to assessing real situations with the help of clues from the environment and help from adults, a simpler format is needed. Following this reasoning, Piaget's experiment for demonstrating egocentricity was altered in one respect. Instead of asking the child to imagine the juxtaposition of objects and mountain peaks as seen by a doll, the task was changed to the simpler one of determining if a naughty boy could hide so he would not be seen by a police officer. Although none of these children in Edinburgh, Scotland, had hidden from a police officer, they had played hide-and-seek games and understood the task immediately. Even 3-year-olds were remarkably successful (Hughes & Donaldson, 1979). When Piagetian problems are presented so that they make "human sense," they are clear to younger children (Donaldson, 1978).

In the following example, Valerie, age 5½, cannot solve Piaget's class inclusion problem with beads, although she can explain the principles of class inclusion to her mother:

> Valerie asked her mother if she loved her more than she loved the kids in her kindergarten. Her mother hesitated, since Valerie's brother was also in the kindergarten, and answered that she loved Valerie and David more than the other kids at the kindergarten. Valerie looked at her mother with a "Silly Mom" kind of look, and explained, "David and I are some of all the kids at the kindergarten—so if you said you loved the kids at the kindergarten you'd be saying you love us too, and you wouldn't have to leave anybody out!" (Rogoff, 1990, p. 5)

The psychologist reports that the next day, Valerie's curious mother tried Piaget's traditional class inclusion problem with Valerie, using red and green wooden beads. When asked to indicate the wooden beads, Valerie pointed to all the beads. But when asked whether there were more red beads or more wooden beads or the same amount, Valerie claimed that there were more red beads (Rogoff, 1990).

Cognitive development is seen as a social and cultural process. The ways that adults demonstrate how a problem is solved are part of learning to think. All cultures initiate children into a myriad of activities through what has been called **guided participation.** When young children learn to help set or clear the table or to sing "Happy Birthday," specific aspects of cultural activity are being transmitted from the more experienced members, adults, to the less experienced members, children.

guided participation The process by which more experienced people transmit cultural information to children.

These children have learned to sing "Happy Birthday" through guided participation.

Katherine Nelson (1986), for example, argues that a knowledge of events is the key to understanding the child's mind. Whereas Piaget tends to focus on what young children don't know, such as categories and numbers, Nelson is interested in what they do know, what they have learned from their own experiences. She believes that a young child's day-to-day experiences become the material for her mental life and problem-solving abilities. Because the child's cognitive processes are based on real-life events, a child's understanding of the world is embedded in social or cultural knowledge.

If development is looked at as a training process, how does a child work toward gaining abilities just beyond reach? To explain this process, Vygotsky provided the concept of the zone of proximal development (ZPD), in which children develop through participation in activities slightly beyond their competence, with the assistance of adults or more skilled children (Vygotsky, 1978). Vygotsky used ZPD to refer to the difference between the child's actual developmental level and the potential level that is guided by adults or older peers. In fact, Vygotsky believed play to be a primary means of moving children toward more advanced levels of social and cognitive skills—a leading activity, which becomes a major source of advanced skills (Nicolopoulou, 1993). As Vygotsky stated,

> In play a child is always above his average age, above his daily behavior; in play, it is as though he were a head taller than himself. As in the focus of a magnifying glass, play contains developmental tendencies in a condensed form; in play, it is as though the child were trying to jump above the level of his normal behavior. (1933/1967, p. 6)

For many researchers, therefore, individual activity develops through social interaction in events that are social or historical practices in particular cultures. Play provides an excellent opportunity to study the way children learn social mores in widely diverse cultures (Rogoff, 1993).

Memory

For some researchers, the information-processing theory described in Chapter 2 is a useful framework for understanding cognitive development. These researchers study memory and problem solving, among other topics, and try to determine how well preschool children remember things. Information-processing researchers recognize different types of memory and different aspects of the process of remembering. When we describe the memory abilities of preschool children, therefore, we need to specify particular types of memory or aspects of remembering.

Psychologists distinguish between *short-term* and *long-term memory*. Short-term memory (sometimes called *working memory*) holds the information that a person has in mind at any one time; it has a limited capacity and a limited duration of about half a minute. One way to test short-term memory is through the digit span task. In this task, people listen to a string of numbers and then repeat them in order. Adults, on average, can repeat seven numbers without mistake. However, 2- and 3-year-olds can repeat only two. Therefore, younger children have more limited short-term memories. This fact is important to keep in mind when we give instructions to young children. If we tell a preschool child to pick up her clothes, comb her hair, brush her teeth, and get dressed, she may not comply because she cannot remember all the commands.

Long-term memory lasts hours, days, months, or years. Taking in a new memory is called *encoding*. Sometimes encoding requires conscious effort (such as studying your textbook), but other times it is automatic (remembering what the weather was like this morning). Older children and adults are good at controlling their attention, so they can choose to encode particular memories while ignoring distracters. Preschool children are not as focused and have more limited attention spans. In a classic study done by Hagen (1972), preschool children and older children were shown a deck of cards. Each card had a picture of an animal and some unrelated object, such as a chair or a telephone. The children were asked to learn all the animals. Later, they were tested for their memories of the animals, and not surprisingly, the older children remembered more than the younger ones. But the children then were asked to remember the other objects that were pictured on the cards. Surprisingly, the preschool children were better at remembering them than were the older children. The older children had concentrated on the animals and had ignored the other pictures. But the preschool children were unable to restrict their attention to just the animals. This finding has implications for teaching young children. They will be less able to focus on the prescribed lesson and will be easily distracted.

Accessing a memory is called *retrieval*. Some memories are easier to retrieve than others. Have you ever been unable to recall someone's name, even though you are certain that you know it? Then later on you do remember the name. This is an example of a retrieval problem, often called the *tip of the tongue phenomenon*. How well do preschool children retrieve memories? Let's now look at two types of retrieval: recognition and recall.

Recognition and Recall Studies of preschool children's memory skills have focused on two different behaviours—recognition and recall. **Recognition** refers to the ability to select from pictures or objects that are currently present or events that are currently happening only those one has seen or experienced before. For example, children may recognize a picture in a book as something they have seen before, but they may be unable to name it or tell us about it. **Recall** refers to the ability to retrieve data about objects or events that are not present or current. It requires the generation of information from long-term memory without the object in view. For instance, if a child who is looking at a picture book is asked what picture comes next and then names it correctly, he is recalling the next picture.

Myers and Perlmutter (1978) have found preschool children's performance on recognition tasks to be quite good, but their recall performance is poor; both forms of remembering improve, nevertheless, between the ages of 2 and 5. In a recognition task in which many objects were shown only once to children between the ages of 2 and 5, even the youngest could correctly point to 81 percent of them, and the older children remembered 92 percent. The study showed that preschool children have considerable proficiency in the recognition skills necessary to encode and retain substantial amounts of information. In recall studies, however, when children between the ages of 2 and 4 were asked to name objects that the experimenter had just shown, the 3-year-olds were able to name only 22 percent of the items and the 4-year-olds only 40 percent—a considerable difference from the scores attained in the recognition task. Preschool children are clearly better at recognition than at recall, but children may perform better on such memory tasks if their caregivers routinely ask many questions that test children's memories (Ratner, 1984).

Rehearsal and Organization Young children's recall difficulties are generally assumed to occur because of their limited strategies for encoding and retrieval (Flavell, 1977; Myers & Perlmutter, 1978). Preschool children do not spontaneously organize or rehearse information that they want to remember, as older children and adults often do. If you give an adult a list to memorize, such as "cat, chair, airplane, dog, desk, car," the adult might first classify the items as "animals," "furniture," and "vehicles" and then repeat (or rehearse) the words quietly before being asked to recall the list. The adult, therefore, has used two memory strategies—**organization** and **rehearsal.** Adults and children, from age 6 on, improve their ability to recall information when taught memory strategies, but it has been found difficult to teach preschoolers to organize and rehearse information.

This does not mean that preschoolers are without any memory strategies. In one study, for example, 18- to 24-month-old toddlers watched an experimenter hide a Big Bird toy under a pillow and then were told to remember where Big Bird had been hidden because they would later be asked where he was. The experimenter then distracted the children with other toys for four minutes. During this time, the children frequently

recognition The ability to correctly identify items previously experienced when they appear again.

recall The ability to retrieve information and events that are not present.

organization and **rehearsal** Strategies for improving recall used mainly by older children and adults.

interrupted their play by talking about Big Bird, pointing at the hiding place, standing near it, or even attempting to retrieve the Big Bird toy (DeLoache, Cassidy, & Brown, 1985). The researchers determined that these were attempts by the toddlers to remember—memory strategies at work. The researchers concluded that these activities resemble and may in fact be precursors of more mature strategies for keeping the material alive in short-term memory.

DeLoache and colleagues determined that preschoolers group spatial—but not conceptual—items into categories when trying to memorize them (DeLoache & Todd, 1988). For example, when very young children were required to remember the location of a hidden object, they frequently used rehearsal-like verbalizations—referring to the hidden toy, to the fact that it was hidden, to the hiding place, and to their having found it. This use of rehearsal techniques suggests that preschoolers can be strategic and deliberately change their behaviour in certain situations to better remember material. Children's use of rehearsal appears to be a genuine precursor to the complex, generalizable, and effective memory strategies of older children (Flavell et al., 1993).

Some researchers have focused on teaching memory strategies—such as study sorting, group naming, or category cuing—to preschool children. Preschoolers were able to learn these techniques and to retain them for several days. Then, after a brief time, they no longer used these strategies, possibly because they forgot them or lost interest in repeatedly performing the strategies and tasks. In addition, learning these memory strategies appeared to have little effect on children's recall abilities (Lange & Pierce, 1992). Similar results have been found in the case of memory strategies mothers use to teach children such skills as remembering the names of characters in stories or the location of zoo animals. While children employed simpler and fewer techniques than their mothers, they did appear to learn about memory strategies in general from them. This finding indicates that children may, with adult guidance, learn to employ some simple strategies that are not yet within their usual strategy repertoire (Harris & Hamidullah, 1993).

Such studies demonstrate that with carefully contrived learning experiences and instruction, young children may learn cognitive skills beyond their current repertoire of abilities. But this learning does not endure—either because children cannot fit the skills comfortably into their current hierarchy of abilities or because they are too busy learning about the world in other, more comfortable ways. It also may be that the skills just beyond the child's cognitive reach are more likely to be used, while those well beyond it will require more time before they are integrated into the child's cognitive behaviours.

The development of memory and language often go hand in hand. Preschool children who are read to and have a greater knowledge of storybooks also have more developed vocabularies (Senechal, LeFevre, Hudson, & Lawson, 1996). This expanded vocabulary will stand them in good stead for school. "The single most important activity for building the knowledge required for eventual success in reading is reading aloud to children" (Anderson, Hiebert, Scott, & Wilkerson, 1985, as cited in Senechal et al., 1996, p. 227). In addition, children are likely to benefit even more from being read to if they also have a broad range of experiences that connect concepts in stories to physical experiences. Children who have watched and handled rabbits and turtles are likely to better understand Aesop's fable about the race.

Preschool children remember a great many things. Try skipping a sentence in a child's favourite storybook or adding a new ingredient to her fruit salad. The child will remember exactly how it was before. Experimental tasks that demonstrate memory in adults may not tap the abilities that children use to enhance memory. But when children are given tasks in a context that is meaningful to them, they have demonstrated what may be rudimentary strategies for remembering. These behaviours can be interpreted as evidence of an early natural propensity to keep what must be remembered in mind (DeLoache, Cassidy, & Brown, 1985). When groups of children who were asked to "remember" or to "play with" toys were compared, the children who played with the toys demonstrated a better memory of them. This result suggests that the act of playing contributed to the children's mental organization of experiencing the toys. Their memory strategy appears to involve perceiving the items through use (Newman, 1990).

Event Scripts and Sequential Understanding It is increasingly clear that children are able to remember information that is ordered temporally, in a time sequence. They appear to structure a series of occurrences into an ordered, meaningful whole. In one study, children were asked to describe how they had made clay pieces two weeks before. When the children were given the opportunity to remake the same clay pieces, they were able to describe how they had worked step by step. It appears that children are able to organize and remember a sequence of actions after a single experience (Smith, Ratner, & Hobart, 1987).

Young children are aware that an event such as a birthday party is composed of an orderly progression of events: a beginning, when the guests arrive with presents; a series of events in the middle, including playing games, singing "Happy Birthday," blowing out the candles, and eating cake and ice cream; and an end, when each guest gets a goodie bag. Children have good memory abilities for repeated events, such as a family dinnertime, grocery shopping, or a day at nursery school. It is as if they have developed a format or script for these routine events (Friedman, 1990; Mandler, 1983; Nelson, Fibush, Hudson, & Lucariello, 1983). When mothers talk to their young children about objects and events that are not immediately present, such as describing the errands to be done after lunch, they help their children to develop scripts and thereby remember the events (Lucariello & Nelson, 1987).

It is highly unlikely that this father can get away with skipping any parts of the storybook he is reading aloud if it is one of his daughter's favourites.

Younger children can remember events only in the order in which they occur. The ability to order and remember information with more flexibility develops with familiarity and over time. Only when children have become extremely familiar with an ordered event can they reverse the sequence of steps (Bauer & Thal, 1990). Scripts, therefore, present a mnemonic device to remember the sequence of an event. They provide an oral rehearsal for the child to enact. Children, as we discussed earlier, may even rehearse these scripts out loud when they are alone. As a recent review stated,

> Life is eventful. People and objects in a young child's world do things; children observe these events and enter into them, thus joining the flow of the world around them. They mentally represent these events (event knowledge). Some of these event representations are generalized and abstract (scripts). This event knowledge, including scripts, of everyday life may be the young child's most powerful mental tool for understanding the world. (Flavell et al., 1993, p. 85)

Theory of Mind

The *theory of mind* is a relatively new focus in the study of children's cognitive development. It was initiated in 1983 by a landmark paper written by Wimmer and Perner. A theory of mind describes a person's understanding of mental states, such as beliefs, thoughts, dreams, and desires. It explores what children understand about their own minds and the minds of other people. Are children aware of how people's beliefs and desires affect their behaviours? Do they understand the connections among beliefs, thoughts, desires, dreams, and reality? Adults use a theory of mind to help them understand and predict behaviour by referring to desires and to beliefs. When do children start to do the same?

Naturalistic Observations   One way that researchers study children's theory of mind is through the naturalistic approach. In the naturalistic approach, researchers study children's everyday talk to see if, and how, they refer to beliefs, thoughts, and desires. For instance, Bartsch and Wellman (1995) examined over 200 000 utterances made by 10 children, studied longitudinally from age 1½ to 6 years. Here is a sample utterance in which a 2½-year-old refers to his desires:

> *Adult:* Ice cream tastes good. It's cold.
>
> *Abe (2 years, 8 months):* I don't want it cold. I want it warm.
>
> *Adult:* You want warm ice cream.
>
> *Abe:* I want you to put hot chocolate on it.
>
> (Bartsch & Wellman, 1995, p. 70)

Even the youngest children (ages 1½ to 2 years) made utterances about desires. They expressed their wants, wishes, fears, and likes in a variety of situations. Common expressions of desires are "I wanna …" "I like …" and "I scared…." Children understand that desires affect behaviour before they appreciate how beliefs affect behaviour. Although 2-year-olds occasionally refer to words related to beliefs (e.g., *think, know,* and *wonder*), they do not appear to understand that these words refer to a person's state of mind (i.e., their mental representations). For example, when 2-year-olds ask, "Know what?" there is no indication that they are asking about the person's state of knowledge. Most likely, they are simply using the expression as a tool to join the conversation. By the time children are 3, though, they talk about beliefs as referring to mental representations. Here is an example:

> (Abe and his father are watching a TV program about snakes with a female narrator.)
>
> *Abe (3 years, 8 months):* Is that a poisonous snake dad?
>
> *Adult:* No
>
> *Abe:* I think if she tells about it … I think if she says it's a poisonous snake … you're gonna be wrong.
>
> *Adult:* You're right, I would be wrong. But it's not a poisonous snake, she just said it wasn't.
>
> *Abe:* It looks like a poisonous snake.
>
> *Adult:* Yeah. But it's not.
>
> (Bartsch & Wellman, 1995, p. 123)

Even though 3-year-olds, like Abe, have some understanding of beliefs, they do not relate beliefs to actions. For example, suppose Abe were asked to explain why someone picked up a poisonous snake. Abe would most likely refer to the person's desires ("because he wanted to") and not to the person's beliefs ("because he didn't know that it was poisonous"). According to Bartsch and Wellman's analyses, children do not use beliefs to explain actions until they are about 4 years old.

Preschool children often do not understand that beliefs are *subjective*—that different people can have different beliefs about the same state of affairs. They assume that beliefs are *objective*—that everyone has the same beliefs, almost as though the beliefs exist out in the world for all to experience. This characteristic is consistent with Piaget's notion that preschool children are egocentric. They even think that mental states, such as dreams, exist in the world outside the mind and can be experienced by more than one person. I remember when my son was 3 and was telling me about one of his dreams. I asked him a question about the dream, to which he replied, "But you should know. You were there" (Digdon).

In summary, naturalistic studies of children's utterances have revealed that children as young as 1½ talk about desires in a variety of settings. An understanding of desires develops at a younger age than an understanding of beliefs. Children do not refer to beliefs as mental representations until they are older (about 3 years old), and it is not until about age 4 that they use beliefs to explain people's actions. Naturalistic studies are valued because they provide a window into the everyday experiences of children in the "real world." As we discussed in Chapter 1, naturalistic studies are ecologically valid. They are not without their criticisms, though (see Astington, 1993). One problem with naturalistic studies is that the researcher does not "control" what the children talk about. In order to study words that are used infrequently, the researcher might have to examine hundreds of thousands of utterances, making the study laborious. Another problem is that a recording of the child's utterance, removed from the full context in which the child made it, may be ambiguous. What exactly did the child mean when she said that?

Controlled Experiments   To address these limitations, researchers such as Janet Wilde Astington at the University of Toronto and Tom Shultz at McGill use controlled experiments, instead of naturalistic studies, to examine children's theory of mind. In an experiment, the researcher presents the child with a task or a made-up situation, and then asks the child specific questions designed to probe their theory of mind.

In one of the early experiments, Tom Shultz examined children's understanding of intentions (Shultz, 1980). Children were shown a shiny penny and a dull penny, arranged side by side on the table in front of them, and then were asked to point to the shiny one. Sometimes they had to do so while wearing special glasses. The children did not know that the glasses had prisms that made the penny on the right appear to be on the left side, and vice versa. Children wearing the glasses mistakenly pointed to the dull penny. They were asked, "Did you mean to do that?" or a child watching was asked, "Did she mean to do that?" Children as young as 3 consistently distinguished between intentional and accidental actions, when explaining both their own behaviour and that of other children.

Preschool children's understanding of intentions is limited, however. For example, they do not understand how intentions relate to pretending (Lillard, 1999). In one of Lillard's experiments, children were shown a troll doll that was made to wiggle across the table. Children were told, "This is Moe, and he is a troll from the land of trolls. Right now, Moe's wiggling. Moe doesn't know what a worm is. He's never heard of a worm. He doesn't even know that worms wiggle. But right now he is wiggling just like a worm—worms wiggle just like that" (Lillard, 1999, p. 984). When asked whether Moe was pretending to be a worm, the majority of 4- and 5-year-olds said yes, often justifying their answer by saying, "He looks like a worm." According to their perspective, even if someone does not intend to pretend to be something, if they are portraying it, they must be pretending to be it.

Preschool children can distinguish between pretend and real beliefs. In one experiment, children were told about a boy who had a cookie and a boy who was pretending he had a cookie (Wellman, 1990). Even 3-year-olds knew which boy could see, touch, eat, or let his friend eat the cookie. They also knew that the first boy's cookie was real and that the second boy's cookie was not real. In another experiment, children were shown two boxes and were told to pretend that there was a friendly puppy in one box and a scary monster in the other (Harris, Brown, Marriott, Whittall, & Harmer, 1991). Children agreed that the puppy and monster were "just pretend," yet they acted differently toward the two; they were more willing to poke their fingers in the box with the pretend puppy than in the one with the pretend monster. Therefore, although in some contexts children know the difference between pretend and real beliefs, in other contexts they act as though pretend entities may be real. This inconsistency can be seen in children who have imaginary friends. The children know that their friend is make-believe, yet they act as though the friend is real.

false beliefs Beliefs that are inconsistent with the real world. They are part of theory of mind.

Several experiments on children's theory of mind have focused on **false beliefs.** As the name suggests, a false belief is one that is inconsistent with the world. False beliefs can affect how people behave. In one experiment, children listened to stories and watched them being acted out with toys (Jenkins & Wilde Astington, 1996). In one story, a boy doll put a toy in a box and went away. While he was gone, another doll took the toy out, played with it, and left it in a basket next to the box. Then the boy doll returned to get his toy. The children were asked where the boy doll would look for the toy. Most children younger than 4 years thought that the boy would look in the basket. The children did not understand that the boy would think that the toy was still in the box, since he was out of the room when the toy was moved. In another task, children were shown a closed Band-Aids box and were asked what they thought was inside. Not surprisingly, they all guessed it had Band-Aids. But when the box was opened, it contained pencils. The children were asked what other children, who had not yet seen inside the box, would think was inside. Would they realize that other children would also expect to see Band-Aids? Surprisingly, many preschool children claimed that other children would expect to find pencils. Over the course of the preschool years, children develop an awareness of false beliefs. Interestingly, children who have more advanced language skills, or who have siblings, understand false beliefs at a younger age than do other children. Perhaps children with siblings have a better understanding of false beliefs because they encounter more of them in teasing interactions with their siblings.

Recently, there has been interest in the effects of culture on theory of mind (Lillard, 1998). Canadian researchers have replicated the findings on false beliefs with preschool children in China (Lee, Olson, & Torrance, 1999). Children in China understand false beliefs at about the same age as do children in Canada. Interestingly, the use of different verbs in Chinese is a clue to whether beliefs are likely to be false. In other cultures, though, it is less clear whether theory of mind is relevant to child development. For instance, children (or adults) in Papua New Guinea rarely comment on reasons for their actions or the actions of others. They do not mention desires and beliefs, and they consider only actions important, not their justification (see Lillard, 1999, for a review of cross-cultural studies on theory of mind).

In summary, results from experiments reveal subtle distinctions in children's theory of mind. For instance, children appear to understand intentions because they can distinguish intentional actions from accidental ones. However, they do not understand the role of intentions in pretending. They think that someone is pretending whenever the person acts a certain way, regardless of the person's intentions or beliefs. Children can distinguish real objects from pretend ones. Yet, at times, they treat pretend objects as though they are real. Preschool children gradually develop an understanding of false beliefs.

Play and Learning

Play is children's unique way of experiencing the world. Play satisfies many needs in a child's life: the need to be stimulated and diverted, to express natural exuberance, to experience change for its own sake, to satisfy curiosity, to explore, and to experiment within risk-free conditions. Play has been called the "work of childhood" because of its central role in the young child's development. It promotes the growth of sensory capacities and physical skills and provides endless opportunities to exercise and expand newfound intellectual and linguistic skills. Play is different from any other kind of activity. By its very nature, playing is not directed toward a goal. As anyone who has observed a busy playground can attest, children expend great energy just for the fun of it. Catherine Garvey (1990) defined play as something that

1. Is engaged in simply for pleasure.
2. Has no purpose other than itself.
3. Players choose to do.
4. Requires players to be "actively engaged" in it.
5. Relates to other areas of life—that is, it furthers social development and enhances creativity.

Question to Ponder

Why do preschool children enjoy pretend play so much?

Types of Play

How children play changes as they develop. Young preschoolers play with other children, talk about common activities, and borrow and lend toys. But their interaction does not include setting goals or making rules for their play. Older preschoolers, however, can play together and help one another in an activity that has a goal. Preschool children like to build and create with objects, to take on roles, and to use props (Isenberg & Quisenberry, 1988). An overview of the types of play in which preschoolers engage, as well as appropriate play materials, is presented in Table 10-1.

There are many ways that children play. Sometimes their play is focused on sensory experience in and for itself. Children will endlessly splash water, ring doorbells, chew grass, bang pots, open bottles, and pluck flower petals just to experience new sounds, tastes, odours, and textures. Children play with motion; running, jumping, twirling, and skipping are just some of the countless forms of play with motion that children enjoy for their own sake. Some children, especially boys, engage in rough-and-tumble play, participating in mock fighting.

Children love to play with language, spouting sayings like "Peter Piper picked a peck of pickled peppers. If Peter Piper picked a peck of pickled peppers, where's the peck of pickled peppers Peter Piper picked?" A major type of play, *sociodramatic play*, involves taking on roles or models—for example, playing house, mimicking a parent going to work, or pretending to be a firefighter, a nurse, an astronaut, or a truck driver. Such play, as we discussed earlier in this chapter, involves not only imitation of whole patterns of behaviour, but also considerable fantasy and novel ways of interaction. See the box "Setting Up Play Centres to Foster Dramatic Play."

Play and Development

Play promotes cognitive, physical, emotional, and social development. In their play with motion, preschool children become aware of speed, weight, gravity, direction, and balance. They also become better at controlling their movements. In their play with objects, they realize that objects have conventional and appropriate uses and properties. In their play with others, children practise social concepts and roles while learning aspects of their culture.

Exploring Physical Objects When preschool children play with all sorts of physical objects—sand, stones, water, and other kinds of toys and materials—they discover and learn about the properties of the objects and about the physical laws that affect the objects. When playing in a sandbox, for example, a child can learn that different objects make different marks in the sand. When bouncing a ball on the floor, a child can learn that throwing the ball harder will make it bounce higher. When building a house with blocks, a child can learn that blocks must balance and be properly supported before they will stay in place. By engaging in constructive play, then, children acquire bits of information that they can use to build their knowledge. This greater knowledge, in turn, lets them learn with increasingly higher levels of understanding and competence (Forman & Hill, 1980). Gradually, they learn to compare and classify objects, and

These sisters are enjoying play with motion.

a

b

c

d

e

Different types of play satisfy different needs and help promote various aspects of development. Some of the major forms of children's play include

(a) sensory play,

(b) play with motion,

(c) rough-and-tumble play,

(d) language play,

(e) dramatic play and modelling, and

(f) constructive play or play with games and rituals.

f

Table 10-1 General Characteristics and Appropriate Play Materials for the Preschool Child

AGE	GENERAL CHARACTERISTICS	APPROPRIATE PLAY MATERIALS
2	Uses language effectively. Large-muscle skills developing, but limited in the use of small-muscle skills. Energetic, vigorous, and enthusiastic, with a strong need to demonstrate independence and self-control.	Large-muscle play materials: Swing sets, outdoor blocks, toys to ride on, pull toys, push toys. Sensory play materials: Clay, fingerpaints, materials for water play, blocks, books, dolls, and stuffed animals.
3	Expanded fantasy life, with unrealistic fears. Fascination with adult roles. Still stubborn, negative, but better able to adapt to peers than at age 2. Early signs of creating products in play.	Props for imaginative play (such as old clothes). Miniature life toys. Puzzles, simple board games, art materials that allow for a sense of accomplishment (for example, paintbrushes, easels, marker pens, crayons).
4	Secure, self-confident. Need for adult attention and approval—showing off, clowning around, taking risks. More able to plan than 3-year-olds, but products often accidental. Sophisticated small-muscle control allows for cutting, pasting, sewing, imaginative block building with smaller blocks.	Vehicles (for example, tricycles, Big Wheels). Materials for painting, colouring, drawing, woodworking, sewing, stringing beads. Books with themes that extend well beyond the child's real world.
5	Early signs of logical thinking. Stable, predictable, reliable. Less self-centred than at 4. Relaxed, friendly, willing to share and cooperate with peers. Realistic, practical, responsible.	Cut-and-paste and artistic activities. Simple card games (for example, Old Maid), table games (for example, Bingo), and board games (for example, Lotto), in which there are few rules and the outcomes are based more on chance than on strategy. Elaborate props for dramatic play.

Source: Hughes, 1991.

they develop a better understanding of concepts—for example, size, shape, and texture. In addition, through active play children develop skills that make them feel physically confident, secure, and self-assured (Athey, 1984).

Play and Egocentrism The egocentrism that Piaget ascribes to preoperational children is particularly evident in their play with others. Children 2 years old will watch other children and seem interested in them, but usually they will not approach them. If they do approach them, the interaction usually centres on playing with the same toy or object (Hughes, 1991). Children 2 years old and younger may seem to be playing together, but they are almost always playing out separate fantasies.

Some have thought that by the time children are 3 years old they begin to understand another child's perspective on the world. Dramatic play reflects this greater social maturity. The play of 3-year-olds reflects an understanding of others' views that allows them to be successful at role-playing games. In role playing, success depends on cooperation among players—if children do not act out their parts, the game does not work. In one study, children were asked to describe how a playmate might feel in a given situation (Borke, 1971, 1973). Children were asked to guess how another

FOCUS ON APPLICATION

Setting Up Play Centres to Foster Dramatic Play

Most day cares and playschools have a number of separate play centres for the children. These centres include an area to play with blocks, a sand table, a reading corner, and a housekeeping centre, among others. Nina Howe and colleagues in Montreal have studied how the set up of the play centres affects the children's play (Howe, Moller, & Chambers, 1994; Howe, Moller, Chambers, & Petrakos, 1993; Howe, Petrakos, Chambers, & Moller, 1995; Petrakos & Howe, 1996). In particular, they were interested in children's dramatic play. In dramatic play, children act out roles in a make-believe world. Many day-care teachers value dramatic play because it facilitates social, emotional, cognitive, and language development. Nina Howe and colleagues found that the physical arrangement of the play centres influenced the extent and type of dramatic play in the following ways:

1. Housekeeping units are one of the most commonly used dramatic play centres, but not all are created equal. Housekeeping units that have three or more types of materials (such as furniture, dolls, toy food, and doll clothes) lead to more dramatic play than do less equipped housekeeping centres.

2. Play centres that include familiar props, such as a toy stove and a broom, are associated with more imitative dramatic play. Children act out adult and child roles commonly associated with the props. But play centres that have "all-purpose" props, such as big boxes, lead to more imaginative, creative use of the props. The boxes can become beds, rocket ships, tiger cages, or submarines.

3. Dramatic play centres can be organized along a number of themes. Howe and colleagues studied the following novel play centres: a bakery, a grocery store, a farm, a train, a restaurant, a pirate ship, an airplane, a pizzeria, a pharmacy, a vet-

---

Dramatic play centres can be organized along a number of themes.

---

erinary clinic, and a hospital. In general, children engaged in more dramatic play in centres that were more familiar to them. The pharmacy, in particular, led to much lower levels of dramatic play and did not engage the children's attention.

4. Play centres could be set up to foster more group play or solitary play. For example, train centres that have single seats lead to more solitary play, but similar centres with double seats lead to more group play. Sometimes teachers prefer solitary play, so that children learn to entertain themselves, but other times they encourage group play, so that children learn appropriate social skills.

5. The pirate play centre and the pizzeria led to more rough-and-tumble play and aggression than did any of the other centres. At the time of the studies, Teenage Mutant Ninja Turtles were popular. The Ninja Turtles were fighters and loved pizza, so in the pizzeria, children pretended they were the fighting Ninja Turtles. It is important to remember that the physical designs of the play centres can influence the extent of rough-and-tumble play. Some encourage more of these behaviours than others.

6. Girls and boys preferred different centres. For the most part, girls played more in the housekeeping centres and boys played more in the novel centres, such as the pirate ships. Therefore, teachers need to ensure that there are sufficient play centres to appeal to both boys and girls. Teachers who want boys to play in housekeeping centres and girls to play on pirate ships may have to explicitly encourage this play, because most children are unlikely to engage in those kinds of play spontaneously.

7. The extent of dramatic play decreases if the same play centres are used week after week, unchanged. Centres need to be changed and embellished from time to time to keep children's interest.

---

child would react to losing a pet, breaking a toy, or attending a birthday party. By age 4, it seems that some children can reliably identify those situations likely to produce happiness, sadness, fear, and anger.

In another study, Shatz and Gelman (1973) asked 4-year-olds to describe to 2-year-olds how a specific toy worked. According to this study, even 4-year-olds understood the necessity of addressing younger children in simple terms. The researchers found that 4-year-olds spoke slowly, used short sentences, employed many attention-getting words, such as *see, look,* and *here,* and often repeated the child's name. However, 4-year-olds did not speak to older children or adults in this way. The study suggests that preschool children have some appreciation of younger children's needs and are able to modify their behaviour to meet those needs.

As with all behaviours, however, social maturity is relative. Children at the age of 3 or even 4 can still be very stubborn and negative. However, by the age of 3, there is a slightly greater tendency for children to be willing to conform to others' expectations. People are more important to 3-year-olds than they were a year earlier, and thus they seek out social interaction. By now, they are more interested in the effects of their behaviours on the world around them and draw considerable satisfaction from showing their products to others—even if the products were accidental rather than intentional (Hughes, 1991).

Dramatic Play and Social Knowledge Older preoperational children are testing their social knowledge in dramatic play. The imitating, pretending, and role taking that occur in dramatic play promote the growth of symbolic representation—the transforming of here-and-now objects and events into symbols. Dramatic play also gives children the opportunity to project themselves into other personalities, to experiment with different roles, and to experience a broader range of thought and feeling. This role playing leads to a better understanding of others, as well as to a clearer definition of one's self (Fein, 1984).

Role playing allows children to experiment with a variety of behaviours and to experience the reactions and consequences of those behaviours. For example, children who play hospital day after day with dolls, friends, or alone will play many different roles: patient, doctor, nurse, visitor. In acting out these roles, children may be motivated by very real fears and anxieties about being immobilized in a hospital bed, being dependent on others, and having their bodies acted upon by others. Whatever the dramatic situation, role playing allows children to express intense feelings, resolve conflicts, and integrate these feelings and conflicts with things they already understand.

Art as Discovery and Problem Solving The interdependence of cognitive and motor skills is apparent in children's art. Here, fine motor coordination works with perceptual, cognitive, and emotional development. The degree of development in these separate areas is evident in the final product. But, no matter how much we examine the end result of the artistic process, the exploratory process itself is what is significant—the daubing, smearing, scribbling, and, finally, representational drawing (Gardner, 1973a). From the moment children take crayons in hand and begin to scribble, at about 18 months, they start working out forms and patterns that will be essential to their later progress. Rhoda Kellogg (1970) has suggested that children start making art by scribbling and by placing their scribbles at different places on the paper. By age 3, they draw shapes in increasingly complex forms. By age 4 or 5, they start to draw representational pictures of houses, people, and other familiar objects.

Once children begin to draw representational objects, their drawings reveal how they think and feel. Goodnow (1977) suggests that children use their drawings as a problem-solving process. They work in specific sequences and have specific rules about space and position of elements in the drawing. For example, when drawing a picture of a girl, they may start at the top by drawing hair; when they have finished that part, they move in sequence down to the next part of the figure. If the hair occupies the space that a later-drawn part, such as the arms, would normally occupy, the children may omit the arms, change the shape of them to fit around the hair, or reposition the arms. Only rarely will they invade the space that the hair already occupies. These rules about space and position carry over into all of the drawings children do.

Children like to handle and manipulate materials in their art. Fingerpaint, clay, mud, sand, and even soapsuds provide opportunities to experiment with a multitude of new shapes, colours, and textures. Children not only gain a fuller sensory experience of combining texture and appearance, but they also learn directly about thickness and thinness, solidity and fluidity, and concentration and dilution.

Paintings reveal how children think and feel. Children use art to solve problems, and they follow specific rules and sequences when drawing and painting.

The Adaptive Role of Cognitive Immaturity

Intelligence is a key aspect of human beings as a species. It allows us to modify our environment to suit our needs and to adapt ourselves in the process. As with our biological abilities, however, humans undergo a long period of cognitive immaturity, or apprenticeship, in which the young depend on adults for care and guidance. It may be that the prolonged period of cognitive immaturity in humans has a specific role in development—a role arrived at through evolution.

Why might cognitive immaturity exist in an adaptive sense for children? One explanation is that prolonged cognitive immaturity may allow for a longer time to practise adult roles and socialization, through play and other means. On the other hand, a completely different explanation may be viable. Perhaps some aspects of younger children's cognitive system are qualitatively different from those of older children and adults to permit younger children to attain social-cognitive milestones, such as attachment or language (Bjorklund & Green, 1992). For example, the limited motor and sensory skills of infants may keep them close to their mothers and reduce the amount of information that they must deal with. This limited environment allows them to construct a simple, readily understandable world from which they can gradually build their cognitive skills.

Young children have an unrealistic optimism in performance expectations and generally overestimate their skills on academic tasks or in comparison with other children. This unrealistic assessment of their abilities would be a handicap in older children or adults, but it may be adaptive in young children. For example, this unrealistic optimism fosters feelings of self-efficacy in children—the belief that they will eventually succeed, perhaps on the next try. This belief provides the motivation to practise skills because children firmly expect to master them and will attempt behaviours they would not otherwise try if they had more realistic conceptions of their abilities (Bjorklund & Green, 1992).

Even egocentrism, which is often presented as a liability for young children, may become an asset. Research, for example, has found that young children learn memory strategies and recall materials better when the target information is related to themselves in some way. Egocentrism may actually enhance children's learning in certain situations because they interpret events according to their own perspectives, which helps them to comprehend and retain these events. Even in terms of language development and play, egocentrism may be perceived as positive. For example, when young children engage in parallel play, they tend to engage in *collective monologues* in which they talk with one another, but not really *to* one another (Piaget, 1955). If they were not engaged in the social situation of play, they would not be so vocal. In this case, egocentrism serves as a technique that gives them access to more socially oriented activities.

According to this viewpoint, therefore, the preoperational child shows adaptive intelligence, rather than intelligence inferior to that of older children and adults. Preoperational thought provides the necessary components—and time—for the development of a fully integrated cognitive system. Consequently, some researchers have labelled as "miseducation" educators' attempts to intensely instruct young children, sometimes beginning as early as infancy; this early instruction, paradoxically, may reduce children's learning performance (Elkind, 1987). For example, an increase in certain cognitive abilities may make language learning more difficult.

The slow maturation of children's cognitive abilities, then, does not merely provide a waiting period for mature cognitive ability; it also provides a protracted period of time during which adaptive limitations may actually increase children's learning potential throughout their development. What were once viewed as preschoolers' cognitive liabilities, such as egocentrism and a poor sense of their overall cognition, actually may be exactly what children need for their particular period of cognitive development. Indeed, researchers have voiced a caution that "we should rethink our efforts to hurry children through a childhood that has uses in and of itself" (Bjorklund & Green, 1992, p. 52).

Early Childhood Education

Schools and programs for preschoolers have become an integral part of educating Canadian children. The changing role of women and such social trends as two-income families, divorce, and single parenthood have accelerated this trend. Early childhood education (ECE) has been promoted as a way to improve both the early learning experiences of poor children and Canada's educational system in order to compete successfully with other countries. In some middle- and upper-class families, the choice of school and of formal and informal educational activities of 3- and 4-year-olds becomes a focus of social competition, as the following anecdote illustrates:

> Not long ago an old friend called to congratulate my wife and me on the birth of our son. During the catch-up conversation, he asked about my then three-year-old daughter's progress. Was she taking gymnastics, ballet, or swimming? Was she enrolled in reading, math, and computer classes? Had I succeeded in placing her name on preliminary lists for testing and admission to selective preschools and private kindergartens? "One can never start too early," he assured. "Oh, and how has she done on early tests?" (Piccigallo, 1988)

In the 1960s, the leaders of the reform movement fostering early childhood programs had ambitious ideas about what 3- and 4-year-olds were likely to gain from schooling. They considered children "competent" to improve their intelligence almost from infancy (Bloom, 1964). A prominent educator claimed that "you can teach any child any subject matter at any age in an intellectually honest way" (Bruner, 1960). Some educators, claiming that "it is easier to teach a one-year-old any set of facts than it is to teach a seven-year-old" (Doman, 1984), translated this belief into instruction of children beginning in the crib.

Some have criticized these views for failing to take into account that the young child is a different kind of learner than the older child. Critics have argued that formal instruction puts excessive demands on young children (Elkind, 1986, 1987), and David Elkind refers to it as "miseducation." Young children may even be harmed by early instruction. Children who are given tasks that are too intellectually demanding are in danger of falling into early patterns of frustration and failure (Ames, 1971). Both short- and long-term risks have been found to be associated with the stresses that formal education places on young children. Fatigue, loss of appetite, decreased efficiency, psychosomatic ailments, and a reduced motivation for learning all have resulted from premature formal schooling (Bjorklund & Green, 1992).

Although some educators believe that 3- and 4-year-olds should be at home, where they will, ideally, receive warmth, security, and continuity in the years before starting school, this option is not open to or desirable to many parents. In addition, research has shown that preschool can offer specific advantages to children. Attending nursery school has been found to foster children's social and emotional development. Compared with children at home, preschool students made advances in sociability, self-expression, independence, and interest in the environment (Mussen, Conger, & Kagan, 1974). In another study, children attending preschool surpassed children who stayed at home on such intellectual tasks as vocabulary, language comprehension, and visual memory (Brand & Welch, 1989). Long-term gains in the ability to learn and in reading have been found in children of both middle-class and poor homes. Some educators feel that a year of preschooling helps many youngsters who would otherwise repeat a grade or require special placement (Featherstone, 1985).

Ultimately, it is the nature of the young child's experience of her surroundings—not whether she attends a formal preschool or spends most of her time at home—that will contribute to her ability to learn. Children learn by observing the consequences of their actions, by putting objects into new forms, and by getting feedback from those around them. Whether they are at home or at school, their surroundings are a powerful presence contributing to the enhancement or retardation of their growth. A carefully planned, well-paced early education program can give children the experiences they need for their cognitive development—especially when this program is designed with children's developmental levels in mind (Zigler, 1987).

Developmentally Appropriate Curriculum

The key concept in defining quality education is *developmental appropriateness*. Because children learn in different ways at different ages, what is acceptable for one age group is inappropriate for another. Obviously, the aim of a developmentally appropriate preschool is to match the school program with the developmental needs and abilities of young children. Within such a setting, the individual needs of each child can be addressed. The developmentally appropriate tasks for 3- and 4-year-olds involve using large- and small-muscle activity to explore their environment. Educators of young children recognize that development cannot be accelerated or skipped. Each stage of development has its own tasks to accomplish (NAEYC, 1996).

How can educators best match their educational programs for young children with their students' developmental needs? The National Association for the Education of Young Children (NAEYC) appointed a commission to study this question and to make recommendations. Their conclusions, based on research findings, are presented in the form of guidelines for teachers of early childhood classrooms. Their guidelines for **developmentally appropriate curriculum** for preschoolers include the following:

developmentally appropriate curriculum A curriculum that matches the developmental needs and abilities of young children.

- In place of an "academic" program, an educational curriculum should include all areas of a child's development—physical, emotional, social, and cognitive.
- Curriculum plans should be based on observations of each child's interests and developmental progress, not the average of the group.
- A learning environment should allow for active exploration and interaction with adults, with other children, and with teaching materials. Highly structured, teacher-directed activities are not encouraged.

- In place of workbooks, dittos, or other abstract materials, young children should be offered concrete activities and materials that are relevant to their lives.
- Adults should respond quickly and directly to children's needs and messages and adapt to children's styles and abilities.

Other guidelines include specific illustrations of appropriate and inappropriate practice for different age levels, from infancy to age 8. For example, stimulating children's skills of 4- and 5-year-olds in all developmental areas fosters the growth of self-esteem, social skills, and language abilities. Learning activities that allow them to be physically and mentally active are considered the appropriate preparation for future learning. In contrast, an emphasis on teaching specific academic skills, such as the rules of reading or mathematics, is considered inappropriate. These are tasks that can be mastered at a later, appropriate level of development. It is noteworthy that, given the wide range of programs currently offered, a large, national organization of educators from the United States could reach such near consensus on basic principles (NAEYC, 1996).

Approaches to Early Education

A number of models for early childhood education have been created. Some schools follow a specific model closely, but most incorporate elements of various approaches. Following are descriptions of four influential models for teaching preschoolers: the Montessori method, formal didactic education, open education, and the Reggio Emilia approach. Each model incorporates an approach to how children learn, as well as beliefs about how people think and behave in our culture.

Montessori Schools Although most **Montessori schools** in Canada and the United States tend to be expensive private schools, the Montessori method took root in quite different surroundings. Dr. Maria Montessori, an energetic and innovative Italian physician, began her experimental educational methods with retarded children and then with socially disadvantaged children from the tenements of Rome. She believed that children who had experienced a difficult, chaotic, or unpredictable home life needed surroundings that emphasized sequence, order, and regularity. The Montessori approach features a prepared environment and carefully designed, self-correcting materials. Each child may select a task to work on individually, returning the materials to the shelf when finished. A typical task involves arranging in sequence a set of graduated cylinders, weights, or smooth- to rough-textured pieces of cloth. Some of the cylinders may have handles to facilitate the fine motor development and finger control necessary for writing. There will be a sound table, where children are introduced to letters and phonics. The children also may learn practical tasks, such as washing dishes, making soup, gardening, and painting a real wall. Classrooms are age mixed, with children from 3 to 7 years. As we have seen earlier in this chapter, groups of mixed age children provide an excellent atmosphere for learning and growing. The older children assist and teach the younger children.

The atmosphere in a Montessori school is one of quiet busyness and confident accomplishment. The teacher arranges the environment but avoids interfering with the learning process; teachers especially avoid injecting any "extraneous" elements, such as praise or criticism. The curriculum develops motor and sensory skills, as well as the ability to order and classify materials. These are considered the basic forerunners of more complex tasks, such as reading and understanding mathematics. Many contemporary educational techniques incorporate some Montessori methods—particularly self-teaching materials, individually paced progress, real-life tasks, and the relative absence of both praise and criticism.

Formal Didactic Education **Formal didactic education,** or the "back-to-basics" approach, uses carefully structured lessons to inculcate a particular set of skills. It is typified by the

---

Question to Ponder

What types of learning environments are most appropriate for preschool children?

Montessori schools Programs emphasizing the use of self-teaching materials, individually paced progress, real-life tasks, and the relative absence of praise and criticism.

---

formal didactic education Programs emphasizing a back-to-basics approach and drill teaching.

In a Montessori school, there is a focus on the development of motor and sensory skills and on the ability to order and classify materials.

Bereiter and Engelmann program (1966) designed for disadvantaged children (later known as the Distar program). To teach the requisite skills in a gradual, sequential order, the two psychologists divided the children into homogeneous, small groups of about five members. The teacher asked a question or offered a sentence, and the children responded by answering the question or repeating the sentence in unison. The children also interacted individually with the teacher, receiving immediate feedback and warm praise for success. Teachers gave frequent positive reinforcement. They taught lessons in 20-minute drill periods, with little time allowed for free play between periods because the psychologists felt that play distracted the children from learning specific facts, principles, and skills.

Research on the Distar program indicated that these children did learn the specific behavioural objectives quickly and well. Long-term results, however, showed little lasting transfer of learned skills to other educational settings. Again, there are several explanations for these results:

1. The follow-up schools for these disadvantaged children might have been so stifling, socially and intellectually, that they could not encourage success in even the brightest, most motivated child.

2. The difference in expectations between the Distar program and the public school was perhaps so great that the particular behaviours could not be sustained.

3. The children might have become overly dependent on the rewards of praise, hugs, and smiles and failed to derive any intrinsic pleasure from the learning and problem-solving process.

At any rate, children in these programs displayed marked initial success, with kindergartners often reading at a grade two level. This early advantage disappeared by at least grade four, when these children became indistinguishable from other "disadvantaged" children.

Open Education **Open education** is an eclectic movement that draws on the work of such diverse theorists as Jean Piaget, John Dewey (1961), and Susan Isaacs (1930). Despite the implications of its name, open education does not signify the absence of

open education Programs emphasizing an integrated day, vertical groupings, and child input in decision making.

structure. Indeed, good open education, as exemplified by the British Infant School, requires extensive planning and preparation. The British Infant School was designed to help children enter the formal English educational system by age 8 or 9 (Plowden, 1967). Some of its main characteristics are the following:

- *The integrated day.* Instead of discrete periods for each subject, children work at continuing projects that employ several skills at once. Setting up a "business office" may entail a field trip for observation, a written report, group discussion, and some artwork or other visual aids.

- *Vertical groupings.* Children of different ages are in the same classroom. Within several years, a child can develop from being the youngest, following and learning from others, to a position of leadership and responsibility.

- *Child input in decision making.* Children in open classrooms often choose from a variety of activities, deciding how they want to participate and for how long. A child's ability to make responsible decisions is respected, and such potential incentives as reward and punishment are minimized. We should note that this is the same sort of philosophy that underlies the Montessori program presented earlier.

The achievement of the British Infant School is impressive; the children equal or surpass the performance of students in more traditional programs. But the school's curriculum planning is extensive, and community support must be strong. Some open classrooms in other educational systems are unsuccessful; the difference seems to lie in the skill and forethought of the planners and teachers.

Reggio Emilia Approach The **Reggio Emilia approach** to early childhood education was spearheaded by Loris Malaguzzi (1920–1994) in a small Italian community after World War II. It quickly attracted international attention and, in the December 2, 1991, issue of *Newsweek* magazine, was acclaimed one of the best approaches in the world to early childhood education. Furthermore, current Canadian textbooks on early childhood education have a strong focus on the Reggio Emilia approach (see Essa, Young, & Lehne, 1998). Why has this approach attracted so much attention? What are the distinguishing features of the Reggio Emilia approach?

> **Reggio Emilia approach** Programs emphasizing in-depth projects that involve considerable use of the visual arts. Children work in small groups, and the teacher consults with them and documents their experiences.

One key element of the approach is that programs are organized around small groups of children working on in-depth projects using visual arts techniques. Through extensive discussions, the teachers and the children choose topics for projects to reflect the children's interests. Children, therefore, have a genuine enthusiasm for the subject matter. For example, a group of children in one Reggio Emilia school carried out a project on snow that examined how snow is produced and how it changes the world around the children (Forman, Lee, Wrisley, & Langley, 1993). The project began several weeks before the first snowfall. Children discussed their memories of snow, how it changed the playground, and how the city responded to huge quantities of snow. The focus was on the children's construction of the experience, rather than on the teacher's telling the children the "correct answers." The teacher facilitated the discussion and recorded the children's ideas and questions.

Teacher documentation of children's ideas is a critical component of the Reggio Emilia approach. Teachers keep meticulous records of children's responses. As projects develop, teachers use the documentation to remind the children of their earlier conceptualization of the project. In this way, the children are able to see contradictions between earlier and later concepts, and they can see how their understanding has evolved. Through the documentation, the children can relive the experience of the project. As well, teachers use the documentation to plan curriculum. The curriculum is called an *emergent curriculum* because it is not fully developed at the outset of the project. Curriculum development is ongoing and is influenced by children's responses and by teachers' extensive consultation with one another and with other professionals, most notably the *atelierista,* who is a specialist in visual arts. The atelierista runs an art studio (called an *atelier*) in the school. Small groups of children regularly work on projects in the atelier. Projects entail a number of artistic endeavours. For example, in the project on snow, children made several drawings: they drew a snow scene at the outset of the project (before the first snowfall) and again after a field trip on a snowy day. They drew their impressions of the sounds of snow, the growth of individual snowflakes, and the process of water changing to ice. According to the Reggio Emilia approach, the visual arts function like symbolic languages, enabling the children to communicate their understanding and interpretation of concepts. For example, one child's before and after drawings of a snow scene depicted a change in the distribution of snow. In the before picture, snow covered everything. In the after picture, more snow was deposited on horizontal surfaces (e.g., the top of cars) than on slanted surfaces (e.g., playground slides), and none was deposited on vertical surfaces (e.g., the sides of buildings). Drawings enabled the child to communicate his new understanding of snow.

In addition to producing individual drawings, the children worked in small groups to create a visual simulation of snow, by sprinkling flour over a city made of wooden blocks, and to make a mural of a snow scene. According to the Reggio Emilia approach, group work is critical because children learn from the varying perspectives of their peers and from the cooperation needed to accomplish a group task.

The Reggio Emilia approach emphasizes learning more than teaching. Teachers spend more time observing, documenting, and facilitating children's learning than they do directing it. Teachers regularly engage children in intellectual conversations about children's understanding of the project. This approach contrasts with that in many preschool programs, in which most of the teacher's conversations with children seem to be about discipline or about evaluating children's performance (Katz, 1993). The Reggio Emilia approach places less emphasis on set class routines or timetables than do many other preschool programs. Work on projects structures the school day. Even lunchtime and naptime may be changed so that they are more compatible with ongoing project work. The timelines for completing a project are open ended. Some projects last for months, much longer than in other types of preschool programs. One of the distinguishing features of the Reggio Emilia approach is that children are encouraged to explore and master topics in greater depth than is typical in preschool curriculums.

At the end of the project, the visual arts are displayed in the school. Alongside the art are write-ups of the comments and questions that the children had during its production. In addition, the displays often include photographs of the children at various stages of production. Therefore, the display attempts to capture the process involved in completing the project, not just the finished product. Children are encouraged to reflect on the process and to share the exhibit with parents and others in the community. There is a strong sense of pride and respect for the children's work. The community celebrates children's learning.

Summary and Conclusions

Cognitive development shows significant change during the preschool years. Children from 2 to 6 years of age develop their ability for symbolic representation—the transformation of physical objects, people, and events into mental symbols. Symbols allow the thought processes of children to become more complex. Symbols also permit the development of concepts such as temporal ordering—past and future.

Not all learning occurs in the preschool or nursery school classroom. Children gain much competence through pretend play. Play provides the opportunity for motor, social, and cognitive experience in the world. Children who have had a good amount of play are better able to understand the concept of conservation—that an object can change shape or form and still remain the same object—and they are more sociocentric, or sensitive to the needs and emotions of others. However, there are limits to preoperational thought. Preoperational children's thought is concrete, irreversible, egocentric, and centred. They focus on the present state of things and are not aware of how things may be transformed. They have difficulty with classification, time, sequence, and spatial relationships.

In recent years, researchers have challenged some of Piaget's conclusions about young children's mental capabilities. These psychologists believe that Piaget underestimated the impact of social experience with adults and other children on the growth of children's thinking. They believe that instruction from adults and solving real problems may well further the development of children's thinking. Piaget's theory focuses on understanding the physical world, rather than the social and cultural world.

One common factor in all the research, however, is that the thinking, memory, and problem solving of younger children is qualitatively different from that of older children. For example, preschoolers show good recognition memory but have poor recall memory. Moreover, it has been found difficult to teach preschoolers strategies to organize and rehearse information. Despite this limitation, preschoolers do seem to have rudimentary memory strategies that relate to meaning, sequence, and function and to their interrelationships. These strategies serve as precursors to the more complex and comprehensive strategies of older children.

Preschool children gradually develop a theory of mind.

Typically, children understand the role of desires in motivating behaviour before they understand the role of beliefs. Young children do not understand false beliefs.

Play offers preschool children opportunities to express themselves freely—without pressure to succeed at something or to produce a product. Play is valuable as self-expression and exploration, and it also furthers social development and fosters creativity. Play takes many forms, from rough-and-tumble play to play with language. All of these forms offer children opportunities to learn socially appropriate behaviours, empathy, rules, and the ability to distinguish pretend from real. Play allows children to manipulate reality, meanings, and their experiences.

Based on a careful review of the skills and abilities of preschool children, cognitive immaturity may be seen as adaptive, rather than as a deficiency. Egocentrism and a lack of awareness of cognition itself may actually allow children to have a longer period of development in which to build and refine developmentally appropriate cognitive skills.

ECE programs are becoming important in Canada. With more women working and a scarcity of high-quality day care, many parents seek preschools or nursery schools as a safe and stimulating environment for their children. Some educators feel that such programs place excessive demands on children before they are ready; others believe that early childhood programs stimulate intellectual, social, and motor development. While educators are divided regarding the benefits of early education for children, they agree that standards and guidelines need to be followed to ensure the optimal environment in which children may grow without stress.

The NAEYC has developed guidelines for educational curricula that match the developmental needs of young children. In general, these guidelines suggest promoting activities that foster motor development, having little structured pre-reading or pre-math activities, providing an open environment with a diversity of ages to encourage exploration and sensitivity, and including responsive, guiding adults.

Several ECE models exist. Among the most influential are the Montessori method, formal didactic education, open education, and the Reggio Emilia approach. The Montessori model is a discovery oriented, self-correcting environment with teachers as guides and an age mix ranging from 3 to 7.

Montessori tasks feature sequence, order, and regularity. In addition to those activities that develop motor, sensory, and practical life skills, there is an introduction to sounds and number, art and music. Traditional, formal approaches teach specific skills in a gradual, sequential order, but the advantages gained tend not to last, possibly because the approaches emphasize rote learning and drill before the children are ready for the concepts. Open education involves planning and forethought for success to occur. It features integrated activities for children to develop several skills simultaneously, much the way they do in the "real world." Again, children of mixed ages participate in the same class and are involved in deciding what to do and for how long. In programs using the Reggio Emilia approach, children work in small groups on in-depth projects that involve the visual arts. Projects are chosen based on the children's interests. Teachers act as facilitators and as recorders of children's learning experiences.

Key Terms and Concepts

centration (p. 308)

classification (p. 310)

developmentally appropriate curriculum (p. 328)

egocentricity (p. 301)

false beliefs (p. 320)

formal didactic education (p. 329)

guided participation (p. 313)

irreversibility (p. 306)

Montessori schools (p. 329)

open education (p. 330)

organization (p. 315)

recall (p. 315)

recognition (p. 315)

Reggio Emilia approach (p. 331)

rehearsal (p. 315)

sociocentric (p. 302)

sociodramatic play (p. 302)

Questions to Review

1. What is the preoperational period of child development? Differentiate between the two stages of preoperational thought.

2. Explain the significance of real and pretend play in the cognitive development of a preschool child.

3. List the limitations of preoperational thought.

4. Discuss the criticisms of Piaget's theory and alternative theories of cognitive development.

5. Describe the memory capabilities of preschool children. Differentiate between recognition and recall. What memory strategies do children use?

6. Describe preschool children's theory of mind.

7. How does play promote cognitive development?

8. How does children's art aid in physical and cognitive development?

9. Discuss the benefits of cognitive immaturity for preschoolers.

10. Discuss different views concerning the benefit of formal education for preschoolers.

11. List and discuss different approaches to early childhood education.

Weblinks

users.sgi.net/~cokids/
Early Childhood Educators' and Family Web Corner
This site has articles on education, position papers, and resources for educators and parents.

www.nlc-bnc.ca/services/eelec.htm
Canadian Children's Literature Service
This site, created by the National Library of Canada, has links to Internet resources on children's literature and a list of award-winning children's books.

www.bestpraceduc.org/people/LevVygotsky.html
Vygotsky's Theory and Education
This U.S. site has a good bibliography of Vygotsky, as well as descriptions of educational programs that are based on his theory. There are also links to other Web sites on Vygotsky.

Early Childhood: Personality and Social Development

Yesterday a child came out to wander
Caught a butterfly inside a jar
Fearful when the sky
Was full of thunder
And tearful at the falling of a star.

JONI MITCHELL
"THE CIRCLE GAME"

Outline

CHAPTER 11

Objectives

By the time you have finished this chapter, you should be able to do the following:

✔ Describe the strong feelings and conflicts that preschool children face.

✔ Understand the difference between fear and anxiety, give some of the sources of these emotions, and describe the ways that children cope with them.

✔ Explain the factors that influence aggressive and prosocial behaviour.

✔ Describe the development of gender schemes during the preschool period and the effects they have on the child's behaviour.

✔ Describe the impact of parenting styles and parents' warmth and control on personality and social development during early childhood.

✔ List some of the ways that brothers and sisters influence social development.

✔ Describe the effects of television on child development.

During the preschool period, young children become socialized. They learn what is expected of them in their family and in their community—what is good and bad behaviour for boys and girls like them. They learn how to handle their feelings in socially appropriate ways. They learn who they are within the social context of their community. In other words, young children learn the norms, rules, and cultural meanings of their society, and they develop a self-concept that may persist throughout their lives. In Chapter 3, we looked briefly at some of these socialization processes. In this chapter, we will examine them in more detail, particularly as they relate to the developmental issues of the preschool period.

There is dramatic growth in the child's self-control and social competence during the four important years from age 2 to age 6. Although 2-year-olds have all the basic emotions of 6-year-olds (or, for that matter, of adults), their expression of these emotions is immediate, impulsive, and direct. They cannot wait to have their desires satisfied. A mother who has promised her 2-year-old an ice cream cone cannot afford the luxury of chatting with a friend outside the ice cream parlour—her child's impatience will interfere with any attempts at conversation. Expressions of dependency, too, are direct and physical at this age. In an unfamiliar setting, a 2-year-old stays close to his mother, clinging to her clothing or returning often to her side. If forcibly separated from her, he may throw himself on the floor, howling with anger, protest, and grief. Children express anger in direct, physical ways at this age. Instead of expressing themselves verbally, 2-year-olds may kick or bite. They may grab a desired toy instead of asking for it.

In contrast, 6-year-olds are much more verbal and thoughtful; they are a little less quick to anger, and they censor or control their behaviour. Their coping patterns are far more diverse than those of 2-year-olds; 6-year-olds can express their anger by kicking a door or a teddy bear, rather than a brother or sister. They may have learned to hold in their anger and to refrain from expressing it outwardly. They may have developed a special assertive posture to defend their rights or a specific fantasy to see them through unpleasant situations. If Mommy is not where they expect her to be, 6-year-olds are unlikely to kick and howl. Instead, they may talk out their anger or fear, or they may express it in a highly disguised form—perhaps by becoming uncooperative and grumpy or by building an elaborate tower of blocks and then knocking it down. In short, most 6-year-olds have become refined in their abilities to cope and have developed their own distinctive styles. There are far more individual variations in methods of coping among 6-year-olds than among 2-year-olds. The personal style that a child develops in these years may be the foundation of a lifelong pattern of behaviour.

Theories Revisited

The socialization of a child during the preschool years is complex, involving the ups and downs of interpersonal relationships and the cumulative effects of countless events. It is no wonder that experts disagree about the major influences and critical interactions and even about the best methods to study the processes. As indicated in Chapter 2, there are a number of theoretical perspectives and issues:

1. The *psychodynamic perspective* emphasizes the child's feelings, drives, and developmental conflicts. Children must learn to cope with powerful emotions, such as anxiety, in socially acceptable ways. Erikson has described the growth of autonomy and the need to balance it with dependency on parents during this period.

2. According to the *social-learning perspective,* social and personality development are primarily products of the environment. The child's behaviour is shaped by rewards and modelling. Sometimes these rewards are external, coming from parents or adults in the environment, and at other times—especially as the child matures—the rewards are internal.

3. The *cognitive development perspective* emphasizes children's own thoughts and concepts as organizers for their social behaviour. Children develop increasingly complex concepts—for example, they learn what it means to be a girl or a boy, a sister or a brother, or a friend. These concepts, in turn, play a major role in directing children's behaviour.

4. Recent studies stress that socialization is *reciprocal* (Eisenberg, Fabes, Shepard, Guthrie, Murphy, & Reiser, 1999). Parents affect children, but children also affect parents; these reciprocal effects are called *bidirectional effects.* Children are born with different temperaments that influence how others respond to them. Furthermore, adult responses to children influence how children behave.

5. Social development is affected by *culture.* According to Bronfenbrenner's ecological model, the cultural level, called the *macrosystem,* has an enormous impact on development because the same behaviour can have different meanings and consequences in different cultural settings. For example, shy or anxious children in China are judged to be socially competent and well adjusted (Chen, Hastings, Rubin, Chen, Cen, & Stewart, 1998). Chinese parents approve of children's shyness and of their inhibited behaviour, and peers are accepting of shy children in China (Chen, Rubin, & Li, 1995). In Canada, however, shy or anxious children are judged to be socially incompetent because assertive and independent behaviour is the cultural norm (Chen et al., 1998). Canadian parents most often respond by punishing shy behaviour in children or becoming overprotective of the children (Chen et al., 1998). Canadian children who are shy and withdrawn are at risk for peer rejection.

6. According to Bronfenbrenner's ecological model, a child's social interactions in one setting (such as the home) can have an effect on her interactions with different people in other settings (such as the day care). Bronfenbrenner referred to these interactions as the *mesosystem.* For example, relationships with siblings can have an effect on those with peers, and vice versa. Researchers at McGill University found that children's popularity in kindergarten was directly related to the quality of

Question to Ponder

How do theories shape the kinds of questions that researchers ask about social development?

their relationships with siblings (Mendelson, Aboud, & Lanthier, 1994a). All of the children in this study had siblings. Children were more likely to be popular with same sex children in kindergarten if they expressed positive feelings toward their siblings and identified with them.

Each of these perspectives has been influential in shaping our understanding of children's social development. In this chapter, we shall discuss research from different perspectives in order to offer a broader understanding of social and personality development in the preschool-age child.

Developmental Issues and Coping Patterns

Children must learn to handle a wide range of feelings in these early years. Some are good feelings, such as joy, affection, and pride. Others, such as anger, fear, anxiety, jealousy, frustration, and pain, are not pleasant at all. Children also must find their own ways of resolving developmental conflicts. They must learn to deal with an awareness of their dependence on others and find ways of relating to the authority figures in their lives. On the other hand, children also must deal with their own feelings of independence or autonomy—their strong drive to do things for themselves, to master their physical and social environments, to be competent and successful. As Erikson (1950) suggests, children who are unable to successfully resolve these early psychosocial conflicts may have difficulty coping later in life.

Preschoolers have intense feelings that they must learn to handle during these early years. Learning that losing a race is not the end of the world may take away some of this child's sadness.

Handling Feelings

The sense of personal and cultural identity that forms between the ages of 2 and 6 is accompanied by many strong feelings that children must learn to integrate into their own personality structures. Finding outlets for these feelings which are acceptable both to themselves and to their parents is no easy task. Children find many solutions to this challenge, but they also experience conflict while doing so.

Fear and Anxiety One of the most important conditions that children must learn to deal with is the stress caused by fear and anxiety. Both children and adults experience these patterns of psychological and physiological stress as unpleasant. The two emotions are not synonymous; a distinction must be made between them. **Fear** is a response to a specific stimulus or situation: for example, a child may fear big dogs or lightning and thunder. In contrast, **anxiety** has a more vague or generalized source. Anxious children experience an overall feeling of apprehension, but they do not know its precise origin. A move to a new neighbourhood or a sudden change in parental expectations, such as the beginning of toilet training, may be the indirect cause of tensions that seem to come from nowhere. Many psychologists believe that anxiety inevitably accompanies socialization, since the child attempts to avoid the pain of parental displeasure and discipline (Wenar, 1990).

fear A state of arousal, tension, or apprehension caused by a specific circumstance.

anxiety A feeling of uneasiness, apprehension, or fear that has a vague or unknown source.

THE CAUSES OF FEAR AND ANXIETY

Fear and anxiety have many causes. Young children may be anxious that their parents will leave them or stop loving them. Parents usually act in a loving and accepting way, but sometimes—frequently as a means of punishment—they withdraw their love, attention, and protection. The withdrawal of love threatens children and makes them feel anxious. Anticipation of other types of punishment, especially physical punishment, is another source of anxiety for young children. Two-year-olds see parents as powerful people; they may have no realistic idea of how far their parents will go in punishing them. When an exasperated parent shouts, "I'm going to break every bone in your body!" the child (who has probably witnessed countless such acts of violence on television) has no way of knowing that the parent's threat is an empty one. The child's own

No child really enjoys going to the doctor. Often a trip to the doctor's office is linked in a child's mind with a painful injection.

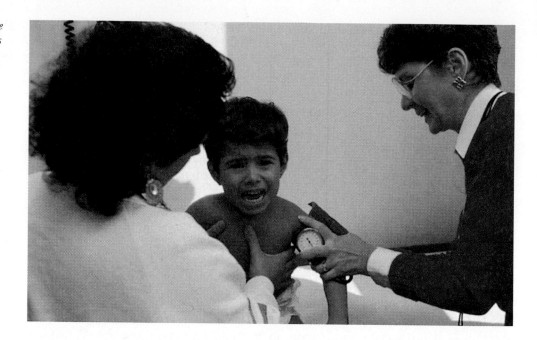

No child really enjoys going to the doctor. Often a trip to the doctor's office is linked in a child's mind with a painful injection.

imagination may increase, or even produce, fear and anxiety. Children often imagine that the birth of a new baby will cause their parents to reject them. Sometimes anxiety results from children's awareness of their own unacceptable feelings, such as anger at a parent or a teacher, jealousy of a sibling or a friend, or neediness in the desire to be held like a baby.

The sources of some fears are easily traced, for example, the fear of the doctor who gives inoculations or the dread inspired by the smell of a hospital or the sound of a dentist's drill. Other fears are not so easy to understand. Many preschoolers develop a fear of the dark at bedtime. This type of fear is frequently related more to fantasies and dreams than to any real events in the child's life. Sometimes these fantasies stem directly from developmental conflicts that the child is currently struggling with; for example, imaginary tigers or ghosts may arise from the child's struggle with dependency and autonomy. In a classic study of children's fears, Jersild and Holmes (1935) found that younger children are most likely to be afraid of specific things, like strangers, unfamiliar objects, loud noises, or falling. In contrast, children at age 5 or 6 show an increased fear of imaginary or abstract things—monsters, robbers, the dark, death, being alone, or being ridiculed. Fifty years later, researchers found most of the same fears in preschool children, except that fears of the dark, of being alone, and of strange sights are now appearing at an earlier age (Draper & James, 1985).

In today's world, there are many sources of fear, anxiety, and stress. Some can be considered a normal part of growing up, for example, being yelled at for accidentally breaking something or being teased by a sibling. Others are more serious, including internal stresses, such as illness and pain, and the chronic long-term stresses of unfavourable social environments, such as poverty, parental conflict or alcoholism, and dangerous neighbourhoods (Greene & Brooks, 1985). Some children must cope with major disasters or terrors, such as earthquakes, floods, and wars. Severe or long-term stressful situations can overwhelm the resources of even the most resilient child (Honig, 1986; Rutter, 1983).

Although fear and anxiety are emotions that we naturally try to avoid and minimize, they are also normal feelings that are necessary for development. In mild forms, they can be a spur to new learning. Some fears—such as a fear of fast-moving cars—are necessary for our very survival and act as part of our physiological arousal system. But others—such as a fear of the bathtub—interfere with daily life and with what our society considers appropriate behaviour. Furthermore, high levels of chronic fear and anxiety are overwhelming and interrupt normal development.

COPING WITH FEAR AND ANXIETY

How can we help children cope with their fears? Using force or ridicule is likely to have negative results, and ignoring children's fears will not make them go away. Children can be gently and sympathetically encouraged to confront and overcome mild fears. However, children may need professional help to cope with somewhat stronger yet unrealistic fears (see Chapter 2).

The best way to help children cope with anxiety and stress is to reduce the amount of unnecessary stress that they must deal with. When children show unusually high levels of tension or have frequent temper tantrums, it is often useful to simplify their lives for a few days by sticking to a routine, specifying clearly what is expected, and helping the child to anticipate coming events. Other helpful strategies include reducing exposure to parental fighting or to violent television shows and protecting children from the teasing and tormenting of neighbourhood bullies. But not all major life stresses can be avoided. Sometimes children must cope with the stress of common events, like the birth of a sibling, moving to a new home, or entering day care, as well as with less common stresses, like death, divorce, or natural catastrophes. Under these circumstances, parents and teachers should try to accomplish the following (Honig, 1986):

1. Learn to recognize and interpret children's stress reactions.
2. Provide a warm, secure base for children to renew their confidence.
3. Allow opportunities for children to discuss their feelings, as a socially shared trauma is easier to handle.
4. Allow immature or regressive behaviour, such as thumb sucking, cuddling a blanket, fussing, or sitting on laps.
5. Help children to give meaning to the event or circumstances by an explanation.

DEFENCE MECHANISMS

In response to more generalized feelings of anxiety—especially those generated in the intense emotional climate of the family, involving issues of morality or sex roles—children learn strategies called **defence mechanisms.** A defence mechanism is an indirect way to disguise or reduce anxiety. By the age of 5 or 6, most children have learned how to hide or disguise their feelings with defence mechanisms. They continue to do so when they are adults. We all employ defence mechanisms (Freud called them *classical ego defences*) as strategies for reducing tensions. A common defence mechanism in young children is **withdrawal.** It is the most direct defence possible: if a situation seems too difficult, the child simply withdraws and goes away from it, either physically or mentally. Another defence mechanism that preschool children use is **regression.** Regression is a return to an earlier or more infantile form of behaviour as a way of coping with a stressful situation. For example, a 5-year-old may suddenly revert to sucking her thumb and carrying around her "blankie"—behaviours given up years before—when her best friend is badly injured in an accident. Another defence mechanism that is common in preschool children is **denial.** Denial is the refusal to admit that a situation exists or that an event happened. Children may react to an upsetting situation, such as the death of a pet, by pretending that the pet is still living in the house and sleeping with them at night.

Children learn some defence mechanisms by observing the behaviour of parents or siblings, but they learn most directly, through their own experience of what defences work best to reduce anxiety without causing other problems. The defence patterns that children adopt are learned thoroughly during the preschool years and may stay with them throughout their lives.

As a result of differences in cultural and family backgrounds, children feel fear and anxiety about different things. A hundred years ago, children feared wolves and bears. Fifty years ago, they worried about goblins and bogeymen. Now their nightmares are populated with extraterrestrials and killer robots. There are also striking cultural

defence mechanisms Any of the techniques people use to reduce tensions that lead to anxiety.

withdrawal A defence mechanism in which a person physically goes away from, or mentally withdraws from, unpleasant situations.

regression Coping with an anxiety-producing situation by reverting to earlier, more immature behaviour.

denial The refusal to admit that an anxiety-producing situation exists or that an anxiety-producing event happened.

differences in the way children express their fears and in how free they are to express them at all. In contemporary Western culture, showing fear is frowned upon—children (especially boys) are supposed to be brave, and most parents worry about a child who is unusually fearful. But this attitude is not universal. Navajo parents believe that it is healthy and normal for a child to be afraid; they consider a fearless child to be ignorant or foolhardy. In a recent study, Navajo parents reported an average of 22 fears in their children, including fears of supernatural beings. In contrast, a group of Anglo-American parents from rural Montana reported an average of 4 fears in their children (Tikalsky & Wallace, 1988).

Distress and Anger Western society not only frowns on the expression of fear, but also expects children to inhibit the display of other negative emotions, such as anger, jealousy, frustration, and distress. Children learn, from a very early age, that open displays of such feelings are unacceptable in public places—and day-care centres and nursery schools count as public places (Dencik, 1989). Although freer displays of emotion are usually permitted at home, most parents expect their children to learn what Kopp (1989) calls *emotion regulation:* the process of dealing with their emotions in socially acceptable ways. As children grow older, their parents' expectations for emotion regulation increase: it is all right for babies to cry loudly when they are hungry, but it is not all right for 6-year-olds to wail bitterly if they must wait a few minutes for a snack. If children have trouble regulating their emotions, they will have difficulties inhibiting their frustration, aggression, and impulsive responses while in emotionally arousing conflicts with peers (Fabes et al., 1999). Preschoolers who cry too frequently are likely to be unpopular with their peers (Kopp, 1989). Learning to manage anger is even more important. Some children who were still having temper tantrums at the age of 10 were followed in a longitudinal study. The researchers found that these children tended to be unsuccessful in adult life as a result of their outbursts of anger: they had difficulty holding jobs, and their marriages often ended in divorce (Caspi, Elder, & Bem, 1987). For most children, though, the problem behaviours of toddlerhood (for example, hitting, biting, and throwing temper tantrums) decline appreciably between the ages of 2 and 5 (Keenan & Shaw, 1997).

Why do some preschool children have more difficulty regulating their emotions? Two factors seem to be important: the child's temperament and how he is socialized. Some children have more difficult temperaments than others in that they are less adaptable and more irritable. The differences are apparent during early infancy and are assumed to be strongly influenced by genetics. Children with more difficult temperaments experience more intense emotions and have more difficulty inhibiting emotional responses (Fabes et al., 1999). Furthermore, parents' reactions to children's expressions of negative emotions affect how children learn to deal with the emotions (Eisenberg et al., 1999). When parents minimize or punish children's emotional reactions, the children have greater difficulty learning to regulate their emotions. We must keep in mind, though, that there are bidirectional effects between parents' responses and children's emotional regulation. Less emotionally regulated children evoke more punitive responses from parents; punitive responses from parents make it more difficult for children to learn to regulate their emotions.

Learning to manage negative emotions is not the same as never having them. Children can come to accept their angry feelings as a normal part of themselves, yet learn to control or redirect their reactions to such feelings. They may use anger as a motivating force, as a way of overcoming obstacles, or as a means of standing up for themselves or others. Whether they choose to accept or to reject their negative feelings, as well as the way in which they express that choice, will have significant consequences in later years. Between the ages of 4 and 8, children start to distinguish between the internal, subjective experiences of emotions and the external expressions of them (Rotenberg & Eisenberg, 1997). For example, they realize that sad children who stop crying because they are told to do so may still be sad. They understand that suppressed emotions are not necessarily eliminated.

Kopp (1992) refers to children's growing ability to control their behaviour as *self-regulation*. In self-regulation, children adopt and internalize a composite of specific standards for behaviour, such as safety concerns, respect for the property of others, and similar rules. Compliance, which is also a component of self-regulation, refers to the child's following the caregivers' requests, such as not to cross the street or run in parking lots. During toddlerhood, parents' requests to perform an action, such as "Pick up your toys," may be met with cries. By the time the child is 3 years old, however, cries occur very infrequently, but resistance behaviour increases—such as refusals or off-task negotiations. By the time the child is 4 years old, there are fewer instances of resistance. Kopp (1992) believes that resistance, in itself, does not disappear as language skills develop; rather, the child is able to introduce self needs in a more socially satisfactory and less emotional way. This is impressive growth in self-regulatory behaviour.

Question to Ponder

Do you think children should be encouraged to express their feelings or to control them?

Affection and Joy In our culture, children must restrain not only their negative feelings, but also their positive emotions. Spontaneous feelings, such as joy, affection, excitement, and playfulness, are dealt with quite differently by 2-year-olds and 6-year-olds. Just as 2-year-olds are direct in expressing distress, they are also likely to be very open in showing positive feelings—they hug people, jump up and down, or clap their hands in excitement. During the course of preschool socialization, we manage to teach children to subdue such open expressiveness. Spontaneous joy and affection become embarrassing; because they are considered "babyish," most children learn to control them. On the other hand, special circumstances, such as birthday parties or baseball games, demand types of emotional expression that are considered inappropriate for everyday life. Children learn all of these social norms.

Sensuality and Sexual Curiosity Two-year-olds are very sensual creatures, deriving great pleasure from sensory experience. They like the feel of messy, gooey things. They are conscious of the softness or stiffness of clothes against their skin. They are fascinated by sounds, lights, tastes, and smells. In infancy, this sensuality was centred on the mouth, but the toddler has a new awareness and fascination with the anal-genital area. Masturbation and sex play are quite common during the preschool period. As children discover that such self-stimulation is pleasurable, some may gradually increase this behaviour; most develop an active curiosity about their bodies and ask many sex-related questions.

Different cultures often elicit anxiety about different things as well as sanctioning different ways of expressing it. This Korean child tries to hide her tearful anxiety rather than "let it all hang out."

Young children are very open about showing positive feelings like joy. But by the age of 6 they have learned to somewhat mask even these feelings.

The ways in which the culture and the family react to this developing sensuality and curiosity will have a powerful effect on children, just as the reactions of others affect the way that children handle hostility and joy. Until recently, mothers in our society were advised to prevent their children from engaging in this kind of exploration (Wolfenstein, 1951). The result was anxiety and guilt in the children, which led them to adopt the various defence mechanisms described by Freud. But sensual exploration is a natural and vital part of every child's experience. Severe restriction of children's sensual feelings and behaviour is likely to cause unnecessary anxiety, guilt, and conflict during adolescence and adulthood.

Coping with Developmental Conflicts

Trying to fit their feelings into the structure of acceptability imposed on them by the outside world is not the only task young children must face during the preschool years. Developmental conflicts also arise as they adjust to their own changing needs. Dependency, autonomy, mastery, and competence are pressing issues in their lives. According to Erikson (1950), the period of early childhood involves an overall psychosocial conflict between the child's initiatives to explore the world and guilt over causing parental displeasure. During this period, children are pulled between their need for autonomy and emotional dependency on their parents. Clearly, during early childhood, issues relating to dependency and autonomy are still being worked out.

Dependency *Dependency* may be defined as any type of activity demonstrating that one person derives satisfaction from another person (Hartup, 1963). It includes the wish or need to be aided, nurtured, comforted, and protected by another, or to be emotionally close to or accepted by that person. Such wishes and needs are normal in people of every age, despite the connotation of weakness or inadequacy that they often carry. Dependency is necessary for the very survival of the young child, who must look to older people for the satisfaction of both physical and psychological needs.

Infants and toddlers show dependency by crying for attention and by seeking close physical contact. By age 4 or 5, children have developed more indirect ways of showing their need for others: they now seek attention by asking questions, by offering to help, by showing off, or even by being disobedient. A study by Craig and Garney (1972) traced developmental trends in expressions of dependency by observing the ways that children at ages 2, 2½, and 3 maintained contact with their mothers in an un-familiar situation. The 2-year-olds spent most of their time physically close to their mothers, staying in the same part of the room and looking up often to make sure that their mothers were still there. The older children (2½- and 3-year-olds) neither stayed as close to their mothers nor checked as often to see if their mothers had left the room. The older the children, the more they maintained verbal contact instead of physical contact. All three age groups made a point of drawing attention to their ac-tivities, but the older children were more inclined to demonstrate them from afar. Other studies have shown similar patterns: distress caused by separation from the mother declines from ages 2 to 3, while distal attachment behaviour, such as show-ing things to the mother from across the room, increases (Maccoby & Feldman, 1972). Note, though, that wide individual differences are always found in every age group.

Dependence and independence are commonly considered opposite types of behaviour. But this is not necessarily the case for the young child. Although children become less dependent (less clingy) as they become older, their independence (or au-tonomy) follows a more complex trajectory. Infants are usually fairly cooperative; for example, they will hold out their arms when their parents are trying to dress them. This behaviour changes abruptly at about the age of 2, when many children suddenly be-come quite uncooperative—parents call this stage the "terrible twos." At 2 years, chil-dren fight to "do it myself," and temper tantrums are frequent when they find that they cannot manage buttons and the sleeve is inside out. When 2-year-olds are asked to do something, they show their independence by saying "No!" As they get older, they become more compliant and cooperative; 3-year-olds are more likely to do what their parents tell them to and are less likely to break rules when their parents are not look-ing (Howes & Olenick, 1986).

Autonomy, Mastery, and Competence As discussed in Chapter 2, the drive toward au-tonomy marks the second stage in Erikson's theory of personality development. Toddlers are discovering their own bodies and are learning to control them. If they are successful in doing things for themselves, they become self-confident. If their efforts at autonomy are frustrated by criticism or punishment, they think that they have failed and feel ashamed and doubtful about themselves. Although autonomy, mastery, and competence

All children need to feel a sense of mastery over their environment. This feeling of mastery may lead to chaos at times but it is still a key aspect of development.

are slightly different drives, they are all part of the same behaviour complex that influences our behaviour throughout life (Erikson, 1963; Murphy, 1962; White, 1959).

INITIATIVE VERSUS GUILT

Erikson suggests that the primary developmental conflict of the years from 3 to 6 is *initiative versus guilt*. In some ways, this conflict is an extension of the toddler's struggle with autonomy. Toddlers gain control and competence starting with their own bodies—feeding, dressing, toileting, handling objects, and getting around. The preschooler is learning how things work, what social situations and relationships mean, and how to influence people in constructive and appropriate ways. Concepts of right and wrong, good and bad, become important; labels such as "sissy," "baby," or "brat" can have devastating effects. The job of the parent or teacher is to guide and discipline the child without creating too much anxiety or guilt. In the confusing and complex social world of the preschool child, initiative can lead either to success and feelings of competence or to failure, frustration, and guilt.

Nearly everyone derives satisfaction from changing the environment to suit herself. For a 3-year-old, this may mean crayoning on a wall or retrieving a toy from a baby sister. Preschoolers are just as pleased with their creations as adults are with theirs. Unfortunately, a youngster's desire to use creativity or initiative sometimes interferes with other people's plans. A little boy's discovery that he can "improve" the vacuum cleaner by filling its tubes with clay does not fit in with his mother's need to keep the house clean. These opposing needs produce conflicts between parent and child and within the child himself.

LEARNING COMPETENCE

What happens when children's attempts at mastery or autonomy meet with constant failure or frustration? What happens when they have little or no opportunity to try things on their own, or when their environment is so chaotic that they cannot see the consequences of their acts? All children have a need for autonomy, a need to master the environment, and a need to feel competent and successful. If these needs are repeatedly blocked, their personality development is likely to be adversely affected. If their efforts at mastery cause too much trouble, they may give up and become passive. Several studies show that such children fail to develop an active, exploratory, self-confident approach to learning, which White and Watts (1973) called the development of *learning competence*. Beyond this, what happens to children who are constantly punished for their independent behaviour and attempts at mastery? Or to children whose parents discourage or frighten them whenever they venture into new activities? Martin Seligman, in his book *The Optimistic Child* (1995), explains how adult reactions to children can affect whether children develop a sense of mastery and competence or a sense of helplessness. Children who often feel helpless are at risk for developing depression. Consider the following example of a father's responding to his 6-year-old son, Ian, who is upset because his older sister, Rachel, made a better Lego rocket than he did:

> *Dad:* Ian, this is really great! I think the rocket you made is wonderful!

> *Ian:* It is not. Rachel's is great. Mine is stupid. I can't even make the wings stay. I'm a dumbo. I never get things right.

> *Dad:* I like it, Ian. I think you are the best rocket maker around.

> *Ian:* Then how come Rachel's is bigger and has wings that are real long and they don't fall off like mine do? I can't do this. I can't do anything right. I hate Legos!

Dad: That's not true Ian. You can do whatever you set your mind to. Here, give me the pieces and let me make it for you. I'll make you one that can fly to the moon and Mars and Jupiter. It will be the fastest rocket ship ever and it will be all yours!

Ian: All right. You make one for me. Mine never work. (Seligman, 1995, p. 13)

The dad's response to Ian, although well intentioned, is undermining Ian's sense of mastery and competence. Instead of trying to bolster Ian's self-esteem, the dad should have acknowledged that Rachel's rocket is better because she is older. When Ian is older, he will be better at building rockets. When the dad built Ian's rocket for him, he showed that Ian was not competent to do so on his own. Ian is likely to develop feelings of helplessness from this interaction.

Another example from Seligman's book reveals how parents can foster mastery and competence. Tamara, an overweight, awkward child, has just finished her first ballet class. She is in tears because she was unable to keep up with the other children.

Tamara: I had a bad day. The other girls did better. I kept falling down and they didn't. Miss Harkum showed us how to skip and move our arms and hands in a real pretty way, but I kept tripping and my hands didn't look the way they were supposed to. It really hurts.

Mom [comforts Tamara]: I'm sorry you had such a hard time today. I know it hurts when you feel like you aren't as good as some of the other girls. Lots of times, Mommy feels disappointed too. Like when I'm at work and don't do as good a job as I'd like to. That makes me feel upset. But you know what I do when that happens? I practice more and most of the time after I keep trying, I do a better job. I have an idea. Let's go and say hello to Miss Harkum and I'll ask her to teach me the dance step and then you and I can go home and practice it together. I bet if we work hard at it, you'll be better at it for your next lesson. How does that sound?

Tamara: Okay, I guess. Will you practice with me tonight after dinner? I want to get good at it, so that I can be a ballerina when I grow up.

Mom: You bet. Let's go talk to Miss Harkum, and then after dinner, we'll push the sofa back and make the living room into your very own dance studio!

Tamara: That'll be fun! I'm gonna practice real hard! (Seligman, 1995, pp. 15–16)

From her mother's response, Tamara is learning to view her failure as temporary. She is learning to persevere and to react to challenges with increased effort, rather than with defeat.

Some children are necessarily restricted in their drives toward autonomy and mastery. Children who have physical handicaps or chronic illnesses may have little opportunity to test their skills in mastering the environment (Rutter, 1979). Children who grow up in dangerous or crowded surroundings and who have to be restrained for their own safety, or children who are supervised by excessively vigilant caregivers, may also learn exaggerated passivity or anxiety (Zuravin, 1985).

Aggression and Prosocial Behaviour

Much of the research on aggression and prosocial behaviour has been conducted from the social-learning perspective. Social-learning research tends to focus on the social processes of reinforcement and modelling that give rise to specific behaviours. Therefore, much of the research will be directed at studying the effects of parents, siblings, peers, and others on producing and maintaining children's social behaviours.

The young child's interactions with others can be either positive or negative. At one point, children may seek closeness or be anxious to help or share. A short time later, they may become angry and hostile. A principal task of socializing young children is to teach them socially acceptable ways of channelling aggressive feelings, and at the same time to encourage positive behaviours such as helping and sharing. Many factors influence the development of aggressive behaviour and of positive or prosocial behaviour.

Psychologists define **aggression** as behaviour intended to hurt or destroy. Aggressive behaviour may be verbal or physical. It may be directed at people or displaced toward animals or objects. **Assertive behaviour,** on the other hand, does not involve an intent to injure others. It is forthright, direct behaviour, such as calmly stating one's rights or initiating vigorous activity, and it need not damage others.

Prosocial behaviour is defined as actions intended to benefit others without the anticipation of an external reward (Eisenberg, 1988). These actions often entail some cost, sacrifice, or risk to the individual. Helping, sharing, cooperating, sympathizing, and being altruistic (showing unselfish concern for the welfare of others) are examples of prosocial behaviour. These actions are frequently a response to positive motivational and emotional states—that is, people behave this way when they feel happy, secure, and empathetic. Aggression, on the other hand, is a common response to anger and hostility.

Types of Aggression and Individual Differences

Psychologists distinguish between two types of aggression (McNeilly-Choque, Hart, Robinson, Nelson, & Olsen, 1996). **Overt aggression** is directed openly at the target. It can be physical or verbal. Hitting and name calling to a person's face are examples of overt aggression. Sometimes overt aggression is called *instrumental* because it is used to attain a desired object or privilege. An example of instrumental overt aggression is pushing another child out of line, so that the aggressor can take his spot in the line. Other times, overt aggression is called *bullying* because it is used to intimidate others, rather than to secure an object or a privilege. **Relational aggression** is a type of indirect aggression whereby a person tries to harm someone by damaging her relationships. Examples of relational aggression are gossiping or telling others not to play with a peer.

Overt aggression and relational aggression are distinct in the sense that about two-thirds of highly aggressive children have problems with one or the other, but not with both (Crick, Casas, & Mosher, 1997). Furthermore, even preschool children can distinguish between the two types of aggression (McNeilly-Choque et al., 1996). Children see overt aggression as "being mean." They interpret relational aggression not as meanness, but rather as a response to anger (which may include other negative emotions, such as jealousy or revenge).

There are age differences in aggression. Overt aggression peaks in toddlers (ages 27 to 29 months) and declines steadily during the preschool years (Tremblay et al., 1996). Relational aggression, on the other hand, begins to increase throughout the preschool years and continues to do so until age 11, at which time it stabilizes (Tremblay et al., 1996).

There are consistent gender differences in type of aggression (Crick et al., 1997). Preschool boys engage in more overt aggression than do preschool girls. Preschool girls use relational aggression more often than do preschool boys. Earlier studies found that boys were more aggressive than girls because the studies neglected to include measures of relational aggression.

Some children are more aggressive than average. A number of factors are associated with the development of aggressive behaviour (Rubin, Hastings, Chen, Stewart,

aggression Hostile behaviour that is intended to injure.

assertive behaviour Forthright, direct behaviour, such as stating one's rights, that does not harm others.

prosocial behaviour Helping, sharing, or cooperative actions that are intended to benefit others.

overt aggression Aggression that is directed openly at the target. It can be physical or verbal.

relational aggression Aggression that is done behind a person's back with the intent of damaging their relationships, for example, gossiping.

Question to Ponder

Why do you think girls use more relational aggression than boys do?

& McNichol, 1998). A child's temperament can contribute to aggression. If he has difficulty regulating his emotions, he will be quicker to anger and will experience more intense anger than other children. He may have difficulty inhibiting his physical responses to anger and be more prone to lash out impulsively. In addition to temperament, parenting is related to individual differences in children's aggression. Parents who are highly directive, intrusive, punitive, and rejecting of their children tend to have children who are more aggressive. Their children may be more aggressive because they learned from interactions with their parents to expect others to be hostile and negative. Other parents of aggressive children are highly permissive. They fail to set limits for their children's behaviour. Children of permissive parents may be more aggressive because they lack appropriate external controls on their behaviour. Interestingly, the same parenting can have different effects on children's level of aggression, depending on the child's temperament and gender. Negative parenting produces higher levels of aggression in boys whose temperaments make it difficult for them to regulate their emotions. Aggression in girls, on the other hand, is influenced mostly by temperament (i.e., by a lack of emotional regulation).

Families have an effect on children's aggression level, as demonstrated by the fact that siblings living in the same Canadian family have more similar levels of aggression than do Canadian children living in different households (Tremblay et al., 1996). The influence of the family on children's aggression levels is greater in families with lower socioeconomic status than it is in families with higher socioeconomic status. Furthermore, children from lower socioeconomic backgrounds had higher levels of both overt and relational aggression, as reported by their mothers, than did children from higher socioeconomic backgrounds. The interpretation of this finding is unclear, though, because it has not been replicated in other studies. For instance, a U.S. study (McNeilly-Choque et al., 1996) found that overt aggression was more common in children from lower socioeconomic backgrounds, but that relational aggression was more common in children from higher socioeconomic backgrounds. Further research is needed to discern whether family background has consistent effects on children's levels of aggression.

In addition, further research is needed to explore the effects of out-of-home care on children's levels of aggression. Interestingly, the Rubin et al. study found that out-of-home care had no effect on children's aggression. However, the researchers stressed that this was a preliminary finding that needed to be replicated by other studies.

High Aggression and Risk for Problems

Preschool girls and boys who are more aggressive than average often have poorer psychological and social adjustment than do their peers (Crick et al., 1997; McNeilly-Choque et al., 1996; Tremblay et al., 1996). Their mothers are more likely to describe them as hyperactive. They are less apt to engage in prosocial behaviours, such as helping others or sharing, than are other children. As well, aggressive children are more likely to be rejected by peers, and children who are more relationally aggressive are more likely to report being lonely than are other children.

A high level of aggression in preschool-age children is the strongest risk factor for aggression, antisocial behaviours, and conduct disorders in later childhood and adolescence (Loeber, 1991). Consequently, highly aggressive preschoolers are being targeted for early interventions to reduce the risks of later problems (Bennet, Lipman, Racine, & Offord, 1998). It is important to note, though, that some highly aggressive preschoolers do not develop later problems (Bennet et al., 1998). Furthermore, some adolescents who have conduct disorders do not have a history of problems with aggression during the preschool years (Loeber & Stouthamer-Loeber, 1998). Therefore, early aggression can be a predictor of later conduct disorders, but it is not an absolute predictor. The risks for developing severe conduct disorders, such as those found in young offenders, include individual factors (e.g., the child's temperament and impulsiveness), family factors (e.g., violence in the home and lack of parental monitoring), school factors (e.g., low achievement and truancy), and societal factors (e.g., living in poverty and experiencing discrimination) (Jaffe & Baker, 1999). We will explore these risk factors in more detail when we discuss young offenders in Chapter 16.

Aggression and Sibling Conflict

Hildy Ross and colleagues at the University of Waterloo observed sibling interactions between children 4½ years old and about 2½ years old and did follow-up observations two years later, when the children were 6½ and 4½ (den Bak & Ross, 1996; Martin & Ross, 1995; Perlman & Ross, 1997; Ross, Filyer, Lollis, Perlman, & Martin, 1994). They documented the extent of overt physical aggression and conflict between the children. Conflicts between siblings were extremely common, averaging 6.4 per hour. Most often, conflicts involved the possession of objects, initiated by either the older or younger siblings, although the older siblings started more of the conflicts than did the younger ones. Other kinds of conflicts initiated by the older siblings involved physical and verbal aggression, bossing, tattling, nagging, and excluding the younger children. Younger siblings started conflicts by interfering with the older siblings' play and by damaging family property.

In general, first-born children were more aggressive toward their siblings than were second-born children. This was due more to birth order than to age. First-born children at age 4½ in the first observation period were compared with second-born children who were 4½ in the follow-up observation. The first-borns were more than twice as aggressive as the second-borns. As well, the first-borns' levels of aggression were more stable. Children who were highly aggressive at age 4½ also tended to be highly aggressive at age 6½. The aggression levels of the second-borns were less stable. The second-borns who were most aggressive at age 4½ had been victimized most often by their older siblings when they were 2½. High levels of aggression in the older children were associated with the younger children's also developing high levels of aggression or, alternatively, with their becoming passive. The older children became even more aggressive and bullied younger children who were passive.

Parent Response to Aggression between Siblings   Martin and Ross (1995) found that even though parents do not approve of aggressive exchanges between their children, they intervene only about half of the time. The other times the children are left to work it out on their own. Some experts on child rearing recommend that children be left to settle their own disputes so that they learn conflict resolution skills. But with no intervention, conflicts are usually resolved by the stronger child winning the fight, regardless of who started it or who was in the right. Parent intervention in fights is associated with changes in how the children behave in conflict situations (Perlman & Ross, 1997). After parent intervention, fighting siblings are more likely to use other-oriented reasoning, to ignore conflict issues, and to comply more frequently. They are less likely to be aggressive, to be oppositional, or to cry.

Parents are more likely to intervene when the older child is aggressive toward the younger one, and especially when the victim of the aggression cries. Parents are more tolerant of aggression in 2-year-olds than in 4- and 6-year-olds. They expect the older children to know better. The most common parent responses to aggression are commands to stop it and questions to clarify the situation. Parent responses have more effect on the aggression levels of 2-year-olds than on those of older children. By the time children are 6 years old, their aggressive behaviours are highly stable, regardless of parent responses (Eron, Huesman, & Zelli, 1991). Therefore, parent responses aimed at reducing aggressive conflicts between siblings are more likely to be effective when the children are toddlers than when they are older.

In general, parents who explain to their children why aggressive responses are inappropriate and who discuss the feelings of victims are more likely to have less aggressive children. But parents who respond to aggression inconsistently, sometimes even encouraging it, have more aggressive children. As well, parents who punish children physically for aggressive conflicts also tend to have more aggressive children. Perhaps the children imitate the parents' aggressive behaviours.

Prosocial Behaviour A number of studies have demonstrated the influence of modelling on prosocial behaviour. In a typical experiment, a group of children observe a person performing a prosocial act, such as putting toys or money into a box designated for "needy children." Other children in a control group watch a model who does not exhibit prosocial behaviour. After watching the generous model, each child is given the opportunity to donate something. The researchers usually find that children who witness another person's generosity become more generous themselves (Eisenberg, 1988).

Because rewards and punishment affect aggression, it is assumed that they also affect helping and sharing. However, this assumption is difficult to prove. Researchers are understandably reluctant to do experiments in which prosocial behaviour is punished, and experiments in which it is rewarded are inconclusive because the results may be due to modelling: when experimenters give a reward, they are also modelling "giving" (Rushton, 1976). The role of learning in prosocial behaviour is better demonstrated by a recent experiment that showed that 4-year-old children who were given many chores to do at home were more likely to be helpful outside of the home (Richman et al., 1988).

Two other procedures that influence prosocial behaviour are **role playing** and **induction.** In role playing, children act out other roles as a way of seeing things from another's point of view. In induction, children are given reasons for behaving in certain ways—for example, they may be told what consequences their actions will have for others. Staub (1971) used both procedures in an experiment with groups of kindergarten children. He subsequently tested them to determine the effectiveness of these procedures. He found that role playing increased the willingness of the children to help others and that its effects lasted for as long as a week. However, induction had little or no effect on the children in Staub's experiment, perhaps because children are unlikely to pay much attention to a lecture from an unfamiliar adult. Induction is more effective when used by parents. Parents who use inductive forms of discipline—for example, who explain to their children the reasons for behaving in certain ways— are more likely to foster prosocial behaviour in their children (Eisenberg, 1988).

More recently, researchers have studied how empathy and the child's experience of emotions affect whether she behaves in a prosocial manner (Eisenberg et al., 1996; Roberts & Strayer, 1996). Children's capacity for empathy is predicted by their role-playing ability and by their ability to express, identify, and regulate their own emotional reactions. Boys who are more empathetic tend to be more cooperative, helpful, and responsible (Roberts & Strayer, 1996). Interestingly, though, empathy is unrelated to prosocial behaviour in girls. Girls are more likely than boys to behave in a prosocial manner, and it seems that they do so regardless of whether they feel empathetic or not. Perhaps, as the researchers suggested, differences in the socialization of girls and boys account for the gender differences in the effects of empathy on prosocial behaviour.

Prosocial behaviour is common among Canadian preschoolers (Landy & Tam, 1996). The majority of parents report that their children engage in helping behaviour "sometimes" to "often" (HRDC & Stats Can, 1996). Furthermore, parents' reports of their children's prosocial behaviour are similar in different provinces and in rural and urban communities.

Carol Thompson, John Barresi, and Chris Moore (1998) at Dalhousie University in Halifax studied how much preschool children share in different situations. All of the children received sticker books and had to decide whether to put stickers in their own books or to share them with a research assistant who also had a sticker book. The children could choose to take the stickers immediately or after a delay. Some of the time, children had to choose between taking stickers for themselves (self-gratification) or taking stickers for themselves and for the research assistant (shared gratification). In this

role playing The acting out of a role in order to see things from another person's perspective.

induction Giving children reasons for behaving in socially desirable ways or for not behaving in undesirable ways.

situation, children could share at no cost to themselves, and even the 3-year-olds shared often. Other times, they had to choose between putting two stickers in their own books or putting one in their book and the other in the research assistant's book. In this situation, sharing incurred some cost to the children. The 3-, 4-, and 5-year-olds all shared, but they did so less often than when there was no cost to themselves. Other times, children had to choose between putting one sticker in their book immediately (self-gratification) or waiting until later and getting both a sticker for themselves and one for the research assistant (delayed shared gratification). Interestingly, the 4- and 5-year-olds were more likely to choose the delayed shared gratification than were the 3-year-olds. The researchers related this age difference to the older children's better understanding of desires and theory of mind (discussed in Chapter 10).

Cooperation is also regarded as a form of prosocial behaviour. Madsen (1971; Madsen & Shapira, 1970) found that American children become less cooperative (or more competitive) as they grow older. When playing a game that can be won only if the two players cooperate (see Figure 11-1), 4- and 5-year-olds often cooperated. Older children, however, tended to compete with each other; as a result, neither player won. Compared with American children, Mexican children and children raised on Israeli kibbutzim were more likely to cooperate, evidently because their cultures place more importance on group goals and less on individual achievement. Madsen suggested that American children are raised to be competitive and that they learn this value so completely that they are often unable to cooperate. Within Canada, Inuit and Hutterite children are socialized to be cooperative rather than competitive with others in their communities (Bonta, 1997).

Peers and Social Skills

Children influence one another in significant ways. They provide emotional support for one another in a variety of situations. They serve as models, they reinforce behaviour, and they encourage complex, imaginative play. In these ways, children help one another to learn a variety of physical, cognitive, and social skills (Asher, Renshaw, & Hymel, 1982; Hartup, 1983). Young boys playing aggressively, for example, may first imitate characters seen on television and then imitate one another. They continue to respond and react to one another in a way that supports and escalates the play—this is sometimes called **social reciprocity** (Hall & Cairns, 1984). Play is often segregated by sex, and groups of girls interact differently than groups of boys (Benenson, Apostoleris, & Parnass, 1997). When in a larger group, girls spend most of the time interacting in pairs, and each pair engages in a different activity. Boys also interact in pairs, but by the time they are 6 years old, boys in pairs interact similarly, and their interactions are coordinated with the overall activity of the larger group.

The Role of Play in Social Skill Development   An early study on peer relations (Parten, 1932–33) identified five levels of social interaction in young children:

social reciprocity The continued interaction between individuals as they respond and react to one another in a way that encourages the prevailing behaviour.

Figure 11-1

In Madsen's game, two children sit at opposite ends of a game board that features a cup at each end, a gutter down each side, and a marble holder with a marble inside. To play the game, the children move the marble holder by pulling on strings; if the marble holder is moved over a cup, a child earns the marble as it drops into the cup. The children must cooperate to earn marbles—if they both pull on the strings at the same time, the marble holder comes apart and the marble rolls into the gutter.

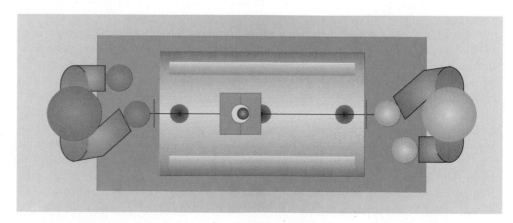

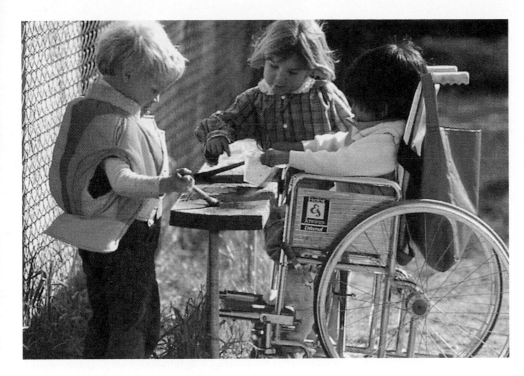

Although these children are sharing materials, they are not yet at the level where they cooperatively play together.

1. *Solitary play,* in which children play alone.
2. *Onlooker play,* in which the child's interaction consists merely of observing other children.
3. *Parallel play,* in which the child plays alongside another child and uses similar toys but does not interact in any other way.
4. *Associative play,* in which children share materials and interact somewhat but do not coordinate their activities toward a single theme or goal.
5. *Cooperative play,* in which children engage in a single activity together, such as building a house with blocks or playing hide-and-seek with a common set of rules.

Different modes of play predominate at given age levels. At age 2, children mostly engage in onlooker and parallel play, whereas at age 4 and 5 they show increasing amounts of associative and cooperative play. In optimal surroundings, 5-, 6-, and 7-year-olds can interact for relatively long periods of time while sharing materials, establishing rules, resolving conflicts, helping one another, and exchanging roles. Unfortunately, some children have trouble interacting with peers even when conditions are optimal.

When we observe children in nursery schools, day-care centres, or kindergartens, it is apparent that some children are popular with their peers, while others are not. These patterns tend to be remarkably stable over the years: children who are rejected by their peers in kindergarten are likely to be rejected in elementary school as well. Later, they are more likely to have adjustment problems in adolescence and adulthood (Parker & Asher, 1987). It is helpful, then, to determine who these children are—those regularly chosen by their peers and those rejected. It has been repeatedly shown that popular children are more cooperative and exhibit more prosocial behaviour during play with their peers. Unpopular children may be either more aggressive or more withdrawn, or they may simply be "out of sync" with their peers' activities and social interactions (Rubin, 1983).

Which comes first: Do rejected children adopt these negative behaviours because they are rejected, or are they rejected because of their behaviour? One researcher videotaped kindergarten boys as they tried to join a play group (Putallaz, 1983). The social skills they demonstrated were used to predict each child's social status in grade one. In this and other studies, popular children were found to have a variety of social skills (Mendelson et al., 1994b). They initiate activity with others by moving into the group slowly, making relevant comments about what's going on, and sharing information. They seem sensitive to the needs and activities of others. They don't force themselves on other children, but they are content to play beside another child. In addition, popular children have strategies for maintaining relationships. They show helpful behaviours; they are good at maintaining communication and sharing information; and they are responsive to other children's suggestions. Finally, children who are destined to be popular have strategies for conflict resolution. Popular children do not necessarily give in when faced with conflict, but they are less frequently involved in aggressive or physical solutions (Asher, 1983; Asher et al., 1982). We see these features presented in Table 11-1.

Popular children are accepted by peers, but this does not mean that their particular friendships are high quality (Mendelson et al., 1994b). Children's friendships are different from general peer acceptance. Kindergarten friends value impulsiveness and high energy in each other. Impulsiveness and high energy strengthen friendships, even though teachers and peers in general perceive these behaviours as negative.

If peer relations are a significant socializing influence in the lives of children—at least by middle childhood—and if the success of these relationships depends on the development of social skills, then it is probably important to help children develop these skills during the preschool period. Adults can help in two ways. First, they can teach social skills directly, by modelling and by induction. Children learn from watching adults interact. The quality of parents' marital relationships is a predictor of behaviour problems in 4- and 5-year-old children (Benzies, Harrison, & Magill-Evans, 1998). Second, adults can offer opportunities for successful social experiences with peers. Children need opportunities to play with other children, as well as appropriate space and materials to support this play. Dolls, clothes for dress-up activities, toy cars and trucks, blocks, and puppets support cooperative play and offer opportunities for interaction. With preschoolers, adult caregivers must be available to help initiate activities, negotiate conflicts, and provide information (Asher et al., 1982). As well, Barbara Lowenthal (1996) outlines different techniques to help special needs preschoolers interact with other children:

1. Arranging the environment so that children play closer to each other, and thus are more likely to interact.

2. Provide opportunities for children to imitate socially competent peers.

3. Have teachers prompt children to engage in particular interactions with other children.

4. Do group activities that encourage affectionate responses (for example, singing the song "If you're happy and you know it, hug your neighbour").

5. Have teachers reinforce children for interacting.

6. Train other children to initiate interaction with the special needs children, and if the special needs children are unresponsive, gently encourage them to participate.

Understanding Self and Others

So far, we have been talking about how children learn the bits and pieces of behaviour—how they learn to share or to be aggressive or to handle their feelings. Children, however, act in a more comprehensive way. They put together all the bits and pieces to form whole patterns of behaviour appropriate for their culture, gender, and family. Experts disagree on just how this integration of patterns of social behaviour occurs. Most agree that as children grow older, they become less dependent on the individual rules, expectations, rewards, and punishments of others, and they become more able to make judgments and to regulate their own behaviour. Cognitive developmental theorists hold that the child's integration of patterns of social behaviour coincides with the development of a concept of self, along with certain social concepts. These concepts then help to mediate the child's behaviour in social situations. The preschool period is an important time for building some of these basic concepts.

Table 11-1 Characteristics of Popular Children in Kindergarten

- Possess a variety of social skills.
- Initiate activity by moving into the group slowly, making relevant comments, and sharing information.
- Are sensitive to the needs and activities of others.
- Don't force themselves on other children.
- Are content to play alongside other children.
- Possess strategies for maintaining friendships.
- Show helpful behaviour.
- Are good at maintaining communication.
- Are good at sharing information.
- Are responsive to other children's suggestions.
- Possess strategies for conflict resolution.
- When faced with conflict, are less likely to use aggressive or physical solutions.

Source: Asher, 1983; Asher et al., 1982.

The Self-Concept

Even the 2-year-old has some self-understanding. As we discovered in Chapter 7, by 21 months the child is able to recognize herself in the mirror; if she sees a red mark on her nose she shows some self-conscious embarrassment. The language of the 2-year-old is full of assertions of possession. In one study of 2-year-olds playing in pairs, most of them began their play with numerous self-assertions. They defined their boundaries and their possessions—"my shoe, my doll, my car." The author of this study asserts that this is a cognitive achievement, not necessarily selfishness: the children are increasing their self-understanding and their understanding of the other child as a separate being (Levine, 1983). A review of other studies of children's self-concepts and social play concluded that children who are most social also have a better-developed self-concept (Harter, 1983). Thus, self-understanding is closely linked to the child's understanding of the social world.

During the preschool years, children develop certain kinds of generalized attitudes about themselves—a positive sense of well-being, for example, or a feeling that they are "slow" or "bratty." Many of these ideas begin to emerge very early, at a nonverbal level. Children may develop strong anxieties about some of their feelings and ideas while being quite comfortable with others. They also develop a set of ideals during these years, and they learn to measure themselves against what they think they ought to be. Often, children's self-evaluation is a direct reflection of what other people think of them. John, for example, was a loveable 2-year-old with a talent for getting into mischief. His older brothers and sisters called him "Bad Buster" whenever he got into trouble. By the age of 7, John was making an effort to maintain his "Bad Buster" reputation. These early attitudes eventually become basic elements of a person's self-concept, but they are difficult to explore later on because they are learned at a less sophisticated verbal level.

Preschool children are fascinated with themselves, and many of their activities and thoughts are centred on the task of learning all about themselves. They compare themselves with other children, discovering differences in height, hair colour, family background, and likes or dislikes. They compare themselves with their parents, learn that they share common traits, and discover behaviours to imitate. As part of their drive to find out about themselves, preschool children ask a variety of questions about where they came from, why their feet grow, whether they are good or bad, and so on.

An awareness of how one appears to others is a key step in the development of self-knowledge. Young preschoolers tend to define themselves in terms of their physical characteristics ("I have brown hair") or possessions ("I have a bike"). Older preschoolers are more likely to describe themselves in terms of their activities: "I walk

Preschoolers are fascinated with themselves. They love to compare themselves with other children, excitedly noting how they are different and how they are similar.

to school," "I play baseball" (Damon & Hart, 1982).

As children learn who and what they are and begin to evaluate themselves as active forces in their world, they are putting together a cognitive theory or personal script about themselves that helps to integrate their behaviour. Human beings need to feel that they are consistent. They do not act randomly; rather, they try to bring their behaviour into line with their beliefs and attitudes. The strongest influence on children's developing self-image is usually their parents because they provide children with the definitions of right and wrong, the models of behaviour, and the evaluations of actions on which children base their own ideas.

Social Concepts and Rules

Preschool children are busy sorting, classifying, and struggling to find meaning in the social world, just as they are in the world of objects. Central to the development of social concepts and rules is a process called **internalization,** in which children learn to make the values and moral standards of their society part of themselves. Some of these values relate to appropriate sex-role behaviour, some relate to moral standards, and some relate to the customary way of doing things.

How do children internalize these rules? At first, they may simply imitate verbal patterns: Jennifer says, "No, no, no!" as she crayons on the wall. She is doing what she wants to do, but at the same time she is showing the beginnings of self-restraint by telling herself that she shouldn't be doing it. In a few more months, she may have the self-control to arrest the impulse she is presently unable to ignore. Cognitive theorists point out that children's attempts to regulate their own behaviour are influenced not only by their developing self-concept, but also by their developing social concepts. Such concepts reflect increased understanding about others, as well as increased understanding about oneself. For example, a preschool child may be learning what it means to be a big brother or sister or to be a friend. The child is also learning about concepts such as fairness, honesty, and respect for others. Many of these concepts are far too abstract for young children, but still they struggle to understand them.

Friendship One area that has been studied a great deal is children's concepts of friendship. A clear cognitive understanding doesn't occur until middle childhood—notions of mutual trust and reciprocity are too complex for the preschool child. Nevertheless, preschool children do behave differently with friends than with strangers, and some 4- and 5-year-olds are able to maintain close, caring relationships over an extended period of time. They may be unable to verbalize what friendship is, but they do follow some of its implied rules (Gottman, 1983).

Young children learning about social concepts often ask the question, "Why did they do that?" A common answer is based on character attribution. For example, the question, "Why did Kevin give me his cookie?" may be answered with, "Because Kevin is a nice boy." As children get older, they are more and more likely to see other people, and also themselves, in terms of stable character attributes (Miller & Aloise, 1989). Some experts believe that caregivers can encourage children to be helpful or altruistic by teaching them that they are kind to others because they want to be—because they are "nice"—and not just because such behaviour is demanded of them (Eisenberg et al., 1984; Grusec & Arnason, 1982; Perry & Bussey, 1984).

Gender Schemes

Among the more significant sets of social concepts and social rules that preschool children learn are those related to gender-appropriate behaviour. As we saw in Chapter 3, children learn some aspects of gender roles by modelling themselves after significant individuals in their lives and by being reinforced for gender-appropriate behaviour. But this is not the whole story. Children are selective in what they imitate and internalize.

internalization Making social rules and standards of behaviour part of oneself—adopting them as one's own set of values.

Question to Ponder

What types of problems might a preschooler who is delayed in the development of self-concept experience in day care or preschool?

Research suggests that children's developing understanding of gender-related concepts—their *gender schemes*—help to determine what attitudes and behaviours they learn. Moreover, these gender-related concepts develop in predictable ways over the preschool period.

By the age of 2½, most children can readily label people as boys or girls, men or women, and they can also answer the question, "Are you a girl or a boy?" (Thompson, 1975). But even though they can classify people as male or female, they may be confused about what the labels mean. Many 3-year-olds believe, for instance, that if a boy puts on a dress, he becomes a girl. They may not realize that only boys can become daddies and only girls can become mommies. But by age 6 or 7, children understand that their gender is stable and permanent for a lifetime, despite superficial changes. The first level of understanding, the one that is achieved between the ages of 2 and 6, is called **gender identity.** Later on, between ages 5 and 7, children are thought to acquire **gender constancy**—the understanding that boys invariably become men and girls become women and that gender is consistent over time and situations (Kohlberg, 1966; Shaffer, 1988).

Recent research has found that 4-year-olds who understand labels for boys and girls display more knowledge of gender stereotypes than children who do not. Moreover, the mothers of children who master these labels endorse more traditional roles for women, as well as for sex roles within the family. These same mothers also initiate and reinforce more sex-typed play with their children (Fagot, Leinbach, & O'Boyle, 1992).

It becomes clear that during early childhood children acquire some sense of the meaning underlying gender stereotypes. When given the opportunity in research settings, 4-year-olds give fierce bear toys to boys and fluffy kitten toys to girls. This research suggests that cultural associations of objects and qualities with one sex or the other do not depend solely on observing or being taught specific associations, such as that dolls are for girls and trucks are for boys. As the researchers concluded,

> Few men keep bears, and cats do not belong only to women. Rather it appears that children, like the rest of us, make inferences on the basis of what they see or know about the nature of things. Children, even at these early ages, may have begun to connect certain qualities with males and other qualities with females. (Fagot et al., p. 229)

Many developmental psychologists believe that children are intrinsically motivated to acquire the values, interests, and behaviours consistent with their own gender. This process is known as *self-socialization.* Children develop concepts of "what boys do" and "what girls do" that might be quite rigid and stereotypical. For example, children may believe that boys play with cars and don't cry and that girls play with dolls and like to dress up. A child will pay more attention to the details of gender-appropriate behaviour and less attention to sex-inappropriate behaviours (Martin & Halverson, 1981).

Do young children actually attend to some things more than to others and remember some things better than others because they are consistent with their gender schemes? Several studies have indicated that they do. In memory tests, for example, boys tend to remember more of the items that are labelled "boy items" and girls remember more "girl items." Children also make memory errors when a story violates their gender stereotypes. They may remember that a boy was chopping wood when, in fact, a girl was chopping wood in the story. Such results indicate that children's developing gender concepts have a powerful influence on their attention and learning (Martin & Halverson, 1981). During the period when concepts of gender stability and consistency are being developed, children tend to have particularly rigid and stereotypical

gender identity The knowledge that one is male or female, and the ability to make that judgment about other people.

gender constancy The concept that gender is stable and stays the same despite changes in superficial appearance.

Children's developing understanding of gender-appropriate behaviour and gender schemes often involves modelling and dramatic play.

concepts of sex-appropriate behaviour. These concepts and rules become organizers that structure the child's behaviour and feelings. If the rules are violated, children may feel embarrassed, anxious, or uncomfortable. Table 11-2 describes the development of gender schemes during early childhood.

The Family Context

Styles of Parenting

Parents use a variety of child-rearing techniques, depending on the situation, the child, and the child's behaviour at the moment. Ideally, parents limit the child's autonomy and instill values and self-control, while taking care not to undermine the child's curiosity, initiative, or competence. To do this, they must balance the parenting dimensions of control and warmth.

Parental control refers to how restrictive the parents are. Restrictive parents limit their children's freedom to follow their own impulses; they actively enforce compliance with rules and see that children fulfill their responsibilities. In contrast, nonrestrictive parents are less controlling, make fewer demands, and place fewer restraints on their children's behaviour and expression of emotions.

Parental warmth refers to the amount of affection and approval the parents display. Warm, nurturing parents smile frequently and give praise and encouragement. They try to restrict their criticisms, punishments, and signs of disapproval. In contrast, hostile parents criticize, belittle, punish, and ignore. They only rarely express affection or approval.

These general styles of parenting affect children's aggression and prosocial behaviour, their self-concepts, their internalization of moral values, and their development of social competence (Becker, 1964; Maccoby, 1984, 1994).

Authoritative, Authoritarian, and Permissive Parents   Many researchers in child development have found Diana Baumrind's (1975) description of parenting styles to be helpful. Baumrind has identified three distinct patterns of parental control: authoritative, authoritarian, and permissive. Although the words *authoritative* and *authoritarian* sound very similar, and despite the fact that both of these types of parents exert firm control over their children's behaviour, these styles are markedly different from each other. Both are also radically different from permissive parenting.

Table 11-2 The Development of Gender Schemes across Early Childhood

LEVELS OF SCHEMES	APPROXIMATE AGE	CHARACTERISTICS OF BEHAVIOUR
Gender identity	2 to 5 years	By 2½, children can label people as boys or girls; they experience confusion about the meaning of being a boy or girl; and they believe gender is changed by surface appearance, for example, changing clothes changes gender.
Gender constancy	5 to 7 years	Children understand that gender is stable and permanent; that boys grow up to become daddies or men and that girls grow up to become mommies or women; and that gender is consistent over time and situations.

Authoritative parents combine a high degree of control with warmth, acceptance, and encouragement of the growing autonomy of their children. Although these parents set limits on behaviour, they also explain the reasoning behind these limits. Their actions do not seem arbitrary or unfair, and as a result, their children are willing to accept these actions. Authoritative parents are willing to listen to their children's objections and to be flexible when appropriate. For example, if a young girl wanted to stay up past bedtime so that she could greet her grandmother at the airport, authoritative parents would be willing to negotiate. Perhaps they would let her go to the airport if she were all ready for bed and if she promised to have a nap or quiet time the following afternoon.

Authoritarian parents are controlling and adhere rigidly to rules. They tend to be low on warmth, although this is not always the case. In the situation that we just described, these parents would probably refuse their daughter's request with a statement like "A rule is a rule." If the child continued to argue or began to cry, the parents would become angry and might impose a punishment—perhaps even a physical punishment. Authoritarian parents issue commands and expect them to be obeyed; they avoid lengthy verbal exchanges with their children. They behave as if their rules are set in concrete and as if they are powerless to change them. Trying to gain some independence from such parents can be very frustrating for the child.

Permissive parents are at the opposite extreme from authoritarians: their parenting style is characterized by few or no restraints placed on the child's behaviour. The issue of staying up later than usual would probably not even arise, because there are no fixed times for going to bed. When permissive parents are annoyed or impatient with their children, they often suppress these feelings. According to Baumrind (1975), many permissive parents are so intent on showing their children "unconditional love" that they fail to perform other important parental functions—in particular, setting limits for their children's behaviour.

Indifferent Parents Baumrind's permissive parents tend to be warm and accepting of their children. Maccoby and Martin (1983) have defined a fourth parenting style, consisting of parents who are low in restrictiveness and also low in warmth: the **indifferent parenting** style. These parents fail to set limits for their children, either because they just don't care or because their own lives are so stressful that they don't have enough energy left over to provide guidance for their children. Concept Summary Table 11-1 summarizes the four parenting styles on the basis of parental control and parental warmth.

authoritative parenting A pattern of parenting that uses firm control with children but encourages communication and negotiation in rule setting within the family.

authoritarian parenting A pattern of parenting that adheres to rigid rule structures and dictates to the children what these rules are; children do not contribute to the decision-making process in the family.

permissive parenting A pattern of parenting in which parents exercise little control over their children but are high in warmth; this parenting style can produce negative results in children, who may have trouble inhibiting their impulses or deferring gratification.

indifferent parenting A pattern of parenting in which parents are not interested in their role as parents or in their children; indifferent parents exercise little control and demonstrate little warmth toward their children.

Authoritative parents encourage the developing autonomy of their children while at the same time setting reasonable limits.

Effects of Different Parenting Styles As shown by Baumrind (1975) and by a number of later researchers, parenting styles have an impact on the personality of the developing child. Baumrind found that authoritarian parents tend to produce withdrawn, fearful children who exhibit little or no independence and are moody, unassertive, and irritable. In adolescence, these children—particularly the boys—may overreact to the restrictive, punishing environment in which they were reared and may become rebellious and aggressive. The girls are more likely to remain passive and dependent (Kagan & Moss, 1962).

Although permissiveness in parenting is the opposite of restrictiveness, permissiveness does not necessarily produce opposite results: oddly enough, the children of permissive parents also may be rebellious and aggressive. In addition, they tend to be self-indulgent, impulsive, and socially inept. In some cases, they may be active, outgoing, and creative (Baumrind, 1975; Watson, 1957).

Children of authoritative parents have been found to be the best adjusted. They are the most self-reliant, self-controlled, and socially competent. In the long run, these children develop higher self-esteem and do better in school than those reared with the other parenting styles (Buri, Louiselle, Misukanis, & Mueller, 1988; Dornbusch, Ritter, Leiderman, Roberts, & Fraleigh, 1987).

The worst outcome is found in the children of indifferent parents. When permissiveness is accompanied by high hostility (the neglectful parent), the child feels free to give rein to his most destructive impulses. Studies of young delinquents show that in many cases their home environments have had exactly this combination of permissiveness and hostility (Bandura & Walters, 1959; McCord, McCord, & Zola, 1959).

Positive, consistent parenting can act as a protective factor for children living in families that have low incomes, inadequate social support, or dysfunction (Landy & Tam, 1996). In these at-risk families, children who had positive parenting did as well socially as other Canadian children. Children in at-risk families who had hostile, inconsistent parenting had social problems, as did children from families that were not at risk who had hostile, inconsistent parenting. This Canadian study showed that parenting makes a difference to children's development.

Cross-Cultural Differences in Parenting Styles We have to be cautious of drawing general conclusions from studies of Baumrind's parenting styles because most of the studies involve Canadian and American families of European or African heritage. What about families from other cultural backgrounds? Would the same conclusions still apply?

Ruth Chao (1994, 1996) has studied American parents of Asian ancestry (Chinese, Japanese, and Korean). Interestingly, these parents most often use a style that is highly controlling, like Baumrind's authoritarian style, yet it is not associated with negative child behaviours. Another example of cross-cultural differences involves Aboriginal families. Traditional Aboriginal child rearing resembles Baumrind's permissive style, yet it does not have a detrimental impact on the development of Aboriginal children (Johnson & Cremo, 1995). Therefore, parenting styles that appear similar on the surface might have quite different effects when they are embedded in different cultural contexts. More and more, developmental psychologists are interested in the effects of context on child development (see, for example, the discussion of Bronfenbrenner's theory in Chapter 2).

In some contexts, cultural differences in parenting style can become a problem if there is rapid assimilation of a minority culture into a larger culture that has very different child-rearing values. For example, Kagitcibasi (1996) studied traditional rural families in Turkey who were faced with rapid modernization and urbanization. The traditional child-rearing goal of Turkish parents stressed obedience. Yet, modern Turkish schools valued autonomy and independent decision making. This difference produced great conflict between the values of the home and the values of the urban society.

Negotiation or Shared Goals Eleanor Maccoby (1979, 1980, 1994) has looked at styles of parenting from a perspective that is similar to Baumrind's, but she has expanded the

Question to Ponder

How do you think parents' value systems influence their styles of parenting?

Concept Summary

Table 11-1 Parenting Styles Combining Warmth and Control

Authoritative	High control High warmth	Accept and encourage the growing autonomy of their children. Have open communication with children; are flexible about rules. Children are found to be the best adjusted—most self-reliant, self-controlled, and socially competent—and have better school performance and higher self-esteem.
Authoritarian	High control Low warmth	Issue commands and expect them to be obeyed; have little communication with children; are inflexible about rules; allow children to gain little independence from them. Children are found to be withdrawn, fearful, moody, unassertive, and irritable; girls tend to remain passive and dependent during adolescence; boys may become rebellious and aggressive.
Permissive	Low control High warmth	Place few or no restraints on child; show unconditional love. Open communication between child and parent; much freedom and little guidance for children; no setting of limits by parents. Children tend to be aggressive and rebellious; also tend to be socially inept, self-indulgent, and impulsive; in some cases, children may be active, outgoing, and creative.
Indifferent	Low control Low warmth	Set no limits for children; lack affection for children; are focused on stress in their own lives and have no energy left for their children. If indifferent parents also show hostility (as in neglectful parents), children tend to show high expression of destructive impulses and delinquent behaviour.

dimensions of this model. She is concerned not only with the effects of parental behaviour on children, but also with the effects of children's behaviour on parents. Parents, of course, are in a better position than children to control the home environment. But the nature of the interaction between the two affects the climate of family life. In some families, parents are highly controlling. At the other extreme, the children are in control. Neither extreme is healthy.

Ideally, neither parents nor children should dominate the family all of the time. Maccoby (1980) focuses on the ways that parents and children interact to achieve a balanced relationship. She points out that as children get older, parents need to go through a process of negotiation with them in order to make decisions. It does not always help to be authoritarian or to be permissive. It is better to help the child develop ways of thinking through problems and of learning the give-and-take of getting along with others. This negotiation can be done in a warm, supportive atmosphere.

Maccoby describes the evolution from parental control to more self-control and self-responsibility by children as they get older. Warmth and emotional support from the parents are important to this evolving relationship because parents engender such feelings in their children. This atmosphere makes interactions between them easier, even in situations requiring the exercising of parental authority. As Maccoby (1980) states,

> Parental warmth binds children to their parents in a positive way—it makes children responsive and more willing to accept guidance. If the parent-child relationship is close and affectionate, parents can exercise what control is needed without having to apply heavy disciplinary pressure. It is as if parents' responsiveness, affection, and obvious commitment to their children's welfare have earned them the right to make decisions and exercise control.

Ideally, parents and children come to agree—through long-term dialogue and interaction—on what Maccoby calls *shared goals*. The result is a harmonious atmosphere in which decisions are reached without much struggle for control. Families that enjoy this balance have a fairly high degree of intimacy, and their interaction is stable and mutually rewarding. Families that are unable to achieve shared goals, however, must negotiate everything—from what to have for supper to where to go on vacation. Despite the need for constant discussion, this too can be an effective family style. But if either the

FOCUS ON DIVERSITY

To Spank or Not to Spank?

CULTURAL DIFFERENCES IN ATTITUDES TOWARD SPANKING

Attitudes toward spanking are not the same around the world (Levinson, 1989). For instance, over 90 percent of parents in the United States spank their children and believe that spanking is a necessary form of discipline (Straus, 1991). But over 70 percent of parents in Sweden believe that children should be brought up without being spanked (Hausser, 1990, as cited in Durrant, 1995). Since Sweden passed a "no spanking law" in 1979, parents can be charged for spanking their children. The attitudes and practices of Canadian parents are less consistent than those of parents in the United States or Sweden. According to Durrant (1995), 75 percent of Canadian parents spank their children, and 70 percent would oppose a law banning spanking. According to data presented in *The Progress of Canada's Children* (CCSD, 1996), more than 55 percent of Canadian children younger than 12 years live with parents who report that they never spank their children.

THE EFFECTS OF SPANKING

It is difficult to make general conclusions about the effects of spanking because the effects vary depending on the context of the spanking, the severity, and the overall relationship between the parent and child. In some situations, spanking is associated with a number of immediate and long-term negative consequences, such as the following:

1. When spanking is harsh and frequent and the parent is hostile to-

---

In some situations, spanking is associated with a number of immediate and long-term negative consequences.

---

ward the child, the child is at risk for a number of problems, including delinquency, school failure, difficulties with peers, and substance abuse (as reviewed in Simons, Whitbeck, Conger, & Chyi-In, 1991). The child is more likely to develop a hostile personality, be easily annoyed, and have an urge to harm people. The child models the parent's aggressive behaviour.

2. When the child who has been spanked defies the punishment or continues to misbehave, there is a danger that the spanking will escalate to abusive levels. The line between spanking and abuse is a fine one. Many incidents of child abuse result from disciplinary methods taken to an extreme (Wolfe, 1987). For instance, a parent who spanks with minimal force may be tempted to increase the force if the child continues to misbehave or defy the punishment. This risk is especially pronounced if the parent is angry.

3. Spanking does not help children to learn to regulate their own behaviour. Instead, children learn to behave well around people who could punish them but misbehave when out of sight (Maccoby, 1994).

In other contexts, however, spanking does not appear to have the same risks or negative impact. For example, Chinese mothers living in the United States tend to favour a more controlling parenting style that includes spanking, especially when the child disobeys the parents (Chao, 1994). The spanking is part of an overall attitude that children need to be trained (known as *Chiao shun*), and this training is done in a supportive, highly involved, and physically close mother–child relationship.

---

parents or the children dominate the situation, there will not be any negotiation, and the family atmosphere will be very unstable. If a parent is highly controlling, preadolescent children soon learn various ways of avoiding the domination. They stay away from home as much as possible. When the children are in control (the parents are permissive and the children are aggressive), the parents avoid the family situation—perhaps by working late. Both of these extremes weaken the socialization process during middle childhood and adolescence; they make it more difficult for children to effect a smooth transition from the family to independence and to close peer friendships. As we shall see in Chapter 14, peer ties are important agents of socialization during middle childhood.

Siblings

The first, and probably the closest, peer group that affects children's personality development is their siblings (their brothers and sisters). Sibling relationships provide experiences for the child that are different from parent–child interactions—they are like "living in the nude, psychologically speaking" (Bossard & Boll, 1960, p. 91). The down-to-earth openness of brothers and sisters gives siblings a chance (whether they want it or not) to experience the ups and downs of human relationships on the most basic level. Siblings can be devotedly loyal to one another, despise one another, and/or form an intense love–hate relationship that may continue throughout their lives. Even when children are far apart in age, they are directly affected by the experience of living with others who are both equal (as other children in the same family) and unequal (differing in age, size, competence, intelligence, attractiveness, and so on). Indeed, siblings are important in helping one another to identify social concepts and social roles by reciprocally prompting and inhibiting certain patterns of behaviour (Dunn, 1983, 1985).

What influence do brothers and sisters have on one another? And how does birth order, or **sibling status,** affect each child's personality? Although previous generations of psychologists have devoted much speculation to the effects on personality of being oldest, youngest, or in the middle, current research does not consistently support these views. In fact, no consistent personality differences have been found solely as a consequence of birth order. This does not mean, however, that the children in a family are similar in personality. In fact, siblings raised in the same family are likely to have very different personalities—almost as different as unrelated children (Plomin & Daniels, 1987). One reason for this tendency is that children have a need to establish distinct identities for themselves (Dreikurs & Soltz, 1964). Therefore, if an older sibling is serious and studious, the younger one may be boisterous. A girl who has four sisters and no brothers may carve out her own niche in the family by taking on a masculine role.

Although birth order seems to have few clear, consistent, and predictable effects on personality, many studies have found effects on intelligence and achievement; here, the oldest child clearly has the edge. On average, the oldest children have higher IQs and achieve more in school and in careers. Only children are also high achievers, although their IQs tend to be slightly lower, on average, than the oldest child in a family of two or three children (Zajonc & Markus, 1975). One explanation for this finding is that only children never have the opportunity to serve as teachers for their younger siblings. Serving as a teacher may enhance a child's intellectual development (Zajonc & Hall, 1986). We should note here that this finding will become significant when we discuss cooperative learning in the next chapter. In cooperative learning, children of all intellectual abilities work jointly on classroom projects. It is believed that as the children serve as teachers for one another, their intellectual development is stimulated.

Nonetheless, differences in IQ based on birth order tend to be small. Larger and more consistent differences appear when researchers look at family size. The more children there are in a family, the lower are their IQs and the less likely they are to graduate from high school. This is true even when other factors, such as family structure and income, are taken into account (Blake, 1989). But we should note that family structure (whether there are two parents or one) and income do have strong effects on IQ and achievement—effects that are noticeably greater than those of birth order or number of siblings (Ernst & Angst, 1983).

First-borns are only children for a year or more; they have their parents' exclusive attention. Then a baby sibling comes along, displacing them from their position of sole importance. Although reactions to the new baby vary, few children show outright hostility to the newcomer—at least at first. They are likely to be curious about the baby and to direct any hostility toward the mother, often by getting into mischief just when she is feeding or diapering the baby (Dunn, 1985). They may also regress to infantile behaviour, such as thumb sucking or wetting their pants. This reaction has been interpreted by psychoanalysts as a defence mechanism, indicating disguised anxiety. More recently, theorists have interpreted it as simple imitation, reflecting interest in the baby, or as a way of competing with the baby for the mother's attention.

sibling status Birth order.

Families provide a powerful context for learning attitudes, beliefs, and appropriate behaviour—sometimes down to the last detail of posture and dress.

In any case, the infantile behaviour is only temporary. By the end of the new baby's first year, it is the younger child who is doing the imitating, and the older child is likely to have gained considerable maturity and independence (Dunn, 1985; Stewart, Mobley, Van Tuyl, & Salvador, 1987).

Older siblings are powerful models; research suggests that children with older siblings of the same sex tend to show stronger sex-typed behaviour than those with older siblings of the opposite sex (Koch, 1956; Sutton-Smith & Rosenberg, 1970). The spacing between siblings also has an important effect on sibling status. The closer in age, the more intense is the influence of the sibling relationship (Sutton-Smith & Rosenberg, 1970). In any case, each child in the family is faced with the task of forming an individual self-concept.

The Effects of Television

Television is not simply an electronic toy or one of many forms of entertainment; rather, it is a pervasive influence in the lives of children—one that has had a major impact on family relationships and traditions since the mid-1950s. The CBC broadcast the first television shows in Canada in September 1952. But at that time, most Canadian households did not yet own television sets—there were a mere 146 000 television sets in all of Canada (*Canada Year Book,* 1997). Interestingly, though, television caught on quickly, so that even by Christmas of 1952, there were an additional 78 000 television sets. And today, there are two or more colour television sets in close to half of all Canadian households (*Canada Year Book,* 1997). On average, Canadian children between the ages of 2 and 11 spend 17.7 hours per week watching television, although there are some regional differences. Children in Newfoundland watch the most television (on average, 23.8 hours per week) and those in British Columbia watch the least (on average, 15.2 hours per week) (*Canada Year Book,* 1997). It is interesting to note that Canadian children generally watch less television than American children, who watch an average of 28 hours per week (American Psychological Association [APA], 1993).

Given how much time children spend watching television, many researchers have wondered how it affects children's development. Perhaps time spent watching television displaces time spent doing other activities. (There are only so many hours in the day!) Tannis MacBeth Williams, at the University of British Columbia, studied this area by comparing three Canadian communities that differed in their exposure to television (Williams, 1986). At the start of her study, the communities differed in the following way: one had no television (nicknamed "Notel"); one had only a single television channel ("Unitel"); and one had four television channels ("Multitel"). By the end of the study (two years later), Notel went from having no television to having one channel; Unitel went from one channel to two; and Multitel remained unchanged, with four channels. The introduction of television in Notel greatly reduced participation in community activities, such as sporting events, dances, suppers, and parties. Children were much more active when there was no television or fewer television choices.

According to Kline (1993), watching television reduces the amount of time children spend reading, playing rhyming games, playing in the street, and eating leisurely family meals. Interestingly, though, it does not reduce the amount of time children spend storytelling or interacting with peers.

Other research has focused on the content of television programs. Some researchers are concerned about the amount of violence on television and its effect on children (Johnson, 1996). Many Canadian children watch American television. Violent acts average 5 per hour on prime time American programming and 20 to 25 per hour on Saturday morning cartoons (Berry & Asamen, 1993). Berry and Asamen reported that preschoolers who regularly watched *Batman* and *Superman* were more likely to get into fights at playschool, were more active, and played less well and less cooperatively with other children.

In a classic study in the United States, 875 boys were studied for 22 years to see if there was any relationship between early television viewing habits and later behaviour (Huesmann, Eron, Lefkowitz, & Walder, 1984). And indeed there was. Boys who watched a lot of violent television when they were 8 years old were more likely than other boys to have antisocial behaviours (like aggression) when they were 30. Singer, Singer, and Rapaczynski (1984) also found a link between violent television and aggression. They studied children of elementary school age over five years and found that television viewing was a major predictor of physical aggression. In an ambitious study, Centerwall (1992) examined homicide rates in Canada, the United States, and South Africa and found that they increased significantly after the introduction of television to a community. There was a 10- to 15-year delay between the introduction of television and elevated homicide rates, perhaps just long enough for television-exposed children to grow up.

In a recent study, Rohrer (1996) interviewed children who had been exposed to televised accounts of Operation Desert Storm, showing the bombing of Iraq. After watching the telecasts of the bombing, many children became anxious, and several expressed fears of being kidnapped and worried that family members would have to fight in the war. In addition, a class of 5-year-olds started playing novel games during class free play—they acted out bombing raids by throwing plastic eggs and making whistling noises. One boy, who was particularly anxious, actually measured the distance between the United States and Iraq on the globe and was alarmed that they were a mere 10.2 centimetres apart. He was not yet cognitively mature enough to understand that 10.2 centimetres stands for thousands of kilometres. He feared that Iraq was close by and that he would soon experience the bombing. This study stresses that children not only react to the violence in regular programming, but also to the violence in brief news flashes that appear from time to time.

Another concern about television is how advertisements affect children. Children are easily deceived by misleading advertising (Huston, Watkins, & Kinkel, 1989). When a commercial succeeds in convincing the child to say, "I want one of those," or "I want some of that," many parents wisely say no. This answer often leads to a conflict between the parent and the child, who may develop a negative attitude toward the parent who refuses to buy a heavily advertised toy (Fabes et al., 1999).

Up to this point in our discussion, it must seem as though researchers have focused only on the potential negative effects of television. But this is not the case. Researchers have also looked for positive effects. For example, Berry and Asamen (1993) reported that preschool children who watched *Mr. Roger's Neighborhood* (similar to the Canadian show *Mr. Dress Up*) were more likely to play cooperatively at play school and to offer to help other children and the teacher. Some children's programming has explicitly tried to counteract stereotypes. For example, *Sesame Street* routinely features children with special needs. Shortly after watching *Sesame Street* with my 4-year-old daughter, I remember overhearing her playing with her dolls. The dolls were excited because one was getting to try out a new wheelchair. The positive portrayal of people with wheelchairs was being imitated in play (Digdon). But, unfortunately, not all television programming is free of negative stereotypes.

Television can also positively affect children by teaching them information that will enhance their school readiness and performance. For instance, in one study, kindergarten teachers were asked to rate how prepared children were for school. They consistently rated children who were regular watchers of *Sesame Street* as being more prepared than other children (Bogatz & Ball, 1971, as cited in Gunter & McAleer, 1990). In a series of studies, Clifford, Gunter, and McAleer (1995) found that school-age children who watched science programs in Britain learned concepts and information that enhanced their performance in school.

Does television teach that aggression is an acceptable response to frustration? Both parents and the government are becoming increasingly concerned about the effects of television violence on children.

Television Format

Unlike other "members of the family," the television set is not responsive or interactive. Television is characterized by rapid-fire visual and auditory stimulation and by visual techniques like zooms, cuts, and special effects. These techniques can be used creatively to capture the child's attention and to structure an educational message, or they can bombard the senses, demanding little thoughtful response on the part of the child. One reviewer suggests that children pay attention to minor superficial impressions but fail to follow much of the storyline or to understand much of the content (Winn, 1983). Others have found that the format can be quite stimulating—it can capture children's attention and create heightened arousal (Rubinstein, 1983; Wright & Huston, 1983).

Although many critics have claimed that the fast-paced, attention-getting stimulation shortens children's attention span and makes them less able to pay attention in other environments, such as the classroom, there is, as yet, no solid evidence to support this view (Anderson & Collins, 1988). However, too much television takes up time children would otherwise spend reading, playing, and interacting with adults in their environments. In this way, especially with its multisensory stimulation, it may encourage passive learning and limit thinking, which is damaging to children's intellectual abilities in the long run.

Some authorities are concerned that the stimulating format of television might capture children's attention so completely that they sit mesmerized in front of the screen. This fear, too, appears to be exaggerated for most preschoolers. Although some sources claim that children watch as much as 30 hours of television a week, this figure is misleading because it refers to the amount of time the television set is turned on. Preschoolers sit in front of the television for 2 to 3 hours per day. However, during this time preschoolers generally do not sit and stare at the screen; in fact, they are looking at the screen only about half the time. The rest of the time they are in and out of the room, engaging in other activities, and talking to parents and siblings. Much of this talk is about the program they are watching (Anderson & Collins, 1988; Huston et al., 1989). The bigger problem with time spent in front of the television—at least in terms of cognitive development—is for older children who actually do watch the television for greatly extended periods of time.

At its best, television can be an educational tool that can expand the horizons of children and encourage them to break away from stereotypical images. The attention-getting, high-action, rapid-pace techniques can help children focus on the information to be learned and seem to do no harm to their cognitive development (Greenfield, 1984; Wright & Huston, 1983). However, these compelling techniques cannot be duplicated in the classroom, and many teachers find themselves frustrated by children who passively wait for education to occur.

Both the content and the format of television may influence children's development.

Summary and Conclusions

Theoretical perspectives provide frameworks for the study of personality and social development during early childhood. The period between 2 to 6 years of age is associated with major transitions in the child's socialization. Children learn the norms and rules of their culture or society; they develop a self-concept that will sustain them throughout life; and they form a set of defence mechanisms that they will use when confronting stress or anxiety.

A key developmental issue of the preschool years is that of handling emotions or feelings. These defence mechanisms assist children in exhibiting the emotions their culture deems appropriate. By the age of 5 or 6 most children use a mixture of defence mechanisms when under stress. A danger of such defences, however, is that they can isolate the child from reality. During the preschool years, it is the role of parents to assist their children in limiting stress. When stress is unavoidable, parents provide a secure base for their children.

In general, our society frowns on uninhibited displays of either positive or negative emotions. Children need to learn to control their joy, as well as their anger. In addition, they must balance their need for autonomy and independence with the dependency and love needs that they have for their parents. Socialization is a process that naturally produces anxiety in those involved.

Aggressive and prosocial behaviours are learned as complex patterns during the preschool years. One of the primary goals of socialization is to teach children ways to channel their aggressive feelings. Aggressive exchanges are common between siblings in the preschool years and tend to be initiated more by the older sibling than by the younger one. Aggressive conflicts are shorter lived when parents intervene. And consistent parent interventions can result in 2-year-olds becoming less aggressive at age 4. But parent interventions have less of an impact on the long-term aggression levels of older children.

Prosocial behaviour, which includes sharing, helping, and so on, is also learned from identifying with models or through a system of rewards and punishments. Some theorists believe that gender differences in prosocial behaviour occur because girls are more likely to be rewarded for nurturing. Therefore, they become more sensitive to the needs and concerns of others. Modelling is most effective in producing prosocial behaviour when children perceive the model as being similar or when the model is powerful, competent, and supportive. Prosocial behaviour develops, as well, through induction and role playing.

Children also learn behaviours from each other. In peer relationships, children model and reinforce each other for what they consider appropriate behaviours. Children who are popular with their peers during the preschool years are likely to remain so in later childhood; children who are bullies in preschool become aggressive older children. Children who lack social skills in early childhood may be aggressive or withdrawn in later childhood and adolescence.

Socialization is also designed to teach children the concepts and rules of the societies in which they live. Children absorb moral standards and values by internalizing society's rules. As these rules are internalized, children develop the self-control necessary to regulate their own behaviour. As children mature, their disputes are characterized by the ability to take another's perspective and by the use of words, rather than physical intervention, to resolve conflicts.

Gender schemes are derived from socialization and genetically based sex differences. By the age of 2½, most children can identify themselves and others as male or female. By age 5 to 7, the child acquires the notion of gender as fixed for a lifetime, despite appearances. Gender schemes help children organize which behaviours they will remember and choose to imitate.

Children also grow and develop in the context of families. Siblings and parents form the first reference group for children. The warmth and control exercised by parents, as well as the basic style of parenting they use, affects the child's personality and social development. The child's position in the family structure, the number of children in the family, and the child's basic personality all influence her IQ and achievement level. Children from the same family may show widely differing personalities because of their individual efforts to assert their uniqueness.

Parents and the discipline they employ in raising their children also have a significant impact on the child's personality, self-esteem, and desire to achieve. An atmosphere of warmth, caring, and firm control within the family—with the parents serving as authoritative guides for the child's behaviour—appears to be most conducive to a child's learning self-discipline and self-regulation. Parents' use of verbal reasoning also encourages children to develop an understanding of social rules and expectations.

One key ingredient in the cognitive and interpersonal skills of today's children is television. Time spent watching television has displaced the time children used to spend reading, being physically active, eating leisurely meals, and playing rhyming games. Exposure to televised violence increases aggression, but certain programming has been found to increase prosocial behaviour and to assist in developing school-related skills.

As with any aspect of the social environment, moderation appears to be the key in parental control, television watching, and peer interactions during the preschool years. Children need time for the growth of self and social understanding to take place—and a safe base from which their initial explorations of the world may occur.

Key Terms and Concepts

aggression (p. 348)

anxiety (p. 339)

assertive behaviour
    (p. 348)

authoritarian parenting
    (p. 359)

authoritative parenting
    (p. 359)

defence mechanisms
    (p. 341)

denial (p. 341)

fear (p. 339)

gender constancy (p. 357)

gender identity (p. 357)

indifferent parenting
    (p. 359)

induction (p. 351)

internalization (p. 356)

overt aggression (p. 348)

permissive parenting
    (p. 359)

prosocial behaviour
    (p. 348)

regression (p. 341)

relational aggression
    (p. 348)

role playing (p. 351)

sibling status (p. 363)

social reciprocity (p. 352)

withdrawal (p. 341)

Questions to Review

1. Describe how theories have affected the study of social development.

2. Discuss the sources of anxiety. Compare and contrast fear and anxiety in the preschool child.

3. Describe defence mechanisms that preschool children use.

4. Discuss different strategies that children might use to cope with anxiety and stress.

5. List several of the strong feelings that preschool children begin to deal with and the ways they learn to handle these feelings.

6. Discuss the developmental conflicts that children must resolve during the preschool years.

7. What is the difference between overt and relational aggression? Why are some children more aggressive than others?

8. What is social reciprocity?

9. List five different levels of social interaction in young children. At what age do these levels apply?

10. What is internalization, and how does it relate to a child's developing self-regulation?

11. What are gender schemes, and how do they apply to socialization?

12. How do parenting styles affect children's personality and social development during middle childhood?

13. How do sibling relationships affect children's personality development?

14. How is television a major socializing force in our society?

Weblinks

www.cmha.ca/
Canadian Mental Health Association
This site has information on publications (both free and for sale), projects, and media releases related to mental health in children and adults. Sample publications are "Embracing Cultural Diversity: A Guide for Canadian Parents" and "Tips for Coping with School Tragedy."

www.canadianparents.com
Canadian Parents Online
This site has articles, surveys, and chat rooms where people can pose questions to experts in child-related disciplines.

www.senate.gov/~dpc/crs/reports/ascii/97-43
Children and Television
This site has a research paper titled "V-Chip and TV Ratings: Helping Parents Supervise Their Children's Television Viewing," written by Marcia Smith. It explores the use of the V-chip in Canada and the United States.

Summing Up...

Early Childhood

Physical

- As ages, rate of growth slows down
- Changes in body proportions—increased leg length and arm length
- Develops lowered centre of gravity
- Experiences bone growth and ossification
- Develops improved cardiovascular functioning
- Develops lateralization and handedness
- Improves in self-care skills

Psychosocial

- Increases self-control (ages 2 to 6)
- Develops a sense of personal and cultural identity (ages 2 to 6)
- Becomes better at regulating emotions
- Expresses dependency through verbal contact (age 6)
- Experiences less separation distress (ages 2 to 3)
- Becomes more compliant and cooperative (ages 2 to 6)
- Addresses the conflict between initiative and guilt (ages 3 to 6)
- Shows less overt aggression (after age 2)
- Takes part in onlooker and parallel play (age 2)
- Takes part in associative and cooperative play (ages 4 and 5)
- Has longer peer interactions, shares more often, becomes better at following rules and resolving conflicts (ages 6 to 7)
- Recognizes self in mirror (age 2)
- Increases self-assertion and evaluation
- Internalizes values and morals
- Forms gender identity (ages 2 to 6)
- Develops gender constancy (ages 5 to 7)

Cognitive

- Enters stage of preoperations: preconceptual (ages 2 to 4); intuitive (ages 5 to 7)
- Improves in use of symbols
- Increases sociodramatic play (age 2)
- Distinguishes between appearance and reality (age 5 or older)
- Improves in short-term memory
- Has more developed recognition memory than recall
- Increases use of memory strategies
- Develops a theory of mind—understands desires (ages 1 to 2) and beliefs (age 3); uses beliefs to explain behaviour (age 4)
- Distinguishes between intentional and accidental actions
- Gradually develops an understanding of false beliefs

Middle Childhood: Physical Development

Then the child turned ten times round the seasons
Skated over ten years frozen streams
Words like "when you're older" must appease him
... and promises of someday make his dreams.

JONI MITCHELL
"THE CIRCLE GAME"

Outline

CHAPTER 12

Objectives

By the time you have finished this chapter, you should be able to do the following:

✔ Describe the physical development of the school-age child.

✔ Describe the changes in fine motor and gross motor skills during middle childhood.

✔ Describe the role of vigorous play in child health and motor development.

✔ Explain rough-and-tumble play and its role in social development for boys.

✔ Identify the major health and safety concerns for school-age children.

✔ Explain the causes and consequences of obesity in middle childhood.

✔ Explain appropriate accommodations schools can make to provide an effective educational and social environment for the physically challenged student.

✔ Identify some key goals for physical education in the elementary school.

School-age children have considerable energy and creative capacities for exploring their world. *Middle childhood* refers to the period from 6 to 12 years—the play and industry years during which children refine their motor and cognitive abilities and become more independent. They begin to branch out from their families and interact more with peers. Their friendship patterns become more established and valued. Children are able to plan and carry out activities in sequence that easily fill their days. In addition, given appropriate training, school-age children are able to learn to swim, ski, dance, or play a musical instrument—as well as to learn many other difficult motor abilities, given the opportunity.

Middle childhood is also a time of increased responsibility. In societies around the world, children of this age are introduced to the tasks and roles of the adult world in a more formal way. In industrial societies, this means school and academic learning for several hours each day. In tribal cultures, the "schooling" may mean an apprenticeship in the gender-specific roles of hunting, gathering, cooking, or weaving (Rogoff, 1990).

School-age children have new physical abilities and coordination—skills they constantly use. Running, jumping, and hopping skills become more mature. New sports, such as soccer, baseball, or tennis, are now open to children because of their improved motor skills. Group sports assume significance because sufficient numbers of individual children now have the talent to participate—both boys and girls. Many children show an intense interest in acquiring and improving the skills necessary to participate in team sports.

The environments where children live give them the opportunity to learn and practise motor skills. Some children during middle childhood have had a wealth of experiences behind them that have allowed them to develop diverse skills. Special classes and activities, such as dance, music, art, or organized sports, also may have provided

Their enhanced motor skills and coordination open the door for school-age children to participate in sports such as tennis.

them with instruction and feedback that have made their efforts more efficient and effective. Other children may have spent time running and playing without instruction or organized activities. They may have developed stamina and the ability to plan their own activities and create their own fun, which the more formal experiences have not encouraged. In either case, the physical development of middle childhood provides children with the readiness to move into more complex or group activities for which their early childhood experiences prepared them.

As we mentioned in Chapter 9, it is important for us to remember that physical, cognitive, and social factors interact to produce individual development. For purposes of clarity, we are focusing in this chapter on physical development, but the various domains of development cannot really be disentangled. When we look at school-age children building a fort, working on building a model, or painting a picture, it is difficult to determine if their growing cognitive skills allow them to plan daily activities or if their new physical abilities allow them to think of new things to do. Because of their new cognitive abilities, for example, they are able to focus their attention for longer periods of time, anticipate the next moves others will make, and monitor the strategies each uses. These skills clearly influence the activities in which they may successfully engage. In either case, the interaction of thinking and action during these years is clear.

In this chapter, we shall present the changes in physical characteristics and motor skills that children go through in these middle years of childhood. We shall discuss the special health and nutrition needs of school-age children and the psychological impact of problems in these areas. We shall then present rough-and-tumble play as a special form of children's vigorous play. Finally, we shall discuss the physical environment of the school as it reflects—or in some cases frustrates—children's motor development.

Physical Growth and Change

As we look at the various aspects of physical development during middle childhood, we can recognize that children follow a similar sequential process. However, each child also emerges as a unique person. Not all children mature at the same rate. Great variation exists in individual development, and this variability increases with age and experience throughout the school years. Some children may be more mature in certain areas than others. For example, one child may have mature physical and motor development for her age and yet be functioning socially at a less advanced level. Another may be socially and cognitively advanced but lag behind peers in motor skills.

Physical Growth during Middle Childhood

During middle childhood, the variation in the growth rate of various parts and systems of the body continues (see Chapter 9). At certain times the growth rate is accelerated, while at other times it is relatively steady. We see the typical profile of growth for one boy presented in Figure 12-1. In general, there is a fairly steady increase in height during middle childhood, which varies from the more rapid pace of growth during infancy and adolescence. From year to year, for the individual child, spurts and slower growth periods alternate. Annual gains are high during infancy, decreasing to a relatively stable 5 to 7.6 centimetres a year during middle childhood. From 5 to 6 years, for example, there is a stretching up in height and a loss of baby fat. During adolescence, a growth spurt occurs that establishes the individual's final height, which stays uniform throughout adulthood.

Variability occurs in the timing and extent to which growth occurs during childhood. Children's growth may be influenced by the environment in which they live, their nutrition, their gender, and basic characteristics inherited from their parents and grandparents. Girls, for example, are slightly shorter and lighter than boys until age 9, when girls' growth accelerates because of hormonal changes that occur earlier in girls

Question to Ponder

Girls' growth spurts typically happen earlier than those of boys. What are the social implications of girls being bigger, on average, than boys at age 11?

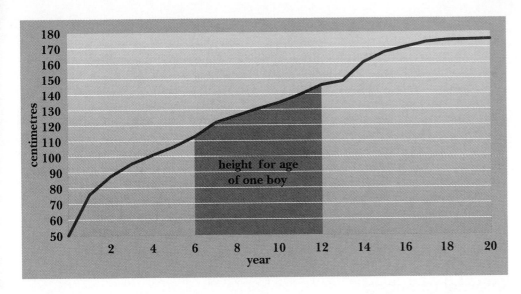

Figure 12-1
The Height of a Boy at
Various Ages
Source: Cratty, B. (1986). *Perceptual and motor development in infants and children.* Englewood Cliffs, NJ: Prentice-Hall, p. 52.

than boys. A girl's growth begins to outpace a boy's growth at that age. We also see that some girls are structurally smaller than other girls. These overall differences in height may affect the child's body image and self-concept—another way in which physical, social, and cognitive development interact.

During middle childhood, therefore, as we can see, growth is slower and more regular than during the first 2 years of life. The average 6-year-old weighs about 20.4 kilograms and is about 1 metre tall. As children enter school, they are in a steady period of growth that continues to around 9 years of age for girls and 11 years for boys, when the adolescent growth spurt begins. Figure 12-2 illustrates the changes in body size and proportion typical of middle childhood.

This period of fairly stable increase in height and weight during middle childhood is associated with a parallel increase in the performance of motor skills. All children

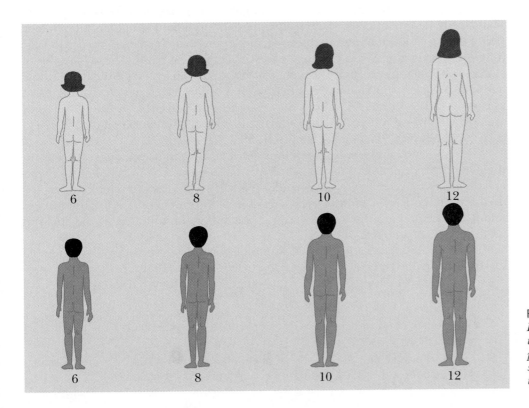

Figure 12-2
During middle childhood, there are tremendous variations in growth patterns, but these changes in body size and proportion are typical of this period.

will become less awkward and more accomplished in activities such as running, jumping, and hopping during this period. However, children who are taller will gain the mechanical advantage of their longer limbs, which may account for some of the variability observed in children's motor skill performance (Nichols, 1990).

One study, conducted in a poor, inner-city community in London, England, found that physical growth was related to children's intellectual development (Dowdney, Skuse, Morris, & Pickles, 1998). Compared with other inner-city children, children who were exceptionally short at age 4 were more likely at age 11 to be short, to experience school failure, and to require speech therapy. None of the exceptionally short children had a disease or medical condition to account for their slow growth. The researchers hypothesized that malnutrition during infancy was likely the cause of both the growth and school problems. Furthermore, the malnutrition may have occurred not just because infants were given a poor diet, but because they had immature motor control over their mouths, which caused them to feed inefficiently and, as they grew up, to require speech therapy.

Internal Changes

As the body grows in the observable dimensions of height and weight, there are also internal changes associated with this growth. During middle childhood, for example, skeletal maturation continues. The long bones of the body lengthen and broaden, and ligaments grow but are not yet firmly attached to the bone. Consequently, school-age children have considerable flexibility in their body movements, although recent research has found that children are less flexible from 5 to 8 years than they were from 3 to 4. In addition, girls are slightly more flexible than boys at all times during childhood (Koslow, 1987). Many adults have marvelled at the 8-year-old who is able to sit on the floor with her feet casually hooked around her neck, or the 9-year-old boy who can sit with legs bent out from the knees at a 45-degree angle.

Skeletal Maturity In middle childhood, bones grow longer as the body lengthens and broadens. But the ligaments are not yet firmly attached. Since the skeleton is not yet mature, early physical training that is overly rigorous may have negative consequences. Many Little League pitchers, for example, have injured their shoulders and elbows. Other young children have suffered wrist, ankle, and knee injuries in their sports or jungle gym activities. Some children suffer from growing pains. These episodes of stiffness and aching caused by skeletal growth are particularly common at nighttime and may be quite painful. Some rapidly growing children experience growing pains as early as 4 years of age. For others, they emerge at adolescence. In either case, they are normal physical responses to growth, and they should be explained to children as such (Nichols, 1990; Sheiman & Slomin, 1988).

Another area of skeletal growth more obvious in school-age children occurs in their teeth. Beginning at 6 to 7 years of age, most children lose all 20 of their primary teeth. When the first few permanent teeth grow in, they often look too big for their mouths until facial growth catches up. Two of the more noticeable landmarks of middle childhood are the toothless smile of a 6-year-old, followed by the "beaver-toothed" grin of an 8-year-old.

As was mentioned earlier with regard to height and weight, there is considerable variability in children's rate of skeletal maturity. Falkner (1962), for example, proposed six different patterns of maturation that are still discussed today. These patterns include the following:

1. An average child who will closely approximate the mean curve for height and weight at stated ages.
2. Early-maturing children who are tall in childhood only because they are more mature than the average; they will not become unusually tall adults.

Although both boys and girls of school age show considerable flexibility in their body movements, girls are slightly more flexible than boys.

3. Early-maturing children who are also genetically taller than average from early childhood. They mature rapidly and remain taller than average throughout their lives.

4. Late-maturing children who are short in childhood but who later evidence reasonable growth. They do not remain unusually small in adulthood.

5. Late-maturing children who are genetically short and who remain short adults.

6. An indefinite group, whose members must often be exposed to medical evaluation. They may be children whose adolescent growth spurt starts unusually early, by age 8 or 9, or their growth may evidence unusual delay and be the cause for parental and medical concern (Cratty, 1986, p. 58).

From these patterns, we can see that skeletal maturity may be used to assess not only children's present maturity, but also future problems and benefits. The early-maturing child in middle childhood may become a valued member of a sports team and therefore become the recipient of adults' coaching. This early start may increase self-esteem and serve as the basis for self-motivation to train hard in order to sustain this success. Late maturers, on the other hand, may not receive this special attention and may be discouraged from participating in sports or athletic training during middle childhood. This sense of discouragement also may have long-term consequences, as the following quote indicates:

> These youngsters are far less likely to persist in sports and games, and may instead turn toward more sedentary endeavours likely to elicit recognition, including music, scientific efforts, computers, and other forms of academics. Less acceptable social compensations than these are also often acted out by the youngster who is immature and inept physically. (Cratty, 1986, p. 66)

Certainly, not all children will become either star athletes or scholars. Many lack outstanding talent in either arena. However, when children are encouraged to follow one path and discouraged from following another, such diverse patterns may develop. Research has found that children as young as 8 have already begun to assign favourable and unfavourable social attributes to various body types, including their own. They are, therefore, aware at this age that various body types exist and know how to rate them. Furthermore, they have been found to show some signs of social retardation if they believe their own body type is not the most socially acceptable—typically, lean and muscular (Cratty, 1986).

Fat and Muscle Tissue Fat deposition increases briefly between birth and 6 months. It then decreases until children are 6 to 8 years of age, with a more marked decrease in boys. During the adolescent growth spurt, boys show a decrease in fat deposition, while girls show an increase—which accounts, in part, for the differing body contours of adult men and women.

During middle childhood, muscles increase in length, breadth, and width (Nichols, 1990). The relative strength of girls and boys is similar during middle childhood but again diverges at adolescence, with boys' strength surpassing that of girls.

Brain Development during Middle Childhood Between 6 and 8 years, the forebrain undergoes a small growth spurt. By age 8, the brain has achieved 90 percent of its adult size. During middle childhood, the corpus callosum, which is the main connecting link between the hemispheres of the brain, also becomes more mature in both structure and function. Interestingly enough, as we will see in Chapter 13, this is also the time when the child moves from one Piagetian stage to another in cognitive development. It is intriguing to note that children typically achieve concrete operations at the same time as their brains are growing more rapidly in substance and connections.

During middle childhood, brain development appears to involve more efficient functioning of various structures in the brain, for example, the frontal lobes of the cortex. The frontal lobe is responsible for thought and consciousness. This part of the brain slightly increases in its surface area because of continuing myelination, which was described in Chapter 6. In addition, lateralization of the brain's hemispheres becomes more pronounced during the school years (Thatcher, Walker, & Guidice, 1987). We now know much about the brain's development—and are on the verge of an explosion of knowledge about brain function and anatomy—because of the development of various medical technologies that allow scientists to explore the brain in increasingly fine detail.

Motor Skill Development

Throughout middle childhood, children continue to grow in the strength, speed, and coordination needed for gross motor skills. This newly acquired physical ability is reflected in their interest in sports and daredevil stunts. They climb trees, use logs as balance beams to cross streams, jump from beam to beam in the frame of an unfinished house. Numerous studies demonstrate the progress of motor development during this period. According to Keogh (1965), at age 7 a boy can throw a ball approximately 10.4 metres. He will probably be able to throw it twice as far by the time he is 10, and three times as far by the time he is 12; his accuracy will improve, as well. Girls make similar progress in throwing and catching skills, although at every age their average throwing distance is shorter than that of boys (Williams, 1983). Sex differences are evident in many other physical skills: all through middle childhood, boys can run faster than girls. After age 11, the difference in running speed widens because boys continue to improve, whereas girls do not (Herkowitz, 1978). However, girls tend to outperform boys in skills that require agility or balance—for example, girls are better at hopping. These sex differences are closely linked to the specific activities children practise. Girls who play baseball develop longer, more accurate throws. Boys and girls who play soccer develop skills at a similar pace.

When we carefully study the makeup of basic movements, such as jumping, the movements of adults and school-age children are the same. The magnitude of the jump or the position from which the individual takes off differs for adults and children, but the jump itself is remarkably uniform (Clark, Phillips, & Peterson, 1989). This research offers support for the view that environmental constraints may affect observed motor behaviours, just as maturation of the central nervous system may affect them (Thelen, 1988). As children mature, they acquire new ways to jump and can jump higher and farther—this may be partly because of increased muscle strength or practice. Despite these changes in magnitude, however, the structure of the jump remains unchanged.

Sex differences in motor skills before the onset of puberty are more a function of opportunity and cultural expectations than of any real physical differences between boys and girls (Cratty, 1986; Nichols, 1990). In general, because of social expectations, girls do better at activities that are expected of girls and boys do better at skills considered more masculine.

The school-age child is capable of controlled, purposeful movement (Nichols, 1990). By the time she enters formal school—usually at around 5 years of age—various locomotor skills, such as running, jumping, and hopping, are well in place. The child can execute these skills with even rhythm and with relatively few mechanical errors—for example, in foot placement or in use of the arms. When we consider the developmental sequence for running, it is amazing to consider how far children have come from tottering 18-month-olds.

Fine Motor Skills Fine motor skills—those skills that enable children to use their hands in increasingly sophisticated ways—also develop

A 12-year-old girl can throw a ball three times as far as she could at the age of 7—one sign of the rapid development of gross motor skills that occurs during this period.

quickly during this period, starting even before a child enters grade one. In preschools, teachers help build writing readiness as they offer children the opportunity to draw, paint, cut, and mould with clay. As their teachers guide them through these activities, children discover how to draw circles, squares, and, finally, triangles. (Children who cannot draw a triangle have difficulty with more complex writing skills.) Each increasingly complex shape requires the improved hand-eye coordination children need to learn in order to write. Children develop most of the fine motor skills required in writing by age 6 or 7. However, some children cannot draw a diamond or master many letter shapes until the age of 8.

The mastery that children develop over their own bodies during this period gives them feelings of competence and self-worth that are essential to good mental health (see also the box "Children's Concepts of Their Bodies"). Controlling their own bodies also helps them win the acceptance of their peers. Awkward, poorly coordinated children are often left out of group activities; they may continue to feel unwanted long after their awkwardness disappears. We see an overview of the physical characteristics of school-age children presented in Table 12-1.

Basic Movement Qualities   In general, virtually all motor performance data for school-age children reflects continuous improvement. Plateaus sometimes appear—or there may be some deceleration—from 7 to 9 years. As motor skills improve, the activities of children also grow to reflect their new physical maturity. Vigorous play develops in intensity, as we will see in subsequent sections of this chapter. Hobbies and crafts also become part of the child's repertoire of behaviours. Arts and crafts, carpentry materials, and the more complex construction sets begin to fill the child's "wish list." For example, Lego sets with built-in motors become more desirable than simple Lego sets. Train layouts become more elaborate.

All of these changes in the quality of movements that the child performs are affected by the following factors: balance, agility, body build, throwing ability, speed, hand precision, and strength and power (Cratty, 1986).

BALANCE

Balance is a combination of several abilities: balancing objects, balancing the body in one position on one foot, and dynamic balance, which involves maintaining balance while crossing a narrow balance beam. An additional skill is maintaining body position in any of the above positions while the eyes are closed.

Between the ages of 6 and 7, most of the fine motor skills needed for writing develop.

FOCUS ON APPLICATION

Children's Concepts of Their Bodies

Remember when you thought your heart was shaped like the classic box of valentine chocolates, or when you were sure, if you tried hard enough, you could look through one ear to see the other? During the early school years, all children conceptualize their internal body organs and functions in a concrete way. They are vitally interested in the workings of their bodies, and based on their observations and the little information they receive, they actively construct what is going on inside. As they grow older and acquire more knowledge and understanding, they learn to describe their bodies in a more sophisticated and abstract way. As you will see, many of their thoughts are remarkably accurate, whereas others are totally outrageous.

In a fascinating study of the thoughts that 6- to 12-year-old children have about the inside of their bodies, Cathleen Crider (1981) found that the typical elementary-school child first identifies the brain, bones, heart, blood, and blood vessels. As you can

---

One 9-year-old described his organs in a global way: "The heart," he said, "is what you breathe in."

---

see from the drawing (Figure 12-3) by a 7-year-old girl, the stomach is absent, but the vegetables that she ate for dinner are present. In the child's mind, nothing is certain about the body interior except the foods she puts into it (Schilder & Wechsler, 1935).

Children's perceptions give them their first clues about their internal organs. They can feel their heart beating; they can feel the hardness of their bones under their skin; they can identify their brain from the inner speech that accompanies thought. Other organs, like the nerves and liver, are not as easy to understand. After having liver for dinner, children may wonder if they have a liver, too. They will be satisfied with their parents' simple answer that they do, and they may feel no need for more information. Similarly, children may understand their bodies' nerves only in terms of the emotional problems of a nervous relative. Even with considerable instruction, it is difficult for them to comprehend other hidden functions of nerves.

Children often use the little information they have about their bodies in inventive ways. For instance, they think

BODY AGILITY

Agility is measured in a variety of ways. It may be the rapidity with which children change direction while running, rhythmic hopping, getting up quickly from a sitting or laying position, or vertical jumps of various types. Agility is related to flexibility, but it is also a function of strength and muscle development.

By the age of 7, many children become interested in arts and crafts, reflecting the continuous expansion of their motor skills.

of body organs, like the stomach and brain, as containers. A child who has already become aware of his stomach describes it in this way: "The stomach is a round thing in our body for holding food. The food goes in your mouth, down your neck, to your stomach. If we didn't have a stomach, the food would go everywhere and it would be a mess" (Crider, 1981, p. 54).

Like every other aspect of development, conceptualization of this kind occurs at different rates for different children. One 9-year-old described his organs in a global way: "The heart," he said, "is what you breathe in. It goes like this. [Child breathes in and out.] The lungs are to breathe in too. Food goes in the stomach, and then it comes in your heart, and then it makes you breathe air.... Your heart moves your stomach." A second 9-year-old had much more sophisticated ideas: "Your heart works by pumping blood out to the vessels," said the child. "Blood goes through your

body, some to your head. It doesn't stop. It keeps on going, but I don't know where it goes" (Crider, 1981, p. 57). Although children's understanding may be sophisticated in one area, it can be simplistic in another. For example, at the same time that a child explains how her stomach "mashes" food and turns it into blood that moves throughout the body, she may conceive of the muscles in only a global sense: muscles "make you strong."

Until children learn to think abstractly—to conceptualize the things they cannot directly perceive—they will continue to construct explanations of what is inside their bodies in these concrete terms. In a child's mind, it makes sense that food collects in the little toe, that the lungs are in the throat, and that the heart is for love. Only when their thought processes pass into the formal operational stage described by Piaget will they be able to understand the real picture of their inner bodies.

Figure 12-3
Drawing of body interior by a 7-year-old girl

BODY BUILD

Movement is also affected by the child's particular body build. Body build is a combination of height, weight, and physique. Build is partly affected by maturation since, as we have already seen, the nature of the body's composition changes as children grow.

THROWING ABILITIES

Children's skill with balls—both in catching and throwing—affects the quality of the movement they perform. Throwing improves as children grow, as does the nature of the hand position they use to catch balls. In general, boys seem to possess better throwing ability than do girls. However, girls who play baseball or softball, and therefore practise throwing and catching skills, appear to do as well as boys in middle childhood.

HAND PRECISION

Children's ability to engage in fine motor skills associated with hand precision is also a primary factor in evaluating their overall quality of movement. A typical measure of this sort of motor skill might involve asking children to drop pennies with precision and speed into a small opening.

STRENGTH AND POWER

Measures of strength and power are difficult to obtain since it is difficult to convince children of 5 to 7 years to exert themselves in ways that may cause even momentary discomfort. A painless way to measure strength in young children is to measure the pressure exerted on a hand dynamometer.

Studies using these measures of movement qualities find that between 5 and 12 years of age, children generally show increments in all areas—moreover, there is considerable

Table 12-1 Characteristics of Physical Development during Middle Childhood

5- to 6-Year-Olds

- Steady increases in height and weight.
- Steady growth in strength for both boys and girls.
- Awareness of large body parts.
- Increased use of all body parts.
- Improvement in gross motor skills.
- Ability to perform motor skills singly.

7- to 8-Year-Olds

- Steady increase in height and weight.
- Steady increase in strength for both boys and girls.
- Increased use of all body parts.
- Refinement in gross motor skills.
- Improvement in fine motor skills.
- Increased variability in motor skill performance but still performed singly.

9- to 10-Year-Olds

- Growth spurt begins for girls.
- Increase in strength for girls accompanied by loss of flexibility.
- Awareness and development of all body parts and systems.
- Ability to combine motor skills more fluidly.
- Improved balance.

11-Year-Olds

- Girls generally taller and heavier than boys.
- Growth spurt begins for boys.
- Accurate judgments in intercepting moving objects.
- Continued combination of more fluid motor skills.
- Continued improvement of fine motor skills.
- Continued increasing variability in motor skill performance.

overlap in these skills. For example, both strength and flexibility contribute to many tasks. As children get older, they become stronger. This improvement may be due to factors other than maturation, such as experience, improvement in skills through practice, or increased willingness to undergo an all-out effort (Cratty, 1986). This is true in tests of muscle strength, as well as in such activities as sustained running, jumping, or competitive swimming.

In general, in tests of strength during middle childhood, there are few, if any, sex differences until the seventh to eighth year, when boys, because of their physical activities, may slightly exceed girls. However, by the end of childhood, the strength of girls may exceed that of boys because girls have already begun their adolescent maturation. Similar findings occur in tests of flexibility, jumping, and throwing.

In general, school-age children show yearly improvements in a variety of skills, including measurable improvements in strength, agility, balance, and velocities in which running and throwing occur. There are also measurable improvements in body mechanics. Body parts become more coordinated (Roberton & Halverson, 1988). These changes result in improvements to the actions themselves, as well as to their outcomes—for example, balls are thrown harder and distances are run faster.

The increased muscle strength of school-age children may be the result not only of maturation, but also of practice in sports, such as competitive running or swimming.

Vigorous Physical Activity

It is important for children to engage in vigorous activity if they are to have normal growth and development. With our current social emphasis on sedentary activities, such as television watching and video game playing, as well as busing to school as opposed to walking or cycling, many children are physically unfit. For them, physical education classes in school or organized sports activities are the only real exercise they get.

Physical educators provide a number of activities to help children be more active. These range from strengthening activities for school-age boys and girls to teaching specific motor skills or the use of particular types of equipment for exercise. In general, such physical education activities should be designed to improve children's self-perceptions and the use of their bodies in performing various motor movements. While physical educators working with young children may teach only one skill at a time, those working with children in middle childhood emphasize activities involving the combination of skills.

During middle childhood, children have fairly short attention spans. Therefore, organized activities and instruction need to be of short duration and to have few rules. Instruction should build sequentially, with children being given the opportunity to practise small "subsets" of the skills before being asked to perform the whole activity or movement.

In addition to these cognitive requirements for motor performance, there are social aspects of children's worlds that influence their ability to participate in sports or in organized vigorous play. For example, one observer of middle childhood notes,

> Socially an egocentric kindergarten child is transformed into a group-centred participant by the fifth or sixth grade. Dependence upon adults is replaced by the growing importance of the peer group for establishing patterns of behaviour. Girls and boys may have developed some perceptions or expectations regarding the suitability of some activities for each sex. (Nichols, 1990, p. 27)

Teachers and adults in general must continue to encourage all children to develop a variety of skills and to design activities so that girls and boys may engage in vigorous physical activity together. In this way, all children may achieve optimal physical development.

Rough-and-Tumble Play

As we have said throughout this chapter, moderate to vigorous physical activity is instrumental to refining and strengthening motor activities during middle childhood. Rough-and-tumble play is one vehicle for this development. The term **rough-and-tumble play** refers to vigorous, playful, and nonaggressive interchanges between children. Examples include play fighting and chasing, as well as somewhat antagonistic behaviours such as teasing, hitting at, poking, pouncing, sneaking up, carrying another child, piling on top of each other, holding, and pushing (Pellegrini, 1988). These behaviours are also accompanied by smiling and laughter.

Clearly, this list of behaviours does not necessarily suggest "nonaggressive" activity. In fact, research has found that the nature of rough-and-tumble play differs depending on certain social or personality factors in the participating children. Since aggressive or socially rejected children have a tendency to interpret social provocations such as those presented above as aggressive, they sometimes turn playful episodes into aggression. Popular, confident children, however, tend to correctly interpret these activities as play and do not turn them into aggression (Pellegrini, 1988). In fact, when popular children engage in rough-and-tumble play, it soon is transformed into games-with-rules, in which protections are developed to avoid hurting children. Popular children, therefore, use rough-and-tumble play groups as opportunities to

rough-and-tumble play Playful and typically nonaggressive activity involving vigorous interchanges between children; examples include play fighting and chasing.

For popular boys, rough play is a way to sharpen their already considerable social skills of negotiating and forging alliances.

model and practise prosocial behaviours—behaviours that encourage social exchanges between children—with other popular children (Pellegrini, 1988). Rough-and-tumble play is also a reasonably safe way for boys to establish and maintain dominance relationships (Pellegrini & Smith, 1998).

Gender Differences in Rough-and-Tumble Play

Interesting gender differences emerge in teachers' and peers' responses to rough-and-tumble play. Whereas teachers associate boys' rough play with social problem solving and social preference, they tend to associate that of girls with antisocial behaviour (Pellegrini, 1989). Popular boys often engage in rough play to have fun and to interact cooperatively with peers. Therefore, for these boys, rough play is a way of practising and developing social skills that are related to their popularity—such as negotiating and forming alliances. Aggressive boys tend to be excluded from rough play by those boys who are popular. For different reasons, girls too are often discouraged from participating in these behaviours. Girls who engage in rough play may be labelled by teachers and peers as antisocial because they engage in what is seen as a male-oriented behaviour.

Finally, while rough-and-tumble play may be perceived somewhat negatively by adults who view it as progressing to aggression, it serves a valuable educational purpose. Rather than leading to increased aggression, rough play often leads to children's engagement in cooperative games with rules. Enhanced social problem solving and popularity are also an outcome for boys who participate. Popular boys can engage in rough-and-tumble play, whereas unpopular boys cannot because they lack the necessary social skills to participate. Disliked or unpopular boys usually cannot discriminate between play and aggression.

Health in School-Age Children

Widespread immunization for infectious diseases—such as polio, diptheria, and measles—has greatly improved the health of Canadian children. In the 1920s, these diseases were the most common causes of childhood death, but today they have been

Question to Ponder

Are gender differences in rough-and-tumble play primarily the result of socialization or of biology?

virtually eliminated (Trovato, 1991). Unfortunately, new infectious diseases, such as AIDS, have arisen, and some infections and respiratory illnesses remain problems for children, including influenza, ear infections, and asthma. In the late 1980s and early 1990s, immunization for whooping cough decreased, resulting in outbreaks of this serious illness (Trovato, 1991).

During middle childhood, some school-related disabilities become more apparent. For instance, per every 1000 children, 17.3 have learning disabilities, 8.4 have behavioural or emotional problems, and 6.9 have mental handicaps (CICH, 1994). Others have vision or hearing problems.

Violence toward children also has become a national concern. Over half of all violent crimes against children are sexual assaults (CICH, 1994).

Health and Illness

Minor illnesses, such as ear infections, colds, and upset stomachs, are prevalent in the preschool period. But during the years from 6 to 12, most children experience fewer of these illnesses. This decrease is partly a result of greater immunity owing to previous exposure. Also, most school-age children know about and practise somewhat better nutrition, health, and safety habits (O'Connor-Francoeur, 1983; Starfield, 1992). Nevertheless, fairly frequent minor illnesses occur. During this period, nearsightedness, or myopia, is often first diagnosed. For example, 25 percent of white, middle-class grade six students have some myopia and have been fitted with glasses.

One author suggests that minor illnesses such as colds are actually of some benefit to the child's psychological development. Although common illnesses certainly disrupt children's school progress, as well as family social roles and work schedules, they and their families generally recover quickly from these interruptions. In the process, children learn to cope with minor stress and to increase their knowledge of themselves. They develop greater empathy and a more realistic understanding of the role of "being sick." Hence, children's illnesses can be seen as a normal part of social and behavioural development (Parmelee, 1986). We shall now briefly discuss two of the more common health problems of middle childhood.

Otitis Media *Otitis media*, or inflammation of the middle ear, is a common disease of infancy and childhood. Many children experience multiple episodes of the disease prior to their third birthday and then continue to have them throughout childhood. Otitis media is associated with a set of symptoms that includes fever, pain, and fluid in the ear. It is also often associated with transient conductive hearing loss; in fact, repeated episodes may lead to chronic auditory impairment (Lonigan, Fischel, Whitehurst, Arnold, & Valdez-Menchaca, 1992). Several studies have found a relation between an early or continued history of otitis media and later problems in language development, including expressive language disorder and poor narrative skills (Feagans, Kipp, & Blood, 1994).

While not all children have severe effects of otitis media, persistent middle-ear infections are a common cause of mild hearing loss—temporary or permanent—and of consequent language delays and disorders (Friel-Patti, 1990). Children who are most at risk to suffer hearing loss are those who lack access to health care or to early treatment to reduce the risk of fluid accumulation in the middle ear.

Obesity Obesity—defined as weighing at least 20 percent more than one's ideal weight—is becoming increasingly common among children: about one-quarter of school-age children are now overweight (Gortmaker, Dietz, Sobol, & Wehler, 1987). What makes this rate of obesity particularly worrisome is that so many of these children will still be overweight when they reach adulthood: nearly 70 percent of obese 10- to 13-year-olds will become obese adults (Epstein & Wing, 1987). Their obesity will predispose them to a number of medical problems, such as heart disease, high blood pressure, and diabetes.

obesity Weighing at least 20 percent more in body weight than would be predicted by one's height.

FOCUS ON APPLICATION

Stress Reactions in Children

Many situations can be stressful to a child: experiencing the divorce of parents or the birth of a new sibling, starting a new school, fighting with peers, having a chronic illness, or failing an exam. *Stress* is loosely defined as any circumstance that affects a child's sense of well-being. It is important to note that the same situation might be stressful for one child but not for another because children's appraisals of situations and of their abilities to cope influence the degrees of stress that they experience (Compas & Epping, 1993; Lazarus & Folkman, 1984). For example, suppose that two children fail exams. One child is devastated and concludes that she is not intelligent enough to pass. She experiences a great deal of stress. But the other child shrugs off the failure, and instead of being defeated by it, is challenged to pass the next exam. This second child experiences far less stress.

Some stressful situations for children are not immediately obvious. For example, some children are involved in so many activities that they have little time to play. According to David Elkind (1981, 1994), hurried, overstructured children are vulnerable to stress reactions. Children need to have a balance between structured activities and free time. Of course, the balance may vary

somewhat for individual children.

Numerous studies have found a link between stress and children's physical and mental health (see, for example, Nosphitz, 1990). Stress is associated with poor adjustment, emotional difficulties, anxiety, depression, behaviour problems, physical illness, accident proneness, learning problems, and a variety of defence mechanisms that we discussed at the beginning of Chapter 11.

Numerous studies have found a link between stress and children's physical and mental health

---

It is important to note, though, that all of these problems are not unique to stress but may be present because of other causes.

One problem that is unique to stress is post-traumatic stress disorder (PTSD). It is associated only with stresses that are "outside the range of usual human experience" (Keppel-Benson & Ollendick, 1993, p. 30). PTSD was originally applied to the psychological problems exhibited by adults who had fought in the Vietnam War. But similar problems have been

observed in children who have experienced different types of trauma, including sexual abuse, natural disasters such as tornadoes, political upheaval and war, serious car accidents, and homicides. The key symptoms of PTSD are the following:

1. The child constantly relives the traumatic event through thoughts, images, dreams, and repetitive play in which he acts out the trauma. All of these experiences are upsetting to the child and are beyond his control.

2. The child avoids situations that remind her of the trauma. The child experiences a numbing of emotions—she feels like a robot. As well, the child loses interest in activities and hobbies that she used to enjoy.

3. The child constantly checks to make sure the traumatic event does not reoccur and is overly anxious.

These symptoms need to be present for at least a month to warrant the diagnosis of PTSD. Other symptoms that are sometimes, but not always, found in children with PTSD are trauma-related fears, feelings of guilt if others were killed in the traumatic event, and behavioural problems.

Genetic factors play an influential role in obesity. The child of one obese parent has a 40 percent chance of becoming obese; the odds leap to 80 percent if both parents are obese. If the child is adopted, it is the weight of her biological parents, rather than of her adoptive parents, that will have the greatest influence on her adult weight (Rosenthal, 1990; Stunkard, 1988).

The fact that childhood obesity is more common now than it was 20 years ago proves that environmental factors are also important because genes do not change that quickly. One environmental factor that has been blamed is television viewing, which has increased steadily over this period. Today, children watch television for 17.7 hours a week on average, and those who watch more tend to be heavier than those who watch less. There are two reasons for the connection between television viewing and obesity: too little physical activity and too much snacking on junk food (Dietz, 1987). Children who sit in front of a television set are not getting the exercise they need to develop their physical skills and to burn off excess calories. At the same time, if they spend their viewing hours munching on potato chips and drinking sweetened beverages, their appetite is diminished for more nutritious and less calorie-heavy foods.

Children should not be placed on drastic weight-loss programs, even if they are seriously overweight, because they need a balanced, nutritious diet to support energy levels and proper growth. Instead of trying to lose weight quickly, they need to develop better eating habits that they can maintain over time. In particular, they should increase their intake of healthy foods, such as fruits and vegetables, and decrease their intake of foods that are high in fats, for example, pizza. Equally important, they must increase their physical activity. As we noted earlier, obesity often runs in families; thus, successful weight-loss programs frequently involve treating the parents as well as the children (Epstein, Valoski, Wing, & McCurley, 1990).

A common belief about obesity is that it causes children to have low self-esteem or feelings of low self-worth. A study conducted in Montreal casts doubt on this belief (Mendelson, White, & Mendelson, 1996). The researchers distinguished between different types of self-esteem: global self-esteem was the child's overall feelings of self-worth. Academic self-esteem was the child's appraisal of his intellectual abilities. Social self-esteem was the child's appraisal of his interpersonal skills. Appearance self-esteem was the child's satisfaction with his physical appearance. Weight self-esteem was the child's satisfaction with his weight. A child could be high on some aspects of self-esteem, but low on others. Interestingly, being overweight lowers a child's weight self-esteem, but it does not affect other types of self-esteem. Nonetheless, dissatisfaction with one's appearance is associated with lowered global self-esteem. Therefore, it is dissatisfaction with appearance, not feelings about one's weight per se, that puts a child at risk for lowered global self-esteem. Overweight children who have positive feelings about their appearance, though not necessarily about their weight, tend to have high global self-esteem.

Television watching has been linked to the increase in numbers of obese children. Children who watch more than 17.7 hours of television a week tend to weigh more than children who watch less.

Physical Fitness

Health is often measured by what it is not, or illness. However, an index of positive health is the degree of physical fitness individuals achieve. The human body was built for movement. Vigorous physical activity is required for the development of a healthy body (Nichols, 1990). The progressively more demanding physical activities that most school-age children perform—combined with physical education classes they take in school—ideally promote favourable attitudes toward an active life that includes vigorous, fun-filled activities. Furthermore, an increasing body of research links health problems such as cardiovascular disease to inactivity during the childhood years. The beginnings of clogged blood vessels, a symptom of cardiovascular disease, have been found in autopsies of children as young as 2 years of age. High cholesterol and triglycerides (a type of fat) have also been found in sedentary children (Nichols, 1990). Exercise reduces all three of these characteristics, which are major risk factors for adult cardiovascular disease. This finding reinforces the need for children to be active and to exercise regularly.

Physical fitness, which refers to the optimal functioning of the heart, lungs, muscles, and blood vessels—does not require children to become master athletes. In order for children to be physically fit, they must engage in sports or exercises that involve four different aspects of conditioning—flexibility, muscle endurance, muscle strength, and cardiovascular functioning. Needless to say, some activities in which children participate are better for accomplishing physical fitness than are others. Soccer, tennis, bicycling, and swimming, for example, exercise the whole body, while baseball does not (Nichols, 1990). In baseball, for the most part one player moves at a time and then for only a brief time.

Given the high number of hours children spend on average in front of the television set or playing video games during middle childhood, it is not surprising that

Chronic Illness and Children's Peer Relationships

Which chronic illnesses, if any, have a detrimental effect on children's peer relationships? Researchers in Halifax are studying the effects of Tourette's syndrome on children's relationships with their school classmates (Bawden, Stokes, Camfield, Camfield, & Salisbury, 1998). Tourette's syndrome is a disorder that involves compulsive movements, called *tics*, and vocalizations. Tics include grimacing, blinking, and head turning, among others. Vocalizations include grunting, throat clearing, and cursing, among others. Children with Tourette's syndrome may seem odd to other children. In addition, many children who have Tourette's also have attention deficit disorder. Do children with Tourette's syndrome have more difficulty interacting with peers than do other children?

The researchers compared 7- to 15-year-old children with Tourette's with a control group of children of similar ages and backgrounds who had insulin-dependent diabetes or who had no illnesses. Children with Tourette's were compared with diabetic children to see whether the detrimental effects of Tourette's were general effects owing

---

Researchers in Halifax are studying the effects of Tourette's syndrome on children's relationships with their school classmates.

---

to chronic illness or effects specific to Tourette's.

The researchers measured children's peer relationships by interviewing each child's classmates. A child's classmates rated him on three measures: social withdrawal, aggression, and likeability. Children who had both Tourette's syndrome and attention deficit disorder were rated as more aggressive, more withdrawn, and less likeable than were diabetic children or children with no illnesses. Children who had Tourette's without attention deficit disorder were rated as more withdrawn than the other two groups of children. Why did the children with Tourette's receive poorer ratings than other children? Their poorer ratings were not related to the severity or duration of their tics, nor were they related to problems interacting with their families. The next step in this research is to discover why children with Tourette's, especially those who also have attention deficit disorder, are at risk for problems in peer relationships. This information is needed so that clinicians can design intervention programs for these children.

---

many children live relatively sedentary lives. In addition, if they are latchkey children who must care for themselves between coming home from school and their parents' return home from work, they may have been warned to stay inside the house or apartment for safety reasons, further increasing the number of hours spent in inactivity.

Accidents and Injuries

Children's motor development changes both their exposure to hazards and their ability to protect their health. As children become more mobile, for example, they are able to interact with their physical environment in ways that increase their risk of accidents and their exposure to illness. During infancy, it is fairly easy to safeguard children. However, as children grow in coordination, size, and strength, they begin to engage in increasingly dangerous activities, including riding on skateboards and bicycles, as well as to participate in team sports involving potentially deadly projectiles and damaging bodily contact (Maddux et al., 1986). Generally, from infancy onward, children's need to perform their newfound skills often conflicts with their need for protection against risks to their health. In addition, their ability to harm themselves often exceeds their ability to foresee the consequences of their actions (Achenbach, 1982). Many children, for example, have been warned against riding their bicycles into the street without looking, but in the excitement of play they may forget—and be seriously injured. According to a recent study in Quebec, bicycle crashes account for about 10 percent of all deaths of 5- to 14-year-old children (Farley, Haddad, & Brown, 1996). Head injuries are present in 60 to 80 percent of the fatalities. Farley et al. carried out a four-year intervention study in Montreal and surrounding communities to get children to wear helmets. The intervention focused on educational activities to fos-

Soccer is a good sport for children because it exercises the whole body, in contrast to a sport like baseball.

ter positive attitudes toward wearing helmets and on improving access to helmets. At the start of the study, only 1.3 percent of children wore helmets. But by the end of the study, 33 percent did. Girls, younger children, children from homes with higher incomes, and children riding on bicycle paths instead of roads wore helmets more often than did other children.

An understanding of motor development and its relationship to accident risk is important, since accidents are the leading cause of death and disability among children. Injuries cause more deaths in children than do the six next most frequent causes combined (cancer, congenital anomalies, pneumonia, heart disease, homicide, and stroke). About half of all deaths in children result from injuries and accidents.

For example, while 1- to 4-year-olds are particularly at risk for poisoning, children from 5 to 9 have higher rates of pedestrian accidents; older children and adolescents are more likely to be injured on recreational equipment such as swings, bicycles, and skateboards. They are also more likely to be injured in sports-related activities. For more information on injuries incurred at school or on playgrounds, see Tables 12-2 and 12-3.

Motor development is not the only determinant of the increased accident risk of school-age children. Young children often are unable to control impulses sufficiently to "listen to" internal rules and statements. Therefore, children at play may not follow rules such as, "Look both ways before you cross the street." They also may be exposed to or take part in environmental hazards such as drugs or violence. Another concern is that children can be persuaded by their friends to be involved in riskier behaviour than they would engage in on their own (Christensen & Morrongiello, 1997). Sally Christensen and Barbara Morrongiello, from the University of Guelph, showed 8- and 9-year-olds pictures that required the children to select a route between a designated start and finish. In each picture, there was a low-risk route and a higher-risk one. For example, there was a picture of a tobogganing hill. Children had to pick a path to the bottom of the hill. One path was called low risk because it was clear of obstacles. Another path was called high risk because there were exposed stumps and trees along it, as well as an open stream at the bottom of it. On their own, 88 percent of the children chose the low-risk path. However, 43 percent of them were later persuaded by a same-sex friend to take the higher-risk path. Boys and girls were equally likely to be persuaded. Interestingly, though, there were differences in the kinds of arguments that boys and girls used to influence their friends. Boys were more likely to appeal to

> ## Table 12-2 Summary of the Injuries Reported at Schools
>
> - Boys were injured more often than girls—61 percent of the injuries happened to boys; 39 percent to girls.
> - The peak ages of injury were 11 years for girls and 13 years for boys.
> - Most injuries happened at lunchtime and on the playground.
> - Injuries were more common in September, October, November, and May than in other months.
> - Sports-related injuries accounted for 44.5 percent of the total number of injuries. The sports with the highest rate of injuries were basketball, football, and soccer.
> - During playing, 32.9 percent of the injuries occurred, and 12.9 percent occurred during walking or running.
> - Collisions caused 35.2 percent of the injuries; falls caused another 33.5 percent of the injuries; children's overexertion caused 14.6 percent of the injuries; and their horseplay and aggression caused 8.9 percent of the injuries. Falls were especially common in younger children. Collisions and overexertion were most common in older children.
> - Fracture was the most common injury, with 44.6 percent of the injuries involving the arms, 26.6 percent the legs, and 20.1 percent the head.
> - No treatment was required for 20.4 percent of the injuries; 24.7 percent required minor treatment without follow-up; 47.6 percent required ongoing outpatient treatment; and 6.3 percent required hospitalization.

Source: Gibson & Klassen, 1996.

> ## Table 12-3 Playground Safety in Kingston, Ontario, and Surrounding Communities
>
> Following is a summary of injuries that happened on playgrounds:
> - Children between the ages of 5 and 9 years accounted for more injuries than any other age group.
> - Most injuries were caused by falling or jumping from a height greater than 1 metre.
> - Almost 40 percent of the injuries required medical treatment.
> - Cuts, swellings, and fractures were the most common injuries.
> - Most injuries affected the head or the arms.
> - All of the playgrounds were inspected for safety, and only 15.4 percent of the playgrounds met all the Canadian Standards Association (CSA) criteria. The inspection focused on the effectiveness of the ground surface covering in absorbing the shock of a child's fall; on the design of the equipment, such as the presence of handrails and guardrails; and on hazards such as sharp edges and small holes.
> - The most common safety violations were inadequate or inappropriate ground surface cover, sharp edges, and small spaces where the children could get their heads or other body parts stuck.

Source: Pickett, Carr, Mowat, & Chui, 1996.

arguments related to fun, whereas girls were more likely to appeal to arguments related to safety. Another interesting finding from this study was that children's knowledge about the hazards along a path or about the possibility of sustaining injuries did not predict whether children would select the risky path. Even children who are aware of the dangers can be convinced by a friend to take the risky path.

Drug Use among School-Age Children We tend to associate drug use with adolescence, but recent studies have found that elementary school children below the age of 12 also try substances such as alcohol, cigarettes, and marijuana. This is especially likely to be true in urban areas, where drugs are more readily available. Early use of alcohol, tobacco, and marijuana is associated with alcohol and other drug abuse in adolescence and adulthood. Although the average age of first use of alcohol and marijuana is 13, pressure to initiate use begins even earlier. Elementary school students report peer pressure to try beer, wine, and liquor, and many succumb to this pressure.

By the time they are 13 years old, many Canadian children have tried smoking

Question to Ponder

How can adults help prevent school-age children from becoming drug abusers?

cigarettes. Interestingly, though, boys tend to try it younger than do girls. For example, 26 percent of 11-year-old boys have tried smoking, whereas only 19 percent of girls have (CICH, 1994). But between the ages of 11 and 13 years, the number of girls who have tried smoking increases rapidly. So by age 13, 50 percent of girls have tried it, compared with 41 percent of boys. Furthermore, 9 percent of 13-year-old girls report smoking every day, whereas only 5 percent of boys report smoking that often.

Many Canadian children also have experimented with alcohol. By the time they are 13 years old, 35 percent of boys and 31 percent of girls have been drunk at least once. In addition, 14 percent of boys and 7 percent of girls drink alcohol at least once a week (CICH, 1994). Most 13-year-olds report that their parents use alcohol—90 percent of 13-year-olds report that their fathers drink at least occasionally, and 75 percent report that their mothers drink at least some alcohol.

In general, this research indicates a tendency for young children to try substances that may produce negative health effects—especially on growing bodies. The research also suggests the effects of modelling behaviour on school-age children—children who try these substances often have seen either peers or family members using them. In addition, this early use of potentially harmful substances suggests the need for education and intervention during middle childhood. By adolescence, habits may be well established.

Since their improved mobility exposes school-age children to greater accident risk, they often need guidance on ways to protect themselves from injury.

Physical Development and the School Environment

We generally think of school in terms of its effect upon children's cognitive or social development, forgetting that schools must also provide for children's physical and motor needs. The effect of the standard Canadian classroom was aptly summarized by a grade one student after her first day at school. When asked how she liked her new school, she replied, "Oh, you mean sit-down school?" She was reacting not to the difference in teachers and schedules, but to being confined to a desk and chair for a whole day. There is no evidence that children learn best by sitting in straight-backed chairs for long periods of time—on the contrary, many studies have shown the limitations of passive, receptive learning.

An example of a positive, open environment may be found in Montessori classrooms, where various stations designed for particular activities are placed about the classroom. There may be a reading corner complete with pillows, a section for carpentry, one for water activities, and so forth. This design allows small children to move around the classroom and integrate activity with learning. Rugs are used as transportable "desks" to make space for children to work individually.

Six-year-old children are still learning with their bodies, still integrating physical and intellectual knowledge. It is artificial to divorce the body from the mind and personality, using it only in gym or at recess. A school can be responsive to a child's physical needs in many ways. In a math class, for example, children might measure a corridor in metres, and then measure it again in terms of their own footsteps or the time it takes them to walk its length. In this way, their knowledge would be both abstract and concrete, both general and personal. Schools might also stress physical expression for its own sake. For example, some British primary schools have set aside a special period for movement expression and exploration (Evans, 1975).

Coping with Physical Challenges

A number of physical conditions that require special considerations in the school environment may affect children during middle childhood. We need to be sensitive to

"Just think of it as a brief interlude in, as opposed to a major disruption of, your life."

physically challenged A term emphasizing the environmental factors that limit a disabled child's access to goods and services, rather than dealing with handicapping conditions themselves; the emphasis is on changes in the environment, such as ramps or language boards, which help the child to adapt.

mainstreaming Requiring that all physically challenged children have access to all education programs provided by schools in the least restrictive setting; this includes physical education classes.

the issue of labelling for children with various physical conditions. The term **physically challenged** is more acceptable today than are the terms *handicapped* or *physically disabled.* While physically challenged may be seen by some as a euphemism, it more accurately reflects the environment that such children confront. It also directs the efforts of the educational system toward changing the environment to meet the needs of such children. Many efforts in special education, therefore, are focused on talking about the environmental challenges facing children, and, consequently, avoiding laying the blame on the particular child's special needs. Building ramps or providing children with adaptive equipment, such as language boards or Braille scanners, is effective environmental intervention that enhances their ability to learn.

In some cases, the child's special needs may make participating in classroom activities difficult. Peer relations and friendships may be difficult to initiate or sustain. In addition, developmental delays may limit the child's ability to effectively interact with more advanced peers. In today's school environment, because of legislation on behalf of children with special needs, most physically challenged children are **mainstreamed,** or taught in the least restrictive setting possible.

What sorts of special needs do physically challenged children have? These problems run from low fitness associated with obesity or poor nutrition, to severe cerebral palsy. Cerebral palsy is a neuromuscular condition caused by damage to areas of the brain. Children with cerebral palsy often are multiply disabled—with uncontrollable body movements and difficulty in producing language. Those children with severe cerebral palsy often require the use of a wheelchair to control their body movements. Some of these children are also learning disabled, while others may be highly intelligent, as the following case indicates:

Mike was a feisty 9-year-old. He had severe cerebral palsy that required his placement in a wheelchair someone else had to push. Speech was difficult for him, and he had to go through extreme body contortions to push the words out. It was difficult for others to watch him. Despite this, he participated fully in classroom discussions. He had a good sense of humour and often laughed at himself. His peers, with the help of sensitive teachers, became comfortable with his condition and vied to help push his wheelchair.

Elementary schools also include children with other physically challenging conditions, such as blindness and deafness, diabetes, and asthma. Children with special needs, like other children, are expected to develop life skills in school that will help them become more independent and as fit as possible. It is also an educational goal that they will develop a good self-concept and learn socially appropriate behaviours that will enable them to optimally interact with peers and adults.

Physical Education

Elementary schools have as their main goal to optimize learning for all children—and to build a foundation of skills that will prepare children for lifelong learning. *Physical education* is defined as a process of carefully planned and conducted motor activities that prepare students for skillful, fit, and knowledgeable performance (Nichols, 1990). Physical education may be carried out in a series of settings in the school: classrooms, gymnasiums, multipurpose rooms, playgrounds, or playing fields.

Physical education is included in traditional elementary school curriculum because physical activity in childhood is associated with a range of beneficial health and fitness outcomes. It improves muscle strength, endurance, and general cardiopulmonary functioning (Pellegrini & Smith, 1998). Physical play prevents obesity by ensuring that surplus energy is not stored as extra fat. In addition, childhood physical activity often fosters attitudes and habits that increase the likelihood of individuals' engaging in regular exercise in adulthood.

There are cognitive as well as physical benefits of physical activity. In a study done in Trois-Rivières, Quebec, some elementary school classes received an extra five hours of physical education per week (Shephard, 1983). Children in these classes had better academic performance than children in classes that did not receive extra physical education. One explanation for their improved academic performance is that exercise made the children more alert. Another explanation is that exercise helped learning because it provided a break from learning. Children learn better when they have several short learning sessions with breaks in between than when they have one longer session. Some of the success of Japanese schools has been attributed to the use of frequent breaks (Stevenson & Lee, 1990). Japanese schools usually have a 10-minute exercise recess every hour.

Question to Ponder

How can a classroom teacher integrate more physical activity into the regular curriculum? Would providing children with more opportunities for physical activity improve their academic performance?

Although children now learn such activities as dancing in physical education classes, even here, much of the time they are engaged in sedentary activities such as watching.

One study found that during the weekly schedule of 140 minutes of physical education in the U.S. elementary schools studied, less than 10 percent of class time was spent on moderate to vigorous physical activity, approximately 24 percent was spent in minimal activity, and 68 percent was spent in sedentary activity (Simons-Morton, Parcel, Baranowski, O'Hara, & Forthofer, 1991). Traditional team sports and games accounted for the bulk of class time, but lifetime activities, such as dancing, calisthenics, jogging, and jump roping, were also represented. In all activities, however, much of the time spent was sedentary, as children often were waiting to participate or watching, rather than actually participating.

Other researchers observed schools, however, where children arrived on the field promptly and became active immediately. In these situations, teachers provided rapid transitions between activities and students were organized into small groups, which maximized equipment sharing and participation, and received extensive individual instruction and reinforcement. More time, consequently, was devoted to physical activity.

FOCUS ON APPLICATION

Keeping the Fun in Sport

Organized sports provide excellent opportunities for children to stay fit. Yet many children choose not to participate in them because they fear that they will perform badly or that they will not make the team (see Smith, Smoll, & Barnett, 1995, for a concise review of the literature). Some children develop high sport anxiety and are especially sensitive to fears of failure and of negative social evaluations. For instance, they worry more about making mistakes, playing badly, and losing than do other young athletes. In addition, they worry that coaches, peers, and parents will criticize poor performance. As a result, the sports are no longer fun and the children are more likely to drop out. One study looked at children who quit competitive swimming (Gould, Feltz, Horn, & Weiss, 1982). The study found that 52 percent of them did so because of the pressure. Another study found that children as

young as 7 years already show high sport anxiety (Orlick & Botterill, 1975).

What can adults do to help prevent children from developing high sport anxiety? Smith, Smoll, and Barnett (1995) described a training program

---

Organized sports provide excellent opportunities for children to stay fit.

---

for coaches that stresses keeping the fun in sport. Although intended for coaches, parents could also use many aspects of the program. The training program focused on increasing positive coaching behaviours and decreasing negative ones. The positive behaviours included (1) reinforcing children for effort and improvement, and not just for good performance (emphasizing

personal effort and improvement rather than winning); (2) encouraging children when they made mistakes, rather than getting angry with them; (3) giving corrective instruction in an encouraging and supportive fashion; and (4) providing technical instruction to improve the children's skill level. The negative behaviours that were targeted for elimination included (1) failing to respond to good performance or effort (nonreinforcement); (2) punishing the children either verbally or nonverbally; (3) instructing the children in a sarcastic or unkind manner; and (4) regimenting behaviours to maintain constant control.

Smith et al. (1995) used this training program with Little League baseball coaches of 10- to 12-year-old boys. They found that boys who played for trained coaches reported learning more and having more fun than did boys who played for other coaches.

Many children stay fit through participation in sports.

Summary and Conclusions

During middle childhood, a pattern of stable physical growth persists that culminates in the adolescent growth spurt. Not only do children grow taller and heavier, but their bodies undergo accompanying internal changes. Bones continue to grow and mature—at different rates in different children. Some children are early maturers who will go through a fairly rapid growth spurt before their growth halts. Others are late maturers whose growth period will last for a longer time, and they will therefore end up taller when their growth halts. Still others more closely resemble the average pattern of growth.

Muscles tend to grow larger and stronger, increasing children's physical strength and endurance. These changes allow the child to engage in progressively more complex, coordinated motor activities. The motor activities of children in middle childhood resemble those of adults in terms of their actual processes; what differs are environmental constraints such as positioning and outcome—for example, the actual distance a ball is thrown.

For each child, the quality of movement is based on some combination of various factors, including balance, body agility, body build, throwing abilities, hand precision, strength, and power. The overall maturity of movement, therefore, varies in children of the same chronological age, since each child will have differing skill levels for each of these factors.

While children perform many of their activities in the school environment, children also engage in vigorous play, including rough-and-tumble play. This rough play also offers an opportunity for vigorous physical exchange between children. While rough play might appear to resemble aggression, it differs in many ways. Rough-and-tumble play also offers boys a chance to practise prosocial skills, such as negotiation and alliance building. It has more positive attributes for boys than for girls, who are perceived as antisocial if they participate in rough play.

Health is an important factor in children's physical development. Healthy children are better able to optimally participate in the physical, cognitive, and social activities of the world around them—including the school environment. Children with physical challenges may require special interventions to take full advantage of their learning opportunities. Some children have significant health problems, such as cerebral palsy, blindness, deafness, or diabetes. Other children have difficulties associated with their behaviours, for example, obesity, lack of physical fitness, or learning disabilities. Still others have acute illnesses that require temporary adaptation. This final category includes disorders such as influenza and otitis media.

As children's motor skills develop and become refined, their world expands commensurably. The entire house and neighbourhood are now open to school-age children. This expanded environment significantly increases the hazards and risks to which they are exposed. A rise in accidents and injuries during this period reflects children's greater mobility and independence. Unfortunately, children's cognitive abilities and impulse control during this period are not as mature as their physical abilities; this disparity also contributes to their increased risks.

School environments often reflect an awareness of the physical needs of elementary school students. Physical education classes, for example, have as their goals in elementary school to increase the motor skills of children, as well as their self-concept and social skills.

In general, children enter this period of middle childhood as "little people," but by its end they more closely resemble adults in size and abilities. Their strength, endurance, and ability to compete now allow them to participate fully in the physical world around them.

Key Terms and Concepts

mainstreaming (p. 392) obesity (p. 385) physically challenged (p. 392) rough-and-tumble play (p. 383)

Questions to Review

1. Describe the development of gross and fine motor skills in middle childhood.
2. How do the different patterns of skeletal maturity affect children's eventual adult height?
3. What environmental and biological factors influence motor skill development during middle childhood?
4. List the factors contributing to the development of basic movement qualities in school-age children.
5. How are children's illnesses a part of normal behavioural development?
6. What is the primary cause of childhood obesity? What is the most advisable treatment for this condition?
7. How does children's motor development influence exposure to hazards and risks in middle childhood?
8. How common are smoking cigarettes and drinking alcohol in 13-year-old children?
9. Describe the components of rough-and-tumble play. How does this play differ from aggression?
10. Describe gender differences in how children respond to rough-and-tumble play.
11. How should the school environment reflect the physical development of children during middle childhood?
12. What sorts of physical challenges do children with physical challenges face in the school environment? What sorts of illnesses and disabilities affect school-age children?
13. What are the main goals of physical education?

Weblinks

www.cich.ca/
Canadian Institute of Child Health
This site has publications, news releases, and project descriptions related to the health of Canadian children.

www.cpha.ca/
Canadian Public Health Association
This association provides information about policies, periodicals, and health resources.

www.cahperd.ca/e/index.htm
The Canadian Association for Health, Physical Education, Recreation and Dance
This nonprofit organization was founded in 1933 to promote the health and well-being of Canadians. The Web site has information on programs and services, as well as a catalogue of resources.

Middle Childhood: Cognitive Development and School Tasks

And so we discovered that education is not something which the teacher does, but that it is a natural process which develops spontaneously in the human being.

MARIA MONTESSORI
THE ABSORBENT MIND

Outline   CHAPTER 13

Objectives

By the time you have finished this chapter, you should be able to do the following:

✔ Compare preoperational thought with concrete operational thought.

✔ Describe how Piaget's concepts of thinking in middle childhood could be applied to education.

✔ Explain cognitive development during middle childhood as it is described by information-processing theorists.

✔ Describe some of the developmental challenges that middle childhood presents for children, parents, and teachers.

✔ Explain the ongoing controversy regarding definitions of intelligence and the uses and abuses of intelligence testing.

✔ Explain the two main types of learning disabilities and the various views on their causes and treatments.

For most children, middle childhood is a time for settling down, for developing more fully those patterns that have already been set. It is a period for learning new skills and refining old ones—from reading and writing to playing basketball, dancing, or skateboarding. Children focus on testing themselves, on meeting their own challenges as well as those imposed by the environment. The child who is successful in these tasks will probably become even more capable and self-assured; the one who is unsuccessful is more likely to develop a feeling of inferiority or a weaker sense of self.

Erikson has referred to middle childhood as the period of *industry*. The word captures the spirit of this period, for it is derived from a Latin term meaning "to build." In this chapter, we shall sample some of the ways in which children build cognitive competencies. We shall also look at school tasks and problems encountered in middle childhood, including the ways in which intelligence and achievement tests are administered and interpreted and some current approaches to understanding learning disabilities.

The development of physical and cognitive competencies and an increased mastery of the environment are only part of a child's developmental tasks during this period. For school-age children, "belonging" is of critical importance. They become very concerned about their status among their peers. This status depends increasingly on the competence and capabilities discussed in this chapter.

Concrete Operational Thought

The thinking of a 12-year-old child is very different from that of a 5-year-old. This difference is due not only to the much larger body of knowledge and information that the 12-year-old has accumulated, but also to the different ways in which the two children think and process information. For Piaget, the elementary school child is in a period of developing concrete operational thought.

Cognitive Abilities of the School Beginner

Starting school is a milestone in the life of any child. The fact that so many cultures have chosen the ages from 5 to 7 years for beginning the systematic education of their young is probably no historical accident. Between ages 5 and 7, many of children's cognitive, language, and perceptual-motor skills mature and interact in a way that makes some kinds of learning easier and more efficient.

In Piaget's theory, the years between ages 5 and 7 mark the transition from preoperational to *concrete operational thought:* thought becomes less intuitive and egocentric and more logical. In Chapter 10, we discussed some of the limitations of preoperational thought when compared to concrete operational thought. However, we also saw that many of these differences relating to cognitive immaturity are actually adaptive for young children. Before age 7, children tend to focus on one aspect of a problem at a time. They focus on the here-and-now and on perceptual evidence, rather than on logical reasoning. Their ability to find relationships between the events and things around them is limited.

Toward the end of Piaget's preoperational stage, the rigid, static, irreversible qualities of children's thought begin to "thaw out," to use Piaget's own terminology. Children's thinking begins to be reversible, flexible, and considerably more complex. They begin to notice one, then another aspect of an object and can use logic to reconcile differences between the two. They can evaluate cause-and-effect relationships, especially if they have the concrete object right in front of them and can see changes occur. When a piece of clay looks like a sausage, they no longer find it inconsistent that the clay was once a ball or that it can be moulded into a new shape, such as a cube. This emerging ability to leap mentally beyond the immediate situation or state lays the foundation for systematic reasoning in the concrete operational stage and, later, in the formal operational stage. We may see the properties of preoperational and concrete operational thought contrasted in Concept Summary Table 13-1.

One difference between preoperational and concrete operational thought can be illustrated by school-age children's use of **logical inference** (Flavell, 1985). Recall Piaget's liquid conservation experiment (Chapter 2). In this experiment, preoperational children consistently judge that a tall, narrow glass holds more liquid than a short, wide one, although both quantities of liquid were shown to be identical at the start. Concrete operational children, in contrast, know that both containers hold the same amount of liquid. They can make logical inferences from what they have seen. Concrete operational children begin to think differently about states and transformations. They can remember how the liquid appeared before it was poured into the tall, thin container. They can think about how its shape changed as it was poured from one glass into the other and can imagine what shape the liquid would have if it were poured back. Concrete operational children, then, not only include the process of transformation in their thinking, but also are aware that the fluid may assume other shapes in different containers, including the original. Their thinking is *reversible*.

In addition, concrete operational children know that differences between similar objects can be quantified, or measured. In Piaget's (1970) matchstick problem, children are shown a zigzag row of six matchsticks and a straight row of five matchsticks placed end to end (see Figure 13-1). When asked which row has more matchsticks, very young children centre only on the distance between the end points of the rows and thus pick the "longer" row with five matchsticks. Concrete operational children, however, can take into account what lies between the end points of the rows and therefore will choose the one with six matchsticks.

Finally, unlike preoperational children, concrete operational children can theorize about the world. They think about and anticipate what will happen; they make

Question to Ponder

What do you think Piaget's theory would say about starting academic learning during the preschool years?

logical inference A conclusion reached through "unseen" evidence; concrete operational children are capable of this type of thinking.

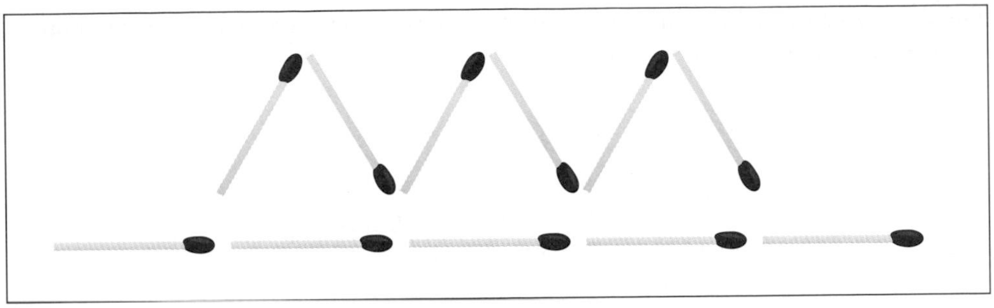

Figure 13-1
Piaget's Matchstick Problem
Concrete operational children realize that the six matchsticks in the zigzag top row will make a longer line than the five matchsticks in the bottom row. Younger children will say that the bottom row is the longest because they tend to centre only on the end points of the two lines and not on what lies between them.

guesses about things and then test their hunches. They may estimate, for example, how many more breaths of air they can blow into a balloon before it pops and will keep blowing until they reach or surpass this mark. *This ability to theorize is limited to concrete objects and social relationships that children can see and test.* Children do not develop theories about abstract concepts, thoughts, or relationships until they reach the stage of formal operations, which begins around age 11 or 12.

Piaget defined *operation* as a reversible mental action. The concrete operational period, therefore, means that children are able to perform reversible mental actions on real, concrete objects but not on abstract ideas.

The transition from preoperational to concrete operational thought does not happen overnight. It is a developmental task that requires years of experience in manipulating and learning about the objects and materials in the environment. To a large extent, children learn concrete operational thought on their own. As they actively explore their physical environment, asking themselves questions and finding the answers, they acquire a more complex, sophisticated form of thinking.

Piaget and Education

As we saw in Chapter 6, infants benefit from stimulation that is presented slightly ahead of their developmental level. Such stimulation promotes cognitive growth.

Concept Summary

Table 13-1 A Comparison of Preoperational and Concrete Operational Thought

STAGE	AGE	THE CHILD'S THINKING IS
Preoperational	2 to 5–7 years	Rigid and static
		Irreversible
		Focused on the here-and-now
		Centred on one dimension
		Egocentric
		Focused on the perceptual evidence
		Intuitive
Concrete Operational	5–7 to 12 years	Flexible
		Reversible
		Not limited to the here-and-now
		Multidimensional
		Less egocentric
		Using logical inferences
		Seeking cause-and-effect relationships

Some researchers believe that appropriate training can also accelerate the cognitive development of preoperational children, hastening their entrance into the level of concrete operations. Training is most effective when children have reached a state of *readiness,* an optimal period that occurs just before they make the transition to the next stage (Bruner, Olver, & Greenfield, 1966).

Many of the basic concepts Piaget presented have been applied to education, especially in the areas of science and math. One such application includes the use of concrete objects for teaching 5- to 7-year-olds. By combining, comparing, and contrasting concrete objects (for example, blocks and rods of different shapes and sizes, seeds that grow in sand, water, or soil), children discover similarities, differences, and relationships.

One method for using objects is to arrange them into simple patterns (see Figure 13-2). Many children who are 5 to 7 years old may still be centring on one particular aspect of objects. Yet a teacher or caregiver may want to teach an abstract concept (say, the number 16), an operation (subtraction), or a relationship (equality). In introducing grade two students to the number concept of 16, for example, a teacher might present several different spatial arrays of 16 cubes—grouped into two towers of 8, one row of 16, four rows of 4, and so on. The teacher could also give verbal cues to the concept of conservation, pointing out, for instance, that the number of cubes remains the same even though the length and width of the rows may change.

There are many other applications of Piaget's concepts. For example, addition and subtraction involve an understanding of reversibility ($5 + 8 = 13$, and $13 - 5 = 8$). Again, children can best learn about these processes by manipulating real objects. Many concepts of time and distance are quite abstract, or they involve the understanding of the relationship between different units of measure. For example, telling time from a clock requires understanding the relationship between minutes and hours. Understanding the basic principles of Piaget's theory of cognitive development makes it easier to develop effective educational lessons and to organize these lessons into a logical sequence. Indeed, Piagetian concepts have been applied to a wide range of curriculum projects, including social studies, music, art, math, and science.

Some educators have noted that Piaget seemed to have a philosophy of learning, as well as a theory of cognitive development. They point to the Piagetian principles that children are active learners, that they construct their own theories about how the world operates, and that they themselves are motivated to change these theories when pieces of information do not fit (Bruner, 1973). These educators warn against structuring education in ways that encourage children to seek praise from the teacher rather than to solve problems for their own sake. They emphasize that children's interest

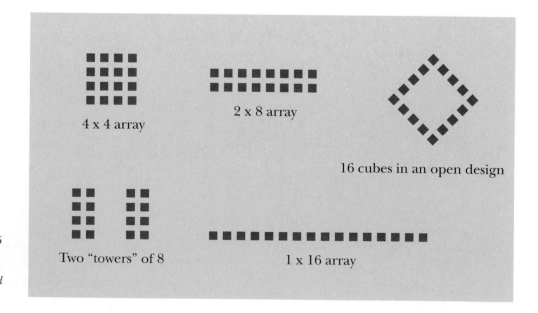

Figure 13-2
Some possible spatial arrays of 16 cubes. By arranging the cubes in different ways, a teacher can help young school children understand the number concept of 16.

4 x 4 array

2 x 8 array

16 cubes in an open design

Two "towers" of 8

1 x 16 array

in learning depends on the intrinsic rewards they find in the encounter with the subject matter itself. Children gain confidence from mastering a problem or discovering a principle.

These educators also point out that, too often, teachers instruct young children by *telling* them instead of *showing* them. They remove the real-life, concrete context of many subjects. They present rules and items for children to memorize by rote without motivating the children to develop an understanding of these rules. Children are then left with an arid body of facts without the structure to connect them and without the ability to apply these facts and principles to other settings. Children, some educators contend, need to learn by doing, by actively exploring ideas and relationships, and by solving problems in a realistic context. We may see the key aspects of Piaget's principles of education presented in Concept Summary Table 13-2.

Piaget was a remarkable observer of the young child; he offered a number of key insights into the child's cognitive development. But there are some aspects of cognitive development that he did not describe and that are important for school learning. Many of these factors come under the heading of what is called the *information-processing perspective*.

Information Processing

In information-processing theory, the different components of the mind—attention, memory, problem solving, and the like—can be studied separately. During middle childhood, many of these processes show considerable development.

Memory

A number of significant developments occur in the memory abilities of concrete operational children. Recall from Chapter 10 that preoperational children do well in recognition tasks but do poorly in recall tasks; they have trouble using memory strategies such as rehearsal. The ability to recall lists of items improves significantly, however, between the ages of 5 and 7. At this time, most children consciously begin the task of memorizing. They look at the material to be remembered and begin to rehearse it—repeating it over and over to themselves. Later, they may also organize the material into categories, and, still later, they may create little stories or visual images to help them remember. This increasingly deliberate use of strategies makes the older child's recall more effective and efficient (Flavell, 1985).

Research conducted in southern Ontario shows that elementary school children can be taught to use more effective strategies than those they would use spontaneously (Willoughby, Porter, Belsito, & Yearsley, 1999). Children in grades two, four, and six were required to learn facts about familiar and unfamiliar animals. An example of a

Concept Summary

Table 13-2   Piaget's Principles Applied to Education

- Children are active learners who construct their own theories about how the world operates.

- Children are motivated to change their theories when pieces of information do not fit.

- Children's interest in learning depends primarily on the intrinsic rewards they gain from contact with the subject matter itself. Teachers' praise may be detrimental to optimal learning.

- Teachers should show rather than tell children what to do.

- Children need to learn by doing, by actively exploring new ideas and relationships, and by solving problems in a realistic format.

Following Piaget, some educators stress that children's interest in learning is encouraged when they have the intrinsic satisfaction of solving a problem or discovering a principle rather than looking to a teacher for praise.

fact about a familiar animal is, "The western spotted skunk mostly eats corn." An example of a fact about an unfamiliar animal is, "The collared peccary eats roots and cacti." To help them remember the facts, children were taught different strategies. In the *elaborative interrogation strategy*, children were told to ask themselves why the fact was true of that particular animal. This strategy improved the learning of children in all grade levels, but it worked better when children were learning facts about familiar animals than about unfamiliar ones. In the *imagery strategy*, children were told to make a picture in their minds that linked the animal to the fact. Children in grades four and six were better than those in grade two at using this strategy to learn facts about familiar animals, and only those in grade six were able to use it to help them learn facts about unfamiliar animals. A third strategy, the *keyword strategy*, was similar to the imagery strategy, except children

FOCUS ON AN ISSUE

Children's Humour: "Why Did the Cookie Cry?"

Children's humour is definitely different—different from adult humour, and often, unique to the child. It is often difficult for adults to see why children find something funny, as the following example indicates:

> One father came home from work to find his 4-year-old son, Corey, dissolved in laughter. Corey would sober himself up and then would repeat "ping pong balls falling on your head" and dissolve into laughter again. He was unable to convey what had been so funny, so the father asked the mother what had happened.

> It turned out that Corey had been watching *Captain Kangaroo* and one of the characters walked into a room, where ping pong balls fell

on his head from the ceiling. Every time the character tried to get up, more balls would fall. Corey thought this was very funny and had been trying to share his experience with his father—to no avail.

Humour may be seen as a form of intellectual play.

This sort of slapstick humour does not appeal to every adult—or even to every child. However, when it does, it is very effective at producing laughter.

What makes something funny? One view is that humour is associated with the discovery and resolution of incongruity (Shultz, 1976). For example, a

child might be asked which of two endings to a question is funnier: *Q:* Why did the cookie cry? *A:* Because its mother was a wafer, or *B:* Because its mother was a wafer so long. For most young children, the question itself is funny without a "punchline" because the notion of a cookie crying is incongruous—it is unexpected.

Humour changes developmentally. During the preschool years, play and humour are often linked. For example, the sheer enjoyment of bouncing on a trampoline or jumping into the water may evoke shouts of laughter—even though nothing truly "funny" is occurring. Children during this age may also find play with words to be funny. For example, 3- and 4-year-olds love to produce such rhymes as "shoe, boo, foo, poo," and so forth—or to use forbidden

were given a keyword to help them make an interactive image. The keyword was a smaller word within the animal name. The keyword for collared peccary was *collar*. Children at all grade levels used the keyword strategy effectively to remember facts about familiar animals. Therefore, providing younger children with a keyword enabled them to benefit from an imagery strategy. However, only the children in grade six were able to use the keyword strategy to help them learn facts about unfamiliar animals. The results of this study suggest that children of elementary school age can be taught to use strategies, and that strategy usage improves learning. To improve children's learning, instruction on strategy usage could be incorporated in the school curriculum.

Question to Ponder

Do you remember being taught learning and study strategies in school? What types of strategies could children be taught to improve their learning?

Metacognition

There are several other information-processing components that become more sophisticated during middle childhood. Children become better able to focus their attention on what they're doing and to keep it focused despite distractions. They gradually improve their problem-solving strategies. They also develop higher-order control processes. Children become better able to monitor their own thinking, memory, knowledge, goals, and actions. They become better able to plan, to make decisions, and to select which memory strategy or problem-solving strategy they want to use. These higher-order processes are called meta processes, or **metacognition.**

In his description of metacognition, Flavell (1985) cites the following example. Preschool and elementary school children were asked to study a group of items until they were certain they could remember them perfectly. After studying the items for a while, the elementary school children said they were ready, and they usually were. When they were tested, they remembered each item without fail. The preschool children did not perform as well, even though they assured the researchers that they knew every item.

Despite the good intentions of the preschoolers to remember and understand the things they studied, they did not have the cognitive ability to do so; they could

metacognition The process of monitoring one's own thinking, memory, knowledge, goals, and actions.

---

words such as "poop" in public (McGhee, 1979).

During middle childhood, children have learned that words are sometimes ambiguous in meaning. Therefore, jokes and riddles such as "Why did the cookie cry?" become a staple of humour. Grade three students usually appreciate jokes like the following:

Judge: Order! Order in the court.
Defendant: Ham and cheese on rye, your honour. (McGhee, 1979)

After the age of 11 or 12, children become increasingly bored with riddles and engage in more sophisticated humour that plays with social expectations, illogical behaviour and events, or words.

Humour may be seen as a form of intellectual play that reflects the cognitive skills and level of thinking of the children engaging in it. Pleasure in cognitive mastery is also involved in more

sophisticated types of humour. Finally, the nature and intensity of children's reactions to potentially humorous events is tied to the context in which they occur. For example, children may laugh at an adult's fall—but only when it isn't their own parent and when it is clear there is no real injury. At that point, they may not only laugh, but also imitate. Other contextual factors that affect humour are gender—boys tell more jokes and engage in more physical humour than do girls—and family exposure—if parents tell jokes and engage in humorous activities, then children do also (McGhee, 1979).

The various types of children's humour are evidence of their growing cognitive capacities, combined with their own creativity. With each advancing stage, children become aware of more incongruities that tickle them. They play with language, tease, tell jokes, and clown. A playful frame of

During middle childhood children love riddles. Then at age 11 or 12, they discover humour in playing with social expectations or in illogical behaviour or events.

mind often helps growing children resolve tension, become more creative, or just plain have fun as they learn to negotiate the complexities of their world.

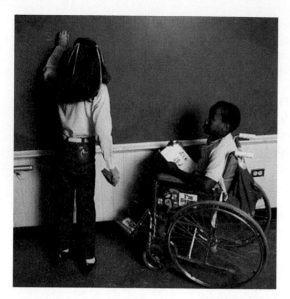

Studies suggest that elementary school children can be taught to use strategies to improve learning.

not monitor their own intellectual processes. This ability to monitor one's own thinking and memory is just beginning at about age 6. These abilities emerge between ages 7 and 10. For example, most children in grade four, when contrasted with children in grade two, are capable of deliberately and efficiently using category organization as a memory strategy. However, their use of these strategies seems to occur more efficiently when the material to be learned is typical or familiar (Hasselhorn, 1992).

Like other aspects of cognitive ability, metacognitive skills develop gradually during middle childhood and adolescence. Just as a 9-year-old has greater metacognitive ability than a 4-year-old, a 15-year-old's self-monitoring skill far surpasses that of the 9-year-old. Because children use these self-monitoring skills in oral communication, reading comprehension, writing, and other cognitive abilities, they are a critical part of cognitive development.

Learning and Thinking in School

Most children enter primary school between the ages of 5 and 7. Once in school, they encounter a number of demands and expectations. Children vary greatly in how well they adapt to these demands.

New Demands and Expectations

Whether schooling starts with nursery school at age 3 or not until grade one at age 6, children must adapt to some changes immediately. They are separated from their parents or caregivers, perhaps for the first time, and must begin to trust unfamiliar adults to ensure their safety and satisfy their needs. At the same time, they must start to become independent and learn to do certain things for themselves. No longer can a little boy sit down and yell, "Put on my boots!" It is time for him to put on his own boots. Even with a favourable student–teacher ratio, children must compete for adult attention and assistance.

The social rules of any classroom are complex. Relationships with classmates involve discovering the right balance between cooperation and competition; relationships with the teacher involve a compromise between autonomy and obedience. One educator has described the school child's situation this way:

> Assigned to classes that may contain strangers, perhaps even adversaries, students are expected to interact harmoniously. Crowded together, they are required to ignore the presence of others. Urged to cooperate, they usually work in competition. Pressed to take responsibility for their own learning, they must follow the dictates of a dominant individual—the teacher. (Weinstein, 1991, pp. 493–494)

Some schools have elaborate codes of behaviour: children must listen when the teacher speaks, line up for recess, obtain permission to go to the bathroom, and raise a hand before speaking. A great deal of time may be spent on enforcing these rules. Psychology students sometimes observe public school classrooms and measure how much time teachers spend on the following activities: (1) teaching a fact or concept; (2) giving directions for a particular lesson; (3) stating general rules of appropriate classroom behaviour; (4) correcting, disciplining, and praising children; and (5) miscellaneous. The results are revealing: in a half-hour lesson, it is not unusual for a teacher to spend only 10 to 15 percent of the time on the first and second categories (Sieber & Gordon, 1981). Research indicates that children learn more in classes where "time on task" is maximized—that is, where the teacher spends at least half the time on actual teaching and less on things like keeping order (Brophy, 1986).

Nonetheless, a considerable amount of time and energy may be put into socializing the children to the highly specific demands of the classroom, demands that are only vaguely connected to intellectual or social growth. Of course, these demands may differ radically from one time or place to another, depending on nationality, customs, and educational philosophy. Regardless of the kind of school that children enter, there is always a tremendous gap between what is acceptable at home and the new demands of the classroom. The greater the gap, the more difficult the adaptation will be. Although children at this age have just begun to internalize the rights and wrongs of family life, they are suddenly expected to adapt to a whole new set of standards. The success with which they make this transition depends on family background, school environment, and the variables of individual development. How well have the children previously coped with dependency, autonomy, authority relationships, the need to control aggression, and the prompting of conscience? Their inner resources may be shaky; nevertheless, we require a flexibility from school beginners that is rarely required of adults.

Attending school makes new demands on children. Now they must follow complex codes of behaviour, such as lining up when travelling in the hallways.

Learning the Basics

Reading Learning to read involves two separate components: (1) **decoding,** translating the print into sounds and words, and (2) **comprehension,** understanding the meaning of what is being read (Adams, 1990). To become skilled readers, children must be able to decode print efficiently, so that they can devote most of their attention to comprehension. In fact, beginning readers often put so much effort into decoding that it detracts from comprehension. How do children learn to read well and to understand what they read?

The answer to this question is at the centre of a major controversy in the teaching of reading in Canada and the United States (Adams, 1990; Simner, 1995; Stanovich & Stanovich, 1995). There are two main approaches to early reading instruction. One approach, called **phonics,** emphasizes decoding. Children are taught to recognize speech sounds, called *phonemes,* alone and in combination. This is called *phonemic awareness.* For example, the children might be taught to look for sound patterns, such as rhymes, and to sound out words. The other approach, **whole language learning,** emphasizes the teaching of reading in a meaningful context. The children might be taught to memorize a few familiar words, called *sight words,* so that they can quickly learn to read familiar texts. There is less emphasis on learning to decode unfamiliar words. And sometimes the children recognize the familiar words, not by sounding out the letters, but from the words' visual patterns or from their contexts. For example, children might recognize the word *grandfather* because it is a long word that starts with a *g.* So when they come across a new word, such as *grandmother,* they might quickly read it as *grandfather* because of its similar appearance, or because it fits with the meaning of the rest of the sentence.

Which method is better? For some children who learn to read with minimal instruction, either method appears to work. But for children who require more intensive instruction, developing phonemic awareness is critical (Simner, 1995). Therefore, these children need either a phonics approach or a whole language approach that incorporates phonemic awareness. Recent research suggests that one aspect of phonemic awareness—the distinction between *onset* and *rime*—is critical to reading (Dombey, 1999). The onset is the beginning sound in a syllable (like *b* in *bat*). The rime is the rest of the sounds in the syllable (like *at* in *bat*). Children can hear that *bat* has an *at* part better than they can hear the separate phonemes *a* and *t.* Children's awareness of onset and rime can help them identify new words that rhyme with words they know.

decoding The process of reading that involves translating print into sounds and words.

comprehension Understanding the meaning of what is being read.

phonics An approach to early reading instruction that teaches children how to decode new words.

whole language learning An approach to early reading instruction that encourages children to recognize words in context, rather than sounding them out.

Interestingly, when parents hear their children make reading errors, they sound out troublesome words by breaking them up into onset and rime (Evans, Barraball, & Eberle, 1998). This type of parent feedback helps children learn to read.

In addition to phonemic awareness, children need motivation to read often. According to Marilyn Jager Adams, a renowned reading expert, "If we want children to learn to read well, we must find a way to induce them to read lots" (1990). Unfortunately, some children do not like to read. According to Juel (1988), a whopping 40 percent of poor readers in grade four would rather clean their rooms than read! By the time they are in grade four, many poor readers have developed negative attitudes toward reading and have lost confidence in their reading abilities.

Early intervention is critical for children who have difficulty reading. In a recent study, grade one children who were reading-delayed received extensive remediation that emphasized phonemic awareness (Vellutino et al., 1996). The majority were able to read at grade level by the end of grade two. This finding led Vellutino et al. to conclude that "the majority of children who might be diagnosed as 'reading disabled' are impaired by experiential and instructional deficits rather than basic cognitive deficits" (p. 629). According to Carter (1984), reading-delayed students can catch up to grade level if they receive remediation before grade three. But if they are not brought up to grade level by then, the chances of their ever catching up are slim, even with special programming.

Writing Writing is more than simply putting words on paper. Writers have to conform to conventions for spelling, punctuation, and grammar. In addition, they have to organize their thoughts and express them in ways that will be clear to their intended audiences. This is no small task for children learning to write.

Ann Cameron and colleagues at the University of New Brunswick have been studying the writing of elementary school children (Cameron, 1995; Cameron, Edmunds, Wigmore, Hunt, & Linton, 1998; Cameron, Hunt, & Linton, 1996; Cameron, Lee, Webster, Munro, Hunt, & Linton, 1995; Cameron & Moshenko, 1996). They have examined whether children engage in sophisticated writing processes such as planning (thinking before writing), goal setting, editing, and revising. And indeed they do.

In one study, children were told to pretend that they were editing stories for a newspaper (Cameron et al., 1998). The stories had surface flaws (errors in spelling,

In recent years there has been a controversy in Canada about how children should be taught to read.

punctuation, and the use of capital letters) and semantic flaws (errors in meaning because of inappropriate or missing words). Even children in grade two could detect about a third of the errors, and by grade six, children could detect over three-quarters of the flaws. Interestingly, Cameron et al. found that children were better at detecting the flaws in other children's writing than in their own. But even so, rewriting and revising improved the children's writing.

A prominent theme in Cameron's research is the need to consider children's writing in its social context. The purpose of the children's writing must be taken into account.

Arithmetic How do children learn to do arithmetic? Jeff Bisanz and colleagues at the University of Alberta and at Carleton University have examined how children solve simple problems that involve adding one-digit numbers, such as 7 + 3 (Bisanz & Bisanz, 1994; Bisanz & LeFevre, 1990; LeFevre, Sadesky, & Bisanz, 1996). They have focused on how children solve the problems, rather than just on the answers they attain. Interestingly, there are a number of ways to solve the problems. One way is to use a counting procedure. To solve 7 + 3, the child first counts to 7, perhaps using her fingers or other objects, and then counts out 3 more to make 10. This procedure requires a lot of effort and is time consuming. In a somewhat shortened procedure, called the *min procedure,* the child simply starts with the bigger number (that is, she does not count it out) and then adds on the smaller number. For example, to solve 7 + 3, the child would start at 7 and count out 3 more to make 10. An even more efficient way to solve the problem is simply to retrieve the answer from memory, rather than working it out. Not surprisingly, younger children rely more on counting procedures, and older children are more apt to use retrieval. It is important to note, though, that children of all ages use a variety of procedures. There is not an orderly, stage-like progression from counting to retrieval. Even young children can use retrieval for some problems (1 + 1), and, surprisingly, even adults do not use retrieval all of the time.

The manner of solving math problems varies with social situations. For instance, school children in Canada might use counting procedures more when teachers stress accuracy. But they might use retrieval more when teachers stress speed. Interestingly, children who work as street vendors in Brazil are extremely accurate in solving math problems related to their businesses (for example, calculating change) (Konner, 1991). But they are unable to solve the same problems out of context, when they are presented with papers and pencils. This finding highlights the importance of Vygotsky's theory of cognitive development, discussed in Chapter 2.

Developing Competent Learners and Critical Thinkers

Learning has been defined as "an activity of the brain, under the direction and control of the individual, that must result in additions to and modifications of long-term memory" (Letteri, 1985). In a rapidly changing world, there is much to learn and too little time to learn it. Certain knowledge now may become obsolete in a decade or less, and thus today's children will have to become lifelong learners in order to adapt to a changing world. Meanwhile, these children need to integrate and organize the barrage of information that comes at them from all sides. They must find order and consistency in the complex and sometimes unstable experiences of their lives. To help children adapt and become lifelong learners, many educators urge teachers to avoid focusing on too many disconnected facts, principles, and rules. Instead, they emphasize that teachers should focus on instructing children how to become self-directed, competent learners and critical thinkers.

One approach that teachers can use is derived directly from what we know about information processing. Children can be taught to be competent learners by learning control processes. For example, problem solving often involves many component control processes, such as focusing on relevant details or analyzing a problem into component parts. Each of these strategies might be taught by using simple exercises.

FOCUS ON APPLICATION

Could a Child Who Has Wandered Off Find the Way Home?

Occasionally, children wander off. Would they be able to find their way back home? Ed Cornell and colleagues at the University of Alberta have been exploring whether children who are taken on unfamiliar routes can retrace their way back to the start (Cornell, Heth, & Broda, 1989; Cornell, Heth, Kneubuhler, & Sehgal, 1996; Cornell, Heth, & Rowat, 1992).

In each of the studies, children were taken on a route that took 12 to 14 minutes to walk at their pace. The route meandered through the University of Alberta campus, passing various buildings, open grassy areas, transit zones, parking lots, neighbouring residential areas, and roadways. After finishing the route, children had to retrace it to get back to the start.

Along the way, there were several intersections, called *choice points*, where the children had to choose between staying on the original path or deviating from it.

Cornell et al. wondered whether children would be better at retracing

---

Children make more errors in the middle of the route.

---

the route if they were given particular types of instructions. Would some instructions be more effective than others? Cornell et al. tested this idea with 6-year-olds and 12-year-olds. A researcher told the children, "We're

going to play follow the leader. I am going to be the leader. I am going to lead us on a short walk through the university. These are the stairs where we will start (pointing)" (Cornell, Heth, & Broda, 1989, p. 757). Some children got only this minimal instruction, but others received one of three sets of additional instructions: (1) some were told that they would have to lead the way back and were advised to pay attention; (2) others were told that they would have to retrace the route, and they were given additional instructions to pay attention to close landmarks pointed out to them during the walk, such as a telephone booth, that could help them remember the route; and (3) the rest of the children, in addition to being told that they would have to

---

Some educators have had remarkable success in as little as 15 or 20 hours of training with initially poor students. The students become more analytical and focused, they become less impulsive, and they earn better grades (Letteri, 1985).

The development of strategy use and cognitive processing skills during middle childhood are significantly affected by children's school experiences. Teachers seem to be responding to children's developing abilities, as well as guiding this development, when they make frequent strategy suggestions to children in grades two and three. Teachers also give direct metamemory guidance to older students. Especially for low and moderate achievers, exposure to a high-strategy teacher is related to better comprehension and use of cognitive processing instruction. However, the infrequent use of strategy suggestions, and the limited efforts most teachers make to instruct children in metacognition, suggests that most children could benefit by receiving more instruction in the use of strategy (Moely et al., 1992).

What sorts of strategies might teachers instruct children in? Educators and psychologists recommend a range of teaching strategies to develop students' thinking. According to Costa, Hanson, Silver, and Strong (1985), children need to develop six kinds of thought. We might call these the "six R's":

1. *Remembering*—recalling a fact, idea, or concept.
2. *Repeating*—following a model or procedure.
3. *Reasoning*—relating a specific instance to a general principle or concept.
4. *Reorganizing*—extending knowledge to a new context for an original solution.
5. *Relating*—establishing a connection between new knowledge and past or personal experience.
6. *Reflecting*—exploring the thought itself and how it occurred.

retrace the route, were told to pay attention to landmarks visible at a distance that were pointed out to them during the walk, such as tall buildings on the skyline.

Interestingly, Cornell et al. found that age mattered more than the type of instructions. The 12-year-olds were better than the 6-year-olds at retracing the route, regardless of the type of instructions. Perhaps this ability reflects a 12-year-old's increased independence. Curiously, neither the 6-year-olds nor the 12-year-olds benefited from being told that they would be required to retrace the route. Just being told to pay attention did not ensure that the children would attend to helpful cues. For instance, the 6-year-olds often paid attention to unreliable cues, such as a dog tied to a tree, not realizing that it might no longer be there on the return trip. Or, they attended to cues that were too common, such as spruce trees

that all looked the same. They knew they were supposed to turn at the tree, but which tree? However, being told to pay attention to close landmarks, like a telephone booth, did help. Both the 6-year-olds and the 12-year-olds were better at finding their way when close landmarks were pointed out to them on the original walk. It seems that children do not spontaneously attend to these landmarks. The 12-year-olds also did better when told about landmarks visible from a distance. However, the distant landmarks did not help the 6-year-olds.

Cornell et al. also examined the parts of the route that seemed to give the children the most trouble. Interestingly, both the 6- and 12-year-olds were more likely to make wrong turns in the middle of the route than at either the beginning or the end. This finding, called a *serial position effect*, has implications for conducting searches

for lost children. If we had to search all possible wrong turns a lost child might make, we would have an immense area to search. According to Syrotuck, as cited in Cornell, Heth, Kneubuhler, and Sehgal (1996), a person who walks just 5 kilometres in any direction could be anywhere within 78 square kilometres. To search an area that size would require approximately 264 searchers over 12 days! Finding that children make more errors in the middle of the route could help searchers prioritize the areas to search. They might concentrate on the middle of the route.

Cornell is currently developing the applications of his research to real-life searches for lost persons. He is working with the RCMP and park rangers in communities in the Rocky Mountains where people have been lost in the bush. He is trying to predict the routes they would most likely take.

Developing these thinking skills requires special teaching strategies. To develop reasoning, teachers need to present interesting problems and materials. The goal is to increase curiosity, to foster questioning, to develop related concepts, to encourage evaluation of alternatives, and to help students construct hypotheses and devise methods of testing them. Teaching students to develop critical thinking is more difficult than simply imparting facts and principles (Costa, 1985).

Success in School

The schoolroom is the most important stage on which children perform during middle childhood. It is at school that children test their intellectual, physical, social, and emotional competencies to find out if they can equal the standards set for them by their parents and teachers and by society as a whole. It is also at school that children gain confidence in their ability both to master their world and to develop social relationships with their peers. The school, in other words, plays a critical role in the healthy development of the child. Unfortunately, how well the school meets the challenge placed before it—to help children maximize all of their personal resources—is open to question.

As a result, there has been a trend toward increased testing of children. A number of school districts now give children regular tests to ensure that the schools are meeting the curriculum goals (see the box "Math Achievement Test Scores in Canadian Elementary Schools"). As well, some tests are given to children in different countries to compare international standards of education. For example, math and science tests were given to students in grades seven and eight from 45 countries between 1994 and 1995 (called "Third International Achievement Tests"). Singapore, Korea, and Japan received the highest rankings of all. The Canadian average was ranked the fifteenth in

In order to do well in school, children need to eat well.

science and sixteenth in math, although results in the provinces differed. Children in British Columbia and Alberta did better on the tests than did children in other parts of Canada.

It is difficult to interpret the results of international comparisons because children in different parts of the world attend school for different amounts of time. Typically, children in Asian countries attend school more days per year and for more hours each day than do children in North America (Frazier & Morrison, 1998). Therefore, it is unclear whether Asian students are doing better owing to more schooling, to better schooling, or to other factors, such as family background and cultural values. Interestingly, a recent study found that increasing the number of school days per year in some communities in the United States improved students' learning (Frazier & Morrison, 1998). Extending the school year may be a promising educational reform in North America. Another recent educational reform is *year-round schooling,* which refers to a rearrangement of the school year without changing the number of school days. Instead of getting two months of summer holidays, children get several shorter holidays throughout the year. The holidays are short enough that children do not forget as much of their school work as they typically do after a two-month holiday. Children in year-round schooling do slightly better than those in regular schools (Kneese, 1996). Year-round schooling has been implemented in a number of Canadian schools. Case studies of three year-round schools in British Columbia indicate that year-round schooling led to positive changes in teacher interactions and planning, which improved the quality of education (Shields & LaRocque, 1998).

According to David McClelland (1955), the reason that some children achieve more than others may relate to the values of the culture in which they are reared. After comparing several periods of history in several different cultures, McClelland concluded that *achievement motivation*—the drive to attain success and excellence—is a cultural value. Within any given society at any time, some groups value achievement more highly than other groups do (deCharms & Moeller, 1962). Different cultures or subcultures also may value different *kinds* of achievement—one group may stress educational goals, whereas another may place more value on financial or social success. Children whose parents stress values that are different from those of the school may bring less motivation to academic tasks. Such children may simply be channelling their need for achievement into other areas.

Underachievement is a widespread problem (Mandel & Marcus, 1996). In many schools, underachievement has been pinpointed as early as grade three. For both achievers and underachievers, attributions (beliefs), self-esteem, and metacognition interrelate to predict reading achievement. Underachievers have qualitatively different beliefs about themselves in the classroom than do achievers. They seem to possess the same metacognitive strategies, but they do not hold the same expectations of success for themselves as achievers do. As the researchers state, "It is as if their knowledge and abilities were disassociated from their beliefs about instrumentality, a key characteristic of metacognition in achievers" (Carr, Borkowski, & Maxwell, 1991, p. 113). Achievers believe they will succeed, and they use the strategies necessary to do so; underachievers do not make the connection between their prior knowledge and internal beliefs about self-efficacy, the ability to succeed at a task.

Success in school is influenced by many other factors. For example, children who are in poor health, who do not get enough to eat, or who are preoccupied with problems at home may do poorly at school tasks. Self-esteem is another important factor. Children's own judgments of their competence seriously affect their performance in school. In one study, 20 percent of school-age children underestimated their actual abilities. These children set lower expectations for themselves and were surprised at their intermittent high grades (Phillips, 1984).

More recently, research has found that children's perceived academic competence was related to the warmth and quality of interaction with their fathers. For boys, fathers tended to be increasingly less easygoing and put more pressure on sons who had high rather than low perceived academic competence. For girls, fathers put more pressure on daughters with low perceived academic competence but assumed a "hands-off" policy with their daughters whose expectations were high. Another finding was that children with lower perceived academic competence do not trust their own ideas and often turn to adults for guidance and assistance in homework (Wagner & Phillips, 1992). In the early grades, children who participate more in class discussions tend to have better school achievement. Mary Ann Evans, at the University of Guelph, found that many children were shy in kindergarten, but by the time they were in grade one, they participated more in class discussions (Evans, 1996). Some children's shyness, though, persisted through grade one. Persistently shy children had poorer verbal skills. They did not have lower self-esteem than other children. Their quietness was due to a lack of verbal skills more than to a lack of self-confidence.

Parental Influences on School Success

In correlational studies, poverty, gender, ethnicity, and family composition have all been linked to poor school performance. Being male, of minority status, poor, and

Children who perform well in school tend to have parents who strongly value education and encourage their child's self-esteem.

FOCUS ON APPLICATION

Math Achievement Test Scores in Canadian Elementary Schools

Children in Canadian elementary schools routinely write academic achievement tests to monitor their progress and to judge the effectiveness of their schools. The interpretation of test performance, though, can be complicated. Suppose students in one school or province consistently do more poorly than others. We cannot automatically conclude that the source of the differences is the schooling. Perhaps the children had different levels of development before they entered school, or perhaps they came from homes or neighbourhoods that differed in the extent to which they supported academic activities. Recent research in Canada has examined ways that family background is associated with children's math scores in different provinces (Wilms, 1996). Here is a summary of the main findings, as reported by Wilms (1996):

- Tests of children's vocabulary at age 4 or 5 predicted how well children did on math tests in grades two, four, and six. Those with better vocabularies did better on the math tests. Therefore, it is important to look at factors related to vocabulary scores.

Children's vocabulary scores were affected by the mother's level of education, the prestige of the father's job, family composition (children living in two-parent families, on average, scored higher than those living in lone-parent families), and family size (children in smaller families, on average, scored higher than those in large families).

Recent research in Canada has examined ways that family background is associated with children's math scores.

- Of all the family background variables, the mother's level of education was the strongest predictor of children's math scores in grades two, four, and six.
- Family background had less of an effect on children's math achievement in Canada than in other countries, such as the United States or the United Kingdom. Social class

differences in math achievement were less evident in Canada than in the United States or the United Kingdom.

- Throughout elementary school, girls, on average, scored slightly higher on math tests than boys did. There was more variation in boys' scores than in girls' scores. Compared with girls, boys were more likely to have either extremely high or extremely low scores.

- Children's math scores were higher in some provinces than in others, after accounting for provincial differences in socioeconomic status. Ontario was consistently below the national average and fell more behind from grades two to six. Quebec was consistently well above the national average and moved further ahead with each advancing grade. British Columbia and Newfoundland were slightly above the national average. The remaining provinces were close to the national average. Differences among Ontario, Quebec, and British Columbia have been found consistently in studies dating back to the 1980s.

coming from a single-parent family have been especially linked with high risk for school failure. Yet, as we noted in Chapter 1, it is inappropriate to assume that because two factors are correlated, one causes the other. It is almost always more complicated than that. For example, in correlational studies, inner-city males have been found to be especially at risk for school failure. This may be because inner-city children often grow up in cultural environments where academic achievement and other types of scholastic success may be devalued (Patterson, Kupersmidt, & Vaden, 1990); where violence produces stress that makes learning difficult (Timnick, 1989); or where effective male role models are unavailable (Garibaldi, 1992). But, certainly, many inner-city males succeed in school, especially if one or more of these circumstances are absent.

Parents play a large role in providing a supportive environment and in encouraging the development of the specific skills that help children succeed. On the negative side, children from homes where there is severe marital distress, paternal criminality, maternal psychiatric disorder, or overcrowding and children who are intermittently placed in foster care are at special risk for school failure. These children lack the appropriate safe environment in which learning optimally occurs (Sameroff et al., 1993).

In contrast, if we look at the parents of children who succeed in school, we find behaviours that almost any parent can accomplish, regardless of economic circumstances. Reviews of the research on school success point to three types of parental variables (Hess & Holloway, 1984):

1. Parents of successful children have realistic beliefs about their child's current abilities yet high expectations for the future. They encourage their children to master age-appropriate tasks both in school and at home. These parents believe in their children and help the children to have confidence and high expectations for themselves.

2. Parent–child relationships are warm and affectionate, and parents have discipline and control strategies that are authoritative rather than authoritarian. Children have limits on their behaviour but feel safe and accepted.

3. Finally, and perhaps most important, these parents talk to their children. They spend time with them, read to them, listen to them, tell them stories, and have lots of conversations with them. They model interest in the world around them and provide some of the conceptual frameworks for understanding social and physical phenomena. They support and enrich their children's exploration and inquiry.

We also must be aware of cultural factors that influence parents' expectations for their children's education. For example, researchers in British Columbia surveyed immigrants from Taiwan, Hong Kong, or mainland China regarding their children's schooling in Canada (Zhang, Ollila, & Harvey, 1998). Ninety-eight percent of them noticed a "difference" or a "great difference" between schooling in Canada and in their homeland. Their perception of Canadian schools was mixed. On the one hand, they perceived Canadian education as more flexible, creative, and autonomous. Canadian teachers and students have more input into curriculum. In Chinese countries, the curriculum is standardized across schools, and students are not given choices in what they learn. On the other hand, Chinese parents perceived Canadian schools as lacking in discipline and as being too indulgent of children. Chinese parents valued homework, although parents from different countries had different expectations about the role of parents in children's homework. Parents from mainland China were more likely than other Chinese parents to expect their children to show initiative by doing their homework on their own. Parents from Hong Kong were more likely to help their children with homework. Chinese parents, in general, had high expectations for their children's school performance. They wanted their children to do well so that they could go to university and make a contribution to society. None of the Chinese parents reported that they wanted their children to make a lot of money, regardless of what they did. In Chinese culture, it is considered indecent to link the value of education to making money. In summary, it is important to be aware of cultural diversity in Canadian schools because parents from different backgrounds may have expectations and values that are not consistent with the mainstream values found in the school. This has been a long-standing problem among some Aboriginal families who feel alienated by mainstream education, which does not incorporate Aboriginal values and culture (Hookimaw-Witt, 1998). We will explore this problem in more detail in Chapter 15 when we discuss why adolescents drop out of school.

Technology in the School Environment

Today's learning environments are in transition as new technology affects the way teaching is—and will be—conducted. While those who were children 30 years ago may have arrived in the classroom relatively unaffected by the then new technology of television, today's children have been extensively exposed to it. As one educator commented,

> For the contemporary child who is just learning to read, it is not television that is new. It is the linear and sequential nature of print on the page that is alien.

A key aspect of the computer's arrival in the classroom is the interaction between student and machine. How well this interaction works is a function of the particular program being used.

As Marshall McLuhan pointed out, one can be absorbed by the glowing screen of television in a way that is not possible with books.... Most children experience the rhythm and tempo of a world vastly different from the one presented in a typical classroom. Compare the excitement of watching a wide screen version of "Batman" to a classroom discussion on history or geography. The disparity of such experiences creates very real tensions. (Kaha, 1990, p. 46)

Not only is technology affecting children's experience at school, but it is also having an impact on how parents relate to the school. For example, many Canadian schools now have voice mail that allows parents and teachers to leave messages for each other 24 hours a day. Interestingly, Cameron and Lee (1998) found that 64 percent of parents felt only mildly comfortable leaving messages by voice mail. For example, one parent commented, "I was so rattled, I'd forget who I was. I don't know if I thought there was some little man there that would automatically know who was calling" (p. 8). However, 27 percent of parents felt that voice mail had improved communication between home and school. Parents of older elementary students (grade five) were more likely to find voice mail helpful than were parents of children in kindergarten.

Another new method of communication between parents and schools is e-mail. Many Canadian schools are getting hooked up to the Internet. Some schools now have their own Web pages that convey information to parents, students, and the larger community. But not all parents have access to the Internet. Schools must find a way to balance the push toward maximizing the use of new technology with the pull of ensuring that all families have equal opportunities to communicate with schools.

Computers, Learning, and Thinking   Computers have arrived in the classroom as well as in homes and in businesses. Now that most schools have computers, educators are struggling to decide how to use them to enhance learning and thinking. As with many new technologies, controversy surrounds the use of computers by children.

To many, the computer seems a beneficent genie, a powerful tool with the capacity to transform our schools and revolutionize children's learning. To others, the computer seems a potentially menacing device, more likely to undermine than improve our educational system, more likely to control than serve children. (Lepper & Gurtner, 1989, p. 170)

How are computers likely to affect the lives of children in the future? First, computers may well become personal tutors and make learning more efficient, effective, and highly motivating for students. With a computer, learning is more individualized to the needs and abilities of the student. Second, computers will serve as multipurpose tools for writing and communication skills. Computers may indeed become a boon to students who do not normally succeed in today's schools. Since computers are machines, they are always fair and impartial. This impartiality will minimize any pernicious effects of teacher prejudice or favouritism that may occur in classroom learning situations (Lepper & Gurtner, 1989).

Computers have been used for *programmed learning*, or *computer-assisted instruction*. In this mode, the computer serves as a surrogate teacher. The computer program structures learning in sequential steps and adjusts the size of the steps to the ability of the individual child. A child who learns quickly can progress rapidly through the program, whereas one who learns more slowly can be given extra opportunities for review. The programs correct children and provide immediate feedback. If they are well designed, children can learn skills such as addition and subtraction or typing.

Another use of computers in the classroom is to foster creativity and inventiveness. One way of doing this is to teach children how to program computers themselves, so that they are responsible for what the computer does. In a programming language called LOGO, children can create complex geometric constructions. They are no longer simply repeating programmed drills; by doing the programming themselves, children discover principles, construct new forms, and analyze structures (Papert, 1980, 1993).

Question to Ponder

How do you think the use of computers affects children's cognitive development?

Another way of enhancing creativity is to let children use computers for writing stories. Children can be taught to type and to use a word processing program. Once they gain the basic skills, they can edit their stories with relative ease. For younger children, there are programs that allow them to construct stories without writing. Even preschoolers can use computer graphics to develop sequences of action for stories and then play back their own creations (Forman, 1985).

How will the use of computers change the social dynamics of the classroom? Will boys use the computers more often than girls? Interestingly, when children are in kindergarten, there is no difference between boys and girls in the use of computers (Bergin, Ford, & Hess, 1993). But by the time children are in grade six, boys enjoy computers more than do girls. Will the use of computers in the classroom give some children advantages over others? For example, will children who do not have access to computers at home be able to keep up with peers who do have computers at home? On a more positive note, will the use of computers make it easier to accommodate the special learning needs of individual children? For example, special computer programs exist to help children with autism, cerebral palsy, hearing impairment, learning disabilities, high IQ (gifted children), and language disorders.

Assessing Individual Differences

Schools measure children's ability and achievement in order to determine their level of development and their readiness to learn new skills. This measuring is accomplished through various forms of intelligence, diagnostic, and achievement tests.

In the 1940s and 1950s, a great effort was made in Canada and the United States to administer tests to school children—IQ tests, achievement tests, personality tests, and career aptitude tests. School files were—and in many cases still are—filled with test scores of varying degrees of accuracy and significance. In the 1960s, many parents and educators reacted against what they considered the abuse of diagnostic tests. More recently, there has again been an increase in the use of diagnostic and achievement tests. But most teachers are now more aware of the dangers of misinterpreting (or overinterpreting) test results and of pinning labels on children. Consequently, they are using the tests with greater caution.

The rationale behind testing is that schools must assess students' abilities in order to plan efficient educational programs. But all too often, the scores have been misused. Teachers and administrators have employed test results to pigeonhole children or to deny some of them access to certain educational opportunities. Almost as frequently, the test results have not been used at all. More than one child has experienced the frustration of entering grade one with reading test scores at the grade three level, only to be assigned to a class in beginning reading because he "has not had that subject yet."

In an approach known as **diagnostic-prescriptive teaching,** however, tests and informal assessments can be a vital aid to education. The idea behind this kind of teaching is that if educators know precisely what an individual child can do, they will be better able to prescribe the next step. The diagnosis does not apply a generalized label but measures a specific, observable behaviour or skill. The child is assessed for what she can do. The testers do not call the student "superior" or "mildly retarded" or "a slow learner"—they simply identify the child's particular knowledge, skills, and abilities at that point in time. Sometimes, the diagnosis is based on classroom observation or a diagnostic lesson; other times, it is based on formal tests called **criterion-referenced tests** (Glaser, 1963).

Because criterion-referenced tests focus on the achievements of an individual, they differ radically from the more familiar **norm-referenced tests,** which are concerned with how one child's score compares with that of another child. Most standard IQ tests, achievement tests, and scholastic aptitude tests are norm referenced. They compare one child's score with the scores of a large number of other children. In other words,

diagnostic-prescriptive teaching A system of teaching in which tests and informal assessments inform educators as to a child's abilities so that they may prescribe appropriate instruction.

criterion-referenced test A test that evaluates an individual's performance in relation to mastery of specified skills or objectives.

norm-referenced test A test that compares an individual's performance with the performances of others in the same age group.

Some forms of diagnostic and achievement tests are important because the school must assess students' abilities in order to plan efficient educational programs.

a criterion-referenced math test describes a child's accuracy and speed in several specific math skills, whereas a norm-referenced test shows that a child is performing at a level higher or lower than the average for her grade or age. Therefore, a norm-referenced test might identify a child as being in the bottom 10 percent of her class in arithmetic skills, but it will say little or nothing about what she does know, why she fails specific items, or what specific skills she needs to acquire so that she may progress. Also, the test reveals nothing about the child's pattern of attention, her level of anxiety when she faces a math question, or any of a number of things that the teacher may need to know in order to help her. The test may merely label the child, in a general way, as a good student or a poor one.

Intelligence Testing

In the field of developmental psychology, perhaps no issue has been more controversial than that of intelligence and intelligence testing. The academic debate has become a public one largely because of the broad impact that intelligence test scores have on educational and social opportunities. When young children are labelled on the basis of IQ scores, the results can be far reaching. IQ scores may affect the extent and quality of children's education, determine the jobs they may have as adults, and put a lasting imprint on their self-image. The emphasis on testing, especially at the elementary and secondary school levels, has resulted in the grouping and rating of students based solely on their test performances. Children, too, are taught to take these tests seriously.

Why do we hold intelligence in such high regard? What are we actually trying to measure? In this section, we shall explore the concept of intelligence, beginning with some early attempts to measure and thus to define it.

Alfred Binet The first comprehensive intelligence test was designed in the late 19th century by Alfred Binet, a French psychologist. He was commissioned by the French government to devise a method of identifying those children who would not profit from a public education. Binet needed a scale that would yield an index of the educability of children. His concept of intelligence focused on such complex intellectual processes as judgment, reasoning, memory, and comprehension. To measure these capabilities, he used test items involving problem solving, word definitions, and general knowledge. Binet believed that intelligence does not remain static but grows and changes throughout life. Test questions, therefore, had to be carefully arranged to reflect this growth. A good test item differentiated between older and younger children. If more than half of the 5-year-olds were able to define the word *ball,* and fewer than half of the 4-year-olds were able to do so, then the definition of *ball* was included on the test for 5-year-olds (Binet & Simon, 1905, 1916). This empirical basis for selecting and ordering items was a landmark in the testing movement. The resulting test score was called a **mental age.**

The Intelligence Quotient According to the concept of mental age, a 4-year-old who could answer most of the questions on the test for 5-year-olds would have a mental age of 5. Later psychologists found a way of conveniently expressing the relationship between mental age and chronological (or "real") age: the **intelligence quotient,** or IQ. Intelligence quotient is calculated by dividing mental age by chronological age and multiplying the result by 100. Therefore, our bright 4-year-old with a mental age of 5 would have an intelligence quotient of 5/4 times 100, or 125. Any child whose mental age and chronological age are equal—in other words, a child whose intellectual development is progressing at an average rate—will have an IQ of 100.

> **mental age** An intelligence test score showing the age group with which a child's performance most closely compares.
>
> **intelligence quotient** An individual's mental age divided by chronological age, multiplied by 100 to eliminate the decimal point.

In 1916, an English version of Binet's test, revised by Lewis Terman at Stanford University, was introduced in the United States. The concept of IQ testing won wide acceptance in the United States and was much used during the 1940s and 1950s. In contrast to Binet, who believed that intelligence was modifiable, many American psychologists believed that as mental and chronological ages increased during development, the ratio between them remained fixed—it was innate (Weinberg, 1989).

Today, with a few exceptions, the ratio IQ that was described earlier has fallen into disuse in favour of a norm-referenced **deviation-IQ test,** which assigns an IQ score by comparing a child's performance on the test with performances of other children of the same age. This measure carries no automatic assumption about whether intelligence is fixed or modifiable. The current Stanford-Binet test, which is widely used, is the direct descendant of Binet's 1905 test. Another IQ test that is widely used in Canada is the Wechsler Intelligence Scale for Children—Third Edition (WISC-III). The WISC-III has been given to large numbers of Canadian children, and Canadian norms now exist for this test. These norms are more appropriate for Canadian children than are the American ones (Beal, Dumont, Cruse, & Branche, 1996).

> **deviation IQ** An IQ score derived from a statistical table comparing an individual's raw score on an IQ test with the scores of other subjects of the same age.

The Nature of Intelligence

The development of sophisticated models for testing and measuring intelligence has stimulated inquiry, both popular and scientific, into the nature of intelligence itself. We shall briefly consider some of the highlights of this continuing debate. You will notice that some of the following arguments might be applied equally well to other human characteristics, such as aggressiveness, self-confidence, and even physical beauty.

Innate and Learned Intellectual Abilities The nature-versus-nurture controversy still sparks fireworks in academic journals and in the popular press. Arthur Jensen (1969) generated a great deal of controversy when he stated his belief that 80 percent of what is measured on IQ tests is inherited, and only 20 percent is determined by a child's environment. Criticism of Jensen's paper (and the data on which it was based) was widespread; some psychologists even took the view that there was no good evidence for any genetic effect on IQ (Kamin, 1974). The current view is a more balanced one—the consensus seems to be that genetic and environmental factors are about equally potent in determining how well a child will do on an IQ test (Weinberg, 1989). But the pendulum may once again be tipping toward the side of those who think that intelligence is largely innate (see, for example, Herrnstein & Murray, 1994). A recent paper on identical twins who were reared apart claims that the heritability of IQ (how much is inherited) is 70 percent (Bouchard, Lykken, McGue, Segal, & Tellegen, 1990).

General and Specific Abilities   Several early theorists, most notably Spearman (1904), believed that intelligence was a single central attribute, reflected in the ability to learn. He drew this conclusion from the fact that children who did well on one kind of test item usually did well on other kinds of test items, too. For example, a child who has a high score on the vocabulary test is also likely to be above average in solving puzzles or doing math problems (Hunt, 1961). Other theorists (Guilford, 1959; Thurstone, 1938) have contended that intelligence is a composite of many different abilities, such as perceptual speed, word fluency, memory, and others. An individual may be good at remembering facts or perceiving similarities, but this does not necessarily mean that he will also do well on tasks involving spatial relationships.

Intelligence tests differ on whether they define intelligence as a unitary attribute or as a composite of several abilities. The WISC-III has separate subtests for information, comprehension, mathematics, vocabulary, digit span, picture arrangement, and others. This test yields a verbal IQ score, a performance (nonverbal) IQ score, and a full-scale score that represents a combination of the two. The current version of the Stanford-Binet test, on the other hand, yields a single score that indicates an overall intelligence level, although individual test items measure a variety of abilities and skills.

One proponent of the view that intelligence is made up of several independent abilities is Howard Gardner (1983, 1993). Gardner reviews the literature of neurology, psychology, and even that of human evolutionary history and comes up with seven "frames of mind"—seven different kinds of intelligence. These are divided into two groups. In the first group are *linguistic intelligence, musical intelligence, logical-mathematical intelligence,* and *spatial intelligence.* The second group includes *kinesthetic intelligence, interpersonal intelligence,* and *intrapersonal intelligence.* Each of these forms of intelligence works with different information and processes the information in different ways. Although a child may be below average in the kinds of intelligence measured by IQ tests (mainly linguistic and logical-mathematical), he may be high in other kinds of intelligence—for example, interpersonal intelligence (the ability to understand the feelings and motivations of others).

Another current view is that of Robert Sternberg (1985). Sternberg has a "triarchic" (three-part) concept of intelligence. The first kind is *contextual intelligence,* which involves adaptation to the environment. If the environment is poor, a person who is high in this type of intelligence may modify the environment or find a better one. The second type is *experiential intelligence,* which involves the capacity to cope with new tasks or situations, as well as with old ones. Coping with new tasks involves the capacity to learn quickly, and coping with old ones involves the capacity to automatize performance so that a minimum of thought and energy is spent on these tasks. Finally, the third type is *componential intelligence,* which corresponds roughly to the abilities measured by IQ tests.

Diagnostic and Achievement Tests

As mentioned earlier, the purpose of tests is to help schools assess the capabilities of students so that educators can design programs to fit individual needs. Because many capabilities cannot be measured by an IQ test, educators must find other ways to assess the diverse skills and strengths of each individual.

Beyond Acquisition of Knowledge   What kind of test to give and how the results should be used depend on educational priorities and how the learning process is viewed. Some theorists believe that the educational system has focused too much on "intelligence" and "achievement" and has ignored a number of equally significant abilities. For example, of the six cognitive abilities defined by Bloom and Krathwohl (1956), only the first two are regularly measured in school. Beginning with the simplest, the six categories are as follows:

1. *Knowledge of facts and principles* refers to the direct recall of information. Such knowledge frequently involves the rote memorization of dates, names, vocabulary words, and definitions—items that are easy to identify and test. Perhaps because of its convenience, this cognitive ability has long been the focus of education.

2. *Comprehension* entails the understanding of facts and ideas. Unfortunately, tests that are successful in measuring recall of facts or principles are often unsuccessful in assessing how well the student actually understands the material.

3. *Application* refers to the need to know not only rules, principles, or basic procedures but also how and when to use them in new situations. This ability is less frequently taught and measured than the previous two.

4. *Analysis* involves the breaking down of a concept, idea, system, or message into its parts, then seeing the relationship between these parts. This ability may be taught in reading comprehension, math, or science classes. Often, however, the end product of the analysis is taught, but the analytical process itself is not.

5. *Synthesis* refers to the putting together of information or ideas—integrating or relating the parts of a whole.

6. *Evaluation* entails judging the value of a piece of information, a theory, or a plan in terms of some criterion, or standard.

Most testing—and most teaching—focuses on ability 1, with occasional attention given to ability 2. Very rarely do teachers give tests that require a student to use the thinking abilities listed in categories 3 through 6. Indeed, many teachers avoid category 6, although, without evaluation, much information may be hollow and superficial.

Limitations of Intelligence Testing In a world where new problems arise and "facts" change every day, it is increasingly important for children to be taught the skills they need to deal with the unknown as well as the known. Therefore, some researchers feel that schools should teach children not *what* to think but *how* to think. Children can be taught how to generate new ideas, how to look at an issue in a new way, and how to identify the key aspects of a problem. These skills, it is claimed, are more useful than the facts and principles that are generally taught and measured (Olton & Crutchfield, 1969).

Some skills or abilities—such as a sense of humour—may be ignored because they are not especially valued in the elementary school. Other skills are ignored because the behaviour involved is too difficult to define. Teachers may feel, for example, that they cannot measure a student's ability to enjoy classical music or to appreciate art. Recent research has suggested that skills that are learned in group educational settings will inevitably provide a less than accurate portrayal of individuals' capacities—they do not adequately or equally challenge all children in the group to learn. The brightest children may not be fully stimulated, while those who have difficulty may be overwhelmed. Furthermore, appropriate assessment of children's abilities requires an understanding of the cultural constraints regulating their use of concepts and reasoning processes (Miller-Jones, 1989).

The tendency of schools to concentrate on measurable abilities reflects the popularity of **behavioural objectives.** These objectives describe the kinds of knowledge and skills expected of a student after a specified amount of instruction. In a sense, they provide a way of testing *schools*, not students. Each June, schools are expected to demonstrate in a tangible way what their students have learned. As valuable as this approach is, great concern with a school's success often means that children spend most of the school day acquiring competencies that can be easily measured. As a result, less tangible competencies, ways of thinking, and personality traits are often overlooked. How does one objectively measure kindness, courage, curiosity, sensitivity, or openness to new experiences?

behavioural objectives The kinds of knowledge and skills expected of a student after a specified amount of instruction; they provide a demonstration of the school's adequacy, as well as the student's.

In schools today, skills that are not easily measured, such as the ability to appreciate art, tend to be ignored.

Cultural Biases and Test Abuses

Psychologists, educators, and parents have criticized diagnostic and achievement tests for various reasons. We have shown that tests do not provide the whole story and that some personal qualities and skills are difficult or impossible to measure using conventional testing methods. In addition, there is the question of the cultural bias of the tests themselves. To show the absurdity of culturally linked intelligence tests, Stephen Jay Gould (1981) gave a class of Harvard students a nonverbal test of innate intelligence designed for World War I army recruits. (A sample of the test is shown in Figure 13-3.) He found that many of his students could not identify a horn as the missing part of a Victrola, despite the test makers' claim that the subjects' "innate" intelligence would guide them to the correct answer.

Some minority groups resent being measured by tests that assume wide exposure to the dominant white culture; they feel that the tests are unfair to those who have different cultural experiences. For example, many Aboriginal children do poorly on tests of verbal IQ, yet these tests do not predict how well the children will do in school (Common & Frost, 1992). The tests do not accurately indicate the children's potential. A number of researchers in Ontario have developed a new test for the assessment of minority students (Samuda, Kong, Cummins, Pascual-Leone, & Lewis, 1989).

Figure 13-3
Segment of the Army Beta Mental Test
This is Part 6 of the Army Beta mental test given to recruits during World War I. They were asked to find the missing parts in the following images. (Answers: 1. mouth; 2. eye; 3. nose; 4. spoon in right hand; 5. chimney; 6. left ear; 7. filament; 8. stamp; 9. strings; 10. rivet; 11. trigger; 12. tail; 13. leg; 14. shadow; 15. bowling ball in right hand; 16. net; 17. left hand; 18. horn of Victrola; 19. arm and powder puff in mirror image; 20. diamond.)

Source: S.J. Gould (1981). *The Mismeasure of Man*. New York: W.W. Norton & Co.

This test measures a child's capacity for learning without relying on measurements of how much the child already knows. Therefore, the test is described as *culture-fair*, or *culture-free*, because it does not give one cultural group an advantage over another.

Research also suggests that minority groups may be victims of a **self-fulfilling prophecy:** they have acquired low expectations about their academic performances on tests designed by the white community, and these low expectations further lower their self-confidence and thus their test scores.

Not only minority children fall victim to the self-fulfilling prophecy, however. Imagine the effect that being labelled "below average" or "a slow learner" has on a child's self-image. Such labelling of students may also affect the administrators of the tests—the teachers. In a famous study, teachers were told that a few children, actually selected at random, possessed previously undetected high abilities and potential. At the end of the school year, it was found that these children showed significantly better achievement than their classmates. Presumably, the teachers had in some way conveyed their expectations to these students that they were especially bright and would do well in school (Rosenthal & Jacobson, 1968). Although this study has been criticized for its methodological faults, the basic finding has been supported by many later studies. People will respond according to the expectations of others.

It is dangerous to underestimate the complexity of the student–teacher relationship and the effect of labelling on children's performances. Labels do persist, and children do tend to live up to them, whether they be "class clown," "good child," "underachiever," or "bright." Insofar as teachers' expectations affect their own behaviour toward children, these expectations apparently do have an influence on children's learning.

It is not always necessary to use tests to assess children's progress. Teachers, parents, and caregivers can learn a good deal about how to proceed by informally observing what children do and say. By merely giving the child a book and listening to him read, a skilled teacher can determine many of the skills that he still has to learn. Perhaps the most dramatic example of the need for caution in the use and interpretation of tests is in the area of learning disabilities.

Learning Disabilities

The term **learning disability** is used to identify the difficulties of a broad category of children who often have no more in common than the label itself. In school systems today, children are described as "learning disabled" when they require special attention in the classroom—that is, when they have trouble learning to read, write, spell, or do arithmetic, despite having normal intelligence. In the absence of any obvious sensory or motor defect (such as poor vision, deafness, or cerebral palsy), these children are described as having learning disabilities. Of learning-disabled children, 80 percent are boys.

Day after day, learning-disabled children face their own inability to do things that their classmates seem to accomplish effortlessly. With each failure, these children become increasingly insecure about their ability to perform. Sometimes, this insecurity leads to a growing sense of hopelessness or helplessness. Classmates tend to avoid choosing the child who does not succeed. Children with learning disabilities have difficulty with social skills, as well as with academic skills. They may become increasingly isolated from peers or even from family members. Some become shy and withdrawn, some boastful, whereas others strike out with impulsive or angry outbursts. Academic confidence is central to the school-age child's self-esteem. It is difficult to find ways in which the learning-disabled child can develop feelings of confidence and, as a result, experience success in other areas.

The study of learning disabilities has been a challenging puzzle with a confusing array of expert opinions on symptoms, causes, and treatments. Many of the classic controversies of child development are evident in the questions raised. Is this child abnormal, deficient, or disabled, or is she just different in temperament and style? Is

self-fulfilling prophecy An expectation that helps to bring about the predicted event, which consequently strengthens the expectation.

Question to Ponder

Do you think Canadian schools should use IQ tests? What do you think are the advantages and disadvantages of using them?

learning disability Extreme difficulty in learning school subjects such as reading, writing, or math, despite normal intelligence and absence of sensory or motor defects.

Question to Ponder

In what ways can computers and other technology be used to assist children with learning disabilities?

dyslexia A learning disability involving reading; unusual difficulty in learning how to read.

dysgraphia A learning disability involving writing.

dyscalculia A learning disability involving mathematics.

attention deficit/hyperactivity disorder (ADHD) A disorder including three subtypes. One subtype involves problems with attention and distractibility. Another involves hyperactivity or excessive movement. Another subtype is the combination of the two.

her problem due to organic dysfunction or to her environment at home or at school? Should she be "treated" medically, "managed" with behavioural management programs, or "educated" creatively?

Before the 1950s, there were "slow readers" and children who did poorly on school tasks, but they were not labelled as learning disabled. If they had no obvious emotional or physical problems, it was assumed that they were simply "dumb." Teachers then began to notice that some children who appeared to be quite bright in other respects nonetheless had trouble with school tasks, especially reading. To explain this disparity, the concept of "minimal brain dysfunction" was introduced. It was assumed that there was something wrong with the child's brain but that the abnormality was too subtle (or "minimal") to show up in other ways. Although many authorities still believe that learning disabilities are caused by some kind of subtle brain abnormality, the label "minimal brain dysfunction" is now seldom used (Silver, 1990).

There are two main groups of learning-disabled children. The first group includes children with **dyslexia** (difficulty in learning how to read); many of these children also have **dysgraphia** (difficulty with writing). Others may have **dyscalculia,** difficulty with math.

The second main group of learning-disabled children has **attention deficit/ hyperactivity disorder (ADHD),** the inability to focus attention on anything long enough to learn it. Many of these children are also hyperactive—they can't sit still, and they are constantly getting into trouble. Children with ADHD are likely to do poorly in a variety of school subjects for the simple reason that they are not spending enough "time on task." Virginia Douglas, a Canadian researcher from McGill University, was one of the first to recognize that hyperactive children often have problems with inattention. Her research in the 1970s prompted the American Psychiatric Association to recognize hyperactivity as a disorder for the first time in 1980 (Diller, 1998).

Dyslexia

Because dyslexic children often confuse letters such as *b* and *d,* or read *star* as *rats,* it was believed for a long time that these children simply "see things backward." But very few of them have anything wrong with their eyes. In other contexts, dyslexic children have no perceptual problems—for example, they have no trouble finding their way around (so they are not deficient in spatial relationships), and they may be exceptionally good at putting together puzzles. Why, then, do they make errors like

Some learning disabilities may be helped by educational management that works on improving specific skills.

confusing *b* and *d*? The answer is that this is a very common kind of error for beginning readers. Most children make reversal errors when they are first learning how to read, but most get through this stage quickly. Dyslexic children remain stuck in the early stages of reading (Richardson, 1992; Vogel, 1989).

Dyslexic children also have problems outside of the school context. In fact, many have a pervasive problem involving the use of language. Many of these children were delayed in learning how to speak, or their speech is at a lower developmental level than that of their age mates. Their difficulty in naming letters and written words is matched by a similar difficulty in naming objects or colours—it takes them longer than usual to pull an ordinary word like *key* or *blue* out of their memory. They also have difficulty in "hearing" the two separate syllables in a two-syllable word, or in recognizing that the spoken word *sat* starts with an *s* sound and ends with a *t* sound (Shaywitz, Shaywitz, Fletcher, & Escobar, 1991; Wagner & Torgerson, 1987). They have pervasive problems with the sound system involved in reading (Snowling, Defty, & Goulandris, 1996). Difficulties with reading are not limited to cognitive effects. They can have an effect on children's self-perceptions and peer acceptance. Dyslexic children in grades one and two perceived themselves as less capable in school and as less accepted by classmates than did other children (Klein & Magill-Evans, 1998).

Although the hypothesized "brain dysfunction" that underlies dyslexia has still not been identified, it is clear that heredity plays a role in the disorder. Many dyslexic children have a parent who had trouble learning how to read as a child or a sibling with the same problem (Scarborough, 1989). It is also interesting to note that dyslexia tends to run in the same families that exhibit left-handedness. However, left-handedness itself is only weakly associated with dyslexia—most dyslexics are right-handed (Hiscock & Kinsbourne, 1987).

The treatment of dyslexia generally involves intensive remedial work in reading and language. Many educational programs for learning-disabled children provide carefully sequenced tutorial instruction in reading. Some programs emphasize high-interest materials; others emphasize early success. Stanton (1981) emphasizes the need to build the child's confidence in any approach. The teacher must first simplify the problem for the child in order to reduce anxiety about the unknown. He must then respond to the child with an attitude of genuineness, unconditional acceptance, and empathy, all of which make the child believe in and expect success. Although no single educational plan seems to work with all children, most programs have some record of success. The graduates of one especially successful program—a British residential school for dyslexic children—are generally able to go on to college. In contrast, the children who attend the least successful programs generally become high school dropouts (Bruck, 1987).

In addition to providing remedial work for children with dyslexia, intervention programs need to consider the impact of the children's disabilities on other members of the families. Other family members may need support because a child's learning disability increases parental stress and alters family functioning and sibling interaction (Dyson, 1996).

For children with attention deficit disorder and hyperactivity, there is no single treatment or approach that "solves" the problem.

Attention Deficit/Hyperactivity Disorder

For every symptom in the broad category of learning disabilities, there are a variety of possible causes. Just as people experience headaches for a number of reasons, an inability to focus attention may arise from any one of several conditions. Some of the suggested causes of ADHD include malnutrition, lead poisoning, organic brain damage, heredity, intrauterine abnormalities, prenatal exposure to drugs like "crack," and lack of oxygen during fetal development or childbirth. Many children with symptoms of learning disabilities are known to have had some irregularity at birth; premature births are common among these children (Buchoff, 1990). According to recent studies in neuroscience, some children with ADHD have abnormalities in the frontal lobes of the cortex, an area of the brain that regulates planful, goal-oriented behaviour (Aman, Roberts, & Pennington, 1998). Recently, researchers have identified a gene—DRD4—that may make some individuals more susceptible to developing ADHD (Rutter et al., 1999a).

An estimated 3 to 5 percent of school-age children have ADHD (American Psychiatric Association, 1994). Boys with ADHD outnumber girls four to one. Just as there is variation in the causes of ADHD, there is variation in its manifestation. There are three subtypes of ADHD: one subtype has problems primarily with inattention. These children do not pay attention to details. Their school work appears messy and careless. They are disorganized and often flit from one unfinished activity to another. They are easily distracted and forgetful, and they have trouble listening to instructions. Another subtype has problems primarily with hyperactivity. They have trouble sitting still and tend to fidget and squirm more than other children the same age. They run, climb, and talk excessively. The last subtype has problems both with inattention and with hyperactivity.

There is no one correct answer to the problems of ADHD children. Some of the "answers" have been learned quite by accident, as illustrated by the history of one type of drug treatment.

Several years ago, it was discovered that some children who displayed symptoms of hyperactivity responded to the drug Ritalin, a stimulant in the amphetamine family. These hyperactive children, whose symptoms had not improved with tranquilizers or depressants, actually calmed down in response to this drug. Ritalin lowered their threshold of sensitivity to events around them and allowed them to focus consistently on one task. The use of Ritalin in Canada quadrupled between 1990 and 1997 (Diller, 1998). Although not all ADHD children improve by taking Ritalin, for those who do improve, the benefits can outweigh the risk of possible side effects when the treatment program is monitored carefully. Not only does their school work get better, but their relationships with family members and peers also improve (Campbell & Spencer, 1988). However, some critics of Ritalin worry about long-term effects of the drug. There may be psychological effects. Children, and parents, may attribute improvements in children's behaviour to Ritalin and become psychologically dependent on the children's taking their pills to control their behaviour. The use of Ritalin in older children and adults is complicated by the fact that the drug produces a high when taken in a larger dosage than prescribed. Will adolescents be tempted to abuse the drug or to sell their medication to others? In 1998, there were media reports of adolescents in Manitoba trafficking in Ritalin. Are there physical effects caused by long-term usage of Ritalin? Cylert, another drug used to treat ADHD, was banned by Health Canada in 1999. Cylert was associated with an increase in fatal liver disease among children on the medication.

An alternative form of treatment for children with ADHD is *educational management,* which takes place both at home and at school. For some children, it can be used instead of medication; for other children, it can be used in addition to medication. In most cases, this method makes an attempt to restructure a child's environment by simplifying it, reducing distractions, making expectations more explicit, and, in general, reducing confusion. The specific educational plan depends on the theoretical position of the therapist or educator. Cruickshank (1977) advocates an instructional program involving various training tasks that require specific skills. Diagnostic tests are used to identify any deficits that the child demonstrates. The program consists of careful, systematic, and progressively more difficult exercises to correct the problems. A program by Ross (1977) focuses more on the development of selective attention. The specific task does not really matter. Instead, by careful management of the instruction and the rewards, the teacher helps the child to listen and to observe more precisely. The child might work on perceptual exercises or on other general skills. Roberts, White, and McLaughlin (1998) offer a number of practical suggestions to teachers of children with ADHD:

- Allow children to have input into class rules and consequences. Children comply more with rules they helped develop.

- Seat ADHD children at the front, close to the teacher's desk. ADHD children seated in the back can be distracted by classmates in front of them.

- Keep the top of the ADHD child's desk free of distraction by removing all items not being used.

- Give short assignments with breaks between them, rather than a long assignment with a longer period of time to complete it.

- Find opportunities to praise the ADHD child more often than he is scolded. Scolding, especially if it is loud and angry, does not improve the behaviour of ADHD children; instead, this type of feedback can worsen the behaviour.

A part of any treatment program is concern for the child's emotional well-being. Untreated, children with ADHD are at risk for poor academic achievement, school suspensions and expulsions, poor peer and family relations, anxiety and depression, aggression, conduct problems and delinquency, early substance abuse, and driving accidents and speeding violations (Barkley, 1997). Of children with ADHD, 30 to 50 percent have symptoms that persist into adulthood (Barkley, 1997).

Some ADHD children have diagnoses for ADHD, as well as for other disorders such as *conduct disorder* or *oppositional-defiant disorder.* Having more than one disorder is called *comorbidity.* The key features of conduct disorder are aggression, destruction of property, deceitfulness or theft, and serious violation of rules (American Psychiatric Association, 1994). Children with oppositional-defiant disorder often lose their tempers, are easily annoyed, argue with adults, defy rules and requests, deliberately annoy other people, and blame others for their mistakes or misbehaviour (American Psychiatric Association, 1994). Children who have both ADHD and conduct disorder are more likely to engage in criminal activity as adults than are children with one or none of the disorders (Babinski, Hartsough, & Lambert, 1999). When researchers study the long-term effects of ADHD, they must distinguish whether the effects come from ADHD, from other comorbid disorders, or from a combination of disorders.

Summary and Conclusions

Piaget proposed that during middle childhood, children enter the concrete operational period of cognitive development. Children are therefore able to make logical inferences, think about physical transformations, perform reversible mental operations, and, in general, form hypotheses about the physical world. Children are able to theorize about persons, objects, and events in their immediate experience. If children are given specific instruction in concrete operational skills when they reach a state of readiness, it appears that they will move out of the preoperational stage earlier.

Piaget proposed that education should recognize and respond to the unique character of thinking in middle childhood. Since children are active learners, he proposed that hands-on, discovery learning should occur. Teachers should guide students and structure the learning experience so that learning itself becomes an intrinsic reward for the child. External reinforcement, such as praise from the teacher, may not produce the most optimal motivation for learning. Children should be encouraged to make inferences about objects and their relationships in the world by themselves—rather than have them made for them.

Piaget did not offer the only theory of cognitive growth in middle childhood. Information-processing theorists describe the children's control processes that provide memory strategies, as well as the higher-order control processes, such as metacognition. The child's monitoring of her own thinking, memory, knowledge, goals, and actions becomes more developed during middle childhood. This development, in turn, leads to more skills in thinking, learning, and understanding that change the way the child can deal with the world.

Schools are a primary site of formal learning for middle childhood. Children learn the basics of reading, writing, and arithmetic. Children can be taught to read with either a phonics method or a whole language approach. Controversy over which approach is better continues. Educators have attempted to determine the optimal ways to encourage competency and critical thinking in learning. Teachers must help children learn control processes and thinking skills, rather than encourage them to memorize rote lists of unrelated facts. Success in school depends on the child's achievement motivation and on the values of the culture in which the child is reared. If the child's subculture or culture emphasizes success in areas other than academ-

ics, the school will not be an important arena for competition for that child. Computers are another tool that educators are employing to teach children. Computer-assisted instruction and the use of computers for programming logic and writing skills are common.

The assessment of individual differences in intelligence and the ability to profit from schooling is a long-standing concern in developmental psychology. In the 19th century, for example, the French psychologist Alfred Binet developed the first intelligence test. This test was later imported to America and translated into English by Lewis Terman, who called his test the Stanford-Binet. The early psychometricians believed that intelligence was a fixed, inherited characteristic. The contemporary view of IQ testing makes no such assumption, but rather believes that children's intelligence is determined by a mix of heredity and environment.

Researchers have also disagreed on the nature of intelligence. Some, like those who designed the Stanford-Binet test, represent IQ as a single attribute, while others, such as the designers of the Wechsler IQ test (WISC-III), measure abilities in multiple areas of cognition. In general, today's theorists suggest that intelligence is not unitary and may consist of as many as seven discrete competencies. They also believe that all aspects of human thinking and problem solving are not tested on standard tests of intelligence.

Intelligence tests often come under fire because of the cultural biases and test abuses associated with them. In general, scores are higher for white, middle-class students and lower for members of minority groups. Moreover, placing children in labelled-ability categories may create a self-fulfilling prophecy because of teachers' expectations for the children's performance.

As with physical and motor development during middle childhood, some children are challenged by learning disabilities. Dyslexia and attention deficit/hyperactivity disorder (ADHD) are two such problems. Dyslexia causes great difficulty for children in learning to read—despite the fact that they have normal intelligence and no sensory or motor defects. It is believed that dyslexia results from some subtle type of brain abnormality that may be inherited. The basic problem for children with ADHD is an inability to focus their attention on material long enough to learn it. Drug therapy using Ritalin has been found helpful for many of these children.

Key Terms and Concepts

attention deficit/hyperactivity disorder (ADHD) (p. 424)

behavioural objectives (p. 421)

comprehension (p. 407)

criterion-referenced test (p. 417)

decoding (p. 407)

deviation IQ (p. 419)

diagnostic-prescriptive teaching (p. 417)

dyscalculia (p. 424)

dysgraphia (p. 424)

dyslexia (p. 424)

intelligence quotient (p. 419)

learning disability (p. 423)

logical inference (p. 400)

mental age (p. 419)

metacognition (p. 405)

norm-referenced test (p. 417)

phonics (p. 407)

self-fulfilling prophecy (p. 423)

whole language learning (p. 407)

Questions to Review

1. How does Piaget's preoperational stage differ from the concrete operational stage characteristic of middle childhood?

2. Explain how Piagetian concepts of learning and cognitive development would be applied to educational practices.

3. How do information-processing theorists view the human mind? Explain some control processes and higher-order control processes that are important in middle childhood as they are defined by information-processing theorists.

4. Describe the new demands and expectations that children face when they enter school, and discuss some of the factors that determine how well they adjust to this transition.

5. What are some strategies that teachers can use to help students become competent learners and critical thinkers?

6. Describe two approaches to teaching children to read.

7. Describe different ways in which computers can be used as educational devices in the classroom.

8. List several factors that determine a child's success in school.

9. What are some of the uses and abuses of intelligence testing?

10. Compare and contrast a criterion-referenced test and a norm-referenced test.

11. Compare and contrast the varying definitions of intelligence.

12. What types of competencies are not usually measured by diagnostic and achievement tests?

13. What are behavioural objectives, and in what sense do they test schools rather than students?

14. Discuss different types of learning disabilities, including their symptoms, causes, and treatments.

Weblinks

www.ctf-fce.ca/
Canadian Teachers' Federation
This excellent site has a wealth of information on hot issues and teaching in Canada, as well as numerous press releases related to education and a list of publications for sale.

www.oise.utoronto.ca/~mpress/eduweb.html
Canadian Education on the Web
This Web site has links to sites related to elementary, secondary, and postsecondary education in Canada. It includes organizations, resources, and online, full text journals.

www.hc-sc.gc.ca/hpb-dgps/therapeut/zfiles/english/publicat/adhd_survey_e.html
Survey of Attention Deficit Hyperactivity Disorder
This site, sponsored by Health Canada, provides a 40-page paper detailing the results of a survey of Canadian physicians about the diagnosis and treatment of ADHD.

Middle Childhood: Personality and Social Development

Then the child moved ten times round the seasons
Skated over ten clear frozen streams
Words like "when you're older" must appease him
... and promises of someday make his dreams.

JONI MITCHELL
"THE CIRCLE GAME"

Outline

CHAPTER 14

Objectives

By the time you have finished this chapter, you should be able to do the following:

✔ Describe different styles of parenting and their effects on children's personality and behaviour.

✔ List several factors that affect a child's ability to cope with stressful events.

✔ Describe the effects of divorce on children.

✔ Describe the factors that can lead to child abuse and list the various types of psychological abuse.

✔ Explain the development of social cognition and moral reasoning during middle childhood.

✔ Summarize the characteristic features of childhood friendships and peer groups.

✔ Explain how children develop racial awareness and how their attitudes toward members of other groups change as they grow older.

✔ Describe the relationship between a child's academic ability, popularity in the peer group, and self-esteem.

It may seem a bit dramatic to say that children have their own culture, but in many ways it is true. The world of the preadolescent child at play is not the world in which adults live. The child's world has its own customs, language, rules, games—even its own distinctive beliefs and values. What is this "culture of childhood," and what role does it play in a child's development?

Many times, children seem to caricature adults. We have seen how a 2-year-old's fierce demands for autonomy resemble those of a tyrannical adult. A 4-year-old's jealousy and rage may strike an all-too-familiar chord. The customs and rituals of middle childhood sometimes mirror elaborate adult social conventions; in some ways, childhood rituals are even more strict and demanding. A child may pay almost superstitious attention to rituals, such as not stepping on sidewalk cracks for fear of breaking someone's back. Rhymes must be said just so, and rigid rules dictate the one right way to play each game. Peer relationships may also be ritualized. Children may make lifelong pledges in private clubs and in "blood brother" fraternities.

Children adopt the rhymes, rituals, stunts, and customs of childhood without help from adults. Some of their games and rituals have been transmitted from older to younger children for countless generations; this occurs in almost every culture. Many childish chants can be traced to medieval times, and some games, such as jacks, go back to the Roman era (Opie & Opie, 1959).

Children seem to derive potency from mastering the bits and pieces of a culture, from learning how to do things correctly. Perhaps the rituals and rules of middle childhood are practice for adulthood, exercises in learning the detailed behaviour that is expected of adults. Perhaps they are a form of security, a familiar framework of rules that allows the child to feel both at home and competent in an otherwise bewildering world. These rules may help children to master intense emotions or to defuse intense peer relationships, such as victim and conqueror. Perhaps they also teach complex social concepts like justice, power, or loyalty. Although we are not certain of the precise purpose of middle childhood's traditions, the phenomenon of a special culture of childhood exists in almost every society.

Continuing Family Influences

Families continue to be one of the most important socializing influences for school-age children. Children acquire values, expectations, and patterns of behaviour from their families, and they do so in a number of ways (see also Chapters 3 and 11). Parents and siblings serve as models for appropriate and inappropriate behaviour, and they reward and punish children's behaviour. Expanding cognitive abilities allow children to learn a wide range of social concepts and rules, both those that are explicitly taught and those that are only implied. Finally, social learning takes place in the context of relationships. Relationships are sometimes close and secure, sometimes anxiety provoking, and sometimes full of conflict.

In this section, we shall examine the family as a context for development. We shall also examine how families are changing and how stress in the family influences personality development in children.

Parent–Child Interactions and Relationships

In the elementary school years, the nature of parent–child interactions changes. Children express less direct anger toward their parents, and they are less likely to whine, yell, or hit than when they were younger. For their part, parents are less concerned with promoting autonomy and establishing daily routines and more concerned with children's work habits and achievement (Lamb, Ketterlinus, & Fracasso, 1992). School-age children need less—but more subtle—monitoring of their behaviour than previously, although parental monitoring is still important. Researchers find, for example, that well-monitored boys receive higher grades than those less monitored (Crosler et al., 1990).

What might be considered optimal parenting? The experts' answers to this question have differed over the years. Contemporary research emphasizes that one primary goal of parental socialization practices is to increase the child's self-regulated behaviour. When a parent relies on verbal reasoning and suggestions, the child tends to negotiate rather than react with defiance (Lamb et al., 1992).

Parental reasoning with the child (or using induction) is related both to prosocial behaviour and to compliance with social rules. Parents who use other-oriented induction—who remind their children of the effect of their actions on others—tend to have children who are more popular and who manifest internalized moral standards. In contrast, when parents use power-assertive socialization, their children do not develop internalized standards and controls. In several studies, for example, children who complied with adult demands when adults were present but not when they were absent were more likely to have parents who used power-assertion. Out-of-sight compliance is associated with parents who use other-oriented induction (Maccoby, 1992).

Parents are more successful in promoting children's self-regulated behaviour if they gradually increase the children's involvement in family decisions. In a series of studies on parental dialogue and discipline, Eleanor Maccoby (1992) concluded that children are best adjusted when their parents foster what she calls *co-regulation*. These parents build cooperation and shared responsibility. They look forward to the teenage years, when they expect their children will make

Parents teach the value of warmth and affection by their own behaviour.

most decisions for themselves. In preparation, they engage in frequent discussions and negotiations with their children. These parents see themselves as building the framework for responsible decision making.

When we look at parents who are sensitive to the developmental stages of their children the concept of *scaffolding* is useful (see Chapter 7). Children learn about the social world in complex social contexts accompanied by parents or by other more competent partners (Rogoff, 1990). Imagine a family attending a large wedding. Socially competent parents help their children anticipate what will happen and discuss expected events and behaviours before arrival. They may discuss the meaning of the event and of specific practices. After arrival, parents cue their children on expectations for age-appropriate behaviour. Only small parts of the broad set of shared meanings for "marriage and weddings" are conveyed at any one time. Of course, children also learn by observing the behaviours of their parents, older siblings, and other more socially advanced wedding guests.

As children grow and mature, the quality of the ongoing parenting relationship continues to be crucial. Family relationships are not one-way, but reciprocal. Youniss (1983) argues that socialization should not be viewed as a process in which control shifts from parents to child as the child becomes more autonomous and self-regulating. Rather, it is a process of mutual or shared coregulation throughout the remainder of the participants' lives—until one or the other ends the relationship. In fact, Maccoby (1992) suggests that enduring parental influence stems from the strength and health of relationships that parents and children have jointly constructed during middle childhood. In some cases, parents' contributing to the coregulation inhibits their children; in other cases, it enables them to grow in autonomy within the relationship. In addition, interactions with parents allow children to practise and refine social skills that will later improve their peer interactions.

In general, when family members have joint goals and shared meanings, or scripts, the family as a whole grows and shows optimal development. Coregulation is not a function of any particular cultural group, but is instead something that occurs in diverse family settings. In some cases, it produces beneficial results; in others, the results are more mixed. When coregulation does not exist within a family, the outcome is likely to be more negative. Children in such a family may be at risk for a variety of social and behaviour problems.

Question to Ponder

What can society do to help families that lack coregulation?

Challenges Faced by Families

Poverty and Households Headed by Mothers Over 1.5 million Canadian children live in poverty (Campaign 2000, 1997). These children must overcome a number of problems:

> It means not having enough food to eat. It means living in houses that are in ill-repair. It means not having warm clothes in the winter. It means not having access to the kinds of play and recreation facilities that children need to grow and develop. It means being less likely to finish high school and even less likely to go to college or university, which means being less likely to find a job. (CICH, 1994, p. 113)

Data from the National Longitudinal Survey of Children and Youth indicate that about 57 000 Canadian families with children do not have enough food (McIntyre, Connor, & Warren, 1998).

Why do so many families live in poverty? Some families are unemployed. Other families are working poor—the parents are employed but their jobs are low paying or part time. Indeed, one-third of Canadian families that experience hunger are dual-wage-earner families in which neither parent earns a living wage (McIntyre et al., 1998). Single-parent families headed by mothers are more likely to be living in poverty

Children in close-knit, adaptable families generally tend to be the best equipped to cope with stressful situations.

than any other type of family. Disturbingly, 89 percent of children under 7 who live with single mothers who have never married are poor (CICH, 1994). In 1991, single mothers accounted for 13 percent of all Canadian families (*Canada Year Book*, 1997). Interestingly, this is about the same percentage as in 1931, but the reasons for single-parent families have changed dramatically. In 1931, most single mothers were widowed, whereas in 1991, most were divorced, were separated, or had never married (*Canada Year Book*, 1997). Poverty is also more common among Aboriginal families than it is among families from other ethnic backgrounds (McIntyre et al., 1998). Nearly 70 percent of Aboriginal families living off reserves have incomes below the poverty line (CCSD, 1996).

Families and Stress Poverty is a source of stress for both parents and children, but there are other life events that are stressful for children and their families—for example, moving to a different town, being left back in school, or suffering a serious illness or injury. What are some of the factors that determine whether or not a child is able to cope constructively?

One factor is the sheer number of stressful situations in a child's life—a child who can deal successfully with a single stressful event may be overwhelmed if she is forced to deal with several all at once (Hetherington, 1984). A second factor is the child's perception or understanding of the event. For example, the first day of school is a major event in a child's life. A child who knows what to expect and who can use this milestone as a sign of her increasing maturity will have less difficulty dealing with this new experience.

The research literature clearly indicates that close-knit, adaptable families with open communication patterns and problem-solving skills are better able to weather stressful events (Brenner, 1984). Social support systems, such as neighbours, relatives, friendship networks, or self-help groups are also valuable.

Stress and coping do not always occur as single events; instead, they often exist as ongoing or transitional processes. A young child who is moving to a new neighbourhood may experience anticipatory anxiety before the move. The child will then have to make immediate short-term adjustments to the new setting, and he will need some long-term coping skills to deal with establishing new relationships and recovering from the loss of old ones. According to the National Longitudinal Survey of Children and Youth, most Canadian children have experienced a move—only one in four 10- and 11-year-olds has never moved. In general, there are no lasting effects of one or two moves. But compared with children who have never moved, children who have moved often (more than three times) are more likely to have difficulties in school, behavioural problems, and substance abuse habits (DeWit, Offord, & Braun, 1998). Children have an even greater risk of these problems if they also come from homes where there are inconsistent and punitive parenting practices and if they have weak attachments to their parents, low academic achievement, and low participation in extracurricular activities.

Many personality traits influence children's ability to cope with stressful environments. Over the past 30 years, Emmy Werner (1989) has studied a group of what she calls *resilient children*. These children, who were born on one of the Hawaiian islands, lived in family environments marred by poverty, parental conflict or divorce, alcoholism, and mental illness. Yet they developed into self-confident, successful, and emotionally stable adults. Most children reared under such conditions do not do well, so Werner was interested in learning how these children managed to thrive in spite of an unfavourable environment. She found that they had been temperamentally "easy" and loveable babies who had developed a close attachment to a parent or grandparent in the first year of life. Later, if that parent or grandparent was no longer available, these children had the ability to find someone else—another adult or even a sibling or a friend—to give them the emotional support they needed. "The resilience literature portrays a hopeful picture of bouncing back from negative experience" (Yawney, 1996, p. 134).

Children of Divorce

Nearly 40 percent of all marriages in Canada now end in divorce (Baker, 1996). An increase in divorce has led to more children with parents who have been divorced (sometimes more than once). Children born in the 1980s were three times more likely by the time they were 6 to have divorced parents than were children born in the 1960s (Ross et al., 1996). Even so, it is important to remember that divorced families are still a minority compared with nondivorced families (referred to as *intact families*). In 1994–1995, 84.2 percent of Canadian children under the age of 12 were living in intact families (Ross et al., 1996).

The breakup of the family affects children in a number of ways. We have seen that both parents have strong effects on the development of their children; however, a divorce means that both parents will no longer be equally available to their children. These children are also part of a family that has been under tension for a long period of time. They know that relationships have been disturbed, and they may have heard the word *divorce* spoken aloud (or shouted) in their homes for months or even years. They have seen one parent leave and may fear that the other parent will also abandon them. They may feel sad, confused, angry, or anxious; they may become depressed or disruptive, or they may do poorly in school. Many children (particularly younger ones) feel that they are to blame for the divorce—that if only they had been better, maybe their parents would not have split up. They may try to bring their parents back together, perhaps by being very good or by fantasizing about a reconciliation (Hetherington, 1989, 1992; Wallerstein, Corbin, & Lewis, 1988). The following case study presents the acting-out behaviour that can accompany hostility between parents.

> Bridget was 12 years old—the middle of three sisters. Her parents had gotten married when the mother discovered she was pregnant. They had fought throughout the marriage, and lately the fighting was constant. Divorce and threats of leaving were regularly heard in the family. Bridget had been an honour student. She began to have serious difficulty with her studies and started to cut classes. Things worsened at home. She left school with three older boys and borrowed her mother's car without permission; the same afternoon, the four were picked up for speeding—160 kilometres away from home. The police called the parents to come and pick up their children.

> Before Bridget's parents saw their daughter, the police youth counsellor said: "You are angry now and what she did was wrong, but you must remember that when children do things like this they are crying for your attention, guidance, and help."

Relationships with both parents change during and after a divorce. Children may become defiant and argumentative; in adolescence, they may emotionally disengage themselves from their families. Or, children may often be forced to become a sounding board for their parents, listening to each parent describe the faults of the other. They may be at the centre of a custody battle and may be asked to choose between parents. The parents may compete for the affection of the children and may try to bribe them with gifts or privileges. The parents themselves are often under considerable stress right after the divorce and may be incapable of providing either warmth or control—they may be less affectionate, inconsistent with discipline, uncommunicative, or unsupportive. Also, children may become upset when their parents start dating or establishing relationships with others. A boy who is living with his mother may take over the role of "man of the house" and may feel threatened when a rival appears on the scene (Hetherington, 1989).

As a group, children from divorced families have a higher rate of problems than do children from intact families. Problems include academic difficulties, behavioural problems, depression, withdrawal, and relationship problems with siblings, peers, or parents. About 20 to 25 percent of children from divorced families have at least one of these problems, compared with 10 percent of children from intact families (Hetherington & Stanley-Hagan, 1999). It is important to note that even though children from divorced families, as a group, have more problems, the majority do not have problems. The way that children respond to divorce is influenced by a number of factors that either increase or decrease the risk for problems. Perhaps the five most important ones are the following:

1. The amount of hostility accompanying the divorce. If there is a great deal of hostility and bitterness preceding or following a divorce, it is harder for children to adjust to the situation. Ongoing legal battles (over custody, for example) or squabbles over the division of property or child care make the situation much more difficult for everyone involved (Rutter & Garmezy, 1983). On the other hand, if a divorce results in considerably less family conflict, children may do better after the divorce than they were while living in a high-conflict intact family (Hetherington & Stanley-Hagan, 1999).

2. The amount of actual change in the child's life. If the child continues to live in the same home, attends the same school, and has the same friends, there tends to be less difficulty in adjusting to separation and divorce. In contrast, if the child's daily life is disrupted in major ways—moving back and forth from one parent's household to the other's, losing old friends, entering a new school—it will be difficult for the child to build self-confidence and to have a sense of order in her world. The more changes there are, particularly right after the divorce, the more difficult the adjustment will be (Hetherington & Camara, 1984).

3. The nature of the parent–child relationship. Long-term involvement and emotional support from a parent—or, better still, from both parents—help the child to make a successful adjustment. In fact, the nature of the ongoing parent–child interaction is much more important than whether or not both parents are present in the home (Rutter & Garmezy, 1983). Parents who are able to maintain an authoritative parenting style are best able to help their children adjust to divorce (Hetherington, Bridges, & Isabella, 1998). Parental distress has an effect on children's adjustment because it makes it more difficult for parents to parent effectively. Parental distress is described as having an indirect effect on child adjustment because its effects are mediated by changes in parenting behaviour.

4. The age of the child at the time of the divorce. Preschool children do not understand that divorce is permanent, and they react with separation anxiety, decreased play and enjoyment, and fear of abandonment (Arnold, 1990). Because they don't understand the concept of time, they will not automatically know what it means to see daddy once a week (Schneider & Zuckerberg, 1996). They often develop reconciliation fantasies that may persist for many years. However, by 10 years after the divorce, many of these children are coping better than are children who were older when their parents divorced (Arnold, 1990). Children who are 6 to 8 years old react to divorce by becoming frightened and angry. They grieve and develop reconciliation fantasies. And 10 years after the divorce, they have feelings of powerlessness and anxiety about independence. Children who are 9 to 12 years old are especially prone to loyalty conflicts and to choosing sides. About half experience a sharp drop in school work. And 10 years later, their memories of the divorce are worse than are those of younger children. Adolescents react to divorce by becoming concerned about their parents' motives and by withdrawing from their parents. Some become depressed and angry. Furthermore, 10 years later, they often worry that they too will have troubled marriages (Arnold, 1990).

5. The child's characteristics. Children who have easy temperaments, who are intelligent, socially well adjusted, and have high self-esteem adapt better to divorce than do other children (Hetherington & Stanley-Hagan, 1999). On the other hand, children who have difficult temperaments, who are not socially well adjusted, or who have low self-esteem tend not to adjust well to divorce. Problems that existed before the divorce are often worsened by the divorce.

While some children adjust to a stepparent and stepsiblings, others greet the family reconfiguration with such emotions as anger, anxiety, or guilt.

Child Abuse

One of the most serious and dramatic examples of family breakdown is the phenomenon of **child abuse**. Instead of encouraging and reinforcing the bond between parent and child, the child abuser destroys the expectations of love, trust, and dependence so essential to the young child. Severe developmental problems frequently result.

We shall define *child abuse*, and distinguish it from neglect, by using the term to refer only to physical and psychological injuries that are *intentionally* inflicted on a child by an adult (Burgess & Conger, 1978). *Neglect*, in contrast, results from parents' or caregivers' failure to act rather than from their injurious actions. The consequences can be equally tragic: children die of neglect as well as of abuse. Here, however, we shall discuss only the physical and emotional damage that is intentionally inflicted on children: extreme psychological punishment, such as constant ridicule or criticism; violent physical punishment resulting in injury or death; and sexual abuse.

It can be difficult to distinguish between child abuse and ordinary punishment. What qualifies as child abuse is a relative question and must be viewed in light of community standards. Historically, many cultures have condoned and even encouraged physical mistreatment that we consider shocking and brutal. It was used to discipline and educate children, to exorcise evil spirits, or to placate the gods. Furthermore, some cultures imbued certain forms of physical cruelty, such as foot binding, skull shaping, or ritual scarring, with a deep symbolic meaning. Traditionally, children were viewed as the property of their parents, and parents had the legal right to treat them in any way they saw fit. Infanticide or the abandonment of unwanted babies was a time-honoured method for desperate adults trying to cope with their children's hunger, illegitimacy, or birth defects (Radbill, 1974). In general, we have different standards now: causing injury or death to a child is considered to be a serious crime. But, sadly, it is not an uncommon one.

The Incidence of Child Abuse In the United States, official reports of child abuse and neglect now number almost one million a year; three children die every day as a result of physical abuse or neglect. These figures may be shocking, but they are not

child abuse Intentional psychological or physical injuries inflicted on a child.

FOCUS ON DIVERSITY

Stepfamilies and Blended Families

According to the National Longitudinal Survey of Children and Youth, 8.6 percent of Canadian children under the age of 12 live in stepfamilies, and 6.1 percent live in blended families (Cheal, 1996). *Stepfamilies* are created when a parent marries someone who does not have children. All of the children in the stepfamily are biologically related to the same parent. The unrelated parent is the stepparent. In *blended families*, the children in the family differ in their relatedness to the parents. The family might include the mother's children from a previous marriage, the father's children from a previous marriage, and children born into the new family. Over 50 percent of blended families in Canada include the mother's children from a previous marriage and children born into the new family (Cheal, 1996).

Do children in stepfamilies and blended families develop differently from other children? Are they at risk for more problems in development? About 20 to 25 percent of children in stepfamilies and blended families have academic, behavioural, or self-esteem problems, compared with 10 percent of children in intact families (Hetherington et al., 1998). Although children in stepfamilies and blended families have a greater risk of problems, it is important to note that the majority (75 to 80 percent) do not have problems and are reasonably well adjusted. As well, it is important to be aware of research issues that complicate the interpretation of studies of children in stepfamilies. First, when researchers find more problems in stepfamilies, it may be unclear whether

the children's problems are due to being in a stepfamily, per se, or whether they are carry-over problems from going through the breakup of their first family. Researchers must distinguish between problems that are associated with stepfamilies and those that are pre-existing. Second, it may be uncertain whether the problems are temporary reactions to the new family arrangement or whether they are enduring. This issue can be addressed by studying the children longitudinally to see how they adjust to family life over time. Researchers are currently addressing these issues (Hetherington et al., 1998).

Children are affected by the quality of parenting and by the stability in the home.

Stepfamilies and blended families are often the result of divorced parents marrying a new spouse. Do children fare better or worse when their parents remarry? The answer to this question is complicated. Children adjust differently to becoming a member of a stepfamily, depending on their gender, temperament, home life prior to the stepfamily, and experiences within the stepfamily (Hetherington & Stanley-Hagan, 1999). Boys tend to adjust better to stepfamilies than girls do. Most stepfamilies have a stepfather, rather than a stepmother, and boys get along better with stepfathers than girls do. Children are affected by the quality

of parenting and by the stability in the home. The problems that surface during a divorce may not disappear when one or both parents remarry. Although some children welcome the arrival of a stepparent, for others, the remarriage is another major adjustment that they must make after adjusting to the divorce. Children may see their dreams of reuniting their parents shattered; they may resent the stepparent's attempt to discipline them or to win their affection. They may see themselves as having a divided loyalty to their parents, or they may worry about being left out of the new family that is forming. Children may also be unhappy about having to share the attention of the custodial parent with the new partner, or they may feel guilty about "abandoning" the non-custodial parent by giving affection to the new stepparent. In some cases, children may have the additional problem of having to get along with stepsiblings (Hetherington et al., 1989). As part of the National Longitudinal Survey of Children and Youth, 44.2 percent of children (ages 10 and 11) living in stepfamilies reported difficulties with family relationships (Cheal, 1996). Only 28.2 percent of children living in intact families reported such problems. As well, compared with children in intact families, children in stepfamilies were more likely to report that they lacked emotional support from parents and that they received erratic punishment. Other studies have reported that the incidence of child abuse is higher in stepfamilies than it is in intact families (Hetherington et al., 1998).

unique to the United States; similar rates have been noted in Australia, Great Britain, and Germany (Emery, 1989). Canada does not keep national statistics on child abuse; however, there are statistics available for Ontario (CCSD, 1996). In 1993, there were 21 investigations of child abuse per 1000 children in Ontario. In nearly 60 percent of the investigations, abuse was confirmed or suspected. In the other 40 percent, allegations of abuse were unsubstantiated.

More than half of physically abused children are abused by their own parents, with mothers and fathers implicated in approximately equal numbers. When someone other than a parent is responsible for the abuse, however, male abusers outnumber females by four to one. For sexual abuse, the proportion of abusers who are male is even higher—nearly 95 percent. You may be surprised to learn that the sexual abuse of a little girl is usually not committed by the child's own father. It is estimated that a stepfather is five times more likely to abuse his stepdaughter than a father is to abuse his daughter (Sedlack, 1989; Wolfe, Wolfe, & Best, 1988).

Although the victim of sexual abuse is likely to be a girl, physical abuse is more often inflicted on a boy. Also, younger children sustain more serious injuries than older ones do; about half of the serious injury or death cases involve children under the age of 3 (Rosenthal, 1988).

Sexual and physical child abuse have long-term effects on the child's emotional well-being. The child's self-esteem has been irreparably damaged, and he or she may find it difficult ever to trust anyone again. Adults who were abused as children are at greater risk of many psychological problems, including depression and alcoholism (Schaefer, Sobieraj, & Hollyfield, 1988).

Approaches to Understanding Child Abuse   The large amount of research that has been done in this area has been centred on three main theoretical explanations of child abuse: psychiatric, sociological, and situational (Parke & Collmer, 1975). Each explanation is useful for explaining some, but not all, incidences of abuse. Most researchers today recognize that there are a number of pathways that lead to abuse (Emery & Laumann-Billings, 1998).

PSYCHIATRIC EXPLANATIONS

The psychiatric model focuses on the personality of the parents. It assumes that abusive parents are sick and require extensive psychiatric treatment. Early theorists looked for psychotic traits in adults who abused children, but they failed to find any. They discovered that clear cases of adult psychosis, such as schizophrenia, account for only a small percentage of incidents of child abuse. Other researchers have attempted to find a cluster of personality traits that might indicate a tendency toward abuse. Parents who have low self-esteem, poor impulse control, prolonged negative mood, a heightened response to stress, or drug and alcohol dependency are at risk for perpetrating child abuse (Emery & Laumann-Billings, 1998). It is important to note, though, that some parents who have these risk factors do not abuse their children. Community support can counteract individual risk factors of the parents (Gabarino & Kostelny, 1992).

One fact that researchers have discovered about child abusers is that many of them were themselves abused as children (Ney, 1988). Although psychologists are not certain why child abuse patterns are passed on from one generation to the next, one plausible explanation is that people who were abused as children had abusive adult models to follow. Their parents may have taught them that needs such as dependency or autonomy are unacceptable—that crying or asking for help is useless, inappropriate, or evidence of an evil nature. One child whose parents were going through therapy to halt their abuse even became distressed when his father no longer beat him. He poignantly asked the social worker, "How come daddy doesn't love me anymore?" Children absorb such lessons deeply and thoroughly at an early age. Another explanation is the genetic link between parent and child. Children of abusive parents may have inherited a tendency toward poor control over aggressive impulses (Emery & Laumann-Billings, 1998).

SOCIOLOGICAL EXPLANATIONS

The sociological model, as defined by Parke and Collmer (1975), focuses not on individual differences but on social values and family organization. One social value significantly related to child abuse is violence. Some suggest that the endless display of brutality and hostility on television teaches parents and children alike that violence is an acceptable way to resolve conflicts. If physical aggression occurs in some family disputes, especially those between husband and wife, it is also likely to occur in parent–child relationships. It is estimated that 40 to 75 percent of children who observe marital violence in their homes are also victims of physical abuse (Emery & Laumann-Billings, 1998).

Poverty, unemployment, and overcrowding also play a role in child abuse. Although physical abuse of children is found at all socioeconomic levels, it is almost seven times more likely to be reported in homes where the annual income is below the poverty line (Sedlak, 1989). This statistic may result partly from the fact that abuse in middle-class homes is less likely to come to the attention of authorities. But it is also true that any kind of family stress—and poverty is unquestionably a source of family stress—increases the risk that a child will be abused. Unemployment is also a source of stress. A parent who is suddenly and unexpectedly out of work may become abusive toward his or her children. Aside from the financial problems, unemployment also lowers the parent's social status and self-esteem. An unemployed father may try to compensate by wielding authority at home through physical domination. In periods of high unemployment, male violence against both wives and children rises.

Another characteristic that is observed in many families troubled by child abuse is social isolation. Parents who abuse their children are often isolated from relatives, friends, and community support systems (Garbarino & Kostelny, 1992). They have difficulty sustaining friendships and rarely belong to any formal organizations. Consequently, they have no one to ask for help when they need it, and they turn their frustration and rage against their children. Some of this isolation is self-imposed. Abusive parents, with their low self-esteem, feel so guilty and unworthy that they avoid contact with others. They also obstruct their children's attempts to form meaningful bonds and relationships with people outside the home.

Sociological explanations also apply to a newly recognized form of abuse—sibling abuse. Many people are unaware of the possibility of sibling abuse because violence between siblings is considered "normal." This viewpoint will likely change though, as people become more aware of the fact that children can be physically injured or terrorized by siblings. All forms of family violence have deleterious effects on children.

SITUATIONAL EXPLANATIONS

The situational model of child abuse, like the sociological model, seeks causes in environmental factors. The situational model concentrates on interaction patterns among family members (Parke & Collmer, 1975). This model recognizes children as active participants in the interaction process. It tries to identify the situations in which abusive patterns develop and to find the stimuli that trigger the abuse. One study attempted to discover distinctive patterns in the everyday interactions of families with incidents of child abuse. The study showed that abusive parents had less verbal and physical interaction with their children than did nonabusive parents. Abusive parents were also more negative and less willing to comply with the requests of other family members (Burgess & Conger, 1978).

Abusive parents also tend to be inconsistent in the behavioural demands they make on their children. They may punish their children for coming home late one day, but they ignore it the next—or they may punish them long afterward, so that the children feel they are being punished for no apparent reason. These parents also tend to have trouble in defining their marital roles. They often fail to allocate responsibility between themselves for important tasks, including discipline of the children. Therefore, their children may be confused by parental inconsistencies and may lack a clear idea of what kind of behaviour will be tolerated. Once the abuse is begun, it tends to perpetuate itself. The parents may justify the abuse as a way of "building character" and may play down the child's injuries. They may shift the blame to the child and justify their behaviour on the grounds that the child is "hateful" or "stubborn" (Belsky, 1980; Parke & Collmer, 1975).

Finally, let us look at the role of the child in abusive families. Parents are usually selective in their abuse, singling out one child for mistreatment. Infants and very young children are the most frequent targets. Those born prematurely and those with physical disabilities or hearing impairment are especially at risk (Stevenson, 1999). Infants and children who are unusually difficult to take care of are at greatest risk. Infants who cry constantly can drive parents to the breaking point. In other cases, there may be a mismatch between the parent's expectations and the child's characteristics—this is basically a problem of incompatibility between parent and child. For example, a physically demonstrative mother may find that her infant does not like to be touched. In other cases, the parent has an unrealistic expectancy of behaviour in the children. For example, a mother may believe her 1-month-old child cries to be nasty or because she hates her mother. A father may become angry when his 2- and 3-year-olds fail to take responsibility for the family garden. Such misconceptions may lead to abuse (Parke & Collmer, 1975; Vasta, 1982).

Some children may be singled out for abuse because they serve as an uncomfortable reminder of their parent's own flaws. Many parents have still not come to terms with the unresolved conflicts from their own childhood years. If their child has a characteristic that they regard as unacceptable in themselves, they may punish this child harshly. These unfortunate children tap a wellspring of self-hatred in their parents. We may see these three explanations contrasted in Concept Summary Table 14-1.

All three of these approaches shed some light on the causes of child abuse. None of them, unfortunately, tells us how to stop it. Programs for preventing child abuse focus on providing parents with social support and teaching them better methods for controlling their children. Although such programs usually succeed in reducing the level of abuse, around 25 percent of the participants continue to abuse their children (Ferleger, Glenwick, Gaines, & Green, 1988). One step that is being taken to improve the effectiveness of interventions is to offer them in the homes of at-risk families. "There is an emerging consensus that home visiting is the most effective of these targeted services" (Stevenson, 1999, p. 91). Sometimes, criminal prosecution of the offenders and removal of the child from the home are the only safe alternatives. Emery and Laumann-Billings (1998) argue that this is the best approach for severe cases of child abuse but that less serious cases might benefit more from family support and parent training than from prosecution. In addition to preventing abuse, interventions are needed to counteract adverse effects of abuse after it has occurred. Abused children who have a close, confiding relationship with an adult are more resilient. Schools can play a positive role. "If an enduring trusting relationship with a schoolteacher can be established and/or specific talents or interests fostered, be they academic, artistic, or recreational, then particular benefits for maltreated children should follow" (Stevenson, 1999, p. 95).

Concept Summary

Table 14-1   Approaches to Understanding Child Abuse

Psychiatric explanations	Parents as causes	Focuses on personality of the parents as being sick and in need of extensive psychotherapy; most child abusers were themselves abused as children; presence of poor parenting models leads to family cycles of violence.
Sociological explanations	Society as cause	Views families as living in a culture of violence reflected in television programming; physical punishment is widely used and can get out of control when the family is under stress; social isolation increases the risk of poor parenting skills; socioeconomic conditions such as unemployment, overcrowding, and poverty increase stress and, therefore, the possibility of abuse.
Situational explanations	Immediate circumstances and patterns of interaction as causes	Seeks environmental causes for the abuse such as dysfunctional family interaction patterns; often, the abused child has some trait the parents consider undesirable and thus becomes the focus for abuse.

Unemployment increases family stress and the risk of child abuse.

Psychological Abuse Physical or sexual abuse is always accompanied by a psychological component. Mistreatment exists in the context of an interpersonal relationship, and this relationship has become psychologically abusive—manipulative, rejecting, or degrading. One researcher states that the psychological accompaniments of child abuse may be even more damaging than the abuse itself (Emery, 1989).

Psychological abuse comes in various forms and may be committed by various people, such as parents, teachers, siblings, and peers. The significant characteristic of these people is that they have power in situations in which the child is vulnerable (Hart, Germain, & Brassard, 1987). For instance, most of us have encountered, at some point in our lives, the sadistic teacher who picks out one particular student in the class and makes this student the victim of a continuing campaign of cruelty.

Psychological abusers have a wide range of techniques. Hart, Germain, and Brassard (1987) have specified six types of psychological abuse used by parents, teachers, siblings, or peers:

1. *Rejection.* This involves refusing the request or needs of a child in such a way as to imply strong dislike for the child. Active rejection, rather than passive withholding of affection, is involved here.
2. *Denial of emotional responsiveness.* This is the passive withholding of affection. Detachment, coldness, or failing to respond to the child's attempts at communication are examples.
3. *Degradation.* Humiliating children in public or calling them "stupid" or "dummy" is degrading. Children's self-esteem is lowered by frequent assaults on their dignity or intelligence.
4. *Terrorization.* Being forced to witness violence to a loved one, or being threatened with violence to oneself, is a terrifying experience for a child. A child who suffers regular beatings or who is told, "I'll break every bone in your body if you don't behave," is being terrorized. A more subtle form of terrorism is demonstrated by the parent who simply walks away from a misbehaving child while they are out in the street, leaving the child unprotected from danger.
5. *Isolation.* A parent who refuses to allow a child to play with friends or to take part in family activities is isolating that child. Some forms of isolation, such as locking a child in a closet, may also be terrorization.
6. *Exploitation.* Taking advantage of a child's innocence or weakness is exploitation. The most obvious example of exploiting a child is sexual abuse.

Psychological abuse is so common that virtually no one grows up without experiencing some form of it. But, in most cases, the abuse is not intense enough or frequent enough to do permanent damage (Hart et al., 1987). What distinguishes the psychologically abused child is that the child is caught in a damaging relationship and is not being socialized in a positive, supportive way. As a consequence, the child may be unable to satisfy needs for dependency, may have to be overly adaptive in order to escape abuse, and may develop neurotic traits or problem behaviours. What is more, the child has learned to exploit, degrade, or terrorize and to expect that relationships are often painful. These are pervasive, long-term consequences.

Social Knowledge

As we have seen, children are continually learning how to deal with the complex social world that exists both inside and outside the family. In middle childhood, they must come to terms with the subtleties of friendship and authority, with expanding or conflicting sex roles, and with a host of social rules and regulations. One way they make these adjustments is through the process of direct socialization: getting rewards for desirable behaviour and punishments for undesirable behaviour, and observing and imitating models. Social learning helps children to acquire appropriate behaviours and attitudes. Another way children learn about the social world involves psychodynamic processes. Children develop anxious feelings in certain situations, and they learn to reduce this anxiety by using a number of defence mechanisms (see Chapter 11).

A third way that children learn about the social world is called **social cognition.** Just as children's understanding of the physical world changes as they mature, so does their understanding of the social world. Social cognition is thought, knowledge, and understanding that involves the social world.

The Development of Social Cognition

As children develop during middle childhood and adolescence, social cognition becomes an increasingly important determinant of their behaviour. It is in middle childhood that children must learn how to deal with some of the complexities of friendship and justice, social rules and manners, sex-role conventions, obedience to authority, and moral law. Children begin to look at the social world around them and gradually come to understand the principles and rules that it follows (Ross, 1981). Cognitive theorists, who believe that all knowledge, whether scientific, social, or personal, exists as an organized system or structure and not as unrelated bits and pieces, have studied this process. The understanding of the world does not develop in a piecemeal fashion; rather, it occurs in a predictable sequence. The development of social cognition progresses in a similar way to other kinds of cognitive development.

As we saw in Chapter 10, preschool children's understanding of the world is limited by their egocentrism. Although by age 7 children have reached "the age of reason" and are able to perform some logical operations, they are still somewhat hampered by their inability to see another person's point of view. Many children in early middle childhood still do not recognize that their point of view is limited to themselves. They are not fully aware that other people have different points of view because of their different backgrounds, experiences, or values. This fact only gradually becomes apparent to the young child.

A first component of social cognition, therefore, is **social inference**—that is, guesses and assumptions about what another person is feeling, thinking, or intending (Flavell, 1985; Flavell et al., 1993). A young child, for example, hears his mother laughing and assumes that she is happy. An adult might hear something forced about the mother's laughter and infer that the woman is covering up her feelings. Although young children cannot make such a sophisticated inference, by age 6 they can usually infer that another person's thoughts may differ from their own. By age 8 or so, they realize that another person can think about their thoughts. By age 10, they are able to infer what another person is thinking while at the same time inferring that their own thoughts are the subject of another person's thoughts. A child might think, "Johnny is angry with me, and he knows that I know he is angry." The process of developing fully accurate social inference is gradual and continues into late adolescence (Shantz, 1983).

A second component of social cognition is the child's understanding of **social relationships.** Children gradually accumulate information and understanding about the obligations of friendship, such as fairness and loyalty, the respect for authority, and the concepts of legality and justice. Researchers at the University of Toronto found that elementary school children's respect for adult authority in decision making depends on the context (Helwig & Kim, 1999). Children acknowledge adult authority in decisions about the choice of movie children should watch, decisions about which school children should attend, and decisions about the school curriculum.

Isolating a child from other children is a form of psychological abuse.

social cognition Thought, knowledge, and understanding that involves the social world.

social inference Guesses and assumptions about what another person is feeling, thinking, or intending.

social relationships Relationships that involve obligations such as fairness and loyalty. The knowledge of these obligations is a necessary part of social cognition.

FOCUS ON AN ISSUE

Canadian Research on Playground Aggression and Bullying

According to surveys, bullying is common in Canadian schools; 19 percent of students reported being bullied at school more than twice a term, and 8 percent reported being bullied at least once a week. As well, 15 percent of children reported that they bullied others more than twice a term, while 9 percent indicated that they bullied others at least once a week (Charach, Pepler, & Ziegler, 1995). To better understand bullying, Debra Pepler, Wendy Craig, William Roberts, and colleagues in Toronto observed interactions among children aged 6 to 11 on school playgrounds (see Craig & Pepler, 1997; Pepler, Craig, & Roberts, 1998). They used naturalistic observation so that they could study aggression in a broader context, documenting events that preceded and followed the aggression. They studied the child's behaviour against the backdrop of the ongoing behaviour of other people around him. Here are some of their main findings:

- There was an average of 6.5 incidents of bullying per hour.

Bullying is common in Canadian schools.

- The same children were often both perpetrators and victims of bullying. Of the children who were observed in more than two bullying episodes, 67.9 percent were observed as both perpetrators and victims, whereas 20 percent were just perpetrators and 12.1 percent were just victims.
- Half of the incidents involved verbal aggression, 29 percent involved physical aggression, and 21 percent involved both verbal and physical aggression.

- Of the bullying episodes, 4 percent involved racial content.
- Boys bullied more than girls did, and 86 percent of the time boys bullied other boys. Girls, on the other hand, bullied other girls only 48 percent of the time.
- There was no age difference in the prevalence of bullying.
- Peers were present in 85 percent of the incidents of bullying. They intervened in 13 percent of the incidents in which they were present. Peers sided more with the bully than with the victim. Peer attention and reinforcement may help to perpetuate bullying.

However, children think that other decisions should be made by consensus: "They should find something that everyone wants to do, that way everyone would be happy" (p. 506). Consensus was preferred for making decisions about what game children would play, decisions about where a family would go on vacation, and decisions about where a school class would go on a field trip. A third aspect of social cognition is the understanding of **social regulations,** such as customs and conventions. Many of these conventions are first learned by rote or imitation. Later, they can become less rigid, depending on the child's ability to make correct social inferences and to understand social relationships.

Culture strongly influences social cognition. In a recent study, children from China and Canada evaluated whether lying or truth-telling was more appropriate (Lee, Cameron, Xu, & Board, 1998). Children heard a story about a child who had done a good deed and who was then asked by a teacher whether he had done it. The Canadian children thought that the child should tell the truth, even though it meant self-promotion. In fact, Canadian culture often values self-promotion. Interestingly, however, the Chinese children thought that it was better for the child to lie and not to admit that he was responsible. This viewpoint is consistent with the Chinese teaching of modesty and self-effacement. It is better to lie than to brag. However, it is not better to lie in all situations. The children also heard a story about a child who had done something naughty and who was asked by a teacher whether she had done it. In this situation, the Chinese children, like the Canadian children, thought that it was better for the child to tell the truth.

Psychologists who study social cognition find that it develops in a predictable sequence—some even call the steps in this sequence *stages*. Most researchers agree that children overcome the worst of their egocentrism by age 6 or 7: they stop focusing on only one aspect of a situation and gradually get better at making social inferences. As we will soon see, these advances make it possible for a child to form lasting and satisfying friendships with other children. They also affect the child's ability to

social regulations The rules and conventions governing social interactions.

- School staff were present in 25 percent of the incidents of bullying. They intervened in 23 percent of the incidents in which they were present. Observers judged that school staff were unaware of bullying in about 80 percent of the incidents. It is difficult for staff to detect all incidents of bullying because they are often brief or difficult to distinguish from rough-and-tumble play or playful teasing. The researchers suggested infrequent and inconsistent teacher responses to bullying may be contributing to its high rate.

- Teachers classified children as aggressive or nonaggressive. Playground observations were consistent with the teachers' classifications. Aggressive children engaged in more physical and verbal aggression. They also tended to be more hyperactive (this is consistent with the discussion in Chapter 13 of the comorbidity of

ADHD and conduct disorders). There was no indication, though, that the aggressive children lacked positive social skills. Their rates of all behaviours—antisocial and prosocial—were higher than those of nonaggressive children. However, aggressive children's prosocial behaviour accounted for a lower proportion of their overall behaviour.

- Compared with nonaggressive children, aggressive children were more likely to send their peers mixed messages by behaving both antisocially and prosocially in the same interaction situation.

- There was no indication that peers were treating aggressive children differently and thus contributing to their aggression. Peers reacted similarly to aggressive and nonaggressive children.

What steps can be taken to reduce the rate of bullying and aggression on Canadian playgrounds? Researchers in Hamilton, Ontario, trained grade five students in conflict resolution and had these trained students intervene in playground disputes (Cunningham, Cunningham, Martorelli, Tran, Young, & Zacharias, 1998). The use of student mediators led to a decline in physical aggression on the playground, and this decline was still evident one year after the program was implemented. In addition, students trained as mediators reported that they engaged in less conflict themselves as a result of the program. The use of student mediators may compensate for the lack of additional adult supervision. Typically, there are only one or two adults to supervise an entire playground, and they may be unaware of less flagrant incidents of aggression.

think about moral issues. We may see these aspects of social cognition presented in Concept Summary Table 14-2.

Moral Judgment

Moral judgment—making decisions about right and wrong—is another area of social cognition. In the process of growing up, most children somehow learn to tell "good" from "bad" and to distinguish between kindness and cruelty, generosity and selfishness. Mature moral judgment, then, involves more than the rote learning of social rules and conventions.

moral judgment The process of making decisions about right and wrong.

There is considerable debate as to how children develop morality. Social-learning theorists believe that children learn it by being rewarded or punished for various kinds

Concept Summary

Table 14-2 Aspects of Social Cognition

Social inference	Children make guesses and assumptions about what another is feeling, thinking, or intending; by age 6, can infer that the thoughts of others differ from theirs; by age 8, realize that another person can think about their thoughts; by age 10, can infer what another is thinking—as well as infer that their thoughts may be the subject of another's thoughts.
Social relationships	Children accumulate information and understanding about obligations of relationships, such as fairness and loyalty, respect for authority, and the concepts of legality and justice.
Social regulations	Children articulate and understand the customs and conventions of society; first learned by imitation and rote; later, social regulations become less rigid.

Developing a sense of right and wrong involves understanding social rules and gaining experience in social relationships.

of behaviour and by imitating models. Psychodynamic psychologists believe that it develops as a defence against anxiety over the loss of love and approval. Cognitive theorists believe that, like intellectual development, morality develops in progressive, age-related stages. Let us take a closer look at cognitive approaches to moral development.

Cognitive Views of Moral Development Piaget defined *morality* as "an individual's respect for the rules of social order and his sense of justice"—justice being "a concern for reciprocity and equality among individuals" (Hoffman, 1970). According to Piaget (1965), children's moral sense arises from the interaction between their developing thought structures and their gradually widening social experience. The moral sense develops in two stages. At the **moral realism stage,** children think that all rules should be obeyed because they are real, indestructible things, not abstract principles. A child at this stage judges the morality of an act in terms of its consequences and is incapable of weighing intentions. For example, a young child will think that the girl who accidentally breaks 12 dishes while setting a table is much guiltier than the girl who intentionally breaks 2 dishes because she is angry with her sister.

Later, children reach the **moral relativism stage.** At this point, they realize that rules are created and agreed on cooperatively by individuals and that rules can be changed as the need arises. This realization leads to awareness that there is no absolute right or wrong and that morality depends not on consequences, but on intentions. We can see these two aspects of morality presented in Concept Summary Table 14-3.

KOHLBERG'S STAGE THEORY

moral realism stage Piaget's term for the first stage of moral development, in which children believe in rules as real, indestructible things.

moral relativism stage Piaget's term for the second stage of moral development, in which children realize that rules are agreements that may be changed if necessary.

Piaget's two-stage theory of moral development was extended by Lawrence Kohlberg (1981, 1984). Kohlberg presented his subjects (children, adolescents, and adults) with a series of morally problematic stories and then asked them questions about the stories. The leading character in each story was faced with a moral dilemma, and the subject being interviewed was asked to resolve this dilemma. Kohlberg was less interested in the specific answers to the problem than in the reasoning behind the answers. Here is one of his stories, which has become a classic:

> In Europe, a woman was near death from a special kind of cancer. There was one drug that the doctors thought might save her. It was a form of radium that a druggist in the same town had recently discovered. The drug was expensive to make, but the druggist was charging 10 times what the

Concept Summary

Table 14-3   Piaget's Concept of Moral Development

Moral realism	Ages 4 to 6	Child believes that rules should be obeyed because they are real, indestructible things, not abstract principles; morality of an action is judged by its consequences—a person who commits more damage is guiltier than a person who commits less damage.
Moral relativism	Ages 7 and older	Child believes that rules are created and agreed on cooperatively; rules can be changed by consensus as the need arises; thus, there is no absolute right or wrong; morality of an action is determined by the intention rather than consequences of action.

FOCUS ON APPLICATION

After-School Care Programs and Children's Social Development

Many Canadian schools now have special programs to care for children before and after school—the equivalent of day care for school-age children. Children in these programs spend considerably more time with groups of peers than do other children. Does this have an impact on their social development and peer relations?

Researchers in Quebec studied kindergarten children (Jacobs, White, Baillargeon, & Betsalel-Presser, 1995) and compared those who attended after-school care with those who went home. A number of differences emerged: the after-school care children participated more in kindergarten and interacted more with other children. But they also were more prone to angry outbursts and aggression and complied less with teacher directives. Interestingly, though, this behaviour did not affect their popularity with peers. However, they were more skilled at joining groups of children already involved in games. They tended to be more controlling and "bossed" their way into the games. Children with less group experience were more passive and tended to hover

by the other children. It took them longer to join in the play.

Why do the after-school care children behave differently from other children? Can we conclude that experience in after-school care caused the differences? Think back to the research design issues raised in Chapter 1 (the concept of quasi-experiments). In a quasi-experiment, as

---

There are wide differences in after-school care programs.

---

in the studies on after-school care, we compare pre-existing groups, but we do not know whether there are other differences between the groups that might affect our results. For example, 92.5 percent of the children in after-school care had extensive day-care experience, but none of the other children had any day-care experience. Therefore, we do not know whether the different behaviour of the after-school care children is because of the after-school care, per se, or because of the lingering effects of day

care. All we know is that the groups differ.

We also have to recognize that there are wide differences in after-school care programs (Jacobs et al., 1995). Some are much more structured than others. Some focus on academics and have set homework times; others focus on extracurricular activities, such as sports and crafts. Researchers are currently exploring factors that relate to the quality of after-school care. Some factors are similar to those associated with quality day care (that is, the safety of the environment), but others are different because school-age children have different developmental needs than preschool children. For example, school-age children have increased needs for privacy. How does the after-school care program accommodate these needs? As well, after-school care programs have to communicate with the school to ensure compatible programming and goals. This communication makes certain that children have smooth transitions between school and after school.

---

drug cost him to make. He paid $200 for the radium and charged $2,000 for a small dose of the drug. The sick woman's husband, Heinz, went to everyone he knew to borrow the money, but he could only get together $1,000, which is half of what it cost. He told the druggist that his wife was dying and asked him to sell it cheaper or let him pay later. But the druggist said, "No, I discovered the drug, and I am going to make money from it." So Heinz got desperate and broke into the man's store to steal the drug for his wife. (Kohlberg, 1969, p. 379)

The person being interviewed was then asked: "Should Heinz have stolen the drug?" "Why?" "Was the druggist right to have charged so much more than it cost to make the drug?" "Why?" "Which is worse, letting someone die or stealing if it will save a life?" "Why?"

The ways that different age groups answered these questions led Kohlberg to the theory that moral reasoning develops in distinct stages. He defined three broad levels of moral reasoning and subdivided these levels into more specific stages (see Table 14-1). Support for his theory was provided by several studies that showed that young boys, at least in Western societies, generally went through these stages in the predicted fashion. In one 20-year longitudinal study of 48 boys, Kohlberg and his associates found

Table 14-1 Kohlberg's Stages of Moral Development

STAGE	ILLUSTRATIVE REASONING
Level I. Preconventional (based on punishments and rewards)	
Stage 1. Punishment and obedience orientation. **Stage 2.** Naive instrumental hedonism.	Obey rules in order to avoid punishment. Obey to obtain rewards, to have favours returned.
Level II. Conventional (based on social conformity)	
Stage 3. "Good-boy" morality of maintaining good relations, approval of others. **Stage 4.** Authority-maintaining morality.	Conform to avoid disapproval or dislike by others. Conform to avoid censure by legitimate authorities, with resulting guilt.
Level III. Postconventional (based on moral principles)	
Stage 5. Morality of contract, of individual rights, and of democratically accepted law. **Stage 6.** Morality of individual principles of conscience.	Abide by laws of land for community welfare. Abide by universal ethical principles.

Note: Stage 6 is rare and does not occur in all versions of Kohlberg's theory.

Source: From *Stages of Moral Development* by Lawrence Kohlberg (unpublished doctoral dissertation, University of Chicago, 1958). ® 1958 by Lawrence Kohlberg. Used by permission. Also adapted from *The Philosophy of Moral Development* by Lawrence Kohlberg (New York: Harper & Row, 1981).

remarkable consistency with these stages (Colby, Kohlberg, Gibbs, & Lieberman, 1983).

Kohlberg's theory has raised many objections. Some researchers have found that it is very difficult to follow Kohlberg's procedures exactly and to agree on how a child's response to the test should be scored (Rubin & Trotten, 1977). Others have attacked Kohlberg's theory on the grounds of **moral absolutism:** it disregards significant cultural differences that determine what is moral in other societies (Baumrind, 1978; Campbell & Christopher, 1996). Kohlberg (1978) himself acknowledged that it is necessary to take into account the social and moral norms of the group to which a person belongs. He has concluded that his sixth stage of moral development may not apply to all people in all cultures.

moral absolutism Any theory of morality that disregards cultural differences in moral beliefs.

Power and Reimer (1978) find other weaknesses in Kohlberg's theory. They point out that Kohlberg's scale measures attitudes, not behaviour, and that there is a great difference between thinking about moral questions and behaving morally. Moral decisions are not made in a vacuum; instead, they are usually made in "crisis situations." No matter how high our moral principles may be, when the time comes to act on them, our behaviour may not reflect our thoughts or beliefs.

GILLIGAN'S OBJECTIONS

Carol Gilligan (1982) claims that Kohlberg based his theory entirely on his work with male subjects and failed to consider the possibility that moral development might proceed somewhat differently in females. In other words, she accuses Kohlberg of sex bias. Gilligan found that girls and women generally score lower than males do on Kohlberg's moral dilemma test. But, she says, this does not mean that their thinking is at a lower level—only that they use different criteria for making moral judgments.

According to Gilligan (1982), girls and boys are taught from early childhood to value different qualities. Boys are trained to strive for independence and to value abstract thinking. Girls, in contrast, are taught to be nurturing and caring and to value their connectedness to others. Gilligan believes that there are two distinct types of moral reasoning: one is based on concepts of abstract justice, and the other is based on human relationships and on caring for other people. The justice perspective is characteristic of male thinking, whereas caring for others is more common in females. Men often focus on rights, whereas women see moral issues in terms of concern for the needs of others. However, Gilligan notes that sex differences in moral reasoning (like other sex differences) are not absolute. Some women make moral judgments from a justice perspective, and some men make them from a caring one.

Gilligan's subjects were mostly adolescents and young adults. Other researchers have looked at younger children and have failed to find a sex difference in moral judgments made by children younger than age 10. However, some 10- or 11-year-old boys give rather aggressive responses to the questions that are asked on these tests—the sort of responses that are hardly ever given by girls. For example, in one study the children listened to a story about a porcupine that, needing a home for the winter, moved in with a family of moles. The moles soon found that they were constantly being pricked by the porcupine's sharp needles. What should they do? Only boys responded to this question with suggestions like "Shoot the porcupine" or "Pluck out his quills." Girls of this age tended to look for solutions that would harm neither the moles nor the porcupine— in other words, caring solutions (Garrod, Beal, & Shin, 1989).

EISENBERG'S VIEW

Nancy Eisenberg (1989a, 1989b) feels that Kohlberg's mistake was not in placing too much emphasis on abstract justice; it was in making the stages too rigid and absolute. She feels that children's moral development is not quite this predictable and narrowly determined. Many factors go into children's moral judgments, ranging from the social customs of the culture in which they are reared to how they feel at a particular moment. Children are capable of making moral judgments at a high level one day and at a lower level the next. They may even make judgments at a higher level for some issues (for example, whether they would help someone who was injured) than for others (for example, whether they would invite someone they didn't like to their birthday party).

With regard to sex differences, Eisenberg also finds that girls between ages 10 and 12 give more caring and empathetic responses than do boys of this age. However, she thinks this stems mainly from the fact that girls mature more rapidly than boys do. By late adolescence, boys have caught up. Eisenberg and her colleagues find few sex differences in the responses of older adolescents (Eisenberg, 1989a; Eisenberg et al., 1987).

Question to Ponder

Should moral education be taught in Canadian schools? If so, who should decide on the curriculum?

Peer Relationships and Social Competence

As the previous discussion indicates, the ability to make moral decisions on the basis of empathy and concern for others is something that develops as children mature. Girls mature a little faster; therefore, they develop empathy at a somewhat earlier age than boys do. Empathy is based on social inference because if you do not know what someone else is feeling, you cannot empathize with him. Social inference and empathy are the foundation on which friendships are built.

Concepts of Friendship

The ability to infer the thoughts, expectations, feelings, and intentions of others plays a central role in understanding what it means to be a friend. Children who can view things from another person's perspective are better able to develop strong, intimate relationships with others.

Using a social cognition model, Selman (1976, 1981) studied the friendships of children aged 7 to 12. His approach was similar to Kohlberg's: tell children a story involving a social dilemma and then ask them questions designed to measure their concepts about other people, their self-awareness and ability to reflect, their concepts of personality, and their ideas about friendship. Here is an example of the kind of story that Selman used:

> Kathy and Debby have been best friends since they were 5. A new girl, Jeannette, moves into their neighbourhood, but Debby dislikes her because she considers Jeannette a showoff. Later, Jeannette invites Kathy to go to the circus on its one day in town. Kathy's problem is that she has promised to play with Debby that same day. What will Kathy do?

This story raises questions about the nature of relationships, about old versus new friendships, and about loyalty and trust. It requires children to think and to talk about how friendships are formed and maintained and to decide what is important in a relationship. In other words, Selman's method provides a way of assessing a child's concepts and thought processes—how the child decides what is important.

Selman (1981) described four stages of friendship. At the first stage (below age 7), friendship is based on physical or geographical considerations and is rather self-centred. A friend is just a playmate—someone who lives nearby, who goes to the same school, or who has desirable toys. At this stage, there is no understanding of the other person's perspective.

At the second stage (ages 7 to 9), the idea of reciprocity and an awareness of another person's feelings begin to form. Friendship is seen mostly in terms of the social actions of one person and the subjective evaluation of these actions by the other. A child at this stage might say that Kathy could go to the circus with Jeannette and remain friends with Debby only if Debby did not object to the change in plans.

At the third stage (ages 9 to 12), friendship is based on genuine give-and-take; friends are seen as people who help each other. Children realize that they can evaluate the actions of their friends and that friends can evaluate their actions in return. The concept of trust appears for the first time. Children at the third stage might realize that the friendship between Kathy and Debby is different from the friendship between Kathy and Jeannette because the older friendship is based on long-standing trust.

At the fourth stage, which occurred only rarely among the 11- and 12-year-olds he studied, children see friendship as a stable, continuing relationship that is based on trust. Children are now capable of looking at the relationship from the perspective of a third party. A child at this level might comment, "Kathy and Debby should be able to understand each other." Selman argues that the key to developmental changes in children's friendships is perspective-taking ability. We can see these stages of friendship presented in Concept Summary Table 14-4.

Not all researchers agree with Selman's model. For example, there is evidence that young children implicitly know more of the rules and expectations of being a friend than they are able to tell an interviewer (Rizzo & Corsaro, 1988). Also, real friendships are quite complicated and are constantly changing. They may involve mutuality, trust, and reciprocity at one time and independence, competitiveness, or even conflict at another. Certain types of conflict may be intrinsic to the nature of friendship. Such complexities are not easily handled by a model that looks only at the cognitive aspects of children's friendships and ignores the emotional aspects (Berndt, 1983).

Functions of Friendship

Children and adults alike benefit from having close, confiding relationships. Through friendships, children learn social concepts and social skills, and they develop self-esteem. Friendship provides a structure for a child's activity in games; it reinforces and solidifies group norms, attitudes, and values; and it serves as a backdrop for individual and group competition (Hartup, 1970a).

Friendship patterns shift during childhood (Piaget, 1965). The "egocentric" pattern of Selman's first stage, typical of preschoolers and younger school-age children,

Concept Summary

Table 14-4 Selman's Stages of Friendship Development

Stage 1	Ages 6 and under	Friendship is based on physical or geographic factors; children are self-centred, with no understanding of the perspectives of others.
Stage 2	Ages 7 to 9	Friendship begins to be based on reciprocity and an awareness of others' feelings; it begins to be based on social actions and evaluation.
Stage 3	Ages 9 to 12	Friendship is based on genuine give-and-take; friends are seen as people who help each other; mutual evaluation of each other's actions occurs; concept of trust appears.
Stage 4	Ages 11 to 12 and older	Friendship is seen as a stable, continuing relationship that is based on trust; children can observe the relationship from the perspective of a third party.

Source: Selman, 1981.

changes during middle childhood, when children begin to form closer relationships, frequently with a few "best" friends. These friendship ties are strong while they last, but they tend to be short-lived. In late childhood and adolescence, group friendships become common. The groups are generally large, with several boys or girls regularly sharing activities.

Two children who are friends may satisfy different needs in each other. One may be dominant, and the other may be submissive. One child may use her friend as a model, and the other child may enjoy teaching her friend the "proper" way to play or dress. In still another case, the relationship may be egalitarian, with neither friend playing a clear or consistent role. The pattern depends on the dominance, dependency, and autonomy needs of each child.

With a friend, children can share their feelings and fears and every detail of their lives. Having a best friend in whom one can confide teaches a child how to relate to others openly and unselfconsciously. However, this pattern of friendship is more common in girls. Boys tend to play in larger groups and to reveal less of themselves to their friends (Maccoby, 1990; Rubin, 1980).

Friendship can also be a vehicle of self-expression. Children sometimes choose friends whose personalities are quite different from their own. An outgoing or impulsive child may choose a more reserved or restrained child as a close friend. The relationship gives each a maximum of self-expression with a minimum of competition, and the pair, as a unit, demonstrates more personality traits than either child could alone (Hartup, 1970a, 1970b). Of course, friends are rarely complete opposites. Friendship pairs that last over a long period of time usually have many shared values, attitudes, and expectations, both within the pair and in relation to others.

Some childhood friendships last throughout life, but more often friendships change. Best friends may move away or transfer to another school, and children may feel a real sense of loss—until they make a new friend. Sometimes, friends become interested in other people who meet their needs in new and different ways, and, sometimes, friends just grow apart or develop new interests. As children mature, they turn to new partners who can provide more satisfactory relationships (Rubin, 1980).

Finally, not all children have friends. Some are consistently unsuccessful in their attempts to form friendships. Children who are rejected by their peers are at risk for later maladjustment. A recent longitudinal study found enduring effects of whether children had a friend or were friendless in grade five (Bagwell, Newcombe, & Bukowski, 1999). The grade five children were reassessed 12 years later, when they were young adults. Those who had been friendless in grade five reported lowered feelings of self-worth, more difficulties in family relationships, and more depression. But we should note that not all children who are rejected by peers are, in fact, friendless. Some research suggests that even a single close friend helps children cope with the negative effects of being disliked and isolated

Friendship pairs allow children to share feelings and fears and to reinforce activities, values, and norms.

Peer groups form wherever children with common values, interests, or goals are thrown together.

from most of their peers (Rubin & Coplan, 1992). Researchers in Montreal studied grade five students who were bullied at school (Hodges et al., 1999). If the bullied children developed a close friendship, they were less likely to be bullied the next year than were bullied children who were friendless. In addition, having a friend protected children from psychological and behavioural problems—such as depression, withdrawal, aggression, and disruptiveness—that are typically associated with being bullied.

The Peer Group

peer group A group of two or more people of similar status who interact with one another and who share norms and goals.

What is a **peer group**? When we use this term, we are not talking about just any "bunch of kids." The size of a peer group is limited by the fact that all of its members must interact with one another. In addition, a peer group is relatively stable, and it stays together for a period of time. Its members share many values, and common norms govern interaction and influence each child. Finally, some degree of status differentiation governs the group's interaction; there is at least a temporary division into leaders and followers.

Developmental Trends in the Peer Group Peer groups are important throughout middle childhood, but a general shift occurs both in their organization and in their significance to the child during the years from 6 to 12.

In early middle childhood, peer groups are relatively informal. They are usually formed by the children themselves, they have few operating rules, and they have a rapid turnover in membership. It is true that many of the group's activities, such as playing games or riding bikes, may be carried out according to precise rules. But the structure of the group itself is quite flexible.

The group takes on a more intense significance for its members when these children reach the ages 10 to 12. Group conformity becomes extremely meaningful to the child, who may be showing an almost religious reverence for rules and norms in other areas of social interaction. Peer pressures assume a coercive influence on the child. Groups also develop a more formal structure. They may have special membership requirements, club meetings, and initiation rites. At this time, division of the sexes becomes very important. Groups are now almost invariably composed of one sex, and each sex maintains different interests and activities and has different styles of interaction (Maccoby, 1990). These strict attitudes about rules, conformity, and sex segregation are common to children's interaction through the latter part of middle childhood, and they are usually not relaxed until mid-adolescence.

Group Formation Children are constantly being thrown together by circumstances—in schools, in camps, and in neighbourhoods. In each case, and generally within a short time, groups form. Role differentiation develops within the group. Common values and interests emerge. Mutual influences and expectations grow, and a feeling of tradition takes shape. The process is almost universal, and some interesting studies have recorded exactly how it happens.

One classic experiment was called the "Red Rover" study (Sherif & Sherif, 1953). The subjects were grade five boys with similar backgrounds who were attending a summer camp. In the first phase of the study, the boys lived in two separate groups for a few days and were watched carefully as they began to form friendships. Just as these budding friendships were starting to solidify, the experimenters split up the friends by dividing the groups along new lines. The second stage of the study lasted for five days. The observers saw that in-group friendships soon formed in the new groups, and a clear hierarchy of leadership—not necessarily related to popularity—quickly emerged. Group names were chosen (the "Red Devils" and the "Bulldogs"), and group rules and norms were developed.

In the final stage, the two groups were brought into direct competition in games that were rigged so that one group was almost never allowed to win. At first, the competition resulted in the quick development of animosity and even open hostility between the groups, with powerful feelings of in-group exclusivity. But the frustrated group's structure soon fell apart. Leadership disintegrated, and intragroup disharmony developed.

A second study, sometimes called the "Robber's Cave" experiment (Sherif, Harvey, White, Hood, & Sherif, 1961), duplicated the circumstances and findings of the first study, with one substantial change. The competition between the groups was now equal. The results showed some interesting aspects of group structure. Equal competition intensified in-group solidarity in both groups, reinforcing norms and expectations. Feelings of exclusivity within each group and a sense of hostility toward the opposing group also grew stronger, just as the experimenters had hypothesized. Another finding was that the hierarchical structures of both groups changed. Leadership shifted as the boys who did best in the current competition rose to new leadership positions. In other words, group roles were shown to be quite strongly related to group goals. When the goals changed, so did the leaders.

In both of these studies, the experimenters had created openly hostile situations, and in each case, they tried to undo the damage before the boys were sent home from camp. In the highly frustrating "Red Rover" condition, the hostility was never completely erased. In the second study, however, the experimenters were better able to control the situation. They theorized that if the two groups were brought together with a common goal, the hostility would break down. This theory was proven to be true when both groups were forced to cooperate on a camp project that involved fixing the food truck so that both groups could eat.

Why are these older, classic studies still worth describing? They were conducted in natural settings, the kinds of situations that almost every child experiences. They also tell us a lot about groups. As the experimenters predicted, the groups formed quickly, and status differentiation seemed to develop almost automatically. Group members found common values and had shared norms; they even named their groups. Most important, when groups were put into competition against each other, feelings of exclusivity and hostility quickly developed. But when the groups were required to cooperate, hostility was reduced. These findings are typical of the way in which groups form and compete in classrooms, in athletic competitions, and in neighbourhood or ethnic rivalries.

Status within the Peer Group If we watch schoolchildren at lunchtime or at recess, we can observe the "natural selection" of roles that takes place in every group. One girl is surrounded by children eager to get her attention. Another, ignored, stands on the fringes of the group. Three boys run by, shouting. A muscular child grabs a smaller child's toy, and the smaller one cries. This kind of scene occurs all over the world, wherever there are children.

Each peer group has some members who are popular and others who are not. Several factors seem to contribute to this difference in social status, some of which we discussed in Chapter 11. Peer acceptance is often related to an individual's overall adjustment; enthusiasm and active participation, ability to cooperate with others, and responsiveness to social overtures all affect acceptance. This kind of attunement (or lack of it) tends to reinforce itself in a circular pattern, owing to its effects on self-esteem and social self-confidence. The good adjustment of well-liked children is bolstered by their popularity; inept children become even more ill at ease when they are ignored or rejected by the group (Glidewell, Kantor, Smith, & Stringer, 1966).

When researchers study children's popularity, how do they determine which children are most popular? It is important to note that they usually rely on the children's own perceptions, rather than on the judgments of adults observing them (for example, see Boivin & Begin, 1986). As well, children's popularity is studied in the context of a particular group, such as the children's class at school. For example, each child in the class is asked to nominate three children she likes most (positive nominations) and three children she likes least (negative nominations). Children differ in the number of nominations they receive, and based on the number and types of nominations, children are labelled *popular, average, rejected, neglected,* or *controversial.* Popular children receive lots of positive nominations and no negative ones. Average children receive more positive nominations than negative ones. **Rejected children** receive numerous negative nominations and few, if any, positive ones. These children's classmates openly dislike them. Neglected children do not receive many nominations at all. They are not mentioned as the most liked, nor as the least liked. They tend to be ignored. Controversial children receive numerous positive nominations and numerous negative ones. They seem to rub some children the right way, but others the wrong way.

In recent years, researchers have been especially interested in children who are rejected by peers (Boivin, Hymel, & Bukowski, 1995). These children, more than any of the others, are at risk for a variety of problems, including mental illness, behavioural disorders, and school failure (Bagwell et al., 1999; Kupersmidt, Coie, & Dodge, 1990). Why are children rejected by peers? Two types of children tend to be rejected: those who are overly aggressive and those who are shy and withdrawn (Rubin, LeMare, & Lollis, 1990). Aggressive children are at risk for acting-out problems, which can take the form of conduct disorders. Withdrawn children are at risk for internalized problems, such as depression (Boivin, Poulin, & Vitaro, 1994). Interestingly, aggressive children often deny having difficulties with peers (Boivin & Hymel, 1997). But withdrawn children's self-perceptions are more negative. Boivin and Hymel (1997) have outlined a model in which children's social withdrawal ultimately leads to loneliness and depression through the mediating effects of peer rejection and victimization. It is important to note, though, that the effects of social withdrawal vary with the children's social contexts, ages, and cultures. In Western cultures, such as those of Canada and the United States, withdrawn children are rejected (Boivin & Hymel, 1997). However, if the children are part of a group of peers in which many of the children are withdrawn, they are more accepted (Stormshak et al., 1999). Older withdrawn children are rejected even more than younger ones. However, in Eastern cultures, such as that of China, withdrawn children under 12 years are not rejected by peers (Chen, Rubin, & Li, 1995). Chinese culture assigns more positive value to shy, sensitive, and inhibited behaviours in young children.

Just as the consequences of children's withdrawn behaviour vary in different contexts, so do the consequences of children's aggressive behaviour (Stormshak et al., 1999). American boys who were aggressive in grade one were more likely to be rejected by their classmates if they were in a class that, as a group, was nonaggressive than if they were in a class in which many children were aggressive. Whether classmates

rejected children Children whose classmates give them numerous negative nominations for popularity and few, if any, positive ones. These children are at risk for such problems as mental illness, behavioural disorders, and school failure.

FOCUS ON AN ISSUE

Nicknames

Remember the good old days in elementary school when you were called everything but the name your parents gave you? You may have been lucky enough to have borne the nickname "Chief" or "Coach" or "Ace," or you may have been unfortunate enough to be called "Dumbo" or "Four-Eyes" or even "Sewage." These labels may seem amusing to adults, but they are a serious matter to children. Recent research has shown that nicknames may teach children about social status, friendship, morality, and the adult world itself.

To get to the bottom of the nickname puzzle, Rom Harre and his colleagues (1980) surveyed thousands of youngsters and adults in the United States, Great Britain, Spain, Mexico, Japan, and the Arab countries. What they found is that children between the ages of 5 and 15 often create separate and secret worlds for themselves and that nicknames may perform important social functions in these worlds.

One of the main reasons children bestow nicknames on one another is to separate "us" from "them." Children who have no nicknames are considered too insignificant to bother with. They tend to be low in popularity and to be isolated from the rest of the group. As Harre and his colleagues (1980) point out, "To be nicknamed is to be seen as having an attribute that entitles one to social atten-

tion, even if that attention is unpleasant. Thus, it may be better to be called 'Sewage' than merely John" (p. 81).

The "Fatties" and "Lamebrains" of the group are used as examples by group leaders to show how people are not supposed to be. They are walking advertisements of violated group standards. These group standards are the children's attempts to internalize society's norms. Through nicknames, children loudly proclaim what is acceptable

---

Children who have no nicknames are considered too insignificant to bother with.

---

to society and what is not. Any behaviour, style, or physical characteristic that does not meet society's standards can become the source of a nickname. So, when children call others "Stinky," "Pimples," or "Eagle Nose," they are trying to internalize the accepted adult norms for cleanliness and appearance.

Unfortunately, for the recipients of these nicknames, the process can be very painful. However, as the researchers found, these children are often willing victims: "It is not necessarily the fattest, stupidest, and dirtiest who acquire the names 'Hippo' or 'Tapeworm-Woman,'

but those who willingly bear the humiliation of being symbols of childhood greed, improvidence, and aversion to washing" (Harre, 1980, p. 81).

Nicknames also express children's own sense of class consciousness, social separateness, and hidden knowledge. Nicknames that are understood by only a small circle of friends make outsiders of those who do not know their meaning. In some cases, nicknames communicate secret information that may be unknown to the children who actually bear the names. In one school, for example, the boys labelled the sexually available girls "Dragoon One," "Dragoon Two," and so on, even though the girls had no idea what these names meant.

Children use nicknames differently in various cultures. Nicknames like "The Lame One" or "The Three-Legged One," which poke fun at physical deformities, are much more common in Arab countries than in England or Japan. The Japanese are more likely to use animal and insect analogies. In any culture, it seems that nicknames help children to build the social reality they take with them into adulthood.

What's in a name? In the case of nicknames, there is a lot more than you might expect.

---

rejected an aggressive child depended on the kind of classroom he was in. Interestingly, this was not the case for children with another common problem—inattentiveness and hyperactivity. Inattentive or hyperactive children were not popular in any of the classes.

Now that researchers have a better understanding of behaviours that put children at risk for rejection, the next step is to work on prevention. The most common treatments for rejected children are based on behavioural programs that attempt to teach the children social skills (Asher & Coie, 1990; Erwin, 1993). In addition to changing the rejected child's behaviour, however, we also have to consider the attitudes of her classmates. Rejected children can become stigmatized, and even if they improve their behaviour, their peers still expect them to act "the old way." Therefore, solving the problem of peer rejection likely involves more than just treating the rejected child.

Peer Group Conformity Conforming to the peer group can be normal, healthy, and often desirable behaviour. As part of their daily behaviour, children conform to peer group standards, as well as to adult expectations. But children sometimes conform excessively to group norms, even when these standards are not helpful to the individual child, to the group as a whole, or to outsiders.

Which children are most strongly influenced by group pressures? There are a few characteristics that appear to be common in high-conforming children. They have feelings of inferiority and low "ego strength" (Hartup, 1970a). They tend to be more dependent or anxious than other children and are exceptionally sensitive to social cues. Children who have these characteristics also tend to monitor their own behaviour and verbal expressions very closely. They are especially concerned with how they appear to others and are constantly comparing themselves with their peers. Watching what others do or say and then adapting to the group norm is common to *self-monitoring children* (Graziano et al., 1987).

Peer pressure can be positive as well as negative. For example, a child who belongs to a group of high academic achievers might feel pressured to complete homework assignments. In fact, children are more likely to conform to peer pressure when it is positive than when it involves antisocial acts, such as drinking, smoking, or stealing. When peer pressure actually involves antisocial acts, boys are more likely than are girls to yield to it (Brown, Clasen, & Eicher, 1986). Children who are unsupervised after school also tend to conform to antisocial peer pressure more than those who are monitored by adults (Steinberg, 1986).

Conformity is especially meaningful to children during late middle childhood, when they are moving away from the security of family life. Preadolescents have a strong need to belong, to feel accepted, and to feel that they are part of a social setting larger than themselves. These needs coexist with an equally strong need for autonomy or mastery. Children try to exert some control over their social and physical environments, to understand the rules and limits, and to find a place within these limits. For this reason, they become very involved in making rules and learning rituals.

At several points in human development, this coexistence of autonomy and acceptance needs is especially important. It is critical for 1½-year-olds, who are just beginning to learn what they can do for themselves. During late middle childhood, these two opposing needs again become paramount. But the balance that the preadolescent works out is different from that of the toddler. For the older child, the peer group often satisfies both the need for acceptance and the need for autonomy.

Prejudice

prejudice A negative attitude formed without adequate reason and usually directed toward people because of their membership in a group.

Conformity within a peer group is normal and often desirable behaviour.

What happens to children as they move away from their families during middle childhood and discover that the norms of the broader culture differ from those at home? Children have this experience when they learn, for example, that their friends do not like spinach or do not go to church. The difference in attitudes can lead to special problems for minority group children, as they struggle to reconcile their own self-image with the unpleasant stereotypes and prejudices that they may encounter. This struggle can affect their behaviour, their school achievement, and their relationships with others. As we saw in our discussion of the *self-fulfilling prophecy* (Chapter 13), people tend to live up (or down) to the expectations of others (Howard & Hammond, 1985).

Prejudice means a negative attitude directed toward people because of their membership in a group, with the group being targeted on the basis of race, religion, national origin, language, or any other noticeable attribute. We tend to think of prejudice as an adult attitude, but racial awareness begins to develop early, during the preschool years (Aboud, 1988). A child develops a rigid sense of two groups—an ingroup and an outgroup. The ingroup contains people judged to be similar to the child, and they are perceived as the "good guys." The outgroup involves people who are different, and they are judged to be the "bad guys." The notions of an ingroup and an outgroup have been used to help understand prejudices based on race, language (French versus English), gender, and body build (slim versus obese) (Powlishta, Serbin, Doyle, & White, 1994).

Why do children develop the notions of an ingroup and an outgroup? In part, social learning can explain these notions. Children learn the prejudices of their families and of their larger cultures. But social learning does not provide a complete explanation because children do not become more prejudiced as they get older. In fact, kindergarten children are more prejudiced than older children (Powlishta et al., 1994). Two Canadian researchers, Anna Beth Doyle and Frances Aboud, have examined other factors related to children's prejudices. In particular, they have found a relationship between prejudices and immature social cognitive development (Doyle & Aboud, 1995). Young children's thinking about people is more rigid and overly simplistic. They tend to "judge a book by its cover." However, older children are much more flexible. For example, they understand that people from different racial backgrounds can be similar in spite of different appearances, sharing interests and personality traits, and that people from the same racial group are not necessarily similar.

> **Question to Ponder**
>
> How can we help children become less prejudiced?

Self-Concepts

As children grow older, their developing social cognition enables them to form a more accurate and complex picture of the physical, intellectual, and personality characteristics of other people. At the same time, they are able to form a more accurate and complex picture of their own characteristics. They compare themselves with their age mates, and they conclude, "I'm better than Chris at sports, but I'm not as good in math as Kerry," or "I may not be as pretty as Courtney, but I'm better at making friends." Children's emerging self-concepts, in turn, provide a "filter" through which they evaluate their own social behaviour and that of others (Harter, 1982).

Self-Image and Self-Esteem

Self-image refers to seeing oneself as an individual with certain characteristics. **Self-esteem** means seeing oneself as an individual with positive characteristics—as a person who will do well in the things that one thinks are important. In addition to developing overall self-esteem, children also develop self-esteem separately for cognitive functioning (for example, how well they do in school and how smart they think they are), social functioning (for example, how popular they are with peers), and physical functioning (for example, how they look and how well they do in sports) (Harter, 1982). A child's self-esteem is not necessarily consistent across these different domains. In addition, the extent to which a particular domain contributes to a child's overall sense of self-esteem varies with age. Children in elementary school base their overall self-esteem most on their cognitive and social functioning (Harter, 1982), whereas adolescents base their overall self-esteem most on physical factors.

> **self-image** Seeing oneself as an individual with certain characteristics.
>
> **self-esteem** Seeing oneself as an individual with positive characteristics—as someone who will do well in the things that one thinks are important.

During the school years, there is a positive correlation between self-esteem and academic performance (Alpert-Gillis & Connell, 1989). This means that children who do well in school tend to have higher self-esteem than children who do poorly. Some teachers have actually tried to improve children's academic performances by trying to boost their self-esteem (Damon & Hart, 1982). But these programs have not succeeded because high self-esteem does not cause high grades (Seligman, 1995); it is high grades that cause high self-esteem. Also, too frequent and inappropriate praise can have inadvertent negative effects.

In moderation, praise can be quite helpful. However, critics have suggested that too much praise, without the appropriate links to achievement or to ethical behaviour, creates children who do not have a real sense of their own strengths and weaknesses. They may begin to think, "I am great no matter what I do." This belief can create confusion and problems for them in peer and school relations (Damon & Hart, 1982), as the following example indicates:

Realistic praise—that is, praise linked to achievement—encourages the growth of self-esteem in children.

Question to Ponder

Do you remember when you were 12 years old? How do you think your personality at that time relates to the way you are today?

Early in my son's kindergarten year, he returned home with a three-by-five index card containing two words: "I'm terrific." Every child in his class had been given a similar card with the same two words. My son told me that his teacher had asked all the children to recite the words in class, to remember them, and to keep the cards for a further reminder. I asked my son what it all meant. He said that he was terrific and that his friends were terrific. He had no particular ideas about why, how, or what they were terrific at. (Damon, 1991, p. 12)

Children cannot be quickly inoculated with self-confidence through facile phrases such as "I'm great" or "I'm terrific." Researchers have recently raised concerns that when children are told that the most important thing in the world is how highly they think of themselves, they are clearly being sent a message that they are at the centre of the universe. This emphasis has been cited as possibly pushing children toward social insensitivity—or self-love. Furthermore, critics contend that without an objective moral referent beyond themselves, children cannot acquire a stable sense of right and wrong—for example, children may deny a misdeed even when caught red-handed because they are convinced of their rightness (Damon, 1991). Teachers, therefore, are encouraged to link praise to behaviour in order to encourage children to develop realistic self-esteem.

The self is therefore seen as a complex, highly individual, attitudinal framework that forms early and that is continually refined throughout the person's life. Since it requires considerable social feedback to develop, one's sense of self is highly sensitive to the culture and historical period in which one lives. For example, Western cultures, such as those of Canada and the United States, emphasize people's uniqueness. Eastern cultures, such as those of China and Japan, emphasize people's connections to others (Matsumoto, 1994). These cultural differences certainly influence the types of self-concepts that individuals develop (Heine & Lehman, 1995; Kitayama, 1993).

Summary and Conclusions

During middle childhood, a "culture of childhood" exists that is composed of customs, rules, games, and rituals. Distinctive beliefs and values also emerge through social play. These games and rituals help children to understand and adapt to the demands of the society in which they live.

Many children today are being raised in households that are experiencing stresses, such as those associated with poverty or divorce. Children, like adults, can often effectively handle some stress in their lives, but they may begin to show the negative effects of stress when multiple situations deteriorate. Various factors have been found to help children cope with multiple stresses. These factors include knowing what to expect, having a supportive and adaptable family, and having a resilient personality. For many children, unfortunately, these factors do not exist in their lives, and they may fall victim to the stress that overwhelms them.

Divorce is a stress that significantly affects the lives of children. They may feel guilty, sad, angry, or anxious. In addition, divorce changes their relationships with their parents—they may have to adjust to the loss of one parent, to the addition of stepparents, and to altered attention from the remaining parent. A child's adjustment to divorce is affected by the amount of hostility the parents show before the divorce, by how much the child's life actually changes because of the divorce, by the nature of relationships with parents after the divorce, and by the age and characteristics of the child.

Another factor that in recent years has affected families in increasing numbers is child abuse. There are three main explanations for child abuse: psychiatric, sociological, and situational. The psychiatric explanation focuses on parents as the cause of abuse, the sociological focuses on the social forces that foster abuse, and the situational looks at the interaction between parents and abused children as the prime causal factor. None of these explanations has clearly established a cause or found a workable solution to the multiple problems associated with child abuse.

Psychological abuse also occurs in children. The various sorts of psychological abuse include rejection, denial of emotional responsiveness, degradation, terrorization, isolation, and exploitation. Exploitation is most clearly seen in cases of sexual abuse.

In addition to the changes in family dynamics and the nature of play, middle childhood also brings considerable advances in social cognition to the child. Social cognition is thought, knowledge, and understanding of the social world in which the child lives. Social cognition includes social inference, meaning assumptions about the feelings of another; social relationships; and social regulations, meaning an understanding of the rules of justice and respect that underlie social functioning.

Moral judgment is also an aspect of social cognition. This term refers to the process of making decisions about right and wrong. Piaget and Kohlberg are cognitive theorists who suggest that moral thinking develops in stages during childhood. According to Piaget, children are first moral realists who believe that rules are physical things and that goodness or badness is determined by an action's consequences, and later they are moral relativists who believe that rules are made by people and thus may be changed by consensus. Children at this stage believe that an act's goodness or badness is determined by the intentions of the person who committed it.

Kohlberg describes three broad levels of moral development, which may be further divided into more specific stages. The first level, the preconventional level, is based on rewards and punishments; the second, the conventional level, is based on social conformity; and the third, the postconventional level, is based on self-chosen ethical principles. Kohlberg's theory has been accused of being culturally and gender specific. It has been described as a white, male, American view of morality. Gilligan states that the morality of boys and girls differs. She argues that boys are justice oriented, while girls are oriented toward caring and empathy in their moral choices.

Peer relationships and social competence are also powerful factors influencing social development during middle childhood. Selman has studied the development of friendship patterns during childhood. In the first stage, at age 6 and under, friendships are self-centred and based on proximity or convenience. In the second stage, at ages 7 to 9, friendships become more reciprocal and are based on an awareness of each other's feelings. In the third stage, at ages 9 to 12, children begin to include trust and the evaluation of each other's actions as the basis for friendship. Finally, in the fourth stage, which begins at age 12, children see friendships as stable, continuing relationships based on trust.

Friendships serve many purposes during middle childhood. Children learn social concepts and skills, and they develop self-esteem through friendships. Friends may complement each other; for example, one may be outgoing and one introspective. Often, they share revelations about themselves. This is more likely to be true for girls than boys. In addition to friendships, as children move through middle childhood, the peer group becomes more important. Peer groups imply shared norms and goals. Group conformity, therefore, becomes increasingly important. Peer groups often form hierarchies based on leadership and followership. When groups compete, feelings of exclusivity and hostility toward the opposing group develop. When competing groups undertake cooperative activities, these negative outcomes seem to be reduced.

The status of children within peer groups is based on their overall adjustment. As perceived by their peers, children are labelled average, popular, neglected, controversial, or rejected. Children who are overly aggressive or withdrawn are more likely to be rejected. Rejected children, more than other children, are at risk for later problems.

The children most susceptible to group pressure are those with low self-esteem who are anxious and monitor themselves very closely. They are more likely to identify with the group's norms as a way of enhancing their self-esteem. Group membership and conformity become especially meaningful to children during late middle childhood.

Prejudice and racial awareness develop early. As children get older, their attitudes toward children of other groups tend to be less rigid. However, in contrast to this cognitive change, older children are more likely to form friendships based on similarity.

Children develop self-esteem separately for cognitive, social, and physical functioning, in addition to their overall self-esteem. During the school years, children who earn higher grades at school tend to have higher self-esteem than children who do poorly. It is the high grades that lead to increased self-esteem, not the other way around. Cultural factors strongly influence the development of self-concept.

Key Terms and Concepts

child abuse (p. 437)

moral absolutism (p. 448)

moral judgment (p. 445)

moral realism stage
   (p. 446)

moral relativism stage
   (p. 446)

peer group (p. 452)

prejudice (p. 456)

rejected children (p. 454)

self-esteem (p. 457)

self-image (p. 457)

social cognition (p. 443)

social inference (p. 443)

social regulations
   (p. 444)

social relationships
   (p. 443)

Questions to Review

1. List several factors that affect children's ability to cope with stressful events.

2. What are the factors that influence the way a child responds to divorce?

3. Discuss three different explanations for child abuse.

4. List different forms of psychological abuse.

5. Explain social cognition and its significance for middle childhood. Include in your discussion three important components of social knowledge.

6. Describe the sequence of the development of social cognition during middle childhood.

7. Explain Kohlberg's cognitive theory of moral development and describe its connection to Piaget's theory of development.

8. List some criticisms of Kohlberg's model.

9. Discuss Gilligan's two methods of moral reasoning.

10. Describe the importance of friendship pairs during middle childhood.

11. Discuss developmental trends in peer groups.

12. Describe some characteristics of peer group formation.

13. How do rejected children differ from other children?

14. Why do children develop prejudices?

15. How is self-esteem related to performance in school?

Weblinks

www.voices4children.org/index.htm
Voices for Children
This Canadian site has a number of parenting resources, as well as descriptions of violence prevention initiatives in Canadian schools.

www.cwlc.ca/
Child Welfare League of Canada
This site has information on child abuse, the Young Offenders Act, foster children, adoption, and other topics.

www.canadiankids.net/
The Canadian Kids Page
This site has links to Internet sites that children created or that were designed for children's use.

Summing Up...

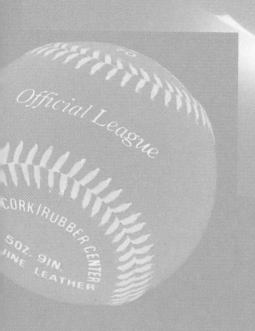

Middle Childhood

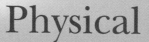

Physical

- Gains height and loses baby fat
- Girls are slightly shorter and lighter than boys until age 9
- Undergoes continued skeletal maturation
- By age 8, brain is 90% of adult size
- Develops maturity in corpus callosum
- Improves in strength, speed, and coordination required for gross motor skills
- Develops fine motor skills

Psychosocial

- Adopts culture of childhood
- Acquires values, expectations, and patterns of behaviour of families
- Develops coping mechanisms for stress
- Develops social cognition—social inferences, understanding of social relationships
- Develops morality—passes from the moral realism stage to the moral relativism stage (age 7 or older)
- Forms friendships—self-centred relationships (younger than 7), reciprocity (ages 7 to 9), genuine give-and-take (ages 9 to 12)
- Develops increased empathy
- Becomes part of more rigid and formal peer group (ages 10 to 12)
- Develops greater overall self-esteem, as well as cognitive, physical, and social self-esteem

Cognitive

- Develops concrete operational thought
- Develops flexible and reversible thought
- Can evaluate cause-and-effect relationships
- Can solve conservation problems
- Significantly improves in memory recall (ages 5 to 7)
- Increases use of memory strategies, such as rehearsal
- Improves in metacognition
- Masters academic tasks

Adolescence: A Time of Transition

The young ...
are full of passion, which
excludes fear;
and of hope, which inspires confidence.

ARISTOTLE
RHETORIC BOOK II

Outline CHAPTER 15

Objectives

By the time you have finished this chapter, you should be able to do the following:

- ✔ Include cultural and historical factors as part of a discussion of adolescent development.

- ✔ Discuss physical maturation during adolescence and describe the way in which cultural ideals influence an adolescent's adjustment to these changes.

- ✔ Discuss the factors that influence an adolescent's emerging sexuality and gender identity.

- ✔ Describe the cognitive changes that occur during adolescence and explain how these changes affect the scope and content of adolescent thought.

Adolescence is a time of enormous change. A person enters adolescence a child and leaves an adult. He changes physically, psychologically, and socially. In traditional cultures, the physical, psychological, and social transitions occur at about the same time and the transitional period is brief. The different spheres of development are in synch; as soon as the child looks like an adult, he is expected to think and behave like one and to take his place as an adult member of the society. Adolescence is a short-lived period.

In Western culture, though, adolescence stretches over the better part of a decade. Physical, psychological, and social developments follow different timetables. The adolescent may mature physically, but she may not yet be given full-fledged adult status. In some contexts, she is expected to act like a child—she is required to attend school and to obey her parents. In other contexts, she is expected to act as responsibly as an adult—she is permitted to look after younger children on her own. Adolescence has an ambiguous beginning and end in our culture, as it does in all modern technological societies (Fox, 1977, 1997; Simmons, 1996). In previous centuries, the physical maturation of puberty occurred later than it does now. Today, a girl has her first menstrual period at an average age of 12½; in the 1880s, the average age was 15½ (Frisch, 1988). When puberty occurred at 15 or 16, the social transition from youth to adult followed closely on the heels of physical change. Now, in Canada and in other industrialized countries, there is an interval of several years between attaining biological maturity and making the social transition to adulthood. Therefore, young people who are mature in a physical sense are nonetheless considered too young for the privileges and responsibilities of full adulthood (Miles, 1995).

In a technologically advanced society where complex jobs go to adults, adolescents experience prolonged dependence. In most cases, the jobs available to them are neither intrinsically interesting nor financially rewarding. This situation prolongs adolescents' dependence on their parents, delays the time when they can fully use their capabilities, and increases their frustration and restlessness, which can lead to conflict and stress. Compared with younger children, adolescents question and contradict their parents more, have more frequent negative moods, and engage in riskier behaviour (Arnett, 1999). However, there are individual differences among adolescents, and some do not have these conflicts. Having no conflict, or only mild to moderate conflict, is considered normal (Arnett, 1999). In the past, psychoanalysts emphasized conflict during adolescence so much that no conflict was considered abnormal (A. Freud, 1958). Because there can be "normal" conflict during adolescence, we must be careful not to excuse adolescent conflicts that are clearly not normal (see the discussion of adolescent suicide in Chapter 16).

Development in a Cultural and Historical Context

Although there are patterns in human development that are common to all societies and to all eras, the process of development is always deeply affected by the social and economic forces of the times. This is especially true of adolescence, when the individual tries to come to terms with social pressures and to strike a balance between internal and external values.

Adolescents are highly sensitive to the society around them—its values, its political and economic tensions, its unwritten rules. They are in the process of forming plans and expectations about their own future, and these expectations will depend in part on the cultural and historical setting in which they live. For example, adolescents who spent their earlier years in a period of economic expansion, when jobs were easy to get and family incomes were increasing, tend to expect similar conditions when they enter the job market. They expect their standard of living to be at least as good as that of their parents. They may be unprepared if the economic conditions that prevailed during their childhood worsen around the time that they enter adulthood (Greene, 1990).

Economic and cultural conditions also can have an impact on the timing of the milestones of growing up. Adolescence may be a brutally short prelude to independence, or it may involve prolonged dependence on the family. In 19th-century Ireland,

In technologically advanced societies, adolescents must wait until they are old enough to obtain jobs that are interesting and financially rewarding. One ritual of "waiting" is hanging out with friends.

for example, potato famines caused widespread poverty and suffering. Young men stayed at home because their labour was needed to keep the families alive. Their growth to adult independence was stunted by terrible economic need. In Canada and the United States, the Great Depression of the 1930s altered plans and conferred unexpected responsibilities on young people coming of age during this period (Elder & Hareven, 1993). There was a tendency to grow up as quickly as possible—young people took on adult tasks and entered the job market sooner than they might have otherwise. In other parts of the world, especially in developing countries, the push for adolescents to enter adult roles remains. For instance, in Somalia, because families are typically large, children are often required to work by age 13 in order to help support the family (Dybdahl, 1996). At this age, girls have been promised for marriage to older men (Barnes & Boddy, 1995).

Rites of Passage

Around the time of puberty, many traditional societies have special rituals, challenges, and celebrations to indicate that the child is now an adult. Anthropologists refer to these symbolic events as **rites of passage,** or transition rituals. The transformation from child to adult is complete and affects all aspects of development—sexuality, identity, societal roles and responsibilities, family relationships, and spirituality (Scott, 1998). All members of the society recognize the transformation. The society guides children into adulthood.

According to Daniel Scott at the University of Victoria (1998), rites of passage are sorely missing in Canadian society, and this absence undermines adolescent development. Canadian adolescents are given mixed messages. Their attainment of adult status is hampered by continued financial dependence, by the need to live with parents long after puberty, by extended schooling, and by the lack of significant community responsibilities. It is difficult for adolescents to understand their place in society because it is ambiguous. Adolescent behaviours in our culture, such as body piercing, tattoos, hair styles, styles of dress, mannerisms, language, and risk taking, are attempts to distinguish themselves from children and adults. These behaviours are remarkably similar to those associated with rites of passage in traditional societies. The difference, though, is that traditional societies embrace these behaviours as part of the transformation into adulthood, whereas our society does not. According to some researchers, celebrations in our society, such as graduation ceremonies and religious confirmations, are important because they help youth feel connected to the society (Markstrom, Berman, Sabino, & Turner, 1998). Troubled youth often miss many of these experiences and feel alienated from society. They need recognition from society for attaining milestones such as completing academic upgrading, developing skills, getting a first job or a new job, opening a bank account, and obtaining a driver's licence. Troubled youths from Aboriginal backgrounds are developing more connection to society by experiencing culturally appropriate rites of passage, such as vision quests, which focus on Aboriginal spirituality and values.

rite of passage A symbolic event or ritual to mark life transitions, such as the one from childhood to adult status.

Question to Ponder

Today's teenagers go through puberty earlier than past generations. What impact do you think earlier puberty has on teenagers' social development?

Adolescence in Contemporary Western Society

In our society, adolescents experience a phenomenon called *age segregation*. Partly because of choices they make and partly due to circumstances over which they have no control, adolescents tend to remain apart both from younger children and from adults. Their separation from younger children deprives them of opportunities to guide and tutor those who are less knowledgeable than themselves. Their separation from the adult world means that they rarely have the opportunity to serve apprenticeships—to learn jobs by working alongside experienced people in responsible positions. Instead, adolescents are separated for many hours every day from the major activities, customs, and responsibilities of the rest of society. Of course, age segregation

Adolescent behaviours in our culture—such as body piercing, tatoos, hair styles, styles of dress, mannerisms, language and risk taking—are attempts by teenagers to distinguish themselves from children and adults.

is not total: adolescents interact with younger children by baby-sitting, caring for younger siblings, or working as camp counsellors. They also help parents with household chores and may hold after-school jobs that, if nothing else, teach them something about the world of work and commerce.

Global Crises Every historical age has had its wars, religious movements, and economic ups and downs, and today is no exception. Although the current period may be less explosive than previous ones, people continue to be distressed by crises at home, in the Middle East, Asia, Eastern Europe, and Africa. Adolescents are—and always have been—especially vulnerable and susceptible to such crises. In general, the state of the world affects adolescents much more than it does younger children (Keppel-Benson & Ollendick, 1993). After all, it is primarily adolescents and young adults who fight in wars, participate in riots, and sustain movements for social reform. It is primarily adolescents and young adults who support radical political and religious movements with their idealism, who lose their jobs during economic downturns, and who are hired during economic booms. The effects of events in the broader society are screened from young children by their families and local communities. These children feel the impact of economic recessions or wars only in a second-hand way, perhaps through their parents' unemployment or long-term absence. But many events of the time have a direct impact on adolescents, who must confront, absorb, and react to them. Other events have an indirect effect, through the mass media.

A Mass Media Society The mass media provide a flood of information and sensations—blending trivial advertising, sensationalized drama, and pressing world issues. Most advertising is meant to sell, not to inform. Television news programs are, to a large extent, a form of entertainment. It is hard even for adult viewers to know what to believe. There is little opportunity for critical analysis of the information or interpretations that are presented.

Most theories of human development emphasize the importance of having an emotionally supportive and responsive environment to promote learning. Individuals of any age learn best when they can act on their environment, perceive the consequences of their actions, and have some power to effect change. But there is no way to alter the events on television, radio, or the movie screen. Some critics suggest that teenagers, with their rapidly developing physical and cognitive capacities, are particularly vulnerable to the passive role of consumer of the mass media. Perhaps they learn casual acceptance of tragedy or brutality or they develop a thirst for excessive raw stimulation. Perhaps they model their behaviour on the trite or bizarre events they see portrayed in movies or on television.

The mass media have increased adolescents' exposure to advertisements. Recently, the Canadian government has turned its attention to the effects of tobacco advertising on the smoking habits of teenagers. In 1988, the federal government passed Bill C-71, which bans all tobacco advertisements directed at young people, because adolescents are clearly not oblivious to the advertisements. For instance, 50 percent of 13- and 14-year-olds are able to recognize four or more cigarette brands with all text and logos removed. And 69 percent can match brand names with the sporting events that they sponsor (Statistics Canada, 1994). Adolescents are aware that advertisements are designed to influence sales, yet they still accept the product claims (Covell, 1995). They are unaware that the advertisements have affected their beliefs and behaviours, although, interestingly, they believe that other people are influenced by advertisements. Girls, more than boys, respond to image-oriented advertisements (Covell, 1995). In these advertisements, smoking is associated with people who are confident, attractive, well dressed, grown-up looking, healthy, and slim. These advertisements appeal especially to 11- to 13-year-old girls, which is of concern because the rate of smoking is increasing in young girls but not in young boys. For example, the number of 15- to 19-year-old girls who smoke daily has increased from 23 percent in 1989 to 25 percent in 1995 (*Canada Year Book*, 1997), whereas the number of boys has remained unchanged at 21 percent. The number of adults who smoke daily has declined.

Work and School

School and work are the main activities of Canadian adolescents (CCSD, 1998). Since the 1980s, youth have been staying in school longer. In 1981, 50 percent of 18-year-olds were still in school, and by 1995, 75 percent were. Along with the longer time youth spend in school, there has been an increase in the number who seek jobs while in school. According to recent Canadian research, working seems not to affect school performance if the adolescent works fewer than 15 hours per week during the school year or works only during the summer (CCSD, 1998). Furthermore, working provides them with spending money, the opportunity to save for postsecondary education, and work experience. However, working more than 15 hours per week during the school year is associated with lower grades. Furthermore, adolescents who work more hours are more likely than other adolescents to smoke and to use alcohol.

The opportunity for adolescents to attain jobs fluctuates from year to year, depending on the economy. During the 1990s, jobs became increasingly scarce owing to recession and loss of low-skilled jobs. The number of adolescents who have never held a job has been growing since the 1990s. Finding summer employment has become difficult. In 1989, 65 percent of teens found summer jobs; in 1997, only 45 percent found them. Many adolescents today are missing the advantages that come with work experience. On a positive note, some adolescents who were unable to find employment during the 1990s have turned to volunteer work. There has been a substantial increase in the number of teens doing volunteer work during the 1990s.

Physical Maturation

Physiologically, adolescence ranks with the fetal period and the first 2 years of life for sheer rate of biological change. Unlike infants, however, adolescents have the pain and pleasure of observing the whole process; they watch themselves with alternating feelings of fascination, delight, and horror as the biological changes occur. Surprised, embarrassed, and uncertain, adolescents constantly compare themselves with others and continually revise their self-image. Both sexes anxiously monitor their development, or lack of it, with knowledge and misinformation, pride and fear, hope and trepidation. Always, there is comparison with the prevailing ideal; trying to reconcile differences between the real and the ideal is one of the problems that adolescents experience during this period of transformation.

Biological Changes

The biological hallmarks of adolescence are a marked increase in the rate of growth, rapid development of the reproductive organs, and the appearance of secondary sex characteristics. Some changes occur in both boys and girls—increased size, improved strength and stamina—but most of them are sex specific.

Hormones The physical changes are controlled by **hormones,** which are biochemical substances secreted in very small amounts by the endocrine glands. The hormones affecting adolescent growth are present in trace amounts from fetal life on, but their output is greatly increased during puberty (see the box "Are Adolescents the Victims of Raging Hormones?"). "Male" hormones and "female" hormones are present in members of both sexes, but males have more of the hormones called *androgens*, the most important of which is *testosterone*, and females have more of the hormones called *estrogen* and *progesterone* (Tanner, 1978).

Each hormone influences a certain set of targets or receptors. For example, the secretion of testosterone causes the penis to grow, the shoulders to broaden, and hair

hormone A biochemical secretion of the endocrine gland that is carried by the blood or other body fluids to a particular organ or tissue and acts as a stimulant or an accelerator.

The onset of puberty requires considerable adaption, whether to a suddenly crackly voice, longer legs, or unfamiliar passions or feelings.

to grow in the genital area and on the face. Similarly, estrogen causes the uterus and the breasts to grow and the hips to broaden. The cells in the target area have the ability to respond selectively to some of the hormones circulating in the bloodstream and to not respond to others: the uterus, for example, selectively responds to estrogen and progesterone. Targeted cells are exquisitely sensitive to minute quantities of the appropriate hormones, even though the hormones are present in such small amounts that it is like detecting a pinch of sugar dissolved in a swimming pool (Tanner, 1978).

The Negative Feedback System for Hormones   The endocrine glands secrete a delicate and complex balance of hormones, the maintenance of which is the job of an area of the brain, the *hypothalamus,* and the *pituitary gland.* The hypothalamus is the part of the brain that initiates the processes of growth and reproduction during adolescence. In the hypothalamus there are minute quantities of chemicals called releasing and inhibiting factors. There is a releasing and inhibiting factor for each of the pituitary's trophic (growth-stimulating) hormones. When the hypothalamus receives a blood-borne chemical message telling it that some hormone is too low, it secretes the appropriate releasing factor into the bloodstream, which, in turn, causes the pituitary gland to produce the hormone. When sufficient quantities of the hormone are detected in the blood, the hypothalamus secretes an inhibiting factor that tells the pituitary gland to stop producing the hormone.

The pituitary is located on the underside of the brain. This gland produces several varieties of hormones, including growth hormone, which controls the overall growth of the body, and some secondary trophic hormones. The trophic hormones stimulate and regulate the functioning of a number of other glands, including the sex glands—the testes in the male and the ovaries in the female. The sex glands have two jobs: to produce sperm or eggs and to secrete androgens or estrogens. The hormones secreted by the pituitary gland and by the sex glands have emotional as well as physical effects upon adolescents.

We can see that there are complex chemical messages constantly being sent through the blood stream among the hypothalamus, the pituitary, and the target organs such as the sex glands. Levels of hormones in the body are controlled by the negative feedback system described above. When low levels of a specific hormone return to the hypothalamus, the appropriate releasing factors are produced and the pituitary secretes the hormone. When sufficient levels are reached, inhibiting factors from the hypothalamus signal the pituitary to stop producing the hormone. In this way, a balance of hormones is achieved within the body. Without this balance, our height, weight, gender characteristics, and reproduction would be seriously affected.

puberty The attainment of sexual maturity in males and females.

menarche The time of the first menstrual period.

Pubescence   Puberty refers to the attainment of sexual maturity in males and females. This maturity is marked in females by the first menstrual period, or **menarche,** and by the first *seminal emission* in males. The period of time that precedes puberty—during which a physical growth spurt occurs—is referred to as *pubescence.* We therefore say that a person is "going through pubescence" but "attains puberty."

The changes of puberty are usually preceded by an increase in body fat; some preadolescents become noticeably pudgy at this time. Both males and females also have fat deposited in the breast area. In females, this fat deposit will be permanent; in males, this is a passing phase. This development is followed, in late childhood or in early adolescence, by a large increase in height. Growth of this magnitude has not occurred since infancy and toddlerhood. Both bones and muscles increase in size, triggered by the

FOCUS ON AN ISSUE

Changing Sleep Habits in Adolescence

Sleep deprivation is becoming a common problem for adolescents, as well as for adults. In a recent study, 87 percent of adolescents report that they are not getting enough sleep (Wolfson & Carskadon, 1998). They are staying up later on school nights—40 percent report that they go to bed after 11:00 p.m.—and are forced to awaken early the next day for school (91 percent were up by 6:30 a.m.). Most are getting far less sleep than 9.2 hours a night, the average amount that is required during adolescence. Even though their sleep needs are high, there has been a change in adolescents' biological clocks so that adolescents have a natural tendency to delay sleep. At this age, more people describe themselves as "night hawks" than as morning people. This change in sleep rhythms does not fit well with most school start times. It also affects sleeping habits on weekends,

when adolescents stay up even later and sleep in the next morning.

Sleep deprivation seems to be having an effect on adolescents' daytime functioning. School performance can be affected by sleepiness. Adolescents

---

School performance can be affected by sleepiness.

---

who are struggling or failing at school (making Cs, Ds, or Fs) report that they get less sleep, have later bedtimes, and have more irregular sleep/wake schedules than do students who are excelling (making As and Bs). However, there are some exceptions—some high-performing students are able to do well on less sleep, but on average, students perform better if they are getting more sleep.

In addition to school performance, other behaviours are associated with differences in sleep habits. Students who get less sleep on school nights are more likely to report depressed mood, daytime sleepiness, and behavioural problems. It is unclear whether lack of sleep causes these other problems or whether the depressed mood and other problems cause the lack of sleep.

What can be done about sleep deprivation of adolescents? One approach is to get adolescents to go to bed earlier, although this approach is not likely to work because their biological clocks are shifted so that they need to go to bed later, not earlier. As well, most adolescents are not told when to go to bed—over 80 percent regulate their own bedtimes. Another approach is to change the start time of school so that it is later and more in synch with adolescents' biological clocks.

---

same set of hormones. In the course of this growth spurt, boys generally lose most of the extra fat that they acquired at its beginning. Girls, however, tend to keep most of the fat that they have acquired, although it ends up being distributed in different places.

During early adolescence, different parts of the body develop at varying rates. The head has pretty much stopped growing by now, as most of its development was completed in the first 10 years of life. Next to reach adult size are the hands and feet; then, there is an increase in leg and arm length. The gangly physique that frequently results at this time may make adolescents feel awkward. The growth of the extremities is followed by growth in body width, with full development of the shoulders coming last.

Another change is the increase in size and activity of sebaceous (oil-producing) glands in the skin, which causes the teenager's face to break out in acne. A new kind of sweat gland also develops in the skin, causing a stronger body odour.

Sex Differences in Pubescence The sexes develop at different rates. On average, girls experience the growth spurt and the other biological changes of pubescence about two years before boys do (see Figure 15-1). However, there is a great deal of variation in the rate of development among members of the same sex. A late-maturing boy or girl may still look like a child, whereas another boy or girl of the same chronological age will have the appearance of a full-grown man or woman. Once the sequence of sexual maturation has begun, it progresses in a fairly predictable order. Keeping in mind the wide individual differences in timing, let us look at the general schedule of physical changes that characterize adolescence.

SEXUAL MATURATION IN MALES

After the growth spurt, the second major biological change is development of the reproductive system. In males, the first indication of puberty is the accelerating growth

FOCUS ON AN ISSUE

Are Adolescents the Victims of Raging Hormones?

The adolescent period in most Western cultures is marked by changes in behaviour and appearance. Historically, most of these changes have been described as negative and have often been attributed to changes in biological factors—especially hormones. Many authors and parents have claimed that adolescents are the victims of their raging hormones. But is this actually true?

From a physiological perspective, hormones act on the brain in two ways. First, sex hormones can influence personality and behaviour by their early effects on brain development. These effects are permanent and therefore are not affected by the change in hormone levels during pubescence. Second, hormones may activate specific behaviours through their effects on the nervous system. These effects tend to be immediate or slightly delayed. Physical and sexual maturation result from an interaction of the hor-

Many authors and parents have claimed that adolescents are the victims of their raging hormones.

monal levels, health factors, and genetics of the developing person. However, there is little support for any direct relationship between levels of hormones during adolescence and the following behaviours (Buchanan, Eccles, & Becker, 1992):

- moodiness
- depression
- restlessness and lack of concentration
- irritability
- impulsiveness
- anxiety
- aggression and behavioural problems

Not all adolescents exhibit dramatic changes in these behaviours, even though all experience hormone increases. Therefore, it is likely that other factors may be involved in producing these behaviours. These factors have been suggested to include changing roles, social or cultural expectations, environmental situations in the home or school, and even the media.

of the testes and scrotum. Approximately one year after this growth has begun, the penis undergoes a similar spurt in growth. In between these two events, pubic hair begins to appear, but it does not attain full growth until after the completion of genital development. During this period, there are also increases in the size of the heart and lungs. Owing to the action of the male sex hormone, testosterone, boys also develop more red blood cells than girls do. This extensive production of red blood cells may be one factor—although certainly not the only one—in the superior athletic ability of the male adolescent over the female.

The first seminal emission (expulsion of semen from the penis) may take place as early as age 11 or as late as age 16. The initial ejaculation usually occurs during a boy's rapid period of growth and may come about during masturbation or in a "wet dream." These first emissions generally do not have enough semen to be fertile (Money, 1980).

One reason girls often feel more mature than boys their own age is that the female growth spurt during puberty occurs about 2 years before the male growth spurt.

Any unflattering description of the adolescent boy invariably includes his awkwardly cracking voice. However, the actual voice change takes place relatively late in the sequence of pubertal changes, and in many boys, it occurs too gradually to be significant as a developmental milestone (Tanner, 1978).

SEXUAL MATURATION IN FEMALES

In girls, the "breast buds" are usually, but not always, the first signal that puberty has begun. There is simultaneous development of the uterus and vagina, with enlargement of the labia and clitoris.

Menarche (the first menstruation), which is probably the most dramatic and symbolic sign of a girl's changing status, actually occurs late in the sequence, after the peak of the growth spurt. Menarche may occur as early as age 9½ or as late as age 16½; the average is about 12½. As we said, previous generations matured more slowly

Where family problems exist during early and middle childhood, for example, family dysfunction increases during adolescence. In dysfunctional families, problems with inappropriate sexual behaviour, running away, aggression, and drug use may occur. However, where parent–child relationships are good before adolescence, relationships generally continue to be good through adolescence as well, and parents continue to have a major positive influence on their children (Buchanan et al., 1992).

This is not to say that hormones have no effect on behaviour. But their effect is often mediated by existing psychological or social factors in the home environment. For example, Udry (1988) reported that the level of testosterone was generally a strong predictor of sexual involvement among 12- to 16-year-old girls. However, its effect was reduced or eliminated by the presence of a father in the home or by the girl's participation in sports. Fathers who are present tend to raise girls' self-esteem in ways that lessen their need to be sexually active. They are also more likely to create, with the mother's guidance and role modelling, situations that stress relationships rather than sexual behaviour in itself. These environmental variables may reduce the potential for sexual involvement and thus override any hormonal effects on behaviour.

The researchers conclude that although additional research is needed in this area, the explanation of raging hormones as a direct cause of adolescent behaviour is a myth. Other cognitive and social factors, including social inference, moral judgment, and a sense of hope for the future, may override any of the immediate, short-term effects of hormones during adolescence. For

Evidently the famous raging hormones of adolescence do not produce moodiness directly as commonly believed.

adolescents, then, biology, or more specifically, hormones, are not destiny.

than girls do today. The acceleration in sexual development is apparently due to improved nutrition and health care. In some parts of the world, menarche still occurs considerably later. The average Czechoslovakian girl has her first period at age 14,

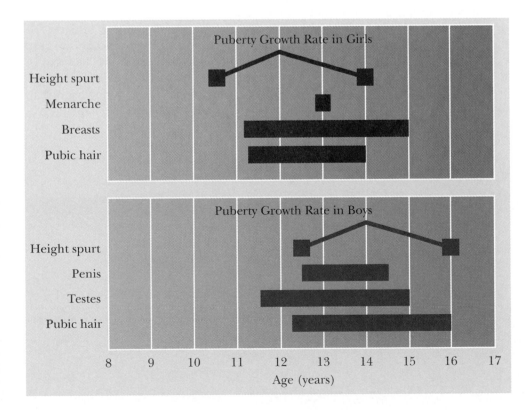

Figure 15-1
Growth Rates and Sexual Development during Pubescence
The peak in the line labelled "height spurt" represents the point of most rapid growth. The bars below represent the average beginning and end of the events of pubescence.

among the Kikuyu of Kenya the average age is 16, and for the Bindi of New Guinea it is 18 (Powers, Hauser, & Kilner, 1989). Menarche generally occurs when a girl has nearly reached her adult height and when she has managed to store a minimum amount of body fat. For a girl of average height, this landmark generally occurs when she weighs around 100 pounds (Frisch, 1988).

The first few menstrual cycles vary tremendously from one girl to another; they also tend to vary from one month to another. In many cases, the early cycles are irregular and anovulatory—an egg is not produced (Tanner, 1978). But it is unwise for a young teenage girl to count on her infertility, as many pregnant 13-year-olds can attest. (We will return to the subject of teenage pregnancies later in this chapter.)

We may see the typical physical changes during pubescence presented in Concept Summary Table 15-1.

Body Image and Adjustment

Young adolescents are frequently fascinated with, and continually appraising, their bodies. Are they the right shape, the right size? Are they coordinated or clumsy? How do they compare with the ideal? Sociologists consider adolescents to be a "marginal group," either between cultures or on the fringe of a dominant culture. Typically, such groups tend to exhibit an intensified need for conformity. For this reason, adolescents can be extremely intolerant of deviation, whether it be a deviation in body type, such as being too fat or too thin, or a deviation in timing, such as being a late maturer. The mass media manipulate this tendency by marketing stereotypical images of attractive, exuberant youths who glide through adolescence without pimples, braces, or awkwardness. Because adolescents are often extremely sensitive about their own physical appearance and spend a lot of time scrutinizing themselves and their friends, the discrepancies between their less-than-perfect self-images and the glossy ideals they see in magazines and on television are often a source of considerable anxiety.

During middle childhood, children become aware of different body types and ideals, and they gain a fairly clear idea of their own body type, proportions, and skills. But in adolescence, body type receives much closer scrutiny. In our society, some young people subject themselves to intense dieting, whereas others embark on rigorous regimens of physical fitness and strength training—weight lifting, athletics, or dancing. In general, girls worry about being too fat or too tall, whereas boys are concerned about being too scrawny (not muscular enough) and too short. The reason weight is important to girls is that they are extremely concerned about social acceptance, and plumpness is frowned on in our society. There are many perfectly normal, even lean, adolescent girls who are medically healthy but who consider themselves

Concept Summary

Table 15-1   Typical Changes in Adolescence

CHANGES IN GIRLS	CHANGES IN BOYS
• Breast development	• Growth of testes and scrotal sac
• Growth of pubic hair	• Growth of pubic hair
• Body growth	• Body growth
• Menarche	• Growth of penis
• Growth of underarm hair	• Change in voice
• Increased output of oil- and sweat-producing glands	• First ejaculation of semen
	• Growth of facial and underarm hair
	• Increased output of oil- and sweat-producing glands

obese and wish to lose weight (see the box "Anorexia and Bulimia"). Yet, other cultures consider plumpness to be a feminine ideal and view thinness in women as unhealthy or as indicating poor family circumstances.

For boys, the primary concern is with physical power that can be exerted on the environment (Lerner, Orlos, & Knapp, 1976). Therefore, height and muscles are important to young males. There are some other interesting differences in the changes that are desired by the two sexes. Girls want very specific changes: "I would make my ears lie back," or "I would make my forehead lower." Boys do not articulate their dissatisfactions this precisely. A typical boy's response is: "I would make myself look handsome and not fat. I would have wavy black hair. I would change my whole physical appearance so that I would be handsome with a good build." Both sexes worry about their skin: almost half of all adolescents voice concerns about pimples and blackheads.

Height, weight, and complexion are the major sources of concern for grade ten students. About two-thirds wish for one or more physical changes in themselves (Peterson & Taylor, 1980). Self-consciousness about one's body diminishes in late adolescence. As shown in a recent longitudinal study, body-image satisfaction is lowest for girls at age 13 and for boys at age 15; after these ages it rises steadily. At every age from 11 to 18, however, it is lower for girls than it is for boys (Rauste-von Wright, 1989; White, Mendelson, & Schliecker, 1995).

Girls' Reactions to Menarche Menarche is a unique event, a milestone on the path to physical maturity. It occurs suddenly and without warning and is heralded by a bloody vaginal discharge. In some parts of the world, it has major religious, cultural, or economic significance (Barnes & Boddy, 1995). It may trigger elaborate rites and ceremonies in some cultures, but in Canada, there is usually no such drama. Nevertheless, for the individual girl it holds considerable significance (Greif & Ulman, 1982).

A study of adolescent girls found menarche to be a memorable event. Only those who were ill prepared or who experienced menarche early described it as especially traumatic or negative. Most often these were girls who had not discussed the onset of menstruation with their mothers or with other women. Some who had a negative experience had received their information from men. But most girls had been prepared by their mothers or female relatives for menstruation and reported a positive reaction to menarche—a feeling that they were coming of age (Ruble & Brooks-Gunn, 1982).

Early and Late Maturers Timing in maturation—whether development is early or late—has engrossed researchers almost as much as adolescence itself. Ill-timed maturation is most likely to be a problem for the late-maturing boy. Because girls mature, on average, two years earlier than boys do, the late-maturing boy is the last to reach puberty and the last to experience the spurt in growth. As a result, he is smaller and less muscular than his age mates, which puts him at a disadvantage in most sports. Other children and adults tend to treat a smaller child as though he were a younger child; therefore, the late maturer has lower social status among his peers and is perceived as being less competent by adults (Brackbill & Nevill, 1981). Sometimes, this perception becomes a self-fulfilling prophecy, and the boy reacts with childish dependency and immature behaviour. In other cases, he may overcompensate and become very aggressive. At any rate, late-maturing boys have a far more difficult adjustment to make than early-maturing males, who tend to accrue all sorts of social and athletic advantages among their peers. From middle childhood on, early-maturing males are likely to be the leaders of their peer groups (Weisfeld & Billings, 1988).

Longitudinal studies reveal interesting, continuing differences related to the timing of maturity's arrival. In their 30s, the

Question to Ponder

Why do you think that so many Canadian girls are unhappy with their body images?

Young adolescents seem to be in love with the image they see in the mirror. In reality they are often very critical of their bodies and can become extremely anxious if they do not conform to an ideal set forth by either their peer group or the wider culture.

FOCUS ON AN ISSUE

Anorexia and Bulimia

ANOREXIA

Anorexia, which literally means lack of appetite, is often referred to as self-starvation. The key symptoms are (1) a refusal to maintain a minimal body weight for age and height—the person is at least 15 percent below normal weight; (2) an intense fear of becoming fat, even though the person is underweight; (3) a distorted body image—the person claims to feel fat even though she is emaciated; and (4) in females, absence of at least three consecutive menstrual periods (American Psychiatric Association, 1994). The person with anorexia is obsessed with limiting calories, often eating only 200 to 900 calories per day. An apple and two slices of bread might be the person's entire daily intake. And some people with anorexia are compulsive exercisers, engaging in several hours of vigorous exercise per day to work off the calories they have consumed.

Anorexia typically develops in girls between the ages of 14 and 18. A period of "normal dieting," which is triggered by the growth spurt during puberty, often precedes anorexia. During this growth spurt, people get taller and heavier, but not necessarily at an even pace. Some people put on weight before they get taller. These people are vulnerable to dieting. For some, dieting will lead to anorexia. Although

this is the typical pattern of anorexia, it is important to note that people with anorexia are a mixed group. Some do not fit this pattern and, instead, develop symptoms before puberty or in early adulthood. In addition, not all people with anorexia are female—5 percent are male (Worrell & Todd, 1996).

Why do people develop anorexia? No single cause explains all cases. Current thinking considers the influence of biological, psychological, and social-cultural factors (Brumberg &

Anorexia is much more common in some societies than in others.

Striegel-Moore, 1993; Smolak, Levine, & Striegel-Moore, 1996). However, it is surprisingly difficult to determine the causes of anorexia because of limitations in the method of study. In a typical study, researchers compare people who have anorexia and who have been starving for several months or years with other people of similar ages and backgrounds who do not have anorexia. People with anorexia differ from others in a number of ways. But can we automatically conclude that these differences caused the anorexia? Or,

are they consequences of the starvation? The starvation itself causes a number of physical and psychological changes. Can you think of another way to study the causes of anorexia? Perhaps researchers could target high-risk individuals and study them before they develop anorexia to see what changes precede the onset of the disorder. Let's now look at some of the biological, psychological, and social-cultural factors associated with anorexia.

The biological factors that have been considered are genetic vulnerability and hormone imbalances. In addition, the starvation leads to a number of physical changes, including slow heart rate, low blood pressure, low body temperature, abnormal metabolism, hair loss from head, growth of fine, black body hair, dehydration, extreme sensitivity to cold, and infertility (Holmes, 1997; Thompson & Sherman, 1993). If anorexia is prolonged, it can cause death, usually from kidney failure or heart damage (Slaby & Dwenger, 1993).

People with anorexia often share a number of psychological characteristics, including moodiness, depression, denial of the problem, and a paralyzing sense of ineffectiveness, even though they are often high achievers. They feel weak, unworthy, and obligated to be perfect. Their self-esteem is low, and they feel alienated from family and friends.

anorexia A type of eating disorder that involves self-starvation, a distorted body image, and sometimes compulsive exercise. It is caused by biological, psychological, and social factors.

early-maturing males still enjoy poise and social success. They tend to be responsible, cooperative, and self-controlled. In contrast to this, they may also be rigid, humourless, and unoriginal. The late maturers show a different pattern. They still show signs of immaturity and overcompensation by being impulsive and assertive, but they are also more perceptive, creative, and tolerant of ambiguity. By their 40s, the conspicuous success of the early maturers has significantly diminished. Early-maturing males tend to have relationship problems and are more likely to experience divorce. Late-maturing males, on the other hand, are more self-accepting and have strong relationships with their spouses and children (Jones, 1965). Livson and Peskin (1980) speculate that because late maturers have to learn how to deal with anxiety over their self-image, they develop more flexibility and better problem-solving skills in adolescence, skills that serve them well when they reach adulthood. Their greater success at relationships may come from the fact that since they were often excluded when young, they attach greater value to relationships as they mature and work harder to keep them.

They are especially uncomfortable eating around others (Crisp, 1984; Gordon, 1990; Thompson & Sherman, 1993). As well, people with anorexia often have disturbed family relationships, especially with their mothers. In healthy families, members are connected yet independent. But the mothers of girls with anorexia often are overinvolved with their daughters, living their lives through their daughters. In such cases, the anorexia appears to be an interpersonal problem, rather than an individual one.

Anorexia is much more common in some societies than in others. It is more prevalent in Canada, the United States, Europe, and Japan. And it is especially rare in China, Malaysia, and New Guinea (Gordon, 1990). This difference between societies has led researchers to consider how social-cultural factors contribute to the disorder (Brumberg & Striegel-Moore, 1993; Gordon, 1990). Societies with higher rates of anorexia share some common features.

First, there is a cultural obsession with thinness and an aversion to obesity. In Canada, the emphasis on low-fat diets and fitness results in society's viewing the early symptoms of anorexia (that is, the calorie restriction and compulsive exercise) as socially desirable. Second, the media portray the ideal female body as prepubescent, or thin as a poker. Third, the roles of women in these societies are often ambiguous, contradictory, and overwhelming. In these societies, women must juggle many roles, and they often feel out of control. Thinness becomes a way to compete and to demonstrate self-control. Interestingly, in more traditional societies in which women have fewer role choices, anorexia is rare. Fourth, meals are no longer social or religious occasions. Fast foods have replaced leisurely family meals. Interestingly, women in other cultures, such as India or Islamic countries, routinely fast, yet the behaviour is part of rich cultural and religious traditions. These women do not go on to develop anorexia.

Within Canada and other countries with high rates of anorexia, some individuals are especially vulnerable because they engage in activities that idealize thin body shapes. Anorexia is more prevalent among models, ballet dancers, gymnasts, figure skaters, wrestlers, and long-distance runners (Gordon, 1990; Thompson & Sherman, 1993). Sometimes, coaches and others involved in elite sport even encourage it (Thompson & Sherman, 1993).

The rate of anorexia has also changed in recent years. It increased rapidly through the 1970s and 1980s, but by 1992, it had started to decline (Colburn, 1995). We can only hope that the decline continues.

BULIMIA

Bulimia is similar in many ways to anorexia, but it is a different ailment. The bulimic personality is also terribly anxious about weighing too much but has an uncontrollable need to eat, especially sweets. To compensate for overeating, bulimics make themselves vomit. Therefore, bulimia is often described as a binge-and-purge pattern of eating.

As with anorexia, most bulimics are female. Bulimia usually afflicts someone in late adolescence, whereas many anorexics are in early or mid-adolescence. Some researchers estimate that about 20 percent of university-age women have engaged in bulimic eating patterns (Muuss, 1986). Several psychologists believe that the prevalence of bulimia among female university students indicates difficulty in adjusting to life away from home. Others contend that bulimics binge on sweets in an attempt to alleviate depression.

Women suffering from bulimia consume huge quantities of carbohydrates in a very short time frame, usually an hour or two. They then feel despondent and out of control. Although bulimia does not have fatal consequences, it is highly self-destructive and requires treatment. Bulimics tend to be more responsive to treatment than anorexics are. The fact that antidepressant drugs are often useful in the treatment of this disorder—even among patients who show no signs of depression—suggests to some researchers that a biochemical abnormality may be involved (Walsh, 1988).

If early maturity is an asset for teenage boys, it is a mixed blessing for girls. In girls, the initial advantage is attached to late maturity. The late-maturing girl matures at about the same time as most of her male peers. She shares the same interests and dating activities with them. She is more popular with her peers than the early-maturing girls are. The early-maturing girl, on the other hand, is taller, develops breasts sooner, and goes through menarche as much as six years before a few of her peers. As a result, she has fewer opportunities to discuss with her friends the physical and emotional changes she is undergoing. There are, however, compensations. The early-maturing girl frequently feels more attractive, is more popular with older boys, and goes out on dates more frequently than her late-maturing age mates (Blyth et al., 1981). In the long term, she is more likely to marry early, have more children, and have less education (Magnusson, 1996). Therefore, early biological maturation changes experiences in other domains.

It is also important to note that the timing of puberty can affect individuals

bulimia A type of eating disorder that involves a binge-and-purge pattern of eating.

There is great variation in the timing of maturation. Very early or late maturation affects an adolescent's status in his peer group.

differently. For example, girls who are serious ballet dancers have more positive body images if they go through puberty late, after age 14 (Brooks-Gunn, 1987). These girls prefer the slim, prepubescent body build because it is closer to the ideal dancer's body. But nondancers have more positive body images if they go through puberty on time, between the ages of 11½ and 14. However, the timing of puberty affects the body images of nondancers less than those of dancers.

Gender Identity and Sexual Practices

Directly related to the biological changes that adolescents must face is the issue of a mature gender identity. This identity includes the expression of sexual needs and feelings and the acceptance or rejection of sex roles. In Chapter 3, we saw how sex roles and sex-role stereotypes are forged long before adolescence, with one crucial period being the preschool years. During middle and late childhood, children associate mostly in same-sex peer groups in a sexually neutral way. With the attainment of puberty and adolescence, the biological changes of physical maturation bring a new interest in members of the opposite sex and a new need to integrate sexuality with other aspects of the personality. During adolescence, young people start entering into relationships in which sex plays a central role.

Developing Sexual Behaviour

The development of sexual consciousness and behaviour is different for girls than it is for boys. In adolescence, girls spend more time fantasizing about romance; boys are more likely to use masturbation as an outlet for their sexual impulses. However, masturbation and fantasizing are common in both sexes (Janus & Janus, 1993). According to one study, about half of adolescent girls and three-quarters of boys masturbate (Hass, 1979). Social-class differences play a part here, or at least they did in the past. The ability to develop a rich fantasy life during masturbation was reportedly more prominent in the middle-class male. Guilt over the "unmanliness" of masturbation was of greater concern to the working-class male. These differences seem to be gradually disappearing. In sexual behaviour, at least, the young middle-class male no longer seems to differ much from the young working-class male (Dreyer, 1982). Class differences in sexual behaviour have traditionally been less significant among females.

The expression of sexuality for both sexes is always dependent on the prevailing norms; it changes as these norms change. Some societies reserve sexuality exclusively for procreation. Others view such restrictions as silly or even as a crime against nature.

Changing Sexual Attitudes Historical changes in social attitudes are perhaps most clearly seen in our responses to our developing sexuality. In large part, adolescents view themselves, as do adults, according to the cultural norms of the time in which they live. Therefore, sexual practices and the quality of sexual relationships vary over time (Brooks-Gunn & Furstenberg, 1989/1997).

Prior to the mid-1960s, most young people felt that premarital sex was immoral, although older adolescent males were under some pressure to acquire sexual experience. Females, in contrast, were under pressure to remain virginal until marriage. By the late 1960s and early 1970s, sexual attitudes had changed considerably. Sorensen (1973) reported the findings of a study on adolescent sexuality. He stated that the majority of adolescents who completed his questionnaires did not think of sex as being inherently right or wrong, but instead judged it in terms of the relationship between the participants. The reactions of both partners to a sexual experience were thought to be equally important; most considered it immoral for one person to force another into a sexual relationship. A majority rejected the traditional "double standard" that gave a great deal of freedom to boys but very little to girls. Almost 70 percent agreed that two people should not have to get married to live together. And 50 percent approved of homosexuality between two consenting individuals—although 80 percent stated that they had never engaged in homosexual acts and would never want to. The subjects in this study clearly distinguished their own attitudes from those of their parents. Although most of the subjects had considerable respect for their parents, they felt that they differed from them a great deal in attitudes toward sex.

By the late 1970s, the sexual revolution was in full swing. In 1979, Chilman reviewed the findings of numerous studies and reported an increasing trend toward sexual liberalization, reflected both by an increase in sexual activity among adolescents and by a change in societal attitudes. Society had become more accepting of a wide range of sexual activities, including masturbation, homosexuality, and unmarried couples living together (Dreyer, 1982; Zgourides, 1996). Hass (1979) reported that 83 percent of the boys and 64 percent of the girls he interviewed approved of premarital intercourse; however, only 56 percent of the boys and 44 percent of the girls had actually experienced sexual intercourse. Note that there was not much difference between boys and girls in sexual activity. This statistic reflects the continuing decline in the double standard. The sexual revolution affected girls' behaviour much more than it did boys': even in the 1940s, 1950s, and 1960s, between one-third and two-thirds of teenage boys had already lost their virginity. During a similar span of years, the proportion of 16-year-old girls who had lost their virginity rose from 7 percent in the 1940s to 33 percent in 1971 and to 44 percent in 1982 (Brooks-Gunn & Furstenberg, 1989/1997).

The sexual revolution was not without problems. Although large numbers of adolescents were having sexual intercourse, many of them did not use birth control. As a result, the rate of pregnancies among teenage girls tripled in the 35 years from 1940 to 1975. Another problem was the spread of sexually transmitted diseases—first syphilis, gonorrhea, and genital herpes, and then, more recently, **AIDS (acquired immune deficiency syndrome)**. Although AIDS is still rare among adolescents, mainly because it often takes years for the symptoms to appear, they have a high rate for other sexually transmitted diseases (Ehrhardt, 1992). The most common sexually transmitted disease among Canadian adolescents is chlamydia (CICH, 1994). This disease, as well as gonorrhea and syphilis, occurs at much higher rates in girls than in boys (CICH, 1994). A recent survey in Nova Scotia indicated that only 27 percent of adolescents were aware that chlamydia is common in adolescence, and only 50 percent knew that an infected person can have no symptoms (Langille, Andreou, Beazley, & Delaney, 1998). Teenagers between the ages of 15 and 19 have the second-highest rate of sexually transmitted diseases in Canada (Sahai & Demeyere, 1996). The highest

The biological changes that occur during adolescence lead to an interest in and the development of a sexual identity.

AIDS (acquired immune deficiency syndrome) A fatal disease caused by a virus. Anyone can be infected through sexual contact or through exposure to infected blood or needles.

rate occurs in 20- to 24-year-olds. Sexually transmitted diseases are much rarer in any other age group. One way for people to reduce the risk of sexually transmitted diseases, besides practising abstinence, is to use condoms. Researchers are now studying the factors that influence people's decisions to use condoms (Gerrard, Gibbons, & Bushman, 1996; Godin et al., 1996; Varnhagen, Svenson, Godin, Johnson, & Salmon, 1991). For instance, Varnhagen et al. found that accessibility to condoms was an issue for teenagers. Both males and females were more comfortable purchasing condoms in washroom vending machines than in stores.

The sexual revolution began to decline by the early 1980s. Young people started being more cautious about sexual activity, and monogamy became fashionable again. During the 1980s, when asked what they thought of the sexual attitudes of the 1960s and 1970s, a sizable proportion viewed these attitudes as "bad." College students in 1980 were more likely than those in 1975 to consider sexual promiscuity "immoral" (Leo, 1984; Robinson & Jedlicka, 1982).

The late 1980s saw a continuation of the trend toward more conservative attitudes in sexual matters, as in other areas of life (Murstein, Chalpin, Heard, & Vyse, 1989). Although young people still see sex as an essential part of a romantic relationship, they are generally not in favour of casual sex (Abler & Sedlacek, 1989). Also, the majority of college students—of both sexes—now say that they would prefer to marry a virgin. Attitudes toward homosexuality also have become more negative again (Williams & Jacoby, 1989).

Sexual Relationships Although society as a whole has become somewhat more conservative with regard to sexual behaviour, teenagers continue to be highly active sexually. According to Health and Welfare Canada, 57 percent of males and 63 percent of females are sexually active between the ages of 15 and 19 (CICH, 1994).

Boys start having sex earlier and tend to have a somewhat different attitude toward it than girls do. For boys, sexual initiation is more likely to be with a casual partner, and they receive more social approval for their loss of virginity than girls do. Boys are also more likely to seek a second experience soon afterward, more likely to talk about their activity, and less likely to feel guilty than girls are (Zelnick & Kantner, 1977).

Several factors influence adolescent sexual behaviour. Chilman (1979) cites education, psychological makeup, family relationships, and biological maturation as being important. Let us consider these four factors in more detail.

Education is related to sexual behaviour partly because those who attain higher levels of education most frequently come from the mainstream middle and upper-middle classes, which tend to hold a more conservative attitude toward sex. This conservative attitude is held especially by adolescents who emphasize careers, intellectual pursuits, and educational goals. Another factor is the relationship between sexual behaviour and academic success or failure in high school: good students are less likely to initiate sexual activity at an early age (Miller & Sneesby, 1988). Perhaps adolescents who are failing academically turn to sexual activity as a way of gratifying their need for success. In the past, this may have been true more for girls than for boys because girls had fewer opportunities for achievement in other areas, such as sports. With the current emphasis on opportunities for women in all aspects of society, including sports, this situation may be changing.

To some extent, the psychological factors associated with early sexual experience for males are different from those for females. Sexually experienced male adolescents tend to have relatively high self-esteem, whereas sexually experienced females tend to have low self-esteem. However, for both sexes, early sexual activity is associated with other problem behaviours, such as drug use and delinquency (Donovan, Jessor, & Costa, 1988).

In the area of family relationships, a number of studies have found that parent–child interactions are related to adolescent sexual behaviour. Both overly restrictive and overly permissive parenting are associated with earlier sexual activity in adolescents; moderate restrictiveness tends to work best with this age group (Miller,

Question to Ponder

How do you think the media influence adolescents' sexual behaviours?

Miceli, Whitman, & Borkowski, 1996). Another significant factor is communication between parents and offspring: adolescents who are sexually active are more likely to report poor communication with their parents. Chilman (1979) is quick to point out, however, that good parent–child relationships will not necessarily prevent young people from experimenting with sex.

According to Chilman, the biological factors that influence early sexual behaviour constitute an important area of research, but these factors are the most frequently overlooked. She argues that adolescents may have become sexually active at an earlier age because of the decline in the average age of puberty. This hypothesis is supported by the fact that individuals who mature early are likely to engage in sexual activity at a younger age than those who mature late. Note, however, that boys reach sexual maturity about two years later than girls do, yet they lose their virginity about a year earlier (Brooks-Gunn & Furstenberg, 1989).

Despite the more conservative attitudes of society toward sex, adolescents are still active sexually.

Sexual Abuse Unfortunately, for a significant number of children and adolescents, their first sexual experiences occur without their consent and in situations of abuse. Cases reported to the police probably represent only a small fraction of the actual number of incidents. In one study, a large, random sample of women was interviewed about childhood and adolescent sexual experiences (Russell, 1983). The results revealed that 32 percent had been sexually abused at least once before the age of 18, and 20 percent had been victimized before the age of 14. Fewer than 5 percent of these women had reported the incidents to the police.

The impact of sexual abuse on children depends on a wide variety of factors— the nature of the abusive act, the age and vulnerability of the victim, whether the offender is a stranger or a family member, whether there was a single incident or an ongoing pattern of abuse, and the reactions of adults in whom the child confides (Kempe & Kempe, 1984). The impact on the individual's sense of identity and level of self-esteem often lasts well into adulthood.

The most common form of sexual abuse occurs between a young adolescent girl and an adult male relative or family friend (Finkelhor, 1984). A stepfather or the mother's boyfriend is more likely to be involved than is the girl's natural father (Wolfe et al., 1988). The mother is usually unaware of the abusive relationship, and the abuse often continues over a period of time and becomes a "secret" between the abuser and the victim.

Adolescent girls who are involved in this kind of sexual abuse may have many symptoms. They often feel guilt and shame, yet they are powerless to break loose from the relationship. They may feel isolated—alienated from their peers and distrustful of adults. Some have learning problems, others have physical complaints, and still others turn to sexual promiscuity. Some girls turn their anger on themselves, and they become depressed or contemplate suicide (Brassard & McNeill, 1987). In any case, their attitudes about intimate relationships have been distorted. Later, as adults, it is difficult for these victims of sexual abuse to establish normal sexual relationships; they may even have difficulty in establishing normal parent–child relationships with their own children.

It is generally difficult for teenage mothers to care for the needs of an infant as well as their own developmental needs.

Teenage Parents

A special topic of concern to researchers studying adolescent sexuality is the incidence of young, unmarried mothers. In 1994, there were 46 753 pregnancies in Canadian women aged 15 to 19—a rate of 48.8 per 1000 (Kalagian, Delmore, Loewen, & Busca, 1998). What is the impact of early parenthood on the teenage girl's later development? There are a number of potentially negative effects. Teenage mothers usually drop out of school prematurely; on average, they work at lower-paying jobs and experience greater job dissatisfaction. They are more likely to become dependent on

FOCUS ON AN ISSUE

What Do Parents in Southern Ontario Think about Sex Education in School?

Should sex education be taught in school? If so, what topics should be addressed, and at what ages should they be discussed? Researchers addressed these questions in a survey of parents in three small communities in southern Ontario: Whitby, Port Hope, and Peterborough (McKay, Pietrusiak, & Holowaty, 1998). Parents were given a list of topics related to sex education and were asked whether schools should teach these topics and at what grade level. Over 6800 parents completed the survey. The majority were mothers between the ages of 30 and 39. Here are the main results:

- When asked whether sex education should be taught at school, 95 percent said yes.

- When asked whether it was important for sex education to respect the different moral beliefs about sexuality that may exist in the community, 81 percent said yes.

- The majority of parents thought that they provided their own children

---

Most parents thought that sex education should begin in early elementary school.

---

with adequate sex education, but that other parents did not.

- Most parents thought that sex education should begin in early elementary school and should focus on the topics of building equal, healthy relationships and helping children and youth avoid sexual abuse. Most respondents believed that these topics should also be discussed in late elementary school, junior high, and senior high. The majority thought that at grades five and six, the topics of puberty and prevention of STDs/AIDS should be introduced and should be readdressed at grades seven and eight, along with the topics of attraction/love/intimacy, communicating about sex, abstinence from sexual activity, reproduction, sexual orientation, birth control, and rape. Most respondents believed that all of these topics, except puberty, should be part of the curriculum for grades nine to twelve, along with the topics of teen parenting and abortion and alternatives.

Question to Ponder

What demographic factors—age of parents, ethnic and religious background, education, and so on—might affect the results of a survey on sex education in schools?

government support. Adolescent mothers must deal with their own personal and social development while trying to adapt to the 24-hour needs of an infant or a small child (Coley & Chase-Lansdale, 1998). Depression is more common in adolescent mothers than it is in older mothers (Deal & Holt, 1998).

The effects of parenthood on the lives of teenage boys may also be negative and long lasting. Owing to pressures that many feel to support their new families, teenage fathers tend to leave school and generally acquire less education than their peers who have not fathered children. They are also more likely to take jobs that require little skill and offer little pay. As the years pass, they are more likely to have marital problems, which often lead to divorce (Card & Wise, 1978).

Often, adolescents who become pregnant encounter strong disapproval at home, or they may already be in conflict with their parents. Yet, if they do not marry, they may have no choice but to continue to live at home in a dependent situation during and after their pregnancy. Consequently, some teenagers are motivated to get married in order to escape this situation and to set up their own households (Reiss, 1971). But teenage marriage is not necessarily the best solution to an adolescent mother's problems. Some researchers believe that even though early motherhood is an obstacle to adult growth, it is in many cases preferable to early motherhood combined with early marriage. Adolescent marriage is more likely to lead to dropping out of high school than is adolescent pregnancy. Similarly, those who marry young are more likely to divorce than those who bear a child and then marry later (Furstenberg, 1976).

The children of teenage parents are also at a disadvantage, compared with children of older parents (Fagot, Pears, Capaldi, Crosby, & Leve, 1998). They may suffer from their parents' lack of experience in handling adult responsibilities and in caring for others. Because these young parents suffer from considerable stress and frustration, they are more likely to neglect or to abuse their children (see the discussion of child abuse in Chapter 14). Children of teenage parents more often exhibit slow behavioural development and cognitive growth (Brooks-Gunn & Furstenberg, 1986; Miller et al.,1996). If adverse factors like poverty, marital discord, and poor education all exist in one family, the child's chances of developing these problems increase.

Some teenage parents, however, do an excellent job of nurturing their young while continuing to grow toward adulthood themselves. To be successful, they almost always need assistance. When pregnant teenagers know more about child development and have more realistic attitudes toward child rearing, their children are less likely to have problems than are those born to teenage mothers who are less cognitively prepared to parent (Miller et al., 1996). Helping young parents and their offspring to thrive and to become productive remains an overriding social concern and challenge.

Many teenage fathers have an especially hard time because of the pressures they feel to drop out of school to support their new family. Often in such situations only low-paying jobs are available.

Cognitive Changes in Adolescence

Although physical maturation and adjustment to sexuality are major steps that take place during adolescence, important cognitive developments also occur at this time. An expansion in capacity and style of thought broadens adolescent awareness, imagination, judgment, and insight. These enhanced abilities also lead to a rapid accumulation of knowledge, which opens up a range of issues and problems that can complicate—and enrich—adolescents' lives.

Abstract Thinking

In Piaget's developmental theory, the hallmark of adolescent cognitive change is the development of formal operational thought. In order to measure this ability, Piaget designed a number of mini science experiments (Inhelder & Piaget, 1958). One experiment involved figuring out what would cause a pendulum to swing faster: the length of the string (short or long); the weight of the object at the end of the pendulum (heavy or light); the force of the push used to set the pendulum in motion (strong or weak); or a combination of factors.

Someone who used formal operational thought would be able to solve the problem by approaching it systematically and testing all possible combinations of factors: (1) short string with heavy object and strong push; (2) short string with heavy object and weak push; (3) short string with light object and strong push; (4) short string with light object and weak push; (5) long string with heavy object and strong push; (6) long string with heavy object and weak push; (7) long string with light object and strong push; and (8) long string with light object and weak push. A person who used formal operational thinking would be able to come up with this solution through an organized system of logic that Piaget called the INRC group. Children in earlier stages have not yet developed the INRC group, so they would be unable to solve the problem.

Someone who uses formal operational thinking is thus able to think more abstractly and to reason about hypothetical situations. For example, Shaffer (1989) describes the results of an interesting study on pretending that people have three eyes: "Suppose that you were given a third eye and that you could choose to place this eye anywhere on your body. Draw me a picture to show where you would place your 'extra' eye and then tell me why you would put it there" (p. 324). Younger children, still in the stage of concrete operations, consistently put the eye on the forehead between the other two eyes. From their concrete experiences, they knew that eyes belonged on the

Figure 15-2
Teenager Conducting an Experiment with a Pendulum
Teenagers who develop formal operational thought are able to solve problems systematically.

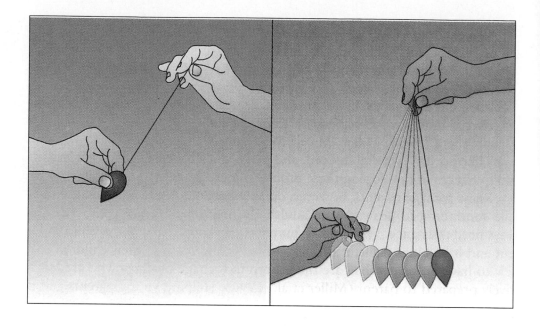

forehead, and they could not imagine other situations. However, older children in the stage of formal operations placed the eye in a variety of unique locations: one child put it in his mouth, so that he could see what he was eating; another put it on a revolving tuft of hair on the top of his head, so that he could quickly look in all directions; and another put it in the palm of his hand, so that he could reach in and see the kinds of cookies in the cookie jar.

Formal operational thinking is more speculative and free from the immediate environment and circumstances. It involves thinking about possibilities, as well as comparing reality with things that might or might not be. Whereas younger children seem to be more comfortable with concrete, empirical facts, adolescents show a growing inclination to treat everything as a mere variation on what *could* be (Keating, 1980). Formal operational thought requires the ability to formulate, test, and evaluate hypotheses. It involves not only manipulation of known, verifiable elements, but also manipulation of those things that are contrary to fact ("Now, let's just suppose for the sake of discussion that ...").

Adolescents also show an increasing ability to plan and to think ahead. In one study (Greene, 1990), a researcher asked grade ten students, grade twelve students, first-year college students, and graduating college students to describe what they thought might happen to them in the future and to say how old they thought they would be when these events occurred. The older subjects could look further into the future than the younger ones could, and the narratives of these older subjects were more specific.

Formal operational thought can therefore be characterized as a second-order process. The first order of thinking is discovering and examining relationships between objects. The second order involves thinking about one's thoughts, looking for relationships between relationships, and manoeuvring between reality and possibility (Inhelder & Piaget, 1958). Three characteristics of adolescent thought are the following:

1. The capacity to combine all variables and find a solution to a problem.
2. The ability to conjecture what effect one variable will have on another.
3. The ability to combine and separate variables in a hypothetical-deductive fashion ("If X is present, then Y will occur") (Gallagher, 1973).

In contrast, information-processing theorists emphasize the adolescent's improvement in those skills referred to as *metacognition*. Metacognition includes several skills, such as the ability to think about thinking, strategy formation, and the ability to plan. Because of these new cognitive skills, teenagers learn to examine and consciously alter their thought processes. For example, they may repeat a number of facts until they have thoroughly memorized them, or they may silently warn themselves not to jump to conclusions without proof.

Teenagers also become extremely introspective and self-absorbed. At the same time, they begin to challenge everything, to reject old boundaries and categories. In so doing, they constantly discard old attitudes and become more creative thinkers (Keating, 1980). In addition to encouraging creativity, thinking about thinking encourages the development of role-taking skills and empathy. True empathy is possible only when persons can imagine what is going on inside the mind of another. In that way, the impact of words, thoughts, and deeds that the other experiences can be understood from that person's perspective.

Adolescents gain cognitive skills that assist their overall problem-solving and decision-making competencies, for example:

> A high school student settles down at her desk to do her homework. She may plan in what order to do the assignments, test herself on a few of the vocabulary items on tomorrow's test to see how much she has to study, check whether the vocabulary flash cards actually are helping her, and switch to a strategy of using each word in a sentence.... Her knowledge that she often makes careless errors leads her to double-check her solutions to some problems. In the opposite direction, her monitoring and self-regulation can lead to new knowledge, as when she learns that her own memory for word meanings is helped more by a meaning-based strategy than rote memorization. (Flavell et al., 1993, p. 153)

The behaviours described above are essentially monitoring and self-regulation activities. The main function of such strategies is to provide people with information about cognitive tasks and about their progress in completing them. Metacognitive skills are monitoring strategies that evaluate the effectiveness of the problem-solving strategies individuals use. Because of their increased cognitive ability, adolescents make greater use of these skills than do younger children.

The notion of a dramatic, qualitative shift as described by Piaget is not shared by all developmental theorists today. Some psychologists contend that the transition is much more gradual, with shifts back and forth between formal operational thought and earlier cognitive modes. For example, Daniel Keating (1976, 1980) believes that the lines drawn between the thinking of children, adolescents, and adults are artificial. He sees cognitive development as a continuous process and suggests that children may have formal operational abilities in some latent form. He asserts, for instance, that some children have the ability to handle abstract thought. Perhaps better language skills and more experience with the world, instead of new cognitive equipment, are responsible for the appearance of these abilities in adolescents.

It is generally agreed that not all individuals are able to think in formal operational terms. Furthermore, adolescents and adults who attain this level do not always maintain it consistently. For example, many people who find themselves facing unfamiliar problems in unfamiliar situations are apt to fall back on a much more concrete type of reasoning. The fact that not all individuals achieve formal operational thought has led some psychologists to suggest that it should be considered an extension of concrete operations, rather than a stage in its own right. Piaget (1972) has even admitted that this may be the case. Nevertheless, he emphasized that elements of this type of thought are essential for the study of advanced science and mathematics.

Information Processing and Intelligence

Many theorists differ in their definitions of the nature of intelligence. Is intelligence what we know, or is it our ability to acquire knowledge? Is intelligence an accumulation of facts and conclusions, or is it the cognitive processes that we use to arrive at these conclusions? In Chapter 13, we discussed current theories of intelligence and ways of measuring intelligence. Many critics of intelligence testing have charged that these tests measure the product, rather than the process, of intellectual behaviour. Piagetian theorists suggest that intelligence tests fail to measure qualitative changes that occur when a child enters a new stage of thought.

In the standard intelligence test, for example, it is difficult to capture the shift from concrete operational thinking to formal operational thinking. Information-processing theorists make a similar argument. They argue that intelligence tests fail to measure process components like attention, memory, problem solving, or decision making.

One major theorist, Robert Sternberg (1984, 1985), has attempted to analyze intelligence into three information-processing components that can be measured separately. For Sternberg, each of these components has a different function:

1. *Metacomponents* are the higher-order control processes for planning and decision making. An example of such processes is the ability to select a particular memory strategy or to monitor how well one is memorizing a list (metamemory).
2. *Performance components* are the processes used to carry out problem solving. These processes include selection and retrieval of relevant information from stored memory.
3. *Knowledge acquisition* (or *storage*) *components* are the processes used in learning new information.

"The metacomponents serve as a strategy construction mechanism, orchestrating the other two types of components into goal-oriented procedures" (Siegler, 1991, p. 69). All of these processes are thought to increase gradually throughout childhood and adolescence. We may see Sternberg's theory, as conceptualized by Siegler (1991), presented in Figure 15-3.

Actually, cognitive development and, hence, the growth of intelligence involve both the accumulation of knowledge and the growth of information-processing components. The two are definitely related. Problem solving is more efficient and effective when one has a larger store of relevant information. Individuals with more efficient storage and retrieval strategies develop a more complete knowledge base.

Adolescents are more efficient and effective at solving problems and making inferences than are school-age children. But they also have a broader range of scripts or schemes that they can draw from. As you will recall, preschool children develop simple scripts for everyday activities. Adolescents develop more complicated scripts for special circumstances (for example, a football game) or procedures (for example, the election of a school president). When they attempt to solve a problem or to understand a social event, they can make inferences about the meaning of such things by drawing from their more elaborate social scripts.

What, then, are the cognitive advances of adolescence? To information-processing theorists, cognitive development in this period includes the following:

1. A more efficient use of separate information-processing components, such as memory retention, and transfer components.
2. The development of more complex strategies for different types of problem solving.
3. More effective ways of acquiring information and storing it symbolically.
4. The development of higher-order (meta) executive functions, including planning, decision making, and flexibility in choosing strategies from a broader base of scripts (Sternberg, 1988).

Changes in Scope and Content of Thought

Basic academic skills and abilities, such as reading comprehension or rote memory, often reach optimal or near-optimal functioning levels during adolescence. Rote

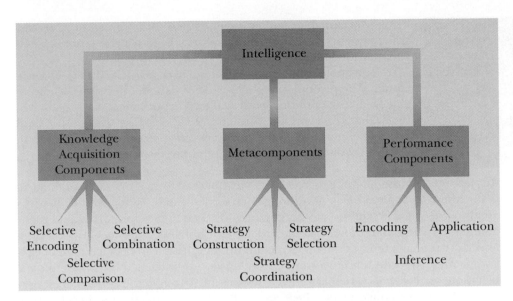

Figure 15-3
Sternberg's Theory of
Intelligence, as Adapted by
Siegler

Source: Siegler, R.S. (1991).
Children's Thinking (2nd ed.).
Englewood Cliffs, NJ: Prentice-Hall.

memory for simple lists of material, for example, reaches adult levels at about age 12 to 14 in most individuals. In contrast, vocabulary continues to improve well into adulthood. Nevertheless, because of greatly improved cognitive skills and the ability to use abstract thinking, adolescents develop a much broader scope and richer complexity in the content of their thoughts. This development influences not only the study of science and math, but also how adolescents examine the social world.

Since the adolescent can now deal with contrary to fact situations, reading and viewing science fiction becomes a new hobby for many teens. Even experimentation with the occult, cults, or altered states of consciousness, caused by anything from meditation to drug-induced states, intrigues adolescents. The ability to understand contrary to fact situations also affects the parent–child relationship during adolescence. Adolescents contrast their "ideal" parent with the "real" parent they see every day. The adolescent becomes highly critical of institutions in general, including the family, and specifically criticizes parents.

Family bickering, therefore, is bound to escalate during early adolescence, as we discussed earlier in this chapter. Many researchers feel that the "battles" that rage over such daily activities as chores, dress, school work, and family meals serve a useful purpose. They allow the adolescent to test his independence in the safety of home, over relatively minor issues. Indeed, negotiation has become one of the prime words in the psychology of adolescence. Many researchers, instead of talking about rebellion and the painful separation of teenagers from their family, now prefer to describe adolescence as a time in which parents and teenagers negotiate new relationships with one another (Flaste, 1988). The teenager must gain more independence in her life; the parents must learn to see their child as more of an equal, with a right to a differing opinion. For most adolescents, the interplay between these competing needs is conducted within a caring, close relationship with their parents. In a recent study, for example, teenagers who had the strongest sense of themselves as individuals were raised in families where the parents offered guidance and comfort—but also permitted their children to develop their own points of view (Flaste, 1988).

Particularly during middle and late adolescence, there may be an increasing concern with social, political, and moral issues. The adolescent begins to develop holistic concepts of society and its institutional forms, along with ethical principles that go beyond those that he has experienced in specific interpersonal relationships. The rational processing of issues is also employed in an effort to achieve internal consistency, as individuals evaluate what they have been in the past and what they hope to become in the future. Some of the swings and extremes of adolescent behaviour occur when young people start taking stock of themselves intellectually. There is a desire to restructure

During middle and late adolescence teenagers exhibit a growing concern about the social, political, and moral issues of their society.

imaginary audience Adolescents' assumption that others are focusing a great deal of critical attention on them.

personal fable Adolescents' feeling that they are special and invulnerable—exempt from the laws of nature that control the destinies of ordinary mortals.

Question to Ponder

Why do you think that adolescents believe that they can take risks and not get caught? Do you think that there is anything that parents or teachers can do to prevent an adolescent from adopting a personal fable?

behaviour, thoughts, and attitudes, either in the direction of greater self-consistency or toward greater conformity with a group norm, a new and individualized image, or some other cognitive model.

The improved cognitive abilities that develop during adolescence certainly help young people to make vocational decisions. They are able to analyze options, both real and hypothetical, and to analyze their talents and abilities. Ginsburg (1972) suggests that it is not until late adolescence that vocational choices become realistic, based in part on candid self-appraisal and valid career options.

Adolescent Self-Insight and Egocentrism One aspect of formal operational thought is the ability to analyze one's own thought processes. Adolescents typically use this ability a great deal. In addition to gaining insight about themselves, they gain insight about others. This ability to take account of others' thoughts, combined with the adolescent's preoccupation with her own metamorphosis, leads to a peculiar kind of egocentrism. Adolescents tend to assume that others are as fascinated by them and their behaviour as adolescents are themselves. They may fail to distinguish between their own concerns and the concerns of others. As a result, adolescents tend to jump to conclusions about the reactions of those around them and to assume that others will be as approving or as critical of them as they are of themselves. Research findings indicate that adolescents are far more concerned than younger children are about having their inadequacies discovered by other people (Elkind & Bowen, 1979).

The adolescent's idea that he is constantly being watched and judged by other people has been called the **imaginary audience** (Elkind, 1967). Adolescents use this imaginary audience as an internal sounding board "to try on" various attitudes and behaviours. The imaginary audience is also the source of much adolescent self-consciousness—of feeling constantly, painfully on display. Because adolescents are unsure of their inner identity, they overreact to others' views in trying to figure out who they really are (Elkind, 1967).

At the same time that they fail to differentiate the feelings of others, adolescents are also very absorbed in their own feelings, believing that their emotions are unique and that no one has ever known, or will ever know, such personal agony or rapture. As part of this type of egocentrism, some adolescents come to believe in a **personal fable**—a feeling they are so special that they must be exempt from the ordinary laws of nature and that they will live forever. This feeling of invulnerability and immortality seems to be the basis for some of the risk-taking behaviour that is so common during this period (Buis & Thompson, 1989). Another type of personal fable is the *foundling fantasy* (Elkind, 1974). Armed with new critical insights, the adolescent suddenly becomes aware of a great number of failings in her parents—and then has trouble imagining how two such ordinary and limited individuals could have possibly produced this sensitive and unique individual. All of this self-absorption can be a great obstacle in learning to see eye to eye with the rest of the world. Fortunately, egocentrism begins to recede by the age of 15 or 16, as adolescents begin to realize that their imaginary audience is not really paying much attention to them and that they are subject to the laws of nature just like everyone else.

Nonetheless, adolescence is an intellectually intoxicating experience. New powers of thought are turned inward to one's own cognitive processes and outward to a world that has suddenly grown more complex. Included in this growth is the capacity for moral reasoning.

Moral Development In Chapter 14, we discussed Kohlberg's theory of the development of moral reasoning. Earlier thinkers, of course, have observed moral development and studied the changes that occur as children grow, especially during adolescence. Kohlberg drew on the developmental theories of J.M. Baldwin (1906), George Mead (1934), and, most directly, Jean Piaget (1965). Although Kohlberg was directly influenced by Piaget, it is Kohlberg's model that has generated the most interest and research.

By looking at individuals in Western society, we can find some validation for many aspects of Kohlberg's theory. By the time they reach their teens, most children in our society have outgrown the first level of moral development (the preconventional level) and have arrived at the conventional level, which is based on social conformity. They are motivated to avoid punishment, are obedience oriented, and are ready to abide by conventional moral stereotypes. They may stay at this "law-and-order" level for the rest of their lives, especially if they receive no stimulation to think beyond it. The final two stages of moral development—morality by social contract and morality as derived from self-chosen ethical principles—require the thought processes of adolescent development. But what is the process of change? Can one teach more advanced moral thought?

Kohlberg and others have set up experimental "moral education" classes for children who come from a variety of social backgrounds. The results, even with juvenile delinquents, suggest that moral judgment can indeed be taught. The classes centre on discussions of hypothetical moral dilemmas. The child is presented with a problem and is asked to give a solution. If the answer is argued at level 4, the discussion leader suggests a level 5 rationale to see if the child thinks it is a good alternative. The students almost always find that this slightly more advanced reasoning is more attractive, and through repeated discussions like this, sooner or later they begin to form judgments at level 5. At this point, the discussion leader might start suggesting level 6 reasoning as an alternative (Kohlberg, 1966).

Adolescence is a time of self-absorption and self-reflection. Sometimes adolescents feel terribly alone and may believe that no one else has ever thought or felt the way they do.

Kohlberg's model and his experiments with moral education show several things. An adolescent's set of values depends partly on cognitive development. These values are, in part, a product of the adolescent's experiences in making moral judgments. If she receives challenging, yet safe, opportunities to consider moral dilemmas at higher levels, adolescence may then be a time of considerable moral development.

Educators, in particular, are concerned with how the moral sense develops during childhood and adolescence. Educators feel that if they could understand it better, they could help to create a better social order. Even though Kohlberg has provided useful descriptions of the stages of moral development, he has not adequately described how a child progresses from one level to another. According to Kohlberg's framework, which is derived from that of Piaget, presenting a child with increasingly complex moral issues creates a disequilibrium in his mind. It would then seem that the consideration of moral paradoxes and conflicts sets up a disturbance that forces the child to make increasingly more mature analyses and judgments about social situations. However, it is not entirely clear if superior moral judgments necessarily lead to superior behaviour, and very little research has been done to date on the relationship between the two.

What we do know is that adolescents are highly receptive both to the culture that surrounds them and to the behaviour of the models they see at home, in school, and in the mass media. We cannot expect them to behave morally if those who serve as their models do not provide an example of moral behaviour.

FOCUS ON AN ISSUE

Why Do Adolescents Drop Out of School?

About 18 percent of Canadian 20-year-olds are school leavers, which means that they have not graduated from high school and are not currently attending school (Clark, 1997). Adolescents who drop out of school often face a future of unemployment or low job satisfaction—a grim scenario for individuals and for society (McCaul, Colardarci, & Davis, 1992). A recent study examined the international problem of school failure by focusing on Canada, Belgium, Japan, Spain, Australia, New Zealand, and the United Kingdom (OECD, 1998). The link between school failure and unemployment was especially strong in Canada—over a third of school dropouts were unemployed in Canada, compared with only 5.6 percent in Japan. As well, the majority of Canadian dropouts do not return to school. Only 25 percent of school leavers are able to return to school to get their diploma and thus better their life circumstances (Clark, 1997). Why do adolescents drop out of school? In the international study, school dropouts in all the countries shared a common profile: they were more likely to come from a low-income home, to speak a language at home that was different from the language of instruction at school, and to have failed a grade (OECD, 1998).

Hymel, Comfort, Schonert-Reichl, and McDougall (1996) reviewed a number of other factors associated with dropping out of school, focusing especially on peer relations. They stress that no single factor predicts all cases—different adolescents drop out of school for different reasons. Therefore, we must be cautious of painting all school dropouts with the same brush. The following factors are associated with dropping out of school for some, but not all, individuals:

1. *Academic difficulties.* School dropouts are more likely to have lower levels of academic ability, poorer achievement and marks, repeated or failed grades, and higher rates of truancy and school transfers.

2. *Unstable families and parent behaviours.* School dropouts are more likely to come from families with low incomes, single-parent or no-parent families, and families that provide less support

---

The link between school failure and unemployment was especially strong in Canada.

---

for educational success. Moreover, the parents are less involved in the schools, have less-strict rules about homework and school attendance, and have lower levels of education.

3. *School atmosphere.* School dropouts are more likely to report that they did not get along with teachers or other students and that they did not feel that they belonged or were safe at school. In addition, the dropout rate is somewhat higher in larger schools than in smaller ones and in system-wide schools than in neighbourhood ones.

4. *Problems interacting with peers.* Children who are rejected by peers in elementary school are at risk for later dropping out of school.

5. *Negative peer group.* School dropouts are more likely to associate with friends who do not value school. As well, they are more likely to have friends who have dropped out of school.

6. *Aggression and antisocial behaviour.* Teachers and peers rate dropouts as being more aggressive than other students. Dropouts are also more likely to be regular users of alcohol and other drugs and to have criminal records.

7. *Combinations of factors.* It is important to consider each factor in the context of the others; sometimes the effects of a factor change depending on which other factors it is combined with. For example, the risk of dropping out of school for adolescents who are both aggressive and low academic achievers is greater than what you would expect considering either factor alone. The two factors interact, so that individuals who have both are especially vulnerable to school dropout. One study found that 64 percent of students who were aggressive and low achievers dropped out of school, compared with 22 percent who were low achievers but not aggressive and 31.3 percent who were aggressive but were not low achievers.

SPECIAL CONCERNS FOR ABORIGINAL STUDENTS

Compared with other Canadian students, Aboriginal students are twice as likely to drop out of school (Wright, 1999). There are many factors that contribute to widespread academic underachievement among Aboriginal students (see Hookimaw-Witt, 1999; Taylor, 1998; and Wright, 1999, for discussions).

First, education in Canada typically includes the values of the larger Canadian culture. Values of mainstream culture are reflected in the focus on competition, individual achievement, set schedules, and punctuality in the schools. This set of values is inconsistent with those of many Aboriginal cultures. For instance, Aboriginal cultures often value cooperation among the group, rather than individual achievement, and they are not as focused on time schedules and punctuality. These values conflict with those students encounter in mainstream school.

Second, in the mainstream Canadian culture, it is typically assumed that education provides the skills required by society in order to achieve economic prosperity. Aboriginal students are less likely to see formal education as the path to a better life. The lack of jobs in many Aboriginal communities means that it is unlikely that those who complete formal school can find jobs in their communities. Furthermore, in Aboriginal cultures, a better life is often defined more in spiritual than economic terms. Formal schooling does not assist people in their quest for spiritual development.

Although the curriculum of mainstream schools aims to prepare students for life in the mainstream society, it fails to prepare them for life in Aboriginal societies. Aboriginal students do not necessarily want to assimilate into mainstream society, so school may seem irrelevant to them.

Exposing Aboriginal children to mainstream education has also come at an enormous cost to their societies. "The introduction of formal schooling placed Inuit in a hopeless dilemma: on the one hand they could maintain their nomadic tradition but this meant leaving their children behind at school, or they could remain near the school and abandon their nomadic tradition" (Taylor, 1998, p. 186). Residential schools, which operated until recently in Canada, separated Aboriginal children from their families and communities. The children were expected to leave behind their language and culture and to adopt those of the mainstream. Furthermore, residential schools portrayed Aboriginal cultures as inferior and primitive. Unfortunately, there are still concerns about racism in schools today.

One of the legacies of residential schools is that many Aboriginal children encountered identity conflicts, which led to the questions, Who am I? What is my culture? Without a clear sense of who they are and where they belong, Aboriginal youth are vulnerable. Is it any wonder that suicide, alcoholism, and drug abuse are more common among Aboriginal youth than in the general Canadian population? Obviously, these problems contribute to dropping out of school.

REDUCING THE RISK OF SCHOOL DROPOUT

A number of Canadian school districts now try to provide special resources to students who are at risk for dropping out. For instance, Rebane and Schonert-Reichl (1994) described a special classroom, called the "Bridge" classroom, for grade nine students at risk for dropping out of school in Vancouver. The goal was to create a democratic classroom and to foster students' feelings of connectedness to one another and to the teacher. The program was effective in greatly increasing student attendance, perhaps a first step in the prevention of dropping out of school. As one of the students commented, "I just hope that I'll be in this class next year. If it wasn't for Bridge class, I wouldn't be in school" (cited in Hymel et al., 1996, p. 13).

A number of districts are trying to address the special needs of Aboriginal students. For example, the Edmonton Public School Board opened an Aboriginal high school, which incorporates Aboriginal cultures into the curriculum. Furthermore, Aboriginal communities are fighting for control over the education of their children and for the freedom to redesign the educational system so that it better meets the needs of Aboriginal students. In British Columbia, the Squamish Nation developed a partnership with Capilano College to create transitional programs for Aboriginal students pursuing postsecondary education. The programs increased the success of Aboriginal students (Wright, 1999).

Summary and Conclusions

Adolescence in contemporary Western society has two key aspects. First, adolescents tend to live in age-segregated societies. They often rely heavily on peers and have little contact with either older adults or younger children. A second characteristic is the significant exposure to the mass media that moulds adolescent thinking and behaviour. Both of these factors play an important role in the experiences and attitudes of adolescents.

Significant biological changes occur during adolescence that culminate in physical and sexual maturity. These changes for both boys and girls include rapid growth, the development of reproductive organs, and the appearance of secondary sex characteristics. Since body image is in part a function of appearance and the individual's response to her body, when the body is altered in major ways, the self-image also changes. Teenagers are both fascinated and concerned by the changes their bodies are undergoing. They constantly compare their bodies with the cultural ideal. Early-maturing boys have definite advantages over late-maturing boys, while for girls early maturity is a mixed blessing.

Sexuality is one of the major issues that adolescents must resolve. The development of sexual culture and behaviour shows considerable gender variability. It is also influenced by prevailing cultural or subcultural norms and values. The sexual revolution of the 1960s and 1970s has largely affected women. Increasing numbers of teenage girls are becoming sexually active, while the percentage of boys who are sexually active has remained fairly constant. In the 1980s and 1990s, adolescents are again becoming more conservative in their sexual attitudes, owing to changes in cultural norms, but also owing to the advent of AIDS. Although many teenagers continue to be active sexually, they are vulnerable to sexually transmitted diseases and pregnancy. Early parenthood puts many pressures on both the mother and father.

Many children and adolescents are the victims of sexual abuse. When children are abused, their self-esteem, sense of identity, and ability to form meaningful relationships may be affected—even into adulthood.

Associated with the new biological maturity and social experiences of the adolescent are increases in cognitive skills. Cognitive changes in adolescence are characterized by the development of formal operational thinking. This type of thinking allows for abstract thinking that is not tied to the immediate, concrete environment. Because of the growth of metacognitive skills, such as monitoring and self-regulation, adolescents are able to think about their own thought processes—and about those of others. Information-processing theorists also state that adolescents gain metacognitive skills that, in turn, influence the effectiveness of their cognitive strategies.

As cognitive skills improve and broaden, adolescents develop the capacity for broader and more complex content to their thoughts. These skills also cause adolescents to become more introspective and self-critical, which leads to a new form of egocentrism during early adolescence. During this period, some adolescents see themselves as performing before an imaginary audience and may believe that a personal fable or script guides their daily path. This egocentrism diminishes in middle and late adolescence, when individuals find that they are not the centre of the world's attention. The imaginary audience becomes, in a sense, a hypothesis about the world, which the young adolescent must test.

Also associated with improved cognitive skills is the ability to develop advanced moral reasoning. Older adolescents are more likely to use conventional arguments or self-chosen ethical principles to judge the morality of actions than are younger adolescents. In general, however, it does not follow that superior moral reasoning necessarily leads to superior moral behaviour.

Adolescence is a crucial transition period during which the child grows into an adult. Many issues that adolescents confront regarding sexuality, morality, commitments, and careers will shape the remainder of their lives. The adolescent is now uniquely able to look to past behaviours, integrate them with present realities, and project into the future the person he will become.

Key Terms and Concepts

AIDS (acquired immune
    deficiency syndrome)
    (p. 479)

anorexia nervosa (p. 476)

bulimia (p. 477)

hormone (p. 469)

imaginary audience
    (p. 488)

menarche (p. 470)

personal fable (p. 488)

puberty (p. 470)

rite of passage (p. 467)

Questions to Review

1. Give several examples of how cultural and historical factors influence the development of adolescence.

2. List the biological changes of males and females during adolescence.

3. What are some examples of how cultural ideals affect body image and adjustment during adolescence?

4. Compare and contrast the experiences of early- and late-maturing males. How do their experiences compare with those of early- and late-maturing females?

5. Discuss the way in which attitudes toward male and female sexuality in our society have changed.

6. List several factors that influence adolescents' sexual behaviour.

7. Describe the sexual revolution and changes in sexual attitudes and behaviour that have since taken place.

8. Describe the impact of sexual abuse on one's sense of identity.

9. Discuss the negative impact of early parenthood on teenage boys and girls.

10. What is formal operational thought? How did Piaget view the adolescent's cognitive changes?

11. How do information-processing theorists describe cognitive development?

12. Describe the impact of cognitive development on changes in the scope and content of adolescent thought.

13. Explain adolescent egocentrism.

14. Discuss Kohlberg's model of moral development and why it fails to adequately describe how a child might progress from one stage of moral development to another.

15. List several cultural factors that shape adolescence in Western society.

Weblinks

www.hc-sc.gc.ca/hppb/childhood-youth/
Childhood and Youth Web Site
This site, sponsored by Health Canada, has information that pertains to all developmental levels, from the prenatal stage to adolescence. It has descriptions of federal programs, community-based programs, centres of excellence, Aboriginal issues, and suicide prevention, among other topics.

www.eating-disorder.org/canadacenters.html
Eating Disorder Treatment Centres in Canada
This site has addresses, phone numbers, and links to Web sites for eating disorder treatment centres in Canada. In addition, it has links to numerous other sites related to eating disorders.

www2.unesco.org/efa/index.html
Education for All
This site, sponsored by the United Nations, reports international trends in education, including those related to school drop-out.

Adolescence: Social and Personality Development

Don't laugh at a youth for his affectations; he is only trying on one face after another to find a face of his own.

LOGAN PEARSALL SMITH
AFTERTHOUGHTS (1921)

Outline

CHAPTER 16

Objectives

By the time you have finished this chapter, you should be able to do the following:

✔ Discuss the major developmental conflicts that adolescents must resolve in order to make a successful transition to adulthood.

✔ Explain the concept of identity status.

✔ Describe the factors and processes that help to shape moral development and the selection of guiding values during adolescence.

✔ Discuss patterns of drug use during adolescence.

✔ Describe how parenting styles and family dynamics continue to influence a child's behaviour during adolescence, and identify key characteristics of successful family functioning during an adolescent's increasing independence.

✔ Name some reference groups that might be important during adolescence and explain their significance.

✔ List the purposes of dating and explain how attitudes toward dating change between early and late adolescence.

In moving from childhood to the status of young adulthood, adolescents frequently display a curious combination of maturity and childishness. This mixture is awkward, sometimes even comical, but it serves an important developmental function. The ways that adolescents cope with the stresses of new bodies and new roles are based on their personality development in earlier years. To meet new adult challenges, they draw on the skills, resources, and strengths that they developed in earlier periods of their lives.

In the preceding chapter, we mentioned that the transitional period between childhood and adulthood varies from culture to culture. In some societies, adult skills are mastered early; new adult members are urgently needed and promptly recruited by the larger community. In Western society, successful transition to adult status, especially occupational status, requires lengthy training. Adolescence in many modern societies is prolonged, stretching from puberty through the second decade of life. Despite their physical and intellectual maturity, adolescents live in limbo, excluded from the meaningful problem-solving work of the larger social group.

On the one hand, prolonged adolescence gives the young person repeated opportunities to experiment with different adult styles without making irrevocable commitments. On the other hand, a decade of adolescence generates pressures and conflicts of its own, such as the need to appear independent and sophisticated despite being economically dependent on one's parents.

Some psychologists argue that adolescents are also under pressure from their parents, who have transferred to them their own compulsions to succeed and to attain a higher social status (Elkind, 1988). The adolescent must cope with all of these inner and outer pressures, confront and resolve significant developmental tasks, and weave the results into a coherent, functioning identity. In this chapter, we shall look at the coping patterns commonly used to meet the dilemmas of adolescence and at the triumphs and tragedies that result. We shall examine how the young person selects values and forms loyalties and, as a consequence, presents a more mature self to society.

Developmental Tasks in Adolescence

Each period in life presents developmental challenges and difficulties that require new skills and responses. Most psychologists agree that adolescents must confront two tasks: (1) achieving a measure of independence or autonomy from one's parents and (2) forming an identity, creating an integrated self that harmoniously combines different elements of the personality.

Adolescence has traditionally been seen as a period of storm and stress, a dramatic upheaval of the emotions. The term *storm and stress* is derived from the name of a German literary movement of the late 18th and early 19th centuries *(Sturm und Drang)*. It was adopted by Anna Freud, the daughter of Sigmund Freud, as a label for the emotional state of adolescents. Anna Freud went so far as to say, "To be normal during the adolescent period is by itself abnormal" (1958, p. 275). The Freudians argue that the onset of biological maturation and increased sexual drive produce conflicts between adolescents and their parents, adolescents and their peers, and adolescents and themselves.

Question to Ponder

Do you think adolescents are more like children or adults?

Independence and Interdependence

According to the prevailing view, adolescents use conflict and rebelliousness as the principal way to achieve autonomy and independence from their parents. The media, especially since the mid-1960s, have focused on the "generation gap" and the turbulent conflict between parents and their children. Stories on this topic may have high drama and great interest, but they have limited support in research. Most of the research literature indicates that the degree of conflict and turbulence in adolescent relations with the rest of the family has been exaggerated.

Just as emotional turmoil is not always part of growing up, conflict is not inevitable between adolescents and their parents. Although the emotional distance between teenagers and their parents tends to increase in early adolescence as adolescents go through the physical changes of puberty (Steinberg, 1988), this does not necessarily lead to rebellion or to rejection of parental values. Bandura (1964) interviewed adolescent boys from middle-class families. He found that by the time the boys reached adolescence, they had already internalized their parents' values and standards of behaviour so thoroughly that there was actually less need for parental control than had been expected. The process of emancipation was substantially complete by the time the boys reached adolescence because the parents had encouraged their sons' independent behaviour starting in early childhood. Note, however, that Bandura's subjects were all middle-class American males; his results may not be applicable to a wider range of adolescents. Socioeconomic and cultural factors will have a great influence on the degree of tension and conflict each teenager experiences. Nevertheless, findings such as Bandura's call into question the Freudian view of inevitable conflict stemming from biological drives.

Clearly, definitions of autonomy that stress freedom from parental influence need to be reconsidered. The concept of independence must take into account the continuing influence of parents on their children during and after adolescence. One theorist (Hill, 1987) has suggested an interesting approach to adolescent independence seeking: Hill defines *autonomy* as self-regulation. Independence involves the capacity to make one's own judgments and to regulate one's own behaviour. "Think for yourself," we often say when we want someone to be independent. Many adolescents go through a process in which they learn to do precisely that. They re-evaluate the rules, values, and boundaries that they previously learned at home and in school.

Contrary to popular belief, adolescence is not inevitably marked by rebellion against parents.

Sometimes, they encounter considerable resistance from their parents, which may lead to conflict. More often, parents work through this process with their children, minimizing the areas of conflict and assisting their adolescents to develop independent thought and self-regulated behaviour (Hill, 1987).

Becoming an adult is a gradual transformation. It requires the ability to be simultaneously independent and interdependent. *Interdependence* can be defined as reciprocal dependence. Work relationships, for example, are interdependent: bosses are dependent on their workers to produce goods, and workers are dependent on their bosses to manage the enterprise so that they all have an income. Interdependence involves long-term commitments and interpersonal attachments that characterize the human condition (Gilligan, 1987). Over time, adolescents develop the ability to combine a commitment to others, which is the basis of interdependence, with a sense of self, which is the basis of independence.

Identity Formation

Before adolescence, we view ourselves according to a collection of different roles—for example, daughter, older sister, friend, student, church member, and flute player. In adolescence, our new cognitive powers of formal operational thought allow us to analyze these roles, to see inconsistencies and conflicts in some of the roles, and to restructure them in order to forge a new identity. This process sometimes requires abandoning old roles and establishing new relationships with parents, siblings, and peers. Erikson (1968) sees the task of identity formation as the major hurdle that adolescents must cross in order to make a successful transition to adulthood.

Sources of Identity Adolescents derive many of their ideas of suitable roles and values from **reference groups.** Reference groups may consist of individuals with whom adolescents are close and whom they see every day, or they may be broader social groups

> **reference group** A social group or collection of people with whom an individual shares attitudes, ideals, or philosophies.

with whom adolescents share attitudes and ideals—such as religious, ethnic, generational, or interest groups. Individuals compare themselves with a reference group, whether broad or narrow, and find their values either confirmed or rejected.

Adolescents must come to terms with a variety of reference groups. Groups that were automatic in childhood—such as the family, the neighbourhood gang, or the church youth group—are no longer as comfortable or fulfilling. An adolescent may feel conflicting loyalties toward her family, ethnic group, and peer group.

Sometimes, adolescents are drawn to the values and attitudes of one person, rather than to those of an entire group. This person, called a **significant other,** might be a close friend, an admired teacher, an older sibling, a movie or sports star, or anyone whose opinions are highly valued. Although the influence of a significant other may be felt at any stage of life, it often has its greatest impact during adolescence, when the individual is actively seeking models.

Therefore, adolescents are surrounded by a bewildering variety of roles offered by a multitude of reference groups and significant others. These roles must be integrated into a personal identity, and the conflicting ones must be reconciled or discarded. The process is made more difficult when there is conflict between roles (for instance, between being a member of a fun-loving peer group and being a good student) or between significant others (for instance, between a boyfriend and an older sister).

Erikson's Concept of Identity Erik Erikson, a clinical psychologist, spent much of his professional life working with adolescents and young adults. His work on the process of establishing "an inner sense of identity" has had an enormous impact on developmental psychologists and on the general public. According to Erikson, the process of self-definition, called *identity formation,* is lengthy and complex. It provides continuity between the individual's past, present, and future. It forms a framework for organizing and integrating behaviours in diverse areas of the individual's life. It reconciles the person's own inclinations and talents with earlier identifications or roles that were supplied by parents, peers, or society. By helping the person to know where he stands in comparison to others in society, it also provides a basis for social comparisons. Finally, an inner sense of identity helps to give direction, purpose, and meaning to a person's future life. It is a rich and full concept presented with numerous examples drawn from personal case studies (Erikson, 1959, 1963, 1968; Waterman, 1985).

The richness of Erikson's concept is somewhat lost when we translate it into research. Unfortunately, as one researcher observed, a lengthy autobiographical interview on an individual's vocational plans, religious beliefs, political ideology, and social roles is too often translated into a one- or two-word categorical label (Archer, 1985).

Modes of Identity Formation In a theory based on Erikson's developmental scheme, James Marcia (1980) has defined four different states or modes of identity formation. The four modes, or *identity statuses,* are **foreclosure, diffusion, moratorium,** and **identity achievement.** These statuses are defined according to two factors: whether or not the individual has gone through a decision-making period called an **identity crisis,** and whether or not the individual has made a commitment to a selected set of choices, such as a system of values or a plan for a future occupation.

Adolescents who are in *foreclosure status* have made a commitment without going through a decision-making period. They have chosen an occupation, a religious outlook, or an ideological viewpoint, but the choice was made early and was determined by their parents or teachers, rather than by themselves. The transition to adulthood occurs smoothly and with little conflict.

Young people who lack a sense of direction and who seem to have little motivation to find one are in *diffusion status.* They have not experienced a crisis, and they have not selected an occupational role or a moral code. They are simply avoiding the issue. Some seek immediate gratification; others experiment in a random fashion with all possibilities (Côté & Levine, 1988).

Adolescents or young adults in *moratorium status* are in the midst of an ongoing

significant other Anyone whose opinions an individual values highly.

foreclosure The identity status of those who have made commitments without going through an identity crisis.

diffusion The identity status of those who have neither gone through an identity crisis nor made commitments.

moratorium The identity status of those who are currently in the midst of an identity crisis.

identity achievement The identity status of those who have gone through an identity crisis and have made commitments.

identity crisis A period of making decisions about important issues—of asking "Who am I and where am I going?"

Teenagers may be drawn to and adopt the values, behaviours, attitudes, and even mannerisms of a friend or peer they look up to.

identity crisis or decision-making period. The decisions may concern occupational choices, religious or ethical values, or political philosophies. Young people in this status are preoccupied with "finding themselves."

Identity achievement is the status attained by people who have passed through the crisis and have made their commitments. As a result, they pursue work of their own choosing and attempt to live by their own moral codes. Although there are healthy and pathological dimensions to all four identity statuses, identity achievement is usually viewed as the most psychologically desirable (Marcia, 1980). We may see these various identity statuses contrasted in Concept Summary Table 16-1.

Effects of Identity Status Research indicates that identity status profoundly influences an adolescent's social expectations, self-image, and reactions to stress. Moreover, cross-cultural research in Canada, the United States, Denmark, Israel, and other societies suggests that Marcia's four statuses are part of the developmental process in several related cultures. Let us look at how the four identity statuses interact with some of the problems of adolescence.

Anxiety is a dominant emotion for young people in moratorium status because of their unresolved decisions. They struggle with a world of conflicting values and choices and are constantly faced with unpredictability and contradictions. These adolescents are often tied to their parents with ambivalent bonds of love and hatred; they struggle for freedom, yet they fear and resent parental disapproval. Many postsecondary students are in the moratorium status. These are the people who are actively seeking information and making decisions.

Adolescents in foreclosure status experience a minimum of anxiety. These adolescents hold to more authoritarian values than those in other statuses, and they have strong, positive ties to significant others, who sometimes follow untraditional paths. They generally operate in a pattern of continuity and stability, although in some areas of life, they may experience uncertainty. Young men in foreclosure status tend to have lower self-esteem than do those in moratorium status, and they are more susceptible to the suggestions of others (Marcia, 1980).

Diffusion status is seen most frequently in teenagers who have experienced rejection or neglect from detached or uncaring parents. These adolescents may become society's dropouts, perhaps turning to drug or alcohol use as a way of evading responsibility. Baumrind (1991) has shown that drug and alcohol abuse is most common in the offspring of what she refers to as "unengaged parents."

In comparison with young people in moratorium, foreclosure, or diffusion status, those who have attained identity achievement have the most balanced feelings toward their parents and family. Their quest for independence is less emotionally charged than that of the moratorium youths, and it is not tainted with the fear of abandonment that bothers individuals in the identity diffusion status (Marcia, 1980).

The proportion of people in identity achievement status increases with age. In junior high and high school, there are far more individuals in diffusion and foreclosure

Concept Summary

Table 16-1   Marcia's Model of Identity Formation

	UNDERGOING IDENTITY CRISIS OR DECISION-MAKING PERIOD	COMMITMENT TO CHOICES
Foreclosure	No	Yes
Diffusion	No	No
Moratorium	Ongoing	Ongoing
Identity achievement	Completed	Completed

statuses than in moratorium and identity achievement statuses. Identity status may also vary according to the aspect of life that is being considered: a high school student may be in foreclosure status in regard to sex-role preference, moratorium status in regard to vocational choice or religious beliefs, and diffusion status in regard to political philosophy.

Sex Differences Marcia and other researchers have noticed a marked difference between males and females in the behaviour and attitudes associated with the various identity statuses. Males in identity achievement and moratorium statuses seem to have a great deal of self-esteem, whereas females in these statuses appear to have more unresolved conflicts, especially regarding family and career choices. Later studies have partially confirmed some of these earlier findings but have presented a more complex picture.

Sally L. Archer (1985), for example, found that for family and career choices, girls of senior high school age were most likely to be in foreclosure status, whereas boys were most likely to be in diffusion status. Furthermore, girls in foreclosure and moratorium statuses expressed a great deal of uncertainty about reconciling conflicts between their family and career preferences. Although both boys and girls said that they planned to marry, have children, and pursue careers, it was primarily the girls who expressed concern about possible conflicts between family and career. When asked how much concern they had, 75 percent of males and 16 percent of females said none, 25 percent of males and 42 percent of females said some, and 0 percent of males and 42 percent of females said they felt a lot of concern about potential conflicts between family and career.

In the other major areas of interest—religious and political beliefs—studies indicate a mixed result. In religion, research indicates that there are no significant differences between the genders. But with respect to political beliefs, there seems to be a significant difference in identity status between older male and female adolescents. Males are more often in identity achievement status than females are, and females are more often in foreclosure status than males are (Waterman, 1985).

Ethnic Minorities Establishing personal identities can be complicated when adolescents need to reconcile ethnic identities with the values of the larger society. Consider, for example, the case of Canadian adolescents who have Lebanese Muslim backgrounds. These adolescents come from religious and cultural traditions that are quite different from those of the larger society (Fahlman, 1983). There are different rules for what they can eat—they are not allowed to eat pork. Sometimes these rules lead to ridicule. There are restrictions on how they can dress—girls are not allowed to wear shorts. This can cause problems in physical education if the teacher does not understand the cultural background. They have set rules about how they can behave—drinking alcohol and taking other drugs are strictly forbidden. Girls are not allowed to date, and they are expected to marry Muslims. Both boys and girls are expected to choose careers that fit their parents' wishes. Considering all of these differences, it is perhaps not surprising that many adolescents of Lebanese Muslim heritage go through a difficult phase when they feel different and out of place and believe that they cannot trust anyone except other Muslims (Fahlman, 1983).

How do adolescents from ethnic minority backgrounds develop a sense of personal identity? According to one theory, they progress through five stages (Atkinson, Morten, & Sue, 1983). In stage one, they identify most with the values of the larger society, rather than with those of their ethnic group. But by stage two, they have become aware of conflicts between the values of the larger society and those of their ethnic group. This is a stage of considerable conflict and confusion. And in stage three, they resolve the conflict by actively rejecting the values of the larger culture and accepting the values of their ethnic group. This stage, however, is also temporary. Stage four follows, a stage of considerable introspection. The adolescents question the values of both cultures. In stage five, the adolescents resolve these conflicts by developing personal identities that select elements from the larger society and the ethnic group. It is important to note, though, that this theory was developed in the

United States. It is unclear whether it would apply to Canadians. The United States has a long history assimilation of ethnic minorities into the larger culture; consequently, the United States is sometimes referred to as a *melting pot*. But in Canada, there is a history of preserving cultural distinctiveness, through *multiculturalism*. Ethnic minorities might have quite different experiences in the two countries.

It is also important to note that the formation of personal identities might differ across ethnic groups. Chinese and Japanese adolescents are especially influenced by social groups, more so than are American adolescents of European heritage (Yeh & Huang, 1996). The Chinese have concepts for two identities: "big me," that is, the connectedness to the group, and "little me," that is, the individual. The individual identity is subordinated to the collective identity.

Adolescence and the Family

Adolescents are very much influenced by their families, even though the old ties may be strained in some instances. Studies over the past 20 years have consistently shown that there is much less conflict between adolescents and their families than was previously believed.

> Survey studies are consistent in reports of conflict in only 15% to 25% of families.... When conflicts do occur, mundane issues predominate. Family chores, hours, dating, grades, personal appearance, and eating habits are the matters of concern.... Study after study has confirmed that parent-adolescent conflicts about basic economic, religious, social, and political values are rare. (Hill, 1987)

The relatively few adolescents who form independent opinions about ideological matters generally do so late in their high school or college years (Waterman, 1985). Moreover, there appears to be a definite time frame to when conflict is likely to occur. Generally, early adolescence is more conflict laden than is later adolescence, by which time both parents and teens have come to grips with potentially difficult autonomy and separation issues. It is important for families to realize that if they can keep open communication and shared views during adolescence, they will successfully negotiate the difficult times.

Impact of the Family on Adolescents

Parents continue to influence not only teenage beliefs, but also teenage behaviour. However, mothers and fathers influence their teenagers in different ways. Although there seems to be little difference between the way adolescent males and females report their family relations (Hauser et al., 1987; Youniss & Ketterlinus, 1987), there seems to be considerable difference between the behaviour and roles of mothers and fathers in adolescent family relations (Steinberg, 1987). Fathers tend to encourage intellectual development and are frequently involved in problem-solving activities and discussions within the family. As a result, both boys and girls generally discuss ideas with their fathers (Hauser et al., 1987). Adolescent involvement with mothers is far more complex. Mothers and adolescents interact in the areas of household responsibilities, school work done at home, discipline in and out of the home, and leisure-time activities (Montemayor & Brownlee, 1987). This involvement may cause greater strain and conflict between mothers and their children. However, it also tends to create greater closeness between adolescents and their mothers than between adolescents and their fathers (Youniss & Ketterlinus, 1987).

In Chapter 7, we discussed the attachment relationship that develops between infants and parents. This relationship continues to be important throughout childhood, adolescence, and even adulthood, although there are age-specific differences in its expression. During adolescence, young people become less dependent on parents, yet at the same time, they derive security from knowing that parents are available (Lieberman, Doyle, & Markiewicz, 1999). Securely attached adolescents develop what researchers call a *working model,* or general belief, that they are worthy, loveable people and that others will be responsive to their needs. They form closer friendships and are more accepted by peers than are adolescents who do not have a secure attachment to parents.

In Chapter 11, we discussed the influence that different parenting styles have on children's psychological makeup (Baumrind, 1975). This influence continues into adolescence. Baumrind's concept of three categories of parenting styles has had considerable support in the research literature. The authoritative parenting style is most likely to yield "normal" or "healthy" adolescent behaviour (Baumrind, 1991; Hill, 1987). We may speculate that the warmth coupled with the sense of confident control administered by the authoritative parent is reassuring for most adolescents. In this instance, the parent provides the experimental adolescent with a "safety net."

Interestingly, though, recent research has shown that authoritative parenting works better in some contexts than in others, depending on the neighbourhood, ethnic background, and peers (Steinberg, Darling, Fletcher, Brown, & Dornbusch, 1995). "The key to understanding the influence of the parenting during adolescence inheres in looking beyond the boundaries of the home and at the broader context in which the family lives" (Steinberg et al., 1995, p. 461). This viewpoint is consistent with Bronfenbrenner's theory, which was described in Chapter 2.

Impact of the Adolescent's Leaving Home

Families must make adjustments as adolescents become increasingly independent and prepare to leave home. Making this adjustment is not an easy task. Parents and children must renegotiate roles. Adolescents require a different support system than younger children do, primarily because adolescents are actively exploring their independence. Separateness and self-assertion are not harmful characteristics for adolescents—they are age appropriate and crucial to development. Some families encourage this development, whereas others oppose it.

Many adolescents today experience the transition from high school to university or college. Adolescents who are securely attached to parents tend to cope better with this transition (LaRose & Boivin, 1998). They are able to become independent from their families and to explore new environments. They are less likely to experience intense loneliness or anxiety. Secure attachment to their mothers reduces the loneliness of adolescents who leave home to attend university or college. Typically, the mother is the preferred attachment figure in times of stress, such as leaving home. Securely attached adolescents are able to turn to their mothers for emotional support. Secure attachment to fathers, however, tends not to reduce the loneliness of adolescents living away from home.

Researchers identify three dimensions in family functioning: *cohesion, adaptability,* and *quality of communication* (Barnes & Olsen, 1985). In most cases, it helps during the separation process if families have moderate but not extreme levels of cohesion and adaptability. It is best if families are somewhat flexible and adaptable but not so loosely structured that they seem chaotic. Also, members should be cohesive without smothering one another. Families adapt best if they can negotiate the changes in a rational fashion, taking into consideration each member's wants and needs. Family cohesiveness can be maintained when parents and the departing adolescent are able to approach one another as equals and to establish a reciprocal relationship (Grotevant & Cooper, 1985). Open communication, which enables family members to talk things out without friction, helps to preserve the cohesion of the family.

Question to Ponder

After completing high school, many adolescents today continue to live with their parents, often for financial reasons. How will this affect young people's social and emotional development?

In general, the greater involvement of mothers in their adolescent children's daily activities, such as homework, tends to make this relationship more complex.

As adolescents grow more independent and prepare to leave home, families have to adjust to the separation.

FOCUS ON AN ISSUE

Out-of-School Care of Young Adolescents

By the time children are in grade six, their out-of-school care varies considerably. Nancy Galambos and Jennifer Maggs at the University of Victoria examined whether types of out-of-school care were associated with differences in the development of self-concepts, peer interactions, and problem behaviours (see Galambos & Maggs, 1991). They compared four groups of adolescents: those who had (1) adult care (parent or nonparent); (2) self-care in the home; (3) self-care in friends' homes; or (4) self-care, and the freedom to "hang out" in the community. They also measured aspects of the parent–adolescent relationships, including the amount of parental warmth and acceptance directed toward the adolescents, the types of discipline used by the parents, and the extent of parent–adolescent conflicts.

The effects of the care seemed to depend more on where the care was given than on whether it was self-care, per se. The experiences of adolescents who had self-care at home resembled more the experiences of adolescents who had adult care than the experi-

---

Self-care is not necessarily associated with negative outcomes.

---

ences of those who had self-care out of the home. Self-care out of the home was associated with greater peer involvement. Girls in self-care who hung out in the community had greater risks of developing problem behaviours, of

having contact with more deviant peers, and of having poor self-images. These risks, though, were reduced if parents were more accepting and less permissive. Boys in self-care who hung out in the community did not have greater risks of developing problem behaviours, having contact with more deviant peers, or having poor self-images. Adolescent–parent relationships influenced boys more. Low parent acceptance and high parent–adolescent conflicts were associated with more problems in boys.

It is important to note that placing adolescents in self-care is just one of many factors that influence their experiences. Self-care is not necessarily associated with negative outcomes or with positive ones. Other factors, such as adolescent–parent relationships, also affect adolescents' experiences.

Values, Ideals, and Moral Development

Selection of a set of guiding values is a key task during adolescence. This process is hardly new to the adolescent, however. The development of a conscience and moral standards begins very early in the socialization process, when the toddler is taught not to pull hair, tell lies, or take toys away from others. Throughout childhood, social-learning techniques—particularly imitation of parental models and receiving rewards and punishments—play an essential role in the child's moral development.

This early training forms only part of the value system of a mature adult. Many psychologists believe that processes like modelling, identification, and rewards and punishment, which teach the young child to distinguish right from wrong, can only go so far. They are satisfactory only as a means of teaching an external morality, which the child then internalizes. But in order to become a mature adult, the individual must eventually reassess and analyze these principles to build a coherent set of values.

Reassessment in Adolescence

Preadolescent children may be unable to construct their own value system, even if they should want to do so. As we saw in our review of middle childhood, cognitive theorists point out that the individual must have the ability to make relative judgments about what is right in order to form a mature system of morality. The 5-year-old, or even the 11-year-old, simply does not have the mental capacity to form a systematic framework of these principles. It is necessary for a person to have the ability to consider all of the possible alternatives, to reason from the specific to the general, to use cause-and-effect logic, to think about the past and the future, and to consider hypothetical alternatives. The ability to perform all of these cognitive tasks is not fully reached until adolescence—or perhaps later or not at all. The newly acquired intellectual abilities of adolescents make the transition to adulthood a period that is marked by changes in ideals, values, and attitudes.

According to Hoffman (1980), moral development occurs in three different, overlapping ways. The first is *anxiety-based inhibition*—socially acceptable behaviour that is induced by fear of punishment. Children learn to associate unacceptable behaviour with punishment issued by parents and others. Eventually, children master this fear of punishment by refraining from the forbidden act. Therefore, they have internalized the rules, and actual punishment is no longer necessary. Second, as children grow older, they also learn *empathy-based concern* for others. This moral perspective combines the human capacity to share feelings with the growing cognitive ability to figure out how someone else is feeling, as well as how one's behaviour may alter other people's inner states. Third, children and adolescents undergo moral development through exercising *formal operational thought*—testing hypotheses, re-evaluating information, and reformulating concepts. (This is a model developed by Kohlberg, which we discussed in Chapters 14 and 15.)

These three types of moral growth are not chronological stages, nor are they mutually exclusive. According to Hoffman, they usually coexist in all adults. But in adolescence, the three types may shift in importance. For example, anxiety-based morality can be severely undermined in the antiauthoritarian, peer-dominated university environment. At the same time, empathy may be eroded by exposure to some of life's harsher realities, leading to moral cynicism in adolescents. In contrast, empathy-based morality may be strengthened through exposure to inspiring leaders and teachers and through intense debates that stimulate intellectual support of empathic views. As well, recent research has shown that individual adolescents often are inconsistent. They may use one type of moral reasoning in some situations but other types in different situations (Wark & Krebs, 1996). Therefore, reaching higher levels of reasoning does not necessarily imply that the lower ones are no longer used.

The moral growth that occurs during adolescence helps teenagers recognize the value of community action and concern for others.

Social Context

The substance of adolescents' values depends heavily on the cultural context and historical period in which they live. At many points in history, there have been groups of adolescents who have taken on the role of the conscience of society. In our own recent history, we can see this phenomenon in the civil rights and antiwar movements, in the feminist struggle for equality, in the environmental crusades, and in Craig Kielburger's mission to end child labour.

According to Baumrind (1987), "Adolescents may construct a moral vision of an ideal world in which inequities are resolved justly and peers nourish and care for each other in mutual love and interdependence." Unfortunately, there is little practical support for such a vision in the real world. Will young people remain committed to moral action, despite the lack of support? Or, will they abandon it and run the risk of becoming cynical and feeling alienated and hostile toward an "imperfect" society?

Decisions about Drug Use

During the transitional period of adolescence, individuals are exposed to a variety of behaviours and lifestyles. They adopt certain behaviours and avoid others. A major decision that they must make is whether or not to participate in patterns of drug use and abuse.

How many adolescents choose to use drugs? Researchers in Ontario have been surveying students in grades seven to thirteen every two years since 1977 (Adalf, Ivis, Smart, & Walsh, 1995, 1996). They asked students which drugs they had used each year. The drugs included tobacco, alcohol, marijuana, glue, other solvents, barbiturates and other tranquilizers, heroin, methamphetamine ("speed"), stimulants, LSD and other hallucinogens, and cocaine. In recent years, crack cocaine, PCP, crystal methamphetamine ("ice"), and MDMA ("ecstasy") also appeared in the survey. The good news from this survey is that drug use was lower in the 1990s than it was in the late 1970s.

But researchers have also detected changing trends in drug use over the course of the 1990s. The reported use of eight drugs has increased significantly between 1993 and 1995 (Adalf et al., 1996). These drugs are marijuana, hallucinogens (such as "magic mushrooms"), glue, cocaine, PCP, methamphetamine, ecstasy, and tobacco.

Marijuana use has increased most—from 12.7 percent in 1993 to 22.7 percent in 1995. The increases in reported drug use were greatest for students in grades nine and eleven. Is this the beginning of a trend toward greater drug usage, or is it a temporary increase? Survey results for 1997 are now being analyzed, and according to one group of researchers, cigarette smoking remained constant between 1995 and 1997, so use of this drug appears to have levelled off (Hobbs, Pickett, Ferrence, Brown, Madill, & Adlaf, 1999).

The survey also asked students what grades they were in when they tried drugs for the first time. Those students who use drugs typically first try alcohol and tobacco in grade seven. They then try marijuana for the first time in grade nine (Adalf et al., 1996).

Why do some students use drugs but others abstain? And why do some adolescents go beyond occasional, experimental use of drugs to substance abuse? The answers to these questions are likely complicated and involve aspects of the individuals, peers, families, and societies. Teens most vulnerable to substance use are those who are easily bored (i.e., score high on a scale of novelty seeking), who affiliate with substance-using peers, and who have substance-using parents (Lynskey, Fergusson, & Horwood, 1998). These factors are part of a general vulnerability for using tobacco, alcohol, or marijuana. In the past, some people thought that the use of alcohol or tobacco caused teens to progress to other drugs, such as marijuana. Recent data do not support this position (Lynskey et al., 1998). Teens use more than one drug because the same vulnerability factors apply to the use of different drugs, not because one drug causes them to progress to other drugs.

A recent study related substance abuse in 10- to 15-year-olds to parenting behaviour (Stice & Berrera, 1995). Young people who rated their parents as having less control over their children's behaviour and as providing less emotional support reported more substance abuse. But we must be cautious of inferring that parenting behaviour caused the substance abuse. The child's substance abuse can also change the parenting behaviour—more substance abuse results in less parental control and less parental support. Effects go from parent to child and from child to parent. Furthermore, the quality of relationship between parents and teens can have indirect effects on teen substance use because it affects teens' affiliation with peers (Bogenschneider, Wu, Raffaelli, & Tsay, 1998). According to Bronfenbrenner's ecological theory (described in Chapter 2), experiences in one microsystem (such as the home) can affect another microsystem (such as the peer group). Bronfenbrenner called these interactions the mesosystem. When teens have responsive mothers who express love and praise, who are available when needed, and who engage in give-and-take discussions, the teens are less oriented toward their peers, which, in turn, results in less adolescent substance use, provided that the mothers have a negative attitude toward substance use (Bogenschneider et al., 1998).

Let us now look at some of the drugs in more detail.

Alcohol Alcohol acts as a depressant; its effects are similar to those of sleeping pills. In small amounts, the psychological effects include lowered inhibitions and self-restraint, heightened feelings of well-being, and an accelerated sense of time. Many drinkers use alcohol to ease tension and to facilitate social interaction. The effects of larger doses include distorted vision, impaired motor coordination, and slurred speech; still larger doses lead to loss of consciousness or even to death. These effects depend not only on the amount of alcohol consumed, but also on individual tolerance. Long-term habitual use of alcohol increases tolerance but eventually causes damage to the liver and the brain.

Probably the most powerful factor in teenage alcohol use is the view that alcohol consumption is a symbol of adulthood and social maturity. Teenagers are constantly reminded by their parents and by the adults they see in advertising, on television, and in movies that drinking is an activity indulged in by the sophisticated and worldly. Drinking

Alcohol is the most widely used drug among adolescents and young adults. Participating in heavy drinking binges during spring break is a popular ritual for many university and college students.

alcohol is common among Canadian adolescents. According to a national survey conducted in 1990, 80 percent of 15- to 19-year-olds report using alcohol (CICH, 1994). A U.S. study has revealed an interesting pattern in adolescent drinking behaviour (National Institute on Drug Abuse, 1989). It is rare for adolescents to drink every day—only one in 20 high school seniors reports doing so. But it is common for adolescents to binge drink, consuming large quantities of alcohol on the weekend and abstaining during the week. Fully 35 percent of high school seniors report having had five or more drinks in a row at least once in the last two weeks, and 32 percent report that most or all of their friends "get drunk" at least once a week.

Heavy drinking in adolescence is of concern because even adolescents can become alcoholics. Researchers in Montreal have been studying boys who are substance abusers by age 13 to identify early risk factors (Dobkin & Tremblay, 1996; Dobkin, Tremblay, & Sacchitelle, 1997). Substance abusers have histories of particular behavioural problems and have less nurturing mothers. Six-year-old boys who are oppositional, hyperactive, and combative are at risk for becoming substance abusers. Interestingly, sons of alcoholic fathers do not have increased risks of substance abuse unless the sons also have disruptive behaviours. The fathers' alcoholism was not the critical risk factor. Earlier studies mistakenly claimed that fathers' alcoholism was crucial because they failed to consider how the sons' behaviours affected their risks for substance abuse (Dobkin et al., 1997).

Tobacco Tobacco use is another habit that the adult world encourages by example. Cigarettes are still a powerfully alluring symbol of maturity to some teenagers. However, as national mortality statistics show and as medical science has long known, cigarette smoking is a serious health hazard. Smoking increases the heart rate, causes shortness of breath, constricts the blood vessels, irritates the throat, and deposits foreign matter in sensitive lung tissues. Years of smoking lead to premature heart attacks, lung and throat cancer, emphysema, and other lung diseases. Moderate smoking shortens a person's life by an average of 7 years (Eddy, 1991).

Even though the health hazards of smoking have been widely advertised in recent years, adolescents continue to smoke. For instance, 1.2 million Canadians between the ages of 15 and 24 smoke, and 99 percent of them smoke daily (DeCivita & Pagani, 1997).

Studies in both Canada and the United States have found that adolescents have easy access to cigarettes, even though it is against the law in both countries for retailers to sell cigarettes to minors (DiFranza, Savageau, & Aisquith, 1996; Dovell, Mowat, Dorland, & Lam, 1996). In a Canadian study, the rate at which retailers sold cigarettes to minors dropped from 46 percent to 6 percent only after stores received educational materials and threats of law enforcement (Dovell et al., 1996). A U.S. study found that retailers sold more often to girls than to boys and more often to adolescents who looked older (DiFranza et al., 1996). This study also examined the effectiveness of "It's the Law" stickers, which remind retailers that it is illegal to sell cigarettes to minors. Interestingly, these stickers had no effect on the number of sales to minors. Our laws seem to send adolescents mixed messages about smoking. On the one hand, it is illegal to sell cigarettes to minors, but on the other hand, it is not illegal for minors to possess cigarettes or to smoke.

Ontario tried to reduce teen smoking by banning it on school properties. According to a survey of school administrators, the ban did not appear to affect teen smoking or attitudes toward smoking in most of the schools (Northrup, Ashley, & Ferrence, 1998). The same numbers of students smoked—they just did so off school property.

Why do adolescents choose to purchase cigarettes and to become smokers? Research has focused on the individual, peers, family, and advertisements. Adolescents who have symptoms of depression or anxiety are at risk for becoming smokers (Patton, Hibbert, Rosier, Carlin, Caust, & Bowes, 1996), as are adolescents who have friends who smoke. The influence of the family, however, is more complicated (see DeCivita & Pagani, 1997, for a review).

The parents of adolescents who smoke tend to be less close to their children,

Many cigarette ads now target teenagers. Adolescent girls smoke more frequently than boys.

provide less monitoring, and are more lax in expressing rules against smoking. Interestingly, the effects of the parents' smoking behaviour depend on the quality of the relationship between the parents and adolescent. Children of smokers are more likely to smoke if they are strongly attached to their parents, but children of nonsmokers are less likely to smoke if they are strongly attached to their parents (Foshee & Bauman, 1992, as cited in DeCivita & Pagani, 1997). Other researchers found that nonsmoking mothers who discussed the negative implications of smoking with their daughters and who punished smoking had daughters who were less likely to smoke or to affiliate with smoking peers (Chassin, Presson, Rose, Sherman, & Todd, 1998). Daughters of smoking mothers viewed their mothers as more tolerant of teen smoking, even though their mothers reported that they disapproved of it. These daughters were very much aware of the mixed messages being sent by their mothers.

Exposure to advertisements also influences the onset of adolescent smoking, even when the effects of family and peers are controlled (Schooler, Feighery, & Flora, 1996), as was discussed in Chapter 15. Similarly, adolescents—more so than adults—are affected by the cost of cigarettes (Hobbs et al., 1999).

Are adolescent smokers likely to still be smoking in their adult years? For many, the answer is yes. For instance, boys who start smoking in adolescence continue to smoke for an average of 16 years, and girls for an average of 20 years (Pierce & Gilpin, 1996). Moreover, adolescents who start smoking before age 13 find it more difficult to quit than do people who start smoking when they are older (Breslau & Peterson, 1996). Furthermore, most smokers start the habit during adolescence. If people make it to adulthood as nonsmokers, there is a good chance that they will remain nonsmokers.

Marijuana After alcohol and nicotine, marijuana is the most widely used drug in Canada and the United States. Marijuana is derived from the leaves of the hemp plant (the botanical name of the hemp plant is *cannabis*). The leaves are coated in a sticky substance that has over 80 chemicals, the most familiar being THC. These chemicals produce a number of psychological effects, including heightened sensitivity to sounds and sights, time distortion (time seems to pass more slowly), splitting of consciousness, a high or euphoria, racing thoughts, and either stimulation or sedation (McKim, 1997).

Most adolescents who use marijuana in Canada and the United States can be described as casual users who take the drug in social settings but rarely when alone, and most are not daily users (McKim, 1997). In some respects, marijuana can be considered a relatively safe drug; it is highly nontoxic (it is nearly impossible to overdose on it), and it is considered less addictive than either nicotine or alcohol. That does not mean, though, that it is harmless. For instance, marijuana impairs driving. Marijuana-intoxicated drivers are so busy attending to internal sensations that they fail to attend adequately to the road. Smoking marijuana causes lung damage and increases the risk of lung cancer. And smoking both marijuana and tobacco increases the risk of early onset lung cancer, before age 42 (Sridhar, Ruab, & Weatherby, 1994). Interestingly, the effects of marijuana smoke on asthma are complicated. For a short while, smoking marijuana seems to improve the symptoms of asthma because it dilates the airways. But with continued usage, it damages the lungs and may actually cause asthma (McKim, 1997).

In the 1960s, researchers noticed that some adolescent users of marijuana seemed to undergo major personality and behavioural changes at around the same time they started using the drug (McGlothlin & West, 1968). They seemed preoccupied with the drug, at the expense of thinking about school, career aspirations, and future goals. They acted childishly and became more introverted. All of these changes have been referred to as the *amotivational syndrome*. Although the presence of this syndrome has been established, it is unclear whether marijuana causes it (McKim, 1997). All the evidence shows is a correlation between the two. And, as noted in earlier chapters, correlation does not imply causation. Perhaps motivational problems cause people to choose to use marijuana, rather than the other way around. Correlational studies do not allow us to determine which interpretation is correct.

Another concern is whether marijuana use is a stepping stone to other "harder" drugs. For instance, one study found that virtually all heroin users had used marijuana before starting heroin (Golub & Johnson, 1994). But this type of evidence does not prove that marijuana caused people to take heroin. To use an analogy, most children drink milk before they drink juice, but this does not mean that drinking milk causes children to drink juice.

Risk Taking in Adolescence

As we have seen, some adolescents engage in a variety of risk-taking behaviours—as a matter of fact, some have called adolescence a time of risk taking. Many adolescents engage in unprotected sex—sometimes with multiple partners—abuse drugs, drive too fast, perhaps engage in violent activities, and generally experiment with a variety of dangerous activities. Often, they engage in these high-risk activities in combination.

Naturally, some teens engage in more of these activities than do others, often accumulating an increasing repertoire as they age (Jessor, Donovan, & Costa, 1992). For other teens, however, the natural increase in energy and intellectual curiosity that accompanies adolescence is harnessed in such activities as sports or put to constructive, rather than potentially destructive, use. For example, many teens become involved in social activism by engaging in environmental clean-ups, by building houses with Habitat for Humanity, or by working with children who are ill or experiencing violence in their lives. Adolescents who engage in high-risk behaviours for destructive purposes are in the definite minority of all adolescents.

When adolescents engage in high-risk behaviours, however, there are various reasons that could be advanced to explain why they do so. For example, adolescents get into trouble because they do not understand the risks they are taking, either because they have too little information or because the message about risks was incomprehensible or unconvincing. A final explanation is that adolescents actually understand the risks but choose to ignore them. Depending on which of these beliefs one holds, the answer to dealing with high-risk behaviour may be very different.

A ready explanation for why adolescents take risks is that they underestimate the likelihood of bad outcomes—in other words, they see themselves as invulnerable. Because of this belief, they focus mainly on the benefits of such high-risk behaviours—the status gained with peers or the exhilarating loss of inhibitions, for example. This explanation ties in with Elkind's (1967) views on imaginary audience and personal fable. Elkind argued that adolescents' personal fables endowed them with a uniqueness so strong that they became convinced they could not die or become addicted or get pregnant.

Over two decades of research on adolescent risk-taking behaviour has determined that there are multiple causes for such behaviours. We may see these causes presented in Figure 16-1. In general, the factors producing high-risk behaviours may be divided into five domains: biology/genetics, the social environment, the perceived environment, personality, and actual behaviour. These factors interrelate to produce the various adolescent high-risk behaviours or lifestyles. Such behaviours and lifestyles, in turn, produce negative or compromising outcomes for the adolescents who engage in them.

What sorts of factors protect adolescents from engaging in such high-risk behaviours? First, it appears that many families use strategies to protect their adolescents from the risks, dangers, and illegitimate opportunities encountered in many high-risk settings. They garner resources, badger public officials and teachers when their child is having difficulty, and provide monitoring against drug use or other destructive behaviours. Often, the family may move their child to what they consider a safer niche, such as a local parochial school, rather than give in to dangerous neighbourhood elements (Jessor, 1993). Enlisting parental involvement in public schools has also been found to be a successful strategy. In general, when self-esteem, a sense of competence, and a sense of belonging to a stable family and social order develop within adolescents, they

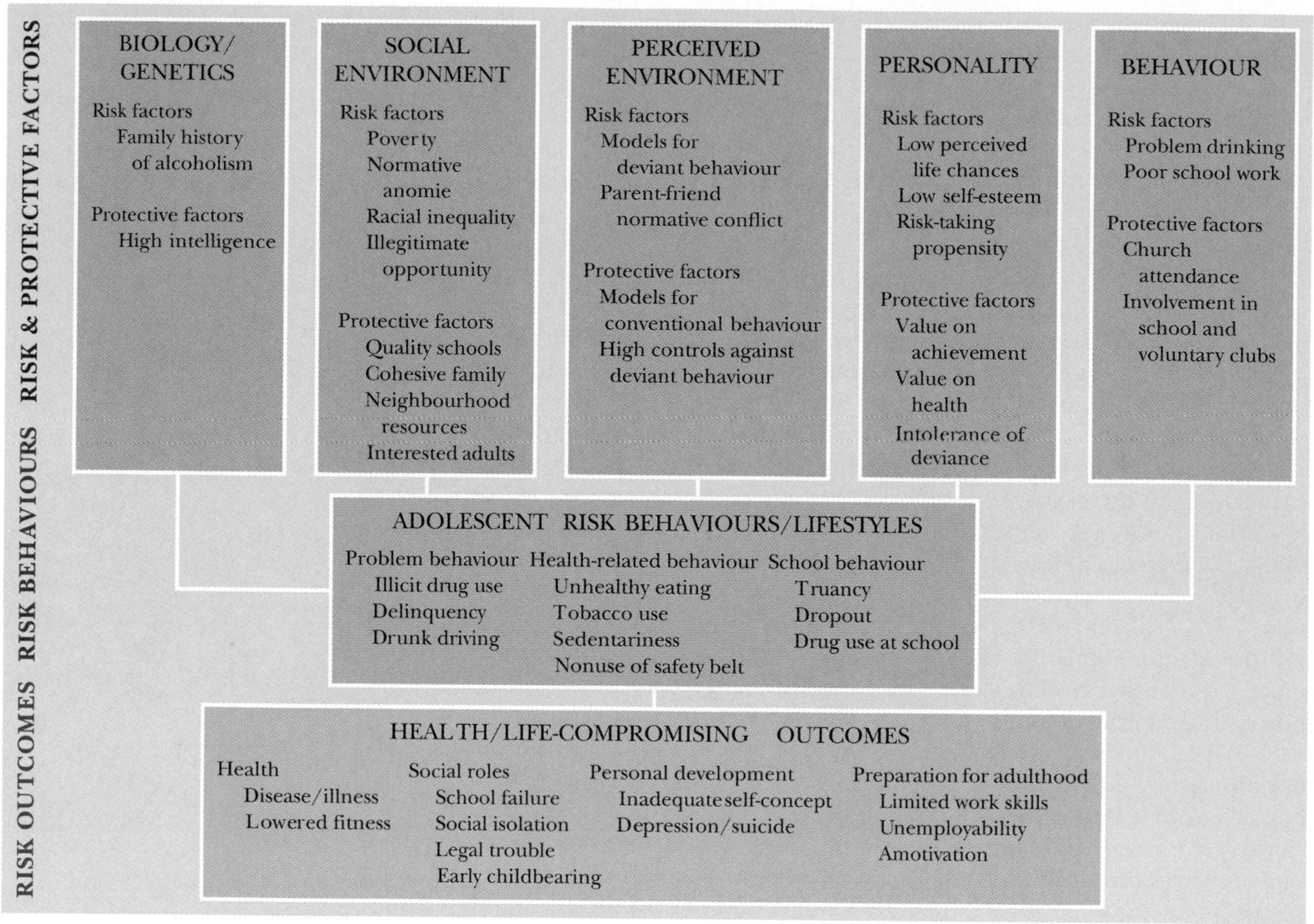

BIOLOGY/ GENETICS	SOCIAL ENVIRONMENT	PERCEIVED ENVIRONMENT	PERSONALITY	BEHAVIOUR
Risk factors Family history of alcoholism Protective factors High intelligence	Risk factors Poverty Normative anomie Racial inequality Illegitimate opportunity Protective factors Quality schools Cohesive family Neighbourhood resources Interested adults	Risk factors Models for deviant behaviour Parent-friend normative conflict Protective factors Models for conventional behaviour High controls against deviant behaviour	Risk factors Low perceived life chances Low self-esteem Risk-taking propensity Protective factors Value on achievement Value on health Intolerance of deviance	Risk factors Problem drinking Poor school work Protective factors Church attendance Involvement in school and voluntary clubs

RISK & PROTECTIVE FACTORS

ADOLESCENT RISK BEHAVIOURS/LIFESTYLES

Problem behaviour	Health-related behaviour	School behaviour
Illicit drug use	Unhealthy eating	Truancy
Delinquency	Tobacco use	Dropout
Drunk driving	Sedentariness	Drug use at school
	Nonuse of safety belt	

RISK BEHAVIOURS

HEALTH/LIFE-COMPROMISING OUTCOMES

Health	Social roles	Personal development	Preparation for adulthood
Disease/illness	School failure	Inadequate self-concept	Limited work skills
Lowered fitness	Social isolation	Depression/suicide	Unemployability
	Legal trouble		Amotivation
	Early childbearing		

RISK OUTCOMES

Figure 16-1
A Conceptual Framework for Adolescent Risk Behaviour

Source: "Risk Behavior in Adolescence: A Psychosocial Framework for Understanding and Action" (p. 27) by Richard Jessor, 1992, in *Adolescents at Risk: Medical and Social Perspectives,* edited by D.E. Rogers and E. Ginzberg, Boulder, CO: Westview Press. Copyright 1992 by Westview Press. Reprinted by permission.

are less likely to feel the need to engage in high-risk behaviours (Jessor, 1993; Quadrel, Fischhoff, & Davis, 1993).

Stress and Coping in Adolescence

Are adolescents a troubled group of people? The answer is some are, but most are not. The majority are well adjusted and have no major conflicts with their parents, peers, or themselves. But an estimated 10 to 20 percent have psychological disturbances that range from mild to severe. Although this proportion may seem high, it is no higher than the proportion of adults who have psychological disturbances (Powers, Hauser, & Kilner, 1989).

Dramatic and extreme rhetoric often characterize the many articles and discussions involving adolescents—for example, articles may claim that all adolescents are depressed or rebellious or potential runaways, or articles may state, "Wait until your child turns 12, then the storm and stress begin." Two problems arise as a consequence of this overstating of the psychological traumas of adolescence. First, all adolescents are viewed as experiencing psychological distress, and second, adolescents who need help are not taken seriously because their behaviour and feelings are considered part of a normal phase of adolescence (Connelly, Johnston, Brown, Mackay, & Blackstock, 1993). It is important to distinguish between normal adolescents and those who are in psychological distress.

Depression In general, studies of psychiatric disorders during adolescence have found a fairly low incidence of moderate to severe depression, but symptoms may be life threatening in those affected (Peterson, Compas, Brooks-Gunn, Stemmler, Ey, &

FOCUS ON APPLICATION

Youth Gambling in Quebec

Gambling among youth is becoming a concern. More children and adolescents gamble on a regular basis than drink alcohol, smoke cigarettes, or take drugs. According to a recent survey in Quebec, 81 percent of children and adolescents (ages 9 to 17), have engaged in gambling. Their preferred types of gambling were card playing, lottery tickets, bingo, sports pools, and sport lottery tickets (Derevensky & Gupta, 1998). Furthermore, 42 percent indicated that they gambled a minimum of once a week. Most gambling took place at home, at a friend's place, or at school. Older adolescents sometimes frequented gambling establishments, such as casinos and bingo halls. As well, 65 percent of children and adolescents gambled with their families, and 73 percent gambled with friends. Interestingly, girls were more likely to gamble with family and boys with friends. Children and adolescents reported that they gambled mainly because of the enjoyment and excitement. They did not report making money as a main motivator until grade eleven.

The popularity of gambling among youth is a concern because gambling is potentially addictive. According to the Quebec survey, 4 to 8 percent of the children and adolescents were pathological gamblers, and another 10 to 15 percent had a very serious gambling problem. Adolescents were two to three times more likely to develop gambling problems than were adults. The following factors are associated with gambling problems in adolescents:

> *Gambling is potentially addictive.*

- Being male.
- Being a high risk taker and sensation seeker.
- Starting gambling young, at about age 9.
- Experiencing depression, high anxiety, and low self-esteem.
- Having lower conformity and self-discipline.
- Engaging in dissociative behaviours

while gambling. These include experiencing the perception of loss of time, trance-like behaviour, feeling like a different person, blackouts, or the feeling of being outside of one's own body.

- Engaging in substance abuse.
- Having antisocial and criminal problems.
- Experiencing academic difficulties.
- Having problems with peer and family relationships.

As can be seen by the above list, gambling problems are associated with difficulties in almost all areas of the young person's life. According to Derevensky and Gupta (1998), adolescents with gambling problems engage in gambling to escape from problems. These researchers strongly advocate developing scientifically validated gambling prevention programs for children and adolescents, awareness and education programs for parents, greater enforcement of laws prohibiting youth from gambling, and a national advertising campaign to discourage youth from gambling.

Grant, 1993). In a recent study, for example, while the results show an increase in measured depression over the teenage years, the percentage of those experiencing depression is consistently low, peaking at age 16 and again at 19, as we see in Table 16-1. As the authors conclude,

> The relatively low rates of moderate and severe depression in this population indicate that the large majority of teenagers do not experience difficulty in this area. The corollary is that those who evidence symptomatology need to be identified and helped. (Connelly et al., 1993, p. 157)

For adolescents who have problems, the symptoms tend to vary according to gender. Troubled teenage boys are likely to engage in antisocial behaviour, such as delinquency and substance abuse. Troubled teenage girls are more likely to direct their symptoms inward and to become depressed (Ostrov, Offer, & Howard, 1989). The symptoms of depression are much more common in girls than in boys from age 14 to adulthood, but not in younger children (Marcotte, 1996). Psychologists have not agreed on the reason for this sex difference, but it may be related to the substantial drop in self-esteem that has been found to occur in girls—but not in boys—around the time they enter junior high school (Bower, 1991). This lowered self-esteem is an effect of sex-role socialization that accompanies puberty in adolescent girls—girls are pressured by peers and by the media to become more attractive and to value relationships above achievements (Connelly et al., 1993). In general, having less effective coping styles and facing more challenges may increase the likelihood of depression among girls as they move through adolescence. This fact may account for the 16- and 19-year peaks in depression in adolescent girls. Interestingly, though, there is one exception to this pattern of sex differences—it is noticeably less, or nonexistent, in studies of college students (Gladstone & Koenig, 1994; Greenberger & Chen, 1996). Female college students have lower rates of depression than do other females the same age, perhaps because females in college encounter more equality in opportunities, status, and channels of self-expression than is typical in other settings.

Ethnic group differences also characterize the incidence of depression in adolescence. For example, Aboriginal teenagers were found to have elevated rates of depression in adolescence (Armstrong, 1993). Homosexual youth also show higher rates of depression, as well as a two- to threefold increase in risk of suicide, than heterosexual adolescents (Connelly et al., 1993). Adolescents' cultural and ethnic backgrounds also affect how they report their depressions. In traditional Chinese culture, bodily complaints are emphasized and affective symptoms are minimized (Zhang, 1995). Open expression of emotions and discussion of psychological issues are discouraged in Chinese culture, and there is a powerful social stigma associated with mental illness.

Depression and the Co-occurrence of Other Disorders It has been well documented that depression in adolescence occurs simultaneously with other disorders. Therefore, depression and anxiety disorders often occur together, as do depression and conduct disorders involving acting-out behaviour. Boys are more likely to have disruptive disorders and depression, whereas girls are more likely to have eating disorders, such as anorexia or bulimia, with depression (Connelly et al., 1993). A high proportion of those attempting suicide are depressed, at least after the attempt. Depressed mood, thoughts of suicide, and substance use are also related (Kandel, Raveis, & Davies, 1991).

For girls, poor body image may lead to eating disorders and then to depression. Elevated risk of depression has been found to be associated with medical illness—the assumption being that depression makes one vulnerable to medical illness. Depression may also cause other problems because of its impact on interpersonal functioning. Poor social functioning may worsen the parent–child relationship during adolescence and may also affect romantic relationships. For example, there is a threefold increase in teen pregnancy among depressed teenage girls (Horwitz, Klerman, Sungkuo, & Jekel, 1991).

Question to Ponder

Why do you think depression is more common in females than in males?

Table 16-1 Percentage of Students by Age and Gender Experiencing None to Mild and Moderate to Severe Depression

MALES				AGE				
Depression	**13**	**14**	**15**	**16**	**17**	**18**	**19**	**Total**
None to mild	96%	97%	93%	88%	93%	94%	89%	93%
Moderate to severe	4%	3%	7%	12%	7%	6%	11%	7%

FEMALES				AGE				
Depression	**13**	**14**	**15**	**16**	**17**	**18**	**19**	**Total**
None to mild	93%	90%	89%	84%	87%	87%	82%	88%
Moderate to severe	7%	10%	11%	16%	13%	13%	18%	12%

Note: Number of students surveyed = 2698

Source: Connelly et al., 1993.

Developmental Processes: Risk and Protective Factors As we noted in Chapter 15, adolescence is a time of great transition. The biological changes of puberty, as well as the social changes related to the move from elementary school to middle and high schools, demand adjustment by adolescents. Factors that place adolescents at risk for depression and stress responses include the following:

- Negative body image, which is believed to lead to depression and eating disorders.
- Increased capacity to reflect on the developing self and the future, which is believed to lead to an increased risk of depression as adolescents dwell on negative possibilities.
- Family dysfunction or parental mental health problems, which are believed to lead to stress responses and depression, as well as to conduct disorders.
- Marital discord or divorce and economic hardship, which lead to depression and stress.
- Low peer popularity, which is related to depression in adolescence and is among the strongest predictors of disorders as adults.
- Poor school achievement, which leads to depression and disruptive behaviour in boys but does not appear to affect girls.

While these factors predict risk for stress, there are counterbalancing factors that help adolescents to cope with the transitions of this period. Good relationships with parents, and by middle adolescence with peers, serve as buffers against the stress of life transitions. The importance of protective, supportive relationships during this difficult time cannot be overestimated, as the following comments indicate:

> Once on a depressed trajectory in development, an individual becomes more likely to stay on this course because of the tendency to both alienate and withdraw from the very social supports that can minimize negative effects. The effects are likely to be especially devastating to a developing adolescent. Imagine the 13-year-old, hospitalized for depression following the death of a parent. The hospitalization removes the adolescent from the peer group and school; family members are likely to visit, but the context is certainly not the same as home. (Connelly et al., 1993, p. 161)

This adolescent experiences unusual—and perhaps stigmatizing—treatment, but also misses important developmental experiences at school with peers. The longer an adolescent is removed from peers, the more difficult is the reintegration process. It may become so stressful in itself that a more isolated, less socially competent, depressed approach to life may be the result.

Adolescents' Coping Responses Adolescents use a variety of coping responses to deal with the stress of their daily lives (see the box "Adolescent Suicide"). In general, research has found that substance use, diversionary responses, and rebellious responses are the major ways adolescents cope with stress. Students at all levels report drinking alcohol, smoking cigarettes, and using drugs as a means of reducing stress. We have already discussed substance use earlier in this chapter. Diversionary responses are also frequently employed. These include shopping, taking a hot bath or shower, going out with friends, sleeping, watching television, and eating. These activities do not directly deal with problems the adolescents are confronting, but rather divert attention away from them. The final category, rebellious responses, includes rebelling against the rules or resorting to violence. Few adolescents who are really stressed out view dealing with the stress "head on" as an option (Mates & Allison, 1992). In this, they differ little from adults in similar situations.

Peers, Friends, and the Social Environment

During adolescence, the importance of peer groups increases enormously. Teenagers seek support from others in order to cope with the physical, emotional, and social changes

FOCUS ON AN ISSUE

Adolescent Suicide

In recent years, there has been growing public concern over the increased rate of adolescent suicide. In 1993, suicide accounted for more deaths among Canadian 15- to 19-year-olds than any other cause except motor vehicle accidents (Wilkins, 1996). Suicide was the reported cause of death in 23 percent of male deaths and in 16 percent of female deaths.

We should note that the statistics on suicide tend to be low estimates of the true prevalence. Suicides have always tended to be underreported because of religious implications, concern for the family, and financial considerations regarding insurance payment restrictions (Garland & Zigler, 1993).

What are the risk factors for adoles-cent suicide? Researchers have studied suicide attempters and have also conducted psychological autopsies of successful suicides in order to determine risk factors. Many adolescents will ex-

---

Over one thousand suicide hotlines offer services to adolescents.

---

perience some or all of these risk factors and never commit suicide. However, although individuals may not always conform to these predictions, they prove useful in designing suicide intervention programs. The generally accepted risk factors for adolescent suicide include the following:

- Psychiatric illness, such as conduct disorder, antisocial personality, depression, or substance abuse.
- A previous suicide attempt (the best single predictor).
- High amounts of depression, hopelessness, and helplessness.
- Drug and alcohol abuse.
- Stressful life events, such as serious family turmoil, divorce, or separation.
- Increased accessibility and use of firearms.

Elkind (1988) attributed the dramatic increase in adolescent suicide to in-

---

of adolescence. Understandably, they are most likely to seek this support from others who are going through the same experience. These "others" are their peers. Studies have shown that adolescents spend at least half of their time with their peers—friends and classmates—and much less time with their families (Csikszentmihalyi & Larson, 1984).

The Influence of Peers

Peer networks are essential to the adolescent's development of social skills. The reciprocal equality that characterizes teenage relationships also helps develop positive responses to the various crises these young people face (Epstein, 1983; Hawkins & Berndt, 1985). Teenagers learn from their friends and age mates the kinds of behaviour that will be socially rewarded and the roles that best suit them. Social competence is a major element in a teenager's ability to make new friends and to maintain old ones (Fischer, Sollie, & Morrow, 1986).

Most adolescents are members of an adolescent peer group. There are two basic types of groups, distinguished by size. The larger, which has between 15 and 30 members, is called a *crowd;* the smaller, which has as few as 3 members or as many as 9, is called a *clique.* The average crowd consists of several cliques. Because of their small number, cliques are highly cohesive. Their members share similar characteristics or reputations—for example, the jocks, the populars, the brains, and the druggies (Brown & Lohr, 1987; Dunphy, 1963).

Sometimes, cliques are based on elements of adult society, such as socioeconomic status or ethnic origin. In joining them, adolescents are seeking another component of identity—the group identity. Interestingly enough, in seeking autonomy from the family, they often end up substituting a group that is quite similar to their parents.

Solitude and Loneliness Although 80 percent of adolescents join peer groups, a significant 20 percent do not. Generally, we think of

Peers serve as audience, critic, and emotional support for their friends' ideas, innovations, and behaviour.

creased pressure on young children to achieve and to be responsible at an early age. Others have blamed the mass media, since there is a significant increase in adolescent suicidal behaviour following television or newspaper coverage of suicides. Fictional stories about suicide have also been found to be associated with an increase in suicidal behaviour (Garland & Zigler, 1993). In general, social imitation—the "copycat suicides"—appear to occur particularly in adolescence, when individuals are most vulnerable to the belief that the future is not in their control or is unlikely to meet their dreams.

PREVENTION EFFORTS

The most prevalent types of suicide prevention efforts are crisis intervention services. Telephone hotlines are the most popular of these services. Currently, over one thousand suicide hotlines offer services to adolescents. A relatively new approach to suicide prevention is curriculum-based prevention or education programs. These programs are most commonly directed at secondary school students, their parents, and educators.

The content of a typical suicide prevention program for students includes a review of the statistics on suicide, a list of warning signs, a list of community resources and how to contact them, and a list of listening skills peers can use to assist friends in gaining help (Garland & Zigler, 1993).

Recently, the American Psychological Association has developed a multiple-front prevention program for teen suicide (Garland & Zigler, 1993). This program includes the following recommendations:

1. Provide professional education for educators and health and mental health-care workers.
2. Restrict access to firearms by passing strict gun control laws.
3. Educate the media about suicide to ensure correct information and appropriate reporting.
4. Identify and treat at-risk youth.

Given the severity of this problem, a comprehensive program such as this, while undoubtedly costly, may offer the best means of preventing adolescent suicide.

---

nonjoiners as loners. Most of us think of being alone as a sad state of affairs that no one would willingly choose. However, this is not necessarily the case. Ancient hermits and modern mystics have sought solitude for purposes of contemplation or to deepen their religious experience. Creative work—in painting, music composition, or writing, for example—is solitary. Creative people often seek to be alone, both to create and to think. Solitude may have many other positive attributes. Some people experience a sense of renewal or healing when they are alone. Also, many seek solitude for the same reasons as the artist or writer—they can think best when alone and can work through their problems at this time (Marcoen, Goossens, & Caes, 1987).

However, there is also a negative side to being alone. This condition can bring on severe feelings of rejection, isolation, depression, and boredom. Hence, there are two ways of experiencing solitude. One is involuntary aloneness, which is perceived as an unhappy state of affairs; the response to involuntary aloneness is to seek the company of others or to turn away from them because of feeling rejected. The other way of experiencing solitude is voluntary aloneness, which is seen as a relief from the pressures of the world—an opportunity for creativity or psychological renewal.

As young people move from late childhood into early adolescence, some experience a feeling of loneliness. Others do not have this experience at any age-specific point in the transit through adolescence, but they feel lonely after arguing with friends or sensing rejection by other peers (Marcoen et al., 1987). Still others voluntarily withdraw from extensive socializing for a period so that they can deal with personal concerns without experiencing public pressure.

The Need for Support Adolescence can be a time of stress. Part of the ability to handle stress grows from finding support in at least one area of engagement. If the changes of adolescence occur in too many areas at one time, they become too difficult to deal with and are a cause of great discomfort. Adolescents who can find security in some environments or relationships are better equipped to deal with discomforts in other aspects of their lives. Gradual changes—in relation to parents and siblings, school, or the peer network—are much easier to deal with than are changes in all of these areas at the same time (Simmons, Burgeson, Carlton-Ford, & Blyth, 1987). Parents, in particular, can be sources of consistent support. A recent study found that the way parents treated junior high students predicted the occurrence of later problems of depression and conduct disorders (Ge, Best, Conger, & Simons, 1996). Parents who were cold and hostile had children who were most at risk for developing depression and conduct disorders.

young offenders Canadians between the ages of 12 and 17 years who are convicted of crimes.

Young Offenders The criminal acts of **young offenders** range in seriousness from shoplifting and vandalism to robbery, rape, and murder. Young offenders range in age from 12 to 17 years; children under 12 cannot be charged with crimes in Canada. Many people these days are under the impression that the number of crimes committed by young offenders is increasing, if not skyrocketing. But between 1991–1992 and 1994–1995, the number of youths tried in Canadian courts actually decreased by almost 6 percent (Onstad, 1997). However, there has been an increase in the number of youths charged with minor physical assaults, such as fighting. It is difficult to determine, though, whether this represents a real increase in these behaviours, or simply more of a willingness to report them and to press charges. The interpretation of problem behaviours, and the method of dealing with them, vary over the years (Jones, 1997; Schlossman & Cairns, 1993). The number of youths charged with murder has been stable for more than 20 years (Onstad, 1997).

At some point in their lives, many, if not most, children engage in some kind of behaviour that could be called delinquent. Shoplifting, for example, is very common, as are minor acts of vandalism—that is, damage to property performed for the pleasure of destruction. The labelling of individuals as delinquents depends on whether they are arrested and on the frequency of these arrests.

Sociologists and psychologists offer quite different explanations for delinquent behaviour. Sociological statistics and theories help to link delinquency to environmental factors, but they do not explain individual psychological factors. A psychological theory of delinquency would maintain that environmental factors do not, in themselves, explain why people commit crimes. Individuals are not delinquent because they are poor or are city dwellers. They may be delinquent because, as individuals, they have repeatedly been unable or unwilling to adjust to society or to develop adequate impulse controls or outlets for anger or frustration.

Perhaps the distinction between sociological and psychological causes of delinquency is artificial (Gibbons, 1976). As we have previously seen, sociological factors often lead to psychological consequences, and vice versa. The sociological influences of crowding, mobility, rapid change, and impersonality contribute to psychological problems. Like the other patterns we have studied in this chapter, delinquency is a form of adjustment to the social and psychological realities of adolescence—an extreme adjustment of which society disapproves. Delinquency satisfies certain special needs for self-esteem; it also provides acceptance within the peer group and a sense of autonomy. For some delinquents, the thrill of high-risk behaviours is the compelling factor. The kinds of personality disturbances we have discussed seem to predispose certain adolescents to delinquent behaviour.

In addition to these individual factors, research has also implicated the media in the development of violent or delinquent behaviours among some especially vulnerable teenagers. Film viewing, for example, may affect the potential juvenile delinquent through the processes known as *social learning* and *instigation*. Identification by the adolescent with the movie and its characters also provides a vehicle by which similar behaviours may occur, as the following example indicates:

On March 24, 1984, a teenager from Rochester, New York, died after shooting himself with a .38 calibre handgun while playing Russian roulette. The movie *The Deerhunter* recently had been shown in the neighborhood. It was known that the youth had a fascination with films, especially violent ones. On the night of the shooting, he was holding a high school beer-drinking party at his home and had been drinking himself. At least 43 deaths have been attributed, at least in part, to the movie, with all victims being male and 20 victims under the age of eighteen. (Snyder, 1991, p. 127)

Understanding adolescent violence is complicated by the fact that there are different developmental paths for youth aggression (Loeber & Stouthamer-Loeber, 1998). One subgroup has an early onset of problems—either during the preschool or elementary school years—that persists into adolescence. A second subgroup has early problems, but their problems are of limited duration, and they seem to outgrow them by adolescence or early adulthood. Finally, a third subgroup of adolescents—called a *late-onset group*—develops problems with aggression for the first time during adolescence. It is important to be aware of the different subgroups when designing interventions. See the box "Prevention of Youth Violence" for further discussion.

Friendships and Relationships

In late childhood, friendship patterns are often based on sharing specific activities, such as playing ball, riding bikes, or using computers. During adolescence, friendships assume more significance. As individuals become more independent of their families, they depend increasingly on friendships to provide emotional support and to serve as testing grounds for new values (Douvan & Adelson, 1966; Douvan & Gold, 1966). With close friends, the younger adolescent is working out an identity. To be able to accept this identity, the adolescent must feel accepted and liked by others.

Adolescents tend to select friends who are from a similar social class and who have similar interests, moral values, and academic ambitions (Berndt, 1982). They become increasingly aware of peer groups and are very concerned about whether their group is "in" or "out." Adolescents know to which group they belong and are usually aware of its effect on their status and reputation. The social status of their group has a measurable effect on their self-esteem: teens who belong to high-status groups tend to have high self-esteem (Brown & Lohr, 1987).

Between ages 12 and 17, adolescents develop the capacity to form closer and more intimate friendships. Over this period of time, they are increasingly likely to

Delinquency satisfies certain special needs for self-esteem and is a way of gaining acceptance within the peer group.

FOCUS ON APPLICATION

Prevention of Youth Violence

The unthinkable happened in Canada—a teen brought a gun to school and killed a classmate. Since this event, there have been public outcries in the media about youth violence. From media accounts, it would be easy to get the impression that youth violence is a far more serious problem today than it was in the past. But is this impression accurate? According to recent statistics, it is not—youth are not considerably more violent today than in the past. In the early 1990s there was a slight increase in the number of 12- to 17-year-olds convicted of violent crimes (mostly for minor assaults), but from 1994 to 1997 there has been a decrease (Canadian Centre for Justice Statistics, cited in Jaffe & Baker, 1999). Furthermore, youth convictions for homicide have not increased. "Murder, manslaughter and attempted murder cases together accounted for less than 1% of cases heard in youth court in 1996–1997" (Jaffe & Baker, 1999, p. 23).

Youth violence does not have to be rampant, though, to be of concern. Even a low rate of violence can have devastating effects on the individuals involved and on society at large. Let us now look at approaches to dealing with youth violence.

Even a low rate of violence can have devastating effects.

THE "GET TOUGHER" MOVEMENT

This approach focuses on tougher penalties for youth who are violent. It assumes that violent youth need strong discipline to turn their lives around. Among its recommendations are amendments to the Young Offenders Act to make it less lenient and the establishment of boot camps for wayward youth. There is a perception that vio-

lent youth are dealt with too leniently by the Canadian justice system. However, this perception is wrong, as "the rate at which violent youth are sentenced to custody is four times higher than the rate for adults and higher than the rate of many Western countries, including the United States, Australia and New Zealand; the custody rate [of Canadian youth] has increased by 26% since 1986" (Jaffe & Baker, 1999, p. 23).

Advocates of the get tougher movement often assume that violent youth are not upset about their violence unless they are caught and punished. Data collected in the National Longitudinal Survey of Children and Youth, though, paint a different picture of violent 10- and 11-year-olds (Sprott & Doob, 1998). Violent children are often unhappy children who contend with other problems, such as poor family relationships and difficulties with peers. "Violent children are part of a group

agree with statements like "I feel free to talk with my friend about almost anything," and "I know how my friend feels about things without his or her telling me." This increased intimacy is reported both by girls (in regard to their friendships with other girls) and by boys (in regard to their friendships with other boys). At the same time that the intimacy of same-sex friendships is increasing, friendships with members of the opposite sex are beginning to occur. Close relationships with opposite-sex friends are reported at an earlier age by girls than by boys (Sharabany, Gershoni, & Hoffman, 1981).

During early adolescence, most interactions with the opposite sex take place in group settings. Many 14- or 15-year-olds prefer this group contact to the closer relationship of dating. "Hanging out" (sitting around and chatting in a café, on a street corner, or in some other public place) is a popular pastime throughout adolescence, and it becomes increasingly "coeducational" as adolescence progresses. This type of interaction is often the first step in learning how to relate to the opposite sex. Early adolescence is a stage of testing, imagining, and discovering what it is like to function in coeducational groups and pairs. It gives adolescents a trial period when they can collect ideas and experiences with which to form basic attitudes about sex roles and sexual behaviour without feeling pressured to become too deeply involved with someone of the opposite sex (Douvan & Adelson, 1966).

For some teenagers, however, dating starts early. In one sample from a small town in the United States, 13 percent of grade six students had already started to date. The proportion rose to over 90 percent in mid- and late adolescence. Bruce Roscoe and his colleagues (Roscoe, Diana, & Brooks, 1987) have listed seven functions that dating serves:

of unhappy children whose lives have gone wrong in many respects. Thus, punitive policies—for example punishment through the justice system—will not lead us to address the most important problems posed by these children" (Sprott & Doob, 1998, p. 27).

THE MOVEMENT TOWARD IN-HOME TREATMENT

Nine communities in Ontario are implementing intensive treatment for young offenders in their homes, based on a type of treatment called multisystemic therapy, which was developed by Scott Henggeler in the United States (Bernfeld, 1998). This intervention treats the violent youth in the context of his family and his community. It is used as an alternative to incarceration. It recognizes a wide range of risk factors for youth violence, including parental neglect, problems with family relationships, poverty, aggression, and criminality in the family. Interventions are problem centred and may involve

several members of the family. Evaluations of the program are promising; it has led to a reduction in the number of youth who are repeat offenders (Bernfeld, 1998).

THE MOVEMENT TOWARD PRIMARY PREVENTION

The goal of primary prevention is to intervene early, so that children do not become young offenders. This approach was adopted by the National Crime Prevention Council (1996). It is based on the assumption that early experiences, especially those in the family, can contribute to later problems. The National Crime Prevention Council, in its *Preventing Crime by Investing in Families* reports (1996, 1997), recommended a number of interventions, including prenatal support to parents to promote healthy development of their babies, early identification and interventions for child abuse, parent training and support for families, early identification and interventions for highly aggressive preschool

children, interventions for children encountering difficulties in elementary school, and initiatives to promote the development of strong communities.

MULTIMEDIA PROGRAMS FOR VIOLENCE PREVENTION

A number of high schools are exploring violence prevention programs for their students. One approach is the computer-based, multimedia program called SMART TALK. SMART TALK has games, simulations, cartoons, animations, and interactive interviews. It teaches adolescents about anger management, about nonviolent ways to resolve disputes, and about recognizing the perspectives of others. After using the program for one month, a school in the United States reported a significant decrease in school violence and an increase in prosocial behaviour (Bosworth, Espelage, & DuBay, 1998).

1. *Recreation*—an opportunity to have fun with a member of the opposite sex.

2. *Socialization*—an opportunity for members of the opposite sex to get to know each other and to develop appropriate techniques of interaction.

3. *Status*—an opportunity to raise one's status within one's group by being seen with someone who is considered desirable.

4. *Mate selection*—an opportunity to associate with members of the opposite sex for the purpose of selecting a husband or wife.

5. *Sex*—an opportunity to engage in sexual experimentation or to obtain sexual satisfaction.

6. *Companionship*—an opportunity to have a friend of the opposite sex with whom to interact and share activities.

7. *Intimacy*—an opportunity to establish a close, meaningful relationship with a person of the opposite sex.

Roscoe and his colleagues questioned adolescents of different ages about their attitudes toward dating. They found that younger adolescents tend to think in terms of immediate gratification; they consider recreation and status to be important reasons for dating. Young adolescents look for dates who are physically attractive, who dress well, and who are liked by others. Older adolescents are less superficial in their attitudes toward dating; they are less concerned about appearance and more concerned about personality characteristics and about the person's plans for the future. Older adolescents consider companionship and mate selection important reasons for dating. For both younger and older adolescents, an interesting sex difference emerged: females consider intimacy to be more important than sex, whereas males consider sex to be far more important than intimacy (Roscoe et al., 1987).

The adolescents' ethnic, religious, or racial backgrounds also can influence dating. Sometimes adolescents are expected to date only people from similar backgrounds. For example, Jewish parents often strongly encourage adolescents to restrict their dating to other Jewish adolescents and to avoid interfaith marriages (Marshall & Markstrom-Adams, 1995). They discourage interfaith marriages because these are not legally binding in the Jewish faith and may jeopardize the socialization of children in the Jewish faith and the passing of the faith to future generations. Depending on where they live, Jewish adolescents have different attitudes toward dating and interfaith marriages. Those who live in Jewish-majority communities in Canada, such as some parts of Montreal, and who attend Jewish schools tend to restrict their dating and to oppose interfaith marriages. However, those who live in Jewish-minority neighbourhoods and who do not attend Jewish schools are less likely to restrict their dating or to believe that interfaith marriages are wrong (Marshall & Markstrom-Adams, 1995).

Personality Integration

Throughout this chapter, we have talked about the needs of adolescents and the different patterns that they create to fill these needs. During early adolescence, teenagers usually feel intense pressure to conform to the norms and expectations of a few or several reference groups. Their self-image is affected by how well they fit in with a group or measure up to their peers. Their value systems often depend on the values of other people (Douvan & Adelson, 1966).

As adolescents grow older, the measuring stick by which they evaluate themselves and those around them changes. Their ideas about the way they fit into the world may come more from their own discoveries about themselves than from other people. Their evaluations may reflect a sincere, idealistic, long-term commitment to certain values, instead of short-term commitments to friends. The development of this new idealism is the reason that the first two years of university or college are often a period of significant transformation. In part, this change in how youths see themselves and others is caused by their exposure to, and reaction to, the university or college atmosphere. Much of the change is also caused by the maturing of their rational processes—the new cognitive tools that they can use to evaluate themselves.

Youths who do not seek postsecondary education often go through the same dramatic transformation during the first few years after high school. In part, their change is also the result of adjusting to a new way of life, as they are socialized into a particular occupation, learn new rules and norms, and watch their old circle of friends dissolve. Yet, older adolescents who enter the workforce frequently develop a more objective and independent outlook. Their measuring stick, like that of the postsecondary student, may become more individualistic.

Although many working youths do not have to face the awkward, artificial period of dependence that confuses postsecondary students, the adjustment process is just as complex. Specific problems centre on teenage unemployment and the dull, repetitive jobs that adolescents are usually given. Cognitive maturity makes meaningful and significant work particularly important at this point of development (Dansereau, 1961; Goodman, 1960). Unemployment or meaningless work offers no challenge and denies individuals the opportunity to see the consequences of their efforts. The lack of significant work can be demeaning and demoralizing because the contrast between an optimal state of biological, cognitive, and social maturity and seemingly trivial tasks is disorienting. Often, adolescents have no armour of numbness or carelessness for protection against frustration and lack of fulfillment. Needs

Question to Ponder

When do you think adolescents are ready to start dating? What do you think are the advantages and disadvantages of dating during adolescence?

Hanging out with friends is typical teenage behaviour.

for personality integration, identity, and self-fulfillment are especially insistent during these years. Therefore, working adolescents, like postsecondary students, are vulnerable and sensitive to an impersonal, technological society.

Summary and Conclusions

Adolescence, as a period of transition, is prolonged in Western society, mainly because of the length of time it takes to learn adult roles. Adolescents must complete developmental tasks in order to achieve the status of adults. These tasks include establishing an integrated identity or self and appropriate independence or interdependence. In completing these tasks, adolescents may go through emotional turmoil—or they may not. Storm and stress are not inevitable aspects of adolescence. For many teenagers, conflicts occur over relatively superficial matters, and they successfully negotiate most disagreements with parents.

In many instances, adolescents follow rules and values they have learned from their parents. Since parental standards have been internalized, little direct instruction or monitoring is needed.

Occasionally during adolescence, individuals may have problems coping with stress. Depression, acting out, rebellion, substance abuse, or suicide may result. Depression is a problem with fairly low prevalence among adolescents, but it is serious in its implications and often occurs in combination with other problems, such as eating disorders or rebellion. More females than males are apt to show the symptoms of depression, and there are significant ethnic differences in the occurrence of depression.

As cognitive development moves into formal operations during adolescence, teenagers are able to see the inconsistencies and conflicts in the roles they play, as well as in the roles others—including parents—play. The resolution of these conflicts helps the individuals to carve out a new identity for themselves. Erikson believed that this establishment of an ego identity was the crucial task of adolescence.

In addition to introspection, adolescents draw their identity from reference groups and significant others. It is challenging at best for adolescents to integrate the diverse messages they receive about themselves into one coherent personality.

James Marcia modified Erikson's work to define four identity statuses that adolescents may pass through in developing their identity. In the first, if adolescents have made

commitments without going through an identity crisis, they are said to be in foreclosure status. If the adolescent has neither completed an identity crisis nor made any commitments, the diffusion status occurs. Those who are both going through an identity crisis and answering questions about commitments are said to be in moratorium status. Finally, those who have successfully resolved their identity crisis and made their commitments are said to be in identity achievement status. Individual identity statuses are influenced by a variety of factors, including social expectations, self-image, and reactions to stress.

Part of the resolution of the identity crisis is the attainment of a personal moral code. In order to choose a set of moral values, the adolescent must have attained formal operational thought. Without it, the adolescent is unable to consider alternatives, use cause-and-effect logic, or think about the past and future. Hoffman proposes that the development of morality is affected by different factors at different ages. In young children, for example, morality develops through anxiety-based inhibition. In middle childhood, empathy-based concern for others is the key factor. Finally, in adolescence, the use of formal operational thought, with its introspection and hypothetical thinking, completes the process. Hoffman believes that it is possible for all three types of moral growth to function in an individual simultaneously.

Drug use and other high-risk behaviours often occur in adolescence for various reasons. These behaviours are, in part, attempts to reduce stress; in other aspects, they are shaped by cognitive functioning. High-risk behaviour may result from cognitive experimentation—or from something diametrically opposed, the pursuit of raw pleasure. Psychoactive drugs from tobacco to crack are used in Canada. Adolescents often see their consumption as an index of adulthood.

Families must adjust to the increasing independence of teenagers as they prepare to move out on their own. Most families get through this transition by renegotiating roles while maintaining cohesion, flexibility, and open communication. As the role of the family declines, the role of peers and significant others increases. The emotional support gained from such relationships is essential for the development of social skills. Peer groups generally take two forms: larger ones are referred to as crowds, while smaller groups are called cliques.

Not all groups are positive. It is possible for adolescents to get in with the "wrong crowd" and move into delinquency. Delinquency is associated with psychological characteristics, such as the need for affiliation and the unwillingness to learn how to control impulsive actions. In general, delinquency is considered to be a personality disturbance that occurs in individuals who are unable to cope with the rapidity of social change in the world in which they live.

Friendships and relationships become the adolescent's lifeline. Adolescents generally choose friends who are similar to them and who share their values. Friendships and dating patterns during early adolescence are usually based on superficial characteristics, such as appearance and status. By late adolescence, commitments and choices are taken more seriously and are more likely to reflect the values of the individual. Dating is likely to occur first in group settings and then move to more intimate settings without a large number of peers.

By the end of adolescence, the individual has established an identity and has either made—or is prepared to make—the commitments to work and love that will sustain her identity during adulthood.

Key Terms and Concepts

diffusion (p. 498)

foreclosure (p. 498)

identity achievement (p. 498)

identity crisis (p. 498)

moratorium (p. 498)

reference group (p. 497)

significant other (p. 498)

young offenders (p. 516)

Questions to Review

1. What are the major developmental challenges of adolescence?

2. Describe the processes of achieving independence and interdependence as they relate to adolescent development.

3. What is the impact of reference groups on the adolescent? How does a significant other influence the teen years?

4. Describe Erikson's concept of identity formation.

5. List and describe four identity strategies that adolescents use to meet the challenge of establishing an identity.

6. Explain why it is important to look at cognitive development when discussing a person's moral development.

7. Describe three different types of moral growth.

8. Describe the way in which open communication and shared goals may help all members of a family negotiate the difficulties that may develop during adolescence.

9. In which risky behaviours do adolescents engage, and how can such high-risk activities be reduced?

10. What sort of coping skills do adolescents use to deal with stresses that they encounter in their daily lives?

11. What are the symptoms of depression in adolescents?

12. What should be done to deal with depression in adolescents?

13. How do peers influence adolescent development?

Weblinks

www.rcmp-grc.gc.ca/html/drugsituation.htm
Drug Situation in Canada
This RCMP Web site has recent information on the use of cocaine, heroin, hashish, liquid hashish, marijuana, and chemical drugs in Canada.

www.cps.ca/english/publications/AdolesMed.htm
Adolescent Medicine
This site, sponsored by the Canadian Paediatric Society, has links to position papers on a range of topics, including emergency contraception, adolescent pregnancy, family-friendly health care, age limits during adolescence, chronic illness, firearm deaths, and eating disorders.

mentalhelp.net/guide/pro03.htm
Mental Health Net
This site has links to numerous important resources dealing with adolescent and child development, as well as to psychology sites such as Psych Info.

Summing Up...

Adolescence

Physical

- Goes through rapid growth and changing body proportions

- Boys experience increase in androgens and girls experience increase in estrogen and progesterone

- Develops secondary sex characteristics

- Attains puberty (girls about 2 years earlier than boys)

- Develops sexual attitudes and behaviour

Psychosocial

- Goes through rites of passage
- Develops greater morality
- Increases risk-taking behaviour
- Reassesses values
- Develops a personal identity
- Has continued attachment to parents but also becomes more independent
- Becomes more dependent on peers for emotional support

Cognitive

- Attains formal operations (Piaget)
- Improves in ability to plan and think ahead
- Improves in metacognition (information processing)
- Becomes more introspective
- Develops greater self-monitoring and self-regulation
- Understands contrary to fact situations
- Becomes influenced by imaginary audience and develops personal fable
- Completes high school

Glossary

accommodation   Piaget's term for the act of changing our thought processes when a new object or idea does not fit our concepts.

adaptation   In Piaget's theory, the process by which infant schemes are elaborated, modified, and developed.

afterbirth   The placenta and related tissues, following their expulsion from the uterus during the third stage of childbirth.

aggression   Hostile behaviour that is intended to injure.

AIDS (acquired immune deficiency syndrome)   A fatal disease caused by a virus. Anyone can be infected through sexual contact or through exposure to infected blood or needles.

alleles   A pair of genes, found on corresponding chromosomes, that affect the same trait.

alphafetoprotein   A protein that when found in elevated levels in the mother's blood sample may indicate abnormalities in the fetus.

amniocentesis   A test for chromosomal abnormalities that is performed during the second trimester of pregnancy; it involves the withdrawal and analysis of amniotic fluid.

amniotic sac   A fluid-filled membrane that encloses the developing embryo or fetus.

anorexia   A type of eating disorder that involves self-starvation, a distorted body image, and sometimes compulsive exercise. It is caused by biological, psychological, and social factors.

anxiety   A feeling of uneasiness, apprehension, or fear that has a vague or unknown source.

Apgar score   An assessment scale of the newborn's physical condition.

aphasia   Language impairment caused by brain damage.

assertive behaviour   Forthright, direct behaviour, such as stating one's rights, that does not harm others.

assimilation   In Piaget's theory, the process of making new information part of one's existing mental structures.

attachment   The bond that develops between a child and another individual as a result of a long-term relationship. The infant's first bond is usually characterized by strong interdependence, intense mutual feelings, and vital emotional ties.

attention deficit/hyperactivity disorder (ADHD) A disorder including three subtypes. One subtype involves problems with attention and distractibility. Another involves hyperactivity or excessive movement. Another subtype is the combination of the two.

authoritarian parenting   A pattern of parenting that adheres to rigid rule structures and dictates to the children what these rules are; children do not contribute to the decision-making process in the family.

authoritative parenting   A pattern of parenting that uses firm control with children but encourages communication and negotiation in rule setting within the family.

autosomes   The chromosomes of a cell, excluding those that determine sex. It includes the first 22 pairs.

base pairs   The "rungs" of the DNA molecule. All DNA has the same four types of bases, and this is enough to provide the codes for all life forms.

behavioural objectives   The kinds of knowledge and skills expected of a student after a specified amount of instruction; they provide a demonstration of the school's adequacy, as well as the student's.

birth   The second stage of childbirth, which is the time between full cervix dilation and the time when the baby is free of the mother's body.

blastula   The hollow, fluid-filled sphere of cells that forms several days after conception.

bonding   Forming an attachment; refers particularly to the developing relationship between parents and infant that begins immediately after birth.

breech presentation   The baby's position in the uterus, such that the buttocks will emerge first; assistance is usually needed in such cases to prevent injury to the mother or the infant.

bulimia   A type of eating disorder that involves a binge-and-purge pattern of eating.

case grammar   The use of word order to express different relationships.

causality   A relationship between two variables in which change in one brings about an effect or result in the other.

centration   The focusing on only one aspect or dimension of an object or situation, which is characteristic of preoperational thought.

cephalocaudal developmental trend   The sequence of growth in which development occurs first in the head and progresses toward the feet.

cesarean section   A surgical procedure used to remove the baby and the placenta from the uterus by cutting through the abdominal wall.

child abuse   Intentional psychological or physical injuries inflicted on a child.

chorion   The protective outer sac that develops from tissue surrounding the embryo.

chorionic villi sampling (CVS)   A prenatal screening test that involves the analysis of fetal cells for genetic disorders. It provides earlier results than amniocentesis but has a greater risk of miscarriage.

chromosome   A DNA molecule; human cells have 23 pairs of chromosomes, making a total of 46.

circular response   A particular form of adaptation in Piaget's theory, in which the infant accidentally performs some action, perceives it, then repeats the action.

classical conditioning   A type of learning in which a neutral stimulus comes to elicit a response by repeated pairings with an unconditioned stimulus.

classification   The dividing of a large group into subgroups that have similar features.

codons   A group of three consecutive base pairs. The sequence of codons controls protein synthesis.

cognition   The process by which we know and understand our world.

competence motivation   A need to achieve in order to feel effective as an individual.

comprehension   Understanding the meaning of what is being read.

conservation   A cognitive ability described by Piaget, in which the child is able to judge changes in amounts based on logical thought instead of mere appearances; thus, she judges that an amount of water will remain the same even when it is poured into a glass of a different shape and size.

content   The meaning of any written or spoken message.

continuity   Development is ongoing, occurring in small steps and not in distinct stages, as a tree grows wider and develops more branches.

convergence   The ability to focus both eyes on one point.

correlations   Relationships between variables. Correlations do not prove cause and effect.

Creole   A new language created by children in communities where the adults do not have a common language. The adults communicate with pidgin, a form of speech that lacks grammar. Children automatically add grammar to pidgin, and a new language is born.

criterion-referenced test   A test that evaluates an individual's performance in relation to mastery of specified skills or objectives.

critical period   The only point in time when a particular environmental factor can have an effect.

cross-language transfer   The learning of a foreign language that improves mastery of the native language.

crossover   The process during meiosis in which individual genes on a chromosome cross over to the opposite chromosome. This process increases the random assortment of genes in offspring.

cross-sectional design   A method of studying development in which a sample of individuals of one age are observed and compared with one or more samples of individuals of other ages.

decoding   The process of reading that involves translating print into sounds and words.

defence mechanisms   Any of the techniques people use to reduce tensions that lead to anxiety.

deferred imitation   Imitation after a delay.

denial   The refusal to admit that an anxiety-producing situation exists or that an anxiety-producing event happened.

dependent variable   The variable in an experiment that changes as a result of manipulating the independent variable.

depth perception   The integration of images from the two eyes to gain information about distance or relative size, and the movement of the head to see the world in three dimensions.

designing experiments   An experiment requires the manipulation of an independent variable in a controlled setting to see whether the independent variable causes changes in a dependent variable. Greatest control is achieved by conducting the experiment in a tightly controlled environment, such as a laboratory. When experiments are properly controlled, they allow researchers to determine the causes of behaviour.

deterministic model   The view that a person's values, attitudes, behaviours, and emotional responses are determined by past or present environmental factors.

development   The changes over time in structure, thought, or behaviour of a person as a result of both biological and environmental influences.

developmentally appropriate curriculum   A curriculum that matches the developmental needs and abilities of young children.

deviation IQ   An IQ score derived from a statistical table comparing an individual's raw score on an IQ test with the scores of other subjects of the same age.

diagnostic-prescriptive teaching   A system of teaching in which tests and informal assessments inform educators as to a child's abilities so that they may prescribe appropriate instruction.

differentiation   In embryology, the process in which undifferentiated cells become increasingly specialized.

diffusion   The identity status of those who have neither gone through an identity crisis nor made commitments.

discontinuity   Development progresses through distinct stages, as a caterpillar transforms into a butterfly.

discrepancy hypothesis   A cognition theory according to which infants acquire, at around 7 months, schemes for familiar objects. When a new image or object is presented that differs from the old, the child experiences uncertainty and anxiety.

disorganized/disoriented attachment A new attachment category that is common in infants who have been abused. Infants act in a contradictory way: they seek closeness to their mothers, yet they fear them and are stressed in their presence.

distal processes The broader context of development, including outside factors that can influence how individuals interact with others. The focus of study is like a wide-angle lens.

DNA (deoxyribonucleic acid) The material that contains the genetic code that regulates the functioning and development of the person.

dominant In genetics, one gene of a gene pair that will cause a particular trait to be expressed.

dyscalculia A learning disability involving mathematics.

dysgraphia A learning disability involving writing.

dyslexia A learning disability involving reading; unusual difficulty in learning how to read. **ecological systems theory** A theory that focuses on how different levels of the environment affect child development and on how the child alters his environment. Development is viewed as a dynamic, two-directional process.

ecological validity The results of a study give an accurate portrayal of the behaviour in the "real world."

ectoderm In embryonic development, the outer layer of cells that becomes the skin, sense organs, and nervous system.

egocentricity Having a self-centred view of the world—viewing everything in relation to oneself.

embryonic period The second prenatal period, which lasts from the end of the second week to the end of the second month after conception. Most of the major structures and organs of the individual are formed during this time.

endoderm In embryonic development, the inner layer of cells that becomes the digestive system, lungs, thyroid, thymus, and other organs.

epiphysis The cartilaginous growth centre at the end of each bone.

episiotomy An incision made to enlarge the vaginal opening during childbirth.

equilibration Piaget's term for the basic process in human adaptation, in which individuals seek a balance, or fit, between the environment and their own structures of thought.

ethnocentrism The tendency to assume that one's own beliefs, perceptions, customs, and values are correct or normal and that those of others are inferior or abnormal.

ethology The study of animal behaviour, often observed in natural settings and interpreted in an evolutionary framework.

exosystem The indirect environmental influences on a child, such as policies in the parent's workplace.

expressive jargon A term used to describe the babbling of an infant when the infant uses inflections and patterns that mimic adult speech.

extrinsic feedback Rewards of praise given for performing a task well.

Fallopian tubes Two passages that open out of the upper part of the uterus and carry the ova from the ovary to the uterus.

false beliefs Beliefs that are inconsistent with the real world. They are part of theory of mind.

false labour Painful contractions of the uterus without dilation of the cervix.

fear A state of arousal, tension, or apprehension caused by a specific circumstance.

fertilization The union of an ovum and a sperm.

fetal alcohol syndrome (FAS) Congenital abnormalities, including small size, low birth weight, certain facial characteristics, and possible mental retardation, resulting from maternal alcohol consumption during pregnancy.

fetal period The final period of prenatal development, lasting from the beginning of the third month after conception until birth. During this period, all organs, limbs, muscles, and systems become functional.

fetoscope A long, hollow needle with a small lens and light source at its end that is inserted into the amniotic sac for observation of the fetus.

fine motor skills Capabilities involving small body movements.

foreclosure The identity status of those who have made commitments without going through an identity crisis.

form The particular symbol used to represent content.

formal didactic education Programs emphasizing a back-to-basics approach and drill teaching.

French immersion School instruction that is mostly in French for English-speaking children.

functional subordination The integration of a number of separate simple actions or schemes into a more complex pattern of behaviour.

gender constancy The concept that gender is stable and stays the same despite changes in superficial appearance.

gender identity The knowledge that one is male or female, and the ability to make that judgment about other people.

genes Strands of DNA that code for a particular trait, such as eye colour.

gene therapy The manipulation of individual genes to correct certain defects.

genetic counselling Counselling that helps potential parents evaluate their risk factors for having a baby with genetic disorders.

genotype The genetic makeup of a given individual.

germinal period   Includes conception, the period of very rapid cell division, and initial cell differentiation. This period lasts approximately two weeks.

gestation period   The total period of time from conception to birth—in humans, about 266 days.

grammar   A complicated set of rules for building words, as well as the rules for combining words to form phrases and sentences.

gross motor skills   Capabilities involving large body movements.

guided participation   The process by which more experienced people transmit cultural information to children.

habituation   The process of becoming accustomed to certain kinds of stimuli and no longer responding to them.

holophrastic speech   In the early stages of language acquisition, the young child's use of single words, perhaps to convey full sentences.

hormone   A biochemical secretion of the endocrine gland that is carried by the blood or other body fluids to a particular organ or tissue and acts as a stimulant or an accelerator.

humanistic psychology   A holistic approach to the study of personality that considers the person's inner thoughts, feelings, goals, and dreams. According to this approach, humans are spontaneous, self-determining, and creative.

identity achievement   The identity status of those who have gone through an identity crisis and have made commitments.

identity crisis   A period of making decisions about important issues—of asking "Who am I and where am I going?"

imaginary audience   Adolescents' assumption that others are focusing a great deal of critical attention on them.

implantation   The embedding of the prenatal organism in the uterine wall after its descent through the Fallopian tube.

imprinting   The instinctual learning process by which newly hatched birds form a relatively permanent bond with the parent in a few hours or days.

independent variable   The variable that experimenters manipulate in order to observe its effects on the dependent variable.

indifferent parenting   A pattern of parenting in which parents are not interested in their role as parents or in their children; indifferent parents exercise little control and demonstrate little warmth toward their children.

induction   Giving children reasons for behaving in socially desirable ways or for not behaving in undesirable ways.

inflections   Changes in form that words undergo to designate number, gender, tense, mood, and case.

insecure ambivalent attachment   A type of insecure attachment characterized by clingy, anxious behaviour and by a lack of exploration.

insecure avoidant attachment   A type of insecure attachment characterized by exceptional independence and indifference toward the attachment figure.

integration   The organization of differentiated cells into organs or systems.

intelligence quotient   An individual's mental age divided by chronological age, multiplied by 100 to eliminate the decimal point.

internalization   Making social rules and standards of behaviour part of oneself—adopting them as one's own set of values.

intrinsic feedback   Feedback that comes from experiencing the natural consequences of performing a task.

***in vitro* fertilization (IVF)**   Fertilization of a woman's egg outside the womb.

irreversibility   The belief that events and relationships can occur in only one direction, which is characteristic of preoperational thought.

iteration   Infants' purposeful repetition, elongation, and pause in sounds that imitate speech.

labour   The first stage of childbirth, typically lasting 12 to 18 hours and characterized by uterine contractions during which the cervix dilates to allow for passage of the baby.

lateralization   The process whereby specific skills and competencies become localized in particular hemispheres of the brain.

learning disability   Extreme difficulty in learning school subjects such as reading, writing, or math, despite normal intelligence and absence of sensory or motor defects.

logical inference   A conclusion reached through "unseen" evidence; concrete operational children are capable of this type of thinking.

longitudinal design   A study in which the same people are observed continually over a period of time.

macrosystem   The environmental influences at the level of the society. They include values, laws, and customs.

mainstreaming   Requiring that all physically challenged children have access to all education programs provided by schools in the least restrictive setting; this includes physical education classes.

malnutrition   An insufficiency of total quantity of food or of certain kinds of food.

maturation   The physical development of an organism as it fulfills its genetic potential.

mean length of utterance (MLU)   The average length of the sentences that a child produces.

mechanistic   A person's development is shaped by factors beyond his control.

mechanistic model   In learning theory, the view of human beings as machines that are set in motion by input (stimuli) and that produce output (responses).

meiosis   The process of cell division in reproductive cells that results in an infinite number of different chromosomal arrangements.

menarche   The time of the first menstrual period.

mental age   An intelligence test score showing the age group with which a child's performance most closely compares.

mesoderm   In embryonic development, the middle layer of cells that becomes the muscles, blood, and excretory system.

mesosystem   The interactions among different microsystems.

metacognition   The process of monitoring one's own thinking, memory, knowledge, goals, and actions.

microsystem   The immediate environments, such as home and school, in which the child spends the most time.

midwife   A childbirth assistant who remains with a mother throughout labour and who can supervise births where no complications are expected; nurse-midwives have had training in hospital programs, where they have studied obstetrics.

miscarriage (spontaneous abortion)   Expulsion of the prenatal organism before it is viable.

Montessori schools   Programs emphasizing the use of self-teaching materials, individually paced progress, real-life tasks, and the relative absence of praise and criticism.

moral absolutism   Any theory of morality that disregards cultural differences in moral beliefs.

moral judgment   The process of making decisions about right and wrong.

moral realism stage   Piaget's term for the first stage of moral development, in which children believe in rules as real, indestructible things.

moral relativism stage   Piaget's term for the second stage of moral development, in which children realize that rules are agreements that may be changed if necessary.

moratorium   The identity status of those who are currently in the midst of an identity crisis.

morphemes   The minimal units of meaning in language that form basic words, prefixes, and suffixes.

morphology   The set of rules for building words that is present in all languages.

mutations   Changes in the sequence of codons within the gene. Mutations may be harmful, beneficial, or inconsequential.

mutuality (synchrony)   The pattern of interchange between caregiver and infant in which each responds to and influences the other's movements and rhythms.

myelination   The formation of the myelin sheath covering the axons of neurons. This sheath increases the speed of transmission and the precision of the nervous system.

"natural" childbirth   A childbirth method that involves the mother's preparation (including education and exercises), limited medication during pregnancy and birth, and the mother's (and perhaps father's) participation during the birth.

naturalistic observations   Recording the ongoing behaviour of children in their natural environments without attempting in any way to change or control the environments.

nature   Stresses the role of heredity and maturation in development.

neonate   A baby in the first month of life.

neurons   Cells in the nervous system that are responsible for communication. They form prenatally and continue to grow, branch, and make connections throughout life.

neuroscience   The interdisciplinary study of the brain and behaviour.

nonsex-linked autosomal trait   Trait caused by genes on the nonsex-determining chromosomes (autosomes).

norm-referenced test   A test that compares an individual's performance with the performances of others in the same age group.

norms   Average development for children of certain ages.

novelty paradigm   A research plan that uses infants' preferences for new stimuli over familiar ones in order to investigate their ability to detect small differences in sounds, patterns, or colours.

nurture   Stresses the role of upbringing and environment in development.

obesity   Weighing at least 20 percent more in body weight than would be predicted by one's height.

object permanence   According to Piaget, the realization in infants at about 18 months that objects continue to exist when they are out of sight, touch, or some other perceptual context.

open education   Programs emphasizing an integrated day, vertical groupings, and child input in decision making.

operant conditioning   A type of conditioning that occurs when an organism is reinforced for voluntarily emitting a response. What is reinforced is then learned.

optimal period   The time during which a behaviour is most easily developed. However, an optimal period does not have the all-or-nothing quality of a critical period.

organismic   A person plays an active role in her development.

organization and rehearsal   Strategies for improving recall used mainly by older children and adults.

overregularization   The generalization of complex language principles, typically by preschool children rapidly expanding their vocabularies.

overt aggression   Aggression that is directed openly at the target. It can be physical or verbal.

ovulation The release of the ovum into one of the two Fallopian tubes; occurs approximately 14 days after menstruation.

ovum The female reproductive cell (the egg or gamete).

peer group A group of two or more people of similar status who interact with one another and who share norms and goals.

perception The complex process by which the mind interprets and gives meaning to sensory information.

perinatology A branch of medicine that deals with the period from conception through the first few months of life.

perineum The region between the vagina and the rectum.

permissive parenting A pattern of parenting in which parents exercise little control over their children but are high in warmth; this parenting style can produce negative results in children, who may have trouble inhibiting their impulses or deferring gratification.

personal fable Adolescents' feeling that they are special and invulnerable—exempt from the laws of nature that control the destinies of ordinary mortals.

phenotype In genetics, those traits that are expressed in the individual.

phonemes The smallest units of sound—vowels and consonants—that combine to form morphemes and words.

phonics An approach to early reading instruction that teaches children how to decode new words.

physically challenged A term emphasizing the environmental factors that limit a disabled child's access to goods and services, rather than dealing with handicapping conditions themselves; the emphasis is on changes in the environment, such as ramps or language boards, which help the child to adapt.

pincer grasp The method of holding objects, developed around the age of 12 months, in which the thumb opposes the forefinger.

pivot grammar A two-word sentence-forming system used by 2-year-olds and involving action words, prepositions, or possessives (pivot words) in combination with x-words, which are usually nouns.

placenta A disk-shaped mass of tissue that forms along the wall of the uterus, through which the embryo receives nutrients and discharges wastes.

polygenic inheritance A trait caused by an interaction of several genes or gene pairs and interactions between genes and environmental influences.

posterior presentation A baby is positioned in the uterus facing the mother's abdomen rather than her back.

prejudice A negative attitude formed without adequate reason and usually directed toward people because of their membership in a group.

premature Having a short gestation period (less than 37 weeks) and/or low birth weight (less than 2.5 kilograms).

productive language The spoken or written communication of children.

prosocial behaviour Helping, sharing, or cooperative actions that are intended to benefit others.

proximal processes Factors that affect an individual's development through his direct interactions with others, such as critical interactions with family or peers. The focus of study zooms in on the details of the interactions.

proximodistal developmental trend The directional sequence of development that occurs from the midline of the body outward.

psychoanalytic tradition Based on the theories of Freud, whose view of human nature was deterministic. He believed that personality is motivated by innate biological drives.

psychosexual stages Freud's stages of personality development.

psychosocial model Erikson's theory that personality arises from the manner in which social conflict is resolved.

puberty The attainment of sexual maturity in males and females.

readiness A point in time when an individual has matured enough to benefit from a particular learning experience.

recall The ability to retrieve information and events that are not present.

receptive language The repertoire of words and commands that a child understands, although she may be unable to say them.

recessive In genetics, one gene of a gene pair that determines a trait in an individual only if the other member of that pair is also recessive.

recognition The ability to correctly identify items previously experienced when they appear again.

reference group A social group or collection of people with whom an individual shares attitudes, ideals, or philosophies.

reflex An unlearned, automatic response to a stimulus. Many reflexes disappear after three or four months.

Reggio Emilia approach Programs emphasizing in-depth projects that involve considerable use of the visual arts. Children work in small groups, and the teacher consults with them and documents their experiences.

regression Coping with an anxiety-producing situation by reverting to earlier, more immature behaviour.

rejected children Children whose classmates give them numerous negative nominations for popularity and few, if any, positive ones. These children are at risk for such problems as mental illness, behavioural disorders, and school failure.

relational aggression Aggression that is done behind a person's back with the intent of damaging their relationships, for example, gossiping.

resilient children Children who develop normally despite exposure to persistent and/or prolonged stress.

rite of passage A symbolic event or ritual to mark life transitions, such as the one from childhood to adult status.

RNA (ribonucleic acid) A substance formed from and similar to DNA. It acts as a messenger in a cell, bringing the genetic code to the site of protein production. It also brings the appropriate amino acids.

role playing The acting out of a role in order to see things from another person's perspective.

rough-and-tumble play Playful and typically nonaggressive activity involving vigorous interchanges between children; examples include play fighting and chasing.

secure attachment The use of the attachment figure as a secure base for exploration.

self-esteem Seeing oneself as an individual with positive characteristics—as someone who will do well in the things that one thinks are important.

self-fulfilling prophecy An expectation that helps to bring about the predicted event, which consequently strengthens the expectation.

self-image Seeing oneself as an individual with certain characteristics.

sensorimotor period Piaget's first stage of cognitive development.

sensory integration The linking of information across sense modalities, for example, the recognition that a mother's voice (auditory information) comes from her face (visual information).

sequential design A combination of cross-sectional and longitudinal research designs in which individuals of several different ages are observed repeatedly over an extended period of time.

sex-linked traits Traits carried by genes on either of the sex-determining chromosomes.

shaping Systematically reinforcing successive approximations to a desired act.

sibling status Birth order.

significant other Anyone whose opinions an individual values highly.

signs The symbols, such as speech and written language, that are used in a culture to influence the behaviour of other people and one's own behaviour. According to Vygotsky, different cultures may use different signs.

social cognition Thought, knowledge, and understanding that involves the social world.

social cognitive theory The belief that people are not passive recipients of reinforcement. From observing the consequences of their own behaviour and that of others, people can anticipate the consequences of future behaviour. Thinking is a part of learning.

social inference Guesses and assumptions about what another person is feeling, thinking, or intending.

socialization The general process by which the individual becomes a member of a social group.

social reciprocity The continued interaction between individuals as they respond and react to one another in a way that encourages the prevailing behaviour.

social referencing In ambiguous situations, infants look to their parents' emotional expressions to learn how to respond.

social regulations The rules and conventions governing social interactions.

social relationships Relationships that involve obligations such as fairness and loyalty. The knowledge of these obligations is a necessary part of social cognition.

sociocentric Emphasizing the shared or social interpretation of a situation, as opposed to an egocentric view, which ignores the reality of others.

sociodramatic play Pretend play in which children take on the personas, actions, and scripts of other persons or objects to play out a temporal drama.

sperm The male reproductive cell (or gamete).

stranger or separation anxiety An infant's fear of strangers or of being separated from the caregiver. Both occur in the second half of the first year and indicate, in part, a new cognitive ability to detect and respond to differences in the environment.

strange situation test A laboratory test procedure used to measure attachment.

structuralism A branch of psychology concerned with the structure of thought and the ways in which the mind processes information.

subtractive bilingualism The learning of a foreign language that interferes with the learning of a native language.

sudden infant death syndrome (SIDS) The sudden death of an apparently healthy infant or child in whom no medical cause can be found in a postmortem examination.

surprise paradigm A research technique used to test infants' memory and expectations. Infants cannot report what they remember or expect, but if their expectations are violated, they respond with surprise. For example, if the doll is not under the cloth where the infants saw it hidden, they are surprised.

symbolic representation The use of a word, picture, gesture, or other sign to represent past and present events, experiences, and concepts.

synapses Sites of communication between neurons.

syntax The rules for combining words to form phrases and sentences.

telegraphic speech The utterances of 1- and 2-year-olds that omit the less significant words and include the words that carry the most meaning.

teratogens The toxic agents that cause birth defects and developmental abnormalities.

teratology The study of developmental abnormalities or birth defects.

toddler The infant in the second year of life who has begun to walk—the child has a somewhat top-heavy, wide stance and walks with a gait that is not solidly balanced or smoothly coordinated.

trimesters The three equal time segments that compose the nine-month gestation period.

twin comparisons Comparing the degree of similarity between identical twins with that between fraternal, same-sex twins.

ultrasound A technique that uses sound waves to produce a picture of the fetus while it is still in the mother's uterus.

umbilical cord The rope of tissue connecting the placenta to the embryo; this rope contains two fetal arteries and one fetal vein.

use The way in which a speaker employs language to give it one meaning as opposed to another.

viable After 24 weeks of development, the ability of the fetus to live outside the mother's body, provided it receives special care.

visual cliff An experimental apparatus that tests depth perception of infants by simulating an abrupt drop-off.

visually guided reach Accurate reaching made possible by the functional integration of visual input.

whole language learning An approach to early reading instruction that encourages children to recognize words in context, rather than sounding them out.

withdrawal A defence mechanism in which a person physically goes away from, or mentally withdraws from, unpleasant situations.

young offenders Canadians between the ages of 12 and 17 years who are convicted of crimes.

zone of proximal development The difference between children's actual performance when they work alone and their potential performance when more knowledgeable adults or peers assist them.

zygote A fertilized ovum.

References

AAP Task Force on Infant Positioning and SIDS. (1992). Positioning and SIDS. *Pediatrics, 89*(6), 1120–1126.

Abel, E. (1990). Fetal alcohol syndrome. Oradell, NJ: Medical Economics Books.

Abel, E. (1992). Paternal exposure to alcohol. In T. B. Sonderegger (Ed.), *Prenatal substance abuse: Research findings and clinical implications.* Baltimore: Johns Hopkins University Press.

Abel, E. (1995). Maternal risk factors in fetal alcohol syndrome: Provocative and permissive influences. *Neurotoxicology and Teratology, 17,* 445–462.

Abler, R. M., & Sedlacek, W. E. (1989). Freshman sexual attitudes and behaviors over a 15-year-period. *Journal of College Student Development, 30,* 201–209.

Abraham, C. (1998, November 28). A world gene hunt targets Canada. *The Globe and Mail,* pp. A1, A10–A11.

Adolph, K. E., Vereijken, B., & Denny, M. A. (1998). Learning to crawl. *Child Development, 69,* 1299–1312.

Aboud, F. (1988). *Children and prejudice.* New York: Basil Blackwell.

Achenbach, T. M. (1982). *Developmental psychopathology.* New York: Wiley.

Adams, M. J. (1990). *Beginning to read.* Cambridge, MA: MIT Press.

Adlaf, E. M., Ivis, F. J., Smart, R. G., & Walsh, G. W. (1995). *The Ontario student drug use survey: 1977–1995.* Toronto: Addiction Research Foundation.

Adlaf, E. M., Ivis, F. J., Smart, R. G., & Walsh, G. W. (1996). Enduring resurgence or statistical blip? Recent trends from the Ontario student drug use survey. *Canadian Journal of Public Health, 87,* 189–192.

Adolph, K. E., Vereijken, B., & Denny, M. A. (1998). Learning to crawl. *Child Development, 69,* 1299–1312.

Aguiar, A., & Baillargeon, R. (1998). Eight-and-a-half-month-old infants' reasoning about containment events. *Child Development, 69,* 636–653.

Ainsworth, M. D. (1967). *Infancy in Uganda: Infant care and the growth of love.* Baltimore: Johns Hopkins University Press.

Ainsworth, M. D. (1973). The development and infant-mother attachment. In B. M. Caldwell & H. N. Ricciuti (Eds.), *Review of child development research* (Vol. 3). Chicago: University of Chicago Press.

Ainsworth, M. D. S. (1983). Patterns of infant-mother attachment as related to maternal care. In D. Magnusson & V. Allen (Eds.), *Human development: An interactional perspective.* New York: Academic Press.

Ainsworth, M. D., Blehar, M., Waters, E., & Wall, S. (1978). *Patterns of attachment.* Hillsdale, NJ: Erlbaum.

Ainsworth, M. D. S., Blehar, M. C., Waters, E., & Wall, S. (1979). *Patterns of attachment.* New York: Halsted Press.

Alpert-Gillis, L. J., & Connell, J. P. (1989). Gender and sex-role influences on children's self-esteem. *Journal of Personality, 57,* 97–113.

Aman, C. J., Roberts, R., Jr., & Pennington, B. F. (1998). A neuropsychological examination of the underlying deficit in attention deficit hyperactivity disorder: Frontal lobe versus right parietal lobe theories. *Developmental Psychology, 34,* 956–969.

American Psychiatric Association. (1994). *Diagnostic and statistical manual* (4th ed.). Washington, DC: Author.

American Psychological Association. (1993). *Violence and youth: Psychology's response: Vol. 1. Summary report of the American Psychological Association Commission on violence and youth.* Washington, DC: Author.

American Psychological Association. (1994). *Diagnostic and statistical manual of mental disorders* (4th ed.). Washington, DC: Author.

Ames, E. W. (1997). *The development of Romanian orphanage children adopted to Canada: Final report.* Ottawa: National Welfare Grants Program, Human Resources Development Canada.

Ames, L. B. (1971, December). Don't push your preschooler. *Family Circle.*

Anderson, D. R., & Collins, P. A. (1988). *The impact on children's education: Television's influence on cognitive development.* Washington, DC: U.S. Department of Education, Office of Educational Research and Improvement.

Anderson, E. S. (1979, March). *Register variation in young children's role-playing speech.* Paper presented at the Communicative Competence, Language Use, and Role-playing Symposium, Society for Research and Child Development.

Andersson, B-E. (1989). Effects of public day-care: A longitudinal study. *Child Development, 60,* 857–866.

Anisfeld, M. (1996). Only tongue protrusion modeling is matched by neonates. *Developmental Review, 16,* 149–161.

Apgar, V. (1953). Proposal for a new method of evaluating the newborn infant. *Anesthesia and Analgesia, 32,* 260–267.

Archer, S. L. (1985). Identity and the choice of social roles. *New Directions for Child Development, 30,* 79–100.

Armitage, S. E., Baldwin, B. A., & Vince, N. A. (1980). The fetal sound environment of sheep. *Science, 208,* 1173–1174.

Armstrong, H. (1993). Depression in Canadian Native Indians. In P. Cappeliez and R. J. Flynn (Eds.), *Depression and the social environment.* Montreal: McGill-Queen's University Press.

Arnett, J. J. (1999). Adolescent storm and stress, reconsidered. *American Psychologist, 54,* 317–326.

Arnold (1990). *Childhood stress.* New York: Wiley.

Artz, S. (1998). Where have all the school girls gone? Violent girls in the school yard. *Child and Youth Care Forum, 27,* 77–110.

Asher, S. R. (1983). Social competence and peer status: Recent advances and future directions. *Child Development, 54,* 1427–1434.

Asher, S. R., & Coi, J. D. (1990). *Peer rejection in childhood.* New York: Cambridge University Press.

Asher, S. R., Renshaw, P. D., & Hymel, S. (1982). Peer relations and the development of social skills. In W. W. Hartup (Ed.), *The young child: Reviews of research* (Vol. 3). Washington, DC: National Association for the Education of Young Children.

Aslin, R. N. (1987). Motor aspects of visual development in infancy. In P. Salapatek & L. Cohen (Eds.), *Handbook of infant perception: Vol. 1. From sensation to perception.* New York: Academic Press.

Aslin, R. N., Pisoni, D. V., & Jusczyk, P. W. (1983). Auditory development and speech perception in infancy. In P. H. Mussen (Ed.), *Handbook of child psychology* (Vol. 2). New York: Wiley.

Aslin, R. N., & Smith, L. B. (1988). Perceptual development. *Annual Review of Psychology, 39,* 435–473.

Athey, I. J. (1984). Contributions of play to development. In T. D. Yawkey & A. D. Pellegrini (Eds.), *Child's play.* Hillsdale, NJ: Erlbaum.

Atkinson, D. R., Morten, G., & Sue, D. W. (1983). *Counseling American minorities: A cross-cultural perspective.* Dubuque, IA: Wm. C. Brown.

Babinski, L. M., Hartsough, C. S., & Lambert, N. M. (1999). Childhood conduct problems, hyperactivity-impulsivity, and inattention as predictors of adult criminal activity. *Journal of Child Psychology and Psychiatry, 40,* 347–355.

Babson, S. G., & Benson, R. C. (1966). *Primer on prematurity and high-risk pregnancy.* St. Louis: Mosby.

Bagwell, C. L., Newcomb, A. F., & Bukowski, W. M. (1998). Preadolescent friendship and peer rejection as predictors of adult adjustment. *Child Development, 69,* 140–153.

Baillargeon, R. (1987). Object permanence in three-and-a-half and four-and-a-half-month-old infants. *Developmental Psychology, 23*(5), 655–674.

Baillargeon, R. (1997). How do infants learn about the physical world? In M. Gauvin & M. Cole (Eds.), *Readings on the development of children.* New York: W. H. Freeman.

Bakeman, R., & Adamson, L. B. (1990). !Kung infancy: The social context of object exploration. *Child Development, 61,* 794–809.

Baker, B. L., & Brightman, A. J. (1989). *Steps to independence: A skills training guide for parents and teachers of children with special needs* (2nd ed.). Baltimore: Paul H. Brookes.

Baker, M. (1996). Families: *Changing trends in Canada* (3rd ed.). Toronto: McGraw-Hill.

Bakermans-Kranenburg, M. J., & van IJzendoorn, M. H. (1993). A psychometric study of the adult attachment interview: Reliability and discriminant validity. *Developmental Psychology, 29,* 870–879.

Baker-Ward, L., Gordon, B. N., Ornstein, P. A., Larus, D. M., & Clubb, P. A. (1993). Young children's long-term retention of a pediatric examination. *Child Development, 64,* 1519–1533.

Baldwin, J. M. (1906). *Mental development in the child and the race: Methods and processes* (3rd ed.). New York: Macmillan.

Bandura, A. (1964). The stormy decade: Fact or fiction. *Psychology in the Schools, 1,* 224–231.

Bandura, A. (1977). *Social learning theory.* Englewood Cliffs, NJ: Prentice-Hall.

Bandura, A. (1986). *Social foundations of thought and action.* Englewood Cliffs, NJ: Prentice-Hall.

Bandura, A., & Walters, R. H. (1959). *Adolescent aggression.* New York: Ronald Press.

Bandura, A., & Walters, R. H. (1963). *Social learning and personality development.* New York: Holt, Rinehart & Winston.

Banks, M., & Dannemiller, J. (1987). Infant visual psychophysics. In P. Salapatek & L. Cohen (Eds.), *Handbook of infant perception: Vol. 1. From sensation to perception.* New York: Academic Press.

Banks, M. S., & Salapatek, P. (1983). Infant visual perception. In P. H. Mussen (Ed.), *Handbook of child psychology* (4th ed.). New York: Wiley.

Barbero, G. (1983). Failure to thrive. In M. Klaus, T. Leger, & M. Trause (Eds.), *Maternal attachment and mothering disorders.* New Brunswick, NJ: Johnson & Johnson.

Barkley, R. A. (1997). Behavioral inhibition, sustained attention, and executive functions: Constructing a unifying theory of ADHD. *Psychological Bulletin, 121,* 65–94.

Barnes, D. M. (1989). "Fragile X" syndrome and its puzzling genetics. *Research News,* 171–172.

Barnes, H. L., & Olsen, D. H. (1985). Parent-adolescent communication and the circumplex model. *Child Development, 56,* 438–447.

Barnes, V. L., & Boddy, J. (1995). *Aman: The story of a Somali girl.* Toronto: Vintage Canada.

Bartsch, K., & Wellman, H. M. (1995). *Children talk about the mind.* New York: Oxford University Press.

Baruch, G. K., & Barnett, R. C. (1986). *Consequences of fathers' participation in family work: Parent role strain and well-being* (Working Paper No. 159). Wellesley, MA: Wellesley College Center for Research on Women.

Bass, J. L., Brennan, P., Mehta, K. A., & Kodzis, S. (1990). Pediatric problems in a suburban shelter for homeless families. *Pediatrics, 85*(1), 33–37.

Bassuk, E. L. (1991, December). Homeless families. *Scientific American,* 66–74.

Bassuk, E. L., & Rosenberg, L. (1990). Psychosocial characteristics of homeless children and children with homes. *Pediatrics, 85*(3), 257.

Bates, J. E. (1987). Temperament in infancy. In J. D. Osofsky (Ed.), *Handbook of infant development* (2nd ed., pp. 1101–1149). New York: Wiley.

Bateson, G. (1955). A theory of play and fantasy. *Psychiatric Research Reports, 2,* 39–51.

Bauer, P. J., & Thal, D. J. (1990). Scripts or scraps: Reconsidering the development of sequential understanding. *Journal of Experimental Child Psychology, 50,* 287–304.

Bauerfeld, S. L., & Lachenmeyer, J. R. (1992). Prenatal nutritional status and intellectual development: Critical review and evaluation. In B. B. Lahey & A. E. Kazdin (Eds.), *Advances in clinical child psychology* (Vol. 14). New York: Plenum Press.

Baumrind, D. (1975). *Early socialization and the discipline controversy.* Morristown, NJ: General Learning Press.

Baumrind, D. (1978). A dialectical materialist's perspective on knowing social reality. *New Directions for Child Development, 2.*

Baumrind, D. (1987). A developmental perspective on adolescent risk-taking in contemporary America. *New Directions for Child Development, 37,* 93–125.

Baumrind, D. (1991). The influence of parenting style on adolescent competence and substance use. *Journal of Early Adolescence, 11*(1), 56–95.

Bawden, H. N., Stokes, A., Camfield, C. S., Camfield, P. R., & Salisbury, S. (1998). Peer relationship problems in children with Tourette's disorder or diabetes mellitus. *Journal of Child Psychology and Psychiatry, 39,* 663–668.

Baydar, N., & Brooks-Gun, J. (1991). Effects of maternal employment and child-care arrangements on preschoolers' cognitive and behavioural outcomes: Evidence from the National Longitudinal Survey of Youth. *Developmental Psychology, 27,* 932–945.

Beal, A. L., Dumont, R., Cruse, C. L., & Branche, A. H. (1996). Practical implications of differences between the American and Canadian norms for WISC-III and a short form for children with learning disabilities. *Canadian Journal of School Psychology, 12,* 7–14.

Beal, C. R. (1987). Repairing the message: Children's monitoring and revision skills. *Child Development, 58,* 401–408.

Beardsley, T. (1996, March). Trends in human genetics: Vital data. *Scientific American,* 100–105.

Beck, A. T. (1972). *Depression: Causes and treatment.* Philadelphia: University of Pennsylvania Press.

Beck, M. (1988, August 15). Miscarriages. *Newsweek,* 46–49.

Becker, J. (1993). Young children's numerical use of number words: counting in many-to-one situations. *Developmental Psychology, 29,* 458–465.

Becker, W. C. (1964). Consequences of different kinds of parental discipline. In M. L. Hoffman (Ed.), *Review of child developmental research* (Vol. 1). New York: Russell Sage Foundation.

Beckwith, L., & Cohen, S. E. (1989). Maternal responsiveness with preterm infants and later competency. In M. H. Bornstein (Ed.), *New directions for child development: Vol. 43. Maternal responsiveness: Characteristics and consequences.* San Francisco: Jossey-Bass.

Bell, S. M., & Ainsworth, M. D. (1972). Infant crying and maternal responsiveness. *Child Development, 43,* 1171–1190.

Bellugi, U. (1970, December). Learning the language. *Psychology Today,* 32–38.

Belsky, J. (1980). Child maltreatment: An ecological integration. *American Psychologist, 35,* 320–335.

Belsky, J. (1996). Parent, infant, and social-contextual antecedents of father-son attachment security. *Developmental Psychology, 32,* 905–913.

Belsky, J., Campbell, S. B., Cohn, J. F., & Moore, G. (1996). Instability of infant-parent attachment security. *Developmental Psychology, 32,* 921–924.

Belsky, J., & Cassidy, J. (1994). Attachment: Theory and evidence. In M. L. Rutter, D. F. Hay, & S. Baron-Cohen (Eds.), *Development through life: A handbook for clinicians.* Oxford: Blackwell.

Belsky, J., Garduque, L., & Hrncir, E. (1984). Assessing performance, competence, and executive capacity in infant play: Relations to home environment and security of attachment. *Developmental Psychology, 20,* 406–417.

Bem, S. L. (1975, September). Androgyny vs. the tight little lives of fluffy women and chesty men. *Psychology Today,* 59–62.

Benbow, C. P. (1986). Physiological correlates of extreme intellectual precocity. *Neuropsychologia, 24,* 719–725.

Bender, B. G., Linden, M. G., & Robinson, A. (1987). Environment & developmental risk in children with sex chromosome abnormalities. *Journal of the Academy of Child and Adolescent Psychiatry, 26,* 499–503.

Benenson, J. F., Apostoleris, N. H., & Parnass, J. (1997). Age and sex differences in dyadic and group interaction. *Developmental Psychology, 33,* 538–543.

Bennett, K. J., Lipman, E. L., Racine, Y., & Offord, D. R. (1998). Annotation: Do measures of externalising behaviour in normal populations predict later outcome? Implications for targeted interventions to prevent conduct disorder. *Journal of Child Psychology and Psychiatry, 39,* 1059–1070.

Bennett, S. C., Robinson, N. M., & Sells, C. J. (1983). Growth and development of infants weighing less than 800 grams at birth. *Pediatrics, 7*(3), 319–323.

Benzies, K. M., Harrison, M. J., Magill-Evans, J. (1998). Impact of marital quality and parent-infant interaction on preschool behavior problems. *Public Health Nursing, 15,* 35–43.

Bereiter, C., & Engelmann, S. (1966). *Teaching disadvantaged children in the preschool.* Englewood Cliffs, NJ: Prentice-Hall.

Berk, L. E. (1985, July). Why children talk to themselves. *Young Children,* 46–52.

Berko, J. (1958). The child's learning of English morphology. *Word, 14,* 150–177.

Berndt, T. (1983). Social cognition, social behavior and children's friendships. In E. T. Higgins, D. Ruble, & W. Hartup (Eds.), *Social cognition and social development: A socio-cultural perspective.* New York: Cambridge University Press.

Berndt, T. J. (1982). The features and effects of friendship in early adolescence. *Child Development, 53,* 1447–1460.

Berney, B. (1993). Round and round it goes: The epidemiology of childhood lead poisoning, 1950–1990. *The Milbank Quarterly, 71*(1), 3–39.

Bernfeld, G. A. (1998). *Intensive in-home treatment of young offenders: Model development & implementation.* Paper presented at the annual meeting of the Canadian Psychological Association, Edmonton.

Berry, G. L., & Asamen, J. K. (1993). *Children and television: Images in a changing sociocultural world.* Newbury Park, CA: Sage.

Bertenthal, B. I., & Campos, J. J. (1987). New directions in the study of early experience. *Child Development, 58,* 560–567.

Bialystok, E. (1999). Cognitive complexity and attentional control in the bilingual mind. *Child Development, 70,* 636–644.

Bickerton, D. (1975). *Dynamics of a Creole system.* New York: Cambridge University Press.

Bigelow, A. E. (1995). The effect of blindness on the early development of the self. In P. Rochat (Ed.), *The self in infancy: Theory and research.* New York: Elsevier Science B.V.

Bigelow, A. E. (1996). Blind and sighted children's spatial knowledge of their home environments. *International Journal of Behavioral Development, 19,* 797–816.

Binet, A., & Kooh, S. W. (1996). Persistence of vitamin D-deficiency rickets in Toronto in the 1990s. *Canadian Journal of Public Health, 87,* 227–230.

Binet, A., & Simon, T. (1905). Methodes nouvelles pour le diagnostic du niveau intellectual des anormaux. *L'Annee Psychologique, 11,* 191–244.

Binet, A., & Simon, T. (1916). *The development of intelligence in children.* (E. S. Kite, Trans.). Baltimore: Williams & Wilkins.

Birch, H. G., & Gussow, J. D. (1970). *Disadvantaged children: Health, nutrition, and school failure.* New York: Harcourt Brace.

Bisanz, G., & Bisanz, J. (1994). Studying the development of academic skills in the 1990's: Implications for assessment. *The Alberta Journal of Educational Research, XL,* 127–146.

Bisanz, J., & LeFevre, J. (1990). Strategic and nonstrategic processing in the development of mathematical cognition. In D. F. Bjorklund (Ed.), *Children's strategies: Contemporary views of cognitive development.* Hillsdale, NJ: Lawrence Erlbaum.

Bjorklund, D. F., & Green, B. L. (1992). The adaptive nature of cognitive immaturity. *American Psychologist, 47(1),* 46–54.

Blake, J. (1989). Number of siblings and educational attainment. *Science, 245,* 32–36.

Bloom, B. S. (1964). *Stability and change in human characteristics.* New York: Wiley.

Bloom, B. S., & Krathwohl, D. R. (1956). *Taxonomy of educational objectives: Handbook I. The cognitive domain.* New York: McKay.

Bloom, L. (1970). *Language development: Form and function in emerging grammars.* Cambridge, MA: MIT Press.

Bloom, L., & Lahey, M. (1978). *Language development and language disorders.* New York: Wiley.

Bloom, L., Lifter, K., & Broughton, J. (1985). The convergence of early cognition and language in the second year of life: Problems in conceptualization and measurement. In M. Barrett (Ed.), *Children's single-word speech.* New York: Wiley.

Blyth, D., Bulcroft, A. R., & Simmons, R. G. (1981). *The impact of puberty on adolescents: A longitudinal study.* Paper presented at the annual meeting of the American Psychological Association, Los Angeles.

Boccia, M., & Campos, J. J. (1989). Maternal emotional signals, social referencing, and infants' reactions to strangers. In N. Eisenberg (Ed.), *New directions for child development: Vol. 44. Empathy and related emotional responses* (pp. 25–50). San Francisco: Jossey-Bass.

Bogenschneider, K., Wu, M., Raffaelli, M., & Tsay, J. C. (1998). Parent influences on adolescent peer orientation and substance use: The interface of parenting practices and values. *Child Development, 69,* 1672–1688.

Bohannon, J. N., Jr., & Hirsh-Pasek, K. (1984). Do children say as they're told? A new perspective on motherese. In L. Feagans, C. Garvey, & R. Golinkoff (Eds.), *The origins and growth of communication.* Norwood, NJ: Ablex.

Boivin, M., & Hymel, S. (1997). Peer experiences and social self-perceptions: A sequential model. *Developmental Psychology, 33,* 135–145.

Boivin, M., Hymel, S., & Bukowski, W. M. (1995). The roles of social withdrawal, peer rejection, and victimization by peers in predicting loneliness and depressed mood in childhood. *Development and Psychopathology, 7,* 765–785.

Boivin, M., Poulin, F., & Vitaro, F. (1994). Depressed mood and peer rejection in childhood. *Development and Psychopathology, 6,* 483–497.

Boland, M. G., & Oleske, J. (1995). The health care needs of infants and children: An epidemiological perspective. In N. Boyd-Franklin, G. L. Steiner, & M. G. Boland (Eds.), *Children, families, and HIV/AIDS.* New York: The Guilford Press.

Bonta, B. D. (1997). Cooperation and competition in peaceful societies. *Psychological Bulletin, 21,* 299-323.

Borke, H. (1971). Interpersonal perception of young children: Egocentrism or empathy. *Developmental Psychology, 5,* 263–269.

Borke, H. (1973). The development of empathy in Chinese and American children between 3 and 6 years of age: A cross-cultural study. *Developmental Psychology, 9,* 102–108.

Borke, H. (1975). Piaget's mountains revisited: Changes in the egocentric landscape. *Developmental Psychology, 11,* 240–243.

Bornstein, M. (Ed.). (1987). *Sensitive periods in development: Interdisciplinary perspectives.* Hillsdale, NJ: Erlbaum.

Bornstein, M. H. (1978). Chromatic vision in infancy. In H. W. Reese & L. P. Lipsett (Eds.), *Advances in child development and behavior* (Vol. 12). New York: Academic Press.

Bornstein, M. H. (Ed.). (1989). *Maternal responsiveness: Characteristics and consequences.* San Francisco: Jossey-Bass.

Bornstein, M. H., & Bruner, J. (1986). *Interaction in human development.* Hillsdale, NJ: Erlbaum.

Bossard, J. H. S., & Boll, E. S. (1960). *The sociology of child development.* New York: Harper & Brothers.

Bosworth, K., Espelage, D., & DuBay, T. (1998). A computer-based violence prevention intervention for young adolescents: Pilot study. *Adolescence, 33,* 785–795.

Bouchard, R. J., Jr. (1987, June 25). *Environmental determinants of IQ similarity in identical twins reared apart.* Paper presented at the 17th annual meeting of the Behavior Genetics Association, Minneapolis, MN.

Bouchard, T. J., Jr., Lykken, D. T., McGue, M., Segal, N., & Tellegen, A. (1990). Sources of human psychological differences: The Minnesota study of twins reared apart. *Science, 250,* 223–228.

Boughton, K., Blower, C., Chartrand, C., Dircks, P., Stone, T., Youwe, G., & Hagen, B. (1998). Impact of research on pediatric pain assessment and outcomes. *Pediatric Nursing, 24,* 31–35.

Bower, B. (1991). Emotional aid delivers labor-saving results. *Science News, 139,* 277.

Bower, T. G. R. (1971, October). The object in the world of the infant. *Scientific American,* 30–38.

Bower, T. G. R. (1974). *Development in infancy.* San Francisco: Freeman.

Bowlby, J. (1960). Separation anxiety. *International Journal of Psychoanalysis, 41,* 89–113.

Bowlby, J. (1973). *Attachment and loss: Vol. 2. Separation.* New York: Basic Books.

Bowlby, J. (1980). *Attachment and loss: Vol. 3. Loss, sadness and depression.* New York: Basic Books.

Bowlby, J. (1982). *Attachment and loss: Vol. 1. Attachment* (2nd ed.). New York: Basic Books.

Bowlby, J. (1988). *A secure base.* New York: Basic Books.

Brackbill, Y. (1979). Obstetrical medication and infant behavior. In J. Osofsky (Ed.), *Handbook of infant development.* New York: Wiley.

Brackbill, Y., & Nevill, D. (1981). Parental expectations of achievement as affected by children's height. *Merrill-Palmer Quarterly, 27,* 429–441.

Bradshaw, J. (1989). *Hemispheric specialization and psychological function.* New York: Wiley.

Braine, M. D. S. (1963). The ontogeny of English phrase structure: The first phase. *Language, 39,* 1–13.

Brainerd, C. J. (1978). The stage question in developmental theory. *The Behavioral and Brain Sciences, 1,* 173–182.

Brand, H. J., & Welch, K. (1989). Cognitive and social-emotional development of children in different preschool environments. *Psychological Reports, 65,* 480–482.

Brassard, M. R., & McNeill, L. E. (1987). Child sexual abuse. In M. Brassard, R. Germain, & S. Hart (Eds.), *Psychological maltreatment of children and youth.* New York: Pergamon.

Braungart-Reiker, J., Garwood, M. M., Powers, B. P., & Notaro, P. C. (1998). Infant affect and affect regulation during the still-face paradigm with mothers and fathers: The role of infant characteristics and parental sensitivity. *Developmental Psychology, 34,* 1428–1437.

Brazelton, T. B. (1969). *Infants and mothers: Differences in development.* New York: Dell.

Brazelton, T. B. (1973). *Neonatal behavioral assessment scale.* London: Heinemann.

Brazelton, T. B., Nugent, J. K., & Lester, B. M. (1987). Neonatal behavioral assessment scale. In J. Osofsky (Ed.), *Handbook of infant development* (2nd ed., pp. 780–817). New York: Wiley.

Brenner, A. (1984). *Helping children cope with stress.* Lexington, MA: D. C. Heath.

Breslau, N., & Peterson, E. L. (1996). Smoking cessation in young adults: Age at initiation of cigarette smoking and other suspected influences. *American Journal of Public Health, 86,* 214–219.

Bretherton, I., & Waters, E. (Eds.). (1985). Growing points of attachment. *Monographs of the Society for Research in Child Development, 50*(1–2, Serial No. 209).

Briggs, G. C., Freeman, R. K., & Yaffe, S. J. (1986). *Drugs in pregnancy and lactation* (2nd ed.). Baltimore: Williams & Wilkins.

Broberg, A. G., Wessels, H., Lamb, M. E., & Hwang, C. P. (1997). Effects of day care on the development of cognitive abilities in 8-year-olds: A longitudinal study. *Developmental Psychology, 33,* 62–69.

Bronfenbrenner, U. (1979). *The ecology of human development: Experiments by nature and design.* Cambridge, MA: Harvard University Press.

Bronfenbrenner, U. (1989). Ecological systems theory. In R. Vasta (Ed.), *Annals of Child Development* (Vol. 6, pp. 187–251). Greenwich, CT: JAI Press.

Bronfenbrenner, U. (1995). Developmental ecology through time and space: A future perspective. In P. Moen, G. H. Elder, Jr., and K. Luscher (Eds), *Examining lives in context: Perspectives on the ecology of human development.* Washington, DC: American Psychological Association.

Bronson, G. (1978). Aversion reactions to strangers: A dual process interpretation. *Child Development, 49,* 495–499.

Bronson, W. C. (1981). Toddlers' behavior with agemates: Issues of interaction and cognition and affect. In L. P. Lipset (Ed.), *Monographs on Infancy* (Vol. 1). Norwood, NJ: Ablex.

Brooks, R. L., & Obrzut, J. E. (1981). Brain lateralization: Implications for infant stimulation and development. *Young Children, 26,* 9–16.

Brooks-Gunn, J. (1987). Pubertal processes and girls' psychological adaptation. In R. M. Lerner & T. T. Foch (Eds.), *Biological-psychosocial interactions in early adolescence.* Hillsdale, NJ: Lawrence Erlbaum.

Brooks-Gunn, J., & Furstenberg, F. F., Jr. (1986). The children of adolescent mothers: Physical, academic, and psychological outcomes. *Developmental Review, 6,* 224–251.

Brooks-Gunn, J., & Furstenberg, F. F., Jr. (1989). Adolescent sexual behavior. *American Psychologist, 44,* 249–257.

Brooks-Gunn, J., & Furstenberg, F. F., Jr. (1989/1997). Adolescent sexual behavior. In M. Gauvin & M. Cole (Eds.), *Readings on the development of children.* New York: W. H. Freeman. Originally published in *American Psychologist, 44,* 249–257.

Brophy, J. (1986). Teacher influences on student achievement. *American Psychologist, 41,* 1069–1077.

Broussard, E. R. (1989). The infant-family resource program: Facilitating optimal development. *Prevention in Human Services, 6*(2), 179–224.

Brown, B. B., Clasen, D. R., & Eicher, S. A. (1986). Perceptions of peer pressure, peer conformity dispositions, and self-reported behavior among adolescents. *Developmental Psychology, 22,* 521–530.

Brown, B. B., & Lohr, M. J. (1987). Peer-group affiliation and adolescent self-esteem: An integration of ego-identity and symbolic-interaction theories. *Journal of Personality and Social Psychology, 52,* 47–55.

Brown, J. L., & Pollit, E. (1996). Malnutrition, poverty, and intellectual development. *Scientific American, 274,* 38–43.

Brown, J. V., Bakeman, R., Coles, C. D., Sexson, W. R., & Demi, A. S. (1998). Maternal drug use during pregnancy: Are preterm and full-term infants affected differently? *Developmental Psychology, 34,* 540–554.

Brown, R. (1965). *Social psychology.* New York: Free Press.

Brown, R. (1973). *A first language: The early stages.* Cambridge, MA: Harvard University Press.

Bruck, M. (1978). The suitability of French immersion programs for language-disabled children. *Canadian Modern Language Review, 34,* 884–887.

Bruck, M., Ceci, S. J., & Hembrooke, H. (1998). Reliability and credibility of young children's reports: From research to policy and practice. *American Psychologist, 53,* 136–151.

Bruck, M. (1987). The adult outcomes of children with learning disabilities. *Annals of Dyslexia, 37,* 252–263.

Brumberg, J. J., & Striegel-Moore, R. (1993). Continuity and change in symptom choice: Anorexia. In G. H. Elder Jr., J. Modell, & R. D. Parke (Eds.), *Children in time and place: Developmental and historical insights.* New York: Cambridge University Press.

Bruner, J. (1983). *Child's talk.* New York: Norton.

Bruner, J., & Haste, H. (Eds.). (1987). *Making sense: The child's construction of the world.* London & New York: Methuen.

Bruner, J. S. (1960). *The process of education.* Cambridge, MA: Harvard University Press.

Bruner, J. S. (1971). *The relevance of education.* New York: Norton.

Bruner, J. S. (1973). *Beyond the information given: Studies in the psychology of knowing.* New York: Norton.

Bruner, J. S., Olver, R. R., & Greenfield, P. M. (1966). *Studies in cognitive growth.* New York: Wiley.

Buchanan, C. M., Eccles, J. S., & Becker, J. B. (1992). Are adolescents the victims of raging hormones: Evidence for activational effects of hormones on moods and behavior at adolescence. *Psychological Bulletin, 111*(1), 62–107.

Buchoff, R. (1990, Winter). Attention deficit disorder: Help for the classroom teacher. *Childhood Education, 67,* 86–90.

Buck, G. M., Cookfair, D. L., Michalek, A. M., Nasca, P. C., Standfast, S. J., Sever, L. E., & Karmer, A. A. (1989). Interuterine growth retardation and risk of sudden infant death syndrome (SIDS). *American Journal of Epidemiology, 129,* 874–884.

Buis, J. M., & Thompson, D. N. (1989). Imaginary audience and personal fable: A brief review. *Adolescence, 24,* 773–781.

Bul, B., & Sabatier, C. (1986). The cultural context of motor development: Postnatal manipulations in the daily life of Bambara babies. *International Journal of Behavior Development, 9,* 440–447.

Bulterys, M. G., Greenland, S., & Kraus, J. F. (1990, October). Chronic fetal hypoxia and sudden infant death syndrome: Interaction between maternal smoking and low hematocrit during pregnancy. *Pediatrics, 86*(4), 535–540.

Burgess, R. L., & Conger, R. D. (1978). Family interaction in abusive, neglectful, and normal families. *Child Development, 49,* 1163–1173.

Buri, J. R., Louiselle, P. A., Misukanis, T. M., & Mueller, R. A. (1988). Effects of parental authoritarianism and authoritativeness on self-esteem. *Personality and Social Psychology Bulletin, 14,* 271–282.

Buss, A. H., & Plomin, R. (1984). *Temperament: Early developing personality traits.* Hillsdale, NJ: Erlbaum.

Cadoret, R. J., Yates, W. R., Troughton, E., Woodworth, G., & Stewart, M. A. (1995a). Adoption study demonstrating two genetic pathways to drug abuse. *Archives of General Psychiatry, 52,* 42–52.

Cadoret, R. J., Yates, W. R., Troughton, E., Woodworth, G., & Stewart, M. A. (1995b). Gene-environment interaction in the genesis of aggressivity and conduct disorders. *Archives of General Psychiatry, 52,* 916–924.

Cameron, C. A. (1995). Making a place for social cognitive processes in writing development. *Issues in Education, 1,* 171–176.

Cameron, C. A., Edmunds, G., Wigmore, B., Hunt, A. K., & Linton, M. J. (in press). Children's revision of textual flaws. *International Journal of Behavioral Development.*

Cameron, C. A., Hunt, A. K., & Linton, M. J. (1996). Written expression as recontextualization: Children write in social time. *Educational Psychology Review, 8,* 125–150.

Cameron, C. A., & Lee, K. (1998). The development of children's telephone communication. *Applied Developmental Psychology.*

Cameron, C. A., & Lee, K. (1999). Emergent use of English grammatical morphemes by Chinese-speaking children. *IRAL, XXXVII,* 43–58.

Cameron, C. A., Lee, K., Webster, S., Munro, K., Hunt, A. K., & Linton, M. J. (1995). Text cohesion in children's narrative writing. *Applied Psycholinguistics, 16,* 257–269.

Cameron, C. A., & Moshenko, B. (1996). Elicitation of knowledge transformational reports while children write narratives. *Canadian Journal of Behavioural Science, 28,* 271–280.

Cameron, C. A., & Wang, M. (in press). Frog, where are you? Children's narrative expression over the telephone. *Discourse Processes.*

Campaign 2000 (1997). *Report Card: Child Poverty in Canada.* Ottawa: Statistics Canada.

Campbell, M., & Spencer, E. K. (1988). Psychopharmacology in child and adolescent psychiatry: A review of the past five years. *Journal of the American Academy of Child and Adolescent Psychiatry, 27,* 269–279.

Campbell, R. L., & Christopher, J. C. (1996). Moral development theory: A critique of its Kantian presuppositions. *Developmental Review, 16,* 1–47.

Campos, J. J., Langer, A., & Krowitz, A. (1970). Cardiac responses on the visual cliff in prelocomotor human infants. *Science, 170,* 196–197.

Campos, J. L., Berenthal, B. I., & Kermoian, R. (1997). Early experience and emotional development: The emergence of wariness of heights. In M. Gauvin & M. Cole (Eds.), *Readings on the development of children.* New York: W. H. Freeman and Company.

Canada Council on Social Development (1998). *Youth at work in Canada: A research report.* Ottawa: Author.

Canada Year Book. (1997). Ottawa: Statistics Canada.

Canadian Council on Social Development. (1996). *The progress of Canada's children, 1996.* Ottawa: Author.

Canadian Hospitals Injury Reporting and Prevention Program. (1994). *CHIRPP News.* Ottawa: Health Canada.

Canadian Institute of Child Health. (1994). *The health of Canada's children: A CICH profile* (2nd ed.). Ottawa: Author.

Capelli, C. A., Nakagawa, N., & Madden, C. M. (1990). How children understand sarcasm: The role of context and intonation. *Child Development, 61,* 1824–1841.

Card, J. J., & Wise, L. L. (1978). Teenage mothers and teenage fathers: The impact of early childbearing on the parents' personal and professional lives. *Family Planning Perspectives, 10,* 199–205.

Carey, S. (1984). Reflections on a decade of French immersion. *Canadian Modern Language Review, 41,* 246–259.

Carlson, C. I., Cooper, C. R., & Spradling, V. Y. (1991, Spring). Developmental implications of shared versus distinct perceptions of the family in early adolescence. *New Directions for Child Development, 51,* 13–30.

Carlson, E. A. (1998). A prospective longitudinal study of attachment disorganization/disorientation. *Child Development, 69,* 1107–1128.

Carpenter, G. (1974). Mother's face and the newborn. *New Scientist, 61,* 742–744.

Carter, L. G. (1984). The sustaining effects study of the compensatory and elementary education. *Educational Researcher,* 4–13.

Case, R. (1992). The role of central conceptual structures in the development of children's scientific and mathematical thought. In

A. Demetriou, M. Shayer, and A. Efklides (Eds.), *Neo-Piagetian theories of cognitive development: Implications and applications for education.* New York: Routledge.

Caspi, A., Elder, G. H., Jr., & Bem, D. J. (1987). Moving against the world: Life-course patterns of explosive children. *Developmental Psychology, 23*, 308–313.

Cassidy, J., & Berlin, L. (1994). The insecure/ambivalent pattern of attachment: Theory and research. *Child Development, 65*, 971–991.

Cassidy, J., Kirsh, S. J., Scolton, K. L., & Parke, R. D. (1996). Attachment and representations of peer relationships. *Developmental Psychology, 32*, 892–904.

Caudill, W., & Weinstein, H. (1969). Maternal care and infant behavior in Japan and America. *Psychiatry, 32*, 12–43.

Ceci, S. J., & Bruck, M. (1993). Suggestibility of the child witness: A historical review and synthesis. *Psychological Bulletin, 113*, 403–439.

Centerwall, B. S. (1992). Television and violence: The scale of the problem and where to go from here. *JAMA, 267*, 3059–3063.

Chan, M. (1987). Sudden Infant Death Syndrome and families at risk. *Pediatric Nursing, 13*(3), 166–168.

Chan, R. W., Raboy, B., & Patterson, C. J. (1998). Psychosocial adjustment among children conceived via donor insemination by lesbian and heterosexual mothers. *Child Development, 69*, 443–457.

Chance, G. W., & Harmsen, E. (1998). Children are different: Environmental contaminants and children's health. *Canadian Journal of Public Health, 89*(Suppl. 1), 9–13.

Chao, R. K. (1994). Beyond parental control and authoritarian parenting style: Understanding Chinese parenting through the cultural notion of training. *Child Development, 65*, 1111–1119.

Chao, R. K. (1996, August). *Cultural reconceptualizations of Chinese parenting.* Paper presented at the XXVI International Congress of Psychology, Montreal.

Chapman, K. L., & Mervis, C. B. (1989). Patterns of object-name extension in production. *Journal of Child Language, 16*, 561–571.

Charach, A., Pepler, D. J., & Ziegler, S. (1995). Bullying at school: A Canadian perspective. *Education Canada, 35*, 12–18.

Charlesworth, W. (1988). Resources and resource acquisition during ontogeny. In K. B. MacDonald (Ed.), *Sociobiological perspectives on human development.* New York: Springer-Verlag.

Chassin, L., Presson, C. C., Rose, J. S., Sherman, S. J., & Todd, M. (1998). Maternal socialization of adolescent smoking: The intergenerational transmission of parenting and smoking. *Developmental Psychology, 34*, 1189–1201.

Chaudham, N. (1998). Child health, poverty and the environment: The Canadian context. *Canadian Journal of Public Health, 89*(Suppl. 1), 26–29.

Cheal, D. (1996). Stories about step-families. In Human Resources Development Canada & Statistics Canada. *Growing up in Canada.* National Longitudinal Survey of Children and Youth. Ottawa: Author.

Chen, X., Hastings, P. D., Rubin, K. H., Chen, H., Cen, G., & Stewart, S. L. (1998). Child-rearing attitudes and behavioral inhibition in Chinese and Canadian toddlers: A cross-cultural study. *Developmental Psychology, 34*, 677–686.

Chen, X., Rubin, K. H., & Li, B. (1995). Depressed mood in Chinese children: Relations with school performance and family environment. *Journal of Consulting and Clinical Psychology, 63*, 938–947.

Chen, X., Rubin, K. H., & Li, Z. (1995). Social functioning and adjustment in Chinese children: A longitudinal study. *Developmental Psychology, 31*, 531–539.

Chesnick, M., Menyuk, P., Liebergott, J., Ferrier, L., & Strand, K. (1983, April). *Who leads whom?* Paper presented at the meeting of the Society for Research in Child Development, Detroit.

Chess, S. (1967). Temperament in the normal infant. In J. Hellmuth (Ed.), *The exceptional infant* (Vol. 1). Seattle: Special Child Publications.

Children's Defense Fund. (1992). *The state of America's children 1992.* Washington, DC: Author.

Chilman, C. (1979). *Adolescent sexuality in changing American society.* Washington, DC: Government Printing Office.

Chisholm, K. (1998). A three year follow-up of attachment and indiscriminate friendliness in children adopted from Romanian orphanages. *Child Development, 69*, 1092–1106.

Chisholm, K., Carter, M. C., Ames, E. W., & Morrison, S. J. (1995). Attachment security and indiscriminately friendly behavior in children adopted from Romanian orphanages. *Development and Psychopathology, 7*, 283–294.

Chomsky, C. (1969). *The acquisition of syntax from 5 to 10.* Cambridge, MA: MIT Press.

Chomsky, N. (1993). On the nature, use, and acquisition of language. In A. I. Goldman (Ed.), *Readings in philosophy and cognitive science.* Cambridge, MA: MIT Press.

Christensen, S., & Morrongiello, B. A. (1997). The influence of peers on children's safety judgments about engaging in behaviors that threaten their safety. *Journal of Applied Developmental Psychology, 18*, 547–562.

Chugani, H. (1994). Development of regional brain glucose metabolism in relation to behavior and plasticity. In G. Dawson & K. Fischer (Eds.), *Human behavior and the developing brain.* New York: Guilford.

Chukovsky, K. (1963). *From two to five* (M. Morton Ed. & Trans.). Berkeley: University of California Press.

Clark, E. V. (1987). The principle of contrast: A constraint on acquisition. In B. Macwhinner (Ed.), *Mechanisms of language acquisition.* Hillsdale, NJ: Erlbaum.

Clark, J. E., & Phillips, S. J. (1985). A developmental sequence of the standing long jump. In J. E. Clark & J. H. Humphrey (Eds.), *Motor development: Current selected research.* Princeton, NJ: Princeton Book Company.

Clark, J. E., Phillips, S. J. & Peterson, R. (1989). Developmental stability in jumping. *Developmental Psychology, 25*(6), 929–935.

Clark, W. (1997, Summer). School leavers revisted. *Canadian Social Trends*, 10–12.

Clarke-Stewart, K. A. (1978). And daddy makes three: The father's impact on mother and young child. *Child Development, 49*, 466–478.

Clarke-Stewart, K. A., & Fein, G. C. (1983). Early childhood programs. In M. Haith & J. Campos (Eds.), *Handbook of child psychology: Vol. 2. Infancy and developmental psychobiology* (4th ed.). New York: Wiley.

Clelland, D. (1999). A review of midwifery in BC, one year after legalization. *Birth Issues, XIII* (4), 35.

Clifford, B. R., Gunter, B., & McAleer, J. (1995). *Television and children.* Hillsdale, NJ: Lawrence Erlbaum Associates.

Cohen, L. B., & Gelber, E. R. (1975). Infant visual memory. In L. B. Cohen & P. Salapatek (Eds.), *Infant perception: From sensation to cognition* (Vol. 1). New York: Academic Press.

Colburn, D. (1995, November 23). Eating disorders down, study suggests. *Edmonton Journal.*

Colby, A., Kohlberg, L., Gibbs, J., & Lieberman, M. (1983). A longitudinal study of moral development. *Monographs of the Society for Research in Child Development, 48* (1–2, Serial No. 200).

Coley, R. L., & Chase-Lansdale, P. L. (1998). Adolescent pregnancy and parenthood: Recent evidence and future directions. *American Psychologist, 53,* 152–166.

Common, R. W., & Frost, L. G. (1992). The implications of the mismeasurement of Native students' intelligence through the use of standardized intelligence tests. In S. Towson (Ed.), *Educational psychology: Readings for the Canadian context.* Peterborough, ON: Broadview Press.

Compas, B. E., & Epping, J. E. (1993). Stress and coping in children and families: Implications for children coping with disaster. In C. F. Saylor (Ed.), *Children and disasters: Issues in clinical child psychology.* New York: Plenum Press.

Conger, R. D., Patterson, G. R., & Ge, X. (1995). It takes two to replicate: A mediational model for the impact of parents' stress on adolescent adjustment. *Child Development, 66,* 80–97.

Connelly, B., Johnston, D., Brown, I. D. R., Mackay, S., & Blackstock, E. G. (1993). The prevalence of depression in a high school population. *Adolescence, 28*(109), 149–158.

Coren, S., & Porac, C. (1980). Birth factors and laterality: The effect of birth order, parental age, and birth stress on four indices of lateral preference. *Behavioral Genetics, 10,* 123–138.

Corkum, V., & Moore, C. (1997). The origins of joint visual attention in infants. *Developmental Psychology, 34,* 28–38.

Cornell, E. H., Heth, C. D., & Broda, L. S. (1989). Children's wayfinding: Response to instructions to use environmental landmarks. *Developmental Psychology, 25,* 755–764.

Cornell, E. H., Heth, C. D., Kneubuhler, Y., & Sehgal, S. (1996). Serial position effects in children's route reversal errors: Implications for police search operations. *Applied Cognitive Psychology, 10,* 301–326.

Cornell, E. H., Heth, C. D., & Rowat, W. L. (1992). Wayfinding by children and adults: Response to instructions to use look-back and retrace strategies. *Developmental Psychology, 28,* 328–336.

Costa, A. (Ed.). (1985). *Developing minds: A resource book for teaching thinking.* Washington, DC: Association for Supervision and Curriculum Development.

Costa, A., Hanson, R., Silver, H., & Strong, R. (1985). Building a repertoire of strategies. In A. Costa (Ed.), *Developing minds: A resource book for teaching thinking.* Washington, DC: Association for Supervision and Curriculum Development.

Coster, G. (1972, November). *Scientific American,* 44.

Côté, J. E., & Levine, C. (1988). A critical examination of the ego identity status paradigm. *Developmental Review, 8,* 147–184.

Covell, K. (1995). The vulnerability of young adolescents to persuasion. In K. Covell (Ed.), *Readings in child development: A Canadian perspective.* Toronto: Nelson.

Cowan, D., et al. (1997). Study of birth defects of Gulf War vets' offspring. *The New England Journal of Medicince.*

Craig, G. J., & Garney, P. (1972). *Attachment and separation behavior in the second and third years.* Unpublished manuscript, University of Massachusetts at Amherst.

Craig, W. M., & Pepler, D. J. (1997). Observations of bullying and victimization in the school yard. *Canadian Journal of School Psychology, 13,* 41–60.

Cratty, B. (1986). *Perceptual and motor development in infants and children.* Englewood Cliffs, NJ: Prentice-Hall.

Cratty, B. J. (1970). *Perceptual and motor development in infants and children.* New York: Macmillan.

Crick, N. R., Casas, J. F., & Mosher, M. (1997). Relational and overt aggression in preschool. *Developmental Psychology, 33,* 579–588.

Crider, C. (1981). Children's conceptions of body interior. In R. Bibace & M. E. Walsh (Eds.), *Children's conceptions of health, illness, and bodily functions.* San Francisco: Jossey-Bass.

Crisp, A. H. (1984). The psychopathology of anorexia nervosa: Getting the heat out of the system. In A. J. Stunkard and E. Stellar (Eds.), *Eating and its disorders.* New York: Raven Press.

Crockenberg, S., & McCluskey, K. (1986). Change in maternal behavior during the baby's first year of life. *Child Development, 57,* 746–753.

Cruickshank, W. M. (1977). Myths and realities in learning disabilities. *Learning Disabilities, 10*(1), 57–64.

Csikszentmihalyi, M., & Larson, R. (1984). *Being adolescent.* New York: Basic Books.

Cunningham, C. E., Cunningham, L. J., Martorelli, V., Tran, A., Young, J., & Zacharias, R. (1998). The effects of primary division, student-mediated conflict resolution programs on playground aggression. *Journal of Child Psychology and Psychiatry, 39,* 653–662.

Damon, W., & Hart, D. (1982). The development of self-understanding from infancy through adolescence. *Child Development, 53,* 841–864.

Dansereau, H. K. (1961). Work and the teen-ager. *Annals of the American Academy of Political and Social Sciences, 338,* 44–52.

Dargassies, S. S. (1986). *The neuromotor and psychoaffective development of the infant* (English language edition). Amsterdam, the Netherlands: Elsevier.

Davis, S. G., Corbitt, A. M., Everton, V. M., Grano, C. A., Kiefner, P. A., Wilson, A. S., & Gray, M. (1999). Are ball pits the playground for potentially harmful bacteria? *Pediatric Nursing, 25,* 151–155.

Day, E. M., & Shapson, S. (1992). A comparison of early and late French immersion programs in British Columbia. In S. Towson (Ed.), *Educational psychology: Readings in the Canadian context.* Peterborough, ON: Broadview Press.

Deal, L. W., & Holt, V. L. (1998). Young maternal age and depressive symptoms: Results from the 1988 national maternal and infant health survey. *American Journal of Public Health, 88,* 266–269.

de Boysson-Bardies, B., Halle, P., Sagart, L., & Durand, C. (1989). A crosslinguistic investigation of vowel formants in babbling. *Journal of Child Language, 16,* 1–17.

DeCasper, A. J., & Fifer, W. P. (1980). Of human bonding: Newborns prefer their mothers' voices. *Science, 208,* 1174–1176.

DeCasper, A. J., & Spence, M. (1992). Auditorily mediated behavior during the perinatal period: A cognitive view. In M. J. Weiss & P. R. Zelazo (Eds.), *Newborn attention: biological constraints and the influence of experience.* Norwood, NJ: Ablex.

DeCharms, R., & Moeller, G. H. (1962). Values expressed in American children's readers: 1800–1950. *Journal of Abnormal and Social Psychology, 64,* 136–142.

DeCivita, M., & Pagani, L. (1997). Familial constraints on the initiation of cigarette smoking among adolescents: An elaboration of social bonding theory and differential association theory. *Canadian Journal of School Psychology, 12,* 177–190.

DeLoache, J. S., Cassidy, D. J., & Brown, A. L. (1985). Precursors of mnemonic strategies in very young children's memory. *Child Development, 56,* 125–137.

Den Bak, I. M., & Ross, H. S. (1996). I'm telling! The content, context, and consequences of children's tattling on their siblings. *Social Development, 5*, 292–309.

Dencik, L. (1989). Growing up in the post-modern age: On the child's situation in the modern family, and on the position of the family in the modern welfare state. *Acta Sociologica, 32*, 155–180.

Dennis, W. (1960). Causes of retardation among institutional children: Iran. *Journal of Genetic Psychology, 96*, 47–59.

Dennis, W. (1973). *Children of the creche.* New York: Appleton-Century-Crofts.

Dennis, W., & Najarian, P. (1957). Infant development under environmental handicap. *Psychological Monographs, 717* (Whole No. 436).

Derevensky, J. L., & Gupta, R. (1998, June). *Youth gambling: Prevalence, risk factors, clinical issues and social policy.* Paper presented at the Annual Convention of the Canadian Psychological Association, Edmonton.

Desjardins, R. N., Rogers, J., & Werker, J. F. (1997). An exploration of why preschoolers perform differently than do adults in audiovisual speech perception tasks. *Journal of Experimental Child Psychology, 66*, 85–110.

de Villiers, P. A., & de Villiers, J. G. (1979). *Early language.* Cambridge, MA: Harvard University Press.

Dewey, J. (1961). *Democracy and education.* New York: Macmillan.

DeWit, D. J., Offord, D. R., & Braun, K. (1998). *The relationship between geographic relocation and childhood problem behaviour.* Ottawa: Human Resources Development Canada.

Diamond, A. (1993). Neuropsychological insights into the meaning of object concept development. In M. Johnson (Ed.), *Brain development and cognition.* Oxford: Blackwell.

Diaz, R. M., & Lowe, J. R. (1987). The private speech of young children at risk: A test of three deficit hypotheses. *Early Childhood Research Quarterly, 2*, 181–184.

Dietz, W. H., Jr. (1987). Childhood obesity. *Annals of the New York Academy of Sciences, 499*, 47–54.

DiFranza, J. R., Savageau, J. A., & Aisquith, B. F. (1996). Youth access to tobacco: The effects of age, gender, vending machine locks, and "It's the Law" programs. *American Journal of Public Health, 86*, 221–224.

Diller, L. H. (1998). *Running on Ritalin.* New York: Bantam Books.

Dobkin, P. L., & Tremblay, R. E. (1996, August). *Predicting boys' early onset substance abuse from individual and family factors.* Paper presented at the XXVI International Congress of Psychology, Montreal.

Dobkin, P. L., Tremblay, R. E., & Sacchitelle, C. (1997). Predicting boys' early onset substance abuse from father's alcoholism, son's disruptiveness, and mother's parenting behavior. *Journal of Consulting and Clinical Psychology, 65*, 86–92.

Dodwell, P., Humphrey, G. K., & Muir, D. (1987). Shape and pattern perception. In P. Salapatek & L. Cohen (Eds.), *Handbook of infant perception.* New York: Academic Press.

Doman, G. (1984). *How to multiply our baby's intelligence.* Garden City, NY: Doubleday.

Dombey, H. (1999). Picking a path through the phonics minefield. *Education 3 to 13, 27*, 12–21.

Donaldson, M. (1978). *Children's minds.* New York: Norton.

Donaldson, M. (1979). The mismatch between school and children's minds. *Human Nature, 2*, 158–162.

Donovan, J. E., Jessor, R., & Costa, F. M. (1988). Syndrome of problem behavior in adolescence: A replication. *Journal of Consulting and Clinical Psychology, 56*, 762–765.

Dornbusch, S. M., Ritter, P. L., Leiderman, P. H., Roberts, D. F., & Fraleigh, M. J. (1987). The relation of parenting style to adolescent school performance. *Child Development, 58*, 1244–1257.

Douvan, E., & Adelson, J. B. (1966). *The adolescent experience.* New York: Wiley.

Douvan, E., & Gold, M. (1966). Modal patterns in American adolescence. In L. W. Hoffman & M. L. Hoffman (Eds.), *Review of child development research* (Vol. 2). New York: Russell Sage Foundation.

Dovell, R. A., Mowat, D. L., Dorland, J., & Lam, M. (1996). Changes among retailers selling cigarettes to minors. *Canadian Journal of Public Health, 87*, 66–68.

Dowdney, L., Skuse, D., Morris, K., & Pickles, A. (1998). Short normal children and environmental disadvantage: A longitudinal study of growth and cognitive development from 4 to 11 years. *Journal of Child Psychology and Psychiatry, 39*, 1017–1029.

Doyle, A. B., & Aboud, F. (1995). A longitudinal study of white children's racial prejudice as a social-cognitive development. *Merrill-Palmer Quarterly, 41*, 209–227.

Draper, T. W., & James, R. S. (1985). Preschool fears: Longitudinal sequence and cohort changes. *Child Study Journal, 15*(2), 147–155.

Dreikurs, R., & Soltz, V. (1964). *Children: The challenge.* New York: Duell, Sloan & Pearce.

Dreyer, P. H. (1982). Sexuality during adolescence. In B. Wolman (Ed.), *Handbook of developmental psychology.* Englewood Cliffs, NJ: Prentice-Hall.

Drotar, D. (Ed.). (1985). *New directions in failure to thrive: Implications for research and practice.* New York: Plenum.

Duncan, R. M., & Pratt, M. W. (1997). Microgenetic change in the quantity and quality of preschoolers' private speech. *International Journal of Behavioral Development, 20*, 367–383.

Dunn, J. (1983). Sibling relationships in early childhood. *Child Development, 54*, 787–811.

Dunn, J. (1985). *Sisters and brothers.* Cambridge, MA: Harvard University Press.

Dunn, J. (1986). Growing up in a family world: Issues in the study of social development of young children. In M. Richards & P. Light (Eds.), *Children of social worlds: Development in a social context.* Cambridge, MA: Harvard University Press.

Dunn, J., & Kendrick, C. (1979). Interaction between young siblings in the context of family relationships. In M. Lewis & L. Rosenblum (Eds.), *The child and its family: The genesis of behavior* (Vol. 2). New York: Plenum.

Dunphy, D. C. (1963). The social structure of urban adolescent peer groups. *Sociometry, 26*, 230–246.

Durrant, J. E. (1995). Culture, corporal punishment, and child abuse. In K. Covell (Ed.), *Readings in child development.* Toronto: Nelson.

Dwyer, T., Ponsonby, A. B., Newman, N. M. & Gibbons, L. E. (1991). Prospective cohort study of prone sleeping position and sudden infant death syndrome. *The Lancet, 337*, 1244–1247.

Dybdahl, R. (1996, August). *The child in context: Exploring childhood in Somalia.* Paper presented at the XXVI International Congress of Psychology, Montreal.

Dyson, L. L. (1996). The experiences of families of children with learning disabilities: Parental stress, family functioning, and sibling self-concept. *Journal of Learning Disabilities, 29*, 280–286.

Edelbrock, C., Rende, R., Plomin, R., & Thompson, L. A. (1995). A twin study of competence and problem behaviours in childhood and early adolescence. *Journal of Child Psychology and Psychiatry, 36,* 775–786.

Eddy, D. M. (1991). The individual vs. society: Is there a conflict? *Journal of the American Medical Association, 265*(11), 1446–1450.

Ehrhardt, A. A. (1992). Trends in sexual behavior and the HIV Pandemic. *American Journal of Public Health, 82*(11), 1459–1461.

Ehrhardt, A. A., Epstein, R., & Money, M. (1968). Fetal androgens and female identity in the early-treated androgenital syndrome. *Johns Hopkins Medical Journal, 122,* 160–167.

Eibl-Eibesfeldt, I. (1989). *Human ethology.* New York: Aldine de Gruyter.

Eimas, P. D. (1974). Linguistic processing of speech by young infants. In R. L. Schiefelbusch & L. L. Lloyd (Eds.), *Language perspectives: Acquisition, retardation, and intervention.* Baltimore: University Park Press.

Eimas, P. D. (1975). Speech perception in early infancy. In Lin L. B. Cohen & P. Salapatek (Eds.), *Infant perception: From sensation to cognition* (Vol. 2). New York: Academic Press.

Eisenberg, A., Murkoff, H. E., & Hathaway, S. E. (1984). *What to expect when you're expecting.* New York: Workman Publishers.

Eisenberg, N. (1988). The development of prosocial and aggressive behavior. In M. Bornstein & M. Lamb (Eds.), *Developmental psychology: An advanced textbook* (2nd ed.). Hillsdale, NJ: Erlbaum.

Eisenberg, N. (1989a). *The development of prosocial moral reasoning in childhood and mid-adolescence.* Paper presented at the April meeting of the Society for Research in Child Development, Kansas City.

Eisenberg, N. (1989b). The development of prosocial values. In N. Eisenberg, J. Reykowski, & E. Staub (Eds.), *Social and moral values: Individual and social perspectives.* Hillsdale, NJ: Erlbaum.

Eisenberg, N., Fabes, R. A., Shepard, S. A., Guthrie, I. K., Murphy, B. C., & Reiser, M. (1999). Parental reactions to children's negative emotions: Longitudinal relations to quality of children's social functioning. *Child Development, 70,* 513–534.

Elbers, L., & Ton, J. (1985). Play pen monologues: The interplay of words and babbles in the first words period. *Journal of Child Language, 12,* 551–565.

Elder, G. H., Jr., & Hareven, T. K. (1993). In G. H. Elder, Jr., J. Modell, & R. D. Parke (Eds.), *Children in time and place: Developmental and historical insights.* New York: Cambridge University Press.

Elder, G. H., Jr., Modell, J., & Parke, R. D. (Eds.). (1994). *Children in time and place: Developmental and historical insights.* New York: Cambridge University Press.

Elder, G., Nguyen, T., & Caspi, A. (1985). Linking family hardship to children's lives. *Child Development, 56,* 361–375.

Elder, J. L., & Pederson, D. R. (1978). Preschool children's use of objects in symbolic play. *Child Development, 49,* 500–504.

Elkind, D. (1967). Egocentrism in adolescence. *Child Development, 38,* 1025–1034.

Elkind, D. (1974). *Children and adolescents: Interpretive essays on Jean Piaget.* New York: Oxford University Press.

Elkind, D. (1981). *The hurried child: Growing up too fast too soon.* Reading, MA: Addison Wesley.

Elkind, D. (1986, May). Formal education and early childhood education: An essential difference. *Phi Delta Kappan,* 631–636.

Elkind, D. (1987). *The miseducation of children: Superkids at risk.* New York: Knopf.

Elkind, D. (1994). *Ties that stress: The new family imbalance.* Cambridge, MA: Harvard University Press.

Elkind, D., & Bowen, R. (1979). Imaginary audience behavior in children and adolescents. *Developmental Psychology, 15,* 38–44.

Elman, J. L., Bates, E. A., Johnson, M. H., Karmiloff-Smith, A., Parisi, D., & Plunkett, K. (1996). *Rethinking innateness: A connectionist perspective on development.* Cambridge, MA: Bradford Books.

Emery, R. E. (1989). Family violence. *American Psychologist, 44,* 321–328.

Emery, R. E., & Laumann-Billings (1998). An overview of the nature, causes, and consequences of abusive family relationships. *American Psychologist, 53,* 121–135.

Entwisle, D. R., & Doering, S. (1988). The emergent father role. *Sex Roles, 18,* 119–141.

Epstein, J. L. (1983). Selecting friends in contrasting secondary school environments. In J. L. Epstein & M. L. Karweit (Eds.), *Friends in school.* New York: Academic Press.

Epstein, L. H., Valoski, A., Wing, R. R., & McCurley, J. (1990). Ten-year follow-up of behavioural, family-based treatment for obese children. *Journal of the American Medical Association, 264,* 2519–2523.

Epstein, L. H., & Wing, R. R. (1987). Behavioral treatment of childhood obesity. *Psychological Bulletin, 101,* 331–342.

Erikson, E. H. (1950). In M. J. E. Senn (Ed.), *Symposium on the healthy personality.* New York: Josiah Macy, Jr., Foundation.

Erikson, E. H. (1959). The problem of ego identity. In E. H. Erikson (Ed.), Identity and the life cycle: Selected papers. *Psychological Issues Monograph* (No. 1).

Erikson, E. H. (1963). *Childhood and society* (2nd ed.). New York: Norton.

Erikson, E. H. (1968). *Identity, youth, and crisis.* New York: Norton.

Ernst, C., & Angst, J. (1983). *Birth order: Its influence on personality.* New York: Springer-Verlag.

Eron, L., Huesman, L., & Zelli, A. (1991). The role of parental variables in the learning of aggression. In D. Pepler & K. Rubin (Eds.), *The development and treatment of childhood aggression.* Hillsdale, NJ: Lawrence Erlbaum Associates.

Erwin, K. (1993). *Friendship and peer relations in childhood.* Chichester, England: Wiley.

Essa, E., Young, R., & Lehne, L. (1998). *Introduction to early childhood education* (2nd Canadian ed.). Toronto: Nelson.

Esterbrook, M. A., & Goldberg, W. A. (1984). Toddler development in the family: Impact of father involvement and parenting characteristics. *Child Development, 55,* 740–752.

Evans, E. D. (1975). *Contemporary influences in early childhood education* (2nd ed.). New York: Holt, Rinehart, & Winston.

Evans, M. A. (1996). Reticent primary grade children and their more talkative peers: Verbal, nonverbal, and self-concept characteristics. *Journal of Educational Psychology, 88,* 739–749.

Evans, M. A., Barraball, L., & Eberle, T. (1998). Parental responses to miscues during child-to-parent book reading. *Journal of Applied Developmental Psychology, 19,* 67–84.

Evers, S., Doran, L., & Schellenberg, K. (1998). Influences on breastfeeding rates in low income communities in Ontario. *Canadian Journal of Public Health, 89,* 203–206.

Fabes, R. A., Eisenberg, N., Jones, S., Smith, M., Guthrie, I., Poulin, R., Shepard, S., & Friedman, J. (1999). Regulation, emotionality, and preschoolers' socially competent peer interactions. *Child Development, 70*, 432–442.

Fagan, J. F., III. (1977). Infant recognition memory: Studies in forgetting. *Child Development, 48*, 66–78.

Fagot, B. I., Leinbach, M. D., & O'Boyle, C. (1992). Gender labeling, gender stereotyping, and parenting behaviors. *Developmental Psychology, 28*(2), 225–230.

Fagot, B. I., Pears, K. C., Capaldi, D. M., Crosby, L., & Leve, C. S. (1998). Becoming an adolescent father: Precursors and parenting. *Developmental Psychology, 34*, 1209–1219.

Fahlman, L. (1983). Culture conflict in the classroom: An Edmonton survey. In E. H. Waugh, B. Abu-Laban, & R. B. Qureshi (Eds.), *The Muslim community in North America*. Edmonton: The University of Alberta Press.

Falkner, F. (1962). The development of children: A guide to interpretation of growth charts and developmental assessments:. A commentary and future problems. *Pediatrics, 29*, 448–486.

Fantz, R. L. (1958). Pattern vision in young infants. *Psychological Record, 8*, 43–47.

Fantz, R. L. (1961, May). The origin of form perception. *Scientific American*, 66–72.

Fantz, R. L., Ordy, J. M., & Udelf, M. S. (1962). Maturation of pattern vision in infants during the first six months. *Journal of Comparative and Physiological Psychology, 55*, 907–917.

Farb, P. (1978). *Humankind*. Boston: Houghton Mifflin.

Farber, J. (1970). *The student as nigger*. New York: Pocket Books.

Farber, S. (1981, January). Telltale behavior of twins. *Psychology Today*, 58–64.

Farley, C., Haddad, S., & Brown, B. (1996). The effects of a 4-year program promoting bicycle helmet use among children in Quebec. *American Journal of Public Health, 86*, 46–51.

Faulkner, M. S. (1996). Family responses to children with diabetes and their influence on self-care. *Journal of Pediatric Nursing, 11*, 82–93.

Feagans, L. V., Kipp, E., & Blood, I. (1994). The effects of otitis media on the attention skills of day-care attending toddlers. *Developmental Psychology, 30*, 701–708.

Featherstone, H. (1985, June). Preschool: It does make a difference. *Harvard Education Letter*, 16–21.

Fedor-Freybergh, P., & Vogel, M. L. V. (1988). *Prenatal and perinatal psychology and medicine*. Carnforth, Lanc: Parthenon.

Fein, G. G. (1981). Pretend play in childhood: An integrated review. *Child Development, 52*, 1095–1118.

Fein, G. G. (1984). The self-building potential of pretend play, or "I gotta fish all by myself." In T. D. Yawkey & A. D. Pellegrini (Eds.), *Child's play*. Hillsdale, NJ: Erlbaum.

Feiring, C., Lewis, M., & Starr, M. D. (1984). Indirect affects and infants' reactions to strangers. *Developmental Psychology, 20*, 485–491.

Ferguson, C., & Snow, C. (1977). *Talking to children: Language input and acquisition*. Cambridge, MA: Cambridge University Press.

Ferleger, N., Glenwick, D. S., Gaines, R. R. W., & Green, A. H. (1988). Identifying correlates of reabuse in maltreating parents. *Child Abuse and Neglect, 12*, 41–49.

The fetal monitoring debate. (1979). *Pediatrics, 63*, 942–948.

Field, T. (1977). Effects of early separation, interactive deficits, and experimental manipulations on infant-mother face-to-face interaction. *Child Development, 48*, 763–771.

Field, T. (1978). Interaction behaviors of primary vs. secondary caretaker fathers. *Developmental Psychology, 14*(2), 183–184.

Field, T. (1986). Models for reactive and chronic depression in infancy. In E. Tronick & T. Fields (Eds.), *New directions for child development: Vol. 34. Maternal depression and infant disturbance*. San Francisco: Jossey-Bass.

Field, T. M. (1979). Interaction patterns of pre-term and term infants. In T. M. Field (Ed.), *Infants born at risk*. New York: Spectrum.

Field, T. (1991). Quality infant day-care and grade school behaviour and performance. *Child Development, 62*, 863–870.

Filipek, P. A. (1999). Neuroimaging in the developmental disorders: The state of the science. *Journal of Child Psychology and Psychiatry, 40*, 113–128.

Fillmore, C. J. (1968). The case for case. In E. Bach & R. T. Harms (Eds.), *Universals of linguistic theory*. New York: Holt, Rinehart & Winston.

Fincher, J. (1982, July/August). Before their time. *Science 82 Magazine*, 94.

Fine, S. (1999, May 24). Playing the odds on conception. *The Globe and Mail*, pp. A1, A6–A7.

Finkel, A. (1995). Origins of the welfare state in Canada. In R. B. Blake & J. Keshen (Eds.), *Social policy in Canada: Historical readings*. Toronto: Copp Clark.

Finkelhor, D. (1984). *Child sexual abuse: New theory and practice*. New York: Free Press.

Fischer, J. L., Sollie, D. L., & Morrow, K. B. (1986). Social networks in male and female adolescents. *Journal of Adolescent Research, 6*(1), 1–14.

Fisher, L., Ames, E. W., Chisholm, K., & Savoie, L. (1997). Problems reported by parents of Romanian orphans adopted to British Columbia. *International Journal of Behavioral Development, 20*, 67–82.

Flaste, R. (1988, October). The myth about teenagers. *New York Times Magazine*, pp. 19, 76, 82, 85.

Flavell, J. H. (1963). *The developmental psychology of Jean Piaget*. Princeton, NJ: Van Nostrand Reinhold.

Flavell, J. H. (1977). *Cognitive development*. Englewood Cliffs, NJ: Prentice-Hall.

Flavell, J. H. (1985). *Cognitive development* (2nd ed.). Englewood Cliffs, NJ: Prentice-Hall.

Flavell, J. H., Flavell, E. R., & Green, F. L. (1987). Young children's knowledge about the apparent-real and pretend-real distinctions. *Developmental Psychology, 23*, 816–822.

Flavell, J. H., Green, F., & Flavell, E. R. (1986). Development of knowledge about the appearance-reality distortion. *Monographs of the Society for Research in Child Development, 212*.

Flavell, J. H., Miller, P. H., & Miller, S. A. (1993). *Cognitive development*. Englewood Cliffs, NJ: Prentice-Hall.

Forman, G. (1985, June). The value of kinetic print in computer graphics for young children. In E. L. Klein (Ed.), *New directions for child development. Children and computers*. San Francisco: Jossey-Bass.

Forman, G., Lee, M., Wrisley, L., & Langley, J. (1993). The city in the snow: Applying the multisymbolic approach in Massachusetts. In C. Edwards, L. Gandini, & G. Forman (Eds.), *The hundred languages of children: The Reggio Emilia approach to early childhood education*. Norwood, NJ: Ablex.

Forman, G. E., & Fosnot, C. (1982). The use of Piaget's constructivism in early childhood education programs. In B. Spodek (Ed.), *Handbook on early childhood education.* Englewood Cliffs, NJ: Prentice-Hall.

Forman, G. E., & Hill, F. (1980). *Constructive play: Applying Piaget in the preschool.* Monterey, CA: Brooks/Cole.

Fox, V. C. (1977/1997). Is adolescence a phenomenon of modern times? In M. Gauvin & M. Cole (Eds.), *Readings on the development of children.* New York: W. H. Freeman. Originally published in *Journal of Psychohistory, 5,* 271–290.

Fraiberg, S. H. (1959). *The magic years.* New York: Scribner's.

Fraiberg, S. H. (1974). Blind infants and their mothers: An examination of the sign system. In M. Lewis & L. Rosenblum (Eds.), *The effect of the infant on its caregiver.* New York: Wiley.

Frankenburg, W. K., & Dodds, J. B. (1967). The Denver developmental screening test. *Journal of Pediatrics, 71,* 181–191.

Frauenglass, M. H., & Diaz, R. M. (1985). Self-regulatory functions of children's private speech: A critical analysis of recent challenges to Vygotsky's theory. *Developmental Psychology, 21,* 357–364.

Frazier, J. A., & Morrison, F. J. (1998). The influence of extended-year schooling on growth of achievement and perceived competence in early elementary school. *Child Development, 69,* 495–517.

Freda, V. J., Gorman, J. G., & Pollack, W. (1966). Rh factor: Prevention of isoimmunization and clinical trial on mothers. *Science, 151,* 828–830.

Freeman, N. H. (1980). *Strategies of representation in young children.* London: Academic Press.

Freiler, C., & Cerny, J. (1998). *Benefiting Canada's children: Perspectives on gender and social responsibility.* Ottawa: Research Directorate, Status of Women.

Freud, A. (1958). Adolescence. In R. S. Eisler, A. Freud, H. Hartmann, & E. Kris (Eds.), *Psychoanalytic study of the child* (Vol. 13). New York: International Universities Press.

Freud, A., & Dann, S. (1951). An experiment in group up-bringing. In R. S. Eisler, A. Freud, H. Hartmann, & E. Kris (Eds.), *The Psychoanalytic study of the child* (Vol. 6). New York: International Universities Press.

Frick, J. E., & Colombo, J. (1996). Individual differences in infant visual attention: Recognition of degraded visual forms by four-month-olds. *Child Development, 67,* 188–204.

Fried, P. A., & Oxorn, H. (1980). *Smoking for two: Cigarettes and pregnancy.* New York: Free Press.

Friel-Patti, S. (1990). Otitis media with effusion and the development of language: a review of the evidence. *Topics in Language Disorders, 11*(1), 11–22.

Frisch, R. E. (1988, March). Fatness and fertility. *Scientific American,* 88–95.

Frost, J. L., & Sunderline, S. (Eds.). (1985). *When children play.* Proceedings of the International Conference on Play and Play Environments, Association for Childhood Education International, Weaton, MD.

Fuller, J., & Simmel, E. (1986). *Perspectives in behavioral genetics.* Hillsdale, NJ: Erlbaum.

Furstenberg, F. (1976). *Unplanned parenthood: The social consequences of teenage childbearing.* New York: Free Press.

Futterweit, L. R., & Ruff, H. A. (1993). Principles of early development: Implications for early intervention. *Journal of Applied Developmental Psychology, 14,* 153–173.

Fuzessy, C. (1999). Biculturalism in postsecondary Inuit education. *Canadian Journal of Native Education, 22,* 201–209.

Gabbard, C., Dean, M., & Haensly, P. (1991). Foot preference behavior during early childhood. *Journal of Applied Developmental Psychology, 12,* 131–137.

Galambos, N. L., & Maggs, J. L. (1991). Out-of-school care of young adolescents and self-reported behavior. *Developmental Psychology, 27,* 644–655.

Galinsky, E. (1980). *Between generations: The six stages of parenthood.* New York: Times Books.

Gallagher, J. J. (1989). A new policy initiative: infants and toddlers with handicapping conditions. *American Psychologist, 44*(2), 387–391.

Gallagher, J. M. (1973). Cognitive development and learning in the adolescent. In J. F. Adams (Ed.), *Understanding adolescence* (2nd ed.). Boston: Allyn & Bacon.

Garbarino, J., & Kostelny, K. (1992). Child maltreatment as a community problem. *Child Abuse and Neglect, 16,* 455–467.

Garber, K., & Marchese, S. (1986). *Genetic counseling for clinicians.* Chicago: Year Book Medical Publishers.

Gardner H. (1973a). *The arts and human development: A psychological study of the artistic process.* New York: Wiley-Interscience.

Gardner, H. (1973b). *The quest for mind: Piaget, Levi-Strauss, and the structuralist movement.* New York: Random House.

Gardner, H. (1983). *Frames of mind.* New York: Basic Books.

Gardner, H. (1993). *Multiple intelligences.* New York: Basic Books.

Gardner, J. M., & Karmel, B. Z. (1984). Arousal effects on visual preference in neonates. *Developmental Psychology, 20,* 374–377.

Gardner, R. (1989). *Sex abuse hysteria: Salem witch trials revisited.* Longwood, NJ: Creative Therapeutic Press.

Garland, A. F., & Zigler, E. (1993). Adolescent suicide prevention: Current research and social policy implications. *American Psychologist, 48*(2), 169–182.

Garmezy, N. (1991). Resiliency and vulnerability to adverse developmental outcomes associated with poverty. *American Behavioral Scientist, 34*(4), 416–430.

Garrod, A., Beal, C., & Shin, P. (1989). *The development of moral orientation in elementary school children.* Paper presented at the April meeting of the Society for Research in Child Development, Kansas City.

Garvey, C. (1977). *Play.* Cambridge, MA: Harvard University Press.

Garvey, C. (1984). *Children's talk.* Cambridge, MA: Harvard University Press.

Garvey, C. (1990). *Play.* Cambridge, MA: Harvard University Press.

Ge, X., Best, K., Conger, R. D., & Simons, R. L. (1996). Parenting behaviors and the occurrence and co-occurrence of adolescent depressive symptoms and conduct problems. *Developmental Psychology, 32,* 717–731.

Ge, X., Cadoret, R. J., Conger, R. D., & Neiderhiser, J. M. (1996). The developmental interface between nature and nurture: A mutual influence model of child antisocial behavior and parent behaviors. *Developmental Psychology, 32,* 574–589.

Gelman, R. (1990). First principles organize attention to and learning about irrelevant data: Number and the animate-inanimate distinction as examples. *Cognitive Science, 14,* 79–106.

Gelman, R., & Gallistel, C. R. (1986). *The child's understanding of number.* Cambridge, MA: Harvard University Press.

Genesee, F. (1976). The suitability of immersion programs for all children. *Canadian Modern Language Review, 32,* 494–515.

Gerrard, M., Gibbons, F. X., & Bushman, B. J. (1996). Relation between perceived vulnerability to HIV and precautionary sexual behavior. *Psychological Bulletin, 119,* 390–409.

Gesell, A. (1940). *The first five years of life: The preschool years.* New York: Harper & Brothers.

Gesell, A., & Ames, L. B. (1947). The development of handedness. *Journal of Genetic Psychology, 70,* 155–175.

Gibbons, D. C. (1976). *Delinquent behavior* (2nd ed.). Englewood Cliffs, NJ: Prentice-Hall.

Gibson, E. J., & Spelke, E. S. (1983). The development of perception. In P. Mussen (Ed.), *The handbook of child psychology: Vol. 3. Cognitive development* (pp. 2–60). New York: Wiley.

Gibson, E. J., & Walk, R. D. (1960, April). The "visual cliff." *Scientific American,* 64–71.

Gibson, H., & Klassen, T. P. (1996). How safe are our schools? *Canadian Journal of Public Health, 87,* 106–107.

Gilligan, C. (1982). *In a different voice: Psychological theory and women's development.* Cambridge, MA: Harvard University Press.

Gilligan, C. (1987). Adolescent development reconsidered. *New Directions for Child Development, 37,* 63–92.

Ginsburg, E. (1972). Toward a theory of occupational choice: A restatement. *Vocational Guidance Quarterly, 20,* 169–176.

Gladstone, T. R. G., & Koenig, L. J. (1994). Sex differences in depression across the high school to college transition. *Journal of Youth and Adolescence, 23,* 643–669.

Glaser, R. (1963). Instructional technology and the measurement of learning outcomes: Some questions. *American Psychologist, 18,* 519–521.

Gleitman, L. R., & Newport, E. L. (1995). The invention of language by children: Environmental and biological influences on language acquisition. In D.N. Osherson (Gen. Ed.), L. R. Gleitman, & M. Liberman (Eds.), *An invitation to cognitive science: Language* (Vol. 1). Cambridge, MA: MIT Press.

Glidewell, J. C., Kantor, M. B., Smith, L. M., & Stringer, L. A. (1966). Socialization and social structure in the classroom. In L. W. Hoffman & M. L. Hoffman (Eds.), *Review of child development research* (Vol. 2). New York: Russell Sage Foundation.

Godin, G., Maticka-Tyndale, E., Adrien, A., Singer, S. M., Willms, D., Cappon, P., & Daus, T. (1996). Understanding use of condoms among Canadian ethnocultural communities: Methods and main findings of the survey. *Canadian Journal of Public Health, 87,* 33–37.

Goldberg, M. C., Maurer, D., & Lewis, T. L. (1996). Influence of a central stimulus on infants' visual fields. *Infant Behavior and Development.*

Goldberg, S. (1972). Infant care and growth in urban Zambia. *Human Development, 15,* 77–89.

Goldberg, S. (1979). Premature birth: Consequences for the parent-infant relationship. *American Scientist, 67,* 214–220.

Goldberg, S. (1983). Parent-infant bonding: Another look. *Child Development, 54,* 1355–1382.

Goldberg, S., & Lewis, M. (1969). Play behavior in the year-old infant: Early sex differences. *Child Development, 40,* 21–31.

Goldberg, S., Lojkasek, M., Gartner, G., & Corter, C. (1988). Maternal responsiveness and social development in preterm infants. In M. H. Bornstein (Ed.), *New directions for child development: Vol. 43. Maternal responsiveness: characteristics and consequences.* San Francisco: Jossey-Bass.

Goldfield, E. C. (1989). Transition from rocking to crawling: Postural constraints on infant movement. *Developmental Psychology, 25*(6), 913–919.

Goldsmith, H. H. (1983). Genetic influence on personality from infancy to adulthood. *Child Development, 54,* 331–355.

Golombok, S., Cook, R., Bish, A., & Murray, C. (1995). Families created by the new reproductive technologies: Quality of parenting and social and emotional development of the children. *Child Development, 66,* 285–298.

Golub, A., & Johnson, B. D. (1994). The shifting of importance of alcohol and marijuana as gateway substances among serious drug abusers. *Journal on Studies on Alcohol, 55,* 507–514.

Goodman, G. S., & Bottoms, B. L. (1993). *Child victims, child witnesses.* New York: The Guilford Press.

Goodman, P. (1960). *Growing up absurd.* New York: Random House.

Goodnow, J. (1977). *Children drawing.* Cambridge, MA: Harvard University Press.

Gopnik, A. (1988). Three types of early word: The emergence of social words, names and cognitive-relational words in the one-word stage and their relation to cognitive development. *First Language, 8,* 49–70.

Gopnik, A., & Meltzoff, A. N. (1987). The development of categorization in the second year and its relation to other cognitive and linguistic developments. *Child Development, 58,* 1523–1531.

Gordon, I. (1969). Early childhood stimulation through parent education. *Final Report to the Children's Bureau Social and Rehabilitation Services Department of HEW.* ED 038-166.

Gordon, R. (1990). *Anorexia and bulimia: Anatomy of a social epidemic.* Oxford: Blackwell.

Gorski, R. A. (1985). The 13th J. A. Stevenson Memorial Lecture. Sexual differentiation of the brain: Possible mechanisms and implications. *Canadian Journal of Physiology and Pharmacology, 63,* 577–594.

Gortmaker, S. L., Dietz, W. H., Jr., Sobol, A. M., & Wehler, C. A. (1987). Increasing pediatric obesity in the United States. *American Journal of Diseases of Children, 141,* 535–540.

Goslin, D. A. (Ed.). (1969). *Handbook of socialization theory and research.* Chicago: Rand McNally.

Gottesman, I. I., & Goldsmith, H. H. (1994). Developmental psychopathology of antisocial behavior: Inserting genes into its ontogenesis and epigenesis. In C. A. Nelson (Ed.), *Threats to optimal development: Integrating biological, psychological and social factors. The Minnesota symposia of child psychology* (Vol. 27, pp. 20–44). Hillsdale, NJ: Erlbaum.

Gottman, J. M. (1983). How children become friends. *Monographs of the Society for Research in Child Development, 48*(3).

Gould, D., Feltz, D., Horn, T., & Weiss, M. (1982). Reasons for discontinuing involvement in competitive youth swimming. *Journal of Sport Behavior, 5,* 155–165.

Gould, S. J. (1981). *The mismeasure of man.* New York: Norton.

Granrud, C. D., Yonas, A., & Petterson, L. (1984). A comparison of monocular and binocular depth perception in 5 and 7 month old infants. *Journal of Experimental Child Psychology, 38,* 19–32.

Gratch, G., & Schatz, J. (1987). Cognitive development: The relevance of Piaget's infancy books. In J. Osofsky (Ed.), *Handbook of infant development* (2nd ed.). New York: Wiley.

Gravelle, K. (1990). *Understanding birth defects*. New York: Franklin Watts.

Gray, D. B., & Yaffe, S. J. (1986). Prenatal drugs and learning disabilities. In M. Lewis (Ed.), *Learning disabilities and prenatal risk*. Urbana: University of Illinois Press.

Gray, V. A., & Cameron, C. A. (1980). Longitudinal development of English morphology in French immersion children. *Applied Psycholinguistics, 1,* 171–181.

Greenberg, M., & Morris, N. (1974, July). Engrossment: The newborn's impact upon the father. *American Journal of Orthopsychiatry, 44*(4), 520–531.

Greenberger, E., & Chen, C. (1996). Perceived family relationships and depressed mood in early and late adolescence: A comparison of European and Asian Americans. *Developmental Psychology, 32,* 707–716.

Greene, A. L. (1990). Great expectations: Constructions of the life course during adolescence. *Journal of Youth and Adolescence, 19,* 289–303.

Greene, A. L., & Brooks, J. (1985, April). *Children's perceptions of stressful life events*. Paper presented at the Society for Research in Child Development, Toronto.

Greenfield, P. (1984). *Mind and media: The effects of television, video games and computers*. Cambridge, MA: Harvard University Press.

Greenough, W. T., Black, J. E., & Wallace, C. S. (1987). Experience and brain development. *Child Development, 58,* 539–559.

Greenspan, S., & Greenspan, N. (1985). *First feelings*. New York: Penguin.

Greenspan, S. I. (1997). *The growth of the mind*. Reading, MA: Perseus Books.

Greif, E. B., & Ulman, K. J. (1982). The psychological impact of menarche on early adolescent females: A review of the literature. *Child Development, 53,* 1413–1430.

Grossman, F. K., Pollack, W. S., & Golding, E. (1988). Fathers and children: Predicting the quality and quantity of fathering. *Developmental Psychology, 24*(1), 82–91.

Grotevant, H. D., & Cooper, C. R. (1985). Patterns of interaction in family relationships and the development of identity exploration in adolescence. *Child Development, 56,* 415–428.

Grusec, J. E., & Arnason, L. (1982). Consideration for others: Approaches to enhancing altruism. In S. Moore & C. Cooper (Eds.), *The young child: Reviews of research* (Vol. 3). Washington, DC: National Association for the Education of Young Children.

Guilford, J. P. (1959). Three faces of intellect. *American Psychologist, 14,* 469–479.

Gunderson, V., & Sackett, G. P. (1982). Paternal effects on reproductive outcome and developmental risk. In M. E. Lamb and A. L. Brown (Eds.), *Advances in developmental psychology* (Vol. 2). Hillsdale, NJ: Erlbaum.

Gunnar, M. R. (1989). *New directions for child development: Vol. 45. Studies of the human infant's adrenocortical response to potentially stressful events*. San Francisco: Jossey-Bass.

Gunter, B., & McAleer, J. L. (1990). *Children and television: The one eyed monster?* London: Routledge.

Guy, K. A. (1997). *Our promise to our children*. Ottawa: Health Canada.

Habbick, B. F., Nanson, J. L., Snyder, R. E., Casey, R. E., & Schulman, A. L. (1996). Foetal alcohol syndrome in Saskatchewan: Unchanged incidence in a 20-year period. *Canadian Journal of Public Health, 87,* 204–207.

Hagen, J. W. (1972). Strategies for remembering. In S. Farnham-Diggory (Ed.), *Information processing in children*. New York: Academic Press.

Hagerman, R. J. (1996). Biomedical advances in developmental psychology: The case of fragile x syndrome. *Developmental Psychology, 32,* 416–424.

Haglund, B., & Cnattingius, S. (1990). Cigarette smoking as a risk factor for sudden infant death syndrome: A population-based study. *American Journal of Public Health, 80,* 29–32.

Hall, W. M., & Cairns, R. B. (1984). Aggressive behavior in children: An outcome of modeling or social reciprocity? *Developmental Psychology, 20,* 739–745.

Halliday, M. (1973). *Exploration in the functions of language*. London: Edward Arnold.

Hammerly, H. (1989). *French immersion: Myths and reality*. Calgary: Detselig.

Handyside, A. H., Lesko, J. G., Tarin, J. J., Winston, R. M. L., & Hughes, M. R. (1992). Birth of a normal girl after in vitro fertilization and preimplantation diagnostic testing for cystic fibrosis. *New England Journal of Medicine, 327*(13), 905–909.

Haqq, C. M., King, C. Y., Ukiyama, E., Falsafi, S., Haqq, T. N., Donahoe, P. K., & Weiss, M. A. (1994). Molecular basis of mammalian sexual determination: Activation of mullerian inhibiting gene expression by SRY. *Science, 266,* 1494–1500.

Harlow, H. F. (1959, June). Love in infant monkeys. *Scientific American,* 68–74.

Harlow, H. F., & Harlow, M. K. (1962, November). Social deprivation in monkeys. *Scientific American,* 137–146.

Harre, R. (1980, January). What's in a nickname? *Psychology Today,* 78–84.

Harris, B. (1979). Whatever happened to little Albert? *American Psychologist, 34,* 151–160.

Harris, J. R. (1998). *The nurture assumption*. New York: The Free Press.

Harrsion, M. J., & Magill-Evans, J. (1996). Mother and father interactions over the first year with term and preterm infants. *Research in Nursing and Health, 19,* 451–459.

Harrsion, M. J., Magill-Evans, J., & Benzies, K. (1999). Fathers' scores on the nursing child assessment teaching scale: Are they different from those of mothers? *Journal of Pediatric Nursing, 14,* 1–8.

Harris, P. L., Brown, E., Marriott, C., Whitall, S., & Harmer, S. (1991). Monsters, ghosts, and witches: Testing and the limits of the fantasy-reality distinction in young children. *British Journal of Developmental Psychology, 9,* 105–123.

Hart, S. N., Germain, R. B., & Brassard, M. R. (1987). The challenge: To better understand and combat psychological maltreatment of children and youth. In M. R. Brassard, R. Germain, & S. N. Hart (Eds.), *Psychological maltreatment of children and youth* (pp. 3–24). New York: Pergamon.

Harter, S. (1982). The perceived competence scale for children. *Child Development, 53,* 87–97.

Harter, S. (1983). Developmental perspectives on the self system. In P. H. Mussen (Ed.), *Handbook of child psychology* (4th ed., Vol. 4). New York: Wiley.

Hartup, W. W. (1963). Dependence and independence. In H. W. Stevenson, J. Kagan, & C. Spiker (Eds.), *Child psychology*. Chicago: National Society for the Study of Education.

Hartup, W. W. (1970a). Peer interaction and social organization. In P. H. Mussen (Ed.), *Carmichael's manual of child psychology* (3rd ed., Vol. 2). New York: Wiley.

Hartup, W. W. (1970b). Peer relations. In T. D. Spencer & N. Kass (Eds.), *Perspectives in child psychology: Research and review*. New York: McGraw-Hill.

Hartup, W. W. (1983). Peer relations. In P. H. Mussen (Ed.), *Handbook of child psychology* (4th ed., Vol. 4). New York: Wiley.

Hartup, W. W. (1989). Social relationships and their developmental significance. *American Psychologist, 44*(2), 120–126.

Hass, A. (1979). *Teenage sexuality: A survey of teenage sexual behavior.* New York: Macmillan.

Hatem-Asmar, M., Blais, R., Lambert, J., & Maheux, B. (1996). A survey of midwives in Quebec: What are their similarities and differences. *Birth, 23,* 94–100.

Hawkins, J. A., & Berndt, T. J. (1985). *Adjustment following the transition to junior high school.* Paper presented at the biennial meeting of the Society for Research in Child Development.

Hawley, R. S., & Mori, C. A. (1999). *The human genome: A user's guide.* Boston: Academic Press.

Hazen, N. L., & Lockman, J. J. (1989). Skill in context. In J. J. Lockman & N. L. Hazen (Eds.), *Action in social context: Perspectives on early development* (pp. 1–22). New York: Plenum.

Health and Welfare Canada. (1993). *Breastfeeding support.* Ottawa: Minister of National Health and Welfare.

Hecox, K. (1975). Electrophysiological correlates of human auditory development. In L. B. Cohen & P. Salapatek (Eds.), *Infant perception: From sensation to cognition* (pp. 151–191). New York: Academia.

Heine, S. J., & Lehman, D. R. (1995). Cultural variation in unrealistic optimism: Does the West feel more invulnerable than the East? *Journal of Personality and Social Psychology, 68,* 595–607.

Helfer, R. (1982). The relationship between lack of bonding and child abuse and neglect. In *Round Table on Maternal Attachment and Nurturing Disorder* (Vol. 2). New Brunswick, NJ: Johnson & Johnson.

Hellige, J. B. (1993). Unity of thought and action: Varieties of interaction between the left and right cerebral hemispheres. *Current Directions in Psychological Science, 2*(1), 21–25.

Helwig, C. C., & Kim, S. (1999). Children's evaluations of decision-making procedures in peer, family, and school contexts. *Child Development, 70,* 502–512.

Hepper, P. (1989). Foetal learning: Implications for psychiatry? *British Journal of Psychiatry, 155,* 289–293.

Herkowitz, J. (1978). Sex-role expectations and motor behavior of the young child. In M. V. Ridenour (Ed.), *Motor development: Issues and applications.* Princeton, NJ: Princeton Book Co.

Herrnstein, R. J., & Murray, C. (1994). *The bell curve.* New York: The Free Press.

Hess, E. H. (1970). Ethology and developmental psychology. In P. H. Mussen (Ed.), *Carmichael's manual of child psychology* (3rd ed., Vol. 1). New York: Wiley.

Hess, R. D., & Holloway, S. D. (1984). Family and school as educational institutions. In R. D. Parke (Ed.), *Review of Child Development Research 7: The Family* (pp. 179–222). Chicago: University of Chicago Press.

Hetherington, E. M. (1984, June). Stress and coping in children and families. In A. Doyle, D. Gold, & D. Moskowitz (Eds.), *New di-*

rections for child development: Vol. 24. Children in families under stress. San Francisco: Jossey-Bass.

Hetherington, E. M. (1989). Coping with family transitions: Winners, losers, and survivors. *Child Development, 60,* 1–14.

Hetherington, E. M. (1992). Coping with marital transitions: A family systems perspective. *Monographs of the Society for Research in Child Development, 57*(2–3, Serial No. 227).

Hetherington, E. M. (1998). Relevant issues in developmental science: Introduction to the special issue. *American Psychologist, 53,* 93–94.

Hetherington, E. M., & Baltes, P. B. (1998). Child psychology and life-span development. In E. M. Hetherington, R. Lerner, & M. Perlmutter (Eds.), *Child development in life-span perspective.* Hillsdale, NJ: Erlbaum.

Hetherington, E. M., Bridges, M., & Isabella, G. M. (1998). What matters? What does not? Five perspectives on the association between marital transitions and children's adjustment. *American Psychologist, 53,* 167–184.

Hetherington, E. M., & Camara, K. A. (1984). Families in transition: The process of dissolution and reconstitution. In R. D. Parke (Ed.), *Review of child development research* (Vol. 7). Chicago: University of Chicago Press.

Hetherington, E. M., Reiss, D., & Plomin, R. (1994). *Separate social worlds of siblings: Impact of nonshared environment on development.* Hillsdale, NJ: Erlbaum.

Hetherington, E. M., & Stanley-Hagan, M. (1999). The adjustment of children with divorced parents: A risk and resiliency perspective. *Journal of Child Psychology and Psychiatry, 40,* 129–140.

Hill, J. P. (1987). Research on adolescents and their families past and present. *New Directions for Child Development, 37,* 13–32.

Hirshberg, L. (1990). When infants look to their parents: II. Twelve-month-olds' response to conflicting parental emotional signals. *Child Development, 61,* 1187–1191.

Hirshberg, L. M., & Svejda, M. (1990). When infants look to their parents: I. Infants' social referencing of mothers compared to fathers. *Child Development, 61,* 1175–1186.

Hirsh-Pasek, K., Nelson, D. G., Jusczyk, P. W., & Wright, K. (1986, April). *A moment of silence: How the prosaic cues in motherese might assist language learning.* Paper presented at the International Conference on Infant Studies, Los Angeles.

Hiscock, M., & Kinsbourne, M. (1987). Specialization of the cerebral hemispheres: Implications for learning. *Journal of Learning Disabilities, 20,* 130–142.

Hobbs, F. M., Pickett, W., Ferrence, R. G., Brown, K. S., Madill, C., & Adlaf, E. M. (1999). Youth smoking in Ontario 1981–1997: A cause for concern. *Canadian Journal of Public Health, 90,* 80–81.

Hodges, E. V. E., Boivin, M., Vitaro, F., & Bukowski, W. M. (1999). The power of friendship: Protection against an escalating cycle of peer victimization. *Developmental Psychology, 35,* 94–101.

Hoffman, M. L. (1970). Moral development. In P. H. Mussen (Ed.), *Carmichael's manual of child psychology* (3rd ed., Vol. 2). New York: Wiley.

Hoffman, M. L. (1980). Moral development in adolescence. In J. Adelson (Ed.), *Handbook of adolescent psychology.* New York: Wiley.

Holden, C. (1980). Identical twins reared apart. *Science, 207,* 1323–1328.

Holmes, D. S. (1997). *Abnormal psychology* (4th ed.). New York: Addison Wesley.

Honig, A. S. (1986, May). Stress and coping in young children. *Young Children*, 50–63.

Honig, A. S. (1980, October). The importance of fathering. *Dimensions*, 33–38, 63.

Hookimaw-Witt, J. (1999). Any chances since residential school? *Canadian Journal of Native Education, 22*.

Horowitz, F. D. (1982). The first two years of life: Factors related to thriving. In S. Moore & C. Cooper (Eds.), *The young child: Reviews of research* (Vol. 3). Washington, DC: National Association for the Education of Young Children.

Horowitz, S. M., Klerman, L. V., Sungkuo, H., and Jekel, J. F. (1991). Intergenerational transmission of school age parenthood. *Family Planning Perspective, 23*, 168–177.

Hoversten, G. H., & Moncur, J. P. (1969). Stimuli and intensity factors in testing infants. *Journal of Speech and Hearing Research, 12*, 687–702.

Howard, J., & Hammond, R. (1985, September 9). Rumors of inferiority. *The New Republic*, 17–21.

Howe, N., & Jacobs, E. (1995). Child care research: A case for Canadian national standards. *Canadian Psychology, 36*, 131–148.

Howe, N., Moller, L., & Chambers, B. (1994). Dramatic play in day care: What happens when doctors, cooks, bakers, pirates and pharmacists invade the classroom? In H. Goelman & E. Vineberg-Jacobs (Eds.), *Play and child care*. New York: SUNY Press.

Howe, N., Moller, L., Chambers, B., & Petrakos, H. (1993). The ecology of dramatic play centers and children's social and cognitive play. *Early Childhood Research Quarterly, 8*, 235–251.

Howe, N., Petrakos, H., Chambers, B., & Moller, L. (1995). Teacher ratings and observations of children's play in dramatic play centres. *International Play Journal, 3*, 113–120.

Howe, R. B. (1995). Evolving policy on children's rights in Canada. In K. Covell (Ed.), *Readings in child development*. Toronto: Nelson.

Howes, C., & Olenick, M. (1986). Family and child care influences on toddler's compliance. *Child Development, 57*, 202–216.

Huesman, R. L., Eron, L., Lefkowitz, & Walder, L. (1984). The stability of aggression over time and generations. *Developmental Psychology, 20*, 1120–1134.

Hughes, F. P. (1991). *Children, play, and development*. Newton, MA: Allyn & Bacon.

Hughes, M., & Donaldson, M. (1979). The use of hiding games for studying the co-ordination of viewpoints. *Educational Review, 31*, 133–140.

Human Resources Development Canada & Statistics Canada. (1996). *Growing up in Canada*. National Longitudinal Survey of Children and Youth. Ottawa: Author.

Hunt, J. M. (1961). *Intelligence and experience*. New York: Ronald Press.

Huston, A. C., Watkins, B. A., & Kinkel, D. (1989). Public policy and children's television. *American Psychologist, 44*(2), 424–433.

Hutcheson, R. H., Jr. (1968). Iron deficiency anemia in Tennessee among rural poor children. *Public Health Reports, 83*, 939–943.

Hwang, C. P., & Broberg, A. (1992). The historical and social context of child care in Sweden. In M. E. Lamb & K. J. Sternberg (Eds.), *Child care in context* (pp. 27–53). Hillsdale, NJ: Erlbaum.

Inhelder, B., & Piaget, J. (1958). *The growth of logical thinking: From childhood to adolescence* (A. Parsons & S. Milgram, Trans.). New York: Basic Books.

In-vitro fertilization comes of age: Issues still unsettled. (1984, June 15–30). *OB/GYN News, 19*(12), 3.

Isaacs, S. (1930). *Intellectual growth in young children*. London: Routledge & Kegan Paul.

Isabella, R. A., Belsky, J., & Von Eye, A. (1989). Origins of infant-mother attachment: An examination of interactional synchrony during the infant's first year. *Developmental Psychology, 25*(1), 12–21.

Isenberg, J., & Quisenberry, N. L. (1988, February). Play: A necessity for all children. *Childhood Education*.

Jacobs, E. V., White, D. R., Baillargeon, M., & Betsalel-Presser, R. (1995). Peer relations among children attending school-age child-care programs. In K. Covell (Ed.), *Readings in child development: A Canadian perspective*. Toronto: Nelson.

Jacobson, J. L., Jacobson, S. W., Schwartz, P. M., Fein, G., & Dowler, J. K. (1984). Prenatal exposure to an environmental toxin. A test of the multiple effects model. *Developmental Psychology, 20*, 523–532.

Jacobson, J. L., & Jacobson, S. W. (1996). Methodological considerations in behavioral toxicology in infants and children. *Developmental Psychology, 32*, 390–403.

Jacobson, J. L., & Wille, D. E. (1984). Influence of attachment and separation experience on separation distress at 18 months. *Developmental Psychology, 70*, 477–484.

Jaeger, E., & Weinraub, M. (1990, Fall). Early nonmaternal care and infant attachment: In search of progress. *New Directions for Child Development, 49*, 71–90.

Jaffe, P. G., & Baker, L. L. (1999). Why changing the YOA does not impact youth crime: Developing effective prevention programs for children and adolescents. *Canadian Psychology, 40*, 22–29.

Janus, S. S., & Janus, C. L. (1993). *The Janus report on sexual behavior*. New York: Wiley.

Jelliffe, D. B., Jelliffe, E. F. P., Garcia, L., & DeBarrios, G. (1961). The children of the San Blas Indians of Panama. *Journal of Pediatrics, 59*, 271–285.

Jenkins, J. M., & Wilde Astington, J. (1996). Cognitive factors and family structure associated with theory of mind development in young children. *Developmental Psychology, 32*, 70–78.

Jensen, A. R. (1969). How much can we boost IQ and scholastic achievement? *Harvard Educational Review, 39*, 1–123.

Jensh, R. (1986). Effects of prenatal irradiation on postnatal psychophysiologic development. In E. P. Riley & C. V. Vorhees (Eds.), *Handbook of behavioral periontology*. New York: Plenum.

Jersild, A. T., & Holmes, F. B. (1935). Children's fears. *Child Development Monograph* (No. 20). New York: Teachers College Press, Columbia University.

Jessor, R. (1993). Successful adolescent development among youth in high-risk settings. *American Psychologist, 48*(2), 117–126.

Jessor, R., Donovan, J. D., & Costa, F. (1992). *Beyond adolescence: Problem behavior and young adult development*. New York: Cambridge University Press.

Jewison, K. (1995). Our students, our future: Innovations in First Nations education in the NWT. *Education Canada, 35*, 4–11.

Jing, Q. C. (1996, August). *China's reform and challenges for psychology*. Paper presented at the XXVI International Congress of Psychology, Montreal.

Johnson, J. E., Christie, J. F., & Yawkey, T. D. (1987). *Play and early childhood development*. Glenview, IL: Scott, Foresman.

Johnson, J. S., & Newport, E. L. (1989). Critical period effects in second-language learning: The influence of maturational state on the acquisition of English as a second language. *Cognitive Psychology, 21,* 60–90.

Johnson, M. (1993). Cortical maturation and the development of visual attention in early infancy. In M. Johnson (Ed.), *Brain development and cognition.* Oxford: Blackwell.

Johnson, M. O. (1996). Television violence and its effects on children. *Journal of Pediatric Nursing, 11,* 94–99.

Johnson, N. & Cremo, E. (1995). Socialization and the Native Family. In K. Covell (Ed.), *Readings in child development.* Toronto: Nelson.

Jones, A. P., & Crnic, L. S. (1986). Maternal mediation of the effects of malnutrition. In E. P. Riley & C. V. Vorhees (Eds.), *Handbook of behavioural teratology.* New York: Plenum.

Jones, H. W., & Park, I. J. (1971). A classification of special problems in sex differentiation. In D. Bergsma (Ed.), *The clinical delineation of birth defects:. Part X. The endocrine system.* Baltimore: The Williams and Wilkins Company.

Jones, Judge P.J. (1997). *Young offenders and the law* (2nd ed.). North York, ON: Captus Press.

Jones, M. C. (1965). Psychological correlates of somatic development. *Child Development, 36,* 899–911.

Juel, C. (1988). Learning to read and write: A longitudinal study of fifty-four children from first through fourth grade. *Journal of Educational Psychology, 80,* 437–447.

Kagan, J. (1971). *Change and continuity in infancy.* New York: Wiley.

Kagan, J. (1994). *Galen's prophecy: Temperament in human nature.* New York: Basic Books.

Kagan, J., & Moss, H. A. (1962). *Birth to maturity: A study in psychological development.* New York: Wiley.

Kagitcibasi, C. (1996, August). *Human development: Cross-cultural perspectives.* Paper presented at the XXVI International Congress of Psychology, Montreal.

Kalagian, W., Delmore, T., Loewen, I., & Busca, C. (1998). Adolescent oral contraceptive use: Factors predicting compliance at 3 and12 months. *The Canadian Journal of Human Sexuality, 7.*

Kalnins, I. V., & Bruner, J. S. (1973). Infant sucking used to change the clarity of a visual display. In L. J. Stone, H. T. Smith, & L. B. Murphy (Eds.), *The competent infant: Research and commentary.* New York: Basic Books.

Kamin, L. (1974). *The science and politics of IQ.* Hillsdale, NJ: Erlbaum

Kandel, D. B., Raveis, V. H., & Davies, M. (1991). Suicidal ideation in adolescence: Depression, substance use, & other risk factors. *Journal of Youth and Adolescence, 20,* 289–309.

Kandel, E. R., Schwartz, J. H., & Jessell, T. M. (1995). *Essentials of neural science and behavior.* Norwalk, CT: Appleton & Lange.

Kantor, A. F., et al. (1979). Occupations of fathers of patients with Wilm's tumour. *Journal of Epidemiology and Community Health, 33,* 253–256.

Kantrowitz, B. (1988, May 16). Preemies. *Newsweek,* 62–67.

Karlson, A. L. (1972). *A naturalistic method for assessing cognitive acquisition of young children participating in preschool programs.* Unpublished doctoral dissertation, University of Chicago.

Karpov, Y. V., & Haywood, H. C. (1998). Two ways to elaborate Vygotsky's concept of mediation: Implications for instruction. *American Psychologist, 53,* 27–36.

Katz, L. (1993). What can we learn from Reggio Emilia? In C. Edwards, L. Gandini, & G. Forman (Eds.), *The hundred languages of children: The Reggio Emilia approach to early childhood education.* Norwood, NJ: Ablex.

Keating, D. (1976). Intellectual talent, research, and development: Proceedings. In D. Keating (Ed.), *Hyman Blumberg Symposium in Early Childhood Education.* Baltimore: Johns Hopkins University Press.

Keating, D. P. (1980). Thinking processes in adolescence. In J. Adelson (Ed.), *Handbook of adolescent psychology.* New York: Wiley.

Keenan, K., & Shaw, D. (1997). Development and social influences on young girls' early problem behavior. *Psychological Bulletin, 121,* 95–113.

Kellogg, R. (1969). *Analyzing children's art.* Palo Alto, CA: National Press Books.

Kellogg, R. (1970). *Analyzing children's art.* Palo Alto, CA: National Press Books.

Kelly, T. (1986). *Clinical genetics and genetic counseling* (3rd ed.). Chicago: Year Book Medical Publishers.

Kempe, R. S., & Kempe, C. H. (1984). *The common secret: Sexual abuse of children and adolescents.* San Francisco: Freeman.

Kendrick, A. S., Kaufmann, R., & Messenger, K. P. (1991). *Healthy young children: A manual for programs.* Washington, DC: National Association for the Education of Young Children.

Keogh, J. F. (1965). *Motor performance of elementary school children.* Monograph of the Physical Education Department, University of California, Los Angeles.

Keppel-Benson, J. M., & Ollendick, T. H. (1993). Posttraumatic stress disorder in children and adolescents. In C. F. Saylor (Ed.), *Children and disasters: Issues in clinical child psychology.* New York: Plenum Press.

Kermis, M. D. (1984). *The psychology of human aging: Theory, research and practice.* Newton, MA: Allyn & Bacon.

Kermis, M. D. (1986). *Mental health in late life: The adaptive process.* Boston: Jones and Bartlett.

Kermoian, R., & Campos, J. J. (1988). Locomotor experience: A facilitation of spacial cognitive development. *Child Development, 59,* 908–917.

Kerns, K. A., Kelpac, L., & Cole, A. (1996). Peer relationships and preadolescents' perceptions of security in the child-mother relationship. *Developmental Psychology, 32,* 457–466.

Kiester, E., Jr. (1977, October). Healing babies before they're born. *Family Health,* 26–30.

Kirkness, V. J. (1999). The critical state of Aboriginal languages in Canada. *Canadian Journal of Native Education, 22,* 1–15.

Kisilevsky, B. S., Hains, S. M. J., Lee, K., Muir, D. W., Xu, F., Fu, G., Zhao, Z. Y., & Yang, R. L. (1998). The still-face effect in Chinese and Canadian 3- to 6-month-old infants. *Developmental Psychology, 34,* 629–639.

Kitayama, S. (1993). *Sociocultural influences in basic psychological processes* (Position Paper). National Institute of Mental Health Behavioral Science Task Force, Socio-Cultural Influences Subcommittee. Washington, DC.

Klahr, D., Langley, P., & Necher, R. (Eds.). (1987). *Production system model of learning and development.* Cambridge, MA: MIT Press.

Klaus, M. H., & Kennell, J. H. (1976). *Maternal-infant bonding.* St. Louis: C. V. Mosby.

Klein, N., Hack, N., Gallagher, J., & Fanaroff, A. A. (1985). Preschool performance of children with normal intelligence who were very low birth weight infants. *Pediatrics, 75,* 531–537.

Klein, S., & Magill-Evans, J. (1998). Perceptions of competence and peer acceptance in young children with motor and learning difficulties. *Physical & Occupational Therapy in Pediatrics, 18,* 39–52.

Klima, E. S., & Bellugi, U. (1966). Syntactic regularities. In J. Lyons & R. J. Wales (Eds.), *Psycholinguistics papers.* Edinburgh: University of Edinburgh Press.

Kline, S. (1993). *Out of the garden: Toys and children's culture in the age of TV marketing.* Toronto: Garamond Press.

Klinnert, M. D., Emde, R. N., Butterfield, P., & Campos, J. J. (1986). Social referencing: The infant's use of emotional signals from a friendly adult with mother present. *Developmental Psychology, 22,* 427–432.

Knight, G. P., Fabes, R. A., & Higgins, D. A. (1996). Concerns about drawing causal inferences from meta-analyses: An example in the study of gender differences in aggression. *Psychological Bulletin, 119,* 410–421.

Knobloch, H., Malone, A., Ellison, P. H., Stevens, F., & Zdeb, M. (1982, March). Considerations in evaluating changes in outcome for infants weighing less than 1,501 grams. *Pediatrics, 69*(3), 285–295.

Knobloch, H., Pasamanick, B., Harper, P. A., & Rider, R. V. (1959). The effect of prematurity on health and growth. *American Journal of Public Health, 49,* 1164–1173.

Knox, S. (1980). Ultra-sound diagnosis of foetal disorder. *Public Health, London, 94,* 362–367.

Koch, H. L. (1956). Sissiness and tomboyishness in relation to sibling characteristics. *Journal of Genetic Psychology, 88,* 213–244.

Koch, R., & Koch, K. J. (1974). *Understanding the mentally retarded child: A new approach.* New York: Random House.

Kohlberg, L. (1966). A cognitive developmental analysis of children's sex-role concepts and attitudes. In E. Maccoby (Ed.), *The development of sex differences.* Stanford: Stanford University Press.

Kohlberg, L. (1966). Moral education in the schools: A developmental view. *School Review, 74,* 1–30.

Kohlberg, L. (1969). Stage and sequence: The cognitive-developmental approach to socialization. In D. A. Goslin (Ed.), *Handbook of socialization theory and research* (pp. 347–480). Chicago: Rand McNally.

Kohlberg, L. (1978). Revisions in the theory and practice of moral development. *New Directions for Child Development, 2.*

Kohlberg, L. (1981). *Essays on moral development: Vol. 1. The philosophy of moral development.* New York: Harper & Row.

Kohlberg, L. (1984). *Essays on moral development: Vol. 2. The psychology of moral development.* New York: Harper & Row.

Kolb, B. (1995). *Brain plasticity and behavior.* Mahwah, NJ: Lawrence Erlbaum.

Komner, M., & Shostak, M. (1987), Timing and management of birth among the !Kung: Biocultural interaction and reproductive adaptation. *Cultural Anthropology, 2,* 11–28.

Konner, M. (1991). *Childhood: A multicultural view.* Boston: Little, Brown.

Kopp, C. B. (1989). Regulation and distress and negative emotions: A developmental view. *Developmental Psychology, 25,* 353–354.

Kopp, C. B. (1992, Spring). Emotional distress and control in young children. In N. Eisenberg & R. Fabes (Eds.), *New Directions for Child Development.* San Francisco: Jossey-Bass.

Korner, A. F. (1987). Preventive intervention with high-risk newborns: Theoretical, conceptual, and methodological perspectives. In J. Osofsky (Ed.), *Handbook of infant development.* New York: Wiley.

Korte, D., & Scaer, R. (1990). *A good birth, a safe birth.* New York: Bantam.

Koslow, R. E. (1987). Sit and reach flexibility measures for boys and girls aged three through eight years. *Perceptual and Motor Skills, 64,* 1103–1106.

Krause, C. M., & Saarnio, D. A. (1993). Deciding what is safe to eat: Young children's understanding of appearance, reality, and edibleness. *Journal of Applied Developmental Psychology, 14,* 231–244.

Kreppner, K., & Lerner, N. (Eds.). (1989). *Family systems and life-span development.* Hillsdale, NJ: Erlbaum.

Kropp, J. P., & Haynes, O. M. (1987). Abusive and nonabusive mothers' ability to identify general and specific emotion signals of infants. *Child Development, 58,* 187–190.

Kuhl, P. K., & Meltzoff, A. N. (1988). Speech as an intermodel object of perception. In A. Yonas (Ed.), *The Minnesota Symposia on Child Psychology: Vol. 20. Perceptual development in infancy* (pp. 236–266). Hillsdale, NJ: Erlbaum.

Kuliev, A. M., Modell, B., & Jackson, L. (1992). Limb abnormalities and chorionic villus sampling. *The Lancet, 340,* 668.

Kupersmidt, J., Coie, J. D., & Dodge, K. A. (1990). The role of poor peer relationships in the development of the disorder. In S. R. Asher & J. D. Coie (Eds.), *Peer rejection in childhood.* New York: Cambridge University Press.

Kutcher, S., Marton, P., & Boulos, C. (1993). Adolescent depression. In P. Cappeliez & R. J. Flynn (Eds.), *Depression and the social environment.* Montreal: McGill-Queen's University Press.

Ladd, G. W., & Ladd, B. K. (1998). Parenting behaviors and parent-child relationships: Correlates of peer victimization in kindergarten? *Developmental Psychology, 34,* 1450–1458.

Ladebauche, P. (1997). Managing asthma: A growth and development approach. *Pediatric Nursing, 23,* 37–44.

Laing, D. (1992). A comparative study of the writing abilities of English-speaking grade 8 students in French-speaking schools. In S. Towson (Ed.), *Educational psychology: Readings for the Canadian context.* Peterborough, ON: Broadview Press.

LaLonde, C. E., & Werker, J. F. (1995). Cognitive influences on cross-language speech perception in infancy. *Infant Behavior and Development, 18,* 459–475.

Lamb, M. E. (1979). Paternal influences and the father's role. *American Psychologist, 34,* 938–943.

Lamb, M. E. (1987). *The father's role: Cross-cultural perspectives.* New York: Wiley.

Lamb, M. E., Ketterlinus, R. D., & Fracasso, M. P. (1992). Parent-child relationships. In M. H. Bornstein & M. E. Lamb (Eds.), *Developmental psychology: An advanced textbook.* Hillsdale, NJ: Lawrence Erlbaum.

Lamb, M., & Lamb, J. (1976). The nature and importance of the father-infant relationship. *Family Coordinator, 4*(25), 379–386.

Lambert, W., & Tucker, G. R. (1972). *Bilingual education of children: The St. Lambert experiment.* Rowley, MA: Newbury House.

Landau, B., & Gleitman, L. R. (1985). *Language and experience: Evidence from the blind child.* Cambridge, MA: Harvard University Press.

Landy, S., & Tam, K. K. (1996). Yes parenting does make a difference to the development of children in Canada. In Human Resources Development Canada & Statistics Canada. *Growing up in Canada*. National Longitudinal Survey of Children and Youth. Ottawa: Author.

Langille, D. B., Andreou, P., Beazley, R. P., & Delaney, M. E. (1998). Sexual health knowledge of students at a high school in Nova Scotia. *Canadian Journal of Public Health, 89*, 85–89.

Langlois, C. (Ed.). (1998). *Growing with your child: Pre-birth to age 5*. North York, ON: Canadian Living and Ballantine Books.

Lapkin, S., Swain, M., & Argue, V. (1983). *French immersion: The trial balloon that flew*. Toronto: OISE.

LaRose, S., & Boivin, M. (1998). Attachment to parents, social support expectations, and socioemotional adjustment during the high school-college transition. *Journal of Research on Adolescence, 8*, 1–27.

Latham, M. C. (1977). Infant feeding in national and international perspective: An examination of the decline in human lactation, and the modern crisis in infant and young child feeding practices. *Annals of the New York Academy of Sciences, 300*, 197–209.

Lazarus, R. S., & Folkman, S. (1984). *Stress, appraisal and coping*. New York: Springer.

Leavitt, L. A., & Goldson, E. (1996). Introduction to special section: Biomedicine and developmental psychology: New areas of common ground. *Developmental psychology, 32*, 387–389.

Leboyer, F. (1976). *Birth without violence*. New York: Knopf.

Lebrun, M., & Freeze, R. (1995). HIV positive students in the Manitoba public school system: Are Manitoba's teachers ready? *Developmental Disabilities Bulletin, 23*, 32–42.

Lee, K., Cameron, C. A., Xu, F., & Board, J. (1998). Chinese and Canadian children's evaluations of lying and truth-telling: Similarities and differences in the context of pro- and anti-social behaviors. *Child Development*.

Lee, K., Olson, D. R., & Torrance, N. (1999). Chinese children's understanding of false beliefs: The role of language. *Journal of Child Language, 26*, 1–21.

LeFevre, J., Sadesky, G. S., & Bisanz, J. (1996). Selection of procedures in mental addition: Reassessing the problem size effect in adults. *Journal of Experimental Psychology: Learning, Memory and Cognition, 22*, 216–230.

Legerstee, M. (1990). Infants use multimodal information to imitate speech sounds. *Infant Behavior and Development, 13*, 343–354.

Legerstee, M. (1991). The role of person and object in eliciting early imitation. *Journal of Experimental Child Psychology, 51*, 423–433.

Legerstee, M. (1997). Contingency effects of people and objects on subsequent cognitive functioning in three-month-old infants. *Social Development, 6*, 307–321.

Legerstee, M., Anderson, D., & Schaffer, A. (1998). Five- and eight-month-old infants recognize their faces and voices as familiar and social stimuli. *Child Development, 69*, 37–50.

Legerstee, M., Pomerleau, A., Malcuit, G., & Feider, H. (1987). The development of infants' responses to people and a doll: Implications for research in communication. *Infant Behavior and Development, 10*, 82–95.

Lehane, S. (1976). *Help your baby learn*. Englewood Cliffs, NJ: Prentice-Hall.

Leichtman, M. D., & Ceci, S. J. (1995). The effects of stereotypes and suggestions on preschoolers' reports. *Developmental Psychology, 31*, 568–578.

Lenneberg, E. (1967). *Biological foundations of language*. New York: Wiley.

Leo, J. (1984, April 9). The revolution is over. *Time*, 74–83.

Lepper, M. R., & Gurtner, J. L. (1989). Children and computers: Approaching the twenty-first century. *American Psychologist, 44*(2), 170–178.

Lerner, R. M., Orlos, J. B., & Knapp, J. R. (1976). Physical attractiveness, physical effectiveness and self-concept in late adolescence. *Adolescence, 11*, 313–326.

Lester, B. M., & Brazelton, T. B. (1982). Cross-cultural assessment of neonatal behavior. In D. Wagner & H. Stevenson (Eds.), *Cultural perspectives on child development*. San Francisco: Freeman.

Letteri, C. A. (1985). Teaching students how to learn. *Theory into Practice*, 112–122.

Leventhal, E. A., Leventhal, H., Shacham, S., & Easterling, D. V. (1989). Active coping reduces reports of pain from childbirth. *Journal of Consulting and Clinical Psychology, 57*, 365–371.

Levine, L. E. (1983). Mine: Self-definition in two-year-old boys. *Developmental Psychology, 19*, 544–549.

Lewinsohn, P. M. (1974). A behavioral approach to depression. In R. J. Friedman & M. M. Katz (Eds.), *The psychology of depression: Contemporary theory and research*. New York: Wiley.

Lewis, M. (1987). Social development in infancy and early childhood. In J. Osofsky (Ed.), *Handbook of infant development*. New York: Wiley.

Lewis, M., & Feinman, S. (Eds.). (1991). *Social influences and socialization in infancy*. New York: Plenum.

Lewis, M., & Feiring, C. (1989). Infant, mother, and mother-infant interaction behavior and subsequent attachment. *Child Development, 60*, 831–837.

Lewis, M., Feiring, C., & Kotsonis, M. (1984). The social network of the young child: A developmental perspective. In M. Lewis (Ed.), *Beyond the dyad: The genesis of behavior*. New York: Plenum.

Lewis, M., & Rosenblum, L. (Eds.). (1974). *The effect of the infant on its caregiver*. New York: Wiley.

Li, D-K., Mueller, B. A., Hickok, D. E., Daling, J. R., Fantel, A. G., Checkoway, H., & Weiss, N. S. (1996). Maternal smoking during pregnancy and the risk of congenital urinary tract anomalies. *American Journal of Public Health, 86*, 249–252.

Lieberman, M., Doyle, A., & Markiewicz, D. (1999). Developmental patterns in security of attachment to mother and father in late childhood and early adolescence: Associations with peer relations. *Child Development, 70*, 202–213.

Lillard, A. (1999). Wanting to be it: Children's understanding of intentions underlying pretense. *Child Development, 69*, 981–993.

Linn, M. C., & Hyde, J. S. (1991). Trends in cognitive and psychosocial gender differences. In R. M. Lerner, A. C. Peterson, & J. Brooks-Gunn (Eds.), *Encyclopedia of adolescence*. New York: Garland.

Lipman, E. L., Offord, D. R., & Dooley, M. D. (1996). What do we know about children from single-mother families? Questions and answers from the National Longitudinal Survey of Children and Youth. In Human Resources Development Canada & Statistics Canada. *Growing up in Canada*. National Longitudinal Survey of Children and Youth. Ottawa: Author.

Lisina, M. I., & Neverovich, Y. Z. (1971). Development of movements and formation of motor habits. In A. Z. Zaporozlets & D. B. Elkonin (Eds.), *The psychology of preschool children*. Cambridge, MA: MIT Press.

...n, N., & Peskin, H. (1980). Perspectives on adolescence from longitudinal research. In J. Adelson (Ed.), *Handbook of adolescent psychology*. New York: Wiley.

Loeber, R., & Stouthamer-Loeber, M. (1998). Development of juvenile aggression and violence: Some common misconceptions and controversies. *American Psychologist, 53*, 221–241.

Londerville, S., & Main, M. (1981). Security of attachment, compliance and maternal training methods in the second year of life. *Developmental Psychology, 17*, 289–299.

Lonigan, C. J., Fischel, J. E., Whitehurst, G. J., Arnold, D. S., & Valdez-Menchaca, M. C. (1992). The role of otitis media in the development of expressive language disorder. *Developmental Psychology, 28*(3), 430–440.

Lorenz, K. Z. (1952). *King Solomon's ring*. New York: Crowell.

Lowenthal, B. (1996, Spring). Teaching social skills to preschoolers with special needs. *Journal of Applied Childhood Education International*, 137–140.

Lozoff, B., Klein, N. K., Nelson, E. C., McClish, D. K., Manuel, M., & Chacon, M. E. (1998). Behavior of infants with iron-deficiency anemia. *Child Development, 69*, 24–36.

Lucariello, J., & Nelson, K. (1987). Remembering and planning talk between mothers and children. *Discourse Processes, 10*, 219–235.

Lynskey, M. T., Fergusson, D. M., & Horwood, L. J. (1998). The origins of the correlations between tobacco, alcohol, and cannabis use during adolescence. *Journal of Child Psychology and Psychiatry, 39*, 995–1004.

Lyons-Ruth, K., Repacholi, B., Alpern, B., & Connell, D. (1991). *Disorganized attachment behavior in infancy: Short-term stability, maternal correlates, and the prediction of aggression in kindergarten.* Symposium presented at the biennial meeting of the Society for Research in Child Development, Seattle.

Maccoby, E. E. (1979, March 15). *Parent-child interaction*. Paper presented at the biennial meeting of the Society for Research in Child Development.

Maccoby, E. E. (1980). *Social development: Psychological growth and the parent-child relationship*. New York: Harcourt Brace Jovanovich.

Maccoby, E. E. (1984). Socialization and developmental change. *Child Development, 55*, 317–328.

Maccoby, E. E. (1990). Gender and relationships: A developmental account. *American Psychologist, 45*, 513–520.

Maccoby, E. E. (1992). The role of parents in the socialization of children: An historical overview. *Developmental Psychology, 28*(6), 1006–1017.

Maccoby, E. E. (1994). The role of parents in the socialization of children: An historical overview. In R. D. Parke, P. A. Ornstein, J. J. Rieser, & C. Zahn-Waxler (Eds.), *A century of developmental psychology*. Washington, DC: American Psychological Association.

Maccoby, E. E. (1995). The two sexes and their social systems. In P. Moen, G. H. Elder, Jr., & K. Luscher (Eds.), *Examining lives in context: Perspectives on the ecology of human development*. Washington, DC: American Psychological Association.

Maccoby, E. E., & Feldman, S. S. (1972). Mother-attachment and stranger-reactions in the third year of life. *Monographs of the Society for Research in Child Development, 37* (1, Serial No. 146).

Maccoby, E. E., & Jacklin, C. N. (1974). *The psychology of sex differences*. Stanford: Stanford University Press.

Maccoby, E. E., & Martin, J.A. (1983). Socialization in the context of the family: Parent-child interaction. In P. H. Mussen (Ed.), *Handbook of child psychology: Vol. 4. Socialization, personality, and social development*. New York: Wiley.

MacFarlane, A. (1978, February). What a baby knows. *Human Nature, 1*, 81–86.

MacKay, W. E. (1972). *The contextual revolt in language teaching: Its theoretical foundations*. Quebec: Centre International de Recherche sur le Bilinguisme.

Maddux, J. E., Roberts, M. C., Sledden, E. A., & Wright, L. (1986). Developmental issues in child health psychology. *American Psychologist, 41*(1), 25–34.

Madsen, M. C. (1971). Developmental and cross-cultural differences in the cooperative and competitive behavior of young children. *Journal of Cross-Cultural Psychology, 2*, 365–371.

Madsen, M. C., & Shapira, A. (1970). Cooperative and competitive behavior of urban Afro-American, Anglo-American, Mexican-American, and Mexican village children. *Developmental Psychology, 3*, 16–20.

Magenis, R. E., Overton, K. M., Chamberlin, J., Brady, T., & Lorrien, E. (1977). Parental origin of the extra chromosome in Down's syndrome. *Human Genetics, 37*, 7–16.

Magnusson, D. N. (1996, August). *The person in developmental research*. Paper presented at the XXVI International Congress of Psychology, Montreal.

Maguire, M. H., & McAlpine, L. (1996). Attautsikut/together: Understanding cultural frames of reference. *The Alberta Journal of Educational Research, XLII*, 218–237.

Main, M., & Solomon, J. (1990). Procedures for identifying infants as disorganized/disoriented during the Ainsworth Strange Situation. In M. T. Greenberg, D. Cicchetti, & E. M. Cummings (Eds.), *Attachment in the preschool years: Theory, research and intervention*. Chicago: University of Chicago Press.

Maizels, M., Rosenbaum, D., & Keating, B. (1999). *Getting to dry: How to help your child overcome bedwetting*. Boston: The Harvard Common Press.

Makin, J. W., & Porter, R. H. (1989). Attractiveness of lactating females' breast odors to neonates. *Child Development, 60*, 803–810.

Mandel, H. P., & Marcus, S. I. (1996). *Could do better: Why children underachieve and what to do about it*. Toronto: HarperPerennial.

Mandell, F., McClain, M., & Reece, R. (1987). Sudden and unexpected death. *American Journal of Diseases of Children, 141*, 748–750.

Mandler, J. M. (1983). Representation. In J. H. Flavell & E. M. Markham (Eds.), *Handbook of child psychology: Cognitive development* (Vol. 3). New York: Wiley.

Mandler, J. M. (1988). How to build a baby: On the development of an accurate representational system. *Cognitive Development, 3*, 113–136.

Mandler, J. M. (1990, May–June). A new perspective on cognitive development in infancy. *American Scientist, 78*, 236–243.

Mandler, J. M., McDonough, L. (1998). On developing a knowledge base in infancy. *Developmental Psychology, 34*, 1274–1288.

Mangelsdorf, S. C., McHale, J. L., Plunkett, J. W., Dedrick, C. F., Berlin, M., Meisels, S. J., & Dichtellmiller, M. (1996). Attachment security in very low birth weight infants. *Developmental Psychology, 32*, 914–920.

Marcia, J. (1980). Identity in adolescence. In J. Adelson (Ed.), *Handbook of adolescent psychology*. New York: Wiley.

Marcoen, A., Goossens, L., & Caes, P. (1987). Loneliness in pre-through adolescence: Exploring the contributions of a multi-dimensional approach. *Journal of Youth and Adolescence, 16*.

Marcotte, D. (1996). Irrational beliefs and depression in adolescence. *Adolescence, 31,* 935–951.

Markstrom, C. A., Berman, R. C., Sabino, V. M., & Turner, B. (1998). The ego virtue of fidelity as a psychosocial rite of passage in the transition from adolescence to adulthood. *Child & Youth Care Forum, 27,* 337–355.

Marshall, S. K., & Markstrom-Adams, C. (1995). Attitudes on interfaith dating among Jewish adolescents. *Journal of Family Issues, 16,* 787–809.

Martin, C. L., & Halverson, C. F., Jr. (1981). A schematic processing model of sex-typing and stereotyping in children. *Child Development, 52,* 1119–1134.

Martin, J. L., & Ross, H. S. (1995). The development of aggression within sibling conflict. *Early Education and Development, 6,* 335–358.

Masataka, N. (1996). Perception of motherese in a signed language by 6-month-old deaf infants. *Developmental Psychology, 32,* 874–879.

Mascola, M. A., VanVunakis, H., Tager, I. B., Speizer, F. E., & Hanrahan, J. P. (1998). *American Journal of Public Health, 88,* 893–895.

Maslow, A. H. (1954). *Motivation and personality.* New York: Harper and Brothers.

Masten, A. S., & Coatsworth, J. D. (1998). The development of competence in favorable and unfavorable environments. *American Psychologist, 53,* 205–220.

Mates, D., & Allison, K. R. (1992). Sources of stress and coping responses of high school students. *Adolescence, 27*(106), 463–474.

Matsumoto, D. (1994). *People: Psychology from a cultural perspective.* Pacific Grove, CA: Brooks Cole.

Mauer, D., & Lewis, T. L. (1993). Visual outcomes after infantile cataract. In K. Simons (Ed.), *Early visual development: Normal and abnormal.* Oxford: Oxford University Press.

Maurer, D., & Maurer, C. (1988). *The world of the newborn.* New York: Basic Books.

Maurer, D., & Mondloch, C. J. (1996, October). *Synesthesia: A stage of normal infancy?* Presented at the meeting of the International Society for Psychophysics, Padua, Italy.

Maurer, D., Nnubia, N., & Lewis, T. L. (1996). *Infant behavior and development.* Norwood, NJ: Ablex Publishing Corp.

McBride, S. L. (1990, Fall). Maternal moderators of child care: The role of maternal separation anxiety. *New Directions for Child Development, 49,* 53–70.

McCall, R. B., Eichorn, D. H., & Hogarty, P. S. (1977). Transitions in early mental development. *Monographs of the Society for Research in Child Development, 42*(3, Serial No. 171), 1–75.

McClelland, D. C. (1955). Some social consequences of achievement motivation. In M. R. Jones (Ed.), *Nebraska symposium on motivation* (Vol. 3). Lincoln: University of Nebraska Press.

McLoyd, V. C. (1998). Socioeconomic disadvantage and child development. *American Psychologist, 53,* 185–204.

McCord, W., McCord, J., & Zola, I. K. (1959). *Origins of crime.* New York: Columbia University Press.

McGhee, P. E. (1979). *Humor: Its origin and development.* San Francisco: W. H. Freeman.

McGlothlin, W. H., & West, L. J. (1968). The marijuana problem: An overview. *American Journal of Psychiatry, 125,* 370–378.

McGraw, M. (1935). *Growth: A study of Johnny and Timmy.* New York: Appleton-Century.

McIlroy, A. (1999, May 25). Fertility clinics face curbs: Ottawa to introduce far-reaching controls on reproductive technology. *The Globe and Mail,* pp. A1, A4.

McIntyre, L. (1996). Starting out. In Human Resources Development Canada & Statistics Canada. *Growing up in Canada.* National Longitudinal Survey of Children and Youth. Ottawa: Author.

McIntyre, L., Connor, S., & Warren, J. (1998). *A glimpse of child hunger in Canada.* Ottawa: Human Resources Development Canada.

McKim, W. A. (1997). *Drugs and behavior: An introduction to behavioral pharmacology* (3rd ed.). Upper Saddle River, NJ: Prentice-Hall.

McKusick, V. A. (1988). *Mendelian inheritance in man: Catalogs of autosomal dominant, autosomal recessive, and X-linked phenotypes* (7th ed.). Baltimore: Johns Hopkins University Press.

McLoughlin, M., Shryer, T. L., Goode, E. E., & McAuliffe, K. (1988, August 8). Men vs. women. *U.S. News & World Report.*

McNeill, D. (1972). *The acquisition of language: The study of developmental psycholinguistics.* New York: Harper & Row.

McNeilly-Choque, M. K., Hart, C. H., Robinson, C. C., Nelson, L. J., & Olsen, S. F. (1996). Overt and relational aggression on the playground: Correspondence among different informants. *Journal of Research in Childhood Education, 11,* 47–67.

Mead, G. H. (1934). *Mind, self, and society: From the standpoint of a social behaviorist.* Chicago: University of Chicago Press.

Mead, M., & Newton, N. (1967). Cultural patterning of perinatal behavior. In S. A. Richardson & A. F. Guttermacher (Eds.), *Childbearing: Its social and psychological aspects.* Baltimore: Williams & Wilkins.

Meadow, K. P. (1975). The development of deaf children. In E. M. Hetherington (Ed.), *Review of child development research* (Vol. 5). Chicago: University of Chicago Press.

Meltzoff, A. N. (1988a). Infant imitation and memory: Nine month olds in immediate and deferred tests. *Child Development, 59,* 217–225.

Meltzoff, A. N. (1988b). Infant imitation after a 1-week delay: Long-term memory for novel acts and multiple stimuli. *Developmental Psychology, 24*(4), 470–476.

Meltzoff, A. N., & Borton, R. W. (1979). Intermodel matching by human neonates. *Nature, 282,* 403–404.

Meltzoff, A. N., & Moore, M. K. (1989). *Imitation in newborn infants: Exploring the range of gestures imitated and the underlying mechanisms.* National Institute of Child Health and Human Development (HD-22514).

Mendelson, B. K., White, D. R., & Mendelson, M. J. (1996). Self-esteem and body-esteem: Effects of gender, age, and weight. *Journal of Applied Developmental Psychology, 17,* 321–346.

Mendelson, M. (1990). Psychoanalytic views on depression. In B. B. Wolman & G. Stricker (Eds.), *Depressive disorders: Facts, theories and treatment methods.* New York: Wiley.

Mendelson, M. J., Aboud, F. E., & Lanthier, R. P. (1994a). Kindergartners' relationships with siblings, peers, and friends. *Merrill-Palmer Quarterly, 40,* 416–435.

Mendelson, M. J., & Aboud, F. E., & Lanthier, R. P. (1994b). Personality predictors of friendship and popularity in kindergarten. *Journal of Applied Developmental Psychology, 15,* 413–435.

Mervis, C. B. (1987). Child-basic object categories and early lexical development. In U. Neisser (Ed.), *Concepts and conceptual development: Ecological and intellectual factors in categorization.* London: Cambridge University Press.

Metcoff, J., Costiloe, J. P., Crosby, W., Bentle, L., Seshachalam, D., Sandstead, H. H., Bodwell, C. E., Weaver, F., & McClain, P. (1981). Maternal nutrition and fetal outcome. *American Journal of Clinical Nutrition, 34,* 708–721.

Mikulincer, M., & Orbach, I. (1995). Attachment styles and repressive defensiveness: The accessibility and architecture of affective memories. *Journal of Personality and Social Psychology, 68,* 917–925.

Miles, B. S. (1995). Are adolescents competent decision makers? In K. Covell (Ed.), *Readings in child development: A Canadian perspective.* Toronto: Nelson.

Miller, B. C., & Sneesby, K. R. (1988). Educational correlates of adolescents' sexual attitudes and behavior. *Journal of Youth and Adolescence, 17,* 521–530.

Miller, C. L., Miceli, P. J., Whitman, T. L., & Borkowski, J. G. (1996). Cognitive readiness to parent and intellectual-emotional development in children of adolescent mothers. *Developmental Psychology, 32,* 533–540.

Miller, P. (1989). *Theories of developmental psychology* (2nd ed.). New York: Freeman.

Miller, P. H., & Aloise, P. A. (1989). Young children's understanding of the psychological causes of behavior: A review. *Child Development, 60,* 257–285.

Miller, R. (1990). *What are schools for? Holistic education in American culture.* Brandon, VT: Holistic Education Press.

Miller-Jones, D. (1989). Culture and testing. *American Psychologist, 44*(2), 360–366.

Minde, K. (1993). Prematurity and serious medical illness in infancy: Implications for development and intervention. In C. H. Zeanah, Jr. (Ed.), *Handbook of infant mental health.* New York: Guilford.

Mock, N. B., Bertrand, J. T., & Mangani, N. (1986). Correlates and implications of breastfeeding practices in Bas Zaire. *Journal of Biosocial Science, 18,* 231–245.

Moen, P., Elder, G. H., Jr., & Luscher, K. (1995). *Examining lives in context: Perspectives on the ecology of human development.* Washington, DC: American Psychological Association.

Money, J. (1980). *Love and love sickness: The science of sex, gender differences and pair-bonding.* Baltimore: Johns Hopkins University Press.

Money, J., & Ehrhardt, A. A. (1972). *Man & woman, boy & girl.* Baltimore: Johns Hopkins University Press.

Monmaney, T. (1988, May 16). Preventing early births. *Newsweek.*

Montagu, M. F. (1950). Constitutional and prenatal factors in infant and child health. In M. J. Senn (Ed.), *Symposium on the healthy personality.* New York: Josiah Macy Jr. Foundation.

Montemayor, R., & Brownlee, J. R. (1987). Fathers, mothers, and adolescents: Gender-based differences in parental roles during adolescence. *Journal of Youth and Adolescence, 16,* 281–292.

Moore, C., Angelopoulos, M., & Bennett, P. (1997). The role of movement in the development of joint visual attention. *Infant Behavior and Development.*

Moore, G. (1984, June). The superbaby myth. *Psychology Today,* 6–7.

Moore, M. K., Borton, R., & Darby, B. L. (1978). Visual tracking in young infants: Evidence for object permanence? *Journal of Experimental Child Psychology, 25,* 183–198.

Morelli, G.A., Rogoff, B., Oppenheim, D., & Goldsmith, D. (1992). Cultural variation in infants' sleeping arrangements: Questions of independence. *Developmental Psychology, 28,* 604–613.

Morrison, S. J., Ames, E. W., & Chisholm, K. (1995). The development of children adopted from Romanian orphanages. *Merrill-Palmer Quarterly, 41,* 411–430.

Morse, D. L., Lessner, L., Medvesky, M. G., Glebatis, D. M., & Novick, L. F. (1991, May Supplement). Geographic distribution of newborn HIV seroprevalence in relation to four sociodemographic variables. *American Journal of Public Health, 81,* 25–29.

Mosher, W. D., & Pratt, W. F. (1990). Fecundity and fertility in the United States, 1965–88. *Advanced Data from Vital and Health Statistics, 192.* Hyattsville, MD: National Center for Health Statistics.

Moss, E., Rousseau, D., Parent, S., & Saintonge, J. (1998). Correlates of attachment at school age: Maternal reported stress, mother-child interaction, and behavior problems. *Child Development, 69,* 1390–1405.

Muckle, G., Dewailly, E., & Ayotte, P. (1998). Prenatal exposure of Canadian children to polychlorinated biphenyls and mercury. *Canadian Journal of Public Health, 89*(Suppl. 1), 20–36.

Muir, D., & Field, J. (1979). Newborn infants orient to sounds. *Child Development, 50,* 431–436.

Muris, P., Steerneman, P., Merckelbach, H., & Meesters, C. (1996). The role of parental fearfulness and modeling in children's fears. *Behavior Research and Therapy, 34,* 265–268.

Murphy, L. B. (1962). *The widening world of childhood: Paths toward mastery.* New York: Basic Books.

Murstein, B. I., Chalpin, M. J., Heard, K. V., & Vyse, S. A. (1989). Sexual behavior, drugs, and relationship patterns on a college campus over thirteen years. *Adolescence, 24,* 125–139.

Mussen, P. H., Conger, J. J., & Kagan, J. (1974). *Child development and personality.* New York: Harper & Row.

Muuss, R. E. (1986, Summer). Adolescent eating disorder: Bulimia. *Adolescence,* 257–267.

Myers, J., Jusczyk, P. W., Kemler-Nelson, D. G., Charles-Luce, J., Woodward, A. L., & Hirsh-Pasek, K. (1996). Infants' sensitivity to word boundaries in fluent speech. *Journal of Child Language, 23,* 1–30.

Myers, N. A., Clifton, R. K., & Clarkson, M. G. (1987). When they were very young: Almost-threes remember two years ago. *Infant Behavior and Development, 10,* 123–132.

Myers, N. A., & Perlmutter, M. (1978). Memory in the years from two to five. In P. Ornstein (Ed.), *Memory development in children.* Hillsdale, NJ: Erlbaum.

Naeye, R. L. (1979). Weight gain and the outcome of pregnancy. *American Journal of Obstetrics and Gynecology, 135,* 3.

Naeye, R. L. (1980). Abruptio placentae and placenta previa: Frequency, perinatal mortality, and cigarette smoking. *Obstetrics and Gynecology, 55,* 701–704.

Naeye, R. L. (1981). Influence of maternal cigarette smoking during pregnancy on fetal and childhood growth. *Obstetrics and Gynecology, 57,* 18–21.

National Association for the Education of Young Children. (1986). *NAEYC position statement on developmentally appropriate practice in early childhood programs: Birth through age eight.* Washington, DC: Author.

National Crime Prevention Council. (1996). *Preventing crime by investing in families: Promoting positive outcomes in children prenatal to six years old.* Ottawa: Ministry of Justice.

National Crime Prevention Council. (1997). *Preventing crime by investing in families: Promoting positive outcomes in children six to twelve years old.* Ottawa: Ministry of Justice.

National Institute of Child Health and Human Development. (1998). Early child care and self-control, compliance, and problem behaviour at twenty-four and thirty-six months. *Child Development, 69*, 1145–1170.

Needleman, H. L., Schell, A., Bellinger, D., Leviton, A., & Alfred, E. N. (1990). The long-term exposure to low doses of lead in childhood. *New England Journal of Medicine, 322*, 83–88.

Nelson, C. A., Henschel, M., & Collins, P. (1993). Neural correlates of cross-modal recognition memory by 8-month-old human infants. *Developmental Psychology, 29*, 411–420.

Nelson, K. (1974). Concept, word and sentence: Interrelations in acquisition and development. *Psychological Review, 81*, 267–285.

Nelson, K. (1981). Individual differences in language development: Implications for development and language. *Developmental Psychology, 17*, 170–187.

Nelson, K. (1986). *Event knowledge: Structure and function in development.* Hillsdale, NJ: Erlbaum.

Nelson, K., Fibush, R., Hudson, J., & Lucariello, J. (1983). Scripts and the development of memory. In M. T. C. Chi (Ed.), *Trends in memory development research.* Basil, Switzerland: Carger.

Nemeth, R. J., & Bowling, J. M. (1985). Son preference and its effects on Korean lactation practices. *Journal of Biosocial Science, 17*, 451–459.

Neville, H. (1995). Developmental specificity in neurocognitive development in humans. In M. Gazzaniga (Ed.), *The cognitive neurosciences.* Cambridge, MA: Bradford.

New, R. (1988). Parental goals and Italian infant care. In R. B. LeVine, P. Miller, & M. West (Eds.), *New directions for child development: Vol. 40. Parental behavior in diverse societies* (pp. 51–63). San Francisco: Jossey-Bass.

Newman, J. (1995). How breast milk protects newborns. *Scientific American, 273*, 76–79.

Newman, L. S. (1990). Intentional and unintentional memory in young children: Remembering vs. playing. *Journal of Experimental Child Psychology, 50*, 243–258.

Newport, E. L. (1990). Maturational constraints on language learning. *Cognitive Science, 14*, 11–28.

Ney, P. G. (1988). Transgenerational child abuse. *Child Psychiatry and Human Development, 18*, 151–168.

Nichols, B. (1990). *Moving and Learning: The elementary school physical education experience.* St. Louis, MO: Times Mirror/Mosby College Publishing.

Nicoladis, E., & Genesee, F. (1996). A longitudinal study of pragmatic differentiation in young bilingual children. *Language Learning, 46*, 439–464.

Nicolopoulou, A. (1993). Play, cognitive development, and the social world: Piaget, Vygotsky, and Beyond. *Human Development, 36*, 1–23.

Nilson, B. F. (1997). *Plans for observing and recording young children.* Boston: Delmar.

Nilsson, L. (1990). *A child is born.* New York: Delacorte.

1997 Declaration of the Environment Leaders of the Eight on Children's Environmental Health. (1998). *Canadian Journal of Public Health, 89*(Suppl. 1), 5–8.

Nnubia, N., Maurer, D., & Lewis, T. L. (1992). The effect of sucking on infants' orientation toward peripheral visual stimuli. *Infant Behaviour and Development, 15*, 603.

Nofstad, P., Fugelseth, D., Qvigstad, E., Zahlsen, K., Magnus, P., & Lindemann, R. (1998). Nicotine concentration in the hair of nonsmoking mothers and size of offspring. *American Journal of Public Health, 88*, 120–123.

Nordentoft, M., Lou, H. C., Hansen, D., Nim, J., Pryds, O., Rubin, P., & Hemmingsen, R. (1996). Intrauterine growth retardation and premature delivery: The influence of maternal smoking and psychosocial factors. *American Journal of Public Health, 86*, 347–353.

Normand, C. L., Zoccolillo, M., Tremblay, R. E., McIntyre, L., Boulerice, B., McDuff, P., Perusse, D., & Barr, R. G. (1996). In the beginning: Looking for the roots of babies' difficult temperament. In Human Resources Development Canada & Statistics Canada. *Growing up in Canada.* National Longitudinal Survey of Children and Youth. Ottawa: Author.

Northrup, D. A., Ashley, M. J., & Ferrence, R. (1998). The Ontario ban on smoking on school property: Perceived impact on smoking. *Canadian Journal of Public Health, 89*, 224–227.

Nosphitz, J. D. (1990). *Stressors and the adjustment disorders.* New York: Wiley.

Nowakowski, R. S. (1993). Basic concepts of CNS development. In M. Johnson (Ed.), *Brain development and cognition.* Oxford: Blackwell.

Nugent, J. K., Greene, S., & Mazor, K. (1990, October). *The effects of maternal alcohol and nicotine use during pregnancy on birth outcome.* Paper presented at Bebe XXI Simposio Internacional, Lisbon, Portugal.

Oates, K., & Shrimpton, S. (1991). Children's memories for stressful and non-stressful events. *Medicine, Science and the Law, 31*, 4–10.

Ochs, E. (1986). Introduction. In B. B. Schieffelin & E. Ochs (Eds.), *Language socialization across cultures.* Cambridge, England: Cambridge University Press.

O'Connor, T. G., Deater-Deckard, K., Fulker, D., Rutter, M., & Plomin, R. (1998). Genotype-environment correlations in late childhood and early adolescence: Antisocial behavioral problems and coercive parenting. *Developmental Psychology, 34*, 970–981.

O'Connor-Francoeur, P. (1983, April). *Children's concepts of health and their health behavior.* Paper presented at the meeting of the Society for Research in Child Development, Detroit.

Odom, S. L., & Brown, W. H. (1993). Social interaction skills for young children with disabilities in integrated settings. In C. A. Peck, S. L. Odom, & D. D. Bricker (Eds.), *Integrating young children with disabilities into community settings.* Baltimore, MD: Brookes.

Oller, D. K., & Eilers, R. E. (1988). The role of audition in infant babbling. *Child Development, 59*, 441–449.

Olshan, A. F., et al. (1990). Birth defects among offspring of firemen. *American Journal of Epidemiology, 131*, 312–321.

Olton, R. M., & Crutchfield, R. S. (1969). Developing the skills of productive thinking. In P. H. Mussen, J. Langer, & M. Covington (Eds.), *Trends and issues in developmental psychology.* New York: Holt, Rinehart & Winston.

Oncker, C. (1996). Nicotine replacement therapy during pregnancy. *American Journal of Health Behavior, 20*, 300–304.

Oni, G. A. (1987, October). Breast-feeding pattern in an urban Nigerian community. *Journal of Biolosocial Science, 19*(4), 453–462.

Onstad, K. (1997, March). What are we afraid of? The myth of youth crime. *Saturday Night*, 46–59.

Onyskiw, J. E., Harrison, M. J., & Magill-Evans, J. E. (1997). Past childhood experiences and current parent-infant interactions. *Western Journal of Nursing Research, 19,* 501–518.

Opie, I., & Opie, P. (1959). *The love and language of school children.* London: Oxford University Press.

Orlick, T. D., & Botterill, C. (1975). *Every kid can win.* Chicago: Nelson-Hall.

Ostrov, E., Offer, D., & Howard, K. I. (1989). Gender differences in adolescent symptomatology: A normative study. *Journal of the American Academy of Child and Adolescent Psychiatry, 28,* 394–398.

Ouellette, E. M., Rosett, H. L., & Rosman, N. P. (1977). Adverse effects on offspring of maternal alcohol abuse during pregnancy. *New England Journal of Medicine, 297,* 528–530.

Palkovitz, R. (1985). Fathers' birth attendance, early contact and extended contact with their newborns: A critical review. *Child Development, 56,* 392–406.

Papert, S. (1980). *Mindstorms: Children, computers and powerful thinking.* New York: Basic Books.

Papert, S. (1993). *The children's machine: Rethinking school in the age of the computer.* New York: Basic Books.

Papoušek, H. (1961). Conditioned head rotation reflexes in infants in the first three months of life. *Acta Paediatrica Scandinavica, 50,* 565–576.

Parke, R. (1996). *Fatherhood.* Cambridge, MA: Harvard University Press.

Parke, R. D. (1979). Perceptions of father-infant interaction. In J. Osofsky (Ed.), *Handbook of infant development.* New York: Wiley.

Parke, R. D. (1981). *Fathers.* Cambridge, MA: Harvard University Press.

Parke, R. D., & Collmer, C. (1975). Child abuse: An interdisciplinary analysis. In E. M. Hetherington (Ed.), *Review of child development research* (Vol. 5). Chicago: University of Chicago Press.

Parke, R. D., & Stearns, P. N. (1993). Fathers and child rearing. In G. H. Elder, Jr., J. Modell, & R. D. Parke (Eds.), *Children in time and place.* Cambridge, MA: Cambridge University Press.

Parke, R. D., & Tinsley, B. J. (1987). Family interaction in infancy. In J. D. Osofsky (Ed.), *Handbook of infant development* (2nd ed., pp. 579–641). New York: Wiley.

Parker, J. G., & Asher, S. R. (1987). Peer relations and later personal adjustment: Are low-accepted children at risk? *Psychological Bulletin, 102,* 357–389.

Parmelee, A. H., Jr. (1986). Children's illnesses: Their beneficial effects on behavioral development. *Child Development, 57,* 1–10.

Parten, M. B. (1932–33). Social participation among preschool children. *Journal of Abnormal and Social Psychology, 27,* 243–269.

Pascalis, O., & de Schonen, S. (1994). Recognition memory in 3-4 day old human neonates. *Neuroreport, 5,* 1721–1724.

Pascual-Leone, J. (1987). Organismic processes for Neo-Piagetian theories: A dialectical causal account of cognitive development. *International Journal of Psychology, 22,* 531–570.

Pascual-Leone, J. (1996). Vygotsky, Piaget, and the problems of Plato. *Swiss Journal of Psychology, 55,* 84–92.

Patterson, C. J., Kupersmidt, J. B., & Vaden, N.A. (1990). Income level, gender, ethnicity, and household composition as predictors of children's school-based competence. *Child Development, 61,* 485–494.

Patterson, M. L., & Werker, J. F. (in press). Matching phonetic information in lips and voice is robust in 4.5-month-old infants. *Infant Behavior and Development.*

Patton, G. C., Hibbert, M., Rosier, M. J., Carlin, J. B., Caust, J., & Bowes, G. (1996). Is smoking associated with depression and anxiety in teenagers? *American Journal of Public Health, 86,* 225–230.

Paulby, S. T. (1977). Imitative interaction. In H. R. Schaffer (Ed.), *Studies of mother-infant interaction.* London: Academic Press.

Paulesu, E., Harrison, J., Baron-Cohen, S., Watson, J., Goldstein, L., Heather, J., Frackowiak, R., & Frith, C. (1995). The physiology of coloured hearing: a PET activation study of colour-word synesthesia. *Brain, 118,* 661–676.

Pederson, D. R., & Moran, G. (1996). Expressions of the attachment relationship outside of the Strange Situation. *Child Development, 67,* 915–927.

Pederson, D. R., Moran, G., Bento, S., & Buckland, G. (1992). *Maternal sensitivity and attachment security: Concordance of home and lab-based measures.* Poster session presented at the International Conference on Infant Studies, Miami, FL.

Pederson, F., et al. (1979). Infant development in father-absent families. *Journal of Genetic Psychology, 135,* 51–61.

Pegg, J. E., & Werker, J. F. (1997). Adult and infant perception of two English phones. *Journal of Acoustical Society of America, 102,* 3742–3753.

Pellegrini, A. D. (1988). Elementary-school children's rough-and-tumble play and social competence. *Developmental Psychology, 24*(6), 802–806.

Pellegrini, A. D. (1989). Elementary school children's rough-and-tumble play. *Early childhood Research Quarterly, 4,* 245–260.

Pellegrini, A. D., & Smith, P. K. (1998). Physical activity play: The nature and function of a neglected aspect of play. *Child Development, 69,* 577–598.

Pelletier, J. (1998). A comparison of children's understanding of school in regular English language and French immersion kindergartens. *The Canadian Modern Language Review,* 239–259.

Pepler, D. J., & Craig, W. M. (1995). A peek behind the fence: Naturalistic observations of aggressive children with remote audiovisual recording. *Developmental Psychology, 31,* 548–553.

Pepler, D. J., Craig, W. M., & Roberts, W. L. (1998). Observations of aggressive and nonaggressive children on the school playground. *Merrill-Palmer Quarterly, 44,* 55–76.

Perlman, M., & Ross, H. S. (1997). The benefits of parent intervention in children's disputes: An examination of concurrent changes in children's fighting styles. *Child Development, 64,* 690–700.

Perrin, J., Guyer, B., & Lawrence, J. M. (1992). Health care services for children and adolescents. In R. E. Behrman (Ed.), *The future of children.* Los Angeles, CA: Center for the Future of Children of the David and Lucile Packard Foundation.

Perry, B. (1995). Incubated in terror: Neurodevelopmental factors in the cycle of violence. In J. Osofsky (Ed.), *Children, youth and violence: Searching for solutions.* New York: The Guilford Press.

Perry, D. G., & Bussey, K. (1984). *Social development.* Englewood Cliffs, NJ: Prentice-Hall.

Peterson, A. C., Compas, B. E., Brooks-Gunn, J., Stemmler, M., Ey, S., & Grant, K. E. (1993). Depression in adolescence. *American Psychologist, 48,* 155–168.

Peterson, A. C., & Taylor, B. (1980). The biological approach to adolescence: Biological change and psychological adaptation. In J. Adelson (Ed.), *Handbook of adolescent psychology.* New York: Wiley.

Peterson, C., & Bell, M. (1996). Children's memory for traumatic injury. *Child Development, 67,* 3045–3070.

Petrakos, H., & Howe, N. (1996). The influence of the physical design of the dramatic play center on children's play. *Early Childhood Research Quarterly, 11,* 63–77.

Pharoah, P. O. D., & Alberman, E. D. (1990). Annual statistical review. *Archives of Disease in Childhood, 65,* 147–151.

Phillips, D. (1984). The illusion of incompetence among academically competent children. *Child Development, 55,* 2000–2016.

Piaget, J. (1926). *The language and thought of the child.* London: Kegan, Paul, Trench & Trubner.

Piaget, J. (1950). *The psychology of intelligence* (M. Percy & D. E. Berlyne, Trans.). New York: Harcourt Brace.

Piaget, J. (1951). *Play, dreams and imitation in childhood.* New York: Norton.

Piaget, J. (1952). *The origins of intelligence in children* (M. Cook, Trans.). New York: International Universities Press. (Original work published 1936)

Piaget, J. (1955). *The language and thought of the child.* New York: World.

Piaget, J. (1962). *Plays, dreams, and imitation.* New York: Norton.

Piaget, J. (1965). *The moral judgment of the child* (M. Gabain, Trans.). New York: Free Press. (Original work published 1932)

Piaget, J. (1970). Piaget's theory. In P. H. Mussen (Ed.), *Carmichael's manual of child psychology* (3rd ed., Vol. 1). New York: Wiley.

Piaget, J. (1972). Intellectual evolution from adolescence to adulthood. *Human Development, 15,* 1–12.

Piccigallo, P. R. (1988, Fall). Preschool: Head start or hard push? *Social Policy, 1988,* 45–48.

Pickett, W., Carr, P. A., Mowat, D. L., & Chui, A. (1996). Playground equipment hazards and associated injuries in Kingston and area. *Canadian Journal of Public Health, 87,* 237–239.

Pierce, J. P., & Gilpin, E. (1996). How long will today's new adolescent smoker be addicted to cigarettes? *American Journal of Public Health, 86,* 253–255.

Pines, M. (1981, September). The civilizing of Genie. *Psychology Today,* 28–34.

Pinker, S. (1994). *The language instinct.* New York: HarperPerennial.

Pinker, S. (1995). Language acquisition. In D.N. Osherson (Gen. Ed.), L. R. Gleitman & M. Liberman (Eds.), *An invitation to cognitive science: Language* (Vol. 1). Cambridge, MA: MIT Press.

Pitcher, E. G., & Schultz, L. H. (1983). *Boys and girls at play: The development of sex roles.* New York: Praeger.

Pleck, J. H. (1985). *Working wives, working husbands.* Beverly Hills, CA: Sage.

Plomin, R. (1983). Developmental behavioral genetics. *Child Development, 54,* 25–29.

Plomin, R. (1990). *Nature and nurture: An introduction to human behavioral genetics.* Pacific Grove, CA: Brooks/Cole.

Plomin, R., & Daniels, D. (1987). Why are children in the same family so different from one another? *Behavioral and Brain Sciences, 10,* 1–60.

Plomin, R., & Rutter, M. (1998). Child development, molecular genetics, and what to do with genes once they are found. *Child Development, 69,* 1223–1242.

Plowden, B. (1967). *Children and their primary schools: A report of the Central Advisory Council for Education in England* (Vol. 1). London: Her Majesty's Stationery Office.

Poest, C. A., Williams, J. R., Witt, D. D., & Atwood, M. E. (1989). Physical activity patterns of preschool children. *Early Childhood Research Quarterly, 4,* 367–376.

Polka, L., & Werker, J. F. (1994). Developmental changes in perception of nonnative vowel contrasts. *Journal of Experimental Psychology: Human Perception and Performance, 20,* 421–435.

Pollock, S. W., & Thompson, C. L. (1995). The HIV-infected child in therapy. In N. Boyd-Franklin, G. L. Steiner, & M. G. Boland (Eds.), *Children, families, and HIV/AIDS.* New York: The Guilford Press.

Pomerleau, A., Bolduc, D., Malcuit, G., & Cossette, L. (1990). Pink or blue: Environmental gender stereotypes in the first two years of life. *Sex Roles, 22*(5/6), 359–367.

Poole, W. (1987, July/August). The first 9 months of school. *Hippocrates,* 66–73.

Power, C., & Reimer, J. (1978). Moral atmosphere: An educational bridge between moral judgment and action. *New Directions for Child Development, 2.*

Powers, S. I., Hauser, S. T., & Kilner, L. A. (1989). Adolescent mental health. *American Psychologist, 44,* 200–208.

Powlishta, K. K., Serbin, L. A., Doyle, A. B., & White, D. R. (1994). Gender, ethnic, and body type biases: The generality of prejudice in childhood. *Developmental Psychology, 30,* 526–536.

Pratt, K. C. (1954). The neonate. In L. Carmichael (Ed.), *Manual of child psychology* (2nd ed.). New York: Wiley.

Prechtl, H., & Beintema, D. (1965). *The neurological examination of the full term newborn infant* (Clinics in Developmental Medicine Series No. 12). Philadelphia: Lippincott.

Purvis, A. (1990, November 26). The sins of the fathers. *Time,* 68.

Putallaz, M. (1983). Predicting children's sociometric status from their behavior. *Child Development, 54,* 1417–1426.

Quadrel, M. J., Fischhoff, B., and Davis, W. (1993). Adolescent (in)vulnerability. *American Psychologist, 48*(2), 102–116.

Queenan, J. T. (1975, August). The Rh-immunized pregnancy. *Consultant,* 96–99.

Qureshi, R. B., & Qureshi, S. M. M. (1983). Pakistani Canadians: The making of the Muslim community. In E. H. Waugh, B. Ab-Laban, & R. B. Qureshi (Eds.), *The Muslim community in North America.* Edmonton: University of Alberta Press.

Radbill, S. (1974). A history of child abuse and infanticide. In R. Helfer & C. Kempe (Eds.), *The battered child.* Chicago: University of Chicago Press.

Radke-Yarrow, M., Cummings, E. M., Kuczynski, L., & Chapman, M. (1997). Patterns of attachment in two- and three-year-olds in normal families and families with parental depression. In M Gauvain & M. Cole (Eds.), *Readings on the development of children* (2nd ed.). New York: W. H. Freeman and Company.

Rahbar, F., Momeni, J., Fumufod, A. K., & Westney, L. (1985). Prenatal care and perinatal mortality in a black population. *Obstetrics and Gynecology, 65*(3), 327–329.

Raizenne, M., Dales, R., & Burnett, R. (1998). Air pollution and children's health. *Canadian Journal of Public Health, 89*(Suppl. 1), 43–48.

Ramey, C. T., & Ramey, S. L. (1999). *Right from birth: Building your child's foundation for life.* New York: Goddard Press.

Raphael-Leff, J. (1991). *Psychological processes of childbearing.* New York: Chapman and Hall.

Ratner, H. H. (1984). Memory demands and the development of young children's memory. *Child Development, 55,* 2173–2191.

Ratner, N., & Bruner, J. S. (1978). Games, social exchange and the acquisition of language. *Journal of Child Development, 5,* 1–15.

Ratner, N. B., & Pye, C. (1984). Higher pitch in BT is not universal: Acoustic evidence from Quiche Mayan. *Journal of Child Language, 11,* 515–522.

Rauste-von Wright, M. (1989). Body image satisfaction in adolescent girls and boys: A longitudinal study. *Journal of Youth and Adolescence, 18,* 71–83.

Reich, P. A. (1986). *Language development.* Englewood Cliffs, NJ: Prentice-Hall.

Reid, M. (1990). Prenatal diagnosis and screening. In J. Garcia, R. Kilpatrick, & M. Richards (Eds.), *The politics of maternity care* (pp. 300–323). Oxford: Clarendon Press.

Reiss, I. L. (1971). *The family system in America.* New York: Holt, Rinehart & Winston.

Renaud, A., Ryan, B., Cloutier, D., Urbanek, A., & Haley, N. (1997). Knowledge and attitude assessment of Quebec daycare workers and parents regarding HIV/AIDS and hepatitis B. *Canadian Journal of Public Health, 88,* 23–26.

Reuhl, K. R., & Chang, L. W. (1979). Effects of methylmercury on the development of the nervous system: A review. *Neurotoxicology, 1,* 21–55.

Rice, S. G. (1990). *Putting the play back in exercise.* Unpublished manuscript.

Richardson, S. O. (1992). Historical perspectives on dyslexia. *Journal of Learning Disabilities, 25*(1), 40–47.

Richman, A. L., LeVine, R. A., New, R. A., Howrigan, G. A., Welles-Nystrom, B., & LeVine, S. E. (1988, Summer). Maternal behavior to infants in five cultures. In R. A. LeVine, P. M. Miller, & M. M. West (Eds.), *New Directions for Child Development: Vol. 40. Personal behavior in diverse societies* (pp. 81–98). San Francisco: Jossey-Bass.

Ricks, S. S. (1985). Father-infant interactions: A review of empirical research. *Family Relations, 34,* 505–511.

Riddel, J., & Moon, M. W. (1996). Children with HIV becoming adolescents: Caring for long-term survivors. *Pediatric Nursing, 22,* 220–227.

Rizzo, T. A., & Corsaro, W. A. (1988). Toward a better understanding of Vygotsky's process of internalization: Its role in the development of the concept of friendship. *Developmental Review, 8,* 219–237.

Roberton, M. A., and Halverson, L. E. (1988). The development of locomotor coordination: longitudinal change and invariance. *Journal of Motor Behavior, 20*(3), 197–241.

Roberts, M., White, R., & McLaughlin, T. F. (1998). Useful classroom accommodations for teaching children with ADD and ADHD. *B.C. Journal of Special Education, 21,* 71–84.

Roberts, W., & Strayer, J. (1996). Empathy, emotional expressiveness, and prosocial behavior. *Child Development, 67,* 449–470.

Robertson, M. (1984). Changing motor patterns during childhood. In J. R. Thomas (Ed.), *Motor development during childhood and adolescence.* Minneapolis, MN: Burgess.

Robinson, I. E., & Jedlicka, D. (1982). Change in sexual behavior of college students from 1965–1980: A research note. *Journal of Marriage and the Family, 44,* 237–240.

Rochat, P. (1989). Object manipulation and exploration in 2- to 5-month-old infants. *Developmental Psychology, 25*(6), 871–884.

Rogers, M. F., White, C. R., Sanders, R., Schable, C., Ksell, T. E., Wasserman, R. L., Bellanti, J. A., Peters, S. M., & Wary, B. B. (1990). Lack of transmission of human immunodeficiency virus from infected children to their household contacts. *Pediatrics, 85,* 210.

Rogoff, B. (1990). *Apprenticeship in thinking: Cognitive development in social context.* New York: Oxford University Press.

Rogoff, B. (1993). Commentary. *Human Development, 36,* 24–26.

Rohrer, J. C. (1996, Summer). "We interrupt this program to show you a bombing": Children and schools respond to a televised war. *J of ACEI,* 201–205.

Romney, J. C., Romney, D. M., & Menzies, H. M. (1995). Reading for pleasure in French: A study of the reading habits and the interests of French immersion children. *The Canadian Modern Language Review, 51,* 474–493.

Roscoe, B., Diana, M. S., & Brooks, R. H., II. (1987). Early, middle, and late adolescents' views on dating and factors influencing partner selection. *Adolescence, 12,* 59–68.

Rose, S. A., Feldman, J., & Wallace, I. (1992). Infant information processing in relation to six-year cognitive outcomes. *Child Development, 63,* 1126–1141.

Rose, S. A., Gottfried, A. W., & Bridger, W. H. (1981). Cross-modal transfer in 6-month-old infants. *Developmental Psychology, 17,* 661–669.

Rosen, K. S., & Rothbaum, F. (1993). Quality of parental caregiving and security of attachment. *Developmental Psychology, 29,* 358–367.

Rosenfeld, A. (1974a, September 7). If Oedipus' parents had only known. *Saturday Review,* 49f.

Rosenfeld, A. (1974b, March 23). Starve the child, famish the future. *Saturday Review,* 59.

Rosenstein, D., & Oster, H. (1988). Differential facial response to four basic tastes in newborns. *Child Development, 59,* 1555–1568.

Rosenthal, E. (1990, January 4). New insights on why some children are fat offers clues on weight loss. *New York Times,* p. B8.

Rosenthal, J. A. (1988). Patterns of reported child abuse and neglect. *Child Abuse and Neglect, 12,* 263–271.

Rosenthal, R., & Jacobson, L. (1968). *Pygmalion in the classroom: Teacher expectation and pupil's intellectual development.* New York: Harper & Row.

Rosett, H. L., Weiner, L., & Edelin, K. C. (1981). Strategies for prevention of fetal alcohol effects. *Obstetrics and Gynecology, 57,* 1–16.

Roskinski, R. R. (1977). *The development of visual perception.* Santa Monica, CA: Goodyear.

Ross, A. O. (1977). *Learning disability, the unrealized potential.* New York: McGraw-Hill.

Ross, D. P., Scott, K., & Kelly, M. A. (1996). Overview: Children in Canada in the 1990's. In Human Resources Development Canada & Statistics Canada. *Growing up in Canada.* National Longitudinal Survey of Children and Youth. Ottawa: Author.

Ross, H. S., Filyer, R. E., Lollis, S. P., Perlman, M., & Martin, J. (1994). Administering justice in the family. *Journal of Family Psychology, 8,* 254–273.

Ross, H. S., & Lollis, S. P. (1987). Communication within infant social games. *Developmental Psychology, 23,* 241–248.

Ross, L. (1981). The "intuitive scientist" formulation and its developmental implications. In J. H. Flavell & L. Ross (Eds.), *Social cognitive development.* Cambridge, England: Cambridge University Press.

Rotenberg, K. J., & Eisenberg, N. (1997). Developmental differences in the understanding of and the reaction to others' inhibition of emotional expression. *Developmental Psychology, 33,* 526–537.

Roug, L., Landberg, I., & Lundberg, L. J. (1989, February). Phonetic development in early infancy: A study of four Swedish children during the first eighteen months of life. *Journal of Child Language, 16*(1), 19–40.

Rovee-Collier, C. (1987). Learning and memory in infancy. In J. Osofsky (Ed.), *Handbook of infant development* (2nd ed.). New York: Wiley.

Rowe, D. C., & Rogers, J. L. (1995). Behavioral genetics, adolescent deviance, and "d": Contributions and issues. In G. R. Adams (Ed.), *Advances in adolescent psychology*. Hillsdale, NJ: Erlbaum.

Rozin, P. (1990). Development in the food domain. *Developmental Psychology, 26*(4), 555–562.

Rozin, P., Hammer, L., Oster, H., Horowitz, T., & Marmara, V. (1986). The child's conception of food: Differentiation of categories of rejected substances in the 1.4 to 5-year range. *Appetite, 7*, 141–151.

Rubin, K. H. (1983). Recent perspectives on social competence and peer status: Some introductory remarks. *Child Development, 54*, 1383–1385.

Rubin, K. H., & Coplan, R. J. (1992). Peer relationships in childhood. In M. H. Bornstein & M. E. Lamb (Eds.), *Developmental psychology: An advanced textbook*. Hillsdale, NJ: Erlbaum.

Rubin, K. H., Fein, G. C., & Vandenberg, B. (1983). In P. H. Mussen (Ed.), *Handbook of child psychology* (Vol. 4). New York: Wiley.

Rubin, K. H., Hastings, P., Chen, X., Steward, S., & McNichol (1998). Intrapersonal and maternal correlates of aggression, conflict, and externalizing problems in toddlers. *Child Development, 69*, 1614–1629.

Rubin, K. H., Hastings, P. D., Steward, S. L., Henderson, H. A., & Chen, X. (1997). The consistency and concomitants of inhibition: Some of the children, all of the time. *Child development, 68*, 467–483.

Rubin, K. H., LeMare, L., & Lollis, S. (1990). Social withdrawal in childhood: Developmental pathways to peer rejection. In S. R. Asher & J. D. Coie (Eds.), *Peer rejection in childhood*. New York: Cambridge University Press.

Rubin, K., & Trotten, K. (1977). Kohlberg's moral judgment scale: Some methodological considerations. *Developmental Psychology, 13*(5), 535–536.

Rubin, Z. (1980). *Children's friendships*. Cambridge, MA: Harvard University Press.

Rubinstein, E. A. (1983). Television and behavior: Conclusion of the 1982 NIMH report and their policy implications. *American Psychologist, 38*, 820–825.

Ruble, D. (1988). Sex-role development. In M. Bornstein & M. E. Lamb (Eds.), *Developmental psychology: An advanced textbook* (2nd ed., pp. 411–460). Hillsdale, NJ: Erlbaum.

Ruble, D. N., & Brooks-Gunn, J. (1982). The experience of menarche. *Child Development, 53*, 1557–1577.

Rudy, L., & Goodman, G. S. (1991). Effects of participation on children's reports: Implications for children's testimony. *Developmental Psychology, 27*, 527–538.

Ruff, H. A., & Rothbart, M. K. (1996). *Attention in early development*. New York: Oxford University Press.

Rushton, T. P. (1976). Socialization and the altruistic behavior of children. *Psychological Bulletin, 83*(5), 898–913.

Russell, D. (1983). The incidence and prevalence of intrafamilial and extrafamilial sexual abuse of female children. *Child Abuse and Neglect, 7*, 133–146.

Russell, M., Martier, S., Sokol, R., Mudar, P., Jacobson, S., & Jacobson, L. (1996). Detecting risk drinking during pregnancy.

A comparison of four screening questionnaires. *American Journal of Public Health, 86*, 1435–1439.

Rutter, M. (1979). Protective factors in children's responses to stress and disadvantage. In M. W. Kent & J. E. Rolf (Eds.), *Primary prevention of psychopathology: III. Social competence in children*. Hanover, NH: University Press of New England.

Rutter, M. (1983). Stress, coping and development: Some issues and questions. In N. Garmezy & M. Rutter (Eds.), *Stress, coping and development in children*. New York: McGraw-Hill.

Rutter, M. (1984). PT conversations: Resilient children. *Psychology Today, 18*(3), 60–62, 64–65.

Rutter, M., & Garmezy, N. (1983). Developmental psychopathology. In P. H. Mussen (Ed.), *Handbook of child psychology* (Vol. 4). New York: Wiley.

Rutter, M., Silberg, J., O'Connor, T., & Simonoff, E. (1999a). Genetics and child psychiatry: I. Advances in quantitative and molecular genetics. *Journal of Child Psychology and Psychiatry, 40*, 3–18.

Rutter, M., Silberg, J., O'Connor, T., & Simonoff, E. (1999b). Genetics and child psychiatry: II. Empirical research findings. *Journal of Child Psychology and Psychiatry, 40*, 19–55.

For the Safety of Canadian Children and Youth. (1997). Ottawa: Health Canada.

Safty, A. (1992). French immersion as bilingual education: New inquiry directions. *Canadian Ethnic Studies, 24*, 60–76.

Safty, A. (1995). French immersion and the making of a bilingual society: A critical review and discussion. In L. W. Roberts & R. A. Clifton (Eds.), *Contemporary Canadian educational issues*. Toronto: Nelson.

Sagi, A., van Ijzendoorn, M. H., Aviezer, O., Donnell, F., & Mayseless, O. (1994). Sleeping out of home in Kibbutz communal arrangement: It makes a difference for infant-mother attachment. *Child Development, 65*, 992–1004.

Sahai, V., & Demeyere, P. (1996). Sexual health: Are we targeting the right age groups? *Canadian Journal of Public Health, 87*, 40–41.

Salkind, N. (1981). *Theories of human development*. New York: D. VanNostrand.

Samuda, R. J., Kong, S. L., Cummins, J., Pascual-Leone, J., & Lewis, J. (1989). Mental capacity testing as a form of intellectual-developmental assessment. In C. J. Hogrefe (Ed.), *Assessment and placement of minority students*. Toronto: Intercultural Social Sciences Publications.

Sasserath, V. J. (Ed.). (1983). *Minimizing high-risk parenting*. Skillman, NJ: Johnson & Johnson.

Savitz, D. A., & Chen, J. (1990). Parental occupation and childhood cancer: Review of epidemiological studies. *Environmental Health Perspectives, 88*, 325–337.

Scarborough, H. S. (1989). Prediction of reading disability from familial and individual differences. *Journal of Educational Psychology, 81*, 101–108.

Scarr, S., & Kidd, K. K. (1983). Behavior genetics. In M. Haith & J. Campos (Eds.), *Manual of child psychology: Infancy and the biology of development* (Vol. 2). New York: Wiley.

Scarr, S., & Weinberg, R. A. (1983). The Minnesota adoption studies: Genetic differences and malleability. *Child Development, 54*, 260–267.

Schacter, F., & Strage, A. (1982). Adult's talk and children's language development. In S. Moore & C. Cooper (Eds.), *The young child: Reviews of research* (Vol. 3 pp. 79–96). Washington, DC: National Association for the Education of Young Children.

Schaefer, M. R., Sobieraj, K., & Hollyfield, R. L. (1988). Prevalence of childhood physical abuse in adult male veteran alcoholics. *Child Abuse and Neglect, 12,* 141–149.

Schaffer, H. R. (1977). *Studies in mother-infant interaction.* London: Academic Press.

Schardein, J. L. (1976). *Drugs as teratogens.* Cleveland, OH: Chemical Rubber Co. Press.

Schieffelin, B. B., & Ochs, E. (1983). A cultural perspective on the transition from prelinguistic to linguistic communication. In R. M. Golinkoff (Ed.), *The transition from prelinguistic to linguistic communication.* Hillsdale, NJ: Erlbaum.

Schilder, P., & Wechsler, D. (1935). What do children know about the interior of the body? *International Journal of Psychoanalysis, 16,* 355–360.

Schlesinger, J. M. (1982). *Steps to language: Toward a theory of native language acquisition.* Hillsdale, NJ: Erlbaum.

Schliecker, E., White, D., & Jacobs, E. (1991). The role of day care quality in the prediction of children's vocabulary. *Canadian Journal of Behavioral Science, 23,* 12–24.

Schlossman, S., & Cairns, R. B. (1993). Problem girls: Observations on past and present. In G. H. Elder, Jr., J. Modell, & R. D. Parke (Eds.), *Children in time and place: Developmental and historical insights.* New York: Cambridge University Press.

Schneider, B. A., Trehub, S. E., & Bull, D. (1979). The development of basic auditory processes in infants. *Canadian Journal of Psychology, 33,* 306–319.

Schneider, M. F., & Zuckerberg, J. (1996). *Difficult questions kids ask about divorce.* New York: Simon & Schuster.

Schooler, C., Feighery, E., & Flora, J. A. (1996). Seventh graders' self-reported exposure to cigarette marketing and its relationship to their smoking behavior. *American Journal of Public Health, 86,* 1216–1221.

Scott, D. G. (1998). Rites of passage in adolescent development: A reappreciation. *Child & Youth Care Forum, 27,* 317–335.

Sears, R. R. (1963). Dependency motivation. In M. R. Jones (Ed.), *The Nebraska symposium on motivation* (Vol. 11). Lincoln: University of Nebraska Press.

Sedlak, A. J. (1989). *Supplementary analyses of data on the national incidence of child abuse and neglect.* Rockville, MD: Westat.

Segal, J., & Yahraes, H. (1978, November). Bringing up mother. *Psychology Today,* 80–85.

Seifer, R., Schiller, M., Sameroff, A. J., Resnick, S., & Riordan, K. (1996). Attachment, maternal sensitivity and infant temperament during the first year of life. *Developmental Psychology, 32,* 12–25.

Seligman, M. E. P. (1995). *The optimistic child: A proven program to safeguard children against depression and build lifelong resilience.* New York: Harper Perennial.

Selman, R. L. (1976). The development of interpersonal reasoning. In A. Pick (Ed.), *Minnesota symposia on child psychology* (Vol. 1). Minneapolis: University of Minnesota Press.

Selman, R. L. (1981). The child as a friendship philosopher. In S. R. Asher & J. M. Gottman (Eds.), *The development of children's friendships.* Cambridge, England: Cambridge University Press.

Senechal, M., Cornell, E. H., & Broda, L. S. (1995). Age-related differences in the organization of parent-infant interactions during picture-book reading. *Early Childhood Research Quarterly, 10,* 317–337.

Senechal, M., LeFevre, J., Hudson, E., & Lawson, E. P. (1996). Knowledge of storybooks as a predictor of young children's vocabulary. *Journal of Educational Psychology, 88,* 520–536.

Serbin, L. A., Cooperman, J. M., Peters, P. L., Lehoux, P. M., Stack, D. M., & Schwartzman, A. E. (1998). Intergenerational transfer of psychosocial risk in women with childhood histories of aggression, withdrawal, or aggression and withdrawal. *Developmental Psychology, 34,* 1246–1262.

Serbin, L. A., & Stack, D. M. (1998). Introduction to the special section: Studying intergenerational continuity and the transfer of risk. *Developmental Psychology, 34,* 1159–1161.

Shaffer, D. R. (1988). *Social and personality development* (2nd ed.). Pacific Grove, CA: Brooks/Cole.

Shaffer, D. R. (1989). *Developmental psychology* (2nd ed.). Pacific Grove, CA: Brooks/Cole.

Shannon, D., & Kelly, D. (1982). SIDS and near-SIDS. *New England Journal of Medicine, 306,* 961–962.

Shantz, C. (1983). Social cognition. In P. H. Mussen (Ed.), *Handbook of child psychology* (Vol. 3). New York: Wiley.

Sharabany, R., Gershoni, R., & Hoffman, J. E. (1981). Girlfriend, boyfriend: Age and sex differences in intimate friendship. *Developmental Psychology, 17,* 800–808.

Shatz, C. (1992). The developing brain. *Scientific American* (9), 61–67.

Shatz, M. (1994). *A toddler's life: Becoming a person.* New York: Oxford University Press.

Shatz, M., & Gelman, R. (1973). The development of communication skills: Modifications in the speech of young children as a function of the listener. *Monographs of the Society for Research in Child Development, 38*(152).

Shaywitz, S. E., Shaywitz, B. A., Fletcher, J. M., & Escobar, M. D. (1991). Reading disability in children. *Journal of the American Medical Association, 265,* 725–726.

Shea, C. H., Shebilske, W. L., & Worchel, S. (1993). *Motor learning and control.* Englewood Cliffs, NJ: Prentice-Hall.

Sheiman, D. L., & Slomin, M. (1988). *Resources for middle childhood.* New York: Garland.

Shephard, R. J. (1983). Physical activity and the healthy mind. *Canadian Medical Association Journal, 128,* 525–530.

Sherif, M., Harvey, O. J., White, B. J., Hood, W. B., & Sherif, C. W. (1961). *Intergroup conflict and cooperation: The robber's cave experiment.* Norman: University of Oklahoma Press.

Sherif, M., & Sherif, C. W. (1953). *Groups in harmony and tension.* New York: Harper & Brothers.

Shields, C. M., & LaRocque, L. J. (1998). Year-round schooling: A catalyst for pedagogical change. *The Alberta Journal of Educational Research, XLIV,* 366–382.

Shirley, M. M. (1931). The first two years: A study of twenty-five babies. *Institute of Child Welfare Monograph, 1*(Serial No. 1). Minneapolis: University of Minnesota Press.

Shore, R. (1997). *Rethinking the brain: New insights into early development.* New York: Family and Work Institute.

Shultz, T. R. (1976). A cognitive-developmental analysis of humour. In A. J. Chapman & H. C. Foot (Eds.), *Humour and laughter: Theory, research, and applications.* London: Wiley.

Shultz, T. R. (1980). Development of the concept of intention. In W. A. Collins (Ed.), *Minnesota Symposium on Child Psychology* (Vol. 13). Hillsdale, NJ: Erlbaum.

Shultz, T. R., Mareschal, D., & Schmidt, W. C. (1994). Modeling cognitive development on balance scale phenomena. *Machine Learning, 16,* 57–86.

Shultz, T. R., Schmidt, W. C., Buckingham, D., & Mareschal, D. (1995). Modeling cognitive development with a generative connectionist algorithm. In T. J. Simon and G. S. Halford (Eds.), *Developing cognitive competence: New approaches to process modeling.* Hillsdale, NJ: Erlbaum.

Sieber, R. T., & Gordon, A. J. (1981). Socialization implications of school discipline or how fast first graders are taught to listen. In *Children and their organizations: Investigations in American culture.* Boston: G. K. Hall.

Siegler, R. S. (1986). *Children's thinking.* Englewood Cliffs, NJ: Prentice-Hall.

Siegler, R. S. (1991). *Children's thinking* (2nd ed.). Englewood Cliffs, NJ: Prentice-Hall.

Sigel, I. (1987). Does hothousing rob children of their childhood? *Early Childhood Research Quarterly, 2,* 211–225.

Silber, S. J. (1991). *How to get pregnant with the new reproductive technology.* New York: Warner Books.

Silver, L. B. (1990, October). Learning disabilities. *Harvard Mental Health Letter, 7,* 3–5.

Simmons, C. V. (1996, August). *Adolescence and education.* Paper presented at the XXVI International Congress of Psychology, Montreal.

Simmons, R. G., Burgeson, R., Carlton-Ford, S., & Blyth, D. A. (1987). The impact of cumulative change in early adolescence. *Child Development, 58,* 1220–1234.

Simner, M. L. (1995). Reply to the ministries' reactions to the Canadian Psychological Association's position paper on beginning reading instruction. *Canadian Psychology, 36,* 333–342.

Simons, R. L., Whitbeck, L. B., Conger, R. D., & Chyi-In, W. (1991). Intergenerational transmission of harsh parenting. *Developmental Psychology, 27,* 159–171.

Simons-Morton, B. G., Parcel, G. S., Baranowski, T., O'Hara, N., & Forthofer, R. (1991). School promotion of healthful diet and exercise behavior: An integration of organizational changes and social learning theory intervention. *American Journal of Public Health, 81,* 986–991.

Simopoulos, A. P. (1983). Nutrition. In C. C. Brown (Ed.), *Prenatal roundtable: Vol. 9. Childhood learning disabilities and prenatal risk* (pp. 44–49). Rutherford, NJ: Johnson & Johnson.

Siqueland, E. R., & DeLucia, C. A. (1969). Visual reinforcement of nonnutritive sucking in human infants. *Science, 165,* 1144–1146.

Skinner, B. F. (1968). *The technology of teaching.* New York: Appleton-Century-Crofts.

Slaby, A. E., & Dwenger, R. (1993). History of anorexia. In A. J. Giannini & A. E. Slaby (Eds.), *The eating disorders.* New York: Springer-Verlag.

Slobin, D. I. (1972, July). They learn the same way all around the world. *Psychology Today,* 71–74ff.

Smith, B. S., Ratner, H. H., & Hobart, C. J. (1987). The role of cuing and organization in children's memory for events. *Journal of Experimental Child Psychology, 44,* 1–24.

Smith, C., & Lloyd, B. (1978). Maternal behavior and perceived sex of infant: Revisited. *Child Development, 49,* 1263–1265.

Smith, R. E., Smoll, F. L., & Barnett, N. P. (1995). Reduction of children's sport performance anxiety through social support and stress-reduction training for coaches. *Journal of Applied Developmental Psychology, 16,* 125–142.

Smith, W. (1987). *Obstetrics, gynecology, & infant mortality.* New York: Facts on File Publications.

Smolak, L., Levine, P. M., & Striegel-Moore, R. H. (1996). *Developmental psychopathology of eating disorders.* Hillsdale, NJ: Erlbaum.

Smotherman, W. P., & Robinson, S. R. (1996). The development of behavior before birth. *Developmental Psychology, 32,* 425–434.

Snow, C. (1989). Understanding social interaction and language acquisition: Sentences are not enough. In M. Bornstein & J. Bruner, *Interaction in human development* (pp. 83–104). Hillsdale, NJ: Erlbaum.

Snowling, M. J., Defty, N., & Goulandris, N. (1996). A longitudinal study of reading in the development of dyslexic children. *Journal of Educational Psychology, 88,* 653–669.

Snyder, S. (1991). Movies and juvenile delinquency: An overview. *Adolescence, 26*(101), 121–132.

Society for Research in Child Development. (1990). *Ethical standards for research with children.* Chicago: Society for Research and Child Development.

Sorensen, R. C. (1973). *Adolescent sexuality in contemporary America: Personal values and sexual behavior, ages 13-19.* New York: World.

Speece, M. W., & Brent, S. B. (1984). Children's understanding of death: A review of three components of a death concept. *Child Development, 55,* 1671–1686.

Spelke, E. S. (1988). The origins of physical knowledge. In L. Weiskrantz (Ed.), *Thought without language* (pp. 168–184). Oxford: Clarendon Press.

Sperry, R. (1970). Perception in the absence of neocortical commissures. In *Perception and its disorders* (Research Publication A.R.N.M.D., Vol. 48). New York: Association for Research in Nervous and Mental Disease.

Sprott, J. B., & Doob, A. N. (1998). *Who are the most violent ten and eleven year olds? An introduction to future delinquency* (Strategic Policy Working Papers). Ottawa: Human Resources Development Canada.

Sridhar, K. S., Ruab, W. A., & Weatherby, N. L. (1994). Possible role of marijuana smoking as a carcinogen in the development of lung cancer at a young age. *Journal of Psychoactive Drugs, 26,* 285–288.

Stanovich, K. E. (1986). *How to think straight about psychology.* Glenview, IL: Scott, Foresman.

Stanovich, K. E., & Stanovich, P. J. (1995). How research might inform the debate about early reading acquisition. *Journal of Research in Reading, 18,* 87–99.

Stanton, H. E. (1981). A therapeutic approach to help children overcome learning difficulties. *Journal of Learning Disabilities, 14,* 220.

Starfield, B. (1992). Child and adolescent health status measures. In R. E. Behrman (Ed.), *The future of children* (pp. 25–39). Los Angeles, CA: Center for the Future of Children of the David and Lucile Packard Foundation.

Statistics Canada. (1994a, October). *Women in the labour force* (Catalogue no. 75-507E). Ottawa: Author.

Statistics Canada. (1994b). *Youth smoking survey* (Catalogue no. 82C0014). Ottawa: Author.

Staub, E. (1971). The use of role playing and induction in children's learning of helping and sharing behavior. *Child Development, 42,* 805–816.

Stechler, G., & Shelton, A. (1982). Prenatal influences on human development. In B. Wolman (Ed.), *Handbook of developmental psychology.* Englewood Cliffs, NJ: Prentice-Hall.

Stein, Z. A., & Susser, M. W. (1976). Prenatal nutrition and mental competence. In J. D. Lloyd-Still (Ed.), *Malnutrition and intellectual development.* Littleton, MA: Publishing Sciences Group.

Steinberg, L. (1986). Latchkey children and susceptibility to peer pressure: An ecological analysis. *Developmental Psychology, 22,* 433–439.

Steinberg, L. (1987). Recent research on the family at adolescence: The extent and nature of sex differences. *Journal of Youth and Adolescence, 16,* 191–198.

Steinberg, L. (1988). Reciprocal relation between parent-child distance and pubertal maturation. *Developmental Psychology, 24,* 122–128.

Steinberg, L., Darling, N. E., Fletcher, A. C., Brown, B. B., & Dornsbusch, S. M. (1995). Authoritative parenting and adolescent adjustment. In P. Moen, G. H. Elder, Jr., & K. Luscher (Eds.), *Examining lives in context: Perspectives on the ecology of human development.* Washington, DC: American Psychological Association.

Sternberg, R. J. (1984). Mechanisms of cognitive development: A componential approach. In R. J. Sternberg (Ed.), *Mechanisms of cognitive development.* New York: Freeman.

Sternberg, R. J. (1985). *Beyond IQ: A triarchic theory of human intelligence.* Cambridge, England: Cambridge University Press.

Sternberg, R. J. (1988) Intellectual development: Psychometric and information processing approaches. In M. H. Bornstein & M. E. Lamb, (Eds.), *Developmental psychology: An advanced textbook* (2nd ed.). Hillsdale, NJ: Erlbaum.

Sternglass, E. J. (1963). Cancer: Relation of prenatal radiation to development of the disease in childhood. *Science, 140,* 1102–1104.

Stevens, E., Blake, J., Vitale, G., & MacDonald, S. (1998). Mother-infant object involvement at 9 and 15 months: Relation to infant cognition and early vocabulary. *First Language, 18,* 203–222.

Stevenson, H. W., & Lee, S. Y. (1990). Contexts of achievement. *Monographs for the Society for Research in Child Development, 55.*

Stevenson, J. (1999). The treatment of the long-term sequelae of child abuse. *Journal of Child Psychology and Child Psychiatry, 40,* 89–111.

Stewart, R. B., Mobley, L. A., Van Tuyl, S. S., & Salvador, M. A. (1987). The firstborn's adjustment to the birth of a sibling: A longitudinal assessment. *Child Development, 58,* 341–355.

Stice, E., & Berrera, M., Jr. (1995). A longitudinal examination of the reciprocal relations between perceived parenting and adolescents' substance use and externalizing behavior. *Developmental Psychology, 31,* 322–345.

St James-Roberts, I., & Plewis, I. (1996). Individual differences, daily fluctuations, and developmental changes in amounts of infant waking, fussing, crying, feeding, and sleeping. *Child Development, 67,* 2527–2540.

Stoel-Gammon, C. (1989). Prespeech and early speech development of two late talkers. *First Language, 9,* 207–223.

Stone, L. J., Smith, H. T., & Murphy, L. B. (Eds.). (1973). *The competent infant: Research and commentary.* New York: Basic Books.

Stormshak, E. A., Bierman, K. L., Bruschi, C., Dodge, K. A., Coie, J. D., and the Conduct Problems Prevention Research Group. (1999). The relation between behaviour problems and peer preference in different classroom contexts. *Child Development, 70,* 169–182.

Straus, M. A. (1991). Discipline and deviance: Physical punishment of children and violence and other crime in adulthood. *Social Problems, 38,* 133–154.

Streissguth, A., & Kanter, J. (1997). *The challenge of FAS.* RJ520.P74C46.

Streissguth, A. P., Barr, H., & MacDonald, M. (1983). Maternal alcohol use and neonatal habituation assessed with the Brazelton scale. *Child Development, 54,* 1109–1118.

Streissguth, A. P., Sampson, P. D., Barr, H. M., Darby, B. L., & Martin, D. C. (1989). I.Q. at age 4 in relation to maternal alcohol use and smoking during pregnancy. *Developmental Psychology, 25*(1), 3–11.

Strong-Boag, V. (1983). Intruders in the nursery: Childcare professionals reshape years one to five, 1920–1940. In J. Parr (Ed.), *Childhood and family in Canadian history.* Toronto: McClelland & Stewart.

Stunkard, A. J. (1988). Some perspectives on human obesity: Its causes. *Bulletin of the New York Academy of Medicine, 64,* 902–923.

Sumner, G., & Speitz, A. (1994). *NCAST caregiver/parent-child interaction teaching manual.* Seattle, WA: NCAST Publications, University of Washington, School of Nursing.

Super, C. M., Herrera, M. G., & Mora, J. O. (1990). Long-term effects of food supplementation and psychosocial intervention on the physical growth of Colombian infants at risk of malnutrition. *Child Development, 61,* 29–49.

Sutton-Smith, B., & Rosenberg, B. G. (1970). *The sibling.* New York: Holt, Rinehart & Winston.

Swain, M. (1978). French immersion, early, late, or partial? *Canadian Modern Language Review, 34,* 577–585.

Swain, M., & Lapkin, S. (1992). Heritage language children in an English-French bilingual program. In S. Towson (Ed.), *Educational psychology: Readings for the Canadian context.* Peterborough, ON: Broadview Press.

Symons, D., & Carr, T. (1995). Maternal employment and early infant social development: Process and policy. In K. Covell (Ed.), *Readings in child development: A Canadian perspective.* Toronto: Nelson.

Symons, D. K. (1998). Post-partum employment patterns, family-based care arrangements, and the mother-infant relationship at age two. *Canadian Journal of Behavioural Science, 30,* 121–131.

Taft, L. I., & Cohen, H. J. (1967). Neonatal and infant reflexology. In J. Hellmuth (Ed.), *The exceptional infant* (Vol. 1). Seattle: Special Child Publications.

Tanner, J. M. (1978). *Foetus into man: Physical growth from conception to maturity.* Cambridge, MA: Harvard University Press.

Tarabulsy, G. M., Tessier, R., Gagnon, J., & Piche, C. (1996). Attachment classification and infant responsiveness during interactions. *Infant Behaviour and Development, 19,* 131–143.

Tardif, T. (1996). Nouns are not always learned before verbs: Evidence from Mandarin speakers' early vocabularies. *Developmental Psychology, 32,* 492–504.

Tellegen, A. D. T., Lykken, D. T., Bouchard, T. J., Wilcox, K., Segal, N. L., & Rich, S. (1988). Personality similarity in twins reared apart and together. *Journal of Social and Personality Psychology, 59,* 1031–1039.

Teller, D., & Bornstein, M. (1987). Infant color vision and color perception. In P. Salapatek & L. Cohen (Eds.), *Handbook of infant perception* (Vol. 1). New York: Academic Press.

Tharp, R. G. (1994). Intergroup differences among Native Americans in socialization and child cognition: An ethnogenetic analysis. In P. M. Greenfield & R. Cocking (Eds.), *Cross-cultural roots of minority child development.* Hillsdale, NJ: Erlbaum.

Thatcher, R. W., Walker, R. A., & Guidice, S. (1987). Human cerebral hemispheres develop at different rates and ages. *Science, 236,* 1110–1113.

Theilgaard, A. (1983). Aggression and the XYY personality. *International Journal of Law and Psychiatry, 6,* 413–421.

Thelen, E. (1988). Dynamical approaches to the development of behavior. In J. A. S. Kelso, A. J. Mandell, & M. F. Shlesinger (Eds.), *Dynamic patterns in complex systems* (pp. 348–369). Singapore: World Scientific Publishers.

Thelen, E. (1989). The rediscovery of motor development: Learning new things from an old field. *Developmental Psychology, 25*(6), 946–949.

Thelen, E. (1992). Development as a dynamic system. *Current Directions in Psychological Science, 1*(6), 189–193.

Thelen, E., & Fogel, A. (1989). Toward an action-based theory of infant development. In J. J. Lockman & N. L. Kazen (Eds.), *Action in social context: Perspectives on early development* (pp. 23–64). New York: Plenum.

Thompson, C., Barresi, J., & Moore, C. (1998). The development of future-oriented prudence and altruism in preschoolers. *Cognitive Development.*

Thompson, R. A. (1990). Vulnerability in research: A developmental perspective on research risk. *Child Development, 61,* 1–16.

Thompson, R. A. (1996). Early sociopersonality development. In W. Damon (Series Ed.) & N. Eisenberg (Vol. Ed.), *Handbook of child psychology: Vol. 3. Social, emotional and personality development* (5th ed.). New York: Wiley.

Thompson, R. A., & Sherman, R. T. (1993). *Helping athletes with eating disorders.* Windsor, ON: Human Kinetics Publishers.

Thompson, S. K. (1975). Gender labels and early sex-role development. *Child Development, 46,* 339–347.

Thomson, G. (1996, November 18). Ban drawstrings on kids' clothes, physicians urge. *Edmonton Journal.*

Thurstone, L. L. (1938). Primary mental abilities. *Psychometric Monographs* (Serial No. 1).

Tikalsky, F. D., & Wallace, S. D. (1988). Culture and the structure of children's fears. *Journal of Cross-Cultural Psychology, 19*(4), 481–492.

Timnick, L. (1989, September 3). Children of violence. *Los Angeles Times Magazine,* 6–12, 14–15.

Tomasello, M., Mannle, S., & Kruger, A. C. (1986). Linguistic environment of one- to two-year-old twins. *Developmental Psychology, 22,* 169–176.

Tout, K., de Haan, M., Campbell, E. K., & Gunnar, M. R. (1998). Social behaviour correlates of cortisol activity in child care: Gender differences and time-of-day effects. *Child Development, 69,*1247–1262.

Tremblay, R. E., Boulerice, B., Harden, P. W., McDuff, P., Perusse, D., Pihl, R. O., & Zoccolillo, M. (1996). Do children in Canada become more aggressive as they approach adolescence? In Human Resources Development Canada & Statistics Canada. *Growing up in Canada.* National Longitudinal Survey of Children and Youth. Ottawa: Author.

Trovato, F. (1991). Early childhood mortality 1926–1986. *Canadian Social Trends,* 6–10. Ottawa: Statistics Canada.

Troy, M., & Stroufe, L. A. (1987). Victimization among preschoolers: The role of attachment relationship history. *Journal of the American Academy of Child Psychiatry, 26,* 166–172.

Turkington, C. (1987). Special talents. *Psychology Today, 21*(9), 42–46.

Turnbull, A. P., & Turnbull, H. R., III. (1990). *Families, professionals and exceptionality: A special partnership* (2nd ed.). Columbus, OH: Merrill.

Tyson, H. (1991). Outcomes of 1001 midwife-attended home births in Toronto, 1983–1988. *Birth, 18,* 14–19.

Udry, J. R. (1988). Biological predispositions and social control in adolescent sexual behavior. *American Sociological Review, 52,* 841–855.

United Nations. (1996). Family challenges for the future. New York: United Nations Publications.

Unland, K. (1999, April 11). Ethics critical in finding genetic basis of illness. *Edmonton Journal,* p. A10.

Uzgiris, I. C. (1984). Imitation in infancy: Its interpersonal aspects. In M. Perlmutter (Ed.), *Minnesota Symposia on Child Psychology: Vol. 17. Parent-child interaction and parent-child relations.* Hillsdale, NJ: Erlbaum.

van Balen, F. (1998). Development of IVF children. *Developmental Review, 18,* 30–46.

Vandell, D. L., & Wilson, C. S. (1987). Infants' interactions with mother, sibling and peer: Contrasts and relations between interaction systems. *Child Development, 58,* 176–186.

Van den Boom, D. C. (1994). The influence of temperament and mothering on attachment and exploration: An experimental manipulation of sensitive responsiveness among lower-class mothers with irritable infants. *Child Development, 65,* 1457–1477.

Vanier, P. (1996). The children of hope. In M. Russell, J. Hightower, & G. Gutman (Eds.), *Stopping the violence: Changing families, changing futures.* Vancouver: Benwell Atkins Ltd.

Varnhagen, C. K., Svenson, L. W., Godin, A. M., Johnson, L., & Salmon, T. (1991). Sexually transmitted diseases and condoms: High school students' knowledge, attitudes and behaviours. *Canadian Journal of Public Health, 82,* 129–132.

Varni, J. W., & Babani, L. (1986). Long-term adherence to health care regimens in pediatric chronic disorders. In N. A. Krasnegor, J. D. Arasteh, & M. F. Cataldo (Eds.), *Child health behavior: A behavior pediatrics perspective.* New York: Wiley Interscience.

Vasta, R. (1982). Physical child abuse: A dual component analysis. *Developmental Review, 2,* 125–149.

Vellutino, F. R., Scanlon, D. M., Sipay, E. R., Small, S. G., Pratt, A., Chen, R., & Denckla, M. B. (1996). Cognitive profiles of difficult-to-remediate and readily remediated poor readers: Early intervention as a vehicle for distinguishing between cognitive and experiential deficits as basic causes of specific reading disability. *Journal of Educational Psychology, 88,* 601–633.

Verma, I. M. (1990, November). Gene therapy. *Scientific American,* 68–84.

Vessey, J. (1999). Psychological comorbidity in children with chronic conditions. *Pediatric Nursing, 25,* 211–214.

Vogel, J. M. (1989). *Shifting perspectives on the role of reversal errors in reading disability.* Paper presented at the April meeting of the Society for Research in Child Development, Kansas City.

Volling, B. L., & Belsky, J. (1993). Parent, infant, and contextual characteristics related to maternal employment decisions in the first year of infancy. *Family Relations, 42,* 4–12.

von Hofsten, C. (1989). Motor development as the development of systems: comments on the special section. *Developmental Psychology, 25*(6), 950–953.

Vorhees, C., & Mollnow, E. (1987). Behavioral teratogenesis. In J. Osofsky (Ed.), *Handbook of infant development* (2nd ed.). New York: Wiley.

Vulliamy, D. G. (1973). *The newborn child* (3rd ed.). Edinburgh: Churchill Livingstone.

Vygotsky, L. S. (1966). *Thought and language.* Cambridge, MA: MIT Press.

Vygotsky, L. S. (1967). Play and its role in the mental development of the child. *Soviet Psychology, 12*, 6–8.

Vygotsky, L. S. (1978). *Mind in society: The development of higher psychological processes* (M. Cole, Y. John-Steiner, S. Scribner, & E. Souberman, Eds.). Cambridge, MA: Harvard University Press.

Wachs, T. D. (1996). Known and potential processes underlying developmental trajectories in childhood and adolescence. *Developmental Psychology, 32*, 796–801.

Wagner, B. M., & Phillips, D. A. (1992). Beyond beliefs: Parent and child behaviors and children's perceived academic competence. *Child Development, 62*, 1380–1391.

Wagner, R. C., & Torgerson, J. K. (1987). The nature of phonological processing and its causal role in the acquisition of reading skills. *Psychological Bulletin, 101*, 192–212.

Wallace, E. (1995). The origin of the social welfare state in Canada, 1867–1900. In R. B. Blake & J. Keshen (Eds.), *Social policy in Canada: Historical readings*. Toronto: Copp Clark.

Wallerstein, J., Corbin, S. B., & Lewis, J. M. (1988). Children of divorce: A ten-year study. In E. M. Hetherington & J. Arasteh (Eds.), *Impact of divorce, single-parenting, and stepparenting on children*. Hillsdale, NJ: Erlbaum.

Wallis, C. (1984, September 10). The new origins of life. *Time*, 46–50, 52–53.

Walsh, B. T. (1988). Antidepressants and bulimia: Where are we? *International Journal of Eating Disorders, 7*, 421–423.

Wark, G. R., & Krebs, D. L. (1996). Gender and dilemma differences in real-life moral judgment. *Developmental Psychology, 32*, 220–230.

Waterman, A. S. (1985). Identity in the context of adolescent psychology. *New Directions for Child Development, 30*, 5–24.

Waters, E., & Deane, K. (1985). Defining and assessing individual differences in attachment relationships: Q methodology and the organization of behavior in infancy and early childhood. *Monographs of the Society for Research in Child Development, 50*(1–2, Serial No. 209).

Watson, G. (1957). Some personality differences in children related to strict or permissive parental discipline. *Journal of Psychology, 44*, 227–249.

Watson, J. B. (1930). *Behaviorism*. New York: Norton.

Watson, J. B., & Raynor, R. (1920). Conditioned emotional reactions. *Journal of Experimental Psychology, 3*, 1–14.

Watson, J. S., & Ramey, C. T. (1972). Reactions to response-contingent stimulation in early infancy. *Merrill-Palmer Quarterly, 18*, 219–227.

Weber, R. A., Levitt, M. J., & Clark, M. C. (1986). Individual variation in attachment security and strange situation behavior: The role of maternal and infant temperament. *Child Development, 37*, 56–65.

Weikart, D. P., Rogers, L., & Adcock, C. (1971). *The cognitively oriented curriculum* (ERIC-NAEYC publication in early childhood education). Urbana: University of Illinois Press.

Weinberg, R. A. (1989). Intelligence and IQ: Landmark issues and great debates. *American Psychologist, 44*(2), 98–104.

Weinraub, M., Clemens, L. P., Sockloff, A., Ethridge, T., Gracely, E., & Myers, B. (1984). The development of sex role stereotypes in the third year: Relationships to gender labeling, gender identity, sex-typed toy preference and family characteristics. *Child Development, 55*, 1493–1503.

Weinstein, C. S. (1991). The classroom as a social context for learning. *Annual Review of Psychology, 42*, 493–525.

Weisfeld, G. E., & Billings, R. L. (1988). Observations on adolescence. In K. B. MacDonald (Ed.), *Sociobiological perspectives on human development*. New York: Springer-Verlag.

Welford, H. (1998). *NCT book of potty training*. London: Thorsons.

Welles-Nystrom, B. (1988, Summer). Parenthood and infancy in Sweden. In R. A. LeVine, P. M. Miller, & M. M. West (Eds.), *New Directions for Child Development: Vol. 40. Parental behavior in diverse societies* (pp. 75–78). San Francisco: Jossey-Bass.

Wellman, H. M. (1990). *The child's theory of mind*. Cambridge, MA: Bradford Books/MIT Press.

Werker, J. F. (1995). Exploring developmental changes in cross-language speech perception. In D. N. Osherson (Ed.), *An invitation to cognitive science: Language* (Vol. 1). Cambridge, MA: MIT Press.

Werker, J. F., & Desjardins, R. N. (1995). Listening to speech in the 1st year of life: Experiential influences on phoneme perception. *Current Directions in Psychological Science, 4*, 76–81.

Werker, J. F., Pegg, J. E., & McLeod, P. J. (1994). A cross-language investigation of infant preference for infant-directed communication. *Infant Behavior and Development, 17*, 323–333.

Werker, J. F., & Tees, R. C. (1999). Influences on infant speech processing: Toward a new synthesis. *Annual Review of Psychology, 50*, 509–535.

Werner, E. E. (1984, November). Resilient children. *Young Children*, 68–72.

Werner, E. E. (1989). Children of the garden island. *Scientific American, 260*(4), 106–111.

West, M. L., & Sheldon-Keller, A. E. (1994). *Patterns of relating: An adult attachment perspective*. New York: Guilford Press.

White, B. L. (1971). *Human infants: Experience and psychological development*. Englewood Cliffs, NJ: Prentice-Hall.

White, B. L., & Held, R. (1966). Plasticity of sensorimotor development in the human infant. In J. F. Rosenblith & W. Allinsmith (Eds.), *Causes of behavior: Readings in child development and educational psychology*. Boston: Allyn & Bacon.

White, B. L., & Watts, J. (1973). *Experience and environment: Major influences on the development of the young child*. Englewood Cliffs, NJ: Prentice-Hall.

White, D. R., Mendelson, B. K., & Schliecker, E. (1995). Adolescent perceptions of self: Is appearance all that matters? In K. Covell (Ed.), *Readings in child development: A Canadian perspective*. Toronto: Nelson.

White, R. W. (1959). Motivation reconsidered: The concept of competence. *Psychological Review, 66*, 297–333.

Whiting, B. B., & Whiting, J. W. M. (1975). *Children of six cultures: A psychocultural analysis*. Cambridge, MA: Harvard University Press.

Wilkins, K. (1996). Causes of death. *Canadian social trends* (Catalogue no. 11-008-XPE, pp. 11-17). Ottawa: Statistics Canada.

Williams, H. G. (1983). *Perceptual and motor development*. Englewood Cliffs, NJ: Prentice-Hall.

Williams, P. L., Innis, S. M., & Vogel, A. M. P. (1996). Breastfeeding and weaning practices in Vancouver. *Canadian Journal of Public Health, 87*, 231–235.

Williams, P. L., Innis, S. M., Vogel, A. M. P., & Stephen, L. J. (1999). Factors influencing infant feeding practices of mothers in Vancouver. *Canadian Journal of Public Health, 90*, 114–119.

Williams, T. M. (1986). *The impact of television: A natural experiment in three communities*. Orlando, FL: Academic Press.

Willoughby, T., Porter, L., Belsito, L., & Yearsley, T. (1999). Use of elaboration strategies by students in grades two, four, and six. *The Elementary School Journal, 99,* 221–231.

Wilms, J. D. (1996). Indicators of mathematics achievement in Canadian elementary schools. In Human Resources Development Canada & Statistics Canada. *Growing up in Canada.* National Longitudinal Survey of Children and Youth. Ottawa: Author.

Wilson, E. O. (1975). *Sociobiology: The new synthesis.* Cambridge, MA: Belknap Press of Harvard University Press.

Wimmer, H., & Perner, J. (1983). Beliefs about beliefs: Representation and constraining function of wrong beliefs in young children's understanding of deception. *Cognition, 13,* 103–128.

Winn, M. (1983). *The plug-in drug* (2nd ed.). New York: Viking.

Winner, E. (1986). Where pelicans kiss seeds. *Psychology Today, 8,* 25–35.

Wolfe, D. A. (1987). *Child abuse: Implications for child development and psychopathology.* Newbury Park, NJ: Sage.

Wolfe, D. A., Wolfe, V. V., & Best, C. L. (1988). Child victims of sexual abuse. In V. B. VanHasselt, R. L. Morrison, A. S. Bellack, & M. Herson (Eds.), *Handbook of family violence.* New York: Plenum.

Wolfenstein, M. (1951). The emergence of fun morality. *Journal of Social Issues, 7*(4), 15–25.

Wolff, P. H. (1966). The causes, controls, and organization of behavior in the neonate. *Psychological Issues, 5* (No. 1, Monograph 17).

Wolfson, A. R., & Carskadon, M. A. (1998). Sleep schedules and day-time functioning in adolescence. *Child Development, 69,* 875–887.

Woodcock, L. P. (1941). *The life and ways of the two-year-old.* New York: Basic Books.

Worrell, J., & Todd, J. (1996). Development of the gendered self. In L. Smolak, M. P. Levine, & R. H. Striegel-Moore (Eds.), *Developmental psychopathology of eating disorders.* Hillsdale, NJ: Erlbaum.

Wright, J., & Huston, A. (1983). A matter of form: Potentials of television for young viewers. *American Psychologist, 38,* 835–843.

Wyatt, P. R. (1985). Chorionic biopsy and increased anxiety. *The Lancet, 2,* 1312–1313.

Yarrow, L. J., Rubenstein, J. L., Pedersen, F. A., & Jankowski, J. J. (1972). Dimensions of early stimulation and their differential effects on infant development. *Merrill-Palmer Quarterly, 18,* 205–218.

Yawney, D. (1996). Resiliency: A strategy for survival of childhood trauma. In M. Russell, J. Hightower, & G. Gutman (Eds.), *Stopping the violence: Changing families, changing futures.* Vancouver: Benwell Atkins Ltd.

Yeh, C. J., & Huang, K. (1996). The collectivistic nature of ethnic identity development among Asian-American college students. *Adolescence, 31,* 645–661.

Ying, J., Braithwaite, J., & Kogon, R. (1998). Needs assessment of child care centres in the former city of Toronto. *Canadian Journal of Public Health.*

Yonas, A., & Owsley, C. (1987). Development of visual space perception. In P. Salapatek & L. Cohen (Eds.), *Handbook of infant perception* (Vol. 2, pp. 80–122). New York: Academic Press.

Young, D. (1982). *Changing childbirth: Family birth in the hospital.* Rochester, NY: Childbirth Graphics.

Youniss, J. (1983). Social construction of adolescence by adolescents and parents. H. D. Grotevant & C. R. Cooper (Eds.), *New directions for child development: Vol. 22. Adolescent development in the family* (pp. 93–109). San Francisco: Jossey-Bass.

Youniss, J., & Ketterlinus, R. D. (1987). Communication and connectedness in mother and father adolescent relationships. *Journal of Youth and Adolescence,* 265–280.

Zajonc, R. B., & Hall, E. (1986, February). Mining new gold from old research. *Psychology Today,* 46–51.

Zajonc, R. B., & Markus, G. B. (1975). Birth order and intellectual development. *Psychological Review, 82,* 74–88.

Zaporozlets, A. V., & Elkonin, D. B. (Eds.). (1971). *The psychology of preschool children.* Cambridge, MA: MIT Press.

Zeanah, C. H., Jr., Mammen, O. K., & Lieberman, A. F. (1993). Disorders of attachment. In C. H. Zeanah, Jr. (Ed.), *Handbook of infant mental health.* New York: Guilford Press.

Zelazo, P. D., & Reznick, J. S. (1991). Age-related asynchrony of knowledge and action. *Child Development, 62,* 719–735.

Zelnick, M., & Kantner, J. F. (1977). Sexual and contraceptive experience of young unmarried women in the United States, 1976 and 1971. *Family Planning Perspectives, 9,* 55–71.

Zeskind, P. S., & Ramey, C. T. (1978). Fetal malnutrition: An experimental study of its consequences on infant development in two caregiving environments. *Child Development, 49,* 1155–1162.

Zgourides, G. (1996). *Human sexuality: Contemporary perspectives.* New York: HarperCollins.

Zhang, D. (1995). Depression and culture—a Chinese perspective. *Canadian Journal of Counselling, 29,* 227–233.

Zhang, C., Ollila, L. O., & Harvey, C. B. (1998). Chinese parents' perceptions for their children's literacy and schooling in Canada. *Canadian Journal of Education, 23,* 182–190.

Zigler, E. F. (1987). Formal schooling for four-year-olds? No. *American Psychologist, 42*(3), 254–260.

Zuckerman, B., & Brown, E. R. (1993). Maternal substance abuse and infant development. In C. H. Zeanah, Jr. (Ed.), *Handbook of infant mental health.* New York: Guilford Press.

Zuravin, S. (1985). Housing and maltreatment: Is there a connection? *Children Today, 14*(6), 8–13.

Name Index

Subject Index

Figures

15 Reprinted from *Analyzing Children's Art* by permission of Mayfield Publishing Company. Copyright 1969, 1970, by Rhonda Kellog **165** Adapted from *Growth and Development of Children, 5th ed.*, by E.H. Watson and G.H. Lowrey (Chicago: Year Book Medical publishers, 1967). **242** © 1992 by Sidney Harris **270** B. Nichols (1990) *Moving and Learning The Elementary School Physical Education Experience.* St.Louis, MO: Times Mirror/Mosby College Publishing **392** Jack Zeigler **422** S.J. Gould (1981). *The Mismeasure of Man.* New York: W.W. Norton & Co.

Photos

3 Photo Courtesy of Health Canada **4** (a) James Stevenson/Science Photo Library (b) Tacke Henstra/Petit Format (c) Myrleen Ferguson (d) Myrleen Ferguson **5** (e) Frank Siteman (f) Elizabeth Crews (g) M. Greenlar **8** Photo Researchers **9** Photo Researchers **10** Photo Researchers **11** Bettmann **14** Paula M. Lerner/Picture Cube **17** Michael Newman/Photoedit **20** Prentice Hall Archives **26** Prentice Hall Archives **31** Photo Courtesy of Health Canada **34** Prentice Hall Archives **35** Erelanson Productions/The Image Bank **36** Shirley Zeiberg **40** (a) Wayne Behling, psilanti Press (b) Monkmeyer Press **43** Laima Druskis **44** Richard Hutchings, Photo Researchers **48** J.R. Holland/Stock Boston **54** Jean-Luc Ducloux **63** Pentagram **64** Jean Claude Revy, Phototake **66** Photo Researchers **72** Bruce Roberts **79** B.W. Hoffmann **81** Frank Siteman, Picture Cube **82** Elizabeth Crews, The Image Works **87** Daemmrich, The Image Works **90** Gale Zucker, Stock Boston **91** Laura Dwight/Photoedit **95** W. Hill, Jr./The Image Works **96** Francis Leroy, Biocosmos/Science Photo Library/Photo Research **101** Porterfield-Chickering/Photo Researchers **103** (a) A. Lennart Nilsson Being Born (b) C. Lennart Nilsson A Child is Born (c) Dr. Landrum B. Shettles (d)-(h) C. Lennart Nilsson Being Born **113** United Nations **114** William McCoy/Rainbow **117** David Young/Wolff/Photoedit **119** Gaye Hilsenrath/Picture Cube **120** Photo Researchers **125** Pentagram **128** Griffin/The Image Works **129** Jim Olive **130** Peter Arnold **133** Heinz Kluetmeier/DOT Pictures **135** Lawrence Migdale **136** Jim Corwin/Stock Boston **138** (top left) Format/Science Source/Photo Researchers (top right) Petit Format/J.M. Steinlein/Photo Researchers (bottom right) Tucker/Monkmeyer Press **144** Crews/The Image Works **146** Alan Carey/The Image Works **149** Al Harvey **150** Mark Richards/Photoedit **155** Pentagram **161** (1) E. Crews/The Image Works (b) Tony Freeman/Photoedit (c) Crews/The Image Works (d) Suzanne Szasz/Photo Researchers (e) Mary Jane Denny/Photoedit **164** M. Siluk/The Image Works **169** C. Errath/Explorer/Photo Researchers **170** SARIE-Camera Press/Pono Press **174** Dr. Joseph J. Campos **177** Shirley Zeiberg **179** John Eastcott **182** Frank Herholdt/Stone **183** Dr. T.G.R. Bower/*Scientific American*, October 1971, p. 38 **186** Dorian Weber/Image Network Inc. **189** Jeffrey W. Myers/Stock Boston **192** Spender Grant/Photo Researchers **195** Dennis O'Clair/Stone **197** (top) Thomas McAvoy/Life Magazine, Time Warner (bottom) Martin Rogers/Stone **199** Crews/The Image Works **202** (right) Zen Radovan/Photoedit (left) United Nations **207** Robert Brenner/Photoedit **208** Shirley Zeiberg **211** J.Berndt **216** Rhoda Sidney **217** (right) Crews/The Image Works (left) National Institute on Aging **223** Peter Southwick/Stock Boston **230** Corroon/Monkmeyer Press **231** Ray Ellin/Photo Researchers **237** Pentagram **239** David Young-Wolff/Photoedit **240** Carol Palmer/Picture Cube **243** Charles Gupton/Stock Boston **248** Ed Malitsky/Picture Cube **253** Alice Kandell/Rapho/Photo Researchers **255** Shostak/Anthro Photo **258** Joseph Schuyler/Stock Boston **260** © Dick Hemingway **263** Robert Brenner/Photoedit **267** Photo Courtesy of Health Canada **268** David Young-Wolff/Photoedit **270** David Young-Wolff/Photoedit **271** Scott Camazine/Photo Researchers **274** George Goodwin/Monkmeyer Press **275** George Goodwin/Monkmeyer Press **276** Jon Love/Image Bank **277** Shirley Zeiberg **279** Greeman/Grishaber/Photoedit **280** Rhoda Sidney/Monkmeyer Press **283** George Zimbel/Monkmeyer Press **289** Bob Daemmrich/Stock Boston **291** Robert Brenner/Photoedit **292** Larry Milvehill/Photo Researchers **294** Michael Peake/Canada Wide **295** Freda Leinwant/Monkmeyer Press **299** Pentagram **302** Teri Stratford **303** A. Griffiths/Woodfin Camp & Associates **311** Tony Freeman/Photoedit **312** Lew Merrim/Monkmeyer Press **313** Ryan VcVay/PhotoDisc **317** J. Zaruba/First Light **321** Lawrence Migdale/Stock Boston **322** (a) George Goodwin (b) Jim Corwin (c) Elizabeth Crews (d) Myrleen Ferguson (e) David Young-Wolff (f) George Goodwin **326** Lawrence Migdale/Photo Researchers **330** George Goodwin/Monkmeyer Press **337** Pentagram **339** Robert Brenner/Photoedit **340** Sarah Putnam/Picture Cube **343** Michael Newman/Photoedit **344** Robert Brenner/Photoedit **345** Anthony Jalandoni/Monkmeyer Press **353** L. Kolvoord/The Image Works **355** B. Daemmrich/The Image Works **357** Wendy Moran **359** Walter Hodges-West Light/First Light **363** Rameshwar Das/Monkmeyer Press **365** Bill Aron/Photoedit **366** Elizabeth Hathon/Stock Market **373** Pentagram **374** Tony Freeman **378** David Young-Wolff/Photoedit **379** Myrleen Ferguson/Photoedit **380** Tessa Macintosh – NWT Archives/Government of NWT Collection **382** Tony Freeman/Photoedit **384** Elizabeth Zuckerman **387** Michael Newman **389** Tony Freeman/Photoedit **391** Renee Lynn/Photo Researchers **393** Margot Granitsas/Photo Researchers **394** Lawrence Migdale/Photo Researchers **395** David Young-Wolff/Photoedit **399** Pentagram **404** Laima Druskis **405** Al Harvey **406** Will McIntyre **407** Frank Siteman/Picture Cube **408** Al Harvey **412** Bob Daemmrich/Stock Boston **413** Michael Newman **416** Zefa/Image Network Inc. **418** Bob Daemmrich/Stock Boston **421** Day McCoy/Rainbow **424** Stephen McBrady/Photoedit **425** George Goodwin/Monkmeyer Press **431** Pentagram **432** Myrleen Ferguson **434** David Young-Wolff/Photoedit **437** John Coletti/Photoedit **442** Michael Newman/Photoedit **443** Myrleen Ferguson **446** Richard Smith/Monkmeyer Press **451** Frank Siteman/Rainbow **452** Bob Carroll **456** Robert W. Ginn/Photoedit **458** Bob Daemmrich/The Image Works **465** Kevin Morris/Stone **466** Don Smetzer/Stone **468** Toml/Photolink/PhotoDisc **470** Rhoda Sidney **472** David Young-Wolff/Photoedit **473** Billy Barnes/Photoedit **475** Willie Hill/The Image Works **478** John Elk III/Stock Boston **479** Steven Frame/Stock Boston **481** (top) George Goodwin/Monkmeyer Press (bottom) Dick Hemingway **483** Tony Freeman/Photoedit **488** Al Harvey **489** Frank Simonetti/Image Network Inc. **495** Al Harvey **497** Rhoda Sidney/Photoedit **498** Bob Daemmrich/Stock Boston **502** Rhoda Sidney/Monkmeyer Press **503** Richard Pasley/Stock Boston **505** Al Harvey **506** Bob Daemmrich/The Image Works **508** Bill Sandford/Canada Wide **514** Monatiuk/Eastcott/Woodfin Camp & Associates **520** Ron Sherman/Stone